HANDBOOKS IN OPERATIONS RESEARCH
AND MANAGEMENT SCIENCE
VOLUME 4

Handbooks in Operations Research and Management Science

Editors

G.L. Nemhauser
Georgia Institute of Technology

A.H.G. Rinnooy Kan
Erasmus University Rotterdam

Volume 4

N·H

ELSEVIER
Amsterdam – London – New York – Oxford – Paris – Shannon – Tokyo

Logistics of Production and Inventory

Edited by

S.C. Graves
Massachusetts Institute of Technology

A.H.G. Rinnooy Kan
Erasmus University Rotterdam

P.H. Zipkin
Columbia University

ELSEVIER
Amsterdam – London – New York – Oxford – Paris – Shannon – Tokyo

ELSEVIER B.V.
Radarweg 29
P.O. Box 211, 1000 AE
Amsterdam, The Netherlands

ELSEVIER Inc.
525 B Street
Suite 1900, San Diego
CA 92101-4495, USA

ELSEVIER Ltd
The Boulevard
Langford Lane, Kidlington,
Oxford OX5 1GB, UK

ELSEVIER Ltd
84 Theobalds Road
London WC1X 8RR
UK

First edition 1993
Reprinted 2002, 2005

Library of Congress Cataloging in Publication Data

Logistics of production and inventory / edited by S.C. Graves, A.H.G.
Rinnooy Kan, P.H. Zipkin.
p. cm. - - (Handbooks in operations research and management science: v. 4)
Includes bibliographical references and index.
ISBN 0-444-87472-0
1. Production control. 2. Inventory control. I. Graves, S.C.
II. Rinnooy Kan, A. H. G., 1949- . III. Zipkin, Paul Herbert.
IV. Series.
TS 157.L63 1993
658.5 - - dc20

92-34645
CIP

ISBN: 9780444874726

Transferred to digital printing 2007

Printed and bound by CPI Antony Rowe, Eastbourne

Preface

Since their beginnings earlier in this century, Operations Research and Management Science have been deeply concerned with the managerial problems raised by production, inventory and distribution – all the activities comprised by the general term *logistics*. OR/MS have contributed greatly, both to our intellectual understanding of the nature of logistics systems and to the resolution of diverse practical problems in the field.

Given this fruitful history, one might suspect that all the major issues and problems in the area would have been resolved by now. This is simply not so. One clear message that emerges from the essays in this book is that logistics remains an active, vibrant subject of inquiry.

There are several reasons for this continued development. First, many logistics systems are extremely complex. It is difficult, both for researchers and managers, to achieve a clear, coherent picture of how such systems work. It has sometimes taken decades to obtain satisfactory solutions to the technical problems inherent in these systems, and even now many such problems remain open. Moreover, we continue to witness the development of fundamentally new approaches to the subject and a lively debate over basic terms, premises and issues.

Second, the practical world of logistics has changed markedly over the past few decades. The physical technologies of production and transportation have evolved considerably – think of flexible manufacturing and overnight air delivery. Even more striking has been the explosion of information technologies, which has utterly transformed the very nature of logistics management. Over that same period, furthermore, the questions that concern managers most deeply have shifted. The intricate problems of day-to-day control, while still important, have yielded center stage to broader issues of performance evaluation and systems design. Taking just one more example, the dimension of quality has become a central focus in virtually all logistics organizations. All these changes have posed, and doubtless will continue to pose, significant new challenges to researchers.

This book presents a broad survey of the state of the art in logistics systems research as viewed by a distinguished group of scholars. The essays collected here, all written specifically for this volume, focus mainly on the key developments of the last decade.

And what a decade it has been! We have witnessed a truly astonishing leap in our understanding of what logistics is all about. In topic after topic, as the following chapters testify, old problems have been tackled with fresh approaches, and entirely new subfields have been born.

Here is an overview of what is to come: the book is divided into four parts, each composed of several chapters. Rather than fully summarize each chapter here (the authors have done that admirably themselves!), we shall provide a broad look at the several parts and their connections.

Part I. Fundamentals. Part I consists of Chapter 1, *Single-Product, Single-Location Models*, by Hau Lee and Steven Nahmias. These basic models truly are fundamental to all that follows; they form the building blocks from which more elaborate models are constructed. Furthermore, such models are widely applied themselves. And, as Lee and Nahmias point out, even these simple formulations have yielded exciting new insights in recent years.

Part II. Multiple Products and Locations. This part includes five chapters, each of which examines complex logistics systems from a different perspective. In Chapter 2 John Muckstadt and Robin Roundy summarize the extraordinary advances that have been achieved (in which they have played central roles) in optimizing the crucial coordination decisions required to manage complex production and distribution systems. Whereas in this approach the world is viewed as deterministic, the next two chapters explicitly focus on stochastic demands. A key issue in this case is how information is collected and used. Awi Federgruen, in Chapter 3, treats the case where all information is centralized, while in Chapter 4 Sven Axsäter examines systems operating in a decentralized mode. Substantial progress has been made in our understanding of both types of systems.

Chapter 5, by Rajan Suri, Jerry Sanders and Manjunath Kamath focuses on the congestion effects resulting from the interaction between randomness and limited processing capacity. Specifically, they consider networks of queues as models of manufacturing systems. Interestingly, such networks were originally formulated to model production systems, but applications languished until fairly recently. Now, the field has become very active, as this chapter documents. Uday Karmarkar, in Chapter 6, combines this style of modeling with basic inventory-control issues, such as lotsizing and order-release planning. This combined approach is quite novel, and it yields a number of new insights.

Part III. Production Planning and Scheduling. This part of the book offers several perspectives on practical modeling methods for implementing production plans over the short and medium term. Here, for the most part, we return to the deterministic picture of Chapter 2 above, but a host of additional factors must now be accounted for, including workforce planning, multiple production resources, and the like. This subject is extraordinarily broad and diverse, and Joseph Thomas and John McClain provide an indispensable overview in Chapter 7. Then, in Chapter 8, Jeremy Shapiro reviews the use of mathematical programming methods in logistics. While such applications are quite venerable, going back to the roots of linear programming, recent developments in solution methods and model-management software have given fresh impetus to the subject.

Chapter 9, by Eugene Lawler, Jan Karel Lenstra, Alexander Rinnooy Kan, and David Shmoys, is a thorough survey of the extensive literature on production sequencing and scheduling. The focus here is on computational complexity; this approach teaches us when such problems can be solved fairly easily and when they are fundamentally difficult. Finally, in Chapter 10, Gabriel Bitran and Devanath Tirupati introduce the concept of hierarchical planning. More than a model per se, this is an approach to constructing a suite of models at different levels of detail to enable managers to cope with truly complex systems.

Part IV. Additional Topics. This last part might well be entitled 'new directions', for indeed each of its chapters covers a topic of intense and largely recent interest. Chapter 11, by Kenneth Baker, is concerned with material requirements planning (MRP) and related methods, which have become the standard control mechanism for discrete-parts manufacturing. This approach has spawned a substantial body of research. The next two chapters treat even newer subjects, both largely inspired by the example of Japanese approaches to logistics management. Harry Groenevelt discusses the Just-in-Time production system, focusing on research efforts to understand it, in Chapter 12. In Chapter 13 Peter Kolesar offers a provocative look at the issue of quality management and a rather sharp critique of research in the area.

New developments in manufacturing technology, and research efforts to come to grips with them, are the subject of Charles Fine's concluding Chapter 14.

S.C. Graves
A.H.G. Rinnooy Kan
P.H. Zipkin

Contents

Part I
Fundamentals

S.C. Graves et al., Eds., *Handbooks in OR & MS, Vol. 4*

Chapter 1

Single-Product, Single-Location Models

Hau L. Lee

Department of Industrial Eng., Stanford University, Stanford, CA 94305-4024, U.S.A.

Steven Nahmias

Decision and Information Sciences, Santa Clara University, Santa Clara, CA 95053, U.S.A.

1. Introduction

Inventory management is one area in which operations research has had a significant impact. At the present time, the total value of inventories in the United States is close to one trillion dollars (Economic Report of the President, February, 1989). Mathematical models form the basis for many of the inventory control systems in use today, whether they be inventories of raw materials, spare parts, cash, or finished goods.

Most mathematical inventory models are designed to address two fundamental issues: when should a replenishment order be placed, and how much should the order quantity be. The complexity of the model depends on the assumptions that one makes about the demand, cost structure, and physical characteristics of the system. In some cases, the operating characteristics of a given policy are analyzed.

The objective of virtually all inventory control models is to minimize costs. In most cases, minimizing costs will result in the same control policy as that obtained by maximizing profits. When uncertainty is present the traditional approach has been to minimize expected costs. The use of the expected value operator is justified from the law of large numbers: as the number of planning periods grows, the arithmetic average of the actual costs incurred will be close to the expected costs. Since most inventory control problems are ongoing, this approach makes sense.

Most inventory control problems in the real world involve multiple products. For example, spare parts systems for military applications may require management of hundreds of thousands of different items. However, it is often true that single product models are able to capture the essential elements of the problem, so that it is not necessary to explicitly include the interaction of different items into the formulation. Furthermore, multiple product models are often too unwieldy to be of much use when the number of products is very large. For this reason, single product models dominate the literature and are used most frequently in practice.

This chapter is concerned with mathematical models for controlling the inventory of a single product. Other chapters in this volume will be concerned with multiple products and special topics.

1.1. History

Although operations research methodology is based on mathematical developments spanning centuries, much of the interest in the application of this methodology had its origins in the logistic support activities which took place during the Second World War. Interdisciplinary teams of scientists would brainstorm problems that were not amenable to traditional analysis. The success of these activities, along with the subsequent discovery of both the simplex method and the electronic computer led to the birth of operations research as a discipline. It is interesting to note that the first work on inventory modeling pre-dates these developments by about thirty years.

Ford Harris [1913] is generally credited with the discovery of the original EOQ (Economic Order Quantity, to be described in Section 2) model. Harris' analysis was the basis for an inventory system that he marketed. Interest in academic circles was sparked by the later studies of R.H. Wilson [1934]. Few papers were published in the next fifteen years, although some interest in mathematical inventory models resurfaced during the war. Landmark papers were published in the early fifties [Arrow, Harris & Marshak, 1951; Dvoretsky, Kiefer & Wolfowitz, 1952a,b] which laid the groundwork for later developments in the mathematical theory of inventories. The monograph by Whitin [1957] was also an important development in presenting the relationship of inventory management issues and classical economic thinking, and was one the first treatments of the (Q, r) model under uncertainty (to be described in Section 5), which later became the cornerstone for many commercial inventory systems.

A number of important scholars turned their attention to mathematical inventory models during the 1950s. Bellman, Glicksberg & Gross [1955] showed how the methods of dynamic programming, a term apparently coined by the first author for describing a class of sequential decision problems, could be used to obtain structural results for a simple version of the periodic review stochastic demand problem. A collection of highly sophisticated mathematical models by Arrow, Karlin & Scarf [1958] provided much of the impetus for later work in this area. At about the same time, Wagner & Whitin [1958] discovered the solution to the dynamic lot sizing problem subject to time varying demand.

The number of papers published today on single product inventory problems is well into the thousands. These papers appear in journals published in the United States including *Management Science*, *Operations Research*, *AIIE Transactions*, *Naval Research Logistics Quarterly*, *Mathematics of Operations Research*, and *Decision Sciences*, to name a few, and many more international journals. Dozens of books have been published on the subject. The study of inventory management models is now part of the required curriculums in both Schools of Industrial Engineering and Schools of Business (where it is integrated with production and operations management). Commercial computer based systems for inventory control have been available for more than twenty-five years and several inventory control systems for the personal computer are now available.

1.2. Motivation

Arrow [1958] presented an interesting discussion of the motives of a firm for holding inventories. He argues that the motives for holding inventories and the motives for holding cash are the same. He refers to Keynes who claimed that there are essentially three motives for holding cash: the transaction, the precautionary, and the speculative.

1.2.1. The transaction motive

The key to the transaction motive is that by producing or ordering large lots, fixed costs may be reduced. Economies of scale can be achieved when the number of set-ups are reduced or the number of transactions are minimized. This fact was evidently recognized by Harris [1913], because the original formulation of the EOQ model incorporates a set-up cost for ordering. Arrow also points to a number of references of work published in the 1920s which explicitly discuss this issue in the light of inventory considerations.

1.2.2. The precautionary motive

The precautionary motive is based on the fact that inventories are often retained as a hedge against uncertainty. As we will see in this chapter, the focus of a major portion of the research in inventory modeling is controlling inventories in the face of stochastic demand. Although demand uncertainty is the most obvious and significant source of uncertainty for most systems, other uncertainties exist as well. There may be uncertainty in the supply. Such a situation occurred in the late 1970s in the United States when there was an oil embargo placed against the United States by members of OPEC. Uncertainty in the order lead time is a common problem. Some costs may be difficult to predict. Holding costs are tied to the rate of inflation. Commodities such as precious metals are subject to considerable price variation. Safety stocks in inventory systems are essentially the same as reserve ratios of cash for banks. Arrow points out that the reserve ratio problem was studied as far back as 1888, and was rediscovered by Eisenhart in 1948 in the context of inventory control.

1.2.3. The speculative motive

There are essentially two speculative motives for holding inventories. If the cost of obtaining or producing the items is expected to rise in the near future, it is clearly advantageous to hold inventories in anticipation of the price rise.

Companies which use commodities whose value may fluctuate could find it advantageous to stockpile inventory. For example, silver is used in the production of photographic film. Although the price of silver has been relatively stable in recent years, it increased suddenly by about a factor of ten during the late 1970s. Increases in labor costs could occur due to negotiated wage increases, changes in the labor pool, changes in the need for specialized help, or strikes.

Inventories may also be retained in advance of sales increases. If demand is expected to increase, it may be more economical to build up large inventories in advance rather than to increase production capacity at a future time. However, it is often true that inventory build-ups occur as a result of poor sales. For this reason, aggregate inventory levels are often used as a means of gauging the health of the economy.

1.3. Types of inventory models

Inventory models come in all shapes, sizes, colors and varieties. In this chapter we will consider models for only a single product at a single location. Even with these restrictions the number of possible models is enormous. In general, the assumptions that one makes about three key variables determines the essential structure of the model. These variables are demand, costs, and physical aspects of the system. We will discuss each of these in turn.

(1) *Demand*. The assumptions that one makes about demand are usually the most important in determining the complexity of the model.

(a) *Deterministic and stationary*. The simplest assumption is that the demand is constant and known. These are really two different assumptions: one, that the demand is not anticipated to change, and the other is that the demand can be predicted in advance. The simple EOQ model is based on constant and known demand.

(b) *Deterministic and time varying*. Changes in demand may be systematic or unsystematic. Systematic changes are those that can be forecasted in advance. Lot sizing under time varying demand patterns is a problem that arises in the context of manufacturing final products from components and raw materials.

(c) *Uncertain*. We use the term uncertainty to mean that the distribution of demand is known, but the exact values of the demand cannot be predicted in advance. In most contexts, this means that there is a history of past observations from which to estimate the form of the demand distribution and the values of the parameters. In some situations, such as with new products, the demand uncertainty could be assumed but some estimate of the probability distribution would be required.

(d) *Unknown*. In this case even the distribution of the demand is unknown. The traditional approach in this case has been to assume some form of a distribution for the demand and update the parameter estimates using Bayes rule each time a new observation becomes available.

(2) *Costs*. Since the objective is to minimize costs, the assumptions one

makes about the cost structure are also important in determining the complexity of the model.

(a) *Averaging versus discounting*. When the time value of money is considered, costs must be discounted rather than averaged. The discount factor, α, is given by $\alpha = (1 + r)^{-1}$ where r is the interest rate. If $C_1, C_2, \ldots$ represents a stream of costs incurred over periods 1, 2, . . . (or expected costs if there is uncertainty), then the present value of the cost stream is given by:

$$\sum_{i=1}^{\infty} \alpha^i C_i .$$

On the other hand, if costs are averaged, then the average cost (again, assuming infinitely many periods in the planning horizon) is given by:

$$\lim_{n \to \infty} \frac{1}{n} \sum_{i=1}^{n} C_i .$$

(b) *Structure of the order cost*. The assumptions that one makes about the order cost function can make a substantial difference in the complexity of the resulting model. The simplest assumption is that the cost of obtaining or producing y items is cy for some constant c. This is known as a proportional order cost and is often assumed when demand is uncertain. However, it is much more realistic to assume that the order cost has both fixed and variable components. That is, it is of the form $cy + K\delta(y)$, where $\delta(y)$ is the Dirac delta function satisfying

$$\delta(y) = \begin{cases} 1 & \text{if } y > 0 , \\ 0 & \text{if } y = 0 . \end{cases}$$

Most deterministic inventory models assume an order cost of this form. The analysis of stochastic models is considerably more complex when a fixed order cost is included, however.

(c) *Time varying costs*. Most inventory models assume that costs are time invariant. Time varying costs can often be included without increasing the complexity of the analysis.

(d) *Penalty costs*. Most stochastic, and many deterministic models, include a specific penalty, p, for not being able to satisfy a demand when it occurs. In many circumstances p can be difficult to estimate. For that reason, in many systems one substitutes a service level for p. The service level is the acceptable proportion of demands filled from stock, or the acceptable proportion of order cycles in which all demand is satisfied.

(3) *Other distinguishing physical aspects*. Inventory models are also distinguished by the assumptions made about various aspects of the timing and logistics of the model. Some of these include:

(a) *Lead time assumptions*. The lead time is defined as the amount of time that elapses from the point that a replenishment order is placed until it arrives.

The lead time is a very important quantity in inventory analysis; it is a measure of the system response time. The simplest assumption is that the lead time is zero. This is, of course, analytically expedient but not very realistic in practice. It makes sense only if the time required for replenishment is short compared with the time between reorder decisions.

The most common assumption is that the lead time is a fixed constant. The analysis is much more complicated if the lead time is assumed to be a random variable. Issues such as order crossing (that is, orders not arriving in the same sequence that they were placed), and independence must be considered.

(b) *Backordering assumptions*. Assumptions are required about the way that the system reacts when demand exceeds supply. The simplest and most common assumption is that all excess demand is backordered. Backordered demand is represented by a negative inventory level. The other extreme is that all excess demand is lost. This latter case, known as lost sales, is most common in retailing environments.

Mixtures of backordering and lost sales have also been explored. Various alternatives exist for mixture models. One is that a fixed fraction of demands is backordered and a fixed fraction lost. Another is that customers are willing to wait a fixed time for their orders to be filled.

(c) *The review process*. Continuous review means that the level of inventory is known at all times. This has also been referred to as transactions reporting because it means that each demand transaction is recorded as it occurs. Modern supermarkets with scanning devices at the checkout counter are an example of this sort of system (assuming, of course, that the devices are connected to the computer used for stock replenishment decisions). The other extreme is periodic review. This means that the inventory level is known only at discrete points when physical stock taking occurs. Most systems are periodic review, although continuous review approximations are common. In continuous review systems one generally assumes that reorder decisions can be made at any time while in periodic review they can be made only at the predetermined times corresponding to the start of periods.

(d) *Changes which occur in the inventory during storage*. Traditional inventory theory assumes that the inventory items do not change character while they are in stock. Some inventories, such as volatile liquids or radioactive materials, experience exponential decay in which a fixed fraction of the inventory is lost each unit of time. Fixed life inventories, such as food or photographic film, are assumed to have constant utility until they reach their expiration date and must be discarded. Finally, inventories may be subject to obsolescence, which means their useful lifetime may not be predictable in advance.

This chapter will present an overview of the major developments and results for single product inventory management. Porteus [1988] in a chapter in an earlier volume discusses stochastic inventory models. Other chapters will be devoted to inventory systems with multiple echelons and to production/distribution systems. This chapter is organized as follows: 1. Introduction; 2.

Models with constant demand rates; 3. Models with deterministic time-varying demand; 4. Periodic review stochastic demand models; 5. Continuous review stochastic demand models; 6. Application of inventory theory in industry.

2. Models with constant demand rates

In this section we introduce a class of models that is based on the simplest demand assumption: demand is deterministic and stationary. We concentrate primarily on the case where the demand rate is constant and not anticipated to change.

Although the assumption of deterministic and stationary demands seems quite restrictive, models requiring that assumption are still important for the following reasons. First, many results are quite robust with respect to the model parameters, such as the demand rate and costs. The Economic Order Quantity (EOQ) model is an excellent example. Second, the results obtained from these simple models are often good starting solutions for more complex models. This point will be more transparent in Section 4.

2.1. The basic EOQ model

The assumptions of the basic EOQ model are:

(1) Demand is known with certainty and fixed at λ units per unit time.

(2) Shortages are not permitted.

(3) Lead time for delivery is instantaneous.

(4) There is no time discounting of money. The objective is to minimize average costs per unit time over an infinite time horizon.

(5) Costs include K per order, and h per unit held per unit time.

The unit holding cost h is composed of the cost of physical storage (e.g., handling, insurance, taxes, warehousing) h' and the cost of capital invested in inventory. Let I be the capital cost per dollar of inventory investment, and c be the unit cost of the item, then $h = h' + Ic$.

Since delivery lead time is instantaneous and demand is known with certainty, one only orders whenever the inventory level hits zero. Suppose the order size is Q. Define the cycle time as the time between two successive arrivals of orders, called T. Note that $T = Q/\lambda$. Since all cycles are identical, the average cost per unit time is simply the total cost incurred in a single cycle divided by the cycle length.

In each cycle, the order cost is K. Consider a cycle from time $t = 0$ to T. The total holding cost incurred in a cycle is

$$h \int_0^T (Q - \lambda t)\,\mathrm{d}t = h(QT - \tfrac{1}{2}\lambda T^2) = \tfrac{1}{2}hTQ\,.$$

Figure 1 describes the inventory level during cycles. It follows that the total average cost per unit time is

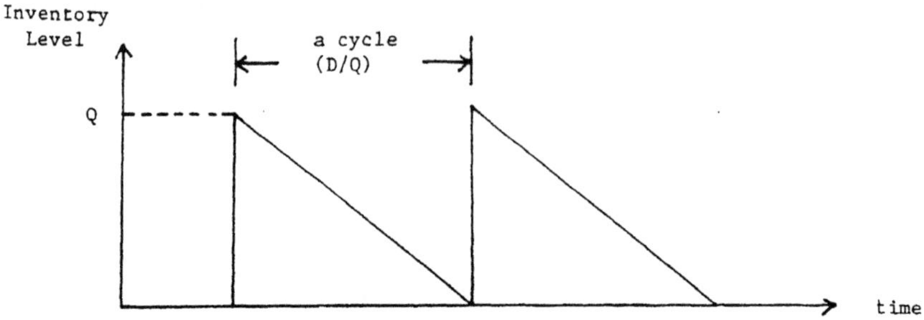

Fig. 1. Inventory level during cycles.

$$C(Q) = (K + \tfrac{1}{2}hTQ)/T = K\lambda/Q + \tfrac{1}{2}hQ\ .$$

$C(Q)$ is convex in Q. To find the Q which minimizes $C(Q)$ we solve $\mathrm{d}C/\mathrm{d}Q = 0$. The optimal solution Q^*, commonly known as the EOQ, is:

$$Q^* = \sqrt{2K\lambda/h}\ . \tag{2.1}$$

When there is a positive lead time of, say, τ time units, then one merely places each order τ units of time before the inventory level hits zero.

Substituting Q^* in the expression for $C(Q)$, one gets $C(Q^*) = \sqrt{2K\lambda h}$. It is easy to show that

$$\frac{C(Q)}{C(Q^*)} = \frac{1}{2}\left[\frac{Q^*}{Q} + \frac{Q}{Q^*}\right].$$

If $Q^*/Q = 2$, then $C(Q)/C(Q^*) = 1.25$. This means that an error of 100% in Q results in an increase in the average costs of only 25%. Hence, if there are errors in the estimation of the cost and demand parameters, the resultant error in Q may not result in a substantial cost penalty. The EOQ formula has thus been found to be extremely insensitive in average costs to errors in parameter estimation [see Hadley & Whitin, 1963; Silver & Peterson, 1985].

A natural extension of the basic EOQ model is the Economic Manufacturing Quantity (EMQ) model (also called EPQ for Economic Production Quantity). In the EMQ model, an order of stock does not arrive instantaneously but instead, stock is produced at a finite rate of ψ per unit time, where $\psi > \lambda$. Here, while production of a batch is underway, stock is accumulating at a rate of $\psi - \lambda$ per unit time. The total time of production in a cycle is Q/ψ, so that the peak level of inventory in a cycle is $(\psi - \lambda)Q/\psi$. The total inventory held in a cycle is thus $(\psi - \lambda)QT/2\psi$. Proceeding as with the EOQ model, we obtain the optimal lot size Q^*, called the EMQ, as:

$$Q^* = \sqrt{2K\lambda\psi/h(\psi - \lambda)}\ . \tag{2.2}$$

As ψ goes to infinity, (2.2) becomes the EOQ.

The EOQ model assumes an average cost per unit time criterion. It ignores the time value of money. It is easy to generalize the model to the case of discounted costs. Let r be the continuous discount factor, and consider the present value of total costs. The resulting EOQ value can be approximated by the use of Maclaurin expansion [see Jesse, Mitra & Cox, 1983; Porteus, 1985b]:

$$Q^* = \sqrt{2K\lambda/(h' + rc)}\,. \tag{2.3}$$

Recall that h' is the component of the inventory cost due to cost of capital only.

As it turns out, (2.3) is exactly the same as (2.1) with I replaced by r. Hadley [1964] compared the above formula with the exact solution of Q^* and found that the approximation is excellent.

When the time horizon is finite, and beginning and ending inventory levels are constrained to be zero, the optimal order sizes within the time horizon have been shown to be all equal to $\lambda T/n^*$ [Schwarz, 1972], where T is the time horizon, and n^* is the smallest integer satisfying

$$T \leqslant \left[\frac{2n(n+1)K}{\lambda(1-\lambda/\psi)h}\right]^{1/2}.$$

Schwarz [1977] showed that if T corresponds to a duration of 5-EOQ's worth of supply, the cost penalty of operating under the optimal finite horizon policy instead of the infinite horizon is only 1%.

In the remainder of this section, we consider several extensions of the basic EOQ model under infinite time horizons.

2.2. *Quantity discounts*

In the basic EOQ model, the unit procurement cost of the item is assumed to be independent of the order size, and hence has been excluded from consideration in the cost function. In many situations, the supplier is willing to charge less per unit for larger orders, thus providing an incentive to increase the lot size. Three types of discount schedules are most commonly used: (1) a continuous discount schedule where the price of the item is a continuous (often linear) function of the order size [Ladany & Sternlieb, 1974; Rosenblatt & Lee, 1985], (2) an all units discount schedule in which the lower unit cost is applied to all of the units in the order [Hadley & Whitin, 1963], and (3) incremental discount which is applied only to the additional units beyond some breakpoint [Hadley & Whitin, 1963; Hax & Candea, 1984]. The example in Table 1 illustrates the distinction between the all units and incremental discount schedules.

With a quantity discount, the cost function for determining the optimal lot size would have to include the average procurement cost. Moreover, the unit

Table 1

Order size Q	All unit discount		Incremental discount	
	Unit cost	Total cost	Unit cost	Total cost
$0 < Q < 100$	1.00	$Q \times 1.00$	1.00	$Q \times 1.00$
$100 \leq Q < 200$	0.98	$Q \times 0.98$	0.98	$100 \times 1.00 + (Q - 100) \times 0.98$
$200 \leq Q$	0.95	$Q \times 0.95$	0.95	$100 \times 1.00 + 100 \times 0.98 + (Q - 200) \times 0.95$

holding cost would change as a result of changing unit cost of the item due to a change of the lot size. With the continuous discount schedule, determining the optimal solution may require solving a transcendental equation, so that the optimal lot size would have to be obtained by numerical search.

For the all units quantity discounts schedule, assume several price breaks $b_1, b_2, \ldots, b_i, \ldots, b_m$, such that if the order lot size Q is within discount interval i, i.e., $b_{i-1} \leq Q < b_i$, then the unit price for each of the Q units is c_i, where $c_i < c_{i-1}$, and m is the number of discount intervals. Let I be the rate per dollar of carrying inventory. The average cost per unit time if discount level i is used is:

$$C_i(Q) = c_i\lambda + K\lambda/Q + \tfrac{1}{2}(h' + Ic_i)Q .$$

It can be shown that the optimal Q^* must be either the EOQ for some discount level, or one of the breakpoints of some discount interval. Hence, to find the Q^*, we can proceed by determining the individual Q_i's that optimize $C_i(Q)$ subject to the constraint $b_{i-1} < Q \leq b_i$, respectively (which should either be the EOQ for discount level i, b_{i-1}, or b_i). Hadley & Whitin [1963] suggested an efficient algorithm for finding Q^*.

For the incremental quantity discounts schedule, suppose the first b_1 units cost c_1 each, the next $(b_2 - b_1)$ units cost c_2 each, and, in general, the units in the (b_{i-1}, b_i) interval cost c_i each, with $c_i < c_{i-1}$ and b_0 defined to be 0. Suppose Q lies in $[b_{i-1}, b_i)$, then the purchase cost of a lot of size Q is given by:

$$P_i = \sum_{j=1}^{i-1} c_j(b_j - b_{j-1}) + c_i(Q - b_{i-1}) .$$

The total cost per unit time for discount schedule i is thus:

$$C_i(Q) = (K + P_i)\lambda/Q + \tfrac{1}{2}(h' + IP_i) .$$

As $C_i(Q)$ has basically the same form as the cost function of the EOQ model, it is straightforward to find the optimal Q_i that minimizes $C_i(Q)$. The overall global optimal Q^* is again obtained by searching over the various intervals.

2.3. Learning effects

Learning effects are said to exist when, as cumulative production volume increases, the unit production cost or time decreases as a result of the experiences gained. The implication to the lot-sizing problem is that the production cost is not constant over time.

When there are learning effects, three modifications for the basic EOQ model are required. First, learning effects can result in lower manufacturing costs [Keachie & Fontana, 1966; Muth & Spremann, 1983; Smunt & Morton, 1985]. Second, learning effects can increase the production rate as the cumulative production volume increases. Hence, the production time for a lot of Q units is no longer linear in Q [Adler & Nanda, 1974; Sule, 1978; Fisk & Ballou, 1982]. Third, the lower manufacturing cost as a result of learning lowers the inventory carrying cost [Wortham & Mayyasi, 1972; Smunt & Morton, 1985]. The second and third effects can only be analyzed in a finite time horizon.

With the presence of learning, one would also have to specify how the effects of learning are carried over from one production cycle to another. Between one production run and another, there will be time when items are not being produced. During this time, it is possible that some 'forgetting' or 'unlearning' will occur, so that at the time of the next production run, the unit manufacturing cost is not the same as that of the last production run. The term 'transmission' of learning is usually used in this context. When there is perfect transmission of learning, then the unit manufacturing cost will decrease at a rate independent of the lot size. Hence, if the holding cost is constant over time, i.e., the third effect of learning does not exist, then the learning effect should have no impact on the optimal EOQ. Most of the studies focus on partial or no transmission of learning. Again, the effect of partial transmission of learning can be meaningfully studied for the finite horizon case. Here we illustrate the case with no transmission of learning.

Let $y(i)$ = cost of the ith unit in a production run of Q, $i \leq Q$. Then the learning curve function specifies that as cumulative production increases by a constant percentage, unit cost decreases by a constant percentage. This relationship gives rise to the following functional form of the learning curve: $y(i) = ai^{-b}$, where a is the cost of the first and b is the rate of cost decrease, $0 < b < 1$.

The cumulative average cost per unit, for a lot size of Q, is:

$$(1/Q) \sum_{i=1}^{Q} y(i) = aQ^{-b}/(1-b) ,$$

which is obtained by approximating $\Sigma_{i=1}^{Q} y(i)$ by $\int_0^Q i^{-b}\, di$.

The optimal Q^* minimizes

$$C(Q) = K\lambda/Q + \tfrac{1}{2}hQ + aQ^{-b}/(1-b) .$$

2.4. Uncertainty in orders received

The basic EOQ model assumes that the amount received is the same as the amount ordered, i.e., Q. In many inventory systems, this may not be the case. Recognizing that production processes are often imperfect so that production yields may be random, there has been considerable interest in inventory models where the amount received is uncertain.

Let Y = the amount received given lot size Q, and $\mathrm{E}(Y \mid Q)$ and $\mathrm{V}(Y \mid Q)$ be the expectation and variance of Y, respectively. Because the beginning of a cycle is a regeneration point for a renewal process, and thus the expected average costs per unit time, $C(Q)$, is the ratio of the expected cost per cycle, and the expected cycle length. The expected cycle length is now given by $\mathrm{E}(Y \mid Q)/\lambda$. We thus have:

$$C(Q) = \frac{K + h\{\mathrm{V}(Y \mid Q) + [\mathrm{E}(Y \mid Q)]^2\}/2\lambda}{\mathrm{E}(Y \mid Q)/\lambda} .$$

The optimal Q^* minimizes $C(Q)$. Explicit expressions for Q^* have been derived for specific forms of the density function of Y, given Q [see Silver, 1976; Shih, 1980].

Recently, Porteus [1986] and Rosenblatt & Lee [1986] have independently incorporated the effect of defective items into the basic EOQ model. An order would initiate the production process to produce Q units. The production process is either in control and defect-free items are produced, or out of control and defective items are produced. Defective items can be reworked instantaneously at a cost. The production process begins in the in-control state after a setup is performed. At some point in time, the process goes out of control, and would remain in that state until the next setup, which corrects the process back in control. Two essentially equivalent assumptions are used: Porteus [1986] assumes that there is a probability q that the process would go out of control while producing one unit of the product; whereas Rosenblatt & Lee [1986] assume that the time between the beginning of the production run (in the in-control state) until the process goes out of control is exponential with mean $1/\mu$. In Rosenblatt & Lee [1986], once the process is out of control, a fraction α of the items produced is assumed to be defective. Let s be the unit rework cost. The total cost functions now consist of the usual setup and holding costs, plus the rework costs. Using approximations based on Maclaurin expansions, Porteus [1986] and Rosenblatt & Lee [1986] obtained explicit modifications to the EOQ and the EMQ formula, respectively:

$$Q^* = \left[\frac{2K\lambda}{h + \lambda q s}\right]^{1/2} ,$$

$$Q^* = \left[\frac{2k\lambda\psi}{h(\psi - \lambda) + \alpha\mu\lambda s}\right]^{1/2} .$$

It can be seen that the above Q^*'s are smaller than the EOQ or the EMQ. Thus, the presence of defective products motivates smaller lot sizes. Numerical results show that, even though the probability of the shift is usually very small, the cost penalty for not incorporating the effects of defective items can be significant. In later work, Lee & Rosenblattt [1987] considered using process inspection during the production run so that the shift to the out-of-control state can be detected and restorations made earlier.

2.5. Pricing and perishability

In the EOQ model, the demand rate λ is assumed to be constant and independent of the lot size. The model can be easily extended to include the effects of marketing policies. Ladany & Sternlieb [1974] formulated such an extension by considering net profit as the objective. The net profit is $\lambda[P - c(Q)]$ minus the ordering and holding costs, where P is the unit selling price and $c(Q)$ is the procurement or unit production cost as a function of Q. The selling price P is modelled as a fixed mark-up of the unit cost, and hence is a function of Q. Also the demand rate λ is a function of the selling price. Normally, for a downward sloping demand curve, λ is decreasing in P. The implication of such a formulation is that the objective function is a much more complex function of the lot size. By making simple assumptions on the form of $c(Q)$ and the relationship of λ and P, closed form expressions for the optimal lot size can be obtained [Ladany & Sternlieb, 1974; Lee & Rosenblatt, 1986]. In general, however, search routines would have to be used to find the optimal lot size.

P may be considered to be a decision variable, instead of a given function of Q. This is the approach taken by Whitin [1955] and Cohen [1977]. In this case, the EOQ is still the optimal lot size, although the optimal price can rarely be expressed in closed form.

The EOQ extensions for perishable items usually assume exponential decay of the items [Ghare & Schrader, 1963; Cohen, 1977]. Let μ be the stock decay rate and $I(t)$ be the one hand inventory at time t. The differential equation describing the time behavior of the inventory level is $\mathrm{d}I(t)/\mathrm{d}t = -\mu I(t) - \lambda$, from which one obtains $I(t)$ as:

$$I(t) = I(0)\exp(-\mu t) - (\lambda/\mu)[1 - \exp(-\mu t)] .$$

Using the boundary condition $I(0) = Q$, one can compute the inventory costs in a cycle. The total cost function should also include the costs of the decayed items. Let c be the unit cost of an item. Using approximations based on the Maclaurin series, the optimal Q^* that minimizes expected costs is:

$$Q^* = \sqrt{2K\lambda/(c\mu + h)} .$$

It can be seen that the optimal lot size is similar to the EOQ, with a modification of the holding costs to include the cost of item decay.

2.6. *Announced price increase*

The basic EOQ model assumes that all cost parameters remain unchanged during the time horizon. Extensions exist which allow these parameters to change after a known future point in time. Most of these studied [e.g., Lev & Soyster, 1979; Lev, Weiss & Soyster, 1981; Aggarwal, 1981; Taylor & Bradley, 1985] focus on the unit cost of the item. In particular, it is assumed that there is an announced price increase at some future point in time. Obviously, after the new price is in effect, the optimal order size should be the new EOQ based on the new price to compute the inventory holding cost. The problem is, what should the ordering policy be between the announcement of the price increase (at time 0) and the time at which the new price becomes effective (at time τ)?

Before the price increase, the ordering policy is the EOQ based on the current price. Depending on whether there exist regular 'scheduled' replenishment orders under the current EOQ between times 0 and τ, different results are obtained [Taylor & Bradley, 1985]. If τ is small so that there does not exist any current EOQ orders between times 0 and τ, then we may want to place a special order just prior to τ, under the current price, to be consumed after τ. The optimal policy is that a special order should be placed if the inventory level just prior to τ is less than some threshold, which is a function of the EOQ model parameters, and the current and new prices, but is independent of τ. Otherwise, no special order should be placed.

Suppose τ is large enough so that there exist current EOQ orders between times 0 and τ, let τ_1 be the time between the first current EOQ order time and τ. If τ_1 is very small or very large, then Taylor and Bradley showed that it is optimal to modify the current EOQ so that the inventory level just prior to τ will be zero, and to place a special order at τ. If τ_1 is of intermediate value, then it is optimal to continue using the current EOQ ordering policy, but place a special order at the time when the last EOQ order is placed prior to τ.

2.7. *Inflation*

Instead of a one-time increase in the future, the EOQ model can also incorporate inflationary conditions. Consider the EOQ model with discount rate r for the time value of money. Suppose there is an inflation rate of ζ, $\zeta < r$, so that all costs are increasing continuously at a rate of ζ per year. Such a formulation is actually equivalent to stating that the 'effective discount rate' is $r - \zeta$. The resulting modified EOQ is thus the same as given by (2.1.3), with r replaced by $r - \zeta$ [see Trippi & Lewin, 1974; Jesse, Mitra & Cox, 1983]. Buzacott [1975] and Kanet & Miles [1985] obtained essentially the same result for the total cost approach. When $\zeta > r$, then the total cost function is unbounded for an infinite horizon, and only the finite horizon analysis is meaningful [Bierman & Thomas, 1977].

2.8. Demand with trends

When demand is deterministic but follows some known trend, the optimal ordering policy is much more complicated. Resh, Friedman & Barbosa [1976] solved the problem for the linear trend case. Suppose time starts at the origin, and the demand rate at time t is given by $\lambda(t) = \lambda t$. Consider first a finite horizon T. Let $t_0, t_1, \ldots, t_{m-1}$ be the replenishment times, and $Q_0, \ldots, Q_{m-1}$ be the respective order quantities. Hence, there are m replenishments throughout T. Define $t_m = T$. Let $y_i(t)$ be the inventory level at t, $t_i \leq t \leq t_{i+1}$, $i = 0, \ldots, m-1$. Then,

$$Q_i = \int_{t_i}^{t_{i+1}} \lambda(t)\,\mathrm{d}t = \lambda(t_{i+1}^2 - t_i^2)/2\lambda$$

and

$$y_i(t) = Q_i - \int_{t_i}^{t} \lambda(u)\,\mathrm{d}u = \lambda(t_{i+1}^2 - t^2)/2\lambda\,.$$

Given m, the total inventory costs in T can then be computed. Resh, Friedman & Barbosa [1976] provided an efficient algorithm to compute the optimal values of t_i's, from which the optimal total cost for a given m can be obtained. Such a cost is shown to be convex in m, so that the optimal m^* can be readily found. Of interest is the infinite horizon case, i.e., when m^* goes to infinity. For a given m^*, there is a range of T such that m^* remains unchanged. For this m^*, Resh, Friedman and Barbosa showed that

$$t_i^* = A_i(2K/\lambda h)^{1/3}\,, \quad i = 1, \ldots, m^* - 1\,, \tag{2.4}$$

where A_i's are constants that are functions of m^* and i only. It can be shown that each t_i^* converges to a limit as m^* tends to infinity. Moreover, (2.4) compares rather strikingly with the EOQ cycle length, which is given by $(2K/\lambda h)^{1/2}$ for demand rate λ. For this reason, Resh, Friedman & Barbosa termed (2.4) as the 'cubic root law' for a growing market, as opposed to the 'square root law' for a stable market.

Barbosa & Friedman [1978] generalized the above result for the case where demand is given by a power form: $\lambda(t) = \lambda t^a$, $a > -2$. An '$(a+2)$ root law' resulted for the optimal replenishment times over an infinite horizon,

$$t_i^* = L_i[(a+2)K/\lambda h]^{1/(a+2)}\,,$$

where L_i is a constant which is a function of i and a.

3. Models with deterministic time-varying demand

As noted above in Section 1.3 it is generally the assumption about demand that is most important in determining the complexity and structure of an inventory model. In this section we generalize the premise of the previous section to allow demand to be time-varying. However, we will retain the assumption that demand is deterministic.

A continuous review model which allowed for time varying demand was considered in Section 2.8. However, since the vast majority of the research on time-varying demand problem assumes periodic review, we will henceforth restrict attention to that case. Let $(r_1, r_2, \ldots, r_n)$ be known requirements for a single product over the next n periods. Periods are defined as times of replenishment opportunity. Let $(y_1, y_2, \ldots, y_n)$ be the order sizes placed in these periods. For convenience we add the assumption that the order lead time is zero. As with the EOQ type models discussed above, the extension to a positive order lead time is not difficult. One merely translates the order backwards by the number of periods in the lead time. Furthermore, since the models described below are often used in MRP (Material Requirements Planning) settings for production, we will use the terms order sizes and production quantities interchangeably.

3.1. *The Wagner–Whitin model*

The original formulation of this problem is due to Wagner & Whitin [1958] (henceforth referred to as WW). They assume:

(1) Shortages are not permitted.

(2) Starting inventory is zero. This assumption may be relaxed by netting out starting inventory from the first period's (or additional periods', if necessary) demand.

(3) Only linear costs of holding and fixed order costs are present. Note that (3) means that the total cost function is *concave*. WW's results hold under the more general assumption:

(3′) The holding cost is a concave function of the ending inventory in each period[1] and the ordering cost is a concave function of the order quantity in each period.

The ending inventory in period t is given by:

$$x_t = \sum_{j=1}^{t} (y_j - r_j) .$$

Let $h_t(x_t)$ be the holding cost incurred in period t and $c_t(y_t)$ the order cost.

[1] WW assume holding cost is based on starting rather than ending inventory.

The objective is to find non-negative order or production quantities $(y_1, y_2, \ldots, y_n)$ to

$$\text{minimize} \quad \sum_{t=1}^{n} [c_t(y_t) + h_t(x_t)]$$

$$\text{subject to} \quad x_t = \sum_{j=1}^{t} (y_j - r_j)\,,$$

$$x_t \geq 0\,, \quad t = 1, \ldots, n\,,$$

$$x_0 = 0\,.$$

The most common form of the cost functions is:

$$c_t(y_t) = K\delta(y_t) + cy_t$$

and

$$h_t(x_t) = hx_t\,,$$

where $\delta(y_t)$ equals 1 if $y_t > 0$, and 0 otherwise.

Wagner and Whitin developed an efficient algorithm for solving this problem which was based on the following observation.

Result. *An optimal ordering policy has the property*

$$y_t x_{t-1} = 0\,, \quad t = 1, 2, \ldots, n\,.$$

This means $y_t > 0$ only if $x_{t-1} = 0$ or in words, ordering takes place only in periods when starting inventory is zero. A little reflection will show that this result means that $y_t = 0,\ r_t,\ r_t + r_{t+1}, \ldots, r_t + r_{t+1} + \cdots + r_n$, are the only permissible values for y_t. If not, it could happen that for some t, $0 < x_{y-1} < r_t$ and ordering would have to occur to avoid shortages.

The optimal policy is then an 'exact requirements' policy and is completely specified by the periods in which ordering is to occur. The optimal policy may be found by finding the shortest path through an acyclic network with nodes labelled $1, 2, \ldots, n+1$ and arcs (i, j) connecting all pairs of nodes with $i < j$. The length of the arc connecting nodes i and j, c_{ij}, is the cost of ordering in period i to satisfy requirements through period $j-1$, where $i < j \leq n+1$, and

$$c_{ij} = c_i\left(\sum_{k=i}^{j-1} r_k\right) + \sum_{k=i}^{j-2} h_k\left(\sum_{l=k+1}^{j-1} r_l\right).$$

Given the values of c_{ij} for $1 \leq i < j \leq n+1$, one may find the optimal order policy by solving either a backwards or forwards dynamic program. The backward formulation is:

$$f_i = \min_{j>i} (c_{ij} + f_j) \quad \text{for } i = 1, \ldots, n ,$$

$$f_{n+1} = 0 .$$

Interpret f_i as the cost of following an optimal policy when i periods remain. The optimal solution is found by re-tracing the optimal values of j. The procedure is best illustrated by example. (This example appears in more detail in Nahmias [1989]).

Example. Suppose $\boldsymbol{r} = (52, 87, 23, 56)$, $c_t(y) = K\delta(y)$, where $K = 75$ for $t = 1, \ldots, 4$, and $h_t(x) = hx$, where $h = 1$ for $t = 1, \ldots, 4$.

Then the dynamic programming equations yield:

$$f_5 = 0 ,$$

$$f_4 = 75 \quad \text{at } j = 5 ,$$

$$f_3 = 131 \quad \text{at } j = 5 ,$$

$$f_2 = 173 \quad \text{at } j = 4 ,$$

$$f_1 = 241 \quad \text{at } j = 2 .$$

The optimal solution is determined in the following manner. Because the minimizing value of f_1 occurs at $j = 2$, one orders in period 1 and again in period 2. Since the minimizing value of f_2 occurs at $j = 4$, one orders in period 2 and not again until period 4. Finally one must order in period 4 to satisfy the requirement in that period. Hence the optimal policy is

$$y_1 = r_1 = 52 ,$$

$$y_2 = r_2 + r_3 = 110 ,$$

$$y_3 = 0 ,$$

$$y_4 = r_4 = 56 .$$

3.2. *Planning horizons*

Wagner and Whitin's work sparked considerable interest in the concave cost dynamic lot size problem. One area of interest is planning horizons. Wagner and Whitin's original observation was the following.

WW Planning Horizon Theorem. *Let $l(t)$ be the last period a set-up occurs for the optimal order policy associated with a t period problem. Then for any problem of length $t^* > t$ it is necessary to consider only periods $l(t) \leq j \leq t^*$ as candidate periods for the last set-up. Furthermore, if $l(t) = t$, the optimal solution to a t^* period problem has $y_t > 0$. In the latter case, periods 1, 2, . . . , $t-1$ constitute a planning horizon.*

What is the advantage of locating a planning horizon? Its identification means that the optimal policy for periods 1, 2, . . . , $t-1$ does not depend upon the demand forecasts beyond period t. When a forward algorithm is used to compute the optimal policy, the computations can go forward from the end of the last planning horizon rather than from period 1.

Additional results on planning horizons for the no backlog case were obtained by Zabel [1969], Eppen, Gould & Pashigian [1969], and Lundin & Morton [1975], and for the backlog case by Blackburn & Kunreuther [1974]. Planning horizons are, we feel, of more theoretical than practical interest. The WW algorithm (forward or backward) is extremely efficient. As one extends the length of the horizon the salient issue is forecast accuracy and not computational efficiency.

3.3. Backordering

Zangwill [1966a] generalizes the work of WW to allow for backordering of demand. When backordering is permitted the fundamental structural result of WW that $y_t > 0$ only if $x_t = 0$, where x_t is the starting inventory of period t, generalizes to $y_t > 0$ only if $x_t \leq 0$. Furthermore an optimal policy still orders exact requirements. That is, there exist integers $0 = S_0 \leq S_1 \leq \cdots \leq S_n = n$ such that:

$$y_t = 0 \quad \text{if } S_{t-1} = S_t \,,$$

and

$$y_t = \sum_{j=1+S_{t-1}}^{S_t} r_j \quad \text{for } 1 \leq t \leq n \,.$$

Backorders occur when $S_t < t$.

Zangwill's analysis permitted general concave holding and shortage costs and a limit on the number of periods a backorder stays on the books. He gave a forward dynamic programming algorithm for computing the optimal policy. An extension of these results to allow for multiple products and echelons appears in Zangwill [1966b].

3.4. *Heuristic methods*

There has been considerable interest in approximate solutions to the basic WW lot sizing model. In some sense this is surprising since dynamic programming efficiently finds the optimal solution. Production lot-sizing plays an important role in MRP and practitioners have shied away from incorporating dynamic programming into their planning systems. Hence there is strong interest in more intuitively appealing heuristic methods. Also, the heuristics often provide more stable solutions in a rolling horizon environment in which demand forecasts are revised periodically. We discuss a number of better known methods.

3.4.1. *The Silver–Meal heuristic*

This method, due to Silver & Meal [1973], is a forward algorithm that requires computing the average cost per period as a function of the number of periods in the current order horizon.

Define $C(T)$ = the average cost of holding and setup per period if the current order spans the next T periods.

If $(r_1, \ldots, r_n)$ are the requirements over the next n periods and all costs are constant, it follows that

$$C(T) = [K + hr_1 + 2hr_2 + \cdots + (T-1)hr_T]/T .$$

The method is to compute $C(T)$ for $T = 1, 2, \ldots,$ stop the first time that $C(T) > C(T-1)$, and set $y_1 = \Sigma_{j=1}^{T-1} r_j$. The process is started again at period T and continues until the end of the horizon is reached.

3.4.2. *Part period balancing*

Part period balancing is generally credited to DeMatteis [1968]. Like the Silver–Meal heuristic, the method finds the length of the horizon to be spanned by the current order. The horizon length is that whose total holding cost most closely matches the set-up cost.

Example. Consider the previous example with

$$\boldsymbol{r} = (52, 87, 23, 56), \qquad K = 75, \qquad h = 1 .$$

(a) Solving by the Silver–Meal heuristic:

Starting in period 1:

$C(1) = 75$

$C(2) = (75 + 87)/2 = 81.$

Stop and set $y_1 = r_1 = 52.$

Starting in period 2:

$C(1) = 75$

$C(2) = (75 + 23)/2 = 49$

$C(3) = [75 + 23 + (2)(56)]/3 = 70.$
Stop and set $y_2 = r_2 + r_3 = 110$.
Finally $y_4 = 56$.
The Silver–Meal solution is $\boldsymbol{y} = (52, 110, 0, 56)$.

(b) Solving by part period balancing:
Starting in period 1:

Order horizon	Total holding cost
1	0
2	87

Since the set-up cost of 75 is closer to 87 than 0, set $y_1 = r_1 + r_2 = 139$ and commence the process again in period 3.

Starting in period 3:

Order horizon	Total holding cost
1	0
2	56

Since the set-up cost of 75 has not yet been reached, set $y_3 = r_3 + r_4 = 79$. The part period balancing solution is thus: $\boldsymbol{y} = (139, 0, 79, 0)$.

For this example, Silver–Meal gives the optimal solution while part period balancing does not. The cost of the optimal solution is $(75)(3) + (1)(23) = 248$. The cost of the part period balancing solution is $(75)(2) + (1)(87 + 56) = 293$.

It has been demonstrated that as the number of periods grows without bound, the relative error of Silver–Meal can be arbitrarily large [Axsäter, 1982] but the relative error of part period balancing is bounded by 3 [Bitran, Magnanti & Yanasse, 1984]. This might suggest that part period balancing is a better heuristic. However, worst-case performance is not necessarily an accurate indicator for the effectiveness of a heuristic. In fact, simulation studies [Silver & Peterson, 1985] indicate that on average Silver–Meal is a better performer. (A more extensive discussion of heuristics is given by Baker in Chapter 11 of this volume.)

3.5. Capacitated lot sizing

Practically speaking, an important generalization of WW is the case where there are upper bounds on the production quantities each period. That is, there are capacities $U_1, U_2, \ldots, U_n$, such that $y_i \leqslant U_i$, for $1 \leqslant i \leqslant n$. Limiting production capacity each period significantly alters the properties of the optimal solution, and the computational complexity of the optimal solution procedure.

Florian & Klein [1971] have discovered a solution procedure based on the following property of an optimal policy: between any two periods in which starting inventory is zero there is at most one period in which production is neither zero nor at capacity. They constructed a solution algorithm based on solving a collection of acyclic network problems. In general, however, the method is quite tedious. Love [1973] also obtained a characterization of the optimal policy under a more general model structure, but his results do not lead to an efficient algorithm in general.

The most computationally efficient method of solving the problem optimally seems to be the one proposed by Baker, Dixon, Magazine & Silver [1978]. They developed a tree search algorithm based on properties of an optimal solution. Still the authors note that, in the worst case, their algorithm is not computationally effective. For example, a typical 24 period problem required the solution of 18 000 different subproblems.

Because of the computational complexity of optimal solution algorithms, approximate methods are of interest. Heuristic methods for solving the capacitated problem have been explored by Dixon & Silver [1981] and Karni [1981]. These heuristics involve determining a feasible solution and subsequently combining lots to reduce setups. Nahmias [1989] considers such a method in the context of material requirements planning.

A number of researchers have considered multi-item lot-sizing subject to capacity constraints. We will not review these methods here but refer the interested reader to Chapter 8 of this volume.

3.6. Convex costs

In the production planning context, concave costs arise much more frequently than do convex costs. The primary reason is that if a fixed set-up cost is present and all other costs are linear (a common situation), then the production cost function is concave. Furthermore, concavity occurs when there are declining marginal costs of production or other scale economies present. There are some cases, however, where costs are convex rather than concave functions. An example is where fixed costs are negligible, and there is a capacity constraint on production. Another example is where there are several sources of limited production which are used in order to ascending costs. This occurs in the generation of electric power. As with the WW model above, the problem is to find non-negative production quantities $(y_1, y_2, \ldots, y_n)$ to:

$$\text{minimize} \quad \sum_{t=1}^{n} C_t(y_t) + h_t(x_t)$$

$$\text{subject to} \quad x_t = \sum_{j=1}^{t} (y_j - r_j),$$

where x_t can be positive or negative. Interpret $C_t(y_t)$ as the cost of producing y_t in period t, $h_t(x_t)$ as the cost of holding x_t in period t if $x_t > 0$, and the cost of backordering x_t in period t if $x_t < 0$. The functions C_t and h_t are assumed to be convex functions of their arguments for $1 \leq t \leq n$.

Veinott [1964] has developed a parametric algorithm for solving this problem. It is based on the observation that if costs are convex, the optimal production quantities are non-decreasing functions of the requirements. Including the additional assumption that the cost functions are piecewise linear with endpoints on the integers assures that the optimal production amounts are also integral.

Assume that backorders are not permitted and suppose $(y_1, \ldots, y_n)$ is an optimal production plan for $(r_1, \ldots, r_n)$. Then Veinott proved that $(y_1, \ldots, y_j + 1, \ldots, y_n)$ is optimal for the requirements schedule $(r_1, \ldots, r_i + 1, \ldots, r_n)$ where $1 \leq i \leq n$ and $1 \leq j \leq n$. Since $y_i = 0$ is almost always optimal for $r_i = 0$, $1 \leq i \leq n$, a solution procedure is to start with a zero requirements vector and increase a component of the requirements vector by one unit and find the component of production that increases by simply comparing the costs of the n possibilities. This process is continued until the original requirements vector is obtained. A more complex procedure is required when backordering is permitted.

3.7. Lot sizing and materials requirements planning

As noted earlier in this section, one of the most important applications of dynamic lot sizing algorithms is Materials Requirements Planning (MRP) systems [see, e.g., Orlicky, 1975, and Chapter 11 of this volume]. Briefly, MRP is the means by which a set of forecasts for an end item (known as the master production schedule) are converted to requirements for raw materials and subassemblies. At each stage of the system production lot sizes must be determined over the appropriate planning horizon.

Several problems arise when considering multi-level lot-sizing problems which are not present in the single-level problem. Capacity constraints may render independent single-level solutions infeasible, thus making multi-level optimization desirable problems related to rolling horizons [Carlson, Jucker & Kropp, 1982] and nervousness [Carlson, Beckman & Kropp, 1979; Kropp & Carlson, 1984] also affect the choice of a lot sizing algorithm. We merely note these issues here and refer the interested reader to Baker's more in depth treatment in Chapter 11 of this volume.

4. Periodic review stochastic demand models

The majority of research in inventory has been focused on stochastic demand models. These models are more sophisticated and usually provide a better description of reality. Because of their importance, we will consider separately discrete time and continuous time cases.

4.1. The newsboy model

The newsboy model is the basis for most discrete time stochastic inventory models. It applies when the product's useful life is only one planning period. This would be the case when a product perishes quickly such as fresh produce, certain short-lived style goods, or newspapers (hence the name 'newsboy' model). It is more interesting for its structural importance than its applicability.

Suppose that the demand during a period is a random variable D which has known Cumulative Distribution Function (CDF) $F(t)$. For convenience we assume that D is purely continuous. Similar results apply when D is discrete or partially continuous and partially discrete. Let $f(t)$ be the density of one period's demand.

There are several ways to define costs. We adopt the traditional one used by Arrow, Karlin & Scarf [1958] and others. Assume it costs c to purchase one unit, inventory remaining at the end of the period costs h per unit and there is a penalty cost of p per unit of unsatisfied demand. Assume $p > c$.

Suppose the initial inventory on hand at the start of the period is $x \geqslant 0$. The decision variable, y, is the inventory on hand *after* ordering. Hence y may be called the order-up-to-point and satisfies $y \geqslant x$. We assume that the delivery time is zero or small enough so that the order can be used to satisfy the demand during the period.

The number of units remaining on hand at the end of the period is the random variable $y - D$, which may be positive or negative. Denote $X^+ = \max\{X, 0\}$. It follows that the cost incurred in the period for a given y is

$$c(y - x) + h(y - D)^+ + p(D - y)^+ ,$$

which is also a random variable. The usual approach in analyzing such problems is to determine the expectation and choose the decision variable to minimize the expected value. This is generally justified by the Law of Large Numbers. If the decision process is repeated many times, then the average cost per period will be minimized.

The expected cost, $G(y, x)$, is

$$\begin{aligned} G(y, x) &= c(y - x) + h \int_0^y (y - t)f(t)\,dt + p \int_y^\infty (t - y)f(t)\,dt \\ &= G(y) - cx , \end{aligned}$$

where

$$G(y) = cy + h \int_0^y (y - t)f(t)\,dt + p \int_y^\infty (t - y)f(t)\,dt .$$

It is easy to show that $G(y)$ is convex in y so that the minimizing value of y, say y^*, occurs where $G'(y^*) = 0$. Taking the derivative and solving gives

$$F(y^*) = \frac{p - c}{p + h} .$$

The optimal solution is: if $x < y^*$ order $y^* - x$, otherwise do not order. This is known as a critical number policy. Since $F(y^*)$ is the probability that demand does not exceed y^*, the optimal solution occurs where this probability is equal to the critical ratio. Note that the critical ratio is often expressed in the form $c_u/(c_u + c_o)$ where c_u is the underage cost (i.e., $p - c$), and c_o is the overage cost (i.e., $h + c$). Also, the assumption $p > c$ guarantees that the critical ratio is a probability.

The newsboy model may be formulated and solved assuming discrete demand and discrete variables, or with the objective of maximizing profit rather than minimizing costs [see Hadley & Whitin, 1963]. One must be careful to properly interpret costs when applying the model in practice, however. (This issue is discussed in Hillier & Lieberman [1987] and Nahmias [1989].)

4.2. *Dynamic models with no set-up cost*

4.2.1. *The basic model*

Most discrete stochastic inventory problems have been formulated as dynamic programs. Bellman, Glicksberg & Gross [1955] appear to be the first to formulate and analyze dynamic inventory models in this fashion. Assume the same cost structure as in the previous section, but suppose demands in successive periods are IID (Independent Identically Distributed) random variables $D_1, D_2, \ldots$ with common CDF $F(t)$ and density $f(t)$. Define $C_n(x)$ as the minimum expected discounted cost when n periods remain and x is the current inventory level. Assume the discount factor, $0 \leqslant \alpha \leqslant 1$ where $\alpha = 1$ only if $n < \infty$. Furthermore assume zero order lead time. Then the functional equations defining an optimal policy are

$$C_n(x) = \min_{y \geqslant x} \left\{ G(y) - cx + \alpha \int_0^\infty C_{n-1}[s(y, t)] f(t) \, dt \right\} \quad \text{for } n \geqslant 1 ,$$

where $G(y)$ is defined in Section 4.1.

The function $s(y, t)$ is known as the transfer function. If excess demand is backordered then $s(y, t) = y - t$ while if excess demand is lost $s(y, t) = (y - t)^+$. One generally assumes the initial condition $C_0(x) = 0$, although the assumption $C_0(x) = -cx$ (meaning that inventory left at the end of the horizon is returned for the purchase price) leads to a stationary optimal policy (see Section 4.2.4 below).

If $C_0(x) = 0$, then the optimal policy has the form

if $x < y_n$ order up to y_n ,
if $x \geq y_n$ do not order ,

where y_n minimizes the bracketed sum above. It is relatively easy to show that

$$y_1 \geq y_2 \geq \cdots \geq y_\infty .$$

If demand is backordered y_1 solves the newsboy model described in the previous section and y_∞ solves

$$F(y_\infty) = \frac{p - (1 - \alpha)c}{p + h} .$$

Similar results apply in the lost sales case.

4.2.2. Extension to include positive order lead time

When a positive order lead time is included, the complexity of the resulting model is much more sensitive to backlogging assumptions. The dynamic programming formulation now requires a multi-dimensional state variable indicating sizes of all outstanding orders. As Karlin & Scarf [1958] proved, however, as long as excess demand is backordered, the optimal policy depends only on the sum of the on-hand and on-order stock. Furthermore, the optimal policy has the same structure as the zero lead time case although the critical numbers are computed differently.

Unfortunately, when there is a positive order lead time and excess demand is lost rather than backordered, the optimal policy is extremely complex. It is a non-linear function of the vector of outstanding orders. The functional equations defining an optimal policy in the lead time lost sales case are

$$C_n(x_0, x_1, \ldots, x_{T-1}) =$$

$$\min_{y \geq 0} \left\{ cy + L(x_0) + \alpha \int_0^{x_0} C_{n-1}(x_0 + x_1 - t, x_2, \ldots, x_{T-1}, y) f(t)\, \mathrm{d}t \right.$$

$$\left. + \alpha C_{n-1}(x_1, x_2, \ldots, y)(1 - F(x_0)) \right\} ,$$

where T = order lead time in periods, x_0 = inventory on hand, x_i = outstanding order scheduled to arrive in i periods for $1 \leq i \leq T - 1$, y = size of the current order, to be delivered in T periods.

The function $L(x_0)$ is the expected holding and shortage cost in one period if inventory at the start of the period is x_0. When all costs are linear

$$L(x_0) = h \int_0^{x_0} (x_0 - t) f(t)\, \mathrm{d}t + p \int_{x_0}^{\infty} (t - x_0) f(t)\, \mathrm{d}t .$$

Because of the complexity of the optimal policy, approximations are important. Morton [1969] suggests the following approximation for the optimal order quantity assuming infinitely many periods remain in the planning horizon

$$y^* = \min\{y_1^*, y_2^*, \ldots, y_{T+1}^*\},$$

where y_i^* solves

$$F^i(y_i^*) = \frac{p - \alpha^{-T}c}{p + h - \alpha^{-T+1}c},$$

where F^i is the CDF of the i-fold convolution of the one period CDF $F(\cdot)$.

Nahmias [1979] using different methods develops approximations for several lead time lost sales inventory models including a positive set-up cost for ordering, uncertainty in the lead time, and partial backordering of demand.

4.2.3. *Lead time uncertainty*

Kaplan [1970] analyzed an extension of the dynamic lead time model to incorporate lead time uncertainty. What makes the random lead time problem difficult is the way one treats order crossing. If orders are placed with one supplier it is unlikely that they would cross in time; that is, an order placed on Monday should arrive before one placed on Tuesday even though the exact arrival times may not be certain. The difficulty is that if orders are not permitted to cross, successive lead times are dependent random variables. Hadley & Whitin [1963] discuss the order crossing problem.

Kaplan's formulation of the problem was quite ingenious. Let

$$p_i = \Pr\{\text{all orders placed } i \textit{ or more} \text{ periods ago arrive in the current period}\}.$$

This formulation guarantees that orders do not cross since the arrival of an order i periods ago forces the arrival of orders placed $i+1$, $i+2, \ldots, m$ periods ago as well. The likelihood that the lead time is i periods, q_i, may be computed from p_i. It is the values of q_i one would observe in a real system.

Kaplan showed that if there is no order set-up cost, the optimal policy is a critical number policy in every period.

4.2.4. *Batch ordering*

Veinott [1965] discovered a forward formulation of the dynamic problem that leads to several interesting results. In particular he showed that under reasonable assumptions about the salvage value and the transfer function, an n period multi-period dynamic inventory problem can be decomposed into n single-period inventory problems.

As above, let $L(y)$ be the expected one-period holding and shortage cost function. For convenience assume zero order lead time.

Let x_n = starting inventory in period n and y_n be the order-up-to point in period n. Then the expected discounted cost for an N period problem may be written

$$f_N = \mathrm{E}\left\{\sum_{n=1}^{N} \alpha^{n-1}[c(y_n - x_n) + L(y_n)]\right\} - \alpha^N c x_{N+1} .$$

This formulation assumes that the stock remaining at the end of the horizon, x_{N+1}, can be returned at the original purchase price of c. If excess demand is backordered, $x_{n+1} = y_n - D_n$ for $1 \leq n \leq N$. Making this substitution and rearranging terms gives

$$f_N = \sum_{n=1}^{N} \alpha^{n-1}\mathrm{E}\{cy_n(1-\alpha) + L(y_n)\} - cx_1 - \sum_{n=1}^{N} \alpha^n c\lambda$$

$$= \sum_{n=1}^{N} \alpha^{n-1} W(y_n) - cx_1 - \sum_{n=1}^{N} \alpha^n c\lambda ,$$

where $\lambda = \mathrm{E}(D_n)$ for $n = 1, 2, \ldots, N$.

If there are no constraints on y, then the optimal policy is the value of y^* minimizing $W(y)$. Because f_N is the sum of N one period expected cost functions, one can find the form of the optimal policy for the multi-period problem as easily as for the one period. Similar results apply when there is a positive order lead time and excess demand is backordered.

This method can often be used to characterize the form of the optimal policy when there are constraints on y. As an example, suppose the minimum order size is M. This problem is common in dry goods inventory control where items are packaged in groups of six or twelve. Then it is easy to find the optimal policy. Consider Figure 2. If $W(y)$ is a strictly convex function of y there is a

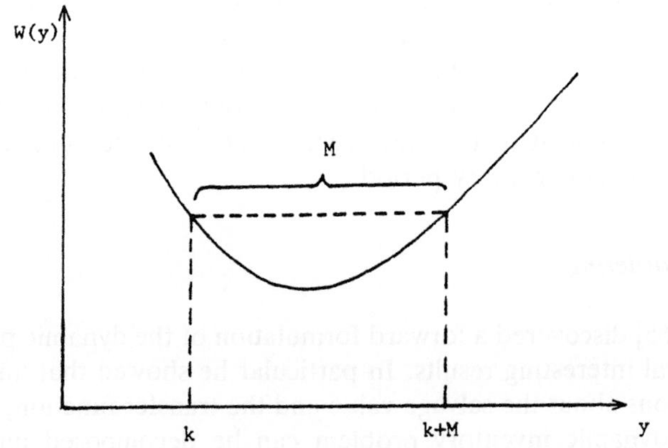

Fig. 2. Optimal policy for batch ordering.

unique value k satisfying $W(k) = W(k + M)$.[2] Suppose in any period that $k < x < k + M$. An order size of one batch brings the inventory level to $x + M > k + M$ and to a necessarily higher cost. Hence it is optimal not to order in this case. If $x < k$ then it is clear that one should order that number of batches that brings the inventory into the interval $[k, k + M]$.

This forward formulation is also useful for characterizing the optimal policy in multiproduct systems with no set-up cost.

4.3. Dynamic models with positive set-up cost

4.3.1. Structure of the optimal policy

A set-up cost for ordering means that the cost of ordering u units is $K\delta(u) + cu$ where

$$\delta(u) = \begin{cases} 0 & \text{if } u = 0\,, \\ 1 & \text{if } u > 0\,. \end{cases}$$

What makes the analysis difficult is that $\delta(u)$ is discontinuous at zero. The form of the optimal policy is easy to derive for a one-period problem, but proving that form is optimal for the multi-period problem is more difficult. The function to be minimized in the newsboy model, $G(y)$, is convex. It appears in Figure 3.

Define S as the value of y at which G is minimized, and s to satisfy $s < S$, $G(s) = G(S) + K$. As above, let x be the starting inventory in a period. If $s \leq x < S$ then $G(x) \leq G(S) + K$ and it is clearly advantageous not to order. If

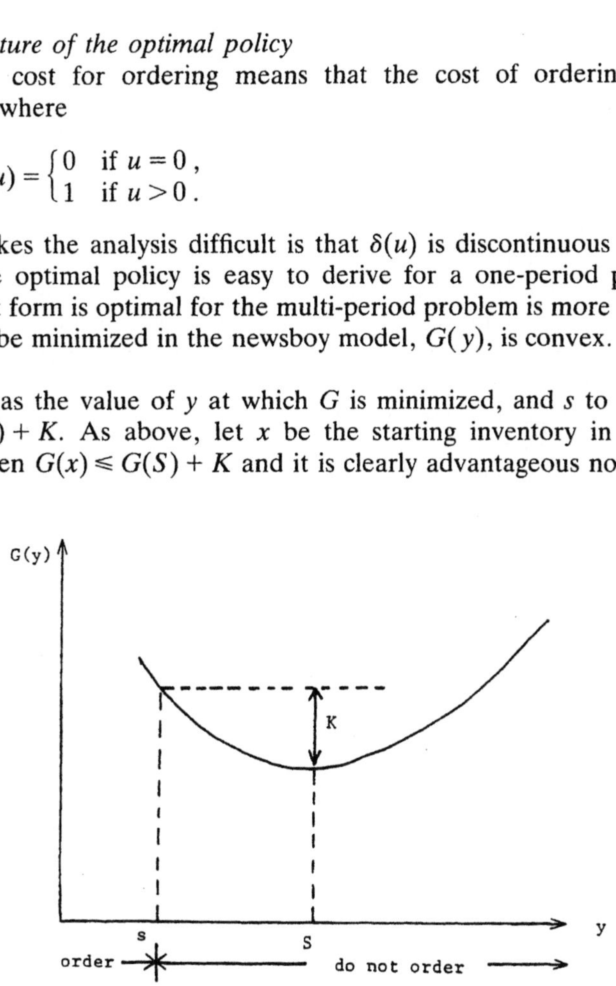

Fig. 3. Optimal policy for the one-period problem with set-up cost.

[2] This holds under somewhat weaker conditions as well. For example if W is strictly quasiconvex.

$x < s$ then $G(x) > G(S) + K$ and it is optimal to order up to S. Hence, the optimal policy is an (s, S) policy:

if $x < s$ order to S (i.e., order $S - x$),
if $x \geq s$ do not order.

The functional equations defining an optimal policy for the multi-period version of the problem are

$$C_n(x) = \min_{y \geq x} \left\{ K\delta(y - x) - cx + G(y) + \alpha \int_0^\infty C_{n-1}(s(y, t))f(t)\, dt \right\}.$$

If we could show that the bracketed term is convex in y, then the arguments above establish that an (s, S) policy is optimal in every period. However, the bracketed term is *not* convex as a function of y. The goal of the analysis is to determine if there is some property possessed by the bracketed term as a function of y for which (s, S) policies remain optimal. This property was discovered by Scarf [1960] and is known as K-convexity. A differentiable function $g(x)$ is K-convex if $K + g(x + y) - g(x) - yg'(x) \geq 0$. Scarf showed that an (s, S) policy is optimal for a K-convex function and established properties of K-convex functions that allowed him to prove inductively that the bracketed term is a K-convex function of y for the case $S(y, t) = y - t$. This property allowed Scarf to show that the form of the optimal policy was (s, S) in every period of a finite horizon problem, although the values of s and S could change from one period to the next. That a stationary (s, S) policy is optimal for the infinite horizon problem was proven by Iglehart [1963].

4.3.2. Generalized (s, S) policies

An order cost function consisting of both proportional and fixed components is a special type of *concave* order cost. More general concave order costs are of interest, since they can be used to describe quantity discounts. Porteus [1971] was able to characterize the form of an optimal policy when the order cost function is concave. For his proof he required the demand density to be a one-sided Polya frequency function. (The definition and the properties of Polya frequency functions are discussed in detail by Karlin [1968].) Porteus calls the optimal policy a generalized (s, S) policy. If the order cost function is piecewise linear concave then the generalized (s, S) policy has the following form. If x is the starting inventory in any period and $y(x)$ the inventory after ordering then there exist $2r$ numbers satisfying $s_r < s_{r-1} < \cdots < s_1 \leq S_1 < S_2 < \cdots < S_r$ such that

$$y(x) = \begin{cases} S_r & \text{for } x < s_r , \\ S_i & \text{for } s_{i+1} \leq x < s_i,\ 1 \leq i \leq r , \\ x & \text{for } x > s_1 . \end{cases}$$

The optimal order-up-to quantity, $y(x)$, is a more complex non-linear function of the starting inventory x when the order cost function is an arbitrary concave function.

4.3.3. Approximations

Optimal (s, S) policies may be computed by either successive approximations using the functional equations [Wagner, O'Hagen & Lund, 1965], by policy iteration methods [Federgruen & Zipkin, 1984], or by Markovian methods [Karlin, 1958]. However, these calculations are generally complex and time consuming. For that reason approximate (s, S) policies are of interest.

Several researchers have suggested methods for computing approximate (s, S) policies. One is based on a continuous review analogue (We discuss continuous review models in the next section.) We will not review all of the methods here but note that Porteus [1985a] has performed a computational comparison of 17 methods. He found that several methods (in particular, two based on his own prior work with Freeland) seemed to perform best. As he notes in his conclusion, stationary (s, S) policies are of only limited interest in practice since the distribution of demand is time varying in most real environments.

From our experience, practitioners seem to favor the continuous review model discussed in the next section and simply recompute the lot size and reorder point on a periodic basis as new estimates of the mean and standard deviation of demand are made. These estimates are generally obtained using a forecasting tool such as simple exponential smoothing.

4.4. Service constraints in periodic review systems

It is often difficult for management to accurately estimate shortage costs. Shortage costs should include both direct costs and indirect costs of shortage. Direct costs include clerical expenses of keeping track of unfilled orders and lost or deferred profit from sales. Indirect costs include disruptions that might result elsewhere in the firm due to shortages of key equipment and loss of customer goodwill. The consequences of loss of customer goodwill are very difficult to gauge. In particular, customers may choose to go elsewhere which means that the pattern of future demand is altered.

Primarily for this reason service levels are very popular in practice. Service levels may be defined in several ways, but two seem to be the most common:

(1) the proportion of periods in which all demand is met;

(2) the proportion of demand satisfied immediately from inventory.

Refer to these as Type 1 and Type 2 measures of service, respectively. One often sees policies determined assuming a Type 1 service level because of its simplicity, but Type 2 service is what one commonly means by service. In order to understand the difference between these two measures consider the following simple example from Nahmias [1989]. Suppose that over ten order cycles the following has occurred:

Order cycle	Demand	Stockouts
1	180	0
2	75	0
3	235	45
4	140	0
5	180	0
6	200	10
7	150	0
8	90	0
9	160	0
10	40	0

Based on a Type 1 service, there were $8/10 = 80\%$ of the periods in which no stockout occurred. However, the Type 2 service measure is much higher. The total number of demands over the ten periods is 1450 (the sum of the entries in column 2) while the total number of demands which could not be met immediately was 55. The proportion of satisfied demands was $1395/1450 = 0.9621$ or slightly more than 96%.

Clearly these measures of service are quite different. As a result, they yield very different operating policies. Other service measures are possible as well. For example one might wish to minimize time weighted backorders or the probability that stockouts do not exceed some critical level.

4.4.1. Service levels when set-up cost is zero

Optimal policies subject to service level constraints for periodic review systems with no order set-up cost are easy to find. Let β_1 be the desired level of Type 1 service and β_2 the desired level of Type 2 service (assume both are expressed as fractions). Because $F(t)$ is the probability distribution of one period's demand and is the probability that demand is less than or equal to t, it follows that the order up to level, say S, should satisfy

$$F(S) = \beta_1$$

for a Type 1 service measure.

For Type 2 service, define $n(S)$ as the expected number of unsatisfied demands at the end of a period when ordering to S. Then

$$n(S) = \mathrm{E}[(D - S)]^+ = \int_S^\infty (x - S) f(x)\,\mathrm{d}x\,,$$

where D is the demand during one period.

If the expected demand per period is λ, then $n(S)/\lambda$ is the expected fraction of demands not satisfied in one period. Since β_2 is the average fraction of demands met in one period, it follows that

$$n(S)/\lambda = 1 - \beta_2\,.$$

When lead time demand is normal with mean λ_T and standard deviation σ_T, $n(S) = \sigma_T L((S - \lambda_T)/\sigma_T)$ where $L(z)$ is the standardized loss integral for which both tables and approximations are available. [See Brown, 1967 for example.]

4.4.2. Service levels when set-up cost is positive

Since set-up costs are common, it is more important to be able to find optimal and suboptimal policies in this case. Unfortunately, computations are just as complex for service levels as they are when penalty costs are used. For this reason approximations are of interest here as well.

One approach for finding approximate (s, S) policies satisfying a service level constraint is to use the (Q, R) approximation assuming continuous review and set $s = R$ and $S = R + Q$. Continuous review policies subject to service level constraints are discussed in the next section.

While the results obtained from this approach are reasonable in many circumstances, more accurate approximations may be required. Several researchers have suggested (s, S) approximations subject to service levels. Their methods are based on the results of Roberts [1962].

Roberts considered an asymptotic analysis of the underlying renewal process. He showed that for the cost model when both K and p were large one could approximate (s, S) by

$$S - s \cong \sqrt{2K\lambda/h} + \mathrm{BT},$$

and

$$p \int_s^\infty (t - s) f(t)\, \mathrm{d}t = \sqrt{2K\lambda h},$$

assuming no discounting and an order lead time of T periods. Interpret λ as the expected value of one period's demand and BT a constant depending only on the length of the lead time. Similar, but somewhat more complex, formulas were obtained for the case where costs are discounted.

Roberts' results were first extended to consider service levels by Schneider [1978] and later refined by Tijms & Groenevelt [1984]. They suggest for a Type 2 service criterion that the reorder level, s, solve

$$\int_s^\infty (t - s)^2 f^{T+1}(t)\, \mathrm{d}t = \eta,$$

where

$$\eta = (1 - \beta_2) 2\lambda [S - s + \lambda_2 / 2\lambda]$$

and

$$\lambda_2 = \int_0^{+\infty} t^2 f(t)\, \mathrm{d}t.$$

Interpret β_2 as the desired service level and $f^{T+1}(t)$ as the density of the $T+1$ fold convolution of one period's demand. Tijms and Groenevelt use these results to obtain approximations for s based on the first two moments of the distribution of one period's demand. The authors present extensive computations and discuss under which circumstances their approach is accurate. Recently Cohen, Kleindorfer & Lee [1988] considered an extension of these results to lost sales and priority classes of demand.

5. Continuous time stochastic demand models

Continuous review has also been referred to as transactions reporting [see, e.g., Hadley & Whitin, 1963], because all demand transactions are recorded as they occur. A supermarket with an optical scanner connected to a centralized inventory control system is an example of such a system. In this system, all transactions are monitored continuously and thus inventory ordering decisions can be made as soon as these transactions occurred. Hence, such a system will be more responsive than the periodic review system, where inventory ordering actions can only take place at the specific review times. Such responsiveness is achieved, however, at the expense of a continuous-time monitoring system.

When the inventory system is monitored on a continuous time basis, the analysis of such system requires the specification of the demand process to the system. Consider a demand process where the interarrival times between demands form a sequence of IID random variables with a finite mean $1/\lambda$, and with density $\psi(\cdot)$ and CDF $\Psi(\cdot)$. Any sequence of IID random variables forms an ordinary renewal process. Assume that the quantity demanded at each occurrence of demand is a random variable. By treating stationary continuous time demand with stationary costs as a limiting case of the periodic review models discussed above, we can argue, heuristically, that an (s, S) policy is optimal. This result can be proved rigorously [see Beckmann, 1961; Hadley & Whitin, 1963.] Hence, the management problem of interest is the determination of the optimal (s, S) values that would minimize some long run average cost measures.

In this section, we will first present the cost model based upon which the (s, S) values are to be found. A heuristic solution procedure to find near-optimal (s, S) values is then described. To compute the exact value of the expected cost components in this cost model, however, we need to find the steady state behavior of several key operating characteristics of the system. One such key characteristic is the inventory position (on hand plus on order). We first show how this operating characteristic can be found in the case of general renewal process demands. We then show how the model can be considerably simplified for the cases of Poisson demands, and the one-for-one ordering policy (where $s = S - 1$). Besides useful to compute the cost function, knowledge of the distribution of the inventory position is often sufficient to determine other characteristics of interest as well. One such characteristic, the waiting time distribution, will be examined.

5.1. The cost function and heuristic models

The long run average cost is often used as the performance measure for a continuous review inventory system. Similar to periodic review models, this cost consists of order, inventory holding, and shortage costs. Let K be the order cost, h be the unit holding cost per unit time, p be the unit shortage cost (for each unit that is backordered or lost as a result of shortage), and p' the cost per unit time that a unit is backordered (for the case of backordering of unmet demands). Then, the average cost C equals:

$$C = KN + pM + hH + p'B , \tag{5.1}$$

where N is the expected number of orders placed per unit time, M is the expected number of units short per unit time, H is the expected on-hand inventory level, and B is the expected backorder level. The problem is then to find N, U, H and B.

Instead of finding the exact values of N, M, H and B, an approach is to find an approximate expression for C in (5.1), and use heuristics to find the optimal values of (s, S). Here we describe simple, yet effective ways to find the optimal (s, S) values in the backorder case where $p' = 0$, and the lost sales case [see Hadley & Whitin, 1963].

Let $Q = S - s$. The (s, S) inventory control system is sometimes referred to as the (Q, r) inventory control system, where the 'r' corresponds to the 's'. The problem is to find optimal values of Q and s. Define a replenishment cycle as the length of time between two successive points in time where orders are placed. The approximate cost function is based on assuming that there is at most one order outstanding, and demands arrive one at a time. It is also based on treating replenishment cycles as renewal cycles so that the order and shortage components of the average cost can be computed as the ratio of the expected order and shortage cost per replenishment cycle and the expected length of a replenishment cycle. Such a treatment, of course, is only an approximation.

Let λ be the average demand per unit time, ζ be the random variable denoting the lead time demand. Suppose unmet demands are backordered. The expected number of replenishment cycles per unit time is λ/Q. In each cycle, the expected number of units backordered is $\mathrm{E}(\zeta - s)^+$, and so the expected units backordered per unit time is $(\lambda/Q)\mathrm{E}(\zeta - s)^+$. The expected ending inventory at the time when an order arrives is $\mathrm{E}(s - \zeta)$, and the expected inventory level after an order arrival is $Q + E(s - \zeta)$. The expected on-hand inventory level is then approximated by the average of these two inventory levels:

$$C = K\lambda/Q + p(\lambda/Q)\mathrm{E}(\zeta - s)^+ + h[s - \mathrm{E}(\zeta) + \tfrac{1}{2}Q] .$$

Setting the first derivatives of C with respect to s and Q, respectively, to 0, we get:

$$Q = \sqrt{2\lambda[K + p\mathrm{E}(\zeta - s)^{+}]/h}\,, \tag{5.2}$$

$$\Pr\{\zeta \geq s\} = Qh/p\lambda\,. \tag{5.3}$$

An iterative procedure can then be used to find the optimal values of s and Q. The procedure starts with using an initial value of Q (e.g., the EOQ) to obtain s from (5.3). From this value of s, a new Q can be computed from (5.2), which can then be used in (5.3) to update s. The procedure ends when the values of s and Q stabilize.

A similar approximate cost function can also be developed for the lost sales case. Here, with at most one order outstanding, the expected ending inventory at the time just before a replenishment order arrives is given by $\mathrm{E}(s - \zeta)^{+}$. The expected inventory level right after the order arrives is $Q + \mathrm{E}(s - \zeta)^{+}$. The average inventory level is obtained by taking the average of the two, i.e., $(Q/2) + \mathrm{E}(s - \zeta)^{+}$. The expected number of shortages in a cycle is $\mathrm{E}(\zeta - s)^{+}$. Hence, the expected quantity demanded in a replenishment cycle is $Q + \mathrm{E}(\zeta - s)^{+}$. The expected number of orders placed per unit time is thus $\lambda/[Q + \mathrm{E}(\zeta - s)^{+}]$. As $\mathrm{E}(\zeta - s)^{+}$ is usually much smaller than Q, one can approximate the expected number of orders placed per unit time by λ/Q. The approximate cost function is thus given by:

$$C = \lambda[K + p\mathrm{E}(\zeta - s)^{+}]/Q + h[\tfrac{1}{2}Q + \mathrm{E}(s - \zeta)^{+}]\,.$$

Setting the derivatives of C with respect to Q and s to zero yield the same expression for Q as in (5.2), and:

$$\Pr(\zeta \geq s) = Qh/(Qh + \lambda p)\,. \tag{5.4}$$

A similar iterative procedure can then be used to obtain the optimal values of s and Q.

There are some interesting observations that one can draw from the heuristic models. First, from (5.2), the optimal value of Q must be larger than or equal to the EOQ, i.e., a larger order quantity is needed as a result of uncertainty in demand and the penalty cost of shortages. The reason for this is as follows. The inventory system will be vulnerable to shortages when we have placed an order and it has not arrived. A larger order quantity would mean that the above situation will happen less frequently. Second, from both (5.3) and (5.4), the optimal value of s is non-increasing in Q. Here the interpretation is that, when the lot size is larger, it is less frequent that the inventory system will run into the position in which it is vulnerable to shortages. Thus, the need to have a higher reorder point for safety purposes is reduced, and so the optimal value of s is smaller.

When there is a service criterion, such as the two service measures of Section 4, the usual way is to add the service requirement and adjust the iterative procedure above. A description of these heuristic methods can be found in Nahmias [1976] and Yano [1985].

5.2. Renewal process demand models

In this section, we focus on the backorder case with $p = 0$. The major concern is then to find the exact values of H and B. It turns out that, in the case of backordered demands and constant lead times, the on-hand inventory level and the backorder level are related to the inventory position. Hence, the steady state distribution of the inventory position in continuous review inventory systems has been an important topic of research.

To see the relationship between the on-hand inventory level and the backorder level with the inventory position, let $V(t)$ and $I(t)$ be the installation inventory level and the inventory position at time t respectively. Let T be the replenishment lead time, which is a constant. Let also $D(t-T, t)$ denote the demand during the interval $(t-T, T]$. Thus, the on-hand inventory level and the backorder level at time t are given by $\max\{V(t), 0\}$ and $\max\{-V(t), 0\}$, respectively. Consider $I(t-T)$. Note first that all the orders outstanding that made up $I(t-T)$ would have arrived by time t, and thus all the items in $I(t-T)$ would contribute to the inventory level $V(t)$. The demands in $(t-T, T]$, however, will deplete this inventory level. Hence, we have the following relationship:

$$V(t) = I(t-T) - D(t-T, t) . \tag{5.5}$$

The relationship above shows that $V(t)$ can be obtained from $I(t-T)$ and $D(t-T, t)$. Under the (s, S) policy, when the inventory position reaches or drops below the reorder level s, an order is immediately placed so that the inventory position is brought back to S. Hence, the inventory position is always between $s+1$ and S. There are several methods from which the steady state distribution of the inventory position can be found.

Sivazlian [1974] traced the transient behavior of the inventory position, and obtained the following result for the unit demand case. Without loss of generality, suppose we are now at time 0, where an order has just been made, bringing the inventory position up to S. Let $Q = S - s$. Denote $\psi^Q(\cdot)$ and $\Psi^Q(\cdot)$ as the density and CDF of the Q-fold convolution of $\psi(\cdot)$, respectively. The convention $\psi^0(0) = 1$, i.e., $\Psi^0(\cdot) = 1$ will be used. Sivazlian shows that, for $n = 1, \ldots, Q$,

$$\Pr\{I(t) = s + n\} = \sum_{k=0}^{\infty} [\Psi^{kQ+Q-n}(t) - \Psi^{kQ+Q-n+1}(t)]$$

Using the Laplace transform of the probability function of $I(t)$ and taking the limit as $t \to \infty$, it can be shown that $\lim_{t\to\infty} \Pr\{I(t) = s + n\} = 1/Q$. The remarkable result is that, in the steady state, the inventory position is uniformly distributed in $[s+1, s+2, \ldots, s+Q]$, and is independent of the distribution of the interarrival times between demands. This simplifies tremendously the derivation of the distribution of on-hand inventory and backorder level from (5.5).

Instead of unit demand, suppose now that the quantity demanded in each demand event is an IID random variable greater than or equal to one, and which has a finite mean. Let the probability function and cumulative distribution of each demand quantity be given by $\phi(\cdot)$ and $\Phi(\cdot)$ respectively. Let also $r(\cdot)$ and $R(\cdot)$ denote its renewal function and the associated distribution function respectively. Under the (s, S) policy, the inventory position at the time when an order is triggered may be below s. The quantity of the difference between s and the inventory position at this time is usually called the undershoot. It turns out that the uniformity of the distribution of the inventory position may no longer hold.

Let the steady state distribution of the inventory position be given by $\pi(x)$, $x \in [s, S]$. Richards [1975] used a simple approach that focused on the expected holding time of the inventory position within each replenishment cycle to obtain:

$$\pi(x) = r(S-x)/[1 + R(S-s)] .$$

He also showed that this distribution is uniform if and only if demands are of unit size.

A similar result for the steady state distribution of the inventory position has also been developed by Tijms [1972] and Sahin [1979], using a different approach. First they obtained the probability function of the inventory position at a given point in time, t. The probability distribution of a replenishment cycle was shown to be

$$1 - \sum_{k=0}^{\infty} [\Psi^k(\cdot) - \Psi^{k+1}(\cdot)]\Phi^k(S-s) ,$$

with expected length given by $[1 + R(S-s)]/\lambda$. Let $m(\cdot)$ denote the renewal density of the cycle. Consequently, $\lim_{x\to\infty} m(x) = \lambda/[1 + R(S-s)]$. Next,

$$\begin{aligned}
&\Pr\{x \leq I(t) \leq x + \mathrm{d}x\} \\
&\quad = \sum_{k=1}^{\infty} [\Psi^k(t) - \Psi^{k+1}(t)]\phi^k(S-x) \\
&\qquad + \sum_{k=1}^{\infty} \int_0^t m(t-u)[\Psi^k(u) - \Psi^{k+1}(u)]\phi^k(S-x)\,\mathrm{d}u .
\end{aligned}$$

Taking the limit of the above expression as $t \to \infty$, one obtains the steady state distribution of the inventory position, which is the same as the one obtained by Richards. Stidham [1974] has also noted that the (s, S) system is a special case of a 'stochastic clearing system' from which the steady state distributions can be obtained.

The uniform distribution of the inventory position can, however, be recaptured by modifying the procurement policy slightly. Consider the following policy, termed the (s, nQ) policy, that orders an amount of nQ, $n = 1, 2, \ldots$, when the inventory position falls to or below s. The value of n is determined so that the inventory position after ordering is between $s+1$ and $S = s + Q$. Here, the inventory position after ordering is itself a random variable, and depends on the magnitude of the undershoot at the time when an order is placed. The (s, nQ) policy and the (s, S) policy are the same when demands are all of unit size. Consider now the embedded Markov chain of the inventory position at the times of customer arrival. Specifically, let W_n denote the time of arrival of the nth customer, $n = 1, 2, \ldots$. Define the stochastic process $\{Y_n, n = 0, 1, 2, \ldots\}$, where $Y_0 = I(0)$, and $Y_n = I(W_n)$, $n = 1, 2, \ldots$. It follows that $\{Y_n\}$ is a finite state discrete Markov chain. The one step transition probability matrix is given by:

$$p_{jk} = \Pr\{Y_{n+1} = k \mid Y_n = j\} = \begin{cases} \sum_{m=1}^{\infty} \phi(mQ + k - j) & \text{if } j < k\,, \\ \sum_{m=0}^{\infty} \phi(mQ + k - j) & \text{if } j \geq k\,. \end{cases}$$

This Markov chain is irreducible if $\phi(1) > 0$. Noting that the matrix $\{p_{jk}\}$ is doubly stochastic, Simon [1968] shows that the stationary distribution of the inventory position immediately following a customer arrival, and consequently, the steady state distribution of the inventory position, is uniform.

Given the steady state distribution of the inventory position, we now turn to the derivation of the steady state distribution of the inventory level from (5.5). Note first that $I(t-T)$ and $D(t-T, t)$ will be independent only if $t - T$ is a customer arrival point or if the customer arrival process is Poisson. Sahin [1979] derived expressions for the transient probability of $V(t)$. Let $V(\infty)$, $I(\infty)$ and $D(\infty)$ denote random variables having the limiting distributions of the inventory level, inventory position, and demand in lead time, respectively. Sahin [1979] proved that $I(\infty)$ and $D(\infty)$ are independent. Therefore, from (5.5), if $I(\infty)$ and $D(\infty)$ exist, we have:

$$V(\infty) = I(\infty) - D(\infty)\,. \tag{5.6}$$

Thus, the distribution of $V(\infty)$ can be obtained from those of $I(\infty)$ and $D(\infty)$ by simple convolution. The distribution of $I(\infty)$ is $\pi(\cdot)$. $D(\infty)$ is related to an equilibrium cumulative renewal process, and has density $g(y)$ given by:

$$g(y) = \lambda\left\{\sum_{k=1}^{\infty} \phi^k(y)\right\} \int_0^T [1 - \Psi(u)][\Psi^{k-1}(T-u) - \Psi^k(T-u)]\,\mathrm{d}u\,,$$
$$y > 0\,,$$

$$g(0) = \lambda \int_0^{\infty} [1 - \Psi(u+T)]\,\mathrm{d}u\,.$$

Zipkin [1986] gave a rigorous treatment of when the relationship given by (5.6) and the independence property would hold. In the case of stochastic lead times, we need to construct a similar relationship as (5.6). Suppose lead time τ is a random variable, and that $D_\tau(\infty)$ denote the lead time demand in the limit, given that the lead time is τ. The standard approach [see Hadley & Whitin, 1963] is then to find the marginal distribution of $D_\tau(\infty)$ over the range of τ. Let $D(\infty)$ denote the variable with such a marginal distribution. We then obtain $V(\infty)$ from (5.6).

The assumptions that justify (5.6) are that orders do not cross and their lead times are independent. One way to ensure this, due to Zipkin [1986], is to focus on the process by which orders arrive. Consider a real-valued, stationary stochastic process $\{U(t): t \in \mathbb{R}\}$ satisfying the following assumptions:

(1) $U(t) \geqslant 0$ and $\mathrm{E}[U(t)] < \infty$;

(2) $t - U(t)$ is nondecreasing;

(3) sample paths of $\{U(t)\}$ are continuous to the right;

(4) $\{U(t)\}$ is independent of the placement and size of orders and of demand process.

Suppose an order is placed at time u and that it arrives at time $z = \min\{t: t - U(t) \geqslant u\}$. This way, it is clear that lead times are nonnegative. Moreover, orders never cross, since if $u_1 < u_2$, then, whenever $\{t - U(t)\}$ passes the value u_1, the process forces the order to arrive at time t, where $t = U(t) + u_1$, but $t - U(t) = u_1 < u_2$, so that the second order cannot arrive at t.

5.3. Poisson demands

In the last section, we have seen how the steady state distribution of the inventory position can be used to compute the steady state distribution of the on-hand inventory and backorder level. An important renewal demand process in inventory modelling is the Poisson process. Continuous time inventory models are relatively straightforward when demand is Poisson. Models with more general lead time assumptions can be studied. Expressions for the cost function can be derived explicitly when demand is Poisson, so that algorithms to find the optimal (s, S) values can be readily found [see Beckmann, 1961; Archibald & Silver, 1978].

As with periodic review, the lost sales case is much more difficult to analyze. The renewal approach of the previous section fails here. The major problem arises in the transition of the inventory position when the on-hand stock becomes zero. When demand occurs and the system is out of stock, the inventory position remains unchanged. Nevertheless, it should be easy to see that the maximum number of outstanding orders at any point in time in lost sales systems is $\lfloor S/(S-s) \rfloor$, where $\lfloor x \rfloor$ denotes the largest integer smaller than or equal to x. Thus, when $S - s > s$ and unmet demands are lost, there can be at most one order outstanding at any point in time. In that case, the inventory position and the inventory level are the same just before a replenishment order is placed. As a result, with Poisson demands, constant lead time, and the values of (s, S) considered satisfying $Q = S - s > s$, exact results for some operating characteristics of the system can be obtained [see Hadley & Whitin, 1963]. When demand arrivals are Poisson and the order quantity from each customer arrival is a random variable (known as compound Poisson, discussed also in Section 5.3), one can obtain exact results for the lost sales case with at most one order outstanding [Archibald, 1981].

When replenishment lead times have the negative exponential distribution, exact results can also be obtained. Order crossing is not a problem in this case. One utilizes the Chapman–Kolmogorov equations for the steady state probabilities as in standard queueing systems. For the simple case where the arrival rates and the replenishment times are independent of the state of the system, Galliher, Morse & Simond [1959] defined the system state as the number of orders outstanding at the instant in question, k, and the number of demands which have arrived since the last order went out, n. Let P_{kn} be the associated steady state probability and $1/\mu$ the mean replenishment lead time. Let $Q = S - s$. Then p_{kn} is the solution to:

$$0 = \lambda p_{k,n-1} + (k+1)\mu p_{k+1,n} - (\lambda + k\mu)p_{kn}\,, \qquad 0 < n < Q\,,$$

$$0 = \mu p_{10} - \lambda p_{00}\,,$$

$$0 = \lambda p_{k-1,Q-1} + (k+1)\mu p_{k+1,0} - (\lambda + k\mu)p_{k0}\,, \quad k > 0\,.$$

The operating characteristics of the inventory system are then obtained, as a function of p_{kn}.

The problem of state dependent lead times can be solved as well when demands are Poisson. Gross & Harris [1971] first analyzed the problem when $S - s = 1$, and later extended their analysis to the general (s, S) system in Gross & Harris [1973]. Each order placed by the inventory system is assumed to be processed by a single server queueing system, where the service rate is state dependent. Two types of dependencies of lead times on system states were considered: (1) the instantaneous probability that an order will finish service in an infinitesimal interval $\mathrm{d}t$ is $\mu(k)\,\mathrm{d}t + \mathrm{o}(\mathrm{d}t)$, where k is the number of outstanding orders, and (2) the service time for an order is exponentially distributed with mean $1/\mu(m)$, where m is the number of outstanding orders just after the previous order has arrived. In both cases, $\mu(m)$ is specified to be μ_1 if $m = 1$, and μ_2 otherwise. The first case is solved by using standard Chapman–Kolmogorov approach as above, whereas the second case is solved by deriving the steady state distribution from the limiting distribution of the imbedded Markov chain generated by the departure points of the service system.

Wijngaard & Van Winkel [1979] considered a more general problem where the Poisson arrival rates and exponentially distributed lead time rates are both dependent of the net inventory level of the system. Their analysis is based on the average behavior of the inventory level in a cycle, which is defined to be the successive points in time when the inventory level hits zero.

5.4. Order-for-order inventory policies

An important class of ordering policies is the order-for-order policy, known also as the one-for-one replenishment policy, or the $(S-1, S)$ policy. This is a special case of the (s, S) policy with $s = S - 1$. Here, any time when a customer demand occurs, an order is made to return the inventory position to S. Such policies are usually used for low-demand items where the order set-up cost is small compared to the shortage and holding costs. When demands are Poisson, explicit results can be obtained for both the stochastic lead time case where orders *can* cross and for the lost sales case. These results are possible because of the strong similarities between these inventory systems and conventional queueing systems.

For an $(S-1, S)$ inventory system, the on-hand inventory at time t is given by $[S - W(t)]^+$, where $W(t)$ is the number of orders in resupply at time t. The number of backorders at time t is $[W(t) - S]^+$. Consider the steady state distribution of $W(t)$. Note that the number of customers in an $M/G/\infty$ queueing system is the same as the number of outstanding orders in an $(S-1, S)$ inventory system with Poisson demands, complete backlog of unsatisfied demands, and arbitrary but independent lead times. Let λ be the Poisson arrival rate, and T be the mean replenishment lead time. By a result due to Palm [1938], the number of customers in an $M/G/\infty$ queueing system, and consequently, the number of outstanding orders in the inventory system, is Poisson with mean λT. Hence, this distribution only depends upon λT, and does not depend on the distribution of the replenishment lead time! Given the distribution of the number of orders in resupply, it is straightforward to develop the performance measures for the inventory system. In the steady state, the on-hand inventory is distributed as $(S - W)^+$, where W is Poisson with mean λT; whereas the number of backorders is truncated Poisson, i.e., $(W - S)^+$.

The number of customers in an $M/G/S/S$ queueing system is the same as the number of outstanding orders in an $(S-1, S)$ inventory system with Poisson demands, arbitrary but independent resupply lead times, and lost sales for shortages. From standard queueing theory, the steady state probability that the number of customers in the queueing system is k, is

$$[(\lambda T)^k/k!] \Big/ \left[\sum_{i=0}^{S} (\lambda T)^i/i!\right] \quad \text{for } 0 \le k \le S .$$

Let W be a random variable with this probability distribution. The probability that the inventory system will have no on-hand stock is the same as the probability that all servers in the queueing system are busy. Hence, the expected order cost per unit time is $K\lambda[1 - \Pr\{W = S\}]$. The expected shortages per unit time is $\lambda \Pr\{W = S\}$, and the expected on-hand stock is again given by $E(S - W)^+ = E(S - W)$. Smith [1977] described ways to obtain optimal values of S for such inventory systems.

Suppose arrivals of customers are Poisson with rate λ. The amount demanded by each customer is an IID random variable with $\phi(j)$ denoting the probability that the demand is j, $j > 0$. Such a demand process is called Compound Poisson, and $\phi(j)$ is sometimes referred to as the compounding distribution. If $\phi(0) > 0$, then we can redefine $\lambda' = \lambda[1 - \phi(0)]$, and $\phi'(j) = \phi(j)/[1 - \phi(0)]$, $j > 0$. This way, we ensure that the probability is zero that the amount demanded from a customer is zero. When $\phi(j) = (1 - \rho)\rho^{j-1}$, $j > 0$, i.e., a geometric compounding distribution, then the demand distribution is called a stuttering Poisson. Denote $p(k; T)$ as the probability that the demand in an interval of length T is k. Then:

$$\begin{aligned} p(k; T) &= \sum_{y=1}^{k} \Pr\{k \text{ demanded from } y \text{ customers}\} \Pr\{y \text{ arrivals in } T\} \\ &= \sum_{y=1}^{k} \phi^y(k)(\lambda T)^y \exp(-\lambda T)/y!\,. \end{aligned} \tag{5.7}$$

Feeney & Sherbrooke [1966] extended Palm's Theorem to the compound Poisson demand case. They assumed that, each time an order is issued as a result of a customer arrival, all the items in that order will be resupplied as a batch, i.e., no order splitting by the supplier is allowed. The order lead times are all IID. Let $h(k)$ be the steady state probability that there are k items in resupply. For the complete backorder case, it can be proven that $h(k) = p(k; T)$. With lost sales two cases are considered. The no partial fill case is one such that, if a customer arrives and finds the number of stock on hand is less than what he/she demands, then *all* the demands are lost. For this case,

$$h(k) = p(k; T) \Big/ \sum_{i=0}^{S} p(i; T)\,, \quad 0 \leq i \leq S\,.$$

The partial fill case is one such that only the portion not satisfied in a customer's demands would be lost. For this case,

$$h(k) = p(k; T)/\Delta(S)\,, \quad 0 \leq k < S\,,$$

$$h(S) = \left\{ \sum_{y=0}^{S} [(\lambda T)^y \exp(-\lambda T)/y!] \sum_{i=S}^{\infty} \phi^y(i) \right\} \Big/ \Delta(S)\,,$$

where $\Delta(S)$ is a normalizing constant.

5.5. Waiting time distributions

Besides average cost, a performance measure of interest is the waiting time distribution of customer orders. The waiting time is the amount of time a customer must wait for his/her order to be fulfilled. For the general renewal demand models, the usual approach to deriving the waiting time distribution is to establish the equivalence of the event that a customer has to wait a certain length of time, to some other event involving demands, the inventory position or the number of orders outstanding, and the waiting time. Because the steady state distribution of the inventory position and the number of orders outstanding can be obtained as in previous subsections, the waiting time distribution can be easily derived.

Suppose $s \geq -1$ so that no customer will ever wait more than the lead time T, assumed to be constant. Consider the probability that a customer arriving at time t would have to wait for more than x time units, i.e., the customer is still waiting at time $t+x$. Note that all the outstanding orders that are part of the inventory position at time $t+x-T$ would have arrived by time $t+x$, and can thus be used to satisfy the customers arriving prior to that time. Hence, the event that a customer arriving at time t will wait for at least x time units is equivalent to the event that demand in $(t+x-T, t]$ is greater than the inventory position at time $t+x-T$. Because the steady state distribution of the inventory position is known (see Section 5.1), one can obtain the distribution of waiting time for the general (s, S) inventory system [Kruse, 1981].

In the case of $(S-1, S)$ inventory policy with Poisson demands, stronger results exist. Higa, Feyerherm & Machado [1975] first studied this problem with stuttering Poisson demands and negative exponential lead times. Unlike other studies assuming compound Poisson demands in this case, it is assumed that each individual item within the same batch has an independent lead time. Waiting time is defined to be the length of time for all demands within a customer order to be met. Let $W(t)$ be the number of items in resupply at time t. The approach is based on observing that the waiting time of a batch of k units arriving at time t is zero if $W(t)+k \leq S$, and is the $(W(t)+k-S)$th order statistic in the set of resupply times for the $W(t)+k$ items. An explicit expression was then developed for this probability distribution by noting that the steady state distribution of $W(t)$ is also compound Poisson. For the constant lead time and Poisson demand case assuming an $(S-1, S)$ policy, the expression can be quite simple. Sherbrooke [1975] showed that the probability that the waiting time is less than or equal to w time units is simply a sum of Poisson probabilities from 0 to $S-1$, where the mean of this Poisson probability is a function of w.

Higa, Feyerherm & Machado's result is not entirely correct when a First-Come-First-Serve (FCFS) discipline is used to satisfy customer demands. Suppose, as before, a customer arrives at time t. While this customer is waiting for his/her order, there could be arrivals after time t. Because of stochastic lead time, the orders generated by these arrivals could have arrived during the waiting time of the customer arriving at t, which could be used to satisfy the customer arriving at time t, under FCFS. Hence, the equivalence of the two events used by Higa, Feyerherm & Machado described above does not hold exactly. Kruse [1980] corrected for this difference with Poisson demands and $(S-1, S)$ policies, and extended it to general IID lead times. A new event equivalence has to be established: the event that a customer arriving at time t would have to wait for more than w time units is equivalent to

$$W(t) - r_1(t, t+w) - r_2(t, t+w) - \delta(w) \geq S ,$$

where $W(t)$ is the number of outstanding orders at time t, $r_1(t, t+w)$ is the amount of outstanding orders generated in $(0, t]$ which are filled by the supplier in $(t, t+w]$, $r_2(t, t+w)$ is the amount of outstanding orders generated in $(t, t+w]$ which are filled by the supplier in $(t, t+w]$, and $\delta(w)$ is 1 if the order triggered by the customer arrives by w, and 0 otherwise. Here, $\Pr\{\delta(w)=1\}$ is the probability that the lead time is less than or equal to w. The waiting time distribution is obtained by using results of infinite-server queueing systems.

The effect of waiting time on customer balking has been studied by Das [1977]. The model assumes Poisson demands, $(S-1, S)$ policies, negative exponential lead times, and that a customer would cancel its order after waiting for a fixed time period. The steady state probabilities of the number of outstanding orders are solved by using Chapman–Kolmogorov equations.

6. Application of inventory theory in industry

Some of the fundamental concepts imbedded in the inventory models described in this volume have been used extensively in practice. With the advance of computer technology, many software systems for the control of inventory have been developed, which have incorporated these concepts. However, it is difficult to assess accurately the extent to which inventory models have been used in industry, because documentation of its use in publicly available literature is rare. In this section, we describe how the inventory models described in previous sections are used in practice, as described in published studies in the literature.

6.1. Use of EOQ

The EOQ model is perhaps the most widely used in practice. In 1961, APICS (American Production and Inventory Control Society), in conjunction with Factory Magazine, surveyed the Society's members, and found that the use of 'modern' analytical techniques such as EOQ was extremely rare [see Factory Magazine, 1961]. A majority of the respondents cited 'pure judgement' as the method used for determining inventory ordering and safety stock decisions. However, the use of analytical methods steadily increased [Factory Magazine, 1966]. In 1973, a similar survey found that 56% of the respondents were using EOQ, and 32% were using some form of statistical analysis for the calculation of the re-order point [Davis, 1975]. In a 1978 survey of manufacturing firms in Arizona, California, Illinois, New York and Pennsylvania, 85% of the respondents reported using EOQ [Reuter, 1978a,b]. Such a finding is reconfirmed by a recent study by Osteryoung, MacCarty & Reinhart [1986], in which 84% of the firms surveyed, which included manufacturing, retail, services and wholesale/distributers, reported using EOQ. Of these firms, 48% reported that the EOQ usage was for finished goods inventory control.

On the other hand, the EOQ has often been criticized. In previous sections, we noted that most of the assumptions required in the derivation of the EOQ formula do not hold. Similar objections have been made about the other inventory models as well. A major problem reported by practitioners is the inability of most firms to accurately assess ordering and carrying costs [Zeitzew, 1979]. Gardner [1980] found that the fundamental problem of inventory practice is accurately estimating the cost parameters. Most of the cost parameters are estimated by standard accounting procedures that generate at best *average* costs, yet it is marginal costs that matter in inventory control. Schonberger & Schniederjans [1984] found two major flaws with inventory models. First, most costs are difficult to estimate. It is also difficult to incorporate the hidden costs such as the quality costs related to large batches, i.e., the longer response time to detect quality problems when batch sizes are large. Second, many inventory models are static. For example, the EOQ analysis assumes costs are stationary. However, many of these costs are dynamic; that is, time varying. Moreover, by proper investments, some of those costs (e.g., set-up costs) can be reduced over time, resulting in smaller lot sizes.

Despite its shortcomings, the basic EOQ model remains the most widely used. It is also the cornerstone of many currently commercially available software packages for inventory control.

6.2. IBM's inventory package IMPACT

In the early sixties, IBM introduced an inventory package called IMPACT (Inventory Management Program and Control Techniques) [IBM, 1967]. The package has steadily gained popularity among wholesalers and retailers, many of which have adapted it to their particular needs. It contains the logic for inventory control, as well as complete inventory file structure and forecasting systems. In the seventies, an enhancement of IMPACT, called INFOREM (Inventory Forecasting and Replenishment Modules) was developed, also by IBM [IBM, 1978]. This new system employs an improved forecasting technique, and includes simulation for forecasting and strategic planning of inventory policies. IMPACT was an important step in the advancement of computerized inventory control systems in industry. Many of the commercially available inventory control software systems actually employ logics similar to those of IMPACT. We describe the extent to which inventory models reviewed in this chapter are used in IMPACT.

IMPACT assumes a periodic review, reorder point, fixed lot size inventory control systems similar to the one of Section 4. The lot size is assumed to be the EOQ. The reorder point is the sum of mean lead time demand plus one review period's demand plus safety stock. Such an operating system is exactly the approximation of (s, S) policies described in Section 4.4.2. The safety stock equals a safety factor multiplied by the standard deviation of the demand in lead time plus a review period. Determination of the safety factor is based on the following assumptions:

(1) demand per period is normally distributed;

(2) a target service level based on the expected amount of demands filled over the expected demand, i.e., the Type 2 service measure used in Section 4.4.1, can be specified;

(3) unmet demands are backordered;

(4) at most one order is outstanding at all times.

The safety factor is chosen to most nearly equate the percentage of demands filled immediately in an order cycle and the prespecified target service level.

Kleijnen & Rens [1978] conducted simulation studies and found that IMPACT often provides overservice; that is, the simulated services using the reorder points of IMPACT are greater than the prespecified targets. Kleijnen and Rens attributed this difference to: (1) unmet demands can be lost, and (2) the approximation of a periodic review system by a continuous review (Q, r) system requires proper adjustment of the reorder point. Actually, the criticism of IMPACT that it does not give good reorder points when unmet demands are lost is unreasonable, because it is a backorder model. It is easy to modify the formulas used in IMPACT to account for lost sales. The adjustment of the reorder point to account for the approximation of periodic review by continuous review is also straightforward. Silver & Peterson [1985] suggest several ways to make such an adjustment.

6.3. *Success stories of application*

There have been several successful applications of inventory models reported in the literature. Most of these reported a significant reduction in inventory investment while maintaining the same level of service to customers. It is interesting to note that in many of these applications simple models were employed, and approximations used extensively. Again, EOQ analysis prevailed. We consider several such applications below.

Many applications were in the manufacturing sector. Liberatore [1979] reported one such application for FMC's Industrial Chemical Group plants. Here, the problem was to find ordering policies for bulk raw materials for a chemical production process. Since the production process is continuous and the product is produced at fairly uniform rate, the environment was ideal for

EOQ analysis. The EOQ was used as the order size, with an appropriate adjustment for full truck loads. A reorder point was used to account for the variability of demand, even though that variability was small. A Type 1 service measure described in Section 4.4.1, giving the probability of stockout in an ordering cycle, was used. This criterion was appropriate because the main cost of shortages in this environment was the cost of a shutdown of the production process, regardless of the amount short.

An (s, S) inventory model was used for managing finished goods for Planters Division of Standard Brands Inc. [Brout, 1981]. Again, the EOQ was used to determine the lot size, whereas the reorder point was computed based on the Type 2 service measure of Section 4.4.1. A similar model has been used for managing materials for aircraft production [Lingaraj & Balasubramanian, 1983]. In this case an EOQ with an adjustment for minimum order size was recommended, coupled with a reorder point based on Type 1 service. Similar (s, S) systems have been employed for managing finished goods at Pfizer Pharmaceuticals [Kleutghen & McGee, 1985].

The military has been a major user of modern inventory models. EOQ was first implemented by the U.S. Air Force in 1952 for the purchase of expendable weapon's system spares [Austin, 1977]. In 1958, the Department of Defense directed all defense procurement and logistics agencies to use the basic EOQ formula. The use of EOQ and simple approximate continuous review models has also resulted in significant cost savings at the U.S. Navy [Gardner, 1987].

Finally, we note that there has been a significant impact of modern inventory models on the management of blood inventories at major blood banks [Brodheim & Prastacos, 1979].

References

Adler, G.L., and R. Nanda (1974). The effects of learning on optimal lot size determination – Single product case. *AIIE Trans.* 6, 14–20.

Aggarwal, S.C. (1981). Purchase-inventory decision models for inflationary conditions. *Interfaces* 11, 18–23.

Archibald, B.C. (1981). Continuous review (s, S) policies with lost sales. *Management Sci.* 27, 1171–1177.

Archibald, B.C., and E.A. Silver (1978). (s, S) policies under continuous review and discrete compound Poisson demand. *Management Sci.* 24, 899–909.

Arrow, K.A. (1958). Historical background, in: K.A. Arrow, S. Karlin and H.E. Scarf (eds.), *Studies in the Mathematical Theory of Inventory and Production*, Stanford University Press, Stanford, CA.

Arrow, K.A., T.E. Harris and J. Marschak (1951). Optimal inventory policy. *Econometrica* 19, 250–272.

Arrow, K.A., S. Karlin and H.E. Scarf (eds.) (1958). *Studies in the Mathematical Theory of Inventory and Production*, Stanford University Press, Stanford, CA.

Austin, L.M. (1977). Project EOQ: A success story in implementing academic research. *Interfaces* 7(4), 1–13.

Axsäter, S. (1982). Worst case performance for lot sizing heuristics. *European J. Oper. Res.* 9, 339–343.

Baker, K.R., P.R. Dixon, M.J. Magazine and E.A. Silver (1978). Algorithm for the dynamic lot-size problems with time varying production capacity constraints. *Management Sci.* 16, 1710–1720.

Barbosa, L.C., and M. Friedman (1978). Deterministic inventory lot size models – A general root law. *Management Sci.* 24, 819–826.

Beckmann, M. (1961). An inventory model for arbitrary interval and quantity distributions of demand. *Management Sci.* 8, 35–57.

Bellman, R.E., I. Glicksberg and O. Gross (1955). On the optimal inventory equation. *Management Sci.* 2, 83–104.

Bierman, H., and L.J. Thomas (1977). Inventory decisions under inflationary conditions. *Decision Sciences* 8, 151–155.

Bitran, G.R., T.L. Magnanti and H.H. Yanasse (1984). Approximation methods for the uncapacitated dynamic lot size problem. *Management Sci.* 30, 1121–1140.

Blackburn, J., and H. Kunreuther (1974). Planning and forecast horizons for the dynamic lot size model with backlogging. *Management Sci.* 21, 251–255.

Brodheim, E., and G.P. Prastacos (1979). The long island blood distribution system as a prototype for regional blood management. *Interfaces* 9(5), 3–20.

Brout, D.B. (1981). Scientific management of inventory on a hand-held calculator. *Interfaces* 11(6), 57–69.

Brown, R.G. (1967). *Decision Rules for Inventory Management*, Dryden Press, Hinsdale, IL.

Buzacott, J.A. (1975). Economic order quantities with inflation. *Oper. Res. Quart.* 26, 553–558.

Carlson, R.C., J.V. Jucker and D.H. Kropp (1979). Less nervous MRP systems: A dynamic economic lot-sizing approach. *Management Sci.* 25 754–761.

Carlson, R.C., S.L. Beckman and D.H. Kropp (1982). The effectiveness of extending the horizon in rolling production scheduling. *Decision Sciences* 13, 129–146.

Cohen, M.A. (1977). Joint pricing and ordering policy for exponentially decaying inventory with known demand. *Naval. Res. Logist. Quart.* 24, 257–268.

Cohen, M.A., P. Kleindorfer and H. Lee (1988). Service constrained (s, S) inventory systems with priority demand classes and lose sales. *Management Sci.* 34, 482–499.

Das, C. (1977). The $(S-1, S)$ inventory model under time limit on backorders. *Oper. Res.* 25, 835–850.

Davis, E.W. (1975). A look at the use of production-inventory techniques: Past and present. *Prod. Invent. Management J.*, December, 1–19.

DeMatteis, J.J. (1968). An economic lot sizing technique: The part-period algorithms. *IBM Syst. J.* 7, 30–38.

Dixon, P.S., and E.A. Silver (1981). A heuristic solution procedure for the multi-item, single-level, limited capacity, lot sizing problem. *J. Oper. Management* 2, 23–39.

Dvoretzky, A., J. Kiefer and J. Wolfowitz (1952a). The inventory problem: I. Case of known distributions of demand. *Econometrica* 20, 187–222.

Dvoretzky, A., J. Kiefer and J. Wolfowitz (1952b). The inventory problem: II. Case of unknown distributions of demand. *Econometrica* 20, 450–466.

Eppen, G.D., F.J. Gould and B.P. Pashigian (1969). Extensions of the planning horizon theorem in the dynamic lot size model. *Management Sci.* 15, 268–277.

Factory Magazine (1961). Exclusive survey of production and inventory control. *Factory Magazine*, April.

Factory Magazine (1966). Exclusive survey shows new directions in production and inventory control. *Factory Magazine*, October.

Federgruen, A., and P. Zipkin (1984). An efficient algorithm for computing optimal (s, S) policies. *Oper. Res.* 32, 1268–1285.

Feeney, G.J., and C.C. Sherbrooke (1966). The $(S-1, S)$ inventory policy under compound Poisson demand. *Management Sci.* 12, 391–411.

Fisk, J.C., and D.P. Ballou (1982). Production lot sizing under a learning effect. *IIE Trans.* 14, 257–264.

Florian, M., and M. Klein (1971). Deterministic production planning with concave costs and capacity constraints. *Management Sci.* 18, 12–20.
Galliher, H.P., P.M. Morse and M. Simond (1957). Dynamics of two classes of continuous-review inventory systems. *Oper. Res.* 7, 362–384.
Gardner, E.S. (1980). Inventory theory and the Gods of Olympus. *Interfaces* 10(4), 42–45.
Gardner, E.S. (1987). A top-down approach to modelling US Navy inventories. *Interfaces* 17(4), 1–7.
Ghare, P.M., and G.F. Schrader (1963). A model for an exponential decaying inventory. *J. Indust. Engrg.* 14, 238–243.
Gross, D., and C.M. Harris (1971). On one-for-one-ordering inventory policies with state-dependent leadtimes. *Oper. Res.* 19, 735–760.
Gross, D., and C.M. Harris (1973). Continuous review (s, S) inventory policies with state-dependent leadtimes. *Management Sci.* 19, 567–574.
Hadley, G. (1964). A comparison of order quantities computed using average annual cost and the discounted cost. *Management Sci.* 10, 472–476.
Hadley, G., and T.M. Whitin (1963). *Analysis of Inventory Systems*, Prentice-Hall, Englewood Cliffs, NJ.
Harris, F.W. (1913). How many parts to make at once. *Factory, The Magazine of Management* 10(2), 135–136, 152.
Hax, A.C., and D. Candea (1984). *Production and Inventory Management*, Prentice-Hall, Englewood Cliffs, NJ.
Higa, I., A.M. Feyerherm and A.L. Machado (1975). Waiting time in an $(S-1, S)$ inventory system. *Oper. Res.* 23, 674–680.
Hillier, F.S., and G.T. Lieberman (1987). *Introduction to Operations Research, 4th edition*, Holden Day, Oakland, CA.
Iglehart, D.L. (1963). Optimality of (s, S) policies in the infinite horizon dynamic inventory problem. *Management Sci.* 9, 259–267.
IBM (1967). *Basic Principles of Wholesale IMPACT – Inventory Management Program and Control Techniques*, E20-8105-1, IBM, White Plains, New York, *revised edition.*
IBM (1978). *INFOREM: Principles of Inventory Management – Application Description*, GE20-0571-1, IBM, White Plains, New York, *revised edition.*
Jesse, R.R., A. Mitra and J.F. Cox (1983). EOQ formula: Is it valid under inflationary conditions? *Decision Sciences* 14, 370–374.
Kanet, J.J., and J.A. Miles (1985). Economic order quantities and inflation. *Internat. J. Production Res.* 23, 597–608.
Kaplan, R. (1970). A dynamic inventory model with stochastic lead times. *Management Sci.* 16, 491–507.
Karlin, S. (1958). Steady state solutions, in: Arrow, Karlin and Scarf (eds.), *Studies in the Mathematical Theory of Inventory and Production*, Stanford University Press, Stanford, CA, Chapter 14.
Karlin, S. (1968). *Total Positivity*, Stanford University Press, Stanford, CA.
Karlin, S., and H.E. Scarf (1958). Optimal inventory policy for the Arrow Harris Marschak dynamic model with a time lag, in: Arrow, Karlin and Scarf (eds.), *Studies in the Mathematical Theory of Inventory and Production*, Stanford University Press, Stanford, CA, Chapter 10.
Karni, R. (1981). Maximum Part Period Gain (MPG) – A lot sizing procedure for unconstrained and constrained requirements planning systems. *Prod. Invent. Management* 22, 91–98.
Keachie, E.C., and R.J. Fontana (1966). Effects of learning on optimal lot size. *Management Sci.* 13, B102–108.
Kleijnen, J.P.C., and P.J. Rens (1978). IMPACT revisited: A critical analysis of IBM's inventory package 'IMPACT'. *Prod. Invent. Management* 19(1), 71–90.
Kleutghen, P.P., and J.C. McGee (1985). Development and implementation of an integrated inventory management program at Pfizer Pharmaceuticals. *Interfaces* 15(1), 69–87.
Kropp, D.H., and R.C. Carlson (1984). A lot sizing algorithm for reducing nervousness in MRP systems. *Management Sci.* 30, 240–244.

Kruse, W.K. (1980). Waiting time in an $S-1$, S inventory system with arbitrarily distributed lead times. *Oper. Res.* 28, 348–352.
Kruse, W.K. (1981). Waiting time in a continuous review (s, S) inventory system with constant lead times. *Oper. Res.* 29, 202–207.
Ladany, S., and A. Sternlieb (1974). The interaction of economic ordering quantities and marketing policies. *AIIE Trans.* 6, 35–40.
Lee, H.L., and M.J. Rosenblatt (1986). The effects of varying marketing policies and conditions on the economic ordering quantity. *Internat. J. Prod. Res.* 24, 593–598.
Lee, H.L., and M.J. Rosenblatt (1987). Simultaneous determination of production cycle and inspection schedules in a production system. *Management Sci.* 33.
Lev, B., and A.L. Soyster (1979). An inventory model with finite horizon and price changes. *J. Oper. Res. Soc.* 30, 43–53.
Lev, B., H.J. Weiss and A.L. Soyster (1981). Optimal ordering policies when anticipating parameter changes in EOQ systems. *Naval. Res. Logist. Quart.* 28, 267–279.
Liberatore, M.J. (1979). Using MRP and EOQ/safety stock for raw materials inventory control: Discussion and case study. *Interfaces* 9(2) Part 1, 1–7.
Lingaraj, B.P., and R. Balasubramanian (1983). An inventory management and materials information system for aircraft production. *Interfaces* 13(5), 65–70.
Love, S.F. (1973). Bounded production and inventory models with piecewise concave costs. *Management Sci.* 20, 313–318.
Lundin, R.A., and T.E. Morton (1975). Planning horizons for the dynamic lot size model: Zabel vs. protective procedures and computational results. *Oper. Res.* 23, 711–734.
Morton, T.E. (1969). Bounds on the solution of the lagged optimal inventory equation with no demand backlogging and proportional costs. *SIAM Rev.* 11, 527–596.
Muth, E.J., and K. Spremann (1983). Learning effects in economic lot sizing. *Management Sci.* 29, 264–269.
Nahmias, S. (1976). On the equivalence of three approximate continuous review inventory models. *Naval. Res. Logist. Quart.* 23, 31–36.
Nahmias, S. (1979). Simple approximations for a variety of dynamic leadtime lost-sales inventory models. *Oper. Res.* 27, 904–924.
Nahmias, S. (1989). *Production and Operations Analysis*, Richard D. Irwin, Homewood, IL.
Orlicky, J. (1975). *Material Requirements Planning*, McGraw-Hill, New York.
Osteryoung, J.A., D.E. McCarty and W.J. Reinhart (1986). Use of the EOQ model for inventory analysis. *Prod. Invent. Management* 27(3), 39–45.
Palm, C. (1938). Analysis of the Erlang traffic formula for busy signal arrangements. *Ericsson Technics* 5, 39–58.
Porteus, E.L. (1971). On the optimality of generalized (s, S) policies. *Management Sci.* 17, 411–427.
Porteus, E.L. (1985a). Numerical comparisons of inventory policies for periodic review systems. *Oper. Res.* 33, 134–152.
Porteus, E.L. (1985b). Undiscounted approximations of discounted regenerative models. *Oper. Res. Lett.* 3, 293–300.
Porteus, E.L. (1986). Optimal lot sizing, process quality improvement and setup cost reduction. *Oper. Res.* 34, 137–144.
Porteus, E.L. (1988). Stochastic inventory theory, in: D. Heyman and M. Sobel (eds.), *Handbooks in Operations Research and Management Science, Vol. II: Stochastic Models.*
Resh, M., M. Friedman and L.C. Barbosa (1976). On a general solution of the deterministic lot size problem with time-proportional demand. *Oper. Res.* 24, 718–725.
Reuter, V.G. (1978a). The big gap in inventory management. *J. Purchasing Mater. Management*, Fall, 17–22.
Reuter, V.G. (1978b). Are we using the inventory management tools. *Indust. Management, May/June*, 26–30.
Richards, F.R. (1975). Comments on the distribution of inventory position in a continuous-review (s, S) inventory system. *Oper. Res.* 23, 366–371.

Roberts, D.M. (1962). Approximations to optimal policies in a dynamic inventory model, in: K.A. Arrow, S. Karlin and H.E. Scarf (eds.), *Studies in Applied Probability and Management Science*, Stanford University Press, Stanford, CA, Chapter 13, pp. 207–299.

Rosenblatt, M.J., and H.L. Lee (1985). Improving profitability with quantity discounts under fixed demands. *IIE Trans.* 17, 388–395.

Rosenblatt, M.J., and H.L. Lee (1986). Economic production cycles with imperfect production processes. *IIE Trans.* 18, 48–55.

Sahin, I. (1979). On the stationary analysis of continuous review (s, S) inventory systems with constant lead times. *Oper. Res.* 27, 717–729.

Scarf, H.E. (1960). The optimality of (s, S) policies in the dynamic inventory problem, in: K.A. Arrow, S. Karlin and P. Suppes (eds.), *Mathematical Methods in the Social Sciences*, Stanford University Press, Stanford, CA.

Schneider, H. (1978). Methods for determining the re-order point of an (s, S) ordering policy when a service level is specified. *J. Oper. Res. Soc.* 29, 1181–1193.

Schonberger, R.J., and M.J. Schniederjans (1984). Reinventing inventory control. *Interfaces* 14(3), 76–83.

Schwarz, L.B. (1972). Economic order quantities for products with finite demand horizons. *AIIE Trans.* 4, 234–237.

Schwarz, L.B. (1977). A note on the near optimality of '5-EOQ's worth' forecast horizons. *Oper. Res.* 25, 533–536.

Sherbrooke, C.C. (1975). Waiting time in an $(S-1, S)$ inventory system – Constant service time case. *Oper. Res.* 23, 819–820.

Shih, W. (1980). Optimal inventory policies when stockouts result from defective products. *Internat. J. Prod. Res.* 18, 677–686.

Silver, E.A. (1976). Establishing the order quantity when the amount received is uncertain. *INFOR* 14, 32–39.

Silver, E.A., and H.C. Meal (1973). A heuristic for selecting lot size quantities for the case of a deterministic time-varying demand rate and discrete opportunities for replenishment. *Prod. Invent. Management* 14, 64–74.

Silver, E.A., and R. Peterson (1985). *Decision Systems for Inventory Management and Production Planning, 2nd edition*, Wiley, New York.

Simon, R.M. (1968). The uniform distribution of inventory position for continuous review (s, Q) policies, Rand Corporation Paper P3938, Santa Monica, CA.

Sivazlian, B.D. (1974). A continuous-review (s, S) inventory system with arbitrary interarrival distribution between unit demand. *Oper. Res.* 22, 65–71.

Smith, S.A. (1977). Optimal inventories for an $(S-1, S)$ system with no backorders. *Management Sci.* 23 522–528.

Smunt, T.L., and T.E. Morton (1985). The effects of learning on optimal lot sizes: Further developments on the single product case. *IIE Trans.* 17, 33–37.

Stidham, S. (1974). Stochastic clearing systems. *Stochastic Process. Appl.* 2, 85–113.

Sule, D.R. (1978). The effect of alternative periods of learning and forgetting on economic manufacturing quantity. *AIIE Trans.* 10, 338–343.

Taylor, S.G., and C.E. Bradley (1985). Optimal ordering policies for announced price increases. *Oper. Res.* 33, 312–325.

Tijms, H.C. (1972). *Analysis of (s, S) Inventory Models*, Mathematisch Centrum, Amsterdam.

Tijms, H.C., and H. Groenevelt (1984). Simple approximations for the reorder point in periodic and continuous review (s, S) inventory systems with service level constraints. *European J. Oper. Res.* 17, 175–190.

Trippi, R.R., and D.E. Lewin (1974). A present-value formulation of the classical EOQ problem. *Decision Sciences* 5, 30–35.

Veinott, A.F. (1964). Production planning with convex costs: A parametric study. *Management Sci.* 10, 441–460.

Veinott, A.F. Jr. (1965). The optimal inventory policy for batch ordering. *Oper. Res.* 13, 424–432.

Wagner, H.M., and T.M. Whitin (1958). Dynamic version of the economic lot size model. *Management Sci.* 23, 89–96.

Wagner, H.M., M. O'Hagen and B. Lund (1965). An empirical study of exactly and approximately optimal inventory policies. *Management Sci.* 11, 690–723.
Whitin, T.M. (1955). Inventory control and price theory. *Management Sci.* 2, 61–68.
Whitin, T.M. (1957). *The Theory of Inventory Management, Revised edition*, Princeton University Press, Princeton, NJ.
Wijngaard, J., and E.G.F. Van Winkel (1979). Average costs in a continuous review (s, S) inventory system with exponentially distributed lead time. *Oper. Res.* 27, 396–401.
Wilson, R.H. (1934). A scientific routine for stock control. *Harvard Business Rev.* 13, 116–128.
Wortham, A.W., and A.M. Mayyasi (1972). Learning considerations with economic order quantity. *AIIE Trans.* 4, 69–71.
Yano, C.A. (1985). New algorithms for (Q, r) systems with complete backordering using a fill-rate criterion. *Naval. Res. Logist. Quart.* 32, 675–688.
Zabel, E. (1964). Some generalizations of an inventory planning horizon theorem. *Management Sci.* 10, 465–471.
Zangwill, W.I. (1966a). A determinsitic multi-period production scheduling model with backlogging. *Management Sci.* 13, 105–119.
Zangwill, W.I. (1966b). A deterministic multi-product multi-facility production and inventory model. *Oper. Res.* 14, 486–507.
Zeitzew, H. (1979). EOQ – Is there a better way? *Purchasing Magazine*, 29–33.
Zipkin, P. (1986). Stochastic leadtimes in continuous-time inventory models. *Naval. Res. Logist. Quart.* 33, 763–774.

Part II
Multiple Products and Locations

S.C. Graves et al., Eds., *Handbooks in OR & MS, Vol. 4*

Chapter 2

Analysis of Multistage Production Systems*

John A. Muckstadt and Robin O. Roundy

School of Operations Research and Industrial Engineering, College of Engineering, Cornell University, Ithaca, NY 14853, U.S.A.

1. Introduction

The control of inventories of physical objects has been the theme of literally thousands of technical and trade journal articles during this century. Since Harris [1915] described the basic trade-offs that need to be made when making these control decisions, numerous models and algorithms have been devised that indicate how basic control parameters should be established. In his work, Harris, to our knowledge, provided the first derivation of the economic lot size formula, or economic order quantity (EOQ) formula. Later Raymond [1931] wrote the first full book on the topic of inventory control in which he explained, without the aid of mathematical theory, how extensions of the now classic EOQ problem could be implemented.

It was not until the 1950s when more serious mathematical analyses of various inventory problems were undertaken. Whitin's [1953] stochastic version of the EOQ model and works by Arrow, Harris, & Marshak [1951], Dvoretzky, Kiefer, & Wolfowitz [1952, 1953] and Arrow, Karlin, & Scarf [1958] provided the mathematical basis for subsequent extensions of the single location model. Also see Chapter 1 of this volume. The first multi-stage models were developed at about the same time. The important works of Clark & Scarf [1960, 1962] and the papers found in the book edited by Scarf, Gilford, & Shelly [1963] generated considerable interest from both academics and practitioners. The often quoted text by Hadley & Whitin [1963] and the survey paper by Veinott [1966] provide excellent summaries of many of these early modeling efforts. While much of this work concentrated on stochastic modeling, there was and currently is a strong interest in developing further extensions of Harris' basic EOQ model.

These extensions include single item, single location models that consider backordering, finite production rates, and quantity discounts of several types, and multi-item models that represent joint replenishment problems and con-

*This research was supported by National Science Foundation grants DMC-85-09131, ECS-8404641 and DMC-8451984, and also by AT&T Information Systems and DuPont Corporation.

straints of many types. Most of these single location models are discussed in some detail by Peterson & Silver [1979]. Recently, efforts in single stage modeling have focused on different issues such as the trade-offs between setup cost reduction and inventory costs [Porteus, 1985, 1986, 1987] and the effects of process quality on inspection and lot sizing policies [Porteus, 1986; Lee & Rosenblatt, 1987; and Muckstadt, 1988].

Other important advances have come from the study of various types of multi-stage systems. These include the extension of the EOQ model to consider serial, assembly, and distribution systems as well as more general system structures. We will examine these other systems in detail in subsequent sections. However, our coverage will by necessity be limited. There are many important contributions that we will not discuss including, for example, the extensive research on systems with nonconstant demands and the research on setup cost reduction. We also will ignore heuristics for multi-stage lot sizing without provable performance bounds, such as the ones developed by Blackburn & Millen [1982], Williams [1981], Crowston & Wagner [1973], Crowston, Wagner, & Henshaw [1972], Crowston, Wagner, & Williams [1973], Graves [1981], Jensen & Khan [1972], McLaren [1976], and many others, some of which are listed in the references. The same applies to the joint replenishment problem; we review only heuristics with provable performance bounds. We refer the reader to Silver & Peterson [1985] for a discussion of other heuristics for the joint replenishment problem.

Our purpose in this chapter is to review optimization based methods for solving low sizing problems for a range of serial, assembly, distribution, and other more general system structures with constant demand rates. Furthermore, we will study only a class of algorithms that has a provable bound on their performance. To be precise, our goal is to present models and algorithms that can be used to determine what we call consistent and realistic reorder intervals for each stage in each of the types of systems we have mentioned. We have chosen to develop our presentation in terms of reorder intervals, that is, the time between placement of orders, rather than in terms of lot size. Although the classic EOQ model is formulated in terms of lot sizes, we believe that there are several important reasons for formulating the model in terms of reorder intervals.

First, in many environments we have examined, we found it easier to think in terms of planning the frequency of production rather than calculating the lot size quantities, because the resources required to manufacture and distribute components, subassemblies, and finished products are generally related to the number of production runs per unit of time rather than just to the lot sizes. For example, the frequency of production dictates the number of setups, planned production orders, requests for tooling and fixtures, and requirements for moving batches of work-in-process inventories. It is easier to think in terms of producing items, say either weekly, monthly, quarterly, or yearly rather than to plan production to optimal lot sizes that indicate production should occur every 2.796 weeks for one item, 3.921 weeks for a second and $\sqrt{\pi}$ weeks for a third.

Second, the mathematical representation of the problem is simplified when the model's decision variables are reorder intervals rather than lot sizes. When the decision variables are production lot sizes, constraints must often be stated to ensure that an adequate supply of each component is available to produce the lot. These constraints, which must be stated in terms of installation stock, are not always easy to work with. As a result, the algorithm for finding the optimal lot sizes can be quite complex. Choosing the decision variables to be the reorder intervals makes the model easy to state and solve.

Third, when the demand pattern for each item and the lead time for inventory replenishment are known exactly, then once the reorder intervals are established it is obviously easy to compute the corresponding lot sizes. However, in most real situations demand forecasts change somewhat from time to time. Consequently, when there are small variations in the demand process, it is generally easier to keep reorder intervals constant and to adjust the lot sizes than to change the frequency of production intervals. Thus from a practical viewpoint, this choice simplifies the subsequent scheduling task and greatly reduces the so-called nervousness found in some MRP systems.

As mentioned, each of the models we will examine ensures that consistent production decisions are made for each stage. By this we mean that the reorder intervals must be determined so that a feasible and cost effective flow of material will occur from stage to stage. Furthermore, the reorder intervals between successive stages should be planned so that schedules can be generated that can be implemented realistically on the shop floor. That is, a solution is not useful when it indicates that a component's reorder interval is $\sqrt{3}$ times longer than that of the assembly into which it is placed. Consequently, we believe that restricting attention to a certain class of solutions is desirable.

The policies considered throughout this chapter are based on ones we have observed in practice. We began our research that led to the material we will present by studying the production control system used in stamping plants for a major U.S. automotive manufacturer. In that environment, we observed that demand for products (doors, body panels, rear decks, etc.) remains relatively constant over a lengthy period of time. The schedules determined by the production planner required each operation or component to be produced exactly once, twice, or four times during each 4-week period. The amount produced in each run was planned to be approximately the same. By having the time between production runs remain constant for an operation or component, the planner could assign a specific operation to time slots on each machine so that, for example, every fourth week the same operation takes place at the same time on the same machine. By restricting the production schedules to the type we have described, the planner could create schedules relatively quickly. His objective was to choose the week, or weeks, in which to perform an operation so that the machine utilization across the 4-week horizon was balanced. The selection of the day and shift on which to run an operation was also guided by the desire to balance the work across shifts, and across days of the week.

The planner also had to coordinate production among stages. To do so, he selected reorder intervals so that production could not occur at an operation unless it also occurred at all of the immediate successor operations. This production tactic was chosen to prevent build up of work-in-process inventory. Thus if production at one operation occurred every second week, then the immediate successor operations had production every week or every second week. Policies of this type are called nested.

Scheduling operations on several hundred machines was obviously a difficult task. It was clear to us that the planner's effectiveness rested heavily on the fact that each operation was scheduled to occur every week, every other week, or every fourth week. If this 1, 2, 4 type of policy had not been followed, the scheduling process would have been considerably more time and resource consuming.

Subsequent to our automative manufacturing study, we examined production planning systems used by manufacturers of reprographic machines, computers and pneumatic tools. In each case we observed that these firms made similar assumptions to those described previously when planning production. In particular, the major portion of products being manufactured had relatively constant demand and the firms used nested policies. Furthermore, these firms were also using policies similar to the 1, 2, 4 type. We found, for example, in one case that production lots were equal to demand expected during 3 months, 6 months, or 1 year.

The assumptions and policies considered in this chapter are guided by these observations. The models we will present restrict attention for the most part to policies that are nested and stationary. By stationary, we mean that the time between production runs at each stage or operation is constant. Although policies of this form are not necessarily optimal [Muckstadt & Singer, 1978; Williams, 1982], they are of significant practical importance. The nestedness assumption is made primarily for ease of presentation. The models can easily be modified to consider nonnested solutions at particular stages or operations. More is said about this generalization by Roundy [1985a, 1986] and Maxwell & Muckstadt [1985]. In Section 9 we explicitly consider the effects of using nonnested policies.

Furthermore, we also consider only solutions for which each stage or operation can produce a multiple of two (i.e., 1, 2, 4, 8, . . . , 2^k, . . . , where k is a nonnegative integer) times per reorder interval for any predecessor stage. We also assume that a *base planning period* exists, such as a shift, day, week, or month, and that all reorder intervals must be an integer multiple of this period. As we have discussed, restricting attention to such solutions greatly simplifies the task of scheduling the actual production for each workcenter. When limiting the choice of a solution to this restricted class of policies, the optimal objective function value does not differ substantially from that obtained when the policy space is unconstrained. In Sections 2 and 3 we prove that, when restricting the solutions to this class, the average cost can never be more than 6% higher than can be achieved following any other nested policy. Other simple policies, such as 3^k or 5^k, do not have as tight a worst-case bound.

The remainder of this chapter is organized as follows. In the next section we introduce some notation and present the powers-of-two extension of Harris' single item, single stage EOQ problem. We then examine several different multi-stage generalizations of the powers-of-two model. In Section 3 we study a system having a serial structure. That section contains some mathematical background that applies to all subsequent models as well as detailed proofs showing why the average annual cost of following the powers-of-two policy cannot exceed the cost for any other policy by more than 6%. In Section 4 we examine a system with an assembly system structure and in Section 5 we discuss a model and an algorithm for a distribution system. Section 6 contains a model of a general system structure. All the other models described in this chapter are special cases of this model. In Section 7 we again examine a general system structure, but we also consider the effect of constraints on available time for setup and production in each workcenter found in a manufacturing and distribution system.

2. Powers-of-two solution for the single item, single stage deterministic lot sizing problem

The purpose of this section is to introduce some basic concepts and nomenclature and to restrict Harris' EOQ problem to a powers-of-two lot-sizing problem. We use the single item, single stage deterministic lot size model to develop the powers-of-two lot-sizing approach because it is so simple and permits us to introduce concepts without cumbersome notation. We will show how optimal powers-of-two solutions can be found and will compare the solution to the one obtained when solving Harris' classic EOQ problem. Many of the ideas put forth here are basic to the more complicated ones that will be subsequently developed in the following sections.

2.1. Harris' EOQ model

We begin by reviewing the classic EOQ problem. Recall that this problem is one of determining the constant reorder quantity that minimizes the average annual cost of purchasing and carrying inventory. The assumptions underlying this problem are as follows:

(1) The demand rate λ is constant and continuous. λ is measured in units per year.

(2) No backordering is allowed.

(3) Production is instantaneous, or equivalently, the production rate is infinite.

(4) A fixed cost K is incurred whenever an order is placed.

(5) An inventory holding charge is incurred proportional to the on hand inventory. For each unit held in stock for one year the holding cost is h dollars.

(6) All other costs are assumed to be independent of the ordering decision.
(7) The lead time is zero.
Based on these assumptions the classic EOQ lot sizing model is given by

$$z = \min_{Q \geq 0} \frac{\lambda K}{Q} + \tfrac{1}{2} hQ \,, \tag{2.1}$$

where Q is the constant reorder quantity. This problem is known to be a useful mathematical approximation for determining lot sizes. However, rather than analyzing it directly, we choose to reformulate it in terms of reorder intervals rather than reorder quantities, where a reorder interval is the time between successive production runs. Obviously there is a relationship between the reorder intervals and the reorder quantities. If T is the reorder interval, then clearly $T = Q/\lambda$. Hence problem (2.1) can be restated in terms of T as follows:

$$z = \min_{T \geq 0} \frac{K}{T} + \tfrac{1}{2} \lambda h T \,. \tag{2.2}$$

We call this problem the economic reorder interval problem. Letting $g = \frac{1}{2}\lambda h$, its solution is

$$T^* = \sqrt{\frac{K}{g}} \tag{2.3}$$

and

$$z^* = 2\sqrt{Kg} \,. \tag{2.4}$$

Thus the optimal solution is to place an order every T^* time units. Since the lead time is zero, the optimal policy is obviously to place and receive an order only when the on-hand inventory level is zero.

It is well known that the average annual cost is relatively insensitive to the choice of T. For example, if $T = 2T^*$, then the corresponding average annual cost exceeds z^* by only 25%. The robustness of the cost to the value of T is an important factor affecting the usefulness of the powers-of-two model.

2.2. Powers-of-two restriction of the economic reorder interval problem

Because the value of T^* can be any positive real number, the solution to problem (2.2) is often impractical to implement. For example, T^* might equal $\sqrt{2}$ weeks. Typically there are practical reasons why orders can be placed only in certain intervals, such as a day, a week, etc. We assume a minimum reorder interval exists, which we called a *base planning period* in Section 1. We denote this base planning period by T_L. It can be a shift, day, week, or other appropriate time period.

We assume that the reorder interval T must be a power of two (i.e., 1, 2, 4, 8, . . . , 2^k, . . . , where k is a nonnegative integer) times the base planning period. That is,

$$T = 2^k \cdot T_L\,, \quad k \in \{0, 1, \ldots\}\,.$$

As we will now see, when restricting ourselves to a policy of this form we can never have a solution whose average annual cost exceeds z^* by more than about 6%.

The powers-of-two reorder interval problem is

$$\begin{aligned} z_c &= \min_{T \geq 0} \frac{K}{T} + gT\,, \\ T &= 2^k T_L\,, \quad k \in \{0, 1, \ldots\}\,. \end{aligned} \tag{2.5}$$

To find its solution we employ a first differencing argument. Let

$$f(T) = \frac{K}{T} + gT\,.$$

Note that if T^* is given by (2.3) and $T = \alpha T^*$, then $f(T) = \frac{1}{2}(\alpha + 1/\alpha) f(T^*)$. Because $f(T)$ is a convex function, we find the solution to problem (2.5) by finding the smallest nonnegative integer value k for which

$$f(2^{k+1} \cdot T_L) \geq f(2^k \cdot T_L)\,.$$

This condition reduces to finding the smallest nonnegative integer k for which

$$2^k \geq \frac{1}{T_L} \sqrt{\frac{K}{2g}} = \frac{1}{\sqrt{2}\,T_L}\, T^*\,. \tag{2.6}$$

In what follows, we assume T_L is chosen such that $T^* \geq T_L$. Because k is chosen to satisfy (2.6), it is clear that

$$\frac{1}{\sqrt{2}}\, T^* \leq 2^k \cdot T_L < \sqrt{2}\, T^*\,. \tag{2.7}$$

Therefore, the optimal power-of-two solution must be close to T^*; it must be at least 0.707 times T^* and no more than 1.41 times T^*. Furthermore, observe that

$$\begin{aligned} f\left(\frac{T^*}{\sqrt{2}}\right) &= f(\sqrt{2}\,T^*) = \left(\sqrt{2} + \frac{1}{\sqrt{2}}\right)\sqrt{Kg} \\ &= \left(\sqrt{2} + \frac{1}{\sqrt{2}}\right)\frac{z^*}{2} \\ &\cong 1.06 z^*\,. \end{aligned} \tag{2.8}$$

Because $f(T)$ is strictly convex,

$$f(2^k \cdot T_L) \leq f(\sqrt{2}T^*) \cong 1.06z^*$$

or

$$\frac{z_c}{z^*} \leq 1.06 .$$

Thus the powers-of-two solution has an objective function value that must be very close to z^*. The average cost of a powers-of-two solution is better yet. If we assume that 2^kT is uniformly distributed over the interval $(T^*/\sqrt{2}, \sqrt{2}T^*)$, then the expected value of z_c/z^* is $\sqrt{0.5}(\frac{3}{4} + \ln 2) \cong 1.0205$.

In summary, the powers-of-two restriction of the economic reorder interval problem produces solutions that are similar in both cost and the values of the reorder intervals to those found when solving problem (2.1). As we will observe, these results hold in even the most general situations we will discuss. This makes the powers-of-two solutions particularly useful, as we shall observe.

3. Serial systems

Perhaps the simplest extension to the single stage economic reorder interval problem is the serial system reorder interval problem. Rather than having a single production stage, we now assume that there are n such stages, as displayed in Figure 1. This graph indicates that each unit that is produced of a single item must go through n distinct stages, beginning with stage n and ending with stage 1. The problem is to determine the reorder intervals for each stage.

The assumptions on which our analysis is performed are relatively obvious extensions of the ones made in the previous sections and account for the presence of n rather than one production stage. We will next introduce some notation and terminology. Some of the notation may seem cumbersome and perhaps unnecessarily complicated to describe this simple problem. We have chosen to introduce it here because it is more easily interpreted in this case and will make the material in subsequent sections more easily understood.

First, we let G represent the directed graph representing the serial production system with $N(G)$ the node set and $A(G)$ the arc set corresponding to G. The graph G is analogous to a bill of material network. The elements of $N(G)$ represent the production stages and the elements in $A(G)$ indicate the precedence constraints implying the order in which operations must be performed. In this serial system $N(G) = \{1, \ldots, n\}$ and $A(G) = \{(n, n-1), (n-1,$

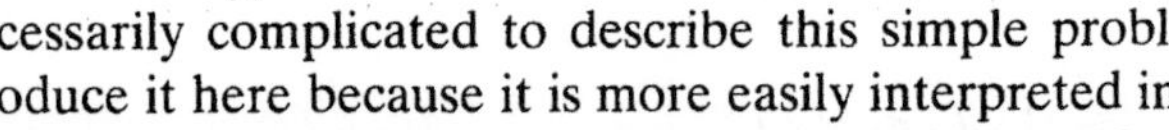

Fig. 1. Graph of a serial system.

$n-2), \ldots, (2, 1)\}$. For each $i \in N(G)$, λ_i represents the total demand rate for the units produced at stage i. Note that λ_i need not be the same for all stages. Several units at stage j could be required to produce one unit at stage $j-1$. However, we will select our units of measure for inventory at the different stages so that $\lambda_i = \lambda$ for all $i \in N(G)$.

Next, let T_i represent the reorder interval for stage i. As in the single stage model, T_i is expressed as a powers-of-two multiple of the base planning period, T_L.

The costs considered in the model are fixed setup costs K_i and holding costs h_i, for all $i \in N(G)$. The holding costs are incremental echelon holding costs, i.e., $h_i = h'_i - h'_{i+1}$ where h'_i is the conventional holding cost at stage i. These echelon holding costs are charged for stage i proportional to the inventory on hand in stage i and all its successor stages. That is, the holding costs for stage i are charged on the inventory on hand in stages 1 through i. Lastly, we let $g_i = \frac{1}{2}h_i\lambda$, the average yearly echelon holding cost for stage i when $T_i = 1$. Before developing the model, we discuss why echelon inventory holding costs are used rather than the usual holding costs. We also discuss the form of the optimal policy.

3.1. Echelon inventory and nested policies

Let us first examine a two stage system to gain an understanding of the importance of using echelon inventory as a basis for charging holding costs and also to establish the form of the policies that will be used.

We restrict our attention to policies that are both stationary and nested, as discussed in Section 1. Although stationary and nested policies need not be optimal for all types of production systems, they are optimal for the serial system we are now examining. To see why a nested policy is optimal consider a two stage system.

Suppose production occurs at time t at stage 2 while no production occurs at stage 1. Suppose that $t' > t$ is the first time following t that production occurs at stage 1. Hence the inventory produced at time t at stage 2 must be held until at least time t' before it is used at stage 1. Consider an alternative production plan in which the production at stage 2 that occurred at t is postponed and is initiated at t' instead. All other production times remain unchanged. Because the number of setups in the two plans is the same and the holding costs are lower in the second one, it is obvious that it is preferable to produce at stage 2 only when production occurs at stage 1.

A formal proof of this assertion is easily constructed for an n stage system by following an argument similar to the one we have stated. We do not present such a proof but state

Theorem 1. *For an n stage serial system it is optimal to follow a nested policy.*

For a proof of this result see Schwarz [1973] or Love [1972].

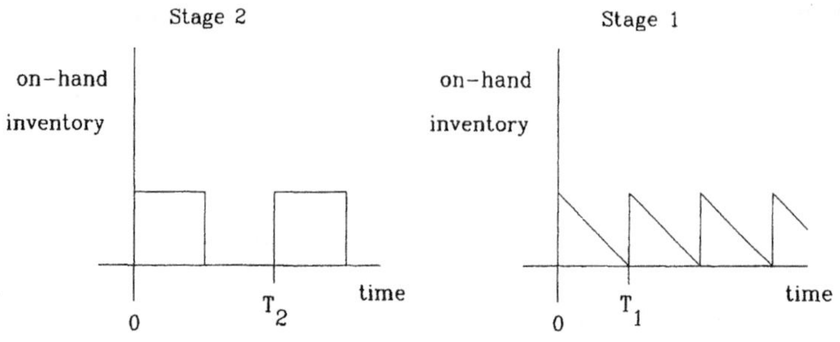

Fig. 2. Graphs of on-hand inventory.

We note, however, that it is possible to have production at stage $i-1$ without having production at stage i. Thus $T_i \geqslant T_{i-1}$.

Returning to our two stage example, suppose that $T_1 = \frac{1}{2}T_2$. Then the on-hand inventory graphs for stages 1 and 2 are given in Figure 2. Note the shapes of these graphs. The graph for stage 1 is the usual saw-toothed curve that is found in the single stage system. However, the graph for stage 2 is not of this form. Furthermore, the average on-hand inventory is not $\frac{1}{2}\lambda T_2$, but is, in this case, $\frac{1}{4}\lambda T_2$. In fact the average on-hand inventory at stage 2 is a function of both T_1 and T_2. On the other hand, the average stock on hand at stage 1 is always $\frac{1}{2}\lambda T_1$, independent of the choice of T_2. The fact that the average on-hand inventory at stage 2 depends on both T_1 and T_2 makes it undesirable to calculate holding costs using the on-hand inventories.

Now suppose we construct the graphs for echelon stock. The echelon stock at stage 1 is the same as the graph of on-hand inventory. The graph of stage 2 echelon stock is quite different. The echelon stock for stage 2 consists of the stock on hand at stage 2, the shaded area in Figure 3, plus the amount on hand at stage 1, represented by triangles a, b, c, and d in the graph. Note that the graph of echelon stock in both stages is saw-toothed in shape.

The average echelon inventory level at stage 2 depends only on T_2. A similar statement applies to stage 1. Thus if inventory costs are charged proportional

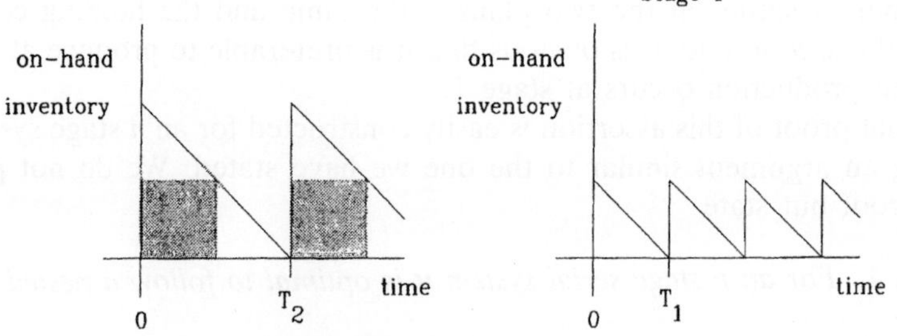

Fig. 3. Graphs of echelon stock.

to echelon inventory levels, then the average costs are $h_2 \cdot \frac{1}{2}\lambda T_2$ and $h_1 \cdot \frac{1}{2}\lambda T_1$ for stages 2 and 1, respectively. This corrects the serious deficiency observed earlier when attempting to charge holding costs based on average on-hand inventory. But what do these costs measure? How do they compare with the holding costs based on on-hand inventory?

Returning to Figure 2, we see that holding costs based on on-hand stock are equal to $(h_1 + h_2) \cdot \frac{1}{2}\lambda T_1$ for stage 1 and $h_2 \cdot \frac{1}{4}\lambda T_2$ for stage 2. The echelon holding cost for stage 1 is $h_1 \cdot \frac{1}{2}\lambda T_1$ and for stage 2 is

$$h_2 \cdot \tfrac{1}{2}\lambda T_2 = h_2 \lambda T_1 = h_2 \cdot \tfrac{1}{2}\lambda T_1 + h_2 \cdot \tfrac{1}{2}\lambda T_1 = h_2 \cdot \tfrac{1}{4}\lambda T_2 + h_2 \cdot \tfrac{1}{2}\lambda T_1 \, .$$

Hence the total carrying costs are the same whether they are calculated using echelon or on-hand inventories. For obvious reasons we choose to use echelon stock as the basis for calculating holding costs.

Clearly, $\frac{1}{2}\lambda T_i$ is the average echelon stock for stage i in any serial system. It is also true that $\frac{1}{2}\lambda T_i$ is the average echelon stock for node $i \in N(G)$ for the more general graphs examined later in this chapter.

3.2. *A reorder interval model and its relaxation*

Using the definitions, assumptions, form of the policies considered, and the echelon inventory method for calculating holding costs, we see that the reorder interval model is

$$\begin{aligned} z_9 = \text{minimize} \quad & \sum_{i \in N(G)} [K_i/T_i + g_i T_i] \, , \\ \text{subject to} \quad & T_i = 2^l T_L \, , \quad l \in \{0, 1, \ldots\} \, , \\ & T_i \geq T_{i-1} \geq 0 \, . \end{aligned} \tag{3.1}$$

This problem is a nonlinear, integer programming problem. The integer decision variable is l. However, due to its special structure we can easily solve it even when G is an arbitrary acyclic graph. As was the case for the single stage system, problem (3.1) turns out to have a very close relationship to its following relaxation:

$$\begin{aligned} z_{10} = \text{minimize} \quad & \sum_{i \in N(G)} [K_i/T_i + g_i T_i] \\ \text{subject to} \quad & T_i \geq T_{i-1} \geq 0 \, . \end{aligned} \tag{3.2}$$

We now characterize the solution to problem (3.2) and show its relationship to problem (3.1).

3.3. *Characterizations of the optimal solution to problems (3.1) and (3.2)*

We begin by establishing the correspondence between the solutions to problem (3.1) and the ordered partitions of the graph G. These relationships are important for the more general graphs we shall discuss subsequently. Consequently, we use definitions that are more general than needed here.

Define a *subgraph* G' of G to consist of a node set $N(G') \subset N(G)$ together with an arc set $A(G') \subset A(G)$ and where $(i, j) \in A(G')$ if and only if $i, j \in N(G')$. An ordered collection of subgraphs $(G_1, \ldots, G_N)$ of G is said to be *ordered by precedence* if for any $1 \leq l < k \leq N$ there does not exist a node $j \in N(G_l)$ and a node $i \in N(G_k)$ such that $(j, i) \in A(G)$. Consequently, there is no node in $N(G_l)$ that precedes any node in $N(G_k)$, $k > l$. We say that a collection of subgraphs $(G_1, G_2, \ldots, G_N)$ forms an *ordered partition* of G if

(i) the node subsets form a partition of $N(G)$, and

(ii) the collection of subgraphs is ordered by precedence.

For a serial system, an ordered partition of G has the form $N(G_1) = \{1, \ldots, n_1\}$, $N(G_2) = \{n_1 + 1, \ldots, n_2\}, \ldots, N(G_N) = \{n_{N-1}, \ldots, n\}$.

Next we define a directed cut of the subgraph G' to be an ordered (binary) partition (G'^-, G'^+) of G'.

Suppose we have a subgraph G'. Consider the following relaxed problem:

$$\begin{aligned} &\text{minimize} \quad \sum_{i \in N(G')} [K_i/T_i + g_i T_i] \\ &\text{subject to} \quad T_i \geq T_{i-1} \geq 0 \quad \text{for all } (i, i-1) \in A(G') . \end{aligned} \tag{3.3}$$

Suppose further that all reorder intervals T_i, $i \in N(G')$, must be equal; that is, $T_i = T$, $i \in N(G')$. The optimal value of T is

$$T = \left[\frac{\sum_{i \in N(G')} K_i}{\sum_{i \in N(G')} g_i} \right]^{1/2} .$$

If we let $K(G') = \sum_{i \in N(G')} K_i$ and $g(G') = \sum_{i \in N(G')} g_i$, then

$$T = [K(G')/g(G')]^{1/2} .$$

Suppose next that we have a feasible solution to problem (3.2), and suppose there are N distinct reorder intervals associated with this solution. We denote these N reorder intervals by $T^*(1) < T^*(2) < \cdots < T^*(N)$. Then for each reorder interval there must correspond a subset of the production stages sharing that value. Let $G_1, \ldots, G_N$ represent the subgraphs that correspond to these N distinct intervals. Because $\cup_{i=1}^N N(G_i) = N(G)$ and the subgraphs are disjoint, these subgraphs form an ordered partition of G. In an optimal solution to problem (3.2) we must also have $T^*(k) = [K(G_k)/g(G_k)]^{1/2}$ for $k = 1, \ldots, N$.

Conversely, let $(G_1, \ldots, G_N)$ be an ordered partition of the graph G. Also, let $T^*(k) = [K(G_k)/g(G_k)]^{1/2}$, $k = 1, \ldots, N$, and assume $T_i^* = T^*(k)$ for all $i \in N(G_k)$. Then this solution is feasible to problem (3.2) if $T^*(1) \leq T^*(2) \leq \cdots \leq T^*(N)$, or equivalently

$$\frac{K(G_1)}{g(G_1)} \leq \frac{K(G_2)}{g(G_2)} \leq \cdots \leq \frac{K(G_N)}{g(G_N)} .$$

The relationship between the optimal solutions to problem (3.2) and the ordered partitions of G is given by:

Theorem 2. *Suppose we have an arbitrary collection of N reorder intervals, $T^*(1), \ldots, T^*(N)$. The following conditions are necessary and sufficient for these reorder intervals to provide an optimal solution to problem* (3.2):

(i) *There exists an ordered partition $(G_1, \ldots, G_N)$ of G such that*

$$T^*(k) = [K(G_k)/g(G_k)]^{1/2} ;$$

(ii) $T^*(1) \leq T^*(2) \leq \cdots \leq T^*(N)$;

(iii) *For each $k = 1, \ldots, N$, there does not exist a directed cut (G_k^-, G_k^+) of G_k for which*

$$\frac{(K(G_k^-)}{g(G_k^-)} < \frac{K(G_k^+)}{g(G_k^+)} .$$

The proof of this theorem can be found in Jackson, Maxwell, & Muckstadt [1988].

Any ordered partition of G that satisfies the three above conditions is an *optimal partition*. These conditions also provide a means for identifying optimal solutions for the more general graphs discussed in the succeeding sections of this chapter. The node sets $N(G_1), N(G_2), \ldots, N(G_N)$ are called *clusters*. Note that the solution to (3.2) can easily be constructed once the clusters are known. In the following section we give an algorithm that solves (3.2) for a serial system by finding the clusters. In Section 6 we show how a standard network algorithm can be used to find the clusters for an arbitrary acyclic graph G.

Now suppose we are given an optimal partition $G_1, \ldots, G_N$ of the serial system graph G. Let $T^*(k)$ be the corresponding optimal solution. Now let us see how we can find the optimal powers-of-two solution to problem (3.1). Let $T_i = T(k)$, $i \in N(G_k)$, $k = 1, \ldots, N$, where we find $T(k)$ by solving

$$\begin{aligned} &\text{minimize} \quad \sum_{i \in N(G_k)} [K_i/T(k) + g_i T(k)] , \\ &\text{subject to} \quad T(k) = 2^l T_L , \quad l \in \{0, 1, \ldots\} . \end{aligned} \tag{3.4}$$

$T(k)$ is found using a first differencing approach as discussed for the single stage case. Thus $T(k) = 2^l T_L$, where l is the smallest nonnegative integer for which

$$2^l \geq \frac{1}{T_L}\left[\frac{K(G_k)}{2g(G_k)}\right]^{1/2} = \frac{1}{\sqrt{2}T_L}\,T^*(k)\,. \tag{3.5}$$

Observe that $T^*(k-1) < T^*(k)$ implies that $T(k-1) \leq T(k)$, assuming that l is chosen using (3.5) for all clusters k. Therefore an optimal solution to (3.5) satisfies the precedence constraint in problem (3.1). Hence this solution is feasible for (3.1). Furthermore, by applying the fact that there are no directed cuts for G_k satisfying the conditions of part (iii) of Theorem 2, we can show that this solution is *optimal* for problem (3.1). The details proving that this ordered partition is optimal can be found in Maxwell & Muckstadt [1985].

3.4. *An algorithm for finding the optimal ordered partition for a serial system*

The following algorithm can be used to find the optimal ordered partition for a serial system. It consists of three main steps. In the first, we find the clusters, or equivalently, an optimal partition of G; in the second, we solve problem (3.2); and in the third, we solve problem (3.1). Given an arbitrary node set C, we define $T^*(C) = [(\Sigma_{i\in C} K_i)/(\Sigma_{i\in C} g_i)]^{1/2}$.

Algorithm 1. *Serial systems.*

Step 1. *Find an optimal partition of* G.

(a) Set $C^i \leftarrow \{i\}$ and $\sigma(i) \leftarrow i-1$ for all $1 \leq i \leq n$, and $S \leftarrow \{1, 2, \ldots, n\}$. Set $j \leftarrow 2$. Note: $\sigma(i)$ is the node that precedes i in the sequence S.

(b) If $T^*(C^j) \geq T^*(C^{\sigma(j)})$, go to Step 1d; otherwise, collapse $C^{\sigma(j)}$ into C^j by setting $C^j \leftarrow C^{\sigma(j)} \cup C^j$, $\sigma(j) \leftarrow \sigma(\sigma(j))$, and $S \leftarrow S\backslash\{\sigma(j)\}$.

(c) If $\sigma(j) > 0$, go to Step 1b.

(d) Set $j \leftarrow j+1$. If $j \leq n$, go to Step 1b.

(e) Re-index the clusters $\{C^i\colon i \in S\}$ so that $S = \{1, 2, \ldots, N\}$ and if $j \in C^i$, $k \in C^l$, and $j < k$ then $i < l$.

Comment: $\{C^k\colon k \in S\}$ are the clusters. The optimal partition is $\{G_k\colon k \in S\}$ where G_k is the subgraph of G induced by C^k. Thus $C^k = N(G_k)$.

Step 2. *Find the Solution to problem* (3.2).

For each cluster C^k, $k \in S$, set

$$T^*(k) = T^*(C^k) = \left[\Big(\sum_{i\in C^k} K_i\Big)\Big/\Big(\sum_{i\in C^k} g_i\Big)\right]^{1/2}.$$

For each $i \in C^k$ set $T_i^* = T^*(k)$.

Step 3. *Find the Solution to problem* (3.4).

For each $i \in C^k$ set $T_i = 2^l T_L$ where $2^l \geq T^*(k)/\sqrt{2}T_L > 2^{l-1}$.

It is sometimes desirable to impose a uniform lower and/or upper bound which applies to all reorder intervals. Suppose we add to problem (3.1) the constraint

$$2^{\underline{l}}T_L \leq T_i \leq 2^{\bar{l}}T_L \quad \forall i \in N(G)\,.$$

If $i \in C^k$, an optimal solution to this version of (3.1) is obtained by selecting $T_i = 2^{\underline{l}}T_L$ if $T^*(k) \leq 2^{\underline{l}}T_L$, $T_i = 2^{\bar{l}}T_L$ if $T^*(k) \geq 2^{\bar{l}}T_L$, and selecting T_i as in Step 3 above if $2^{\underline{l}}T_L \leq T^*(k) \leq 2^{\bar{l}}T_L$. If this is done all claims of optimality and near-optimality made in the following still apply.

An alternate procedure for performing Step 3 is found by Roundy [1986]. This procedure has the advantage of producing policies that are within 2% of optimal, rather than the 6% bound that results from Step 3 above. However, this procedure requires that T_L be treated as a variable. For many systems the base planning period is determined by the times at which information is reported and acted upon, and cannot be treated as a variable.

The relaxation (3.2) of problem (3.1) was first formulated and solved in a more general setting by Schwarz & Schrage [1975]. The system myopic policies they proposed use a rounding scheme that is similar to Step 3, but they do not use the same values of T^*.

3.5. *Analysis of worst-case behavior of the algorithm*

To establish the worst-case behavior of the algorithm we calculate an upper bound on the optimal objective function value to problem (3.1) and compare it to a lower bound. The lower bound is found by solving problem (3.2), as we will subsequently demonstrate. We carry out this worst-case analysis for the serial system in detail. A similar analysis can be performed for other graph structures. However, we will not conduct this analysis for these cases but will only assert the conclusions that would result from such an analysis.

Suppose we have an optimal partition of G found using the algorithm described in the previous section. Let $(G_1, \ldots, G_N)$ represent this partition. Then

$$T_i^* = T^*(k) \quad \text{for all } i \in N(G_k)\,,$$

where

$$T^*(k) = [K(G_k)/g(G_k)]^{1/2}\,,$$

$$z_{10} = \sum_{k=1}^{N} 2\sqrt{K(G_k) \cdot g(G_k)}\,.$$

Recall that $T(k)$, $k = 1, \ldots, N$, represents the optimal solution to problem (3.1), where

$$T(k) = 2^l \cdot T_L ,$$

and l is the smallest nonnegative integer satisfying

$$2^l \geq \frac{1}{\sqrt{2}T_L} \sqrt{\frac{K(G_k)}{g(G_k)}} = \frac{1}{\sqrt{2}T_L} T^*(k) .$$

Then

$$\frac{T^*(k)}{\sqrt{2}} \leq T(k) < \sqrt{2}T^*(k) .$$

Let

$$f_i(T_i) = \frac{K(G_k)}{T_i} + g(G_k) \cdot T_i , \quad i \in N(G_k) .$$

Because $f_i(\cdot)$ is convex and

$$f_i\left(\frac{T^*(k)}{\sqrt{2}}\right) = f_i(\sqrt{2}T^*(k)) = \left(\sqrt{2} + \frac{1}{\sqrt{2}}\right)\sqrt{K(G_k) \cdot g(G_k)} ,$$

we have

$$f_i(T(k)) \leq \left(\sqrt{2} + \frac{1}{\sqrt{2}}\right)\sqrt{K(G_k) \cdot g(G_k)} .$$

Hence the solution to problem (3.1) satisfies

$$\begin{aligned} z_9 &= \sum_{k=1}^{N} \left\{ \sum_{i \in N(G_k)} [K_i / T(k) + g_i T(k)] \right\} \\ &\leq \left(\sqrt{2} + \frac{1}{\sqrt{2}}\right) \sum_{k=1}^{N} \sqrt{K(G_k) \cdot g(G_k)} \\ &= \tfrac{1}{2}\left(\sqrt{2} + \frac{1}{\sqrt{2}}\right) z_{10} , \end{aligned}$$

so that

$$\frac{z_9}{z_{10}} \leq 1.06 .$$

This is the same result we obtained in the single stage model and one that holds for all the models discussed in this chapter.

We now show that z_{10} is a lower bound on the long run minimum average cost attainable for a nested policy. This result also holds for more general cases as well.

Let $z(t)$ represent the minimal holding and setup costs incurred over an interval of length t given a nested production plan is followed. We will show that

$$z_{10} \leq \lim_{t\to\infty} z(t)/t .$$

Let $n_i(t)$ be the number of setups for stage i through time t, and let τ_{ik} represent the time at which the kth setup occurs for stage i. We assume $\tau_{i0} = 0$, $i \in N(G)$. Because the production plan is nested,

$$\tau_{ik} = \tau_{i-1,k'}$$

for some $k' \geq k$, $k = 1, \ldots, n_i(t)$.

Now let h_i' represent the holding cost per year for on-hand inventory held at stage i. If τ_i represents the sequence of setup times for stage i over the horizon of length t, we define $I_i(u; \tau_i, n_i(t))$ to be the on-hand inventory at stage i at time u, $u \in [0, t]$, given policy τ_i and $n_i(t)$ setups over the interval of length t. Furthermore, let $E_i(u; \tau_i, n_i(t))$ represent the corresponding echelon inventory at time u, $u \in [0, t]$. Thus the total holding cost during the interval is

$$\sum_{i\in N(G)} h_i' \int_0^t I_i(u; \tau_i, n_i(t))\, dt . \tag{3.6}$$

As we discussed earlier, (3.6) can be restated as

$$\sum_{i\in N(G)} h_i \int_0^t E_i(u; \tau_i, n_i(t))\, dt . \tag{3.7}$$

Let us temporarily ignore the fact that we must follow a nested policy. Because there are $n_i(t)$ setups for stage i, it is easy to prove that the time between setups should be equal if holding costs are to be minimized at stage i. The echelon holding costs over the planning period for stage i, assuming equally spaced setups of length $T_i = t/n_i(t)$ time units, is $g_i T_i t$. Because this is a lower bound on echelon holding costs for stage i,

$$h_i \int_0^t E_i(u; \tau_i, n_i(t))\, du \geq g_i T_i t .$$

The setup cost for stage i over $[0, t]$ is $n_i(t) \cdot K_i = (t/T_i)K_i$. Thus

$$z(t) = \underset{n_i(t),\tau_{ik}}{\text{minimum}} \sum_{i\in N(G)} \left(n_i(t) \cdot K_i + h_i \int_0^t E_i(u; \tau_i, n_i(n))\, du\right) .$$

Given that τ_i is nested

$$z(t) \geq \underset{T_i}{\text{minimum}} \left\{ \sum_{i \in N(G)} \left(\frac{K_i}{T_i} + g_i T_i \right) \cdot t \colon T_i \geq T_{i-1} \geq 0 \right\}$$
$$= z_{10} \cdot t \,.$$

Thus $z_{10} \leq z(t)/t$ for all $t > 0$ and therefore $z_{10} \leq \lim_{t \to \infty} z(t)/t$.

3.6. Summary

A number of key ideas introduced in this section will re-appear in several later sections. For this reason we summarize some of the most important elements of the analysis we have just described.

The problem of finding a powers-of-two stationary nested policy with minimal cost was formulated as the nonlinear integer program, problem (3.1). The variables in this problem are the reorder intervals. A near-optimal policy was obtained by solving the continuous relaxation of this problem, and rounding off the reorder intervals to get a feasible, stationary, nested powers-of-two policy.

Two facts about the solution to the continuous relaxation, problem (3.2), are noteworthy. The first is that the bill of material network G is partitioned into subgraphs. The set of nodes or stages in a given subgraph was called a *cluster*. All stages in a cluster use the same reorder interval. Local optimality implies that the reorder interval for the stage in cluster C is $[(\Sigma_{i \in C} K_i)/(\Sigma_{i \in C} g_i)]^{1/2}$. Thus finding the clusters is equivalent to solving problem (3.1).

The second fact is that the solution to problem (3.2) was shown to be a lower bound on the average cost of any feasible policy for the original system, including policies that are neither powers-of-two nor stationary. We showed that the cost of the feasible policy we compute is within 6% of the solution of problem (3.1). Because nested policies are optimal in serial systems, our heuristic is guaranteed to compute a policy whose cost is at most 6% above the cost of an optimal policy.

Optimization problems similar to problems (3.1) and (3.2) will appear in every section of this chapter. The relationship between them, the policies, and bounds on the cost performance of those policies is similar in every section.

4. Assembly systems

We next consider a multi-stage system in which a single finished product is assembled from a set of parts. Each part could be manufactured in several stages and could also be assembled from several other parts. Such systems are called assembly systems and have bill of material networks that are arborescences. Figure 4 is an example of a graph G of this type of system. For ease of discussion, we assume that each node in $N(G)$ represents the fabrication of a part. Hence node i corresponds to the stage in which part i is manufactured.

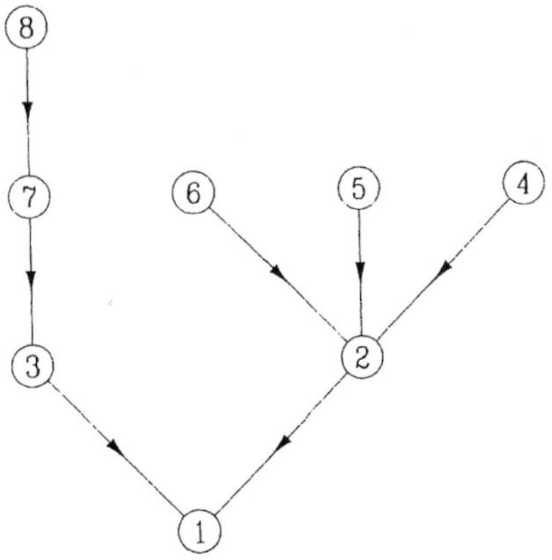

Fig. 4. An assembly system.

We assume that each part $i > 1$ is consumed at a unique *direct successor* stage. We define part 1 to be the finished product. It has no successor stage; instead, it is consumed by external demand, which, as before, is constant, continuous, and must be met without backlogging.

The other assumptions made in Section 2 regarding costs and machine times hold here as well. Furthermore, our goal is to determine reorder intervals for each part so that the long-run average annual setup plus holding costs are minimized.

4.1. *Stationary nested power-of-two policies and their costs*

As before, we restrict attention to stationary nested powers-of-two policies. In Section 3 we argued that nested policies are optimal for serial systems. Each stage of an assembly system has either no external demand and a unique successor, or no successor and external demand. Therefore, the same argument could be used to show that nested policies are optimal for assembly systems.

Let us introduce some additional notation. Let s_i be the direct successor of component i, p_i be the set of direct predecessors of component i, S_i be the set composed of i and all of its successors, direct or indirect, and let P_i be similarly defined. We assume without loss of generality that if $j \in p_i$, then one unit of j is consumed for each unit of i ordered.

Recall that the *echelon holding cost* for part i is h_i and is the amount by which the holding cost of part i exceeds the sum of the holding costs of its direct predecessors. It is assumed that the echelon holding costs of all of the parts are positive. The *echelon inventory* E_i^t of part i at time t is the sum of the inventories of all j, $j \in S_i$. Using the same argument in Section 3, the total rate at which holding costs are being incurred at time t is $\Sigma_i h_i E_i^t$.

Let the stages of the assembly system be numbered 1 through n. We denote the powers-of-two policy by $\mathcal{T} = (T_i, 1 \leq i \leq n)$. Recall that a *nested* policy is a policy in which an order is placed at the successor of stage i simultaneously with every order at i. Hence in this case, $\mathcal{T}$ is nested if and only if

$$T_i \geq T_{s_i} \quad \text{for all } i\,. \tag{4.1}$$

It is easy to show that an optimal policy is nested and has the following property.

The Zero-Ordering Property. *Orders are placed at stage i only when the inventory of i is zero.*

In the sequel we will restrict attention to stationary nested powers-of-two policies that satisfy the Zero-Ordering Property. This implies that the average cost of $\mathcal{T}$ can be written as

$$c(\mathcal{T}) = \sum_i (K_i/T_i + g_i T_i) \tag{4.2}$$

where $g_i = \frac{1}{2}h_i\lambda$ and λ is the demand rate.

4.2. Structural results and computation

The problem of finding an optimal stationary nested powers-of-two policy can therefore be written as

$$\text{minimize} \quad \sum_i (K_i/T_i + g_i T_i)$$

$$\text{subject to} \quad T_i \geq T_{s_i} \quad \text{for all } i\,, \tag{4.3}$$

$$T_i = 2^l T_L\,, \quad l = 0, 1, 2, \ldots, \quad T_L > 0\,. \tag{4.4}$$

We call this problem (4.3) and solve it using the approach of Section 3. The first step in solving it is to relax (4.4) and solve

$$\begin{aligned} &\text{minimize} \quad \sum_i (K_i/T_i + g_i T_i) \\ &\text{subject to} \quad T_i \geq T_{s_i} \quad \text{for all } i\,. \end{aligned} \tag{4.5}$$

This is done for two reasons. First, it will give us a set of approximate reorder intervals that we will round off to integer powers-of-two. Second, it will give us a lower bound on the average cost of an arbitrary policy for this problem. The lower bound is used in evaluating our heuristic.

As we discussed in Section 3, the solution to problem (4.5) partitions the network G of Figure 4 into connected subgraphs. The nodes in these connected subgraphs are sets of stages whose costs induce them to place orders simultaneously. As before, we call these node sets *clusters*. We define the *root* of a cluster C to be the unique state $i \in C$ satisfying $C \subseteq P_i$.

Let C^i be the cluster whose root is stage i, $K(C^i) \equiv \Sigma_{j \in C^i} K_j$ be the total setup cost for cluster i, and $g(C^i) \equiv \Sigma_{j \in C^i} g_j$ be the total echelon holding cost for cluster i. For $j \in C^i$ we define $K(j) \equiv \Sigma_{k \in P_j \cap C^i} K_k$ and $g(j) \equiv \Sigma_{k \in P_j \cap C^i} g_k$. If $i \neq j \in C^i$ and we were to partition cluster i by letting j be the root of a new cluster, the total setup cost of the new cluster rooted at j would be $K(j)$ and the total holding cost would be $g(j)$. The following lemma is the assembly system analog of Theorem 2 in Section 3.

Lemma 1. *$\mathcal{T} = (T_i^*: 1 \leq i \leq n)$ solves problem (4.5) if and only if there is a partition of the stages into clusters C^i that satisfies the following conditions:*

C^i is the node set of a connected subgraph of graph G with root i ,

$$T_n^* = T^*(i) \quad \text{for all } n \in C^i \text{ and for all clusters } i\,, \tag{4.6}$$

$$T^*(i) = (K(C^i)/g(C^i))^{1/2} \quad \text{for all clusters } i\,, \tag{4.7}$$

$$K(C^i)/g(C^i) \geq K(C^j)/g(C^j) \quad \text{whenever } s_i \in C^j\,, \tag{4.8}$$

$$K(j)/g(j) < K(C^i)/g(C^i) \quad \text{for all } j \in C^i,\ j \neq i\,. \tag{4.9}$$

Equation (4.9) states that if we try to split cluster i in two by letting j be the root of a new cluster, the constraint $T_j^* \geq T_k^*$, $k = s_j$, will be violated. To see this, suppose that we split cluster i. Note that the total setup cost of the portion of cluster i that does not contain j is $K(C^i) - K(j)$ and the total holding cost is $g(C^i) - g(j)$. Because $K(j)/g(j) < K(C^i)/g(C^i)$, (4.6) and (4.7) imply that

$$T_j^{*2} = K(j)/g(j) < (K(C^i) - K(j))/(g(C^i) - g(j)) = T_k^{*2}\,, \quad k = s_j\,.$$

We are now ready to give an algorithm for computing the clusters. This algorithm is known as the *minimum violators algorithm* and was developed to solve the statistical problem of isotonic regression [Thompson, 1962; Best & Chakravarty, 1988]. Once the clusters have been identified, Steps 2 and 3 of Algorithm 1 are used to compute solutions to problems (4.5) and (4.3).

Algorithm 2. *The minimum violators algorithm.*

Step 1. Create a singleton cluster for each component in the system. Let the set Q initially consist of roots of all clusters other than the one containing the final product. (Subsequently, the set Q will be the set of roots of clusters C^i for which we do not know that (4.8) holds.) Let $r = \{1\}$ (Subsequently, r will be the set of roots of the clusters that solve problem (4.5).)

Step 2. If Q is empty, then stop; the clusters C^i, $i \in r$, are optimal.

Otherwise, find a cluster $i \in Q$ for which $K(C^i)/g(C^i)$ is minimal. In the event that there is a tie, choose a cluster C^i for which $|S_i|$ is minimal. Let $s_i \in C^j$.

Step 3. Remove i from Q. If $K(C^i)/g(C^i) \geq K(C^j)/g(C^j)$, then add i to r and go to Step 2. If $K(C^i)/g(C^i) < K(C^j)/g(C^j)$, then collapse cluster i into cluster j ($C^j \leftarrow C^j \cup C^i$) and go to Step 2.

The minimum violators algorithm can be implemented in $O(n \log n)$ time by using an appropriate data structure for $\{K(C^i)/g(C^i): i \in Q\}$. At each iteration of the algorithm we remove the member of this set that lexicographically minimizes $(K(C^i)/g(C^i), |S_i|)$. In many of the iterations we alter the value of one of the elements of the set. Using a heap (or any of several other data structures), these two operations can both be performed in $O(\log n)$ time [Aho, Hopcroft & Ullman, 1974]. Because the number of iterations is at most $n-1$, the overall running time of the algorithm is $O(n \log n)$. Another algorithm for computing clusters for this problem is found in Schwarz & Schrage [1975]. That algorithm can also be implemented to run in $O(n \log n)$ time.

The proof that the minimum violators algorithm computes the optimal clusters is based on Equations (4.6)–(4.9). The main ideas are as follows.

It is easily verified that the algorithm maintains the following two properties:

$$\bigcup_{i \in Q \cup r} C^i = N(G)$$

$$K(C^i)/g(C^i) \geq K(C^j)/g(C^j) \quad \text{for all } i \in Q\,,\ j \in (r \backslash \{1\})\,. \tag{4.10}$$

Furthermore, the value of $\min_{i \in Q} K(C^i)/g(C^i)$ is nondecreasing as the algorithm progresses. Consequently, if $K(C^i)/g(C^i) \geq K(C^j)/g(C^j)$ in Step 3, then $j \in r$; if $K(C^i)/g(C^i) < K(C^j)/g(C^j)$, then $j \in Q \cup \{1\}$. Therefore, once $i \neq 1$ is added to r in Step 3, no changes are made to C^i.

When the algorithm terminates the preceding paragraph implies that (4.8) holds. The proof that (4.9) holds is found in Roundy [1985b]. Equations (4.6) and (4.7) follow from Step 2 of Algorithm 1, which is used to compute the T_n^*'s.

By substituting (4.6) and (4.7) into the objective function of (4.5), we see that the solution to problem (4.5) is

$$z^* \equiv \sum_{i \in r} 2\sqrt{K(C^i)g(C^i)}\,. \tag{4.11}$$

As was done for the serial system in Section 3, it can be shown that z^* is a lower bound on the average cost of any feasible solution to the original lot sizing problem. When the reorder intervals T_i^* computed by the minimum violators algorithm are rounded off to an integer powers-of-two times T_L, the cost of the resulting policy computed is known to be within 6% of optimal or, if the roundoff procedure that treats T_L as a variable is used, is within 2% of optimal.

5. Distribution systems

We now consider another special type of graph G called a distribution network. Figure 5 contains an illustration of this type of network. The nodes correspond to stages, and the arcs indicate the direction in which material flows through the system. Material enters the system at stage 1, and moves down through the different levels of the system until it is consumed by external demand. Each stage $i > 1$ is supplied by a unique *predecessor stage*, so the distribution network G is an arborescence.

External demand can occur at any or all of the stages. The demand rate at stage i is positive if i has no successors in the network. Again the basic assumptions made in Section 2, and the costs defined there, apply to this case as well. Additionally, the objective is to find a feasible policy for an infinite time horizon which approximately minimizes the long-run average order and holding costs. This model and similar models have been addressed by several authors [Schwarz, 1973; Graves & Schwarz, 1977; and Williams, 1981, 1983].

5.1. *Policies*

As before, we restrict ourselves to stationary nested powers-of-two policies. For the systems of Sections 3 and 4, nested policies were optimal. However for distribution systems, optimal nested policies can be seriously sub-optimal. Suppose for example that our distribution system consists of three stages. Stage one (the factory) supplies two outlets, stages two and three. The factory is in Albany, outlet one is in New York City, and outlet two is in Singapore. The Singapore outlet has very low demand and a very high order cost. For such a system it might be reasonable to place orders at the factory and at the New York outlet on a weekly basis, and to place orders at Singapore less often, say, once every 32 weeks. However if a nested policy were followed, an order could not be placed at the factory unless a simultaneous order were placed at Singapore. A nested policy would incur either high inventory costs at the factory due to a long reorder interval there, or high order costs at the Singapore outlet due to a low reorder interval there, or both.

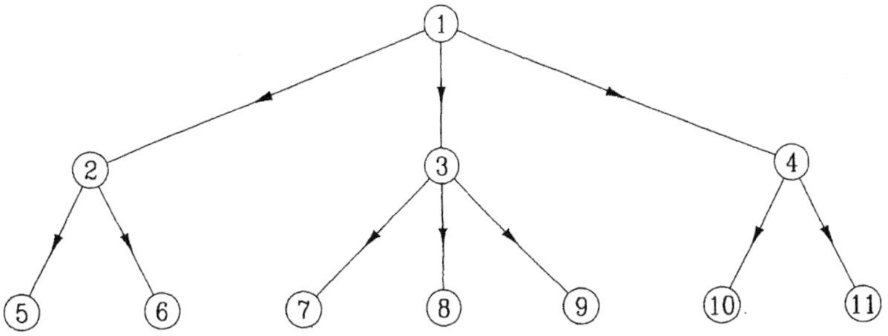

Fig. 5. A distribution system.

As this example illustrates, nested policies tend to become seriously sub-optimal when relatively high order costs are combined with relatively low demand rates. The model of this section is intended for use in situations where all of the stages have fairly high and stable demands. For systems that have stages with low, stable demands and relatively high order costs, the methods of Section 9 are more appropriate. For stages that have sporadic demand, or stages for which the inventory is replenished at pre-determined points in time that are beyond our control, our models are not appropriate. These cases will normally be handled by a different model, possibly one that is based on reorder points and/or order quantities.

5.2. Formulation

As we did in Section 4, we denote a stationary nested powers-of-two policy by $\mathcal{T} = (T_i: 1 \leq i \leq n)$. Note that stage $i > 1$ in the graph G is supplied by a unique *predecessor stage* p_i. The set of *successor stages* S_i of i includes i and all stages that are directly or indirectly supplied through stage i. Because we consider only nested policies, we required that

$$T_{p_i} \geq T_i \quad \text{for all } i > 1\,, \ (p_i, i) \in A(G)\,. \tag{5.1}$$

The *echelon inventory* at stage i at time t is E_i^t, the sum of the inventories at all stages j, $j \in S_i$. Because the *echelon holding cost* h_i at stage i is given by $h_i = h_i' - h_{p_i}'$ where h_i' is the conventional holding cost at stage i, the rate at which holding costs are accumulating at time t is $\Sigma_i h_i E_i^t$. The demand for the echelon inventory at stage i is $\lambda_i > 0$, the sum of the external demand rates at the stages j, $j \in S_i$.

As before, we assume that the Zero-Ordering Property of Section 4 holds, i.e., that no stage places an order when its inventory level is positive. As in Sections 3 and 4, if $\mathcal{T}$ is a stationary nested powers-of-two policy that satisfies the Zero-Ordering Property, then the echelon inventory at stage i follows the traditional sawtooth pattern with a minimum level of zero and a maximum level of $\lambda_i T_i$. Therefore, the average cost incurred by $\mathcal{T}$ is

$$\sum_i (K_i/T_i + g_i T_i) \tag{5.2}$$

where $g_i = \frac{1}{2}\lambda_i h_i$ as usual. Therefore the problem of finding an optimal stationary nested powers-of-two policy can be written as

$$\text{minimize} \quad \sum_i (K_i/T_i + g_i T_i) \tag{5.3}$$

$$\text{subject to} \quad T_{p_i} \geq T_i \quad \text{for all } i > 1\,, \tag{5.4}$$

$$T_i = 2^{l_i} T_L\,, \quad l_i = 0, 1, 2, \ldots, \; T_L > 0\,. \tag{5.5}$$

We call this problem (5.3).

5.3. Solution

As in earlier sections, we relax (5.5), solve the resulting problem, and then round off the reorder intervals to a powers-of-two times T_L. We will show that the relaxation of problem (5.3) can be solved by the algorithm of Section 4 via a simple transformation.

The only difference between the relaxation of (5.3) and problem (4.5) is the form of the constraint (5.4). In both cases the constraint takes on the form $T_i \geq T_j$ whenever $(i, j) \in A(G)$. But here the arcs are oriented away from the root of the arborescence, whereas in Section 4 they were oriented towards the root.

We transform the relaxation of problem (5.3) into an instance of problem (4.5) as follows. Let $U_n = 1/T_n$. Then the relaxation can be rewritten as

$$\text{minimize} \quad \sum_i (g_i/U_i + K_i U_i) \tag{5.6}$$

$$\text{subject to} \quad U_i \geq U_{p_i} \quad \text{for all } i > 1 \, . \tag{5.7}$$

The problem, which we call problem (5.6), is of the form of problem (4.5). The roles of the setup cost K_i and the holding cost coefficient g_i have been interchanged. The orientation of the arcs in the distribution network has been reversed to convert it into the bill of material network of an assembly system. Thus, in the language of Section 4, p_i is the successor of i. The clusters that solve problem (5.6) also solve the relaxation of problem (5.3). They can be computed by applying Algorithm 2 of Section 4 to problem (5.6). Then the reorder intervals that solve problem (5.3) are calculated as in Algorithm 1, Steps 2 and 3.

5.4. Performance analysis

This algorithm computes nested policies, and the ratio of the cost of an optimal nested policy to the cost of an optimal policy can be arbitrarily high. However, the cost of the policy computed by our algorithm can be shown to be within 6% of the cost of an optimal nested policy or, if the base period is treated as a variable, within 2% of the cost of an optimal nested policy.

6. A model of general multistage production–distribution systems

In this section we present a model for establishing reorder intervals in general multistage production–distribution systems. By this we mean that the graph G that describes the system is an arbitrary acyclic directed graph.

Our analysis is based on the assumptions made in Section 2. We also continue to assume that only nested and stationary policies are of interest. Because the output rate for all final products is assumed to be constant and continuous, we let λ_i represent the stationary, continuous demand rate for echelon stock for node (operation) i, $i \in N(G)$. As before, h_i represents echelon holding costs, K_i represents the fixed setup costs, and $g_i = \frac{1}{2} h_i \lambda_i$.

Based on these definitions and our assumptions we state the general multi-stage production–distribution system model as

$$\begin{aligned} &\text{minimize} \quad \sum_{i \in N(G)} [K_i / T_i + g_i T_i] \\ &\text{subject to} \quad T_i = 2^{l_i} T_L, \quad i \in N(G), \\ &\qquad T_i \geq T_j, \quad (i, j) \in A(G), \\ &\qquad l_i \text{ integer}, \quad i \in N(G). \end{aligned} \tag{6.1}$$

6.1. Solving problem (6.1)

Problem (6.1) is a large-scale, nonlinear, integer programming problem. In practical situations, the sets $N(G)$ and $A(G)$ could contain many thousands of elements. Consequently, in these cases an optimal solution to problem (6.1) cannot be directly obtained using a standard branch and bound algorithm. To circumvent this problem, we solve it using a two-step procedure. Before presenting the details, we discuss the objectives and approach followed in each step.

In the first step we solve a relaxed version of problem (6.1) to establish what groups of operations must have identical reorder intervals. The mathematical formulation of this relaxed problem, which we call problem (6.2), is

$$\begin{aligned} &\text{minimize} \quad \sum_{i \in N(G)} [K_i / T_i + g_i T_i] \\ &\text{subject to} \quad T_i \geq T_j \geq 0, \quad (i, j) \in A(G). \end{aligned} \tag{6.2}$$

In Maxwell & Muckstadt [1985] it is proven that if the solution to problem (6.2) indicates that $T_i = T_j$ for $(i, j) \in A(G)$, then operations i and j share a common reorder interval in the solution to problem (6.1). However, the solution to problem (6.2) may not indicate all the operations that should have the same reorder interval in the solution to problem (6.1). For example, the solution to problem (6.2) might state that $T_i = 1.001 T_j$ for some $(i, j) \in A(G)$, so that operations i and j would most likely share a common reorder interval in the solution to problem (6.1). Thus a second step is needed to find the optimal solution to problem (6.1).

The second step of the algorithm uses the solution to problem (6.2) to find the optimal solution to problem (6.1). This is done using Step 3 of Algorithm 1.

6.1.1. *Solving problem (6.2)*

The Kuhn–Tucker conditions. The solution to problem (6.2) is obtained by recognizing that its solution must satisfy its associated Kuhn–Tucker conditions. Because problem (6.2) has a strictly convex objective function and the constraint set is convex, it has a unique optimal solution.

Let us introduce some additional notation. Let $(T_i^*: i \in N(G))$ solve problem (6.2), and let

$P_G(i)$ = direct predecessor set for node i in graph G,

$S_G(i)$ = direct successor set for node i in graph G

θ_{ij} = multiplier for constraint $T_i \geq T_j$ in problem (6.2).

Using these definitions, we can state the Kuhn–Tucker conditions as follows:

$$-K_i/T_i^{*2} + g_i - \sum_{j \in S_G(i)} \theta_{ij} + \sum_{j \in P_G(i)} \theta_{ji} = 0\,, \quad i \in N(G)\,, \tag{6.3}$$

$$\begin{cases} T_i^* \geq 0\,, & i \in N(G)\,, \\ T_i^* - T_j^* \geq 0\,, & (i,j) \in A(G)\,, \end{cases} \tag{6.4}$$

$$\theta_{ij} \geq 0\,, \quad (i,j) \in A(G)\,, \tag{6.5}$$

$$\theta_{ij}(T_i^* - T_j^*) = 0\,, \quad (i,j) \in A(G)\,. \tag{6.6}$$

Observe that condition (6.3) implies that in any optimal solution

$$T_i^* = \left[K_i \Big/ \Big(g_i - \sum_{j \in S_G(i)} \theta_{ij} + \sum_{j \in P_G(i)} \theta_{ji}\Big)\right]^{1/2}.$$

Thus T_i^* is similar to the solution found for the reorder interval in the classic EOQ problem discussed in Section 2; if $\Sigma_{j \in P_G(i)} \theta_{ji} = \Sigma_{j \in S_G(i)} \theta_{ij}$, then T_i^* equals the reorder interval in the EOQ problem. Since multiplier θ_{ij} represents the price for deviating from the economic reorder interval, $\Sigma_{j \in S_G(i)} \theta_{ij}$ measures the subsidy and $\Sigma_{j \in P_G(i)} \theta_{ji}$ measures the penalty to i's holding cost induced by i's successor and predecessor operations, respectively.

Also, observe that the multiplier θ_{ij} corresponds to arc $(i,j) \in A(G)$ and hence appears in exactly two constraints of the type (6.3). Furthermore, the sign of θ_{ij} is different in these two constraints, so that

$$\sum_{i \in N(G)} \left[-\sum_{j \in S_G(i)} \theta_{ij} + \sum_{j \in P_G(i)} \theta_{ji}\right] = 0\,. \tag{6.7}$$

Thus, if the T_i^* are chosen to be equal, we find, by summing over the constraints of type (6.3), that

$$T_i^{*2} = \Big(\sum_{i \in N(G)} K_i\Big) \Big/ \Big(\sum_{i \in N(G)} g_i\Big), \quad i \in N(G).$$

Let this common value of T_i^{*2} be represented by $D(G)$. Assume the T_i^* are chosen to be equal. If there exists θ_{ij} satisfying (6.3) and (6.5), all the Kuhn–Tucker conditions will be satisfied and the optimal solution will have been obtained. Otherwise, all the T_i^* cannot be equal. Finding the optimal solution to problem (6.2) in this case requires subdividing G until all the Kuhn–Tucker conditions are satisfied.

6.1.2. Directed and maximal cuts

The subdivisions of G are called *directed cuts*. A directed cut is a split of G into two separate acyclic directed graphs, G^+ and G^-, so that

(1) $N(G)$ is partitioned into $N(G^+)$ and $N(G^-)$, and

(2) For all $(i, j) \in A(G)$ either

 (a) $i, j \in N(G^+)$, and these (i, j) constitute $A(G^+)$,

 (b) $i, j \in N(G^-)$, and these (i, j) constitute $A(G^-)$, or

 (c) $i \in N(G^+)$ and $j \in N(G^-)$.

The directed cut reflects a partition of $N(G)$ into two sets of clusters of nodes or operations, $N(G^+)$ and $N(G^-)$. Each operation in $N(G^+)$ will have a reorder interval of the same length, and each operation in $N(G^-)$ will share a common reorder interval. The notion of a directed cut implies that conditions (6.5) are satisfied, that is, the common reorder interval for operations in $N(G^+)$ must be at least as large as that for the operations in $N(G^-)$.

Define the value of a directed cut (G^+, G^-) to be

$$v(G^+, G^-) = \sum_{i \in N(G^+)} \{K_i / D(G) - g_i\}.$$

By definition of $D(G)$, $v(G^+, G^-) = \Sigma_{i \in N(G^-)} \{g_i - K_i/D(G)\}$. Suppose $T^*_{G^+}$ and $T^*_{G^-}$ represent the common reorder intervals for the operations in $N(G^+)$ and $N(G^-)$, respectively, and suppose that $T^*_{G^+} = T^*_{G^-} = \sqrt{D(G)}$. As is clear from the definition of a directed cut, the nodes in G^+ precede those in G^- in the graph G. Because of this property, if $T^*_{G^+}$ is increased above $\sqrt{D(G)}$ or $T^*_{G^-}$ is decreased below $\sqrt{D(G)}$, the resulting solution remains feasible. Furthermore, note that the rate of decrease of the objective function, evaluated at $T^{*2}_{G^+} = D(G)$, when $T^*_{G^+}$ increases, is $v(G^+, G^-)$. Similarly, $v(G^+, G^-)$ measures the rate of change or gradient of the objective function as $T^*_{G^-}$ decreases. Consequently, if $v(G^+, G^-) > 0$, then the current solution cannot be optimal and the T_i^* cannot all assume the same value in the optimal solution.

We observe that there are many possible directed cuts that can be constructed corresponding to a graph G. Finding the best directed cut corresponds

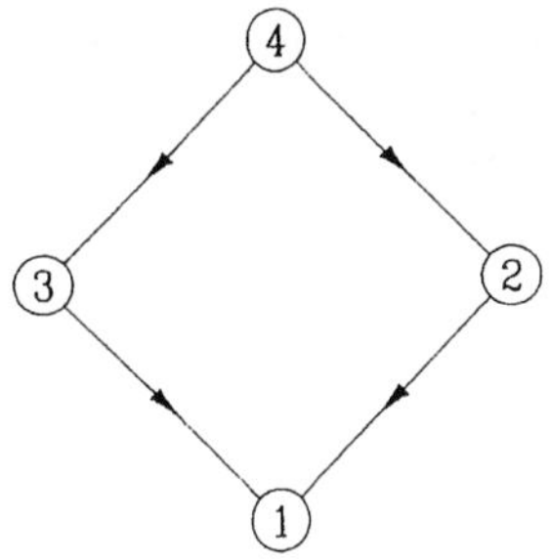

Fig. 6. Example graph.

to finding the one having the maximal value, that is, the one yielding the maximal rate of decrease in cost evaluated at the current value of $T_i^* = \sqrt{D(G)}$. If the value of the maximal cut is nonpositive, then the optimal solution is $T_i^* = \sqrt{D(G)}$ for all $i \in N(G)$.

Consider the graph G given in Figure 6. Suppose $K_1 = 4$, $K_2 = 1$, $K_3 = 6$, $K_4 = 1$, and $g_i = 1$ for all $i = 1, \ldots, 4$. Assuming the reorder intervals are equal, $D(G) = (\Sigma K_i)/(\Sigma g_i) = 3$. Observe that there are four possible directed cuts associated with this graph,

$$\begin{aligned}
&N(G^+) = \{4\}, && N(G^-) = \{3,2,1\}, && v(G^+, G^-) = -\tfrac{2}{3}, \\
&N(G^+) = \{4,3\}, && N(G^-) = \{2,1\}, && v(G^+, G^-) = \tfrac{1}{3}, \\
&N(G^+) = \{4,2\}, && N(G^-) = \{3,1\}, && v(G^+, G^-) = -\tfrac{4}{3}, \\
&N(G^+) = \{4,3,2\}, && N(G^-) = \{1\}, && v(G^+, G^-) = -\tfrac{1}{3}.
\end{aligned}$$

The maximal cut (G^+, G^-) has value $\frac{1}{3}$ with $N(G^+) = \{4, 3\}$ and $N(G^-) = \{2, 1\}$.

6.1.3. Finding the maximal cut

The problem of finding the maximal cut for the graph G corresponding to the solution $T_i^* = \sqrt{D(G)}$ for all $i \in N(G)$ is related to the problem of calculating the multipliers that satisfy the Kuhn–Tucker conditions (6.3). Assume there are n nodes in G numbered 1 through n. Let $a_i = K_i/D(G) - g_i$ for $i = 1, \ldots, n$. Then the multipliers satisfying (6.3), given $T_i^* = \sqrt{D(G)}$, correspond to flows in a transshipment network having n nodes and having supply available for shipment at nodes for which $a_i < 0$ and requirements for supply at nodes for which $a_i > 0$. Nodes having $a_i = 0$ are transshipment nodes. If the flow satisfying the constraints (6.3) also satisfies the nonnegativity requirements (6.5), the graph G does not need to be subdivided; however, if no such solution exists, then at least one $\theta_{ij} < 0$.

To determine the maximal cut, we solve a minimum flow problem on a graph G', which is related to G as follows.

Graph G' has two nodes in addition to those found in G. The first new node, which we call node 0, is a source node; the second new node, labeled node $n+1$, is a sink node. The other n nodes correspond to those found in G. Furthermore, if $(i, j) \in A(G)$, then $(i, j) \in A(G')$; G' has another $2n$ arcs in the form $(0, i)$ and $(i, n+1)$ for $i \in N(G)$. Associated with each arc $(i, j) \in A(G')$ is a lower bound, $l(i, j)$, on the flow θ_{ij} over that arc. For all $(i, j) \in A(G)$, let $l(i, j) = 0$; for arcs of the form $(0, i) \in A(G')$, let $l(i, j) = 0$; for arcs $(i, n+1) \in A(G')$, let $l(i, n+1) = a_i = K_i/D(F) - g_i$.

The graph G' corresponding to the graph G given in Figure 6 is shown in Figure 7. The numbers on the arcs represent the lower bounds on the flows.

The addition of the source node to the transshipment network ensures that a flow that satisfies conditions related to (6.3) and (6.5) exists. In particular, by adding this node, conditions (6.3) become, for each $i \in N(G)$,

$$\theta_{0i} + \sum_{j \in P_G(i)} \theta_{ji} - \sum_{j \in S_G(i)} \theta_{ij} = a_i .$$

The flow $v = \sum_{i=1}^{n} \theta_{0i}$ measures the total requirement in the original transshipment network that cannot be satisfied without reversing the orientation on at least one arc, that is, by making at least one $\theta_{ij} < 0$. If $v = 0$, then a feasible flow satisfying (6.3) and (6.5) exists.

The sink node appended to the original network serves a different purpose. Each arc $(i, n+1)$ has a corresponding lower bound on its flow. If the lower bound is positive, that is, $a_i > 0$, then a node i has a requirement in the original network. If $a_i < 0$, node i has a supply in the original network. In this latter case, the negative lower bound on the arc $(i, n+1)$ indicates that the natural supply orientation of this arc has been reversed. Thus the negative lower bound indicates that a flow can exist from node $n+1$ to i that cannot exceed $-a_i$.

By adding both the source and sink nodes, we can rewrite (6.3) as

$$\theta_{i,n+1} + \sum_{j \in S_G(i)} \theta_{ij} = \theta_{0i} + \sum_{j \in P_G(i)} \theta_{ji} .$$

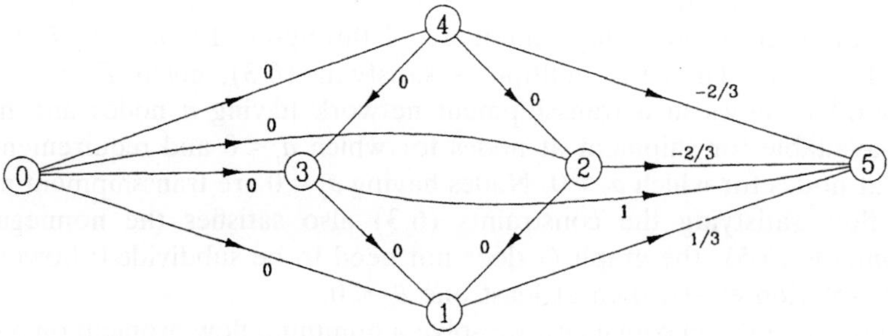

Fig. 7. Graph of G'.

The minimum flow problem, called problem (6.8), that yields the maximum cut for the graph G is

$$v = \min \sum_{i=1}^{n} \theta_{0i}$$

$$\text{subject to} \quad \theta_{i,n+1} + \sum_{j\in S_G(i)} \theta_{ij} = \theta_{0i} + \sum_{j\in P_G(i)} \theta_{ji}\,, \quad i = 1, \ldots, n\,, \qquad (6.8)$$

$$\theta_{ij} \geq l(i, j)\,, \quad (i, j) \in A'(G')\,.$$

The definition of $D(G)$ implies that $\Sigma_i\, a_i = 0$. Equation (6.8) implies that $\Sigma_i\, \theta_{0i} = \Sigma_i\, \theta_{i,n+1}$. Therefore $v = 0$ if and only if $\theta_{0i} = 0$ and $\theta_{i,n+1} = a_i$ for all i, i.e., (6.3) and (6.5) have a solution.

Problem (6.8), like the classic maximum flow problem, can be solved efficiently for very large graphs. An algorithm exists to solve it that is at worst of order n^3. The solution identifies the maximum directed cut as follows:

$$0 \in N(G'^{+})\,,$$

$$n + 1 \in N(G'^{-})\,,$$

$$v = \sum_{i\in N(G'^{+})} \sum_{j\in N(G'^{-})} l(i, j)$$

$$= \sum_{i\in N(G'^{+})-\{0\}} a_i \geq 0\,.$$

The maximal cut (G^{+}, G^{-}) is $(G'^{+} - \{0\}, G'^{-} - \{n+1\})$. Note that if $v = 0$, then G need not be subdivided further.

6.1.4. An algorithm for solving problem (6.2)

The solution to problem (6.2) is found using an algorithm that is based on the concept of a directed cut. The algorithm operates as follows. To begin, assume that all operations share a common reorder interval. Problem (6.8) is then solved to correspond to this feasible solution. If $v = 0$, the Kuhn–Tucker multipliers are nonnegative and the solution is optimal; if not, G must be divided into graphs G^{+} and G^{-}, which are determined by solving problem (6.8). The process is then repeated separately on G^{+} and G^{-} until no further splitting of the graphs is needed, that is, until the solutions to the corresponding problem (6.8) indicate that nonnegative multipliers exist that satisfy all the Kuhn–Tucker conditions.

Formally, we state the algorithm as follows.

Algorithm 3. *The divide and conquer algorithm.*

Step 0. Assume all reorder intervals are identical.

Step 1. If no directed cut (G^+, G^-) has a positive value, that is, if no directed cut has $\Sigma_{i\in N(G^+)} (K_i/D(G) - g_i) > 0$, then STOP.

Step 2. Find the maximal cut, by solving problem (6.8), and divide G into two separate subgraphs G^+ and G^-. Apply the divide and conquer algorithm to each of the graphs G^+ and G^-.

In the event that problem (6.8) has more than one maximal cut, any one of the maximal cuts may be selected in Step 2.

This algorithm constructs a set of subgraphs which we denote $\{G_k, 1 \leq k \leq N\}$. The clusters are $\{N(G_k), 1 \leq k \leq N\}$. Steps 2 and 3 of Algorithm 1 are now used to obtain the reorder intervals that solve problems (6.2) and (6.1). A proof that the divide and conquer algorithm does solve problem (6.2) to optimality can be found in Maxwell & Muckstadt [1985].

In the event that the reorder intervals T_i, $i \in N(G)$, are constrained to satisfy

$$2^{\underline{l}} T_L \leq T_i \leq 2^{\bar{l}} T_L ,$$

the modified roundoff procedure described in Section 3.4 can be used. All claims of optimality and near-optimality made in this section apply to the constrained version of the problem as well. This is also true of the models of Sections 4, 5 and 7–9.

6.3. *Computational complexity of the algorithm*

The solution of problem (6.2) is constructed by solving a sequence of minimum flow problems – problem (6.8). Each solution to problem (6.8) generates either two or no leaf vertices. However, there can be no more than n leaf vertices in the final binary tree, where n represents the number of nodes in G. Because the number of steps required by the algorithm for finding the optimal solution to problem (6.8) is at worst proportional to n^3, the algorithm for solving problem (6.2) is an order n^4 or less algorithm.

6.4. *An example problem*

The problem used in this section to illustrate the algorithm was obtained from a supplier of components to the U.S. automotive industry. Figure 8 shows the product structure graph G corresponding to this problem. The graph shows that there are 4 finished products, which correspond to nodes 1, 2, 4, and 6. Each of the 94 nodes in the graph represents an operation. Those nodes represented by triangles indicate the acquisition of raw materials. Squares indicate operations having positive setup times and circles operations requiring no setup time.

Observe that G represents neither a pure assembly nor a pure distribution system. Some raw materials are used in the production of more than one

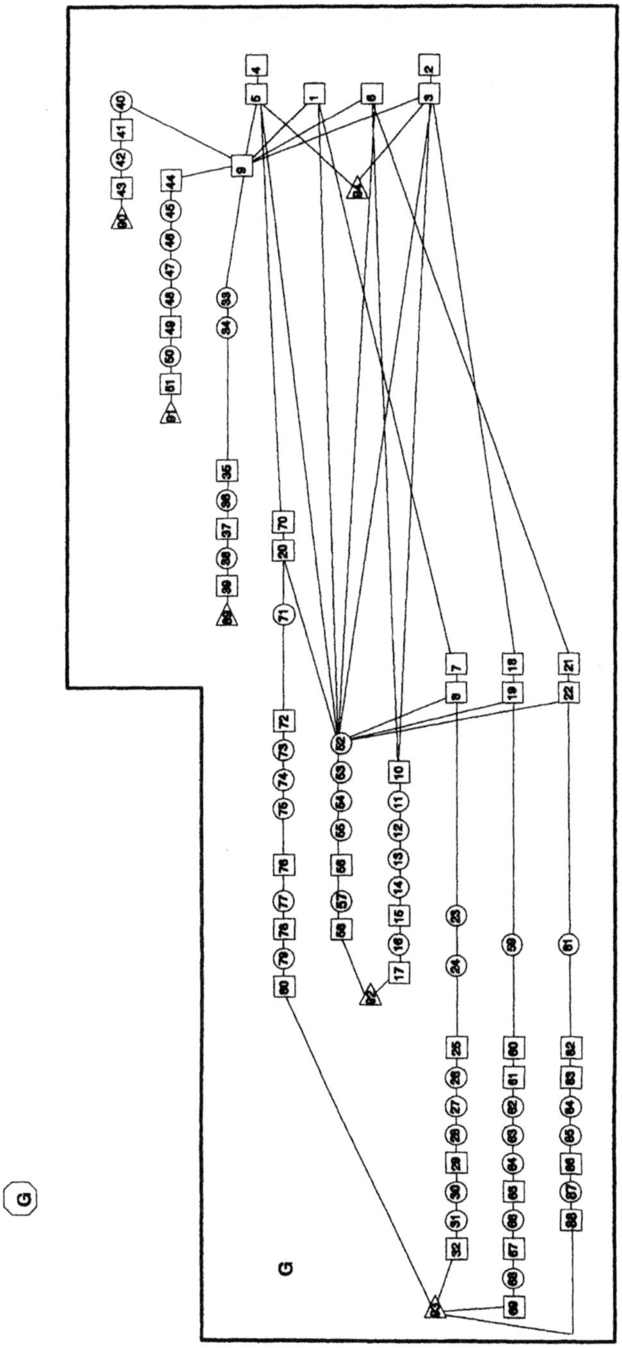

Fig. 8. Product structure graph *G*.

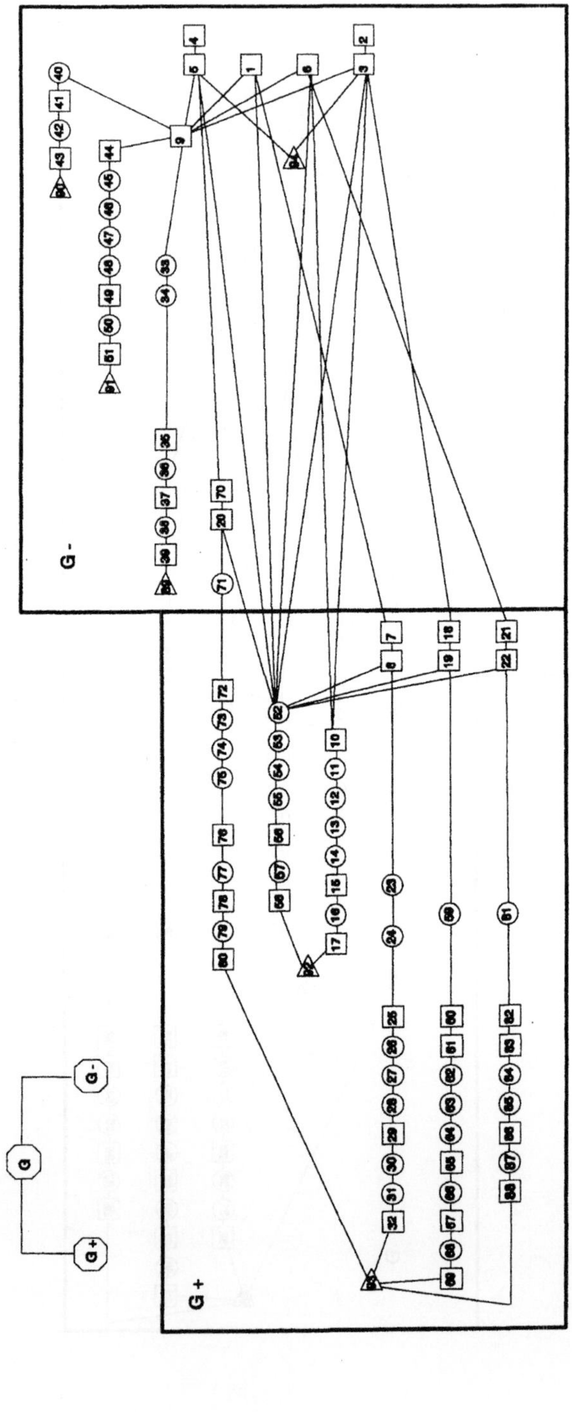

Fig. 9. Graphs G^+ and G^-.

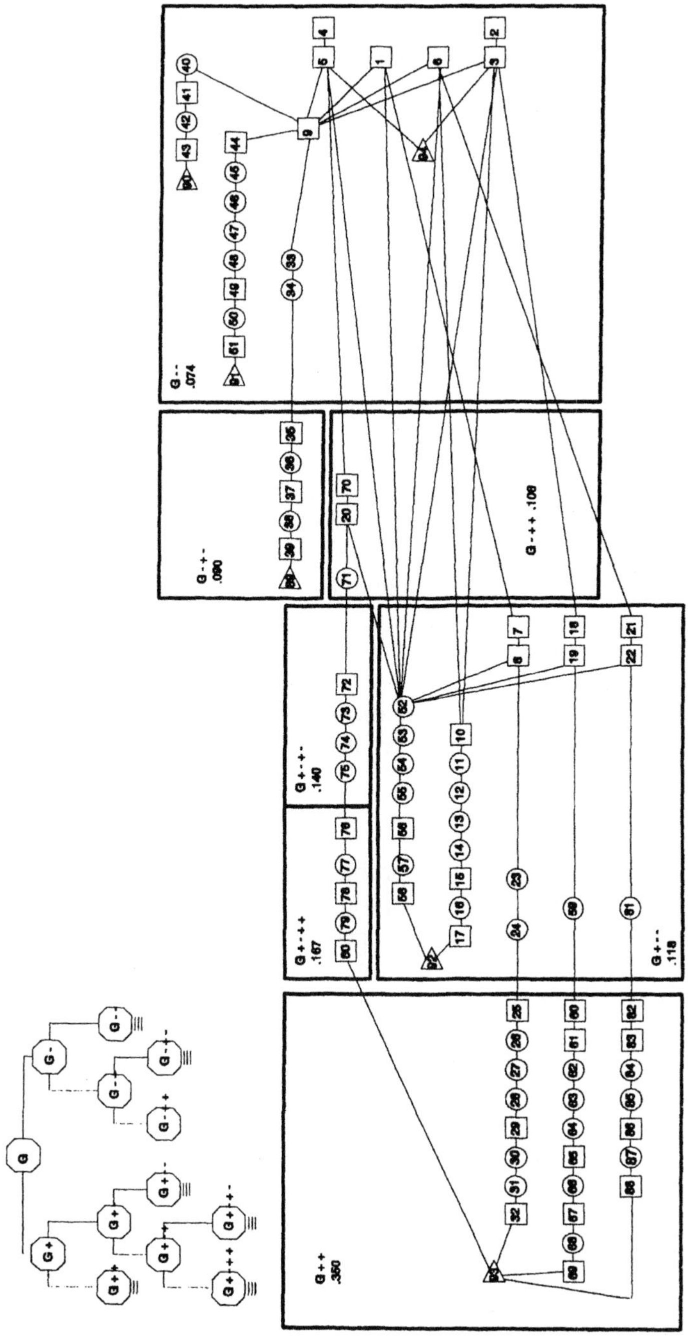

Fig. 10. Optimal solution to the relaxed problem.

component. Some components are used in more than one assembly or subassembly. For example, the component completed at operation 52 is used in 8 different ways. Furthermore, the subassembly at operation 3 requires 5 different components. Thus this graph G represents a relatively complex production environment.

The reorder intervals for each operation were obtained using Algorithm 3. Figure 9 gives the first partition of G into G^+ and G^-. Underlining of a leaf vertex in the solution tree indicates that the leaf vertex is in a permanent state. Because all leaf vertices are underlined in the tree shown in Figure 10, the optimal reorder intervals for problem (6.2) have been found. The reorder interval for operations in G^{--} is 0.074 years, in G^{-+-} is 0.090 years, in G^{-++} is 0.106 years, in G^{+--} is 0.118 years, in G^{+-+-} is 0.140 years, in G^{+-++} is 0.167 years, and in G^{++} is 0.350 years. Thus, for example, operations 76 through 80, the elements of G^{+-++}, should have the same reorder interval and should be produced about once every 2 months. Note that the magnitude of the values of the reorder intervals correspond to an ordering of the sets $G^{\alpha_1 \cdots \alpha_n}$. Furthermore, observe that the magnitude of most of these reorder intervals is similar, indicating that more operations might share common reorder intervals in the solution to problem (6.1).

This solution to problem (6.2) shows that the operations should initially be divided into 7 distinct groups. Problem (6.1)'s solution indicates that the operation should be combined further. A base planning period of a day was used. The optimal solution indicates that the operations in G^{++} should be on a cycle that is 128 days long. Those in G^{+-++} and G^{+-+-} should have reorder intervals equal to 64 days. The operations in sets G^{--}, G^{-+-}, G^{-++}, and G^{+--} should all have the same reorder interval of 32 days.

6.5. *Summary*

In this section, we studied the problem of determining consistent and realistic reorder intervals in a general production–distribution system environment. A mathematical model was developed whose special structure permits its solution using a standard network flow algorithm. As in earlier sections, attention was restricted to policies that are nested, stationary, and a powers-of-two multiple of a base planning period. As before, if we follow a powers-of-two policy, the total cost cannot be more than 6% higher than can be achieved following any other nested policy.

7. Constrained work centers

To this point we have assumed that the reorder intervals were chosen independent of available resource levels. In this section we consider planning problems occurring when the production facility is divided into work centers, each of which is assumed to have a limited production capacity, expressed in total annual standard hours. Since the total run time of all jobs processed through the work center is unaffected by lot sizing/reorder interval decisions we deduct the projected total annual run time from the production capacity. The result is an estimate of the total annual standard hours available for performing other work center functions, in particular, for performing setups within the work center. The remainder of the assumptions on which we base the following model are the same as those made for the models developed earlier in Section 2 of this chapter. Notational differences are minor and will be identified as we proceed.

We assume that each operation i in the production/distribution graph is associated with one and only one work center. Following the concepts and the notation of Section 3, we assume that the work centers form a partition of the node set of the graph G. Let W_h denote the subgraph of G formed from the node set $N(W_h)$, consisting of all the operations in work center h, and the arcset $A(W_h)$, consisting of all arcs of the form (i, j) where $i, j \in N(W_h)$ and $(i, j) \in A(G)$, for $h = 1, \dots, H$, where H is the number of distinct work centers. Let $\eta(i)$ index the work center associated with operation i.

Let L_i denote the setup time required by operation i, measured in standard hours, for all $i \in N(G)$. We also assume that the setup cost for operation i is directly proportional to L_i. This assumes that work center groupings are closely aligned with labor classifications and that material and energy costs involved in setting up operations are not significant. Let c_h denote the setup labor rate in work center h. By assumption, then, $K_i = c_h L_i$ for all operations i in work center h, $h = 1, \dots, H$. Finally, let b_h represent the total annual time available for performing setups in work center h, $h = 1, \dots, H$.

The general (relaxed version) multiple work center capacitated planning problem that we examine is given by

$$\begin{aligned} \text{minimize} \quad & \sum_{i \in N(G)} [c_{\eta(i)} L_i / T_i + g_i T_i] \\ \text{subject to} \quad & T_i \geq T_j \geq 0\,, \quad (i, j) \in A(G)\,, \\ & \sum_{i \in N(W_h)} L_i / T_i \leq b_h\,, \quad h = 1, 2, \dots, H\,. \end{aligned} \tag{7.1}$$

The powers-of-two formulation of this problem includes restrictions of the form $T_i = 2^l T_L$, $l \in \{0, 1, \dots\}$, $i \in N(G)$.

Before examining this problem, we make an observation that is the basis of the solution procedure we will discuss. Recall the necessary and sufficient conditions given in Section 3.3 for solving the following problem:

$$\begin{aligned} \text{minimize} \quad & \sum_{i \in N(G)} (K_i / T_i + g_i T_i) \\ \text{subject to} \quad & T_i \geq T_j \geq 0\,, \quad \text{for all } (i, j) \in A(G)\,. \end{aligned} \tag{7.2}$$

Now suppose we have a new problem with $\bar{K}_i = \alpha K_i$ and $\bar{g}_i = \beta g_i$ for each $i \in N(G)$, $\alpha > 0$, $\beta > 0$. Suppose we have an optimal solution to problem (7.2), i.e., an optimal partition $(G_1, \ldots, G_N)$ of G. This partition is also optimal for the new problem as well. This result easily follows from the conditions of Theorem 2 presented in Section 3.3. We call this the invariance property of the optimal partition of G. Thus the optimal partition of G is invariant under positive scaling of both setup and holding costs. Thus uniform increases or decreases in labor rate, overhead or interest rates do not change the optimal partition. It may, however, change the value of the optimal reorder intervals.

7.1. *Single work center*

The case of a single work center is particularly easy to solve because of the invariance property. The relaxed version of the capacitated single work center problem can be written as follows:

$$\begin{aligned} &\text{minimize} \quad \sum_{i \in N(G)} [cL_i/T_i + g_i T_i] \\ &\text{subject to} \quad T_i \geq T_j \geq 0\,, \quad (i, j) \in A(G)\,, \\ &\qquad\qquad \sum_{i \in N(W)} L_i/T_i \leq b\,, \end{aligned} \tag{7.3}$$

where the subscript h indexing different work centers has been dropped. We assume $c > 0$.

Let α denote the Lagrange multiplier for the capacity constraint. Dualizing this constraint, and letting $\alpha' = \alpha + c$, yields the following relaxed problem:

$$\begin{aligned} &\text{minimize} \quad \sum_{i \in N(G)} [\alpha' L_i/T_i + g_i T_i] \\ &\text{subject to} \quad T_i \geq T_j \geq 0\,, \quad (i, j) \in A(G)\,. \end{aligned} \tag{7.4}$$

We seek a value of $\alpha' \geq c$ ($\alpha \geq 0$) such that the solution to this uncapacitated problem satisfies the omitted capacity constraint and satisfies it with equality if $\alpha' > c$ ($\alpha > 0$).

We find the optimal solution as follows. First, find the optimal partition for problem (7.4) with $\alpha' = c$. If the associated solution satisfies the capacity constraint, then stop; the solution is optimal for the capacitated problem. Otherwise, the capacity constraint is binding. Based on the invariance property, the same partition is optimal for all positive values of α'. Suppose the partition is $(G_1, \ldots, G_N)$. The optimal reorder intervals for problem (7.4) as a function of α' are given by

$$T^*(k, \alpha') = (\alpha' L(k)/g(k))^{1/2}\,, \tag{7.5}$$

where $L(k) = \Sigma_{i \in N(G_k)} L_i$ and $g(k) = \Sigma_{i \in N(G_k)} g_i$, $k = 1, \ldots, N$. The capacity used as a function of α' is given by

$$\sum_{k=1}^{N} \sum_{i \in N(G)} L_i / T(k, \alpha') = \sum_{k=1}^{N} L(k) / [\alpha' L(k) / g(k)]^{1/2}$$
$$= \sum_{k=1}^{N} \frac{[L(k) g(k)]^{1/2}}{\sqrt{\alpha'}} .$$

Substituting for the left-hand side in the capacity constraint and solving for α' yields

$$\alpha'^* = \left[\frac{\Sigma_{k=1}^{N} [L(k) g(k)]^{1/2}}{b} \right]^2 . \tag{7.6}$$

Thus, a closed form solution is available for the single work center problem, problem (7.4), given the optimal partition for the problem. Note that α'^* must be greater than c in the above expression because, by assumption, the constraint is violated at $\alpha' = c$. Clearly the capacity used is a decreasing function of α', $\alpha' \geqslant c$.

Let U denote the capacity utilization ratio when $\alpha' = c$ $(\alpha = 0)$:

$$U = \frac{\Sigma_{k=1}^{N} \Sigma_{i \in N(G_k)} L_i / T^*(k, c)}{b}$$
$$= \sum_{k=1}^{N} \frac{[L(k) g(k)]^{1/2}}{\sqrt{c} \cdot b} . \tag{7.7}$$

Rewriting (7.6) in terms of the utilization ratio, U:

$$\alpha'^* = cU^2 , \quad \text{or} \quad \alpha^* = cU^2 - c . \tag{7.8}$$

Similarly, the optimal reorder intervals for the capacitated problem, $\{T^*(k)\colon k = 1, \ldots, N\}$, satisfy

$$T^*(k) = T^*(k, \alpha'^*) = T^*(k, c) \cdot U . \tag{7.9}$$

The optimal reorder intervals for the relaxed version of the single work center constrained problem are simply the natural $(\alpha = 0)$ reorder intervals scaled by the capacity utilization ratio (when $U > 1$).

7.2. *The powers-of-two single work center problem*

Before extending the solution technique to handle multiple work centers, we consider the relation between the relaxed version of the single work center problem and the powers-of-two version. The powers-of-two formulation of the single work center planning problem is given by:

$$\text{minimize} \quad \sum_{i \in N(G)} [cL_i/T_i + g_iT_i]$$

$$\text{subject to} \quad \sum_{i \in N(G)} L_i/T_i \leq b ,$$

$$T_i \leq T_j , \quad (i, j) \in A(G) ,$$

$$T_i = 2^{l_i}T_L , \quad l_i \in \{0, 1, 2, \dots\} , \ i \in N(G) .$$

By analogy with the uncapacitated problem discussed earlier, consider the powers-of-two solution given by $T_i = T(k)$ for all $i \in N(G_k)$, $k = 1, \dots, N$, and let $T(k) = 2^{l(k)}T_L$, where $l(k)$ is the smallest value of l satisfying

$$2^l \geq \frac{1}{T_L}\left[\frac{\alpha'^* L(k)}{2g(k)}\right]^{1/2} . \tag{7.10}$$

We now investigate the feasibility and cost performance of this solution using some of the results developed previously.

By (7.5) and (7.10), $l(k)$ satisfies

$$2^{l(k)} \geq \frac{T^*(k)}{\sqrt{2} \cdot T_L} > 2^{l(k)-1} ,$$

so that

$$\frac{T^*(k)}{\sqrt{2}} < T(k) \leq \sqrt{2} \cdot T^*(k) . \tag{7.11}$$

We examine the cost performance of the powers-of-two solution first. Let

$$f_k(T) = \sum_{i \in N(G_k)} [cL_i/T + g_iT] = cL(k)/T + g(k)T ,$$

the cost associated with a common reorder interval T for subgraph G_k. By convexity,

$$f_k(T(k)) \leq \max\{ f_k(T^*(k)/\sqrt{2}), f_k(\sqrt{2}T^*(k))\} .$$

Assuming the capacity constraint is binding ($U \geq 1$), we have

$$\begin{aligned}
f_k(\sqrt{2}T^*(k)) &= \frac{cL(k)}{\sqrt{2}T^*(k)} + g(k)\sqrt{2}T^*(k) \\
&= \frac{cL(k)}{\sqrt{2}T^*(k,c)\cdot U} + g(k)\sqrt{2}T^*(k,c)\cdot U \\
&= \sqrt{cL(k)g(k)}\left[\frac{1+2U^2}{\sqrt{2}U}\right]
\end{aligned} \tag{7.12}$$

and

$$\begin{aligned}
f_k(T^*(k)/\sqrt{2}) &= \sqrt{cL(k)g(k)}\left[\frac{2+U^2}{\sqrt{2}U}\right] \\
&\leq f_k(\sqrt{2}T^*(k)),
\end{aligned} \tag{7.13}$$

because $U \geq 1$.

Let F_b denote the cost associated with the powers-of-two solution given a capacity of b:

$$\begin{aligned}
F_b &= \sum_{k=1}^{N} \sum_{i \in N(G_k)} \left[\frac{cL_i}{T(k)} + g_i T(k)\right] \\
&= \sum_{k=1}^{N} f_k(T(k)) \\
&\leq \sum_{k=1}^{N} \sqrt{cL(k)g(k)}\left[\frac{1+2U^2}{\sqrt{2}U}\right].
\end{aligned} \tag{7.14}$$

Suppose $\{T(k)\colon k = 1, \ldots, N\}$ is feasible for the powers-of-two single work center problem. Then F_b is an upper bound on the minimal cost for that problem. Let Z_b denote the minimal cost of the relaxed version of the single work center problem:

$$\begin{aligned}
Z_b &= \sum_{k=1}^{N} \sum_{i \in N(G_k)} \left[\frac{cL_i}{T^*(k)} + g_i T^*(k)\right] \\
&= \sum_{k=1}^{N} f_k(T^*(k)) \\
&= \sum_{k=1}^{N} \sqrt{cL(k)g(k)}\left[\frac{1+U^2}{U}\right].
\end{aligned} \tag{7.15}$$

Z_b can be shown to be a lower bound on the minimal cost for the powers-of-two single work center problem using the method developed in Section 3. It follows that

$$\frac{F_b}{Z_b} \leqslant \frac{(1+2U^2)}{\sqrt{2}(1+U^2)} . \tag{7.16}$$

As $U \to \infty$ this bound converges to $\sqrt{2}$. That is, the proposed powers-of-two solution cannot exceed the solution to the relaxed version of the single work center problem by more than 41%. Table 1 tabulates the bound for a variety of values of U. Observe that for a 20% overutilization in the constrained case ($U = 1.2$) the powers-of-two cost is bounded to within approximately 12% of the cost of the solution to the relaxed problem.

Next, let us turn our attention to the feasibility of the proposed powers-of-two solution. Observe that the second condition of Theorem 2 implies that the constraints $T_i \geqslant T_j$, $(i, j) \in A(G)$, will be satisfied by the solution $\{T(k): k = 1, \ldots, N\}$. Using the fact that $T(k) \geqslant T^*(k)/\sqrt{2}$, $k = 1, \ldots, N$, worst-case analysis reveals that

$$\sum_{k=1}^{N} \sum_{i \in N(G_k)} L_i/T(k) \leqslant \sqrt{2} \cdot b , \tag{7.17}$$

that is, the powers-of-two solution can exceed capacity by at most 41%. This analysis assumes that for each set G_k in the partition, $T(k)$ takes on the smallest possible value. In reality, we would expect that $T(k)$ would be larger than $T^*(k)$ for some of the sets G_k and smaller than T_k for others. If the number of sets in the partition is large, we would anticipate that the powers-of-two solution would utilize roughly the same amount of capacity as the solution to the relaxed problem.

To illustrate, suppose $T(k)$ is uniformly distributed over the interval $[T^*(k)/\sqrt{2}, \sqrt{2}T^*(k)]$. Then the expected amount of capacity required by the powers-of-two solution is

$$\mathrm{E}\left[\sum_{k=1}^{N} \sum_{i \in N(G_k)} L_i/T(k)\right] = \sum_{k=1}^{N} L(k)\mathrm{E}[1/T(k)]$$

$$= \left[\sum_{k=1}^{N} L(k)/T^*(k)\right]\sqrt{2}\log 2 = b(\sqrt{2}\log 2) , \tag{7.18}$$

Table 1
Cost bound for the powers-of-two solution

U	Bound on F_b/Z_b
1.0	1.061
1.1	1.094
1.2	1.124
1.5	1.197
2.0	1.273
5.0	1.387

because $\{T^*(k): k=1, \ldots, N\}$ satisfies the constraint exactly. Assuming the $\{T(k): k=1, \ldots, N\}$ are independent, then the strong law of large numbers implies

$$\lim_{N\to\infty} \sum_{k=1}^{N} \sum_{i\in N(G_k)} L_i/T(k) = \sqrt{2}\log 2 \cdot b \approx 0.980 \cdot b\,.$$

Hence, in a probabilistic sense, for a large number of sets in the optimal partition, we would anticipate that the powers-of-two solution would be feasible. A more rigorous analysis of this conjecture appears impractically difficult. Computational experience with the algorithm, described by Jackson, Maxwell, & Muckstadt [1988], suggests that for practical problems the powers-of-two solutions are close to feasible.

Roundy [1986] describes an extension to this algorithm that guarantees feasibility of the powers-of-two solution by adjusting the length of the base planning period, T_L. For his algorithm, the cost of the powers-of-two solution cannot exceed the solution to the relaxed version by more than 44%. In practice, the base planning period is often determined by the information system reporting cycle and in these cases it is not easily subject to change. For example, in most manufacturing facilities visited by the authors we observed MRP type planning systems in which T_L was either a week or a month. That is, these planning systems generated production requirements for each week or month over some time horizon. Thus reorder intervals were constrained to be some multiple of these time intervals.

7.3. The multiple work center planning algorithm

There are several ways in which the multiple work center capacitated planning problem could be solved. We propose a technique that takes advantage of the ease by which single work center problems can be solved. The idea behind the algorithm is that there are two useful Lagrangian relaxations of the multiple work center problem. We propose an iterative algorithm that alternates between these two relaxations.

One approach to using Lagrangian relaxation on the multiple work center problem is to dualize all the capacity constraints. Let α_n denote the Lagrange multiplier on the capacity constraint for work center h, $h=1, \ldots, H$. If $\alpha'_h = \alpha_h + c_h$, $h=1, \ldots, H$, and α' denotes the vector of coefficients $(\alpha'_1, \ldots, \alpha'_H)$, then one possible relaxation of the multiple work center is given by

$$\begin{aligned} &\text{minimize} \quad \sum_{i\in N(G)} [\alpha'_{\eta(i)} L_i/T_i + g_i T_i] \\ &\text{subject to} \quad T_i \geq T_j \geq 0\,, \quad (i,j)\in A(G)\,. \end{aligned} \tag{7.19}$$

We seek a vector $\alpha' \geqslant (c_1, \ldots, c_H)$ such that the capacity constraints which are omitted from problem (7.19) are satisfied by the solution to problem (7.19). Furthermore, if $\alpha'_h > c_h$, the constraint for work center h must be satisfied with equality. Unfortunately, the optimal partition for this relaxed problem is not necessarily invariant to the choice of α' because the scaling factors are not common across all operations. Let the optimal partition for this problem be denoted $(G_1^{\alpha'}, \ldots, G_{N(\alpha')}^{\alpha'})$ for a given vector α'. Let the optimal set of reorder intervals be given by $\{T^*(k, \alpha'): k = 1, \ldots, N(\alpha')\}$ and let $U_h^{\alpha'}$ denote the corresponding capacity utilization ratio for work center h:

$$U_h^{\alpha'} = \frac{1}{b_h} \sum_{k=1}^{N} \Big(\sum_{i \in N(W_h) \cap N(G_k^{\alpha'})} L_i \Big) \Big/ T^*(k, \alpha') \tag{7.20}$$

for $h = 1, \ldots, H$.

An alternative approach to using Lagrangian relaxation on the multiple work center problem is to dualize all the consistency constraints that link different work centers together. That is, eliminate constraints of the form $T_i \geqslant T_j$, where $(i, j) \in A(G)$ and $\eta(i) \neq \eta(j)$. Let θ_{ij} denote the Lagrange multiplier on such a linking consistency constraint and let

$$\kappa_i(\theta) = \sum_{\substack{j \in N(G) \\ (j,i) \in A(G) \\ \eta(j) \neq \eta(i)}} \theta_{ji} - \sum_{\substack{j \in N(G) \\ (i,j) \in A(G) \\ \eta(i) \neq \eta(j)}} \theta_{ij} .$$

Then, an alternative Lagrangian relaxation of the multiple work center capacitated problem is given by the following problem:

$$\begin{aligned} &\text{minimize} && \sum_{i \in N(G)} [c_{\eta(i)} L_i / T_i + g_i T_i + \kappa_i(\theta) T_i] \\ &\text{subject to} && T_i \geqslant T_j \geqslant 0 , \quad (i, j) \in A(W_j) , \\ &&& \sum_{i \in N(W_h)} L_i / T_i \leqslant b_h , \quad h = 1, 2, \ldots, H . \end{aligned} \tag{7.21}$$

For a given vector of multipliers, $\theta = (\theta_{ij})$, this latter relaxation is separable by work center. The single work center subproblem, for a given vector θ, is given by:

$$\begin{aligned} &\text{minimize} && \sum_{i \in N(W_h)} [c_h L_i / T_i + (g_i + \kappa_i(\theta)) T_i] \\ &\text{subject to} && T_i \geqslant T_j \geqslant 0 , \quad (i, j) \in A(W_h) , \\ &&& \sum_{i \in N(W_h)} L_i / T_i \leqslant b_h , \end{aligned} \tag{7.22}$$

for work center h, $h = 1, \ldots, H$.

Observe that for a given vector θ, this single work center subproblem is identical in form to the single work center problem examined previously. Letting $\bar{\alpha}_k$ denote the Lagrange multiplier for the single work center capacity constraint and letting $\bar{\alpha}'_h = \bar{\alpha}_h + c_h$, the *uncapacitated* version of the single work center subproblem can be written:

$$\begin{aligned} &\text{minimize} \quad \sum_{i \in N(W_h)} [\bar{\alpha}'_h L_i / T_i + (g_i + \kappa_i(\theta)) T_i] \\ &\text{subject to} \quad T_i \geq T_j \geq 0\,, \quad (i, j) \in A(W_h)\,. \end{aligned} \tag{7.23}$$

Therefore, by the invariance property, given an optimal partition to problem (7.23) for any value of $\bar{\alpha}'$, a closed form solution to the capacitated subproblem, problem (7.22), is available immediately. Denote the optimal value of the Lagrange multiplier by $\bar{\alpha}^*_h(\theta)$, a function of θ because the definition of the subproblem depends on the vector θ.

In the following, we note that if an optimal partition is available for problem (7.19), which was used to define the vector θ, then this partition induces an optimal partition on each of the single work center uncapacitated subproblems.

Theorem 3. *For a given vector of Lagrange multipliers α' on the work center capacity constraints, let $(G_1^{\alpha'}, \ldots, G_{N(\alpha')}^{\alpha'})$ be an optimal partition of (7.19) and let θ be a corresponding vector of optimal Lagrange multipliers on the consistency constraints linking work centers. Let $\mathrm{RP}_h(\theta)$ be the single work center capacitated problem of type (7.21) for work center h which is formed using this vector θ. Then, the ordered partition of G, $(G_1^{\alpha'}, \ldots, G_{N(\alpha')}^{\alpha'})$, induces an optimal partition on the subgraph W_h for problem $\mathrm{RP}_h(\theta)$, $h = 1, \ldots, H$.*

The proof of this theorem can be found in Jackson, Maxwell, & Muckstadt [1988].

If an optimal partition is available for problem (7.19), then the solution to problem (7.21) can be obtained in closed form without explicit knowledge of the vector of multipliers, θ, on the linking consistency constraints. That is, under the conditions of the proposition, for $h = 1, \ldots, H$,

$$\bar{\alpha}^*_h(\theta) = \max\{0, \alpha'_h [U_h^{\alpha'}]^2 - c_h\}\,. \tag{7.24}$$

The proof of this fact can be found in Jackson, Maxwell, & Muckstadt [1988].

To this point we have specified two relaxations of the multiple work center capacitated problem. The first relaxed problem, problem (7.19), can be solved by the modified network algorithm described in Maxwell & Muckstadt [1985], which was discussed in Section 6, for any given vector $\alpha = (\alpha_1, \ldots, \alpha_H)$. A by-product of that algorithm is a vector of Lagrange multipliers on all the consistency constraints $\{T_i \geq T_j\colon (i, j) \in A(G)\}$. That is, the solution to problem (7.19) implies the existence of a vector of Lagrange multipliers on the constraints linking the work centers: $\theta = (\theta_{ij}: (i, j) \in A(G), \eta(i) \neq \eta(j))$. These multipliers can be used to define an alternative relaxation of the problem, referred to as problem (7.21). This relaxed problem is separable and can be used to define a new vector of multipliers, $\bar{\alpha}(\theta)$, on the capacity constraints. The subproblems of problem (7.21) and problem (7.22) can be solved using Equation (7.24) without explicit knowledge of the vector θ. The following algorithm is iterative in nature; it alternates between solving (7.19) to get a new vector of capacity utilization ratios, $\alpha' = (U_1^{\alpha'}, \ldots, U_H^{\alpha'})$, and solving (7.21) to get a new vector of capacity multipliers, α.

The Multiple Work Center Planning Algorithm.

Step 0. Pick an initial nonnegative vector α^0.

Step 1. On iteration n, for vector α^n, solve problem (7.19) using the algorithm described in Section 6. Obtain an optimal partition, $(G_1^{\alpha^n}, \ldots, G_{N(\alpha^n)}^{\alpha^n})$, and a solution $\{T_i^{*\alpha^n}\}$. Let θ^n denote a vector of Lagrange multipliers on the consistency constraints associated with this solution. It is not necessary to obtain this vector explicitly.

Step 2. For each work center h, compute the capacity utilization ratio:

$$U_h^{\alpha^n} = \frac{\sum_{i \in N(W_h)} L_i / T_i^{*\alpha^n}}{b_h} . \tag{7.25}$$

For a pre-specified tolerance ε, if $U_h^{\alpha^n} - 1 < \varepsilon$ for all h such that $\alpha_h^n = 0$ and $|U_h^{\alpha^n} - 1| < \varepsilon$ for all h such that $\alpha_h^n > 0$, $h = 1, \ldots, H$, then stop; the solution from Step 1 is ε-optimal.

Step 3. For each work center h, $h = 1, \ldots, H$, let

$$\theta_h(\theta^n) = \max\{0, (\alpha_h^n + c_h)[U_h^{\alpha^n}]^2 - c_h\} . \tag{7.26}$$

Let $\alpha(\theta^n)$ denote the resulting vector of Lagrange multipliers on the capacity constraints.

Step 4. Let $\alpha^{n+1} = \alpha^n + \gamma^n(\alpha(\theta^n) - \alpha^n)$ where γ^n is an appropriately chosen step size parameter $(0 < \gamma^n \leq 1)$. Set $n \leftarrow n + 1$ and go to Step 1.

Step 1 of the algorithm requires most of the computational effort. The computational complexity of this problem depends on the structure of the graph G. For arbitrary acyclic graphs the computational effort is at worst $O(n^4)$, where n is the number of nodes in the graph. If G has a special structure, such as the ones described in other sections of this chapter, computation time may be proportional to $n \log n$.

There are many possible strategies for choosing the step size γ^n in Step 4. To date, we have been unable to identify a strategy that guarantees convergence of the algorithm. However, the naive strategy of halving the current step size after a pre-specified number of iterations was effective in the test cases reported in Jackson, Maxwell, & Muckstadt [1988].

8. Joint order costs

In all earlier sections we have assumed that there is an order cost K_i for stage i in the system, and that if S is the set of items being ordered at a given point in time, then the total order cost incurred at that point in time is $\Sigma_{i \in S} K_i$, i.e., the order cost is a modular function of the set of items being ordered. In many situations this is not a realistic assumption. In this section we survey several different models in which the total order cost incurred depends in a more complicated way on the set of items being ordered at a given point in time.

8.1. The joint replenishment problem

Perhaps the simplest way in which the cost of ordering can fail to be modular is through a joint order cost. Consider a single facility that stocks a number of different items. Each item i has a traditional order cost K_i, a holding cost rate h_i, and deterministic demand which occurs at a constant continuous rate λ_i. However, in addition, there is a joint order cost K_0 which is incurred every time an order is placed for any item. This order cost is in addition to the order costs for the individual items being ordered. Therefore, if at a given point in time an order is placed for the items in the set $S \neq \emptyset$, the total order cost incurred is $K_0 + \Sigma_{i \in S} K_i$. The objective is to schedule orders for the items over an infinite time horizon so as to minimize the long-run average order and holding cost, while meeting the demand for all items without shortages.

The joint replenishment system can be viewed as a special case of the assembly system discussed in Section 4. This is accomplished by modeling the joint order cost K_0 as a separate stage. Consider the assembly system illustrated in Figure 11. In this system stages i, $i \geq 1$, correspond to the items of the joint replenishment system, and stage 0 corresponds to the joint order cost. The order costs and the holding cost coefficients for stages $i \geq 1$ are K_i and $g_i = \frac{1}{2}\lambda_i h_i$, respectively. For stage 0 the order cost is K_0 and the holding cost coefficient is $g_0 = 0$.

For assembly systems nested policies are optimal. For the joint replenishment system of Figure 11, the nestedness constraint implies that an order must be placed at node 0 (i.e., the joint order cost must be incurred) whenever any of the items is ordered. Therefore for the joint replenishment system, the nestedness constraint forces the joint order cost to be incurred at the appropriate points in time, and is a necessary condition for feasibility.

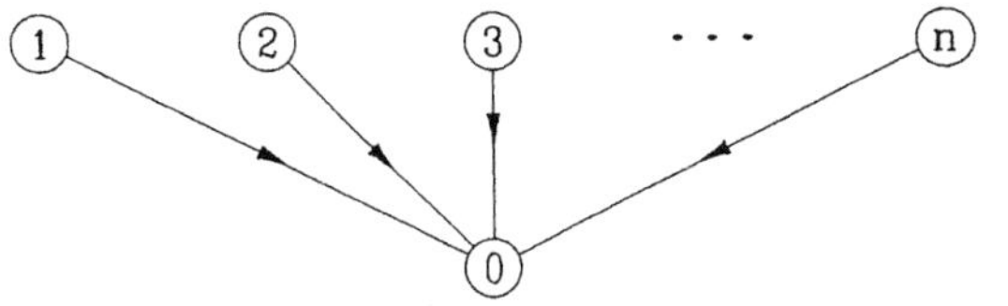

Fig. 11. Joint replenishment system.

If the algorithms of Section 4 are applied to the system of Figure 11, they will compute policies whose cost is within 6% of optimal if a fixed base planning period is used, and within 2% of optimal if the base planning period is a variable [Jackson, Maxwell, & Muckstadt, 1985]. However, for these systems a much simpler and more efficient algorithm is available for solving the relaxation of the planning problem – problem (4.5). The algorithm is given below. In Step 2 we set $K/g = \infty$ if $g = 0$.

Algorithm 4. *Simple joint replenishment systems.*

Step 1. Sort the items so that $K_i/g_i \leq K_{i+1}/g_{i+1}$ for all $i \geq 1$. Set $K \leftarrow K_0$, $g \leftarrow 0$, and $k \leftarrow 0$.

Step 2. If $k = n$ or $K/g < K_{k+1}/g_{k+1}$, then go to Step 4. Otherwise go to Step 3.

Step 3. Set $k \leftarrow k+1$. Set $K \leftarrow K + K_k$ and $g \leftarrow g + g_k$. Go to Step 2.

Step 4. Set $T_i^* = \sqrt{K/g}$ for all $i \leq k$, and set $T_i^* = \sqrt{K_i/g_i}$ for all $i > k$. The optimal clusters are $\{0, 1, \ldots, k\}$, $\{k+1\}$, $\{k+2\}, \ldots, \{n\}$.

The running time of this algorithm is limited by the time required to perform the sort in Step 1. This can be done in $O(n \log n)$ time. The algorithm is based on the idea that the joint order cost will be incurred once every T_0 time units. There are two types of items: those that order every T_0 time units and those that order less frequently. The items that order less frequently do so because their natural reorder interval, based on their own order and holding costs, is longer than T_0. The items that order every time the joint order cost is incurred have natural reorder intervals shorter than T_0. If $\{i: 1 \leq i \leq k\}$ is the set of items that order once every T_0 time units then local optimality implies that

$$T_0 = \left[\left(K_0 + \sum_{1 \leq i \leq k} K_i\right) \Big/ \left(\sum_{1 \leq i \leq k} g_i\right)\right]^{1/2}.$$

Via the transformation of Section 5, the problem of finding a good nested policy for a one-warehouse, multi-retailer inventory system can be transformed into the problem of finding a good policy for a two-stage assembly system. The only essential difference between a two-stage assembly system and a joint replenishment system is that assembly systems typically have a positive holding cost coefficient associated with node 0. This can be compensated for by changing the statement $g \leftarrow 0$ in Step 1 to $g \leftarrow g_0$. With this change, the above algorithm can be used to find nested policies in one-warehouse, multi-retailer distribution systems, or to find policies for two-level assembly systems. The performance bounds obtained in Sections 4 and 5 apply to two-level assembly and distribution systems, respectively.

8.2. The family model

In this subsection we consider an extension of the general lot sizing model of Section 6. The system considered there is modeled by an acyclic, directed graph representing a bill of material network G with node set $N(G)$ and arc set $A(G)$. Node $i \in N(G)$ corresponds to stage i of the system. Part i is stocked at stage i. Part I has order cost $K_i \geq 0$, echelon holding cost rate $h_i \geq 0$, and demand rate $\lambda_i \geq 0$. Associated with each arc $(i, j) \in A(G)$ is a *gozinto parameter* γ_{ij}. Whenever an order for q units of part j is placed it is instantly delivered, and $\gamma_{ij} q$ units of part i are simultaneously consumed.

This system, which we studied in Section 6, is now enhanced by allowing order costs to be associated with families of components. To illustrate, consider an injection molding machine on which we produce Lego blocks. The blocks come in three different sizes and in three different colors, making nine parts in all. There are three molds, one for each size of block. Whenever we finish a batch of one of the nine parts the cavity in the mold needs to be cleaned. The cost of doing this is K_c. When we switch the machine from one block size to another, the mold currently on the machine needs to be removed and another one must be mounted. The cost of doing this is K_m.

Let i index the parts, let k index the molds, and let I_k be the set of parts that are produced using mold k. Let part i be produced once every T_i days, and let mold k be loaded onto the machine once every T_k days, where the T's are powers of two. If the batches are sequenced appropriately, the average order cost incurred per day is $\Sigma_i K_c / T_i + \Sigma_k K_m / T_k$. The order intervals are constrained to satisfy $T_k \leq T_i$ for all $i \in I_k$.

This example motivates the following extension to the model of Section 6. Let F be a collection of sets $f \subset N(G)$ called *families*. We assume that $|f| \geq 2$ for all $f \in F$. Associated with each family $f \in F$ is an order cost $K_f > 0$. We assume that the order cost K_f is incurred every time an order is placed for one or more of the items $i \in f$.

We model the joint setup costs K_f, $f \in F$ as follows. Given the bill of material network G of Section 6, we define the *extended bill of material network* G' to be the network with node set $N(G') = N(G) \cup F$ and arc set $A(G') = A(G) \cup \{(i, f): i \in f, f \in F\}$. The nodes $f \in F$ are referred to as *order cost nodes*, and the arcs (i, f), $i \in f, f \in F$ are referred to as *order cost arcs*. The nodes in $N(G)$ are referred to as *inventory nodes*, and the arcs in $A(G)$ are *inventory arcs*. Associated with each order cost node $f \in F$ is an order cost K_f, an echelon holding cost $h_f = 0$, and an echelon demand rate $\lambda_f = 0$. Associated with each order cost arc (i, f) is a gozinto parameter $\gamma_{ij} = 0$. Because the order cost K_f must be incurred every time any of the items $i \in f$ is ordered, all feasible policies satisfy

$$T_f \leq T_i \quad \text{for each } i \in f\,, \ f \in F\,. \tag{8.1}$$

We say that a policy is *nested on order cost arcs* if it satisfies (8.1). All feasible policies are nested on order cost arcs.

Following Section 6, we define a *stationary nested power-of-two policy* for the extended bill of material network G' to be a vector $\mathcal{T} = (T_i: i \in N(G'))$ satisfying

$$T_i = 2^{l_i} T_L\,, \quad l_i \text{ integer}\,, \ T_L \text{ positive for all } i \in N(G') \tag{8.2}$$

and

$$T_i \geq T_j \quad \text{for all } (i, j) \in A(G')\,. \tag{8.3}$$

An optimal stationary nested powers-of-two policy is found by solving

$$\begin{aligned} &\text{minimize} \quad C(\mathcal{T}) = \sum_{i \in N(G')} \left[\frac{K_i}{T_i} + g_i T_i \right] \\ &\text{subject to} \quad (8.2), (8.3)\,. \end{aligned} \tag{8.4}$$

This problem is clearly of the same form as the corresponding problem in Section 6, and the algorithms presented there can be applied to it. They compute a policy whose cost is known to be within 2% or 6% of the cost of an optimal nested policy, depending on how the roundoff operation is performed. See Roundy [1986].

In the extended bill of material network, order cost nodes have holding cost coefficients of zero. This leads to the concern that the solution to the relaxation of (8.4) may have $T_i^* = \infty$ for some i. If one or more stages i has order cost $K_i = 0$, then there is also a possibility that the solution to the relaxation of (8.4) may have $T_i^* = 0$. The following mild conditions on an extended bill of material network G' guarantee that all reorder intervals in the solution to the relaxation of (8.4) are positive and finite.

(1) G is an acyclic directed network.

(2) If no arcs emanate from node i in G, then $K_i > 0$.

(3) If no arcs lead into node i in G, then $g_i > 0$.

We conclude this subsection by pointing out that order cost families can be combined with the capacity-constrained models of Section 7. To return to the injection molding machine we discussed at the beginning of the subsection, let us now suppose that a mold can be used on either of two different machines. It is used to make parts 1 and 2 on machine a, and it is used to make parts 3 and 4 on machine b. We wish to model the cost of mounting the mold on each of the machines, and also to model the fact that the mold is only available for a limited amount of time. We can accomplish this by creating two families, $\{1, 2\}$ and $\{3, 4\}$. The cost of mounting the mold on machine a is associated with family $\{1, 2\}$, and the cost of mounting it on machine b is associated with $\{3, 4\}$. A constrained workcenter is created to model the availability of the molds. If the time required to clean the mold is negligible, the workcenter consists of the families $\{1, 2\}$ and $\{3, 4\}$. If the time required to clean the mold is significant, the workcenter includes the nodes 1, 2, 3, and 4 in addition to the families $\{1, 2\}$ and $\{3, 4\}$.

8.3. Multi-item distribution systems

There are two interesting and important special cases of the model of Section 8.2 for which extremely efficient algorithms have been developed. The first of these is a one-warehouse, n-retailer distribution system through which I items are distributed. Each item is stocked at each location, i.e., at the warehouse and at each retailer. Each item-location pair has its own order cost, echelon holding cost rate, and demand rate. In addition there is a joint order cost associated with each of the retailers. The order cost for retailer j is incurred whenever an order is placed at retailer j, regardless of which items comprise the order.

The extended bill of material network G of this system is illustrated in Figure 12. Stages 1, 2, and 3 correspond to the inventories of items 1, 2, and 3, respectively, at the warehouse. Stages 4, 5, and 6 correspond to the inventories of the three items at retailer one, and items 7 through 12 correspond to the inventories at retailers two and three. These nodes are all inventory nodes with positive order costs, positive echelon holding costs, and positive demand rates. The arcs connecting them are inventory arcs that represent the movement of material through the system. Their gozinto parameters are all equal to one.

Stage 13 is an order cost node that represents the joint order cost at retailer one. Its demand rate and echelon holding cost rate are both zero, and its order cost is the joint order cost. The arcs adjacent to 13 are order cost arcs with gozinto parameters of zero. Stages 14 and 15 are similar.

This model is clearly a special case of the family model of Section 8.2, and the algorithm of that section can be used to find a good nested policy for it. We now describe a much more efficient $O(n \log n)$ algorithm that finds the optimal clusters for this problem. As before, once the clusters have been found, Steps 2 and 3 of Algorithm 1 are used to obtain the reorder intervals. See Muckstadt & Roundy [1987].

Let $W \subset N(G)$ be the set of nodes corresponding to the inventories of the I items held at the warehouse (nodes 1, 2, 3 in Figure 12). Let $R \subset N(G)$ be the set of nodes corresponding to the inventories held at the different retailers (nodes 4 through 12 in Figure 12), and let $J \subset N(G)$ be the set of joint order

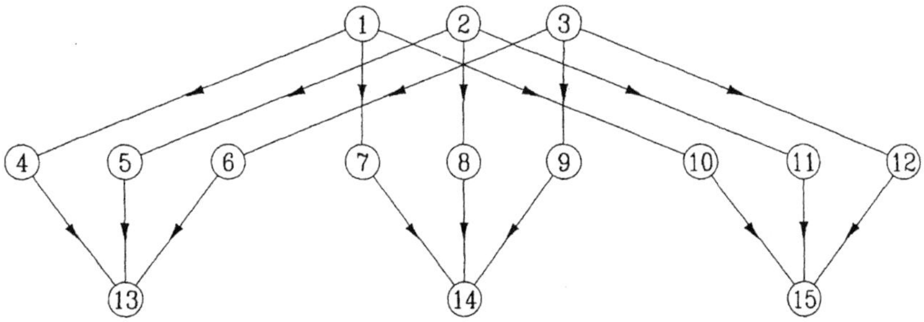

Fig. 12. A three-item, three-retailer system.

cost nodes (nodes 13, 14, and 15). Recall that s_i (respectively, p_i) is the set of direct successors (respectively, predecessors) of i in G.

The following observations are important in understanding the algorithm. The first two observations concern the one-warehouse, multi-retailer subsystems and the joint replenishment subsystems of RP. For a given node $j \in J$, consider the joint replenishment subsystem whose graph is the subgraph of G induced by the node set $\{j\} \cup p_j$. Consider the clusters that are optimal for this subsystem, when it is considered in isolation from the rest of G. Algorithm 4 can be used to compute these clusters. Among these clusters, let L_j be the cluster that contains node j. Each node $i \in p_j - L_j$ is in a singleton cluster $\{i\}$. Let $\tau^j = (\Sigma_{i\in L_j} K_i)/(\Sigma_{i\in L_j} g_i)$, and let $\tau^r = K_r/g_r$ for all $r \in R$. The key property of L_j is the following.

Observation 1. *If $r \in L_j - \{j\}$ and $i \in P_j - L_j$, then $\tau^r \leq \tau^j < \tau^i$.*

Similarly, consider the clusters that are optimal for the one-warehouse, multi-retailer subsystem whose graph is the subgraph induced by $\{w\} \cup s_w$ for some $w \in W$. The clusters that are optimal for this subsystem are also computed using Algorithm 4 via the transformation of Section 5. Let V_w be the cluster that contains w, and let $\tau^w = (\Sigma_{i\in V_w} K_i)/(\Sigma_{i\in V_w} g_i)$. The following observation holds.

Observation 2. *If $r \in S_w - V_w$ and $i \in V_w - \{w\}$, then $\tau^r < \tau^w \leq \tau^i$.*

The final observation is the key to understanding the algorithm used to solve RP.

Observation 3. *The optimal clusters for the graph G of Figure 12 can be classified into four types. There is a special cluster called the* major cluster, *abbreviated MC. Let*

$$\tau_{\mathrm{MC}} = \Big(\sum_{i\in \mathrm{MC}} K_i\Big) \Big/ \Big(\sum_{i\in \mathrm{MC}} g_i\Big) . \tag{8.5}$$

The other three cluster types are: the one-warehouse, multi-retailer clusters V_w, $w \in W$ for which $\tau^w > \tau_{\mathrm{MC}}$; the joint replenishment clusters L_j, $j \in J$ for which $\tau^j < \tau_{\mathrm{MC}}$; the one-node clusters $\{r\}$ for which $r \in R$, $\tau^r > \tau_{\mathrm{MC}}$, $r \notin V_w$ for any $w \in W$; and the one-node clusters $\{r\}$ for which $r \in R$, $\tau^r < \tau_{\mathrm{MC}}$, $r \notin L_j$ for any $j \in J$.

Observation 3 implies that the optimal clusters and reorder intervals for G can easily be determined once τ_{MC} is known. One way to interpret what the algorithm does is to view it as a parametric search for τ_{MC} and MC. It first determines what nodes would be in MC if τ_{MC} were infinitely large (as determined by Observation 3). The value of τ_{MC} is then continuously lowered from ∞ to its optimal value, and the algorithm performs the sequence of changes in the membership of MC that Observation 3 requires. Every time the membership of MC changes, the right-hand side of (8.5) is updated. The algorithm determines that the optimal value of τ_{MC} has been found when (8.5) holds. The algorithm has then established the optimal membership of MC.

The algorithm is given below. Step 2 requires that we solve the joint replenishment subproblems and the one-warehouse, multi-retailer subproblems referred to in Observations 1 and 2 above.

Algorithm 5. *Multi-item, one-warehouse multi-retailer systems.*

Step 1. Let $\tau^r = K_r/g_r$, $r \in R$. Sort these values and list them from the largest to the smallest.

Step 2. For all $j \in J$, solve the joint-replenishment problem formed by the graph $G(\{j\} \cup p_j)$. For all $w \in W$, solve the corresponding one-warehouse, multi-retailer problem over the graph $G(\{w\} \cup s_w)$. Let $\tau^j = (\Sigma_{i \in L_j} K_i)/(\Sigma_{i \in L_j} g_i)$ for all $j \in J$ and $\tau^w = (\Sigma_{i \in V_w} K_i)/(\Sigma_{i \in V_w} g_i)$ for all $w \in W$.

Step 3. Insert τ^j and τ^w, $j \in J$, $w \in W$, into the previously generated list of τ^r, $r \in R$. If $\tau^r = \tau^w$, place τ^r before τ^w in the list. If $\tau^j = \tau^r$, put τ^j in the list ahead of τ^r.

Step 4. Set the major cluster MC $= W$.

Step 5. Set $\tau_{MC} = (\Sigma_{i \in MC} K_i)/(\Sigma_{i \in MC} g_i)$. If either the list is empty or the largest remaining number τ^n on the list satisfies $\tau^n \leq \tau_{MC}$, go to Step 6. Otherwise:

(a) Remove the largest remaining number τ^n from the list.
(b) If $n \in R$ and $(w, n) \in A(G)$, then;
  (i) if $n \in V_w$, set MC$\leftarrow$MC $\cup \{n\}$;
  (ii) if $n \not\in V_w$, create the cluster $\{n\}$ and set MC$\leftarrow$MC $- \{n\}$. (Note: n may have entered MC via Step 5d, or n may not be in MC.)
(c) If $n \in W$, create the cluster V_n and set MC$\leftarrow$MC $- V_n$.
(d) If $n \in J$, set MC$\leftarrow$MC $\cup L_n$.
(e) Go to Step 5.

Step 6. The major cluster MC has been determined. If τ^j remains on the list for some $j \in J$, L_j is a cluster. If τ^j remains on the list for some $r \in R \cap P_j$ and $r \not\in L_j$, then $\{r\}$ is a separate cluster. The remaining τ^n on the list do not correspond to clusters.

The optimal clusters are MC, plus the clusters identified in Steps 5b(ii), 5c, and 6. As before, once the clusters have been found the reorder intervals are computed using Steps 2 and 3 of Algorithm 1.

Some explanatory comments are in order. All $w \in W$ are initially in MC. Nodes $w \in W$ leave MC only through Step 5c. By Observation 2, whenever Step 5a is executed, we have $w \in$ MC. Nodes $r \in R$ leave MC only through Steps 5c and 5b(ii). By Observation 2 and Step 5b, whenever we execute Step 5c we have $V_n \subset$ MC. Nodes $r \in R$ join MC only in Steps 5b(i) and 5d. When

Table 2
Problem data

Node i	1	2	3	4	5	6	7	8	9	10	11	12	13	14	15
K_i	1	4	3	2	1	1	1	1	2	1	1	3	2	5	1
g_i	8	1	1	1	3	5	1	1	1	2	6	1	0	0	0

Step 5b(ii) is executed, either node n has joined MC via Step 5d, or node n is not in MC and the composition of MC does not change.

We now give a numerical example. The system consists of three items stocked at three retailers and one warehouse. The graph for this system is displayed in Figure 12 and the data for the problem are given in Table 2. The solutions to the one-warehouse, three-retailer problems and joint replenishment problems are as follows:

$$n = 1: \quad V_1 = \{1, 4, 7, 10\}, \quad \tau^1 = \tfrac{5}{12},$$

$$n = 2: \quad V_2 = \{2\}, \quad \tau^2 = 4,$$

$$n = 3: \quad V_3 = \{3, 12\}, \quad \tau^3 = 3,$$

$$n = 13: \quad L_{13} = \{13, 5, 6\}, \quad \tau^{13} = \tfrac{1}{2},$$

$$n = 14: \quad L_{14} = \{14, 7, 8, 9\}, \quad \tau^{14} = 3,$$

$$n = 15: \quad L_{15} = \{15, 11\}, \quad \tau^{15} = \tfrac{1}{3}.$$

The list generated in Step 3 is:

n	2	14	12	3	9	4	8	7	13	10	1	15	5	6	11
τ^n	4	3	3	3	2	2	1	1	$\frac{1}{2}$	$\frac{1}{2}$	$\frac{5}{12}$	$\frac{1}{3}$	$\frac{1}{3}$	$\frac{1}{5}$	$\frac{1}{6}$

The optimal clusters are:

$$N(G_1) = \{11, 15\} \quad \text{with } T^*(1) = \sqrt{\tfrac{1}{3}},$$

$$N(G_2) = \{5, 6, 10, 13\} \quad \text{with } T^*(2) = \sqrt{\tfrac{1}{2}},$$

$$\text{MC} = N(G_3) = \{1, 4, 7, 14\} \quad \text{with } T^*(3) = \sqrt{\tfrac{9}{10}},$$

$$N(G_4) = \{8\} \quad \text{with } T^*(4) = 1,$$

$$N(G_5) = \{9\} \quad \text{with } T^*(5) = \sqrt{2},$$

$$N(G_6) = \{3, 12\} \quad \text{with } T^*(6) = \sqrt{3},$$

$$N(G_7) = \{2\} \quad \text{with } T^*(7) = 2.$$

The second system for which an efficient solution algorithm has been developed generalizes the multi-item, one-warehouse, multi-retailer system. In this system a number of items are distributed through a distribution network. The locations of the distribution network are indexed by l, $0 \leq l < L$. All goods enter the system at location $L-1$. Each location $l < L-1$ receives its supply of all items it stocks from a unique *predecessor location* $\varphi(l) > l$. Identifying locations with nodes and predecessor–successor relationships with arcs yields the location arborescence illustrated in Figure 13.

The set of items stocked in the system is $\mathcal{J}$. At location l, each item $J \in \mathcal{J}$ has a constant demand rate (possibly zero) and a linear echelon holding cost rate. At each location, external demand can occur for any or all of the items. When an order for a set of items is placed at a location l, the required amounts of inventory are instantly transferred from location $\varphi(l)$ to location l.

Order costs are associated with subsets $f(i)$, $1 \leq i \leq I$ of $\mathcal{J}$ called *families*. We assume that

$$\text{if} \quad f(i) \cap f(i') \neq \emptyset \quad \text{then} \quad \text{either } f(i) \subset f(i') \quad \text{or } f(i') \subset f(i) . \tag{8.6}$$

Because items interact only through families, we assume without loss of generality that family $F(I)$ contains all of the items. For convenience we also assume that each individual item constitutes a separate family.

To illustrate, suppose that the items stocked are 1 (ice cream), 2 (frozen meat), and 4 (canned peas). The cost of providing a truck is incurred every time an order is placed. This cost is associated with the family $\{1, 2, 4\}$. If either or both of items 1 and 2 are ordered, the truck will have to be refrigerated. The incremental cost of providing a refrigerated truck is associated with the family $\{1, 2\}$. In addition, there is an administrative cost for each distinct item included in the shipment. This cost is associated with each of the families $\{1\}$, $\{2\}$, and $\{4\}$.

For each family $F(j)$, we define the *successor* $\beta(j)$ of j by letting $F(\beta(j))$ be the minimal family that properly contains the family $F(j)$. The uniqueness of $\beta(j)$ follows from (8.6). The family arborescence is defined by associating nodes with families and arcs with predecessor–successor relationships. Figure 14 shows the family arborescence for the simple, three-item example described above.

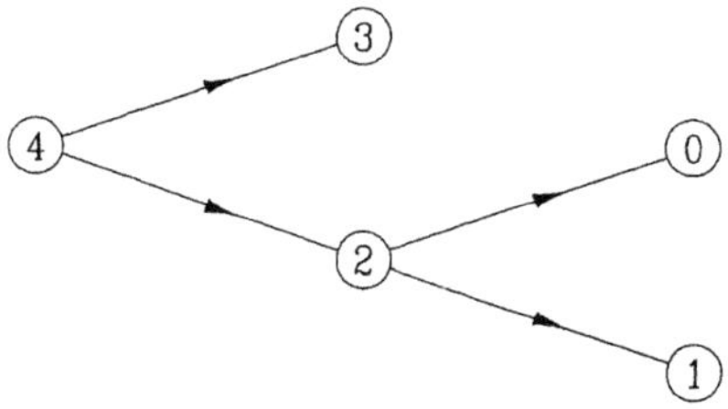

Fig. 13. The location arborescence.

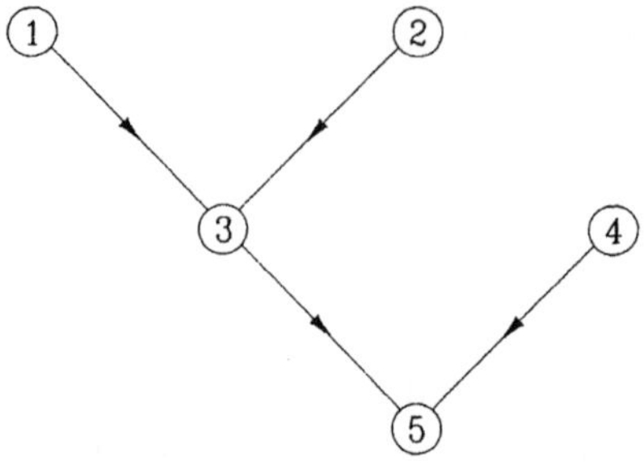

Fig. 14. The item arborescence.

We index the location-family pair $(F(i), l)$ by $n \equiv i + lI$. Associated with each such pair is an order cost $K'_n = K'_{i+lI}$. The cost K'_{i+lI} is incurred at every point in time at which an order is placed for any item in $F(i)$ at location l. Thus, if $S \subset \mathcal{I}$ is the set of items ordered at location l at time t, the total order cost incurred at location l is $\Sigma_{F(i)\cap S \neq \emptyset} K'_{i+lI}$. The extended bill of material network G of this system is defined as follows. The node set of G is $N(G) \equiv \{i + lI: 1 \leqslant i \leqslant I, 0 \leqslant l < L\}$, the set of all location-family pairs. The arc set $A(G)$ of G consists of all *inventory arcs* of the form $(i + \varphi(l)I, i + lI)$, and of all order cost arcs of the form $(i + lI, \beta(i) + lI)$. G is illustrated in Figure 15. Because $I = 5$ and $13 = 3 + 2 \times 5$, node 13 corresponds to item 3 and location 2. Note that the nodes in each column of Figure 15 correspond to a location and that the nodes in each row correspond to a family.

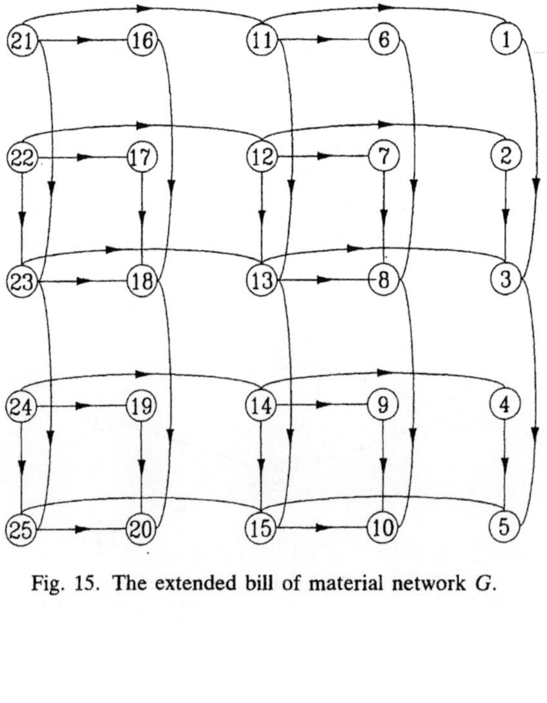

Fig. 15. The extended bill of material network G.

For this system an $O(LID \log LI)$ algorithm has been developed where D is the depth of the item arborescence depicted in Figure 14 [Roundy, 1987]. For most real-world systems D will seldom exceed five.

8.4. *Models with submodular ordering costs*

Given a finite set of stages N^* let $P(N^*)$ be the set of all subsets of N^*. The function $\bar{K}: P(N^*) \to \mathbb{R}$ is said to be *submodular* if $\bar{K}(S) + \bar{K}(T) \geq \bar{K}(S \cap T) + \bar{K}(S \cup T)$ for all $S, T \in P(N^*)$. $\bar{K}$ is said to be *monotone* if $0 = \bar{K}(\emptyset)$ and $\bar{K}(S) \leq \bar{K}(T)$ whenever $S \subset T$. In this section we consider a model in which the cost of placing an order is a monotone submodular function of the set of items being ordered.

The model we consider is an extension of the models of Section 6 and Section 8.2. We are given a circuitless bill of material network G with node set $N(G)$ and arc set $A(G)$. Each node corresponds to a stage at which a single part is stocked. As before, echelon holding cost rates and demand rates are associated with each stage. The assumptions that time is continuous, orders are instantly delivered, demand is deterministic and constant, and stockouts are not allowed apply to this model as well.

The model of this subsection differs from our earlier models in that our order costs are determined by a submodular function $\bar{K}$ mapping $P(N(G))$ into $\mathbb{R}$. Whenever an order is placed the total order cost incurred is $\bar{K}(S)$ when S is the set of items being ordered at that point in time. By contrast, the systems we studied in Sections 3–7 had order costs of the form $K(S) = \Sigma_{n \in S} K_n$. These order costs satisfy $K(S) + K(T) = K(S \cup T) + K(S \cap T)$, i.e., they are *modular*. The systems considered in Sections 8.1 and 8.3 are special cases of the family model of Section 8.2. In this model, $\bar{K}(S) = \Sigma_{f \in F:\, f \cap S \neq \emptyset} K_f$. Because $K_f \geq 0\ \forall f$, this is a submodular order cost function. Other interesting examples of submodular order costs are given by Zheng [1987].

The task of finding a nested powers-of-two policy for systems of this type can be formulated as a nonlinear integer program (NIP) similar to the ones we have formulated in earlier sections. The approach used to compute a policy is also similar to the approach we have used in earlier sections, and the same results on the relative cost of the policies computed apply [Queyranne, 1985; Zheng, 1987; Federgruen, Queyranne & Zheng, 1989]. We first relax the integrality constraints in NIP and solve a continuous optimization problem. We then round off the resulting order intervals to powers-of-two using Step 3 of Algorithm 1. The continuous relaxation of the NIP is solved using a direct analog of the divide and conquer algorithm of Section 6. In the divide and conquer algorithm of Section 6, a maximum flow problem was solved in each iteration. For this model a maximal polymatroidal network flow problem is solved at each iteration. This polymatroidal network flow problem has special structure, and Zheng [1987] has developed a special-purpose algorithm for solving it. The algorithm has a running time of $O(n^4 d)$. Here d is the time required to answer the following question: given j, $1 \leq j \leq n$, and a vector

$x = (x_i \geq 0: 1 \leq i \leq n)$ that satisfies $\Sigma_{i \in S} x_i \leq \bar{K}(S)$ for all $S \subset N(G)$, find the largest amount by which x_j can be increased without violating any of the inequalities $\Sigma_{i \in S} x_i \leq \bar{K}(S)$, $S \subset N(G)$. In practice one would hope that the systems being modeled have special structure which allows this computation to be performed easily.

For the special case of a joint replenishment system with submodular costs, in which the network G has no arcs, a much more efficient algorithm exists. Before describing the algorithm we consider what the average cost of a powers-of-two policy is. Suppose that we are given clusters $C_1, C_2, \ldots, C_N$, that all nodes $i \in C_k$ place orders once every $T(k)$ days, that $T(k) = 2^{l(k)} T_L$, $l(k)$ integer, and that $T(k) \leq T(k+1)$ for all k. The average holding cost incurred per day is clearly $\Sigma_{k=1}^{N} g(C_k) T(k)$ where, as before, $g(C_k) = \Sigma_{i \in C_k} g_i$. Let $T(N+1) = \infty$ and let $\bar{C}_k = \cup_{l \leq k} C_l$. On the average, once every $[1/T(k) - 1/T(k+1)]^{-1}$ days an order is placed for the items in $\bar{C}_k$ and no others. Therefore, the average order cost incurred is

$$\sum_{k=1}^{N} \bar{K}(\bar{C}_k)\left[\frac{1}{T(k)} - \frac{1}{T(k+1)}\right].$$

Thus the average cost of the policy is

$$\sum_{k} [(\bar{K}(\bar{C}_k) - \bar{K}(\bar{C}_{k-1}))/T(k) + g(C_k)T(k)],$$

where $\bar{C}_0 = \emptyset$.

As before, we initially ignore the integrality constraints and compute clusters by solving a convex, nonlinear optimization problem. In the solution to this problem, the reorder interval for nodes in cluster C_k is

$$T^*(k) = [(\bar{K}(\bar{C}_k) - \bar{K}(\bar{C}_{k-1}))/g(C_k)]^{1/2}. \tag{8.7}$$

For a given set of clusters $C_1, \ldots, C_N$, $\bar{C}_l = \cup_{k \leq l} C_l$, and for each node set $S \subseteq C_l$, we define $\bar{K}_l(S) = \bar{K}(S \cup \bar{C}_{l-1}) - \bar{K}(\bar{C}_{l-1})$.

The function $\bar{K}_l$ is itself a monotone submodular function on the subsets of C_l. The algorithm used to compute the clusters is similar to the divide and conquer algorithm of Section 6. It starts with all nodes in a single cluster, and successively splits clusters into smaller clusters, until the final set of clusters has been identified. The algorithm follows.

Algorithm 6. *Joint replenishment systems with submodular order costs.*

Step 0. Set $N \leftarrow 1$, $l \leftarrow 1$, $C_1 \leftarrow \{1, 2, \ldots, n\}$.

Step 1. Find a maximal vector $X = (X_i: i \in C_l)$ satisfying $\Sigma_{i \in S} X_i \leq \bar{K}_l(S)$ for all $S \subseteq C_l$ and $X_i \leq U_i^l$ for all $i \in C_l$, where $U_i^l = g_i \bar{K}_l(C_l)/g(C_l)$.

Step 2. Set $A \leftarrow \text{sat}(X)$ where sat(X) is the (unique) maximal subset of C_l satisfying $\Sigma_{i \in \text{sat}(X)} X_i = \bar{K}_l(\text{sat}(X))$.

Step 3. If $A = C_l$, then set $l \leftarrow l + 1$ and go to Step 4 (C_l is one of the clusters). If $A \neq C_l$, then set $N \leftarrow N + 1$, $C_{m+1} \leftarrow C_m$ for each $m > l$, $C_{l+1} \leftarrow C_l \backslash A$, and $C_l \leftarrow A$.

Step 4. If $l = N + 1$ and go to Step 5. Otherwise go to Step 1.

Step 5. Compute $T^*(k)$ for each cluster k using (8.7). Then compute the reorder intervals T_i of the items using Step 3 of Algorithm 1.

The running time of this algorithm depends on the amount of time required to perform Steps 1 and 2. In practice one would hope that the function $\bar{K}$ has special structure which enables these computations to be performed easily. For a more complete discussion of this model and algorithm, see Zheng [1987].

9. Nonnested policies

In Sections 3–8, we have restricted ourselves to stationary nested powers-of-two policies. For the systems of Sections 3 and 4, nested policies were optimal. However for the other systems we have considered, optimal nested policies can be seriously sub-optimal. Suppose for example that we are modeling a three-stage distribution system. Stage one (the factory) supplies two outlets, stages two and three. The factory is in Albany, outlet one is in New York City, and outlet two is in Singapore. The problem data is in Table 3 below. The time units are weeks. The demand rate λ at the Singapore outlet is very low, and the order cost K there is very high.

A reasonable policy for this system is to place orders at the factory and at the New York outlet on a weekly basis, and to place orders from Singapore approximately once every $\sqrt{K/\lambda} > 1$ weeks. However, if a nested policy were followed, an order could not be placed at the factory unless a simultaneous order were placed in Singapore. A nested policy would incur either high inventory costs at the factory due to a long reorder interval there, or high order costs at the Singapore outlet due to a low reorder interval there, or both. For several sets of problem parameters, the effectiveness of an optimal nested policy is illustrated in Table 4. The effectiveness is the ratio of the cost of an optimal policy to the cost of an optimal nested policy.

As this example illustrates, nested policies tend to become seriously sub-optimal when relatively high order costs are combined with relatively low demand rates. In this model, n retailers with order costs of K and demand rates

Table 3
Problem data

	1: Factory	2: New York	3: Singapore
Order cost	1	1	K
Demand rate	0	2	λ
Echelon holding cost	1	1	1

Table 4
Effectiveness of optimal nested policies

	K		
	2	32	∞
$\frac{1}{2}$	96%	75%	58%
$\frac{1}{32}$	82%	44%	17%
0	73%	29%	0%

of λ have the same effect as one retailer with an order cost of nK and a demand rate of $n\lambda$. Therefore no individual retailer needs to have an uncommonly high order cost for nested policies to perform poorly.

9.1. *Algorithm for one-warehouse, multi-retailer systems*

Consider a single warehouse (stage 0) which supplies a number of retailers (stages 1 through n). The order cost at stage i is K_i, the echelon holding cost rate at stage i is h_i, and the demand rate at retailer $i \geq 1$ is λ_i. The bill of material network is illustrated in Figure 16. As before, we seek to minimize the total order and inventory costs subject to the constraint that all demand must be met without stockouts.

In earlier sections we restricted attention to stationary nested powers-of-two policies which satisfy the Zero-Ordering Property. In this section we drop the assumptions of stationarity and nestedness, and study powers-of-two policies that satisfy the Zero-Ordering Property. This means that orders are placed at equal intervals of time which are powers-of-two multiples of T_L, and that the inventory at a stage is zero every time an order is placed there.

Let orders be placed at stage i once every T_i days. Let $g_i = \frac{1}{2}h_i\lambda_i$ and let $g^i = \frac{1}{2}h_0\lambda_i$. Let $T = (T_0, \ldots, T_n)$ be a powers-of-two policy satisfying the Zero-Ordering Property. For the purpose of computing holding costs, we separate the inventory at the warehouse into n categories, according to the retailer to which it will be shipped. Let $h_i(T_0, T_i)$ be the average annual cost of holding inventory at the warehouse that is destined to be shipped to retailer i, and of holding inventory at retailer i. We will show that

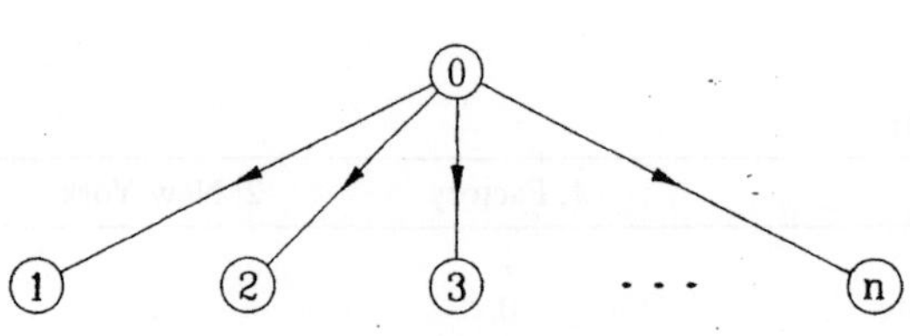

Fig. 16. One-warehouse, multi-retailer system.

$$h_i(T_0, T_i) = g_i T_i + g^i(T_0 \vee T_i), \tag{9.1}$$

where $\vee$ denotes the maximum.

Case 1. $T_i \geq T_0$. In this case the warehouse places an order simultaneously with every order at the retailer. Therefore no inventory for retailer i is ever held at the warehouse, and the only costs to be considered are the costs at the retailer. As in the familiar single-item model,

$$h_i(T_0, T_i) = (g_i + g^i)T_i,$$

which agrees with (9.1) if $T_i \geq T_0$.

Case 2. $T_i < T_0$. In this case it is convenient to use the echelon method of computing order costs. We consider only those goods that will eventually be consumed by external demand at retailer i. The total system inventory of these goods follows the familiar sawtooth inventory pattern with an order interval of T_0. The inventory at retailer i follows a sawtooth inventory pattern with order interval T_i. Therefore the average cost of holding all inventory in the system that is destined to be consumed at retailer i is

$$h_i(T_0, T_i) = g_i T_i + g^i T_0,$$

which agrees with (9.1) when $T_i \leq T_0$.

Therefore the average cost of a powers-of-two policy is given by

$$c(\mathscr{T}) = \sum_{i\geq 0} \frac{K_i}{T_i} + \sum_{i\geq 1} [g_i T_i + g^i(T_0 \vee T_i)]. \tag{9.2}$$

Since we are considering powers-of-two policies satisfying the Zero-Ordering Property, the only constraint on the order intervals is

$$T_i = 2^{l_i} T_L, \quad l_i \text{ integer}, \quad T_L > 0. \tag{9.3}$$

Therefore, the problem of finding an optimal powers-of-two policy is the problem of minimizing (9.2) subject to (9.3).

We use the same basic approach that we have used in earlier sections. We first relax (9.3) and minimize (9.2) over all nonnegative $\mathscr{T}$ [Roundy, 1985a]. We then round-off the reorder intervals thus computed to integer powers of two. We use Step 3 of Algorithm 1 if T_L is fixed, and we use the algorithm in Roundy [1985a] if T_L is variable. In the former case the cost of the policy is within 6% of the minimum of (9.2), and in the latter case the cost of the policy is within 2% of the minimum of (9.2).

It is possible to show that the minimum of (9.2) is in fact a lower bound on the average cost of any feasible policy whatsoever. In Sections 5 and 6 we computed policies whose costs were close to the cost of an optimal nested policy, but optimal nested policies can be far from optimal. The policies we compute in this section have costs that are close to the cost of an optimal policy.

What remains is to show how (9.2) can be efficiently minimized. The intuition behind the algorithm is as follows. There are three kinds of retailers. Those retailers who place orders less frequently than the warehouse does are in category G. If $\mathcal{T}^* = (T_i^*: 1 \leq i \leq n)$ minimizes (9.2), then local optimality and (9.2) dictate that

$$T_i^* = \sqrt{K_i/(g_i + g^i)} > T_0^* \quad \text{if } i \in G. \tag{9.4}$$

Those retailers who place orders more frequently than the warehouse does are in category L. Local optimality and (9.2) dictate that

$$T_i^* = \sqrt{K_i/g_i} < T_0^* \quad \text{if } i \in L. \tag{9.5}$$

Finally, those retailers who place orders simultaneously with the warehouse are in category E. Local optimality and (9.2) dictate that they place orders once every

$$T_0^* = \sqrt{\left[K_0 + \sum_{i \in E} K_i\right] \Big/ \left[\sum_{i \in E} (g_i + g^i) + \sum_{i \in L} g^i\right]} \tag{9.6}$$

days. The algorithm searches for sets G, L, and E that satisfy (9.4)–(9.6). It is given below.

Algorithm 7. *Nonnested policies for one-warehouse multi-retailer systems.*

Step 1. Calculate the reorder cycles $\tau_i' = [K_i/(g^i + g_i)]^{1/2}$ and $\tau_i = (K_i/g_i)^{1/2}$, and sort them to form a nondecreasing sequence of $2n$ numbers. Call this sequence S. Label each reorder cycle with the value of i and with an indicator showing whether it is the conventional reorder cycle τ_i' or the echelon reorder cycle τ_i.

Step 2. Set $E = G = \emptyset$, $L = \{1, \ldots, n\}$, $K = K_0$, and $H = \Sigma_{i \geq 1} g^i$.

Step 3. Let τ be the largest element of S. If $\tau^2 \geq K/H$ and $\tau = \tau_i$ is an echelon reorder cycle, remove τ from S and update E, L, K, and H by $E \leftarrow E \cup \{i\}$, $L \leftarrow L \backslash \{i\}$, $K \leftarrow K + K_i$ and $H \leftarrow H + g_i$. Then go to Step 3. If $\tau^2 > K/H$ and $\tau = \tau_i'$ is a conventional reorder cycle, remove τ from S and update E, G, K, and H by $E \leftarrow E \backslash \{i\}$, $G \leftarrow G \cup \{i\}$, $H \leftarrow H - g^i - g_i$ and $K \leftarrow K - K_i$, and go to Step 3. Otherwise, the current sets G, L, and E are optimal. Go to Step 4.

Step 4. Set $T_0^* = (K/H)^{1/2}$. Then $T_i^* = T_0^*$ for all retailers $i \in E$, and T_i^* for retailers not in E is given by (9.4) and (9.5).

The sort in Step 1 requires $O(n \log n)$ comparisons. All other phases of the algorithm require a number of operations that is linear in n.

9.2. The extended bill of material network

We return momentarily to the three-node example at the beginning of Section 9. In this example, we could conceptually separate the inventory at the factory into two categories; the inventory that will be shipped to New York and the inventory that will be shipped to Singapore. We could then assign separate reorder intervals to these two categories of inventory. At the factory we could order inventory bound for New York once per week, and order inventory bound for Singapore approximately once every $\sqrt{K/\lambda}$ weeks. In this way we would succeed in managing the system effectively while preserving much of the structure of stationary nested powers-of-two policies.

This is essentially what the algorithm of Section 9.1 does. We can interpret it as an algorithm which computes nested policies on a modified bill of material network. The bill of material network in Figure 16 is modified in the following way. We split the warehouse into $n+1$ different stages, labeled 0, $n+1$, $n+2, \ldots, 2n$. Stage 0 represents the joint order cost at the warehouse. Stage i, $1 \leq i \leq n$, represents retailer i, and stage $n+i$, $1 \leq i \leq n$, represents the inventory at the warehouse that will be shipped to retailer i. The bill of material network associated with this system is illustrated in Figure 17. Table 5 lists the data associated with each stage. Note that relative to the network of Figure 17, the policies of Section 9.1 and Table 5 are nested. Also note that the sum of the average costs associated with the stages corresponds to the total average cost of the policy $\mathcal{T}$, given by (9.2).

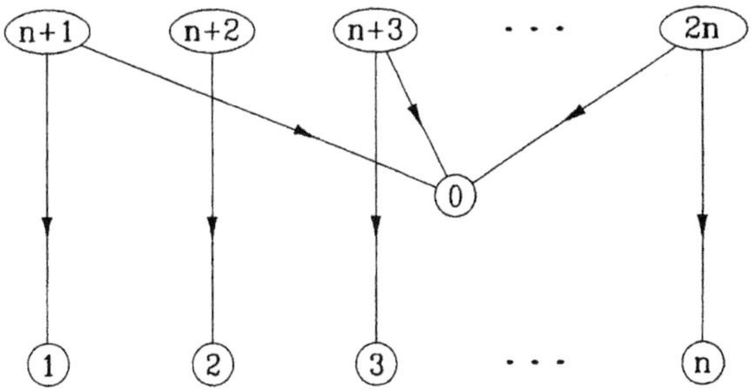

Fig. 17. Nonnested policies for one-warehouse, multi-retailer systems.

Table 5
Data for the stages

Stage index	Order cost	Holding cost coefficient	Reorder interval	Average cost
0	K_0	0	T_0	K_0/g_0
$i, 1 \leq i \leq n$	K_i	g_i	T_i	$K_i/T_i + g_i T_i$
$n+i, 1 \leq i \leq n$	0	g^i	$T_0 \vee T_i$	$g^i(T_0 \vee T_i)$

This example illustrates our approach to overcoming the limitations of nested policies. We transform the original bill of material network into an expanded network in which nested policies are near-optimal. This is accomplished by partitioning the inventory at each stage into classes according to the way in which the goods will be routed through the system. We treat these different classes of inventories as if they were distinct stages, and allow them to be controlled by different reorder intervals. This approach allows us to compute policies that are known to be near-optimal for systems with general bill of material networks.

We now describe a procedure for transforming an arbitrary bill of material network into an expanded network on which nested policies are near-optimal. Assume that we are given a bill of material network G with node set N and arc set A. This network may contain order cost nodes and order cost arcs (see Section 8.2). The following data are associated with the network. For each node $i \in N$ there is an order cost $K_i \geq 0$, an echelon holding cost $h_i \geq 0$, and a demand rate $\lambda_i \geq 0$. For each arc $(i, j) \in A$ there is a gozinto coefficient $\gamma_{ij} \geq 0$. This data is sufficient to define an instance of the production planning problems of Sections 3–6 and Section 8, with the exception of the submodular cost models of Section 8.4. We make the following assumptions.

Property 1. *G is an acyclic directed graph.*

Property 2. *If no arcs emanate from node i in G, then $K_i > 0$.*

Property 3. *If no arcs lead into node i in G, then $g_i > 0$.*

As mentioned in Section 8.2, these properties guarantee that the reorder intervals will be positive and finite.

In this subsection it is convenient to use the *external demand rates* D_i, $i \in N(G)$, for the nodes rather than the total demand rates λ_i, $i \in N(G)$, that we use elsewhere. The external and total demand rates are related via the equation

$$\lambda_i = D_i + \sum_{(i,j) \in A(G)} \gamma_{ij} \lambda_j \quad \forall i \in N(G) .$$

An arc $(i, j) \in A(G)$ is an *inventory arc* if $\gamma_{ij} > 0$, and it is an *order cost arc* if $\gamma_{ij} = 0$. A *common part node* is a node with more than one emanating inventory arc, or a node with one emanating inventory arc and with a positive external demand rate. The constraint that a nested policy must be followed can cause trouble at common part nodes.

The algorithm we use to transform the bill of material network is iterative in nature. We say that node *i precedes* node *j* in a network if there is a directed path from *i* to *j* in the network. At each iteration the procedure selects a common part node *i* that does not precede any other common part node in the network. It then makes local changes to the network by splitting node i into several different nodes, none of which is a common part node. The algorithm terminates when no common part nodes are left.

The iterative step of the algorithm is illustrated in Figure 18. There is a joint order cost associated with the family $\{2, 3\}$, which is represented by node 0. All arcs not adjacent to node 0 are inventory arcs. Initially, node 2 is the only common part node. Nodes 2, 3, and 4 have positive external demand rates.

The iterative step of the algorithm is as follows. Let node i be the common part node selected (node 2 in the example). Node i is split into a number of different nodes. For every inventory arc (i, j) emanating from node i there is a new *inventory node* $n(i, j)$ (nodes 5 and 6 in the example). The inventory of i that will be used to make part j is associated with $n(i, j)$. Node $n(i, j)$ inherits a copy of each arc leading into node i, and it inherits the arc (i, j) leading out of node i. The order cost and the external demand rate for node $n(i, j)$ are both zero, and $n(i, j)$ inherits the echelon holding cost rate of node i. If $D_i > 0$ then there is a new *demand node* $n(i, d)$ (node 7 in the example). The inventory of i that will be used to satisfy the external demand at i is associated with $n(i, d)$. Node $n(i, d)$ inherits a copy of each arc leading into node i. The order cost for node $n(i, d)$ is zero, and $n(i, d)$ inherits the holding cost rate and the external demand rate of node i. Finally, a node $n(i, K)$ (node 8 in the example) is used to account for the order cost. The holding cost rate and the external demand rate for node $n(i, K)$ are zero, and $n(i, K)$ inherits the order cost of node i. Node $n(i, K)$ also inherits all order cost arcs leading out of node i. We create a new order cost arc from each new inventory node $n(i, j)$ to node $n(i, K)$, and from the new demand node $n(i, d)$ (if there is one) to node $n(i, K)$. Figure 18b shows the network at the end of the iteration.

Note that none of the nodes created during the iterative step is a common part node. However, in the example of Figure 18, node 1 has become a common part node. The next iteration will split node 1 into several nodes. Figure 18c displays the result. In this network there are no common part nodes, so the procedure terminates. Another example of how a bill of material network is transformed by this algorithm is given in Figure 19. In this figure, initially all arcs are inventory arcs.

The iterative step of the algorithm preserves Properties 1–3 listed above, so the algorithm produces a network and associated data that can be interpreted as a bill of material network. Let G be the original bill of material network, and let G^* be the transformed bill of material network. Recall that in all bill of material networks, policies must be nested on setup arcs in order to be feasible. We have discussed how inventories are associated with the nodes of G^*. Using this association, one can easily show that any feasible policy for G corresponds to a feasible policy for G^* that has the same cost, and vice versa. Therefore either of these networks can be used to model the system being studied. Policies that are nested in G are nested in G^*, but not vice versa. The advantage of G^* lies in the following fact: whereas an optimal nested policy can be far from optimal, there is always a policy that is nested in G^* and is

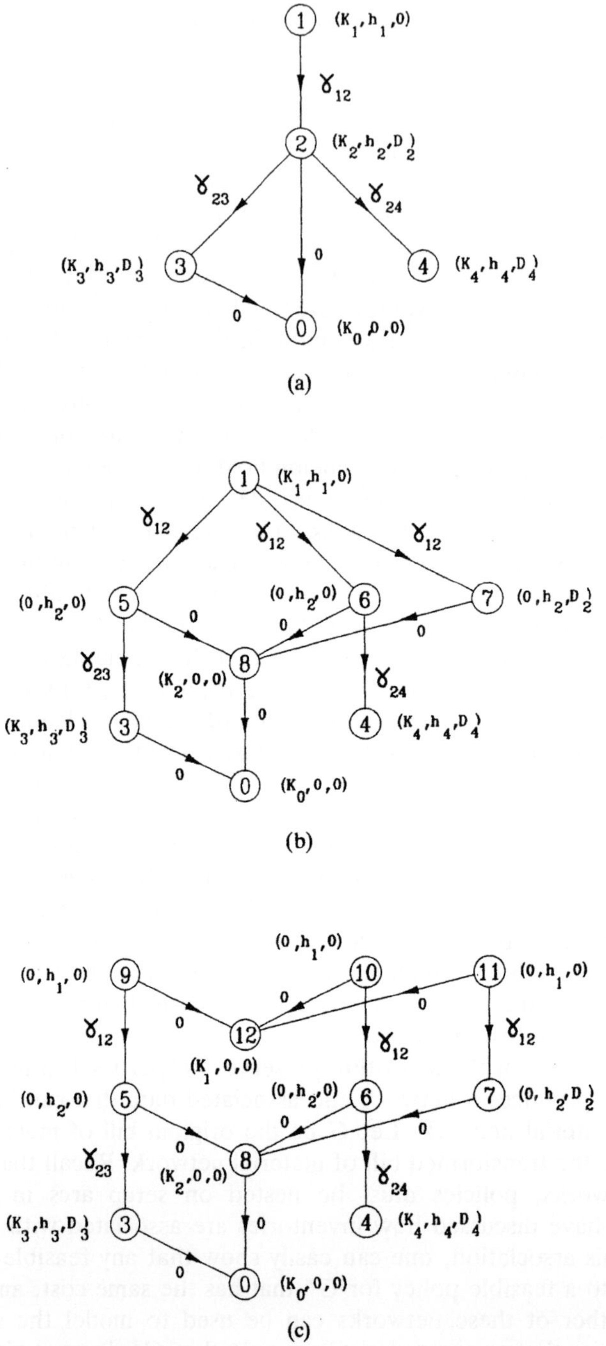

Fig. 18. The transformation from G to G^*: (a) G; (b) end of first iteration; (c) G^*. *Legend*: (Order Cost, Echelon Holding Cost, External Demand Rate).

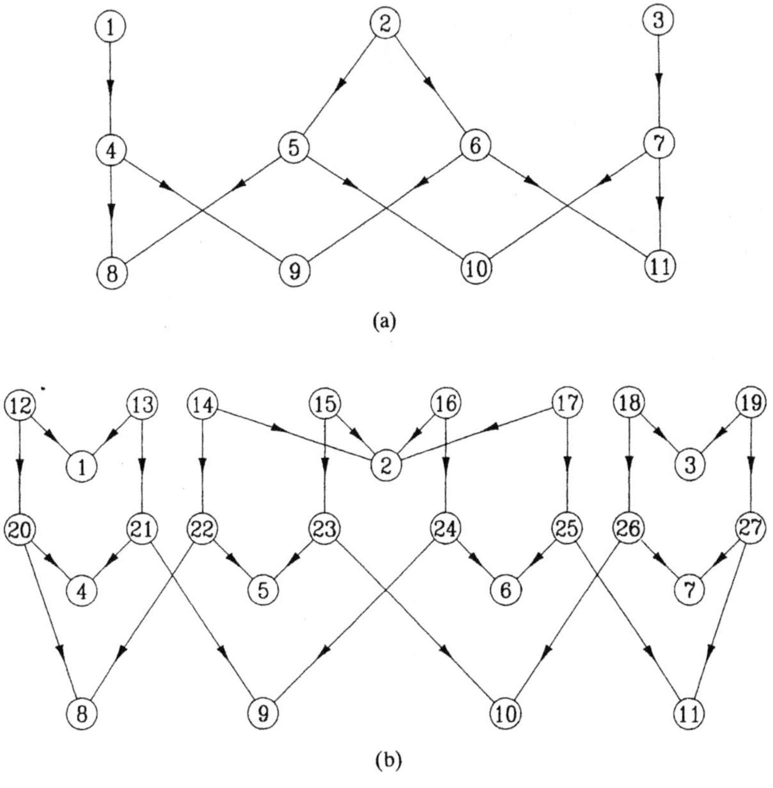

Fig. 19. The networks G and G^*: (a) G; (b) G^*.

within 6% of optimal. More precisely, the solution of the continuous relaxation of the lot sizing problem (problem 6.2) for G^* is a lower bound on the cost of any feasible policy whatsoever [Roundy, 1986]. Consequently, by applying the algorithms of Section 6 to G^*, we can compute a policy that is within 6% of optimal if the base planning period is fixed, and within 2% of optimal if it is variable.

The network G^* is very sparse. For example, if G has no order cost families then each node of G^* has at most two emanating arcs, so $|A(G^*)| \leq 2|N(G^*)|$. However, in the worst case, $|N(G^*)|$ is exponential in $|N(G)|$. Let $F(G)$ be the set of finished products in G, i.e., the set of stages or nodes in G that have positive external demand, and let R_{ij} be the number of directed paths from node i to node j in G. It can be shown that if there are no order cost families then $|N(G^*)| \leq |N(G)| + \Sigma_{i \in N(G), j \in F(G)} R_{ij}$. In most real-world bill of material networks $|R_{ij}|$ is O(1). For this reason, a quick and crude estimate of $|N(G^*)|$ is $|N(G)| \times (F+1)$ where F is the average over all $i \in N(G)$ of the number of finished products that require part i. For the industrial system illustrated in Section 6, $|N(G)| = 94$, $|F(G)| = 4$, $|N(G^*)| = 282$, $|N(G)| \times (F+1) = 294$, and $|R_{ij}| \leq 2$ for all $i, j \in N(G)$.

Zheng [1987] has proposed using a different network G^{**} in place of G^*. The networks G^* and G^{**} are equivalent in terms of the policies computed, their costs, and the lower bound. The advantage of G^{**} is that it is bipartite and has the same number of nodes as G^*. The disadvantage of G^{**} is that it can have as many as $\frac{1}{2} \times |N(G)| \times |N(G^*)|$ arcs, whereas G^* has fewer than $2 \times |N(G^*)|$ arcs.

Nonnested policies can easily be combined with submodular order costs of the type considered in Section 8.4. See Queyranne [1985], Zheng [1987], and Federgruen, Queyranne & Zheng [1989] for details. Capacity constraints of the type considered in Section 7 are also easily incorporated.

10. Other extensions

In this section we briefly describe other related research, including extensions of the models that we have discussed and improved algorithms for computations. We begin with extensions to the models.

10.1. Lead times

Suppose that there is a positive, deterministic lead time for preparing a shipment at the originating stage, for transportation from one stage to another, and for receiving the shipment at the destination stage. We assume that these lead times are dependent only on the two stages involved. In particular they are independent of the quantity of the order. Lead times of this sort can often be incorporated without causing a drop in the performance of the policies we have discussed, or a significant amount of extra computation.

For the serial, assembly, and single-item distribution systems discussed in Sections 3–5, we handle lead times by initially ignoring them. After a schedule has been computed, the orders at each stage are simply translated forward or backward in time by an appropriate amount. The theorems on the worst-case relative cost of the resulting schedule still apply.

The multi-item distribution systems discussed in Section 8.3 can be handled similarly. Assume that the lead time for processing and shipping an order is a function only of the two locations involved; it is independent of which items are ordered and of the order quantities. Once again, we initially ignore the lead times. After a schedule has been computed, the orders at each location are translated forward or backward in time by an appropriate amount.

For systems with arbitrary bill of material networks, such as those discussed in Sections 6 and 8.2, lead times can be handled in a similar way without causing a decrease in system performance if the lead times are 'balanced' [Roundy, 1986]. This condition holds if the bill of material network G has no cycles, but it is likely to fail for networks with cycles unless some very special structure, such as the structure of multi-item distribution systems, is present.

10.2. *Finite production rates*

Often a stage is a manufacturing operation, and production occurs at a finite rate. Recently several researchers have constructed detailed models of the finiteness of the production rate, the way in which material is transferred from one stage to another, and the impact that this has on intervening inventories. The impact is clearly larger if the production rates are small compared to the echelon demand rates. Schwarz & Schrage [1975] consider an assembly system of the type discussed in Section 4 under the assumption that material is transferred from one stage to another only after a batch is completed. Karimi [1987] studied a two-stage serial system with finite production rates and continuous transfer of material from one stage to another. Szendrovits [1975] studied serial systems in which a single reorder interval T is used at all stages, and material is transferred between stages in transfer batches of size b, $1 \leq b \leq T\lambda$, where λ is the demand rate. Atkins, Queyranne, & Sun [1989] have obtained policies that are within 6% of optimal for assembly systems with finite production rates in which the processing rate at the successor of node n is not less than node n's processing rate, for all n.

10.3. *Bounds on the reorder intervals*

As was mentioned earlier, any of the lot sizing models considered herein can be enhanced by adding the constraint

$$2^{\underline{l}} T_L \leq T_i \leq 2^{\bar{l}} T_L \quad \forall i \in N(G) .$$

The only change required in the algorithms is the simple alteration to the roundoff procedure described in Section 3.4. All claims of optimality and near-optimality can be shown to apply.

In many cases one would like the lower and/or upper bound on T_i to be different for different values of i. Recently Zheng [1987] has provided a general algorithm for solving this problem which is similar in spirit to the divide and conquer algorithm. He has also shown that the policies computed in this way have provably near-optimal costs. Best & Chakravarty [1987] have developed efficient algorithms for the continuous relaxation of the lot sizing problem for serial systems.

10.4. *Fixed batch sizes*

Anily & Federgruen [1987] have studied a multi-item, two-level system in which the top level consists of a single stage which produces a single generic part in batches of fixed size. The second level consists of a step in which the generic part is transformed into any of several different parts, each of which has constant demand. Traditional holding costs apply at all stages. Order costs are also present, but the way in which they are modeled is nonstandard. They present efficient algorithms for computing policies that are known to be within 6% of optimal.

10.5. *Algorithms for special bill of material structures*

There are several other algorithms that have been devised for solving the continuous relaxation of the lot sizing problem (problem 6.2) for different bill of material networks G. Some of these were developed for the problems of isotonic regression and precedence-constrained single-machine scheduling [Roundy, 1986]. For serial networks a linear-time algorithm exists [Ayer, Brunk, Ewing, Reid & Silverman, 1955; Best & Chakravarty, 1987]. For series-parallel digraphs on $O(n \log n)$ algorithm exists [Lawler, 1978]. For the assembly system of Section 4, a linear-time algorithm based on median-finding was recently developed by Queyranne [1987]. An $O(n \log n)$ algorithm for arbitrarily directed trees has been developed by Jackson & Roundy [1985].

10.6. *Efficient algorithms for systems with fixed base planning periods*

The divide and conquer algorithm of Section 6 for solving the continuous relaxation (6.2) of the lot sizing problem (6.1) can be described as follows. We first assume that all of the stages are in a single cluster. We compute the reorder interval $\tau = [(\Sigma_i K_i)/(\Sigma_i g_i)]^{1/2}$ that this cluster would use. We then set the reorder intervals of all stages equal to τ and we attempt to prove that all stages are in a single cluster by finding a feasible dual solution for (6.2). Dual solutions correspond to feasible flows in a certain network. If we find a feasible solution, we know that we were correct in assuming that one cluster contains all of the stages. If we do not find one, we find a minimal cut which divides the nodes of G into two classes; those nodes i for which $T_i^{*2} \geq \tau$ and those nodes i for which $T_i^{*2} < \tau$, where $(T_i^*: 1 \leq i \leq n)$ solves (6.2). This information allows us to decompose the original problem (6.2) into smaller subproblems of the same type.

The computations described above can be performed for any value of τ. In particular, if T_L is given and we use $\tau = 2^{l+1/2}$, the algorithm will tell us which stages i satisfy $T_i^{*2} \geq \tau$ and which ones satisfy $T_i^{*2} < \tau$. By repeating this computation for selected integer values of l, we can identify integers l_i, $i \in N(G)$ such that $2^{l_i - 1/2} T_L \leq T_i^* < 2^{l_i + 1/2} T_L$, without ever finding the exact value of T_i^*. The round-off procedure (Step 3 of Algorithm 1) will select $T_i = 2^{l_i} T_L$, which determines our policy.

This idea is due to Zheng [1987]. Assuming that the number of different values of l that we need to consider is uniformly bounded, he has obtained improved running times for many of the models discussed herein.

References

Aho, A.V., J.E. Hopcroft and J.D. Ullman (1974). *The Design and Analysis of Computer Algorithms*, Addison-Wesley, Reading, MA.

Anily, S., and A. Federgruen (1987). Structured partitioning problems: Part II. Applications to capacitated two-stage multi-item production/inventory models, Research Paper, Faculty of Commerce, University of British Columbia, Vancouver, BC.

Arrow, K.J., T. Harris and J. Marschak (1951). Optimal inventory policy. *Econometrica* 19, 250–272.

Arrow, K.J., S. Karlin, and H. Scarf (1958). *Studies in the Mathematical Theory of Inventory and Production*, Stanford University Press, Stanford, CA.

Atkins, D., M. Queyranne, and D. Sun (1989). Lot sizing policies for finite production rate assembly systems, Research Paper, Faculty of Commerce, University of British Columbia, Vancouver, BC.

Ayer, M., H.D. Brunk, G.M. Ewing, W.T. Reid and E. Silverman (1955). An empirical distribution function for sampling with incomplete information. *Ann. of Math. Stat.* 26, 641–647.

Best, M.J., and N. Chakravarty (1987). Active set algorithms for isotonic regression: A unifying framework, Research Report CORR 87-24, Faculty of Mathematics, University of Waterloo, Waterloo, IA.

Best, M.J., and N. Chakravarty (1988). Active set algorithms for isotonic regression when the underlying graph is an arborescence, Research Report CORR 88-18, Faculty of Mathematics, University of Waterloo, Waterloo, IA.

Blackburn, J.D., and R.A. Millen (1982). Improved heuristics for multi-stage requirements planning systems. *Management Sci.* 28, 44–56.

Caie, J.P., and W.L. Maxwell (1981). Hierarchical machine load planning, in: L.B. Schwarz (ed.), *Multi-Level Production/Inventory Control Systems. Theory and Practice*, North-Holland, New York, Chapter 5.

Clark, A., and H. Scarf (1960). Optimal policies for a multi-echelon inventory problem. *Management Sci.* 19, 517.

Clark, A., and H. Scarf (1962). Approximate solutions to a simple multi-echelon inventory problem, in: K. Arrow, S. Karlin and H. Scarf (eds.), *Studies in Applied Probability and Management Science*, Stanford University Press, Stanford, CA, Chapter 5.

Crowston, W.B., and M.H. Wagner (1973). Dynamic lot size models for multi-stage assembly systems. *Management Sci.* 20, 14–21.

Crowston, W.B., M.H. Wagner and A. Henshaw (1972). A comparison of exact and heuristic routines for lot size determination in multi-stage assembly systems. *AIIE Trans.* 4, 313–317.

Crowston, W.B., M.H. Wagner and J.F. Williams (1973). Economic lot size determination in multi-stage assembly systems. *Management Sci.* 19, 517–527.

Dvoretzky, A., J. Kiefer and J. Wolfowitz (1952). The inventory problem: I. Case of known distributions of demand; II. Case of unknown distribution of demand. *Econometrica* 20, 187–222, 450–466.

Federgruen, A., M. Queyranne and Y.S. Zheng (1989). Simple power of two policies are close to optimal in a general class of production/distribution networks with general joint setup costs, Working Paper #89-MSC-012, Faculty of Commerce, University of British Columbia, Vancouver, BC.

Graves, S.C. (1981). Multi-stage lot sizing: An iterative procedure, in: L.B. Schwarz (ed.), *Multi-Level Production/Inventory Control Systems. Theory and Practice*, North-Holland, New York, Chapter 4.

Graves, S.C., and L.B. Schwarz (1977). Single cycle continuous review policies for arborescent production/inventory systems. *Management Sci.* 23, 529–540.

Hadley, G., and T.M. Whitin (1963). *Analysis of Inventory Systems*, Prentice-Hall, Englewood Cliffs, NJ.

Harris, F. (1915). *Operations and Cost*, Factory Management Series, A.W. Shaw Co., Chicago, IL, pp. 48–52.
Jackson, P.L., and R.O. Roundy (1985). Constructive algorithms for planning production in multi-stage systems with stationary demand, Technical Report 632, School of Operations Research and Industrial Engineering, Cornell University, Ithaca, NY.
Jackson, P.L., W.L. Maxwell and J.A. Muckstadt (1985). The joint replenishment problem with powers of two restriction. *AIIE Trans.* 17, 25–32.
Jackson, P.L., W.L. Maxwell and J.A. Muckstadt (1988). Determining optimal reorder intervals in capacitated production–distribution systems. *Management Sci.* 34(8), 938–958.
Jensen, P.A., and H.A. Khan (1972). Scheduling in a multi-stage production system with setup and inventory costs. *AIEE Trans.* 4, 126–133.
Kalymon, B.A. (1972). A decomposition algorithm for arborescence inventory systems. *Oper. Res.* 20, 860–874.
Karimi, I.A. (1987). Optimal cycle times in a two-stage serial system with setup and inventory costs, Technical Report, Department of Chemical Engineering, Northwestern University, Evanston, IL.
Lambrecht, M. and J. Vander Eecken (1978). A facilities in series capacity constrained dynamic lot-size model. *European J. Oper. Res.* 2, 42–49.
Lawler, E.L. (1978). Sequencing jobs to minimize total weighted completion time subject to precedence constraints. *Ann. Discrete Math.* 2, 75–90.
Lee, H.L., and M.J. Rosenblatt (1987). Simultaneous determination of production cycle and inspection schedules in a production system. *Management Sci.* 33(9), 1125–1137.
Love, S.F. (1972). A facilities in series inventory model with nested schedules. *Management Sci.* 18, 327–338.
Maxwell, W.L., and J.A. Muckstadt (1981). A model for planning production in an *N* stage system, Technical Report 508, School of Operations Research and Industrial Engineering, Cornell University, Ithaca, NY.
Maxwell, W.L., and J.A. Muckstadt (1985). Establishing consistent and realistic reorder intervals in production–distribution systems. *Oper. Res.* 33(6), 1316–1341.
McLaren, B.J. (1976). A study of multiple level lot sizing techniques for material requirements Planning Systems, Unpublished Ph.D. Dissertation, Purdue University, West Lafayette, IN.
Muckstadt, J.A. (1985). Planning component delivery intervals in constrained assembly systems, in: S. Axsäter, C. Schneeweiss and E. Silver (eds.), *Multi-Stage Production Planning and Inventory Control*. Springer, Berlin.
Muckstadt, J.A. (1988). Establishing reorder intervals and inspection policies when production and inspection processes are unreliable, Technical Report 774, School of Operations Research and Industrial Engineering, Cornell University, Ithaca, NY.
Muckstadt, J.A. and R.O. Roundy (1987). Multi-item, one-warehouse, multi-retailer distribution systems. *Management Sci.* 33(12), 1613–1621.
Muckstadt, J.A., and H.M. Singer (1978). Comments on single cycle continuous review policies for arborescent production/inventory systems. *Management Sci.* 24, 1766–1768.
Peterson, R., and E. Silver (1979). *Decision Systems for Inventory Management and Production Planning*, Wiley, New York.
Porteus, E.L. (1985). Investing in reduced setups in the EOQ model. *Management Sci.* 31, 998–1010.
Porteus, E.L. (1986). Optimal lot sizing, process quality improvement and setup cost reduction. *Oper. Res.* 34(1), 137–144.
Porteus, E.L. (1987). Setup reduction and increased effective capacity. *Management Sci.* 33(10), 1291–1301.
Queyranne, M. (1985). A polynomial-time submodular extension to Roundy's 98% effective heuristic for production/inventory systems, Working Paper 1136, University of British Columbia, Vancouver, BC.
Queyranne, M. (1987). Finding 94%-effective policies in linear time for some production/inventory systems, Working Paper, University of British Columbia, Vancouver, BC.

Raymond, F.E. (1931). *Quantity and Economy in Manufacture*, McGraw-Hill, New York.

Roundy, R.O. (1985a). 98% Effective integer-ratio lot-sizing for one warehouse multi-retailer systems. *Management Sci.* 31(11), 1416–1430.

Roundy, R.O. (1985b). 94%-Effective lot-sizing in multi-stage assembly systems, Technical Report 674, School of Operations Research and Industrial Engineering, Cornell University, Ithaca, NY.

Roundy, R.O. (1986). A 98% effective lot-sizing rule for a multi-product, multi-stage production inventory system. *Math. Oper. Res.* 11, 699–727.

Roundy, R.O. (1987). Computing nested reorder intervals for multi-item distribution systems, Technical Report 751, School of Operations Research and Industrial Engineering, Cornell University, Ithaca, NY.

Scarf, H., D. Gilford and M. Shelly (1963). *Multistage Inventory Models and Techniques*, Stanford University Press, Stanford CA.

Schwarz, L.B. (1973). A simple continuous review deterministic one-warehouse *N*-retailer inventory problem. *Management Sci.* 19, 555–566.

Schwarz, L.B., and L. Schrage (1975). Optimal and system-myopic policies for multi-echelon production/inventory assembly systems. *Management Sci.* 21, 1285–1294.

Silver, E.A., and R. Peterson (1985). *Decision Systems of Inventory Management and Production Planning, 2nd edition*, Wiley, New York.

Szendrovits, A.Z. (1975). Manufacturing cycle time determination for a multi-stage economic production quantity model. *Management Sci.* 22(3), 298–308.

Thompson, W.A. (1962). The problem of negative estimates of variance components. *Ann. Math. Stat.* 33, 273–289.

Veinott Jr., A.F. (1966). The status of mathematical inventory theory. *Management Sci.* 12(11), 745–777.

Veinott Jr., A.F. (1969). Minimum concave cost solution of Leontief substitution models of multi-facility inventory systems. *Oper. Res.* 17, 262–291.

Whitin, T.M. (1953). *The Theory of Inventory Management*, Princeton University Press, Princeton, NJ.

Williams, J.F. (1981). Heuristic techniques for simultaneous scheduling of production and distribution in multi-echelon structures: Theory and empirical comparisons. *Management Sci.* 27, 336–352.

Williams, J.F. (1982). On the optimality of integer lot size ratios in economic lot size determination in multi-stage assembly systems. *Management Sci.* 28, 1341–1349.

Williams, J.F. (1983). A hybrid algorithm for simultaneous scheduling of production and distribution in multi-echelon structures. *Management Sci.* 29, 77–105.

Zheng, Y.-S. (1987). Replenishment strategies for production/distribution networks with general joint setup costs, Ph.D. Thesis, Columbia University, New York.

S.C. Graves et al., Eds., *Handbooks in OR & MS, Vol. 4*

Chapter 3

Centralized Planning Models for Multi-Echelon Inventory Systems under Uncertainty

A. Federgruen

Graduate School of Business, Columbia University, New York, NY 10027, U.S.A.

1. Introduction and summary

The previous chapter addressed planning models for production and distribution systems with multiple products and/or locations, allowing for rather general interdependencies between different items, locations and production/distribution stages as well as quite general cost structures. The most serious restriction of these models is the assumption that demands for all items occur at a *constant* and *deterministic* rate and that the lead times are either zero or constant and deterministically known as well. These assumptions may be valid in certain environments, e.g., assembly plants for intermediate products which operate with deterministic and regular schedules. In most settings however, sales volumes are subject to a considerable degree of nonstationarity (due to seasonal and periodic fluctuations, promotions and trends, e.g.) as well as uncertainty, even in the presence of the most sophisticated forecasting systems. Similar uncertainties and nonstationarities often prevail with respect to production and distribution lead times.

In this chapter we discuss planning models for multi-echelon systems which allow for uncertain and nonstationary demand and lead time processes. We confine ourselves to so-called PUSH systems with a *central decision maker*, who possesses continuously or periodically updated information about all inventories of all products at all relevant facilities and production stages; all replenishment decisions in the system are determined *centrally* on the basis of this information. The next chapter (Chapter 4) deals with planning models for systems with *decentralized* control (PULL systems), in which some replenishment decisions are made by *local* managers on the basis of *local* information only.

Recall that for almost all multi-item models with deterministic, constant rate demands (Chapter 2) we do not have efficient algorithms for the determination of fully optimal strategies. The same situation prevails, for the more complex models discussed in this chapter. (A special class of discrete-time single-product facilities-in-series models, introduced by Clark & Scarf [1960], provides an interesting exception to this general rule and is discussed in Section 2.) More importantly, the complexity of the structure of fully optimal strategies makes them unattractive, even if such strategies could be computed efficiently.

In the last 5–10 years, the focus has shifted – and with considerable success – towards the identification of close-to-optimal, but not necessarily fully optimal, policies of relatively *simple* structure, which are easy to compute and to implement. Also, accurate and easily computable *approximations* of the *total system-wide cost* have been developed for use in design and parametric studies.

Most approximation approaches start with an exact formulation of the planning problem as a dynamic program or Markov decision problem. As pointed out above, the large dimension of the associated state (and action) spaces precludes, in general, exact solution of these dynamic programs. The exact model is therefore replaced by an approximate one through the application of one or more manipulations of the problem, like those used in large scale mathematical programming (relaxations, restrictions, projections, cost approximations, cf. Geoffrion [1970]). These distinctions are important, because the properties of an approximation depend on the types and sequence of manipulations applied.

If only relaxations are used, for example, the resulting approximation is a *lower-bound* on the true optimal cost of the problem. (We use the term relaxation in the general sense popularized by Geoffrion [1970], i.e., any approximation of a minimization model which results in a lower-bound, e.g., expansions of the feasible set and/or replacements of the objective function by lower-bound objectives.) This fact is very helpful in assessing optimality gaps for any heuristic strategy, since the cost of an appropriately constructed feasible strategy provides an upper bound on the optimal cost. (As is the case with most mathematical programming approximation methods, such as Lagrangian relaxation, the heuristic strategy is usually based on the solution of the approximate model.) If the difference between upper and lower bounds is small, we can conclude *both* that the approximation is accurate *and* that the constructed policy is a good one.

Another approach is first to *restrict* the policy space to a more convenient and qualitatively appealing class. If determination of an optimal strategy within the chosen class is still intractable and the restriction is followed by one or more relaxations, the result is a lower bound, not on the original problem, but on the minimum cost among all policies within the class, so that optimality gaps may be assessed with respect to the chosen class of strategies only.

We complete this introduction with an outline of the remainder of this chapter. In Section 2 we describe the above mentioned *exact* analysis for a discrete-time facilities-in-series model, giving separate treatment to finite horizons and infinite horizon settings, with expected average costs, or expected total discounted costs as the (system-wide) objective. We also discuss approximation methods for settings with more complex cost structures.

The remainder of this chapter is devoted to the treatment of tree-structured distribution (production) networks, i.e., 'distribution' systems in which *every* facility (item) has a unique supplier. To our knowledge, no adequate exact or approximate methods have been obtained for more general network topologies. Certain assembly systems have been studied, i.e., systems in which each intermediate product is used as a component of a unique end-item. In particular, when all distribution and/or production costs are assumed to be linear, and under some additional assumptions, it can be shown that such systems may be transformed into equivalent series systems, for which the methods of Section 2 can be used. We discuss the (somewhat limited) literature on assembly systems at the end of Section 2.

Section 3 discusses *distribution* systems, using two-echelon (i.e., one-warehouse-multiple-retailer) systems as the basic network structure, with extensions to systems with an arbitrary number of echelons treated at the end. An important distinction within this class of models is that between systems where inventory *is* carried at the central warehouse and systems *without* central inventories. The latter applies, e.g., when the depot does *not* represent a physical location at all, but rather a centralized ordering function; here detailed decisions about shipments to ultimate destinations do not need to be made at the time a system-wide order is placed (with an outside supplier), but can be postponed till some time later. Even if the central warehouse does correspond to a physical location it acts as a transshipment center rather than a stocking point. Rosenfield & Pendrock [1980] refer to systems with centralized stock as 'uncoupled' and to systems without central stock as 'coupled', respectively. Section 4 discusses an alternative class of models for coupled systems.

2. Facilities in series and assembly systems

2.1. A discrete-time model of facilities in series

Consider a system with a single item and N facilities, where facility i supplies stock to facility $i+1$, for $i = 1, \ldots, N-1$. The first facility in the series, facility 1, replenishes its stock by placing orders of unrestricted size with an outside supplier, see Figure 1. Stocks are reviewed and decisions made periodically. Instantaneous, perfect information about inventories at all levels is assumed. Orders from the outsider supplier and transfers from one level to the next may each require a (level-specific) lead time before reaching their respective destinations. Demands for the product occur at the lowest echelon only.

To facilitate the presentation below, we assume that all lead times are *fixed* (integer multiples of the review period). This assumption can be relaxed, as discussed below. Unfilled demand at the lowest echelon is backordered, incurring in each period a penalty cost which is assumed to be proportional with the size of the end-of-the-period backlog.

Inventory carrying costs are assumed to be proportional to the end-of-the-period inventories, at cost rates which may vary by period and by echelon, but are nondecreasing in the echelon index. (The latter assumption is standard; in most applications, holding cost rates consist primarily of the cost of capital, and are thus increasing with the cumulative value added.) We therefore assess

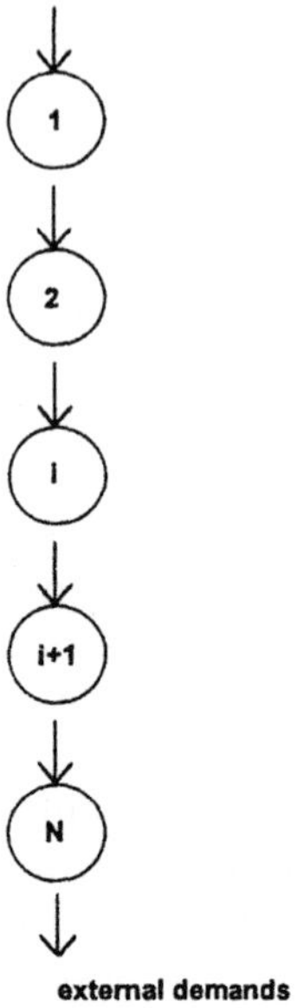

Fig. 1.

holding costs on 'echelon inventories' where the inventory of the ith echelon is defined as the stock at facilities i, $i+1, \ldots, N$ or in transit between them. The cost of transfers between levels is assumed to be linear, while an order to the outside supplier involves a fixed cost as well as a proportional cost. An efficient *exact* analysis of the system can only be given when the transfer costs between levels are linear (or convex); if *fixed* transfer costs are incurred as well, only *approximate* methods have been proposed as discussed below.

Clark & Scarf [1960], assuming a *finite* planning horizon, show that an optimal policy for this system can be computed by decomposing the problem (exactly) into N separate single-location problems which can be specified and solved recursively for echelons $l = N, N-1, \ldots, 1$. The model and solution method were originally suggested by Clark [1958].

The problem for the lowest echelon includes only its 'own' costs, ignoring all others. A slight modification of a critical-number (see Chapter 2) policy solves this problem: if the inventory position at the bottom echelon is below some order-up-to-level, it is increased to the latter, provided the next facility up (facility $N-1$) has sufficient stock; if this facility does *not* have enough stock, ship as much as possible. We refer to such policies as *modified base stock* policies.

The problem for each intermediate echelon i $(1 < i < N)$ includes the echelon's inventory holding cost, the cost of shipments from the previous echelon $(i-1)$ and a convex *induced penalty cost* which assesses the difference between the 'expected costs at all lower echelons $l = i+1, \ldots, N$ under the given echelon inventory at echelon i' and 'the *minimum* value of these expected costs, under an *unlimited* echelon inventory at echelon i'. In other words, the induced penalty cost describes the increase in expected costs at echelons $i+1, \ldots, N$ due to insufficient inventory at echelon i. The optimal policy and expected cost function for echelon $(i+1)$ for each period are used to define these induced penalty cost functions. As for the lowest echelon, modified base-stock policies are optimal for all intermediate facilities as well.

Finally, the problem for the first facility is of the same type as that of the intermediate levels, with the exception that its order-cost function includes fixed-cost components. It follows that an (s, S)-type policy is optimal at this level, i.e., in each period the system-wide inventory position is increased to an order-up-to-level S, whenever the starting position is at or below a reorder level s, see Chapter 1.

In describing the analysis of the above model we consider the special case of two echelons, i.e., $N=2$. (Such a system can be thought of consisting of a depot and one retailer. We use superscripts d and r to distinguish between them.) This merely simplifies the notation and exposition. The general case with $N>2$ echelons can be handled inductively and recursively, see Clark & Scarf [1960] or Gross, Soland & Pinkus [1981] for details. We also start with the *finite* horizon case.

We specify the sequence of events somewhat differently from that in Clark and Scarf, in accordance with what has become common usage. Holding as well as penalty costs are incurred *after* demand in each period. Also, orders and shipments arrive, following their respective lead times, at the beginning of a period, i.e., *after* costs are assessed in the prior period, and *before* the current decisions. (This change does not affect the analysis in any essential way, and slightly simplifies computations.) This formulation follows Federgruen & Zipkin [1984b].

The index n will denote the number of periods *remaining* until the end of the planning horizon, i.e., we number time periods backward. The cost data of the problem are:

K_n = fixed cost to place an order with the outside supplier, in period n;
c_n^d = variable cost rate for outside orders placed in period n;
c_n^r = cost rate for shipments to the retailer which start in period n;
h_n^d = holding cost rate for total system inventory in period n (the depot echelon holding cost rate);
h_n^r = additional holding cost rate for inventory held at the retail outlet in period n (the retailer echelon holding cost rate);
p_n^r = penalty cost rate for backorders at the retail outlet at the end of period n.

We assume that these cost factors are nonnegative and that they are related in ways to preclude it being optimal never to order. Other parameters are:

α = discount factor, $0 \leq \alpha \leq 1$;
l = lead time for shipments, a nonnegative integer;
L = lead time for outside orders, a nonnegative integer;
u_n = demand in period n, a nonnegative random variable;
$u_n^{(i)} = \sum_{l=0}^{i-1} u_{n+l}$ = i-period demand starting in period n;

$\mu_n = \mathrm{E}(u_n) < \infty$,
$\mu_n^{(i)} = \Sigma_{l=0}^{i-1} \mu_{n+l} = \mathrm{E}(u_n^{(i)})$, $n, i = 0, 1, \ldots$.

Demands in different periods are assumed independent.

The evolution of the system is described by several state and action variables. (Our formulation already includes the standard transformation, as in Clark and Scarf, which eliminates state variables representing individual outstanding shipments.)

The variables are:

x_n^r = inventory at the retail outlet, plus shipments currently in transit, at the beginning of period n;
v_n^d = echelon inventory at the depot
= inventory at the depot, plus x_n^r, at the beginning of period n;
z_n = shipment from the depot to the retail outlet, initiated in period n;
y_n = order size in period n;
y_n^i = outstanding order placed i periods ago at the beginning of period n, $i = 1, \ldots, L$;
$\tilde{y}_n = (y_n^1, \ldots, y_n^L)$.

The actions are constrained by the inequalities

$$y_n \geqslant 0\,, \qquad z_n \geqslant 0\,, \qquad x_n^r + z_n \leqslant v_n^d + y_n^L\,.$$

The following equations specify the dynamics of the system:

$$x_{n-1}^r = x_n^r + z_n - u_n\,, \qquad v_{n-1}^d = v_n^d + y_n^L - u_n\,,$$
$$\tilde{y}_{n-1} = (y_n, y_n^1, \ldots, y_n^{L-1})\,.$$

To formulate system-wide inventory costs, we (temporarily) need more detailed descriptors of the system: at the beginning of period n, let w_n^d = inventory at the depot, w_n^r = inventory at the retail outlet, and s_n^i = outstanding shipment placed i periods ago for $i = 1, \ldots, l$. At the end of the nth period, system-wide inventory equals

$$w_n^d + y_n^L + \sum_{i=1}^{l-1} s_n^i + [w_n^r + s_n^l - u_n]^+$$
$$= v_n^d + y_n^L + \{-(w_n^r + s_n^l) + [w_n^r + s_n^l - u_n]^+\}\,.$$

Our current decisions affect the expressions in brackets only l periods later. We shall thus treat the corresponding expected costs through the first l periods as constants, and in period n count expected costs occurring l periods later. Under this standard accounting scheme (see Chapter 1) the relevant one-period expected holding costs for system-wide inventory are

$$h_n^d\,\mathrm{E}\{v_n^d + y_n^L - \alpha^l(x_n^r + z_n - u_n^{(l)}) + \alpha^l[x_n^r + z_n - u_n^{(l+1)}]^+\}\,.$$

Similarly, we assign to period n expected penalty and holding costs at the outlet occurring l periods later,

$$\alpha^l \, \mathrm{E}(h_n^r[x_n^r + z_n - u_n^{(l+1)}]^+ + p_n^r[u_n^{(l+1)} - x_n^r - z_n]^+)\,,$$

treating prior such costs as constant.

Let A^r denote all the constant costs mentioned above. The one-period holding and penalty costs may thus be represented by

$$D_n(v_n^d + y_n^L) + R_n(x_n^r + z_n)\,,$$

where

$$\begin{aligned} D_n(v) &= h_n^d v\,,\\ R_n(x) &= \alpha^l\{-h_{n+l}^d(x - u_n^{(l)}) + p_{n+l}^r \, \mathrm{E}[u_n^{(l+1)} - x]^+ \\ &\quad + (h_{n+l}^d + h_{n+l}^r)\, \mathrm{E}[x_n - u_n^{(l+1)}]^+\}\,. \end{aligned}$$

Finally, let

$$\begin{aligned} c_n^d(y) &= \text{order cost function in period } n\\ &= \begin{cases} 0 & \text{if } y_n = 0\,,\\ K_n + c_n^d y_n & \text{if } y_n > 0\,. \end{cases} \end{aligned}$$

We may now state the finite-horizon dynamic program:

$\hat{g}_n(\tilde{y}_n, v_n^d, x_n^r)$ = minimum total discounted expected costs with n periods remaining, if the system begins in state $(\tilde{y}_n, v_n^d, x_n^r)$, excluding costs represented by A^r.

Then, dropping the index n in all cost functions and state and action variables:

$$\begin{aligned} \hat{g}_0 &= 0\\ \hat{g}_n(\tilde{y}, v^d, x^r) &= \min_{y,z} \{c^d(y) + D(v^d + y^L) + c^r z + R(x^r + z)\\ &\quad + \alpha \, \mathrm{E}\hat{g}_{n-1}[(y, y^1, \ldots, y^{L-1}), v^d + y^L - y,\\ &\qquad x^r + z - u]:\\ &\qquad y \geq 0, z \geq 0, x^r + z \leq v^d + y^L\}\,, \quad n \geq 1\,. \end{aligned} \tag{2.1}$$

(Because of the transformation, the effective planning horizon is shifted from $n = 0$ to $n = l$, so (2.1) represents a different numbering of time periods.)

The main result of Clark and Scarf is that program (2.1) can be decomposed into a pair of simpler programs. The first of these programs involves the outlet alone:

$$g_0^r = 0\,,$$
$$g_n^r(x^r) = \min_{z \geq 0} \{c^r z + R(x^r + z) + \alpha\, \mathrm{E} g_{n-1}^r(x^r + z - u)\}\,, \quad n \geq 1\,. \tag{2.2}$$

Since R is convex and $c^r z$ is linear, a critical-number policy solves this problem. Let $x_n^{r\,*}$ denote the critical number for period n. Now define the induced penalty cost functions:

$$\hat{P}_n(x) = \begin{cases} 0\,, & x \geq x_n^{r\,*}\,, \\ c^r(x - x_n^{r\,*}) + [R(x) - R(x_n^{r\,*})] & \\ \quad + \alpha\, \mathrm{E}[g_{n-1}^r(x - u) - g_{n-1}^r(x_n^{r\,*} - u)]\,, & x < x_n^{r\,*}\,. \end{cases}$$

(These functions are easily shown to be nonnegative and convex.)

The second dynamic program is the following:

$$\hat{g}_0^d = 0$$
$$\hat{g}_n^d(\tilde{y}, v^d) = \min_{y \geq 0} \{c^d(y) + D(v^d + y^L) + \hat{P}_n(v^d + y^L) + \alpha\, \mathrm{E}\hat{g}_{n-1}^d[(y, y^1, \ldots, Y^{L-1}), v^d + y^L - u]\}\,, \quad n \geq 1\,. \tag{2.3}$$

Current decisions in problem (2.3) affect the costs only L periods later. Moreover we have $v_{n+L}^d = (v_n^d + y_n^L + \cdots + y_n^1) - u_n^{(L)}$. As before, we can thus treat the expected costs in the first L periods of the planning horizon as constants, and in period n assign the expected echelon holding and induced penalty costs L periods later. This accounting scheme allows us, once again, to represent (2.3) as a dynamic program in the *single* state variable $X_n^0 = v_n^d + y_n^L + \cdots + y_n^1$, the system-wide inventory position. Because of the form of $c^d(\cdot)$ and the convexity of D and P_n, an (s, S) policy solves this problem [cf. Scarf, 1960] in each period n.

In particular, Clark and Scarf show

$$\hat{g}_n(\tilde{y}, v^d, x^r) = \hat{g}_n^d(\tilde{y}, v^d) + g_n^r(x^r)\,, \tag{2.4}$$

and an optimal policy for the system consists of an optimal (s, S) policy for (2.3) as the (outside) order policy and a modified base-stock policy derived from (2.2) as the shipment policy. These results can be proved by induction with respect to the horizon length $n = 1, 2, \ldots$.

The above decomposition and structural results greatly simplify the original problem: note that a single dynamic program with $(L + 2)$-dimensional state space is solved by a *pair* of dynamic programs with one-dimensional state spaces only! The computational effort is nevertheless significant. First, as in all finite horizon dynamic programs, a set of recursive functional equations needs to be solved. In particular, the solution of (2.3) can only be obtained numerically by discretizing the (one-dimensional) state space. Moreover, each evaluation of the induced penalty cost functions $\hat{P}_n(\cdot)$ in (2.3) entails, in general, a numerical integration over the retailer outlet's optimal cost function $g^r_n(\cdot)$. In fact, when $L>0$, the one-dimensional representation of (2.3) requires the use of functions $P^L_n(\cdot)$ defined by $P^L_n(x) = \mathrm{E}\hat{P}_n(x - u^{(L)}_n)$, thus requiring an additional level of numerical integration.

For many single item models, significant computational simplifications may be achieved by considering *infinite* planning horizons (with stationary data) rather than *finite* horizons. Federgruen & Zipkin [1984b] show that similar simplifications can be achieved for two-echelon problems. They show first that the decomposition of the original dynamic program with $(L+2)$-dimensional state space into two one-dimensional dynamic programs extends to the infinite horizon case, both under the criterion of discounted costs and that of long-term average costs. Moreover, these two one-dimensional dynamic programs may again be interpreted as single-facility models.

The infinite-horizon extension IH is established as follows. First, employing standard results about the relationships between infinite horizon and finite-horizon value functions and optimal policies in single item models (see Chapter 1), one can show that the induced penalty functions $\hat{P}_n(\cdot)$ converge (uniformly) to a limit function $P(\cdot)$, defined by

$$P(x) = \begin{cases} 0 & \text{if } x \geqslant x^{r*}\,, \\ (1-\alpha)c^r(x - x^{r*}) + [R(x) - R(x^{r*})] & \text{if } x < x^{r*}\,, \end{cases}$$

where x^{r*} is the infinite-horizon optimal order-up-to-level for the retailer.

Clearly, $P(\cdot)$, like the $\hat{P}_n(\cdot)$ functions, is nonnegative and convex. Note moreover, that in contrast to the $\hat{P}_n$, P does not involve optimal cost functions and requires no integration, except possibly to evaluate R. Define a program similar to (2.3) but with P replacing the $\hat{P}_n$:

$$\begin{aligned} g^d_0 &= 0\,, \\ g^d_n(\tilde{y}, v^d) &= \min_{y \geqslant 0}\{c^d(y) + D(v^d + y^L) + P(v^d + y^L) \qquad (2.5)\\ &\quad + \alpha\,\mathrm{E}g^d_{n-1}[(y, y^1, \ldots, y^{L-1}), v^d + y^L - u]\}\,, \quad n \geqslant 1\,, \end{aligned}$$

and, by analogy with (2.4), define $g_n(\tilde{y}, v^d, x^r) = g^d_n(\tilde{y}, v^d) + g^r_n(x^r)$. Intuitively, since $\{\hat{P}_n\} \to P$ (uniformly) as n becomes large, significant differences between the programs (2.3) and (2.5) recede infinitely far into the future.

Indeed, it can be shown [see Federgruen & Zipkin, 1984b] that (i) the differences $\{\hat{g}^d_n - g^d_n\}$ converge uniformly to the zero function, and (ii) the functions $g^r_n(g^d_n)$ represent n-period cost functions in a *stationary* single item inventory model with full backlogging, convex one-step expected inventory cost functions and linear (fixed plus linear) order cost functions and a simple order-up-to-policy with order-up-to-level x^{r*} [(s^d, S^d) policy] is therefore optimal in the infinite horizon version IH^r [IH^d] of this model. (This contrasts with the functions $\hat{g}_n^d$ which represent n-period cost functions in a *nonstationary* model.) Most importantly, the stationary system-wide policy that specifies orders according to this (s^d, S^d) policy and shipments to the retail outlet according to the (modified) critical number policy with order-up-to-level x^{r*} is optimal for IH. All of the above results apply both under the criterion of discounted costs (with discount factor $\alpha < 1$) and that of long-term average costs [where $\alpha = 1$ in (2.2) and (2.5)].

We conclude with a description of what is required to compute this optimal policy. The critical number x^{r*} is the global minimum of the convex, differentiable function $(1-\alpha)c^r x + R(x)$ and hence solves the equation $(1-\alpha)c^r + R'(x) = 0$. Due to the supplier lead time of L periods, the infinite horizon depot model IH^d has a one-step expected cost function:

$$\begin{aligned} \mathrm{E}\, D(x - u^{(L)}) + \mathrm{E}\, P(x - u^{(L)}) &= h^d(x - \mu^{(L)}) + \mathrm{E}\, P(x - u^{(L)}) \\ &= h^d(x - \mu^{(L)}) \\ &\quad + \int_{x - x^{r*}}^{\infty} [R(x-t) - R(x^{r*})]\, \mathrm{d}F^{(L)}(t)\,, \end{aligned}$$

with $F^{(i)}(\cdot)$ the cdf of $u^{(i)}$.

Federgruen & Zipkin [1984b] show that for Normal one-period demand distributions, this function may be obtained in closed form as a function of the univariate and *bivariate* Normal cumulative distributions (which are available in most standard computer libraries). Closed form expression may be obtained for Erlang demands as well. Finally the computation of an optimal (s^d, S^d) policy requires the application (to a discrete version of IH^d) of one of several algorithms, e.g., Veinott & Wagner [1965], Federgruen & Zipkin [1984d], or Zheng & Federgruen [1991].

The above analysis may be extended to incorporate *lead time uncertainty*, as long as the random lead times are generated by an exogenous supply process which is independent of the demand process and with the property that orders are received in the sequence in which they are placed; see Zipkin [1986a, 1986b] for a formal description of such lead time processes. Under these assumptions, the extension to random lead times reduces to taking expectations over the marginal distributions of L and l in all relevant expressions above.

Other variations of the basic Clark and Scarf model include Fukuda [1961] who includes an option of disposing of stocks, Rosling [1987a] who derives bounds for the optimal reorder levels, and Axsäter & Lundell [1984] who treat a continuous-review version of the model.

2.2. Extensions

In this subsection we discuss a number of extensions of the basic series model above.

2.2.1. Fixed shipment costs

We consider first the complications that arise in such a series system when the shipment costs *between* facilities consist of fixed as well as variable components (like the outside order costs). To simplify the exposition, we confine ourselves to a finite horizon problem with two facilities, a depot and a retailer. Thus, let K_n^r = fixed cost of a shipment to the retail outlet in period n.

In attempting to extend the decomposition method above, note first that (2.2) must be adapted as follows. (Let $\delta(x) = 1$ if $x > 0$ and $\delta(x) = 0$ otherwise.)

$$g_n^r(x^r) = \min_{z \geq 0} \{K^r \delta(z) + c^r z + R(x^r + z) + \alpha\, \mathrm{E} g_{n-1}^r(x^r + z - u)\}\,, \quad n \geq 1 \tag{2.6}$$

Now, a sequence of (s, S) policies solves (2.6); see Scarf [1960] and Chapter 1. Let (s_n^r, S_n^r) denote the optimal policy parameters. We have seen that, with linear shipment costs, the expected cost consequences of insufficient inventory at the depot are described by an induced penalty cost function $\hat{P}_n(\cdot)$ which depends *only* on the echelon inventory $(v_n^d + y_n^L)$. With fixed-plus-linear costs, the induced penalty $\hat{P}_n$ is a function of both the echelon inventory and the retail outlet's own inventory position x_n^r. For $\hat{P}_n = 0$ if $v_n^d + y_n^L \geq x_n^r > s_n^r$ (since in this case no shipment is prescribed by the (s_n, S_n)-policy while $\hat{P}_n > 0$ if $x_n^r \leq s_n^r$.

We conclude that no *exact* decomposition of the dynamic program into two separate 'single location' problems can be achieved in the presence of fixed shipment costs. Indeed no efficient, exact solution method is known for this model. On the other hand, approximate solution methods may be designed by replacing the induced penalty cost functions $P_n(x_n^d + y_n^L, x_n^r)$ by appropriate approximations which depend on the echelon inventory position only. Clark & Scarf [1962] suggest the use of the following lower and upper bound approximate functions

$$\underline{P}_n(v_n^d + y_n^L) \leq P_n(v_n^d + y_n^L, x_n^r) \leq \bar{P}_n(v_n^d y_n^L)\,.$$

$\bar{P}_n$ is obtained by charging the induced penalty

$$\{c^r(x - S_n^r) + [R(x) - R(S_n^r)] + \alpha\, \mathrm{E}[g_{n-1}^r(x - u) - g_{n-1}^r(S_n^r - u)]\}\,, \tag{2.7}$$

whenever $x = v_n^d + y_n^L < S_n^r$ (regardless of the value of x_n^r). Likewise, if (2.7) is charged only when $x = v_n^d + y_n^L < s_n^r$ a lower bound function $\underline{P}_n(\cdot)$ is obtained, which is a function of $(v_n^d + y_n^L)$ only. Replacing $\hat{P}_n(\cdot)$ in (2.3) by $\underline{P}_n(\cdot)$ or $\bar{P}_n(\cdot)$ we obtain two sequences $\{\bar{g}_n^d(\cdot)\}$ and $\{\underline{g}_n^d(\cdot)\}$, respectively, with $\underline{g}_n^d \leq \hat{g}_n^d \leq \bar{g}_n^d$. Therefore

$$\underline{g}_n \stackrel{\text{def}}{=} \underline{g}_n^d + g_n^r \leq \hat{g}_n \leq \bar{g}_n^d + g_n^r \stackrel{\text{def}}{=} \bar{g}_n .$$

Hochstädter [1970] extends this approach to certain settings with multiple retailers.

2.2.2. *Assembly systems*

Assembly networks arise in particular when modelling production systems in which a number of components are acquired from outside vendors, to be assembled, typically in several stages, into subassemblies and then finally into a single end product. Assembly networks are therefore trees with the node at the root corresponding with the single end item, the leaves corresponding with the externally acquired components, and all other nodes with intermediate products (sub-assemblies). Assembly networks generalize facilities-in-series systems in that each facility (node) has at most one successor node but may have *more* than *one* predecessor node.

No exact or approximate solution methods appear to be known for the general case with *fixed costs* for ordering the primary components from (the) outside supplier(s). On the other hand when all order and assembly cost functions are *linear*, Rosling [1987b] showed that an assembly system may be transformed into an equivalent series system, provided the initial stock levels satisfy some simple conditions, which hold automatically under any optimal policy, after at most finitely many periods. (This condition is therefore completely unrestrictive when minimizing long-run average costs over an infinite planning horizon.) All carrying, outsider order and assembly costs in the equivalent system remain linear (as does the backlogging cost for the final product); it is therefore optimal to employ modified base-stock policies in each period (of a finite or infinite horizon model) and for all nodes, as above.

The equivalent series model is obtained by computing the *echelon lead time* for each item, i.e., the sum of that item's lead time and those of all of its successors. All items are now placed *in series*, starting with the end product, in descending order of their echelon lead times. This ordering guarantees that, if item i is the successor of item j, then i is placed below j (even if the assembly procedure for item i has zero lead time). Now, renumber the items such that the item on the ith echelon from the top has index i. Without loss of generality we choose the units in which the items are measured, such that a *single* unit of any item is required in the assembly of its successor. At the beginning of the planning horizon, for all $i = 1, \ldots, N$ let

X_i^l = the echelon inventory of item i, ordered at most l periods earlier, i.e., all units on hand of item i (whether by itself or as components of successor items or in process of being assembled as such) plus all units 'ordered' in the last l periods;

M_i = the echelon lead time of item i.

The condition with respect to the initial stocks, allowing for the transformation of the assembly system into an equivalent facilities-in-series system, specifies that for all $i = 1, \dots, N-1$ and $m = 0, \dots, M_i - 1$:

$$X_i^m \leq X_{i-1}^m .$$

Rosling's work builds on that of Schmidt & Nahmias [1985], who considered the simplest of all assembly networks, where *two* components are purchased from outside vendors, to be assembled into a single end item. Assuming linear order and assembly costs (as in Rosling), Schmidt and Nahmias characterize the optimal policy under *all* possible combinations of initial component's and end product's stock. Under inappropriately matched initial inventories, the optimal policy may have a tediously complex structure, but only in the initial periods of the planning horizon.

Carlson & Yano [1986] consider special cases of assembly systems in which a number of externally purchased components are assembled in a single operation into a single end product. (Such systems may therefore be represented as a two-level arborescence.) Unlike Rosling, they address order and assembly costs *with* fixed (setup) components, which amounts to a *complete* generalization of Clark and Scarf's two echelon model. Carlson and Yano assume that the *periods* with assembly runs are *predetermined* (by some other model). Theirs may thus be viewed as a restriction approach, see Sections 3.2 and 4.1. All remaining decisions, i.e., assembly quantities in the predetermined assembly periods, and order epochs and quantities for the components, are determined within the model on the basis of heuristics.

3. Arborescence distribution systems

In this section we consider single-item discrete-time multi-echelon distribution systems which have the form of an *arborescence*, i.e., each location has a unique supplier. The same models may be applied to multi-stage production processes, in which each product is manufactured in batches from a single input product or raw material. Arborescences generalize series systems (see Section 2), in that the same supply facility may be used by several (parallel) destinations.

As in Section 2, we start with a two-echelon system: the top echelon consists of a depot which supplies a collection of outlets $\{1, \dots J\}$ where exogenous, random demands for a single commodity must be filled. (The demand processes may be correlated across outlets). The remaining model assumptions are identical to those in the one-depot-one-retailer models of Section 2. In particular let

L = lead time for outside orders (a nonnegative integer);
l_j = lead time for shipments from the depot to retailer j, $j = 1, \ldots, J$ (a nonnegative integer);
$c_t(y)$ = cost to order a quantity y in period t
= 0 if $y = 0$, $K_t + c_t^d y$ if $y > 0$;
h_{jt} = unit cost of holding inventory at location j from period $t + l_j$ to period $t + l_j + 1$;
p_{jt} = unit penalty cost for demand backordered at location j from period $t + l_j$ to period $t + l_j + 1$;

(The time shifts applied in the last two definitions simplify the notation below. Linear shipment costs between the depot and the outlets can be included by a suitable redefinition of p_{jt} and h_{jt}.)

u_{jt} = demand at location j in period t, $u^t = (u_{jt})_{j=1}^J$;
$\hat{u}_{jt} = \Sigma_{s=t}^{t+l} u_{js}$, with cdf $\hat{F}_{jt}(\cdot)$ and mean $\hat{\mu}_{jt}$.

We also assume that for each period t, the distributions of the demand variables $(\hat{u}_{jt}, j = 1, \ldots, J)$ are identical up to a linear transformation, i.e., there exists a cdf $\Phi(\cdot)$ such that $\hat{F}_{jt}(u) = \Phi((u - \hat{\mu}_{jt})/\hat{\sigma}_{jt})$ for appropriate constants $\hat{\mu}_{jt}$ and $\hat{\sigma}_{jt}$. This holds, e.g., when all one-period demands are normal. Finally, let $\hat{M}_t = \Sigma_j \hat{\mu}_{jt}$ and $U_t = \Sigma_j u_{jt}$.

To simplify the exposition, we assume as before that all lead times are deterministic. Random lead times, may however be treated as well under the general assumptions stated in Section 2.

As mentioned in the introduction, we distinguish between systems *with* central inventories at the depot and systems *without* central stock.

3.1. Systems without central inventories

Centralized ordering among the outlets offers two distinct advantages, even in the absence of centralized stock. First, there are economies of scale in the order costs. Note also that one could choose to decide the future allocations at the same time as the order. Postponing the allocations permits one to observe the demands in the intervening L periods, and thus to make better informed allocations. Eppen & Schrage [1981] coined the phrase *statistical economies of scale* for this effect.

Consider first the problem of minimizing total expected costs over a finite planning horizon of T periods. (Costs in future periods may be discounted by appropriate specification of the cost parameters above.) Analogous to the notation employed in Section 2, let

y_t = the size of the order placed by the depot at the beginning of period t;
x_{jt} = the inventory *position* of location j at the beginning of period t, $x^t = (x_{jt})$;
z_{jt} = allocation to location j in period t, $z^t = (z_{jt})$.

As before, for $t \leq T - l_j$ we charge to outlet j in period t, the expected carrying and backlogging costs at the end of period $t + l_j$, which are a function of $(x_{jt} + z_{jt})$ only, and can thus be denoted as:

$$q_{jt}(x_{jt} + z_{jt}) = \begin{cases} h_{jt}\mathrm{E}[x_{jt} + z_{jt} - \hat{u}_{jt}]^+ \\ \quad + p_{jt}\mathrm{E}[\hat{u}_{jt} - x_{jt} - z_{jt}]^+ , & t \leq T - l_j , \\ 0 , & t > T - l_j . \end{cases}$$

The problem may be formulated as a dynamic program: the state of the system at the beginning of period t is given by the $J + L$-dimensional vector $(x^t, \tilde{y}^t)$, where $\tilde{y}^t = (y_{t-L}, \ldots, y_{t-1})$. The actions taken in period t must satisfy

$$y_t \geq 0 , \qquad \sum_{j=1}^{J} z_{jt} = y_{t-L} , \tag{3.1a}$$

$$z_{jt} \geq 0 , \quad j = 1, \ldots, J . \tag{3.1b}$$

If in period t action (y_t, z^t) is taken in state $(x^t, \tilde{y}^t)$, the state in the next period is determined as follows:

$$x^{t+1} = x^t + z^t - u^t , \qquad \tilde{y}^{t+1} = (y_{t-L+1}, \ldots, y_{t-1}, y_t) .$$

With the definitions above we can state the recursive functional equations, whose solution provides the optimal policy for the problem. Let

$f_t(x^t, \tilde{y}^t)$ = minimum total expected value of all cost components that are charged to periods t through T.

$f_1(\cdot\,,\cdot)$ includes the expected value of all costs over the planning horizon which can be influenced by our decisions. We have:

$$\text{(P)} \quad f_t(x^t, \tilde{y}^t) = \min_{y_t, z^t} \Big\{ c_t(y_t) + \sum_{j=1}^{J} q_{jt}(x_{jt} + z_{jt}) + \mathrm{E}f_{t+1}[(x^t + z^t - u^t), (y_{t-L+1}, \ldots, y_t)] : (y_t, z^t) \text{ satisfy } (3.1) \Big\} \tag{3.2}$$

and $f_T(\cdot\,,\cdot) = 0$.

The state space of this dynamic program has dimension $J + L$ and there is no obvious way to decompose the model into smaller ones. For any but the smallest values of J, L and T, clearly, exact solution of the equations is impractical.

3.1.1. Approximation by relaxation

We first consider an approximation to the dynamic program (P) obtained by merely relaxing the nonnegativity constraints (3.1b) (and hence enlarging the feasible action sets). Let $\tilde{f}_t(\cdot\,,\cdot)$ denote the value-functions in this approximate dynamic program (P'):

$$(\mathrm{P}')\quad \tilde{f}_t(x^t,\tilde{y}^t)=\min_{y_t,z^t}\Big\{c_t(y_t)+\sum_{j=1} q_{jt}(x_{jt}+z_{jt}) + \mathrm{E}\tilde{f}_{t+1}[(x^t+z^t-u^t),(y_{t-L+1},\ldots,y_t)]: (y_t,z^t) \text{ satisfy (3.1a)}\Big\}, \tag{3.3}$$

with, once again, $\tilde{f}_T(\cdot\,,\cdot)=0$. Note that $\tilde{f}_t \leqslant f_t$ $(t=1,\ldots,T)$ and in particular $\tilde{f}_1 \leqslant f_1$.

We first describe this relaxation approach for the special case where in each period the same holding and backlogging cost rate applies to all outlets, i.e., $p_{jt}=p_t^0$ and $h_{jt}=h_t^0$ for all $J=1,\ldots,J$ and all $t\geqslant 1$. In this case, the success of the relaxation approach is based on the following two observations:

(a) the value-functions $\tilde{f}_t$ depend on the *vector* of inventory positions x^t only via its *sum* X_t;

(b) in each period it is *optimal* to choose z^t *myopically* – so as to achieve the minimum in the single-constraint allocation problem

$$R_t(x^t, y_{t-L}) \overset{\text{def}}{=} \min \sum_{j=1}^{J} q_{jt}(x_{jt}+z_{jt}) \quad \text{s.t.} \quad \sum_{j=1}^{J} z_{jt}=y_{t-L} \tag{3.4}$$

(i.e., to minimize the expected value of the carrying and backlogging costs that are charged to the current period only).

The two observations may be verified by induction with respect to t. Note that $\tilde{f}_{t+1}=0$ satisfies (a). Assume that for some $t<T$, $\tilde{f}_{t+1}=\tilde{f}_{t+1}(X_{t+1},\tilde{y}^{t+1})$, and substitute in (3.3):

$$\begin{aligned}\tilde{f}_t(x^t,\tilde{y}^t) &= \min_{y_t,z^t}\Big\{c_t(y_t)+\sum_J q_{jt}(x_{jt}+z_{jt}) + \mathrm{E}\tilde{f}_{t+1}[(X_t+y_{t-L}-U_t),(y_{t-L+1},\ldots,y_t)]\Big\} \\ &\quad \text{s.t. (3.1a)} \\ &= \min_{y_t\geqslant 0}\{c_t(y_t)+\mathrm{E}\tilde{f}_{t+1}[(X_t+y_{t-L}-U_t),(y_{t-L+1},\ldots,y_t)]\} \\ &\quad + \min_{z^t}\Big\{\sum_j q_{jt}(x_{jt}+z_{jt}): \sum_j z_{jt}=y_{t-L}\Big\}.\end{aligned} \tag{3.5}$$

Thus, the minimizations over y_t and z^t separate. The minimization over z^t is precisely the 'myopic' allocation problem (3.4), thus showing that observation (b) holds in period t.

Also, the optimality conditions of (3.4) can be manipulated [Zipkin, 1982] to yield the following (where λ is the Lagrange multiplier, and using $\hat{F}_{jt}^{-1}(u) = \hat{\mu}_{jt} + \hat{\sigma}_{jt}\Phi^{-1}(u)$ for all u),

$$\sum_{j=t}^{J} \hat{\sigma}_{jt}\, \Phi_{jt}^{-1}\left(\frac{p_t^0 + \lambda}{p_t^0 + h_t^0}\right) = X_t + y_{t-L} - \hat{M}_t\,. \tag{3.6}$$

(The term in parentheses is the critical ratio that always appears in such constrained newsboy problems.) Hence,

$$\lambda = -p_t^0 + (p_t^0 + h_t^0)\Phi[(X_t + y_{t-L} - \hat{M}_t)/\tilde{S}_t]\,, \tag{3.7}$$

where $\tilde{S}_t = \Sigma_j^J \hat{\sigma}_{jt}$.

Note too that $\lambda = \partial R_t/\partial y_{t-L}$. Thus, R_t can be obtained by integrating (3.7): Letting

$$\tilde{G}_t(U) = \Phi[(U - \hat{M}_t)/\tilde{S}_t]\,,$$
$$R_t(X_t, y_{t-L}) \equiv p_t^0[\hat{M}_t - (X_t + y_{t-L})] + (p_t^0 + h_t^0)\int_{-\infty}^{\hat{X}_t + y_{t-L}} \tilde{G}_t(U)\,\mathrm{d}U\,. \tag{3.8}$$

Observe that R_t has the form of a one-period expected holding-and-penalty cost function at a single location (which we may consider to be the depot). (In particular, R_t is strictly convex in $X_t + y_{t-L}$.) It depends *only* on the total (echelon) inventory in the system X_t, *not* its distribution among the locations. In particular, substituting (3.8) into (3.5), it follows that $\tilde{f}_t$ is equal to a function that depends on x^t only via X_t, i.e., observation (a) holds for period t as well, thus completing the induction step of the proof.

When the holding and backlogging cost parameters fail to be identical for all outlets, the two results [(a) and (b)] continue to hold as close approximations rather than exactly. This can be verified by induction, as follows: assuming again that $\tilde{f}_{t+1} = \tilde{f}_{t+1}(X_{t+1}, \tilde{y}^{t+1})$, (3.5) continues to apply so that the minimizations over y_t and z^t continue to separate. The Lagrange multiplier associated with the myopic allocation problem, i.e., the optimization problem over z^t, now takes the form

$$\sum_{j} \hat{\sigma}_{jt}\Phi^{-1}\left(\frac{p_{jt} + \lambda}{p_{jt} + h_{jt}}\right) = X_t + Y_{t-L} - \hat{M}_t\,. \tag{3.6'}$$

This equation can no longer be solved in closed form, but the right-hand side of (3.7) continues to be usable as a close *approximation* of λ with p_t^0 and h_t^0

weighted averages of the $\{p_{jt}\}$ and $\{h_{jt}\}$ numbers, derived by any one among several interpolation methods. This implies that the right-hand side of (3.8) continues to be useable as an approximation of R_t. Using this approximation instead of the exact function R_t and substituting it into (3.5) we obtain an approximation for $\tilde{f}_t$ which depends on x^t only via X_t, see observation (a).

The closed-form representation of $R_t(x_t, y_{t-L})$ via the *single* variable function $\tilde{R}_t(X_t, y_{t-L})$ permits us to represent the dynamic program (P′) by one in which the state of the system in any period t is of dimension $(L+1)$ (instead of $L+J$), namely $(X_t, \tilde{y}_t)$:

$$\tilde{f}_t(X_t, \tilde{y}^t) = \min_{y_t \geq 0} \{c_t(y_t) + \tilde{R}_t(X_t + y_{t-L}) + \mathrm{E}\tilde{f}_{t+1}(X_{t+1}, \tilde{y}^{t+1})\} \tag{3.9}$$

Recall that $\tilde{R}_t$ may be interpreted as the one-step expected cost function of a single location (with back order cost rate p^0_t, holding cost rate h^0_t and demand distribution $\tilde{G}_t(\cdot)$). This means that the same accounting device invoked in Section 2 and the beginning of this section, can be applied to achieve a further reduction of the state space of (3.9). Reformulate (3.9) by counting in period t the expected penalty and holding costs previously represented in period $t+L$. (Recalling the earlier transformation, these costs are actually incurred in period $t+L+l$. We thus ignore the expected penalty and holding costs previously charged to periods $t = 1, \ldots, L$ since these are not affected by any orders placed during the planning horizon.) Let

$$\bar{U}_t = \sum_{s=t}^{t+L-1} U_s \,,$$

with cdf $\bar{G}_t$, and

$$X^{\Delta}_t = X_t + \sum_{s=t-L}^{t-1} y_s$$

= the system-wide inventory position
= the sum of all inventory levels at the outlets, plus stock in transit between the depot and the outlets, plus all stock on order from the outside supplier.

Viewed from period t, the initial inventory in period $(t+L)$ will be $X_{t+L} = X^{\Delta}_t - \bar{U}_t$. The expected cost in period $t+L$ is thus

$$\begin{aligned} P_t(X^{\Delta}_t + y_t) &= \mathrm{E}_{\bar{U}_t}\tilde{R}_{t+L}(X^{\Delta}_t - \bar{U}_t + y_t) \\ &= p^0_{t+L}[(\hat{M}_{t+L} + \mathrm{E}(\bar{U}_t)) - (X^{\Delta}_t + y_t)] \\ &\quad + (p^0_{t+L} + h^0_{t+L}) \int_{-\infty}^{X^{\Delta}_t + y_t} H_t(U)\,\mathrm{d}U \,, \end{aligned} \tag{3.10}$$

where $H_t = \bar{G}_t * \tilde{G}_{t+L}$. (The second equality follows from (3.7) and by reversing the order of integration.) The dynamic program (3.9) is thus equivalent to one with the *single* state variable X_t^Δ. Let

$g_t(X_t^\Delta)$ = minimum total expected ordering costs in period t through T, and (approximate) penalty and holding costs represented in (3.9) in periods $t + L$ through T, given the system starts period t in state X_t^Δ.

To simplify the notation, assume hereafter that $l_j = l$ for all $j = 1, \ldots, J$. Then $g_{t-L-l+1} = 0$, and for $t \leqslant T - L - l$:

$$g_t(X_t^\Delta) = \min_{y_t \geqslant 0} \{c_t(y_t) + P_t(X_t^\Delta + y_t) + \mathrm{E}g_{t+1}(X_t^\Delta + y_t - U)\} . \quad (3.11)$$

It is easily verified that the functions $P_t(\cdot)$ are convex; it follows [Karlin, 1960] that for the approximate problem (3.11), a simple order-up-to-policy is optimal if the order cost function is linear, while an (s, S) policy is optimal [Scarf, 1960], if these order cost functions contain fixed components as well. The approximate dynamic program is thus easily solvable. Also, (3.11) provides a *lower bound* $g_1(X_1^\Delta)$ (since it was derived from the original problem by *relaxing* the allocation variables' nonnegativity constraints only) and generates a feasible order policy of a simple structure. To obtain a complete feasible strategy for all system-wide decisions, one needs to complement this order policy with an appropriate allocation policy. One possible choice is to allocate any arriving order y_{t-L} so as to achieve the optima in the myopic allocation problems (3.4) (now with the constraints $z_{jt} \geqslant 0$ reimposed to guarantee feasibility). Note, however, that the solution to (3.11) results in a lower bound on the true expected cost under *any* policy. We are therefore free to search for a tractable low-cost allocation policy without being restricted to the myopic allocation policies per se. In Section 3.1.3. we discuss appropriate choices for these allocation policies, as well as the performance of the resulting combined ordering/allocation strategies.

Recall, the approximate dynamic programs (3.11) may be interpreted as a single-location inventory problem with full backlogging, a fixed order leadtime of $L + l$ periods, order cost functions $c_t(\cdot)$, linear carrying and penalty costs with unit rates h_{t+L}^0 and p_{t+L}^0 for costs charged to period t, and one-period demands that are independent (across time). The cdf of the demand in period t is *almost* $\bar{G}_t * \bar{G}_{t+L}$, the distribution of system-wide demands in periods t through $t + L + l$, but not quite. In fact, the *mean* of the demand distribution H_t is equal to that of $\bar{G}_t * \bar{G}_{t+L}$, but its variance is

$$\begin{aligned}
\operatorname{var}(H_t) &= \operatorname{var}(\bar{G}_t) + \operatorname{var}(\tilde{G}_{t+L}) \\
&= \sum_{s=t}^{t+L-1} \operatorname{var}(U_s) + \Big(\sum_{s=t+L}^{J} \hat{\sigma}_{jt+L}\Big)^2 \\
&\geqslant \sum_{s=t}^{t+L-1} \operatorname{var}(U_s) + \sum_{s=t+L}^{t+L+l} \operatorname{var}(U_s) = \operatorname{var}(\bar{G}_t * \bar{G}_{t+L}) ,
\end{aligned}$$

with equality holding if and only if the $\hat{u}_{jt+L}$ $(j = 1, \ldots, J)$ are perfectly correlated. In the special case where $\sigma_{jt} = \sigma$ for all j and t, and the u_{jt} are independent over j as well as t, we obtain

$$\mathrm{var}(H_t) = [LJ + (l+1)J^2]\sigma^2 > (L + l + 1)J\sigma^2 = \mathrm{var}(\bar{G}_t * \bar{G}_{t+L}) .$$

The larger variance of H_t reflects the increased uncertainty in a system with decentralized outlets and less than perfectly correlated demands, as compared to a system in which all such demands are pooled at the depot. Note also that for fixed total lead time $L + l$, the difference between the distributions H_t and $\bar{G}_t * \bar{G}_{t+L}$ decreases as L increases. That is, the *statistical economies of scale* are greater when L is larger, relative to $L + l$.

The above approximation approach may similarly be applied to models with an infinite planning horizon and the total discounted cost or the long-run average cost criterion; see Sections 3.1 and 4.1 of Federgruen & Zipkin [1984c].

3.1.2. Approximation by restriction

A different approach to approximating the dynamic programs begins with a *restriction* of the order-policy set to some attractive class. We describe this approach for models with an infinite planning horizon and the long-run average cost criterion.

The specific restrictions that have been considered all determine the order as a function of X^{Δ}, the system-wide inventory position, as above. Moreover, the stochastic process $\{X_t^{\Delta}\}$ is regenerative at replenishment epochs under any of the classes of order policies considered; see, e.g., Ross [1970]. A sequence of subsequent relaxations results in a lower bound for the total costs in a replenishment cycle, which is *independent* across cycles and *identically* distributed for all cycles. The ratio (expected approximate cycle costs)/(expected cycle length), when optimized over the given class of policies, gives us a lower bound on the true cost of the best policy in this class. (This ratio represents the average cost per unit time in a renewal–reward process with replenishment epochs as renewals and the approximate cycle costs as costs per renewal, see Ross [1970].) This optimization also generates a specific feasible order policy which, when complemented with an appropriate allocation policy, results in a feasible overall strategy. As before, we refer to Section 3.1.3 for a discussion of appropriate choices for these allocation policies. Below we describe two examples of restriction approaches, tailored to the special case of normal demands (i.e. $\Phi(\cdot)$ is the cdf of the standard normal) and back-logging and holding-cost rates that are *identical* across outlets. We refer to Federgruen & Zipkin [1984c, Section 4.2] for a detailed treatment of more general parameter settings.

We first need the following supplementary notation. Dropping the time index t throughout, let

$u_j^{(i)}$ = i-period demand at location j ($i = 1, 2, \ldots$);
$U^{(i)}$= i-period system-wide demand;
$\mu_j^{(i)} = i\mu_j = \mathrm{E}(u_j^{(i)})$ and $[\sigma_j^{(i)}]^2 = i\sigma_j^2 = \mathrm{var}(u_j^{(i)})$; (3.12)
$\mu \quad = \Sigma_j \mu_j$; $\sigma = \Sigma_j \sigma_j$ and $\tilde{\sigma}^2 = \mathrm{var}(U)$ (note $\tilde{\sigma} \leq \sigma$);
$\xi_j \quad = x_j + z_j$ ($j = 1, \ldots, J$).

Recall that the one-step expected holding and backlogging costs are:

$$q_j(\xi_j) = \mathrm{E}\{p_j[u_j^{(l+1)} - \xi_j]^+ + h_j[\xi_j - u_j^{(l+1)}]^+\}$$

$$= p_j[\mu_j^{(l+1)} - y_j] + (p_j + h_j) \int_{-\infty}^{y_j} \Phi\left[\frac{u - \mu_j^{(l+1)}}{\sigma_j^{(l+1)}}\right] du .$$

Several auxiliary cost functions related to the $q_j(\cdot)$ will be needed. First, analogous to (3.4):

$$R(\xi) = \min \sum q_j(\xi_j) \quad \text{s.t.} \quad \sum \xi_j = \xi ,$$

$$q_j^{(\tau)}(\xi_j) = p_j[\mu_j^{(l+1+\tau)} - \xi_j] + (p_j + h_j) \int_{-\infty}^{\xi_j} \Phi\left(\frac{u - \mu_j^{(l+1+\tau)}}{(l+1+\tau)^{1/2}\sigma_j}\right) du , \quad \tau \geq 0 , \tag{3.13}$$

$$R^{(\tau)}(\xi) = \min \sum_j q_j^{(\tau)}(\xi_j) \quad \text{s.t.} \quad \sum_j \xi_j = \xi , \tag{3.14}$$

and for any positive integer m, let

$$R(y; m) = \frac{1}{m} \min \sum_{\tau=0}^{m-1} \sum_j q_j^{(\tau)}(\xi_j) \quad \text{s.t.} \quad \sum_j \xi_j = \xi . \tag{3.15}$$

One convenient class of policies are the regular-interval critical-number policies, under which an order is placed every m periods, so as to increase the system-wide inventory position X^{Δ} to the critical number $v^{\#}$ (whenever $X^{\Delta} \leq v^{\#}$) and *no* order is placed when $X^{\Delta} > v^{\#}$. An alternative class of policies (already encountered in the relaxation approaches discussed above) are the (s, S)-policies, under which an order is placed so as to increase the system-wide inventory position X^{Δ} to the critical number S whenever, at the beginning of a period, it has dropped below a level s. In this section, we restrict ourselves to regular-interval critical number policies; the analysis below is quite easily extended to address (s, S) policies, see Federgruen & Zipkin [1984c] for details.

Note that after at most finitely many replenishment epochs, $X^{\Delta} \leq v^{\#}$ throughout. In view of the long-run average cost criterion, we assume without loss of generality that this condition holds. Consider now a period in which an order arrives and must be allocated. Let C denote the expected backlogging and holding costs charged until the next such period; then, $C = \sum_{\tau=0}^{m-1} \sum q_j^{(\tau)} (x_j + z_j)$; see (3.13). Now, relax the nonnegativity constraints $z_j \geqslant 0$ ($j = 1, \ldots, J$). Note, in view of this relaxation, the current choice of the allocation vector z in no way affects the achievable values of the vector ξ at future allocation (i.e., order arrival) periods, and hence does not influence costs beyond the next m periods. The optimal allocation policy therefore solves (3.15) with $\xi = x + y^L$ (where y^L is the order that was placed L periods ago, and has just arrived to the depot). No closed form expression for the resulting cost $mR(x + y^L; m)$ appears to exist, but it can be bounded below by solving (3.14) separately for every $\tau = 0, 1, \ldots, m-1$, and each such problem does possess a closed form expression, see (3.8):

$$R^{(\tau)}(\xi) = p[(l+1+\tau)\mu - \xi] + (p+h) \int_{-\infty}^{\xi} \Phi\left[\frac{u - (l+1+\tau)\mu}{(l+1+\tau)^{1/2}\sigma}\right] du . \tag{3.16}$$

Note that $\xi = x + y^L$ at the beginning of a period in which an order arrives (i.e., L periods after *placement* of an order) may be written as

$$\xi = v^{\#} - U^{(L)} .$$

Since demands are independent over time, C is bounded below by

$$\begin{aligned} \underline{C} &\overset{\text{def}}{=} K + \sum_{\tau=0}^{m-1} \mathrm{E}R^{(\tau)}(v^{\#} - U^{(L)}) \\ &= K + \sum_{\tau=0}^{m-1} P^{(\tau)}(v^{\#}) , \end{aligned} \tag{3.17}$$

where, analogous to (3.10),

$$\begin{aligned} P^{(\tau)}(v) &= p[(L+l+1+\tau)\mu - v] \\ &\quad + (p+h) \int_{-\infty}^{v} \Phi\left(\frac{u - (L+l+1+\tau\mu)}{\sqrt{L\tilde{\sigma}^2 + (l+1+\tau)\sigma^2}}\right) du . \end{aligned}$$

We conclude that $\underline{C}/m = (K/m) + (1/m) \sum_{\tau=0}^{m-1} P^{(\tau)}(v^{\#})$ represents a lower bound for the total average costs under this policy. To find the $(m, v^{\#})$ policy which minimizes the lower bound, we may proceed as follows. First, note that the functions $P^{(\tau)}(\cdot)$ functions are convex so that $(\underline{C}/m)$ is convex in $v^{\#}$. For fixed m, differentiating $(\underline{C}/m)$ with respect to $v^{\#}$ yields the following equation for $v^{\#}$:

$$\frac{1}{m}\sum_{\tau=0}^{m-1}\Phi\left[\frac{v^{\#}-(L+l+1+\tau)\mu}{\sqrt{(l+1+\tau)\sigma^2+L\tilde{\sigma}^2}}\right]=\frac{p}{p+h}\,. \tag{3.18}$$

(This equation has a unique solution $v^{\#}(m)$.) The minimum over m may now be found by direct search methods. (See Federgruen & Zipkin [1984c] for more details.)

3.1.3. Allocation policies; performance of the approximation methods

Whatever approximation method is used, the order policy needs to be complemented with a feasible allocation policy to achieve a complete (feasible) policy. In this section we briefly discuss some possible choices for the allocation policy. The reader is referred to Federgruen & Zipkin [1984c] for a systematic and detailed treatment. We confine our remarks to infinite planning horizon models with stationary data, and cost parameters that are identical across the locations (i.e., $p_j = p$ and $h_j = h$ for all $j = 1, \ldots, J$).

The *myopic* allocation policy, optimal for the relaxed problems in Section 3.1.1, is one possible choice; every incoming order is allocated so as to minimize the expected cost in the very first period in which the allocations have an impact, i.e., in the period where the shipments arrive at their destinations; in other words, the allocation vector z is determined so as to achieve the minimum in (3.14) with $\tau = 0$ and with the nonnegativity constraints $z \geqslant 0$ reimposed. Many efficient solution methods exist for this (continuous) knapsack problem with separable convex objective, see, e.g., Zipkin [1980], Groenevelt [1985], or Federgruen & Groenevelt [1986]. As shown in Federgruen & Zipkin [1984a], this policy works well when the fixed order cost K is zero (small) or when $K > 0$ and the coefficients of variation of the outlets' demands $\{\sigma_j/\mu_j\}$ are (roughly) equal.

When an $(m, v^{\#})$ order policy is used, it is (in general) significantly better to choose the allocation vector z so as to minimize the sum of all expected costs, not just in the period when the allocations arrive at their destinations, but including all $(m-1)$ subsequent periods, i.e., until shipments resulting from the next order are received. We refer to this interval of m periods as the *allocation cycle* and to the corresponding policy as the *cycle allocation policy*. This implies that the vector z be chosen so as to achieve the minimum in $R(x + y^L; m)$ ((3.15)), with the nonnegativity constraints $z \geqslant 0$ reimposed. Alternatively, when (s, S) order policies are used, a simple variant of (3.15) needs to be solved (again with constraints $z \geqslant 0$ added) to reflect the random length of the replenishment cycle. The above mentioned numerical methods can be applied to these problems as well, but some of the computations become significantly more complex.

A third (computationally simpler) alternative is to minimize the expected costs in *one* of the periods of the allocation cycle, as opposed to the entire cycle (*cycle allocation policies*) or the very first such period (*myopic allocations*). Assume, e.g., that the τth period in the cycle is selected; the allocation vector z is then chosen to achieve the minimum in $R^{(\tau)}(x + y^L)$, see (3.14) and will be referred to as the *τ-allocation vector*. It is easily verified from the Karush-Kuhn-Tucker conditions that at optimality the stockout probabilities at the outlets at the end of the selected τth period of the allocation cycle, i.e., the ratios

$$\left\{\frac{x_j + z_j - (l+1+\tau)\mu_j}{(l+1+\tau)^{1/2}\sigma_j}\right\}_{j=1}^{J}, \tag{3.19}$$

are *equalized* to the extent possible. When these ratios are *exactly* equalized, we say that inventories are fully balanced for period τ in the allocation cycle, and

$$\frac{x_j + z_j - (l+1+\tau)\mu_j}{(l+1+\tau)^{1/2}\sigma_j} = \frac{x + y^L - (l+1+\tau)\mu}{(l+t+\tau)^{1/2}\sigma} \quad \text{for all } j .$$

If the coefficients of variation of the outlets' demands (σ_j/μ_j) are equal, then the same allocation vector z achieves the minimum in *any* of the problems $R^{(\tau)}(x + y^L)$ for *any* $\tau \geqslant 0$ and hence in $R(x + y^L; m)$ as well; in other words, the three types of allocation all result in the *same* allocation vector. This equivalence fails to hold when the coefficients of variation are unequal. If a τ-allocation policy is chosen, it appears appropriate to choose the period τ as the period in which it would be most valuable to have (close to) balanced inventories. If we expect the system to be full of stock [i.e., $x + y^L - (l+1+\tau)\mu \gg 0$], then balance is of no particular importance; almost all locations will have sufficient stock, and (with equal cost parameters) it does not matter where the holding costs are incurred. Similarly when the system as a whole is confronted with backlogs [$x + y^L - (l+1+\tau)\mu \ll 0$] it is again of little importance whether the backlogs are equally spread or not. Balance is most beneficial in the period when the system is expected to *run out* of stock, i.e., when $x + y^L - (l+1+\tau)\mu$ is close to zero. The τ-allocation policy chooses τ accordingly, see Federgruen & Zipkin [1984c, Section 3.3]. The principle of constructing allocation policies so as to control *balance* of inventories was first hinted at in Clark & Scarf [1960]; see Zipkin [1984] for a more formal treatment.

The above methods follow the suggestions in Federgruen & Zipkin [1984a,c]. The earlier approach by Eppen & Schrage [1981] *restricts* the order policies to the $(m, v^{\#})$ class. Their cost approximation is related to but different from (3.17); they select $v^{\#}$ under the assumption that stockouts occur only in the last period of the allocation cycle, and they accordingly choose a τ-allocation policy with $\tau = m - 1$.

The performance of the above approximation methods may be gauged by (i) computing the (system-wide) cost approximation, and (ii) determining the method's order and allocation policy and evaluating the associated long-run cost via simulation. (Even the *exact evaluation* of this policy is analytically intractable.) The policy's average cost value is clearly an *upper bound* (UB) for the *minimum* achievable costs. As pointed out in Section 1, if the cost approximation is obtained by relaxations only (i.e., using the methods of Section 3.1.1), it represents a lower bound (LB) for the minimum costs. If a restriction approach is followed, the cost approximation represents a lower bound for the minimum cost within the restricted class of strategies only. In any case, if UB and LB are close, this implies both that the cost approximation is accurate and that the constructed policy is *close-to-optimal* either in a global sense or with respect to the restricted class of policies. Federgruen & Zipkin [1984c, Section 5] apply this evaluation method systematically to all of the above described approximation methods. The overall conclusion is that these methods generate cost approximations and policies that come within a few percentage points of the optima.

3.2. Systems with central inventories

We now consider systems in which central inventories may be kept at the depot. All other model assumptions as described at the beginning of Section 3 remain unaltered. For the sake of brevity, we restrict ourselves to models with an infinite planning horizon, stationary data and identical cost rates for all outlets. We describe two approximation approaches, one based on *relaxation* (of constraints describing feasible action sets) and one based on *restriction* to a class of strategies.

3.2.1. Approximation by relaxation

Our first approximation approach, following Federgruen & Zipkin [1984b], is based on the exact analysis of the one-depot-one-retailer system in Section 2, now extended to the case of J outlets. We therefore return to the notation of Section 2, with the following additions. For all $j = 1, \ldots, J$ let

x_j^r = inventory at outlet j (at the beginning of a given period);
z_j = allocation to outlet j (at the beginning of a given period);
u_j = one period demand at outlet j, with mean μ_j, and standard deviation σ_j.

We use x, z and u to denote the corresponding *vectors*, and X^r, Z and U to denote their sums. All demand-related notation is defined in the multiple-retailer outlet infinite-horizon models of Section 3.1.2. In particular demands are normally distributed.

In systems *with* central inventories, there are *three* types of decisions that need to be taken at the beginning of each period:

(i) the size y of the order placed with the outside supplier (if any);
(ii) the amount Z to be withdrawn from the depot's inventory;
(iii) its allocation z among the outlets. (Recall that in systems *without* central stock only the first and last decisions are needed, since the total allocation Z necessarily equals y^L, the size of the incoming order.)

In the dynamic programming formulation, the system therefore has state $(\tilde{y}, v^d, x^r)$ and action (y, Z, z). The actions need to satisfy the constraints

$$y \geq 0\,, \qquad Z \geq 0\,, \qquad x^r + z \leq v^d + y^L\,,$$
$$\sum_j z_j = z\,, \quad z \geq 0\,. \tag{3.20}$$

The dynamics of the system are given by the identities

$$v^d \leftarrow v^d + y^L - U\,, \qquad x^r \leftarrow x^r + z - u\,, \qquad \tilde{y} \leftarrow (y^{L-1}, \ldots, y^1, y)\,.$$

Finally, total one-period costs are given by

$$c^d(y) + D(v^d + y^L) + c^r Z + \sum_j R_j(x_j^r + z_j),$$

where

$$R_j(x) = -h^d(x - \mu_j^{(l)}) + p^r \mathrm{E}[u_j^{(l+1)} - x]^+ + (h^d + h^r)\mathrm{E}[x - u_j^{(l+1)}]^+\,.$$

Analogous to the approach in Section 3.1.1, *relax* the constraints $z \geq 0$ in (3.20). As argued above, *after* this relaxation the current choice of the vector z in no way affects the achievable future values of the vector $x^r + z$ and hence future costs. In the relaxed problem, it is thus optimal to choose z so as to minimize current costs only, i.e., to solve the *myopic allocation* problem

$$\min_z \sum_{j=1}^{J} R_j(x_j^r + z_j) \quad \text{s.t.} \quad \sum_j z_j = Z\,. \tag{3.21}$$

As demonstrated above, the minimal cost of (3.21) can be written as $R(X^r + Z)$, where

$$R(x) = -h^d(x - \mu^{(l)}) + p^r \mathrm{E}[u^{(l+1)} - x]^+ + (h^d + h^r)\mathrm{E}[x - u^{(l+1)}]^+\,,$$

and $u^{(l+1)}$ denotes, *not* system-wide demand in $l+1$ periods, but rather a normal random variable with the same mean $\mu(l+1) = (l+1)\,\Sigma_j \mu_j$ and a different (larger) standard deviation $\sigma^{(l+1)} = (l+1)^{1/2}\,\Sigma_j\,\sigma_j$. Once again, the vector x^r affects the problem only through its sum X^r. The relaxed problem thus reduces to the *one-retailer* (infinite horizon) problem discussed in Section 2, and the results there can therefore be invoked to determine an optimal policy. See Federgruen & Zipkin [1984b] for further details.

The optimal cost of the relaxed problem provides (once again) a *lower bound* for the true optimal cost of the original problem, since it was obtained by relaxing some of the constraints (3.20) which describe the feasible action sets in the original problem. Analogous to the approximation methods in Section 3.1, the order and withdrawal policies need to be complemented with an appropriate *allocation policy*. For the latter, we may choose the *myopic allocation policy*, which in each period determines the allocation vector z by solving (3.21), with the nonnegativity constraints $z \geq 0$ reimposed:

$$\min_{z} \sum_{j=1}^{J} R_j(x_j^r + z_j) \quad \text{s.t.} \quad \sum z_j = Z \,, \quad z \geq 0 \,. \tag{3.22}$$

As pointed out above, this policy performs well in systems *without* central stock when the outlets' demands have (close to) equal coefficients of variation; Federgruen & Zipkin [1984b] argue that the myopic allocation policy performs, if anything, even better in systems *with* central stock (and equal coefficients of variation). With significantly unequal coefficients of variation, alternative allocation policies are needed, e.g., appropriate modifications of the policies in Section 3.1.3.

When comparing the cost of the relaxed problem with that arising under the combined order-, withdrawal and allocation policy note that the relaxed problem reproduces exactly the costs represented by the functions $c^d(\cdot)$, $D^L(\cdot)$ and $c^r z$. Any error arises in the approximation of $\Sigma_j R_j(x_j + z_j)$ via $R(X^r + Z)$. This approximation would be exact if the constraints $z \geq 0$ were never binding. The accuracy of the approximation as a whole, therefore, depends on how often these constraints are essential and the resulting effects of relaxing the binding constants on the total cost of (3.21). As before, call a replenishment cycle a sequence of periods starting with the arrival of an order at the depot and ending just before the next order arrives. A cycle consists of some 'ample-stock periods', when the depot has enough stock to ship up to the critical number x^{r*}, one period when the depot has positive but less-than-ample stock (the 'allocation period'), and finally some 'empty periods' when the depot has no stock, so $z = 0$. (Not every cycle, of course, need have all three kinds of periods. In particular, in systems designed to have high service levels, i.e., with high values of p^r, most cycles consist of ample-stock periods only.)

Let x_j^{r*} denote the critical number for outlet j alone (i.e., x_j^{r*} minimizes R_j), and $x^{r*} = (x_j^{r*})_{j=1}^J$. A direct calculation shows $\Sigma_j x_j^{r*} = x^{r*}$. Suppose a cycle begins with

$$x^r \leq x^{r*} \,. \tag{3.23}$$

If there is ample stock in the first period, we have $z = x^{r*} - x^r \geq 0$, and it is straightforward to show that the solution to both (3.21) and (3.22) is

$$z = x^{r*} - x^r \,. \tag{3.24}$$

In particular, $z \geq 0$ is essential in (3.22). The only way (3.23) could fail in subsequent periods of the cycle, furthermore, is if some demands were negative, events that have positive, but very low probability under appropriate choices of Normal distributions describing the outlets' demands. It is easy to show that under the proposed policy, from any initial state, we shall arrive at a cycle where (3.23) holds, with probability 1, after a finite number of periods. Subject to the qualification expressed earlier about negative demands, therefore, (3.23) will hold in *all* periods of *all* subsequent cycles, and hence $z \geq 0$ is inessential in all but a finite number of periods with ample stock.

In the allocation period, $z \geq 0$ may be essential and it (almost surely) will be essential in the empty periods. Observe, however, that $z \geq 0$ is inessential in (3.22) if and only if the solution to (3.22) satisfies the following condition:

$$[x_j^r + z_j - \mu_j^{(l+1)}]/\sigma_j^{(l+1)} = [X^r + Z - \mu^{(l+1)}]/\sigma^{(l+1)} = 0\,,$$
$$j = 1, \ldots, J\,, \tag{3.25}$$

see our discussion in Section 3.1.3. For given $(X^r + Z)$, roughly speaking, the cost of (3.22) increases with deviations from (3.25). (Compare Zipkin [1984] for a more formal treatment.) The process described by these differences during the allocation and empty periods evolves in just the same way as it does during an entire cycle of a system without central stock operating under an (s, S) policy. In both cases the system starts with (3.25) nearly satisfied; for the remainder of the cycle the differences are generated by the demand process only. Also, the cost functions in the two cases have the same form. And, as shown empirically in Federgruen & Zipkin [1984a], the cost effects of such 'imbalances' are quite small in the case of no central stock, so they must be small here as well.

All of these observations taken together suggest that the overall approximation provided by the relaxed problem should indeed be very accurate.

Equation (3.24) expresses a remarkable fact: under the proposed policy the shipments to individual outlets are the same as if each outlet followed its own critical-number policy, and the depot simply satisfied the resulting orders when there is enough stock to do so (in ample-stock periods). The only periods in a cycle requiring an explicit allocation decision is the allocation period (hence the name). Thus, even though the original model describes a system under centralized control (PUSH-system), a maximally decentralized policy should perform very well. This situation contrasts markedly with the case of no central stock, where no such interpretation is possible. Rosenfield & Pendrock [1980] among others have noticed before that centralizing some inventory *permits* some decentralization of decision making, but we believe the discussion above provides the first strong evidence that such an approach is economically effective. We emphasize, however that our construction of the cost functions for the relaxed problem to determine the depot's order policy uses data on the individual outlets in a nontrivial way.

3.2.2. *Approximation by restriction*

In this subsection we give a brief outline of possible restriction approaches for models with central stock. We first consider the approach in Federgruen &

Zipkin [1991]. The same two classes of order policies may be used as in Section 3.1.2 for systems without central stock, i.e., the $(m, v^{\#})$ and (s, S)-policies. As before, the parameters $v^{\#}$, s and S relate to critical levels of the system-wide aggregate inventory position, which now includes depot inventories as well. The discussion below confines itself to $(m, v^{\#})$ policies; the adaptations required in treating (s, S) policies are relatively minor.

As in the relaxation method of Section 3.2.1, shipments may be conceived of as being decided in two steps. First, a total *withdrawal* quantity is determined in each period; this is the total amount to be withdrawn from the depot's stock for shipment to all the demand points. The withdrawal is calculated according to a modified base-stock policy: just enough stock is withdrawn to raise the sum of the echelon inventories of the demand points to the base-stock level $x^{r\#}$, provided the depot has that much stock on hand; otherwise, all the depot's stock (if any) is withdrawn. Second, the stock withdrawn is *allocated* among the demand points. To describe a full policy of this form thus requires three parameters, m, $x^{d\#}$ and $x^{r\#}$ (or s, S and $x^{r\#}$).

We now outline the basic approach used to estimate the overall system-wide cost of a policy of this type. As before, define a *cycle* as m consecutive periods, numbered $0, \ldots, m-1$, starting with the *arrival* of an order at the depot. The following random variables [adapted from Jackson, 1988] are central to the analysis:

τ = the *depot-runout* period during a cycle, the first period during a cycle in which system-wide demand exceeds stock on hand at the depot;
ε = the *excess*, the amount by which demand exceeds stock in period τ.

(If demand never exceeds on-hand stock, then we define $\tau = m$. We refer to period $\tau + 1$ as the 'allocation period', i.e., the period when the depot does not have enough stock to withdraw up to $x^{r\#}$; after the withdrawal in period $\tau + 1$ the depot has no stock until the beginning of the next cycle.)

Suppose we condition on τ and ε. In periods 0 through τ, the total inventory position at the demand points after shipments is $x^{r\#}$. As before, while the exact one-step expected total inventory carrying and backlogging costs at all the demand points is a function of the *vector* of their *inventory positions*, it is possible to derive an approximation $R(y)$ which is a function of y, the total inventory position, only. Thus, $R(x^{r\#})$ provides an approximation of these costs in periods $0, \ldots, \tau$. In period $\tau + 1$ the inventory position is $x^{r\#} - \varepsilon$, so $R[x^{r\#} - \varepsilon)$ approximates the total cost. One can also develop analogous functions $R_t(y)$, approximating the expected costs t periods from now, starting with inventory position y, assuming no intervening shipments, where $R_0 = R$. For periods $s = \tau + 1, \ldots, m-1$, therefore, $R_{s-\tau-1}(x^{r\#} - \varepsilon)$ provides an approximation of the cost. In sum, total costs at the demand points in a cycle are approximated by

$$(\tau + 1)R(x^{r\#}) + \sum_{t=0}^{m-\tau-2} R_t(x^{r\#} - \varepsilon) .$$

Federgruen & Zipkin [1991] have developed three approaches to estimate the distribution of (τ, ε), and hence to calculate the expectation of the expression above. They evaluate the accuracy of the three approaches by numerical comparisons with simulated joint distributions. The most sophisticated of the three approaches (which is in fact exact up to approximating one-period demands by a mixture of Erlang distributions) generates quite accurate estimates; the other two approaches are computationally simpler at the expense of a somewhat reduced though arguably still acceptable precision.

In all three of these methods the conditional distribution $(\varepsilon \mid \tau)$ is approximated by a random variable and it turns out that $E_\varepsilon R_t(x^{r\#} - \varepsilon)$ is then a function of the same form as R_t. The other components of the average cost in a cycle (the depot's echelon holding cost and the average ordering costs) are easy to compute as well. The computation of the overall cost estimate is thus quite simple; it is in fact considerably simpler than that of the relaxation method in Section 3.2.1, and optimization over the parameters $(m, v^{\#}, x^{r\#})$ is relatively simple as well.

The resulting cost approximation, order and withdrawal policy need again to be complemented with an appropriately specified allocation policy. See the corresponding discussion in the previous subsections.

Kim [1978] and Jackson [1988] describe a similar restriction approach for the special case of our model where the depot lead time $L = 0$. In this restriction approach the system-wide replenishment strategy is completely specified except for the choice of certain critical parameters: an $(m, v^{\#})$ or (s, S) order policy, and a shipment policy which increases each retailer's inventory position to a critical level $x_j^{r\#}$ for as long as possible, i.e., until the runout period, and allocates the remaining depot stock ε at the beginning of the run-out period so as to minimize the expected costs in the remainder of the cycle. A different approach is used for the characterization of the excess and runout-time variables ε and τ.

3.3. *Extensions*

In this section we discuss several extensions of the basic models in Sections 3.1 and 3.2.

3.3.1. *Systems with more than two levels*

Consider a distribution system with 3 or more levels which is of the form of an 'arborescence', i.e., each location has a unique supplier. As in Section 3.1 assume stock is held at the lowest echelon only and all costs for internal shipments, i.e., *between* levels of the system, are linear in the shipment volumes. As discussed in Federgruen & Zipkin [1984a], the relaxation approach of Section 3.1.1 can easily be adapted to this more general network structure. Consider, e.g., a three-level system and refer to an intermediate facility and its dependent outlets as a 'subsystem'. The relaxation method of Section 3.1.1 replaces each subsystem by a single location with a one-period expected holding and shortage cost function of exactly the same form as that of an individual outlet, and with linear replenishment costs. Thus, if the relaxation method is first applied to each of the subsystems, an approximate model results which is of the exact same form as the two-level model considered in Section 3.1. The latter may now be approximated via any of the methods discussed in that section. For a general arborescence network structure, the same relaxation approach may be applied repeatedly.

The three-level model may be used to represent a multi-product multi-location system. An order at the highest level represents production of an intermediate good or an order of a raw material. This resource is allocated among the several end items at the second level while at the third-level products are allocated among locations. (Each 'location' at the lowest level thus represents a product-location pair. Alternatively, the second level might represent shipment of the intermediate product to locations, where it is subsequently used to manufacture the various end items.

3.3.2. Capacity constraints

The models of Sections 3.1 and 3.2 assume that orders of unlimited size may be placed in each period and that unlimited amounts may be shipped from the depot to the outlets. (In a production setting this amounts to assuming unlimited production capacity in each period.) The assumption of limitless capacity, while a reasonable approximation in some situations, is a poor one in others.

For single-location models with linear order costs, Federgruen & Zipkin [1986a,b] show that a modified base-stock policy is optimal: follow a base-stock policy when possible; when the prescribed order quantity exceeds the capacity, order to capacity. If the order costs have a fixed (as well as a variable) component, it might be reasonable to expect that a similarly modified (s, S)-policy is optimal. However, Wijngaard [1972] gives an example where *no* modified (s, S) is optimal.

Consider now the following extensions of the models in Sections 3.1 and 3.2.

(G1) A system without central stock; linear order costs and a *finite* order capacity (but unlimited shipment capacities).

(G2) A system with central stock, linear order costs, a finite order capacity and/or finite *total* shipment capacity.

Minor extensions of the proofs in Federgruen & Zipkin [1986a,b] reveal that the relaxation approaches for our basic models (Sections 3.1.1 and 3.2.1) can be adapted fairly simply to both (G1) and (G2). In both cases a modified base-stock policy is the optimal order policy in the relaxed model, and for (G2) the optimal withdrawal policy has the same form. The restriction approaches in Sections 3.1.2 and 3.2.2 are easily adapted to (G1) and (G2) as well.

No results appear to be known for other situations with limited order or shipment capacities. For example, if there are upper bounds on the shipments to *individual* outlets, none of the approximation methods above can be used. (This is the case, *unless* appropriate closed form expressions can be found for the optimal values of certain allocation problems, e.g., the myopic allocation problems, now with additional upper bounds on the allocation variables, see, e.g., (3.4). However, we know of no such results.) If the depot order costs have a *fixed* (as well as variable) component, the relaxation methods fail, as no simply-structured order policy is guaranteed to optimize the relaxed models.

3.3.3. *Models with transshipments or redistribution*

In some distribution systems, stock may be transferred *between* facilities that belong to the same echelon. For example, in one-warehouse multiple-retailer systems, *transshipments* may be planned *between* the different outlets. Karmarkar & Patel [1975] and Karmarkar [1981] developed qualitative results as well as optimization algorithms for *single-period*, *single-echelon* models of this kind. (See their references for earlier work in this area.)

Some of these qualitative results have been extended to multi-period problems by Tan [1974], Karmarkar [1981] and Showers [1981a,b]. Laakso & Thomopoulos [1979] give heuristic analyses of certain aspects of such problems. Jonsson & Silver [1984] consider a one-warehouse multiple-retailer system without central stock (as in Section 3.1), restricting themselves to $(m, v^{\#})$ order policies but allowing for transshipments to occur in *one* specific (transshipment) period of each cycle of m periods. The transshipment quantities in such a period are determined so as to generate a distribution of inventory positions which minimize system-wide costs until the end of the cycle.

All of the above papers consider transshipments as an *anticipatory* mechanism to rebalance inventories among the outlets. In many practical systems, transshipments are only used as an emergency measure, by which stockouts are filled with units from locations with positive inventories (if available). Klein [1990] shows that when the holding and backlogging cost rates are identical across locations, all of the approximation methods of Section 3.1 may be extended to incorporate such nonanticipating transshipments. In addition to relaxations and/or restrictions, a further approximation is required in the representation of the system dynamics. A detailed numerical study indicates that the resulting cost approximations remain highly accurate, and the (properly modified) order and allocation policies remain close-to-optimal. (Similar extensions can, at least in theory, be achieved for systems with central stock, as in Section 3.2.) This numerical study also exhibits that allowing for nonanticipating transshipments can reduce system-wide costs by a significant percentage, while improving the service level provided to customers: nonanticipating transshipments succeed in eliminating a significant part of the additional costs incurred by a geographically dispersed network of outlets as opposed to one which is concentrated in a single location.

3.3.4. *Correlated demands*

In the models of Sections 3.1 and 3.2, demands are allowed to be dependent across outlets in accordance with a general correlation structure. (With normal demands, this is easily described by a general multi-variate normal distribution.) In fact this correlation structure plays an important role in the cost approximations (and hence in the generated policies) as discussed above. On the other hand, the models in Sections 3.1 and 3.2 do assume that demands are independent over time. Recall from Chapter 2 that, even in single-location, single-item systems, the analysis becomes cumbersome when demands are correlated over time. (An exact representation usually requires incorporation of one or more sufficient statistics of the demand history into the state description, thus resulting in multidimensional dynamic programs even for such single-item systems; see however Miller [1986]; and Lovejoy [1988] for some exceptions.) Approximation methods based *only* on relaxations of feasible action sets (as in Sections 3.1.1 and 3.2.1) thus remain intractible.

On the other hand, correlated demands are fairly simply incorporated into the *restriction* approaches of Sections 3.1.2 and 3.2.2. A specific model based on this approach has been developed by Erkip, Hausman & Nahmias [1984].

3.3.5. More complex cost structures

One restriction of the models in Sections 3.1 and 3.2 is the assumption that all distribution costs are linear, with the possible exception of the outside order cost. In many practical settings fixed cost components are incurred for shipments from the depot to the outlets as well. Sometimes the cost structure even fails to be separable, as economies of scale may be exploited by combining several shipments or procurements. For such nonseparable cost structures, it is often true that complete economies of scale prevail, in the sense that the marginal cost increase, due to the addition of an extra location in the distribution effort of a given group of outlets, is less than if the same location were added to a subset of this group. (This property is usually referred to as submodularity, see Federgruen & Zheng [1988b] for a discussion of such cost structures.) In other settings, even this submodularity may fail to hold, e.g., when goods are distributed from the depot to the outlets by a fleet of vehicles, and deliveries are combined into routes.

We are not aware of any stochastic, multi-period, multi-location models capable of handling these complex cost structures. Efficient methods for models with such cost structures are available only when demands are assumed to arise at *constant deterministic rates*; see Chapter 3.

The following *hierarchical* approach may be adopted to capture both complicating factors, i.e., (i) complex cost structures, and (ii) general stochastic demand processes: solve first one of the above models with constant deterministic demand rates (set equal to their assumed *expected* values). The strategies generated by the approximation methods for these models invariably prescribe replenishments to each facility at constant time intervals (usually power-of-two multiples of some common base period). Next, solve a stochastic model as in Sections 3.1 or 3.2 restricted to $(m, v^{\#})$ order policies and periodic shipments to all outlets, choosing all replenishment cycles (i.e., the value of m and the outlet's replenishment frequencies) in accordance with the cycle lengths obtained from the first (deterministic) model, and minimizing holding and shortage costs only.

To our knowledge, this approach has not been tested thoroughly; but, as mentioned above, it appears to be the only available approach for stochastic multi-location models with fixed inter-facility transfer costs.

4. An alternative model for coupled systems

An alternative model for *two-echelon* distribution systems *without* central stock, goes back to Silver [1965]. Here the assumption is that orders are received instantaneously by the depot, i.e., $L = 0$; alternatively if L is positive, one assumes that any order to the outside supplier is to be allocated among the outlets, the very moment it is placed by the depot. This restriction eliminates the possibility of exploiting the statistical economies of scale mentioned in Section 3 (and hence the need to allocate incoming orders), by effectively eliminating the first lead time component (L). Contrary to the model in Section 3.1, Silver's allows for *all* shipment and order cost functions to consist of *fixed* (as well as variable) components. It therefore provides an alternative to the hierarchical two-model approach suggested in Section 3.4.

Silver [1965] as well as all subsequent papers on this type of model, assumes that inventories are monitored continuously rather than periodically, but this distinction is not essential. In fact, Federgruen and Zipkin have used continuous-time analogs of their models in some applications and Naddor [1975] treats a periodic review analog of the Silver model. The earlier papers by Veinott [1965], Bessler & Veinott [1966] and Ignall & Veinott [1969] may all be viewed as periodic analogs of Silver's model, in the absence of *any* economies of scale, i.e., linear costs throughout. (They may therefore also be viewed as special cases of the models in Section 3.1. On the other hand, these models allow for joint constraints in inventory positions.) These three papers show that myopic policies are optimal under various assumptions; and it is of interest that the (approximate) myopia results for the more general models of Section 3.1 are reminiscent of theirs. Sobel [1987] extends the results in these three papers to demand processes which are correlated across outlets as well as time, following a general autoregressive moving-average structure.

Returning to Silver's model, demands are assumed to be generated by independent unit or compound Poisson processes. The model can be formulated as a semi-Markov decision problem; once again, in view of the dimensionality of the state space, exact solution methods are computationally intractible. Moreover, Ignall [1969] showed that an optimal rule may fail to have a simple form (even in the case of *two* outlets) and would therefore be hard or impossible to implement, even if it could be computed with reasonable resources.

The proposed *approximation* methods may again be partitioned into those based on *relaxations* and those starting with a *restriction* of the policy space.

Since the vast majority of the literature on the Silver model is based on the restriction approach, and relaxation approaches have started to appear only recently, we treat the former first.

4.1. Restriction approaches

Most of the literature confines the policy space to so-called (s, c, S)- or *can-order* policies: three parameters S_j, c_j, and s_j are specified for each location j with $s_j \leq c_j \leq S_j$. An order (to the outside supplier) is triggered by location j when its inventory position falls to or below the *reorder level* s_j; any location $i \neq j$ whose inventory position is at or below its *can-order level* c_i, is included in this order, and the inventory position of each location k included in the order is increased to the *order-up-to-level* S_k. (Silver's original model considered only the special cases where all can-order levels are set equal to either (i) the reorder levels c, or (ii) the order-up-to levels S. The former case amounts to managing each item by itself ignoring opportunities to exploit economies of scale. The class of can-order policies was first introduced by Balintfy [1967] in a random yield but deterministic demand model.)

For the special case of unit Poisson demands, Silver [1974] provides an iterative method to compute a suboptimal policy of this form. Thompstone & Silver [1975] present a heuristic method for the special case of compound Poisson demands and zero lead times, by using a transformation of the compound Poisson distribution into an 'equivalent' unit Poisson distribution. Solution methods for the most general case are due to Silver [1981] and Federgruen, Groenevelt & Tijms [1984]. See also Peterson & Silver [1979].

All of the above methods employ *decomposition* as an additional type of approximation, i.e., the multi-location model is decomposed into J single-location problems with iteratively adapted characteristics. (Decomposition techniques are common to many mathematical programming solution methods or evaluation and control methods for queueing networks.) Each single-location problem has *normal* replenishment opportunities at the location's demand epochs. The fixed cost of a *normal* order is given by the fixed depot order cost plus the fixed shipment cost to this specific location. In addition there are *special* replenishment opportunities where the fixed order costs are limited to the fixed shipment cost only; these opportunities arise at epochs generated by an independent Poisson process which is an approximation of the superposition of the order processes triggered by the other locations. (It is this representation of the superposition of these order processes, which represents the approximate element in the decomposition method.) For each location, the mean time between consecutive 'special replenishment opportunities' (and hence the parameter of the Poisson process representing these special epochs) is adapted iteratively. In Federgruen, Groenevelt & Tijms [1984], an optimal (s, c, S) rule is found for each of the single location problems via a specialized and highly efficient policy-iteration method. (The latter generalizes the policy iteration methods in Federgruen & Zipkin [1984a, 1985] for finding optimal

(s, S) policies in ordinary single location problems.) Silver [1974], Thompstone & Silver [1975] and Silver [1981] employ heuristic evaluation and search methods for the single location problems. The numerical study by Federgruen, Groenevelt & Tijms [1984] suggests that the algorithm presented there, provides accurate (approximate) evaluations of the average cost of (s, c, S) policies as well as other performance measures of interest. On the other hand, in this restriction approach no bounds are obtained for the optimality gap of the generated (s, c, S) policies.

Analogous to the approaches in Section 3.1.2, one could restrict oneself to policies which determine when to place an order and of what size on the basis of the *aggregate* inventory position only. Indeed Renberg & Planche [1967] in a lesser known paper adopt a restriction approach of this type: an order is placed when the aggregate inventory position falls to or below some system-wide reorder point R and all locations' inventory positions are increased to specific order-up-to levels $\{S_j: j = 1, \ldots, J\}$. In the absence of fixed shipment costs and as shown in Section 3.1, the aggregate inventory position represents an adequate proxy for the system state (the vector of the outlets' inventory positions) and indeed a perfect state description in the relaxed model ibid. The same is true when it is optimal to replenish all outlets with (roughly) equal frequencies. In other settings the restriction appears undesirable, even though it is quite commonly used in practice: e.g., IBM's IMPACT system is based on this type of restriction approach, see Kleijnen & Rens [1978] or Vollmann, Berry & Whybark [1984]. See also Pantumsinchai [1988] for a (not altogether conclusive) numerical comparison between $(Q, S_1, \ldots, S_j)$ and (s, c, S) policies.

4.2. Relaxation approaches

Observe that in the Silver model, the need for centralized control arises exclusively because of the fixed cost that is incurred for orders to the outside supplier. Note also that if this *nonseparable* cost structure were replaced by a *separable lower bound* cost structure, the problem would decompose into J independent single location problems. As pointed out in the introduction of this section, such an approximation is referred to as a *relaxation*, since it results in a *lower bound* for the minimum achievable cost value.

A *separable lower bound* cost structure is obtained when allocating the fixed (depot) order cost K in fixed proportions $(\alpha_1, \alpha_2, \ldots, \alpha_J)$ with $\Sigma_{j=1}^{J} \alpha_j = 1$ and $\alpha_j \geq 0$ $(j = 1, \ldots, J)$. (Note that under the approximate cost structure, the fixed costs incurred under *any* replenishment strategy are less than under the exact cost structure.) In the resulting relaxed model it is clearly optimal to manage each location separately according to an (s, S) policy and the optimal (s, S) policy is easily found for each of the locations $j = 1, \ldots, J$ with one of the algorithms discussed above (see also Chapter 1). Thus, for $j = 1, \ldots, J$ let

k_j = fixed shipment cost for location j;
$T_j(s, S)$ = expected time between consecutive orders by location j under an (s, S) policy;
$C_j(s, S)$ = expected long run average holding and shortage costs for location j, under the (s, S) policy.

We thus obtain the following solution of the relaxed problem:

$$(\mathrm{LB}_\alpha){:}\sum_{j=1}^{J} \psi_j(\alpha_j)\,,$$

where

$$\psi_j(\alpha_j) \overset{\mathrm{def}}{=} \min_{s,S} \left\{ \frac{(\alpha_j K + k_j)}{T_j(s, S)} + C_j(s, S) \right\}.$$

Note that the functions $\psi_j(\cdot)$ are piecewise linear and *concave* and may be evaluated with the above mentioned standard algorithms for the determination of optimal (s, S) policies in single location models. For *each* allocation vector α, we thus obtain a lower bound (LB_α) for the minimum achievable cost value. The *best* such bound is clearly given by

$$\begin{aligned}(\mathrm{LB}){:}\ \max\ & \sum_j \psi_j(\alpha_j)\\ \text{s.t.}\ & \sum_j \alpha_j = 1\,,\\ & \alpha_j \geq 0\,, \quad j = 1, \ldots, J\,.\end{aligned}$$

Evaluation of (LB) thus reduces to maximizing a separable concave objective subject to a single constraint, an optimization problem which is mathematically of the exact same structure as (say) the myopic allocation problems discussed in Sections 3.1.1 and 3.1.3. (See there for an enumeration of efficient solution methods.) The above construction of the lower bound (LB) bears considerable similarity to the lower bounds obtained for mathematical programs via the popular technique of Lagrangian relaxation. (LB_α) has the additional advantage of being *separable* in α.

The above presentation is distilled from Federgruen & Zheng [1989]. The lower bound (LB) was however first presented by Atkins & Iyogun [1987, 1988]. (The latter suggest employing the α-vector which maximizes the lower bound in the deterministic, constant demand rate analog of this model. Federgruen and Zheng show that the true value of (LB) may be efficiently computed.)

When computing (LB) we obtain the vector α^* maximizing (LB_α) and the corresponding J-tuple of (s, S) pairs. This vector of (s, S) policies represents a *feasible* system-wide replenishment strategy. For significant values of K it is however unlikely to be efficient since nearly all orders generated under this strategy are made for *one* location only, i.e., the locations are managed independently. Federgruen, Groenevelt & Tijms [1984] have shown that even the *best* independent control policy can be significantly more expensive than various heuristic coordinated strategies.

The following procedure generates a vastly superior replenishment strategy instead. For the allocation vector α^*, determine an optimal $(m_j, v_j^{\#})$ policy for each location $j = 1, \ldots, J$, treating m as a *continuous* time-variable. (It is empirically known that in single-location problems, optimal (m, v) policies come close to being globally optimal.) Next, round the vector of replenishment cycles $(m_m\colon j = 1, \ldots, J)$ to a neighboring power-of-two vector $(m_j^*\colon j = 1, \ldots, J)$, i.e., a vector in which all components are power-of-two multiples of a common base period, and implement the resulting $\{(m_j^*, v_j^{\#})\colon j = 1, \ldots, J\}$ policy. This rounding procedure is standard in constructing feasible strategies from lower bounds for the deterministic, constant demand rate models of Chapter 2 where it can be shown to result in very minor cost increases (2% or 6% at *worst*, depending upon the exact implementation of the rounding procedure, see Chapter 2). Note that the vector m^* consists of few *distinct* components. This together with the nestedness of the replenishment intervals in a power-of-two vector, induces a large degree of joint replenishments among the different locations.

Atkins & Iyogun [1988] use different heuristics for the determination of the vector of replenishment interval $(m_j\colon j = 1, \ldots, J)$: (i) $m_j = m$ for *all* locations, with m for *all* locations, with m the *best* common interval value, or (ii) $m_j = m$ for all locations j with $\alpha_j^* > 0$, and m_j chosen as an (integer) multiple for all other locations j, i.e., with $\alpha_j^* = 0$. Atkins and Iyogun show in a limited numerical study that their heuristic strategies outperform the (s, c, S) policies of Section 4.1 except for settings in which the fixed order cost K is small. In their sample, the cost value of these policies is on average 12% higher than the specific (suboptimal) lower bound computed in their method. Moreover it appears that the relaxation methods of Atkins & Iyogun [1988] and Federgruen & Zheng [1989] are, in addition, computationally simpler than the methods of Section 4.1.

The relaxation approach has the additional advantage of being applicable to more general joint cost structures; indeed, as shown in Federgruen and Zheng, it is applicable to any joint cost structure which satisfies the general economies-of-scale (submodularity) property defined in Section 3.3. The only change occurs in the specification of the lower bound (LB). Under a general submodular cost structure, the separable concave objective $\Sigma_j \psi_j(\cdot)$ is to be maximized over a more general polyhedron, which is however still of a special (polymatroidal) structure allowing for highly efficient solution methods, see Federgruen & Groenevelt [1986], and Groenevelt [1985]. (See Chapter 2 for a discussion of the deterministic, constant demand rate, counterpart of this joint replenishment model under such general joint cost structures.)

References

Atkins, D., and P. Iyogun (1987). A lower bound for a class of inventory/production problems. *Oper. Res. Lett.* 6, 63–67.

Atkins, D., and P. Iyogun (1988). Periodic versus can-order policies for coordinated multi-item inventory systems. *Management Sci.* 34, 791–795.

Axsäter, S., and P. Lundell (1984). In-process safety stocks, Proceedings of 23rd Conference on Decision and Control, Las Vegas, NV, pp. 839–842.

Balintfy, J.L. (1967). On a basic class of multi-item inventory problems. *Management Sci.* 10, 287–297.

Bessler, A.A., and A.F. Veinott (1966). Optimal policy for a dynamic multi-echelon inventory model, *Naval. Res. Logist. Quart.* 13, 355–389.

Carlson, R.C., and C.A. Yano (1986). Safety stocks in MRP-systems with emergency setups for components. *Management Sci.* 32, 403–412.

Clark, A. (1958). A dynamic, single-item, multi-echelon inventory model, Report, Rand Corporation, Santa Monica, CA.

Clark, A. (1972). An informal survey of multi-echelon inventory theory. *Naval. Res. Logist. Quart.* 19, 621–650.

Clark, A.J., and H. Scarf (1960). Optimal policies for a multi-echelon inventory problem. *Management Sci.* 6, 475–490.

Clark, A.J., and H. Scarf (1962). Approximate solutions to a simple multi-echelon inventory problem, in: K.J. Arrow, S. Karlin and H. Scarf (eds.), *Studies in Applied Probability and Management Science*, Stanford University Press, Stanford, CA, pp. 88–110.

Eppen, G., and L. Schrage (1981). Centralized ordering policies in a multiwarehouse system with leadtimes and random demand, in: L. Schwarz (ed.), *Multi-Level Production/Inventory Control Systems: Theory and Practice*, North-Holland, Amsterdam, pp. 51–69.

Erkip, N., W. Hausman and S. Nahmias (1984). Optimal and near-optimal policies in multi-echelon inventory systems with correlated demands, Presented at the TIMS XXVI International Meeting, Copenhagen, Denmark, June 17–21.

Federgruen, A., and H. Groenevelt (1986). The greedy procedure of resource allocation problems: Necessary and sufficient conditions for optimality. *Oper. Res.* 34, 909–919.

Federgruen, A., H. Groenevelt and H. Tijms (1984). Coordinated replenishments in a multi-item inventory system with compound Poisson demands and constant lead times. *Management Sci.* 30, 344–357.

Federgruen, A., G. Prastacos and P. Zipkin (1986). An allocation and distribution model for perishable products. *Oper. Res.* 34, 75–83.

Federgruen, A., and Y.S. Zheng (1988a). The joint replenishment problem with general joint cost structures: General solution methods and performance bounds, Working Paper, Graduate School of Business, Columbia University, New York, to appear in *Oper. Res.*

Federgruen, A., and Y.S. Zheng (1988b). Minimizing submodular set functions: Efficient algorithms for special structures with applications to joint replenishment problems, Working Paper, Graduate School of Business, Columbia University, New York.

Federgruen, A., and Y.S. Zheng (1989). Coordinated multi-item inventory systems with stochastic demands and general joint cost structures, in preparation.

Federgruen, A., and P. Zipkin (1984a). Approximation of dynamic, multi-location production and inventory problems. *Management Sci.* 30, 69–84.

Federgruen, A., and P. Zipkin (1984b). Computational issues in an infinite-horizon, multi-echelon inventory model. *Oper. Res.* 32, 818–836.

Federgruen, A., and P. Zipkin (1984c). Allocation policies and cost approximation for multilocation inventory systems. *Naval. Research Logist. Quart.* 31, 97–131.

Federgruen, A., and P. Zipkin (1984d). An efficient algorithm for computing optimal (s, S) policies. *Oper. Res.* 32, 1268–1286.

Federgruen, A., and P. Zipkin (1985). Computing optimal (s, S) policies in inventory models with continuous demands. *Adv. in Appl. Probab.* 17, 424–443.

Federgruen, A., and P. Zipkin (1986a). An inventory model with limited production capacity and uncertain demands, I. The average cost criterion. *Math. Oper. Res.* 11, 193–207.

Federgruen, A., and P. Zipkin (1986b). An inventory model with limited production capacity and uncertain demands, II. The discounted cost criterion. *Math. Oper. Res.* 11, 208–216.

Federgruen, A., and P. Zipkin (1991). Approximations for dynamic two-echelon inventory systems with centralized stocks, in preparation.

Fukuda, Y. (1961). Optimal disposal policies, *Naval. Res. Logist. Quart.* 8, 221–227.

Geoffrion, A. (1970). Elements of large-scale mathematical programming. *Management Sci.* 16, 652–691.

Groenevelt, H. (1985). Two algorithms for maximizing a separable concave function over a polymatroid feasible region, Working Paper, Graduate School of Management, University of Rochester, Rochester, NY.

Gross, D., R. Soland and C. Pinkus (1981). Designing a multi-product, multi-echelon inventory system, in: L. Schwarz (ed.), *Multi-Level Production/Inventory Control Systems: Theory and Practice*, North-Holland, Amsterdam, pp. 11–49.

Hochstädter, D. (1970). An approximation of the cost function for a multi-echelon inventory model. *Management Sci.* 16, 716–727.

Ignall, E. (1989). Optimal continuous review policies for two product inventory systems with joint set-up costs. *Management Sci.* 15, 277–279.

Ignall, E., and A. Veinott (1969). Optimality of myopic inventory policies for several substitute products. *Management Sci.* 15, 284–304.

Jackson, P. (1988). Stock allocation in a two-echelon distribution system or 'What to do until your ship comes in'. *Management Sci.* 34, 880–895.

Jonsson, H., and E. Silver (1984). Analysis of an extreme case of a PUSH control system, Working Paper, Faculty of Management, The University of Calgary, Calgary, Alta.

Karlin, S. (1960). Dynamic inventory policy with varying stochastic demands. *Management Sci.* 6, 231–258.

Karmarkar, U.S. (1981). The multiperiod, multilocation inventory problem. *Oper. Res.* 29, 215–228.

Karmarkar, U., and N. Patel (1975). The one-period, *N*-location distribution problem. *Naval. Res. Logist. Quart.* 24, 559–575.

Kim, T. (1978). Two-echelon order point periodic inventory system with performance constraints, Working Paper, Dept. of Industrial and Operations Engineering, University of Michigan, Ann Arbor, MI.

Kleijnen, J., and P. Rens (1978). IMPACT revisited: A critical analysis of IBM's inventory package – IMPACT. *Prod. Invent. Management J.*, first quarter.

Klein, R. (1990). Multilocation inventory systems with transshipments in response to stockouts, Ph.D. dissertation, Columbia University, New York.

Laakso, C., and N. Thomopoulos (1979). Safety stocks and service levels for the multi-warehouse case. *Prod. Invent. Management J.*, second quarter, 72–84.

Lovejoy, W. (1988). Myopic policies for inventory models with dependent parameter-adaptive demand processes, Working Paper, Graduate School of Business, Stanford University, Stanford, CA.

Miller, B. (1986). Scarf's state reduction method, flexibility and a dependent demand inventory model. *Oper. Res.* 34, 83–90.

Naddor, E. (1975). Optimal and heuristic decisions in single and multi-item inventory systems, *Management Sci.* 21, 1234–1249.

Pantumsinchai, P. (1988). A comparison of two joint ordering inventory policies, Working Paper, Department of Management, De Paul University, Chicago, IL.

Peterson, R., and E. Silver (1979). *Decision Systems for Inventory Management and Production Planning*, Wiley, New York.

Renberg, B., and R. Planche (1967). Un Modèle pour la Gestion Simultanée des *n* Articles d'un Stock. *Rev. Inform. Rech. Opér.* 1 (6), 47–59.

Rosenfield, D., and M. Pendrock (1980). The effects of warehouse configuration design on inventory levels and holding costs. *Sloan Management Rev.* 24 (4), 21–33.

Rosling, K. (1987a). Bounds on the optimal reorder levels in a serial multi-echelon inventory model. Working Paper, Department of Management and Economics, Linköping Institute of Technology, Linköping Institute of Technology, Linköping, Sweden.

Rosling, K. (1987b). Optimal inventory policies for assembly systems under random demands. Working Paper, Department of Management and Economics, Linköping Institute of Technology, Linköping, Sweden.

Ross, S. (1970). *Applied Probability Models with Optimization Applications*, Holden-Day, San Francisco, CA.

Scarf, H. (1960). The optimality of (s, S) policies in the dynamic inventory problem, in: K. Arrow, S. Karlin and P. Suppes (eds.), *Mathematical Methods in the Social Sciences*, Stanford University, Stanford, CA.

Schmidt, C.P., and S. Nahmias (1985). Optimal policy for a two-stage assembly system under random demand. *Oper. Res.* 33, 1130–1145.

Showers, J. (1981a). Optimal policies for a multiperiod inventory model with transshipments, Working Paper, Bell Laboratories, Holmdel, NJ.

Showers, J. (1981b). Heuristic policies for a multiperiod inventory model with transshipments, Working Paper, Bell Laboratories, Holmdel, NJ.

Silver, E. (1965). Some characteristics of a special joint-order inventory model. *Oper. Res.* 13, 319–322.

Silver, E. (1974). A control system for coordinated inventory replenishment. *Internat. J. Prod. Res.* 12, 647–671.

Silver, E. (1981). Establishing reorder points in the (S, c, s) coordinated control system under compound Poisson demand. *Internat. J. Prod. Res.* 9, 743–750.

Sobel, M. (1987). Dynamic affine logistics models, SUNY Stony Brook Working Paper, Stony Brook, NY.

Tan, F. (1974). Optimal policies for a multi-echelon inventory problem with periodic ordering. *Management Sci.* 20, 1104–1111.

Thompstone, R., and E. Silver (1975). A coordinated inventory control system for compound Poisson demand and zero lead time. *Internat. J. Prod. Res.* 13, 581–602.

Veinott, A. (1965). Optimal policy for a multiproduct dynamic nonstationary inventory problem. *Management Sci.* 12, 206–222.

Veinott, A., and H. Wagner (1965). Computing optimal (s, S) inventory problems. *Management Sci.* 11, 525–552.

Vollmann, T., W. Berry and D. Whybark (1984). *Manufacturing Planning and Control Systems*, Dow, Jones-Irwin, Homewood, IL, pp. 549–560.

Wijngaard, J. (1972). An inventory problem with constrained order capacity, TH-report 72–WSK-63, Eindhoven University of Technology, Eindhoven, Netherlands.

Zheng, Y.S., and A. Federgruen. (1991). Finding optimal (s, S) policies is about as simple as evaluating a single policy. *Oper. Res.* 39, 654–655.

Zipkin, P. (1980). Simple ranking methods for allocation of one-resource. *Management Sci.* 26, 34–43.

Zipkin, P. (1982). Exact and approximate cost functions for product aggregates. *Management Sci.* 28, 1002–1012.

Zipkin, P. (1984). On the imbalance of inventories in multi-echelon systems. *Math. Oper. Res.* 9, 402.

Zipkin, P. (1986a). Stochastic leadtimes in continuous-time inventory models. *Naval. Res. Logist. Quart.* 33, 763–774.

Zipkin, P. (1986b). Inventory service-level measures: Convexity and approximation. *Management Sci.* 32, 975–981.

S.C. Graves et al., Eds., *Handbooks in OR & MS, Vol. 4*

Chapter 4

Continuous Review Policies for Multi-Level Inventory Systems with Stochastic Demand

Sven Axsäter

Luleå University of Technology, S-951 87 Luleå, Sweden

1. Introduction

1.1. Multi-level inventory systems

When products are distributed over a large geographical region it is often practical to have several local stocking locations that are reasonably close to the final customers. These local inventories may, in turn, be customers of a higher level stocking site, for example a central warehouse. The total inventory system is then a network of different facilities. The system in Figure 1.1 is a two-level (or two-echelon) *arborescent* system (each inventory has a single predecessor).

In the special case when there is just a single retailer we have a *serial* system. In this chapter we shall only deal with serial and arborescent systems. Such structures are especially common in distribution systems but are also important in certain production systems.

Inventory systems of this type are usually managed in practice using adaptations of single-location models. Such inventory models are well known and relatively easy to implement. But it has been shown [Muckstadt & Thomas, 1980] that special multi-level methods may reduce the total costs substantially (in some cases by about 50 per cent) compared to an application of single-level techniques.

Multi-level methods that are designed to take advantage of the system structure will, of course, require some centralized information and control. In a

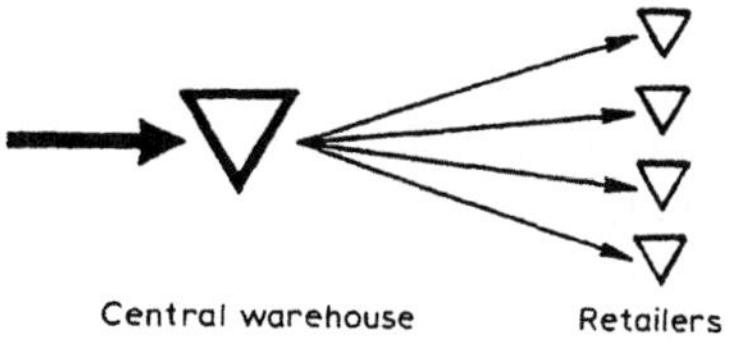

Fig. 1.1. Two-level arborescent system.

completely centralized system all control actions should be carried out by a central decision unit and be based on costs and inventory positions at all facilities. But such a system is usually associated with several disadvantages. Although the technology has improved dramatically, the data movement may lead to additional costs. Furthermore, the control policy will be very complex. It is therefore, in general, more suitable to limit the degree of centralization. Multi-level methods can consequently in most cases best be described as methods for coordination of local decentralized inventory control systems.

Inventory control in multi-level systems is a very promising application area. Many companies and other organizations should be able to reduce their inventory costs considerably by applying more appropriate control policies. Multi-level inventory control is also, as we shall see, a very interesting and challenging research area.

The system in Figure 1.1 has only two levels. In practice it is quite common for inventory systems to have more than two levels. It is usually relatively straightforward, though, to extend techniques for two-level systems to systems with more than two levels as long as the material flow still has the same hierarchical structure. It is more difficult to handle situations with different flow structures, for example when lateral replenishments from stocking sites at the same level are possible.

The fundamental problem in connection with two-level inventory systems is to find the best balance between central stock (at the warehouse) and local stock (at the retailers). It is clear that inventories at different levels will support each other. For example, with a large central inventory, orders from the retailers will very seldom be delayed, and it may be possible to reduce the local safety stocks. Retailer inventory is advantageous in the sense that it is closer to the customers. The central inventory, on the other hand, can in a way provide service to customers at all locations. The optimal solution of a multi-level inventory problem will depend on system structure, demand distributions, leadtimes, costs etc. In some cases it is appropriate to have a large central inventory, but it is also quite common with situations where there should hardly ever be inventory on hand at the central warehouse.

It is also important to note that quite different physical systems may lead to identical, or at least very similar, multi-level inventory systems. We have so far discussed distribution of products that are consumed by customers. Historically, several of the most important models have been developed in connection with military applications where the inventory items very often are repairable. But, as we shall see, consumable and repairable items can be handled in essentially the same way. Furthermore, in some production systems a number of different end products are all produced from a common basic module. Assume that we wish to determine suitable inventory levels in such a system. If in Figure 1.1 we let the central warehouse represent the inventory of the basic module while the retailers correspond to the inventories of the different end products, it is easy to see that the underlying multi-level inventory model is essentially the same as before. The different stocks do not contain identical items any longer, though, and they are normally situated at the same place.

In this chapter we shall only deal with continuous review policies. This means that the inventory levels are followed continuously and that replenishments may be ordered at any time. If the demand is Poisson (or compound Poisson) it is easy to realize that it is sufficient to consider those moments of time when demands occur. In case of low demand there are relatively few such events, and it is usually suitable to apply continuous review policies. On the other hand, in case of very high demand, continuous review can lead to high information costs and it may be more practical to review the inventory system periodically (see Chapter 3). This means that continuous review policies are of special interest for inventory items that naturally have a low demand like, for example, spare parts.

1.2. Control policies and performance criteria

When dealing with a relatively low stochastic demand it is usually assumed that the demand process is Poisson (or occasionally compound Poisson). There are two sound reasons for this assumption. First, it is in many situations a quite realistic assumption (for example when the demand emanates from failures of electronic equipment) and second, it simplifies the analysis considerably. It is also, in general, assumed that only the retailers (see Figure 1.1) face customer demand and that demand that cannot be met directly is backordered.

The leadtime to replenish the central warehouse is assumed to be either a constant or a stochastic variable with a given distribution. The retailer replenishment leadtimes are always stochastic due to occasional stockouts at the central warehouse. Given that the warehouse has stock on hand the leadtime (transportation time) may be constant or stochastic.

Furthermore we assume that there are linear inventory carrying costs both at the warehouse and at the retailers. Obviously there are also carrying costs while items are under transportation to the warehouse or from the warehouse to some retailer. These holding costs are not affected by the inventory control policy, though, and will therefore be disregarded. Besides the holding costs there is either a backorder cost (e.g., proportional to the time delay for a customer) or some standard service constraint. Note that since there is no direct customer demand at the warehouse, there are no costs or constraints associated with shortages there. Such shortages will, however, delay deliveries to the retailers and in that way have an impact on customer service.

In case of low demand, high holding costs and moderate ordering or set-up costs it is quite often optimal to let all deliveries be one-for-one. Such policies have therefore been studied extensively in the literature on multi-stage inventory systems. A very important and simplifying consequence of such policies is that Poisson demand at the retailers will give a demand process at the warehouse that is also Poisson. In many practical situations, however, ordering costs are sufficiently high to motivate deliveries in batches.

In general, a control policy should be based on the state of the whole inventory system. For example, a decision to send a batch from the warehouse to a certain retailer should depend on the inventory status at all retailers.

General centralized control policies of this type are difficult to implement. It is also difficult to determine the optimal policy. It is therefore usually assumed that the inventory control is partly *decentralized*. In case of one-for-one deliveries each inventory is following an $(S-1, S)$-policy, i.e., when the inventory position (inventory on hand plus outstanding orders minus backorders) declines to $S-1$ an order for a new item is immediately issued so that the inventory position always equals S. This means that each stocking location is controlling its own inventory. In this sense the inventory control is decentralized. Note, however, that the determination of the optimal inventory positions for all stocking locations is centralized. In case of batch deliveries each inventory is similarly assumed to follow a (Q, R)-policy, i.e., when the inventory position declines to R a batch of size Q is ordered.

Backorders at all locations are filled on a first-come-first-serve basis. This is not necessarily most economical but simplifies the analysis and is also in a sense a 'fair' policy.

1.3. Consumable or repairable items

Let us consider a situation where the items are repairable. The central warehouse in Figure 1.1 is then a repair depot with an inventory of spare items and the retailers are local operating sites that also maintain inventories of spare items. Assume that $(S-1, S)$-policies are applied at all locations. When an item fails at a site this item is immediately sent to the depot for repair. At the same time the failed item is replaced by a spare item from the local inventory (if there is no inventory on hand the failed item is replaced as soon as a replacement arrives from the depot). The local site does also order a replacement from the depot in order to maintain its inventory position. If there is stock on hand at the depot, this unit is delivered immediately; otherwise, the request is backordered.

It is easy to realize that the described inventory system is almost identical to the situation we have described before with consumable items. A demand will initiate replenishments both at a local inventory and at the central inventory. The replenishment leadtime at the repair depot is the time to transport the failed item from the site to the depot and the repair time at the depot. The replenishment leadtime at the site corresponds exactly to the case with consumable items, i.e., it is the stochastic waiting time at the depot due to stock-outs plus the transportation time from the depot to the site. This means that we can analyze the service performance of the system in exactly the same way independently of whether the items are repairables or consumables. The structure of the cost function may, however, be somewhat different when dealing with repairables, since it is often natural to charge holding costs to the total system inventory consisting of items in operation, in stock, in repair or in transit. Note also that the assumption that the demands occur according to Poisson processes may be less accurate in case of repairable items. The demand for spares at the sites should normally depend on the actual number of working items. When the number of shortages at the site exceed the number of available spares, the number of working items will drop below the normal requirements. This 'error' in the description of the demand process can, of course, be disregarded if there are many working items and the occurrences of such shortages are infrequent.

A review of repairable item inventory control is given by Nahmias [1981].

1.4. Overview of chapter

The purpose of this chapter is to present and discuss available models dealing with continuous review policies for multi-level inventory systems. We shall try to emphasize the main characteristics of different approaches but will sometimes not give a complete description of the considered models. Furthermore, we shall concentrate on two-level systems and consumable items. Generalizations to more than two levels will be discussed shortly in connection with the two-level models. Most of the considered models can also be used in connection with repairable items as explained in Section 1.3.

Section 2 will be completely devoted to the important special case of one-for-one ordering policies. More general batch-ordering policies are analyzed in Section 3. Finally, in Section 4 we give some concluding remarks concerning available models and the need for future research.

2. One-for-one replenishments

2.1. Framework

Let us again consider the material flow in Figure 1.1. The retailer demand is Poisson and all locations apply $(S-1, S)$-policies. We introduce the following notations:

N = number of retailers,
L_i = transportation time for an item to arrive at retailer i from the warehouse, i.e., the leadtime provided the warehouse has stock on hand,
L_0 = replenishment leadtime for the warehouse. The assumption of a constant L_0 can easily be relaxed as we shall discuss in Section 2.2,
λ_i = demand intensity at retailer i,

$$\lambda_0 = \sum_{i=1}^{N} \lambda_i = \text{demand intensity at the warehouse,}$$

S_i = order-up-to inventory position at retailer i,
S_0 = order-up-to inventory position at the warehouse,
I_i = inventory on hand at retailer i in steady state, random variable,
I_0 = inventory on hand at the warehouse in steady state, random variable,
B_i = number of backorders at retailer i in steady state, random variable,

B_0 = number of backorders at the warehouse in steady state, random variable,
W_i = time delay due to stock-outs at retailer i in steady state, random variable,
W_0 = time delay due to stock-outs at the warehouse in steady state, random variable,
O_i = number of outstanding orders at retailer i in steady state, random variable,
O_0 = number of outstanding orders at the warehouse in steady state, random variable.

2.2. *The METRIC approach*

Consider first the central warehouse. At time $t + L_0$ all replenishments that were ordered prior to time t have been delivered. The outstanding orders at time $t + L_0$, i.e., the orders that have not yet been delivered, are therefore those orders that have occurred between t and $t + L_0$. Since the demand is Poisson, the number of outstanding orders has a Poisson distribution with mean $\lambda_0 L_0$.

The number of outstanding orders can also be interpreted as the occupancy level in an M/D/∞ queueing system. According to a famous theorem by Palm [1938], the steady-state occupancy level in the more general M/G/∞ system is Poisson with mean λL where λ is the arrival rate and L is the average service time. Palm's theorem means that our assumption of a constant leadtime L_0 is unnecessarily restrictive. We can relax this assumption and assume that the leadtimes for the replenishment of the warehouse are independent stochastic variables with mean L_0 and any distribution.

It is now easy to determine the average number of backorders at the warehouse. Backorders occur as soon as the number of outstanding orders exceeds the inventory position S_0. The average number $\mathrm{E}(B_0)$ is obtained as

$$\mathrm{E}(B_0) = \sum_{j=S_0+1}^{\infty} (j - S_0) \frac{(\lambda_0 L_0)^j}{j!} \exp(-\lambda_0 L_0) . \tag{1}$$

But $\mathrm{E}(B_0)$ is the average 'length of the queue' of retailer orders and applying Little's well-known formula we obtain the average 'waiting time' $\mathrm{E}(W_0)$ due to stock-outs at the warehouse as

$$\mathrm{E}(W_0) = \mathrm{E}(B_0)/\lambda_0 . \tag{2}$$

In complete analogy with (1) we can also determine the average inventory level $\mathrm{E}(I_0)$ on hand at the warehouse

$$\mathrm{E}(I_0) = \sum_{j=0}^{S_0-1} (S_0 - j) \frac{(\lambda_0 L_0)^j}{j!} \exp(-\lambda_0 L_0) . \tag{3}$$

The *average leadtime* for the replenishment of retailer i is

$$\bar{L}_i = L_i + \mathrm{E}(W_0)\,. \tag{4}$$

So far our analysis is exact, but we shall now introduce the METRIC approximation [Sherbrooke, 1968]. The replenishment leadtimes for retailer i are stochastic variables. If these stochastic variables were independent, we could apply Palm's theorem to characterize the inventory process at each retailer. These leadtimes are evidently not independent, though, since they depend on the inventory situation at the warehouse. The METRIC approximation is to disregard the correlation between successive leadtimes, and then apply Palm's theorem as an approximation. Thus we replace the real stochastic leadtime by its mean $\bar{L}_i$. It is then easy to analyze how different service measures depend on the inventory positions S_0 and S_i. The average number of backorders $\mathrm{E}(B_i)$, the average time delay for a delivery $\mathrm{E}(W_i)$ and the average inventory $\mathrm{E}(I_i)$ are, for example, easy to determine in complete analogy with (1), (2) and (3).

$$\mathrm{E}(B_i) = \sum_{j=S_i+1}^{\infty} (j - S_i)\,\frac{(\lambda_i \bar{L}_i)^j}{j!}\,\exp(-\lambda_i \bar{L}_i)\,, \tag{5}$$

$$\mathrm{E}(W_i) = \mathrm{E}(B_i)/\lambda_i\,, \tag{6}$$

$$\mathrm{E}(I_i) = \sum_{j=0}^{S_i-1} (S_i - j)\,\frac{(\lambda_i \bar{L}_i)^j}{j!}\,\exp(-\lambda_i \bar{L}_i)\,. \tag{7}$$

Let us now assume that our objective is to choose a policy that minimizes the average holding and delay cost per time unit in the long run. We introduce the following additional notations:

h_i = holding cost per unit and time unit at retailer i,
h_0 = holding cost per unit and time unit at the warehouse,
β_i = delay cost per unit and unit time at retailer i,
C = average cost per time unit in steady-state.

The average cost per time unit can be expressed as:

$$C = h_0\mathrm{E}(I_0) + \sum_{i=1}^{N} h_i\mathrm{E}(I_i) + \sum_{i=1}^{N} \lambda_i\beta_i\mathrm{E}(W_i) \tag{8}$$

or equivalently

$$C = h_0\mathrm{E}(I_0) + \sum_{i=1}^{N} h_i\mathrm{E}(I_i) + \sum_{i=1}^{N} \beta_i\mathrm{E}(B_i)\,, \tag{9}$$

i.e., β_i can also be interpreted as the backorder cost per unit and time unit.

Note that the holding and delay costs at a retailer are independent of the inventory positions at other retailers. The holding cost at the warehouse is a function of S_0 only. This means that for given S_0 we can optimize C with respect to each S_i separately. Furthermore, C is convex in S_i. We denote the optimal S_i (for given S_0) by $S_i^*(S_0)$. The cost function $C(S_0, S_1^*(S_0), \ldots, S_N^*(S_0))$ is not necessarily convex in S_0, though, but it is relatively easy to find good upper and lower bounds for both S_0 and S_i. Consequently when optimizing the system we have to consider all values of S_0 within the bounds, while it is sufficient to look for a local minimum due to the convexity when determining the corresponding $S_i^*(S_0)$.

The sketched optimization procedure can be carried out in essentially the same way also when using an exact cost function or other approximations (see Sections 2.3 and 2.4). The optimization of batch ordering systems (see Section 3) can also be handled in a similar way. We shall therefore in the rest of the chapter concentrate on different procedures for evaluating policy costs.

The METRIC approach may also include a joint optimization of inventory policies for several items. A common problem is, for example, to minimize the backorder costs with respect to a budget on total inventory investment over all items. Such optimization problems are usually solved by Lagrangean techniques.

The METRIC approximation has many advantages and it has been used successfully in practice. There are especially many military applications involving high-value, repairable items, for which one-for-one policies are appropriate. The extension to more than two levels is straightforward and it is possible to apply the same technique also when the demand is compound Poisson. Feeney & Sherbrooke [1966] have extended Palm's theorem to compound Poisson demand. Their result is, however, true only when the service time is the same for each of the units in a demand batch. Since stochastic leadtimes are replaced by their means it is also easy to extend the approximations to the case when the transportation times are stochastic.

An important question is, of course, how good the approximation is in different situations. The numerical example in Table 2.1 gives an idea of the errors. The METRIC approximation underestimates the backorders (waiting times) by about 4 per cent for retailer 1 and about 19 per cent for retailer 2. For retailer 2 the error is considerable. The difference in accuracy for the two retailers is understandable. Consider two consecutive orders from retailer 1. Between these orders there are on the average 9 orders from retailer 2. Therefore there is not much correlation between the inventory on hand at the

Table 2.1
Accuracy of the METRIC-approximation and Graves' two-parameter approximation in a numerical example. $N = 2$, $L_0 = L_1 = L_2 = 2$, $\lambda_1 = 0.1$, $\lambda_2 = 0.9$, $\lambda_0 = \lambda_1 + \lambda_2 = 1$, $S_0 = 2$, $S_1 = 1$ and $S_2 = 4$

	$E(B_1)$	$E(W_1)$	$E(B_2)$	$E(W_2)$
Exact solution (Section 2.4)	0.0311	0.311	0.153	0.170
METRIC-approximation	0.0297	0.297	0.124	0.138
Graves' two-parameter approximation (Section 2.3)	0.0322	0.322	0.176	0.195

warehouse at these two events, and the METRIC approximation is reasonable. For retailer 2 we have the opposite situation. A very high correlation can be expected and this is clearly illustrated by our example. To summarize, the METRIC approximation will, in general, work well as long as the demand at each retailer is low relative to the total demand, for example in a case with many small retailers.

The errors in the METRIC approximation may also lead to an incorrect allocation of stock, when the approximation is part of an optimization procedure. In a numerical study by Graves [1985] the METRIC approximation led to the wrong stockage decision in 11.5 per cent of the considered cases.

2.3. Graves' two-parameter approximation

The METRIC approximation led to a description of the number of outstanding orders at retailer i as a Poisson distributed random variable with mean $\lambda_i \bar{L}_i$ [see (5) and (7)]. Since the Poisson distribution is completely characterized by its mean, the METRIC approximation can in a sense be regarded as a single-parameter approximation. A natural way of improving the approximation is to fit a distribution that is characterized by two parameters instead of one.

Graves [1985] determines both the mean $(\lambda_i \bar{L}_i)$ and the variance of the number of outstanding orders, $\mathrm{Var}(O_i)$:

$$\mathrm{Var}(O_i) = \left(\frac{\lambda_i}{\lambda_0}\right)^2 \mathrm{Var}(B_0) + \left(\frac{\lambda_i}{\lambda_0}\right)\left(\frac{\lambda_0 - \lambda_i}{\lambda_0}\right) \mathrm{E}(B_0) + \lambda_i L_i \,, \tag{10}$$

The average backorder level $\mathrm{E}(B_0)$ is obtained according to (1) and $\mathrm{Var}(B_0)$ can be determined by

$$\mathrm{Var}(B_0) = \sum_{j=S_0+1}^{\infty} (j - S_0)^2 \frac{(\lambda_0 L_0)^j}{j!} \exp(-\lambda_0 L_0) - (\mathrm{E}(B_0))^2 \tag{11}$$

(Graves gives a recursive procedure for $\mathrm{Var}(B_0)$ at S_0 in terms of $\mathrm{Var}(B_0)$ at $S_0 - 1$.)

Given the average $\mathrm{E}(O_i) = \lambda_i \bar{L}_i$ and the variance $\mathrm{Var}(O_i)$ Graves fits a negative binomial distribution.

$$\Pr(O_i = j) = \binom{r + j - 1}{j} p^r (1 - p)^j \,, \quad j = 0, 1, 2, \ldots \,, \tag{12}$$

where r and p are positive parameters $(0 < p < 1)$ such that

$$\mathrm{E}(O_i) = r(1 - p)/p \,, \tag{13}$$

$$\mathrm{Var}(O_i) = r(1 - p)/p^2 \,. \tag{14}$$

We can then in complete analogy with (5)–(7) determine alternative and, in general, more accurate estimates of $E(B_i)$, $E(W_i)$ and $E(I_i)$.

Considering the numerical example in Table 2.1 we note that Graves' approximation overestimates backorders and waiting times while the METRIC approach underestimates these measures. Although, there are still considerable errors in the estimates in this example, Graves has shown that his approximation will give very accurate results when used for determining optimal inventory policies. In his numerical study a wrong decision was obtained only in 0.9 per cent of the considered cases compared to 11.5 per cent when applying the METRIC approximation. Slay [1984] has independently studied the negative binomial distribution in this setting.

2.4. Exact solution

When determining various performance measures exactly one possible approach is to first find the exact steady-state distributions of the inventory levels. Given these distributions it is relatively easy to determine average costs that are functions of inventory levels and/or backlog sizes.

Let us first assume that all L_i are identical ($L_i = L_1$). Following Graves [1985] the aggregate outstanding orders (for all retailers) at time $t + L_1$, $O(t + L_1)$, can then be expressed as

$$O(t + L_1) = \sum_{i=1}^{N} O_i(t + L_1) = B_0(t) + D(t, t + L_1)\,, \tag{15}$$

where $D(t, t + L_1)$ is the total demand between t and $t + L_1$. Note that $B_0(t)$ and $D(t, t + L_1)$ are independent and both variables are also independent of S_i ($i = 1, 2, \ldots, N$). $D(t, t + L_1)$ is Poisson. $B_0(t)$ can be expressed as

$$B_0(t) = [O_0(t) - S_0]^+\,, \tag{16}$$

where $[x]^+$ denotes the nonnegative part of x. We know that $O_0(t)$ is Poisson in steady-state and independent of S_0.

In order to determine the steady-state distribution of $O(t + L_1)$ we need to convolve the steady-state distributions of $B_0(t)$ and $D(t, t + L_1)$. Given the steady-state distribution of O we can determine the distribution of the outstanding orders at retailer i as

$$\Pr(O_i = j) = \sum_{k=j}^{\infty} \Pr(O = k) \binom{k}{j} \left(\frac{\lambda_i}{\lambda_0}\right)^j \left(\frac{\lambda_0 - \lambda_i}{\lambda_0}\right)^{k-j} \tag{17}$$

since the conditional distribution of O_i is binominal, due to our assumption that warehouse backorders are filled on a first-come-first-serve basis. Given this distribution it is easy to determine various costs at the retailer like holding and backorder costs [see (5)–(7)].

This derivation is relatively straightforward but the computational effort is considerable due to the necessary convolutions. It is possible to generalize the model in various ways (for example by allowing different L_i's). The first derivation of the exact steady-state distributions was carried out by Simon [1971]. Kruse [1979] extended Simon's model to more than two echelons, and Shanker [1981] showed that the model can permit compound Poisson demand. Svoronos and Zipkin [1991] considered stochastic transportation times that are generated exogenously but that preserve order of replenishment.

A different and, in general, more efficient approach is to directly focus on the average costs associated with a stockage policy [Axsäter, 1990a]. Let us again consider the cost function (8). Denote expected retailer inventory carrying and stockage costs incurred to fill a unit of demand at retailer i by $\Pi_i^{S_i}(S_0)$. The average warehouse holding costs per unit depend on the stockage level S_0 only and are denoted $\gamma(S_0)$. The average costs can consequently be expressed as

$$C = \sum_{i=1}^{N} \lambda_i \Pi_i^{S_i}(S_0) + \lambda_0 \gamma(S_0) . \tag{18}$$

Let us now make the following simple but important observation. Any unit ordered by facility i $(0 \leqslant i \leqslant N)$ is used to fill the S_ith demand at this facility following this order (hereafter referred to as its demand). The observation is an immediate consequence of the ordering policy and of our assumption that delayed demands and orders are filled on a first-come-first-serve basis. When an order is triggered there are always already $S_i - 1$ units that are either in stock or on order, and these units will fill the next $S_i - 1$ demands.

We let $g_i^{S_i}(\cdot)$ denote the density function of the Erlang (λ_i, S_i) distribution of the time elapsed between the placement of an order and the occurrence of its assigned demand unit,

$$g_i^{S_i}(t) = \frac{\lambda_i^{S_i} t^{S_i - 1}}{(S_i - 1)!} \exp(-\lambda_i t) . \tag{19}$$

The corresponding cumulative distribution function $G_i^{S_i}(t)$ is

$$G_i^{S_i}(t) = \sum_{k=S_i}^{\infty} \frac{(\lambda_i t)^k}{k!} \exp(-\lambda_i t) \tag{20}$$

An order placed by retailer i arrives after $L_i + W_0$ time units where W_0, as before, is the random delay at the warehouse. We shall first evaluate the expected retailer carrying and delay costs by conditioning on $W_0 = t$. If the S_ith demand occurs before $L_i + t$ there is a delay, and if the demand occurs after $L_i + t$ we get a holding cost because the item must wait for the demand at the retailer. The *conditional* expected cost is denoted $\pi_i^{S_i}(t)$ (independent of S_0) and can be expressed as

$$\pi_i^{S_i}(t) = \beta_i \int_0^{L_i+t} g_i^{S_i}(s)(L_i + t - s)\,\mathrm{d}s + h_i \int_{L_i+t}^{\infty} g_i^{S_i}(s)(s - L_i - t)\,\mathrm{d}s\,, \quad S_i > 0\,, \tag{21}$$

$$\pi_i^0(t) = \beta_i(L_i + t)\,. \tag{22}$$

It is possible to simplify (21) into

$$\pi_i^{S_i}(t) = \exp(-\lambda_i(L_i + t))\,\frac{h_i + \beta_i}{\lambda_i} \sum_{k=0}^{S_i-1} \frac{(S_i - k)}{k!}(L_i + t)^k \lambda_i^k + \beta_i(L_i + t - S_i/\lambda_i)\,. \tag{23}$$

Since the time between the placement of a warehouse order and the occurrence of the S_0th demand is Erlang (λ_0, S_0), $\Pi_i^{S_i}(S_0)$ can be obtained as

$$\Pi_i^{S_i}(S_0) = \int_0^{L_0} g_0^{S_0}(L_0 - t)\pi_i^{S_i}(t)\,\mathrm{d}t + (1 - G_0^{S_0}(L_0))\pi_i^{S_i}(0)\,, \quad S_0 > 0\,, \tag{24}$$

$$\Pi_i^{S_i}(0) = \pi_i^{S_i}(L_0)\,. \tag{25}$$

Axsäter [1990a] derives the following recursive relationship from (24):

$$\Pi_i^{S_i}(S_0 - 1) = \frac{\lambda_i}{\lambda_0}\Pi_i^{S_i-1}(S_0) + \frac{\lambda_0 - \lambda_i}{\lambda_0}\Pi_i^{S_i}(S_0) + \frac{\lambda_i}{\lambda_0}(1 - G_0^{S_0}(L_0))(\pi_i^{S_i}(0) - \pi_i^{S_i-1}(0))\,, \quad S_i, S_0 > 0\,. \tag{26}$$

It is also possible to show that

$$\Pi_i^0(S_0) = G_0^{S_0}(L_0)\beta_i L_0 - G_0^{S_0+1}(L_0)\frac{\beta_i S_0}{\lambda_0} + \beta_i L_i\,. \tag{27}$$

Furthermore, for large values of S_0 we have

$$\Pi_i^{S_i}(S_0) \approx \pi_i^{S_i}(0)\,. \tag{28}$$

Consequently, starting with a large $\bar{S}_0$ such that (28) is valid we can apply (26) and (27) recursively for $\bar{S}_0 - 1$, $\bar{S}_0 - 2, \ldots, 1$. Since the coefficients in (26), λ_i/λ_0 and $(\lambda_0 - \lambda_i)/\lambda_0$, are both positive numbers between zero and one this recursion will not cause any numerical difficulties.

Finally, we determine in complete analogy with (21) the average holding cost per unit $\gamma(S_0)$ for $S_0 > 0$ ($\gamma(0) = 0$) as

$$\gamma(S_0) = h_0 \int_{L_0}^{\infty} g_0^{S_0}(s)(s - L_0)\,\mathrm{d}s\,. \tag{29}$$

This expression can be simplified into

$$\gamma(S_0) = \frac{h_0 S_0}{\lambda_0}(1 - G_0^{S_0+1}(L_0)) - h_0 L_0(1 - G_0^{S_0}(L_0))\,. \tag{30}$$

Altogether this means that we have a simple recursive procedure for evaluation of the exact costs. This approach can be used for any costs that are functions of the delays experienced by the customers, or the unit's storage time at each of the facilities. The extension to more than two levels is straightforward.

2.5. Extensions

Muckstadt [1973] has provided an important extension of the METRIC framework to include a hierarchical or indentured parts structure (MOD-METRIC). We shall illustrate the basic idea in Muckstadt's approach by an extension of our model.

Let us consider a group of n items ($j = 1, 2, \ldots, n$) that are controlled according to our previous model. The demand for item j at retailer i is denoted λ_{ij} and the stockage levels at the retailer and the warehouse are S_{ij} and S_{0j}. The average replenishment delays at the retailers $\mathrm{E}(W_{ij})$ are then easily obtained according to (1)–(6) if we use the METRIC approximation. Let us furthermore assume that the considered items are modules that are exclusively used when repairing a certain assembly. Retailer i has a stock of such assemblies that is used to replace assemblies that come in for repair. The demand for repairs is Poisson with rate $\lambda_i^a = \sum_{j=1}^n \lambda_{ij}$, i.e., it is assumed that the assembly is repaired by exchanging *exactly one* of the modules. If the needed module is available, the repair time is T_i but due to occasional shortages of modules the average repair time (including waiting time for modules) is obtained as

$$\bar{T}_i = T_i + (1/\lambda_i^a) \sum_{j=1}^{n} \lambda_{ij}\mathrm{E}(W_{ij})\,. \tag{31}$$

Given the inventory policy for the assembly, it is now easy to analyze holding and shortage costs if we use the METRIC approximation and replace the stochastic repair time by its mean $\bar{T}_i$. This means that we can analyze how different inventory policies for the assembly *and the modules* will affect the inventory situation for the assembly.

Muckstadt's model is much more comprehensive than our simple example. For details we refer to the original paper and to Muckstadt [1979]. Sherbrooke [1986] has extended Grave's approximation to the multi-indenture problem.

Another interesting variation of the basic model is to allow *lateral transshipments*. Lee [1987] assumes that the lower level stocking sites (the retailers in our model) are grouped into a number of disjoint pooling groups such that members of each group are independent and, in a sense, share their stocks. When a demand at a site cannot be met directly due to a stock-out, and there are units available in the pooling group, the demand is met by an emergency lateral transshipment from another location in the group with stock on hand. Only if all members of the group are out of stock is the request directed to the upper level. Lee's model is closely related to the model in Graves [1985]. A different approach is suggested in Axsäter [1990b].

3. Batch-ordering policies

3.1. Complexity of general ordering policies – Need for approximations

So far we have assumed that all locations in Figure 1.1 apply $(S-1, S)$-policies. Although there are many important applications of such policies, it is also very common that large ordering costs more or less prohibit one-for-one replenishments. This means that we should look for an efficient batch ordering policy. But, in general, it is more difficult to evaluate general batch ordering policies. The main source of the difficulties is the fact that a retailer demand will no longer immediately trigger a corresponding retailer order. Assume that the retailer demand is Poisson and that retailer i orders in batches of size Q_i. This means that every Q_ith demand at the retailer will trigger an order, and the demand from the retailer at the warehouse is therefore an Erlang renewal process with Q_i stages. Consequently, the demand process at the central warehouse is a superposition of N such Erlang processes instead of the simple Poisson process in the case of one-for-one ordering where N is the number of retailers. There are two important cases when the more complicated demand process at the central warehouse degenerates, and it is relatively easy to evaluate a policy exactly. One case is when the retailers apply one-for-one ordering policies and it is only the warehouse that orders in batches. This means, of course, that the demand at the warehouse is still Poisson. The other case is when there is just one retailer, i.e., a serial system. The demand process at the warehouse is then an Erlang process and we know that exactly every Q_ith system demand will trigger a retailer replenishment order. In the general case it is usually practical to use various approximations when evaluating the costs. Several different types of approximations have been suggested in the literature.

3.2. Serial systems

Let us first consider the case when there is just a single retailer. We assume that both echelons apply inventory policies of the continuous (R, Q) type. When the inventory position declines to R a batch of size Q is ordered. The control parameters are (R_1, Q_1) at the retailer and (R_0, Q_0) at the warehouse where we choose to express R_0 and Q_0 in units of retailer batches. Thus, $R_0 = 2$, $Q_0 = 5$ means that the warehouse orders $5Q_1$ units when the inventory position declines to $2Q_1$. We shall namely assume that all deliveries are in full batches, and this means that the inventory position at the warehouse should always be an integer multiple of Q_1.

We know from Section 2 how to evaluate the costs in the one-for-one case (exactly or approximately). Let $C(S_0, S_1)$ be the exact cost per time unit for a certain policy (S_0, S_1). Recall now that when following an (S_0, S_1)-policy an item ordered by the warehouse will be used to fill the S_0th demand at the warehouse following this order, and in the same way an item ordered by the retailer will be used to fill the S_1th demand at the retailer following the order. This means that an item arriving at the warehouse will continue immediately to the retailer if S_0 demands have already occurred; if not, it will stop at the warehouse until the S_0th demand occurs. Consider now a batch that is ordered by the warehouse in the batch-ordering case. This batch consists of Q_0 sub-batches of size Q_1. The first sub-batch (the one that is delivered first to the retailer) is released from the warehouse when $(R_0 + 1)Q_1$ demands have occurred, the next subbatch when $(R_0 + 2)Q_1$ demands have occurred etc. The first unit in a sub-batch will in the same way be used to fill the $(R_1 + 1)$th retailer demand after the retailer order; the second unit will fill the $(R_1 + 2)$th demand etc. It is now obvious that each unit will face costs corresponding to different one-for-one policies and following Axsäter [1991a] we obtain the holding and delay costs per time unit by taking the average over the batch,

$$C = (1/Q_0Q_1) \sum_{j=R_0+1}^{R_0+Q_0} \sum_{k=R_1+1}^{R_1+Q_1} C(jQ_1, k) . \tag{32}$$

The average number of orders per time unit are at the warehouse λ_0/Q_0Q_1 and at the single retailer λ_0/Q_1 so it is easy to add the ordering costs to the cost expression in (32). This means that batch ordering policies in the serial case can be evaluated based on the analysis of one-for-one ordering policies.

De Bodt & Graves [1985] have developed an interesting approximate method for the serial case. Their model, which does not assume Poisson demand, is closely related to classical standard models for single-stage systems. They assume that the reordering decision at the warehouse is based on the *echelon stock* instead of the *installation stock*, i.e., on the sum of the inventory positions at the warehouse and at the retailer. Let us denote the reorder point by E_0, expressed in units since the echelon stock is not necessarily an integral multiple of Q_1. Q_0 is still expressed in units of retailer batches. The following additional notations are used in the model:

d = expected demand per time unit,
$f(x \mid l)$ = probability density function for leadtime demand, where l denotes the length of the leadtime,
e_0 = h_0 = echelon holding cost at the central warehouse,
e_1 = $h_1 - h_0$ = echelon holding cost at the retailer,
a_0 = ordering cost at the warehouse,
a_1 = ordering cost at the retailer,
b = backorder cost per unit; note that the backorder cost is no longer based on the time delay.

De Bodt and Graves also assume that the policy is nested in the sense that when an order quantity Q_0 arrives at the warehouse an order quantity Q_1 is immediately sent to the retailer. This process is termed a *joint replenishment*. Other *normal replenishments* by the retailer are triggered when the retailer inventory position reaches the reorder point R_1. It is assumed that there is always stock on hand at the warehouse for the normal replenishments. This assumption is normally valid if Q_1 is large compared to the standard deviation of the demand during L_0. We are now ready to estimate the expected costs per time unit. The ordering costs are

$$d\left(\frac{a_0}{Q_0 Q_1} + \frac{a_1}{Q_1}\right). \tag{33}$$

The echelon holding costs at the warehouse are obtained as:

$$e_0\left(\frac{Q_0 Q_1}{2} + \int_0^{\infty} (E_0 - x) f(x \mid L_0)\, \mathrm{d}x\right). \tag{34}$$

When determining the holding costs at the retailer we have to consider both normal and joint replenishments and weigh the costs in proper proportions:

$$e_1\left(\frac{Q_1}{2} + \frac{Q_0 - 1}{Q_0} \int_0^{\infty} (R_1 - x) f(x \mid L_1)\, \mathrm{d}x + \frac{1}{Q_0} \int_0^{\infty} (E_0 - x) f(x \mid L_0 + L_1)\, \mathrm{d}x\right). \tag{35}$$

The expression for the backorder cost is similar:

$$\frac{bd}{Q_1}\left(\frac{Q_0-1}{Q_0}\int_{R_1}^{\infty}(x-R_1)f(x\mid L_1)\,\mathrm{d}x\right.$$

$$\left.+\frac{1}{Q_0}\int_{E_0}^{\infty}(x-E_0)f(x\mid L_0+L_1)\,\mathrm{d}x\right) \tag{36}$$

By summing (33)–(36) we obtain the total expected cost. Note that if $Q_0 = 1$ the problem collapses to the classical one-stage problem.

For a given value of Q_0 it is possible to optimize the system with respect to E_0, Q_1 and R_1 via an iterative procedure. This solution is very similar to that for a single-stage system. Given E_0, Q_1 and R_1 the cost is unimodal in Q_0 and it is easy to find the best choice of Q_0. A possible heuristic optimization procedure is then to start with an initial value of Q_0 and iterate between finding the best choice for E_0, Q_1 and R_1 for a given Q_0 and finding the best choice for Q_0 for given E_0, Q_1 and R_1. This procedure will obtain improved solutions at each step and will converge but not necessarily to the global optimal solution. In order to guarantee optimality it is necessary to evaluate all possible values of Q_0, and for each value determine the best choices of E_0, Q_1 and R_1.

De Bodt & Graves [1985] give also solution procedures for serial systems with more than two stages. Their computational studies indicate that the approximate model is very accurate. For example, when evaluating 768 test problems with Poisson demand in the two-stage case the average percentage absolute error in the safety stock was 2.7% at the warehouse and 1.4% at the retailer. The average percentage error for the backorder estimate was 0.4%. When considering a three-stage system the errors were even less. The exact solution of the test problems were obtained according to Graves & De Bodt [1984].

3.3. *Arborescent systems*

We shall now return to the general case with $N > 1$ retailers but make the simplifying assumption that all retailers are identical. Let $L_i = L_1$, $\lambda_i = \lambda_1$, $h_i = h_1$, $\beta_i = \beta_1$, $Q_i = Q_1$ and $R_i = R_1$ for $i = 2, 3, \ldots, N$. The warehouse uses an installation stock policy (R_0, Q_0) with R_0 and Q_0 expressed in units of retailer batches. We shall also for simplicity assume that $R_0 \geqslant -1$ although this is not necessarily optimal in the batch ordering case. The case when $R_0 < -1$ must be handled in a different way.

Let us first consider the simple case when $Q_1 = 1$. This means that each system demand (at any retailer) will trigger a retailer order, and the demand at the warehouse is still Poisson. It is then easy to evaluate different policies exactly. This was first recognized by Simon [1971]. Following Axsäter [1991a] we can easily express holding and delay costs in almost complete analogy with (32):

$$C = (1/Q_0) \sum_{j=R_0+1}^{R_0+Q_0} C(j, R_1 + 1) , \tag{37}$$

where $C(S_0, S_1)$ as before is the cost when using one-for-one policies at both echelons with inventory positions (S_0, S_1). The first unit in the warehouse batch will now be released for delivery to a retailer at the $(R_0 + 1)$th demand after the order, the second unit after $R_0 + 2$ demands etc. Each unit ordered by a retailer will be used to fill the $(R_1 + 1)$th demand following this order.

In the general case with $Q_1 > 1$ it is more difficult to calculate the costs exactly. A warehouse batch consists now of Q_0 sub-batches of size Q_1 and the kth sub-batch will be used to fill the $(R_0 + k)$th retailer order following the order from the warehouse. The jth retailer order will occur after a number i of system demands. It is evident that i is stochastic and that $i \geq j$. Furthermore $E(i) = jQ_1$. Let p_{ij} denote the probability that the ith demand will trigger the jth retailer order. If we know these probabilities we can express the exact cost in analogy with (32) and (37) as

$$C = (1/Q_0Q_1) \sum_{j=R_0+1}^{R_0+Q_0} \sum_{k=R_1+1}^{R_1+Q_1} \sum_{i=j}^{\infty} p_{ij} C(i, k) . \tag{38}$$

The only obstacle is the computational effort of calculating the probabilities p_{ij}. It is, in general, practical to use a simple approximation instead of the exact probabilities. A very simple approximation can be obtained by assuming that exactly every Q_1th demand generates a retailer order, i.e.,

$$p'_{ij} = \begin{cases} 1 & \text{if } i = jQ_1 , \\ 0 & \text{otherwise} . \end{cases} \tag{39}$$

Note that (39) is exact in the serial case. Another possibility is to assume that each demand triggers a retailer order with probability $1/Q_1$ leading to a negative binomial distribution. For $j > 0$

$$p''_{ij} = \begin{cases} 0 & \text{for } i < j , \\ \binom{i-1}{j-1} \left(\frac{Q_1 - 1}{Q_1} \right)^{i-j} \left(\frac{1}{Q_1} \right)^{j} & \text{for } i \geq j , \end{cases} \tag{40}$$

and $p''_{00} = 1$.

The approximation (40) is reasonable when there are many retailers, but it is in contrast to (39) not exact in the serial case ($N = 1$). Axsäter [1991a] therefore suggests that a weighted average with weights $1/N$ and $(N - 1)/N$ of the costs obtained when applying (39) and (40) is used as an improved approximation. He also gives an exact method that is quite efficient for small values of N. An extension to non-identical retailers is given by Axsäter [1991b].

Other approaches for evaluation of general batch-ordering policies in arborescent systems can be described as decomposition techniques similar in spirit to Sherbrooke's [1968] METRIC approach. Each facility is approximated as a single-location inventory system, but the parameters describing these systems are dependent on the other facilities. The first such approach was by Deuermeyer & Schwarz [1981]. See also Schwarz, Deuermeyer & Badinelli [1985]. They approximate the mean and variance of the warehouse leadtime demand D_0 by

$$\mathrm{E}(D_0) = \frac{\lambda_0 L_0}{Q_1} + \frac{(1 - Q_1)}{2Q_1}, \tag{41}$$

$$\mathrm{Var}(D_0) = \frac{\lambda_0 L_0}{Q_1^2}. \tag{42}$$

Then they fit a normal distribution to these parameters when estimating holding costs and the average delay at the warehouse. The leadtime distribution at a retailer is also approximated by a normal distribution but when fitting this distribution the stochastic leadtime is replaced by its mean obtained as L_1 plus the average delay at the warehouse.

Lee & Moinzadeh [1987a,b] and Moinzadeh & Lee [1986] approximate the demand process at the warehouse by a Poisson process. This approximation is usually reasonable in the case of many retailers with fairly equal demand but less suitable when there are only a few retailers. Using this assumption they determine the distribution of the total number of outstanding orders at all retailers. Next the mean and variance of the number of outstanding orders at a single retailer are obtained by an approximate random disaggregation scheme. They then use different two-moment approximations of the distribution of outstanding orders at the retailer. This approximation is closely related to the approach by Graves [1985] in the one-for-one case (see Section 2.3). Moinzadeh & Lee [1986] have also suggested a power approximation scheme for determination of the optimal batch size.

Svoronos & Zipkin [1988] use a different type of second-moment approximation. The mean and the variance of the warehouse leadtime demand are determined as

$$\mathrm{E}(D_0) = \frac{\lambda_0 L_0}{Q_1} \tag{43}$$

and

$$\mathrm{Var}(D_0) = \frac{\lambda_0 L_0}{Q_1^2} + \frac{N}{Q_1^2} \sum_{k=1}^{Q_1 - 1} (1 - \exp(-\alpha_k \lambda_1 L_0) \cos(\beta_k \lambda_1 L_0)) / \alpha_k, \tag{44}$$

where

$$\alpha_k = 1 - \cos(2\pi k / Q_1), \qquad \beta_k = \sin(2\pi k / Q_1).$$

Given the mean and the variance they then fit a shifted Poisson distribution to these parameters. By using this approximate distribution it is easy to calculate $E(B_0)$ and $E(I_0)$ [see (1) and (3)]. We can also apply Little's formula to obtain the average delay at the warehouse due to stockouts:

$$E(W_0) = \frac{Q_1}{\lambda_0} E(B_0) . \tag{45}$$

Then they derive an approximate expression for $\mathrm{Var}(W_0)$ that is based on an extension of Little's theorem to higher moments and is exact for $Q_1 = 1$, i.e., Poisson demand at the warehouse. Given $E(W_0)$ and $\mathrm{Var}(W_0)$ they proceed to approximate the mean and variance of the retailer leadtime demand D_1:

$$E(D_1) = \lambda_1(E(W_0) + L_1) , \tag{46}$$

$$\mathrm{Var}(D_1) = \lambda_1(E(W_0) + L_1) + \lambda_1^2 \mathrm{Var}(W_0) . \tag{47}$$

Next they approximate the distribution of D_1 by a negative binomial distribution. This approximation is the same as the one used by Graves (Section 2.3) in the one-for-one ordering case.

In order to obtain the distribution of the inventory level they finally convolve the inventory position distribution (uniform over $R_1 + 1, R_1 + 2, \ldots, R_1 + Q_1$) minus the leadtime demand distribution. Note that this step is trivial in the one-for-one case since the inventory position is constant. Given the distribution

Table 3.1
Problem description and optimal policies. From Svoronos & Zipkin [1988]. $L_0 = L_1 = 1$, $h_0 = h_1 = 1$

Problem number	λ_1	N	β	Q_1	Q_0	R_0	R_1
1	0.10	4	20.00	4	1	−1	0
2	0.10	4	20.00	4	4	−1	−1
3	0.10	4	5.00	4	1	−1	−1
4	0.10	4	5.00	4	4	−2	−1
5	0.10	32	20.00	4	1	1	−1
6	0.10	32	20.00	4	4	0	−1
7	0.10	32	5.00	4	1	−1	−1
8	0.10	32	5.00	4	4	−2	−1
9	1.00	4	20.00	4	1	0	2
10	1.00	4	20.00	4	4	−1	2
11	1.00	4	5.00	4	1	−1	1
12	1.00	4	5.00	4	4	−1	0
13	1.00	32	20.00	4	1	8	1
14	1.00	32	20.00	4	4	6	1
15	1.00	32	5.00	4	1	7	0
16	1.00	32	5.00	4	4	5	0

Table 3.2
Exact and approximate average total cost per time unit. SAx I: According to (38) and (39); SAx II: Weighted average with weights $1/N$, and $(N-1)/N$ of (38) and (39), and (38) and (40), respectively; S&Z: Svoronos & Zipkin

Problem number	Exact cost	SAx I		SAx II		S&Z	
		Cost	Rel. dev.	Cost	Rel. dev.	Cost	Rel. dev.
1	9.62	9.62	0.00	9.62	0.00	9.62	0.00
2	14.03	14.01	0.00	14.02	0.00	14.02	0.00
3	6.52	6.52	0.00	6.52	0.00	6.52	0.00
4	11.03	10.53	−0.05	10.88	−0.01	11.27	0.02
5	68.53	67.29	−0.02	68.57	0.00	68.53	0.00
6	71.08	69.83	−0.02	71.10	0.00	71.08	0.00
7	52.16	52.16	0.00	52.16	0.00	52.16	0.00
8	53.89	53.44	−0.01	53.85	0.00	53.89	0.00
9	16.11	15.34	−0.05	16.12	0.00	15.77	−0.02
10	18.57	18.33	−0.01	18.62	0.00	18.21	−0.02
11	11.14	11.14	0.00	11.14	0.00	11.14	0.00
12	13.95	13.57	−0.03	14.03	0.01	13.72	−0.02
13	111.70	108.00	−0.03	113.09	0.01	111.67	0.00
14	112.74	108.86	−0.03	114.11	0.01	112.55	0.00
15	78.72	75.65	−0.04	79.69	0.01	78.63	0.00
16	79.45	76.76	−0.03	80.33	0.01	79.28	0.00

of the inventory level it is finally straightforward to calculate $E(I_1)$ and $E(B_1)$.

It is always difficult to compare the performance of different approximations since their accuracy may change considerably for different types of problems. The performances of different methods have been compared on a set of test problems in Svoronos & Zipkin [1988] and in Axsäter [1991a]. Omitting problems with $Q_1 = 1$, that are easily solved exactly, the remaining problems are given in Table 3.1. For each problem we consider the optimal reorder points R_0 and R_1 determined by Svoronos & Zipkin [1988] for the given order quantities Q_0 and Q_1.

For these problems the approximation methods of Svoronos and Zipkin and of Axsäter are very accurate. The results are presented in Table 3.2 together with the exact cost as derived by Axsäter [1991a]. The performance of the methods by Deuermeyer and Schwarz and by Lee and Moinzadeh have also been evaluated by Svoronos & Zipkin [1988]. They obtained considerable errors in the cost estimates, though. For some of the problems the relative deviation from the exact cost exceeded one hundred per cent.

4. Conclusions

In this chapter we have considered various methods for control of multi-level inventory systems with Poisson (or compound Poisson) demand. As long as the material flow has the simple hierarchical structure in Figure 1.1 we have very good methods for evaluation and optimization of one-for-one policies. We can also handle some special batch-ordering systems (e.g., serial systems) very efficiently. In nearly all other situations, e.g., general batch-ordering, lateral transshipments etc., we have reason to believe that the methodology could still be improved and generalized.

Among the many interesting research topics, we note the need for more efficient techniques for general batch-ordering systems. From a practical point of view it would also be very interesting to evaluate in a more systematic way under what circumstances simple heuristics can replace more accurate but also more complex methods. There are still many open research problems concerning more complex material flow patterns like different types of lateral transshipments. Furthermore, it is not clear when it is worth the effort to apply more general centralized policies instead of the essentially decentralized (R, Q)-policies that we have considered in this chapter.

Although there is a need for further research in the area, it is also clear that the presently available methodology could be used more in practice. Simple approximations would probably give very significant savings compared to the inventory control methods that are applied by most companies today. A recommendation to practioners is therefore that they, as a first step, should evaluate the potential of multi-level techniques in a simulation study, which usually is relatively easy to carry out.

References

Axsäter, S. (1990a). Simple solution procedures for a class of two-echelon inventory problems. *Oper. Res.* 38, 64–69.

Axsäter, S. (1990b). Modelling emergency lateral transshipments in inventory systems. *Management Sci.* 36, 1329–1338.

Axsäter, S. (1991a). Exact and approximate evaluation of batch-ordering policies for two-level inventory systems. *Oper Res.*, to appear.

Axsäter, S. (1991b). Evaluation of (R, Q)-policies for two-level inventory systems with Poisson demand, Working Paper, Luleå University of Technology, Sweden.

De Bodt, M.A., and S.C. Graves (1985). Continuous review policies for a multi-echelon inventory problem with stochastic demand. *Management Sci.* 31, 1286–1295.

Deuermeyer, B., and L.B. Schwarz (1981). A model for the analysis of system service level in warehouse/retailer distribution systems: The identical retailer case. In: L.B. Schwarz (ed.) *Multi-Level Production/Inventory Control Systems*, Stud. Management Sci., Vol. 16, North-Holland, Amsterdam, pp. 163–193.

Feeney, G.J., and C.C. Sherbrooke (1966). The $(S-1, S)$ inventory policy under compound Poisson demand. *Management Sci.* 12, 391–411.

Graves, S.C., and M.A. De Bodt (1984). An exact model for a serial production/inventory system with Poisson demand and continuous review, Sloan School of Management, Massachusetts Institute of Technology.

Graves, S.C. (1985). A multi-echelon inventory model for a repairable item with one-for-one replenishment. *Management Sci.* 31, 1247–1256.

Kruse, W.K. (1979). An exact *N* echelon inventory model: The simple Simon method, Technical Report, U.S. Army Inventory Research Office, Philadelphia.

Lee, H.L. (1987). A multi-echelon inventory model for repairable items with emergency lateral transshipments. *Management Sci.* 33, 1302–1316.

Lee, H.L., and K. Moinzadeh (1987a). Two-parameter approximations for multi-echelon repairable inventory models with batch ordering policy. *IIE Trans.* 19, 140–149.

Lee, H.L., and K. Moinzadeh (1987b). Operating characteristics of a two-echelon inventory system for repairable and consumable items under batch ordering and shipment policy. *Naval Res. Logist. Quart.* 34, 365–380.

Moinzadeh, K., and H.L. Lee (1986). Batch size and stocking levels in multi-echelon repairable systems. *Management Sci.* 32, 1567–1581.

Muckstadt, J.A. (1973). A model for a multi-item, multi-echelon, multi-indenture inventory system. *Management Sci.* 20, 472–481.

Muckstadt, J.A. (1979). A three-echelon, multi-item model for recoverable items. *Naval Res. Logist. Quart.* 26, 199–221.

Muckstadt, J.A., and L.J. Thomas (1980). Are multi-echelon inventory methods worth implementing in systems with low-demand rates? *Management Sci.* 26, 483–494.

Nahmias, S. 1981. Managing repairable item inventory systems: A review, in: L.B. Schwarz (ed.), *Multi-Level Production/Inventory Control Systems*, Stud. Management Sci., Vol. 16, North-Holland, Amsterdam, pp. 253–277.

Palm, C. (1938). Analysis of the Erlang traffic formula for busy signal assignment. *Ericsson Technics* 5, 39–58.

Schwarz, L.B., B.L. Deuermeyer and R.D. Badinelli (1985). Fill-rate optimization in a one-warehouse *N*-identical retailer distribution system, *Management Sci.* 31, 488–498.

Shanker, K. (1981). Exact analysis of a two-echelon inventory system for recoverable items under batch inspection policy. *Naval Res. Logist. Quart.* 28, 579–601.

Sherbrooke, C.C. (1968). METRIC: A multi-echelon technique for recoverable item control. *Oper. Res.* 16, 122–141.

Sherbrooke, C.C. (1986). VARI-METRIC: Improved approximation for multi-indenture, multi-echelon availability models. *Oper. Res.* 34, 311–319.

Simon, R.M. (1971). Stationary properties of a two-echelon inventory model for low demand items. *Oper. Res.* 19, 761–777.

Slay, F.M. (1984). VARI-METRIC – An approach to modeling multi-echelon resupply when the demand process is Poisson with a gamma prior, Working note AF 301-3, Logistics Management Institute, Washington, DC.

Svoronos, A., and P. Zipkin (1988). Estimating the performance of multi-level inventory systems. *Oper. Res.* 36, 57–72.

Svoronos, A., and P. Zipkin (1991). Evaluation of one-for-one replenishment policies for multi-echelon inventory systems. *Management Sci.* 37, 68–83.

S.C. Graves et al., Eds., *Handbooks in OR & MS, Vol. 4*

Chapter 5

Performance Evaluation of Production Networks

Rajan Suri and Jerry L. Sanders

University of Wisconsin-Madison, Department of Industrial Engineering, 1513, University Avenue, Madison, WI 53706, U.S.A.

Manjunath Kamath

Oklahoma State University, School of Industrial Engineering and Management, 322 Engineering North, Stillwater, OK 74078, U.S.A.

1. Introduction

1.1. *Motivation: The role of performance evaluation*

The decade of the 1980s has brought with it the widespread recognition of the importance of manufacturing in maintaining a firm's competitiveness [Hayes, Wheelwright & Clark, 1988; Dertouzos, Lester & Solow, 1989]. As a result, most industrial corporations are now devoting a lot of effort to constantly improving their manufacturing methods and systems. Effective analysis and improvement of manufacturing systems has thus become an important activity in the survival of the modern firm. During the lifetime of a particular manufacturing facility, the firm responsible for it goes through many phases of decision making, from an analysis of initial feasibility through detailed design of the facility, installation and startup, operation of the system, ongoing improvements, and finally obsolescence of the facility [Suri, 1988a]. Typical decisions that must be made for a manufacturing system include: the products to be manufactured, the number and types of equipment to be used, process plans and part routings, tooling and fixtures, material handling methods including number and types of transporters, facility layout, and buffer sizes. Typical performance measures used to evaluate these decisions include physical measures such as production rates, equipment utilization, work in process, and part flow times, as well as financial measures such as return on investment, payback period, and net present value. As a starting definition of performance evaluation (PE) we say it is 'a methodology (including techniques and tools) for determining the performance measures that can be expected to result from a given set of decisions'.

Of course, manufacturing systems analysis is not a new field. The use of factories for manufacturing has been well established since the industrial revolution, and as any industrial engineer knows, the formal study of manufacturing systems is at least as old as Taylor's studies begun in the 1880s [Emerson & Naehring, 1988]. A modern manufacturing system, however, can be quite different from the more traditional system. It is most often a complex system consisting of many interconnected components of hardware and software. Due to this greater complexity, decision making for such a system can be very difficult compared to, say, a traditional job shop. This complexity is due to several factors that are elaborated in Suri [1988a], but briefly they are: the high degree of interconnection and integration, leading to 'global' effects of seemingly 'local' decisions; increased sharing of resources in order to improve efficiency; little 'slack' in the system; and fewer 'humans in the loop'. Because of such factors, even experienced manufacturing personnel have difficulty in perceiving the consequences of a given decision. For such systems, the role of PE as defined above becomes even more critical in providing techniques and tools which will aid manufacturing managers in making their decisions while attempting to achieve their goals with respect to performance measures such as those above.

In order to keep the preceding comments in line with modern manufacturing concepts, it should be mentioned that at the same time there is a trend to reduce complexity in manufacturing [e.g., see Schonberger, 1982]. In other words, an alternative view one might take is to question the need for complexity, and try to reduce it, rather than simply provide tools to analyze and deal with the complex systems [Suri & Shimizu, 1989]. In view of this one might ask whether this trend would eliminate the need for many of the modeling approaches discussed in this article and elsewhere in this Handbook.

Indeed this raises an issue that is critical to the success of research and development in this applications area. In order to build on and improve the modeling approaches described below, for PE of manufacturing systems, it is not enough for the analyst to have an understanding of modeling techniques such as stochastic processes and queueing theory. It is necessary that the analyst has a good understanding of manufacturing systems too. In fact, it is suggested in Suri [1988a] that many of the recent fundamental developments in manufacturing systems have come from outside the traditional analysis community, and part of the reason for this may have been a preoccupation with modeling rather than a concern for the underlying manufacturing issues. As authors of a basic chapter on this topic, we feel a great responsibility to communicate to potential researchers in this field the importance of maintaining a strong connection with actual manufacturing systems while working on models and techniques for PE of these systems.

Returning now to the question posed above, namely, the relevance of various analysis approaches in light of the trend to simplicity, this is discussed in detail in Suri [1988a]. Also discussed is the trend towards just-in-time (JIT) systems and its impact on the need and relevance of analysis. It is shown there that, with appropriate understanding of the new issues that emerge with these trends, PE techniques and tools can be used to complement and improve the application of these trends, rather than be displaced by them. On the other hand, examples are also given to show that ignoring the ultimate needs of the manufacturing enterprise can lead to a whole generation of models and journal publications that become irrelevant to the very subject they purport to assist.

1.2. Overview of PE approaches

The title of this chapter refers to 'production networks' (PN). This terminology is nonstandard, but intentional, in order to clarify the class of manufacturing systems what we address. In general terms, they fall into the category of discrete manufacturing systems, where products are worked on individually or in 'batches' (as opposed to continuous systems such as an oil refinery or chemical processing plant), and furthermore to systems where products tend to visit several different workstations, in varying sequences, before they are completed. Thus the system can be viewed as a 'network' of workstations: hence the term PN.

We should also clarify the approaches that we will cover under the topic of PE. In order to do this, it is useful to introduce a classification of methods. Broadly speaking, the main approaches to PE of discrete manufacturing systems can be placed in three categories.

(i) *Static (allocation) models*. These simply add up the total amount of work allotted to each resource, and estimate the performance from these totals. Such a model tends to be somewhat simple as it ignores most of the dynamics, interactions, and uncertainties typically seen in a manufacturing system. However, it can be useful as a rough initial estimator of system size and performance. For example, the 'rough cut capacity planning' module of a typical material requirements planning (MRP) system uses such an approach. Many planning analyses are also based on such a model, often enhanced with Linear Programming techniques to optimize the decisions in the model. For example, such a model could be used for selecting the product mix and corresponding equipment to maximize profit based on a budget constraint. Usually, due to the use of mathematical programming methods in conjunction with the models, such models fall in the realm of deterministic optimization methods, and also do not exploit the 'network structure' of the manufacturing system, so they will not be covered in this chapter. See Chapter 8 for more on these approaches.

(ii) *Aggregate dynamic models (ADMs)*. Such models do account for some of the dynamics, interactions, and uncertainties in the system, but in an aggregate way. Typically, they use analytical techniques from stochastic processes, queueing theory, queueing networks, and reliability theory. Some of the assumptions in these models may be restrictive for certain manufacturing configurations. The performance measures estimated are often only the steady state averages. Still, these models tend to give reasonable estimates of performance and (relative to alternative approaches) are very efficient. There have been major advances in the development and application of these models in the last two decades, and they are becoming popular in industry for rapid decision making. More background and perspective will be given on these below as they are the subject of this chapter.

(iii) *Detailed dynamic models*. These approaches model the manufacturing system in considerable detail, in some cases, to the level of detail desired by the analyst. They can be further divided into two categories: *deterministic* and *stochastic*. Detailed deterministic models include scheduling approaches [e.g., see Graves, 1981 for a review] and Petri Nets [Kamath & Viswanadham, 1986]. Detailed stochastic models include Monte Carlo simulation [Law & Haider, 1989] and stochastic Petri Nets [Balbo, Chiola & Franceschinis, 1989]. Simulation models deserve special mention since simulation is becoming a widely used tool in industry. In the current context, this refers to computer-based discrete event simulation. These models can mimic the operation of the system in as much detail as required by the analyst. Thus they can be made very accurate, but the price to be paid is in terms of model development time and computer time each time the model is run. Combined with visual animation, these models can be powerful tools for communicating the results of an analysis. Still, for industrial problems, such an approach typically requires one to three orders of magnitude more effort than a queueing model, as shown by actual case studies [Anderson, 1987; Brown, 1988]. This is a major reason behind the development and extension of the analytical models discussed in the body of this chapter. Related to simulation approaches are the emerging sample-path based approaches such as perturbation analysis (see Suri [1989a] for an up-to-date review) and likelihood ratio methods [Glynn, 1989; Reiman & Weiss, 1989; Rubinstein, 1989] which provide efficient means for sensitivity analysis of the detailed dynamic models; sensitivity analysis can be a valuable addition to a PE study.

Further discussion on the above categorization, as well as an extensive set of references on performance evaluation of discrete manufacturing systems can also be found in a recent survey by Leung & Suri [1990]. In addition, two recent books on this subject are Buzacott & Shanthikumar [1992b] and Viswanadham & Narahari [1992].

1.3. *Aims and scope of the chapter*

The aims of this chapter are: (i) to serve as an advanced introduction to the subject – for example, it could be the starting point for a researcher or graduate student beginning work on this topic, or it could be used to accompany a graduate course in this area; (ii) to provide a fairly exhaustive view of the subject, along with an organization that assists the reader in comprehending the field; and (iii) to serve as an up-to-date reference for teachers, researchers and practitioners of operations research and management science.

In terms of scope of the chapter, using the classification above, we will deal primarily with ADMs. Our reason for focusing on ADMs is, in the context of this chapter and its potential educational use, our firm belief that they represent a class of methods that will occupy a significant portion of the PE methodology in the coming decade. The forces behind this are, first, the fact that analytical models usually provide more insight and understanding of a system (as contrasted with, say, simulation models), and second, they enable rapid PE of alternative decisions, a fact that results in significant strategic advantage (both these points are elaborated below). A final reason for not spending time on the other approaches is that some of them are covered in depth in the other chapters in this Handbook.

As an additional comment on the scope of the chapter, using the classification in Suri [1985a], our view of PE is that it is concerned mainly with *evaluative* models, i.e., those that predict system performance given a set of decisions, as opposed to *generative* models, which find a set of decisions to meet a given set of performance criteria.

Several articles identify a correspondence between the three major modeling approaches above and the stages of manufacturing decision making. Specifically, they can be related, respectively, to feasibility studies, aggregate decisions, and detailed decisions – see, e.g., Stecke [1985], Suri [1985b], and Gershwin, Hildebrant, Mitter & Suri [1986]. These decisions could refer to either the design phase or the operation phase of a facility [Suri, 1988a]. For instance, in the operation phase they might refer to decisions with a time horizon of (respectively) years, weeks to months, and minutes to days. A decision support system that integrates various phases of decision making should ideally combine these various approaches and use the one appropriate to the particular decision being reviewed. Such a *hierarchical* approach has been suggested by several authors [e.g., see Hax & Meal, 1975; Kimemia & Gershwin, 1983; Suri & Whitney, 1984; Gershwin, Hildebrant, Mitter & Suri, 1986, and Stecke, 1985]. As we are concerned only with one of the modeling approaches, we will not consider such hierarchical approaches, except for two special cases: hierarchical queueing network models, and integrated modeling environments, both covered in Section 8. A current review of hierarchical approaches can be found in Chapter 10.

1.4. A perspective on the development and use of aggregate dynamic models

The development of ADMs for manufacturing dates back to a few seminal papers by Koenigsberg for cyclic systems (see the review in Koenigsberg [1982]) and Jackson [1963] for job shops. These models were developed as attempts to provide analytic formulas that would predict the performance of manufacturing systems. As such, some initial successes were achieved. For example, as we will discuss later, the work of Jackson [1963] showed that under suitable assumptions the performance of a complex job shop could be predicted just from available formulas for single queues. Despite some of this progress, these models gained popularity only in the academic and research world, and, due to the perceived restrictive nature of some of the assumptions in the models, they did not find their way into the mainstream of manufacturing analysis in industry. In particular, they were viewed as overly theoretical and less accurate tools than, say, simulation models. This situation has changed considerably in the last few years. For one, similar models have enjoyed over a decade of success in the field of computer systems performance modeling – there are whole textbooks on this topic, such as Sauer & Chandy [1981], and many available software tools [e.g., see BGS Systems, 1982, and Lazowska, Zahorjan, Graham & Sevcik, 1984]. A second, more important factor is that it has now been recognized how, especially in the competitive environment of modern manufacturing, ADMs can play a strategically important role. The key lies in the fact that ADMs allow rapid analysis of many different manufacturing alternatives, enabling a firm to constantly explore ways of remaining competitive, and also enabling the firm to make rapid decisions and gain greater decision leverage [Suri, 1989b]. This remains true even though ADMs provide a more 'rough' analysis than, say, simulations [Suri & Diehl, 1987]. As noted in Suri [1989b], the role of ADMs is to provide insight on the key factors in a day or so, as compared with a detailed analysis of all the factors that may well take a few months. This has impact on both the design and the operation phases of manufacturing systems. In the design of a new facility, such a rapid analysis can provide early feedback to the process and equipment designers. In the operation of an existing plant, it can lead to better planning decisions and exploration of many alternative operating options. Finally, ADMs have been shown to support modern competitive manufacturing strategies such as Time-Based Competition and Kaizen [Suri & DeTreville, 1991, 1992]. With this recognition, recently ADMs have seen a marked increase in use in industry: as examples of this, Alcoa and IBM have used ADMs effectively in the design of new factories [Nymon, 1987; Brown, 1988], and DEC, Pratt & Whitney, and Siemens have used ADMs in improving their operational decisions [Anderson, 1987; Harper & O'Loughlin, 1987; Suri, 1988b].

1.5. Classification of systems

While detailed explanation of the classifications will be given in the sections that follow, we give a brief overview of the main categories here. An ADM in its simplest form consists of a set of stations, each of which may have one or more servers, and a set of jobs that visit the stations requiring service. This models a manufacturing system where each station represents a set of functionally identical resources (such as machines, operators, cranes, etc.), which we will henceforth just call 'servers', and each job represents a workpiece or batch of workpieces. The workpieces have a specified routing which requires them to visit the stations in a given sequence, requiring operations to be performed on them from one of the servers at the station visited, and the operation times at each station are also specified. These specifications need not be deterministic; they may be in terms of parameters of probability distributions, for example, if machine failures are to be modeled. Thus a job is characterized by its (possibly stochastic) routing and service times. The network model may be 'open', which means that jobs arrive from an external source and depart from the network when completed, or it may be 'closed' which means that a fixed number of jobs circulates in the network. The model may be 'single class' which means that all jobs are assumed to be statistically identical (in terms of their routing and service requirements), or it may be 'multiple class' where each class of jobs has its own characteristics. A multiple class model may have some classes open and other closed, in which case the network is called 'mixed'. Each station is characterized by the number of servers, the maximum queue space available ('finite buffer') or 'infinite buffer' if queue space is assumed to be unlimited, the service discipline, e.g., first-come-first-serve (FCFS) or shortest processing time (SPT). A special case is a 'tandem' network in which all the jobs enter the system at the first station, visit each station in order, and leave the system after visiting the last station. While many additional classifications exist, this will serve as an introduction to the main categories.

1.6. Overview of typical analysis outputs

Except for the simplest of systems, ADMs usually provide estimates only of steady state performance measures (PMs), and often just average values are estimated (as opposed to say, entire distributions, or a 95% percentile, etc.). The PMs estimated fall primarily into the category of physical PMs rather than financial PMs. This chapter will deal only with physical PMs. Typical PMs estimated by an ADM include (all of these are steady state averages): utilization of each server; throughput (or production rate); flow time of a job through the system; queue length at a station; and work-in-process (WIP) in the system. These are among the primary physical PMs of interest to manufacturing personnel and, even though only steady state average values are estimated, they can be quite valuable in manufacturing decision making [Brown, 1988; Suri, 1989b].

1.7. Structure of the chapter

We begin in Section 2 by studying a single workcenter with multiple identical machines. This 'single queue system' has been the starting point for analytical results on production networks, and also serves as a building block for more complex systems. At the beginning of that section we also establish the main notational conventions which will be used throughout the chapter. Then we cover the results for a large number of cases of this single queue system, many of which are then referenced later in the chapter. Section 3 considers the simplest topological configuration of a network – a tandem production line. Section 4 covers tree-structured manufacturing systems, also known as assembly networks. Sections 5 and 6 survey open networks and closed networks, respectively, allowing for general network structures. Then, Section 7 considers, for the first time, multiple levels of resources: in this case, queueing for machines *and* operators (also known as machine–operator interference models). Finally, Section 8 gives an overview of certain advanced topics and mentions potential research areas.

2. Workcenter with identical machines and a single queue

2.1. System definition

In this section, we consider queueing models of a workcenter consisting of identical machines. The machines are identical in that each can process any of the arriving jobs and we assume here that they do so one at a time. Jobs arrive at the workcenter from external sources, and if all machines are busy processing jobs, the arriving job has to wait. Jobs waiting for service form a single queue which feeds all machines (see Figure 2.1). When a machine finishes the processing of its current job, it chooses another job from those that are waiting, in accordance with a prescribed scheduling discipline. A commonly employed scheduling discipline is FCFS (first-come-first-served), where jobs are served by the workcenter in the order of their arrival.

The study of this single queue system is useful and interesting for two major reasons. First, this simple queueing system is the starting point for all analysis. Hence, a large body of results is available for this system. Understanding the dynamics of the queueing phenomenon is easier in the context of this simple model. Secondly, this simple queueing system is a building block for most

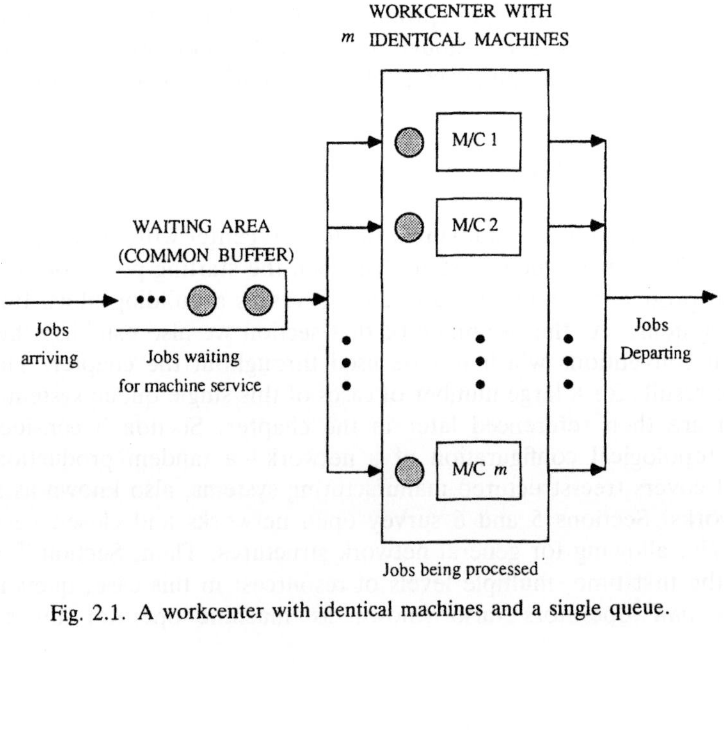

Fig. 2.1. A workcenter with identical machines and a single queue.

other analyses. For example, the task of modeling and analyzing production systems usually involves systems having multiple resources (workcenters, transporters, robots, etc.). This complex structure of multiple interacting resources can be modeled using queueing networks (see Sections 5 and 6). Several useful analysis techniques have been developed for queueing networks by incorporating simple single queue models as submodels in queueing network models.

The queueing system described above can be characterized using a standard shorthand form, $A/S/m/N/K/Z$, known as Kendall's notation. In this notation, A specifies the interarrival-time distribution, S the service-time distribution or the probability distribution for the time it takes to process a job, m the number of parallel (identical) servers or machines, N the restriction on system capacity or the maximum number of jobs (waiting and being processed) that can be simultaneously present in the workcenter, K the size of the external source or calling population, and Z the scheduling or service discipline. It is common practice to omit the symbol N if no restriction is imposed on system capacity and symbol K if the calling population is infinite. If the scheduling discipline is FCFS then the symbol Z is usually omitted. Some standard symbols for the interarrival-time and service-time distributions are:

M = Exponential (Markovian) distribution,
D = Deterministic (constant time),
E_k = Erlang type k ($k = 1, 2, \ldots$),
H_k = Hyperexponential distribution of order k ($k = 1, 2, \ldots$),
G = General (an arbitrarily specified distribution).

A symbol GI often used to specify interarrival times is a shorthand for 'General, Independently distributed interarrival times'. When the interarrival-time distribution is exponential, the arrival process is a Poisson process and we say the queue has Poisson arrivals.

Example. The queue M/D/2/10 represents a work center with two identical machines where the arrival process is Poisson, the processing time for all jobs is the same fixed (deterministic) value, a maximum of ten jobs can be present in the system at a time, the source of jobs is infinite, and the scheduling discipline is FCFS.

Notation. We use the following notation. The squared coefficient of variation (SCV) of a random variable (r.v.) is defined as the variance of the r.v. divided by the square of its mean. Hereafter, 'system' includes the workcenter and buffer.

{Input or given quantities}
m : number of machines in the workcenter,
N : maximum number of jobs allowed in the system,
λ : mean arrival rate of jobs to the system,
c_a^2 : interarrival-time SCV,

τ : mean service time of a job at a machine,
c_s^2 : service-time SCV.

{Output or computed quantities – all are steady-state performance measures}
ρ : utilization of a machine,
c_d^2 : interdeparture-time SCV,
p_n : probability that there are n jobs in the system,
q_n : probability that an arriving job sees n jobs in the system,
L_q : average number of jobs waiting (in the buffer) for service,
L : average number of jobs in the system,
W_q : average time a job spends waiting (in the buffer) before beginning service,
W : average time spent by a job in the system from arrival to departure.

Additional notation will be defined as needed.

Departure process. Information about the discharge or departure process of a workcenter queueing model can be useful if the workcenter is a part of a manufacturing network. In this case if, after visiting this workcenter, jobs are required to visit other workcenters, then the departures from this workcenter will become arrivals to other workcenters. As we will see later in this chapter, departure process information plays a key role in the development of analysis techniques for certain general network models.

General service-time distributions. The assumption of exponential service times makes an exact analysis of single queue models possible in most cases. Hence, a majority of the queueing models used to analyze modern production networks make this assumption. This assumption is usually not satisfied by production systems such as a flexible manufacturing system (FMS) in which the machining times are known quite accurately. Another example is an automatic assembly station in which the assembly time is typically fixed (deterministic) except when a station 'jam' occurs, when a repair process is required. In such cases the exponential service-time models often do not represent reality faithfully, and the analysis using an exponential assumption can sometimes be misleading especially when the service time SCV is near zero or larger than the 1.0 value for the exponential distribution [e.g., see Kamath & Sanders, 1987]. Some recently developed tools and techniques for analyzing production systems [Buzacott & Shanthikumar, 1985; Kamath, Suri & Sanders, 1988; Segal & Whitt, 1989] use queueing models such as the GI/G/1 and GI/G/m queues that allow non-exponential service time distributions. It should be noted that the assumption of exponential service times is only one of the assumptions that is typically made when production networks are analyzed using queueing models; some of the other common assumptions concern the arrival process, scheduling discipline, and queue capacity.

For the discussion in Sections 2.2 and 2.3 we will assume that the scheduling discipline is FCFS and source is infinite. In Section 2.2 we consider systems with no restrictions imposed on the capacity, that is, $N = \infty$. Section 2.3 contains results for systems with a finite buffer or finite N. In both sections, single-serve systems ($m = 1$) are considered separately. In Section 2.4 we present some results for systems where the source is finite. We conclude Section 2 with a brief discussion of results for non-FCFS queueing disciplines.

2.2. Systems without buffer constraints

In this section, we consider systems with no restrictions imposed on the buffer capacity, i.e., $N = \infty$. We start by reviewing some general relations that hold for these systems.

General relations. The following relations hold for a parallel server queueing system for general interarrival-time and service-time distributions. That is, for a $G/G/m$ queue ($m \geq 1$), we have [Tijms, 1988]

$$\rho = \frac{\lambda\tau}{m} \qquad (G/G/m)\,, \tag{2.1}$$

$$W = W_q + \tau \qquad (G/G/m)\,, \tag{2.2}$$

$$L = L_q + m\rho \qquad (G/G/m)\,. \tag{2.3}$$

The machine utilization ρ is usually less than 1.

Little's formula [Little, 1961; Stidham, 1974], possibly the most widely used result in queueing theory, relates mean arrival rate, average system time, and average number of customers (jobs) in a queueing system. For a queueing system, Little's result simply states that

$$\textit{Average number of customers in system} = (\textit{Mean arrival rate}) \times (\textit{Average system time})\,.$$

If any two of these quantities are known, the third is automatically determined. For a $G/G/m$ queue we have

$$L = \lambda W\,. \tag{2.4}$$

Applying Little's result to the jobs waiting in the buffer, we obtain

$$L_q = \lambda W_q\,. \tag{2.5}$$

Note. Multiplying both sides of relation (2.2) by λ and using Little's result yields relation (2.3). The quantity $m\rho$ is the average number of jobs in service. Hence, relation (2.1) can be obtained by applying Little's result to jobs in service.

For most queueing systems discussed below, we give an exact formula or an approximation only for W_q, which is the average waiting time of jobs before beginning service. The related congestion measures, L_q, W, and L can be easily obtained by applying Little's result, Equation (2.5) and general relations (2.2) and (2.3).

2.2.1. Single-server queues

A useful relation for general single-server queues (G/G/1) concerns the server utilization and the probability that the queueing system is empty.

$$p_0 = 1 - \rho \qquad (\mathrm{G/G/1}). \tag{2.6}$$

The M/M/1 *queue.* The most basic and widely used single-server model is the M/M/1 queue. The interarrival times and service times are exponentially distributed with means $1/\lambda$ and τ, respectively. Owing to the memoryless (or Markovian) property of the exponential distribution, an exact analysis of this queue is possible and a complete set of results can be found in standard texts on queueing [Gross & Harris, 1985; Kleinrock, 1975]. We present below formulas for the steady-state performance measures for this queue. Assume $\rho < 1$ here.

The machine utilization is given by the general equation (2.1). The average waiting time of jobs is given by

$$W_q = \frac{\tau\rho}{1-\rho} \qquad (\mathrm{M/M/1}). \tag{2.7}$$

The steady-state probability that there are n jobs in the system is

$$p_n = (1-\rho)\rho^n, \quad n \geq 0 \qquad (\mathrm{M/M/1}). \tag{2.8}$$

Erlangian and hyperexponential queueing models. We shall consider in this section single server queueing models where the interarrival times (or service times) are Erlang type k (E_k) or hyperexponentially (H_k) distributed. These probability distributions have a greater modeling flexibility than the exponential distribution. It is convenient to consider the Erlang type k as being made up of k identical exponential phases, although the arrival or service mechanism may not actually contain a sequence of phases. When $k = 1$ we have an exponential distribution (SCV = 1) and as k approaches ∞, the Erlang becomes deterministic (SCV = 0). Hence, the Erlang type k distribution can model situations with SCV ≤ 1. The hyperexponential distribution is a mixture of exponentials of different means and always has a SCV ≥ 1.

For the Erlang service model, $M/E_k/1$, and Erlang arrival model, $E_k/M/1$, exact analysis is possible by treating the Erlang as a sum of exponential phases. In the Erlang service model, the average waiting time of jobs is

$$W_q = \frac{k+1}{2k} \frac{\tau\rho}{(1-\rho)} \qquad (\mathrm{M/E}_k/1)\,. \tag{2.9}$$

Additional results for this model and formulas for the Erlang arrival model can be found in Gross & Harris [1985].

An approach usually referred to as the method of phases or stages, approximates a general interarrival-time (or service-time) distribution by one that is built up from a combination of Erlang and hyperexponential components (e.g., see Neuts [1981] for details).

The M/G/1 *queue.* The M/G/1 queueing model can be adapted to many situations involving non-exponential service times. The arrivals are Poisson and the distribution of service times (job processing times in our case) can be arbitrary (but specified). However, an imbedded Markov chain [Gross & Harris, 1985, pp. 252–254] can be constructed for the M/G/1 queueing model thus allowing the utilization of Markov-chain theory in the analysis. Formula for the average waiting time of jobs is given below and its use is illustrated next:

$$W_q = \left(\frac{1+c_s^2}{2}\right)\left(\frac{\tau\rho}{1-\rho}\right) \qquad (\mathrm{M/G/1})\,. \tag{2.10}$$

Equation (2.10) is often referred to as the Pollaczek–Khintchine (PK) formula.

Automatic assembly station example. Consider an automatic assembly station where all jobs require precisely the same assembly operation to be done, which takes τ time units. There is only one machine at this station and it is jam-free. Assume that the jobs (assemblies) arrive according to a Poisson process with rate λ per unit time. The machine utilization ρ is given by Equation (2.1), and is equal to $\lambda\tau$ (assume <1). As the machine is jam-free, there is no variation in its service time, and hence the service time SCV is zero. The automatic assembly station can be modeled by the M/D/1 queue, and the formula for average waiting time follows from (2.10):

$$W_q = \frac{1}{2}\left(\frac{\tau\rho}{1-\rho}\right) \qquad (\mathrm{M/D/1})\,. \tag{2.11}$$

If we had made the assumption that the service time is exponential (as pointed out earlier, a common assumption) then we would have used equation (2.7) to calculate the average waiting time which yields a value for the waiting time that is exactly twice the value given by Equation (2.11). Hence, an exponential assumption would give rise to 100% error in the value of the waiting time as well as work-in-process (WIP) in this case. Note that the exponential assumption leads to a service time SCV of 1.0. This simple example brings not only the effect of the service-time variability on the waiting time and queue length, but also the need to correctly model the service-time variability.

The GI/G/1 *queue.* In general the GI/G/1 queue, in which the interarrival and service times both have general probability distributions, is very difficult to analyze. Early work on the GI/G/1 queue includes that of Lindley [1952] who published an integral equation for the stationary distribution of the waiting time in queue of an arbitrary customer. However, Lindley's work yielded useful analytical solutions only in some special cases. Over the last twenty-five years considerable effort has been devoted to the development of approximations and inequalities for the GI/G/1 queue. The works of Kingman [1962] and Marshall [1968] laid the foundation for the development of approximations for the GI/G/1 queue. The interested reader is referred to Gelenbe & Pujolle [1987], Kobayashi [1974], Marchal [1985], Reiser & Kobayashi [1974], Shanthikumar & Buzacott [1980], and Tijms [1988] for details regarding various approximations that have been proposed for the GI/G/1 queue.

Next some GI/G/1 approximations that require only the first two moments of the inter-arrival-time and service-time distributions are presented. These two-moment GI/G/1 approximations are proving to be useful in developing analysis methods for networks of queues with general service-time servers [Kuehn, 1979; Whitt, 1983; Kamath, Suri & Sanders, 1988].

The mean arrival rate and the interarrival-time SCV are used to partially characterize the general interarrival-time distribution, while the mean service time and the service time SCV partially specify the service time process. It is assumed that $\rho < 1$. The main congestion measure which is the average waiting time (or delay in queue) is approximated by the simple formula [Kuehn, 1979; Whitt, 1983; Shanthikumar & Buzacott, 1980]:

$$W_q = \left(\frac{c_a^2 + c_s^2}{2}\right)\left(\frac{\tau\rho}{1-\rho}\right) \qquad (\mathrm{GI/G/1})\,. \tag{2.12}$$

The above expression is exact for the M/M/1 and M/G/1 queueing models. When the arrival process is Poisson, that is, the interarrival-time distribution is exponential, $c_a^2 = 1$, then (2.12) reduces to the PK formula (2.10) for the M/G/1 queueing model. If the service time distribution is also exponential, $c_s^2 = 1$ and (2.12) reduces to (2.7) for the M/M/1 model. A refinement of the approximation for W_q developed by Kraemer & Langenbach-Belz [1976] which yields improved approximations especially when $c_a^2 < 1$ is as follows:

$$W_q = g\left(\frac{c_a^2 + c_s^2}{2}\right)\left(\frac{\tau\rho}{1-\rho}\right) \qquad (\mathrm{GI/G/1})\,, \tag{2.13}$$

where $g \equiv g(\rho, c_a^2, c_s^2)$ is defined as

$$g(\rho, c_a^2, c_s^2) = \begin{cases} \exp\left(\dfrac{-2(1-\rho)}{3\rho} \dfrac{(1-c_a^2)^2}{(c_a^2+c_s^2)}\right), & c_a^2 < 1, \\ \exp\left(-(1-\rho) \dfrac{(c_a^2-1)}{(c_a^2+4c_s^2)}\right), & c_a^2 > 1. \end{cases}$$

The factor g tends to be significantly less than 1 when ρ, c_a^2, and c_s^2, are relatively small [Whitt, 1985].

As we will see later in this chapter (Sections 5 and 6), the GI/G/1 queueing model forms the building block in the development of analysis techniques for queueing networks with general service time servers. In a queueing network, the departures from a node or a server often are arrivals to the other nodes in the network. Hence, departure process results for the GI/G/1 queueing model will be useful in deriving information regarding these internal arrival processes. The departure process of a GI/G/1 queue is approximated by a renewal process partially characterized by the first two moments of the interdeparture-time. By flow conservation, the mean of the interdeparture-time is just the mean of the interarrival-time, so that the departure rate equals the arrival rate. The SCV the interdeparture time, c_d^2, is given by

$$c_d^2 = c_a^2 + 2\rho^2 c_s^2 - 2(1-\rho)\lambda W_q \qquad (\text{GI/G/1}). \tag{2.14}$$

This expression is originally due to Marshall [1968].

Kuehn [1979] used formula (2.14) together with the simple approximation for W_q, (2.12), to yield the following approximation for the departure process of a GI/G/1 queue

$$c_d^2 = (1-\rho^2)c_a^2 + \rho^2 c_s^2 \qquad (\text{GI/G/1}). \tag{2.15}$$

The interdeparture-time SCV as given by the above expression is just a convex combination of the interarrival-time SCV and service-time SCV. Under light load conditions (values of server utilization close to zero), Equation (2.15) yields c_d^2 approximately equal to interarrival-time SCV, whereas under heavy load conditions (server utilization close to 1), when the server or machine is almost always busy, Equation (2.15) gives c_d^2 approximately equal to service-time SCV. This intuitively appealing expression was suggested as a direct heuristic by Sevcik, Levy, Tripathi & Zahorjan [1977].

Just-in-time (JIT) example. The following example is from Suri [1988b]. In a flexible workcell consisting of a single robot capable of working on a variety of parts, raw material – at the rate of one lot every H hours – is delivered to the cell on a JIT basis from a neighboring plant. However, because the deliveries are never exactly on time, a standard deviation of S_H hours around the delivery time can be expected. Next, plotting a histogram of the cycle times for the variety of parts the robot will make indicates that the average cycle time for a lot is C hours, and the standard deviation of the cycle times is S_C hours. By using the simple formula (2.12) we can quickly determine a rough-cut answer for the average waiting time for a lot at the cell. (Note: $\lambda = 1/H$, $c_a^2 = (S_H/H)^2$, $\tau = C$, $c_s^2 = (S_C/C)^2$, and $\rho = C/H$.)

$$W_q^{\text{lot}} = \left(\frac{\left(\frac{S_H}{H}\right)^2 + \left(\frac{S_C}{C}\right)^2}{2}\right)\left(\frac{C^2}{H - C}\right).$$

Now, the average lead time for the lot is given by $C + W_q^{\text{lot}}$.

Even the simple approximation presented above can provide insight in the planning of a JIT implementation. Suppose the raw material is delivered once each shift ($H = 8$ hours) and the analysis of part cycle times indicates that $C = 6$ hours and $S_C = 2$ hours. Currently, the plant supplying the raw material does only a fair job of adhering to the eight-hour delivery schedule. Past delivery records indicate that $S_H = 4$ hours. What would the reduction in the lead time be if the material supply could be made more reliable, for instance with only one hour standard deviation ($S_H = 1$ hour)? The prediction is that, because $S_H = 4$ hours, a lead time of roughly 9.25 hours is required for each lot produced by the robot cell. However, if S_H is reduced to 1 hour, the lead time is reduced to approximately 7 hours – an improvement of almost 25%. We have, therefore, been able to quantify the benefit of more reliable supply.

2.2.2. *Multi-server queues*

Multi-server queues are in general more difficult to analyze than their single-server counterparts. In this section we first present the exact formulas for the tractable model of the M/M/m queue and then describe approximations for the GI/G/m queueing model.

The M/M/m *queue*. The commonly used parallel-server single queue model is the M/M/m queue. A detailed analysis of this queue can be found in standard texts on queueing [Gross & Harris, 1985; Kleinrock, 1975; Ross, 1989]. The formulas for the steady-state (congestion) measures for this queue are presented next.

The probability of an empty system is given by

$$p_0 = \left[\sum_{n=0}^{m-1} \frac{(m\rho)^n}{n!} + \frac{(m\rho)^m}{m!(1-\rho)}\right]^{-1} \quad (\text{M/M/}m)\,. \tag{2.16}$$

The probability that there are n jobs in the system is given by

$$p_n = \begin{cases} \dfrac{(m\rho)^n}{n!}\, p_0\,, & 1 \leqslant n \leqslant m \\[2ex] \dfrac{(m\rho)^n}{m^{n-m} m!}\, p_0\,, & n \geqslant m \end{cases} \quad (\text{M/M/}m)\,. \tag{2.17}$$

The average waiting time of jobs is

$$W_q = \left[\frac{\tau(m\rho)^m}{m!(1-\rho)^2} \right] p_0 \qquad (\mathrm{M/M}/m)\,. \tag{2.18}$$

The GI/G/*m queue.* An approximation for the congestion measure, W_q, for the GI/G/m model is obtained by modifying the exact formula for the M/M/m model. Let $W_q^{(\mathrm{M/M}/m)}$ be the mean delay time for the M/M/m queue as given by (2.18). A simple approximation for W_q, in the case of the GI/G/m model is

$$W_q = \left(\frac{c_a^2 + c_s^2}{2} \right) W_q^{(\mathrm{M/M}/m)} \qquad (\mathrm{GI/G}/m)\,. \tag{2.19}$$

This approximation is based on heavy-traffic limit theorems (see [Whitt, 1983] and references therein). For the M/G/m model ($c_a^2 = 1$), (2.19) is known to be usually an excellent approximation [Whitt, 1983]. The approximation can be improved by using a correction factor similar to the factor g for the GI/G/1 queue [see Whitt, 1989]. Other waiting time approximations for this general multi-server queue can be found in Tijms [1988] and Marchal [1985].

The renewal process approximation for the SCV of the interdeparture-time, c_d^2, as given in Whitt [1983] is,

$$c_d^2 = 1 + (1-\rho^2)(c_a^2 - 1) + \frac{\rho^2(c_s^2 - 1)}{\sqrt{m}} \qquad (\mathrm{GI/G}/m)\,. \tag{2.20}$$

For single-server queues, $m = 1$ and (2.20) agrees with (2.15). For the M/M/m queueing model ($c_a^2 = 1$ and $c_s^2 = 1$), (2.18) yields $c_d^2 = 1$. This is indeed true as the departure process is known to be Poisson for the M/M/m queue [Burke, 1956].

2.3. Workcenter with a finite buffer

This section contains results for a workcenter with a finite capacity of N jobs (total of buffer and servers). Since there can be no more than N jobs (or customers) in the system, if an arriving job finds that there are already N jobs in the system, then it does not enter the system. In a manufacturing context if jobs represent production orders then jobs arriving when the system is full are assumed to be lost. On the other hand if jobs represent parts or workpieces coming from other sections of a production line to a workcenter, then the jobs attempting to enter this workcenter when it is full are blocked at the source. In this case, the source or portion of the production line that is attempting to release a job will normally be shut down until the destination workcenter is ready to accept a new job. Analysis of finite capacity systems is important since, such systems are frequently encountered in industry. As in Section 2.2 single-server systems ($m = 1$) are considered separately.

With regard to the congestion measures of the expected time spent by a job in the system or expected waiting time in the buffer, it makes more sense to calculate these for a job that actually entered the system. Hence, while applying Little's formula to finite buffer systems, the arrival rate that should be used is not the mean arrival rate but rather the mean rate of jobs actually entering the system. Let λ_{eff} denote this rate. For a G/G/m/N queue we have

$$L = \lambda_{\text{eff}} W \tag{2.21}$$

and for jobs waiting in the buffer

$$L_q = \lambda_{\text{eff}} W_q \,. \tag{2.22}$$

The mean arrival rate and λ_{eff} are related through the probability that an arriving job sees the system full in steady state. That is,

$$\lambda_{\text{eff}} = \lambda(1 - q_N) \qquad (\text{G/G}/m/N)\,, \tag{2.23}$$

as $(1 - q_N)$ is the fraction of arrivals that actually enter the system. If the arrival process is Poisson, then the arrival time probability $q_N = p_N$, as Poisson arrivals see time averages [Wolff, 1989]. The general relations (2.1) and (2.2) still hold for a G/G/m/N queue, but the load factor ρ defined by (2.1) is not restricted to be less than 1. This is because a finite capacity queueing system is always stable since customers are lost if the limit determined by the total capacity of the system is exceeded. Relation (2.3) needs to be modified as follows:

$$L = L_q + \lambda_{\text{eff}} \tau \qquad (\text{G/G}/m/N)\,. \tag{2.24}$$

2.3.1. Single-server queues with finite capacity

We start this section by presenting exact formulas for the tractable model of the M/M/1/N queue. Next, we briefly discuss the M/G/1/N queue and give some references that contain an analysis of the queueing system.

The M/M/1/N *queue*. This finite capacity queue with Poisson arrivals and exponential servers, can be analyzed easily [see, e.g., Gross & Harris, 1985; Ross, 1989]. The probability that the system is empty in steady state is given by

$$p_0 = \begin{cases} \dfrac{1-\rho}{1-\rho^{N+1}}\,, & \rho \neq 1 \\ \dfrac{1}{N+1}\,, & \rho = 1 \end{cases} \qquad (\text{M/M/1}/N) \tag{2.25}$$

and the probability that the system is full in steady state (or the long-run fraction of arrivals that are rejected) is

$$p_N = \begin{cases} \dfrac{\rho^N(1-\rho)}{1-\rho^{N+1}}, & \rho \neq 1 \\ \dfrac{1}{N+1}, & \rho = 1 \end{cases} \qquad (\mathrm{M/M/1}/N). \tag{2.26}$$

The average number of jobs in the system is given by

$$L = \begin{cases} \dfrac{\rho}{1-\rho} - \dfrac{(N+1)\rho^{N+1}}{1-\rho^{N+1}}, & \rho \neq 1 \\ N/2, & \rho = 1 \end{cases} \qquad (\mathrm{M/M/1}/N). \tag{2.27}$$

The other congestion measures can be readily obtained by the use of Little's formula, general relation (2.2), and

$$\lambda_{\mathrm{eff}} = \begin{cases} \lambda\left(\dfrac{1-\rho^N}{1-\rho^{N+1}}\right), & \rho \neq 1 \\ \lambda\left(\dfrac{N}{N+1}\right), & \rho = 1 \end{cases} \qquad (\mathrm{M/M/1}/N). \tag{2.28}$$

The M/G/1/N *queueing system.* An imbedded Markov chain analysis for this queueing system can be performed in a way similar to that of the unlimited waiting room case. The restriction on the capacity leads to a finite number of steady-state probabilities, p_n. Given the specific service-time distribution, the stationary equation of the imbedded Markov chain can be numerically solved for all the probabilities. These probabilities can then be used to derive the congestion measures. A detailed description of the analysis is contained in Gross & Harris [1985] and Tijms [1988].

2.3.2. Multi-server queues with finite capacity

The M/M/m/N *queue.* This parallel-server exponential model with finite capacity can be analyzed easily and we present below a summary of the results. In the formulas given below, we will assume that $\rho \neq 1$. We start with the steady-state probability of an empty system, which is

$$p_0 = \left[\sum_{n=0}^{m-1} \frac{(m\rho)^n}{n!} + \frac{(m\rho)^m}{m!}\,\frac{(1-\rho^{N-m+1})}{(1-\rho)}\right]^{-1} \qquad (\mathrm{M/M}/m/N). \tag{2.29}$$

The probability that the system is full (or an arriving job is rejected) is given by

$$p_N = p_0\left[\frac{(m\rho)^m}{m!}\,\rho^{N-m}\right] \qquad (\mathrm{M/M}/m/N). \tag{2.30}$$

The average number of jobs waiting in the buffer is

$$L_q = p_0\left(\frac{(m\rho)^m}{m!}\,\frac{\rho}{(1-\rho)^2}\right)(1-\rho^{N-m+1}-(1-\rho)(N-m+1)\rho^{N-m})\,. \tag{2.31}$$

Expressions for other congestion measures can be derived in a straightforward manner using relations (2.21)–(2.24).

The M/G/*m*/*N* *queueing system.* Some approximations for this finite capacity M/G/*m* queueing system are described in Tijms [1988]. For the special case when $N = m$ (that is, no queueing allowed) some exact results are available [Gross & Harris, 1985]. In fact, for the M/G/*m*/*m* queue, the steady-state probabilities are independent of the form of the service-time distribution, i.e., they depend only on the mean service time.

The GI/G/*m*/*N* *queueing system.* For a discussion on some bounds and approximations for this queueing system, and some recent references see Stoyan [1983], Tijms [1988], and Wolff [1989].

2.4. *Finite source queueing models*

We now consider a queueing model where the calling population of jobs is finite, say of size K. A typical application of this queue is the machine–repairman model (see Section 7 for details). In the machine–repairman model, the calling population is the (K) machines, the (m) repairmen are the servers, and an arrival corresponds to a machine breakdown. We present below results only for the exponential machine–repairman model, (M/M/m/ · /K), where the service times of the m servers (or repair times) are exponentially distributed with mean τ, and the time a machine spends working before it breaks down is also exponential with mean $1/\lambda$.

Using standard birth–death theory, the steady-state probabilities can be easily derived [see, e.g., Gross & Harris, 1985] and are

$$p_n = \begin{cases} \binom{K}{n}(\lambda\tau)^n p_0\,, & 0 \leq n < m \\ \binom{K}{n}\dfrac{n!}{m^{n-m}m!}(\lambda\tau)^n p_0\,, & m \leq n \leq K \end{cases} \qquad (\mathrm{M/M}/m/\cdot/K)\,, \tag{2.32}$$

where p_0 is found by equating the sum of the probabilities to 1 and is

$$p_0 = \left[\sum_{n=0}^{m-1}\binom{K}{n}(\lambda\tau)^n + \sum_{n=m}^{K}\binom{K}{n}\frac{n!}{m^{n-m}m!}(\lambda\tau)^n\right]^{-1} \qquad (\mathrm{M/M}/m/\cdot/K)\,. \tag{2.33}$$

The average number of customers in system or machines down for repair can be easily obtained using the definition of expected value as

$$L = \sum_{n=0}^{K} np_n \qquad (\mathrm{M/M}/m/\cdot/K) . \tag{2.34}$$

Additional results for this queueing model and a discussion of other more general machine–repairman models can be found in Section 7.

2.5. Non-FCFS scheduling disciplines

Thus far, in all the workcenter queueing models considered, jobs belong to a single class (that is, are of the same type) and proceed to service on a first-come-first-served (FCFS) basis. In modern production systems such as an FMS, jobs belonging to several classes are simultaneously present in the system [Suri & Hildebrant, 1984]. Furthermore, in several manufacturing applications, job-related priority scheduling schemes have to be devised and implemented in order to provide preferential service to certain classes of jobs. In priority scheduling disciplines, jobs with the highest priorities are selected for processing ahead of those with lower priorities, independent of the time at which they joined the queue. By increasing the priority of a job class, the throughput (manufacturing lead time) of jobs belonging to this class can be increased (reduced). Hence, in production systems, modeling of priority scheduling disciplines is essential when exploring the effects of various product mixes and control strategies.

Priority queues are in general more difficult to model than nonpriority systems. Gross & Harris [1985] state that as long as the scheme of priorities is in no way a function of the relative size of the processing time, then the steady-state probabilities and congestion measures (only average values) are independent of the scheduling discipline. However, several manufacturing scheduling disciplines such as 'the shortest processing time (SPT) rule' depend on service times. The literature on such priority queues and related models is enormous. Gelenbe & Pujolle [1987], Gross & Harris [1985], and Wolff [1989] have results for certain priority models and several references on this topic.

3. Tandem production line

3.1. System definition

We begin by defining a synchronous line as a number of machines connected in series with synchronized part transfer between machines [Leung & Kamath, 1991]. With this, we define a tandem production line as a series arrangement of manufacturing/assembly stages, where each production stage consists of a single machine, several identical machines in parallel, or a synchronous line.

Between each pair of stages is a buffer of a specified size. A job visits all stages sequentially from the first stage to the last with no loops or rework and hence the name, tandem production line. Tandem production lines are also referred to as transfer lines and flow lines in the literature [Buzacott, 1972; Muth, 1979]. As examples of our definition, in the two-stage transfer line considered by Buzacott & Hanifin [1978] and the automatic transfer line modeled by Ohmi [1981], each stage is itself a *synchronous line* and not a single machine or a set of parallel machines.

The particular tandem production line configuration that will be considered in this section is an asynchronous line consisting of a single machine at each stage. The queueing network model is then an open tandem queueing model or a series arrangement of M single server machines (Figure 3.1). The output of machine i ($i = 1, 2, \ldots, M-1$) forms the input of the next machine in line, which is, machine $i+1$. New jobs are processed first by machine 1 and jobs depart from the system after they are processed by machine M. Based on the type of new job input to machine 1, two types of models can be defined. We define a *Type 1* model as one which assumes that the first machine has an inexhaustible supply of new jobs to process. On the other hand, if new jobs arrive from an external source to the first machine (see Figure 3.1), then we will call the model a *Type 2* model. In this case, an infinite input queue is sometimes allowed upstream of the first machine. In both models, there is a finite buffer between two adjacent machines where in-process parts temporarily wait if the downstream machine is busy. An assumption that is always made is that there is unlimited buffer space for the last machine to release its finished jobs.

A machine is said to be *blocked* if it is unable to release the job that it just finished processing, due to unavailability of space in the destination buffer. Blocking reduces the productivity of a manufacturing/assembly system by forcing machines to be idle during the period of time they are blocked. Two common definitions of blocking exist in the literature [Altiok & Stidham, 1982; Suri & Diehl, 1986]. The description above is the definition of what Suri & Diehl [1986] call *transfer-blocking*. In the second case, a machine or server is not allowed to start service until space is available in the destination buffer. Suri & Diehl [1986] call this the *service-blocking* definition. Generally, transfer-blocking is appropriate for models of production lines (hence it is also called *manufacturing blocking*), while service-blocking is appropriate for models of communication networks where the service process involves transmission of data to the destination station (hence the alternative name *communication*

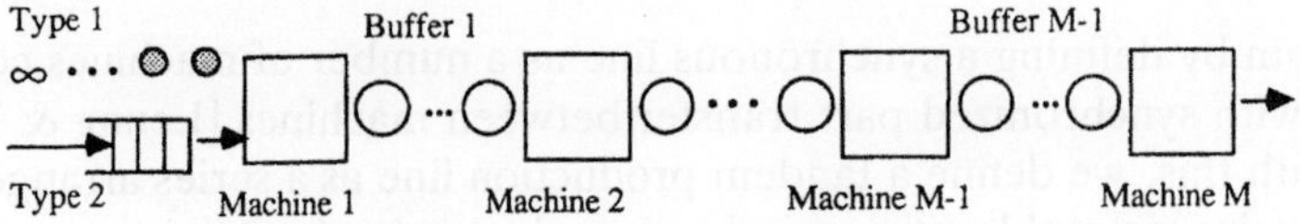

Fig. 3.1. A tandem queueing model.

blocking). Except in special cases, these two definitions of blocking are not equivalent [see Altiok & Stidham, 1982].

The blocking phenomenon makes the solution of such queueing network models nontrivial. In such models, one is interested in determining the effects of service time variability and blocking due to finite buffers on the system performance measures including production rate, work-in-process, and job flow time. The variability of service times can arise from machine breakdowns and repairs in fixed cycle production systems [Buzacott, 1967; Gershwin & Schick, 1983; Gershwin, 1987a,b] or simply from randomness in processing times.

Early works in the analysis of tandem production lines with finite capacity buffers are summarized in a review paper by Koenigsberg [1959]. Although the problem of blocking in such production networks has been studied by researchers for several years, closed form solutions of such models are not available except for a few special cases. If processing times at each machine are assumed to be exponential (or geometric), exact analytical solutions are available only for cases involving a small number of stages and buffers [see, e.g., Gershwin & Berman, 1981; Gershwin & Schick, 1983]. These cases will be discussed in Section 3.2. An important reason for the difficulty in studying models with blocking is the state-space explosion; the number of states grows combinatorially with the number of stages and buffer sizes in the network model [Gershwin, 1987a] and in the exponential/geometric case the resulting Markovian models become intractable. The following is an example of a fixed cycle transfer line from Gershwin [1987a] that shows the great size of the state space even for a system of moderate size.

Consider an M-machine line, where each machine can be in one of two states: operational or failed. Let the capacity of buffer i, the buffer in front of machine $i+1$, be B_i. Buffer i can be in the $B_i + 1$ states, $n_i = 0, 1, 2, \ldots, B_i$, where n_i is the number of jobs in buffer i. A Markov chain representation of the M-machine line with $M - 1$ buffers has a state space of size

$$2^M \prod_{i=1}^{M-1} (B_i + 1) .$$

A 20-machine line with 19 buffers, each of capacity 10 has over 6.41×10^{25} states.

Since an exact analytic solution is difficult to obtain, several approximation methods and numerical techniques have been proposed by researchers for M-stage open tandem queueing models with blocking [Brandwajn & Jow, 1988; Buzacott, 1967; Choong & Gershwin, 1987; Dallery, David & Xie, 1988, 1989; Gershwin, 1987a,b; Perros & Altiok, 1986; Pollack, Birge & Alden, 1985]. More references are contained in a comprehensive bibliography on queueing networks with blocking published by Perros [1984]. Some results on reversibility properties of transfer lines are in Muth [1979] and Yamazaki, Kawashima & Sakasegawa [1985]. The topic of approximations for general finite buffer tandem models is the subject of Section 3.3.

3.2. Solution of two-stage and three-stage transfer lines

3.2.1. Two-stage transfer lines

Based on the review of work on two-stage transfer lines reported in Gershwin & Berman [1981], the two-stage transfer line systems that have been studied and for which results are available can be classified into three main categories.

(i) The processing times at the machines are random and machines do not fail. Most models assume exponential processing times. In this category, both Type 1 and Type 2 models have been considered [see, e.g., Foster & Perros, 1980].

(ii) The second category includes models that assume deterministic processing times, but that allow random machine failures. In other words, this category includes fixed cycle production lines with unreliable machines. Almost all models are Type 1. A majority of the models assume geometrically distributed times to failures and times to repair.

(iii) The third category is one in which machine processing times are random and machines fail randomly. The failure and repair processes are assumed to be exponential. Again a Type 1 model is assumed.

The literature on two-stage models is enormous: the article by Gershwin & Berman [1981] has extensive references. Due to the vastness of literature, only two-stage models belonging to the third category will be described in the remaining part of this subsection. Furthermore, these models seem to be the most general. Such models were studied by Buzacott [1972] and Gershwin & Berman [1981]. In both papers, a continuous time Markov chain was used to represent a two-stage transfer line. The solution of the Markov chain model yielded steady-state system probabilities which were then used to evaluate the measures of performance such as production rate and average in-process inventory.

In Gershwin & Berman's [1981] model (Figure 3.2), the state of the transfer line system is given by the 3-tuple, (n, α_1, α_2), where n, $n = 0, 1, \ldots, B+1$, is the number of jobs in the interstage buffer plus the number of jobs in machine 2 and the binary variable α_i, $i = 1, 2$, is defined to be 1 when machine i is operational and 0 when machine i is failed or under repair. The steady-state probability that the system is in state (n, α_1, α_2) is denoted by $p(n, \alpha_1, \alpha_2)$. The two-stage line is completely characterized by seven parameters, which are, inter-stage buffer size B, machine i mean service time, τ_i, $i = 1, 2$, and the failure and repair rates for machine i, p_i and r_i, $i = 1, 2$, respectively. As stated

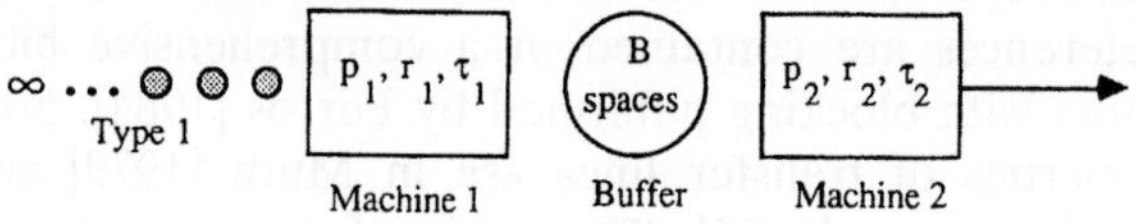

Fig. 3.2. A two-stage transfer line.

before, the service, failure, and repair times are assumed to be exponential. It is also assumed that machines fail only while processing jobs. Machine 1 is *blocked* if it is operational and if there is no room in the buffer to put the finished job. (As Altiok and Stidham [1982] point out, this leads to a service-blocking assumption, which according to them does not seem to represent the physical reality of blocking in production lines.) Machine 2 is *starved* if it is operational and has no jobs to process in the buffer and machine 2. Machine 1 is never starved and machine 2 is never blocked.

Gershwin and Schick then proceed to define the balance equations satisfied by the steady state system probabilities, $p(n, \alpha_1, \alpha_2)$. They present a set of explicit expressions for the probability distribution $p(n, \alpha_1, \alpha_2)$ and outline an algorithm to calculate the same. This distribution is then used in a straightforward manner to calculate the following system performance measures: (i) utilization (efficiency) of machine i which is the long run fraction of time machine i is processing jobs, (ii) production rate of the system, and (iii) average in-process inventory which is the average number of jobs in the buffer plus the average number of jobs in machine 2.

The main difference between Buzacott's model and that of Gershwin and Berman is that in Buzacott's failure model, the probability of failure is independent of the amount of processing time, while in Gershwin and Berman's model, the longer the processing of a job takes, the more likely it is that the machine fails before the processing is complete. In other words, in Buzacott's model, the time between successive breakdowns of a machine, measured in number of job processing cycles completed, has a geometric distribution. In Buzacott & Hanifin's [1978] terminology, Gershwin and Berman model *time dependent failures*, while Buzacott models *operation dependent failures*. Also, Buzacott makes a simplifying assumption that the characteristics of machine 1 and machine 2 are identical. In addition to an exact analysis, Buzacott also presents simple approximations for the two-stage line by combining the results of some previous works. Buzacott & Kostelski [1987] present a recursive solution to this model, based on solutions from Yao & Buzacott [1985c].

3.2.2. *Three-stage transfer lines*

The three-stage transfer line analyzed by Gershwin & Schick [1983] falls into category 2 described in Section 3.2.1. It is a Type 1, fixed production cycle transfer line. All three machines have equal and deterministic processing times. Time is scaled so that a machine cycle takes exactly one time unit. Machines are assumed to have geometrically distributed times between periods of failure and times to repair. For machine i, $i = 1, 2, 3$, the average operating time, expressed in cycles, between failures is $1/p_i$ and the mean time to repair is $1/r_i$ cycles. Machines are assumed to fail only while processing jobs.

Figure 3.3 shows the three-stage transfer line modeled by Gershwin & Schick [1983]. The line parameters are the capacities of the interstage buffers, B_i, $i = 1, 2$, and the failure and repair rates for machine i, p_i and r_i, $i = 1, 2$, and 3,

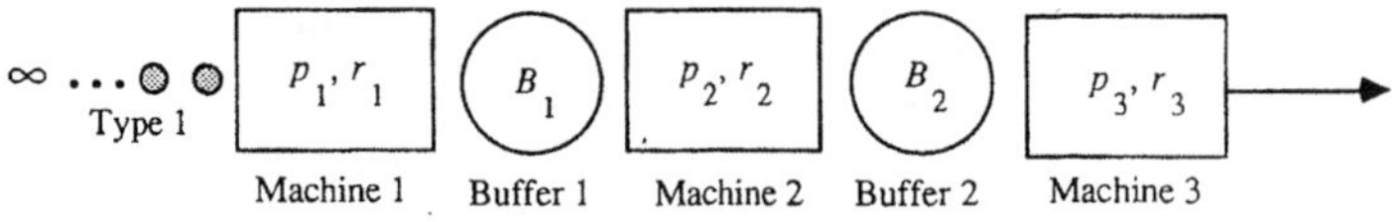

Fig. 3.3. A three-stage transfer line.

respectively. The state of the three-stage line at any time can be completely described by the 5-tuple, $(n_1, n_2, \alpha_1, \alpha_2, \alpha_3)$ where n_i, $0 \leq n_i \leq B_i$, for $i = 1, 2$ is defined to be the number of jobs in buffer i, and α_i, the machine i $(i = 1, 2, 3)$ condition, is defined to be 1 when machine i is operational and 0 when machine i is failed or under repair. The dynamic behavior of the 3-stage line is modeled as a discrete Markov chain and the failure and repair probabilities are used in obtaining the state transition probabilities of the Markov chain. A large portion of Gershwin & Schick [1983] deals with the development of an algorithm for calculating the steady-state probabilities of large scale structured Markov chains such as the one used to model the transfer line.

As in the two-stage case, the steady-state probabilities, $p(n_1, n_2, \alpha_1, \alpha_2, \alpha_3)$, are then used to calculate the following important performance measures: (i) utilization (efficiency) of machine i, which is the steady-state probability that a job emerges from the machine during any given cycle, (ii) production rate of the system (per machine cycle) which is equal to the utilization or efficiency of a machine, since the machine cycles are fixed and equal, and (iii) average level of buffer i. Forced down (starvation and blockage) probabilities and related quantities are also calculated in Gershwin & Schick [1983] and Gershwin [1987a]. In Gershwin & Schick [1983], the authors mention that the algorithm for the solution of the Markov chain model exhibits certain numerical problems for large buffer sizes. This coupled with the large storage and computer time requirements make the method impractical for large buffers. Reliability of the results has been verified for cases with buffer sizes equal to 15. Gershwin and Schick also consider a two-stage line of a similar type.

A three-stage line that falls into category 3 (exponential processing times, exponential failure and repair processes) was analyzed by Altiok & Stidham [1983]. They show that the service completion process at each machine has a phase-type distribution and then proceed to develop a continuous Markov chain model of the three-stage line. A search procedure is also developed to find the allocation of buffer capacities of the three-stage line that maximizes a total profit function.

3.3. *M-machine case – Approximations*

Most decomposition methods used to approximately analyze M-machine lines with finite buffers fall into one of the following two classes.

(i) The behavior of the M-machine line is approximated by the behavior of a set of two-machine lines, so that results available for two-machine lines can be used. The methods developed are based on probability theory and Markov chain theory. In Section 3.3.1 we will discuss Gershwin's decomposition method and its extensions that belong to this set of approximations.

(ii) The second class of approximations decomposes the M-machine line into M single machine (server) lines. That is, the behavior of the tightly coupled (because of finite buffers) system of M single server queues in series, is approximated by the behavior of M single server queues operating independently. The service times for the individual queues are revised to approximately capture the interactions with the neighboring queues in the original M-machine line. The approximation methods in this category use a variety of single server queueing models from an infinite capacity Markovian queue to finite capacity GI/G/1 queueing model. Some of these approximation methods are summarized in Section 3.3.2.

A recent approximation method suggested by Brandwajn & Jow [1988] is similar in spirit to that of Gershwin's. Although their method uses the solution of a two-stage system as a building block, they do not decompose the original line into a set of two-stage lines. Their algorithm proceeds by iterating over pairs of adjacent stations and hence using results available for a two-stage system. In their model, the processing time at a station can have a state-dependent exponential distribution. That is, the mean processing time can depend on the number of jobs present at this station.

3.3.1. Gershwin's decomposition technique

The M-stage transfer line considered by Gershwin [1987a] is identical in characteristics to the three-stage line studied by Gershwin & Schick [1983]. It is a Type 1 fixed cycle line with the fixed processing time same for all machines and which is taken as the time unit. The machines have geometrically distributed working time and repair time distributions. The extension of the method used for the three-stage line to this general case is difficult because of the enormous size of the state space. Exact methods are not available for lines with more than three machines [Gershwin, 1987a]. Hence, Gershwin [1987a] has proposed an approximate decomposition technique.

The basic assumption behind the decomposition technique is that for each buffer in the M-machine line, two hypothetical machines can be described, whose behavior closely models the upstream and downstream part of the line. That is, a single M-machine line is approximated by a set of $(M-1)$ two-machine lines, $L(i)$ for $i = 1, 2, \ldots, M-1$. The buffer in the two-machine line $L(i)$ has the same capacity as the ith buffer in the M-machine line. It is further assumed that the machines in the two-machine lines have geometric working time and repair time distributions. Then for every two-machine line, four parameters must be chosen (two failure rates and two repair rates). These four parameters are chosen so that the performance of the upstream (downstream) machine of the ith two-machine line $L(i)$ closely matches that of the line upstream (downstream) of the buffer i in the original M-machine line. A set of polynomial equations are derived to determine four parameters per two-machine line or a total of $4(M-1)$ parameters. An iterative scheme is used to solve the polynomial equations. Gershwin shows through experimental results that the decomposition technique is very accurate but, he also reports certain convergence problems with the iteration algorithm. Some cases where the algorithm failed to converge contained examples of long lines ($M > 20$). The performance measures of the two-machine lines yield the performance measures of the original M-machine line.

Dallery, David & Xie [1988] proposed a simpler algorithm than that of Gershwin [1987a] to iteratively solve for the parameters of the two-machine lines. Dallery, David and Xie actually replace the original set of polynomial equations by an equivalent one and develop a computationally attractive iterative algorithm to solve the new set of equations. Further, in the cases examined in Dallery, David & Xie [1988], the algorithm always converged.

In another paper, Gershwin [1987b] proposed a method to extend his decomposition method to M-machine lines where machines are allowed to have different processing times. The basic idea is to transform the original line (with different processing times) to a line in which all machine processing times are identical so that the decomposition technique described above can be used for the new line. This is done by replacing every machine but one by a hypothetical two-machine line. The behavior of the resulting line is an approximation of the behavior of the original line. Gershwin [1987b] shows through numerical examples that this method provides good results but again reports some convergence problems. In another article, Choong & Gershwin [1987] adapt Gershwin's [1987a] method to transfer lines with random processing times. The transfer line model analyzed by Choong and Gershwin is an extension of Gershwin & Berman's [1981] two-stage line model with unreliable machines (see Section 3.2.1). A different decomposition approach is in Liu & Buzacott [1989].

Dallery, David & Xie [1989] have developed a new approximation method for analyzing M-machine lines with unreliable machines and finite buffers. They approximate the flow of discrete parts in a transfer line by a *continuous flow*. Their article also contains a review of earlier works on continuous flow modeling of transfer lines. First, they consider a Type 1 fixed cycle line with the fixed processing time same for all machines and where the machine failure and repair times are exponential (a line model similar to that in Gershwin [1987a]). The decomposition method presented is very similar to Gershwin's technique described above. Next, using Gershwin's idea [1987b] they extend their decomposition method to nonhomogeneous lines where machines may have different processing times. Justification for the use of continuous flow models, for performance analysis of discrete lines, is in Alvarez, Dallery & David [1991] and Suri & Fu [1991].

3.3.2. Decomposing the line into individual queues

Early work on this approach includes Hillier & Boling [1967]. Most approximation methods that fall into this category assume exponential processing times. In general, machine failures are not included. The most common assumptions made regarding the arrival of jobs to the first machine and buffer size in front of the first machine are, (i) Poisson arrivals, a finite capacity buffer at the first machine, and jobs arriving when this buffer is full are lost [Altiok, 1982; Perros & Altiok, 1986; Pollock, Birge & Alden, 1985], and (ii) Poisson arrivals and an infinite capacity buffer at the first machine [Foster & Perros, 1980]. The basic assumption behind most approximation methods in this category is that a solution of a model with modified machine service times (modified to handle blocked times approximately) is an approximate solution to the model with blocking.

Altiok [1982] decomposes a finite buffer tandem line with exponential service times into individual finite capacity queues which are analyzed in isolation. The input process to each queue is assumed to be Poisson. In revising the service times it is assumed that each queue can be blocked only by the immediate destination queue, that is, a single queue cannot block more than one upstream queue. The effective service time (actual service time + blocked time) of a machine is approximated by a two-stage Coxian distribution. Each queue is then analyzed as an $M/C_2/1/N$ queue except the last which is analyzed as an $M/M/1/N$ queue. Takahashi, Miyahara & Hasegawa [1980], suggested a similar method for approximately analyzing open queueing networks with finite buffers, Poisson arrivals, and exponential processing times. Perros & Altiok [1986] extend Altiok's [1982] approximation to allow blocking to be backlogged over any number of successive queues. Again, their modified or effective service times have a phase-type or Coxian distribution. The network is decomposed into individual single queueing systems with revised buffer capacities, and modified arrival and service processes. The individual queues are analyzed in isolation and solution is obtained via iteration. They present two cases, one in which the buffer of the first machine is unlimited in size and the other in which it has a finite capacity. Pollock, Birge & Alden [1985] extended this idea of modifying service times to analyze M-machine lines with general processing time distributions at the machines.

4. Tree-structured manufacturing systems (assembly networks)

4.1. System definition; Practical examples

This class of models arises from manufacturing settings where components from the output of two or more processes are required in order for the next process to begin its work. For example, in order for a complete automobile to emerge from the manufacturing operation at some point both an engine and a body must come together to be assembled. The station that performs the engine-body mating process is necessarily dependent on inputs from the engine assembly operations and the body manufacturing facility. Examples of this type are found everywhere because in principle every assembly operation is of this type. Even an operation as simple as inserting a screw in a computer cover depends on a supply of computers (sans screw in the cover) and the supply of screws. The implication is that the assembly operation cannot begin until all required subassemblies or components have arrived. Hence the start time of the assembly operation is often regarded as a random variable which depends on the maximum of the arrival times of the subassemblies or components. Performance analysis of these systems is very difficult analytically. If small buffers (in-process inventories) are added to reduce idle time of the assembly process, then the situation becomes more tractable from a production planning view point but even more problematic analytically. If very large buffer stocks of components are assumed then the assembly process is effectively decoupled from the component production process. In most cases, however, this is an unreasonable assumption and one is forced to deal with the problem in its full complexity.

In major development processes involving the construction (assembly) of complex aircraft, or ships, major subassemblies are themselves the object of development activity and hence the total assembly leadtime of the entire ship or aircraft must necessarily depend on the merging of unique subassemblies. The leadtime models have the same character as project planning models for projects with stochastic activity times. The time frame is considerably longer for these project planning environments than those associated with the usual manufacturing process. In a standard discrete parts manufacturing environment we may consider models which describe many assemblies in various stages of manufacturing and assembly in a network of stations.

Alternatively, the models may describe a network such as the one described above but where the stations consist of two or more merging assembly processes where the feed processes have deterministic cycle times but where the stations are subject to random breakdowns and random repair times. One can obviously complicate this situation by assuming that the cycle times of the feed processes are themselves random.

In these models, questions arise regarding the ideal time between releases of individual jobs or components into the assembly network, estimation of production leadtimes, in-process inventories and station utilizations. In addition, if parts are to be ordered from external vendors, then the problem of setting order times must be considered in the analysis to account for impact of stochastic order leadtimes on the leadtimes of each completed assembly. Generally the use of equilibrium conditions is out of the question in these models since, at least for small lots, the transient response of the network must be incorporated in the models.

4.2. *Solutions and approximations – Infinite buffers*

In this section, we examine a class of manufacturing systems such as those described in the previous section which have the property that repeated merges of sub-assemblies must occur in a timely fashion in order for the next stage of

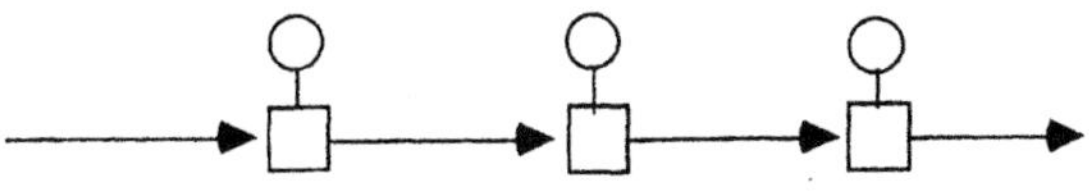

Fig. 4.1. Multi-stage assembly line.

the manufacturing to continue (Figure 4.2). In this section, we further assume that all interstage buffers are large enough to prevent blocking. These systems are most often encountered in assembly applications. However, many of the intermediate steps may require fabrication as well as assembly. As an extreme example of this class of systems we would see the tree stripped of all of its 'branches' and as a consequence we would have an asynchronous flow line where at each node parts buffers are assumed to be sufficiently large to prevent delivery delays (Figure 4.1). In the more general case at each node of the network, delays could be caused in delivery of components from any of the incoming branches.

In early contributions to the modeling of this type of system, Harrison [1973] showed that an assembly station with two input streams whose interarrival times were governed by independent renewal arrival processes and where there is no limit on the number of parts waiting in either queue has the property that the waiting time process does not converge in distribution to a nondefective limit, or in simple terms, there is no equilibrium distribution. This result has implications for analytical modeling since it shows that the simplest model is unreasonable and additional operational assumptions are required. Latouche [1981] showed that if the processes are Poisson and the assembly station has exponential service times then, if the excess number of one type of part over the other is bounded, the waiting time process is stable.

Analytical performance modeling of assembly networks is difficult primarily because in order for an assembly to move through a processing stage one or more additional parts or subassemblies must be present at the same time in order to complete the operation. As a consequence we have the following relationships.

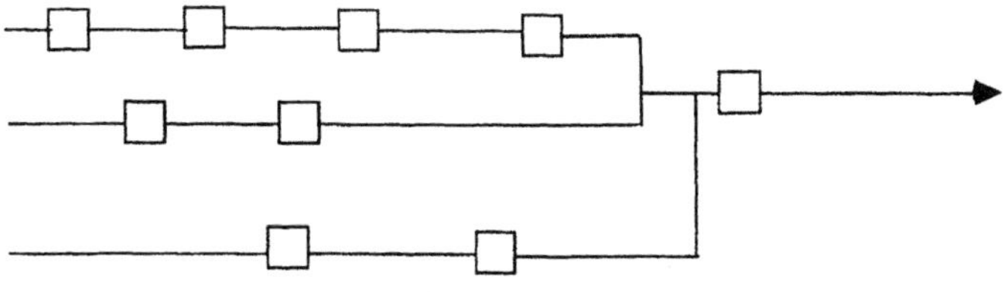

Fig. 4.2. Tree-structured manufacturing system.

In a simple station where (as in Figure 4.1) parts are being added to an assembly we have

$$F_{ij} = S_{ij} + P_{ij} , \tag{4.1}$$

$$S_{ij} = \max(F_{i-1,j}, F_{i,j-1}, A_{ij}) , \tag{4.2}$$

where F_{ij} is the finish time for assembly j at station i, S_{ij} is the start time for assembly j at station i and P_{ij} is the processing time for assembly j at station i. A_{ij} is the time at which the parts for assembly j are available at station i. The formulation presented in (4.1) and (4.2) contrasts with flow line analysis where it is common to assume that parts or components to be added at an individual station are kept there in quantity so that A_{ij} is usually 0. In addition, in most manufacturing systems analysis, the emphasis is on the performance of the total collection or network of assembly or manufacturing stations but in this formulation we are tracking the individual piece or assembly through the network. This particular formulation is appropriate where the manufacturing system is low volume and/or where the final product is large and expensive. This formulation is also appropriate where component and final product delivery leadtimes are of special interest. In more complex networks such as the one depicted in Figure 4.2 the relationship for S_{ij} may be more complex because an operation may require more than one subassembly as well as parts from the station in order to begin the operation at station i.

This formulation is used by Saboo & Wilhelm [1986] – see also Ahmadi-Marandi [1982] – in which a recursive procedure is developed to estimate the mean and the variance of the times at which events take place in the assembly network. All random variables are assumed to be normally distributed (although they may be correlated). Approximations by Clark [1961] are used to obtain the moments of the maximum of two bivariate normal variates.

Specifically, Saboo and Wilhelm begin with the Fundamental Assumption that all operation start and finish times are mutually related by the multivariate normal distribution and that operation times are normally distributed and are mutually independent. If X and Y are normal random variates with parameters (μ_1, σ_1) and (μ_2, σ_2), respectively, and correlation $\rho = r(x, y)$ then the moments $Z = \max(X, Y)$ are given by

$$\begin{aligned} \mathrm{E}[Z] &= \mu_1 \Phi(\alpha) + \mu_2 \Phi(-\alpha) + a\phi(\alpha) , \\ \mathrm{E}[Z^2] &= (\mu_1^2 + \sigma_1^2)\Phi(\alpha) + (\mu_2^2 + \sigma_2^2)\Phi(-\alpha) + (\mu_1 + \mu_2)a\phi(\alpha) , \\ \mathrm{Var}[Z] &= \mathrm{E}[Z^2] - \mathrm{E}^2[Z] , \end{aligned} \tag{4.3}$$

where $a^2 = \sigma_1^2 + \sigma_2^2 - 2\rho\sigma_1\sigma_2$, $\alpha = (\mu_1 - \mu_2)/a$, $\Phi(\alpha)$ = standard normal CDF evaluated at α, and $\phi(\alpha)$ = standard normal PDF evaluated at α.

This procedure is extended to three or more variates via the relation $\max(U, V, W) = \max(U, \max(V, W))$ and hence if $\max(V, W)$ is assumed to be normally distributed, then the moments of $\max(U, V, W)$ can be approximated by using Clark's procedure twice. The correlation $r[U, \max[V, W]]$ is calculated as

$$r[U, \max[V, W]] = \sigma_1 \rho_1 \Phi(\alpha) + \sigma_2 \rho_2 \Phi(-\alpha) / \mathrm{Var}^{1/2}[M] ,$$
$$\text{where } M = \max[V, W] , \ \rho_1 = r[U, V] , \ \rho_2 = r[U, W] . \tag{4.4}$$

These methods are developed into a seven-step procedure by Wilhelm and Ahmadi-Marandi to estimate finish times and leadtimes for assembly networks. The procedure requires the expansion of Equation (4.2) in terms of the properties of earlier operations. All of the moments required to estimate the mean and variance of F_{ij} are known or can be estimated recursively from earlier stages in the system except the correlation coefficient $r = r(F_{i-1,j}, F_{i,j-1})$. All the required moments to estimate r are assumed to be known from the practical context or can be obtained from earlier stages except for $r(F_{i-2,j}, F_{i,j-2})$ and it is assumed that this correlation is associated with random variables that are sufficiently 'remote' that this correlation can be assumed to be zero. Some care must be taken with these procedures because of the number of approximations and assumptions used since they are likely to be useful in 'large' systems where the procedure is applied over and over again in a recursive fashion and as a result errors may cumulate over a large number of stations.

From these estimates, one can derive the estimated completion times (and the variance of the completion times) of assemblies at each stage of the manufacturing process. Further it is possible to set the delivery leadtimes for components (or kits) at each stage of the assembly process in a way that will yield appropriate final product delivery times.

This basic model has been extended in a number of ways by Wilhelm and his coauthors. In Wilhelm [1986a] and Saboo & Wilhelm [1986] considerations of the transient performance of the assembly network, the impact of the spacing of release times of jobs into the network and the impact of vendor leadtime safety margins are incorporated in the analytic models and the results are compared with simulation results. In Wilhelm, Saboo & Johnson [1986] the basic models are extended to incorporate random operation times and the effects of parallel stations. In Wilhelm [1986b] the normality assumptions are extended to consider the lognormal distribution. In Wang & Wilhelm [1985] a set of recursive models are used to extend the analysis to include the effects of finite buffers, routing and sequencing aspects. The accuracy of all of these models are reported by the authors to be excellent and the run time advantages are reported to range from a factor of two up to a factor of 100 faster than the time to obtain the same results from simulation.

4.3. Solutions and approximations – Finite buffers

Hopp & Simon [1989] have examined the case of two 'up-stream' stations feeding a single assembly station AM (see Figure 4.3) with separate buffers $B1$ and $B2$ for parts from the two feed stations $M1$ and $M2$. They assume that the assembly station is never blocked and that the upstream machines continue to work so long as empty space exists in the queues that they feed. The assembly station and the feed stations are all assumed to have exponential service times. They begin by showing this system (shown in Figure 4.3) is equivalent (stochastically) to a three-stage transfer line with finite buffers between the stages. They derive bounds for the average throughput and inventories and they develop a method to approximate the steady-state throughput. They compare the results to earlier work by Lipper & Sengupta [1986]. Their method provides performance bounds and the throughput approximations are claimed to be easier to calculate than the method of Lipper and Sengupta, but the Hopp and Simon results are limited to two input processes. A variation of this system is also analyzed by Flatto & Hahn [1984]. Ammar [1980] analyzes assembly networks with deterministic service times, and finite buffers where the assembly stations are subject to random breakdown with random repair times. Liu & Buzacott [1990] provide approximations and analysis of an automotive assembly system. Buzacott & Shanthikumar [1992b] give a detailed treatment of Flexible Assembly Systems. Gershwin [1991] analyzed assembly/disassembly networks with unreliable machines and finite buffers. Mascolo, David & Dallery [1991] approximate such a system by a continuous flow model.

In summary it appears that, while some progress has been made in this difficult area, a good deal more work is required before routine performance analysis of manufacturing systems with this structure can be undertaken without the aid of simulation tools.

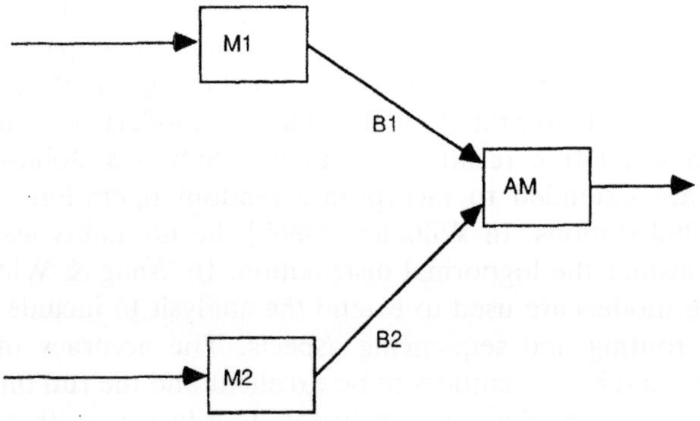

Fig. 4.3.

5. Open networks of queues

5.1. System definition

While open queueing network theory has been applied in a number of practical settings including the analysis of computer systems and telecommunication networks, in manufacturing, perhaps the most common setting for this analysis is the job shop environment. Here the system consists of a number of separate processing departments each involving machines or stations of a certain type and capability. Jobs arrive at random from the environment and each has a given set of processing requirements that specify the routing through the stations which the job must follow. If the distribution of processing times at each station is the same for any possible arriving job then we have a single customer class. If the set of arriving customers can be grouped into classes each of which has its own routing and common distribution of processing times at each station, then we have a multi-class network. Here, as in most production networks, the more important system performance criteria include the leadtime for each job class (mean time in the network), the station utilizations, and the mean work in process for each job class.

5.2. Single class analysis

Among the earliest attempts to provide queueing network models that can be used to analyse job shop environments are the exponential network results of Jackson [1963]. The elegance of the results of this analysis have given rise to a variety of attempts to generalize the results to approximate the behavior of networks of $GI/G/m$ stations where the input process to each station is assumed to be (approximately) a renewal process characterized by the mean and the variance of the interarrival times of customers. The station service times are assumed to have general distributions but are assumed to be characterized by the mean and variance of the service times. Two early papers in this line of research are Reiser & Kobayashi [1974] and Kuehn [1979]. Shanthikumar & Buzacott [1981] were the first to apply this approach to manufacturing job shop control.

Continued work in this area has led to a large volume of papers culminating in a fairly comprehensive paper by Whitt [1983] and in the development of software for routine analysis of open networks, [e.g., Whitt, 1983; Suri, Diehl & Dean, 1986; Bitran & Tirupati, 1988; and Suri & DeTreville, 1991].

5.2.1. Jackson networks and product form

Following Heyman and Sobel [1982] we define a *Jackson network* to be a collection of queues with exponential service times in which the customers travel from node to node according to transition probabilities given by a Markov chain. Specifically the network consists of M service facilities numbered $1, 2, \ldots, M$. We assume that station i contains m_i identical servers,

$m_i \geq 1$. Customers who arrive from outside the network arrive at facility i according to a Poisson process with rate λ_i, $i = 1, 2, \ldots, M$. When a customer receives service at station i it leaves the network with probability p_{i0} or goes immediately to station j with probability p_{ij}, $\Sigma\, p_{ij} = 1$. These transition probabilities are assumed to be independent of past events in the network. Customers are served at each facility according to a FCFS discipline. Service times at each facility i are i.i.d. exponential with mean $1/\mu_i$, $i = 1, 2, \ldots, M$. Visits to successive service facilities are made according to the Markov chain with transition matrix $P = \{p_{ij}\}$ where $p_{00} = 1$ by definition. P is called the routing matrix for the network and the state labeled 0 represents the 'outside'. Define P_0 as the P matrix with row 0 and column 0 removed.

Let a_i represent the asymptotic mean arrival rate at station i. We see that the a_i must satisfy

$$a_i = \lambda_i + \sum_{j=1}^{M} p_{ji} a_j\,, \quad i = 1, 2, \ldots, M\,. \tag{5.1}$$

These equations are called the 'traffic equations'. In vector form we have

$$\boldsymbol{a} = \lambda + \boldsymbol{a}\boldsymbol{P}_0\,,$$

where $\boldsymbol{a} = (a_1, a_2, \ldots, a_M)$, $\lambda = (\lambda_1, \lambda_2, \ldots, \lambda_M)$, and if $1 - p_{i0} \leq 1$ for all $i \neq 0$, then there is a unique solution for $\boldsymbol{a}$ which is nonnegative.

Now due to the Markov properties of the system let $s = (s_1, s_2, \ldots, s_M)$, represent the state of the system where the number of customers at facility i is s_i. Then define $p(s)$ to be the steady-state probability that the system is in state s (assuming that the steady state exists). Then we have the following.

Jackson's Theorem. *If $\rho_i = a_i/(\mu_i m_i) < 1$ for each facility, then $p(s) = \Pi\, p_i(s_i)$, where*

$$p_i(n) = \begin{cases} \dfrac{p_i(0)a_i^n}{\mu_i^n n!} & \text{if } n \leq m_i\,, \\[2ex] \dfrac{p_i(0)a_i^{m_i}\rho_i^{n-m_i}}{\mu_i^{m_i}(m_i)!} & \text{if } n \geq m_i\,, \end{cases} \tag{5.2}$$

where $n = 0, 1, \ldots,$ and $p_i(0)$ is a normalizing constant.

We can see that except for the fact that it was necessary to solve the traffic equations (5.1) for the a_i, Jackson's Theorem effectively decomposes the entire network for us because Equation (5.2) is just the set of steady-state probabilities for an M/M/m_i queue. This network node decomposition allows us to treat each facility as an independent service facility and to use the familiar machinery of M/M/m queues, as in (2.17), to examine the behavior at each facility. (One has to be a bit careful about the use of Jackson's Theorem. It tells us that at a given instant the stationary distribution for the system has the property that the random variables associated with the number of individuals at each of the stations are independent at a given instant of time. It does not say for example that $X_1(t)$ is independent of $X_2(t+1)$ and more specifically it does not say that the waiting times at each of the stations are independent random variables.)

For modeling a network with a single job class this class of models has the great advantage that the analysis is simple and exact (under the assumptions stated). From a manufacturing systems perspective, however, it has some drawbacks. Specifically, the assumption of exponential service time at each station is almost always violated in a manufacturing environment. Since for an exponential distribution, the service time distribution at a station is completely captured by a single parameter (the mean service time) there is no way to incorporate information about the variance of the service time in the model. In addition, as noted above, the waiting times at each station are correlated in the general case and the obvious estimates (expected time in station multiplied by the expected number of visits to the station) of expected flow times that are provided by Jackson network models can be in error by 40% or more.

If the correlations between waiting times at each pair of stations can be neglected, we can obtain the estimated mean flow time in the network from the following procedure (see Shanthikumar & Buzacott [1984] for an examination of this procedure). Since the entire network is decomposed into sets of M/M/m queues with known arrival and mean service times for each station we can calculate a vector $\boldsymbol{W}$ which contains the mean time spent at each station directly from the individual station models. From this we can obtain the total expected system leadtime for customers that begin their first service at each of the possible stations in the network by calculating the vector

$$\boldsymbol{T} = [\boldsymbol{I} - \boldsymbol{P}_0]^{-1}\boldsymbol{W} . \tag{5.3}$$

The matrix $N = [\boldsymbol{I} - \boldsymbol{P}_0]^{-1}$ is known as the 'fundamental' matrix and the typical element from this matrix, say n_{ij}, can be shown to be the expected number of visits to station j by a customer who enters the system at station i before that customer exits the system. As a consequence, T_i is the total expected time in the system for a job that begins its stay in the network at station i.

Station utilizations and other station performance measures such as expected queue lengths can be obtained from the formulas provided in Section 2.

5.2.2. Node decomposition for networks of GI/G/m *queues*

In the case of networks of more general stations or facilities where one cannot assure the conditions of Poisson arrival streams and exponential service times the problem is naturally much more complex and no general exact network theory exists. However one may effect an approximate network decomposition composed of a set of facility models which are approximate

GI/G/m models linked together by sets of traffic equations similar to those required for Jackson networks.

As in the section above, we will confine our attention to the open network case (closed network examples will be treated in Section 6). We will assume (following Whitt [1983]) that all of the assumptions required by Jackson networks are satisfied except those related to the distributions of service times and interarrival times. We will also use the notation of the previous section except when additional parameters are required by the distributional assumptions.

Customers who arrive from outside the network arrive at facility i according to a renewal process with mean rate λ_{oi}, $i = 1, 2, \ldots, M$. Service times at each facility i are i.i.d. with mean $1/\mu_i$, $i = 1, 2, \ldots, M$.

In addition we require c_{oj}^2, c_{sj}^2 for each facility j in the network where these parameters represent respectively the squared coefficient of variation of the interarrival times for station j for arrivals from outside the network and the squared coefficient of variation of the service times of servers at station j. We also need the number of service channels m_j at station j and the mean service rate μ_j for servers at station j. Hence each station can now be described by the parameters $\{c_{oj}^2, c_{sj}^2, \lambda_{oj}, \mu_j, m_j\}$. From these parameters we can obtain the input–output characteristics of each facility and EW, the expected steady-state response time for each facility.

5.2.2.1. An overview of the analysis process. In most regards, the approximate decomposition analysis of networks of GI/G/m queues proceeds along the same lines as the analysis of Jackson networks. Some obvious extensions are required. Since both arrival and departure processes are assumed to be (approximately) renewal processes we require methods for estimating the parameters (mean and variance of interevent times) of processes that are formed by merging other renewal processes and we need to be able to estimate the parameters of processes that are obtained by splitting renewal processes. Finally since we will be using both the mean and the variance (or the coefficient of variation) of each random process in the system we will obtain not only the traffic equations of Jackson networks that estimate the composite mean arrival rates to each station but a second set of equations that will be solved to provide the variability of the arrival process to each station. We will take these issues up in order in the following three sections.

5.2.2.2. Merging of arrival streams. If the arrival stream to a facility is made up of the merging of a series of k streams each with arrival rate λ_i, $i = 1, \ldots, k$, then we need to calculate the arrival rate λ and the squared coefficient of variation of interarrival times c^2 for the merged stream.

Clearly the composite mean arrival rate is $\lambda = \Sigma\, \lambda_i$.

The value of c^2 is approximated by

$$c^2 = w \sum_i \left(\lambda_i \Big/ \sum_i \lambda_i\right) c_i^2 + 1 - w\,, \tag{5.4}$$

where $w = [1 + 4(1-\rho)^2(\nu - 1)]^{-1}$, $\nu = [\Sigma_i (\lambda_i/\Sigma_k \lambda_k)^2]^{-1}$, c_i^2 is the squared coefficient of variation of interarrival times for stream i, and ρ is the load factor of the station to which the streams are arriving.

These approximations are based on an extensive series of investigations undertaken by Albin [1982] and Whitt [1982] and are the result of forming a convex linear combination of two separate approximation methods referred to as the Stationary Interval method and the Asymptotic Method. Whitt [1983] has further simplified these approximations to obtain the equations above which are linear in the component c_i^2.

5.2.2.3. Splitting of departure streams. If a departure stream with interdeparture process coefficient of variation c^2 from a facility is split into k streams of customers where customers go to stream i with probability p_i then the coefficient of variation of stream i is

$$c_i^2 = p_i c^2 + 1 - p_i\,. \tag{5.5}$$

This result is exact when the departure process is renewal and the p_i's represent independent events (Markov routing). The mean flow rate in stream i is clearly λp_i where λ is the mean arrival rate of the original arrival stream to the station.

5.2.2.4. Departures. If a facility is not saturated (i.e., $\rho < 1$) and it is in steady state, then the mean input rate is equal to the mean output rate. Consequently the mean interdischarge time is known when the mean input rate is known. The variance of the interdischarge time however is not so easy to obtain. Whitt [1983] uses the following approximate expression for the coefficient of variation of the interdeparture times of GI/G/m facilities:

$$c_d^2 = 1 + (1-\rho^2)(c_a^2 - 1) + \frac{\rho^2}{\sqrt{m}}(c_s^2 - 1)\,. \tag{5.6}$$

This reduces to $c_d^2 = (1-\rho^2)c_a^2 + \rho^2 c_s^2$ for the GI/G/1 queue and the reader may refer to Section 2 for the origin of these approximations.

5.2.2.5. Traffic and traffic variability equations. If one uses all of these relations given above plus the knowledge that customers cannot be created or destroyed in the network then one can obtain two sets of simultaneous linear equations to be solved respectively for the internal traffic (arrival) rates λ_i and the internal traffic variability coefficients c_{ai}^2. Specifically we have

$$\lambda = \lambda_0(I - P_0)^{-1}\,, \tag{5.7}$$

where λ_0 is the vector of external arrival rates, λ is the vector of composite arrival rates and P_0 as before is the routing matrix.

The squared coefficient of variation of composite arrival process at each station is obtained from the following equations:

$$c_{aj}^2 = a_j + \sum_{i=1}^{M} c_{ai}^2 b_{ij} , \tag{5.8a}$$

where

$$a_j = 1 + w_j\Big[(q_{0j}^2 c_{0j}^2 - 1) + \sum_{i=1}^{M} q_{ij}[(1 - p_{ij}) + p_{ij}\rho_i^2 x_i]\Big] , \tag{5.8b}$$

$$b_{ij} = w_j p_{ij} q_{ij}(1 - \rho_i^2) , \tag{5.8c}$$

and where

$$q_{ij} = (\lambda_i/\lambda_j)p_{ij} ,$$

$$x_i = 1 + m_i^{-0.5}(\max[c_{si}^2, 0.2] - 1) , \qquad \nu_j = \Big[\sum_{i=0}^{M} q_{ij}^2\Big]^{-1} ,$$

$$w_j = [1 + 4(1 - \rho_j)^2(\nu_j - 1)]^{-1} .$$

At this point we have all of the building blocks to completely analyse a single class open network of queues (subject to the assumptions given in the beginning of the section).

The mean and coefficient of variation of both the interarrival times and the station service times are now known and by assuming each station to be a GI/G/m queue, one can calculate all of the usual queueing information for each station (such as mean total time in station, mean number in the queue, mean number in station, busy and idle probabilities etc., see Section 2.2.2). Using the routing matrix P_0 one can calculate total expected time in system, expected total number of customers in the system etc.

5.3. Multiple class analysis

5.3.1. Product form networks

Perhaps the most comprehensive reference on the exact analysis of product form networks is the paper of Baskett, Chandy, Muntz & Palacios [1975] which considers an extremely broad class of such systems encompassing open, closed, and mixed networks with both a single customer class and multiple customer classes. They examine four classes of stations that incorporate cases of first-come-first-served, last-come-first-served, processor sharing and preemptive-resume service disciplines. They examine cases involving state-dependent arrival and service rates as well as service time distributions that generalize the standard exponential assumptions to include service time distributions that have rational Laplace transforms. It should be noted that not all possible combinations of these generalizations are analyzed. In fact, for stations where the service discipline is FCFS the service time of all jobs must have an exponential distribution that is identical for all job types, hence multiclass FCFS networks cannot be handled with the analysis approach of the article. Nevertheless some very complex multiclass networks can be analyzed and perhaps the principal result of the paper is that for a broad range of systems the equilibrium state probabilities can be written as a 'product form'

$$P(s) = Cd(s)f_1(x_1)\cdots f_N(x_N)\,,$$

where C is a normalization constant, d is a constant that depends on the state s, f_i is a function that depends on the type of station (one of four possible types) identified as station i, and x_i is a state vector describing the state of station i. The explicit form of the f functions is given for all of the four admissable station classes. The numerical values of the parameters in the equilibrium probabilities must be obtained either by solving the standard equilibrium equations or by formulating a somewhat simpler set of balance equations referred to as the 'independent balance equations'. Formulating and solving these equations directly can be a formidable task. This problem and the restriction to single customer classes for FCFS stations makes this approach of somewhat limited value for manufacturing systems.

5.3.2. Non-product form networks

Whitt [1983] provides an approximate analysis of multiple customer class queueing networks in the form of an input aggregation which he calls 'inputs by classes and routes'. Each customer class is assumed to have its own route through the network and that route is assumed to be deterministic. Each class may have its own service rate at each station. This set of information is converted into the parameters of a single aggregate customer class and the analysis requirement is effectively reduced to that of the previous section. Once the aggregate network has been analyzed then individual customer classes can be segregated and congestion measures and response times for each individual class can be extracted from the aggregate network performance.

Bitran & Tirupati [1988] have developed an improved approach to estimating the interaction between classes in estimating EW for multiple class network problems. Once again they assume deterministic routing but they do not aggregate the arrival and service time parameters in the same way as Whitt. They split the analysis at a station of the network into calculations for a single product (say product i) and they accumulate the properties of the remaining products into a single aggregate product. As a result they derive an improved expression for the coefficient of variation of the departure stream from each station. They show that this new approximation provides an improvement over Whitt's method and they show that it leads to improved systems analysis performance for the network parameters. Results are given for 10 different network examples with 13 stations and 10 products each. Comparison with simulation results show that the improved approximation yields estimates of the total number of jobs in the network that average within 5% of the simulation results for all 10 examples when compared to average errors of the order of 20% + using Whitt's analysis. They also provide further improvements that use Erlang rather than Poisson interarrival assumptions at each station. These more general assumptions result in better accuracy, albeit at the cost of more complex formulae. In Bitran & Tirupati [1991] they extend their approach to allow overtime at stations.

Harrison & Nguyen [1990] have developed an entirely different approach to modeling of open queueing networks which is based on heavy traffic limits of (multiclass) single server stations [see Reiman, 1984]. These approximations are based on diffusion approximations and their associated reflected Brownian motion processes. The modeling process is again based on two moment approximations but the machinery is quite different than the usual queueing network formulas. The equilibrium distribution for W, the total time in the system is obtained by solving partial differential equations associated with what is called the Basic Adjoint Relation. They report success only with one- and two-dimensional systems to date but the results for this approach, called Q-Net, is really quite good even for systems where the heavy traffic assumptions are not met. In the case of higher dimensional systems a product form assumption is inserted and the resultant approach is referred to as Π-Net. This seems to produce equations for most networks that are fairly similar to those found in QNA. In fact, QNA often produces better results than the Π-Net models on the examples provided in the paper. Wein [1990a,b] has applied this class of analysis to the consideration of optimal scheduling of stations in some simple (two station) multiclass queueing networks. The results obtained outperform standard scheduling rules such as SPT and FCFS by performance margins of 30% or more in the examples provided. More complex networks are analyzed in Wein [1991]. Analysis of networks of infinite server stations is in Glynn & Whitt [1991]. Sojourn time distributions are approximated in Fleming & Simon [1991].

This very general approach to the analysis of queueing networks appears to be quite promising because of the ease with which it can handle multiple classes of customers and general routing assumptions. However, because of the complexity associated with solving the partial differential equations associated with the Q-Net approach it does not yet appear to be a practical tool for manufacturing systems problems. It remains to be seen whether the approximate method (Π-Net) offers fundamental advantages that are not found in the more classical approaches described earlier.

5.4. *Applications to manufacturing systems*

As reviewed by Koenigsberg [1982], some of the earliest work on queueing networks arose from attempts to provide analytic formulas that would predict the performance of manufacturing systems, such as the work of Jackson [1963] for job shops. Many of the advances in queueing network theory and algorithms then took place in the context of computer systems performance modeling. However, the 1980s saw a resurgence in manufacturing modeling using queueing network models. In the context of open networks, fundamental developments include those by Buzacott [1982], Shanthikumar & Buzacott [1981], who model dynamic job shops, and Buzacott & Shanthikumar [1985] who extend such models to shops with SPF (shortest processing time) service discipline. Yao & Buzacott [1985b] further extend the models to the situation where waiting areas are limited. Karmarkar [1987] uses a simple model to provide insight on lot sizing and lead time issues in job shops; more complex cases are analyzed in Karmarkar, Kekre & Kekre [1985a], Zipkin [1986], and Calabrese & Hausmann [1991].

Case studies documenting the use of open network models in manufacturing also began to appear more frequently in the late 1980s [e.g., Chen, Harrison, Mandelbaum, Van Ackere & Wein, 1988], particularly with the availability of commercially supported software packages such as QNA [Whitt, 1983], ManuPlan [Suri, Diehl & Dean, 1986] and MPX [Suri & DeTreville, 1991], along with their PC-based versions [Suri, Tomsicek & Derleth, 1990; Suri & DeTreville, 1992]. In fact, it can now be said that queueing network analysis has found its way out of the academic/research environment into the mainstream of manufacturing analysis. We find, for instance, applications at major corporations such as Alcoa [Nymon, 1987], Digital Equipment [Harper & O'Loughlin, 1987], IBM [Dietrich & March, 1985; Brown, 1988], Kodak [Karmarkar, Kekre, Kekre & Freeman, 1985b], Pratt & Whitney [Suri, 1988b], and Siemens [Anderson, 1987], as well as at many smaller firms [Suri, 1989b; DeTreville, 1991]. Indeed, Suri [1989b] and Suri & DeTreville [1992] explain why, in the competitive context of modern manufacturing, the use of queueing network analysis assumes strategic importance in manufacturing decision-making, and they document this with several industrial case studies.

6. Closed networks of queues

6.1. System definition

A closed network is one where the number of jobs of each class present in the network is fixed. Typically in such a model, one of the stations is a 'load/unload' station: when a job arrives at that station it is removed from the network and another job of the same class is entered in its place. Thus the time for a particular job to return to this station is its flow time, and the production rate of this station models the throughput of the network. Such a model can represent a flexible manufacturing system (FMS) or automatic assembly system where parts require specific fixtures or pallets before they can be put into the manufacturing system, and the fixed number of jobs in the network models the limited number of pallets/fixtures.

As an example, consider the FMS in Figure 6.1. This consists of a load/unload station and several numerically controlled machines, all linked by an automated material handling system. Workpieces are mounted on fixtures and placed on pallets at the load/unload station. The material handling system can transport workpieces from machine to machine, in any desired sequence. When the required operations have been completed, the workpiece is returned to the load/unload station. Thus an FMS can be considered as an automated job shop. If the system is operated such that, whenever a workpiece is dismounted at the unload station, another workpiece is mounted in its place, then the number of workpieces in the system remains fixed and we can represent the FMS by a closed queueing network model. A great deal of the manufacturing-related work on closed networks was stimulated by the performance analysis of FMSs [e.g., Solberg, 1977]. Although specific context-related references will follow in this section, some general references on FMS modeling, which themselves contain further references, are Buzacott & Yao [1986], Choobineh & Suri [1986], Seidmann, Schweitzer & Shalev-Oren [1987], and Stecke & Suri [1985, 1986, 1988, 1989].

If we wish to represent different types of fixtures for different part types, we can enhance the above-described model by using multiple classes; this will be discussed later in the section. However, throughout this section we will assume that the buffer sizes at all stations equal or exceed the number of jobs in the network, so that there is no blocking; models with blocking will be considered in Section 8.

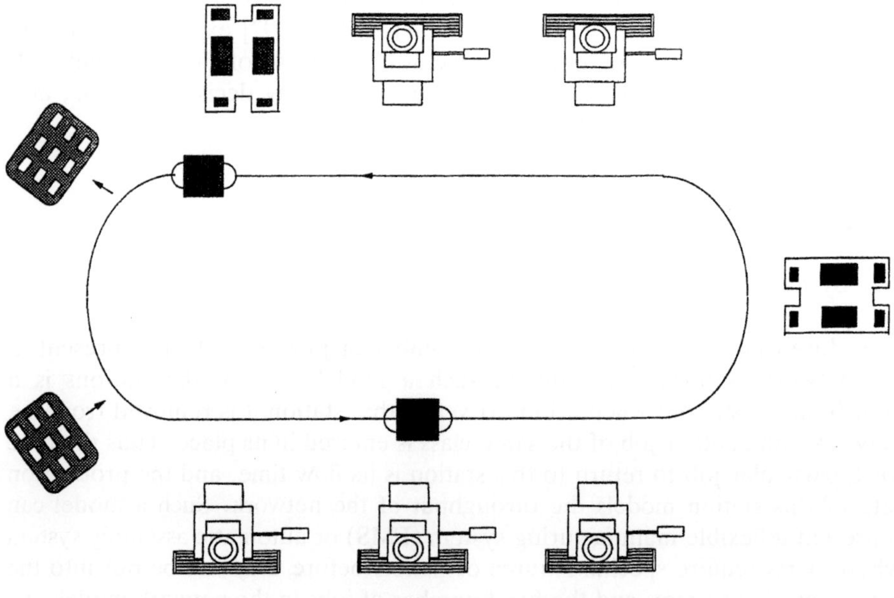

Fig. 6.1. Flexible manufacturing system.

6.2. Single class analysis

6.2.1. Systems with exponential service times

The simplest case of a closed network model is a single class model similar to the open Jackson network described in Section 5. It is assumed that all stations have exponentially distributed service times. The service discipline is FCFS everywhere. It is also assumed that after finishing service at station i, jobs go to station j with probability p_{ij}. Finally, instead of having a vector of arrival rates (λ_i) from external sources as in the open model, here we are given the value of N = number of circulating jobs. Thus the given parameters for this network are:

M = number of stations,
m_i = number of servers at station i,
N = number of jobs in the network,
τ_i = mean service time of a job at station i,
p_{ij} = probability that a job goes from station i to station j.

A slightly more general model is obtained by allowing the service *rate* parameter of the exponential distribution to depend on the number of jobs present at the station. In this case, instead of the parameters m_i and τ_i above, we are given α_{ni} = the service rate of station i when n jobs are present. Such a station is called a *load-dependent server*. The first model is a subset of this one, since we can represent a multiple server station simply by assigning $\alpha_{ni} = n/\tau_i$ for $n \leq m_i$ and $\alpha_{ni} = m_i/\tau_i$ for $n > m_i$. We will begin here by considering the case where there is only one server at each station, and return to the general model later.

Because the number of jobs is fixed, this network is always stable. As in the open network, let $\boldsymbol{n} = (n_1, n_2, \ldots, n_M)$ denote the state of the network, where n_i = number of jobs present at station i. We will only consider the steady state performance measures for this network, the main ones being:

ρ_i = utilization of a server at station i,
a_i = production rate (rate of completion of jobs) at station i,
L_i = average number of jobs present at station i,
W_i = average time spent by a job (waiting and service) per visit to station i,
$P(\boldsymbol{n})$ = probability that the state of the network is $\boldsymbol{n}$,
P_{ni} = probability that there are n jobs at station i.

In addition, two important performance measures result from identifying the load/unload station, say station 0.

X_0 = system throughput ($=a_0$ from above),
W = average time spent in the system by a job.

From the definitions above, we see that W equals the average time between returns to station 0. Since there are no external arrivals and the system is stable, the production rate at each station equals the arrival rate to it, and so, analogous to the open network case, from simple flow conservation considerations we get the following set of traffic equations:

$$a_i = \sum_{j=1}^{M} p_{ji} a_j \,. \tag{6.1}$$

Now however, without the λ_i values which were known and appeared in the equations for the open network, Equations (6.1) only determine the relative values of the a_i and so the actual value of the system throughput needs to be determined by additional analysis. Such a network was analyzed by Gordon & Newell [1967a] who derived the analytic form of the joint probability distribution for the number of jobs at each station, and showed that it too has a product form:

$$P(\boldsymbol{n}) = \frac{1}{G} \prod_{i=1}^{M} (y_i)^{n_i} \,, \tag{6.2}$$

where

$$\begin{aligned} y_i &= v_i \tau_i \,, \\ v_i &= \text{any set of values satisfying (6.1)} \,, \\ G &= \text{a normalization constant (see below)} \,. \end{aligned} \tag{6.3}$$

The normalization constant is defined by requiring the probabilities of all possible states to sum to unity. Although the above holds for any set of values v_i which satisfy (6.1) – since the relative magnitude of the v_i values is offset by the magnitude of the resulting normalization constant – for the manufacturing case it is useful to define v_i by $a_i = v_i X_0$, so that $v_0 = 1$ (i.e., for the load/unload station). The v_i are called *visit ratios*. They can be interpreted as the average number of visits to station i by each new job. Now, provided the matrix of routing probabilities defines an irreducible chain, solution of the resulting equations

$$v_i = \sum_{j=1}^{M} p_{ji} v_j \quad \text{for } i \neq 0 \,, \qquad v_0 = 1 \tag{6.4}$$

provides a set of unique values for the v_i. In principle, we could now compute the value of G and then compute relevant performance measures from the $P(\boldsymbol{n})$ values.

However, computation of the normalization constant apparently requires summing over all possible system states. Since the number of states equals $\binom{M+N-1}{N}$ this would appear to require a great deal of computational effort even for moderately sized networks. Thus, even after the discovery of the product form solution, the practical usage of closed network models remained severely limited until the development of efficient computational algorithms.

6.2.2. *Computational algorithms*

6.2.2.1. Convolution. The development of computational algorithms for closed queueing networks was initiated by Buzen [1973]. From the discussion surrounding (6.2) we see that

$$G = \sum_{n \in S(N,M)} \prod_{i=1}^{M} (y_i)^{n_i}, \tag{6.5}$$

where

$$S(N, M) = \left\{ \boldsymbol{n} \mid \sum_{i=1}^{M} n_i = N \text{ and } n_i \geq 0 \ \forall i \right\}.$$

Buzen defined the quantities

$$g(n, m) = \sum_{n \in S(n,m)} \prod_{i=1}^{m} (y_i)^{n_i} \tag{6.6}$$

and

$$G(n) = g(n, M).$$

Note that with these definitions, the normalization constant G equals $G(N)$. Buzen then showed that the $g(n, m)$ values could be computed by a simple recursion, namely

$$\begin{aligned} &g(n, m) = g(n, m-1) + y_m g(n-1, m) \quad \text{for } m > 1 \text{ and } n > 0, \\ &g(n, 1) = y_1^n \quad \text{for } n = 0, 1, \ldots, N, \\ &g(0, m) = 1 \quad \text{for } m = 1, 2, \ldots, M. \end{aligned} \tag{6.7}$$

Thus for the network with all single server stations, G can be computed extremely efficiently in $O(NM)$ operations, by an easily implemented algorithm. Buzen further showed that many of the common performance measures are simple functions of the values computed during the recursion. For instance,

$$\begin{aligned} &X_0 = \frac{G(N-1)}{G(N)}, \\ &\rho_i = y_i X_0, \\ &P_{ni} = y_i^n \frac{G(N-n) - y_i G(N-n-1)}{G(N)}. \end{aligned} \tag{6.8}$$

Buzen [1973] also generalized the computation of G and the performance measures for the load-dependent case. The details are omitted here, but we note that the computational effort is just $O(NM^2)$ and that algorithm is also easy to implement. Buzen's algorithms are also known as *convolution* algorithms because the steps can be interpreted as the convolution of probability distributions. With the development of these convolution algorithms the popularity of closed network models increased significantly, particularly for computer systems modeling (e.g., see Spragins [1980] and that entire issue of *IEEE Computer*). Along with this increased usage came development of alternative computational algorithms as well as algorithms for more complex models. Both these topics will be covered in sections below.

Example. An example of a manufacturing modeling tool based on the above network model, which uses the Buzen algorithm, is CAN-Q [Solberg, 1977]. This tool is most suited to evaluate FMS configurations, although some applications to other manufacturing systems are also reported. CAN-Q provides quick estimates of performance measures such as throughput and utilizations, and can even be implemented on a hand calculator. Although the early developments of computational algorithms for closed networks occurred in the computer systems modeling community, Solberg's work on CAN-Q can also be viewed as one of the pioneering efforts since it spurred the study of computational algorithms by the manufacturing modeling community. These enhanced the modeling capabilities for manufacturing applications and are described in sections below.

6.2.2.2. Mean value analysis. Although the convolution algorithm is simple and efficient, it does suffer from some numerical problems – since it uses sums of quantities raised to high powers, it can result in 'floating point overflow' or 'underflow' problems during the computations. In fact, this can be easily seen by subjecting a tool such as CAN-Q to extreme cases (e.g., systems with large N and high utilizations). Several 'renormalization' methods are available to correct the numerical behavior of the algorithm, but they result in a more complex implementation. A second, more fundamental impediment to the use of convolution algorithm is that it does not lend itself naturally to heuristic extensions for more general system models. Both these shortcomings are addressed by an alternative approach termed *mean value analysis* (MVA) developed by Reiser & Lavenberg [1980]. Although their development was for multiclass networks, we will first describe it for the single class network with single-server stations.

The starting point for MVA is the proof of the relation

$$W_i(N) = \tau_i + L_i(N-1)\tau_i\,, \quad i = 1, \ldots, M\,, \tag{6.9}$$

where $W_i(n)$ denotes the value of the measure W_i in a network with n circulating jobs (and similarly for other measures).

This equation has an appealing interpretation. To see this, note that the total time a job spends at a station (on average) is comprised of its own service time – the first term on the RHS of (6.9) – plus its waiting time. Thus the term $L_i(N-1)\tau_i$ must be the average waiting time. Due to the memoryless property of the exponential distribution, this means that the average number of jobs ahead of an arriving job is $L_i(N-1)$ – which equals the mean number of jobs present at that station for a network with $N-1$ jobs on it. Thus (6.9) can be interpreted as saying that a job circulating in the network 'sees' a network in equilibrium with itself removed. This result is also known as the arrival theorem [Sevcik & Mitrani, 1979].

The relation (6.9) allows the development of an efficient computational algorithm. Suppose we have computed the values of $L_i(N-1)$, for $i = 1, \ldots, M$. Then we can obtain the values of $L_i(N)$, $i = 1, \ldots, M$, as follows. First we calculate $W_i(N)$ $i = 1, \ldots, M$, from (6.9). Next, by Little's Law applied to the whole network, we have

$$X_0(N) = N \Big/ \sum_{i=1}^{M} v_i W_i(N)\,, \tag{6.10}$$

where the v_i values are obtained as before, from (6.4). Finally, applying Little's Law to each station gives

$$L_i(N) = X_0(N) v_i W_i(N)\,, \quad i = 1, \ldots, M\,. \tag{6.11}$$

Thus we have a way of computing the values $L_i(N)$ given those of $L_i(N-1)$. In order to start this recursion, we only need to note the trivial relation

$$L_i(0) = 0\,, \quad i = 1, \ldots, M\,. \tag{6.12}$$

Starting with this set of values, we can use Equation (6.9), (6.10) and (6.11) to calculate $L_i(1), L_i(2), \ldots, L_i(N)$. Since each step involves $O(M)$ operations, the whole algorithm takes $O(NM)$ operations. At the end of the algorithm we obtain three of the main performance measures, namely X_0, L_i, and ρ_i (which equals $\nu_i \tau_i X_0$, see (6.8) and (6.3)). As can be seen from the form of the three equations used in the iterations, this algorithm is likely to have good numerical properties. However, it only provides the three performance measures stated.

To obtain more detailed performance measures, such as P_{ni}, and/or to analyze load-dependent stations, more elaborate forms of MVA are given in Reiser & Lavenberg [1980] and Reiser [1981]. These involve an iteration on certain marginal probabilities – the $P_{ni}(N)$ values are derived from $P_{ni}(N-1)$. Here there is a greater possibility of numerical problems, but a simple 'renormalization' procedure can be included in each step of these algorithms.

6.2.2.3. Additional developments. Since the introduction of the two basic methods for computing performance measures, namely convolution and MVA, there has been a good deal of research on additional algorithms. This was motivated primarily by the need to find more efficient methods for networks with multiple classes of customers. We will therefore defer discussion on these developments to the section on multiclass networks.

6.2.3. Approximations for non-exponential distributions

6.2.3.1. Flow-equivalence, aggregation, and decomposition. For networks with non-exponential service times, most of the approximations available are based on variations of the 'flow equivalent' approach, which is also related to the terms 'aggregation' and 'decomposition'. Thus we begin by describing these concepts. The seminal paper in this area is one by Chandy, Herzog & Woo [1975a], which showed the following interesting result, reminiscent of Norton's Theorem for electrical networks. Consider a closed network with exponential service times, M stations (which can be load-dependent) and N jobs, which we call network $\mathcal{N}$. Now 'short out' one of the stations in the network, say station m, so that all jobs going to that station are immediately routed back to the rest of the network (the correct manner of doing this, given the routing probabilities, is in Chandy, Herzog & Woo [1975a]). Call this network $\mathcal{N}^{(-m)}$ to denote the shorting out of station m. Now let $\mathrm{TP}(n)$ be the throughput, measured at the 'shorting loop', for network $\mathcal{N}^{(-m)}$ when it has $n = 1, \ldots, N$ jobs in it. Next, consider a new network with just two stations in it. The first is station m, with its original characteristics. Station 2 is a load-dependent station, with parameters $\alpha_{n2} = \mathrm{TP}(n)$ for $n = 1, \ldots, N$. (This is termed the *flow-equivalent server* for the network $\mathcal{N}^{(-m)}$.) Then it turns out that for this new network, the steady-state distribution of the number of jobs at the first station, as well as the throughput at this station, are identical to the values they would have in the original network $\mathcal{N}$. In other words, as far as station m is concerned, replacing the rest of the network by this 'aggregate' representation (a single flow-equivalent server), has no effect on its steady-state performance measures.

Related to this result are the ideas of exact and approximate decomposition [Courtois, 1977]. Consider now a general network (not necessarily product form), and replace a subsystem in this network by its flow-equivalent server. (If the subsystem is not analytically tractable, the parameters for this server might be found by simulation.) Then, in informal terms [e.g., see Agrawal, 1985], the approximate decomposition principle states that if the state transitions within the subsystem occur at a much greater rate than interactions between the subsystem and the rest of the system, not much error is introduced by this replacement. Of course, the 'Norton's Theorem for queueing networks' above is an instance of exact decomposition. However, in that case notice that there is no restriction on the state transition rates at all! This curious result is a consequence of the special form of the transition equations for product form networks and is explained at length in Courtois [1977].

6.2.3.2. Approximate models. The above concepts give rise to a host of approximation methods for non-exponential networks. The basic idea is to replace one or more subnetworks by flow-equivalent servers, and then to analyze the resulting network. To see the relation between the various alternative terms used for this in the literature, separating a network into multiple subnetworks is called *decomposition* and modeling a subnetwork by one station is called *aggregation*. Often, analysis of the network of aggregate stations produces some inconsistencies or deficiencies in the performance measures, which suggest modifications to the decomposition or aggregation steps. In this way, an iteration procedure can be developed which successively refines the accuracy of the model. Thus the two key steps in most of the methods below are (i) the development of the equivalent server, and (ii) the refinement step (if any).

Example. The simplest instance of the above approach is the case where only step (i) is applied. An early application of such an approach is in Brandwajn [1974] for a computer system model. As a manufacturing example of this, Buzacott & Shanthikumar [1980] model an FMS with a random arrival process and N pallets. In such a case it is likely that in practice the number of jobs in the FMS would not be fixed at N, but rather, would have an upper limit of N. They decompose the system into a waiting area for arriving jobs, and the subnetwork of FMS stations. The FMS subnetwork is analyzed as a closed network and its throughput rates for $n = 1, \ldots, N$ jobs define a flow-equivalent server. The arrival process and this aggregate server then define a simple birth–death process which can be analyzed to get the behavior at the waiting area.

Several researchers have proposed methods to analyze networks with general service times using the two-stage method above. Chandy, Herzog & Woo [1975b] use a method that uses M submodels, each consisting of one station and a flow-equivalent server for the complementary subnetwork. They iterate between these submodels to achieve certain consistency criteria. Marie [1978] extends this procedure by using a more sophisticated submodel. In a slightly different approach, Shum & Buzen [1977] use an $M/G/1/N$ queue to represent each general service time station, and use the queue length distribution of this queue to estimate the network throughput. The arrival parameters for the $M/G/1/N$ queues are obtained iteratively. In a similar vein, an 'exponentialization' approach is developed by Yao & Buzacott [1986a], where all servers with general service times are replaced by servers with exponential service times and appropriate state-dependent service rates. Approximate decomposition approaches based on diffusion approximations for $GI/G/1$ queues were proposed by Kobayashi [1974] and Reiser & Kobayashi [1974]. Shanthikumar & Gocmen [1983] improved upon these methods, although their iteration scheme is quite computation intensive and may fail to converge for systems with service time SCVs greater than unity. Kamath, Suri & Sanders [1988] also use GI/G/1 approximations for closed networks. Their algorithm is efficient and convergent, but applies only to closed loop systems – such systems will be discussed in Section 6.3. Another decomposition approach is the isolation method of Labetoulle & Pujolle [1980].

The above methods are based mainly on the convolution approach. Reiser [1979] showed how the basic MVA algorithm could be easily modified to account for non-exponential service times. The idea is to replace the basic MVA relation (6.9) by a heuristic modification such as

$$W_i(N) = \tau_i + \beta_i L_i(N-1)\tau_i\,, \quad i = 1, \ldots, M\,. \tag{6.13}$$

Here β_i is a 'correction factor' that modifies the queue length seen by an arriving job, according to the service time characteristics for station i. Several variations of this correction are possible, and manufacturing applications of it will be discussed in Section 6.4.

A completely different approach to approximations for closed queueing networks uses the maximum entropy principle. In general, entropy maximization is a method for estimating a probability distribution from an undetermined set of linear equations about the probabilistic states of the system. The maximum entropy principle states that from all distributions which satisfy the constraints, we should select the distribution which maximizes the entropy of the system. The intuitive justification for this is that this distribution is best supported by the information conveyed by the constraints, and which is least biased with respect to the information that is missing. We will not review the method any further here, but indicate some relevant references. A good treatment of the maximum entropy formalism can be found in Shore & Johnson [1980, 1981]. Applications to networks of queues are in Ferdinand [1970] and Kouvatsos [1985]. For the interested reader, these papers, in turn, contain references to other material that provides additional insight into this approach.

A much simplified model that exhibits macroscopic behavior consistent with a closed network has been proposed by Spearman [1991]. A good review of many other approximation methods can be found in Agrawal [1985].

6.3. Closed loop systems

The queueing model discussed herein is that of a special class of closed queueing networks known as cyclic queueing networks. The model has M stations or servers numbered $1, 2, \ldots, M$ and arranged in tandem with the output of the last station or server, M, fed back to the first station (Figure 6.2). The queueing discipline at each server is FIFO (first-in-first-out). A fixed number of customers, say N, perpetually circulate in the system and cyclically visit stations $1, 2, \ldots, M$. The model data includes values for M and N and the service time parameters at the M servers. The primary performance measure is

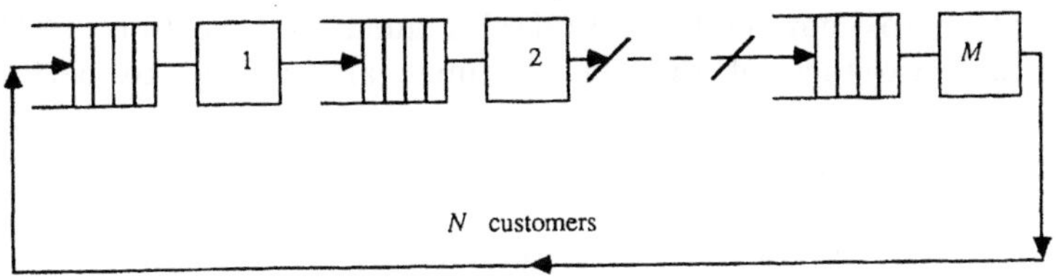

Fig. 6.2. A closed loop system.

the network throughput which is the average arrival rate of customers to a server and the same for all servers by virtue of the network structure.

In the following discussion, we will restrict ourselves to a model where each station is a single server station. We shall also ignore any blocking effects due to limited buffers. In other words, between any pair of adjacent stations, we assume that there is sufficient waiting room for $(N-1)$ customers.

Applications of this closed loop model have been found in several areas related to manufacturing such as production lines, inspection operations, and maintenance and repair facilities [Koenigsberg, 1982], and in a class of assembly systems known as asynchronous automatic assembly systems [Kamath & Sanders, 1986, 1987; Kamath, Suri & Sanders, 1988].

6.3.1. *Closed loop systems with exponential servers*

Here we consider the case where the service time at station i is exponentially distributed with mean τ_i. Now the model falls into the class of product form models for which a well-developed theory exists. A review of the theory and applications of cyclic queues with exponential servers is contained in Koenigsberg [1982]. Exact solution of this closed exponential model can be easily obtained by applying standard methods available for product form networks (see Section 6.2). Some results for customer response time distributions in cyclic exponential queueing networks are contained in Boxma, Kelly & Konheim [1984].

6.3.2. *Closed loop systems with general servers*

Here the service time at station i, $i = 1, 2, \ldots, M$, has a general probability distribution. The network no longer has a product form structure. An exact solution for this general server case may not be possible. However, several approximate methods are available [Agrawal, 1985; Kamath, Suri & Sanders, 1988; Shanthikumar & Gocmen, 1983; Shum & Buzen, 1977; Whitt, 1984b]. Here we describe one such method that was primarily developed to analyze closed cyclic queueing models of asynchronous automatic assembly systems in Kamath & Sanders [1986, 1987] and Kamath, Suri & Sanders [1988]. In this case the service time is typically fixed (deterministic) except when a station 'jam' occurs, when there is a repair time distribution. Such a system is not modeled well by the exponential case. The method below is an extension of the node decomposition method in Section 5.2 and is based on well developed two-moment approximations for the GI/G/1 queue (see Section 2.2.1). Only the mean and variance of the service times are needed to perform the calculations.

Following the notation in Section 5.2, for station i, τ_i and c_{si}^2 are the mean and the SCV of service times, respectively, c_{ai}^2 the interarrival-time SCV, c_{di}^2 the interdeparture-time SCV, ρ_i the utilization, and W_{qi} the average waiting time. λ is the throughput or production rate of the closed loop system. We first outline the approximation method which can be classified as a parametric decomposition method [Kuehn, 1979; Whitt, 1984b] and then present the solution only for the balanced case.

In the closed loop system under consideration, the arrival process to each station is the departure process of the preceding station in line and the last queue feeds into the first. Using this information about the flow of customers together with the two-moment renewal approximation to the departure process of a GI/G/1 queue (formula (2.15)), closed form expressions are derived for c_{ai}^2. The arrival rate to each queue is the unknown network production rate λ. The interdependency among the various station queues is approximately captured by these rate and variability parameters. Next, the queues are treated (approximately) as being stochastically independent and for each queue, the expected waiting time, W_{qi}, is computed using an approximate formula for GI/G/1 queues [formula (2.12) or (2.13)]. Using Little's result a relationship is established between the total number of customers in the system and the mean flow times at the individual GI/G/1 nodes through the unknown network production rate. In the unbalanced system case, writing this relationship in an equation form gives us a nonlinear equation in a single unknown. In Kamath, Suri & Sanders [1988], an efficient bisection scheme was developed to find the solution (root) of this equation. In the case of a balanced system, the relationship yields a quadratic equation when the simple formula (2.11) for the waiting time approximation is used. We present below the solution for a balanced system.

All stations have the same parameters, i.e., $\tau_i = \tau$ and $c_{si}^2 = c_s^2$ for $i = 1, 2, \ldots, M$. It is easy to see that the following equalities hold because of the symmetric nature of the cyclic model:

$$c_{a1}^2 = c_{a2}^2 = \cdots = c_{aM}^2 = c_a^2 \tag{6.14}$$

and

$$c_{d1}^2 = c_{d2}^2 = \cdots = c_{dM}^2 = c_d^2 \,. \tag{6.15}$$

In a closed cyclic network since each arrival process is the departure process from the previous queue and because of equalities (6.14) and (6.15), the following equality holds:

$$c_d^2 = c_a^2 \,. \tag{6.16}$$

Focusing on a particular queue (station) and using formula (2.15) and equality above, we have

$$c_a^2 = c_s^2 .$$

The queues representing the M stations in the closed loop system are now analyzed separately. Let ρ be the (unknown) station utilization (which is the same for all stations in this case). Thus the expected equilibrium waiting time of a customer in queue at station i [using formula (2.12)] is then

$$W_{qi} = c_s^2 \frac{\tau\rho}{1-\rho}, \quad i = 1, 2, \ldots, M . \tag{6.17}$$

Little's result applied to the entire closed loop system gives

$$N = \lambda \sum_{i=1}^{M} (W_{qi} + \tau) . \tag{6.18}$$

Using (6.3–6.4) and rewriting the above relationship in the form of an equation we have

$$\rho^2(M - Mc_s^2) - \rho(M + N) + N = 0 . \tag{6.19}$$

The above equation can be solved explicitly for ρ to get

$$\rho = \begin{cases} \dfrac{N}{N+M} & \text{if } c_s^2 = 1 , \\[2ex] \dfrac{\sqrt{(M+N)^2 + 4MN(c_s^2 - 1)} - (M+N)}{2M(c_s^2 - 1)} & \text{if } c_s^2 \neq 1 . \end{cases} \tag{6.20}$$

Once ρ is known the production rate is given by

$$\lambda = \frac{\rho}{\tau} . \tag{6.21}$$

The above analysis used the simple formula (2.12) for the GI/G/1 waiting time approximation. This works well for large systems [Kamath & Sanders, 1987]. For small systems (say less than ten stations and one customer per station), more accurate results can be obtained by using the refined GI/G/1 approximation (2.13). Also, a correction factor derived in Kamath, Suri & Sanders [1988], which accounts for the fixed number of customers (N) in the system, considerably improves the accuracy of performance prediction for small systems. The use of these refined approximations leads to a nonlinear equation and efficient solution algorithms have been developed in Kamath, Suri & Sanders [1988].

6.4. *Multiple class analysis*

In this section we consider closed networks with multiple classes of customers. First we will discuss networks for which exact solutions are known, after which we will consider approximations for more general systems. A great deal of the development of this area has come from performance analysis of computer systems, and some general references on this are Sauer & Chandy [1981], Lavenberg [1983], and Lazowska, Zahorja, Graham & Sevcik [1984].

6.4.1. *Product form solution*

6.4.1.1. Theory. A very general category of multiple class closed networks which exhibit a product form solution was stated by Baskett, Chandy, Muntz & Palacios [1975]. These networks are known as BCMP networks, after the four authors, and have already been described in Section 5. They allow various combinations of service time distributions and service disciplines. However, in the case where the service discipline is FCFS, the service time distribution must be exponential with the same (possibly load-dependent) rates for all classes. The cases where different classes may have different mean service times, and the product form is retained, involve service disciplines that would be unusual for manufacturing – such as immediate pre-emption of service. These conditions severely restrict the applicability of the BCMP model to manufacturing systems, and in most cases one has to resort to approximate solutions of more realistic models.

Some generalizations of the class of product form networks are possible, including deterministic routings [Kelly, 1975] and more general service times than in the original BCMP paper [e.g., Kelly, 1976; and Barbour, 1976]. Also, the concepts of *insensitivity* [Schassberger, 1978] and *reversibility* [Kelly, 1979] are useful in understanding the properties of product form networks.

6.4.1.2. Computational algorithms. The convolution algorithm was developed for multiclass networks by Reiser & Kobayashi [1976], while computation of performance measures using the MVA algorithm is in Reiser & Lavenberg [1980] and Reiser [1981]. Although both convolution and MVA are relatively efficient in the single class case, their computational requirements are less satisfactory for multiclass networks. This is because their needs grow exponentially with the number of classes. Specifically, in a network with M single-server stations and K classes, with N_k customers in class k, both algorithms require of the order of $MK\,\Pi_{k=1}^{K}(N_k+1)$ operations to compute the main performance measures. They are also space-intensive, with convolution requiring $2\,\Pi_{k=1}^{K}(N_k+1)\,2\,\Pi_{k=1}^{K}(N_k+1)$ storage locations, and MVA taking $M\,\Pi_{k=1}^{K}(N_k+1)$ storage locations [Bruell & Balbo, 1980; Reiser & Lavenberg, 1980]. Agrawal [1985] gives an example showing how these numbers grow rapidly with the number of classes. For example, a network with 15 stations, 5 classes, and 10 customers in each class requires about 48 million operations, and 322 000 locations (convolution) or 1.4 million locations (MVA). These numbers all increase substantially if the stations are load-dependent.

This computational burden has been addressed through three avenues of developments. The first exploits networks with special structure. The second uses approximations – some based on analysis and others heuristic, see Zahorjan [1983] for a detailed treatment of this topic. The third supplies performance bounds instead of point estimates. These are now discussed.

6.4.1.2.1. Networks with special structure. Balsamo & Iazeolla [1982] introduced an extension of Norton's Theorem which is computationally advantageous if one only needs to compute performance measures for a small subnetwork of the whole network. The LBANC (Local Balance Algorithm for Normalizing Constants) and CCNC (Coalesce Computation of Normalizing Constants) algorithms were proposed by Chandy & Sauer [1980] to reduce the storage requirements during computation. The tree-convolution method [Lam & Lien, 1983] and tree-MVA method [Hoyme, Bruell, Afshari & Kain, 1982] are efficient for sparse networks, for example, where each class tends to stay in a sub-area of the network. RECAL (Recursion by Chain Algorithm) developed by Conway & Georganas [1986] is particularly efficient when the number of classes is large compared with the number of stations. De Souza e Silva & Lavenberg [1989] developed a DAC (Distribution Analysis by Chain) algorithm which can compute joint queue-length distributions more efficiently than other approaches.

6.4.1.2.2. MVA-based methods. A large number of approximation techniques for multiclass networks are based on variations of MVA. First we describe methods for reducing the computational requirements by producing approximate solutions for product form networks. One of the earliest of these is the so-called Schweitzer–Bard (SB) approximation, proposed by Schweitzer [1979] and extensively tested by Bard [1979]. Consider the multiclass version of the MVA equation (6.9) which is

$$W_{ik}(N) = \tau_{ik} + \sum_{j=1}^{K} L_{ij}(\boldsymbol{N} - \mathbf{1}_k)\tau_{ik}\,, \quad i = 1, \ldots, M\,, \tag{6.22}$$

where the second subscript now refers to the class, $\boldsymbol{N}$ is the vector of class populations, and $\mathbf{1}_k$ is the unit vector in the kth direction. (Thus $\boldsymbol{N} - \mathbf{1}_k$ is the population vector that has one less customer of class k.) Note here that the service time parameter (τ_{ik}) multiplying the summation term has the *fixed* subscript k – this will be significant when we discuss nonproduct form networks below. In order to reduce the number of computations, the SB method proposes the approximation

$$L_{ij}(\boldsymbol{N} - \mathbf{1}_k) = \begin{cases} L_{ij}(\boldsymbol{N})\,, & j \neq k\,, \\ \dfrac{N_k - 1}{N_k}\, L_{ik}(\boldsymbol{N})\,, & j = k\,, \end{cases} \tag{6.23}$$

which says intuitively that the number of customers of class j in the equilibrium distribution for a network with one less customer of class k is simply the equilibrium number when $j \neq k$, and smaller by the ratio of $(N_k - 1)/N_k$ when $j = k$. Obviously this is a very simplistic approximation, and improvements to it will be discussed below. Nevertheless it performs reasonably [Schweitzer, Seidmann & Shalev-Oren, 1986]. The idea now is that instead of iterating from zero population up to the vector of full populations, we simply note that with (6.23) the MVA equation (6.22), along with the multidimensional versions of (6.9)–(6.11) now define a set of nonlinear equations in the unknowns $L_{ij}(\boldsymbol{N})$. These can be solved simply by iterating through the Equations (6.23), (6.9)–(6.11), or else by any other fixed point solution scheme. For large networks, convergence is often achieved much faster through the fixed point iteration, as compared to working up the vector of populations with the exact algorithms.

Due to the simplistic form of the approximation (6.23), the SB algorithm can occasionally perform poorly (as much as 30% off the exact values) for so-called 'stress cases'. Such examples can be found in Chandy & Neuse [1982] who also proposed the *Linearizer* algorithm as a way of obtaining improved estimates. The basic idea is still to iterate at a given population, but at the same time they iteratively develop an improved estimator for $L_{ij}(\boldsymbol{N} - \boldsymbol{1}_k)$.

6.4.1.2.3. Asymptotic expansions. A powerful analytical technique, based on a completely different approach, was introduced by McKenna & Mitra [1982, 1984]. This uses asymptotic expansions for integral representations of the performance measures, and is particularly efficient for large networks.

6.4.1.2.4. Bounds. In some cases where large networks are being analyzed, the use of bounding techniques, rather than exact solutions, may be preferable. Such techniques provide upper and/or lower bounds on various performance measures, with substantially less computational effort. If the bounds are acceptably tight, then it may be that the additional computational effort of an exact solution is not justifiable.

The simplest bounds are obtained from *asymptotic bound analysis* (ABA) and only require a few arithmetic operations [Muntz & Wong, 1974; Kleinrock, 1976; Denning & Buzen, 1978]. ABA bounds are, however, typically very loose. A much improved set of bounds, also requiring just a few arithmetic operations, was developed by Zahorjan, Sevcik, Eager & Galler [1982], and called *balanced job bounds* (BJBs). These bound the performance measures of the original network by two networks, both of which have balanced resource usage, and whose performance can be computed very simply. A more sophisticated set of bounds is provided by the *performance bound hierarchy* (PBH) which is a hierarchy of successively more accurate upper and lower bounds with the exact solution as its limit [Eager & Sevcik, 1983]. This provides the analyst with a sequence of trade-offs between computational effort and accuracy.

6.4.2. Non-product form networks

6.4.2.1. Flow-equivalent approaches. This is the first of the techniques we will discuss for dealing with nonproduct form networks. The results on flow-equivalent representations, by Chandy, Herzog & Woo [1975a], were derived for multiclass networks, so in principle the approximation procedures based on aggregation and decomposition that were discussed previously, could be applied to multiclass networks as well. In practice, however, there is a computational problem. Suppose we are interested in approximating a nonproduct form network, and we derive a multiclass flow-equivalent server for a subsystem in that network. Note that the service rate function of this server will be of the form $\mu(n_1, n_2, \ldots, n_K)$ where n_K is the number of customers of class k present at the server, i.e., the service rate for the server depends on the number of customers of each class. The problem is that the computational complexity for solving a network with such servers is very great. Therefore, to use aggregation and decomposition procedures for multiclass networks, one usually has to incorporate them along with additional approximations. One such approximation, proposed independently by Brandwajn [1982] and Lazowska & Zahorjan [1982] is to replace the varying values of n_k above by a fixed value for all but one class. Thus the K-dimensional function $\mu(n_1, n_2, \ldots, n_K)$ is replaced by K one-dimensional functions. The fixed values used are the average number of each class present in the subsystem. This decomposes the network into K single class networks which need to be solved via an iterative process to ensure consistency.

6.4.2.2. MVA extensions. Nonproduct form networks can also be analyzed via heuristic extensions of MVA. The starting point for these is the multiclass MVA equation (6.22), which lends itself nicely to intuitively reasonable approximations. A major drawback to the product form solutions is that they do not apply in a multiclass network where classes may have different service parameters at an FCFS station. This however, is the norm in manufacturing. An obvious heuristic modification of (6.22) is to replace the fixed service time parameter in the summation (τ_{ik}) by the service time parameter for each class. This has the intuitive explanation that the estimated number of each class, $L_{ij}(N - \mathbf{1}_k)$, is multiplied by its mean service time (τ_{ij}). The resulting equation is

$$W_{ik}(N) = \tau_{ik} + \sum_{j=1}^{K} L_{ij}(N - \mathbf{1}_k)\tau_{ij}, \quad i = 1, \ldots, M. \tag{6.24}$$

Example. The above approximation was used by Suri & Hildebrant [1984] to analyze FMS performance. They also describe how the analysis tool was implemented and used as part of a decision support system for an FMS at Hughes Aircraft Co. Their implementation actually incorporated two other approximations as well: the SB approximation for $L_{ij}(N - \mathbf{1}_k)$, and another one to account for multiple server stations. Even with the three approximations, the predictions from their algorithms were off only 10%–15% from detailed simulations. However, as they also showed, the set of approximations enabled a very efficient implementation, from both CPU time and memory considerations. These approximations were further enhanced by Shalev-Oren, Seidmann & Schweitzer [1985] whose algorithm showed excellent performance in the context of FMSs with priority scheduling.

Another obvious extension of the above approximation, to account for non-exponential distributions, is to modify the summation term by a correction factor as already shown in equation (6.13). This idea was introduced by Reiser [1979] in the context of communication networks and was used by Cavaille & Dubois [1982] for analyzing FMS behavior.

6.5. *Special properties of closed networks*

Closed networks, because of their structure, enjoy various interesting properties, which will be discussed in this section. These properties can be useful for qualitative analysis of the networks, for a priori statements about impact of parameter changes, for network optimization, or purely as aids to providing insight into the network behavior.

6.5.1. *Monotonicity and second order properties*

In general, monotonicity of a performance measure, say $Y(\theta)$, where θ is any parameter of the network, implies that Y is always nondecreasing (or always non-increasing) in θ. Intuitively, monotonicity assures us that the network is 'well-behaved' with respect to that parameter. For example, one would expect that if the processing power of a station is increased, then the throughput of the network should increase (or at least, not decrease). This however, is not always the case, as shown by a simple counterexample in Suri [1985c]. Thus the question is, under what circumstances do we get the intuitively expected (monotonic) behavior?

This question has been studied by several researchers for various types of closed networks. Suri [1985c] begins by looking at monotonicity of throughput with respect to the number of jobs in a single class product form network, and then shows that several other intuitively desirable properties follow once this monotonicity is assured – examples of such properties are, well-behaved partial derivatives with respect to service time parameters. He also derives various sufficient conditions for this throughput monotonicity to hold. Related results for product form networks, and various alternative methods of proof, can be found in Robertazzi & Lazar [1985], Yao [1985], Shanthikumar & Yao [1987], and Van der Wal [1989].

The broadest available result on monotonicity is due to Adan & Van der Wal [1989], and states that the throughput of a single class closed queueing network with general service times is nondecreasing in the number of jobs. Note, in particular, that the network need not have a product form solution for this result.

As discussed at length in Suri [1985c], monotonicity has many practical uses in network design and analysis. It can be used in conjunction with performance bound analysis, in parameter optimization, and in understanding the robustness of queueing network models. Examples of the use of monotonicity in development of optimization algorithms for FMS are in Vinod & Solberg [1985], Dallery & Frein [1986], and Lee, Srinivasan & Yano [1989].

Monotonicity and the resulting optimization algorithms are useful in searching for parameter values satisfying the first-order optimality conditions. However, usually one requires certain second-order properties (e.g., convexity) to hold for the objective function, at least locally, in order to verify that an optimum has been found. Second-order properties have traditionally been very difficult to establish, even for simple queueing systems. Recently however, Shanthikumar & Yao [1989, 1992] have developed tools based on sample-path analysis that have provided a host of results on second-order properties for queueing networks. In particular, they define and use the notion of *strong stochastic convexity* and are able to establish results for fairly general classes of networks. Examples are concavity or convexity with respect to job populations, server allocation, and service times. In many cases their methods allow them to derive the properties for nonproduct form networks (e.g., a cyclic network with general service time distributions). Shanthikumar & Yao [1989] also provide a survey of existing results and alternate methods of proof for second-order properties, as well as several references to optimization and control applications. In the manufacturing context, several authors have developed algorithms for optimizing the performance of a manufacturing system based on a queueing network model for the system. In addition to the references in the previous paragraph, Stecke & Solberg [1985] and Yao [1985] look at workload allocation, while Yao & Shanthikumar [1986, 1987] consider workload, server allocation and buffer allocation. These qualitative properties are also useful in establishing the simplified model of Spearman [1991].

6.5.2. Sensitivity analysis and robustness

An important question in the application of queueing network models is, how sensitive are the performance predictions to errors in parameter estimates? Open network models can be quite sensitive to such errors [Brumfield, 1982] – intuitively this is understandable since queue lengths become unbounded as utilization levels approach unity. On the other hand, it turns out that the main performance measures for closed networks are actually quite robust to parameter errors; in fact, in general the errors seem to be attenuated, not magnified. This is a rather desirable property and conducive to practical use of such models. In order to establish such a property, we first need expressions for the sensitivity of performance measures to parameters. Hence the connection between the seemingly opposite properties in the subsection title, namely sensitivity and robustness!

Expressions for parameter sensitivities for closed networks have been derived by Williams & Bhandiwad [1976], Gordon & Dowdy [1980], Suri [1983] and Tay & Suri [1985]. As an example of the robustness of performance predictions, consider a system from Tay & Suri [1985]. Here 10 different parameters (visit ratios and mean service times) can *each* be estimated with a 5% error. Yet the throughput prediction will still be within 10% of the true value, and all utilizations will be within 20%.

A deeper use of the robustness results is made by Suri [1983]. It had been widely observed that queueing network models worked well even for systems that did not conform to the classical assumptions (i.e., conditions for product form). For example, Spragins [1980] states, 'The amazing thing is that they have been successful despite the fact; that a number of the most common assumptions . . . are often seriously violated for real systems'. As one way of explaining this phenomenon, Buzen [1976] advanced the concept of *operational analysis*, subsequently extended by Denning & Buzen [1978] for queueing networks, which showed that most of the performance measures for queueing networks could be derived from a set of assumptions involving no statement of the underlying probability distributions. However, one of these assumptions, denoted homogeneous service times (HST), was viewed as being overly restrictive. Suri [1983] shows that the performance measures are in fact extremely robust to violations in HST. This provides analytical insight into the success of closed network models for performance prediction in real systems.

7. Queueing models for machine–operator interference

7.1. Machine–operator interference problem

Automatic or semi-automatic machines require operator service for a variety of tasks including loading and unloading of parts, scheduled maintenance, clearing of part jams, and more major machine repairs. The operators may also be required to perform ancillary duties such as feeding part hoppers in assembly systems. With the increasing level of automation today, it is common for an operator to be responsible for tending several machines. When a machine requires the services of an operator and finds all operators busy servicing other machines, the machine must wait to be serviced. This waiting time is known as *interference time* in the literature [Benson & Cox, 1951; Palesano & Chandra, 1986; Stecke, 1982; Stecke & Aronson, 1985]. Interference or waiting for operator service is undesirable as it decreases the productivity of a machine and consequently that of the production system. The amount of interference is a function of the distribution of the operator service times, the distribution of production times of machines, the number of machines, and the number of operators. The operator walking times between machines and the order in which the machines are tended will also have an effect on the interference time.

The machine interference problem has received the attention of several researchers over the last few decades [Ashcroft, 1950; Benson & Cox, 1951; Stecke, 1982; Stecke & Aronson, 1985]. An expository introduction to various machine interference problems and brief descriptions of models, charts, and solution techniques are contained in the review paper by Stecke & Aronson [1985]. In Stecke [1982] and Stecke & Aronson [1985], several deterministic and probabilistic models available for the interference problem are reviewed. The probabilistic models reviewed include the binomial probability analysis method, queueing theoretic approaches, and simulation models. Information regarding models that explicitly consider operator walking times and various types of tending (or operator service) disciplines such as cyclic, alternating cyclic, distance priority, etc. is contained in Stecke [1982] and Stecke & Aronson [1985].

In this section, only queueing models that are used for interference calculations will be described. First, the classical machine–repairman model is described and the results are summarized. This is followed by a discussion on the generalization of this classical model. Next, a closed queueing network model of the machine–operator system is presented. This alternative model will be advantageous in situations when the operator service times and the machine production times have general probability distributions. We then present a discussion on models that can handle different types of machine stoppage. We conclude this section with a brief look at the modeling of general production networks that exhibit instances of interference.

7.2. Preliminaries

Definitions. A *failed* or a *down* machine is defined as one either waiting for operator service or being serviced by an operator. The *production time* of a machine is its 'up' time between successive periods of breakdown. Operator service process is also known as the *repair process*. (This is due to historical reasons when the main operator task was repair.)

Notation.

{Given parameters}
K = number of machines,
m = number of operators,
τ = average repair (operator service) time,
λ = machine breakdown rate ($1/\lambda$ is the average production time of a machine).

{Performance measures to be predicted}
p_n = steady state probability that there are n failed machines,
L = average number of failed machines,

L_q = average number of machines waiting for operator service,
A = machine availability or the long run proportion of time a machine is available,
I = average interference time which is the amount of time a failed machine has to wait on the average before receiving operator service,
O_e = operator efficiency or the long run proportion of time an operator is busy or working.

Basic performance relations. *Machine availability.* From standard reliability theory for a system with repair [Barlow & Proschan, 1975], we have

$$A = \frac{\text{average production time}}{\text{average production time} + \text{average down time}} . \tag{7.1}$$

If on the average there are L failed machines, then on the average, $(K - L)$ are running and each has a breakdown rate of λ. Hence, the mean rate of arrivals, say λ_{eff}, into the system is

$$\lambda_{\text{eff}} = \lambda(K - L) . \tag{7.2}$$

Dividing the numerator and denominator of the RHS of (7.1) by λ_{eff}, and using Little's result (see Section 2) the machine availability can also be defined as

$$A = \frac{\text{avg. \# of running machines}}{\text{avg. \# of running machines} + \text{avg. \# of failed machines}} . \tag{7.3}$$

Since the denominator of (7.3) is just K, the total number of machines, another definition for machine availability is

$$A = 1 - \frac{L}{K} . \tag{7.4}$$

Operator efficiency. This is given by

$$O_e = \frac{\text{average numbers of busy operators}}{\text{number of operators}} \tag{7.5}$$

or

$$O_e = \frac{L - L_q}{m} . \tag{7.6}$$

Average interference time. Using λ_{eff} (Equation (7.2)) and Little's result we can get the average interference time as

$$I = \frac{L_q}{\lambda_{\text{eff}}} . \tag{7.7}$$

Assumptions. Unless stated otherwise, the following assumptions are made.

(A1) Any one of the failed machines requires only one of the m operators to repair it. Repair times are independent of the number of failed machines.

(A2) Machines fail independently and randomly. All repair times and production times are independent.

(A3) The operators attend to failed workstations in the order they failed or, alternatively, the machines are tended in a totally random order.

(A4) The repair times include the time required for an operator to walk to a machine in need of service.

7.3. *Classical machine–repairman model*

This classical model assumes that the production time of a machine is exponential with mean $1/\lambda$ and operator service time is exponential with mean τ for each operator and each machine. This can be modeled as a finite source multi-server exponential queueing system, where the operators are the servers and machines are the customers. An arrival corresponds to a machine breakdown. Since the number of machines is finite, we have a finite source (of size K). We now use the results for the $\mathrm{M/M}/m/\cdot/K$ queueing system presented in Section 2.4.

The steady-state probabilities p_n and average number of failed machines, L are given by formulas (2.32) and (2.34), respectively. Now, the machine availability A is obtained using formula (7.4). L_q, the average number of (failed) machines waiting for operator service is given by

$$L_q = \sum_{n=m}^{K} (n - m)p_n , \tag{7.8}$$

where p_n is given by formula (2.32). The average interference time I can be obtained using formula (7.7).

7.4. *Models with general distributions*

General production time distribution and exponential repair times. An important invariance result was shown for the $\mathrm{G/M}/m/\cdot/K$ queue by Bunday & Scraton [1980]. For this queueing system they showed that the steady-state probabilities are insensitive to the distributional form of G. In other words, the probability distribution given by (2.32) and (2.33) are valid for any finite source system with exponential service or repair times, independent of the form of the production time distribution. The only requirement is that the production times of a machine should be independent with a mean $1/\lambda$. Hence, the formulas derived in the previous section are valid for a non-exponential production time case.

Exponential production time distribution and general repair times. The queueing model for this case is the $\mathrm{M/G}/m/\cdot/K$ queue. For the special case of $m = 1$, i.e., K identical machines handled by a single operator, this queueing system has been solved using an imbedded Markov chain approach [Takacs, 1962]. Any interested reader is also referred to Tijms [1988] for a detailed analysis of the finite source M/G/1 queue using a regenerative process approach. For the multiple operator case some approximations for the steady-state probabilities are contained in Tijms [1988].

General production time and repair time distributions. Few results are available for this case which is the most general case of the machine–repairman problem. The model is a GI/G/m/ · /K queue. For this general case, viewing the machine–repairman model as a closed queueing network may lead to the development of some useful approximations. This alternative view is presented next.

7.5. *A closed queueing network model*

Because of the finite customer population, the machine–operator interference model can be visualized as a two-stage cyclic queueing network model (Figure 7.1). The number of customers circulating in the network is fixed and is equal to K, the number of machines. One of the stages corresponds to running machines (i.e., those that can fail but are in a working state). We refer to this stage as *Stage* 1. This stage has K identical parallel servers. This parallel server node can be replaced by an infinite server or delay node as customers do not have to wait in queue at this stage. The other stage, *Stage* 2, is an m-server node with a common queue. This stage corresponds to the pool of operators. Customers waiting in the common queue correspond to the failed machines waiting for operators to become available. A customer movement from Stage 2

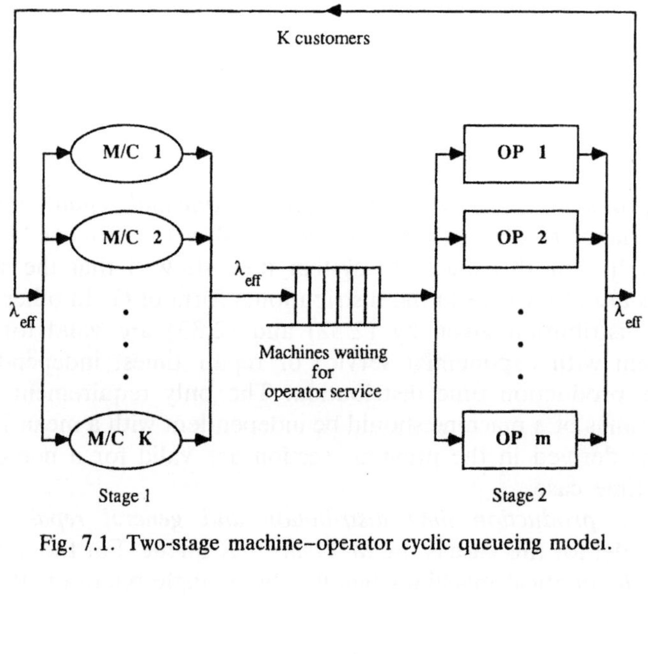

Fig. 7.1. Two-stage machine–operator cyclic queueing model.

to Stage 1 corresponds to the completion of a repair operation and a customer departure from Stage 1 corresponds to the stoppage or breakdown of a machine.

The service time distribution of a server in Stage 1 is the production time distribution of the machines, while that of a server in Stage 2 is the repair time distribution. We will consider the steady-state solution. The probability of finding n customers at Stage 2 is p_n and average interference time I is just the expected waiting time in queue at Stage 2. Machine availability is the utilization of a server in Stage 1 and operator efficiency is the utilization of a server in Stage 2. Hence, the solution of the closed queueing network model directly yields the desired performance measures. The mean arrival rate to each stage or the unknown network throughput rate is λ_{eff}. Estimating the values of p_n may not be required because most solution techniques for closed networks (see Section 6) directly yield a value for the network throughput rate which in our case is λ_{eff}. This in conjunction with a waiting time result for the queue at Stage 2 would suffice to determine the basic performance measures. The problem is thus reduced to solving a closed queueing network with general service time FIFO servers. Approximate methods of solving such a network are discussed in Section 6.

7.6. *Different types of stoppage*

In the interference models considered so far, we implicitly assumed that either (i) the machines experience only one type of stoppage or (ii) the machines experience different types of stoppage and the stoppage modeled is an 'aggregate' of the different types. In this section, we describe briefly certain models that (explicitly) consider different types of stoppage.

Benson & Cox [1951] provide solutions to the following problems involving different types of stoppage. (i) A single operator attending a number of machines which are liable to two types of stoppage, the time to stoppage exponentially distributed with mean $1/\lambda_1$ or $1/\lambda_2$ depending on whether the stoppage is of the first or second type and the operator service times exponential with mean τ_1 (type 1 stoppage) or τ_2 (type 2 stoppage). For this problem their results seem to suggest that the choice between attending machines with long and short stoppages is of little importance. (ii) A team of m operators attending a particular number of machines each of which can experience m types of stoppage. Each operator is trained to attend only one type of stoppage. The time to stoppage is exponentially distributed with mean $1/\lambda_r$ if the stoppage is of type r, $r = 1, 2, \ldots, m$. The repair time for a stoppage of the rth type is distributed exponentially with mean τ_r.

Kelly [1976] considers an example machine interference problem which is closely related to the second problem described above. He considers closed queueing network models of machine–operator interference. His example system contains K identical machines and two operators with different skills.

Machines may experience two types of stoppage and the type of stoppage determines which operator attends to the machine. The assumptions on the production times of machines and stoppages themselves are quite general and are (i) the production time distribution of a machine can be arbitrary, (ii) the current production time and the reason for the current machine stoppage may depend upon previous production times and previous reasons for stoppage for that machine, and (iii) the reason for a machine stoppage may also depend upon the current production time. Each operator attends to the machines that are waiting for his service in the order of their stopping. The operator service times are distributed exponentially with mean τ_1 (operator 1) or τ_2 (operator 2). For further details see Kelly [1976].

Interference problems with multiple types of stoppage are also studied by Palesano & Chandra [1986]. Their system has a single operator and a group of identical machines, each subject to r ($r \geqslant 2$) types of stoppage and the time between type i ($i = 1, 2, \ldots, r$) stoppages is exponential. The operator service time can be either deterministic, exponential, Erlang, or hyperexponential and the mean service time can depend on the type of stoppage. The operator uses a nonpreemptive fixed-priority rule to service the failed machines. Palesano and Chandra perform an imbedded Markov chain analysis and develop a numerical method for obtaining the steady-state performance measures. They also perform a sensitivity analysis of the performance measures to the type of the service time distribution. One of their observations is that the average interference time becomes insensitive to the type of service time distribution and the order of priorities as the operator efficiency approaches unity.

7.7. *Production network models and interference*

The queueing models used to solve interference problems, such as the classical machine–repairman model, assume that information (e.g., the mean) about machine production time or the time to the next request for operator service is known. Some probability based models [Stecke, 1982] that calculate interference, require the probability that a machine is down or failed at any given moment. When machines are part of a production network, these (probabilities and mean times) have to be calculated from other system parameters. In this situation, a simultaneous solution of the machine interference problem and the production network model is called for. An example of this situation can be found in Bulgak, Kamath & Sanders [1989], Kamath [1989], and Kamath & Sanders [1991], where one of the problems considered is the determination of the performance of an automatic assembly system for a given assignment of operators.

Next, we present a different perspective on the production network problem which has an interference problem as one of its components. If the machines and operators are viewed as resources, then, in the event of a machine stoppage, the job currently occupying the machine would be using two resources, the machine and an operator, at the same time. In the product form network terminology, the queueing network, with machines and operators as resources and jobs as customers, has an instance of *simultaneous resource possession* (SRP) [De Souza e Silva & Muntz, 1987; Jacobson & Lazowska, 1982; Pattipati & Kastner, 1988]. Any network with SRP falls into the category of nonproduct form queueing networks and in general this network can be solved only approximately.

Practical solutions to the machine–operator interference problem have been implemented and used in a few cases. For instance, the MPX package models multiple classes of operators tending multiple classes of machines [Suri & DeTreville, 1991]. The solution approach (similar to that in Section 7.5) consists of decomposing the network into two levels: the machine–operator problem is analyzed as a multiple class closed network; this generates PMs that are used to modify the machine service times in the open network. Application of this to an industrial example with operators is in DeTreville [1991].

8. Advanced topics

8.1. General networks with finite buffers

Limited buffer space is a reality in any manufacturing system, as well as in computer systems and communication networks. Thus the topic of performance analysis of networks with finite buffers has received a lot of attention from researchers. Perros [1984] provides a bibliography of 75 papers, Suri & Diehl [1986] also have a large bibliography, and the collection in Perros & Altiok [1989] provides a set of very recent papers. Even so, despite all the research effort devoted, a fairly robust and universal solution to the blocking problem has eluded analysts – we will elaborate on this point below.

8.1.1. Types of blocking

In a finite buffer system, the number of jobs that can queue for a station may be limited. In this case, when the buffer is full, and another job tries to depart from its current server and queue for that station, we say 'blocking' is occurring: the job that is attempting to join the full buffer is called the blocked job, and the server from which the blocked job is trying to depart is also said to be blocked. The unsuspecting reader starting on this topic should immediately be alerted to the fact that many different definitions of blocking exist, and it is possible to make a grave mistake by modeling the wrong type of blocking. The key is how the blocked job is treated. The two most common types of blocking are: *transfer blocking* (also called manufacturing blocking) where a job, after completing service, attempts to go to the next queue, but if it is blocked it stays at its current server which cannot serve another job and thus is also blocked; and *service blocking* (also called communication blocking) where a job must announce its destination before starting service, and service cannot begin if the destination buffer is full, and again the blocked job stays at its current server which gets blocked. Other types of blocking include the case where service must be restarted if the destination buffer is full, and where the job that is blocked is lost (disappears from the network). We will primarily cover work relating to transfer blocking (the most common in manufacturing), and block-and-recirculate – a particular case of the restarting situation which can represent certain material handling systems. In the remainder of this section, we will first cover the cases where exact solutions are available, then divide our coverage of approximations into those for open and closed networks. Due to the complexity and diverse nature of the approaches, we cannot do justice to each approach in the space here, so our coverage will necessarily be brief. We will mention some recent references, as well as papers that themselves have a good bibliography.

8.1.2. Exact solutions

In general, the occurrence of blocking destroys the product form solution, making analytical solutions intractable even for the case of exponential service times – the state space becomes unmanageably large. However, there are a few special situations where the solutions are tractable. The key here is whether the 'reversibility' property is retained [Kelly, 1979]. If it is, then the product form solution is available, along with the possibility of efficient computational algorithms. Some of the early work along these lines was by Yao & Buzacott [1985b] in the context of FMSs, particularly those with a centralized material handling system – Yao [1989] gives an up to date review. More recent developments include those of Akyildiz [1989] and Onvural [1989], who also provide extensive references.

8.1.3. Approximations for finite buffers in open networks

The most rigorously analyzed open configuration with finite buffers is the case of the tandem network. This has been covered in detail in Section 3, so here we shall deal only with approaches for more general configurations. The most common approaches involve decomposition and aggregation methods (see Section 6.2.3) where the finite buffer system is replaced by a pseudo-equivalent system with unlimited buffers and modified parameters for the servers [Takahashi, Miyahara & Hasegawa, 1980; Jun & Perros, 1989; Takahashi, 1989; Schweitzer & Altiok, 1989]. Daskalaki & Smith [1989] also consider routing in finite buffer networks. In some cases, special methods are used for specific topologies, e.g., Konheim & Reiser [1976, 1978], or special blocking definitions [Boxma & Konheim 1981]. Finally, a completely different approach is provided through the use of the maximum entropy formalism [Kouvatsos & Xenios, 1989], also see Section 6.2.3.2. The analysis of open networks with acyclic job routing is much easier, but any recirculation or cyclic routing usually makes the approximations poor (see also Section 8.1.6).

8.1.4. Approximations for finite buffers in closed networks

The analog of the open tandem network, for closed systems, is the closed loop system or cyclic network (see Section 6.3). Cyclic networks with blocking are analyzed by Gordon & Newell [1967b], Suri & Diehl [1986], Kamath [1989], and Onvural & Perros [1990]. More general networks are again analyzed by decomposition and/or aggregation methods [Suri & Diehl, 1986; Dallery & Frein, 1989]. Other approaches involve heavy traffic limit theorems [Kogan & Krichagina, 1989] and maximum entropy methods [Kouvatsos & Xenios, 1989].

8.1.5. Bounds and qualitative properties

Recently there has been much attention on the qualitative properties of queueing networks (see Sections 6.4.1.2.4 and 6.5). This attention has extended to finite buffer systems as well. Van Dijk [1989] derives performance bounds for such networks, and provides other recent references on bounding methods. Monotonicity properties are studied by Adan & Van der Wal [1989] and Shanthikumar & Yao [1989, 1992] who also consider second-order properties and convexity for finite buffer systems.

8.1.6. Remarks

In concluding this subsection it can be said that, for general networks with limited buffers, no single solution technique exists that is efficient, applies to a wide class of systems, and is robust (i.e., works well over a wide range of configurations and parameter values). This is in contrast to networks with unlimited buffer space: for example, for general open networks, Whitt [1983] and Bitran & Tirupati [1988] provide solution techniques that are both efficient and robust, and this is also evident to the extent that many industrial applications have been reported (Section 5.4). No such widespread use is found for general finite buffer solution algorithms. While the problem of finding a 'universal' finite buffer solution technique remains an open one, it is interesting to speculate on the reasons that make it difficult. First, blocking by its very nature means that the status of one station can seriously affect the service at another station, which destroys the 'pseudo-independence' of stations that is exploited by most of the efficient techniques. Attempts at decomposition and aggregation, therefore, become elaborate and require many special cases to be considered. Second, whenever one station blocks two or more stations, one needs to make sequencing decisions for the order of the unblocking. These decisions can have major effect on the performance, which means that this type of analysis needs to consider a greater level of sequencing detail than for the case of unlimited buffers. In fact, minor changes in topology or unblocking rules can have large effects on performance, a situation that always pushes the limits of analysis. Finally, there is also the possibility of deadlock with blocking, and it seems difficult to incorporate its effects efficiently in analytical models for the general case. For all these reasons, we see the development of a robust and efficient general purpose analyzer for networks with finite buffers as a continuing challenge for the indefinite future.

8.2. Kanban and related production control systems

Along with the influence of Japanese manufacturing techniques [e.g., Schonberger, 1982] have come several schemes to assist in the shop floor implementation of JIT. Probably the most well known of these is the Kanban system [Schonberger, 1983]. Performance analysis of Kanban systems has attracted the attention of the OR/MS community [see the review in Uzsoy & Martin-Vega, 1990]. Related to this is the analysis of various other production control schemes which interface with the new Kanban methods. We will therefore review related schemes here as well.

Essentially, Kanban is a card, or other form of signal, which instructs an upstream workstation to begin working on the next job. (Hence the alternative term 'pull system'.) In the more complex Dual Kanban system [Schonberger, 1983], Kanban are also used to signal material handling tasks. As in the previous sections, we will only review network-related ADMs below; other techniques to analyze pull systems (deterministic models, inventory models, petri nets, and simulation) are reviewed in Uzsoy & Martin-Vega [1990].

Suri & DeTreville [1986] analyze the behavior of a simple Kanban system, focusing on modeling the learning effects described in the JIT literature. Seidmann [1988] uses a semi-Markov decision program to compare alternative pull policies. Karmarkar and Kekre [1989] provide insight into batching policies for Kanban systems using Markov models of elementary systems, while more complex models are considered by Groenevelt & Karmarkar [1988]. Kanban-related production control policies are analyzed in Glassey & Resende [1988], Deleersnyder, Hodgson, Muller & O'Grady [1989], Karmarkar [1989], Mitra & Mitrani [1990, 1991], and Spearman & Zazanis [1992]. Models that address both MRP and Kanban systems are in Buzacott [1989] and Buzacott & Shanthikumar [1992a]. CONWIP, an alternative pull system, is analyzed in Spearman, Woodruff & Hopp [1990]. Much of the remaining work on analytical models is very recent, and still in the form of working papers; we have only covered articles that have appeared in the open literature.

Since Kanban policies essentially restrict the number of jobs in the system, their analysis is related to closed network models with blocking (since the non-availability of a Kanban can shut down a station). However, the blocking mechanism induced by Kanban is different from the other ones mentioned in Section 8.1.4. Still, it is possible that many approaches referenced in Section 8.1.4 could be applicable, with minor modifications, to performance analysis of Kanban systems. We feel here a responsibility to communicate to the OR/MS community the importance of 'not missing the boat' in modeling Kanban systems. To view Kanban (and JIT) as merely an inventory control policy is to ignore most of the benefits of JIT. As elaborated in Suri & DeTreville [1986], the major effects of JIT and Kanban come from the longer term learning and organizational changes induced by these mechanisms, not from the performance obtained with a given set of parameters. Ignoring this aspect will lead OR/MS publications on Kanban to the same fate as the EOQ formula.

8.3. *Simulation and other dynamic models*

As stated in Section 1, in this chapter we only deal in some depth with analytical models related to queueing networks. Here we simply summarize other types of dynamic models used for production network analysis. From an industrial applications point of view, the most widely used method is discrete event simulation, and a number of software packages are available for this [Law & Haider, 1989]. A large number of industrial applications of simulation can be found in the annual *Proceedings of the Winter Simulation Conference*, published each December. Related to simulation, and of more interest to the research community, are some recent techniques for sensitivity analysis based on sample-path approaches [Ho, 1987]. These include perturbation analysis [see the review in Suri, 1989a] and likelihood ratio methods [Glynn, 1989; Reiman & Weiss, 1989; Rubinstein, 1989]. Suri & Dille [1985] give a detailed example illustrating the use of such sensitivity analysis methods for decision making in an FMS.

Another approach involves the use of Petri net models. A Petri net is a formal mathematical language and set of symbols used to model a discrete event system. Although originally Petri nets were used primarily to analyze qualitative or logical questions (e.g., 'is there a possibility of deadlock with this control rule?') more recently, stochastic Petri net models have been used for performance analysis as well [Holliday & Vernon, 1987]. Examples of manufacturing applications include modeling of FMS [Kamath & Viswanadham, 1986; Viswanadham & Narahari, 1992] and Kanban systems [Di Mascolo, Frein, Dallery & David, 1989]. Other analytical models include algebraic models [Cohen, Dubois, Quadrat & Viot, 1985; Olsder, Resing, De Vries, Keane & Hooghiemstra, 1988] and formal language models [Inan & Varaiya, 1989; Ramadge & Wonham, 1989]. An up-to-date overview and bibliography of many of these other approaches can be found in Leung & Suri [1990].

8.4. *Hierarchical, hybrid, and integrated models*

This subsection covers models of systems that are much more complex than the ones discussed in earlier sections. In manufacturing, it is common for a workpiece to require multiple resources, such as a machine, an operator, and a fixture. This becomes difficult to analyze, and often simulation models must be used for performance analysis. One set of approximation schemes that has been proposed, however, uses hierarchical queueing network models. A special case of these, namely machine–operator interference models, has already been discussed in Section 7, and involves a two-level hierarchy. Pattipati & Kastner [1988] present a three-level hierarchical model for the analysis of a large and complex electronics facility. Such models bear a relation to the literature on 'simultaneous resource possession' in computer systems modeling, and a good review of various approaches can be found in Agrawal [1985].

In some cases, complex systems can be analyzed using hybrid models, which are models composed of more than one type of technique. Shanthikumar & Sargent [1983] describe and classify a number of hybrid simulation/analytic models, while Balbo, Bruel & Ghanta [1986] combine queueing network models with Petri nets.

Generally, during the life cycle of a manufacturing system, or during the course of an analysis project, no single performance analysis tool will serve all purposes. Therefore, a set of tools or 'toolbox' is more appropriate. Rather than work with a number of independent tools, each with their own data and models, some recent efforts have been made to develop integrated tools for manufacturing analysis [Anderson, Diehl, Shimizu & Suri, 1988; Suri & Tomsicek, 1988]. The benefits of integration include consistency of data across models, eliminating the need to build new models from scratch, and rapid exploration of multiple alternatives [Shimizu, 1991]. Manufacturing applications of such integrated tools are documented in Shimizu & Van Zoest [1988] and Desruelle, Gujar & Hammer [1990].

8.5. Research issues

We could state here a long list of network configurations that remain unsolved, or for which current approximations remain unsatisfactory. Such a list can, however, be easily derived by the researcher who carefully reads each of the preceding sections along with some of the key references. Therefore, we prefer to keep our remarks here at more of a fundamental level, in terms of general directions for the community, and also add a few somewhat subjective observations on what we consider to be important future directions of this field.

A critical observation that can be made about this subject is that industrial application of ADMs in manufacturing remain relatively limited – this is in contrast with other OR tools such as Linear Programming whose use is widespread. Although tools based on queueing network models are beginning to see greater use in manufacturing (see Section 5.4), we feel their potential remains largely untapped. This has an important implication for our community: it means we need to devote more effort (and provide greater incentives) to applying the modeling methods described in this chapter, and to publicizing the successful applications.

Given the recent successes of JIT and other Japanese manufacturing techniques, as well as the industrial awareness and acceptance of the need for those methods, a good strategy would seem to be for researchers to find analysis tools to assist in and complement the implementation of those techniques. One area that has already attracted attention is that of Kanban or pull systems, as discussed in Section 8.2. However, we restate our earlier remark that by simply modeling the control policy we risk missing many of the effects of JIT. In their recent review of models for Kanban systems, Uzsoy & Martin-Vega [1990] list the major benefits of JIT and then state: 'The large number of unquantifiable factors among those listed above and their intimate interrelation has rendered the development of mathematically based decision support tools for JIT environments difficult.' We see this not as an insurmountable task, but as a challenge for the modeling community: if our work is to remain relevant to the latest trends in manufacturing, then we must find better ways to quantify and model the benefits of JIT and related methods. For instance, one the benefits of JIT is the longer term learning that takes place on the shop floor, and a simple model in Suri & DeTreville [1986] gives insight into the benefits of JIT as well as the potential pitfalls of poor implementation of JIT. Also, extensive studies in Mody, Suri, Sanders & Tatikonda [1991], Mody, Suri, Sanders & Van Zoest [1991] and Mody, Sanders, Suri, Contreras & Rao [1991], based on ADMs, show the benefits of JIT implementation, including some of the so-called unquantifiable factors. Taking this idea a step further, any ways of using ADMs to support manufacturing *strategy* are likely to receive more attention than simply analyzing operational details [Suri & DeTreville, 1991].

Another way for expanding the use of these models is to integrate them with existing mainstream organizational procedures. Two important areas for which integration seems feasible in the short term are Manufacturing Resource Planning (MRP II) systems, and costing systems. Initial steps in integrating with MRP II systems have been discussed [Karmarkar, 1989; Luber, 1990; Buzacott & Shanthikumar, 1992a], but this requires better analysis of tree-structured assembly systems (Section 4), multi-period models, as well as analysis of the distribution of leadtimes [e.g., Shanthikumar & Buzacott, 1984; Seidmann & Nof, 1985; Shanthikumar & Sumita, 1988]. Integrating with costing systems involves improved modeling of total system costs, including overheads, so that the full benefits of various alternatives can be quantified [e.g., Fu, Falkner, Suri & Garlid, 1988; Mody, Suri, Sanders & Tatikonda, 1991].

A technical problem that deserves being singled out here is that of modeling general networks with blocking. As discussed in Section 8.1.6, the problem of finding a good and fairly universal approximation procedure for such networks remains unsolved. At the same time, buffer sizing is important in many modern automated systems, as well as in JIT systems. Related to this is the general problem of modeling material handling systems (such as automatic guided vehicle systems), where blocking is also an important issue. While a few analytical inroads have been made into these areas, currently simulation is the major technique used to study the performance of such systems.

A general approach to such complex systems is to look for qualitative results. Initial successes in this area are represented by Shanthikumar & Yao [1989, 1992] and Glasserman & Yao [1991, 1992a,b].

Finally, instead of trying to extend our analytical models for more and more complex systems, there is an alternative: that is, to simplify the manufacturing systems so that they can be analyzed by well-understood models. Much of the basis for success of JIT and related methods comes from simplification, such as, reducing the number of levels of assembly, cutting down the number of components using group technology, and simplifying layouts using cellular manufacturing [Schonberger, 1982, 1986]. Here we refer to a particular type of simplification, that which comes from *analyzability*. This is not just a hypothesis: Suri & Shimizu [1989] term this approach Design for Analysis, argue why it is worth investigating, and give several examples of industrial situations where such a methodology has resulted in competitive advantage. The research agenda related to this approach is therefore twofold: (i) what are the manufacturing building blocks, and ways of combining them, that result in systems that are analyzable with known models; and (ii) in which directions should we push the frontiers of our modeling abilities to make the set of such building blocks more universal. It should also be noted that if this approach gains acceptance, it intimately binds performance analysis with design, and it would accomplish our stated goal of having our community play a more active and strategic role in design and manufacturing decisions.

In conclusion, in the last two decades there has been an exponential (!) growth in performance analysis techniques for production networks, and it is also encouraging to see some industrial applications of these methods. However, there is much to be done to bring these techniques and tools to the point where they are in everyday use by manufacturing and industrial engineers. We see this as the most important challenge for the performance analysis community during the decade of the 1990s.

Acknowledgements

Several researchers provided us with valuable feedback on an earlier version of this chapter. In particular, we would like to acknowledge useful comments from John Buzacott, Ramki Desiraju, Bor-Ruey Fu, Ying-Tat Leung, Chandu Rao, Avi Seidmann, Kathy Stecke, Kalluru Venkateswar, and David Yao.

References

Adan, I, and J. Van der Wal (1989). Monotonicity of the throughput of a closed queueing network in the number of jobs. *Oper. Res.* 37(6), 953–957.

Agrawal, S.C. (1985). *Metamodeling: A study of approximations in queueing models*, Research Reports and Notes, Computer Systems Series, MIT Press, Cambridge, MA.

Akyildiz, I.F. (1989). Exact analysis of queueing networks with rejection blocking, in: H.G. Perros and T. Altiok (eds.), *Queueing Networks with Blocking*, Elsevier, Amsterdam, pp. 19–32.

Albin, S.L. (1982). Poisson approximations for superposition arrival processes in queues. *Management Sci.* 28(2), 126–137.

Altiok, T. (1982). Approximate analysis of exponential tandem queues with blocking. *European J. Oper. Res.* 11, 390–398.

Altiok, T., and S. Stidham Jr (1982). A note on transfer lines with unreliable machines, random processing times, and finite buffers. *IIE Trans.* 12(2), 125–127.

Altiok, T., and S. Stidham Jr (1983). The allocation of interstage buffer capacities in production lines. *IIE Trans.* 15(4), 292–299.

Alvarez, R., Y. Dallery and R. David (1991). An experimental study of the continuous flow model of transfer lines with unreliable machines and finite buffers. *IMACS-IFAC Symposium: Modeling and Control of Technological Systems 91*, Lille, France.

Ammar, M.H. (1980). Modelling and analysis of unreliable manufacturing assembly networks with finite storage, MIT Laboratory for Information and Decision Sciences, Report LIDS-TH-1004.

Anderson, K.R. (1987). A method for planning analysis and design simulation of CIM systems. *Proc. 1987 Winter Simulation Conf.*, IEEE Computer Society Press, pp. 715–720.

Anderson, K.R., G.W. Diehl, M. Shimizu and R. Suri (1988). Integrating spreadsheets, system modeling, and animation for rapid computer-aided design of manufacturing systems. *Proc. 1988 University Programs in Computer-Aided Engineering, Design and Manufacturing (UPCAEDM) Conf.*

Ashcroft, H. (1950). The productivity of several machines under the care of one operator. *J. Roy. Statist. Soc. B* 12(9) 145–151.

Balbo, G., S.C. Bruel and S. Ghanta (1986). Combining queueing network and generalized stochastic Petri net models for the analysis of some software blocking phenomena. *IEEE Trans. Software Engrg.* 12(4), 561–576.

Balbo, G., G. Chiola and G. Franceschinis (1989). Stochastic Petri net simulation for the evaluation of flexible manufacturing systems. *Proc. 1989 European Simulation Multiconference*, pp. 5–12.

Balsamo, S., and G. Iazeolla (1982). An extension of Norton's theorem for queueing networks. *IEEE Trans. Software Engrg.* 8(4), 298–305.

Barbour, A.D. (1976). Networks of queues and the method of stages. *Adv. Appl. Probl.* 8, 584–591.

Bard, Y. (1979). Some extensions to multiclass queueing network analysis, in: M. Arato (ed.), *Performance of Computer Systems*, North-Holland, Amsterdam.

Barlow, R.E., and F. Proschan (1975). *Statistical theory of Reliability and Life Testing: Probability Models*, Holt, Reinhart, and Winston, New York.

Baskett, F., K.M. Chandy, R.R. Muntz and F.G. Palacios (1975). Open, closed, and mixed networks of queues with different classes of customers. *J. ACM* 22(2), 248–260.

Benson, F., and D.R. Cox (1951). The productivity of machines requiring attention at random intervals. *J. Roy. Statist. Soc. B* 13(1), 65–82.

BGS Systems, Inc. (1982). *BEST/1 User's Guide*, Waltham, MA.

Bhat, U.N. (1972). *Elements of Applied Stochastic Processes*, Wiley, New York.

Bitran, G.R., and D. Tirupati (1988). Multiproduct queueing networks with deterministic routing: Decomposition approach and the notion of interference. *Management Sci.* 34(1), 75–100.

Bitran, G.R., and D. Tirupati (1991). Approximations for networks of queues with overtime. *Management Sci.* 37(3), 282–300.

Boxma, O.J., F.P. Kelly and A.G. Konheim (1984). The product form of the sojourn time distributions in cyclic exponential queues. *J. ACM* 31(1), 128–133.

Boxma, O.J., and A.G. Konheim (1981). Approximate analysis of exponential queueing systems with blocking. *Acta Inform.* 15, 19–66.

Brandwajn, A.E. (1974). A model of a time-sharing virtual memory system solved using equivalence and decomposition methods. *Acta Inform.* 4(1), 11–47.

Brandwajn, A.E. (1982). Fast approximate solution of multiprogramming models, Proc. 1982 ACM SIGMETRICS Conf. on Measurement and Modeling of Computer Systems, Seattle, August 1982, *Performance Evaluation Rev.* 11(4), 141–149.

Brandwajn, A., and Y.L. Jow (1988). An approximation method for tandem queues with blocking. *Oper. Res.* 36(1), 73–83.

Brown, E. (1988). IBM combines rapid modeling technique and simulation to design PCB factory-of-the-future. *Ind. Eng.* 20(6), 23–26.

Bruell, S.C., and G. Balbo (1980). *Computational Algorithms for Closed Queueing Networks*, Elsevier, New York.

Brumfield, J.A. (1982). Operational analysis of queueing phenomenon, Ph.D. Thesis, Dept. of Computer Sciences, Purdue University, West Lafayette.

Bulgak, A.A., M. Kamath and J.L. Sanders (1989). Research on the dynamics and design optimization of automatic assembly systems. *Proc. 15th Conf. on Production Research and Technology*, SME, 275–283.

Bunday, B.D., and R.E. Scraton (1980). The G/M/*r* machine interference model. *European J. Oper. Res.* 4, 399–402.

Burke, P.J. (1956). The output of a queueing system. *Oper. Res.* 4, 699–704.

Buzacott, J.A. (1967). Automatic transfer lines with buffer stocks. *Internat. J. Prod. Res.* 5(3), 183–200.

Buzacott, J.A. (1972). The effect of station breakdowns and random processing times on the capacity of flow lines with in-process storage. *AIIE Trans.* 4(4), 308–312.

Buzacott, J.A. (1982). 'Optimal' operating rules for automated manufacturing systems. *IEEE Trans. Automat. Control*, 80–86.

Buzacott, J.A. (1989). Queueing models of Kanban and MRP controlled production systems. *Engrg. Costs Prod. Econom.* 17, 3–20.

Buzacott, J.A. (1990). Abandoning the moving assembly line: Models of human operators and job sequencing. *Internat. J. Prod. Res.* 28(5), 821–839.

Buzacott, J.A., and L.E. Hanifin (1978). Models of automatic transfer lines with inventory banks – A review and comparison. *AIIE Trans.* 10(2), 197–207.

Buzacott, J.A., and D. Kostelski (1987). Matrix-geometric and recursive algorithm solution of a two-stage unreliable flow line. *IIE Trans.* 19(4), 429–438.

Buzacott, J.A., and J.G. Shanthikumar (1980). Models for understanding flexible manufacturing systems. *AIIE Trans.* 12, 339–350.

Buzacott, J.A., and J.G. Shanthikumar (1985). On approximate queueing models of dynamic job shops. *Management Sci.* 31(7), 870–887.

Buzacott, J.A., and J.G. Shanthikumar (1992a). A general approach for coordinating production in multiple-cell manufacturing systems. *Prod. Oper. Management* 1(1), 34–52.

Buzacott, J.A., and J.G. Shanthikumar (1992b). *Stochastic Models of Manufacturing Systems*, Prentice-Hall, Englewood Cliffs, NJ.

Buzacott, J.A., and D.D. Yao (1986). Flexible manufacturing systems: A review of analytical models. *Management Sci.* 32(7), 890–905.

Buzen, J.P. (1973). Computational algorithms for closed queueing networks with exponential servers. *Commun. ACM* 16(9), 527–531.

Buzen, J.P. (1976). Operational analysis: The key to the new generation of performance prediction tools. COMPCON Fall 1976, Washington, DC, 166–171.

Calabrese, J.M., and W.H. Hausman (1991). Simultaneous determination of lot sizes and routing mix in job shops. *Management Sci.* 37(8), 1043–1057.

Cavaille, J.B., and D. Dubois (1982). Heuristic methods based on mean value analysis for flexible manufacturing systems performance evaluation. *Proc. 21st IEEE Conf. on Decision and Control*, Orlando, Florida, pp. 1061–1065.

Chandy, K.M., U. Herzog and L. Woo (1975a). Parametric analysis of queueing networks. *IBM J. Res. Develop.* 19(1), 36–42.

Chandy, K.M., U. Herzog and L. Woo (1975b). Approximate analysis of general queueing networks. *IBM J. Res. Develop.* 19(1), 43–49.

Chandy, K.M., and D. Neuse (1982). Linearizer: A heuristic algorithm for queueing network models of computing systems. *Commun. ACM* 25(2), 126–134.

Chandy, K.M., and C.H. Sauer (1980). Computational algorithms for product form queueing networks. *Commun. ACM* 23(10), 573–583.

Chen, H., J.M. Harrison, A. Mandelbaum, A. Van Ackere and L.M. Wein (1988). Empirical evaluation of a queueing network model for semiconductor wafer fabrication. *Oper. Res.* 36, 202–215.

Choobineh, F., and R. Suri, eds. (1986). *Flexible Manufacturing Systems: Current Issues and Models*, Industrial Engineering & Management Press, Atlanta, GA.

Choong, Y.F., and S.B. Gershwin (1987). A decomposition method for the approximate evaluation of capacitated transfer lines with unreliable machines and random processing times. *IIE Trans.* 19(2), 150–159.

Clark, C.D. (1961). The greatest of a finite set of random variables. *Oper. Res.* 9(2), 145–162.
Cohen, G., D. Dubois, J.P. Quadrat and M. Viot (1985). A linear-system-theoretic view of discrete-event processes and its use for performance evaluation in manufacturing. *IEEE Trans. Automat. Control* 30, 210–220.
Conway, A.E., and N.D. Georganas (1986). RECAL – A new efficient algorithm for the exact analysis of multiple-chain closed queueing networks. *J. Assoc. Comput. Mach.* 33(4), 768–791.
Courtois, P.J. (1977). *Decomposability: Queueing and Computer System Applications*, Academic Press, New York.
Dallery, Y., R. David and X.L. Xie (1988). An efficient algorithm for analysis of transfer lines with unreliable machines and finite buffers. *IIE Trans.* 20(3), 280–283.
Dallery, Y., R. David and X.L. Xie (1989). Approximate analysis of transfer lines with unreliable machines and finite buffers. *IEEE Trans. Automat. Control* 34(9), 943–953.
Dallery, Y., and Y. Frein (1986). An efficient method to determine the optimal configuration of a flexible manufacturing system. *Proc. 2nd ORSA/TIMS Conf. on Flexible Manufacturing Systems*, Ann Arbor, MI, pp. 269–282.
Dallery, Y., and Y. Frein (1989). A decomposition method for the approximate analysis of closed queueing networks with blocking, in: H.G. Perros and T. Altiok (eds.), *Queueing Networks with Blocking*, Elsevier, Amsterdam, pp. 19–32.
Daskalaki, S., and J.M. Smith (1989). Real-time routing in finite queueing networks, in: H.G. Perros and T. Altiok (eds.), *Queueing Networks with Blocking*, Elsevier, Amsterdam, pp. 313–324.
Deleersnyder, J.-L., T.J. Hodgson, H. Muller and P.J. O'Grady (1989). Kanban controlled pull systems: An analytical approach. *Management Sci.* 35(9), 1079–1091.
Denning, P.J., and J.P. Buzen (1978). The operational analysis of queueing network models. *ACM Comput. Surveys* 10(3), 225–261.
Dertouzos, M.L., R.K. Lester, R.M. Solow and the MIT Commission on Industrial Productivity (1989). *Made in America: Regaining the Productive Edge*, MIT Press, London.
De Souza e Silva, E., and S.S. Lavenberg (1989). Calculating joint queue-length distributions in product-form queueing networks. *J. Assoc. Comput. Mach.* 36(1), 194–207.
De Souza e Silva, E., and R.R. Muntz (1987). Approximate solutions for a class of nonproduct form queueing networks. *Performance Evaluation* 7, 221–242.
Desruelle, P., R. Gujar and R. Hammer (1990). Design of a circuit board manufacturing module using a consistent sequence of PC-based analysis tools. *Proc. Manufacturing Intl. '90 Conf.*, ASME Press.
DeTreville, S. (1991). FMS: Finnish manufacturing systems. *Manuf. Syst.* 9, 14–17.
Dietrich, B.L., and B.M. March (1985). An application of a hybrid approach to modeling a flexible manufacturing system. *Ann. Oper. Res.* 3, 263–276.
Di Mascolo, M., Y. Frein, Y. Dallery and R. David (1989). Modeling of Kanban systems using Petri nets. *Proc. Third ORSA/TIMS Conf. Flexible Manufacturing Syst.*, Elsevier, Amsterdam, pp. 307–312.
Disney, R., and D. Koenig (1985). Queueing networks: A survey of their random processes. *SIAM Rev.* 27, 335–403.
Eager, D.L., and K.C. Sevcik (1983). Performance bound hierarchies for queueing networks. *ACM Trans. Comp. Syst.* 1(2), 99–115.
Emerson, H.P., and D.C.E. Naehring (1988). *Origins of Industrial Engineering: The Early Years of Profession*, Industrial Engineering & Management Press, Atlanta, GA.
Ferdinand, A.E. (1970). A statistical mechanical approach to systems analysis. *IBM J. Res. Develop.* 14, 539–547.
Flatto, L., and S. Hahn (1984). Two parallel queues created by arrivals with two demands. I. *SIAM J. Appl. Math.* 44(5), 1041–1053.
Fleming, P.J., and B. Simon (1991). Interpolation approximations of sojourn time distributions. *Oper. Res.* 39(2), 251–260.
Foster, F.G., and H.G. Perros (1980). On the blocking process in queue networks. *European J. Oper. Res.* 5, 276–283.

Fu, B.R., C. Falkner, R. Suri and S. Garlid (1988). Combining economic analysis and system modeling to evaluate test strategies for circuit board assembly lines, in: J.A. Edosomwan and A. Ballakur (eds.), *Productivity and Quality Improvement in Electronics Assembly*, Industrial Engineering & Management Press, Atlanta, GA, pp. 479–506.

Gelenbe, E., and G. Pujolle (1987). *Introduction to Queueing Networks*. Wiley, New York.

Gershwin, S.B. (1987a). An efficient decomposition method for the approximate evaluation of tandem queues with finite storage space and blocking. *Oper. Res.* 35(2), 291–305.

Gershwin, S.B. (1987b). Representation and analysis of transfer lines with machines that have different processing rates. *Ann. Oper. Res.* 9, 511–530.

Gershwin, S.B. (1991). Assembly/disassembly systems: An efficient decomposition algorithm for tree-structured networks. *IIE Trans.* 23(4), 302–314.

Gershwin, S.B., and O. Berman (1981). Analysis of transfer lines consisting of two unreliable machines with random processing times and finite storage buffers. *AIIE Trans.* 13(1), 2–11.

Gershwin, S.B., R.R. Hildebrant, S.K. Mitter, and R. Suri (1986). A control perspective on recent trends in manufacturing systems. *IEEE Control Syst. Mag.* 6, 3–15.

Gershwin, S.B., and I.C. Schick (1983). Modeling and analysis of three-stage transfer lines with unreliable machines and finite buffers. *Oper. Res.* 31, 354–380.

Glasserman, P., and D.D. Yao (1991). Algebraic structure of some stochastic discrete event systems, with applications. *Discrete Event Dynamic Systems: Theory and Applications* 1, 7–35.

Glasserman, P., and D.D. Yao (1992a). Monotonicity in generalized semi Markov processes. *Math. Oper. Res.* 17(1), 1–21.

Glasserman, P., and D.D. Yao (1992b). Generalized semi-Markov processes: Antimatroid structure and second-order properties. *Math. Oper. Res.* 17(2), 444–469.

Glassey, C.R., and M.G.C. Resende (1988). Closed-loop release control for VLSI circuit manufacturing. *IEEE Trans. Semiconductor Manuf.* 1, 36–46.

Glynn, P.W. (1989). Likelihood ratio derivative estimators for stochastic systems. *Proc. 1989 Winter Simulation Conf.*, IEEE Computer Society Press, pp. 374–380.

Glynn, P.W., and W. Whitt (1991). A new view of the heavy-traffic limit theorem for infinite-server queues. *Adv. in Appl. Probab.* 23(1), 188–209.

Gordon, K.D., and L.W. Dowdy (1980). The impact of certain parameter estimation errors in queueing network models. *Proc. Performance '80, Toronto, Canada, Performance Evaluation Rev.* 9(2), 3–9.

Gordon, W.J., and G.F. Newell (1967a). Closed queueing systems with exponential servers. *Oper. Res.* 15, 254–265.

Gordon, W.J., and G.F. Newell (1967b). Cyclic queueing systems with restricted length queues. *Oper. Res.* 15, 266–277.

Graves, S.C. (1981). A review of production scheduling. *Oper. Res.* 29(4), 646–675.

Groenevelt, H., and U.S. Karmarkar (1988). A dynamic Kanban system case study. *Prod. Invent. Management J.* 29, 46–50.

Gross, D., and C.M. Harris (1985). *Fundamentals of Queueing Theory*, Wiley, New York.

Harper, R., and M.J. O'Loughlin (1987). Manufacturing process analysis – Tools and applications. *Proceedings of the 1987 Winter Simulation Conference*, IEEE Computer Society Press, pp. 731–737.

Harrison, J.M. (1973). Assembly like queues. *J. Appl. Probab.* 10, 354–367.

Harrison, J., and V. Nguyen (1990). The QNET method for two-moment analysis of open queueing networks. *Queueing Syst.* 6, 1–32.

Hax, A.C., and H.C. Meal (1975). Hierarchical integration of production planning and scheduling, in: M.A. Geisler (ed.), *Logistics*, North-Holland, Amsterdam.

Hayes, R.H., S.C. Wheelwright and K.B. Clark (1988). *Dynamic Manufacturing: Creating the Learning Organization*, The Free Press, New York.

Heyman, P., and M.J. Sobel (1982). *Stochastic Models in Operations Research*, McGraw-Hill, New York.

Hillier, F.S., and R.W. Boling (1967). Finite queues in series with exponential or Erlang service times – A numerical approach. *Oper. Res.* 15, 286–303.

Ho, Y.C. (1987). Performance evaluation and perturbation analysis of discrete event dynamic systems. *IEEE Trans. Automat. Control* 32, 563–572.

Holliday, M.A., and M.K. Vernon (1987). A generalized timed Petri net model for performance analysis. *IEEE Trans. Software Engrg.* 13, 1297–1310.

Hopp, W.J., and J.T. Simon (1989). Bounds and heuristics for assembly-like queues. *Queueing Syst.* 4, 137–156.

Hoyme, K.P., S.C. Bruell, P.V. Afshari and R.Y. Kain (1982). A tree-structured MVA algorithm, Tech. Report 82-17, Computer Science Dpartment, University of Minnesota, Minneapolis, MN.

Inan, K.M., and P.P. Varaiya (1989). Algebras of discrete event models. *Proc. IEEE* 77, 24–38.

Jackson, J.R. (1963). Jobshop-like queueing systems. *Management Sci.* 10, 131–142.

Jacobson, P.A., and E.D. Lazowska (1982). Analyzing queueing networks with simultaneous resource possession. *Commun. ACM* 25(2), 142–151.

Jun, K.P., and H.G. Perros (1989). Approximate analysis of arbitrary configurations of queueing networks with blocking and deadlock, in: H.G. Perros and T. Altiok (eds.), *Queueing Networks with Blocking*, Elsevier, Amsterdam, pp. 259–279.

Kamath, M. (1989). Analytical performance models for automatic assembly systems, Ph.D. thesis, Dept. of Industrial Engineering, University of Wisconsin-Madison.

Kamath, M., and J.L. Sanders (1986). Analysis of asynchronous automatic assembly systems with bottleneck stations. *SYSTEMS I Conf. Papers*, SME, Chicago, IL.

Kamath, M., and J.L. Sanders (1987). Analytical methods for performance evaluation of large asynchronous automatic assembly systems. *Large Scale Syst.* 12(2), 143–154.

Kamath, M., and J.L. Sanders (1991). Modeling operator/workstation interference in asynchronous automatic assembly systems. *Discrete Event Dynamic Systems: Theory and Applications* 1, 93–124.

Kamath, M., R. Suri, and J.L. Sanders (1988). Analytical performance models for closed-loop flexible assembly systems. *Internat. J. Flexible Manuf. Syst.* 1, 51–84.

Kamath, M., and N. Viswanadham (1986). Applications of Petri net based models in the modeling and analysis of flexible manufacturing systems, *Proc. IEEE 1986 Internat. Conf. Robotics Automation*, IEEE Computer Society Press, pp. 312–317.

Karmarkar, U.S. (1987). Lot sizes, lead times and in-process inventories. *Management Sci.* 33, 409–418.

Karmarkar, U.S. (1989). Capacity loading, release planning and master scheduling with WIP and lead times. *J. Manuf. Oper. Management.*

Karmarkar, U.S., and S. Kekre (1989). Batching policy in Kanban systems. *J. Manuf. Syst.* 9(4), 317–328.

Karmarkar, U.S., S. Kekre and S. Kekre (1985a). Lot sizing in multi-item multi-machine job shops. *IIE Trans.* 17, 290–292.

Karmarkar, U.S., S. Kekre, S. Kekre and S. Freeman (1985b). Lotsizing and lead time performance in a manufacturing cell. *Interfaces* 15, 1–9.

Kelly, F.P. (1975). Networks of queues with customers of different types. *J. Appl. Probab.* 12, 542–554.

Kelly, F.P. (1976). Networks of queues. *Adv. Appl. Prob.* 8, 416–432.

Kelly, F.P. (1979). *Reversibility and Stochastic Networks*, Wiley, New York.

Kimemia, J.G., and S.B. Gershwin (1983). An algorithm for the computer control of production in flexible manufacturing systems. *IIE Trans.* 15(4), 353–362.

Kingman, J.F.C. (1962). Some inequalities for the GI/G/1 queue. *Biometrika* 49, 315–324.

Kleinrock, L. (1975). *Queueing Systems Vol. 1: Theory*. Wiley, New York.

Kleinrock, L. (1976). *Queueing Systems Vol. 2: Computer Applications*, Wiley, New York.

Kobayashi, H. (1974). Application of the diffusion approximation to queueing networks I: Equilibrium queue distributions. *J. ACM* 21, 316–328.

Koenigsberg, E. (1959). Production lines and internal storage – A review. *Management Sci.* 5, 401–433.

Koenigsberg, E. (1982). Twenty five years of cyclic queues and closed queue networks: A review. *J. Oper. Res. Soc.* 33, 605–619.

Koenigsberg, E., and A. Mamer (1982). The analysis of production systems. *Internat. J. Prod. Res.* 20, 1–14.

Kogan, Ya.A., and E.V. Krichagina (1989). Closed exponential queueing networks with blocking in heavy traffic, in: H.G. Perros and T. Altiok (eds.), *Queueing Networks with Blocking*, Elsevier, Amsterdam, pp. 217–225.

Konheim, A.G., and M. Reiser (1976). A queueing model with finite waiting room and blocking. *J. Assoc. Comput. Mach.* 23(2), 328–341.

Konheim, A.G., and M. Reiser (1978). Finite capacity queueing systems with applications in computer modeling. *SIAM J. Comput.* 7(2), 210–229.

Kouvatsos, D.D. (1985). Maximum entropy methods for general queueing networks, in: D. Poltier (ed.), *Modelling Techniques and Tools for Performance Analysis*, North-Holland, Amsterdam, pp. 589–608.

Kouvatsos, D.D., and N.P. Xenios (1989). Maximum entropy analysis of general queueing networks with blocking, in: H.G. Perros and T. Altiok (eds.), *Queueing Networks with Blocking*, Elsevier, Amsterdam, pp. 281–309.

Kraemer, W., and M. Langenbach-Belz (1976). Approximate formulae for the delay in the queueing system GI/G/1. *Proc. 8th Internat. Teletraffic Congress*, Melbourne, pp. 235–1/8.

Kuehn, P.J. (1979). Approximate analysis of general queueing networks by decomposition. *IEEE Trans. Comm.* 27, 113–126.

Labetoulle, J., and G. Pujolle (1980). Isolation method in a network of queues. *IEEE Trans. Software Engrg.* 6(4), 373–381.

Lam, S.S., and Y.L. Lien (1983). A tree convoluted algorithm for the solution of queueing networks. *Commun. ACM* 26(3), 203–215.

Latouche, G. (1981). Queues with paired customers. *J. Appl. Probab.* 18, 684–690.

Lavenberg, S.S. (ed.) (1983). *Computer Performance Modeling Handbook*, Academic Press, New York.

Law, A.M., and S.W. Haider (1989). Selecting simulation software for manufacturing applications: Practical guidelines and software survey. *Ind. Eng.* 21, 33–46.

Lazowska, E.D., and J. Zahorjan (1982). Multiple class memory constrained queueing networks, Proc. 1982 ACM SIGMETRICS Conf. on Measurement and Modeling of Computer Systems, Seattle, August 1982, Performance Evaluation Rev. 11(4), 130–140.

Lazowska, E.D., J. Zahorjan, G.S. Graham and K.C. Sevcik (1984). *Quantitative System Performance: Computer System Analysis Using Queueing Network Models*, Prentice-Hall, Englewood Cliffs, NJ.

Lee, H.F., M.M. Srinivasan and C.A. Yano (1989). An algorithm for the minimum cost configuration problem in flexible manufacturing systems, in: K.E. Stecke and R. Suri (eds.), *Proc. 3rd ORSA/TIMS Conf. on Flexible Manufacturing Systems: Operations Research Models and Applications*, Elsevier, Amsterdam, pp. 85–90.

Leung, Y.T., and M. Kamath (1991). Performance analysis of synchronous production lines. *IEEE Trans. Robotics and Automation* 7(1), 1–8.

Leung, Y.T., and R. Suri (1990). Performance evaluation of discrete manufacturing systems. *IEEE Control Syst. Mag.*, 77–86.

Lindley, D.V. (1952). The theory of queues with a single server. *Proc. Cambridge Philos. Soc.* 48, 277–289.

Lipper, E.H., and B. Sengupta (1986). Assembly-like queues with finite capacity: Bounds, asymptotics and approximations. *Queueing Syst.: Theory Appl.* 1, 67.

Little, J.D.C. (1961). A proof for the queueing formula $L = \lambda W$. *Oper. Res.* 9, 383–387.

Liu, X.-G., and J.A. Buzacott (1989). A zero-buffer equivalence technique for decomposing queueing networks with blocking, in: H.G. Perros and T. Altiok (eds.), *Queueing Networks with Blocking*, Elsevier, Amsterdam, pp. 87–104.

Liu, X.-G., and J.A. Buzacott (1990). Approximate models of assembly systems with finite inventory banks. *European J. Oper. Res.* 45(2–3), 143–154.

Luber, A. (1990). Rapid modeling systems: A practical alternative to MRP II rough cut capacity planning. *P & IM Rev.*, March.

Marchal, W.G. (1985). Numerical performance of approximate queueing formulae with application to flexible manufacturing systems. *Ann. Oper. Res.* 3, 141–152.

Marie, R. (1978). Modelisation par reseaux de files d'attente, Ph.D. thesis, Université de Rennes, France.

Marshall, K.T. (1968). Some inequalities in queueing. *Oper. Res.* 16, 651–665.

Mascolo, M.D., R. David and Y. Dallery (1991). Modeling and analysis of assembly systems with unreliable machines and finite buffers. *IIE Trans.* 23(4), 315–330.

McKenna, J., and D. Mitra (1982). Integral representations and asymptotic expansions for closed Markovian queueing networks: Normal usage. *Bell Syst. Tech. J.* 61(5), 661–683.

McKenna, J., and D. Mitra (1984). Asymptotic expansions and integral representations of moments of queue lengths in closed Markovian networks. *J. ACM* 31(2), 346–360.

Mitra, D., and I. Mitrani (1990). Analysis of a Kanban discipline for cell coordination in production lines. I. *Management Sci.* 36(12), 1548–1566.

Mitra, D., and I. Mitrani (1991). Analysis of a Kanban discipline for cell coordination in production lines. II: Stochastic demands. *Oper. Res.* 39(5), 807–823.

Mody, A., J.L. Sanders, R. Suri, F. Contreras and P.C. Rao (1991). *International Competition in the Bicycle Industry: Keeping Pace with Technological Change*, The World Bank, Washington DC.

Mody, A., R. Suri, J.L. Sanders and M. Tatikonda (1991). *International Competition in the Printed Circuit Board Industry: Keeping Pace with Technological Change*, The World Bank, Washington, DC.

Mody, A., R. Suri, J.L. Sanders and D. Van Zoest (1991). *International Competition in the Footwear Industry: Keeping Pace with Technologial Change*, The World Bank, Washington, DC.

Muntz, R.R., and J. Wong (1974). Asymptotic properties of closed queueing network models. *Proc. 8th Ann. Princeton Conf. on Information Science and Systems*, Princeton University.

Muth, E.J. (1979). The reversibility property of production lines. *Management Sci.* 25(2), 152–158.

Neuts, M.F. (1981). *Matrix-Geometric Solutions in Stochastic Models*, Johns Hopkins University Press, Baltimore.

Nymon, J. (1987). Using analytical and simulation modeling for early factory prototyping. *Proceedings of the 1987 Winter Simulation Conference*, IEEE Computer Society Press, pp. 721–724.

Ohmi, T. (1981). An approximation for the production efficiency of automatic transfer lines with in-process storages. *AIIE Trans.* 13(1), 22–28.

Olsder, G.J., J.A.C. Resing, R.E. De Vries, M.S. Keane and G. Hooghiemstra (1988). Discrete event systems with stochastic processing times. *Proc. 27th IEEE Conf. Decision and Control.* IEEE Computer Society Press.

Onvural, R. (1989). On the exact decomposition of deadlock free closed queueing networks with blocking, in: H.G. Perros and T. Altiok (eds.), *Queueing Networks with Blocking*, Elsevier, Amsterdam, pp. 73–83.

Onvural, R.O., and H.G. Perros (1990). Approximate throughput in cyclic queueing networks with blocking. *IEEE Trans. Software Engrg.* 15, 800–808.

Palesano, J., and J. Chandra (1986). A machine interference problem with multiple types of failures. *Internat. J. Prod. Res.* 24(3), 567–582.

Pattipati, K.R., and M.P. Kastner (1988). A hierarchical queueing network model of a large electronics test facility. *Inform. Decision Tech.* 14(1), 45–64.

Perros, H.G. (1984). Queueing networks with blocking: A bibliography. *Performance Evaluation Rev., ACM SIGMETRICS* 12, 8–12.

Perros, H.G., and T. Altiok (1986). Approximate analysis of open networks of queues with blocking: Tandem configurations. *IEEE Trans. on Software Engrg.* 12(3), 450–461.

Perros, H.G., and T. Altiok (eds.) (1989). *Queueing Networks with Blocking*, Elsevier, Amsterdam.

Pollock, S.M., J.R. Birge and J.M. Alden (1985). Approximation analysis for open tandem queues with blocking: Exponential and general service distribution, Technical Report 85-30. Department of Industrial and Operations Engrg., The University of Michigan, Ann Arbor, MI.

Ramadge, P.J., and W.M. Wonham (1989). The control of discrete event systems. *Proc. IEEE* 77, 81–98.
Reiman, M (1984). Open queueing networks in heavy traffic. *Math. Oper. Res.* 9, 441–458.
Reiman, M.I., and A. Weiss (1989). Sensitivity analysis for simulations via likelihood ratios. *Oper. Res.* 37, 830–844.
Reiser, M. (1979). A queueing network analysis of computer communication networks with window flow control. *IEEE Trans. Comm.* 27, 1199–1209.
Reiser, M. (1981). Mean-value analysis and convolution method for queue-dependent servers in closed queueing networks. *Performance Evaluation* 1, 7–18.
Reiser, M., and H. Kobayashi (1974). Accuracy of the diffusion approximation for some queueing systems. *IBM J. Res. Develop.* 18, 110–124.
Reiser, M., and H. Kobayashi (1976). Queueing networks with multiple closed chains: Theory and computational algorithms. *IBM J. Res. Develop.* 19, 283–294.
Reiser, M., and S.S. Lavenberg (1980). Mean-value analysis of closed multichain queueing networks. *J. ACM* 27, 313–322.
Robertazzi, T.G.', and A.A. Lazar (1985). On the modeling and optimal flow control of the Jacksonian network. *Performance Evaluation* 5, 29–43.
Ross, S.M. (1989). *Introduction to Probability Models*. Academic Press, Orlando, FL.
Rubinstein, R.Y. (1989). Sensitivity analysis and performance extrapolation for computer simulation models. *Oper. Res.* 37, 72–81.
Saboo, S., and W.E. Wilhelm (1986). An approach for modeling small-lot assembly networks. *IIE Trans.* 18, 322–334.
Sauer, C.H., and K.M. Chandy (1981). *Computer System Performance Evaluation*, Prentice-Hall, Englewood Cliffs, NJ.
Schassberger, R. (1978). The insensitivity of stationary probabilities in networks of queues. *Adv. Appl. Prob.* 10, 906–912.
Schonberger, R.J. (1982). *Japanese Manufacturing Techniques: Nine Hidden Lessons in Simplicity*, The Free Press, New York.
Schonberger, R.J. (1983). Applications of single-card and dual-card Kanban. *Interfaces* 13(4) 56–67.
Schonberger, R.J. (1986). *World Class Manufacturing: The Lessons of Simplicity Applied*, The Free Press, New York.
Schweitzer, P. (1979). Approximate analysis of multiclass closed networks of queues, Presented at the International Conference, Stochastic Control and Optimization, Amsterdam, The Netherlands.
Schweitzer, P.J., and T. Altiok (1989). Aggregate modeling of tandem queues without intermediate buffers, in: H.G. Perros and T. Altiok (eds.), *Queueing Networks with Blocking*, Elsevier, Amsterdam, pp. 47–72.
Schweitzer, P.J., A. Seidmann and S. Shalev-Oren (1986). The correction terms in approximate mean value analysis. *Oper. Res. Lett.* 4(5).
Segal, M., and W. Whitt (1989). A queueing network analyzer for manufacturing. *Proc. 12th Internat. Teletraffic Congress*, Torino, Italy, June 1988, pp. 1146–1152.
Seidmann, A. (1988). Regenerative pull (Kanban) production control policies. *European J. Oper. Res.* 35, 401–413.
Seidmann, A., and S.Y. Nof (1985). Unitary manufacturing cell design with random product feedback flow. *IIE Trans.* 17, 188–193.
Seidmann, A., P.J. Schweitzer and S. Shalev-Oren (1987). Computerized closed queueing network models of flexible manufacturing systems: A comparative evaluation. *Large Scale Systems* 12, 91–107.
Sevcik, K.C., A.I. Levy, S.K. Tripathi and J.L. Zahorjan (1977). Improving approximations of aggregated queueing network subsystems, in: K.M. Chandy and M. Reiser (eds.), *Computer Performance*, North-Holland, Amsterdam, pp. 1–22.
Sevcik, K.C., and I. Mitrani (1979). The distribution of queueing network states at input and output instants, in: *Performance of Computer Systems*, North-Holland, New York, pp. 319–335.

Shalev-Oren, S., A. Seidmann and P.J. Schweitzer (1985). Analysis of flexible manufacturing systems with priority scheduling: PMVA. *Ann. Oper. Res.* 3, 115–139.
Shanthikumar, J.G., and J.A. Buzacott (1980). On the approximations to the single server queue. *Internat. J. Prod. Res.* 18, 761–773.
Shanthikumar, J.G., and J.A. Buzacott (1981). Open queueing network models of dynamic job shops. *Internat. J. Prod. Res.* 19, 255–266.
Shanthikumar, J.G., and J.A. Buzacott (1984). The time spent in a dynamic job shop. *European J. Oper. Res.* 17, 215–226.
Shanthikumar, J.G., and M. Gocmen (1983). Heuristic analysis of closed queueing networks. *Internat. J. Prod. Res.* 21, 675–690.
Shanthikumar, J.G., and R.G. Sargent (1983). A unifying view of hybrid simulation/analytic models and modeling. *Oper. Res.* 31(6), 1030–1052.
Shanthikumar, J.G., and U. Sumita (1988). Approximations for the time spent in a dynamic job shop with applications to due date assignment. *Internat. J. Prod. Res.* 26, 1329–1352.
Shanthikumar, J.G., and D.D. Yao (1987). Stochastic monotonicity of the queue lengths in closed queueing networks. *Oper. Res.* 35, 583–588.
Shanthikumar, J.G., and D.D. Yao (1989). Second-order stochastic properties in queueing systems. *Proc. IEEE* 77(1), 162–170.
Shanthikumar, J.G., and D.D. Yao (1992). Spatiotemporal convexity of stochastic processes and applications. *Probab. Engrg. Inform. Sci.* 6, 1–16.
Shimizu, M. (1991). Application of an integrated modeling approach to design and analysis of manufacturing systems. *Adv. Manuf. Engrg.*, to appear.
Shimizu, M., and D. Van Zoest (1988). Analysis of a factory of the future using an integrated set of software for manufacturing systems modeling. *Proc. 1988 Winter Simulation Conf.*, IEEE Computer Society Press, pp. 671–677.
Shore, J.E., and R.W. Johnson (1980). Axiomatic derivation of the principle of maximum entropy and the principle of minimum cross-entropy. *IEEE Trans. Inform. Theory* 26(1), 26–37.
Shore, J.E., and R.W. Johnson (1981). Properties of cross-entropy minimization. *IEEE Trans. Inform. Theory* 27(4), 472–482.
Shum, A.W., and J.P. Buzen (1977). The EPF technique: A method for obtaining approximate solutions to closed queueing networks with general service times. *Proc. 3rd Internat. Sympos. on Measuring, Modelling and Evaluating Comput. Systems*, Bonn, Germany. North-Holland, Amsterdam, pp. 201–220.
Solberg, J.J. (1977). A mathematical model of computerized manufacturing systems. *Proc. 4th Internat. Conf. Production Research*, Tokyo, Japan.
Spearman, M.L. (1991). An analytic congestion model for closed production systems with IFR processing times. *Management Sci.* 37(8), 1015–1029.
Spearman, M.L., D.L. Woodruff and W.J. Hopp (1990). CONWIP: A pull alternative to Kanban. *Internat. J. Prod. Res.* 28(5), 879–894.
Spearman, M.L., and M.A. Zazanis (1992). Push and pull production systems: Issues and comparisons. *Oper. Res.* 40(3), 521–532.
Spragins, J. (1980). Analytical queueing models: Guest editors introduction. *IEEE Computer* 13(4), 9–11.
Stecke,, K.E. (1982). Machine interference: The assignment of machines to operators, in: G. Salvendy (ed.), *Handbook of Industrial Engineering*, Wiley, New York.
Stecke, K.E. (1985). Design, planning, scheduling, and control problems of flexible manufacturing systems. *Ann. Oper. Res.* 3, 3–12.
Stecke, K.E., and J.E. Aronson (1985). Review of operator/machine interference models. *Internat. J. Prod. Res.* 23(1), 129–151.
Stecke, K.E., and J.J. Solberg (1985). The optimality of unbalancing both workloads and machine group sizes in closed queueing networks of multi-server queues. *Oper. Res.* 33(4), 882–910.
Stecke, K.E., and R. Suri (1985). *Flexible Manufacturing Systems: Operations Research Models and Applications*, J.C. Baltzer, Basel, Switzerland.

Stecke, K.E., and R. Suri (1986). *Proceedings of the Second ORSA/TIMS Conference on Flexible Manufacturing Systems: Operations Research Models and Applications*, Elsevier, Amsterdam.
Stecke, K.E., and R. Suri (eds.) (1988). *Flexible Manufacturing Systems: Operations Research Models and Applications II*, J.C. Baltzer, Basel, Switzerland.
Stecke, K.E., and R. Suri (1989). *Proceedings of the Third ORSA/TIMS Conference on Flexible Manufacturing Systems: Operations Research Models and Applications*, Elsevier, Amsterdam.
Stidham, S. (1974). A last word on $L = \lambda W$. *Oper. Res.* 22, 417–421.
Stoyan, D. (1983). *Comparison Methods for Queues and Other Stochastic Models* (English edition, edited and revised by D.J. Daley), Wiley, New York.
Suri, R. (1983). Robustness of queueing network formulas. *J. ACM* 30(3), 564–594.
Suri, R. (1985a). An overview of evaluative models for flexible manufacturing systems, *Ann. Oper. Res.* 3, 13–21.
Suri, R. (1985b). Quantitative techniques for robotic systems analysis, in: S.Y. Nof (ed.), *Handbook of Industrial Robotics*, Wiley, New York, Chapter 31.
Suri, R. (1985c). A concept of monotonicity and its characterization for closed queueing networks. *Oper. Res.* 33, 606–624.
Suri, R. (1988a). A new perspective on manufacturing systems analysis, in: W.D. Compton (ed.), *Design and Analysis of Integrated Manufacturing Systems*, National Academy Press, Washington, DC, pp. 118–133.
Suri, R. (1988b). RMT puts manufacturing at the helm. *Manuf. Engrg.* 100(2), 41–44.
Suri, R. (1989a). Perturbation analysis: The state of the art and research issues explained via the G/G/1 queue. *Proc. IEEE* 77, 114–137.
Suri, R. (1989b). Lead time reduction through rapid modeling. *Manuf. Syst.* 7, 66–68.
Suri, R., and S. DeTreville (1986). Getting from 'Just-in-Case' to 'Just-in-Time': Insights from a simple model. *J. Oper. Management* 6(3), 295–304.
Suri, R., and S. DeTreville (1991). Full speed ahead: A look at rapid modeling technology in operations management. *OR/MS Today* 18, 34–42.
Suri, R., and S. DeTreville (1992). Rapid modeling: The use of queueing models to support time-based competitive manufacturing, in: G. Fandel (ed.), *Proceedings of the German/U.S. Conference on Recent Developments in Operations Research*, Springer, Berlin.
Suri, R., and G.W. Diehl (1986). A variable buffer-size model and its use in analyzing closed queueing networks with blocking. *Management Sci.* 32(2), 206–224.
Suri, R., and G.W. Diehl (1987). Rough-cut modeling: An alternative to simulation. *CIM Rev.* 3, 25–32.
Suri, R., G.W. Diehl and R. Dean (1986). Quick and easy manufacturing systems analysis using MANUPLAN. *Proc. Spring IIE Conf.*, Dallas, TX, IIE, Norcross, GA, pp. 195–205.
Suri, R., and J.W. Dille (1985). A technique for on-line sensitivity analysis of flexible manufacturing systems. *Ann. Oper. Res.* 3, 381–391.
Suri, R., and B.R. Fu (1991). On using continuous flow lines for performance estimation of discrete production lines, in: B.L. Nelson, W.D. Kelton and G.M. Clark (eds.), *Proceedings of the 1991 Winter Simulation Conference*, pp. 968–977.
Suri, R., and R.R. Hildebrant (1984). Modeling flexible manufacturing systems using mean-value analysis. *J. Manuf. Syst.* 3(1), 27–38.
Suri, R., and M. Shimizu (1989). Design for analysis: A new strategy to improve the design process. *Res. Engrg. Des.* 1, 105–120.
Suri, R., and M. Tomsicek (1988). Rapid modeling tools for manufacturing simulation and analysis. *Proc. 1988 Winter Simulation Conference*, IEEE Computer Society Press, pp. 25–32.
Suri, R., M. Tomsicek and D. Derleth (1990). Manufacturing systems modeling using ManuPlan and SimStarter: A tutorial. *Proc. 1990 Winter Simulation Conference*, IEEE Computer Society Press, pp. 168–176.
Suri, R., and C.K. Whitney (1984). Decision support requirements in flexible manufacturing. *J. Manuf. Syst.* 3(1), 61–69.
Takacs, L. (1962). *Introduction to the Theory of Queues*, Oxford Univ. Press, Oxford.

Takahashi, Y. (1989). Aggregate approximation of acyclic queueing networks with communication blocking, in: H.G. Perros and T. Altiok (eds.), *Queueing Networks with Blocking*, Elsevier, Amsterdam, pp. 33–46.

Takahashi, Y., H. Miyahara and T. Hasegawa (1980). An approximation method for open restricted queueing networks. *Oper. Res.* 28(3), 594–602.

Tay, Y.C., and R. Suri (1985). Error bounds for performance prediction in queueing networks. *ACM Trans. Comput. Syst.* 3(3), 227–254.

Tijms, H.C. (1988). *Stochastic Modelling and Analysis: A Computational Approach*, Wiley, New York.

Trivedi, K.S. (1982). *Probability and Statistics with Reliability, Queueing, and Computer Science Applications*, Prentice-Hall, Englewood Cliffs, NJ.

Uzsoy, R., and L.A. Martin-Vega (1990). Modelling Kanban-based demand-pull systems: A survey and critique. *Manuf. Rev.* 3(3), 155–160.

Van der Wal, J. (1989). Monotonicity of the throughput of a closed exponential queueing network in the number of jobs. *OR Spektrum* 11, 97–100.

Van Dijk, N.M. (1989). A simple bounding methodology for non-product-form queueing networks with blocking, in: H.G. Perros, and T. Altiok (eds.), *Queueing Networks with Blocking*, Elsevier, Amsterdam, pp. 3–17.

Vinod, B., and J.J. Solberg (1985). The optimal design of flexible manufacturing systems. *Internat. J. Prod. Res.* 23(6), 1141–1151.

Viswanadham, N., and Y. Narahari (1992). *Performance Modeling of Automated Manufacturing Systems*, Prentice-Hall, Englewood Cliffs, NJ.

Wang, L., and W.E. Wilhelm (1985). Management of component accumulation in small-lot assembly systems, Working Paper 1985–005, Department of Industrial and Systems Engineering, Ohio State University.

Wein, L.M. (1990a). Optimal control of a two-station Brownian network. *Mth. Oper. Res.* 15, 215–242.

Wein, L.M. (1990b). Scheduling networks of queues: Heavy traffic analysis of a two-station network with controllable inputs. *Oper. Res.* 38, 1065–1078.

Wein, L.M. (1991). Brownian networks with discretionary routing. *Oper. Res.* 39(2), 322–340.

Whitt, W. (1982). Approximating a point process by a renewal process: Two basic methods. *Oper. Res.* 30, 125–147.

Whitt, W. (1983). The queueing network analyzer. *Bell Syst. Tech. J.* 62, 2779–2815.

Whitt, W. (1984a). Approximations to departure processes and queues in series. *Naval Res. Logist. Quart.* 31, 499–521.

Whitt, W. (1984b). Open and closed networks of queues. *AT&T Bell Lab. Tech. J.* 63, 1911–1979.

Whitt, W. (1985). The best order of queues in series. *Management Sci.* 31(4), 475–487.

Whitt, W. (1989). Approximations for the GI/G/m queue. *Adv. Appl. Probab.*, to appear.

Wilhelm, W. (1986a). A model to approximate transient performance of the flowshop. *Internat. J. Prod. Res.* 24(1), 33–50.

Wilhelm, W. (1986b). The application of lognormal models of transient operations in the flexible manufacturing environment. *J. Manuf. Syst.* 5(4), 253–266.

Wilhelm, W., and S. Ahmadi-Marandi (1982). A methodology to describe the operating characteristics of assembly systems. *IIE Trans.* 14(3), 204–213.

Wilhelm, W., S. Saboo and R. Johnson (1986). An approach for designing capacity and managing material flow in small-lot assembly lines. *J. Manuf. Syst.* 5(3), 147–160.

Williams, A.C., and R.A. Bhandiwad (1976). A generating function approach to queueing network models of multiprogrammed computer systems. *Network* 6, 1–22.

Wolff, R.W. (1989). *Stochastic Modeling and the Theory of Queues*, Prentice-Hall, Englewood Cliffs, NJ.

Yamazaki, G., T. Kawashima and H. Sakasegawa (1985). Reversibility of tandem blocking queueing systems. *Management Sci.* 31(1), 78–83.

Yao, D.D. (1985). Some properties of the throughput function of closed networks of queues. *Oper. Res. Lett.* 3(6), 313–317.

Yao, D.D. (1989). Modeling flexible manufacturing systems using product form queueing networks, in: J.A. White and I.W. Pence (eds.), *Progress in Materials Handling and Logistics – Vol. I*, Springer, Berlin, pp. 223–235.

Yao, D.D., and J.A. Buzacott (1985a). Queueing models for a flexible machining station. Part I: The diffusion approximation. *European J. Oper. Res.* 19, 233–240.

Yao, D.D., and J.A. Buzacott (1985b). Modeling the performance of manufacturing systems. *Internat. J. Prod. Res.* 23, 945–959.

Yao, D.D., and J.A. Buzacott (1985c). Queueing models for a flexible machining station, Part II: The method of Coxian phases. *European J. Oper. Res.* 19, 241–252.

Yao, D.D., and J.A. Buzacott (1986a). The exponentialization approach to flexible manufacturing systems models with general processing times. *European J. Oper. Res.* 24, 410–416.

Yao, D.D., and J.A. Buzacott (1986b). Models of flexible manufacturing systems with limited local buffers. *Internat. J. Prod. Res.* 24, 107–118.

Yao, D.D., and J.G. Shanthikumar (1986). Some resource allocation problems in multi-cell systems. *Proc. 2nd ORSA/TIMS Conf. on Flexible Manufacturing Systems*. Ann Arbor, MI. Elsevier, Amsterdam, pp. 245–256.

Yao, D.D., and J.G. Shanthikumar (1987). Optimal server allocation in a system of multi-server stations. *Management Sci.* 33(9), 1173–1180.

Zahorjan, J. (1980). The approximate solution of large queueing network models, Ph.D. Dissertation (Tech. Rep. CSRG-122), Univ. of Toronto, Toronto, Canada.

Zahorjan, J., K.C. Sevcik, D.L. Eager, and B.I. Galler (1982). Balanced job bound analysis of queueing networks. *Commun. ACM* 25(2), 134–141.

Zipkin, P.H. (1986). Models for design and control of stochastic, multi-item batch production systems. *Oper. Res.* 34, 91–104.

S.C. Graves et al., Eds., *Handbooks in OR & MS, Vol. 4*

Chapter 6

Manufacturing Lead Times, Order Release and Capacity Loading

Uday S. Karmarkar

Center for Manufacturing and Operations Management, William E. Simon Graduate School of Business Administration, University of Rochester, Rochester, NY 14627, U.S.A.

Manufacturing lead times are a critical measure of manufacturing performance that have not received a great deal of attention in the literature. Lead times are affected by many factors including capacity, loading, batching and scheduling, and themselves affect many aspects of costs, and control. The interaction between lead times and order release mechanisms is discussed and models relating them are described. In addition, models incorporating lead times in capacity planning and design decisions are also surveyed and some directions for research are discussed.

1. Introduction

By 'manufacturing lead time' for a work order in a manufacturing facility, we mean the time taken from the time production is authorized, to the time it is completed and the material is available for use to fill demand by the customer or the next stage. It could be asserted that lead times are one of the most important measures of manufacturing performance, since many costs can be related directly to them. Furthermore, lead times are affected by various levels of manufacturing control and are also needed to set control parameters such as lead time offsets in MRP systems. The central role of lead times has been underlined by the recent influence of Japanese manufacturing techniques such as the 'just-in-time' philosophy. Some of the models discussed below put some analytical substance into the JIT mystique. Unfortunately, it cannot yet be said that the models are far enough along to replace faith completely with logic. There are many areas where modelling efforts fall far short of capturing the manifold impact of lead times. In these cases, empirical studies could well be very valuable.

Certainly, firms would seem to have the incentive to keep a close watch on lead times. But paradoxically, despite its pervasive impact, it is unusual to find effective measurement and use of lead time data in practice. For example, a recent survey of manufacturing control and costing systems practice [Karmarkar, Lederer & Zimmerman, 1990] revealed that lead time was neither widely measured nor used as a performance index. This is particularly surprising given the ease of collecting this data. In the academic literature too, the development of techniques for modelling the relationships between lead times and costs and between lead times and control, has been surprisingly limited. One of the few survey papers on the subject is that of Tatsiopoulos & Kingsman [1983]. Much of the work described is fairly recent, and there are many opportunities for extending our state of knowledge and our understanding of control techniques. While an attempt has been made to cover the literature reasonably well, there are bound to be serious omissions. For completeness, some papers have been listed in the references even though they are not reviewed or discussed. In the effort to convey what I feel are the crucial ideas there is a tendency to focus on the work with which I am most familiar. For all this my apologies.

In the next sub-sections we describe the costs associated with manufacturing lead time, and then discuss the relationship to control procedures, and order release in particular. Some simple models connecting lead time to manufacturing control are described to explicate the basic relationships. In subsequent sections, control and decision models incorporating lead time related costs are discussed in greater detail. In terms of the optimization paradigm, Section 1 deals with lead time related terms in objective functions. Section 2 addresses system models or constraint sets which capture the effect of decisions on lead times. Sections 3 and 4 describe decision models which combine lead time related objective functions with lead time models, and perform some optimization or policy determination.

1.1. Lead times and manufacturing performance

The most obvious cost related to lead times is that of holding work-in-process (WIP) inventories. Little's law provides the relationship between WIP and lead time at the aggregate level. Morton, Lawrence, Rajagopolan & Kekre [1988] consider the revenue cash flows obtained on completion of an order, and directly obtain a lead time related expression as an approximation to the present values of the cash flows. For example, the discount factor in a continuous time model, for a cash flow occurring T time units away is given by e^{-rT}, where r is a discount rate. On expanding and discarding higher order terms, the value of a cash flow of c is approximated by $c(1-rT)$. If the cash flow is proportional to the output quantity, the resulting expression is essentially equivalent to the holding cost of WIP. Rummel [1989] undertakes an empirical study of approximating present values of cash flows in batch manufacturing, and shows that for batching decisions at least, models based on lead times give good results, while traditional setup and cycle inventory cost models do not. Costs of WIP have been used in modelling capacity planning [Kekre, 1984], batching decisions [Bertrand, 1985; Karmarkar, 1987a; Karmarkar, Kekre & Kekre, 1985; Rummel, 1989] and scheduling decisions [Morton, Lawrence, Rajagopolan & Kekre, 1988; Dobson, Karmarkar & Rummel,

1992]. The weighted mean flow time criterion in scheduling accommodates WIP costs, and has a long history [Conway, Maxwell & Miller, 1967]. However, the inclusion of these costs in batching and planning models is a rather recent occurrence.

Another quantifiable inventory consequence of lead time is the level of safety stocks in finished goods inventories. This relationship is conventionally represented as follows: if D is a random variable representing demand per period, and T is the lead time measured as the (stochastic) number of periods required for manufacturing to replenish finished goods, then safety stocks are related to the variance of demand over lead time given by $[\mathrm{E}(D)]^2 \cdot \mathrm{Var}(T) + \mathrm{E}(T) \cdot \mathrm{Var}(D)$. This type of safety stock or reorder point model makes certain tacit assumptions about the nature of the stochastic processes involved. For example, the variance depends on the correlation characteristics of the demand distribution. Furthermore, there is actually a second lead time effect that affects safety stocks. The demand variance must actually be estimated by forecasting, and an added component of variance due to forecasting error is introduced. This component grows larger as lead times increase, since forecasts become less accurate, especially if the demand process has a 'drift'. Wecker [1979] derives the appropriate expressions for the case of exponentially smoothed forecasts of such a process. He shows that the variance of demand over lead time increases with the cube of mean lead time so that the consequences for safety stock are worse than the conventional expression would suggest. Alternative models of the safety stock consequences of lead times are possible, based on modelling the distribution of demand during lead time. For a recent discussion of these issues see Eppen & Martin [1988] and Graves [1988c].

Note that in determining safety stock levels for finished goods in pull systems, the variability of lead times is a factor in addition to the expected lead time. In push systems too, where releases are determined by lead time offsets, lead time variability requires setting safety times which are computed analogously to safety stocks [Whybark & Williams, 1966; Yano, 1987a,b]. These safety times essentially engender early releases as protection against variance in completion times. Just as with safety stocks against multiple item orders, the effect is more pronounced when many items have to be coordinated for assembly. The safety times now have to cover the extreme value distribution of the lead times for all the parts to be assembled. The result of using safety times is that on most occasions (on average), orders are released and completed before they are required, and either finished goods or WIP inventories are increased. Furthermore, in push or MRP systems, long lead times act analogously to the pull system case, by increasing the probability of schedule changes within the lead time 'fence'. The effect of these changes on component level schedules is to create 'nervous' behavior which can be costly (see [Blackburn, Kropp & Millen, 1985] for a discussion of these effects).

The mirror image of the problem of determining safety times and release times, is the problem of setting due dates. The latter occurs when the order is to be delivered as soon as possible, and its lead time and completion date cannot be predicted accurately. The variability inherent in the prediction of lead time requires a tradeoff between negotiating or promising a date that is too far away, so that delivery and payment are delayed, and one that is so close that it is not met, with the corresponding loss of goodwill or with explicit penalties. Seidmann & Smith [1981], Bertrand [1983a], and Baker & Bertrand [1981, 1982] are some papers dealing with this problem.

One of the less easily quantified costs of lead time is due to the effect on quality management. A tangible aspect of these costs is the number of non-conforming parts produced. If the lead time between production and testing is large, then the number of pieces in-process before testing is also proportionally large, and so is the number of bad parts in the system. A more subtle effect is that on the control of process quality. With larger lead times between production and testing, there is a delay introduced in the feedback from testing to adjustment of process parameters. Such a delay can make the control process more unstable, so that if there is a problem with output quality due to a shift in process output, it takes longer to bring the process back in control. In the terminology of feedback control theory, a first-order process with a delay in the feedback, acts like a second-order process, since the delay acts like an additional time constant. See Kuo [1987] or a similar text for details. The effect is not unlike trying to adjust a shower, when there is a delay between turning a valve, to the time a temperature change occurs.

The sequencing and scheduling literature has long considered lead time related measures such as makespan and weighted flow times. The makespan measure appears to be most applicable to cases where a fixed set of tasks is to be completed, and the completion point is associated with a revenue flow. An example of this might be a custom shop that does one project at a time; say a ship builder or a builder of specialized assembly machines. In manufacturing environments where new orders may be released at any time, the makespan measure does not seem to be very appropriate. Weighted flow time is of course a direct lead time measure that could be related to WIP or other holding costs. If due dates and release dates have already been fixed, then tardiness measures are also related to lead time reduction.

Clearly, long lead times have an adverse effect on responsiveness to customer demands. With the production to stock of standard items, the cost of lead times appears in safety stocks as described above. With production to order, the delivery date must be negotiated further into the future, and this affects competitive positioning negatively. In effect, the customer's use or consumption of the product is delayed, and if there is another supplier with a shorter lead time, the customer will switch. Presumably, lead times must be inversely related to market share or price premiums, or both (i.e., to total revenue). Li [1991a,b] models time competition. Certainly, managers are observed in practice to act as though shorter lead times confer a competitive advantage [for example, Karmarkar, Kekre & Kekre, 1987]. There has been some discussion of these issues in a service industry setting, generally with an emphasis on pricing issues [e.g., Dolan, 1978; Koenigsberg, 1985; DeVaney &

Frey, 1982]. Kekre & Udayabhanu [1988] consider prioritization of customer orders and the effect on lead times to customers.

While some of these consequences are not easy to model analytically, it seems apparent that lead time is a convenient proxy for many costs. Schmenner [1988] finds that overall manufacturing performance improvements are strongly correlated with lead time reductions, although the nature of his survey does not reveal the causal connections with costs and revenues. From the viewpoint of new research, empirical or analytical work relating lead times to various costs and benefits would be very valuable.

1.2. *Manufacturing lead times and order release*

Lead times have a close relationship with manufacturing control activities. It is especially convenient to associate lead time with a production order or work order. An 'order' consists of an item or part number, a quantity to be produced, a due date and a release or start date after which production may be started. Order release is generally taken to mean the level of control between planning and scheduling or execution. In many facilities there is a well defined organizational procedure by which physical production activities are initiated by order release, often involving the generation of documentation and work orders. Figure 1 shows an example of a hierarchical control structure of the 'push' type, in which order release represents the communication between

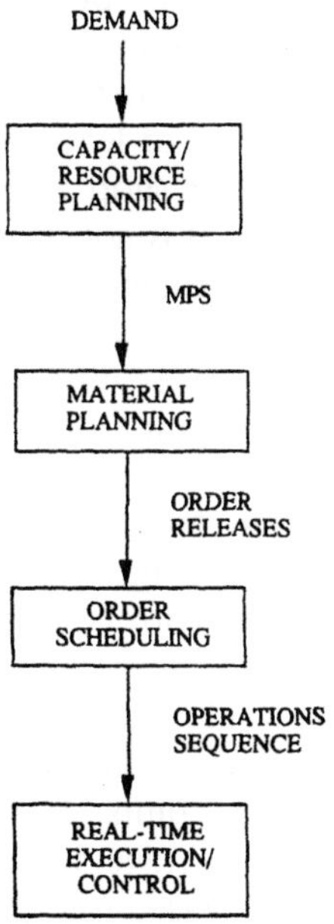

Fig. 1. An example of a hierarchical view of manufacturing control.

material planning and detailed scheduling levels. However, by looking at different levels of decision making and organization of facilities, one can also interpret capacity planning and detailed scheduling decisions as control activities analogous to order release. In other words, master scheduling can be interpreted as order release at the end-item level, and detailed schedules as order releases at the job-step or operation level.

The effect of lead times on order release mechanisms is straightforward. In 'push' systems, order releases are made to satisfy future requirements, and releases must therefore be offset from requirements by the lead time taken to manufacture. In 'pull' systems, releases are triggered by changes in inventory (or backorder) levels. Inventory remaining at the point of triggering must be adequate to cover demand till replenishment. The setting of the trigger inventory levels order point is thus based on lead time, as was discussed in the previous section. There are many models available which discuss the setting of trigger points or reorder points for pull systems given lead times [for example, see Johnson & Montgomery, 1974; Hax & Candea, 1984; Silver & Peterson, 1985]. In the deterministic case, if lead times are known, the setting of release time is simply an offset from the required completion time. The calculation of safety times when lead times are stochastic, was mentioned above.

The effect in the other direction – that of order release method on lead times – is more complex, much less studied and less understood. Traditional release models of both push and pull varieties, tend to ignore this relationship, taking lead times to be given and independent of order release parameters. In fact, order releases load production facilities, and the nature of this loading process relative to available capacity is the primary determinant of lead times in the facility. Yet MRP systems, for example, take the production lead time for a part number as a constant independent of other releases, and of shop loading. The fallacy here is in thinking of lead time as an attribute of a part. Rather it is a property of a facility or shop that depends on total load and capacity, and can thus vary over time. It is not surprising that MRP systems are not associated with 'just-in-time' performance, even though it could be argued that they were intended to be exactly that. In a similar manner, many pull control schemes (e.g., order point, order quantity) make the same error of taking lead times as given, independent of other items and releases, and independent of batching and loading. Such systems may sometimes be rescued by the averaging effects of random triggering, in relatively stable demand environments. However, their shortcomings are quickly apparent when there are systematic demand changes or correlations, as with seasonality. For example, in a seasonal environment, as demand rises, items controlled by independent (OP, OQ) systems will start to trigger simultaneously. The resulting surge on production facilities causes lead time increases which were not accounted for in setting reorder points. Hax & Meal [1975] discuss the problems that occur in this environment, and develop methods for adjusting production quantities and releases based on planned load and inventory status.

1.3. Models of order release mechanisms

The distinction between push and pull used above, is based on triggering mechanism [Karmarkar, 1987a]. Pyke [1987] develops a more extensive view of the terms 'push' and 'pull', considering issues such as the location of triggering and batching decisions, in addition to the mechanism alone. A somewhat different kind of 'pull' release mechanism is based on the amount of work-in-process in the facility, rather than on a finished goods buffer. Clearly, this is a way of relating releases to lead times very directly. Such mechanisms have been extensively developed and studied by Bertrand [1981, 1983b], Bemelmans [1985], Bertrand & Wortmann [1981] and their colleagues. Bechte [1982], Kettner & Bechte [1981], Wiendahl [1987], Wiendahl & Springer [1988] and their colleagues, have studied these methods as 'load oriented production control'. More recently, Spearman & Zazanis [1988] have analyzed this type of release mechanism, described as 'constant WIP'. They show that this release mechanism is more robust than mechanisms based on capacity utilization which attempt to keep utilization and output at some target level. The 'JIT' technique of physically limiting the amount of inventory on the shop floor, and the techniques of work flow control are related to this method.

Kanban systems are pull systems which maintain constant levels of total on-hand and in-process inventory at each production stage [Kimura & Terada, 1981; Sugimori, Kusunoki, Cho & Uchikawa, 1977; Monden, 1981; Huang, Rees & Taylor, 1983; Schonberger, 1983]. The relationships between Kanban systems and pull systems of the base stock type has been discussed by Karmarkar [1991]. Models of Kanban systems include those of Bitran & Chang [1987], Karmarkar & Kekre [1989], Deleersnyder, Hodgson & O'Grady [1987], Mitra & Mitrani [1988] Seidmann [1988] and Zipkin [1989]. The constant WIP methods are clearly closely related. Denardo & Tang [1988] have developed models of control policies based on buffer restitution. Depending on the quality withdrawn from the buffer, some proportion is replenished in the next control period. In a sense this is a particularization of a Kanban type of pull policy. Deleersnyder [1988] develops models of Kanban type release mechanisms, but with more flexibility in the information mechanism. In particular, the conventional Kanban scheme only pulls on the immediately preceding facility. Deleersnyder permits information on withdrawal at a production stage to be transmitted to more than one preceding stage, in effect, letting triggering information jump a stage or more. The simultaneous effect of keeping WIP constant as in Kanban systems, and allowing triggering information to jump stages, is a generalization of both the Kanban and constant WIP methods.

We have mentioned that push and pull methods can be combined. Tandem push and pull schemes are discussed by Pyke [1987] who models specific examples of such systems and examines their performance. He also discusses mixed or two level schemes, where for example, 'normal' orders might be triggered in a push manner with 'expedite' orders for the same stage being triggered in a pull manner. This scheme is implemented with two reorder points. Tandem pull and push systems have also been implemented in practice as 'synchro-MRP' and JIT-MRP [Hall, 1983].

Another approach to combining push and pull mechanisms, is to add a push component to a pull system through setting of control parameters in the pull system. This is not a particularly new idea. Whenever a safety stock level, base stock, or reorder point is changed based on demand forecasts, a push element has been added to a pull system. More elaborate techniques for adapting short term pull mechanisms based on longer term (push) planning, are provided within hierarchical control schemes. Hax & Meal [1975], Hax & Golovin [1978], Bitran & Hax [1977], all describe ways of adjusting order point, order quantity control systems, through changing batching and release rules. However, there is no explicit recognition of lead times and WIP in these models. Lead times are explicitly considered in other pull schemes such as the Kanban and base stock systems. Groenevelt & Karmarkar [1988] describe a 'dynamic' Kanban system in which card quantities, or equivalently the total WIP inventory target is changed as demand levels (and hence loading and lead times) change. In other words, forecasts of future demand (the push component) are used to change the triggering parameters in the system. Their scheme also has a two level trigger mechanism by which backorders are treated differently from normal stock replenishment. This system has been implemented successfully in practice. Karmarkar [1986a] describes a scheme for the integration of MRP and Kanban systems, where the gross requirement at the component level, produced by MRP computations, is used to dynamically determine card quantities at the cell level. Thus WIP as well as order release are affected by both push and pull mechanisms. As an analogy with the previous example, here the MRP system is essentially providing forecasts of demand at the part level based on end item schedules.

Going beyond these combinations of push and pull methods, Buzacott [1988] has developed an order release model that includes MRP and Kanban release methods as special cases as well as backlogging and make-to-order mechanisms. This model specifically accounts for the lead times inherent in not only the production and replenishment process but also in demand queues and transaction queues. Other models of input control based on lead time estimates include Glassey & Resende [1988] and Leachman, Solorzano & Glassey [1988] which consider the effects of queues and bottlenecks on lead times.

2. Lead time prediction, estimation and evaluation models

The components of lead times in a manufacturing facility are queue time, processing time and move or transportation time. The queues include waiting for move operations as well as queues for nonproduction tasks such as order processing, quality control and document generation. It is especially important to include the time from the instant an order is triggered, to the point that it is actually started into production. This time may involve no physical material in queue, but does have an impact on the lead time experienced at the finished goods or customer stage. Hence, while it may not affect WIP, it can affect finished goods safety stocks, and may also affect raw material inventory, or vendor inventory requirements.

In discussing the lead time models that have appeared in the literature, it is useful to draw a distinction between synchronous and asynchronous systems. We use the former term to refer to production systems which have a paced regular production schedule, where production at different stages is coordinated very closely, so that queues in the system are small or non-existent. The latter term refers to facilities where stages or departments are not completely coordinated, because the heterogeneity or complexity of flows in the system, or intrinsic process uncertainty makes this either difficult or impossible. A flow line which is paced so that each stage has the same cycle time is an example of a synchronous system. A multi-product batch flow process with complex flows and queues, is an example of the latter case. A custom job shop is an extreme case of an asynchronous process. The point of this distinction is that processes with queues are different from those without, in that queues represent the large part of lead time and WIP in asynchronous systems. Thus lead time management in these systems focuses on the management of queues. In synchronous systems on the other hand, lead times are primarily due to processing times, cycle stock holding times, and batch consolidation times. Since it is not always convenient to categorize formal models in this way, we note that synchronous systems are typically modelled as static deterministic models, while asynchronous systems are modelled either as dynamic deterministic models or as stochastic models.

In the following we discuss models for the estimation of lead times or for the evaluation of lead times under various assumptions about system characteristics. The lead time estimates from these models can be used to compute costs due to say WIP or safety stocks. In subsequent sections we will describe optimization and control models that use lead time related costs in their objective functions.

2.1. *Deterministic static models*

Sugimori, Kusunoki, Cho & Uchikawa [1977] give the following expression characterizing performance of a Kanban cell:

$$(1 + a)D(T_{\text{wait}} + T_{\text{proc}})/Q = N\,,$$

where

D = average output rate (units/time),
T_{wait}, T_{proc} = average wait and processing times,
Q = container size or batch size,
N = number of cards or containers in the cell,
a = safety or 'fudge' factor.

Note that this is simply Little's law with a safety factor of $(1 + a)$. Note that the expression could be rewritten in terms of average lead time T in the cell, as

$$T = QN/(1 + a)D .$$

The safety factor accounts for the fact that the actual number of cards in Kanban cell is closer to the maximum of WIP and not the average. The maximum WIP level is driven by the variance of lead time in the cell as well as the variance in demand, exactly like a base stock or safety stock level. Although these effects are not explicitly captured in this relationship, the safety factor does emphasize that variance reduction (level loading) will leave the card level close to the average WIP. Furthermore, the quantity QN includes on-hand inventory in addition to in-process inventory including queues, and the safety factor is accounting in physical terms for finished inventories as well. With this interpretation, T should be taken to include holding time in finished inventory (say, T_{fg}), as well as in queue and in process, and N should be taken as the total number of cards in the cell and in finished inventory.

I have found the following simple model pedagogically useful in describing the determinants of lead times in an idealized production system. Consider a synchronous production line with N stations in series producing a family of very similar (identical) products which are produced in a fixed batch size. Suppose that batches are transferred only when processing at a station is completed; i.e., transfer batch size equals the process batch size. Then let

D = actual production rate (units/time),
Q = batch size for all products (units),
t = setup time between batches (time),
P = nominal production rate at all stations (units/time),
T' = cycle time at a station = $(t + Q/P)$,
L = total manufacturing lead time = NT',
WIP = NQ.

Given synchronous operation, there are no queues in the system, and a batch leaves the end of the line once every cycle. Therefore,

$$D = (Q/T') = PQ/(Pt + Q) .$$

Thus, the output rate increases with the batch size, asymptotically reaching the nominal processing rate P. The lead time L and WIP are both linearly increasing in Q. These relationships are depicted in Figure 2a,b. If we eliminate Q, L can be expressed in terms of D as

$$L = Nt/(1 - (D/P)) = Nt/(1 - u)$$

which is graphed in Figure 2c. While these relationships apply to a rather simple system, they illustrate concepts which carry through to more complex

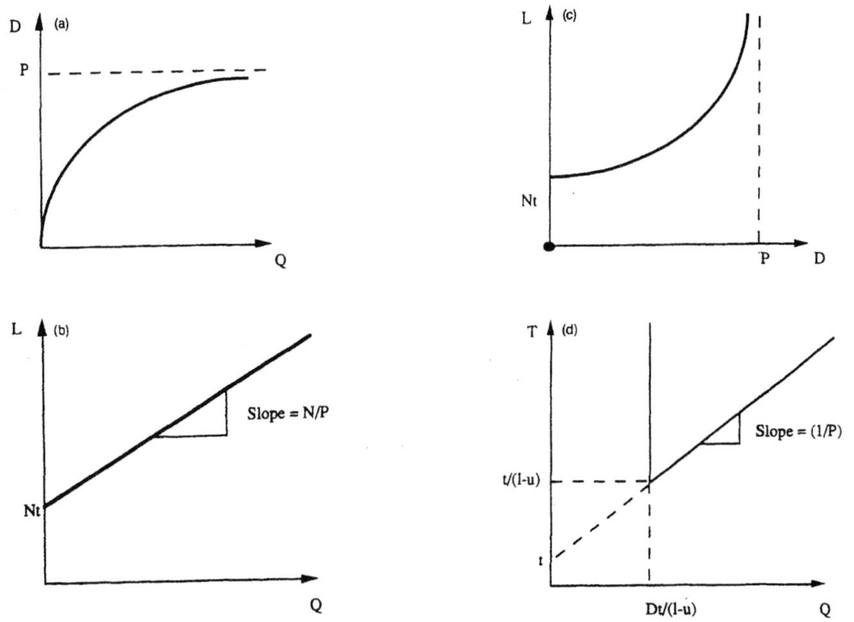

Fig. 2. (a) Output D as a function of batch size Q for a synchronous process model; (b) Leadtime L as a function of batch size Q for a synchronous process model with N stations each with processing rate P, and setup time t; (c) Leadtime L as a function of output D for a synchronous process model with N stations each with processing rate P, and setup time t; (d) Station cycle time T as a function of batchsize Q with a fixed output rate D, for a synchronous process model.

scenarios. Thus it is generally the case that lead times, WIP and output increase with batch sizes and that lead times increase rapidly with capacity utilization, because of the larger batch sizes. The effects of setup time and reductions thereof are also apparent. Another way to state the relationship graphed in Figure 2a, is to describe output in terms of WIP. Substituting $Q = \text{WIP}/N$ in the equation for D above gives

$$D = P(\text{WIP})/(NPt + \text{WIP}) .$$

The shape of the relationship between WIP and output D is the same as in Figure 2a, showing saturation of output rate as WIP increases. A similar relationship can be shown for average output or processing rate and WIP for queueing models discussed in the next section. These relationships are the motivation for so-called 'clearing functions' [Karmarkar, 1989], described in Section 4.1.

A slightly different view of these relationships is obtained if D is kept constant and Q varied. Define 'effective utilization' as

$$u = D/P ,$$

then to obtain an output rate D, the batch size Q and station cycle time T' must satisfy

$$Q \geqslant Dt/(1-u)\,, \qquad T' \geqslant t/(1-u)\,.$$

As Q is increased below this lower limit, but output kept fixed at D, the cycle time must be increased, and idle time is incurred at each station so that lead time and WIP still increase linearly with Q. The relationship between lead time and Q is graphed in Figure 2d.

These relationships are basically the same as the traditional 'rotation cycle' version of the multiproduct capacitated lot size problem (CLSP), for the case in which time is a binding constraint. In this situation, the rotation cycle time T is given by

$$T = \sum_i t_i + \sum_i Q_i/P_i$$

and since $Q_i = D_i \cdot T$,

$$T = \sum_i t_i \Big/ \Big(1 - \sum_i u_i\Big)\,,$$

where

t_i = the setup time for the ith product,
Q_i = the batch size for the ith product,
P_i = the processing rate for the ith product,
D_i = the demand rate for the ith product,
u_i = the utilization by the ith product = D_i/P_i.

Sugimori, Kusunoki, Cho & Uchikawa give this formula for 'lead time' in a press shop which is presumably a synchronous environment.

In fact, in any static lot sizing formulation, the lead time for production is related to the cycle time for each product (i.e., the common cycle time divided by the number of batches of that product per cycle) or more generally, to Q/D where the production batch size is Q. Note that the cycle stock cost (usually written as $hQ/2$) can also be thought of as proportional to the average time spent in finished goods inventory. Furthermore, on reversing the direction of material flow in a static lot size problem, cycle stocks can be interpreted as queues fed by material arriving at a fixed rate, which is then processed in batches. Surveys of the large literature on the static lot size problem are given by Elmaghraby [1978] and Bahl, Ritzman & Gupta [1988].

In the case of multi-stage static deterministic problems, the lead time for a product is equal to the total echelon stock for the product divided by the demand rate. Early discussions of the multi-stage problem include Crowston, Wagner & Williams [1973], and Schwarz & Schrage [1975]. These models assume as with the simple model described earlier, that batches are completed before being moved to the next stage. The work of Goyal & Szendrovits [1986], Drezner, Szendrovits & Wesolowsky [1989], Moily [1986] and others allows the movement of transfer batches that are smaller than process batches, which can reduce lead times substantially. It should be noted that most analyses of static lot sizing do not explicitly consider the cycling of products on resources, and so do not accurately represent lead times created by the contention for resources, due to which products must wait for their turn in the cycle. Nor do they consider the consequences of lead times on costs such as safety stocks. However appropriately modified, they can provide the tools to model lead times and their consequences. Extensions of these models in this direction would constitute a valuable research contribution.

2.2. Deterministic dynamic models

Deterministic dynamic lot sizing models can be interpreted in terms of lead times in the same way as the static models. Again many dynamic lot sizing models do not represent the cycling of products on machines and resources, but content themselves with set up costs as a device for limiting the use of resources. Some models enforce capacity constraints in terms of total processing time across items in a discrete time period or 'bucket' as in a linear program [e.g., Manne, 1958; Lasdon & Terjung, 1971]. However, this does not capture the loss of capacity due to mismatches in arrival and processing. When cycling on machines is explicitly represented [e.g., Jaikumar, 1974; Geoffrion & Graves, 1976; Graves, 1980; Karmarkar & Schrage, 1985] the problem appears to be much more difficult to solve. No standard approach seems to have emerged as yet. Furthermore, again, the literature in this area does not explicitly model or consider lead time related costs.

Correct representation of lead times in a dynamic (deterministic) complex facility, requires the modelling of operations at the detailed scheduling level. In effect, the start and finish times of each operation on each job released to the facility must be determined, and this process is analogous to project scheduling calculations as in PERT and CPM. It is necessary to include the effects of resource constraints, and this can be done by specifying the order in which operations will be executed on resources. This type of formulation is used by Balas [1969], Fisher [1974], Fisher, Lageweg, Lenstra & Rinnooy Kan [1983], and Dobson & Karmarkar [1986]. For example suppose that two jobs require operations i and j respectively to be done on a common resource (machine) k; define

s_{ik} = the start time of operation i on resource k; similarly for j,
f_{ik} = the finish time of operation i on resource k,
$X_{ijk} = 1$ if i precedes j on k; 0 otherwise.

Then to the usual precedence constraints for operations within each job, we add constraints of the form

$$s_{ik} \geq f_{jk} - M(1 - X_{jik}) ,$$
$$X_{ijk} + X_{jik} = 1 .$$

The first type of constraint enforces the relation between start and finish times across jobs, while the other requires that one or the other precedence direction must be chosen for each pair of operations i, j. This is the 'disjunctive graph' formulation of Balas for sequencing at machines. Alternative formulations of sequence selection are discussed by Dobson & Karmarkar [1986]. Once this order is fixed for each resource (machine) and operation, a set of precedence relationships between operations across jobs is created, in addition to the precedences between operations within a job. These additional relationships link the individual jobs together into a large network. The sequences chosen on machines are feasible if and only if this large network is acyclic. It is then possible to either work forward from release or start dates for jobs to determine early start and finish times (forward scheduling), or to work backwards from due dates to determine late start and finish times (backward scheduling).

This network formulation is imbedded in optimization models in the references cited above. More simply, if the order of processing operations on resources is not known, the order can be determined in the course of simulating the progress of jobs through the shop by using a dispatching rule such as first come first served (FCFS), shortest processing time (SPT), due date (DD) or many others [e.g., see Conway, Maxwell & Miller, 1965]. While such simulations have been used to actually produce shop schedules, they can also be used to estimate lead times. Morton, Lawrence, Rajagopolan & Kekre [1988], Rachamadugu & Morton [1981], Vepsalainen & Morton [1988] and Dobson, Karmarkar & Rummel [1992] describe the use of such global estimates in local shop scheduling. They can also be used in order to release decisions.

An approximation to forward scheduling in the sense described above, is so-called 'Input/Output Control', which is often presented as an adjunct to MRP, designed to cure its problems with erroneous lead time information [Wight, 1970; Karni, 1981; Lankford, 1982]. This method uses discrete time periods or 'buckets' in contrast to continuous time models above. Orders arrive at a resource at the start of a time period, and are added to the previous queue of unfinished work. During the time period, the orders are completed according to some specified sequence by priority, arrival sequence or other rule. At the end of the period, completed orders move to the next resource, while unfinished work is carried in the queue to the next period. This method cannot deal with the exact timing of arrivals at resources, and also needs some rule (as in the cases above) for determining which of the queued orders is processed next.

2.3. Stochastic static models

In complex dynamic (asynchronous) manufacturing facilities, the lead time experienced by a job is largely due to queue time. It has been suggested that the queue time can be as great as 80 to 95% of the total time spent in the facility. While the formation of queues and the resulting delays can be modelled by the deterministic dynamic formulations discussed above, queueing models have proved to be an effective way of describing certain kinds of manufacturing facilities. For example, if a facility produces a fixed set of items, and if the mix of output required does not change too rapidly, then the facility will display reasonably stable behavior with respect to queues and delays. In other words, the delay at each work center (machine, department) can be reasonably well represented by the equilibrium solution given by a queueing model. The question remains open as to what is 'reasonable'. However, there is a growing body of favorable empirical evidence on the ability of queueing models to represent manufacturing facilities. Models of single machines or work centers have been in the literature for some time [Conway, Maxwell & Miller, 1965]. There is also a large literature on queueing network models of multi-center facilities [Solberg, 1977; Buzacott & Shanthikumar, 1980; Suri, 1981; Karmarkar, Kekre & Kekre, 1985; Seidmann, Schweitzer & Shalev-Oren, 1987; Zipkin, 1986; Bitran & Tirupathi, 1988]. For reviews of these, see Suri, Sanders & Kamath [1993], Buzacott & Yao [1986]. Here, we describe some simple queueing models for the purpose of illustrating how the relationships between lead time and various design and operating parameters of manufacturing systems can be modelled.

Consider a one machine model representing a machine or resource in a large multi-center shop. To facilitate comparison with the deterministic static case, define:

D = average output of material (units/time),
P = average processing rate (units/time),
Q = batch size,
T = average time in system,
u = effective utilization = D/P.

Suppose that there are no setups between jobs, so that average processing rate per batch is (P/Q), the average processing time (service time) per batch is (Q/P) and the average arrival rate of batches is (D/Q). Then for an M/M/1 queue,

$$T = (Q/P)/(1-u) .$$

Figure 2 shows the well-known relationship between T and D for a fixed Q. In a synchronous system, we would have $T = Q/P$ since there would be no queue time. Thus the formula illustrates that queueing delays scale up lead time by a factor $1/(1-u)$ that goes up with utilization. The formula also shows the linear dependence of lead time on batch sizes. Of course, without set up inefficiencies, the batch size can be driven to a minimum (batch size of 1). When we add a set up time t, between batches, we have

x = average processing time per batch $= t + (Q/P)$,
P' = effective processing rate $= PQ/(Pt + Q)$,

which is analogous to the deterministic case (Figure 3). The M/M/1 formula now gives

$$T = (t + (Q/P))/(1 - (D/P) - (tD/Q)) .$$

The relationship between lead time and batch size is now linear only asymptotically for large Q. It shows the effect of set up inefficiencies as batches become small, when the denominator of the expression becomes small. With large Q, the dependence of the denominator on Q decreases, and the linearity of the numerator prevails. Figure 3 shows the dependence of T on Q for fixed D. Note the similarity to Figure 2d. The usual condition for stability becomes

$$D/P + tD/Q < 1 ,$$

or

$$Q > Dt/(1-u)$$

which is similar to the deterministic state case of Section 2.1, except that the bound cannot be attained.

The heterogeneous multi-item case of the batching model, using an M/G/1

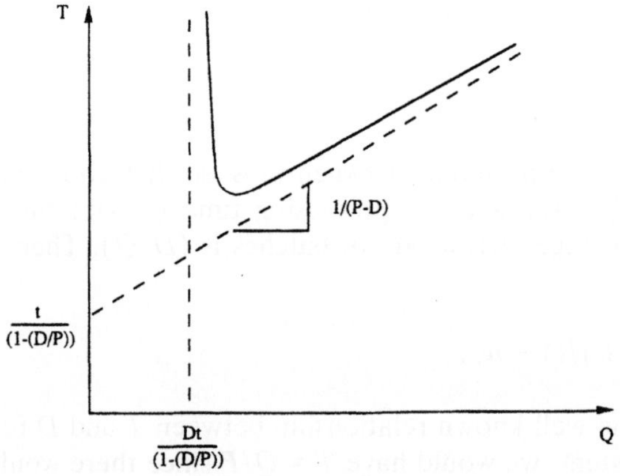

Fig. 3. Average lead time or time in system T as a function of batch size Q for an asynchronous process model.

queueing model is discussed by Bertrand [1985], Zipkin [1986], Karmarkar [1988] and Karmarkar, Kekre & Kekre [1992]. Harel & Zipkin [1984, 1987] establish some basic convexity properties for performance measures in M/G/1 queues. Zipkin and Bertrand model a manufacturing system as network of M/G/1 queues, and Karmarkar, Kekre & Kekre [1985] develop a model of a network of M/G/*c* queues with batching. Seidmann, Schweitzer & Nof [1984] develop a model of a flexible manufacturing cell, and examine the impact of batch sizes on lead times. They show that as larger batches are used, average lead time increases, but the coefficient of variation can decrease, and the distribution of lead time becomes more symmetric (Normal).

In addition to the effect of batch size, other queueing models have considered the effect of system design, process characteristics and shop floor policies. These include multi-class prioritized queues [e.g., Seidmann, Schweitzer & Shalev-Oren, 1986], queues with batching and prioritization [Calabrese, 1988] queues with blocking to represent finite buffers [e.g., Schweitzer & Altiok, 1988] and models with machine failure [e.g., Vinod & Solberg, 1984]. Among the several general purpose queueing network models available for modelling manufacturing systems are CAN-Q [Solberg, 1977], QNA [Whitt, 1983], PMVA [Shalev-Oren, Seidmann & Schweitzer, 1985], MANUPLAN [Suri & Diehl, 1985], and X-FLO [Karmarkar, Kekre & Kekre, 1985; Bacon & Choudhuri, 1987].

Most, if not all of the queueing network models, provide average lead time information, but not accurate variability estimates. The model of Seidmann & Nof [1985, 1989] is one notable exception. They obtain the entire distribution of lead time in a cell as a function of batch size. It is shown that with small batches, the distribution is skewed. With large batches, it tends to normality, and the coefficient of variation reduces. Another exception is the work of Arreola-Risa & Lee [1988] who have developed a fairly general model for the lead time distribution in a G/G queueing system based on a busy period approximation. They derive a distribution described as 'exponential-normal' with a skewed fat-tailed form like a Gamma distribution. Sumita & Kijima [1984] have numerically explored the effect of batching and obtained exact results that quantitatively correspond to other heuristic models. Shanthikumar & Sumita [1988] show that the time spent in a job shop is asymptotically exponentially distributed. However, the results in both these papers depend on some rather strong assumptions. While it is possible to get heuristic estimates for the variability of time spent at one work center, estimating the variance of total lead time is complicated by possible correlations between different queues, which are difficult to model accurately.

The stochastic element in these queueing models bears some discussions. Some authors explicitly consider the manufacturing system being modelled as having stochastic behavior. However, my own view is that these methods could just as well be considered as applying to completely deterministic but complex environments, where the probabilistic model is used to represent lack of knowledge, and heterogeneity, rather than intrinsically stochastic behavior.

Thus, the arrival rate at a work center might be completely deterministic, in the sense that all the information can be conceivably computed or determined. However, the cost of determining arrival times exactly and then using that information might be high relative to the benefits obtainable. In such a case, treating the arrivals as a random process is simply a modelling approximation to simplify analysis. Similarly, the 'randomness' in processing times may be a way of modelling heterogeneity in the mix of items being processed at a machine, even when there is no randomness in actual processing times. In another example, probabilistic routing may simply be a way of modelling the average behavior of a large class of items with somewhat different routings which have been lumped together to reduce the size of the problem. On the other hand, there are also many situations where processing times, arrival times and routings have intrinsic variability in them, and phenomena such as machine failure, machine repair, yield and rework routing which are intrinsically stochastic. Again, the real issue lies in how well queueing models represent real phenomena.

2.4. Stochastic dynamic models

One sense in which these problems can be dynamic is that there is no stability to the mix produced by the facility. In this case, the queueing models do not apply. If in addition, demand occurrence or other factors are not known with certainty, the resulting problem is stochastic and dynamic. Due to the dynamic nature of the problem, the progress of each individual task through the shop cannot be determined on the basis of stable delay distributions. Rather, the probability distribution for each task or operation must be estimated. The problem of determining distributions for start and finish times for operations, and completion times for jobs, is basically similar to stochastic project schedules. However, in order to represent lead times due to contention, it is necessary to add resource constraints. There appears to be little available in the literature with respect to the general problem. The notion of first fixing the sequence on machines and then evaluating the resulting consequences, is less useful here since the sequence is bound to depend on the actual sample path that is observed. However, if we make the assumption that sequences on resources will be kept fixed, then the computation of start and finish time distributions is identical to the stochastic project network model. A recent paper on that topic is by Dodin & Elmaghraby [1985].

One of the basic computations that is required in this model is the determination of the distribution for an event that can occur only when two or more other events have occurred. Since these extreme value distributions are difficult to calculate, there have been some attempts to use approximations and bounds. Wilhelm & Ahmadi-Marandi [1982] develop computational methods for estimating the early start times for assembly tasks given lead time distributions for the components. They use approximations for extreme value distributions developed by Clark [1961]. Agnihothri, Karmarkar & Kubat

[1982] develop upper and lower bounds for completion time related objectives based on the minimum of lead time distributions.

Graves [1986, 1988a] has developed a discrete period stochastic model which might be thought of as an input–output model. In his model the output of a department or cell in a period is a function of the total work in process in the department, in that a certain fraction of the total work waiting in a period can be completed. This implies that processing rate rises with work in process in a linear manner. Thus, the lead time for a product is (by Little's law) fixed, and the model does not indicate the lead time consequences of releases. Rather it requires that planned lead times (i.e., release policies) be realistic for the model to be valid. In other words, unrealistically low planned lead times lead to high implied processing rates, which can be detected as being unrealistic. In this sense, the model could have a diagnostic role with respect to lead time and release policies. A drawback of the model is that the assumed linear relationship between processing rates and WIP does not tally with well-known results from deterministic and stochastic models which suggest that the output rate 'saturates'. However, the linearity of the assumption allows fairly large and complex models to be developed and for the parameters of the system to be estimated efficiently.

2.5. Factors determining lead times

The models described above give valuable qualitative insights about the factors that determine lead times, and by which lead times can be controlled and managed. The queueing models have proved to be especially useful in this sense.

There is a relation between capacity utilization and lead times that is a well-known phenomenon for queues. However, the static deterministic models show that it also holds for the synchronous case. The source of this effect for the latter case is that high levels of capacity utilization imply large lot sizes to minimize set up time. The large lot sizes cause delays for individual batches themselves, and also cause the cycle time for resources to increase. This effect is exacerbated in the case of asynchronous facilities by congestion phenomena and queueing delays. Capacity utilization is determined by the total loading of the facility as well as by the number of products, mix, grouping of products, assignment to cells, choice of equipment, route selection and load planning over time.

The single workcenter queueing models suggest that for asynchronous facilities, in addition to capacity utilization (traffic intensity), queueing delays and queue lengths depend on

- Variability in the arrival process;
- Variability in service times;
- Batch size as in Figures 2d and 3.

Note that batching can affect all of these. For example, batch sizes across heterogeneous items can be adjusted so as to reduce the variance of processing times across items. This is akin to imposing synchronous or paced behavior on the machine by choice of batch size. As a consequence, the departure stream from the machine is also more regular, thereby (possibly) producing less variability at downstream machines. Furthermore, if arrival processes are highly variable, batching them can decrease the variability of interarrival times. At the same time, if an arrival stream is caused by the combination of two different item arrivals, it is possible that larger batches for one of them can increase arrival variability. More generally, these models indicate the benefits of uniform arrivals and processing times in a way suggestive of concepts like level loading of facilities, uniform schedules and synchronous manufacturing.

In addition to batch sizes, the triggering pattern of order release methods across different items, affects both total load, and the variability of arrivals at machines. Order release mechanisms are therefore a major factor in control of lead times. At the level of individual operations, scheduling theory has traditionally focused on sequencing. However, queueing models suggest that changing the sequence (the queue discipline) will not have an impact on average delays across all items, if the discipline is 'work-conserving'. There will of course be an effect on the lead time of a given order, but only with a compensating effect on another. The implication for so-called 'repetitive manufacturing' where a set of parts is produced for assembly at a relatively constant rate, is that lot sizing and release policies could be more important than sequencing considerations [in this context see Bacon & Choudhuri, 1987]. If we consider a make-to-stock environment, however, then safety stock considerations may make it preferable to give a high cost item priority over another so as to reduce its lead time, even though average WIP and lead times do not change. Finally, in a make-to-order context, customer priorities and due date requirements may make sequencing extremely important.

The effect of setup time on lead time is seen to be linear for the synchronous case with an upper bound due to capacity limits. In the case of facilities with queues, *for fixed batch sizes*, the effect is linear for small values of setup time t but rises explosively for large t. Of course, the effect of setup time reductions must be considered in conjunction with batching policies, which have a favorable leveraging effect on the value of setup time reduction. The joint effect is linear for the synchronous case (see Figure 2d) and approximately linear for the asynchronous. The latter will be discussed in a later section.

Finally, lead time models provide a different way of thinking about bottlenecks. The traditional definition of a bottleneck is the resource with the highest utilization, since total throughput will be limited by that resource. This is a useful definition in situations where production efficiency, capacity utilization and throughput maximization are the key criteria. However, the recognition of lead time as a measure of manufacturing performance suggests that a bottleneck might be alternatively defined as any resource that has a long delay associated with it. By this definition, there might be several bottlenecks of varying degrees. Note that delay-causing is not the same as rate-limiting. The models indicate that the longest delay is not necessarily at the most highly utilized resource; with synchronous operation, utilization can be very high without long delays. Furthermore, utilization itself depends on batching policy. The dynamic models suggest further refinements: bottlenecks need not be fixed, but could shift over time, depending on load and mix as well as on the distribution of work in the shop. If bottlenecks are resources that cause delays, then the dynamic network models can reveal which machines actually lie on the critical path for a particular job. This is still another way to define bottlenecks at the level of individual jobs.

3. Order release models

Order releases can be thought of as having three parameters associated with a given part number: a release quantity, a start or release time, and a due date. A more sophisticated release procedure might specify a transfer batch size, if the release quantity can be broken into smaller pieces for material handling purposes [for example see Dobson, Karmarkar & Rummel, 1988]. There may also be priority levels or costs associated with the release, depending upon source of the requirement. Order release models appear in the traditional production and inventory literature under several guises. With deterministic static demand and no production variations, timing is not an issue, since the start time of each batch is known into the future. The resulting model is some version of the static CLSP or ELSP [e.g., Elmaghraby, 1978]. Similarly with variable but known demand, and fixed lead times, (if this can occur) releases might be determined by MRP calculations or by deterministic dynamic lot size models. The timing of releases becomes an issue when either demand or manufacturing lead times or both are variable. In this section we restrict our attention to models of order release, which take lead time costs and lead time effects into account. These models will broadly follow the categorization used in the previous section.

3.1. *Deterministic static models*

We have already said that these models implicitly consider lead time costs in the sense that the cycle stock cost term can be interpreted as the lead time cost of finished inventory. However, most of these models do not explicitly consider setup times and their impact on cycle times and hence cycle stocks. Instead, they use setup costs as a proxy for the opportunity costs of resource usage. The problem with this is that a fixed setup cost, treated as an attribute of an individual item, cannot represent these opportunity costs (or dual prices for capacity), which depend on the *set* of items being produced. While there are some situations in which there are real setup costs which limit batch sizes (from below), in many cases, batch sizes are bounded by production capacity limits which demand that batch sizes be large enough to leave enough production time to meet demand.

Among the static lot size models which consider setup times directly are those of Sugimori, Kusunoki, Cho & Uchikawa [1977] and Dobson [1987]. However, most of these do not explicitly consider lead time related costs. The Sugimori paper is the exception in that it takes lead time reduction as measured by the cycle time, to be the objective. Magee [1956] is an early paper that identifies the safety stock consequences of batch sizes and the resulting cycle times although it does not present an explicit analytical model. Unfortunately, the paper does not seem to have been paid much attention subsequently, in the technical literature.

Karmarkar & Lele [1989] describe a case study with an approximate analysis of the safety stock consequences of batching policy. They assume that safety stocks are held against a lead time equal to the cycle time for each product, and that a rotation cycle production policy is followed. The standard deviation of demand over a lead time of T is taken to be given by scaling up the standard deviation per period by a factor of T^b, where $0.5 \leq b \leq 1.0$. The service level to be provided is given and safety stocks are set at the corresponding multiple of the standard deviation of demand over lead time. This is not a very sophisticated model; the interaction between batching and safety stocks is ignored, and the production rotation cycle is rigidly followed. The standard deviation heuristic is simplistic and has scaling problems. However, the resulting analysis is instructive. In the absence of setup costs, the optimal policy is simply to minimize batch size and cycle time and use up all production capacity. This is because both safety stocks and cycle stocks increase with batch size (or cycle time). For the data sets considered, the safety stock costs were significantly larger than the cycle stocks, often by an order of magnitude. The implications are quite different from the conventional EOQ analysis.

In the presence of real setup costs (due to say material losses in starting a batch) the tradeoff is between stock holding and the setup costs. The average cost per time is given by an expression of the form

$$\sum_i k_i h_i T^b + \sum_i h_i D_i T + \sum_i K_i / T ,$$

where the first term represents safety stocks, the second, cycle stocks and the third the setup costs; k_i is a constant for each item depending on service level and standard deviation of demand per period, and h, D and K represent holding cost rates, demand rates and fixed setup costs respectively. Furthermore, there is a lower bound on T imposed by production time, as described in Section 2.1 and shown in Figure 2d. Note that this model differs from the usual (Q, R) models in that the effect of triggering and batching on lead times and hence on safety stocks is explicitly considered. The costs of safety stocks are concave in T for $b < 1$, while the setup costs are convex; however, the total cost function is typically well behaved. If the setup costs are high enough, the cycle time is forced to be larger than the previous case (the lower bound) and there is some enforced idleness (or unused excess capacity). There are thus some implications for capacity decisions which are discussed in a later section.

It should be possible to extend existing CLSP models in this direction to include the effects of lead times. However, as discussed in Section 2.1, it is necessary that these models correctly represent occupation of the resource, including the effect of setup time so that the relationship between batching policy and lead times is captured.

3.2. Deterministic dynamic models

There appear to be relatively few models in this category that relate lead time costs to both batching and timing release parameters. MRP is in effect a deterministic dynamic release method, but it begs the question with respect to lead times by assuming them to be fixed and requiring them to be provided exogenously. It is thus ignoring the consequences of releases. It could be said that methods such as rough cut planning and input–output analysis are adjuncts that try after the fact to discover these consequences. It is also not apparent what costs or objectives are being considered in MRP calculations.

In Section 2.2 we noted that most conventional deterministic lot size models do not represent resource occupation explicitly. Those that do – the 'product cycling' models – by and large have not considered lead time related costs. Unlike the previous section, the dynamic nature of these models appears to make it inappropriate to consider safety stock implications while remaining in a deterministic framework. The lead time related costs that it is possible to consider are WIP costs, and possibly lateness or tardiness costs. In order to incorporate some element of WIP costs, it seems necessary to model multi-stage production processes, so that the inventory between stages is represented. There do not appear to be any dynamic product cycling models in the literature that consider multiple production stages.

Karni [1981] develops an optimization model of input–output analysis. Batch sizing is not considered in this model so that it is aimed primarily at determining release times, and possibly discovering due date violations. Dynamic programming is used to solve a single work station problem.

The detailed network models are potentially usable in setting release dates and perhaps release quantities. They have been used in this manner as evaluation or simulation tools and have been used to develop detailed scheduling methods. However, there do not appear to be any optimization models of release decisions based on this paradigm. Interestingly, the literature in network models has in the past, not considered the effect of batching. Karmarkar [1987b] shows that batching of releases affects performance measures such as weighted flow times and makespan, in quite general settings. However, no optimization model is presented.

Dobson, Karmarkar & Rummel [1987], Santos & Magazine [1985], Naddef & Santos [1984] have developed models of batching at a single machine with weighted flow time as an objective. These can be thought of as release models although they are perhaps more appropriate for the scheduling level. To give a simple example of batching in this context, consider the following. Suppose that there are two kinds of items to be processed at a machine. Each item requires 1 time unit to setup and 1 to process per piece. Suppose that 8 pieces of each kind are to be made and that it is desired to minimize the total flow time for the items. Now if each piece were available for use as soon as it was processed, the solution would be to process first one item, and then the other, in batches of 8. This has been described as the *item flow* or *item availability* case in the papers above. However, suppose that a piece is available only when the batch of which it is part is completed. This is termed the *batch flow* or *batch availability* case. For this case, labelling the item types A and B, the flow times for different batching and release sequences are as follows:

Sequence	Total flow time
$A,B,A,B,\ldots,A,B$	336
$AA,BB,\ldots,BB$	216
$AAAA,BBBB,\ldots$	200
$8A$'s, $8B$'s	216

We see that the flow time goes through a minimum as the batch size is increased; this behavior is analogous to that in Figure 3. However, note that the deterministic case reveals another facet of the problem. If we were to release the items as $5A$, $5B$, $3A$, $3B$, the total flow time would be 196; i.e., a dynamic release policy gives better results. Dobson, Karmarkar & Rummel [1987] suggest that this can be thought of in the following way: when there are more items waiting (unprocessed), the machine is in effect busier and processing should be done more efficiently. Larger batches increase the effective processing rate. As the number of items waiting declines, smaller batches become viable. Alternatively, the external or implicit 'cost' of a setup is greater with many items waiting, leading to larger batch sizes initially.

To obtain a simple stylized model that captures this, consider a single kind of item being processed at a machine. For simplicity assume that the processing batch size is to be kept constant. Define:

d = total quantity to be processed (units),
n = number of batches,
Q = batch size = d/n,
P = processing rate (units/time),
t = setup time per batch,
T_i = flow time for the ith batch, $i = 1, \ldots, n$.

Then

$$T_1 = (t + Q/P)\,, \qquad T_i = i(t + Q/P)\,,$$

and the total flow time weighted by the batch size for n batches is

$$C(n) = \sum_i iQ(t + Q/P)\,.$$

The number of batches which results in the minimum cost is given by the n that satisfies

$$C(n) \leq C(n-1) \quad \text{and} \quad C(n) \leq C(n+1) .$$

Substituting for $C(n)$ and simplifying gives the condition

$$n(n-1) \leq (d/Pt) \leq n(n+1) .$$

As a first approximation, treating n as a continuous variable,

$$n^2 = (d/Pt) .$$

From which we obtain an approximation for the batch size as

$$Q = (dPt)^{1/2} .$$

Dobson, Karmarkar & Rummel [1987] and Santos & Magazine [1985] show that if the restriction of fixed batch sizes is removed, the size of the first batch is approximated by

$$Q = (2dPt)^{1/2} .$$

The exact optimum varies from this by a small additional term. Once this batch is completed, the quantity waiting is reduced to $d' = d - Q$. Hence, the second batch, applying the same result, is smaller. Surprisingly, with the exact formula, the batches decrease exactly linearly in size.

These formulae have a resemblance to the usual EOQ model. However, it should be recognized that the setting here is quite different. The quantity to be processed is finite, and there is no continuous stream of demand as in the EOQ model. Furthermore, there are no costs involved in this formula and the objective function is different from the EOQ model. Interestingly, the last formula is also very similar to a batching heuristic to minimize waiting time, developed from a queueing model by Karmarkar, Kekre & Kekre [1985]. That result, discussed in the next section, will shed some light on the similarities to, and differences from the EOQ model.

Morton, Lawrence, Rajagopolan & Kekre [1988] have developed a batching model based on the implicit cost of using a machine or resource. These costs are essentially shadow prices determined at a 'higher' planning level, based on the extent to which the resource is utilized. The costs are then used to compute an effective setup cost used in batch size calculations. Since the costs vary over time, the batch sizes also vary dynamically. It appears that there are close similarities between this approach and the results above. Morton & Singh [1988] show by use of a queueing model that the implicit cost or price of using a resource is related to the busy period. It could be said that the models above use the queue length d as an index of cost, and queue lengths are related to busy periods, which suggests the connection between the approaches.

Dobson, Karmarkar & Rummel [1987] use the one item model to develop effective heuristics for the multi-item case. Elsewhere [Dobson, Karmarkar & Rummel, 1989] they extend the single item model to the case of multiple heterogeneous resources with different setup and run characteristics. Again, while stylized, the model suggests some interesting qualitative ideas. In the case where setup times are equal across machines, work is allocated to them in proportion to their production rates. However, when setups vary, it is possible for some machines to be allocated no work.

Santos [1988] has developed an extensive taxonomy for batching problems with lead time related measures of performance. He also analyzes several new extensions of the problem, including two facilities in series. The latter models allow the exploration of the effect of bottlenecks on batching policies. While bottlenecks tend to determine batching, with a finite job set, a bottleneck may have no queue at the start. Instead, there may be a 'gating' machine at which released jobs are queued. As the queue dependent batching formulae above then suggest, initially, the batches will be determined by the gating machine, and subsequently by the bottleneck machine.

The interaction between batching and lead times with multiple machines has begun to receive some attention. Baker [1988] and Baker & Pyke [1988] have developed models of 'lot streaming' where transfer batches are used to reduce lead times by moving material on to succeeding operations. This technique is also called 'overlapping'. Baker develops both simple models that illustrate the concept and LP models that can compute the optimal 'streaming' policy at least for small examples. It also appears that static (i.e., fixed lot) policies are almost as effective as dynamic policies, which bodes well for applications.

While the results obtained to this point are from simple models, often with just one item and one or two machines, they provide new insights and evidence to support existing conjectures. Heuristics developed from these models have been found to be very effective in developing detailed dynamic scheduling methods [e.g., Dobson, Karmarkar & Rummel, 1988]. However, there do not seem to be any direct applications as yet to order release decisions. This appears to be a very critical area for the development of new methods that have potential practical uses, since they would apply to the asynchronous facilities where both MRP and pull methods have limited value.

3.3. *Static stochastic models*

The various queueing models described in Section 2.3 provide a description of the lead time behavior of manufacturing systems with certain characteristics. The models appear to fit systems which are asynchronous and subject to congestion phenomena and queues, but are nevertheless reasonably stable in an aggregate sense. In my opinion, these models are highly suitable for many systems which were previously modelled using multistage dynamic deterministic lot size models of the Wagner–Whitin type. Queueing models and queueing network models have been used successfully to model order release processes in both push and pull systems, including batching decisions, alternative triggering rules, and priority rules.

The use of queueing models to analyze batching policies can be thought of as the third development in lot sizing models after the static [Harris, 1915] and dynamic [Wagner & Whitin, 1958; Manne 1958] deterministic approaches. Some of the early models were those of Bertrand [1985], Karmarkar, Kekre & Kekre [1985], Karmarkar [1987a], and Zipkin [1986]. A key difference between these models and the traditional lot sizing approach is that they consider WIP and lead time related costs. In this author's experience, WIP, safety time and safety stock related costs greatly exceed cycle stock costs in typical asynchronous facilities. Furthermore, the setup costs of the EOQ model do not succeed as a proxy for the opportunity costs of capacity usage. These issues of cost modelling are directly addressed and established by Rummel [1989].

Karmarkar [1987a] presents a model analogous to the EOQ formalism, but with the difference that the setup cost term is replaced by WIP inventory costs. The argument is made that in facilities with congestion and queues, capacity utilization is never 100%. In such a case, the usual concept of a hard capacity constraint as in LP or multi-item lot size models does not apply. Rather the costs of capacity utilization are experienced in terms of queues, delays and WIP that discourage full utilization. These costs can be thought of as an interior penalty function that enforces capacity constraints. In fact the capacity constraints turn out to be equivalent to the usual stability condition for queues. A single item, single machine version of the lot size model can be written as

$$\min_{Q\geq 0} khDT + hQ/2$$

$$\text{subject to} \quad T = (t + (Q/P))/(1 - (D/P) - (tD/Q)),$$

where the variables are as defined earlier in Section 2.3. Here the first term in the objective function represents the costs of work in process, assuming that its average holding cost is kh for $k \leq 1$, where h is the holding cost for finished goods inventory. The second term is the usual cycle stock cost. The constraint gives the average time in the production system as a function of the batch size Q following the model of Section 2.3. For convenience consider the special case of $k = \frac{1}{2}$. This yields a simple solution for the optimal lot size of

$$Q = 2Dt/(1-u).$$

The solution for arbitrary k is given by Karmarkar & Rummel [1986] and interestingly, it turns out to be very close to the above for a wide range of k, when the effective utilization $u = D/P$ is over 0.5. First note that the lot size involves no costs. Also the relationship to D and t is quite different from that in the EOQ model in being linear rather than concave. The batch size formula is very similar to that in the rotation cycle model. On substituting the optimal batch size back into the objective function, the cost of the optimal policy is given by

$$hDt/(1-u) + hDt(1+u)/(1-u)^2 ,$$

where the first term represents cycle stock costs and the second, WIP costs. For a utilization level of $u = 0.8$, it is apparent that the WIP costs are about 9 times the cycle stock costs. Even for $u = 0.5$, the WIP costs are 3 times the cycle stock costs. When there are several such queues in series, these proportions add up. Furthermore, it can be determined that at the optimum, the queue time in the system is a large proportion of the total lead time. In other words in asynchronous facilities with queues, the preponderance of queue times is apparently to be expected.

The multi-item extension of this model, using an M/G/1 model is discussed by Karmarkar [1987a] and Karmarkar, Kekre & Kekre [1984]. In the latter, a batching model similar to the above is formulated, except that the objective function only includes queue time. While this was done for convenience in simplifying the derivations, the answers are qualitatively useful since the queue costs are the large part of total costs. A closed form expression for the batch size could not be derived, but the lot size for the ith item is shown to be given by Q_i

$$Q_i = (2Wt_iP_i)^{1/2} ,$$

where W is a measure of the average work waiting in queue given the optimal lot size. Note that with the replacement of W for d, this is the same as the formula obtained by Dobson, Karmarkar and Rummel for the deterministic case, as described in the previous section. However, now the static job set is replaced by continuous arrivals, and that unlike d, W does not diminish over time as items are processed. Now W is itself a function of parameters such as t and P. Although exact closed form expressions for W and Q are not available, it is shown that approximately,

$$W = 2\sum_i t_iu_i/(1-u)^2 ,$$

and

$$Q_i = 2\alpha_iP_it_i/(1-u) ,$$

where

$$u = \sum_i u_i \quad \text{and} \quad \alpha_i = \Big(\sum_j t_ju_j/t_i\Big)^{1/2} .$$

Note that each factor α_i is homogenous of degree 0 in the vector of setup times, so that if all the setup times double, α_i remains the same. Furthermore, if the ith product dominates the utilization of the machine, α tends to 1. Thus despite the square root in the expression for α, the parametric form for the batch size is actually somewhat similar to the rotation cycle results. The batch size is positive homogeneous of degree 1 in the vector of setup times; i.e., if all the setup times are doubled, all the batch sizes double. However, if the utilization of the ith item or its setup time is very small relative to other items, then the batch size for that item indeed varies as the square root of its setup time, for small perturbations. In this situation the behavior is more like the square root formula. This approximation establishes the connections between the deterministic static, deterministic dynamic and stochastic static cases. Karmarkar, Kekre and Kekre also show that the batch size that minimizes average lead time also comes close to minimizing the variability of lead time. Finally, they investigate the sensitivity of queue times to various parameters, and show that they are approximately linear in setup times.

These lot size models are extended to networks of queues by Karmarkar, Kekre & Kekre [1985] and Zipkin [1986]. The validation of the queueing model as well as the derived lot sizing policy on a simulation of a manufacturing cell is described by Karmarkar, Kekre, Kekre & Freeman [1985]. Bacon & Choudhuri [1987] describe tests of an order launch approach using a release policy derived; from this model. They tested the efficacy of this approach against the performance of a commercial scheduling package (OPT) for a relatively stable (repetitive) batch shop. The simpler order release approach appeared to do as well as or better than detailed scheduling for this case, on the basis of measures such as WIP, lead times and average tardiness relative to a given schedule.

These models have considered the impact of batching on WIP, but not other lead time costs. There are a few models in the literature that consider safety stock implications as well. Cohen and Lee consider the impact of lead times on inventories and distribution systems. Harel & Zipkin [1984, 1987] establish convexity results for performance measures related to this issue.

Graves [1980] presents a discrete period, stochastic demand product cycling model that appears to be the only investigation of that problem. In the model occupancy of the (single) machine is represented in terms of cycling of products so that two products cannot be made in one period. Hence, the lead time effects of batching due to waiting for a turn in the cycle, are captured. This lead time is then reflected in the safety stocks that must be held against the stochastic demand. An exact solution is not obtained, but effective heuristics based on the two product case, are developed. The model uses setup costs rather than setup times, but it appears that this would not be a difficult extension. This could be thought of as a model of a synchronous production facility facing stochastic demand, which creates some variability in the production cycle. This is a more rigorous model than the heuristic approach based on a rotation cycle, described in Section 3.1.

If the production facility is more complex, it will exhibit congestion phenomena and queueing behavior. A 'Kanban' cell that combines a production facility with finished product inventory, requires consideration of both lead time and demand variability effects. Karmarkar & Kekre [1986] develop models of single card, dual card and two-stage Kanban systems based on Markov chain approximations. The models combine decisions on the number of cards (containers) in the cell as well as batch size. The objective function is taken to be the sum of expected holding and backorder costs. This model captures lead time effects on safety stocks and also considers how batching affects this relationship. The paper shows that the effect of batch size on cost for a fixed card count is qualitatively similar to the curve in Figure 2b. In other words the lead time effect of batch size seems to dominate the eventual effect (through inventory levels) on holding and shortage costs. When batch size is fixed and card count changes, the effect on costs is analogous to changing stock level in a Newsboy problem. In two stage systems there are triggering effects between stages which are illustrated in the paper, but no general insight is delivered. Simultaneous optimization of batch size and card count is also illustrated; however the approximations in the model mean that it cannot produce practical numerical results. Zipkin [1989] also presents a Markovian model of a multistage Kanban system and investigates the effect of the number of cards in each stage. The credibility of the qualitative results from these models is enhanced by similar results obtained by Shen [1987] from a SLAM simulation of a two-stage Kanban system. Deleersnyder, Hodgson & O'Grady [1987], Mitra & Mitrani [1988] and Seidmann [1988] present Markovian or regenerative models of Kanban systems. Other simulation studies of card count and batch size choice and other factors in Kanban systems have been done by Huang, Rees & Taylor [1983] and Philipoom, Rees, Taylor & Huang [1987a,b].

4. Capacity and planning decisions

While the emphasis upto this point has primarily been on the order release level, decisions at other hierarchical levels have significant implications for lead times and the resulting costs. As with the order release process, models of these decisions must also incorporate lead time effects in constraints and objective functions. In this section, models incorporating lead time effects are surveyed briefly. The intent is to provide a connection with the order release level and to point out some interesting research directions.

4.1. Capacity planning

Capacity planning models formulate the problem in terms of filling capacity 'buckets' representing available capacity in discrete time periods. Linear programming models have been a natural vehicle for modelling these decisions.

Such models do have lead time implications. For example, if capacity is exceeded in a particular period, a planning model will reassign production to a period in which there is idle capacity. In effect, an early release of those requirements has been made. On the other hand, in these models, the capacity constraint is a hard limit that is either binding or not. However, we have seen from both queueing and sequencing models, that in asynchronous facilities, queues and delays occur even when utilization of facilities is below 100%. These queues and delays result in WIP and other lead time related costs. Most planning models do not account for the WIP implications of the loading decisions made in the models; certainly the LP formulations do not.

Kekre [1984a] and Kekre & Kekre [1984] attempt to capture this issue by adding a WIP term to the objective function of the usual LP planning model. They propose that the WIP level be computed by using a queueing network model. It is assumed that each period in the planning model is long enough so that the average WIP given by the queueing model is an adequate approximation. This type of formulation has obvious problems in that an equilibrium queueing model is being used within a non-stationary discrete period model. In particular, what happens in the transition between periods is not clear. Nevertheless, the approach points out a very important consideration in making planning decisions for complex facilities. The intuitive insight from their analysis is that the WIP (or lead time) costs create a strong incentive to smooth production across periods, in terms of avoiding high utilization levels in any period. This smoothing goes beyond the shifting of production to meet hard capacity constraints.

Cohen & Lee [1986] have used queueing models to analyze the behavior of multi-stage production distribution systems. In particular, they are concerned with lead time effects, where lead times at one stage have an impact on the next. An example is the effect on distribution systems of replenishment times which include manufacturing lead time.

Graves [1986] describes an application of the WIP clearing model by Graves described in Section 2.5. The model is applied to a service facility to investigate workforce planning decisions, and the effect of loading. Graves & Fine [1988] describe an extensive application of the model to a manufacturing facility. Here, the model is extended to allow consideration of several features peculiar to the facility under consideration, including release policies. The parameters of the model are fitted to observed data by regression methods. The model is then used to investigate the effect of various planning and loading policies and the effect of changes in mix. The model is not imbedded in an optimization procedure, although this appears to be possible.

Karmarkar, Kekre & Kekre [1987] describe the application of a queueing network model to the analysis of shift and overtime policies in a manufacturing cell. The alternatives are evaluated by enumeration, and the queueing model is used to provide estimates of work-in-process inventories and cell lead times. This model can only evaluate static policies and does not apply in a seasonal planning context.

One way to capture lead time and WIP effects in a deterministic planning model, uses the construct of a 'clearing function' [Karmarkar, 1989]. Such a function describes the amount of output 'cleared' from a manufacturing facility as a function of its work-in-process. I have initially suggested using a function of the basic form

$$\text{output rate } D = P[\text{WIP}/(\text{WIP} + k)]\,,$$

where P is the nominal (maximum) production rate of the facility, and k is a parameter that determines the clearing rate. This clearing function displays the saturating phenomenon that occurs not only in queueing models but even in deterministic synchronous models, where there is some processing inefficiency leading to batching. For examples see the simple models in Sections 2.1 and 2.3 and in Figure 2a.

The clearing function idea is useful in understanding other models as well. Figure 4 shows the form of the saturating clearing function given above, and also shows the model due to Graves in which $D = \alpha$ WIP for some α between 0 and 1. The figure also shows the clearing function corresponding to the usual capacity constrained planning model, in which $D = P$. The conventional model provides no lead time implications, and has WIP $= 0$ irrespective of output level. In the Graves model, lead time is constant and is treated as a 'planned' parameter. WIP is proportional to output rate; WIP $= D/\alpha$. In the saturating model, WIP levels determine outputs, and the lead time experienced depends on WIP level, which in turn depends on how the facility is loaded. With uniform loading, it is shown that the equilibrium levels of WIP and average lead time are analogous to those given by a simple queueing model. For the case above, it is shown that for a uniform release level and output rate of D

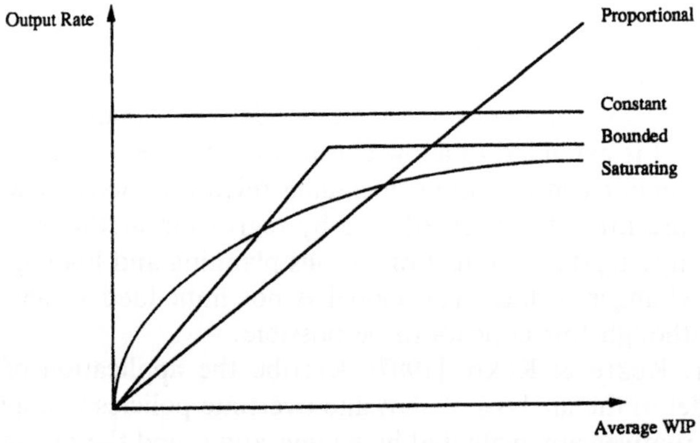

Fig. 4. Clearing functions relating output rate to work-in-process (WIP) for the saturating (Karmarkar), bounded (Input–Output control), constant (LP) and proportional (Graves) output models.

such that $D + k \geqslant P$, the equilibrium WIP level is given by

$$\text{WIP} = (D + k - P)[u/(1 - u)]\,, \quad \text{where } u = D/P\,.$$

It is straightforward to adapt clearing functions for a discrete period dynamic planning model that directly models WIP as well as finished inventories [Karmarkar, 1989]. Since lead times and output vary with loading, the emphasis shifts to release plans, facility loading and WIP, rather than production plans and finished inventories as in the conventional LP planning models. Since the model is deterministic, it is amenable to solution using mathematical programming techniques and can be extended to multiple products and multiple facilities. These developments proceed apace.

4.2. Capacity and design evaluation

Queueing network models have been used for performance evaluation in many studies. They provide a picture of the relationship between capacity, loading and mix and the resulting work-in-process and lead time consequences. Solberg [1977] is an early example of the application of closed queueing network models to manufacturing system analysis. Seidmann, Schweitzer & Nof [1988] develop a probabilistic model of a cell with feedback flow. Bitran & Tirupati [1988] develop a multi-class model that has been applied to capacity planning decisions in several examples. Chen, Harrison, Mandelbaum, Van Ackere & Wein [1988] use a model based on diffusion approximations to represent a wafer fabrication facility. Karmarkar, Kekre & Kekre [1987] in addition to shift policies, also consider alternative machine configurations. A thorough review of the application of queueing models to the representation of manufacturing facilities can be found in Buzacott & Yao [1986] and Suri, Sanders & Kamath [1993].

Kekre & Lafond [1988] model lead times in an automative manufacturing plant with parallel flows to assess how lead time variability affects predetermined production sequences. The exiting stream from the parallel processes has a different sequence from the entering stream due to lead time variations. As a result, subsequent assembly operations cannot be prescheduled. Furthermore, there are random rework instances which lead to feedback flows, which can also cause sequence changes.

It should be noted that most if not all of these are performance evaluation models and do not involve optimization. One exception is the model by Vinod & Solberg [1985] which imbeds a queueing network model in an enumeration scheme. Similarly, Kekre [1984b] develops an enumeration scheme for the design of a batch manufacturing facility, and describes the application to a real data set. The results from the model are compared to a heuristic in use; reassuringly the model gives superior results.

Karmarkar and Lele use the product cycling model described in Section 3.1 to analyze additions to capacity. Deliberate maintenance of excess capacity allows the reduction of cycle times and concomitant reductions in safety and cycle stocks. These can justify the addition of extra shifts or of equipment and machine capacity. In addition, the excess capacity can also provide protection against 'surge' demands. They use a LP model to illustrate that with tight capacity and seasonal demands, a relatively small surge in demand can take a long time to 'clear'. In practice, this is seen as a persistent backorder condition that starts when a demand surge empties certain inventories. The need to respond to surges can justify a strategic investment in capacities.

Banker, Datar & Kekre [1988] use an M/G/1 model to develop an imputed cost of capacity, when the limitation on capacity usage is due to queues and lead times rather than absolute constraints. Morton & Singh [1988] relate the cost of capacity to busy period length.

5. Research opportunities

The development of manufacturing control models incorporating lead times and their consequences is recent. For some reason, the connections between order release, planning and capacity decisions and lead times have not been examined extensively in the past. This is not only true of practice but also of the technical literature. For example, till recently, there was little to be found on issues such as the connection between batching and queueing or batching and sequencing. There has been a tendency to take lead times as given, and the consequences of lead times such as WIP, rarely if ever appear in objective functions. The recent appearance of concepts such as 'zero inventory', JIT, Kanban, setup time reduction, EOQ of 1, and so on, underline the absence of lead time related methods from our repertoire. To the researcher in manufacturing methods, this is as they say, a problem and an opportunity.

There are more unresolved issues here than can be listed; I will simply pick on some that seem interesting and valuable.

– In terms of modelling manufacturing facilities, aggregate models of lead time and WIP behavior are not readily available. There is a need for an approach that will work at a planning level, so that facility loading under seasonal demand can be analyzed. The technical problem here is that planning models tend to be in discrete time while queueing and scheduling models are in continuous time. Graves' model is an attempt to bridge this gap, but it assumes planned lead times. The 'clearing function' model of Section 4.1 is aimed at this situation, but requires more development and validation.

– Some aspects of lead time related costs (like WIP) are easy to model. Others are more difficult. I suspect that quality consequences and responsiveness to demand changes and surges are two important directions.

– In modelling safety stock costs, lead time variability needs to be estimated. It is just as important for safety time, due date setting and release triggering decisions. Currently, the only work available seems to be that of Seidmann, Schweitzer & Nof [1985], and Arreola-Risa & Lee [1988]. I would conjecture that queues in most manufacturing facilities tend to be correlated. For example, if one area is seeing a higher load than normal due to a higher rate of release, so probably are many others. If a job is delayed in a queue created by a failure, the resulting surge will create queues for the job through its subsequent route as well. One can guess that lead time distributions will tend to be fat-tailed and skewed. Some empirical work on this issue would be very useful.

– There seem to be reasonably effective batching models using queueing networks, and reasonable progress on batching in sequencing and scheduling (although there is no shortage of new problems). However, there appears to be no good practical scheme for release batch sizing in a moderately dynamic environment. Queueing models seem to work well as order release rules for MRP in stable shops [e.g., Bacon & Choudhuri, 1987]. However, they will not do for more dynamic situations. Scheduling models work for small shops but are not tractable for very large shops or long horizons. Perhaps an aggregate capacity pricing scheme such as that proposed by Morton & Singh [1988] could provide a tractable dynamic release procedure.

– There are several new models of release policies in the literature [e.g., Deleersnyder, Denardo & Tang]. Some of these do not presently account for issues such as batching or prioritized releases. There are also opportunities for the analysis of other release models which are already in use in practice. For example, there are several kinds of multi-level Kanban mechanisms that look like priority class schemes.

– There appear to be no models which capture lead time behavior with dynamic (i.e., time varying) stochastic demands. There are obviously many such situations in practice. For example, in Groenevelt & Karmarkar [1988], we describe a 'dynamic Kanban' system in which the parameters of the system are changed in response to forecasts. While the system has proved to be very effective in practice, there is a need for formal models that analyze the problem.

References

Ackerman, S.S. (1963). Even-flow, a scheduling method for reducing lateness in job shop. *Management Tech.* 3, 20–31.

Agnihothri, S.R., U.S. Karmarkar and P. Kubat (1982). Stochastic allocation rules. *Oper. Res.* 30, 545–555.

Arreola-Risa, A., and H.L. Lee (1989). Inventory control in a pull production–distribution system, Tech. Rep. Univ. of Washington.

Bacon, R.E., and A.N. Choudhuri (1987). A manager's dilemma: Lot sizing and/or finite scheduling, Working Paper Series No. CMOM 87-08, William E. Simon Graduate School of Business Administration, Univ. of Rochester, Rochester, NY.

Bagchi, U., and J.C. Hayya (1984). Demand during lead time for normal unit demand and Erlang lead time. *J. Oper. Res. Soc.* 35, 131–135.

Bagchi, U., J.C. Hayya and J.K. Ord (1984). Modeling demand during lead time. *Decision Sci.* 15, 157–176.

Bahl, H.C., L.P. Ritzman and J.N.D. Gupta (1987). Determining lot sizes and resource requirements: A review. *Oper. Res.* 35, 329–345.
Baker, K.R. (1984a). Sequencing rules and due-date assignments in a job shop. *Management Sci.* 30, 1093–2004.
Baker, K.R. (1984b). The effects of input control in a simple scheduling model. *Oper. Management* 4, 99–112.
Baker, K.R. (1987). Lot streaming to reduce cycle time in a flow shop, Working Paper No. 203, The Amos Tuck School of Business Administration, Dartmouth College.
Baker, K.R., and J.W.M. Bertrand (1981). A comparison of due-date selection rules. *AIIE Trans.* 13, 123–131.
Baker, K.R., and J.W.M. Bertrand (1982). An investigation of due-date assignment rules with constrained tightness. *J. Oper. Management* 3, 109–120.
Baker, K.R., and J.J. Kanet (1983). Job shop scheduling with modified due dates. *J. Oper. Management* 4, 11–22.
Baker, K.R., and D.F. Pyke (1988). Algorithms for the lot streaming problem, Working Paper No. 233, The Amos Tuck School of Business Administration, Dartmouth College.
Balas, E. (1969). Machine sequencing via disjunctive graphs: An implicit enumeration algorithm. *Oper. Res.* 17, 941–957.
Banker, R.D., S.D. Datar and S. Kekre (1988). Relevant costs, congestion and stochasticity in production environments. *J. Account. Econ.* 10, 171–197.
Bechte, W. (1982). Controlling manufacturing lead time and work-in-process inventory by means of load-oriented order release. *25th Ann. Internat. Conf. Proc. Amer. Prod. Invent. Control Society*, October, 1982, APICS, Falls Church, VA, pp. 67–72.
Bemelmans, R. (1985). Capacity oriented production planning in case of a single bottleneck. *Engrg. Costs Prod. Econom.* 9, 135–140.
Bertrand, J.W.M. (1981). The effect of workload control on order flow-times. *Proc. IXth IFORS Conference on Operations Research*, North-Holland, Amsterdam.
Bertrand, J.W.M. (1983a). The effect of workload dependent due-dates on job shop performance. *Management Sci.* 29, 799–816.
Bertrand, J.W.M. (1983b). The use of workload information to control job lateness in controlled and uncontrolled release production systems. *J. Oper. Management* 3, 67–78.
Bertrand, J.W.M. (1985). Multiproduct optimal batch sizes with in-process inventories and multiwork centres. *IEE Trans.* 17, 157–163.
Bertrand, J., and J. Wortmann (1981). *Production Control and Information Systems for Component Manufacturing*, Elsevier, Amsterdam.
Bitran, G.R., and L. Chang (1987). A mathematical programming approach to a deterministic Kanban system. *Management Sci.* 33, 427–441.
Bitran, G.R., E. Haas and A.C. Hax (1981). Hierarchical production planning: A single stage system. *Oper. Res.* 29, 717–743.
Bitran, G.R., and A.C. Hax (1977). On the design of hierarchical production planning systems. *Decision Sci.* 8, 23–55.
Bitran, G.R., and D. Tirupati (1987). Trade-off curves, targeting, and balancing in manufacturing networks, Working Paper 87-08-05, Univ. of Texas at Austin, Department of Management.
Bitran, G.R., and D. Tirupati (1988). Multiproduct queueing networks with deterministic routing: Decomposition approach and notion of interference. *Management Sci.* 34, 75–100.
Blackburn, J.D., D.H. Kropp and R.A. Millen (1985). MRP system nervousness: Causes and cures. *Engrg. Costs Prod. Econom.* 9, 141–149.
Boxma, O.J., A.H.G. Rinnooy Kan and M. Van Vliet (1990). Machine allocation problems in manufacturing networks. *European J. Oper. Res.* 45, 47–54.
Buzacott, J.A. (1988). Kanban and MRP controlled production systems, Working Paper, Univ. of Waterloo, Waterloo, Canada.
Buzacott, J.A., and J.G. Shanthikumar (1980). Models for understanding flexible manufacturing systems. *AIIE Trans.* 12, 339–350.
Buzacott, J.A., and D.D. Yao (1986). Flexible manufacturing systems: A review of analytical models. *Management Sci.* 32, 890–905.

Calabrese, J.M. (1988). Lot sizing and priority sequencing to minimize manufacturing cycle time and work-in-process inventory, Working Paper, Department of IE-EM, Stanford University, Palo Alto, CA.

Chen, H., J.M. Harrison, A. Mandelbaum, A. Van Ackere and L.M. Wein (1988). Empirical evaluation of a queueing network model for semiconductor wafer fabrication. *Oper. Res.* 36, 202–215.

Clark, C.E. (1961). The greatest of a finite set of random variables. *Oper. Res.* 9, 145–162.

Cohen, M.A., and H.L. Lee (1988). Strategic analysis of integrated production–distribution systems: Models and methods. *Oper. Res.* 36, 216–228.

Conway, R.W. (1965). Priority dispatching and job lateness in a job shop. *J. Ind. Engrg.* 16, 228–237.

Conway, R.W., W.L. Maxwell and L.W. Miller (1967). *Theory of Scheduling*, Addison-Wesley, Reading, MA.

Crowston, W.B., M. Wagner and J.F. Williams (1973). Economic lot size determination in multi-stage assembly systems. *Management Sci.* 19, 517–527.

Davis, W.J., and S.J. Stubitz (1987). Configuring a Kanban system using a discrete optimization of multiple stochastic responses. *Internat. J. Prod. Res.* 25, 721–740.

Deleersnyder, J.L. (1988). Stochastic models for evaluating the effects of information flow structures on the hybrid push–pull system performance, Paper presented at the 5th Euro Summer Institute on Production Planning and Control.

Deleersnyder, J.L., T.J. Hodgson and P.J. O'Grady (1987). Kanban controlled pull systems: An analytic approach, NCSU-IE, Tech. Rep. #87-8, North Carolina State University.

Dempster, M.A.H., M.L. Fisher, L. Jansens, B.J. Lageweg, J.K. Lenstra and A.H.G. Rinnooy Kan (1983). Analysis of heuristics for stochastic programming: Results for hierarchical scheduling problems. *Math. Oper. Res.* 8, 525–537.

Denardo, E.V., and C.S. Tang (1988). Pulling a Markov production line, Working Paper No. 357, Western Management Science Institute, Anderson Graduate School of Management, Los Angeles, CA.

DeVaney, A., and N.G. Frey (1982). Backlogs and the value of excess capacity. *Amer. Econom. Rev.* 72, 441–451.

Dobson, G. (1987). The economic lot-scheduling problem: Achieving feasibility using time-varying lot sizes. *Oper. Res.* 35, 764–771.

Dobson, G., and U.S. Karmarkar (1986). Large scale shop scheduling formulation and decomposition, Working Paper Series No. QM 86-31, W.E. Simon Graduate School of Business Administration, Univ. of Rochester.

Dobson, G., and U.S. Karmarkar (1989). Reversed CLSP and flow time minimization, Working Paper, William E. Simon Graduate School of Business Administration, Univ. of Rochester.

Dobson, G., U.S. Karmarkar and J.L. Rummel (1987). Batching to minimize flow time on one machine. *Management Sci.* 33, 784–799.

Dobson, G., U.S. Karmarkar and J.L. Rummel (1992). A closed loop automatic scheduling system (CLASS). *Prod. Planning Control* 3(2), 130–140.

Dobson, G., U.S. Karmarkar and J.L. Rummel (1989). Batching to minimize flow times on parallel heterogeneous machines. *Management Sci.* 35(5), 607–613.

Dodin, B.M., and S.E. Elmaghraby (1985). Approximating the criticality indices of the activities in PERT networks. *Management Sci.* 31, 207–223.

Dolan, R.J. (1978). Incentives mechanisms for priority queueing problems. *Bell J. Econom.* 9, 421–436.

Drezner, A., A.Z. Szendrovits and G.O. Wesolowsky (1989). Multi-stage production with variable lot sizes and transportation of partial lots. *European J. Oper. Res.* 17, 227–237.

Ebrahimpour, M., and B.M. Fathi (1985). Dynamic simulation of a Kanban production inventory system. *Internat. J. Oper. Prod. Management* 5, 5–14.

Elmaghraby, S.E. (1978). The economic lot scheduling problem (ELSP): Review and extensions. *Management Sci.* 24, 587–598.

Eppen, G.D., and R.K. Martin (1988). Determining safety stock in the presence of stochastic lead time and demand. *Management Sci.* 34, 1380–1390.

Fisher, M.L. (1974). Optimal solution of scheduling problems using Lagrangian multipliers, Part I. *Oper. Res.* 21, 1114–1127.
Fisher, M.L., B.J. Lageweg, J.K. Lenstra and A.H.G. Rinnooy Kan (1983). Surrogate duality relaxation for job shop scheduling. *Discrete Appl. Math.* 5, 65–75.
Fleischmann, B. (1990). The discrete lot-sizing and scheduling problem. *European J. Oper. Res.* 44(3), 347–348.
Geoffrion, A., and G. Graves (1976). Scheduling parallel production lines with changeover costs: Practical application of a quadratic assignment/LP approach. *Oper. Res.* 24, 595–610.
Glassey, C.R., and M.G.C. Resende (1988). Closed-loop release control for VLSI circuit manufacturing. *IEEE Trans. Semicond. Manuf.* 1, 36–46.
Goyal, S.K., and A.Z. Szendrovits (1986). A constant lot size model with equal and unequal sized batch shipments between production stages. *Engrg. Costs. Prod. Econ.* 10, 203–210.
Grassman, W. (1983). The convexity of the mean queue size of the M/M/c queue with respect to the traffic intensity. *J. Appl. Probab.* 20, 916–919.
Graves, S.C. (1980). The multi-product production cycling problem. *AIIE Trans.* 12, 233–240.
Graves, S.C. (1986). A tactical planning model for a job shop. *Oper. Res.* 34, 522–533.
Graves, S.C. (1988a). Extensions to a tactical planning model for a job shop, Working Paper No. 20-9688, Massachusetts Institute of Technology, Alfred P. Sloan School of Management.
Graves, S.C. (1988b) Determining the spares and staffing levels for a repair depot. *J. Manuf. Oper. Management* 1, 227–241.
Graves, S.C. (1988c). Safety stocks in manufacturing systems. *J. Manuf. Oper. Management* 1, 67–101.
Graves, S.C., and C.H. Fine (1988). A tactical planning model for manufacturing subcomponents on mainframe computers. *J. Manuf. Oper. Management* 2, 4–34.
Groenevelt, H., and U.S. Karmarkar (1988). A dynamic Kanban system case study. *Prod. Invent. Management J.* 29, 46–50.
Hackman, S.T., and R.C. Leachman (1989). A general framework for modeling production. *Management Sci.* 35(4), 478–495.
Halim, A.H., S. Miyazaki and H. Ohta (1991). A batch-scheduling problem to minimize actual flow time of parts with multi-due-date under JIT environment, Working Paper College of Engineering, Univ. of Osaka Prefecture, Osaka, Japan.
Hall, R.W. (1983). *Zero Inventories*, Dow, Jones-Irwin, Homewood, IL.
Han, M.-H., and L.F. McGinnis (1988). Shop operating characteristics curves for shop control, Working Paper, Texas A&M University, Department of Industrial Engineering.
Harel, A., and P. Zipkin (1984). Strong convexity results for queueing systems with applications in production and telecommunications, Working Paper No. 84-32, Graduate School of Business, Columbia University, New York.
Harel, A., and P. Zipkin (1987). The convexity of a general performance measure for multiserver queues. *J. Appl. Probab.* 24, 725–736.
Harris, F.W. (1915). Operations and cost. In: *Factory Management Series A*, Shaw & Co., Glastonbury, CT, pp. 48–52.
Hax, A.C., and D. Candea (1984). *Production and Inventory Management*, Prentice-Hall, Englewood Cliffs, NJ.
Hax, A.C., and J.J. Golovin (1978). Hierarchical production planning systems, in: A.C. Hax (ed.), *Studies in Operations Management*, North-Holland, Amsterdam.
Hax, A.C., and H.C. Meal (1975). Hierarchical integration of production planning and scheduling, in: M.A. Geisler (ed.), *Logistics*, Stud. in Management Sci., Vol. 1, North-Holland, Amsterdam.
Hopp, W.J., M.L. Spearman and D.L. Woodruff (1988). Causes of long lead times in manufacturing systems, Tech. Rep. 88-28, Department of Industrial Engineering and Management Sciences, Northwestern University, Evanston, IL.
Huang, P.Y., L.P. Rees and B.W. Taylor (1983). A simulation analysis of the Japanese Just-in-Time technique (with Kanbans) for a multiline, multistage production system. *Decision Sci.* 14, 326–344.

Jacobs, F.R., and D.J. Bragg (1986). The repetitive lots concept: An evaluation of job flow considerations in production dispatching, sequencing and batch sizing, IRMIS Working Paper #505, Graduate School of Business, Univ. of Indiana.
Jaikumar, R. (1974). An operational optimization procedure for production scheduling. *Comput. Oper. Res.* 1, 191–200.
James, I., S. Kekre and N.S. Lafond (1988). Asynchronous parallel paint systems: Sequencing and control issues in JIT environment. *Proc. 1988 Internat. Conf. on Computer Integrated Manufacturing*, Troy, New York, May 23–25.
Johnson, L.A., and D.C. Montgomery (1974). *Operations Research in Production Planning, Scheduling and Inventory Control*, Wiley, New York.
Jonsson, H., and E.A. Silver (1985). Impact of processing and queueing times on order quantities. *Mater. Flow* 2, 221–230.
Kanet, J.J. (1986). Towards a better understanding of lead times in MRP systems. *J. Oper. Management* 6, 305–315.
Karmarkar, U.S. (1986a). Integrating MRP with Kanban pull systems, Working Paper No. QM 86-15, William E. Simon Graduate School of Business Administration, Univ. of Rochester.
Karmarkar, U.S. (1986b). Kanban systems, Working Paper No. 86-12, William E. Simon Graduate School of Business Administration, Univ. of Rochester.
Karmarkar, U.S. (1987a). Lot sizes, lead times and in-process inventories. *Management Sci.* 33, 409–418.
Karmarkar, U.S. (1987b). Lot-sizing and sequencing delays. *Management Sci.* 33(3), 419–423.
Karmarkar, U.S. (1988). Hierarchical decomposition of closed loop MRP systems, Working Paper, William E. Simon Graduate School of Business Administration, Univ. of Rochester.
Karmarkar, U.S. (1989). Capacity loading, release planning and master scheduling with WIP and lead times. *J. Manuf. Oper. Management* 2(2), 105–123.
Karmarkar, U.S. (1991). Push, pull and hybrid control schemes. *Tijdschrift voor Economie en Management* 26, 345–363.
Karmarkar, U.S., and Jinsung Yoo (1991). The stochastic dynamic product cycling problem, Working Paper No. QM 9103, William E. Simon Graduate School of Business Administration, Univ. of Rochester, Rochester, NY.
Karmarkar, U.S., and S. Kekre (1989). Batching policy in Kanban systems. *J. Manuf. Syst.* 8, 317–328.
Karmarkar, U.S., S. Kekre and S. Kekre (1992). Multi-item batching heuristics for minimization of queueing delays. *European J. Oper. Res.* 58, 99–111.
Karmarkar, U.S., S. Kekre and S. Kekre (1985). Lot sizing in multi-item multi-machine job shops. *IIE Trans.* 17, 290–292.
Karmarkar, U.S., S. Kekre and S. Kekre (1987). Capacity analysis of a manufacturing cell. *J. Manuf. Syst.* 6, 165-175.
Karmarkar, U.S., S. Kekre, S. Kekre and S. Freeman (1985). Lot sizing and lead time performance in a manufacturing cell. *Interfaces* 15, 1–9.
Karmarkar, U.S., P.J. Lederer and J.L. Zimmerman (1990). Choosing manufacturing production control and cost accounting systems, in: R.S. Kaplan (ed.), *Measures for Manufacturing Excellence*, Harvard Business School Press, Cambridge, MA, Chapter 12, pp. 353–396.
Karmarkar, U.S., and M. Lele (1989). The manufacturing-marketing interface: Strategic and operational issues, Working Paper, William E. Simon Graduate School of Business Administration, Center for Manufacturing and Operations Management.
Karmarkar, U.S., and J.C. Rummel (1990). The basis for costs in batching decisions. *J. Manuf. Oper. Management* 3(2), 153–176.
Karmarkar U.S., and L. Schrage (1985). The deterministic dynamic product cycling problem. *Oper. Res.* 33(2), 326–345.
Karni, R. (1981). Dynamic algorithms for input–output planning of work station loading. *AIIE Trans.* 13, 333–342.
Kekre, S. (1984a). Management of job shops, Unpublished Ph.D. Thesis, William E. Simon Graduate School of Business Administration, Univ. of Rochester.

Kekre, S. (1984b). Some issues in job shop design, Unpublished Ph.D. Thesis, William E. Simon Graduate School of Business Administration, Univ. of Rochester.
Kekre, S. (1987). Performance of a manufacturing cell with increased product mix. *IIE Trans.* 19(3), 329–339.
Kekre, S. and S. Kekre (1985). Work-in-process considerations in job shop capacity planning, Working Paper, GSIA, Carnegie-Mellon University.
Kekre, S., and N. Lafond (1988). Stochastic dynamic flow analysis of asynchronous parallel manufacturing process: Model formulation and empirical analysis, CMT No. 88–106, Center for Management of Technology, Carnegie Mellon University.
Kekre, S., and V. Udayabhanu (1988). Customer priorities and lead times in long term supply contracts. *J. Manuf. Oper. Management* 1, 44–66.
Kettner, H., and W. Bechte (1981). New production control methods by load-oriented order release. *J. German Engrg. Assoc.* 11, 459–466.
Kimura, O., and H. Terada (1981). Design and analysis of pull systems: A method of multi-stage production control. *Internat. J. of Prod. Res.* 19, 241–253.
Koenigsberg, E. (1985). Queue system with balking: A stochastic model of price discrimination. *RAIRO Rech. Opér.* 19, 205–219.
Krajewski, L.J., B.E. King, L.P. Ritzman and D.S. Wang (1987). Kanban, MRP and shaping the manufacturing environment. *Management Sci.* 33, 39–57.
Kuo, B.C. (1987). *Automatic Control Systems 5th edition*, Prentice-Hall, Englewood Cliffs, NJ.
Lankford, R. (1982). Input/output control: Making it work. *APICS 25th Conf. Proc.*, October, pp. 419–420.
Lasdon, L.S., and R.C. Terjung (1971). An efficient algorithm for multi-item scheduling. *Oper. Res.* 19, 946–969.
Leachman, R.C., M. Solorzano and C.R. Glassey (1988). A queue management policy for the release of factory work orders, Working Paper, Univ. of California at Berkeley, Engineering Systems Research Center.
Lee, H.L., and M.A. Cohen (1983). A note on the convexity of performance measures of M/M/*c* queueing systems. *J. Appl. Probab.* 20, 920–923.
Lee, Y.-J., and P. Zipkin (1991). Tandem queues with planned inventories, Working Paper Graduate School of Business, Columbia University, New York.
Li, L. (1991a). The role of inventory in delivery-time competition, Working Paper, Yale School of Organization and Management, Yale University, New Haven, CT.
Li, L. (1991b). Competing against time, Working Paper, Yale School of Organization and Management, Yale University, New Haven, CT.
Magee, J.F. (1958). Guides to inventory policy, part II. *Harv. Bus. Rev.* 34, 103–116.
Manne, A.S. (1958). Programming of economic lot sizes. *Management Sci.* 4, 115–135.
Marlin, P.G. (1986). Manufacturing lead time accuracy. *J. Oper. Management*, 179–202.
Melnyk, S.A., and G.L. Ragatz (1988). Order review/release and its impact on the shop floor. *Prod. Invent. Management J.* 29, 13–17.
Mitra, D., and I. Mitrani (1988). Analysis of a novel discipline for cell coordination in production lines, I, Working Paper, AT&T Bell Laboratories.
Miyazaki, S., H. Ohta and N. Nishiyama (1988). The optimal operation planning of Kanban to minimize the total operation cost. *Internat. J. Prod. Res.* 26, 1605–1611.
Moily, J.P. (1986). Optimal and heuristic procedures for component lot-splitting in multistage manufacturing systems. *Management Sci.* 32, 113–125.
Monden, Y. (1981). Adaptable Kanban system helps Toyota maintain Just-in-Time production. *Ind. Eng.* 13, 29–46.
Morton, T.E., S.R. Lawrence, S. Rajagopolan and S. Kekre (1988). SCHED-STAR; A price based shop scheduling module. *J. Manuf. Oper. Management* 1, 131–181.
Morton, T.E., and M.R. Singh (1988). Implicit costs and prices for resources with busy periods. *J. Manuf. Oper. Management* 1, 305–322.
Morton, T., and A. Vepsalainen (1987). Priority rules and leadtime estimation for job shop scheduling with weighted tardiness costs. *Management Sci.* 33, 1036–1047.

Naddef, D., and D. Santos (1984). Batching algorithms for single operation problems, Working Paper, Department of Combinatorics and Optimization, Univ. of Waterloo, Canada.

Ornek, M.A., and P.I. Collier (1988). The determination of in-process inventory and manufacturing lead time in multi-stage production systems. *Internat. J. Oper. Prod. Management* 8, 74–80.

Philipoom, P.R., L.P. Rees, B.W. Taylor and P.Y. Huang (1987a). An investigation of the factors influencing the number of Kanbans required in the implementation of the JIT technique with Kanbans. *Internat. J. Prod. Res.* 25, 457–472.

Philipoom, P.R., L.P. Rees, B.W. Taylor and P.Y. Huang (1987b). Dynamically adjusting the number of Kanbans in a Just-in-Time production system using estimated values of leadtime. *IIE Transactions* 19, 199–207.

Pochet, Y., and L.A. Wolsey (1991). Solving multi-item lot-sizing problems using strong cutting planes. *Management Sci.* 37(1), 53–67.

Pyke, D.F. (1987). Push and pull in integrated production–distribution systems under stochastic demand, Unpublished Ph.D. Dissertation, Wharton School of Management, Univ. of Pennsylvania.

Rachamadugu, R.V., and T.E. Morton (1981). Myopic heuristics for the single machine weighted tardiness problem, Working Paper No. 28-81-82, Graduate School of Industrial Administration, Carnegie-Mellon University.

Rummel, J.L. (1989). Cost models for batching decisions, Unpublished Ph.D. Thesis, William E. Simon Graduate School of Business Administration, Univ. of Rochester.

Salomon, M. (1990). Deterministic lotsizing models for production planning, Unpublished Ph.D. Thesis, Erasmus University, Rotterdam.

Salomon, M., L. Kroon, R. Kuk and L.N. Van Wassenhove (1989). The discrete lotsizing and scheduling problem. *Management Rep. Ser.* 30, Rotterdam School of Management, The Netherlands.

Santos, C. (1988). Batching in manufacturing systems, Ph.D. Thesis, University of Waterloo.

Santos, C., and M. Magazine (1985). Batching in single operation manufacturing systems. *Oper. Res. Lett.* 4(3), 99–103.

Sarkar, D., and W. Zangwill (1990). Variance paradoxed in production, Working Paper AT&T Bell Laboratories, Holmdel, NJ.

Schmenner, R.W. (1988). Behind labor productivity gains in the factory. *J. Manuf. Oper. Management* 1(4), 323–338.

Schonberger, R.J. (1983). Application of single-card and dual-card Kanban. *Interfaces* 13, 56–67.

Schrage, L. (1982). The multiproduct lot scheduling problem, in: M.A.H. Dempster, J.K. Lenstra and A.H.G. Rinnooy Kan (eds.), *Deterministic and Stochastic Scheduling* (NATO Advanced Study Institutes Series), Reidel, Dordrecht.

Schwarz, L.B., and L. Schrage (1975). Optimal and system myopic policies for multi-echelon production and inventory assembly systems. *Management Sci.* 21, 1285–1296.

Schweitzer, P.J., and T. Altiok (1988). Aggregate modelling of tandem queues with blocking, in: G. Iazeolla, P.J. Courtois and O.J. Boxma (eds.), *Computer Performance and Reliability*, Proc. 2nd Internat. Workshop on Applied Mathematics and Performance/Reliability Models of Computer/Communication Systems, Elsevier, Amsterdam, pp. 135–149.

Seidmann, A. (1988). Regenerative pull (Kanban) production control policies. *European J. Oper. Res.* 35, 401–413.

Seidmann, A., and S.Y. Nof (1985). Unitary manufacturing cell design with random product feedback flow. *IIE Trans.* 17, 188–193.

Seidmann, A., and S.Y. Nof (1989). Operational analysis of an autonomous assembly robotic station. *IEEE Trans. Robotics Automat.* 5, 15.

Seidmann, A., P.J. Schweitzer and S. Shalev-Oren (1987). Computerized closed queueing network of flexible manufacturing system: A comparative evaluation. *Large Scale Syst.* 12, 91–107.

Seidmann, A., P.J. Schweitzer and S.Y. Nof (1985). Performance evaluation of a flexible manufacturing cell with random multiproduct feedback flow. *Internat. J. Prod. Res.* 23, 1171–1184.

Seidmann, A., and M.L. Smith (1981). Due date assignment for production systems. *Management Sci.* 27, 571–581.

Shalev-Oren, S., A. Seidmann and P. Schweitzer (1985). Analysis of flexible manufacturing systems with priority scheduling: PMVA. *Ann. Oper. Res.* 6, 115–139.

Shantikumar, J.G., and U. Sumita (1988). Approximations for the time spent in a dynamic job shop with applications to due date assignment. *Internat. J. Prod. Res.* 26, 1329–1352.

Shen, H.N. (1987). Simulation of a two stage Kanban system using SLAM, Working Paper No. 87-03, Center for Manufacturing and Operations Management, William E. Simon Graduate School of Business Administration, Rochester, New York.

Silver, E.A., and R. Peterson (1985). *Decision Systems for Inventory Management and Production Planning, 2nd edition*, Wiley, New York.

Singhal, V.R., and A.S. Raturi (1989). The effect of inventory decisions and parameters on the opportunity cost of capital. *J. Oper. Management* 9(3), 406–420.

Smith, V.L., and P.J. Bunce (1985). A model for shop makespans and lead times. *J. Oper. Res. Soc. (UK)* 36, 473–487.

Solberg, J.J. (1977). A mathematical model of computerized manufacturing systems, in: *Proc. 4th Internat. Conf. on Production Research*, Tokyo, Japan.

Solberg, J.J. (1980). *CAN-Q User's Guide*, School of IE, Purdue University, W. Lafayette, IN.

Spearman, M.L., W.J. Hopp and D.L. Woodruff (1989). A hierarchical control architecture for constant work-in-process (CONWIP) production systems. *J. Manuf. Oper. Management* 2(3), 147–171.

Spearman, M.L., and M.A. Zazanis (1988). Push and pull production systems: Issues and comparisons, Tech. Rep. 88-24, Department of Industrial Engineering and Management Sciences, Northwestern University.

St. John, R. (1985). The cost of inflated planned lead times in MRP systems, *J. Oper. Management* 5, 119–128.

Sugimori, Y., K. Kusunoki, F. Cho and S. Uchikawa (1977). Toyota production system and Kanban system materialization of Just-in-Time and respect-for-human system. *Internat. J. Prod. Res.* 15, 553–564.

Sumita, U., and M. Kijima (1986). On optimal bulk size of single-server bulk-arrival queueing systems with set-up times – Numerical exploration via the Laguerre transform. *Selecta Statist. Canad.* VII, *Bulk Queues*, 77–108.

Suri, R. (1981). New techniques for modeling and control of flexible automated manufacturing systems, in: *Proc. IFAC*, Kyoto, Japan.

Suri, R., and G.W. Diehl (1985). MANUPLAN – A precursor to simulation for complex manufacturing systems, *Proc. 1985 Winter Simulation Conference*, San Francisco, CA., pp. 411–420.

Suri, R., J.L. Sanders and M. Kamath (1993). Performance evaluation of production networks, in: S.C. Graves, A.H.G. Rinnooy Kan and P.H. Zipkin (eds.), *Handbooks in Operations Research and Management Science, Vol. 4, Logistics of Production and Inventory*, North-Holland, Amsterdam, Chapter 5.

Suzaki, K. (1985). Work-in-process management: An illustrated guide to productivity improvement. *Prod. Invent. Management* 26, 101–110.

Tatsiopoulos, I.P. (1982). Manufacturing lead-times: A key control factor for the production/marketing integration in small component-manufacturing firms, NATO ARI, No. 14, *Efficiency of Manufacturing Systems*, Amsterdam, pp. 3–6.

Tatsiopoulos, I.P., and B.G. Kingsman (1983). Lead time management. *European J. Oper. Res.* 14, 351–358.

Van Wassenhove, L., and C.N. Potts (1991). Integrating scheduling with batching and lotsizing: A review of algorithms and complexity, Working Paper 91/10/TM, INSEAD, Fontainebleau, France.

Vepsalainen, A.P.J., and T.E. Morton (1988). Improving local priority rules with global lead time estimates. *J. Manuf. Oper. Management* 1, 102–118.

Vickson, R.G., and M.J. Magazine and C.A. Santos (1991). Batching and sequencing of components at a single facility, Tech. Paper 185-MS-1989, Faculty of Engineering, Univ. Waterloo, Waterloo, Canada.

Vinod, B., and J.J. Solberg (1984). Performance models for unreliable flexible manufacturing systems. *Omega* 12, 299–308.

Vinod, B., and J.J. Solberg (1985). The optimal design of flexible manufacturing systems. *Internat. J. Prod. Res.* 23, 1141–1151.

Wagner, H.M., and T.M. Whitin (1958). Dynamic version of the economic lot size model. *Management Sci.* 5, 89–96.

Wecker, W.E. (1979). The variance of cumulative demand forecasts, Working Paper, Graduate School of Business, Univ. of Chicago.

Weeks, J.K. (1979). A simulation of predictable due dates. *Management Sci.* 25, 363–373.

Wein, L.M. (1988). Due-date setting and priority sequencing in a multiclass M/G/1 queue, Working Paper, Sloan School of Management, M.I.T.

Whitt, W. (1983). The queueing network analyzer. *Bell System Tech. J.* 62, 2779–2815.

Whybark, D.C., and J.G. Williams (1966). Material requirements planning under uncertainty. *Decision Sci.* 7, 595–606.

Wiendahl, H.P. (1987). *Load-Oriented Production Control*, Hanser Verlag, Munich Vienna.

Wiendahl, H.P. (1989). The throughput diagram – An universal model for the illustration, control and supervision of logistic processes. *Annals of CIRP* 37, 465–468.

Wiendahl, H.P., and G. Springer (1988). Manufacturing process control on the basis of the input/output chart – A chance to improve the operational behaviour of automatic production systems. *Internat. J. Adv. Manuf. Tech.* 3, 55–69.

Wight, O. (1970). Input/output control a real handle on lead time. *Prod. Invent. Management J.* 11(3), 9–31.

Wilhelm, W.E. (1987). On the normality of operation times in small-lot assembly systems. *Internat. J. Prod. Res.* 25, 145–149.

Wilhelm, W.E., and S. Ahmadi-Marandi (1982). A methodology to describe operating characteristics of assembly systems. *IIE Trans.* 14, 204–213.

Yano, C.A. (1987a). Setting planned lead times in serial production systems with tardiness costs. *Management Sci.* 33, 95–106.

Yano, C.A. (1987b). Stochastic leadtimes in two-level assembly systems. *IIE Trans.* 19, 371–378.

Zipkin, P. (1989), A Kanban-like production control system: Analysis of simple models, Working Paper No. 89-1, Columbia Business School, New York, NY.

Zipkin, P.H. (1986). Models for design and control of stochastic, multi-item batch production systems. *Oper. Res.* 34, 91–104.

Part III
Production Planning and Scheduling

S.C. Graves et al., Eds., *Handbooks in OR & MS, Vol. 4*

Chapter 7

An Overview of Production Planning

L. Joseph Thomas and John O. McClain

Johnson Graduate School of Management, Cornell University, Ithaca, NY 14853-4201, U.S.A.

1. Introduction

1.1. Production planning, scheduling and dispatching – Definitions

Production planning is the process of determining a tentative plan for how much production will occur in the next several time periods, during an interval of time called the *planning horizon*. Production planning also determines expected inventory levels, as well as the workforce and other resources necessary to implement the production plans. Production planning is done using an aggregate view of the production facility, the demand for products, and even of time (using monthly time periods, for example). The selection of the level of aggregation is important and is discussed below.

Production scheduling is more detailed than production planning, coupling individual products with individual productive resources, using smaller time units or even continuous time. Despite its greater detail, even a production schedule typically cannot be implemented exactly. Last minute changes are imposed by machine breakdowns, worker absences, new rush orders, and other disruptions. In real-time, implementation of a production plan or schedule is often called *dispatching*. These decisions are an important part of the operation of a productive facility. They must keep the production plan on track, and *feedback* of the actual, current situation helps the next plan to be (approximately) achievable.

Production planning is affected by higher-level decisions that constrain production. *Fixed resources* limit production. Fixed resources may include plant, equipment, and workforce. However, in some situations, it may be feasible to change the amount of equipment (through leasing) or workforce (through hiring, firing, and overtime) as part of the aggregate production plan. Management must decide which resources are truly fixed, and which are variable within the intermediate term as part of the production plan.

For well over 30 years, the operations research literature has addressed the topic of this chapter under many different names, such as (1) aggregate production and work-force planning, (2) production and employment smoothing, (3) planning production, inventories, and work force, and (4) production and employment scheduling. This chapter reviews some of that literature, concentrating on recent contributions, and discusses practical problems related to the use of OR tools for production planning. We often lean on other chapters in this book for more detailed coverage of individual topics. A unifying theme of this chapter is *aggregation* in production planning, in which at least one of the following three items is viewed in an aggregated manner: production facilities, products, or time unit.

In our experience, most companies do not have a *unique* production plan. Rather, there are several plans made at different levels of aggregation, using different planning horizons. Thus this chapter discusses many different models.

The remainder of this section discusses costs to be minimized, levels of aggregation, and connections to other chapters in this book. Section 2 analyzes several different production planning environments and the type of models that are appropriate. Section 3 discusses tieing different levels of production planning together and reviews some literature on economic effects of production smoothing. Section 4 examines the plethora of recent optimization-type models for production planning. Section 5 presents our view of some of the current practical questions in production planning and describes some research questions that should be addressed. Since this chapter was completed in spring 1989, most of the literature reviewed is from 1988 and before. However, a few additions have been made to include some more recent references, and those articles also contain literature reviews.

1.2. Decisions to be made and costs to be minimized

Production planning must determine the planned level of production for each aggregate product category, in each time period during the planning horizon. Further, production planning may determine the planned level for certain resources, such as workforce, again by resource category. Examples of resource categories are different skill levels of workers, overtime or extra shifts, and subcontracting.

We assume that a forecast of demand can be developed, by product categories, as in input to the production plan. The quality of the forecast varies widely in practice, but some forecast, with an estimate of its accuracy, is always needed. In Section 2, we will separately discuss three forecast situations: (1) if seasonality is dominant, (2) if growth (or decline) is dominant, and (3) if uncertainty is substantial.

At the aggregate level, there are three basic ways of responding to changes in demand: holding a relatively constant production rate and using inventory to satisfy demand peaks (a 'production smoothing' strategy), using changes in level of production to follow demand closely (a 'chase' strategy), or turning away some demand permanently. Production smoothing can use either early production (with an associated inventory cost) or late production (with an associated cost due to possible customer dissatisfaction). There are many ways to change the level of production, including subcontracting, hiring, and overtime, for example, and the specific models to be used depend on the alternatives available. Using combinations of the 'chase' and 'smoothing' strategies, managers face a very large number of possible production plans to meet demand. Demand should be turned away if the marginal cost of production exceeds the marginal benefit, defined to include the future loss due to unhappy customers.

The costs to be used as a basis for comparing alternative production plans include:

(1) Costs of oversupply, including inventory holding costs, obsolescence, etc.

(2) Cost of not satisfying demand (or not satisfying demands on time).

(3) Regular production cost, by product category.

(4) Costs of alternative methods of production, using overtime or subcontracting, for example.

(5) Costs of changing the level of production, perhaps by subcontracting or hiring additional workers.

Regular production cost can take many mathematical forms, depending on the particular situation. Often, production cost is treated as linear in volume of the aggregated product. If setup cost or time is important, even when viewed from an aggregate perspective, they may be included in the objective function. Many papers have been written to deal with different forms of production cost, especially convex and concave costs. Some of these papers will be discussed in subsequent sections.

The cost of changing production and the cost of not satisfying demand are both difficult to obtain in practice. The cost of not satisfying demand is discussed in many OR papers. Estimating this cost is complicated by the fact that 'customer service' means such different things in different settings [see Lalonde, Cooper & Noordewier, 1988]. The cost of disrupting stability by changing levels of production is found to be quite high by Hayes & Clark [1985]. The value of a stable workforce in today's world has been discussed by many authors recently [e.g., see Bolt, 1983]. If reasonable cost estimates cannot be obtained, management can establish policy constraints.

All of the costs are, in fact, difficult to estimate. Average costs contain fixed costs that do not vary with the decisions at hand. True marginal costs are difficult to obtain, and which costs are marginal changes through time. Recently there has been a surge of interest in ways to estimate manufacturing costs and measure manufacturing performance. These important issues are discussed by Kaplan [1983, 1988], and Johnson & Kaplan [1987], among others.

Subcontracting as a means of changing production level raises two important issues. Why does the supplier firm have capacity, when presumably they are also experiencing high demand, and why are their marginal costs of production lower than that of the customer firm? Subcontracting has not been examined to any extent in the literature, probably because of these questions. Kamian & Li [1990] do address these issues, and point out the extensive information needs if firms are to coordinate production schedules using subcontracting.

1.3. The choice of parameters

Several important decisions are made before the production planning model (or set of models) is structured. We have identified six decisions:

(1) The time unit (months, weeks, shifts);

(2) The time horizon (one year, two years, . . .);

(3) Level of aggregation of the products (one aggregate product, a few product categories, or full detail);

(4) Level of aggregation of the production resources (one plant or multiple resources);

(5) Frequency of replanning (every basic time unit or less often);

(6) Number and structure of production plans (e.g., a one-year plan, a three-month plan, and a one-week plan, the last one released to the plant).

Time unit

Aggregate production planning is typically modelled using weeks or months as the time unit. The larger the unit, the less the computational difficulty. The smaller the time unit, the smaller the problem that remains to be solved at the detailed level. (It is not necessarily true that the smaller the time unit, the easier the detailed production schedule is to develop.) Some companies use unequally sized time units: several short periods (e.g., weeks), followed by several longer periods (e.g., months).

Time horizon

There is a natural range of values for the planning horizon (time interval covered by the plan) in most practical situations. If seasonality is a significant factor, a planning horizon of one year or more should be used. With increasing demand, the planning horizon may be significantly longer. Usually the production plan is made to take effect after a shorter period of time; the time interval before the plan is often called a 'frozen horizon'. Decisions within that period are (almost) firm and were determined in a previous production plan.

Level of aggregation – Products

The philosophy of aggregation is to focus attention on the major cost sources, developing a plan that can be carried out simply and economically. To do this the model is structured to deal with relatively large costs and important resources. The difficulty of the detailed problem that remains depends on our choice of level of aggregation. The appropriate level of aggregation depends on the nature of the costs, the product line, and the stability of the situation.

Most aggregate planning models in the research literature assume that there is one 'aggregate product'. The Modigliani & Hohn [1955] model, for example, uses a single aggregate product. Many authors, including Charnes, Cooper & Mellon [1955] and Bergstrom & Smith [1970] discuss multi-item aggregate production planning models. The extreme version of this approach is to build a 'monolithic model' that integrates all of the planning features into a detailed plan that is not aggregated by product (see [Graves, 1982] and Chapter 8 for discussions of alternative approaches, with references).

If an aggregate approach is used, the problem of disaggregation remains. The common approach to that problem is to build a consistent set of models that connects aggregate and detailed plans. (See Chapter 10 and the references therein for a discussion of these approaches.)

Level of aggregation – Facilities

Most aggregate planning models treat the facility as if there were a single resource. Holt, Modigliani, Muth & Simon [1960] treat the work force as the single resource, thereby assuming that all potential levels of the work force can fit within the plant. It is possible to include several resources (types of labor, work centers, raw material availability, and so on). This was done by Dzielinski, Baker & Manne [1963], Dzielinski & Gomory [1965], Gorenstein [1970], Lasdon & Terjung [1971], Billington, McClain & Thomas [1983], Ozden [1987], and many other authors. Some of these models will be discussed in Section 4. Again, 'monolithic' models are at the extreme, attempting to look at each product and each significant resource.

Frequency of replanning

'Plans' are by their nature not implemented exactly in their original form. Although plans are made over a fairly long planning horizon, re-planning occurs frequently and the plans are used in a 'rolling' mode. That is, a T-period plan is formed and implementation is begun. However, after an interval τ shorter than T a new plan is derived. That is, only the first τ periods of any plan are implemented. Baker [1977] discusses the effectiveness of 'rolling schedules', and McClain & Thomas [1977] study the use of rolling schedules when the seasonality of demand is the dominant factor. More recently, Sridharan, Berry & Udayabhanu [1988] discuss schedule stability when using rolling plans.

Planning horizon theorems (to be discussed in Sections 2 and 4) are an attempt to discover when replanning will be necessary. In practice, replanning is done frequently because of changes in the data (forecast revisions, modified schedules, machine breakdowns, and so on). System 'nervousness', discussed in Chapter 11, *can* occur if replanning is too frequent.

Levels of plans before implementation

Industrial companies we have observed often have several plans, at different levels of aggregation, rather than just an 'aggregate' plan and a detailed schedule. A one-year plan may be highly aggregated as to time unit, products and facilities, and be used to plan additions to workforce and overall level of operation. A one-month plan and a one-week plan would use increasingly more detail. Both might involve smaller time units and ending conditions consistent with longer-term plans.

The levels of aggregation depend on how many plans there are, and the choices depend on the situation. Developing an appropriate set of models is related to the hierarchical planning literature discussed in Chapter 10. Once the set of models is developed, maintaining an information system that feeds back current actual information to the planning models is essential, as discussed in Chapter 11.

1.4. Connection to other chapters

The three chapters we depend on most heavily are Chapter 8, 'Mathematical Programming Models and Methods for Production Planning and Scheduling' by Shapiro, Chapter 10, 'Hierarchical Production Planning' by Bitran and Tirupati, and Chapter 11, 'Requirements Planning', by Baker. Some of the issues in Sections 1, 2, and 5 of our chapter are analyzed in Chapter 6, 'Manufacturing Lead Times, Order Release, and Capacity Loading', by Karmarkar, Chapter 9, 'Sequencing and Scheduling: Algorithms and Complexity', by Lawler, Lenstra, Rinnooy Kan and Shmoys, and Chapter 12, 'The Just-in-Time System' by Groenevelt. Chapter 2, 'Analysis of Multistage Production Systems' by Muckstadt and Roundy, contains models discussed in our Section 4. Also, Chapter 14, 'Developments in Manufacturing Technology and Economic Evaluation Models', by Fine, examines optimal replacement of technological equipment, and, thus, changes in capacity and capability.

1.5. Other reviews

Aggregate production planning has been reviewed several times before. Hax [1978] and Hax & Candea [1984] give a complete review of literature up to the mid 70's. Gelders & Van Wassenhove [1981] review many different solution procedures. An historical view of the problem area can be obtained by examining Silver [1967] and Simon & Holt [1954]. Many of the issues are discussed in very current terms in these articles, and additional references are given.

2. Cost tradeoffs in production planning

2.1. Introduction and general results

Production plans are usually a mix of two pure production strategies, which are to 'chase' (produce just before each period's demand) or to 'smooth' (use inventory or backorders to level production). When choosing a strategy, cost tradeoffs must be made. An initial cost that is incurred if a manager wants to follow a 'chase' strategy is the *investment cost of extra fixed capacity*. The more demand varies, the greater the need for extra fixed capacity such as equipment. Some models of the aggregate production and work force planning problem assume that fixed capacity cannot be changed and deal instead with ways of temporarily adding capacity: overtime, extra shifts and subcontracting. Others deal with hiring and firing to change capacity, assuming that labor is the only constraining resource.

The use of overtime and the amount of capacity are related to the unemployment in a country. Brennan, Browne, Davies, O'Kelly & Gault [1982], studying the EEC, argued that reduced use of overtime could create jobs, but would require more investment in fixed plant capacity. The solution to the problem discussed here has societal implications. From a company's viewpoint, the decision to add new fixed plant capacity requires a longer time horizon and can be thought of as a higher level decision, constraining the production plan. We will discuss this issue further in Section 3. Here, we will assume a known plant capacity, perhaps modifiable by changes in workforce. (In fact, in real factories, the 'capacity' is difficult to determine exactly, but a close approximation is usually available.)

Given a capacity limit, tradeoffs can be made among the costs of inventory, overtime, hiring/firing, and so on. For example, inventory should be carried only so long as the cost of carrying inventory for that length of time is less than the cost of reducing the production rate and restoring it later. Cost tradeoffs are discussed in detail following a brief description of graphical planning methods.

Graphical representation

Graphical representation of the aggregate planning problem helps to identify some of the critical elements and to display some options. Typically this method requires that there is only one aggregate product. This allows demand and production to be displayed on a single graph.

Two methods will be discussed briefly. The *cumulative requirements* method computes the total demand from the present time to each of the future time periods. If there are requirements for inventory (safety or cycle stock, for example) these are added to the total demand (separately for each period). The result is the cumulative requirements for each period; an example is shown as the bottom plot in Figure 2.1. Production plans may be shown on the same graph. The plots of cumulative production shown in Figure 2.1 begin above the horizontal axis. The intercept is the initial inventory, which represents excess production from previous periods (including the current period). Plan 1 has the same production rate in periods 1 to 4, as revealed by the constant slope of its cumulative plot. The production rate is then reduced for periods 5 and 6.

In this representation, demand satisfaction is assured by requiring that the cumulative production curve lies above the cumulative requirements curve. Inventory in excess of the required amount is equal to the vertical distance between the production and requirements curves. Changes in production rate show as changes in the slope of the production curve. The advantage of this representation is that it shows clearly the points at which plans are equivalent in total production, because the production curves meet, as is the case with

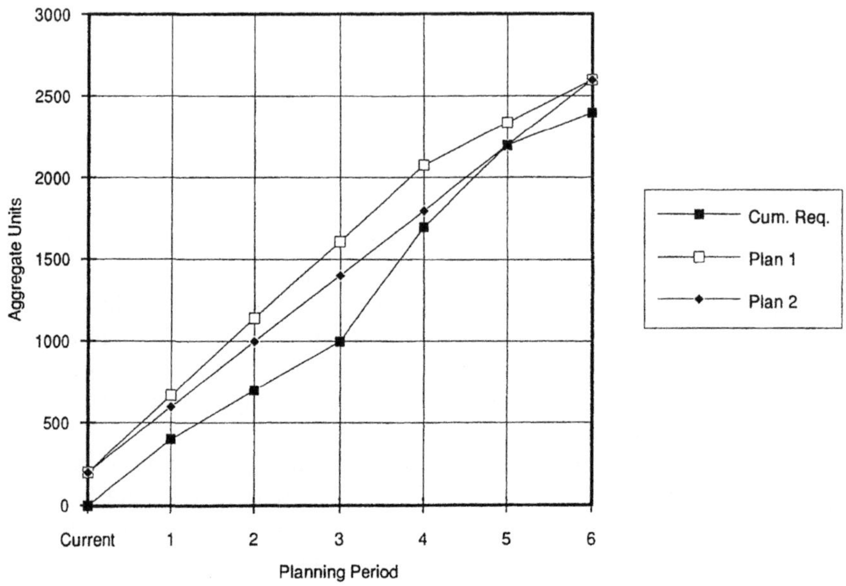

Fig. 2.1. Cumulative requirements and production.

plans 1 and 2 in period 6. The disadvantage is that it is difficult to read production quantities (or anything else) directly from the graph.

The second method is *period requirements*, as shown in Figure 2.2. Each period's production, demand, and inventory may be shown as a vertical bar.

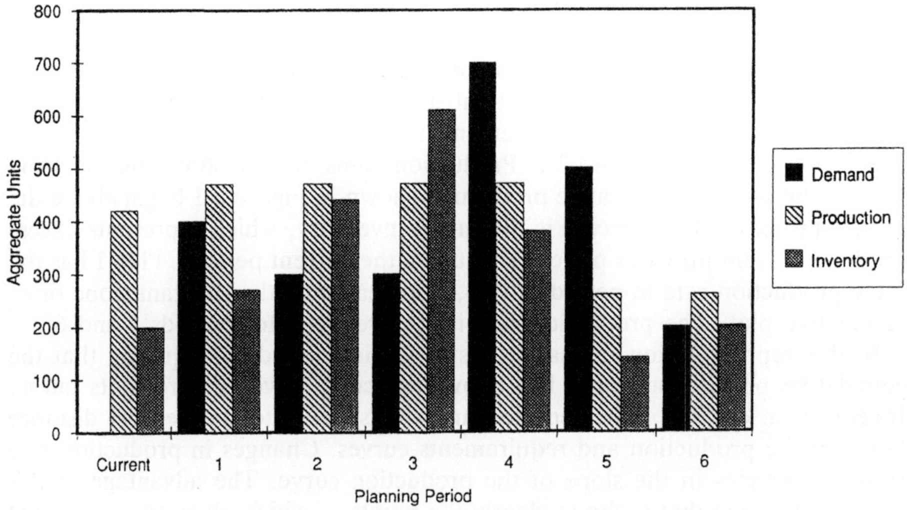

Fig. 2.2. Production and inventory plans.

The production values are much easier to read. However, it is more difficult to represent alternative plans with this method since each plan requires at least two sets of bars (production and inventory), so the chart becomes cluttered quickly. Nonetheless, many people find this method easier to understand.

Both of these methods are better suited for teaching or presentations than for actual analysis. For example, it is easy to explain with either figure why the initial production rate of plan 1 cannot be maintained indefinitely; unless demand increases substantially, production must be cut to avoid a large inventory buildup. We can also illustrate the value of biting the bullet when it comes to layoffs – the sooner production is reduced, the less the change will cost. For example, Figure 2.1 shows that plan 2 achieves less inventory than plan 1 by starting with a lower production rate. However, by the end of the horizon plan 1 has the lower production rate because a large reduction is needed for the last two periods to get rid of the excess inventory. Clearly there is something wrong with plan 1; it has too much inventory and also requires a larger workforce reduction than plan 2. Thus the immediate layoff of a few workers in plan 2 is superior to the delayed action of plan 1.

Plan 2 is of interest for another reason – it has the lowest constant production rate that can be maintained over the planning horizon if demand is to be met. (It is a 'smooth' plan. A 'chase' plan would begin at the initial inventory intercept, move directly to the 'Cum. Req' line, and follow that line thereafter.) Period 5, where plan 2 touches the cumulative requirements curve, is sometimes called a natural planning horizon. (An observer standing on the horizontal axis at the current period and whose height equals initial inventory, would not be able to see the requirements curve beyond period 5.) Although this plan is not necessarily optimal (that depends on the costs), it is clearly of interest when considering production smoothing. If the current actual production rate is lower than plan 2's rate, an increase in production will be needed before period 5. On the other hand, if production is currently above the rate of plan 2, probably it should be decreased immediately.

Economic guidelines

Kunreuther & Morton [1974] describe economic guidelines for aggregate planning with a single product under the assumption that costs are linear. In this section three fundamental parameters n^*, k^* and m^* are developed through examples that show how costs can sometimes be reduced by modifying existing production plans.

For the first example, suppose that a company plans to increase production temporarily, perhaps to accommodate a large one-time order; should the company use overtime or should they hire workers and lay them off once the demand has been satisfied? Using overtime would cost PC_O where P is the added production and C_O is the overtime premium (per aggregate production unit). The cost of temporary hiring depends on how many periods n the new production level would be maintained, since the production per period, P/n divided by the production p per employee per period, determines the number who are hired. If the hiring and layoff costs of temporary workers is C_{HF}, then the cost of this policy is PC_{HF}/np. (The regular payroll cost is ignored since it must be paid under both options.) The hiring/layoff option is less expensive when $n \geqslant C_{HF}/(npC_O) \equiv n^*$. (Technically, n^* is the integer part of this ratio if the company works with discrete time periods.)

The following economic guideline is based on the parameter n^* [see McClain, Thomas & Mazzola, 1992].

(1) Temporary production increases of n^* or fewer periods duration should be accomplished through overtime. For longer time spans, temporary hiring is cheaper.

A second tradeoff concerns the use of overtime in combination with hiring or layoffs. For example, consider the situation in Figure 2.3. This company plans a layoff to take effect in period 2 and destined to remain in effect until period 7. However, the magnitude of the layoff is so large that overtime will be needed for a minor increase in demand in period 5. Could costs be reduced by postponing the layoff? Let k denote the number of periods between the layoff and the overtime. As an alternative plan, suppose the layoff of one employee were postponed one period, resulting in an extra p units of production. These units would be carried in inventory for $k-1$ periods, and then be used to reduce overtime. The saving of overtime cost is pC_O, but inventory cost increases by $(k-1)pC_I$. This is a net saving if $(k-1) \leqslant C_O/C_I \equiv k^*$. In this argument, both regular payroll and hiring/layoff are fixed costs.

The parameter k^* is used in the following guidelines.

(2) If overtime would be needed within k^*+1 periods after a layoff, it would be less expensive to reduce the magnitude of the layoff until

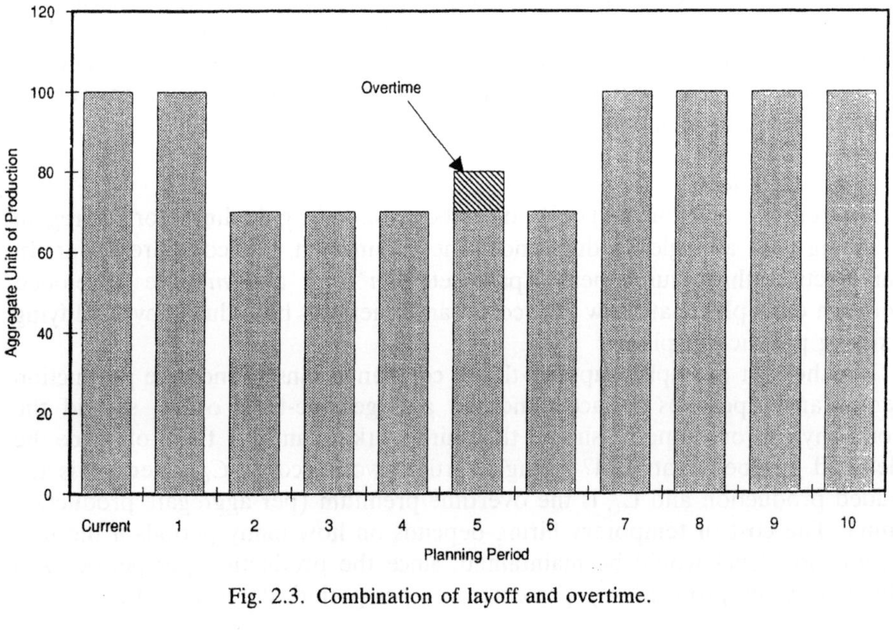

Fig. 2.3. Combination of layoff and overtime.

either the layoff or the overtime is eliminated. A similar argument suggests not using overtime within k^* periods after hiring; hire earlier instead. (The latter does not apply to hiring in period 1.)

The fundamental production smoothing decision is a tradeoff between inventory (smooth production) and changes in the productive capacity, usually thought of as hiring and firing. Kunreuther and Morton pointed out that this is actually a nonlinear tradeoff even if the costs are linear. For example, suppose that capacity is currently in excess of demand. Then a worker who produces p aggregate units each period causes inventory of p units in period 1, $2p$ by the end of period 2 and so on. Inventory cost of this worker's output would be $C_I m(m+1)p/2$ through period m. This cost could be avoided if the worker were laid off for those m periods, providing that demand could still be met. This layoff would cause a net saving if $m < m^* + 1$ periods, where m^* is the largest integer less than $-0.5 + (0.25 + 2C_{HF}/pC_I)^{0.5}$.

The parameter m^* occurs in several guidelines.

(3) A planned workforce reduction should remain in effect for at least $m^* + 1$ periods. One that lasts for fewer than $m^* + 1$ periods can be improved by having a smaller layoff and postponing re-hiring. Similarly, a temporary workforce increase should last for at least $m^* + 1$ periods. If this guideline is violated a better plan is to hire fewer workers, but hire them sooner. Obviously this part of the guideline does not apply to period 1.

Another implication of this analysis is that inventory should not be held for more than $m^* + 1$ consecutive periods. It would be less expensive to reduce production immediately and then increase it again later.

(4) Planned inventory should be at the minimum allowable level at least once in every $2(m^* + 1)$ periods. If a plan violates this rule, it can be improved by an immediate layoff.

These guidelines have a great deal to say about the kinds of plans that should be considered. For example, McClain & Thomas [1977] considered the case of production planning over a horizon with significant seasonal demand variation. In this case, it can be determined by examining the costs alone whether or not a company should consider a policy of annual workforce changes to match the seasonal demand cycle. If $2(m^* + 1)$ is greater than one full season, the hiring/firing guidelines just described cannot be met within one season, so a constant workforce level should be maintained and a production smoothing policy followed in which inventory is built up during slow periods and used to satisfy demand during the peak seasons.

(5) Two seasonal layoffs should be at least $2(m^* + 1)$ periods apart. If $2(m^* + 1)$ exceeds one year, workforce should not vary seasonally.

The guidelines also suggest how much data is needed. For example, to consider plans that vary the production rate by hiring and firing, one should have at least $2(m^* + 1)$ periods of data. (That is, the 'forecast horizon' must be at least $2(m^* + 1)$ periods.) Without at least this much data, a plan that has both hiring and layoffs cannot meet the economic guidelines.

Planning horizon theorems

How many periods are needed for a production plan? The answer to this question depends on several factors, including the adequacy of the demand forecasts. It is difficult to make plans for periods where demand is totally unknown. On the other hand, multiple periods are needed so that decisions that affect future plans can be compared.

Planning horizon theorems are one method of addressing this issue. (See Section 4.3 for more discussion of this topic.) For example, Kunreuther & Morton [1974] studied the effect of assuming zero ending inventory. (No inventory at the end of the plan could be tantamount to going out of business in some circumstances.) They discovered a special condition that guarantees that zero ending inventory is optimal for some planning horizons. Their condition requires that demand be relatively low in the period after the horizon. L. Miller [1979] found another condition that applies when demand is increasing at the end of the horizon. Unfortunately, there is no guarantee that either of these conditions will exist for a given application. In fact, if a planning horizon is found in this manner for a given company, there is no guarantee that the same company will ever find another. Thus, planning horizon theorems may be of limited use in some situations.

Discussion

There are a number of tools available for evaluating aggregate production plans. The methods discussed in this subsection all assume that demand is deterministic. Graphical methods make no assumptions on the structure of the costs and demands, and are quite easily implemented with simple spreadsheet computer programs. The economic guidelines may be used in conjunction with graphical or spreadsheet approaches. However, these all have the limitation of assuming that there is only one aggregate product. Moreover, the economic guidelines are based on the rather severe assumption that all costs are linear. (Versions that depart from linearity are more complicated.) If one is willing to assume linearity, then linear programming (LP) can be used to find optimal plans quickly. With LP it is easy to incorporate multiple aggregate products and additional factors such as learning effects of new employees. LP and other methods are discussed more fully in Sections 2.5 and 4.

2.2. *If cycles dominate the planning problem*

Aggregate production and workforce planning was originally devised to deal with seasonality (annual cycles) in demand. Demand seasonality is the most common cause of significant, predictable workload cycles. However, in some industries such as agriculture, seasonality is caused by the nature of the production process itself. Other cycles sometimes exist, but they are usually less pronounced and more difficult to forecast. Of course, some seasonal planning methods can be used if cycles are present for any reason.

Production planners use many methods in the face of seasonal demand variations. Some (e.g., produce to inventory, vary production, etc.) have already been introduced. In addition, demand management through promotions, pricing, order promising, or other methods can sometimes reduce demand fluctuations. Vacation planning for the employees allows production to fluctuate without seasonal layoffs or overtime [Lamont, 1975]. A third strategy applied during low demand intervals is to focus efforts on training, experimenting with new production methods, or other activities that are useful but that reduce the output rate.

Dividing the workforce into 'permanent' and 'seasonal' (or temporary) groups is common in some environments. The seasonal workers are retained during the time of peak workload.

In addition to these strategies, companies employ the strategies discussed earlier – inventory, overtime and workforce changes. The economic guidelines described in Section 2.1 may be applied in special ways when demand varies seasonally. For example, McClain & Thomas [1977] point out that the maximum number of hiring/firing intervals that should be considered for a seasonal plan of length T periods is d^*, where

$$d^* = \text{Integer part of } T/(2(m^* + 1)) .$$

This is a direct result of the Kunreuther & Morton [1974] property that temporary workforce changes (either hiring or layoffs) should be at least $m^* + 1$ periods apart.

Seasonal planning illustrates the difficulty of assigning costs to inventory, hiring/firing, and overtime in an aggregate plan. For example, if the product mix is deliberately changed during the slow periods in favor of items that have low inventory cost, then how do you assign a unit cost of holding inventory? The marginal cost depends on the quantity held. As inventory accumulates, production shifts toward the more expensive units to avoid overproduction of the others. Multi-product models (e.g., linear programming) allow a resolution of this issue by grouping the aggregate products using both holding cost and seasonal pattern.

2.3. *If growth (or decline) of demand dominates the planning problem*

If demand is continuously growing, 'production smoothing' will not help. The problem becomes one of adding capacity, perhaps of different types, to stay ahead of demand. There may be cyclical fluctuations around the growing mean demand, and inventory may be an option in smoothing these. Examples of this type of problem include electricity generation and planning for computer needs; in both cases, the product (really a service) cannot be inventoried. Thus the problem is to develop a capacity plan that exceeds demand.

For example, in electric power generation, 'capacity' may require high investment cost but low marginal cost, such as nuclear power stations, or more moderate investment with high marginal cost, such as gas turbines. The decision-maker would like to postpone the large investment in low-marginal-cost units as long as possible. Short-term fluctuations are met by the low-investment units, at high marginal cost. The planning problem is to determine when to add the low-marginal-cost units. The shortfall of demand minus 'base capacity' (base capacity = capacity of low-marginal-cost units) determines the capacity needed in high marginal cost units. (Capacity must equal or exceed demand.) Electricity generation has daily, weekly, and annual cycles, as well as a long-term growth pattern. In oversimplified form, in Figure 2.4 we ignore daily and weekly cycles and illustrate the demand and 'base capacity' that might constitute a several-year plan.

Many different forms of the capacity expansion problem exist. We will give only a few references. Bean & Smith [1985] analyze an infinite horizon capacity planning problem. They assume an (essentially) arbitrary time path for demand, do not allow inventory, and require that capacity be no less than demand. They use an infinite horizon dynamic programming formulation and develop conditions for the existence of *forecast horizons* (a period of time over which forecasts are needed) and *decision horizons* (the period of time covered by the optimal first decision, which is also the first decision when considering only a problem of length equal to the forecast horizon). In developing these conditions, they lean heavily on a previous paper, Bean & Smith [1984].

Bean & Smith's [1985] cost model includes only the discounted fixed cost of adding the capacity. Multiple types of capacity are available. Production cost is assumed to be constant regardless of the type of facility, and underutilization of capacity is undesirable only because fixed costs should be postponed as long as possible. The dynamic programming formulation, not given here, uses times of installation, by capacity type, as decision variables. Aronson, Morton & Thompson [1984] also analyze planning horizons in this situation when inventory is not an option.

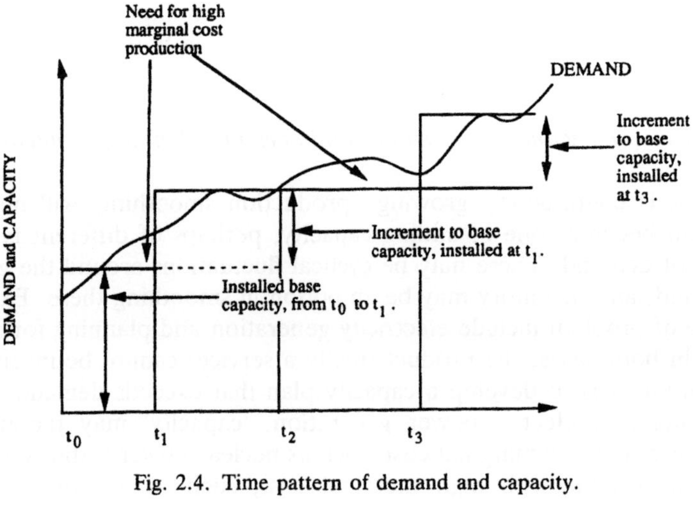

Fig. 2.4. Time pattern of demand and capacity.

Discussions of electricity generation capacity in particular are given by Levin, Tishler & Zahavi [1983], Price & Sharp [1984], and Sherali, Staschus & Huacuz [1987]. Many managerial discussions of the capacity planning problem are given in industry-specific managerial journals. (For example, journals that focus on management of computer systems have many such articles, including Burd & Kassicieh [1987].)

When inventory is feasible, nondecreasing demand still presents a special situation even if capacity is fixed. Several authors deal with models with nondecreasing demand, including Zangwill [1966] and Korgaonker [1977], and some of their references. Korgaonker includes production, inventory, and smoothing costs. All costs are concave or piecewise concave, and capacity is fixed. He finds the minimum cost plan by showing that the problem is equivalent to finding the shortest route through an acyclic network. Luss [1982] presents a review of many approaches and problems. Freidenfelds [1981] also presents models of several types.

Forecast horizons are important in capacity planning problems when growth of demand dominates, with or without inventory as a possibility. When seasonality exists and inventory is allowed, the forecast horizon for the production planning problem is likely to be roughly one year. In the case of growing demands and capacity planning, the forecast horizon may be very long, and changing from using four to using five years of forecasts may significantly affect the first decision.

2.4. *Dealing with significant uncertainty*

Substantial uncertainty in demand requires some changes in thinking for aggregate planning. In addition to production smoothing, the aggregate planning problem becomes one of determining the appropriate amount of safety stock and/or excess capacity to have. These problems fall in the purview of Chapters 1 and 11. However, we will make a few comments appropriate to this chapter.

If production smoothing is employed, safety stock is usually needed only in periods of peak demand – inventory that results from production smoothing performs the safety stock role at other times. (Hax & Meal [1975], e.g., discuss adding safety stock to aggregate plans in a hierarchical planning setting.)

The detailed composition of the safety stock depends on the situation. For example, Thomas & Weiss [1986] analyze a situation where customer service policy dictates that products must be completed within a short period of time after the demand. Further, there were many items, some with high and predictable demand, others with low and unpredictable demand. In this situation, stock should be concentrated in items that are easiest to forecast. This has the effect of reserving capacity for last-minute production of items that have greater demand uncertainty. This initially counterintuitive result (hold safety stock in low-variability-of-demand items) illustrates the effect that the service policy has on the appropriate composition of safety stock to add to an aggregate plan. Sox, McClain & Thomas [1992] give further analysis of this concept.

In planning, *safety time* refers to implementing some portions of a plan earlier because of uncertainty of demand. For example, safety time may be needed in planning for additions to fixed capacity because of uncertainty either in the forecast or in the time to install capacity. In this case the long lead time for installing additional capacity makes the forecasting problem more difficult. The tradeoff is lost sales versus idle capacity. If there is a chance that growth may not materialize, then the cost and risk of overcapacity is greater and the analogy to safety time disappears.

Even if uncertainty truly dominates seasonality and growth, aggregate plans can still be developed in many situations. This is particularly true in make-to-order or assemble-to-order environments. [For a discussion of these terms, see Vollmann, Berry & Whybark, 1992].

For make-to-order factories, Cruickshanks, Drescher & Graves [1984] discuss production smoothing in a single-stage manufacturing process with a production lead time of L_0 periods. An order arrives and delivery is promised within L_1 periods, where $L_1 \geqslant L_0$. The difference, $L_1 - L_0$, is called a 'planning window'. Choosing L_1 is an aggregate planning decision. The authors find that, as expected, variation in production declines as the planning window increases, and that a small increase in the planning window can give a large reduction in the production variation. However, larger L_1 values cause more inventory and longer delivery times for customers.

Assemble-to-order is a strategy for dealing with long manufacturing lead times. Components are manufactured according to forecasts, but finished goods are assembled to order. If there is a high degree of commonality of use for the components, their demand forecasts represent an aggregation of the demands for the end products. Generally, this reduces the forecast error. Even so, producing components to stock does incur a risk of 'building the wrong stuff'. Commonality reduces this risk.

J. Miller [1979] discusses 'hedging the master schedule' in this situation, producing more safety stock in the early stages of production and less as the forecast improves through time. In one industrial example with which we are familiar, production took nine months, and the nine-month forecast was poor. However, rather than just hedging the schedule, this company reduced the lead time to three months, making the 'hedging' problem dramatically easier. Reducing lead time and/or hedging the master schedule help to reduce uncertainty and thereby decrease the quantity of safety stock needed.

Another way to deal with uncertainty and smooth production is discussed in the MRP literature as 'demand management'. Rather than smoothing production, a 'demand management' module places orders against a known capacity, in effect dealing with uncertainty by varying quoted lead time. This general approach is common for high-dollar-value (big-ticket) items such as mainframe computers or airplanes. A production rate is determined, and, when a sales person books an order, the new order takes its place in the queue and is assigned a delivery date. The length of the backlog (the queue) is used as an input to management decisions about production. If the backlog becomes sufficiently large, an increase in the production rate can be considered. If the backlog becomes too small, actions to increase the demand rate (promotions, low-interest loans, 'free' options, and so on) can be taken.

Demand management is discussed by Vollmann, Berry & Whybark [1992] and by Guerrero [1987]. In a similar vein Baker [1984] discusses 'input control' and its effect. Sasser [1976] discusses matching supply and demand in a service setting, where inventory is not an option, and Connell, Adam & Moore [1985] give a health care example of aggregate planning.

In general, the effect of uncertainty is to enhance the value of inventory as a planning tool – it simultaneously helps to avoid production-change costs and poor customer service. However, other strategies such as lead-time reduction or demand management can reduce the need for inventory. The appropriate choice depends on the situation, particularly the service norms for the industry and company under study.

2.5. The historical literature

Several different approaches to aggregate production-workforce planning were proposed in the late 50's and 60's, and several articles were written comparing the performance of these methods. Since Hax [1978] and Silver [1967] review these in detail, we will give only a brief description.

One early line of research, described in Holt, Modigliani, Muth & Simon [1960], analyzed data from a paint factory to study changes in production and changes in workforce. Their approach is often referred to by the author's initials as 'HMMS'. The theoretical underpinning and related topics are described in earlier articles by the authors and others, including Modigliani & Hohn [1955] and Simon [1956].

The HMMS cost model is quadratic. Taking first derivatives results in a set of simultaneous linear equations that can be solved for a set of 'linear decision rules'. A linear decision rule is one in which decisions for production and workforce in each period are linear functions of demand and previous production or workforce values.

The HMMS cost model [Holt, Modigliani, Muth & Simon, 1960, p. 58] is

$$\min \sum_{t=1}^{T} C_t$$

subject to

$$C_t = C_1 W_t + C_{13} \qquad \text{(Regular payroll costs)}$$

$$+ C_2(W_t - W_{t-1} - C_{11})^2 \qquad \text{(Hiring and layoff cost)}$$

$$+ C_3(P_t - C_4W_t)^2 + C_5P_t - C_6W_t + C_{12}P_tW_t \quad \text{(Overtime costs)}$$

$$+ C_7(I_t - C_8 - C_9S_t)^2 , \quad \text{(Inventory-connected costs)}$$

$$I_t = I_{t-1} + P_t - S_t \quad \text{for } t = 1, 2, \ldots, T ,$$

where, for each period t,

I_t = net inventory (can be negative),
P_t = production,
W_t = work force,
S_t = units ordered (demand).

Taking first derivatives results in a set of linear equations that can be solved for linear decision rules (LDR) of the following form

$$P_t = \sum_{j=0}^{11} \alpha_j S_{t+j} + 1.005W_{t-1} + 153.0 - 0.464I_{t-1} , \tag{1}$$

$$W_t = 0.742W_{t-1} + 2.00 - 0.010I_{t-1} + \sum_{j=0}^{11} \beta_j S_{t+j} , \tag{2}$$

in which α_j and β_j are functions of the costs, and were found to decrease in magnitude with j. (See Holt, Modigliani, Muth & Simon [1960, p. 61]. The numbers in Equations (1) and (2) reflect the costs estimated for the factory used as an example in that reference.)

The linear decision rule has been shown to have the important characteristic that if demands are random variables, the LDR derived by inserting expected demand into the cost function is optimal if the objective is to minimize expected costs.

Many authors have generalized the HMMS models, going beyond the single, aggregate product, or adding other decisions to production and workforce levels in each period. Bergstrom & Smith [1970], Hausman & McClain [1971], Welam [1975], and Ozden [1987], among others, have analyzed multiple aggregate items, each of which may have a different seasonal pattern. Welam [1978] develops an interactive method to reduce the number of small changes to the decision variables. Damon & Schramm [1972] add marketing and finance decision variables, and Peterson [1971] allows shipments to differ from orders, with a quadratic cost penalty for deviating. Several authors, including Krajewski, Mabert & Thompson [1973] and Kriebel [1967], have discussed the cost approximations. Schwarz & Johnson [1978] have analyzed the empirical performance of linear decision rules, and several authors have compared, empirically, different approaches to the aggregate production planning problem [Eilon, 1975; Guenther, 1982; Lee & Khumawala, 1974].

Two other methods of generating linear decision rules are 'search methods' and 'managerial coefficients'. Jones [1967], Chang & Jones [1970], and Taubert

[1968] develop rules based on arbitrary (non-quadratic) cost models. Search procedures are used to find the linear decision rules that (approximately) minimize costs. The advantage is that any form of cost model can be used. (The disadvantage is that it is very difficult to build any cost model of a company, as we will discuss below.)

Bowman [1963] argued that a manager has a good feel for the appropriate rule to use, but that he or she may overreact to change. Bowman built a rule using regressions over past actual decisions, to show that a model of a manager's decision process can sometimes outperform the manager. Now that expert systems and artificial intelligence are finding application in operations management (see Bell [1989] and references therein, for a discussion), perhaps Bowman's approach will resurface, in different form.

The final category is linear programming. Early models include Bowman [1956], who proposed a transportation-type LP for aggregate planning. Posner & Szwarc [1983] develop a non-iterative method for this formulation.

Hanssman & Hess [1960] proposed a more complex formulation, and many authors, for example Von Lanzenaur [1970], Thomas [1970], and Goodman [1973, 1974], expand the formulation to include multiple stages of manufacture, marketing variables, and multiple objectives (goal programming) respectively. (The goal programming papers linearize an initially quadratic objective function. Deckro & Smith [1984] use goal programming and deal directly with the nonlinear objective.) There are many other mathematical programming approaches to production scheduling, but many of these are large, monolithic programs that give more detailed information. These will be discussed in Section 4.

2.6. *Validity of the 'costs'*

Cost models are difficult to build for any operations decisions. This is particularly true for aggregate planning where some costs that are fixed in the short run may become modifiable for this intermediate-term decision. The idea of using 'relevant costs' [see Matthews & Meyers, 1976] is hard to implement. In general, accounting numbers can give information inappropriate to some production decisions. Kaplan [1983, 1988] and Johnson & Kaplan [1987] discuss the issue of accounting for manufacturing and give ideas for developing appropriate measures. A manager should develop cost estimates that represent true economic opportunity costs, in so far as possible. These estimates should be reviewed (and perhaps revised) in light of the model that uses the estimates *and* the decisions that result.

3. The relationship of aggregate planning to the economy and to detailed scheduling

Aggregate production planning is surrounded by higher and lower levels of plans. Good aggregate plans can be disaggregated to give good detailed plans.

Overall policy guidance is given to an 'aggregate planner' by higher levels of planning in the organization. In this section we examine several planning methods and their connection to aggregate planning. MRP-II (see Chapter 11) is one method of business planning for production that includes aggregate plans. Section 3.2 discusses aggregate planning and MRP-II. Hierarchical production planning (see Chapter 10) research analyzes ways to develop a set of models often including an aggregate planning model, so that the output from a higher level model provides good (or even optimal) input to the lower planning level. Hierarchical production planning and aggregate planning are discussed in Section 3.3. Section 3.4 examines some of the literature on how to disaggregate plans, and when this can be done in an optimal manner.

Section 3.1 begins with some discussion of the highest level of production smoothing. Does production smoothing exist at a national level, on the average? Do inventories cause recessions or are swings in nationwide inventories the result of a changing economy? Inventory analysis at a national level is an important macroeconomic issue. We will not attempt to summarize this literature, but we will provide a few references on the question of whether production smoothing, using aggregate inventories, exists on a national level as a result of many individual firms' individual decisions.

3.1. Economic impact of inventories and production smoothing

The decisions under consideration in this chapter have major effects on both companies and economies. As stated above, overtime use affects both unemployment and capital expenditures. Also, if firms use production smoothing, swings in demand for products should be absorbed to some extent by inventories. This would imply that variation in production at the national level should be less than variation in sales. Unfortunately, that appears not to be the case. This has caused a significant controversy (and many articles) in the economics literature.

Blinder [1986] refers to previous empirical work of his to state that variation of production exceeds variation of sales, in the data studied. He devised a model to suggest that cost shocks might help to explain the apparent anomaly. Ashley [1985] discusses two motives for holding inventory: to buffer against uncertainty and for smoothing. The motives can have different effects on aggregate inventory. Ashley also discusses the effect of price stickiness and inventory on each other.

West [1986] develops and examines a test of the production-smoothing model. The model is 'nearly always' rejected. However, Ghali [1987] examines the validity of this and other tests of the production-smoothing hypothesis when seasonally adjusted aggregated data are used, and finds that '...the relative size of the variances of the seasonally adjusted production and sales does not offer valid tests of the production-smoothing hypothesis. In addition, aggregating over firms in which the seasonal patterns differ may distort tests...'.

Baghana & Cohen [1987] attempt to combine the economic and operations research views of production inventories in the case where the product is distributed through a multi-echelon (three-layer) system. (Authors back to Forrester [1963], and as recently as Sterman [1989], have noted that separately acting agents in a multi-echelon structure can cause the demand seen by the production units to have dramatically larger variance than sales. Even after some smoothing, the production variance could exceed the sales variance.) Including a setup (ordering) cost at the retail level, Baghana & Cohen [1987] find that the actions of the middle agent can have significant effect. Inventories can have a smoothing effect, but all actors must be considered. In their analysis, all three layers act independently. If an entire system is owned by one company, solutions can be obtained that should reduce overall costs, and, in many cases, smooth production. As more companies reduce inventory using 'Just-in-Time', and as real-time information becomes available across firms, one might expect the production variance to become less than or equal to that of sales.

3.2. MRP-II and production planning

MRP-II (Manufacturing Resource Planning) is a business planning system that makes a connection between aggregate-level planning and detailed plans (see Chapter 11). In MRP-II both aggregate and detailed production planning are included. The planning approach considers capacity at several levels of aggregation. Figure 3.1, from Vollmann, Berry & Whybark [1992], shows two levels of capacity planning: 'resource planning' and 'detailed capacity planning'. These are used in three levels of production planning: production planning, master production scheduling, and material and capacity (detailed) plans. Different patterns exist in different implementations of MRP-II, but this pattern is illustrative.

Capacity planning in MRP-II literature often implies the detailed capacity planning of Figure 3.1. (Currently, in 1992, finite-capacity scheduling is having a resurgence.) In this chapter we are dealing with aggregate plans that are closer to 'resource planning' in Figure 3.1. In applications there are often several plans of different time horizons and levels of aggregation; it is unclear (and unimportant) to decide which plan is *the* aggregate plan. In addition to texts such as Vollmann, Berry & Whybark [1992] and McClain, Thomas & Mazzola [1992], capacity planning in MRP-II is discussed in many articles. For example, Schmitt, Berry & Vollmann [1984] describe 'capacity planning using overall factors'. Hosni & Alsebaise [1987] examine capacity planning in a job-shop setting.

A master production schedule (MPS) typically is given for a month (or less), with a plan that looks several months into the future. Chung & Krajewski [1984] discuss how far to look ahead for the MPS. Lee, Adam & Ebert [1987] analyze the effect of forecast errors in master production scheduling, and Sridharan, Berry & Udayabhanu [1988] discuss MPS stability in rolling-horizon planning.

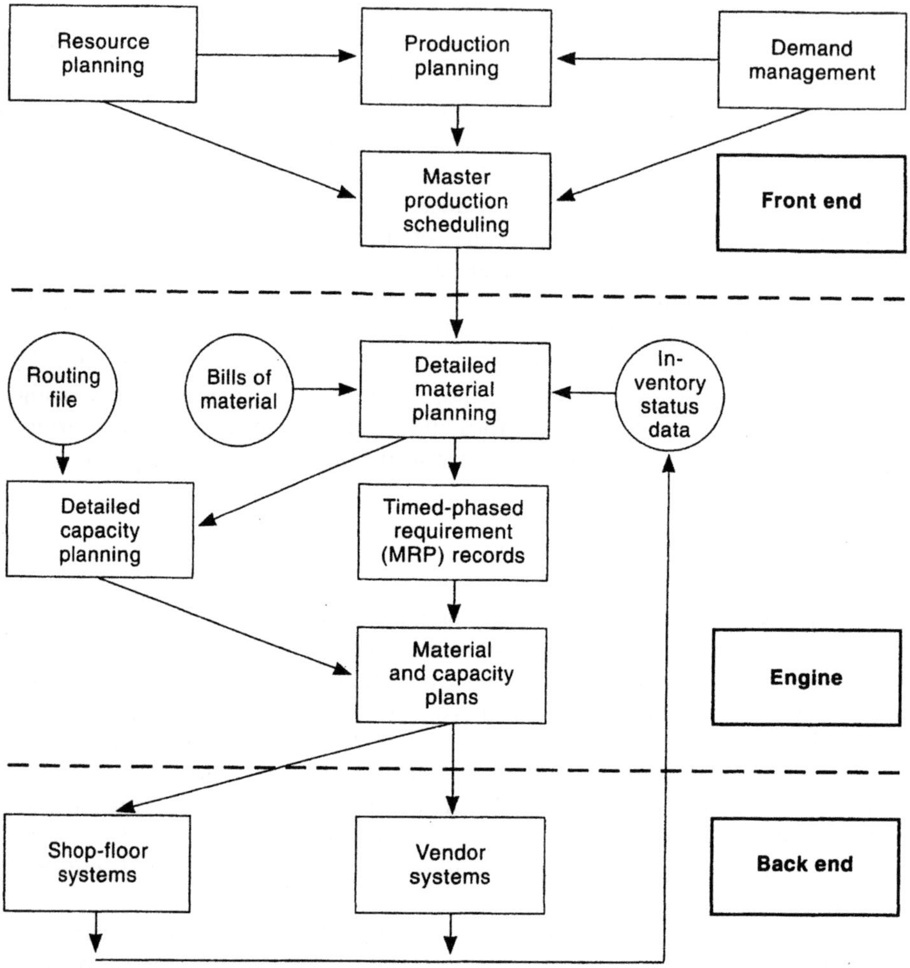

Fig. 3.1. Manufacturing planning and control system. Reproduced from Vollmann, Berry and Whybark (1992). *Manufacturing Planning and Control Systems, 3rd edition*, Irwin, Homewood, IL, Fig. 1.1, with permission.

'Production planning' in Figure 3.1, and the associated 'resource planning', involve adding or deleting resources rather than just living within them. Resources could mean overtime or new plants. This level is not written about extensively in MRP research literature.

Other articles that tie 'aggregate planning' and 'MRP' together include Lee, Steinberg & Khumawala [1983] and Meal & Whybark [1987].

In summary, aggregate planning must consider the details of how the product is put together. This can be done with MRP-II or with large mathematical programs, as discussed in Section 4. The production plan that takes place for a longer time horizon and a higher level of aggregation still must be solved to generate the master production schedule. OR tools can be used and/or a periodic master production scheduling meeting can be used. The basic tradeoffs among inventory, capacity and production-level changes remain.

3.3. *Production planning as part of hierarchical planning*

'Hierarchical planning' (see Chapter 10) is a method of tieing together models that might be used by different levels of the organization, with different levels of detail. Bitran & Hax [1977] discuss the design of hierarchical production planning (HPP) systems. Gelders & Van Wassenhove [1982] give two examples of HPP systems and state that in their opinion such systems must always include managerial judgment as an input. By its nature aggregate production planning lies in a hierarchy of decisions that includes policy direction from above as well as the problem of disaggregating the plan into a detailed schedule. Hax & Meal [1975] postulate seasonal planning (an aggregate planning problem) as a decision below 'plant-product assignment' (with capacity considerations) and above family scheduling and item scheduling.

Several HPP papers present explicit models of a production system and deal directly with a production plan that precedes detailed planning. Bitran, Haas & Matsuo [1986] examine a situation where end-of-season uncertainty is a dominant consideration, and they give an aggregate and detailed model. Bitran, Haas & Hax [1981, 1982] present a single-stage and two-stage model of the production operations in a HPP setting. Maxwell, Muckstadt, Thomas & Vander Eecken [1983] discuss an aggregate plan that contains a more complete model of multi-stage manufacturing, but for a single plant, with known capacity. The correct set of models is situation dependent, just as 'aggregate production planning' or 'production planning' have situation-dependent meanings.

3.4. *Disaggregation of aggregate plans*

Aggregate plans use an aggregate view of products, facilities and time. There is no guarantee that a 'feasible' aggregate plan will allow construction of a feasible detailed schedule. Disaggregation is a key topic in hierarchical production planning. Actually, 'disaggregation' is probably a misnomer. The real problem is how to aggregate in such a way that the resulting plans can be disaggregated to produce good schedules. Both practical and theoretical methods of aggregating products (and disaggregating the production plan) depend on the structure of costs, demands, and constraints.

Several authors have analyzed disaggregation of aggregate production plans, including Zoller [1971], Gelders & Kleindorfer [1975], and Gaalman [1977]. Zipkin [1980] examines bounds on the effect of aggregating variables in linear programs, and Rogers, Plante, Wong & Evans [1991] analyze aggregation and disaggregation in optimization models. Zipkin [1982] extends Gaalman's analysis of quadratic-cost production-planning models and shows that good single-item approximations can be developed for fairly general cost functions. Zipkin [1982] also examines a two-stage production situation and reduces the product line to a small number of aggregate products.

Axsäter [1981, 1986] develops conditions for 'perfect aggregation' and includes multi-stage production (with components being used in other products). Aggregate feasibility can co-exist with detailed infeasibility if either (a) more components are required than are available, or if (b) some production capacity constraints are violated. (Production capacity constraints probably eliminate the possibility of obtaining perfect aggregation.)

Practical methods of aggregation have been discussed by several authors including Hax & Meal [1975]. They have product *families* (which share a major setup cost) and product *types* (groups of families that have similar seasonal patterns). In individual application, managers depend on the fact that certain restrictions are 'soft' constraints. For example, once in a while a unit can be expected to produce more than 'capacity'. Still, managers should present a master production schedule that is feasible if the demand load is an 'average' type of load. Then the actual implementation should be at least close to the plan, even though some orders may be late. Production plans should be achievable on the average, so that when a plant falls behind it has the capacity to catch up.

4. Mathematical programming methods

Graphical representation of aggregate planning allows us to view the production and inventory possibilities, but imprecisely, without reference to costs, and for a single product. Mathematical programming methods allow us to be more precise, minimize the costs (to the extent we can correctly model the costs), and include multiple aggregate products. The models can include many different types of constraints and consider them simultaneously. Because of these powerful modelling and optimization capabilities, mathematical programming models have been used in many practical situations and researched extensively. In this section we will examine aggregate models, Section 4.1, monolithic models, Section 4.2, and some single-product models that trace their history to the Wagner–Whitin [1958] dynamic programming model.

4.1. LP and MILP: Aggregate models

Bowman [1956] gives a transportation LP for aggregate planning. Variables are regular-time production, in period i for use in period j, and overtime production. Backorders can be allowed, at a cost. Other LP models can also include variables to change the available workforce or other variable capacity. Also, more than one aggregate product may be used. One formulation of a multi-item LP with hiring, firing and backorders, is given in Hax [1978].

The model decision variables are:

X_{it} = units of product type i to be produced in period t,
W_t = regular work force hours available in period t,
O_t = overtime work force hours used in period t, constrained to be no more than a fraction p of W_t,
H_t = hours of regular work force hired in period t,
F_t = hours of regular work force fired in period t,
I_{it}^+ = units of inventory for product type i at the end of period t,
I_{it}^- = units backordered for product type i at the end of period t.

Each unit of X_{it} uses k_i hours of workforce, in either regular time or overtime. The cost to be minimized includes the sum of the following linear cost terms:

Variable manufacturing cost:	$v_{it}X_{it}$,
Inventory holding cost:	$c_{it}I_{it}^+$,
Backorder cost:	$b_{it}I_{it}^-$,
Regular payroll cost:	r_tW_t,
Overtime payroll cost:	o_tO_t,
Hiring cost:	h_tH_t,
Firing cost:	f_tF_t,

The LP formulation is

$$\min z = \sum_i \sum_t (v_{it}X_{it} + c_{it}I_{it}^+ + b_{it}I_{it}^-) + \sum_t (r_tW_t + o_tO_t + h_tH_t + f_tF_t)$$

subject to

$$X_{it} + I_{i,t-1}^+ - I_{i,t-1}^- - I_{it}^+ + I_{it}^- = d_{it}, \quad i = 1,\ldots,N, \ t = 1,\ldots,T,$$

$$\sum_i k_iX_{it} - W_t - O_t \leq 0, \quad t = 1,\ldots,T,$$

$$W_t - W_{t-1} - H_t + F_t = 0, \quad t = 1,\ldots,T,$$

$$-pW_t + O_t \leq 0, \quad t = 1,\ldots,T,$$

$$X_{it}, I_{it}^+, I_{it}^- \geq 0, \quad i = 1,\ldots,N, \ t = 1,\ldots,T,$$

$$W_t, O_t, H_t, F_t \geq 0, \quad t = 1,\ldots,T.$$

At an aggregate level, LP's of this type are relatively small and easy to solve. Other extensions are possible, including nonlinear costs (which may be approximated using piecewise linear functions) and multiple resource constraints. At some point, the line between aggregate LP's and 'monolithic' models blurs. Wagner, Vargas & Kathuria [1993] discuss the interesting issue of how good the optimal objective function value of the aggregate LP is as an estimate of the optimal value for the detailed model's objective function. They present an estimation process that performs well in predicting the detailed model's objective function using the aggregate model's objective function.

Linear cost models have been analyzed by many authors. For a single, aggregate item, Lippman, Rolfe, Wagner & Yuan [1967b] consider monotone increasing (or decreasing) demand and provide an efficient solution technique. (In Lippman, Rolfe, Wagner & Yuan [1967a], they analyze models with more general cost functions.) McClain & Thomas [1977] study 'rolling horizon' LP's, and they analyze performance in the face of stochastic demand. LP's do not deal directly with uncertainty, but they can provide a good solution that can be modified to account for uncertainty. See Dzielinski, Baker & Manne [1963] and Hax & Meal [1975] for some further discussion. L. Miller [1979] provides some economic tradeoff information using an LP model. Tang, Adulbhan & Zubair [1981] present an example, with piecewise linear costs. Thomas [1971] adds marketing variables to the LP and uses a decomposition procedure for solution.

Models can be developed that introduce setup cost or time, but those MILP models are often more appropriate at a detailed level. Van Wassenhove & DeBodt [1983] present a medium-term smoothing example with setup cost and report significant improvement over the previously used method.

Akinc & Roodman [1986] give an aggregate MILP model where capacity adjustments can be added or deleted, at a fixed cost. A Benders' decomposition solution procedure is used. The model can be used as a heuristic procedure, with the manager specifying components to include in the procedure. As with many decomposition routines, the procedure can be terminated before optimality, to gain speed.

4.2. *LP and MILP: Monolithic models*

The possibilities for including references in this section are endless; we will only give a few. For additional references see Chapter 8 and the references included in some of the articles given here. One well-known optimization-type approach, OPT, is not discussed because the details of the optimization method are proprietary. See Goldratt [1980] and Jacobs [1983] for a description of the general approach.

Billington, McClain & Thomas [1983] give one formulation of a monolithic model that includes 'recipe' information (what components go into what products, in a multi-stage production system). There are potentially several constraining resources. The formulation is given below.

$$\text{minimize} \quad \sum_i \sum_t (H_i I_{it} + \text{cs}_i X_{it}) + \sum_k \sum_t (\text{co}_{kt} O_{kt} + \text{cu}_{kt} U_{kt})$$

subject to

$$I_{i,t-1} + y_i P_{i,t-L_i} - I_{i,t} - \sum_j a_{ij} P_{jt} = d_{it} \quad \text{for all } i,\ T\ ,$$

$$\sum_i (b_{ik} P_{it} + s_{ik} X_{it}) + U_{kt} - O_{kt} = \text{CAP}_{kt} \quad \text{for all } k,\ T\ ,$$

$$P_{it} - qX_{it} \leq 0 \quad \text{for all } i, T ,$$

$$I_{it}, P_{it}, U_{kt}, O_{kt} \geq 0 , \quad X_{it} = 0 \text{ or } 1 \quad \text{for all } i, k, T .$$

The variables and parameters are:

I_{it} = ending inventory of product i in period t, with unit cost H_i ,
X_{it} = a setup variable for item i in period t, with setup cost cs_i and setup time s_{ik},
O_{kt} = overtime on facility k in period t, with unit cost co_{kt},
U_{kt} = undertime on facility k in period t, with unit cost cu_{kt},
y_i = yield of item i,
L_i = minimal lead time, in periods, for producing item i,
P_{it} = production of item i in period t,
a_{ij} = the number of units of item i required to produce one unit of item j,
d_{it} = external (independent) demand for item i in period t,
b_{ik} = the time required on facility k by one unit of item i,
CAP_{kt} = the time available (capacity) on facility k in period t,
q = a large number.

Some extensions to the formulation are discussed in Billington, McClain & Thomas [1983]. Billington, McClain & Thomas [1986] discuss solution techniques for the special case of a single constrained facility, without setup time but with setup cost. McClain, Thomas & Weiss [1989] analyze the LP version and exploit the special structure of the model. The large number of 'recipe' constraints can be dealt with very efficiently, after pricing out the capacity constraints. Trigeiro, Thomas & McClain [1989] analyze the problem with a single constrained facility with setup time and find that setup time is a more difficult extension than setup cost.

Hackman & Leachman [1989] present a framework that allows more general models of production to be built. Their framework is more flexible than MILP models in that time can be modelled continuously. Thus, lead times need not be integer multiples of some basic period, removing one major difficulty associated with using MILP (or MRP) for a multi-period model with time lags. They use 'rates' and a set of time epochs (not necessarily equally spaced). The authors more completely model lead times by breaking the lead time into two components: a 'transfer/input' lag is the time to move inventory to and prepare it for use at a production location, and an 'output' lag is time needed before produced items are available to move to other locations (time for paint to dry, e.g.). Hackman & Leachman [1989] compare their frameworks to MILP models, MRP, and project management models.

There are many articles that focus on lot-sizing in both multi-stage and single-stage production. Elmaghraby [1978] reviews the single-stage literature. Maes & Van Wassenhove [1986] present some optimization-based heuristics for the single-stage problem. Gascon & Leachman [1988] give a dynamic programming formulation. Recent articles include Campbell & Mabert [1991], Davis

[1990], Pochet & Wolsey [1991], Salomon, Kroon, Kuik & Van Wassenhove, and Zipkin [1991].

Maxwell & Muckstadt [1986] and Afentakis & Gavish [1986] present breakthroughs in dealing with the multi-stage lot-sizing problem. (Also see references in those articles.) Several early and important papers, including Dzielinski, Baker & Manne [1963], Dzielinski & Gomory [1965], Gorenstein [1970], and Lasdon & Terjung [1971] present methods that approximately incorporate setup times and solve realistically large problems. Toczylowski & Hindi [1991] examine aggregate scheduling in the special case of a several-machine FMS.

We expect both LP and MILP formulations of production planning to be implemented in more situations in the future. MILP solution techniques have improved, and setup time is often still a key problem in practice. (Setup *cost* is a fictional number in some situations). As 'just-in-time', with setup time reduction, is implemented, LP models become more realistic as a means of developing a production plan, to be given to a just-in-time line for implementation. As Spence & Porteus [1987] point out, setup reduction also provides additional effective capacity, thereby allowing a changed production plan.

4.3. The Wagner–Whitin legacy

The optimization models discussed in Sections 4.1 and 4.2 are LP and MILP models that easily consider multiple aggregate items. Many dynamic programming models for single-item production planning have been developed, notably Wagner & Whitin [1958]. This model uses discrete demand, for a finite horizon. The cost model in Wagner and Whitin includes a linear production cost and a setup cost. Typically, setup costs are not considered at an aggregate level, especially when using a single aggregate product. However, the notion of planning horizons, discussed in the papers mentioned in this section, is important in aggregate planning.

Wagner & Whitin [1958] developed a planning horizon theorem that started a small industry. The planning horizon theorem allows the single-item production planning problem to be broken into several smaller problems by determining periods in which production must be positive. Many authors worked on using nonlinear costs, finding all planning horizons that exist and including backorders. Eppen, Gould & Pashigian [1969] is one example of this literature, and an important paper that gives computationally efficient algorithms is Federgruen & Tzur [1991]. Other references are given in Chapter 1. Heuristic methods for the dynamic lot-sizing problem are discussed in Chapter 11.

Wagner and Whitin present a dynamic programming formulation similar to the following:

$$f_t(I_{t-1}) = \min_{x_t \geq 0} \{s_t \delta(x_t) + h_t(I_{t-1} + x_t - d_t) + f_{t+1}(I_{t-1} + x_t - d_t)\} ,$$

where d_t, x_t, I_t, h_t and s_t = demand, production, inventory, unit holding cost and setup cost in period t, $t = 1, \ldots, T$ (I_0 and I_T are known constants, $I_0 < \Sigma\, d_t$),

$$f_T(I_{T-1}) = s_T \delta(I_T + d_T - I_{T-1}) , \qquad x_T = I_T + d_T - I_{T-1} ,$$

$$\delta(x) = \begin{cases} 1 & \text{if } x > 0 , \\ 0 & \text{otherwise} , \end{cases}$$

and $f_t(I_{t-1})$ = the minimum cost of satisfying demand from t to T, given initial inventory I_{t-1}.

In this deterministic, periodic review situation it is easy to show that the optimal solution will consist of production in period 1 for periods 1 to $k_1 - 1$, then production in period k_1 for k_1 to $k_2 - 1 \geq k_1$ and so on. Production always occurs when inventory is zero, and production equals the sum of a sequential set of demands. (Initial inventory is netted against the first set of demands.) Using this property, a forward algorithm can be developed that considers only in which periods to produce, which reduces the state space dramatically. Furthermore, the planning horizon theorem allows us to limit the search further and to know when the first period decision will not change as new periods are added to the problem.

Planning horizons and related work have already been mentioned in earlier sections. Bean & Smith [1985] analyze *forecast horizons*, the period of time over which forecasts must be obtained to guarantee the optimality of the first-period decision, in a capacity expansion problem. Planning horizons for the Modigliani & Hohn [1955] model and generalizations are studied by Kleindorfer & Lieber [1979] using convex, separable costs, and by Lee & Orr [1977] using a storage capacity constraint.

Several final comments should be made about Wagner & Whitin [1958] and successors. First, it is not really an aggregate planning method, since many of the articles assume no capacity constraint. Typical example problems have zero production in several periods. Second, Wagner–Whitin dynamic programs have been used by many authors to address lot-sizing in multi-stage manufacturing, for items at all stages of manufacture. This is also not an appropriate use of the model; local costs (inventory and setup) cannot be used since the solution affects the decisions at other levels of the product structure. Blackburn & Millen [1982] study ways to modify the costs so that the Wagner–Whitin dynamic program can be used as an appropriate heuristic for the multi-level lot-sizing problem. (As mentioned above, Maxwell & Muckstadt [1985], and Afentakis & Gavish [1986], present efficient optimal algorithms for some multi-stage situations.) However, Wagner and Whitin's contribution is very important not only as a step on the research path, but also because many solution methods to production planning problems have Wagner and Whitin dynamic programs as a subproblem [Graves, 1981, e.g.], and an efficient solution technique is needed.

5. Summary: Practical considerations and some research questions

This section concludes the paper with two important practical topics (labor-force considerations, Section 5.1, and decision-maker considerations, Section 5.2) and with our view of some of the research needs in this area (Section 5.3). Sections 5.1 and 5.2 briefly discuss implications of the facts that these decisions are made about people and by people. Both research findings and personal and social values should affect the decisions. Section 5.3 describes research topics on the appropriate relation of production planning to the rest of the organization.

5.1. Labor-force considerations

Productivity has improved significantly in production settings in recent years. In the United States, manufacturing productivity gain has exceeded that of the service sector by a significant margin. Several authors have studied aggregate planning including productivity improvements though time as an explicit factor. For example, Ebert [1976] models productivity as improving with cumulative production. Khoshneivis & Wolfe [1983a,b] develop models in which production level changes can reduce productivity, and productivity otherwise improves with cumulative production. Khoshneivis & Wolfe [1986] build a three-part optimization methodology for a model with worker experience classes, learning, and retrogression. The authors' notion of productivity reductions following work-force disruptions fits both with the Hayes & Clark [1987] conclusions mentioned earlier and our opinion.

When production shifts are used, or when multiple production lines may be used, production may be limited to a few possible levels. Many 'production switching heuristics' have been studied, in which production changes among a few levels, based on the amount of inventory. Oliff & Leong [1987] present one recent paper and Oliff & Burch [1985] discuss the application of the methodology in a hierarchical planning system. Mellichamp & Love [1978] also discuss production switching heuristics and give several earlier references. Virgin [1980] questions the cost comparisons given in Mellichamp & Love [1978], arguing that a large fixed-cost base hides the differences among solutions.

All of the aggregate production planning models make decisions of great importance to the individuals who make the product. For example, it is difficult to establish an extra shift for a short period of time and obtain effective production. It reduces morale to hire and fire (or lay off) workers frequently. The work force in a company is a vital asset; a dedicated labor force is of strategic long-term value. That value is hard to estimate, but we believe it usually exceeds inventory costs. Stable employment, with overtime kept within some bounds through time, will lead to a more loyal work force. We are not suggesting that layoffs are never appropriate. Occasionally, longer-term competitive difficulties mandate a work force reduction, to protect the organization and most of the jobs. Since the value of a dedicated work force is very difficult to estimate precisely, models and their output should be used as an input to the final decision, rather than to make the decision.

5.2. Decision-maker considerations

Aggregate-level decisions are made by people. People, research shows, deal with numbers and optimization less well than computer models do, but can include qualitative factors more effectively. Bowman's [1963] early work was based on a belief that managers know how to analyze production problems but tend to overreact.

Several other authors have studied individual decision makers and their response to information and their relative ability compared to models. Chervany & Dickson [1974] show that the form of presentation of information affected the quality of aggregate planning decisions. Those given simple descriptive statistics made better decisions than those given standard data formats, but they had less confidence and took longer. Moskowitz [1972] found that linear decision rules outperformed people, but the gap narrowed when forecasts were poor. Future research may help us better understand the interaction of format and quality of information with decision-makers.

Finally, aggregate planning decisions properly involve people from marketing, finance, and purchasing, as well as production. Any management technique (such as weekly or monthly 'master scheduling meetings') that keeps everyone aware of the plan and, to the extent possible, in agreement, is probably at least as important as the models used to help develop the plan.

5.3. Research needs: Some current and future problems

Production planning must be based on a firm's strategic plans, particularly those policies regarding customer service. The capacity of a production facility, the form of customer service to be given, and the way in which the intermediate-term production plan is developed must be determined together. For example, if enough capacity is purchased, a firm may be able to give fast make-to-order service and maintain very little inventory. Cruickshanks, Drescher & Graves [1984] and Thomas & Weiss [1986] present models, in different settings, that would allow a firm to analyze these areas simultaneously. Research (and practice) tieing service, capacity and production planning together in different settings is needed, particularly as the importance of 'time-based competition' increases. (See Blackburn [1990], for a discussion of time-based competition.)

One type of cross-functional model that has been analyzed but not widely used in practice includes production and marketing variables. Leitch [1974] analyzes an HMMS type of model with marketing variables and finds a solution where an attempt is made to shift demand, using marketing effort, to nonpeak periods. Thomas [1971] also discusses this idea. If it would work, this seems to be a good idea, and many firms offer incentives for buying at non peak times. Empirical research that considers the effectiveness, cost, and value to production of demand shifting would be useful. In general, cross-functional research, tieing production planning with other functional areas, is ripe for research. (Hausman & Montgomery [1990] and Karmarkar [1993] are recent examples.)

Another cross-functional area of research is in the relation of product and process design (engineering) to production planning. Product and process design can dramatically alter the ease of manufacture, but it can also affect how difficult it is to ramp production up or down, and how difficult the problem of disaggregating production plans is to solve. Since connecting design and manufacturing is now widely recognized as crucial to success, we would expect systematic efforts to understand the joint effects. Shortening the product development cycle, from idea to design to manufacture, has become a major factor in the international competitive arena. Companies that can respond quickly to new needs can maintain reasonable margins. Research on two fronts is needed: (1) how best to organize this design effort, and (2) how to measure and plan the capacity of the design effort, or, in other words, to perform an aggregate plan for design.

Aggregate production planning's place in the hierarchy of decisions is a changing thing. New research will be needed for the foreseeable future on how best to plan and implement production. Some research suggestions are given in Abraham, Dietrich, Graves, Maxwell & Yano [1985]. New models, better information, and new marketplace conditions will require different approaches and new empirical validation.

For example, efforts are underway to build real-time manufacturing control systems. See Voelcker, Requicha & Conway [1988], Conway & Maxwell [1991], and Roundy, Maxwell, Herer, Tayur & Getzler [1989]. These models would add items to a schedule by examining inventory levels, existing schedules, availability of time to produce components, and inventory of components. The existing schedule may have come from a production planning model such as an MILP model. How well the real-time schedule can do and how often to solve the large production planning model are empirical questions. This issue is discussed further in Thomas [1993].

Research on the best way to develop a set of models including production planning can proceed in several ways. In limited situations, an optimal set of models may be developed, in the sense that the solution to an aggregate model and the disaggregation(s) thereof may give the solution that would be obtained by solving a large monolithic model. This is discussed in Chapter 10.

In most situations, how to choose an appropriate set of models will be an empirical question. Simulation studies can examine the issue in particular situations, and perhaps, eventually, some large empirical study can ascertain the best among a few alternative ways of breaking up the task. Until then, we feel that anecdotal examples of successful implementations that lead to reduced cost can add to everyone's understanding, even though such research does not give definitive answers. Case studies of this type could include behavioral effects of management techniques and decisions that lead to worker loyalty and to cooperative decision making across functional areas.

References

Abraham, C., B. Dietrich, S. Graves, W. Maxwell and C. Yano (1985). Factory of the future: A research agenda for models to plan and schedule manufacturing systems, Report of Ad Hoc Committee.

Afentakis, P., and B. Gavish (1986). Optimal lot-sizing algorithms for complex product structures. *Oper. Res.* 34(2), 237–249.

Akinc, U., and G.M. Roodman (1986). A new approach to aggregate production planning. *IIE Trans.* 18, 88–94.

Aronson, J.E., T.E. Morton and G.L. Thompson (1984). A forward algorithm and planning horizon procedure for the production smoothing problem without inventory. *European J. Oper. Res.* 15(3), 348–365.

Ashley, R.A., and D. Orr (1985). Further results on inventories and price stickiness. *Amer. Econ. Rev.* 75(5), 964–975.

Axsäter, S. (1981). Aggregation of product data for hierarchical production planning. *Oper. Res.* 29(4), 744–756.

Axsäter, S. (1986). On the feasibility of aggregate production plans. *Oper. Res.* 34(5), 796–800

Baghana, M.P., and M.A. Cohen (1987). Inventory policies and production smoothing, Working Paper, Wharton School.

Baker, K. (1977). An experimental study of the effectiveness of rolling schedules in production planning. *Decision Sci.* 8(1), 19–27.

Baker, K.R. (1984). The effects of input control in a simple scheduling model. *J. Oper. Management* 4(2), 99–112.

Baker, K.R., and W.W. Damon (1977). A simultaneous planning model for production and working capital. *Decisions Sci.* 8(1), 95–108.

Bean, J., and R. Smith (1984). Conditions for the existence of planning horizons. *Math. Oper. Res.* 9, 391–401.

Bean, J.C., and R.L. Smith (1985). Optimal capacity expansion over an infinite horizon. *Management Sci.* 31(12), 1523–1532

Bell, C.E. (1989). Maintaining project networks in automated artificial intelligence planning. *Management Sci.* 35(10), 1192–1214.

Bergstrom, G.L., and B.E. Smith (1970). Multi-item production planning – an extension of the HMMS rules. *Management Sci.* 16(10), B614–B629.

Billington, P., J.O. McClain and L.J. Thomas (1983). Mathematical programming approaches to capacity-constrained MRP systems: Review, formulations and problem reduction. *Management Sci.* 29(10), 1126–1141.

Billington, P., J.O. McClain and L.J. Thomas (1986). Heuristics for multi-level lot sizing with a bottleneck. *Management Sci.* 32(8), 989–1006.

Bitran, G., E. Haas and A. Hax (1981). Hierarchical production planning: A single stage system. *Oper. Res.* 29(4), 717–743.

Bitran, G., E. Haas and A. Hax (1982). Hierarchical production planning: A two-stage system. *Oper. Res.* 30(2), 232–251.

Bitran, G., E. Haas and H. Matsuo (1986). Production planning of style goods with high setup costs and forecast revisions. *Oper. Res.* 34(2), 226–236.

Bitran, G., and A. Hax (1977). On the design of hierarchical production planning systems. *Decision Sci.* 8(1), 28–55.

Blackburn, J., and R. Millen (1982). Improved heuristics for multistage requirements planning systems, *Management Sci.* 28(1), 44–56.

Blackburn, J. (1990). *Time-Based Competition*, Richard D. Irwin, Homewood, IL.

Blinder, A.S. (1986). Can the production smoothing model of inventory behavior be saved? *Quart. J. Econom.* 101(3), 431–453.

Bolt, J.F. (1983). Job security: Its time has come. *Harv. Bus. Rev.* 61(6), 115–123.

Bowman, E.H. (1956). Production scheduling by the transportation method of linear programming. *Oper. Res.* 4, 100–103.

Bowman, E.H. (1963). Consistency and optimality in managerial decision making, *Management Sci.* 9(2), 319–321.

Brennan, L., J. Browne, B.J. Davies, M.E.J. O'Kelly and A.R. Gault (1982). An analysis of the overtime decision. *Internat. J. Oper. Prod. Management* 2(3), 19–36.

Burd, S.D., and S.K. Kassicieh (1987). Logic-based decision support for computer capacity planning. *Inform. Management* 13(3), 125–133.

Campbell, G., and V. Mabert (1991). Cyclical schedules for capacitated lot sizing with dynamic demands, *Management Sci.* 37(4), 409–427.

Chang, R.H., and C.M. Jones (1970). Production and workforce scheduling extensions, *AIIE Trans.* 2, 326–333.

Charnes, A., W.W. Cooper and B. Mellon (1955). A model for optimizing production by reference to cost surrogates. *Econometrica* 23, 307–323.

Chervany, N.L., and G.W. Dickson (1974). An experimental evaluation of information overload in a production environment. *Management Sci.* 20(10), 1335–1344.

Chung, C.H., and L.J. Krajewski (1984). Planning horizons for master production scheduling. *J. Oper. Management* 4(4), 389–406.

Connell, B.C., E.E. Adam Jr and A.N. Moore (1985). Aggregate planning in health care foodservice systems with varying technologies. *J. Oper. Management* 5(1), 41–55.

Conway, R., and W. Maxwell (1992). *PRS Production Planning System: User's Guide*, C-Way Associates, Lansing, New York.

Cruickshanks, A.B., R.D. Drescher and S.C. Graves (1984). A study of production smoothing in a job shop environment, *Management Sci.* 30(3), 368–380.

Damon, W.W., and R. Schramm (1972). A simultaneous decision model for production, marketing, and finance, *Management Sci.* 19(2) 161–172.

Davis, S. (1990). Scheduling economic lot-size production runs, *Management Sci.* 36(8), 985–998.

Deckro, R.F., and J.E. Hebert (1984). Goal programming approaches to solving linear decision rule based aggregate production planning models, *IIE Trans.* 16(4), 308–315.

Dzielinski, B.P., C.T. Baker and A.S. Manne (1963). Simulation tests of lot size programming, *Management Sci.* 9(2), 229–258.

Dzielinski, B.P., and R.E. Gomory (1965). Optimal programming of lot sizes, inventory and labor allocations, *Management Sci.* 11, 874–890.

Ebert, J.R. (1976). Aggregate planning with learning curve productivity. *Management Sci.* 23(2), 171–182.

Eilon, S. (1975). Five approaches to aggregate production planning. *AIIE Trans.* 7, 118–131.

Eppen, G.D., F.J. Gould and B.P. Pashigian (1969). Extensions of the planning horizon theorem in the dynamic lot size model. *Management Sci.* 15(5), 268–277.

Federgruen, A., and M. Tzur (1991). A simple forward algorithm to solve general dynamic lot sizing models with n periods in $O(n \log n)$ or $O(n)$ time. *Management Sci.* 37(8), 909–925.

Forrester, J. (1963). *Industrial Dynamics*, MIT Press, Cambridge, MA.

Freidenfelds, J. (1981). *Capacity Expansion: Analysis of Simple Models with Applications*, Elsevier, New York.

Gaalman, J.G. (1978). Optimal aggregation of multi-item production smoothing models, *Management Sci.* 24(16), 1733–1739.

Gascon, A., and R. Leachman (1988). A dynamic programming solution to the dynamic, multi-item, single-machine scheduling problem. *Oper. Res.* 36(1), 50–56.

Gelders, L., and P.R. Kleindorfer (1975). Coordinating aggregate and detailed scheduling in the one-machine job shop – II – computation and structure. *Oper. Res.* 23(2), 312–324.

Gelders, L.F., and L.N. Van Wassenhove (1981). Production planning: A review. *European J. Oper. Res.* 7, 101–110.
Gelders, L.F., and L.N. Van Wassenhove (1982). Hierarchical integration in production planning: Theory and practice. *J. Oper. Management* 3(1), 27–36.
Ghali, M.A. (1987). Seasonality, aggregation and the testing of the production smoothing hypothesis. *Amer. Econ. Rev.* 77(3), 464–469.
Goldratt, E. (1980). OPT-optimized production timetable, Creative Output, Milford, New York.
Goodman, D.A. (1973). A new approach to scheduling aggregate planning of production and work force. *AIIE Trans.* 5, 135–141.
Goodman, D. (1974). A goal programming approach to aggregate planning of production and work force. *Management Sci.* 20(12), 1569–1575.
Gorenstein, S. (1970). Planning tire production. *Management Sci.* 17(2), B72–B81.
Graves, S.C. (1981). Multi-stage lot sizing: An iterative procedure, in: L. Schwarz (ed.), *Multi-level Production/Inventory Systems: Theory and Practice*, North-Holland, New York.
Graves, S.C. (1982). Using Lagrangean techniques to solve hierarchical production planning problems. *Management Sci.* 28(3), 260–275.
Guenther, H.O. (1982). A comparison of two classes of aggregate production planning models under stochastic demand. *Engrg. Costs Prod. Econom.* 6, 89–97.
Guerrero, H. (1987). Demand management strategies for assemble-to-order production environments, Research Paper Series 87-28, University of Notre Dame, Center for Research in Business.
Hackman, S.T., and R.C. Leachman (1989). A general framework for modelling production. *Management Sci.* 35(4), 478–495.
Hanssmann, F., and S.W. Hess (1960). A linear programming approach to production and employment scheduling. *Management Tech.* 1, 46–51.
Hausman, W.H., and J.O. McClain (1971). A note on the Bergstrom–Smith multi-item production planning model. *Management Sci.* 17(11), 783–785.
Hausman, W.H., and D.B. Montgomery (1990). Making manufacturing market driven, Research Paper 1003, Department of IE and EM, Stanford University.
Hax, A.C. (1978). Aggregate production planning, in: J. Moder and S. Elmaghraby (eds.), *Handbook of Operations Research*, Van Nostrand Reinhold, New York.
Hax, A.C., and D. Candea (1984). *Production and Inventory Management*, Prentice-Hall, Englewood Cliffs, NJ.
Hax, A.C., and H.C. Meal (1975). Hierarchical integration of production planning and scheduling, in: Murray Geisler (ed.), *TIMS Stud. in Management Sci., Vol. 1, Logistics*, pp 53–69.
Hayes, R.H., and K.B. Clark (1985). Explaining observed productivity differentials between plants: Implications for operations research. *Interfaces* 15(6), 3–14.
Holt, C.C., F. Modigliani, J.F. Muth and H.A. Simon (1960). *Planning Production, Inventories and Work Force*, Prentice-Hall, Englewood Cliffs, NJ.
Hosni, Y.A., and A. Alsebaise (1987). Capacity planning in a job-shop environment. *Comput. Ind. Eng.* 13, 96–99.
Jacobs, F.R. (1983). The OPT scheduling system: A review of a new production scheduling system. *Prod. Invent. Management* 24(3), 47–51.
Johnson, H.T. and R.E. Kaplan (1987). *Relevance Lost: The Rise and Fall of Management Accounting*, Harvard Business School Press, Cambridge, MA.
Jones, C.H. (1967). Parametric production planning. *Management Sci.* 13(11), 843–866.
Kahn, J.A. (1987). Inventories and the volatility of production. *Amer. Econom. Rev.* 77(4), 667–679.
Kamien, M., and L. Li (1990). Subcontracting, coordination, flexibility, and production smoothing in aggregate planning. *Management Sci.* 36(11), 1352–1363.
Kaplan, R.E. (1983). Measuring manufacturing performance: a new challenge for management accounting research. *Account. Rev.* 58(4), 686–705.
Kaplan, R.E. (1988). One cost system isn't enough. *Harv. Bus. Rev.* 88(1), 61–66.

Karmarkar, U. (1993). Research in manufacturing strategy: A cross-functional perspective, in: Sarin, R. (ed.), *Perspectives in Operations Management: Essays in Honor of Elwood S. Buffa*, Kluwer, Hingham, MA.

Khoshnevis, B., and P.M. Wolfe (1983a). An aggregate production planning model incorporating dynamic productivity. Part I. Model development. *IEE Trans.* 15(2), 111–118.

Khoshnevis, B., and P.M. Wolfe (1983b). An aggregate production planning model incorporating dynamic productivity: Part II. Solution methodology and analysis. *IIE Trans.* 15(4), 283–291.

Khoshnevis, B., and P.M. Wolfe, (1986). A short-cycle product aggregate planning model incorporating improvement curve productivity. *Engrg. Costs Prod. Econom.* 10(3), 217–233.

Kleindorfer, P.R., and Z. Lieber (1979). Algorithms and planning horizon results for production planning problems with separable costs. *Oper. Res.* 27(5), 874–887.

Korgaonker, M.G. (1977). Production smoothing under piecewise concave costs, capacity constraints, and nondecreasing requirements. *Management Sci.* 24(3), 302–311.

Krajewski, L.J., V.A. Mabert and H.E. Thompson (1973). Quadratic inventory cost approximations and the aggregation of individual products, *Management Sci.* 19(11), 1229–1240.

Krajewski, L., and L. Ritzman (1977). Disaggregation in manufacturing and service organizations. *Decision Sci.* 8(1), 1–18.

Kriebel, C.H. (1967). Coefficient estimation in quadratic programming models. *Management Sci.* 13(8), B473–B486.

Kunreuther, H.C., and T.E. Morton (1974). General planning horizons for production smoothing with deterministic demands. *Management Sci.* 20(7), 1037–1046.

Lalonde, B., M. Cooper and T. Noordewier (1988). *Customer Service: A Management Perspective*, Council of Logistics Management, Oak Brook, IL.

Lamont, G. (1975). Census forecasting: An answer to nursing unit staffing and bed utilization problems, in: *Examination of Case Studies in Nurse Staffing*, National Cooperative Services for Hospital Management Engineering, Richmond, VA.

Lasdon, L.S., and R.C. Terjung (1971). An efficient algorithm for multi-item scheduling. *Oper. Res.* 19(4), 946–969.

Lee, D.R., and D. Orr (1977). Further results on planning horizons in the production smoothing problem. *Management Sci.* 23(5), 490–498.

Lee, T.S., E. Adam Jr and R. Ebert (1987). An evaluation of forecast error in master production scheduling for material requirements planning systems. *Decision Sci.* 18(2), 292–307.

Lee, W.B., and B.M. Khumawala (1974). Simulation testing of aggregate production planning models in an implementation methodology. *Management Sci.* 20(6), 903–911.

Lee, W.B., E. Steinberg and B.M. Khumawala (1983). Aggregate versus disaggregate production planning: A simulated experiment using LDR and MRP. *Internat. J. Prod. Res.* 21(6), 797–811.

Leitch, R.A. (1974). Marketing strategy and the optimal production schedule. *Management Sci.* 21(3), 302–312.

Levin, N., A. Tishler and J. Zahavi (1983). Time step vs. dynamic optimization of generation-capacity-expansion programs of power systems. *Oper. Res.* 31(5), 891–914.

Lippman, S.A., A.J. Rolfe, H.M. Wagner and J.S.C. Yuan (1967a). Optimal production scheduling and employment smoothing with deterministic demands. *Management Sci.* 14(3), 127–158.

Lippman, S.A., A.J. Rolfe, H.M. Wagner and J.S.C. Yuan (1967b). Algorithm for optimal production scheduling and employment smoothing. *Oper. Res.* 15, 1011–1029.

Luss, H. (1982), Operations research and capacity expansion problems: A survey, *Oper. Res.* 30(5).

Maes, J., and L. Van Wassenhove (1986). Multi-item single level capacitated dynamic lot sizing heuristics, Parts I and II. *IIE Trans.* 18, 114–129.

Matthews, J.P., and S.L. Meyers (1976). Relevant costing under aggregate production planning. *Managerial Plan.* 24(5), 38–41.

Maxwell, W., and J. Muckstadt (1985). Establishing consistent and realistic reorder intervals in production-distribution systems. *Oper. Res.* 33(6).

Maxwell, W., J. Muckstadt, L.J. Thomas and J. Vander Eecken (1983). A modeling framework for planning and control of production in discrete parts manufacturing and assembly systems. *Interfaces* 13(6), 92–104.

McClain, J.O., and L.J. Thomas (1977). Horizon effects in aggregate production planning with seasonal demand. *Management Sci.* 23(7), 728–736.
McClain, J.O, L.J. Thomas and J.B. Mazzola (1992). *Operations Management: Production of Goods and Services, 3rd edition*, Prentice-Hall, Englewood Cliffs, NJ.
McClain, J., L.J. Thomas and E. Weiss (1989). Efficient solutions to a linear programming model for production scheduling with capacity constraints and no initial stock. *IIE Trans.* 21(2), 144–152.
Meal, H.L., and D.C. Whybark (1987). Material requirements planning in hierarchical planning systems. *Internat. J. Prod. Oper. Management* 25(7), 947–956.
Mellichamp, J.M., and R.M. Love (1978). Production switching heuristics for the aggregate production planning problem. *Management Sci.* 24(12), 1242–1252.
Miller, J. (1979). Hedging the master schedule, in: *Disaggregation Problems in Manufacturing and Service Organizations*, Martinus Nijhoff, Boston, MA.
Miller, L.W. (1979). Using linear programming to derive planning horizons for a production smoothing problem, *Management Sci.* 25(12), 1232–1244.
Modigliani, F., and F.E. Hohn (1955). Production planning over time and the nature of the expectation and planning horizon. *Econometrica* 23, 46–66.
Moskowitz, H. (1972). The value of information in aggregate production planning: A behavioral experiment, *IIE Trans.* 4(4), 290–297.
Oliff, M.D., and E.E. Burch (1985). Multiproduct production scheduling at Owens–Corning Fiberglas. *Interfaces* 15(5), 25–34.
Oliff, M.D., and G.K. Leong (1987). A discrete production switching rule for aggregate planning. *Decision Sci.* 18(4), 582–597.
Ozden, M. (1987). An aggregate production planning approach with multiple product groups and resource limitations, Working Paper, Miami University, OH.
Peterson, R. (1971). Optimal smoothing of shipments in response to orders. *Management Sci.* 17(9), 597–607.
Pochet, Y., and L. Wolsey (1991). Solving multi-item lot-sizing problems using strong cutting planes. *Management Sci.* 37(1), 53–67.
Posner, M.E., and W. Szwarc (1983). A transportation type aggregate production model with backordering. *Management Sci.* 29(2), 188–199.
Price, D.H.R., and J.A. Sharp (1984). Demand forecasting and aggregate planning in the electrical supply industry. *Internat. J. Oper. Prod. Management* 4(4), 48–56.
Rogers, D., R. Plante, R. Wong and J. Evans (1991). Aggregation and disaggregation techniques and methodology in optimization. *Oper. Res.* 39(4), 553–582.
Roundy, R., W. Maxwell, Y. Herer, S. Tayur and A. Getzler (1991). A price-directed approach to real-time scheduling of production operations. *IIE Trans.* 23(2), 149–160.
Salomon, M., L. Kroon, R. Kuik and L. Van Wassenhove (1991). Some extensions of the discrete lot sizing and scheduling problem. *Management Sci.* 37(7), 801–812.
Sasser, W. (1976). Match supply and demand in service industries. *Harv. Bus. Rev.* 54, 133–140.
Schmitt, T., W. Berry and T. Vollmann (1984). An analysis of capacity planning procedures for a material requirements planning systems. *Decision Sci.* 15, 522–541.
Schwarz, L.B., and R.E. Johnson (1978). An appraisal of the empirical performance of the linear decision rule for aggregate planning. *Management Sci.* 14(4), 844–848.
Sherali, H.D., K. Staschus, and J.M. Huacuz (1987). An integer programming approach and implementation for an electric utility capacity planning problem with renewable energy sources. *Management Sci.* 33(7), 831–847.
Silver, E. (1967). A tutorial on production smoothing and work force balancing. *Oper. Res.* 15(6), 985–1010.
Simon, H.A. (1956). Dynamic programming under uncertainty with a quadratic criterion function. *Econometrica* 24, 74–81.
Simon, H., and C. Holt (1954). The control of inventories and production rates: A survey. *Oper. Res.* 2, 289–301.
Sox, C.R., J.O. McClain and L.J. Thomas (1992). Jellybeans: Storing capacity to satisfy demands within a specified leadtime, Working Paper, JGSM, Cornell University.

Spence, A., and E. Porteus (1987). Setup reduction and increased effective capacity. *Management Sci.* 33(10), 1291–1301.
Sridharan, S., W. Berry and V. Udayabhanu (1988). Measuring master production schedule stability under rolling planning horizons. *Decision Sci.* 19(1), 147–166.
Sterman, J.D. (1989). Modeling managerial behavior: Misperceptions of feedback in a dynamic decision making experiment. *Management Sci.* 35(3), 321–339.
Tang, J.C.S., P. Adulbhan and T. Zubair (1981). Aggregate production planning for a heavy manufacturing industry. *European J. Oper. Res.* 7(1), 22–29.
Taubert, W.H. (1968). A search decision rule for the aggregate scheduling pattern. *Management Sci.* 14(6), B343–B359.
Thomas, L.J. (1971). Linear programming models for production-advertising decision. *Management Sci.* 17(8), B474–B484.
Thomas, L.J. (1993), Stockless and fast production: Review and research agenda, in: R. Sarin (ed.), *Perspectives in Operations Management: Essays in Honor of Elwood S. Buffa*, Kluwer, Hingham, MA.
Thomas, L.J., and E.N. Weiss (1986). Incorporating marketing and capacity planning and detailed production scheduling, in: B. Lev (ed.), *TIMS Studies in the Management Sciences: Production Management: Methods and Applications*, North Holland, Amsterdam, pp. 207–230.
Toczylowski, E., and K. Hindi (1991). Aggregate capacitated lot-size scheduling for a class of flexible machining and assembly systems. *IIE Trans.* 23, 259–266.
Trigeiro, W., L.J. Thomas and J.O. McClain (1989). Capacitated lot-sizing with setup times. *Management Sci.* 35(3), 353–366.
Van Wassenhove, L.N., and M.A. DeBodt (1983). Capacitated lot sizing for injection moulding: A case study. *J. Oper. Res. Soc.* 34(6), 489–501.
Vergin, R.C. (1980). On a new look at production switching heuristics for the aggregate planning problem. *Management Sci.* 26(11), 1185–1186.
Voelcker, H.B., A.A.G. Requicha and R.W. Conway (1988). Computer applications in manufacturing. *Ann. Rev. Comput. Sci.* 3, 349–388.
Vollmann, T.E., W.L. Berry and D.C. Whybark (1992). *Manufacturing Planning and Control Systems, 3rd edition*, Irwin, Homewood, IL.
Von Lanzenaur, C.H. (1970). Production and employment and scheduling in multistage production systems. *Naval. Res. Logist. Quart.* 17, 193–198.
Wagner, H.M., V.A. Vargas and N.N. Kathuria (1993). The accuracy of aggregate LP production planning models, in: R. Sarin (ed.), *Perspectives in Operations Management: Essays in Honor of Elwood S. Buffa*, Kluwer, Hingham, MA.
Wagner, H.M., and T.M. Whitin (1958). A dynamic version of the economic lot size model. *Management Sci.* 5, 89–96.
Welam, U.P. (1975). Multi-item production smoothing models with almost closed form solutions. *Management Sci.* 21(9), 1021–1028.
Welam, U.P. (1978). An HMMS type interactive model for aggregate planning. *Management Sci.* 24(5), 564–575.
West, K.D. (1986). A variance bounds test of the linear quadratic inventory model. *J. Political Econ.* 94(2), 374–401.
Wilson, B., T. Shaftel and R. Barefield (1991). A mathematical programming approach to production decisions in the emerging aquaculture industry. *Decision Sci.* 22(1), 194–205.
Zipkin, P. (1991). Computing optimal lot sizes in the economic lot scheduling problem, *Oper. Res.* 39(1), 56–63.

S.C. Graves et al., Eds., *Handbooks in OR & MS, Vol. 4*

Chapter 8

Mathematical Programming Models and Methods for Production Planning and Scheduling

*Jeremy F. Shapiro**

Sloan School of Management, Massachusetts Institute of Technology, Cambridge, MA, U.S.A.

1. Overview

Mathematical programming is a rich formalism from which powerful optimization models for production planning and scheduling can be constructed and solved. Imbedded in easy-to-use decision support systems, the models can provide production managers with the means to analyze their problems more globally, thereby increasing net revenues or reducing costs.

We have chosen to distinguish between production planning problems, which are tactical in nature, and scheduling problems, which are operational in nature. Models for production planning tend to employ aggregate data, seek to describe large segments of the production environment, and typically consider planning horizons of one month to one year. By contrast, models for production scheduling tend to employ detailed data, seek to describe smaller segments of the production environment, and consider planning horizons of a few hours to several days or a few weeks.

Recently, we have seen a renewed interest in applications of mathematical programming to production planning and scheduling. The interest is due in large part to recent advances in information technology which allow managers to acquire and organize production data on a timely basis. As a result, many managers are actively seeking decision support systems based on models to help them unravel the complex interactions and ripple effects inherent in these data.

A major concern throughout this chapter is to present models and solution methods that either have already been applied to actual production planning and scheduling problems, or which show reasonable promise for practical application in the near future. In this regard, we will attempt to convey how the art as well as the science of modeling building and algorithm construction

*This review was supported in part by a grant from the Leaders in Manufacturing program at MIT.

should be employed in specific problem solving situations. The formalism of mathematical programming is often only the point of departure for analyzing large scale problems. To it we add approximation, aggregation and heuristic methods designed to foster the computation of a 'good' or 'good enough' solution in an acceptable length of time.

A major objective when creating a mathematical programming model for production planning or scheduling is to develop effective approaches for coordinating or integrating a broad range of production activities. The result may be a large scale model that is difficult to assemble, optimize or interpret as a single, *monolithic* entity. Thus, an important focus of this chapter will be an exposition of mathematical programming decomposition methods that allow large scale models to be broken down into manageable sub-models, and then systematically reassembled. These methods show considerable promise for time critical scheduling applications, especially when the methods have been adapted for and implemented on parallel computers. In any event, beyond their demonstrated and potential practical importance, decomposition methods are extremely useful as pedagogical devices for explaining model construction and analysis.

The mathematical programming models we will consider fall into several categories: linear programming, network optimization, mixed integer programming, nonlinear programming, dynamic programming, multiple criteria optimization, and stochastic programming. The form of these models will be implicitly reviewed as we develop specific production planning and scheduling applications throughout the chapter. We assume the reader has some acquaintance with the field; for background, the reader is referred to Nemhauser, Rinnooy Kan & Todd [1989], Schrage [1986], Shapiro [1979a], and Williams [1985].

The plan of this chapter is as follows. In Section 2, we discuss models for lot-sizing and one-machine sequencing problems. These relatively simple models represent building blocks that we employ in later sections to construct larger, more comprehensive models. Lagrange multiplier and decomposition methods are presented in Section 3. These methods are used throughout the remainder of the chapter to analyze large-scale models.

The following three sections, Sections 4, 5, and 6, are devoted to mathematical programming models for three distinct types of production planning and scheduling problems: process manufacturing, discrete parts manufacturing, and job-shop scheduling. In practice, of course, one cannot always classify a production problem as fitting cleanly in one of these categories. At a paper mill, for example, the production of pulp and the operations of the paper machines can be viewed as process manufacturing activities, but conversion of the paper to meet the requirements of specific orders (sizes, coatings, etc.) resembles job-shop scheduling.

Space and time constraints prevent us from considering production planning and scheduling environments that are not adequately described by these three main model types. In particular, we will not cover models for flexible manufacturing systems and refer the reader to Buzacott & Yao [1986]; see also Stecke

[1983]. Nor will we cover the growing body of literature on the application of graph and network optimization techniques to the production of printed circuit boards (PCB) and very large-scale integrated (VSLI) chips; see, for example, Feo & Hochbaum [1986] and Ball & Magazine [1988].

Section 7 contains a brief discussion of stochastic programming extensions to the deterministic models of earlier sections. In Section 8, we discuss the important role that mathematical programming models can play in coordinating manufacturing with other company activities. The chapter concludes with a section devoted to future directions for mathematical programming applications to production planning and scheduling.

Our reference citations are intended to be representative rather than encyclopedic. This is a necessity rather than a convenience since the number of articles and books on the subject published over the past 30 years is enormous. Preference in most instances is given to recently published articles. Interested readers can easily develop their own reference lists by working backward from these recent papers.

2. Simple models

We characterize simple models for production planning and scheduling as those with the property that they can be optimized by a computer in at most a few seconds, for the majority of practical applications. Moreover, the problems addressed by simple models are primitive or elementary ones that reflect only myopic planning concerns. Two examples that we discuss below are: a dynamic programming model for production planning of a single item; and, a traveling salesman problem formulation of one machine scheduling problems.

The class of simple models includes those that can be optimized by polynomially bounded list processing algorithms. The class also includes some models, such as those for the traveling salesman problem, from the class of combinatorial models called NP-complete for which polynomially bounded algorithms do not, in all likelihood, exist [see Papadimitrou & Stieglitz, 1982]. However, for the vast majority of practical applications, optimization of traveling salesman problems, knapsack problems and several other NP-complete problems, can be carried out very quickly, at least to a good approximation. Of course, other NP-complete models, such as the general zero–one programming model, can often be relatively difficult to optimize, and we will not consider them in the category of simple models.

From another perspective, the simple models we discuss here will serve mainly as elements in large-scale model synthesis. This is their primary importance. Conversely, a practitioner would be hard pressed to utilize these simple models on a stand alone basis to support production decision making. This is because, for example, production and inventory decisions about an individual product are difficult to isolate from those for other products, or, decisions about scheduling an individual machine are difficult to isolate from those for other machines that can process some or all of the same product.

2.1. *Single item dynamic lot-size models*

A classic production problem is to determine an optimal balance between set-up costs and inventory carrying costs. On the one hand, a production manager prefers long production runs to spread out set-up costs. On the other hand, he/she would like to make frequent, smaller runs that match demand, thereby reducing inventory carrying costs to a minimum. The problem is complicated by demands and production costs that vary from period to period. The basic dynamic lot-size model [Wagner & Whitin, 1958] formally optimizes these conflicting decisions for individual production items. This model is also discussed by Baker in his chapter in this volume on Requirements Planning.

Parameters
f = set-up cost (\$),
c_t = variable production cost (\$/unit),
h = inventory carrying cost (\$/unit/period),
r_t = demand in period t (units),
M_t = upper bound on production in period t (units).

Decision variables
y_t = inventory at the end of period t,
x_t = production during period t,

$$\delta_t = \begin{cases} 1 & \text{if production occurs during period } t, \\ 0 & \text{otherwise.} \end{cases}$$

Dynamic lot-size model

$$v = \min \sum_{t=1}^{T} \{f\delta_t + c_t x_t + h y_t\} \tag{2.1}$$

subject to

$$y_t = y_{t-1} + x_t - r_t \quad \text{for } t = 1, \ldots, T\,, \tag{2.2}$$

$$x_t - M_t \delta_t \leq 0 \quad \text{for } t = 1, \ldots, T\,, \tag{2.3}$$

$$y_0 \text{ given}\,, \tag{2.4}$$

$$y_t \geq 0\,, \quad x_t \geq 0\,, \quad \delta_t = 0 \text{ or } 1\,. \tag{2.5}$$

This is a very simple mixed integer programming model. The objective function (2.1) is the sum of set-up, variable production, and inventory holding costs over the T period planning horizon. The Equations (2.2) state that inventory at the end of period t equals inventory at the beginning of period t (ending inventory of period $t-1$) plus product in period t minus demand in period t. The constraints (2.3) relate production x_t in period t to setting-up in that period. The quantity M_t may be either a physical limitation on production in period t, or simply a very large number representing a bound above which it would be non-optimal to produce (for example, $M_t = \Sigma_{s=t}^{T} r_t$).

As we shall see, the dynamic lot-size model can be represented as a dynamic programming problem, and as a network optimization problem, as well as a mixed integer programming model. Our purposes in presenting multiple representations is to review the different modeling and optimization methods, and to reveal, at least by example, the manner in which one representation can be transformed into another.

As stated, demand in each period must be satisfied by some combination of starting inventory and production since ending inventory y_t is constrained to be non-negative, i.e., no backlogging is required. The model could easily be extended to allow backlogging by substituting

$$y_t = y_t^+ - y_t^-$$

with $y_t^+ \geqslant 0$, $y_t^- \geqslant 0$. The unit holding cost h is then associated with y_t^+ and a unit backlogging penalty cost, say p, with y_t^-.

Another simple model enhancement that is sometimes worthwhile is to constrain final inventory y_T to lie in some set. Otherwise, the optimization model will tend to run inventories to zero at the end of the planning horizon, even though production and sale of the item will continue for the foreseeable future. Alternatively, the term $-gy_T$ could be added to the objective function where $g > 0$ is a reward per unit (negative unit cost) for terminal inventories.

A more extensive enhancement is to consider part or all of demand r_t to be tied to specific orders with specific due dates. We consider the following example. Suppose demand consists entirely of orders of size w_t for $k = 1, \ldots, K$, where each order has a target completion (shipping) date t_k. Suppose further that every order must be complete before it is shipped. Finally, suppose an order is allowed to be completed one or two periods after the due date t_k, with penalties p_{k1} and p_{k2}, respectively.

We extend the formulation (2.1)–(2.5) to include the situation just described. Let $K_t = \{k \mid t_k = t\}$. Let β_{k_0}, B_{k_1}, β_{k_2} denote zero–one variables that take on values of one only if order k is completed in periods t_k, $t_k + 1$, $t_k + 2$, respectively. With this new notation and variables, we change Equations (2.2) to

$$y_t = y_{t-1} + x_t - \sum_{k \in K_t} w_k \beta_{k_0} - \sum_{k \in K_{t-1}} w_k \beta_{k_1} - \sum_{k \in K_{t-2}} w_k \beta_{k_2} \,. \tag{2.6}$$

In addition, for each order k, we add the multiple choice constraint

$$\beta_{k_0} + \beta_{k_1} + \beta_{k_2} = 1 . \tag{2.7}$$

Lastly, we add to the objective function the penalty term

$$\sum_{k=1}^{K} p_{k1}\beta_{k_1} + p_{k2}\beta_{k_2} . \tag{2.8}$$

In discussing the last enhancement to the dynamic lot-size model, we were somewhat cavalier about assigning penalty values for late orders. Unless such penalties are actually contractual dollar amounts, the situation being modeled is an example of a multiple criteria optimization problem; namely, how to balance avoidable costs against customer service. The penalty approach we outlined is one of many developed by specialists in multiple criteria methods [see Steuer, 1986].

An alternative formulation of this problem would be to set goals for customer service. For example, suppose, instead of penalties, that management set a policy that at least 90% of the orders must be completed by their due dates; and that no more than 2% of the orders may be shipped two periods after the due date. This policy would be modeled by the constraints

$$\sum_{k=1}^{K} \beta_{k_0} \geq (0.90)K ,$$

$$\sum_{k=1}^{K} (\beta_{k_0} + \beta_{k_1}) \geq (0.98)K .$$

The single item dynamic lot-size model (2.1)–(2.5) can be reformulated and optimized as a dynamic programming model. Let $G^t(y)$ = minimal cost of meeting demands in periods $t, t+1, \ldots, T$ when inventory at the beginning of period t is y.

We let Y^t denote the set of beginning inventory states that we need to consider for period t. For example, we might let

$$Y^t = \left\{ y: 0 \leq y \leq \sum_{s=t}^{T} r_s + \bar{y}_T \right\} ,$$

where $\bar{y}_T$ is an upper bound on inventory at the end of the planning horizon.

The G^t functions satisfy the following recursive relationship for all $y \in Y^t$:

$$G^t(y) = \min\{ f\delta_t + c_t x_t + h(y + x_t - r_t) + G^{t+1}(y + x_t - r_t)\} \tag{2.9}$$

$$\begin{aligned} \text{subject to} \quad & x_t \geq \max\{0, r_t - y\} , \\ & x_t - M_t\delta_t \leq 0 , \\ & x_t \geq 0 , \quad \delta_t = 0 \text{ or } 1 , \end{aligned}$$

where $G^{T+1}(y)$ is given for all y.

The recursion (2.9) is solved by backward iteration starting with $t = T$ and continuing until $G^1(y_0)$ has been computed. Since the state space in each period is continuous, some finite discretization is in general required to perform these computations. The result, as we shall shortly see, is a representation of the model and optimization algorithm as the problem of finding a shortest route in a network.

First, we discuss a special property of the dynamic lot-size model. Using an induction argument, one can show that the functions $G^t(\cdot)$ are concave. This property can be used to prove the following result due to Wagner & Whitin [1958]; see also Wagner [1969].

Dynamic lot-size theorem. *If initial inventory $y_0 = 0$, and the M_t are nonbinding upper bounds on production in each period, an optimal solution to the dynamic lot-size model can be characterized by the condition*

$$x_t y_{t-1} = 0 \quad \text{for } t = 1, \ldots, T .$$

This result implies further that an optimal production strategy must satisfy $x_t > 0$ only when $y_{t-1} = 0$ in which case x_t equals one of the quantities

$$r_t, r_t + r_{t+1}, \ldots, \sum_{s=t}^{T} r_s .$$

Unfortunately, the condition that starting inventory equals zero (or $\Sigma_{t=1}^{s} r_t$ for any s) is not realistic in the sense that if we were considering a real-life inventory system, we would in all likelihood find y_0 to be some random amount at the start of a planning horizon. Adjusting to the initial transient caused by positive inventory may require several periods.

We return now to consider in more detail how one computes optimal solutions with the recursion (2.6). According to the dynamic lot-size theorem, when initial inventory is zero, we can solve the dynamic lot-size model by a simple dynamic programming model that considers producing in lot amounts equal to demand of the next k periods for appropriate values of k. Since the simplifying assumption may not hold, and also for the purposes of exposition, we ignore the consequences of the theorem in illustrating the dynamic programming approach.

Example 2.1. Consider a five period problem with demands $r_1 = 695$, $r_2 = 177$, $r_3 = 511$, $r_4 = 425$, $r_5 = 468$. Suppose that the set-up cost is \$800, and that the unit holding cost is \$1. We assume for simplicity that the variable production cost is constant over time and therefore can be ignored (the total variable cost of production is a fixed amount). The complexity of a dynamic programming formulation of this problem is directly proportional to the scale used in describing demand. Thus, it is often desirable and necessary to re-scale the data. In general, computational schemes of dynamic programming rely on formalized methods for aggregation and approximation of the data [Larson,

1982]. For our example, we choose the basic unit of inventory and demand to be 100 units and dollars to be \$100. This gives us the following demands (rounding off to the nearest 100) $r_1 = 7$, $r_2 = 2$, $r_3 = 5$, $r_4 = 4$, $r_5 = 5$. The set-up cost is 8, and the inventory holding cost is 1. We consider two cases: starting inventory = 0 and starting inventory = 3.

Figure 2.1 depicts this problem as a shortest route problem in a network where the nodes correspond to starting inventory states in each period and the arcs correspond to feasible state transitions. For exponential convenience, not all nodes and arcs that should be considered are actually shown in the figure. The arc 'lengths' are the immediate costs. Consider, for example, the choice of an optimal immediate decision at the start of period 3 when starting inventory equals 2 units. The numbers beneath the nodes at the end of period 3 are the $G_4(y)$ values previously computed by backward iteration. The decision choices are to set-up and make any number of units between 3 and 12, with associated transitions to ending inventory states ranging from 0 to 9. The length of the arc from this node to node 3 is 11 corresponding to a set-up cost (8) plus an inventory holding cost (3) on three units of ending inventory. Comparing the 10 decision options, the optimal immediate decision from the indicated state is to set-up and manufacture 7 units, thereby making the transition to $2 + 7 - 5 = 4$ units of ending inventory.

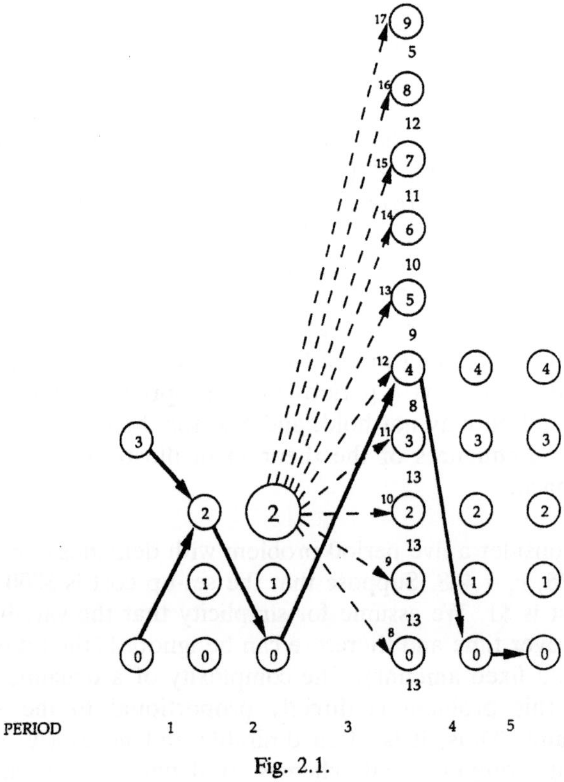

Fig. 2.1.

The solid dark arcs represent shortest routes from the two possible initial inventory states. The implied optimal production strategy when starting inventory is 3 units, for example, is: $x_1 = 6$, $x_2 = 0$, $x_3 = 9$, $x_4 = 0$, $x_5 = 5$. Note that the optimal routes for both cases follow the pattern predicted by the dynamic lot-size theorem; namely, produce only when inventory falls to zero.

The dynamic lot-size model has been studied and generalized by several authors. Zangwill [1966, 1969] extended the dynamic lot-size theorem to include the case of backlogging. Crowston, Wagner & Williams [1973] extended the model and the analysis to a multi-stage and multi-product assembly system in which each product may have many predecessors, but only one successor (multi-item assembly systems are discussed again in Section 5.2). Over an infinite planning horizon, and under mathematical assumptions similar to those made for the dynamic lot-size model and theorem, they prove that the optimal lot size at each stage is an integer multiple of the lot size at the successor stage. Karmarkar, Kekre & Kekre [1987] generalized the model to allow long production runs for a given item that last more than one period. In such an event, only one set-up need be charged for production of that item. Lee & Zipkin [1989] generalized the model to incorporate make-or-buy decisions in each period.

Love [1972] gave a dynamic programming approach and algorithm for the multi-stage serial manufacturing system in which each product may have exactly one predecessor and one successor. Crowston & Wagner [1973] gave a similar but more general dynamic programming approach and algorithm for finite horizon, multi-stage assembly planning.

2.2. *The time dependent traveling salesman problem and one machine sequencing*

The traveling salesman problem (TSP) is a classical and well studied combinatorial optimization problem. Simply stated, the TSP is concerned with finding a tour of a set of cities such that every city is visited exactly once and the total distance traveled is minimal. The TSP admits several distinct zero–one integer programming formulations [see Lawler, Lenstra, Rinnooy Kan & Shmoys 1985]. Its relevance here is to optimizing the sequence of several jobs processed on a single machine. In Section 6, we discuss job shop scheduling problems that correspond roughly to multiple TSP models, one for each machine, with linking precedence constraints.

For our purposes, the TSP formulation that we prefer is one consisting of a shortest route problem with additional constraints requiring each node (city) to be visited exactly once. We discuss this formulation and then show how it can be adapted to one machine scheduling.

Consider a network with nodes $0, 1, 2, \ldots, N$, directed arcs (i, j) for all i and $j \neq i$, and associated arc lengths c_{ij}. Node 0 corresponds to the starting city. For technical purposes, we define a new node with the label $N + 1$ which is located identically with node 0 but corresponds to terminating there. Thus, the arc costs $c_{i,N+1} = c_{i0}$ for all i. As shown in Figure 2.2, we consider N replications of the nodes $1, 2, \ldots, N$ each replication indexed by t. The TSP can be expressed as the problem of sending one unit of flow from node 0 to node $N+1$ so that the distance traveled is minimized (this is a shortest route problem), but with the additional constraints that each node type i must be visited exactly once.

Consider now the problem of sequencing $N+1$ jobs on a single machine [Picard & Queyranne, 1978]. For $i = 0, 1, 2, \ldots, N$, we associate with job i: an integer processing time p_i, an integer due date d_i, an integer changeover time h_{ij}, and a tardiness cost $c_i(t)$ for completing the job by time t. We assume the machine is currently (that is, at time $t = 0$) set-up for job 0. Two examples of $c_i(t)$ are

$$\text{(a)} \quad c_i(t) = \begin{cases} 0 & \text{if } t \leq d_i , \\ \alpha_i & \text{if } t > d_i , \end{cases}$$

$$\text{(b)} \quad c_i(t) = \alpha_i \max\{0, t - d_i\} + \beta_i \max\{0, d_i - t\} .$$

Note that the tardiness function (b) includes the possibility of penalizing

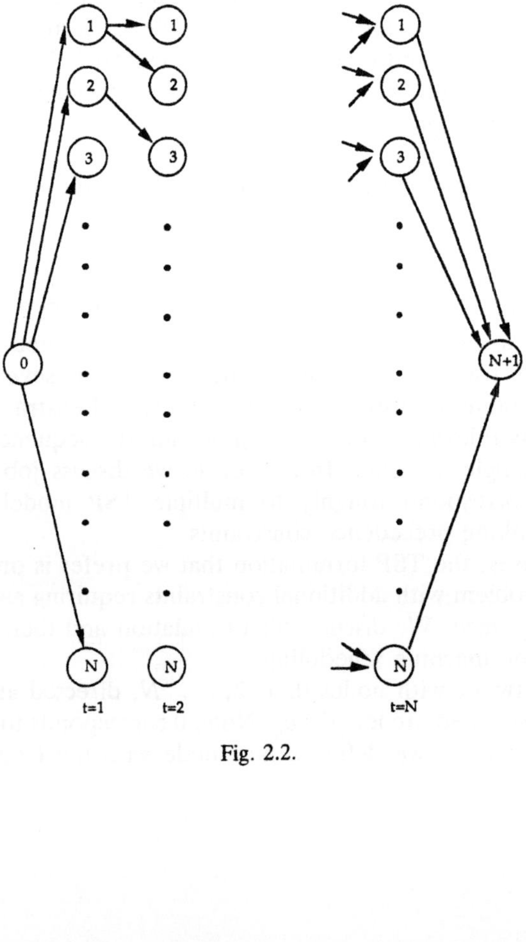

Fig. 2.2.

($\beta_i > 0$) or rewarding ($\beta_i < 0$) early completion of job i. Also associated with each job i and all other jobs j are changeover costs f_{ij}. The problem is to sequence the N jobs so as to minimize the sum of changeover and tardiness costs.

We modify the TSP formulation as follows. Node type i corresponds to job i with node 0 corresponding to the current configuration of the machine. Let T denote an upper bound on the time to complete all jobs, and replicate T times the nodes type 1 through N. For future reference, let T^* denote a lower bound on the completion of all jobs. Finally, let node $N+1$ correspond to completion of all jobs.

The model contains several types of arcs. Node 0 is connected to nodes j for all $j \neq 0$ at time $p_0 + h_{0j}$ by arcs of length $c_{0j0} = f_{0j} + c_0(p_0)$. Each node j at each time t ($t \geq p_0 + h_{0j}$) is connected to node k for all $k \neq j$ at time $t + p_j + h_{jk}$ by an arc with length $c_{jkt} = f_{jk} + c_j(t + p_j)$. In addition, each node i at time t is connected by an arc to node i at time $t+1$ with arc length $c_{iit} = 0$; these arcs are needed in those cases when it is necessary or advantageous to delay processing certain jobs. Finally, each node i at each time t for $t \geq T^*$ is connected to node $N+1$ by an arc with zero length. We assume for simplicity that we do not constrain the terminal configuration of the machine.

Example 2.2. We illustrate the construction with a numerical example given by the data in Tables 2.1, 2.2, and 2.3. The machine is initially set up to perform job 0. Without loss of optimality, we assume that job 0 is performed first and therefore the changeover times and costs from other jobs to job 0 can be ignored.

Table 2.1
One machine sequencing problem

i	Processing time p_i	Due date d_i	Late penalty α_i	Early reward β_i
0	2	2	10	0
1	3	10	6	0
2	1	9	12	−1
3	2	8	8	−2

Table 2.2
One machine sequencing problem changeover times (h_{ij})

From i	To j: 0	1	2	3
0	–	1	1	0
1	–	–	0	2
2	–	1	–	1
3	–	1	2	–

Table 2.3
One machine sequencing problem changeover costs (f_{ij})

From i	To j: 0	1	2	3
0	–	4	3	3
1	–	–	1	5
2	–	2	–	3
3	–	2	6	–

A network representation of the problem is given in Figure 2.3. Note that not all nodes over the planning horizon $T = 13$ are included. Certain machine configurations at certain points in time cannot be achieved (spanned) by feasible sequences of jobs. Moving from left to right, each path to a node i at time t is extended to nodes j $(j \neq i)$ at time $t + p_i + h_{ij}$ with an arc length $c_i(t + p_i) + f_{ij}$. Taking $t = 8$ as the earliest possible completion time for all jobs, we connect all spanned nodes from then on to node 4 (all jobs completed) with a cost of zero.

An algebraic statement of the zero–one integer program for optimizing the problem of Figure 2.3 is the following. We let *Xijt* correspond to the arc beginning at node i at the time $t - p_i - h_{ij}$ and ending at node j at time t. We let *Yi4t* correspond to the arc beginning at node i at time t and ending at node 4. All variables are constrained to take on values of zero or one. The model is

$$\begin{aligned}\min\ & 3\,X032 + 4\,X013 + 3\,X023 - 3\,X215 - 6\,X315 - 2\,X235 + X126 \\ & - 2\,X326 + X128 + 5\,X138 + X238 + 4\,X329 + 2\,X2110 \\ & + 5\,X1310 + 3\,X2310 + 14\,X2111 + 18\,X3111 \\ & + 7\,X1211 + 15\,X2311 + 22\,X3212 + 19\,X1213 + 38\,X2113 \\ & + 11\,X1313 + 39\,X2313\end{aligned}$$

subject to

(1) $X032 + X013 + X023 = 1,$

(2) $-X032 + X315 + X326 = 0,$

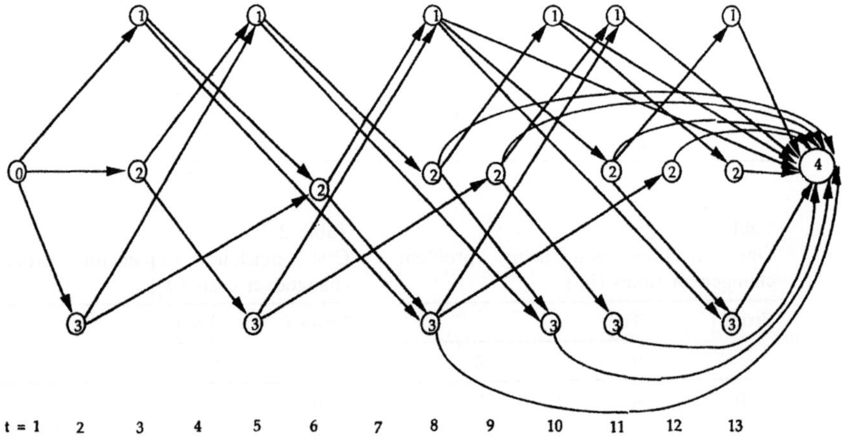

Fig. 2.3.

$$
\begin{aligned}
&(3)\quad -X013 + X126 + X138 = 0,\\
&(4)\quad -X023 + X235 + X215 = 0,\\
&(5)\quad -X215 - X315 + X128 + X1310 = 0,\\
&(6)\quad -X235 + X329 + X318 = 0,\\
&(7)\quad -X126 - X326 + X238 + X218 = 0,\\
&(8)\quad -X1211 + X1313 - X318 - X218 + Y148 = 0,\\
&(9)\quad -X128 + X2110 + X2310 + Y248 = 0,\\
&(10)\quad -X138 - X238 + X3212 + X311 + Y348 = 0,\\
&(11)\quad -X329 + X2111 + X2311 + Y249 = 0,\\
&(12)\quad -X2110 + X1213 + Y1410 = 0,\\
&(13)\quad -X1310 - X2310 + Y3410 = 0,\\
&(14)\quad -X2111 - X3111 + Y1411 = 0,\\
&(15)\quad -X1211 + X2113 + X2313 + Y2411 = 0,\\
&(16)\quad -X2311 + Y3411 = 0,\\
&(17)\quad -X3212 + Y2412 = 0,\\
&(18)\quad -X2113 + Y1413 = 0,\\
&(19)\quad -X1213 + Y2413 = 0,\\
&(20)\quad -X1313 - X2313 + Y3413 = 0,\\
&(21)\quad Y148 + Y248 + Y348 + Y249 + Y1410 + Y3410 + X1411\\
&\qquad + Y2411 + Y3411 + Y2412 + Y1413 + Y2413 + Y3413 = 1,\\
&(22)\quad X013 + X215 + X315 + X2110 + X2113 + X218 + X217\\
&\qquad + X317 + X3110 = 1,\\
&(23)\quad X023 + X126 + X326 + X128 + X329 + X1211 + X3212\\
&\qquad + X1213 = 1,\\
&(24)\quad X032 + X235 + X138 + X238 + X1310 + X2310 + X2311\\
&\qquad + X1313 + X2313 = 1.
\end{aligned}
$$

The constraints (1) through (21) in this model describe a shortest route problem; namely, one unit of flow leaves node 0 and arrives at node 4 with conservation of flow at every intermediate node. The constraints (22)–(24) are degree constraints imposing the condition that each node type i, for $i = 1, 2, 3$, must be visited exactly once by the shortest route path. The optimal solution corresponds to performing the jobs in the sequence 0, 3, 1, 2, with a total cost of -2.

From this example, the reader may have the impression that the zero–one integer programming model for optimizing the machine sequencing problem is quite complex. As we have just noted, however, it is mainly a shortest route model with side constraints. Now, shortest route models have special structure that allows them to be solved very efficiently by polynomially bounded algorithms without requiring solution of a zero–one integer program [see Ahuja, Magnanti & Orlin, 1989]. Thus, if we were able to treat the degree constraints in an indirect manner and optimize only the shortest route model, the machine sequencing problem would be easy to optimize. Rigorous methods for accomplishing this are the topic of the next section.

3. Lagrange multiplier and decomposition methods

In this section, we review Lagrange multiplier and associated price-directed decomposition methods; see Geoffrion [1974], Shapiro [1979a,b], or Fisher [1981] for more details. These methods will be applied to several large scale production planning and scheduling models in the sections that follow. Since the material in this section is concerned primarily with mathematical analysis, the reader who is more interested in model building may wish to skim it.

Resource-directed decomposition, also known as Benders' decomposition, is another relevant and important method, especially for mixed integer programming models. Unfortunately, space limitations prevent us from reviewing this method; the reader is referred to Shapiro [1979a] or Nemhauser & Wolsey [1988].

Decomposition methods for large-scale mathematical programming models, and for complex models with special structures that can be algorithmically exploited, were thoroughly studied during the period 1960–1975. A few applications have been successfully implemented. But, despite their attractive features, practitioners have shown little interest in the methods. Nevertheless, for reasons we are about to explain, the methods are worth examining here in detail.

A primary reason for the lack of applications is that decomposition methods can be inefficient on serial computers when compared with a monolithic (nondecomposition) approach. The imminent availability of commercial parallel computers should greatly renew interest in decomposition methods because the methods can exploit parallel architectures by distributing sub-models to separate processors. The methods allow solutions from these sub-models to be re-assembled in a rigorous manner to find a globally optimal solution. The combination of decomposition methods and parallel computers is particularly alluring for time critical decision support applications such as production scheduling. An important added feature of decomposition methods for these applications is that they provide objective function bounds on how far the best known solution is from optimality.

A second reason for the lack of applications is that decomposition methods need to be tailored to a particular application. This means first that greater effort is required to implement the software than that required by a monolithic method. Moreover, since decomposition methods perform best when provided with good starting information, the user must involve himself/herself more heavily in initialization procedures. Similarly, automatic re-start procedures should be implemented so that those sub-models that have changed since the most recent optimization can be given the greatest attention. Tailoring is also required to fully exploit the sub-model approximations and associated bounds provided by a decomposition approach. In short, the successful implementation and use of a decomposition method may require more work than a monolithic method, but it offers the potential for more flexible and efficient computation, particularly on a parallel computer.

In addition to the potential afforded by parallel computers, decomposition methods are excellent pedagogical tools for presenting and examining production planning and scheduling models, particularly in describing how the models can be constructed as syntheses of smaller sub-models. The methods mechanize concepts of economic equilibria by providing a rigorous means for computing them, thereby providing us with insights into the supply and demand forces that abound in many production environments.

3.1. *Theory*

We begin our mathematical development by considering the mathematical program

$$\text{(P)} \quad v = \min cx$$
$$\text{subject to} \quad Ax \geqslant b\,,$$
$$x \in X\,,$$

which we refer to as the primal problem. The constraints in (P) have been partitioned into the easy to solve implicit constraints $x \in X$, and the more difficult to solve, or complicating, constraints $Ax \geqslant b$. The matrix A is $m \times n$. For the vast majority of cases of interest to us here, the set X is finite and can be enumerated as $\{x^t \mid t = 1, \ldots, T\}$. For example, X might consist of the finite set of zero–one solutions of an integer program, or the finite set of extreme points of a linear programming model. For the machine sequencing model given in the previous section, X corresponds to the set of shortest route equations [constraints (1) through (21)], whereas $Ax \geqslant b$ corresponds to the degree constraints (22)–(24).

An alternate form of (P) that we will sometimes employ is

$$\text{(P}'\text{)} \quad v = \min c_1x_1 + c_2x_2$$
$$\text{subject to} \quad A_{01}x_1 + X_{02}x_2 \geqslant b_0\,,$$
$$x_1 \in X_1\,, \quad x_2 \in X_2\,,$$

where

$$X_1 = \{x_1 \mid A_{11}x_1 \geqslant b_1, x_1 \geqslant 0\}\,, \qquad X_2 = \{x_2 \mid A_{22}x_2 \geqslant b_2, x_2 \geqslant 0\}\,.$$

The model (P′) is no more than a structured linear program. Note that it would decompose into two separate models if it were not for the linking constraints $A_{01}x_1 + A_{02}x_2 \geqslant b_0$.

Returning to model (P), we attempt to eliminate the complicating constraints by pricing them out, or dualizing them, and placing them in the objective function. The result is the *Lagrangean function* defined for any

m-vector $u \geq 0$,

$$L(u) = ub + \min(c - uA)x$$
$$\text{subject to} \quad x \in X .$$

Optimization of the Lagrangean produces the solution $x(u) \in X$. A central question is: when is $x(u)$ optimal in (P)?

The answer to this question is related to the following conditions. We say $x \in X$, $u \geq 0$ satisfy the *global optimality conditions* for (P) if

(i) $L(u) = ub + (c - uA)x$,
(ii) $u(Ax - b) = 0$,
(iii) $Ax \geq b$.

The global optimality conditions are sufficient conditions for optimality as demonstrated by the following theorem that we state without proof.

Theorem 1. *If $x \in X$, $u \geq 0$ satisfy the global optimality conditions, then x is optimal in* (P).

The global optimality conditions are not necessary in the following sense. For a given x optimal in (P), there may be no $u \geq 0$ such that the global optimality conditions hold. This is frequently the case when X is a discrete or otherwise nonconvex set. It is easy to demonstrate, however, that $L(u) \leq v$ regardless of the structure of X.

A second important question is: how should we choose u? The answer is to search for the best lower bound; namely to solve

$$\text{(D)} \quad d = \max L(u)$$
$$\text{subject to} \quad u \geq 0 .$$

We call this the *dual problem*. L is a concave function of u and therefore (D) is a well behaved mathematical program. Clearly, $d \leq v$; if $d < v$, we say there is a *duality gap*.

The following theorem tells us that we need to consider only optimal solutions to (D) in attempting to solve (P) via the global optimality conditions.

Theorem 2. *If $x \in X$, $u \geq 0$ satisfy the global optimality conditions, then u is optimal in* (D). *Moreover, $d = L(u) = v$; that is, there is no duality gap.*

To summarize, a goal of Lagrangean analysis is to compute some $u \geq 0$ that is optimal in (D), and then seek an $x \in X$ such that the global optimality conditions hold at that optimal u. If X is not convex, which is the case with integer programming and combinatorial models, this goal may not be met for any optimal u and any $x \in X$. These are the primal models for which there is a duality gap. Geoffrion [1974] discusses properties of integer programming models and duality gaps associated with Lagrangian analysis.

In general, complex integer programming models will often have duality gaps, but the Lagrangean constructions can be useful even when they arise. First, the bounds from the Lagrangean can be employed in a branch and bound scheme for optimizing (P); see Shapiro [1979a,b]. Second, the Lagrangean analysis may produce a feasible solution $x \in X$ to (P) (conditions (i) and (iii) hold), but the complementary slackness condition (ii) may fail to hold. In such an event, the quantity $u(Ax - b) > 0$ is an upper bound on the duality gap. If it is sufficiently small, the search for an optimal solution to (P) can be abandoned.

Imbedded in a branch and bound scheme, the Lagrangean analysis just described is complementary to heuristic methods for mixed integer programming and other combinatorial optimization models. Optimizing the Lagrangean will only rarely produce a feasible or provably optimal solution to (P). By contrast, problem specific heuristics applied to each sub-model in a branch and bound search are intended to yield good feasible solutions to (P). If v^* is the cost of the best known solution found by the heuristic, the quantity $v^* - L(u^*)$ is a bound on the objective function error if we decide to terminate with this solution, where u^* is the computed dual solution that produces the greatest known dual lower bound. A heuristic may even employ information from the Lagrangean; for example, the heuristic may be based in part on the relative importance of the variables x_j as measured by the reduced cost values $c_j - ua_j$ where u is a 'good' dual solution. Heuristics and Lagrangean analyses have been employed in this manner by Christofides, Alvarez-Valdes & Tamarit [1987] for a job-shop scheduling model, and by Aftentakis & Gavish [1986] for a discrete parts manufacturing model.

Moreover, if branch and bound continues, the *surrogate constraint*

$$(c - u^*A)x \leq v^* - u^*b$$

added to (P) will serve to limit the search for a better solution [e.g., see Karwan & Rardin, 1979].

Example 3.1. We illustrate the Lagrangean decomposition technique by applying it to the following production planning problem. Customers indexed by j have demand d_j for a single product which may be supplied by any of a number of factories. Factory i has capacity M_i to make the product. If factory i is selected to make any of the product, a fixed cost $f_i > 0$ is incurred. In addition, the variable cost per unit of manufacturing the product at factory i and then transporting it to customer j is $c_{ij} > 0$. The objective is to select a set of factories with sufficient capacity to meet total demand so as to minimize the sum of fixed and variable costs.

A mathematical statement of the production location model is

$$v = \min \sum_i \sum_j c_{ij} x_{ij} + \sum_i f_i y_i \tag{3.1}$$

$$\text{subject to} \quad \sum_i x_{ij} \geq d_j \quad \text{for all } j , \tag{3.2}$$

$$\sum_j x_{ij} - M_i y_i \leq 0 \quad \text{for all } i , \tag{3.3}$$

$$x_{ij} \geq 0 , \quad y_i = 0 \text{ or } 1 . \tag{3.4}$$

We dualize this mixed integer program by pricing out the constraints (3.2) and placing them in the objective function. The resulting Lagrangean is

$$L(u) = \sum_j u_j d_j + \min \sum_i \sum_j (c_{ij} - u_j) x_{ij} + \sum_i f_i y_i$$

$$\text{subject to} \quad x_{ij},\ y_i \text{ satisfy (3.3), (3.4)} . \tag{3.5}$$

Further inspection of this computation reveals that

$$L(u) = \sum_j u_j d_j + \sum_i L_i(u) ,$$

where

$$L_i(u) = \min \sum_j (c_{ij} - u_i) x_{ij} + f_i y_i$$

$$\text{subject to} \quad \sum_i x_{ij} - M_i y_i \leq 0 , \tag{3.6}$$

$$x_{ij} \geq 0 , \quad y_i \geq 0 .$$

Still further inspection reveals that each $L_i(u)$ can be computed by a simple analysis. In words, (3.6) is the problem of deciding whether or not to use factory i to make any product, when the 'net revenue' per unit of product produced there for customer j is $-(c_{ij} - u_j)$. From the perspective of factory i, its favored customer is customer j_i such that its unit net revenue Δ_i is greatest; namely

$$\Delta_i = -(c_{ij_i} + u_{j_i}) = \max_j - (c_{ij} - u_j) . \tag{3.7}$$

Clearly, if $\Delta_i \leq 0$, there is no incentive for factory i to make the product. Even if $\Delta_i > 0$, the factory has an incentive only if $\Delta_i M_i$, the total variable net revenue that can be achieved by devoting the facility's entire capacity M_i to the product, exceeds the fixed cost f_i.

In summary, we solve (3.6) by the rule:

If $\Delta_i M_i > f_i$, set $y_i = 1$, $x_{ij_i} = M_i$ and $x_{ij} = 0$, for $j \neq j_i$ where j_i is the index optimal in (3.7). In this case $L_i(u) = \Delta_i M_i - f_i$.

If $\Delta_i M_i \leq f_i$, set $y_i = 0$, $x_{ij} = 0$ for all j. If this case, $L_i(u) = 0$.

To further illustrate the technique, we consider the numerical problem in Table 3.1 involving 2 customers and 8 potential factories for manufacturing and distributing the product to the customers. Suppose the demand of customer 1 is for 31 units and the demand of customer 2 is for 28 units.

We demonstrate that the dual solution $u_1 = 60$, $u_2 = 50$ leads to an optimal solution to the model (3.1)–(3.4) with this data via optimization of the Lagrangean. Later on in this section we discuss how the dual variables can be computed to try to achieve this result. The computations are displayed in Table 3.2. For example, for plant 2, $\Delta_2 = u_1 - c_{21} = 15$ from (3.7). Since $M_2 \Delta_2 = 17 * 15 = 255 > 45 = f_2$, we produce the product there. The company receives a net revenue of 210 from customer $j_2 = 1$ for each unit produced, and the entire capacity of plant 2 is utilized in producing 17 units which are shipped to customer 1. The solution given in Table 3.2 is optimal in the model (3.1)–(3.4)

Table 3.1
Production planning example

i	c_{ij}		M_i	f_i
	$j = 1$	$j = 2$		
1	21	73	14	40
2	45	41	17	45
3	86	50	8	27
4	105	35	6	20
5	110	54	12	39
6	42	22	9	30
7	38	26	13	42
8	63	65	15	46

Table 3.2
Calculation of Lagrangean function production planning example

i	Δ_i	j_i	$M_i \Delta_i$	f_i	y_i	X_{i1}	X_{i2}
1	39	1	546	40	1	14	0
2	15	1	255	45	1	17	0
3	0	2	0	8	0	0	0
4	15	2	90	20	1	0	6
5	−4	2	−48	39	0	0	0
6	28	2	252	30	1	0	9
7	24	1	312	42	1	0	13
8	−3	1	−45	46	0	0	0
			Total satisfied demand			31	28

with this data by appealing to the global optimality conditions; namely conditions (2) and (3) of the conditions hold for $u_1 = 60$, $u_2 = 50$ and the primal solution computed by optimizing the Lagrangean. The cost of this solution is 1982.

3.2. Algorithms

We consider briefly two algorithmic methods for optimizing the dual problem (D). The first is an ascent method called *subgradient optimization*. Suppose L has been evaluated at $u \geqslant 0$. Let $x \in X$ satisfy

$$L(u) = ub + (c - uA)x$$
$$= cx + u(b - Ax)\,.$$

Define $\tau = b - Ax$; this m-vector is called a *subgradient* of L at u. At those points where L is differentiable, the subgradient is unique and equals the gradient. The function L is not everywhere differentiable, however, and we must resort to methods of nondifferentiable optimization. See Lemarechal [1989] for a review of these methods, and for a thorough discussion of subgradient optimization algorithms.

Any subgradient points into the half space containing all optimal solutions. That is, if u^* is optimal in (D), $(u^* - u)\tau \geqslant 0$. This property is sufficient to ensure convergence of the following algorithm despite the fact that τ may not actually point in a direction of increase of L at u.

The algorithm is to choose a sequence $\{u^k\}$ of dual solutions by the formula

$$u_i^{k+1} = \max\left\{0,\, u_i^k + \frac{\alpha_k(d - L(u^k))}{\|\tau^k\|^2} \cdot \tau_i^k\right\} \quad \text{for } i = 1, \ldots, m\,,$$

where $0 < \varepsilon_1 < \alpha_k < 2 - \varepsilon_2 < 2$ for $\varepsilon_1 > 0$ and $\varepsilon_2 > 0$, and $\|\cdot\|$ denotes Euclidean norm. It can be shown that the u^k converges under weak conditions to an optimal dual solution u^*. The difficulty, however, is that we do not know the value of d. Thus, we must guess at d and therefore subgradient optimization is essentially a heuristic method.

Example 3.2. We illustrate the subgradient optimization algorithm using the problem of Example 3.1. Suppose we did not know the result of Example 3.1 and chose to evaluate the Lagrangean L at the point $(u_1, u_2) = (40, 60)$. Computation of L produces the solution given in Table 3.3.

Thus, the solution produced by optimizing the Lagrangean at this dual point spans, in effect, the wrong demands at locations 1 and 2. It produces a lower bound equal to 1488 on an optimal solution to the production location model with the data of Example 3.1. The implied direction of descent of L at (40, 60)

Table 3.3
Calculation of Lagrangean function at non-optimal dual solution production planning example

i	j_i	y_i	X_{i1}	X_{i2}
1	1	1	14	0
2	2	1	0	17
3	2	1	0	8
4	2	1	0	6
5	2	1	0	12
6	2	1	0	9
7	2	1	0	13
8	2	0	0	0
Total satisfied demand			27	52

is given by the subgradient

$$\begin{pmatrix} \tau_1 \\ \tau_2 \end{pmatrix} = \begin{pmatrix} d_1 - \sum_i x_{i1} \\ d_2 - \sum_i x_{i2} \end{pmatrix} = \begin{pmatrix} 31 - 14 \\ 28 - 65 \end{pmatrix} = \begin{pmatrix} 17 \\ -37 \end{pmatrix}.$$

The situation is depicted in Figure 3.1 where the bullseye is the optimal dual solution of Example 3.1, and the solid dot labeled 1 is the current dual solution. (Of course, in applying the subgradient optimization algorithm, we do not know the location or value of an optimal solution.) We see from the figure that the subgradient points in a reasonable direction. We use the formula (3.8) to select a step length in that direction. To do so, we must select values for the parameters α_k and d. In practice, this selection requires artistry, a topic that is beyond the scope of this chapter. For convenience, let us suppose that

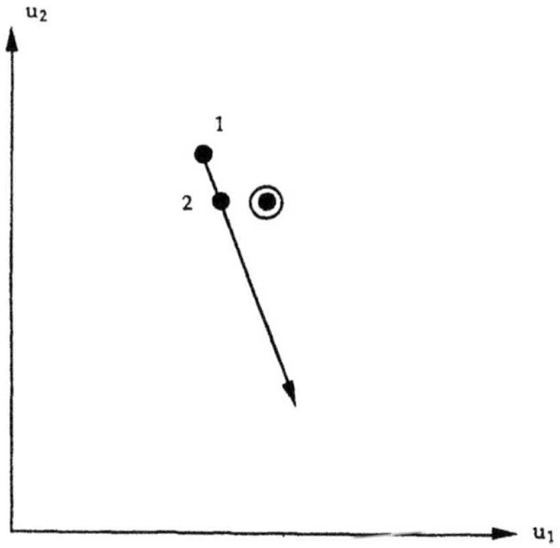

Fig. 3.1. Dual ascent step.

we select $\alpha_k = 0.5$ and guess that the maximal value d of L on the nonnegative orthant is 2100. Then, the new dual solution

$$u_1 = \max\left(0, 40 + \frac{0.5 \cdot (2100 - 1432)}{1658} \cdot 17\right) = 43.43\,,$$

$$u_2 = \max\left(0, 60 - \frac{0.5 \cdot (2100 - 1432)}{1658} \cdot 37\right) = 52.55\,.$$

This is the dot labeled with 2 in Figure 3.1.

The other algorithm we discuss for optimizing the dual problem (D) is generalized linear programming, which is also known as Dantzig–Wolfe decomposition. This approach pre-dates, and in a sense anticipates, the development of general mathematical programming dual methods. Since $X = \{x^t \mid t = 1, \ldots, T\}$, we may write

$$L(u) = \min_{t=1,\ldots,T} \{ub + (c - uA)x^t\}\,.$$

This representation of L permits us to express (D) as the linear program

$$\begin{aligned} d = {} & \max w \\ & \text{subject to} \quad w \leqslant ub + (c - uA)x^t \quad \text{for } t = 1, \ldots, T\,, \\ & \qquad\qquad\quad\; u \geqslant 0\,, \end{aligned}$$

because, for any $u \geqslant 0$, the value achieved by w, say $w(u)$, equals $L(u)$. Taking the dual of this LP, we obtain

$$\begin{aligned} d = {} & \min \sum_{t=1}^{T} (cx^t)\Omega_t \\ & \text{subject to} \quad \sum_{t=1}^{T} (Ax^t)\Omega_t \geqslant b\,, \\ & \qquad\qquad\quad\; \sum_{t=1}^{T} \Omega_t = 1\,, \\ & \qquad\qquad\quad\; \Omega_t \geqslant 0\,. \end{aligned}$$

The difficulty with this representation of the dual problem is that the number T of solutions in X will generally be too large to allow explicit enumeration. Generalized linear programming proceeds by generating solutions implicitly. Thus, suppose we have somehow obtained the solutions $x^t \in X$, $t = 1, \ldots, K$ where K is a reasonable, practical number. The method begins by using the simplex method to solve the LP:

GLP master model

$$d^K = \min \sum_{t=1}^{K} (cx^t)\Omega_t$$

$$\text{subject to} \quad \sum_{t=1}^{K} (Ax^t)\Omega_t \geq b\,, \qquad \text{(constraint rows)}$$

$$\sum_{t=1}^{K} \Omega_t = 1\,, \qquad \text{(convexity row)}$$

$$\Omega_t \geq 0\,.$$

Let Ω_t^K, $t = 1, \ldots, K$, denote optimal values, let u^K denote optimal LP dual variables for the constraint rows, and let θ^K denote an optimal dual value for the convexity row. Note that $d^K \geq d$ since columns have been omitted in the master model.

The next step is to solve the *Lagrangean sub-model* $L(u^K)$ to obtain the solution $x^{K+1} \in X$ that satisfies

$$L(u^K) = u^K b + (c - u^K A)x^{K+1}$$
$$= u^K b + \min_{x \in X} (c - u^K A)x\,.$$

Note that we have reverted to the original definition of L involving minimization over the set X in its given form.

There are two possible outcomes of the Lagrangean optimization.

Case 1.

$$L(u^K) - u^K b = (c - u^K A)x^{K+1} < \theta^K\,.$$

In this case, the solution x^{K+1} is represented by a new column in the master model with variable Ω_{K+1}. The new column will cause the master model solution to change since its reduced cost in the previously optimal LP is negative; namely

$$cx^{K+1} - uAx^{K+1} - \theta^K < 0\,.$$

Case 2.

$$L(u^K) - u^K b = (c - u^K A)x^{K+1} = \theta^K\,.$$

Note that $L(u^K)$ cannot be greater than θ^K since the basic columns in the master model price out to zero. In this case, we have

$$L(u^K) = u^K b + \theta^K = d^K \geq d \geq L(u^K)\,,$$

where the second equality follows from LP duality. Thus, $L(u^K) = d$ and u^K is optimal in the dual.

Convergence of the generalized programming method to Case 2 is finite since we have assumed there are only a finite number of possible columns to be added. As discussed above, when an optimal u^* has been obtained, we seek an $x \in X$ such that the global optimality conditions hold at u^*. The form of an optimal solution when the method has converged at iteration K sheds light on the cause of a duality gap. If the set X is discrete (nonconvex), and more than one Ω_t^K in the master model is positive, then the solution obtained by taking the convex combination

$$\sum_{t=1}^{K} \Omega_t^K x^t$$

may not lie in X. In short, dualization of (P) is equivalent to convexification of (P) [see Magnanti, Shapiro & Wagner, 1976], and Lagrangean decomposition may fail to solve (P) if it is nonconvex. Geoffrion [1974] coined the term *Lagrangean relaxation* for this decomposition method because it effectively relaxes the set X to its convex hull (the smallest convex set containing X).

Assuming the data in A and b are rational, any duality gap produced by the method could be resolved, at least theoretically, if we constrained the Ω_t variables in the master model to be integer, and hence zero or one. Using number theoretic constructions, Bell & Shapiro [1977] and Shapiro [1990] demonstrated for the zero–one integer programming and traveling salesman problems how to successively strengthen the Lagrangean until the duality gap is driven to zero.

Example 3.3. We illustrate generalized linear programming by applying it to the numerical problem of Example 3.1. We initialize computation with the five solutions given in Table 3.4.

Table 3.4

i	Solution 1			Solution 2			Solution 3			Solution 4			Solution 5		
	y_i	X_{i1}	X_{i2}	y_i	X_{i1}	X_{i2}	y_i	X_{i1}	X_{i2}	y_i	X_{i1}	X_{i2}	y_i	X_{i1}	X_{i2}
1	0	0	0	1	14	0	1	0	14	1	7	7	1	14	0
2	0	0	0	1	17	0	1	0	17	1	8	9	1	0	17
3	0	0	0	1	8	0	1	0	8	1	4	4	1	0	8
4	0	0	0	1	6	0	1	0	6	1	3	3	1	0	6
5	0	0	0	1	12	0	1	0	12	1	6	6	1	0	12
6	0	0	0	1	9	0	1	0	9	1	5	4	1	0	9
7	0	0	0	1	13	0	1	0	13	1	6	7	1	0	13
8	0	0	0	1	15	0	1	0	15	1	8	7	0	0	0

The first four solutions are extreme solutions (no plants produce the product, or all plants produce the product). The fifth solution is the solution of Example 3.2. The data for the GLP master model derived from this solution is given in Table 3.5.

The GLP master model is

$$\min 0L1 + 5803L2 + 4777L3 + 5297L4 + 3028L5$$

$$\text{subject to} \quad 94L2 + 47L4 + 14L5 \geq 31\,,$$

$$94L3 + 47L4 + 65L5 \geq 28\,,$$

$$L1 + L2 + L3 + L4 + L5 = 1\,,$$

$$Lt \geq 0\,, \quad t = 1, 2, 3, 4, 5\,.$$

Optimizing the GLP master model produces dual variables $u_1 = 61.73$, $u_2 = 33.29$ on the demand constraints and $\theta = 0$ on the convexity row. Optimizing the Lagrangean at this point produces the primal solution: $y_1 = y_2 = y_6 = y_7 = 1$; $x_{11} = 14$, $x_{21} = 17$, $x_{61} = 9$, $x_{71} = 13$. The lower bound is 1505.06. This solution translates into a new column with cost = 2088, $d_1 = 53$, $d_2 = 0$. The new column has a reduced cost of -1340.69 and should therefore be added to the master model.

Re-optimization of the master model produces dual variables $u_1 = 39.37$, $u_2 = 38.10$ and $\theta = 0$. Optimizing the Lagrangean produces the solution: $y_1 = 1$, $y_6 = 1$, $y_7 = 1$; $x_{11} = 14$, $x_{62} = 9$, $x_{72} = 13$. This solution translates to a new column with cost = 942, $d_1 = 14$, $d_2 = 22$. The column prices out negatively and is again added to the master model.

Further re-optimization of the master model produces dual variables $u_1 = 56.75$, $u_2 = 48.51$ and $\theta = 919.76$. Optimization of the Lagrangean produces the optimal primal solution to the original problem given in Example 3.1. As before, the primal and dual solutions satisfy the global optimality conditions establishing the primal solution's optimality. Note that the dual solution that yields the optimal primal solution in this example is not the same as the one in Example 3.1. That is, it is an alternative optimal dual solution.

Table 3.5
Master model data

t	cx^t	d_1^t	d_2^t
1	0	0	0
2	5803	94	0
3	4777	0	94
4	5297	47	47
5	3028	14	65

Example 3.4. The previous examples in this section illustrated the application of Lagrangean decomposition to a problem (P) for which it works perfectly; namely, an optimal solution to (P) is discovered and proven optimal by appeal to the global optimality conditions. As we indicated earlier, this will not always be the case. For example, if we change the demands in the production planning example to $d_1 = 35$ and $d_2 = 29$, a duality gap results. In particular, the maximal lower bound $d = 2299.61$ whereas the cost of an optimal integer programming solution is 2307.

We return to the alternate primal problem (P′). For $u \geqslant 0$,

$$L(u) = ub + F_1(u) + F_2(u)\,,$$

where

$$\begin{aligned} &F_i(u) = \min(c_i - uA_{0i})x_i \\ &\text{subject to} \quad x_i \in X\,, \quad \text{for } i = 1, 2\,. \end{aligned}$$

Thus, the optimization of (P′) separates. Moreover, since the sub-models i are LP's, LP duality ensures that the global optimality conditions will hold for some u. For (P′) the master model becomes

$$\begin{aligned} d^K = \min \sum_{t=1}^{K} (c_1 x_1^t)\Omega_t + \sum_{t=1}^{K} (c_2 x_2^t)\beta_t \\ \text{subject to} \quad & \sum_{t=1}^{K} (A_{01}x_1^t)\Omega_t + \sum_{t=1}^{K} (A_{02}x_2^t)\beta_t \geqslant b\,, \\ & \sum_{t=1}^{K} \Omega_t = 1\,, \\ & \sum_{t=1}^{K} \beta_t = 1\,, \\ & \Omega_t \geqslant 0\,, \quad \beta_t \geqslant 0\,. \end{aligned}$$

Letting Ω_t^K, β_t denote optimal values and u^K, θ_1^K, θ_2^K denote optimal LP variables for the master model, we optimize the two LP sub-models $F_1(u^K)$. If

$$F_1(u^K) = \theta_1^K \quad \text{and} \quad F_2(u^K) = \theta_2^K$$

the method terminates. In this case, since (P′) is an LP,

$$x_1^* = \sum_{t=1}^{K} (x_1^t)\Omega_t^K \quad \text{and} \quad x_2^* = \sum_{t=1}^{K} (x_2^t)\beta_t^K$$

are optimal solutions in (P′). Otherwise, we add a column to one or both of the two sets in the master model and re-optimize it.

4. Process manufacturing models

The first significant applications of mathematical programming were to oil refinery, food processing and steel manufacturing planning. See Dantzig [1963] for a discussion of these early industrial applications, and Bodington & Baker [1990] for a history of applications in the petroleum industry. Through the years similar types of models have been developed and applied to process manufacturing of other products such as chemicals, paper, soap, and industrial gases. Historically, these modeling applications have been mainly for tactical planning; for example, determining an optimal monthly production plan for a chemical plant. However, due to advances in computer and process control technologies, many process manufacturing companies have introduced or are now considering scheduling systems based in part on mathematical programming models.

Process manufacturing planning and scheduling problems are characterized by the following features: (1) large capital investments in machines and plants that must be operated near capacity if investments are to be profitably utilized; (2) for each stage of production, product transformation activities that are smooth and continuous (although not necessarily linear) as long as the equipment associated with a stage remains in the same major configuration; (3) time consuming and sometimes costly change-overs that occur whenever equipment undergoes an alteration in its major configuration.

Process manufacturing planning models ignore changeovers, and treat products grouped into aggregated families. Process manufacturing scheduling models explicitly consider changeovers and consider products in greater detail, including the shipment of specific orders for specific products to specific customers. In the paragraphs that follow, we discuss first process manufacturing planning models, and then process manufacturing scheduling models.

4.1. Oil refinery example

We begin by considering a numerical example of an oil refinery planning model. The processing stages of the refinery are depicted in Figure 4.1. The first stage at the left performs a distillation of two crudes CR1 and CR2. The outputs of the distillation, $P1$ and $P2$, are transformed by different recipes to produce intermediate products $P3$ and $P4$. The final stage is blending the four intermediate products $P1$, $P2$, $P3$, $P4$ into the final products $F1$ and $F2$.

Table 4.1 is a tabular display of a linear programming model to optimize production over a single period which we consider to be 72 shifts (24 days)

Table 4.1
Statement of the refinery model

	BYCR1	BYCR2	DLCR1	DLCR2	TAP1	TAP2	TBP1	TBP2	*B*1*P*1	*B*1*P*2	*B*1*P*3	*B*1*P*4	*B*2*P*3	*B*2*P*4	SLF1	SLF2	RHS
REV	−20	−22	−1.20	−1.25	−0.50	−0.52	−0.61	−0.68							31	33	
MBCR1	−1		1														=0
MBCR2		−1		1													=0
MBP1			−0.48	−0.49	1		1		1								=0
MBP2			−0.46	−0.48		1		1		1							=0
MBP3					−0.55	−0.59	−0.65	−0.60			1		1				=0
MBP4					−0.37	−0.34	−0.31	−0.38				1		1			=0
CYVA					1	1											⩽72
CYVB							1	1									⩽72
MBF1									−1	−1	−1	−1			1		=0
QAF1									−15	−17	−24	−30			20		⩽0
MBF2													−1	−1		1	=0
QAF2													−21	−30		25	⩽0
LB															105	45	
UB	180	160													135	80	

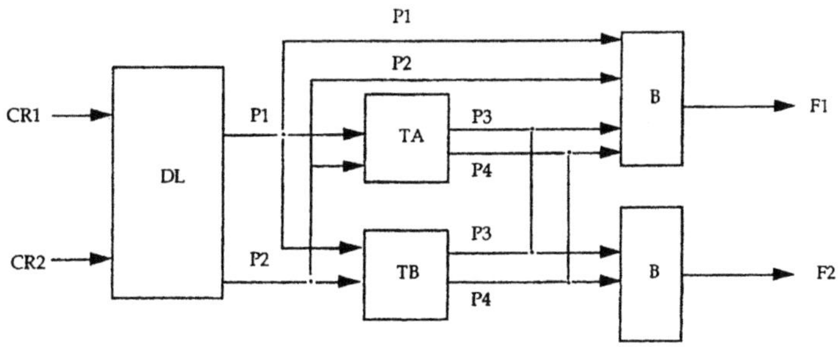

Fig. 4.1.

long. The decision variables in this model are:

BYCRi = quantity of crude i to buy,
DLCRi = quantity of crude i to distill,
TAPi, TBPi = activity levels for transformation A, B,
$BiPj$ = blending activity levels in unit i of product P_j,
SLFi = quantity of finished product i to sell.

The first row (REV) is the net revenue to be maximized over that period. The costs of acquiring crudes and transforming them to finished products are subtracted from the gross revenues accruing from the sale of finished products. Note that no cost is associated with blending; this cost is netted out of the unit sales price of the finished products.

The first six constraints of the model are material balance (MB) equations on the crudes CR1 and CR2 into the distiller, and the intermediate products that result from the distillation and the two process operations TA and TB. The following two inequalities reflect capacity available (CYV) for the operations TA and TB over the 72 shift period. The next four rows are material balance and quality constraints (QA) (e.g., octane rating) on the final products $F1$ and $F2$. For example, the QAF1 inequality states that the quality of the blended product $F1$ must be at least 20. Finally, there are upper bound constraints on the quantities of crudes that can be bought, and upper and lower bounds on the quantities of finished products that can be sold.

The linear programming model just discussed assumes that all transformation activities are linear and additive. Although this assumption has been accepted through the years by practitioners responsible for implementing refinery planning models, important nonlinearities do occur. Advanced modeling techniques involving mixed integer programming and/or nonlinear programming can be applied to achieve greater accuracy in describing operations.

Mixed integer programming constructs can capture nonlinearities if they can be described by separable functions. For example, Figure 4.2 depicts the nonlinear cost of the process transformation activity TAP1 as a function of crude 1 (CR1) input to that process. The quantity F is the fixed cost of setting-up the process activity, m_1 is the conditional minimum operating level

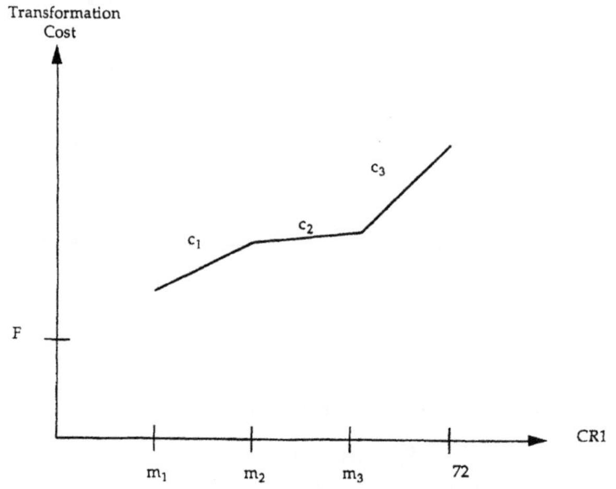

Fig. 4.2.

for the process, c_1 is the initial unit cost of operations, c_2 is a reduced unit cost of operations that prevails once level m_2 has been reached, and c_3 is the increased unit cost of operating in the range m_3 to 72 that is very close to capacity.

The nonlinear characteristics of chemical processing activities may be too complex to easily allow the type of mixed integer programming approximation just presented. In particular, if cross-product terms involving decision variables are important to accurately describe a chemical process, the formalisms of nonlinear programming are probably required. These points are discussed again in Section 4.3.

Example 4.1. We illustrate the price-directed decomposition method discussed in Section 3 by applying it to the process planning problem depicted in Figure 4.1 and modeled in Table 4.1. Specifically, we decompose the model by splitting it into two parts; one part consists of the distillation and transformation activities and constraints, and the other consists of the blending activities. We note that this decomposition is based on the block diagonal form of the matrix in Table 4.1

$$\begin{matrix} D & T \\ 0 & B \end{matrix}$$

where B consists of the lowest four rows (excluding lower and upper bounds) and the right-most eight columns of the matrix. The master model is associated with D and T, whereas the sub-model is associated with B.

The master model is initialized with the four feasible blending solutions shown in Table 4.2; note that these solutions satisfy the blending constraints

Table 4.2
Trial blending solutions

	Solution			
	1	2	3	4
$B1P1$	60	0	0	32
$B1P2$	0	65	45	32
$B1P3$	0	65	45	32
$B1P4$	60	0	45	32
$B2P3$	40	30	30	35
$B2P4$	40	30	50	45

Table 4.3
Intermediate product requirements

	Solution			
	1	2	3	4
BP1	60	0	0	32
BP2	0	65	45	32
BP3	40	95	75	67
BP4	100	30	95	77
Gross revenue	6360	6010	6925	6608

(see MBF1 and MBF2). The four solutions are directly translated to the associated our product inputs and gross revenue outputs shown in Table 4.3. We use these data in constructing the master model

$$\max 6360\, L1 + 6010\, L2 + 6825\, L3 + 6608\, L4 - 20\,\mathrm{CR1} - 22\,\mathrm{CR2}$$
$$- 1.2\,\mathrm{DLCR1} - 1.25\,\mathrm{DLCR2} - 0.5\,\mathrm{TAP1} - 0.52\,\mathrm{TAP2}$$
$$- 0.61\,\mathrm{TBP1} - 0.68\,\mathrm{TBP2}$$

subject to

(1) $-\mathrm{CR1} + \mathrm{DLCR1} = 0\,,$
(2) $-\mathrm{CR2} + \mathrm{DLCR2} = 0\,,$
(3) $60\, L1 + 32\, L4 - 0.48\,\mathrm{DLCR1} - 0.49\,\mathrm{DLCR2} + \mathrm{TAP1} + \mathrm{TBP1} = 0\,,$
(4) $65\, L2 + 45\, L3 + 32\, L4 - 0.46\,\mathrm{DLCR1} - 0.48\,\mathrm{DLCR2} + \mathrm{TAP2} + \mathrm{TBP2} = 0\,,$
(5) $40\, L1 + 95\, L2 + 75\, L3 + 67\, L4 - 0.55\,\mathrm{TAP1} - 0.59\,\mathrm{TAP2} - 0.65\,\mathrm{TBP1} - 0.6\,\mathrm{TBP2} = 0\,,$
(6) $100\, L1 + 30\, L2 + 95\, L3 + 77\, L4 - 0.37\,\mathrm{TAP1} - 0.34\,\mathrm{TAP2} - 0.31\,\mathrm{TBP1} - 0.38\,\mathrm{TBP2} = 0\,,$
(7) $\mathrm{TAP1} + \mathrm{TAP2} \leqslant 72\,,$
(8) $\mathrm{TBP1} + \mathrm{TBP2} \leqslant 72\,,$
(9) $\mathrm{CR1} \leqslant 180\,,$
(10) $\mathrm{CR2} \leqslant 160\,,$
(11) $L1 + L2 + L3 + L4 = 1\,.$

The last constraint in this model requires that the weights $L1$, $L2$, $L3$, $L4$ on the four blending strategies sum to one. This convexification provides the master model with a useful but incomplete description of the blending capabilities of the refinery.

The decomposition proceeds by optimizing the master model. The solution is:

Objective function value = 1512.31900

Variable	Value	Reduced cost
$L1$	0.000000	117.867400
$L2$	0.544085	0.000000
$L3$	0.000000	52.819460
$L4$	0.455915	0.000000
CR1	180.000000	0.000000
CR2	37.518890	0.000000
DLCR1	180.000000	0.000000
DLLR2	37.000000	0.000000
TAP1	69.049250	0.000000
TAP2	0.000000	0.567981
TBP1	21.145720	0.000000
TBP2	50.854280	0.000000

Row	Slack or surplus	Dual prices
(1)	0.000000	21.327400
(2)	0.000000	22.000000
(3)	0.000000	23.630510
(4)	0.000000	24.314690
(5)	0.000000	24.738380
(6)	0.000000	28.444320
(7)	2.950755	0.000000
(8)	0.000000	0.657178
(9)	0.000000	1.327402
(10)	122.481100	0.000000
(11)	0.000000	1226.069000

The values of the weights imply a blending strategy $B1P1 = 14.592$, $B1P2 = 49.942$, $B1P3 = 49.952$, $B1P4 = 114.592$, $B2P3 = 32.280$, $B2P4 = 36.840$. This strategy, along with the solution listed above, represent a feasible solution to the original LP model with net revenue equalling 1512.319. Optimizing the master model also produces: $\pi_1 = 23.631$, $\pi_2 = 24.315$, $\pi_3 = 24.738$, $\pi_4 = 28.444$, where π_i = shadow price on product BPi. These represent the master model's best estimate of the unit cost to provide each of these products to the blending activities. The decomposition continues by solving the sub-model in which the blending activities are charged these unit prices for the products they consume. The sub-model is:

$$\max 31\,F1 + 33\,F2 - 23.631\,B1P1 - 24.315\,B1P2 - 24.738\,B1P3 - 28.444\,B1P4 - 24.738\,B2P3 - 28.444\,B2P4$$

subject to

(1) $F1 - B1P1 - B1P2 - B1P3 - B1P4 = 0$,

(2) $-5\,B1P1 - 3\,B1P2 + 4\,B1P3 + 10\,B1P4 \geqslant 0$,

(3) $F2 - B2P3 - B2P4 = 0$,

(4) $-4\,B2P3 + 5\,B2P4 \geqslant 0$,

(5) $F1 \geq 105$,
(6) $F1 \leq 135$,
(7) $F2 \geq 45$,
(8) $F2 \leq 80$.

The optimal solution to the sub-model is

Objective function value = 1440.98100

Variable	Value	Reduced cost
$F1$	135.000000	0.000000
$F2$	80.000000	0.000000
$B1P1$	60.000000	0.000000
$B1P2$	0.000000	0.438000
$B1P3$	75.000000	0.000000
$B1P4$	0.000000	2.968000
$B2P3$	44.444440	0.000000
$B2P4$	35.555560	0.000000

The solution suggests the new strategy

$$\begin{pmatrix} \text{BP1} \\ \text{BP2} \\ \text{BP3} \\ \text{BP4} \end{pmatrix} = \begin{pmatrix} 60 \\ 0 \\ 119.44 \\ 35.56 \end{pmatrix}$$

to add to the master model with gross revenue = 6825 and variable $L5$. Since the primal problem is a maximization, optimization of the sub-model (Lagrangean) provides an upper bound on the optimal primal problem objective function. Adding the constant term to the above value (see Section 3), we obtain an upper bound of 1728.

The new master model optimal solution is:

Objective function value = 1529.45400

Variable	Value	Reduced cost
$L1$	0.000000	17.710450
$L2$	0.439749	0.000000
$L3$	0.000000	192.848000
$L4$	0.480502	0.000000
$L5$	0.079749	0.000000
CR1	180.000000	0.000000
CR2	40.124490	0.000000
DLCR1	180.000000	0.000000
DLCR2	40.124490	0.000000
TAP1	72.000000	0.000000
TAP2	0.000000	0.332096
TBP1	13.900010	0.000000
TBP2	58.099990	0.000000

Row	Slack or surplus	Dual prices
(1)	0.000000	21.327740
(2)	0.000000	22.000000
(3)	0.000000	23.663310
(4)	0.000000	24.281200
(5)	0.000000	32.340550
(6)	0.000000	32.927430
(7)	0.000000	5.807140
(8)	0.000000	6.955549
(9)	0.000000	1.327744
(10)	119.875500	0.000000
(11)	0.000000	371.546600

Note that the new master model activity associated with the variable $L5$ is used to advantage in maximizing net revenues. Note also that the master model has revised its estimates of the shadow price charges on rows 3, 4, 5, and 6 for the immediate products BP1, BP2, BP3, BP4.

The communication between the master model and the sub-model continued for four iterations until an optimal solution to the original model was computed. Figure 4.3 depicts the net revenue of the feasible solution found by the master model at each iteration. It also depicts the upper bound determined by the sub-model at each iteration. Note that the lower bounds are monotonically increasing, but that the upper bounds are not monotonically decreasing. At the fourth iteration, the lower and upper bounds converged on the optimal LP value.

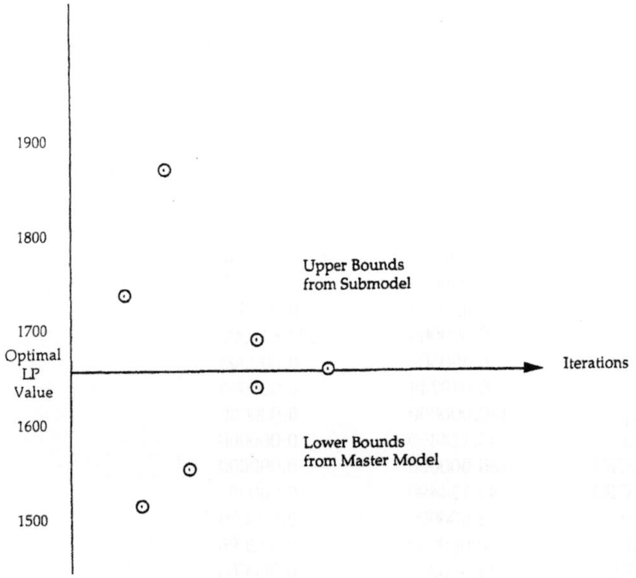

Fig. 4.3.

4.2. Successive linear programming

Nonlinearities arise in refining, petrochemical and other process manufacturing models due to a variety of factors. A major factor is the need to model properties or qualities of product flows as well as the flows themselves. For example, when intermediate products are combined in a tank or pool, nonlinear relationships are required to capture pool qualities. Mathematically, the simplest form of the pooling problem arises when streams of intermediate products are blended on the basis of quality–volume relationships of the form

$$v_p = \sum_i v_i\,, \qquad q_p = \Big(\sum_i q_i v_i\Big)\Big/ v_p\,,$$

where v_i and q_i represent the volume and quality respectively of incoming stream i. The volume of the pool is represented by v_p. The expression for q_p, the quality of the pool, is a nonlinear function of the volume v_i.

Note that if p were a final product constrained, say, to be above some level q, then the relationship $q_p \geqslant q$ could be linearized simply by multiplying both sides of the inequality thereby creating

$$\sum_i (q_i - q)v_i \geqslant 0\,.$$

This is the type of constraint we had on the blended final products in the refinery model displayed in Table 4.1. The difficulty occurs, and thus the need for nonlinear programming techniques, when the intermediate pooled products are themselves pooled in downstream operations.

Nonlinearities may also arise in blending final products if the qualities of the components streams affect the qualities of the blended product in a nonlinear manner. Baker & Lasdon [1985] cite the example of gasoline blending where the octane contribution of components depends radically on the presence of lead in the blend. Nonlinear process yields may similarly occur as functions of operating conditions of the process unit. Finally, costs may prove to be nonlinear functions of operating variables such as throughput or severity. As we pointed out in Section 4.1, however, many of these nonlinearities can be approximated as piecewise linear functions. Zero–one variables are required to capture any nonconvexities in these curves.

Linear programming approximation techniques for capturing nonlinearities in process manufacturing have proven effective for over 20 years. Baker & Lasdon [1985] provide a survey of the more popular methods. They discuss two specific approaches. One is a successive linear programming modeling technique based on first order Taylor series expansions of the nonlinear functions. The expansions are systematically updated based on user supplied tolerances on the range of the expansions and the optimal values of variables in successive linear programming approximations.

In some instances, however, the nonlinearities are not available in functional form to be expanded in Taylor series. Rather, the nonlinear relationships are implicitly captured by process simulation models. An approach suggested for this case is to use the process simulators to identify trial production strategies for various units in a plant, and to construct a plant model that allows convex combinations of these strategies in the spirit of price-directed decomposition. Another approach is to employ the simulators to compute function values and approximate derivatives which become input data to successive linear programming models. The reader is referred to Biegler [1985], Biegler & Hughes [1985], and Lasdon, Waren & Sarkar [1988] for more details.

4.3. Scheduling models

The planning models discussed above were not concerned with sequencing operations in a process manufacturing environment. In this section, we discuss a detailed model that addresses the timing of configuration changes and the management of inventories. The model suggested is appropriate, for example, for optimizing the production schedule over a given planning horizon of one or several linked paper machines in a mill, or for optimizing production in an industrial gases plant.

Indices

$i = 1, 2, \ldots, N$	time periods
$r = 0, 1, 2, \ldots, R$	configuration states,
j	process manufacturing slates,
J_r	slates available under configuration r,
$k = 1, 2, \ldots, K$	products,

$Q = (r1, r2)\colon r1 \neq r2,\ r1, r2, = 0, 1, 2, \ldots, R,$

T	time indices for production targets.

The slates in this model are recipes that transform inputs to output products. The chemical plant can be operated in each of $R + 1$ major configurations. For each configuration, we assume that a finite number of slates are available to be operated at positive activity levels, and that changing from one slate to another within the configuration is instantaneous and costless. The set Q of two-tuples are all the indices of all pairs of configuration states for which major changeovers may occur.

Parameters

c_j = rate at which direct cost is incurred using slate j (\$/hr),

f_{rv} = cost of changing the configuration from r to v (\$),

d_{ik} = cumulative target production for product k at the end of period i for $i \in T$ (#),

p^{+}_{ik} = penalty for each unit of product k exceeding the target at the end of period i (\$/#),

p_{ik}^- = penalty for each unit of product k falling below the target at the end of period i (\$/#),
a_{jk} = rate at which product k is produced by slate j (#/hr),
m_{iw} = quantity of raw material w available in period i (#),
q_{jw} = rate at which raw material w is consumed by slate j (#/hr),
t_i = time when period i ends,
t_{rv} = changeover time from configuration r to configuration v (hrs).

Variables
x_{ij} = time that slate j is used in period i,

$$y_{irv} = \begin{cases} 1 & \text{if configuration } v \text{ is run in period } i \text{ and} \\ & \text{configuration } r \neq v \text{ is run in period } i-1, \\ 0 & \text{otherwise,} \end{cases}$$

$$z_{ir} = \begin{cases} 1 & \text{if configuration } r \text{ is run in period } i, \\ 0 & \text{otherwise,} \end{cases}$$

s_{ik}^+ = surplus cumulative production of product k above target at the end of period $i \in T$,
s_{ik}^- = unmet cumulative production of product k below target at the end of period $i \in T$.

Process manufacturing scheduling model

$$\min \sum_{i=1}^{N} \sum_{r=0}^{R} \sum_{j \in J_r} c_j x_{ij} + \sum_{i=1}^{N} \sum_{(r1,r2) \in Q} f_{r1,r2} y_{i,r1,r2} + \sum_{i \in T} \sum_{k=1}^{K} (p_{ik}^+ s_{ik}^+ + p_{ik}^- s_{ik}^-) \tag{4.1}$$

subject to

$$\sum_{r=1}^{R} \sum_{j \in J_r} q_{jw} x_{ij} \leq m_{iw}, \quad i = 1, \ldots, N, \tag{4.2}$$

$$\sum_{i=1}^{g} \sum_{r=1}^{R} \sum_{j \in J_r} a_{jk} x_{ij} + s_{gk}^- s_{gk}^+ = \sum_{i=1}^{g} d_{ik}, \quad k = 1, \ldots, K, \; g \in T, \tag{4.3}$$

$$\sum_{r=0}^{R} \sum_{j \in J_r} x_{ij} + \sum_{(r1,r2) \in Q} t_{r1,r2} y_{i,r1,r2} = t_i - t_{i-1}, \quad i = 1, \ldots, N, \tag{4.4}$$

$$\sum_{i \in J_r} x_{ij} - (t_i - t_{i-1}) z_{ir} \leq 0, \quad r = 0, \ldots, R, \; i = 1, \ldots, N, \tag{4.5}$$

$$\sum_{r=0}^{R} z_{ir} = 1, \quad i = 1, \ldots, N, \tag{4.6}$$

$$y_{i,r1,r2} \geq z_{i-1,r1} + z_{i-1,r2} - 1 \quad \text{for all } (r1, r2) \in Q \text{ and } i = 1, \ldots, N, \tag{4.7}$$

$$x_{ij} \geq 0, \quad y_{i,r1,r2} = 0 \text{ or } 1, \quad z_{ir} = 0 \text{ or } 1, \quad s^+_{ik} \geq 0, \quad s^-_{ik} \geq 0. \tag{4.8}$$

A brief explanation of the mixed integer programming model is the following. The objective function (4.1) is comprised of direct manufacturing costs, changeover costs, and penalty costs for being above or below cumulative production targets at certain specified points in time. The relations (4.2) state that production in each time period is constrained by the amount of raw materials available for that period and the rate at which they are consumed. The Equations (4.3) relate cumulative production to the production targets. Note that $r = 0$ corresponds to the shut-down configuration for which there is no production; hence this term has been omitted from (4.3).

The Equations (4.4) constrain production and changeover time in each time period to equal the time available. The constraints (4.5) and (4.6) effectively select one major configuration for each period, and restrict the slates that may be used to that configuration. The constraints (4.7) provide the correct relation between the changeover variables and the configuration selection variables; namely, a changeover from configuration $r1$ to configuration $r2$ is allowed ($z_{i-1,r1} = 1$ and $z_{i-1,r2} = 1$) only if the changeover variable $y_{i,r1,r2} = 1$ thereby forcing the changeover costs and times to be incurred.

The number of constraints and variables in this model is dependent on NR^2. Thus, if there are 4 major configurations and if one wishes to determine hourly plans for a week, the model will have in excess of $168 * 16 = 2688$ constraints and zero–one variables. This is a large mixed integer programming model. Moreover, most of the variables and constraints are not active in the sense that very few major configuration changes will actually take place over the planning horizon.

An iterative modeling approach under investigation is intended to greatly reduce difficulties due to size by beginning with a coarse time grid and refining time periods where optimization indicates the model is undecided about the major configuration it designs for a particular period. Reoptimization of a refined model can be quite rapid because the optimal solution for a parent model becomes a feasible solution in its refined descendant. In many instances, the major goal of the model analysis would be to determine the timing of the next (that is, the first) major change in configuration.

Figure 4.4 depicts an implementation using realistic data for industrial gas production. The planning horizon consists of 32 periods with targets on production at the end of periods 16 and 32. Five major configuration states, including shut-down, are allowed; the system is initially in configuration state 1. Four runs were made with iterative refinement of the time periods. The numbers below the axis indicate the configuration in each time period. The final run indicates that the current configuration should not be changed until 8 periods into the planning horizon, and then the change should be to configura-

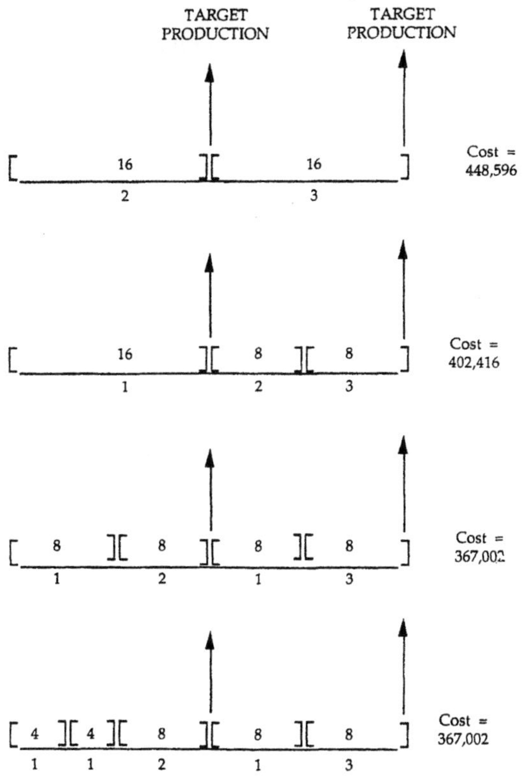

Fig. 4.4.

tion 2. Although we have shown a linear sequence of approximations, the refinement should be elaborated in a tree structure in the manner of branch-and-bound.

4.4. *Process synthesis*

The models for process manufacturing discussed above assume that the number, type and configuration of the physical units of the manufacturing environment are fixed and given. Process synthesis is concerned with selecting and configuring units in order to minimize the sum of amortized investment and operating costs. Mathematical programming models for optimizing and operating this class of problems are complex because they must incorporate: (1) nonlinear equations characterizing chemical processes and equilibria, and (2) zero–one integer programming variables and constraints describing logical equipment design choices for the configuration which in turn determines the equilibrium that will be produced by the equipment.

Several nonlinear programming methods have been applied to the computation of chemical equilibria. Wall, Greening & Woolsey [1986] presented an algorithm based on geometric programming principles ([see Duffin et al. 1967]; geometric programming has found wide application to engineering design problems). Heyman [1990] discussed the application of other nonlinear programming algorithms to this problem.

Kocis & Grossman [1987] developed and tested a decomposition method for the nonlinear mixed integer programming models describing process synthesis. The method resembles Benders' method for (linear) MIP. The master model in their scheme selects the zero–one design variables, whereas the sub-model is a nonlinear program that determines the chemical equilibrium implied by this design choice. Linearizations involving optimal Lagrange multipliers of the nonlinear model about the equilibrium are fed back to the master model which is then resolved.

Biewar & Grossman [1987] extended design analysis in another important direction; namely, to evaluate how the equipment might be scheduled under expected operating conditions. They consider the case of a plant with several batch stages in sequence with one unit per stage. The problem they address is to determine the sizes of the batch equipment, the production schedule, and intermediate storage capacities to meet specified demand so as to minimize total investment cost. Mixed integer programming and nonlinear programming models are again used to perform the optimization.

5. Discrete parts manufacturing models

In this section, we consider syntheses and generalizations of the simple dynamic lot-size model considered in Section 2. The problems addressed by the generalized models remain ones in which items are intermittently produced with associated set-up costs, and stored in inventory with associated holding costs until they are needed. The generalized models, however, take into account production capacities to be shared by the individual items. The models also address plans for coordinating the timing and sizing of production runs of items produced at each of several manufacturing stages. The models discussed in this section are applicable to production planning and scheduling problems in the automobile, aircraft, computer and electronics industries, to name only a few. An extensive review of discrete parts manufacturing models can be found in Bahl, Ritzman & Gupta [1987].

The model we will consider in Section 5.1 extends the scope of decision making from the timing and sizing of production runs for a single item to that of many items sharing production capacity. A further generalization considered in Section 5.2 leads to models for determining the timing and sizing of runs for items in a multi-stage production environment. Finally, in Section 5.3, we consider a model possessing a hierarchical structure in which families of items can be grouped together into types for aggregate planning purposes. As we shall demonstrate, decomposition methods are useful for exploiting the structure of individual sub-models that make up the various large-scale models.

5.1. Multiple-item, single-stage models

Manne [1958] was the first to propose a model for this class of problems. The model and the optimization approach was further developed by Dzielinski & Gomory [1965], and specialized and applied to tire manufacture by Lasdon & Terjung [1971]. For expositional convenience, the version we present here assumes that there is only one type of capacity (e.g., machine hours, labor hours) to be shared in producing items in each period.

Indices

i = items ($i = 1, 2, \ldots, I$),
j = trial production strategies,
J_i = index set of trial production strategies for item i,
t = time periods ($t = 1, 2, \ldots, T$).

Parameters

c_i = set-up cost for item i (\$),
a_i = set-up resource utilization for item i (hrs),
b_i = resource utilization rate for item i (hrs/unit),
h_i = unit holding cost for item i (\$/unit/period),
y_{i0} = initial inventory of item i (units),
r_{it} = demand for item i in period t (units),
q_t = shared resource availability in period t (hrs),
M_{it} = upper bound on production of item i in period t (units).

Variables

x_{it} = quantity of item i produced in period t,
y_{it} = quantity of item i held in inventory at the end of period t,

$$\delta_{it} = \begin{cases} 1 & \text{if } x_{it} > 0, \\ 0 & \text{otherwise.} \end{cases}$$

Implicit in the definition of the problem is the fact that all periods are of the same length (e.g., one week). The model will assume that demand must be met in each period from inventory or production; no backlogging is allowed. Variable production costs have been ignored since they can be assumed to be the same in every period and therefore represent an unavoidable cost. Finally, note that we have included both a set-up cost and a set-up resource utilization for each item. The set-up cost might equal the cost of unusable production at the beginning of a run. The set-up resource utilization might be lost time in adjusting a machine for a new item to be produced.

Multi-item, single-stage discrete parts manufacturing model

$$v = \min \sum_{i=1}^{I} \left\{ c_i \sum_{t=1}^{T} \delta_{it} + h_i \sum_{t=1}^{T} y_{it} \right\} \tag{5.1}$$

subject to

$$\sum_{i=1}^{I} a_i\delta_{it} + b_i x_{it} \leq q_t \quad \text{for } t = 1, \ldots, T. \tag{5.2}$$

For $i = 1, 2, \ldots, I$

$$y_{it} = y_{i,t-1} + x_{it} - r_{it} \quad \text{for } t = 1, \ldots, T, \tag{5.3}$$

$$x_{it} - M_{it}\delta_{it} \leq 0 \quad \text{for } t = 1, \ldots, T, \tag{5.4}$$

$$x_{it} \geq 0, \quad y_{it} \geq 0, \quad \delta_{it} = 0 \text{ or } 1. \tag{5.5}$$

This is an MIP model of potentially very large size. It has $(2I+1)T$ constraints and $3IT$ variables; thus, if $I = 500$ and $T = 10$, we have a model with 10 010 constraints and 15 000 variables. Of course, the constraints (5.3) and (5.4) are quite simple, and for each I constitute an algebraic representation of the single item dynamic lot-size model discussed in Section 2 [see (2.2) and (2.3)]. For future reference, we define the set

$$N_i = \{(x_{it}, y_{it}, \delta_{it}) \text{ that satisfy (5.3), (5.4), (5.5)}\}.$$

A price-directed decomposition or Lagrangean relaxation approach for this model is to dualize on the capacity constraints (5.2), thereby allowing the individual items to be optimized separately. Following the development in Section 3, for any $\pi = (\pi_1, \pi_2, \ldots, \pi_T) \geq 0$, we construct the Lagrangean

$$L(\pi) = -\sum_{t=1}^{T} q_t\pi_t + \min \sum_{i=1}^{I}\sum_{t=1}^{T} \{(c_i + a_i\pi_t)\delta_{it} + (b_i\pi_t)x_{it} + h_i y_{it}\}$$
$$\text{subject to} \quad (x_{it}, y_{it}, \delta_{it}) \in N_i \quad \text{for all } i. \tag{5.6}$$

This function can be re-written as

$$L(\pi) = -\sum_{t=1}^{T} q_t\pi_t + \sum_{i=1}^{I} F_i(\pi),$$

where

$$F_i(\pi) = \min \sum_{t=1}^{T} \{(c_i + a_i\pi_i)\delta_{it} + (b_i\pi_{it})x_{it} + h_i y_{it}\}$$
$$\text{subject to} \quad (x_{it}, y_{it}, \delta_{it}) \in N_i. \tag{5.7}$$

In words, each $F_i(\pi)$ is a dynamic lot-size model defined over the set N_i of exactly the form discussed in Section 2.1. To reflect the price π_t being charged for shared resource in period t, the set-up costs associated with the δ_{it} have been expanded to $c_i + a_i \pi_t$. In addition, a time-dependent variable production cost term $b_i \pi_t$ has been added. Thus, if $\pi_3 > 0$ for the example depicted in Section 2.2, arcs connecting beginning inventory in period 3 to ending inventory in period 3 associated with setting up and producing the item would be 'longer' (more costly), and the dynamic programming recursion would seek a shorter path.

Based on our development in Section 3, we can state the three main properties of the Lagrangean construction.

Property 1 (Optimality test). *The solution* $(x_{it}(\pi), y_{it}(\pi), \delta_{it}(\pi))$ *that is optimal in the Lagrangean* $L(\pi)$ *is optimal in the multi-item model* (5.1)–(5.5) *if*

$$\sum_{i=1}^{I} a_i \delta_{it}(\pi) = b_i x_{it}(\pi) \leq q_t \quad \text{for } t = 1, 2, \ldots, T$$

with equality on constraint t *if* $\pi_t > 0$.

Property 2. *For any* $\pi \geq 0$, $L(\pi) \leq v$.

Property 3. *If* $\pi \geq 0$ *produces an optimal solution to the model according to the optimality conditions of Property* 1, *then* π *is optimal in the dual problem*

$$\begin{aligned} & d = \max L(\pi) \\ & \text{subject to} \quad \pi \geq 0 . \end{aligned} \tag{5.8}$$

Moreover, if the optimality conditions hold, we have $v = d$.

There is no guarantee, however, that the optimality conditions can be made to hold for *any* dual vector $\pi \geq 0$. This is because the multi-item model is a mixed integer program, a class of nonconvex models for which duality gaps $(v - d > 0)$ are common. To ensure convergence to an optimal solution to the model, we would need to imbed the dual methods in a branch-and-bound procedure [see Shapiro, 1979a,b]. As we shall see below, for this particular model, it is possible to characterize the difficulty in applying Lagrangean methods due to the model's nonconvexity.

The price-directed generalized linear programming approach discussed in Section 3 can be specialized for this application. In particular, suppose for each i that we have the trial production strategies $(x_{itr}, y_{itr}, \delta_{itr}) \in N_i$ for $r = 1, 2, \ldots, R_i$, where R_i is the number of such strategies for item i. For $t = 1, 2, \ldots, T$, let

$$\beta_{itr} = a_i \delta_{itr} + b_i x_{itr}$$

and let

$$C_{ir} = c_i \sum_{t=1}^{T} \delta_{itr} + h_i \sum_{t=1}^{T} y_{itr} .$$

Given this data, we construct the master model

$$\min \sum_{i=1}^{I} \sum_{r=1}^{R_i} C_{ir} \Omega_{ir} \tag{5.9}$$

subject to

$$\sum_{i=1}^{I} \sum_{r=1}^{R_i} \beta_{itr} \Omega_{ir} \leq q_t \quad \text{for } t = 1, 2, \ldots, T , \tag{5.10}$$

$$\sum_{r=1}^{R_i} \Omega_{ir} = 1 \quad \text{for } i = 1, 2, \ldots, I , \tag{5.11}$$

$$\Omega_{ir} \geq 0 . \tag{5.12}$$

In words, this linear program is intended to select a schedule r for each item from among the trial schedules generated thus far so as to minimize total cost without exceeding available capacity. Of course, there is no guarantee that a pure (unique) strategy will be selected for each item since more than one Ω_{ir} may take on fractional values between zero and one. This is a serious deficiency of the approach. However, with the reader's indulgence, we delay addressing it until after we have discussed how the optimal LP dual variables for the master model can be employed in generating effective new production strategies.

Let π_i denote the shadow prices on the resource constraints (5.10) and let Φ_i denote the shadow prices on the convexity rows (5.11). For each i, we use the π_t in solving $F_i(\pi)$ given in (5.6). This is a single-item dynamic programming calculation of the type discussed in Section 2.2. If $F_i(\pi) < \Phi_i$, we add a column to the master model corresponding to the production strategy with this value. If $F_i(\pi) = \Phi_i$, we do not add a column to the master model. If no new columns can be added to the master model because the latter condition obtains for all i, then the generalized linear programming method terminates. All earlier master models (that is, those admitting new columns) are called non-optimal. Termination or convergence to an optimal master model must occur in a finite number of steps because there are only a finite number of feasible solutions to each of the $F_i(\cdot)$ models.

We return now to the central issue in applying generalized linear programming to a structured mixed integer programming model such as the multi-item model: namely, how to interpret solutions from an optimal or non-optimal master model. Let Ω_{ir}^* denote optimal values to any optimal or non-optimal master model. We say that the master model produces a *pure strategy* for item i

if $\Omega_{ip}^* = 1$ for some p and $\Omega_{ir}^* = 0$ for all $r \neq p$. Conversely, we say that the master model produces a *mixed strategy* for item i if $\Omega_{ir}^* > 0$ for two or more strategies r; this implies $\Omega_{ir}^* < 1$ for these strategies. Obviously, when the master model suggests a mixed strategy for item i, we are in a quandary about which strategy to employ.

The difficulty is that each time we solve the master model, we can expect mixed strategies to occur for a certain number of items in our multi-item model. If this number is small, say less than 5% of the items, the difficulty may not be serious. For items with mixed strategies, we may choose the strategy that was assigned the highest weight Ω_{ir}^*. The resulting infeasibility or lack of optimality will probably be negligible relative to the accuracy of the demand data.

We can calculate a bound on the maximal number of items that will have mixed strategies in the master model based on properties of the simplex method. In particular, assuming $I > T$, a simple counting argument establishes that the number of mixed strategies cannot exceed T. Thus, if $I = 500$ and $T = 10$, the number of items with mixed strategies cannot exceed 10 or 2%. This is an extreme case, however, because we assumed only one resource to be shared in each period. For example, if $I = 500$, $T = 20$, and the number of shared resources in each period is 10 (different types of machines, labor categories, raw materials, etc.), the potentially maximal number of items that may have mixed strategies equals 200, or 40% of the total number of items. Although the actual percentage of mixed strategies would probably be lower, the percentage could easily be difficult to handle in the heuristic manner just outlined.

A subtle but important point regarding the validity of the dynamic lot-size theorem for a single item discussed in Section 2.1 in the context of the multi-item model (5.1)–(5.5) and the model decomposition is the following. Due to the capacity constraints (5.2), it may not be optimal or even feasible to limit production of any given item to those periods when inventories have fallen to zero. However, by the Lagrangean decomposition (5.7), the interaction between items due to constraints (5.2) have been eliminated, and the dynamic lot-size theorem is valid for computing the $F_i(\pi)$ for all i. In this sense, the dual decomposition is deficient because it fails to provide structure for generating shortest route paths in the dynamic programming network, and therefore columns for the master model (5.9) – (5.12), that violate the Theorem. This deficiency is an unavoidable result of the discrete, non-convex nature of the scheduling sub-models.

Lasdon & Terjung [1971] applied a version of the multi-item model to the production of automobile tires. Recently, Eppen & Martin [1987] have developed variable redefinition procedures for this class of models that produce tighter linear programming and Lagrangean relaxations. They report on successful experiments with models consisting of up to 200 items and 10 time periods. Trigeiro, Thomas & McClain [1989] reported on computation experience using Lagrangean relaxation on very large models of this type.

5.2. Multiple-item, multiple-stage models

The models we shall discuss in this subsection are mixed integer programming generalizations of the single-stage models discussed in the previous subsection. They are applicable to a wide range of discrete parts manufacturing problems although, thus far, they have found little application to real world problems. The lack of application is due in part to the size and complexity of the models which make them difficult to construct and optimize. This technical difficulty should gradually disappear as computer technology continues to improve.

In addition, the practical use of these production models should benefit from recent research into stronger mixed integer programming model formulations and more efficient mixed integer programming algorithms. Crowder, Johnson & Padberg [1983] reported on successful computational experience with cutting plane and other procedures for achieving tighter formulations of pure integer programs. Van Roy & Wolsey [1986, 1987] developed valid inequalities and reformulations for mixed integer programs. Martin [1987] developed a theory of variable redefinition for mixed integer programs that creates or exposes special structure which can be exploited by tailored solution algorithms. These general integer and mixed integer programming procedures have direct application to the types of models discussed here; for example, see Barany, Van Roy & Wolsey [1984], Eppen & Martin [1987], or Martin, Rardin & Campbell [1990].

However, the barrier to use of these models is more than a mathematical or technical one. Materials Requirements Planning systems have found widespread use in industry during the past ten years. The models we discuss here must be conceptually and practically integrated with MRP if they are to have a significant future.

At the moment, the outlook for new modeling applications is promising because many manufacturing managers have come to realize the limitations of their MRP systems. These systems are, in fact, no more than informational programs that provide materials requirements from predetermined master schedules. Moreover, although some MRP systems will calculate capacity loadings that result from a detailed schedule, the systems make no attempt to determine an effective master schedule by allocating capacity resources in an optimal or efficient manner. The models discussed here are intended to fill this planning vacuum. But, the vast majority of manufacturing managers need to be educated about their practical relevance.

At the core of any MRP system, and of mathematical programming models for discrete parts manufacturing problems, is the product structure. A typical product structure is depicted in Figure 5.1. Each box refers to an item to be produced and the number in the box is the index of that item. A chain links each item to all other items that require it. For example, item 17 is linked to items 12, 8, 5, and 2. Each item is associated with exactly one level in the product structure; this level equals the length of the longest chain beginning at

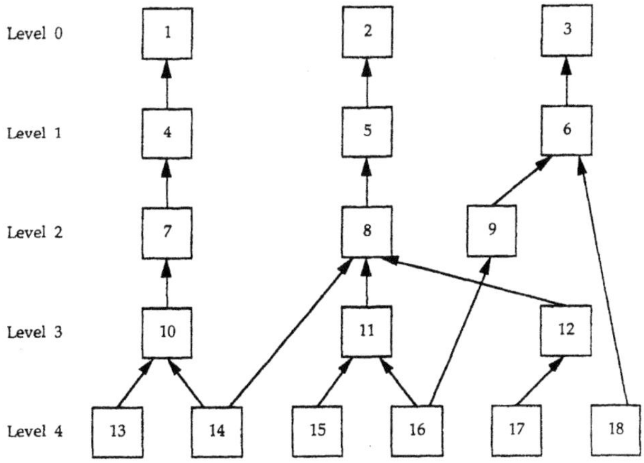

Fig. 5.1.

the item. The levels are indexed 0 to $L-1$ where items at level 0 are called finished goods and items at level $L-1$ are called raw materials.

With this background, we can state a mathematical programming model for optimizing over general product structures. The model statement follows Billington, McClain & Thomas [1983]; see also Chapman [1985].

Indices

$i = 1, \ldots, M$	index of finished goods,
$i = M+1, \ldots, N$	index of intermediate products,
$t = 1, \ldots, T$	index of planning periods,
$k = 1, \ldots, K$	index of facilities.

Parameters

h_i = inventory of holding cost (\$ per unit of item i),
cs_i = set-up cost (\$ per set-up of item i),
co_{kt} = overtime cost (\$ per unit of capacity in period t at facility k),
L_i = minimum lead time for item i,
f_i = yield of item i (fraction),
a_{ij} = number of units of item i required for the production of one unit of item j,
r_{it} = demand for item i in period t,
b_{ik} = capacity utilization rate of item i at facility k (capacity units per unit),
s_{ik} = set-up utilization of facility capacity k by item i (capacity units),
CAP_{kt} = capacity of facility k at time t (units of capacity),
q_{it} = upper bound on the production of item i that can be initialized in period t (units).

Variables

y_{it} = inventory of item i at the end of period t,
δ_{it} = 1 if item made in period t, 0 otherwise,
o_{kt} = overtime capacity at facility k in period t,
x_{it} = production of item i initialized in period t.

Multi-stage, multi-item discrete parts manufacturing model

$$v = \min \sum_{i=1}^{N} \sum_{t=1}^{T} (h_i y_{it} + \mathrm{cs}_i \delta_{it}) + \sum_{k=1}^{K} \sum_{t=1}^{T} (\mathrm{co}_{kt} o_{kt}) \tag{5.13}$$

subject to

$$y_{1,t-1} + f_i x_{i,t-Li} - y_{it} - \sum_{j=1}^{N} a_{ij} x_{jt} = r_{it}\,,$$
$$i = 1, \ldots, N,\ t = 1, \ldots, T\,, \tag{5.14}$$

$$\sum_{j=1}^{N} (b_{ik} x_{it} - s_{ik} \delta_{it}) - o_{kt} \leq \mathrm{CAP}_{kt}\,, \quad k = 1, \ldots, K,\ t = 1, \ldots, T\,, \tag{5.15}$$

$$x_{it} - q_{it} \delta_{it} \leq 0\,, \quad i = 1, \ldots, N,\ t = 1, \ldots, T\,, \tag{5.16}$$

$$\delta_{it} = 0 \text{ or } 1\,, \quad x_{it} \geq 0\,, \quad y_{it} \geq 0\,, \quad o_{kt} \geq 0\,. \tag{5.17}$$

The objective function (5.13) represents avoidable inventory set-up, and overtime costs that we seek to minimize. The constraints (5.14) are generalized inventory balance constraints. Ending inventory of each item i in each period t equals starting inventory plus net production (recall f_i is the yield factor) of the item in period $t - L_i$ (recall L_i is the lead time) minus internal and external demand for the item in that period. Here the lead time L_i should equal the minimal lead time that is required to produce or otherwise acquire the item. Capacity restrictions and set-up constraints are given in (5.15) and (5.16).

The multi-item and multi-stage model can easily attain an enormous size; if $N = 1000$, $T = 13$, and $K = 50$, the model would have 26 650 constraints, 52 650 continuous variables and 26 000 zero–one variables. We will discuss two distinct decomposition approaches for breaking up the model into manageable sub-models. One is a nested decomposition scheme proposed by Chapman [1985] that we will discuss in the paragraphs that follow. The other is a hierarchical planning approach that will be discussed in the next subsection. Although both approaches require further basic research and computational experimentation, they offer considerable promise as effective means for dealing with the size and complexity of monolithic mixed integer programming models to support MRP.

The nested decomposition approach is based on two observations about the model. First, if the set-up variables δ_{it} are fixed at zero–one values, the residual sub-model is a linear program. This is the starting point for Benders' decomposition method. The second observation, which we discuss in detail below, is that the generalized inventory balance equations (5.14) possess dynamic Leontief structures. It is easier to optimize over such structures than over ordinary linear programming equations. Thus, if we were to apply Lagrangean relaxation on the capacity constraints (5.15) in the linear programming sub-model, the special structures could be exploited. The resulting decomposition scheme is depicted in Figure 5.2.

A Leontief substitution model is a linear program

$$\begin{aligned} &\min cx \\ &\text{subject to} \quad Ax = b\,, \\ &\qquad\qquad\quad x \geq 0\,, \end{aligned}$$

where $b \geq 0$ and A is an $m \times n$ matrix ($n \geq m$) of rank m with the property: any $m \times m$ invertible sub-matrix B is of the form $B = I - Q$ where the nonnegative matrix Q has the property that Q^n goes to zero as n goes to infinity. This property implies that any basis B has an inverse B^{-1} consisting of nonnegative elements. This in turn implies that an optimal basis B for any $b \geq 0$ is optimal for all $b \geq 0$ since $B^{-1}b \geq 0$.

A dynamic generalization is

$$\begin{aligned} &\min \sum_{t=1}^{T} (c_t x_t) \\ &\text{subject to} \quad A_t x_t = b_t + R_{t-1} x_{t-1} \quad \text{for } t = 1, \ldots, T\,, \\ &\qquad\qquad\quad x_t \geq 0 \quad (x_0 \text{ given})\,, \end{aligned}$$

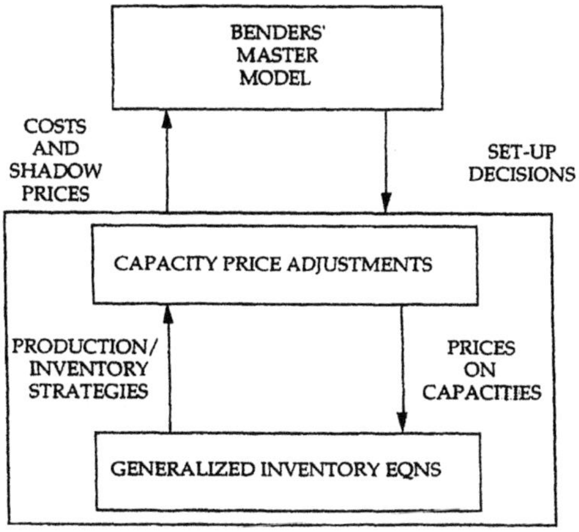

Fig. 5.2.

where A_t is a Leontief substitution matrix and R_t is nonnegative. It can be shown that this multi-period linear programming model can be optimized by computing an optimal basis for each A_t and then computing $x_t = (x_{Bt}, x_{Nt})$ for each t by

$$x_{Bt} = B^{-1}(b_t + R_{t-1}x_{t-1}),$$

$$x_{Nt} = 0.$$

Classic references to dynamic Leontief substitution models and their application to production models are Dantzig [1955] and Veinott [1969].

Now the generalized production/inventory balance equations (5.14) can be viewed as a dynamic Leontief system with substitution, except possibly for transient conditions due to initial inventories and initial production decisions with positive lead times. Looking at (5.14), we can see that net demand for item i

$$r_{il} - y_{i,0} - x_{i,1-L_i}$$

and

$$r_{it} - x_{i,1-L_i} \quad \text{for } t = 2, \ldots, L_i$$

may be negative, thereby destroying the direct application of the Leontief substitution properties. Indeed, we would expect and hope that net demand for some items are negative in early periods, thereby relieving us of the need to produce items in those periods.

Chapman [1985] gives a procedure for indentifying the transients at the start of the planning horizon. Moreover, the residual Leontief substitution systems in this case have a simple structure allowing a solution to be computed without matrix inversion. The algorithm for accomplishing this scans each column of the constraint set exactly once to determine a primal optimal basis and corresponding shadow prices. Calamaro [1985] reports on computational experience with this algorithm and the nested decomposition scheme of Figure 5.2.

The multi-item and multi-stage model allows general product structures and the imposition of capacity constraints. A number of authors have developed algorithmic approaches to restricted, easier versions of the model. Assembly systems have product structures for which each item in the product structure has at most one successor. For uncapacitated assembly systems, Afentakis, Gavish & Karmarkar [1984] developed a Lagrangean relaxation approach that allows production of each item in the product structure to be scheduled separately by a dynamic programming algorithm. The efficiency of their model construction and the decomposition relies upon variables, constraints and costs associated with echelon stock which is defined to be the number of units of an item held explicitly in inventory and implicitly in inventory as parts of its successors. Aftentakis & Gavish [1986] have extended this approach by showing how a general product structure can be transformed to an equivalent assembly structure.

Aftentakis, Gavish & Karmarkar [1984] and Aftentakis & Gavish [1986] employed subgradient optimization of the Lagrangean relaxations which were imbedded in tailored branch-and-bound approaches for globally optimizing the multi-stage models. They also used forward heuristics for generating good solutions. As a result, they were able to report efficient computational results for general multi-stage problems with up to 40 items in which the upper bounds (from the heuristics) and the lower bounds (from the Lagrangean relaxation) are within a few small percentage points.

5.3. *Hierarchical planning*

We saw in the previous two subsections how large scale, monolithic mixed integer programming models for discrete parts manufacturing could be usefully decomposed. In the process, we were able to identify and exploit special structures contained within these monolithic models. Even with the decompositions, however, the models remained monolithic in terms of the treatment of individual items. Specifically, all items in the discrete parts manufacturing models presented above were treated as separate and equal entities to be produced in batches and stored in inventory. No recognition of the possibility for aggregating items into large units for planning or scheduling purposes were made.

Our objective in this section is to discuss how mathematical programming models and decomposition methods can be extended to capture and exploit natural aggregations that occur in many manufacturing environments. For ease of exposition in developing and analyzing the hierarchical model, we will consider a single stage manufacturing system. Our discussion follows closely the development in Graves [1982].

The qualitative basis for considering item aggregation is the concept of *hierarchical planning* [Hax & Meal, 1975]. Using this concept for the single stage system, items may be aggregated into *families*, and families into *types*. A *type* is a collection of items with closely similar seasonal demand patterns and production rates. A *family* is a set of items within a type such that the items in the family share a common setup. In the mixed integer programming model that we develop below, we consider that the *planning function* of the model is to determine time-dependent resource requirements to satisfy aggregate demand for types over a tactical *planning horizon*. We consider that the *scheduling function* of the model is to determine how to allocate these resources over a shorter, *scheduling horizon*.

The hierarchical approach has three advantages over the discrete parts model considered in the previous subsections. First, the aggregation serves to further reduce the dimensionality of the models, both as monolithic and decomposed mixed integer programs. Second, the hierarchical model requires less detailed demand data since demands need only be forecasted for types over the planning horizon [see Axsäter, 1981] for further discussion of aggregation methods in production planning). The third advantage is that the submodels of the decomposed hierarchical model will, or at least should, correspond to the organizational and decision-making echelons of the manufacturing firm.

With this background, we can present a mathematical statement of the model. We employ the notation used in the multi-item multi-stage model presented in the previous section. The main differences are in the definitions of the entities to be produced and the treatment of time. In particular, these are changes in the definitions and meanings of the index sets.

Indices

$i = 1, \ldots, I$ index of types,
$j = 1, \ldots, N$ index of families,
J_i = set of families belonging to type i,
P = length of planning horizon,
p = index of periods in planning horizon,
T = length of scheduling horizon (measured in planning horizon periods),
t = index of periods in scheduling horizon,
k = number of scheduling periods in a planning period.

Figure 5.3 illustrates how we differentiate the length and period definitions for the planning horizon and the scheduling horizon. For $P = 4$@4-week months, $T = 2$@4-week months, and $k = 4$ weeks in a month, the scheduling periods are indexed by $t = 1, \ldots, kT = 8$, and $p = 1, 2, 3, 4$.

Hierarchical planning model

$$v = \min \sum_{p=1}^{P} \left(\mathrm{co}_p o_p + \sum_{i=1}^{I} h_i y_{ip} \right) + \sum_{j=1}^{N} \sum_{t=1}^{kT} (\mathrm{cs}_j \delta_{jt}) \tag{5.18}$$

subject to

$$y_{1,p-1} + x_{ip} - y_{ip} = r_{ip}\,, \quad i = 1, \ldots, I,\ p = 1, \ldots, P\,, \tag{5.19}$$

$$\sum_{i=1}^{I} b_i x_{ip} - o_p \leq \mathrm{CAP}_p\,, \quad p = 1, \ldots, P\,, \tag{5.20}$$

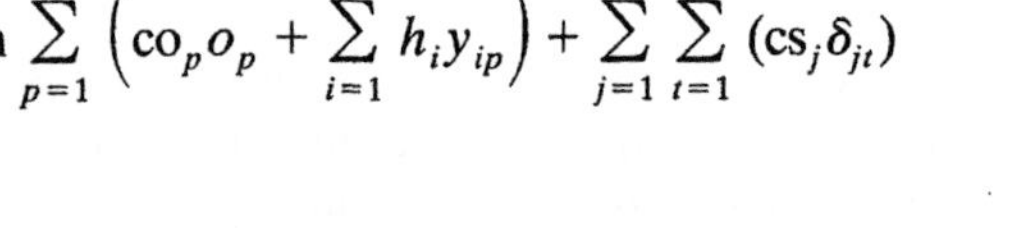

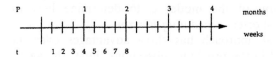

Fig. 5.3. Scheduling and planning horizons.

$$\sum_{j \in J_i} z_{j,kp} - y_{ip} = 0\,, \quad i = 1, \ldots, I,\ p = 1, \ldots, P\,, \tag{5.21}$$

$$z_{j,t-1} + x_{jt} - z_{jt} = r_{jt}\,, \quad j = 1, \ldots, I,\ t = 1, \ldots, kT\,, \tag{5.22}$$

$$x_{jt} - q_{jt}\delta_{jt} \leq 0\,, \quad i = 1, \ldots, N,\ t = 1, \ldots, kT\,, \tag{5.23}$$

$$x_{ip} \geq 0\,, \quad y_{ip} \geq 0\,, \quad o_p \geq 0\,, \tag{5.24}$$

$$\delta_{jt} = 0 \text{ or } 1\,, \quad x_{jt} \geq 0\,, \quad z_{jt} \geq 0\,. \tag{5.25}$$

The objective function (5.18) in this formulation consist of two terms. The first corresponds to avoidable capacity and inventory holding costs associated with the aggregate planning problem over the longer planning horizon consisting of P periods. The second corresponds to avoidable set-up costs associated with the detailed scheduling problem over the shorter scheduling horizon consisting of T periods. As we discussed, the time periods in the time summation for the scheduling problem are a refinement of the time periods used in the planning problem.

The constraints (5.19) and (5.20) describe inventory balance and capacity decisions for the planning problem. The constraints (5.21) link aggregate inventories of types to more detailed inventories of families in each type category. Constraints (5.22) and (5.23) describe inventory balance and set-up decisions for the scheduling problem. Demands for types and demands for families are implicitly linked by the relation

$$\sum_{j \in J_i} \sum_{t=k(p-1)+1}^{kp} r_{jt} = r_{ip} \quad \text{for } p = 1, 2, \ldots, T\,.$$

In words, this relation says that the sum of demands for families j in type i used in (5.22) during the scheduling periods falling in the pth planning period equals the aggregate demand used in (5.19).

The hierarchical planning model can be effectively decomposed by pricing out the linking constraints (5.21). Letting π_{ip} denote the dual variable on each of these constraints, and π the IT-vector with components π_{ip}, the resulting Lagrangean separates as follows

$$L(\pi) = A(\pi) + \sum_{i=1}^{I} \sum_{j \in J_i} F_j(\pi)\,,$$

where $A(\pi)$ is a linear programming model for optimizing the planning problem

$$A(\pi) = \min \sum_{p=1}^{P} \left\{ \mathrm{co}_p o_p + \sum_{i=1}^{I} (h_i - \pi_{ip}) y_{ip} \right\} \qquad (5.26,$$

subject to (5.19), (5.20), (5.24)

and the $F_j(\pi)$ for each family item j is a single item dynamic lot-size model of the type discussed in Section 2.2.

$$F_j(\pi) = \min\left\{ \sum_{k=1}^{kT} (\mathrm{cs}_j \delta_{jt}) + \sum_{p=1}^{P} \pi_{ip} z_{j,kp} \right\} \tag{5.27}$$

subject to (5.22), (5.23), (5.25) .

Note that, in the dynamic lot-size sub-model (5.27), the decomposition has induced holding prices π_{ip} on inventories of families at the end of the aggregate period p. Unlike previous instances of this sort of model, however, these holding prices might be negative as well as positive. A negative holding price on type i items in planning period p would indicate that, from a planning viewpoint, scheduling production to create inventories of families in the stated type in the stated planning period has global benefits.

The same algorithmic procedures discussed in Section 3, and in Section 5.1 above, for determining the dual variables π_{ip} are available for this decomposition. Since the dynamic lot-size sub-models involve integer variables, the dual decomposition method will suffer from duality gaps between the hierarchical planning model and its dual model. Graves [1982] discusses methods for overcoming duality gaps and choosing dual variables, and reports on computational experience with test models.

6. Job-shop scheduling

Job-shop scheduling problems involve jobs consisting of a variety of machine operations to be processed on a number of machines. Moreover, there may be precedence constraints on the sequencing of operations associated with a given job. For example, these might be finishing operations on paper produced at a paper mill or castings produced at a foundry, or, maintenance and repair operations on jet engines. As we shall see, the complexity of job-shop scheduling leads to large and difficult combinatorial optimization models. Thus, the practical use of models and associated analytical and heuristic methods should be to identify demonstrably good schedules, rather than to persist in trying to find an optimal solution.

6.1. Basic model

We consider a combinatorial optimization model proposed by Lageweg, Lenstra & Rinnooy Kan [1977] and a number of other authors for a large class of job-shop scheduling problems. This model is comprised of a number of jobs, each consisting of a number of operations to be processed on preassigned machines. The objective is to minimize the total length of time required to finish all jobs. In so doing, the model must simultaneously sequence the processing of operation assigned to each machine and ensure that the precedence relations among operations of each job are obeyed. Extensions of the basic model are considered in the following section.

Indices and index sets
i = jobs, $i = 1, \ldots, I$,
n_i = number of operations in job i,
j = operations, $j = 1, \ldots, N = \Sigma_{i=1}^{I} n_i$,
k = machine, $k = 1, \ldots, K$,
k_j = machine on which operation j is to be performed,
$J_k = \{j \mid k_j = k\}$ = operations assigned to machine k,
$R_k = |J_k|$ = number of jobs assigned to machine k,
r = machine sequence order, $r = 1, \ldots, R_k$.

The assumption for this class of job-shop scheduling problems is that the operations in a given job are to be processed sequentially; that is, operation $j-1$ must be completed before operation j may begin. Thus, there is a total ordering of the operations of each job. For notational purposes, we assume that the operations of job i are indexed by $j = N_{i-1} + 1, \ldots, N_i$, where

$$N_i = \sum_{g=1}^{i} n_g .$$

Parameters
p_j = processing time for operation j,
T = upper bound on total processing time.

Variables
t_j = start time for operation j,

$$x_{jg} = \begin{cases} 1 & \text{if operation } j \text{ performed before operation } g \\ 0 & \text{if operation } g \text{ performed before operation } j \end{cases} \quad \text{for } j,\ g \in J_k,$$

T = total processing time for all jobs.

Job-shop scheduling model

$$v = \min F \tag{6.1}$$

subject to

for $i = 1, \ldots, I$

$$t_j \geq t_{j-1} + p_{j-1} \quad \text{for } j = N_{i-1} + 2, \ldots, N_i , \tag{6.2}$$

$$F \geq t_{N_i} + p_{N_i} , \tag{6.3}$$

for $k = 1, \ldots, K$

$$\left.\begin{array}{l} t_g \geq t_j + p_j x_{jg} - T(1 - x_{jg}) \\ t_j \geq t_g + p_g(1 - x_{jg}) - T x_{jg} \end{array}\right\} \quad \text{for all } j,\ g \in J_k\,, \tag{6.4}$$

$$x_{jg} = 0 \text{ or } 1 \quad \text{for all } j,\ g \in K_j\,, \tag{6.5}$$

$$F \geq 0\,, \qquad t_j \geq 0 \quad \text{for } j = 1, \ldots, N\,. \tag{6.6}$$

The objective function (6.1) is to minimize the time to complete all jobs. The variable time F is, by (6.3), equal to the maximum of the completion times of the I jobs. The constraints (6.2) state that the start times of operation j for $j = 2$ through $j = n_i$ for each job i must occur after operation $j-1$ has been completed. The start time for operation 1 is not constrained by this total precedence ordering.

The start times t_j of operations are also constrained by the sequence of operations to be performed on each machine k. Specifically, for each pair of operations j, g assigned to machine k, the constraints (6.4) state that either operation j will precede operation g, or that operation g will precede operation j. For example, if $x_{jg} = 1$, then the first of two constraints is binding ($t_g \geq t_j + p_j$), whereas if $x_{jg} = 0$, then the second of the two constraints is binding ($t_j \geq t_g + p_g$).

To sum up, the start time t_j of operation j is constrained both by the total precedence ordering on the operations of its job, and by the sequencing order of operations from a variety of jobs on the machine k_j on which j is processed. The former constraints (6.2) and (6.3) are the simple constraints of a network optimization type found in critical path method models [see Schrage, 1986]. The latter constraints (6.4) are logical constraints of a type referred to in the literature as disjunctive [Roy & Sussmann, 1964; Balas, 1979].

The result is a mixed integer programming model of great size and complexity. If $I = 10$, $n_i = 10$ for all i, $K = 8$, and $R_k = 25$ for all k, the model would have 2580 constraints, 201 continuous variables, and 240 zero–one variables. To try to circumvent extreme computational difficulties, several researchers have proposed solution techniques based on combinations of branch-and-bound schemes, heuristics and lower bounds based on easy to optimize relaxations of the job scheduling model [see Lageweg, Lenstra & Rinnooy Kan, 1977; Adams, Balas & Zawack, 1988]. A central construct is the disjunctive graph which consists of a node for each operation j with an associated weight p_j, plus a dummy node 0 for the start of all operations, and a dummy node $N+1$ for the completion of all operations. For each consecutive pair of operations $j-1$ and j of the same job, there is a directed conjunctive arc. For each pair of operations assigned to the same machine, there is a (undirected) disjunctive edge. The major task in optimizing a given job-shop scheduling problem is to pick a direction for each edge thereby determining an order for the pair of operations. If all the edges have been ordered, and an acyclic network results, the time associated with the implied schedule is computed by finding the longest path, based on the node weights, in the directed network. If the resulting network is cyclic, the implied schedule is infeasible.

Example 6.1. Figure 6.1 taken from Lageweg, Lenstra & Rinnooy Kan [1977] depicts a 3 job, 8 operation, disjunctive graph. The jobs are: (1) 1, 2, 3; (2) 4, 5; (3) 6, 7, 8. The eight operations correspond to the nodes in the network. The directed arcs (the ones with one head) are called *conjunctive* arcs and reflect the sequence in which operations of a job are to be performed. The machine assignments are: machine (1) 1, 4, 7; machine (2) 2, 5, 6; machine (3) 3, 8. The undirected arcs (the ones with two heads) are called *disjunctive* arcs and reflect the fact that both operations must be performed on the same machine. The numbers next to the nodes are the processing times of the operations. Figure 6.2 is an acyclic network representing a feasible (and optimal) schedule. The longest path is 0, 1, 4, 7, 8, 9 with time equal to 14.

In a typical branch-and-bound scheme, a sub-problem would be characterized by a subset of disjunctive arcs that have been resolved with respect to order (direction); the directed network including these arcs and all the conjunctive arcs must be acyclic. The method proceeds to try to fathom this subproblem (that is, find its best completion, or establish that all completions will have higher objective function value than an optimal solution) by optimizing easy to solve relaxations of the residual job-shop scheduling problem, thereby determining lower bounds. If lower bounding fails to fathom a subproblem, two or more new subproblems are created from it by branching on one or more disjunctive arcs. Knowledge about scheduling conflicts and other problem specific information is used in making the branching decisions. These analytic and experimental approaches are reviewed and extended in Lageweg, Lenstra & Rinooy Kan [1977].

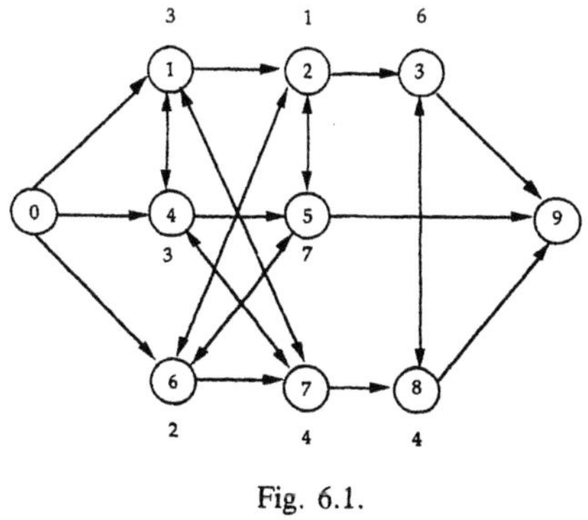

Fig. 6.1.

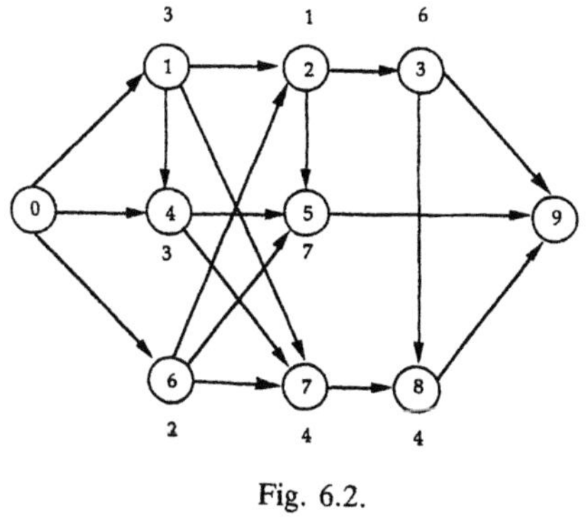

Fig. 6.2.

Example 6.2. For completeness, we give the mixed integer programming formulation of the job-shop scheduling problem of Example 6.1. This formulation is

$$\min F$$

subject to

$$
\begin{array}{rl}
(2) & F - T3 \geqslant 6, \\
(3) & F - T5 \geqslant 7, \\
(4) & F - T8 \geqslant 4, \\
(5) & T2 - T1 \geqslant 3, \\
(6) & T3 - T2 \geqslant 1, \\
(7) & T5 - T4 \geqslant 3, \\
(8) & T7 - T6 \geqslant 2, \\
(9) & T8 - T7 \geqslant 4, \\
(10) & -103\,X14 - T1 + T4 \geqslant -100, \\
(11) & 103\,X14 + T1 - T4 \geqslant 3, \\
(12) & -103\,X17 - T1 + T7 \geqslant -100, \\
(13) & 104\,X17 + T1 - T7 \geqslant 4, \\
(14) & -103\,X47 - T4 + T7 \geqslant -100, \\
(15) & 107\,X47 + T4 - T7 \geqslant 4, \\
(16) & -101\,X25 + T5 - T2 \geqslant -100, \\
(17) & 104\,X25 - T5 + T2 \geqslant 7, \\
(18) & -101\,X26 - T2 + T6 \geqslant -100, \\
(19) & 102\,X26 + T2 - T6 \geqslant 2, \\
(20) & -107\,X56 - T5 + T6 \geqslant -100, \\
(21) & 102\,X56 + T5 - T6 \geqslant 2, \\
(22) & -106\,X38 - T3 + T8 \geqslant -100, \\
(23) & 104\,X38 + T3 - T8 \geqslant 4.
\end{array}
$$

An optimal solution to this model is:
objective function value = 14.0000000

Variable	Value
*X*14	1.000000
*X*17	1.000000
*X*47	1.000000
*X*25	1.000000
*X*26	1.000000
*X*56	0.000000
*X*38	1.000000
F	14.000000
*T*3	4.000000
*T*5	6.000000
*T*8	10.000000
*T*2	3.000000
*T*1	0.000000
*T*4	3.000000
*T*7	6.000000
*T*6	4.000000

6.2. Extensions to the basic model

We discuss briefly a number of important extensions to the basic model presented in the previous subsection. The extensions consider:
- partial ordering of precedences,
- assignment of operations to machines,
- changeover times,
- alternative objective functions,
- resource allocation.

Partial ordering of precedences
The precedences governing the processing of operations $j = N_{i-1}, \ldots, N_i$ of job i may constitute a partial rather than a total ordering as we assumed in developing the basic model. The partial ordering can be described by the relation P where jPg indicates that operation g may begin only after operation j has been completed. The job-shop model of the previous subsection may be easily modified to accommodate the partial order. We simply replace the constraints (6.2) by the constraints

$$t_g - t_j \geqslant p_j \quad \text{for all } jPg \text{ in the partial order}.$$

Assignment of operations to machines
We assumed in the basic model that each operation is assigned a priori to a machine. The implication is that only one machine can perform the operation, or possibly that the choice of machine for each operation is obvious. In the more general situation, there would be a set, which we denote by K_j, of machines that can perform the operation. In this case the assignment of operations to machines must be added to the basic model as decision options.

The extension requires that we add constraints and variables. First, we define new variables

$$y_{jk} = \begin{cases} 1 & \text{if operation } j \text{ is assigned to machine } k, \\ 0 & \text{otherwise.} \end{cases}$$

Then for each operation j for which there is a choice of machine, we add the constraint

$$\sum_{k \in J_k} y_{jk} = 1 .$$

In addition, the constraints (6.4) for each pair of operations j and g that *might* (are allowed to) be assigned to the same machine k are required to hold only if $y_{jk} = 1$ *and* $y_{gk} = 1$. This condition can be enforced by changing (6.4) to

$$t_g \geqslant t_j + p_j x_{jgk} - T(1 - x_{jgk}) - T(2 - y_{jk} - y_{gk})$$

and

$$t_j \geq t_g + p_j(1 - x_{jgk}) - Tx_{jgk} - T(2 - y_{jk} - y_{gk}) .$$

Here, the zero–one variable x_{jgk} has a physical interpretation only if operations j and g are actually assigned to machine k. If the number of combinations of possible operations and machines is large, this extension causes the already difficult MIP formulation of the basic model to become even more difficult.

Changeover times

In general we can expect the time to schedule an individual machine will be affected by changeover times p_{jg} that depend on the specific consecutive pairs (j, g) encountered in a sequence of operations on the machine. Since, however, a zero–one variable is required to capture each changeover option, a direct mixed integer programming extension of the basic model that included changeovers would be excessively large.

A less monolithic mixed integer programming approach appears necessary for this class of problems. We saw in Section 2.2 how to model such changeover times on a single machine as a time-dependent traveling salesman problem. Ignoring precedence constraints for the moment, the resulting sequencing/scheduling problem with changeovers, including the assignment of operations to machines, can be viewed as a collection of traveling salesman problems, one for each machine, linked together by assignment constraints. The traveling salesmen problems can, in principle, be used to generate sequencing schedules for each machine. Feasible sequencing must then be assembled to satisfy the precedence constraints by using dual decomposition methods. This is an area of current research.

Alternative objective functions

The objective function in the basic model was to minimize the time to complete all jobs. A more general objective would be to associate a tardiness cost function $C_i(t_{N_i} + p_{N_i})$ (see Section 2.2) with completing each job by $t_{N_i} + p_{N_i}$, and to minimize their sum over all jobs. We point out, however, that this relatively straightforward extension of the basic job-shop scheduling mixed integer programming model is a serious complication for the disjunctive graph optimization approach. This is because the job-shop scheduling problem no longer reduces to a longest path problem once all disjunctive edges have been oriented. With the more general objective function, we are in effect seeking to compute simultaneously the longest path for each job.

More general objectives would involve a combination of job completion times and avoidable costs to be minimized. For example, in the case discussed above, in which each operation j may be assigned to a machine in a set K_j, differentiated costs for processing operation j on different machines could be captured by adding an appropriate term to the objective function. This term might take the form

$$\sum_{j=1}^{N_I} \sum_{k \in K_j} c_{jk} y_{jk} ,$$

where c_{jk} is the cost of processing operation j on machine k.

Resource allocation

A somewhat simpler version of the job-shop scheduling problem is to treat the machine scheduling part of the problem as resource utilization constraints, rather than detailed sequencing constraints as we treated them in the model (6.1) through (6.6). This model, called the project scheduling with resource constraints model, has been studied by Christofides, Alvarez-Valdes & Tamarit [1987] and by Talbot & Patterson [1978]. Christofides, Alvarez-Valdes and Tamarit [1987] applied Lagrangean relaxation methods and, at the same time, develop stronger mixed integer programming formulations of the project scheduling with resource constraints model. Fisher [1973a,b] proposed a similar Lagrangean relaxation for this class of models.

7. Treatment of uncertainty

The mathematical programming models considered thus far have been strictly deterministic. The models treated all parameters of the future – demand, production rates, yields, lead times, and so on – as if they were known with certainty. This was clearly a simplifying, perhaps even a heroic, assumption, although only certain key parameters will be highly uncertain in a given application.

The fact that the models we have discussed do not explicitly treat critical uncertainties does not seriously detract from their usefulness in many if not most cases. Sensitivity analyses and multiple optimization runs under various parameter settings can usually provide the insights needed to plan effectively for an uncertain future. Moreover, developing explicit descriptions of the uncertainties may be difficult, time consuming and costly. Since production managers have only recently begun to seriously consider using deterministic mathematical programming models to support their planning and scheduling activities, it would be imprudent to suggest that their attention should be directed immediately at the sophisticated and more difficult to understand stochastic models that we discuss in this section.

Nevertheless, some production planning and scheduling applications would undoubtedly benefit greatly from explicit modeling of key uncertainties. This is the situation, for example, in the manufacture of style goods (e.g., dinnerware, clothing). Typically, a company with a product line of 100 distinct style goods items might expect only 5 to 10 times to ultimately experience heavy sales, but it is difficult to forecast in advance which items these will be. Another example where uncertainty is critical is in the manufacture of semiconductor wafers where the yields of certain production stages have high variance, especially in the early periods of production.

Ignoring for the moment issues of model size and computational complexity, stochastic programming with recourse models [see Wets, 1983, or Wagner, 1969] are an extension of the deterministic models discussed above that permit production planning and scheduling uncertainties to be explicitly modeled and evaluated. These models consider simultaneously multiple scenarios of an uncertain future. Optimal contingency plans for each scenario are computed along with here-and-now strategies that optimally hedge against these plans. Such hedging strategies cannot in general be identified by any deterministic model.

Bitran, Haas & Matsuo [1987] presented a stochastic mixed integer programming model for production planning of style goods with high set-up costs and forecast revisions. The model is a stochastic generalization of the multi-item discrete parts production model considered in Section 5.2. The key element of uncertainty in their model is demand for the style goods which is concentrated in the last period of the year; forecasts of demands are revised each period. The objective of their model is to determine a production plan that maximizes expected profit. The objective function includes selling price, salvage value, and the costs of material, inventory holding costs, set-up costs, and the loss of goodwill by not being able to satisfy demand. Using the model's hierarchical structure (see Section 5.4), Bitran, Haas & Matsuo formulate a deterministic approximation to the stochastic model that gives good results under certain assumptions about problem structure.

Hiller [1986] generalized the multi-stage discrete parts manufacturing model of Section 5.3 to a stochastic programming model with recourse for the case when demand for finished goods is uncertain. This model rationalizes the computation of safety stocks at all stages in a multi-stage environment taking into account capacity constraints that limit the buildup of such stocks. This stochastic programming model also provides new insights into the risks faced by a production manager (de-valued inventory or lost sales). The model's structure allows such risks to be constrained; parametric analyses of expected costs versus various measures of risk can also be computed. Beale, Forrest & Taylor [1980] reported on computational experiments with a similar class of models.

We return briefly to a discussion of approaches for dealing with the size and complexity of stochastic programming models for production planning and scheduling which are generalizations of large scale deterministic models that are complex in their own right. Again, decomposition methods are available for breaking up large, monolithic models. In particular, Benders' decomposition method applied to a stochastic programming with recourse model allows the model to be decomposed into a master model involving here-and-now decisions, plus a sub-model for each scenario of the uncertain future [Birge, 1985]. Bienstock & Shapiro [1988] reported on a successful implementation of such a decomposition for a capacity expansion planning model; they also discuss how to combine Benders' decomposition applied to mixed integer programming with its application to stochastic programming. Gassman [1990] reported on a general purpose computer code for stochastic programming based on a nested version of Benders' decomposition method.

8. Coordinating production with other company activities

Mathematical programming models provide management with analytic tools that allow company activities to be much more broadly coordinated than they were in the days before the information revolution. The implications to manufacturing firms goes beyond opportunities for more effective production planning and scheduling. Using decision support systems based on mathematical programming models, management can also make more effective decisions about purchasing, distribution, marketing and strategic plans from the perspective of the manufacturing engine that drives the firm. In this section, we review briefly several applications that indicate how models have promoted improved coordination within manufacturing firms.

Purchasing is an important, but generally neglected functional area that admits useful analysis by models. Bender, Brown, Isaac & Shapiro [1985] reported on the application of mixed integer programming models to support vendor contract selection at IBM. The models consider a family of parts; as many as 100 parts have been evaluated by a single model. Contract selection is difficult because a buyer must consider simultaneously multiple vendors and contracts. Each vendor will offer one or more contracts for one or more parts with volume price breaks, fixed costs, and even resource constraints (machine time, labor). The purchasing decisions are driven by parts requirements that are obtained automatically from an MRP system. The objective is to minimize acquisition, in-bound transportation and inventory costs over multiple period planning horizons of a few months to three years.

The initial application of the modeling system was to the acquisition of parts for mainframe computers. Subsequently, the system has been used to develop purchasing plans for parts from a range of products. The system has also been employed as a negotiating tool with vendors whose quoted prices exclude them from an optimal solution.

Coordination of production plans with distribution plans for firms with multiple production sites in a second important area where models have proven useful. Klingman, Phillips, Steiger & Young [1987] reported on an ambitious and successful project at Citgo Petroleum Company in which large scale linear programming refinery models were linked to a network optimization model for evaluation decision regarding short-term distribution, pricing, inventory and exchange agreements. These models were imbedded in an integrated information and corporate planning system whose use has contributed significantly to marketing and refining profits.

Brown, Shapiro & Singhal [1992] reported on the successful implementation and testing of a tactical production/distribution planning model for an industrial gases company with multiple plants. Given monthly demand forecasts for products by customer locations, the model determines simultaneously which customers to allocate to each plant, how much of each product should be made by each plant, and the production slates and lengths of time slates are run at each plant, so as to minimize total production and distribution costs. The production sub-model in this application was derived from chemical engineering models that describe optimal plant configurations under a variety of output rates for each product. This sub-model was subsequently transformed into an individual plant production scheduling model that runs on a mini-computer in the plant.

Van Roy [1989] reported on a mixed integer programming model for solving complex multi-level production and distribution problems faced by a petrochemical company. Propane and butane are produced at refineries, shipped in bulk to plants for bottling, and then distributed to customers. The final distribution may either be direct or via depots and breakpoints. The model addressed the problem of locating bottling plants and depots, determining production levels at the refineries and the plants, determining inventories at the plants and the depots, selecting customer assignments to plants or depots, and determining aggregate transportation and driver requirements, at minimal cost. Advanced mixed integer programming modeling techniques were used to speed the computation.

Shapiro [1984] discussed a model for optimizing manufacturing and distribution plans for a nationwide consumer products company. This model takes into account manufacturing costs and capacities, warehouse locations, and distribution costs in computing a strategy that minimizes the total cost of products delivered to markets with fixed demands. Using quantitative marketing models developed by Little [1975], Covert [1987] extended a version of the consumer model to incorporate marketing and sales plans. In the extension, demand is considered endogenous (variable) and created by various marketing and sales strategies regarding prices, promotion, advertising, and so on. The objective of the model becomes maximization of net revenues which equals gross revenues from variables sales minus marketing and sales costs to create optimal demand, and minus manufacturing and distribution costs to meet these demands.

Brown, Geoffrion & Bradley [1981] implemented and tested a large scale mixed integer programming for coordinating yearly production and sales plans for manufacturers with limited shared tooling. The objective function in this model is maximization of net revenues equalling gross revenues minus production and inventory holding costs. Product mix decisions are allowed within a range of forecasted demand. Their model is appropriate for companies that make cast, extruded, molded, pressed or stamped products.

Lagrangean relaxation methods (see Section 3) were used to efficiently extract demonstrably good solutions to this model. The sub-models in the dual decomposition consisted of: (1) network optimization models to determine monthly production plans for tools and tool/machine combinations; and (2) dynamic lot-size models (see Section 2.2) to determine production plans for each item. A planning system based on the model was implemented and used regularly at a large manufacturing company.

Models for analyzing strategic planning issues in a manufacturing firm require aggregate production planning and scheduling sub-models. The types of options to be evaluated by such a model include plant and infrastructure capacity expansion, mergers, acquisitions, long term raw materials contracts, new technologies, new markets, and so on. Dembo & Zipkin [1983] discussed methods for aggregating refinery models such as the one discussed in Section 4.1 so that they may be used in strategic analyses. Hiller & Shapiro [1986] showed how to incorporate manufacturing learning effects into capacity expansion planning.

Nonlinear mixed integer programming models for capacity expansion planning of electric utilities have received considerable attention [e.g., Noonan & Giglio, 1977; Bloom, 1983]. Bienstock & Shapiro [1988] devised and implemented a stochastic programming with recourse model that explicitly treats uncertainties regarding demand, fuel costs, and environmental restrictions.

9. Future directions

In previous sections, we discussed a broad range of production planning and scheduling applications of mathematical programming. When implemented, some of the models discussed can easily consist of thousands of constraints and tens of thousands of variables. Many linear and mixed integer programming models of this size have been optimized, at least to a small error tolerance, by commercial codes on today's computers. Decomposition methods for large scale models are conceptually appealing and, for selected applications, have already proven themselves effective in extracting good solutions in a reasonable length of computing time.

However, major improvements in optimization algorithms and methods must still be actively sought, especially for time critical applications. And, although mathematical programming models provide a rich and powerful foundation for analyzing production planning and scheduling problems, the scientific community has not yet demonstrated that they can be routinely generated and optimized in a flexible, reliable and interpretable manner. Interest in applying the models is growing significantly, if only because recent advances in information technology have finally made it possible to acquire the necessary data on a timely basis. Thus, the moment appears ripe for pursuing basic and applied research developments that will permit the promise of mathematical programming models to be better realized.

We can identify five areas of research and technological development that should have a large impact on mathematical programming applications over the next five to ten years:

• Mixed integer programming model formulations and solution methods,
• Explicit modeling of uncertainty,
• Advances in computer hardware,
• Advances in modeling, optimization and associated data base management software,
• Integration of mathematical programming with knowledge-based systems.

Each of these areas is discussed briefly in the paragraphs that follow.

MIP modeling formulations and solution methods

The central role played by mixed integer programming in production planning and scheduling models is evident from the applications reviewed in the previous sections. In Section 5, we discussed the promising new research on stronger mixed integer programming formulations that have already led to computational breakthroughs on some models. We have also seen a growing number of applications of Lagrangean relaxation (dual decomposition) methods. When combined with heuristics for determining feasible solutions, these methods have proven successful in rapidly determining demonstrably good solutions to complex models. Moreover, new heuristic methods based on simulated annealing [e.g., Hajek, 1988] have recently produced promising results for certain classes of combinatorial optimization models. Once the research community reaches an understanding of how to fully integrate these three complementary approaches to mixed integer programming – model formulation, Lagrangean relaxation, and heuristics – we can expect to achieve significantly more effective computational schemes for determining demonstrably good solutions to production planning and scheduling models.

Explicit modeling of uncertainty

Modeling uncertainty by stochastic programming generalizations of deterministic mathematical programming models was discussed in Section 7. Stochastic programming with recourse offers a rigorous formalism for evaluating the impact of uncertainty on production planning and scheduling plans. However, a great deal of artistry and problem specific analysis is required to effectively employ the formalism since it can easily produce complex models.

An area of current and future research is to develop hybrid models in which mathematical programming is combined with Monte Carlo simulation. For a richly elaborated, multi-stage probability tree, the idea of this approach is to sample paths in the tree using simulation, rather than to explicitly analyze all paths and their associated contingency planes. New paradigms must be created for characterizing properties of the best here-and-now strategy uncovered by the hybrid approach.

Another area of future research is to seek a synthesis of the resource allocation and sequencing capabilities of linear and mixed integer programming with the descriptive capabilities of models of networks of queues [Harrison, 1988]. Network queueing models have been successfully applied to job-shop scheduling problems [Wein, 1990].

Advances in computer hardware

The advance in microprocessor performance over the past five years has been called 'The Attack of the Killer Micros', Howe [1990]. Starting at a level of 1 MIP (million instructions per second) in 1985, the processing speed of commercially available microprocessors has risen to a current level of 40 MIPS. Performance is expected to significantly exceed 100 MIPS by 1993, and may reach as high as 1000 MIPS by 1995.

As a result of these developments, large scale mathematical programming models can be effectively generated and optimized on desktop workstations, thereby greatly increasing the ease and flexibility of using models, and greatly decreasing the cost. For example, Shapiro, Singhal & Wagner [1992] report on a PC based system for integrated manufacturing and distribution planning that has optimized models with more than 20 000 constraints. To a certain extent, the future has already arrived. A major computer manufacturer is offering a desktop workstation that can perform large scale optimizations at more than half the speed of a mainframe computer. The workstation's selling price is approximately 1% of the mainframe's price.

Although increases in the speed of computation will improve the performance of algorithms for optimizing mixed integer programming models for production scheduling, the computational complexity of these models guarantees that their optimization will remain a challenge to researchers and practitioners for the foreseeable future. A simple example illustrates why this is so. A scheduling model with 200 zero–one variables is small by today's standards, but the number of possible solutions of these variables, 2^{200}, greatly exceeds the number of atoms in the universe. Of course, any reasonable branch-and-bound method would reduce the number of solutions explicitly tested to at most a few hundred. The point is that sheer computational power cannot outstrip the exponential growth as a function of the number of variables of performing a branch-and-bound search. Algorithmic ingenuity and computing flexibility will always be required to create effective computational schemes.

In this regard, large scale linear and mixed integer programming computation should be greatly enhanced by computations carried out on coarse grained parallel computers. These are computers consisting of a dozen to several hundred independent processors. Each processor has significant computing power and memory in its own right – the advances in microcomputer performance are highly relevant here – and it is efficiently linked to other processors and large shared memories. One advantage of implementing decomposition or mixed integer programming branch-and-bound methods on such a computer is greatly increasing computing power since decomposition submodels or linear programming subproblems can be optimized in parallel. Coarse grained computing also offers greater flexibility in applying algorithmic strategies [see Brown, Shapiro & Waterman, 1988]. For example, one can run multiple branch-and-bound search strategies for mixed integer programming in parallel, and then concentrate on those strategies and areas of the branch-and-bound tree that yield good solutions. Although, in principle, one could program a serial computer to do the same thing, the distributed computing environment of a coarse grained machine facilitates the implementation and testing of such a scheme.

Modeling, optimization, and data management software

In many respects, the process of moving forward form a production manager's problems and his/her data base to an appropriate and correct family of mathematical programming models is more difficult than the process of optimizing the model. For this reason, the science and art of model generation has recently attracted a great deal of attention [Brown, Northup & Shapiro, 1986; Geoffrion, 1987; Brooke, Kendrick & Meeraus, 1988; Fourer, Gay & Kernighan, 1990]. Space does not permit a discussion of the central issues and proposed approaches. We simply mention that these researchers and others are studying symbolic, object-oriented, nonprocedural computer implementation approaches to model generation that should enhance the development of flexible and effective decision support systems based on mathematical programming model.

The flexibility and power of today's microprocessors have stimulated the development of many new linear and mixed integer programming systems. Llewellyn & Sharda [1990] reported on more than 40 commercially available pc-based systems. Several of these systems can handle models of very large size.

The production planning and scheduling models discussed in this chapter structure the manner in which data should be arranged to support decision making even when the models are not generated and optimized. To a large extent, the current interest in better model generation software is a reflection of the need to rationalize and streamline the acquisition, transformation and organization of data acquired from transactional data bases for input to models. Dolk [1988] discussed these developments from the perspective of model management systems and their connection to relational data management systems.

Integration with knowledge-based systems

A great deal has been spoken and written about the potential integration of knowledge-based (that is, expert systems) with mathematical programming models. Very little has been achieved from a formal viewpoint, although a number of ad hoc implementations have been reported in the literature. Formalisms of model generation discussed in the previous paragraph may soon provide the missing links for insightful integrations of the two technologies.

An expert system could prove very useful in determining the most effective mathematical programming model to generate for a given production planning or scheduling problem. An expert system would also be very useful in explaining or interpreting an optimal solution to such a model. Finally, for time-critical applications requiring a large scale model, computation could be significantly speeded up by having an expert system direct the branch-and-bound search or other solution algorithms. These three potential areas of integration require the automation of expertise about *two* domains: the real-world production planning and scheduling domain, and the domain of relevant models.

References

Adams, J., E. Balas and D. Zawack (1988). The shifting bottleneck procedure for job-shop scheduling. *Management Sci.* 34, 391–401.

Afentakis, P., and B. Gavish (1986). Optimal lot-sizing algorithms for complex product structures. *Oper. Res.* 34, 237–249.

Afentakis, P., B. Gavish and U. Karmarkar (1984). Computationally efficient optimal solutions to the lot-sizing problem in multistage assembly systems. *Sci. Management* 30, 222–239.

Ahuja, R., T.L. Magnanti and J.B. Orlin (1989). Network flows, in: G.L. Nemhauser, A.H. Rinnooy Kan and M.J. Todd (eds.), *Handbooks in Operations Research and Management Science, Vol. 1, Optimization*, North-Holland, Amsterdam, Chapter 4.

Axsäter, S. (1981). Aggregation of product data for hierarchical production planning. *Oper. Res.* 29, 744–756.

Bahl, H.C., L.P. Ritzman and J.D.N. Gupta (1987). Determining lot sizes and resource requirements: A review. *Oper. Res.* 35, 329–345.

Baker, T.E., and L.S. Lasdon (1985). Successive linear programming at Exxon. *Management Sci.* 31, 264–274.

Balas, E. (1979). Disjunctive programming. *Ann. Discrete Math.* 5, 3–51.

Ball, M.O., and M.J. Magazine (1988). Sequencing of insertions in printed circuit board assemblies. *Oper. Res.* 36, 192–201.

Barany, I., T.J. Van Roy and L.A. Wolsey (1984). Strong formulations for multi-item capacitated lot-sizing. *Management Sci.* 30, 1255–1261.

Beale, E.M.L., J.J.H. Forrest and C.J. Taylor (1980). Multi-time-period stochastic programming, in: M.A.H. Dempster (ed.), *Stochastic Programming*, Academic Press, New York, Chapter 23.

Bell, D.E., and J.F. Shapiro (1977). A convergent duality theory for integer programming. *Oper. Res.* 25, 419–434.

Bender, P.S., R.W. Brown, M.H. Isaac and J.F. Shapiro (1985). Improving purchasing productivity at IBM with a normative decision support system. *Interfaces* 15, 106–115.

Biegler, L.T. (1985). Improved infeasible path optimization for sequential modular simulators-II: The optimiztion algorithm. *Comput. Chem. Engrg.*, 257–267.

Bieger, L.T., and R.R. Hughes (1985). Feasible path simulation with sequential modular simulators. *Comput. Chem. Engrg.*, 379–394.

Bienstock, D., and J.F. Shapiro (1988). Optimizing resource acquisition decisions by stochastic programming. *Management Sci.* 34, 215–229.

Biewar, D.B., and I.E. Grossmann (1987). Incorporating scheduling in the optimal design of multiproduct batch plants, Paper presented at Annual AIChE Meeting, New York.

Billington, P.J., J.O. McClain and L.J. Thomas (1983). Mathematical approaches to capacity-constrained MRP systems: Review, formulation and problem reduction. *Management Sci.* 29, 1126–1141.

Birge, J.R. (1985). Decomposition and partitioning methods for multistage stochastic linear programs. *Oper. Res.* 33, 989–1007.

Bitran, G.R., E.A. Haas and H. Matsuo (1987). Production planning of style goods with high setup costs and forecast revisions. *Oper. Res.* 34, 226–236.

Bloom, J.A. (1983). Solving an electricity generating capacity expansion planning problem by generalized Benders' decomposition. *Oper. Res.* 31, 84–100.

Bodington, J.E., and T.E. Baker (1990). A history of mathematical programming in the petroleum industry. *Interfaces* 20(4), 117–132.

Brooke, A., D. Kendrick and A. Meeraus (1988). *GAMS: A User's Guide*, Scientific Press, Palo Alto, CA.

Brown, G.G., A.M. Geoffrion and G.H. Bradley (1981). Production and sales planning with limited shared tooling at the key operation. *Management Sci.* 27, 247–248.

Brown, R.W., W.D. Northup and J.F. Shapiro (1986). A modeling and optimization system for business planning, in: G. Mitra (ed.), *Computer Methods to Assist Decision Making*, North-Holland, Amsterdam.

Brown, R.W., J.F. Shapiro and V.M. Singhal (1990). Production allocation modeling system: Optimizing for competitive advantage in a mature manufacturing industry. Working Paper, Sloan School of Management, MIT, Cambridge, MA.

Brown, R.W., J.F. Shapiro and P.J. Waterman (1988). Parallel computing for production scheduling. *Manuf. Syst.* 6, 56–64.

Buzacott, J.A., and D.D. Yao (1986). Flexible manufacturing systems: A review of analytical models. *Management Sci.* 32, 890–905.

Calamaro, J.P. (1985). Implementation of a multi-stage production planning system, S.M. Thesis, Operations Research Center, Massachusetts Institute of Technology.

Chapman, P.T. (1985). Decision models for multi-stage production planning, Technical Report No. 186, Operations Research Center, Massachusetts Institute of Technology.

Christofides, N., R. Alvarez-Valdes and J.M. Tamarit (1987). Project scheduling with resource constraints: A branch and bound approach. *European J. Oper. Res.* 29, 262–273.

Covert, K.B. (1987). An optimization model for marketing and production planning, S.M. Thesis, Sloan School of Management, Massachusetts Institute of Technology.

Crowder, H.E., E.L. Johnson and M. Padberg (1983). Solving large-scale zero–one linear programming problems. *Oper. Res.* 31, 803–834.

Crowston, W.P., and M.H. Wagner (1973). Dynamic lot-size models for multistage assembly systems. *Management Sci.* 20, 13–21.

Crowston, W.P., M.H. Wagner and J.F. Williams (1973). Economic lot-size determination in multistage assembly systems. *Management Sci.* 19, 517–527.

Dantzig, G.B. (1955). Optimal solution of a dynamic Leontief model with substitution. *Econometrica* 23, 295–302.

Dantzig, G.B. (1963). *Linear Programming and Extensions*, Princeton Univ. Press, Princeton.

Dembo, R.S., and P. Zipkin (1983). Construction and evaluation of compact refinery models, in: B. Lev (ed.), *Energy Models and Studies*, North-Holland, Amsterdam, pp. 525–540.

Dolk, D. (1988). Model management systems for operations research: A prospectus, in: G. Mitra, (ed.), *Mathematical Models for Decision Support*, Springer, Berlin, pp. 347–374.

Duffin, R.J., E.L. Peterson and C.M. Zener (1967). *Geometric Programming*, Wiley, New York.

Dzielinski, B., and R. Gomory (1965). Optimal programming of lot sizes, inventories, and labor allocations, *Management Sci.* 11, 874–890.

Eppen, G.D., and R.K. Martin (1987), Solving mutli-item capacitated lot-sizing problems using variable reduction. *Oper. Res.* 35, 832–848.

Feo, T.A., and D.S. Hochbaum (1986). Lagrangean relaxation for testing infeasibility in VSLI routing. *Oper. Res.* 34, 819–831.

Fisher, M.L. (1973a). Optimal solution of scheduling problems using Lagrange multipliers: Part I. *Oper. Res.* 21, 1114–1127.

Fisher, M.L. (1973b). Optimal solution of scheduling problems using Lagrange multipliers: Part II, in: S. Elmagrahby (ed.), *Symposium on the Theory of Scheduling and Its Applications*, Springer, Berlin, pp. 294–318.

Fisher, M.L. (1981). The Lagrangean relaxation method for solving integer programming problems. *Management Sci.* 27, 1–18.

Fourer, R., D.M. Gay and B.W. Kernighan (1990). A modeling language for mathematical programming. *Management Sci.* 36, 519–554.

Gassman, H.I. (1990). MSLiP: A computer code for multistage stochastic linear programming. *Math. Programming* 47, 407–423.

Geoffrion, A.M. (1974). Lagrangean relaxations for integer programming, in: M.L. Balinski (ed.), *Math. Prog. Study 2: Approaches to Integer Programming*, North-Holland, Amsterdam, pp. 82–114.
Geoffrion, A.M. (1987). An introduction to structured modeling. *Management Sci.* 33, 547–588.
Graves, S.C. (1982). Using Lagrangean techniques to solve hierarchical production planning problems. *Management Sci.* 28, 260–275.
Hajek, B. (1988). Cooling schedules for optimal annealing. *Math. Oper. Res.* 13, 311–329.
Harrison, J.M. (1988). Brownian models of queueing networks with heterogeneous customer populations, in: W. Fleming and P.L. Lions (eds.), *Stochastic Differential Systems, Stochastic Control and Applications*, Springer, Berlin, pp. 147–186.
Hax, A.C., and H.C. Meal (1975). Hierarchical integration of production planning and scheduling, in: *North-Holland/TIMS Stud. in Management Sci., Vol. 1, Logistics*, Elsevier, New York, pp. 53–69.
Heyman, D.P. (1990). Another way to solve complex chemical equilibria. *Oper. Res.* 38, 355–358.
Hiller, R.S. (1986). Stochastic programming approximation methods, with applications to multistage production planning, Ph.D. dissertation, Operations Research Center, Massachusetts Institute of Technology.
Hiller, R.S., and J.F. Shapiro (1986). Optimal capacity expansion when there are learning effects. *Management Sci.* 32, 1153–1163.
Howe, C. (1990). Personal communication.
Karmarkar, U., S. Kekre and S. Kekre (1987). The dynamic lot-sizing problem with startup and reservation costs. *Oper. Res.* 35, 389–398.
Karwan, M.H., and R.L. Rardin (1979). Some relationships between Lagrangean and surrogate duality in integer linear programming. *Math. Programming* 17, 320–334.
Klingman, D., N. Phillips, D. Steiger and W. Young (1987). The successful deployment of management science throughout Citgo Petroleum Corporation. *Interfaces* 17, 4–25.
Kocis, G.R., and I.E. Grossmann (1987). Relaxation strategy for the structural organization of process flow sheets. *I&EC Res.* 26.
Lageweg, B., J.K. Lenstra and A.H.G. Rinnooy Kan (1977). Job shop scheduling by implicit enumeration. *Management Sci.* 24, 441–450.
Larson, R.E. (1990). *Principles of Dynamic Programming*, Dekker, New York.
Lasdon, L.S., and R.C. Terjung (1971). An efficient algorithm for multi-item scheduling. *Oper. Res.* 19, 946–969.
Lasdon, L.S., A.D. Waren and S. Sarkar (1988). Interfacing optimizers with planning languages and process simulators, in: G. Mitra (ed.), *Mathematical Models for Decision Support*, Springer, Berlin, pp. 238–262.
Lawler, E.L. (1978). Sequencing jobs to minimize total weighted completion time subject to precedence constraints. *Ann. Discrete Math.* 34, 75–90.
Lawler, E.L., J.K. Lenstra, A.H.G. Rinooy Kan and D.B. Shmoys, eds. (1985). *The Traveling Salesman Problem: A Guided Tour of Combinatorial Optimization*, New York.
Lee, S.-B., and P.H. Zipkin (1989). Nondifferentiable optimization, in: G.L. Nemhauser, A.H.G. Rinnooy Kan and M.J. Todd (eds.), *Handbooks in Operations Research and Management Science, Vol. 1, Optimization*, North-Holland, Amsterdam, Chapter 7.
Lemarechal, C. (1989). Nondifferentiable optimization, in: G.L. Nemhauser, A.H.G. Rinnooy Kan and M.J. Todd (eds.), *Handbooks in Operations Research and Management Science, Vol. 1, Optimization*, North-Holland, Amsterdam, Chapter 7.
Little, J.D.C. (1975). Brandaid: A marketing mix model, Part I, Structure. *Oper. Res.* 23, 628–655.
Llewellyn, J., and R. Sharda (1990). Linear programming software for personal computers: 1990 survey. *OR/MS Today* 17(5), 35–46.
Love, S.F. (1972). A facilities in series inventory model with nested schedules. *Management Sci.* 18, 327–338.
Magnanti, T.L., J.F. Shapiro and M.H. Wagner (1976). Generalized linear programming solves the dual. *Management Sci.* 22, 1195–1203.
Manne, A.S. (1958). Programming of economic lot sizes. *Management Sci.* 4, 115–135.

Martin, R.K. (1987). Generating alternative mixed-integer programming models using variable redefinition. *Oper. Res.* 35, 820–831.
Martin, R.K., R.R. Rardin and B.A. Campbell (1990). Polyhedral characterization of discrete dynamic programing. *Oper. Res.* 38, 127–138.
Nemhauser, G.L., A.H.. Rinnooy Kan and M.J. Todd, eds. (1989). *Handbooks in Operations Research and Management Science, Vol. 1, Optimization*, North-Holland, Amsterdam.
Nemhauser, G.L., and L.A. Wolsey (1988). *Integer and Combinatorial Optimization*, Wiley, New York.
Noonan, F., and R.J. Giglio (1977). Planning power generation: A nonlinear mixed integer model employing Benders' decomposition. *Management Sci.* 23, 946–956.
Papadimitrou, C.H., and K. Stieglitz (1982). *Combinatorial Optimization: Algorithms and Complexity*, Prentice-Hall, Englewood Cliffs, NJ.
Picard, J.C., and M. Queyranne (1978). The time-dependent traveling salesman problem and application to the tardiness problem in one-machine scheduling. *Oper. Res.* 26, 86–110.
Roy, B., and B. Sussmann (1964). Les problemes d'ordonnancement avec constaintes disjonctives, Note DS No. 9 bis, SEMA.
Schrage, L. (1986). *Linear, Integer and Quadratic Programming with LINDO, 3rd edition*, Scientific Press, Palo Alto, CA.
Shapiro, J.F. (1979a). *Mathematical Programming: Structures and Algorithms*, Wiley, New York.
Shapiro, J.F. (1979b). A survey of Lagrangean techniques for discrete optimization. *Ann. Discrete Math.* 5, 113–138.
Shapiro, J.F. (1984). Practical experience with optimization models, in: T.H. Naylor, and C. Thomas (eds.), *The Future of Optimization Models for Strategic Planning*, North-Holland, Amsterdam, pp. 67–78.
Shapiro, J.F. (1990). Convergent duality for the traveling salesman problem, Working Paper OR 204-89, Operations Research Center, Massachusetts Institute of Technology.
Shapiro, J.F., V.M. Singhal and Stephen N. Wagner (1992). Optimizing the value chain. *Interfaces* 22, to appear.
Stecke, K.E. (1983). Formulation and solution of nonlinear integer production planning problems for flexible manufacturing systems. *Management Sci.* 289, 273–288.
Steuer, R.E. (1986). *Multiple Criteria Optimization: Theory, Computation and Application*, Wiley, New York.
Talbot, F.B., and J.H. Patterson (1978). An efficient integer programming algorithm with network cuts for solving resource constrained scheduling problems. *Management Sci.* 24, 1163–1174.
Trigiero, W.W., L.J. Thomas and J.O. McClain (1989). Capacitated lot sizing with setup times. *Management Sci.* 35, 353–366.
Van Roy, T.J. (1989). Multi-level production and distribution planning with transportation fleet optimization. *Management Sci.* 35, 1443–1453.
Van Roy, T.J., and L.A. Wolsey (1986). Valid inequalities for mixed 0–1 programs. *Discrete Appl. Math.* 14, 199–213.
Van Roy, T.J., and L.A. Wolsey (1987). Solving 0–1 programs by automatic reformulation, *Oper. Res.* 35, 45–57.
Veinott, A.F. (1969). Minimum concave cost solution of Leontief substitution model of multi-facility inventory systems. *Oper. Res.* 17, 262–291.
Wagner, H.M. (1969). *Principles of Operations Research, 1st edition*, Prentice-Hall, Englewood Cliffs, NJ.
Wagner, H.M., and T.M. Whitin (1958). Dynamic version of the economic lot size model. *Management Sci.* 5, 89–96.
Wall, T.W., D. Greening and R.E.D. Woolsey (1986). Soling complex chemical equilibria using a geometric-programming based technique. *Oper. Res.* 34, 345–355.
Wein, L.M. (1990). Scheduling networks of queues: Heavy traffic analysis of a two-station network with controllable inputs, *Oper. Res.* 38, 1065–1078.
Wets, R.J.B. (1983). Stochastic programming solution techniques and approximation schemes, in: A. Bachem, M. Grötschel and B. Korte (eds.), *Mathematical Programming State-of-the-Art*, Springer, Berlin, pp. 506–603.

Williams, H.P. (1985). *Model Building in Mathematical Programming, 2nd edition*, Wiley, New York.

Zangwill, W.I. (1966). A deterministic multi-period production scheduling model with backlogging. *Management Sci.* 13, 105–119.

Zangwill, W.I. (1969). A backlogging model and multi-echelon model of a dynamic economic lot-size production system – a network approach. *Management Sci.* 15, 506–527.

S.C. Graves et al., Eds., *Handbooks in OR & MS, Vol. 4*

Chapter 9

Sequencing and Scheduling: Algorithms and Complexity

Eugene L. Lawler
University of California, Berkeley, CA, U.S.A.

Jan Karel Lenstra
Eindhoven University of Technology, Eindhoven, The Netherlands and CWI, Amsterdam, The Netherlands

Alexander H.G. Rinnooy Kan
Erasmus University, Rotterdam, The Netherlands

David B. Shmoys
Cornell University, Ithaca, NY, U.S.A.

Sequencing and scheduling as a research area is motivated by questions that arise in production planning, in computer control, and generally in all situations in which scarce resources have to be allocated to activities over time. In this survey, we concentrate on the area of deterministic machine scheduling. We review complexity results and optimization and approximation algorithms for problems involving a single machine, parallel machines, open shops, flow shops and job shops. We also pay attention to two extensions of this area: resource-constrained project scheduling and stochastic machine scheduling.

PART I. PRELIMINARIES

Sequencing and scheduling is concerned with the *optimal allocation of scarce resources to activities over time*. Of obvious practical importance, it has been the subject of extensive research since the early 1950's, and an impressive amount of literature has been created. Any discussion of the available material has to be selective. We will concentrate on the area of deterministic machine scheduling. We will also pay attention to two extensions of this area that are of particular interest in the context of production planning, namely resource-constrained project scheduling and stochastic machine scheduling.

The chapter is organized as follows. Part I gives a brief overview of the many types of sequencing and scheduling problems that have been investigated, and then describes the types of algorithms and the concepts of complexity theory that we will use throughout. Next, the class of deterministic machine scheduling problems that we will consider is introduced. Parts II, III and IV deal with the single machine, parallel machine and multi-operation problems in this class, respectively. Finally, Part V is devoted to the two generalizations of the deterministic machine scheduling model.

Each of the thirteen sections in Parts II–V starts with the full treatment of a relatively simple but crucial result. After this highlight, we review the other results that have been obtained for the subclass under consideration, in the style of two previous surveys by Graham, Lawler, Lenstra & Rinnooy Kan [1979] and Lawler, Lenstra & Rinnooy Kan [1982].

1. Sequencing and scheduling problems

The theory of sequencing and scheduling, more than any other area in operations research, is characterized by a virtually unlimited number of problem types. Most research has traditionally been focused on *deterministic machine scheduling*. Our presentation reflects this emphasis. It already allows for more than enough variety, as the reader will soon realize, but it is also based on some restrictive assumptions.

The first restriction concerns the type of resource. A *machine* is a resource that can perform at most one activity at any time. The activities are commonly referred to as *jobs*, and it is also assumed that a job is worked on by at most one machine at any time. It is not hard to think of more general scheduling situations in which, at one point in time, a resource serves several jobs and a job uses several resources. That leads us into the area of *resource-constrained project scheduling*, which is the subject of Section 15.

The second restriction concerns the *deterministic* nature of the problems. All the information that defines a problem instance is known with certainty in advance. Deterministic scheduling is part of combinatorial optimization. Indeed, all the techniques of combinatorial optimization have at some point been applied to scheduling problems. It is an obvious extension to assume that some of the problem data are subject to random fluctuations. The area of *stochastic machine scheduling* is briefly reviewed in Section 16.

In studying the allocation of machines to jobs, we are concerned with scheduling at the detailed, *operational* level. We will pay no attention to tactical decisions, such as the determination of due dates, or to strategical decisions, such as the acquisition of machines.

Further, we will restrict ourselves to the minimization of a *single optimality criterion* which is *nondecreasing in each of the job completion times*. This excludes nonregular criteria, which involve, e.g., the earliness of the jobs or the number of setups, and multicriteria scheduling, which is a relatively unexplored area.

We also have to exclude a number of other areas, each of which would be worth a survey of its own: periodic scheduling, cyclic scheduling, scheduling with fixed starting times, and scheduling with sequence-dependent processing times. The latter area is closely related to the traveling salesman problem and its extensions.

General references on sequencing and scheduling are the classic book by Conway, Maxwell & Miller [1967], the introductory textbooks by Baker [1974] and French [1982], the expository articles collected by Coffman [1976], and the proceedings volume edited by Dempster, Lenstra & Rinnooy Kan [1982]. There are several survey papers that complement the present chapter. We mention the review of the broad area of production planning by Graves [1981], the introductory survey of precedence-constrained scheduling by Lawler & Lenstra [1982], the tutorial on machine scheduling by Lawler [1983], the NP-completeness column on multiprocessor scheduling by Johnson [1983], the annotated bibliography covering the period 1981–1984 by Lenstra & Rinnooy Kan [1985], the discussions of new directions in scheduling by Lenstra & Rinnooy Kan [1984], Blazewicz [1987] and Blazewicz, Finke, Haupt & Schmidt [1988], and the recent overviews of single-machine scheduling by Gupta & Kyparisis [1987] and of multiprocessor and flow shop scheduling by Kawaguchi & Kyan [1988].

References on resource-constrained project scheduling and stochastic scheduling will be given in Sections 15 and 16. For the scheduling areas that are not covered in this chapter, we refer to the bibliography by Lenstra & Rinnooy Kan [1985]. In addition, we mention the survey of due date determination rules by Cheng & Gupta [1989], the reviews on scheduling with nonregular criteria by Raghavachari [1988] and Baker & Scudder [1990], the results in that area by Garey, Tarjan & Wilfong [1988], the survey on bicriterion single-machine scheduling by Dileepan & Sen [1988], and the book on the traveling salesman problem edited by the present authors [Lawler, Lenstra, Rinnooy Kan & Shmoys, 1985].

2. Algorithms and complexity

Practical experience makes it clear that some computational problems are easier to solve than others. For some scheduling problems, algorithms have been known for decades that are capable of solving instances with thousands of jobs, whereas for other problems, the best algorithms strain to cope with only a handful of jobs. Complexity theory provides a mathematical framework in which computational problems can be studied so that they can be classified as 'easy' or 'hard'. In this section, we will review the main points of this theory. The reader is referred to the survey articles by Karp [1975], Lenstra & Rinnooy Kan [1979], Shmoys & Tardos [1993], and Stockmeyer [1992], and to the textbook by Garey & Johnson [1979] for a more extensive treatment of this subject.

A computational problem can be viewed as a function f that maps each input x in some given domain to an output $f(x)$ in some given range. Although there may be many ways to represent the input domain for a particular problem, these specifics will be largely unimportant. We will be interested in studying the time required to compute $f(x)$ as a function of the length of the encoding of the input x, denoted $|x|$. For a more precise discussion, a mathematical model of an algorithm, a Turing machine, is commonly used, but it will suffice to think in terms of any standard programming language. In considering an algorithm that computes $f(x)$ on input x, we will measure its efficiency by an upper bound $T(n)$ on the number of steps that the algorithm takes on any input x with $|x| = n$. We will not be concerned with the precise form of the function T but rather with its asymptotic order. For this purpose, we say that $T(n) = O(g(n))$ if there exist constants c and n_0 such that $T(n) \leq cg(n)$ for all $n \geq n_0$. We will consider a problem 'easy' if there exists an algorithm for its solution which has running time $T(n) = O(n^k)$ for some constant k; that is, $T(n)$ is bounded by a polynomial function of n.

Most of the problems in which we are interested are optimization problems, where, for input x, the output $f(x)$ is the smallest value in a range of feasible integral values. It will be convenient to focus on *decision* problems, where the output range is {yes, no}. For any minimization problem f, there is an associated decision problem, the output of which answers the question 'Is $f(x) \leq k$?' for any given k. If the decision problem is easy, then one can typically apply binary search over k to obtain an algorithm for f with polynomially bounded running time. Let P denote the class of decision problems that can be solved in polynomial time.

Unfortunately, for a majority of the problems that we shall encounter, no polynomial-time algorithm is known. It is an important open question if any of these problems can be solved in polynomial time. Nonetheless, a beautiful theory developed by Cook [1971], Karp [1972] and Levin [1973] has provided a means of giving strong evidence that no such algorithm exists for a particular problem.

When a scheduling problem is formulated as a decision problem, e.g., 'Is there a feasible schedule that completes within the deadline d?', there is an important asymmetry between those inputs whose output is 'yes' and those whose output is 'no'. Note that a 'yes' answer can be certified by a small amount of information: the schedule that meets the deadline. Given this *certificate*, the 'yes' answer can be verified in polynomial time. Let NP denote the class of decision problems where each 'yes' input x has a certificate y, such that $|y|$ is bounded by a polynomial in $|x|$ and there is a polynomial-time algorithm to verify that y is a valid certificate for x. The class NP contains an enormous number of problems from a wide range of fields, including optimization, number theory, coding theory, and graph theory. Many of these problems are not known to be solvable in polynomial time. One of the major open problems of modern mathematics is whether P equals NP, and it is generally conjectured that this is not the case.

An NP-*complete* problem is, roughly speaking, a hardest problem in NP, in that if it would be solvable in polynomial time, then each problem in NP would be solvable in polynomial time, so that P would be equal to NP. Thus, the NP-completeness of a particular problem is strong evidence that a polynomial-time algorithm for its solution is unlikely to exist. The principal notion in defining NP-completeness is that of a *reduction*. For two decision problems P and Q, we say that P reduces to Q (denoted $P \propto Q$) if there exists a polynomial-time computable function τ that transforms inputs for P into inputs for Q such that x is a 'yes' input for P if and only if $\tau(x)$ is a 'yes' input for Q. A problem is NP-complete if it is in NP and every problem in NP reduces to it. An optimization problem will be called NP-*hard* if the associated decision problem is NP-complete.

Cook showed that a natural problem from logic is NP-complete by exhibiting a 'master reduction' from each problem in NP to it. Given one NP-complete problem P, it is a much easier task to prove the NP-completeness of the next one, say Q: one need only prove that $Q \in \mathrm{NP}$ and that $P \propto Q$. The *clique* problem is the following problem from graph theory: given a graph $G = (V, E)$ and an integer k, does there exist a set of vertices $C \subset V$ such that $|C| = k$ and for each distinct pair u, $v \in C$, $\{u, v\} \in E$? Cook showed that the clique problem is NP-complete. The wide applicability of the notion of NP-completeness was observed by Karp, who proved that 21 basic problems are NP-complete.

Although we have thus far ignored all questions of encoding the inputs, there is one distinction that will play an important role in our discussion. The natural way to encode integers is to use a binary notation; e.g., $5 = \langle 101 \rangle$. However, one may also consider a unary notation; e.g., $5 = \langle 11111 \rangle$. There is an exponential gap between the lengths of both encodings. In the clique problem, there are no large integers to be encoded, and so this distinction is unimportant, but this is not always the case. In the *partition* problem, the input consists of n numbers $a_1, \ldots, a_n$, and the question is if there exists a subset $S \subset \{1, \ldots, n\}$ such that $\Sigma_{j \in S} a_j = \Sigma_j a_j/2$. This problem is NP-complete under a binary encoding. On the other hand, it can be solved by dynamic programming in $\mathrm{O}(n \Sigma_j a_j)$ time, which is polynomial under a unary encoding; the method is therefore called a *pseudopolynomial-time* algorithm. There are also 'number problems' that are NP-complete, even when the numbers are encoded in unary. In the *3-partition* problem, the input consists of $3n$ integers $a_1, \ldots, a_{3n}$, and the question is if there exists a partition of $\{1, \ldots, 3n\}$ into n 3-element sets $S_1, \ldots, S_n$ such that $\Sigma_{j \in S_i} a_j = \Sigma_j a_j/n$ for $i = 1, \ldots, n$. This problem remains NP-complete under a unary encoding and is therefore called *strongly* NP-*complete*.

The NP-hardness of an optimization problem suggests that it is impossible to always find an optimal solution quickly. However, it may still be possible to use an *approximation algorithm* to find solutions that are provably close to the optimum. For a minimization problem f, a ρ-*approximation algorithm* ($\rho > 1$) delivers a solution with value at most $\rho f(x)$ for each input x. Some NP-hard problems have a *polynomial approximation scheme*, which is a family of algorithms $\{A_\epsilon\}$ such that, for each $\epsilon > 0$, A_ϵ is a polynomial-time $(1+\epsilon)$-approximation algorithm. The running time of A_ϵ may depend not only on the input size but also on the value of ϵ. If it is bounded by a polynomial in $|x|$ and $1/\epsilon$, then the family is called a *fully polynomial approximation scheme*.

The notions presented thus far have all been based on a *worst-case* analysis of the running time or the quality of the solution delivered. It would be desirable to understand the behavior for 'typical' inputs. To do this it appears necessary to assume a probability distribution over the inputs. We shall also discuss results that can be obtained through this sort of *probabilistic* analysis.

3. A class of deterministic machine scheduling problems

Suppose that m machines M_i $(i = 1, \ldots, m)$ have to process n jobs J_j $(j = 1, \ldots, n)$. A *schedule* is an allocation of one or more time intervals on one or more machines to each job. A schedule is *feasible* if no two time intervals on the same machine overlap, if no two time intervals allocated to the same job overlap, and if, in addition, it meets a number of specific requirements concerning the machine environment and the job characteristics. A schedule is *optimal* if it minimizes a given optimality criterion. The machine environment, the job characteristics and the optimality criterion that together define a problem type are specified in terms of a three-field classification $\alpha \mid \beta \mid \gamma$, which is introduced in this section.

3.1. Job data

In the first place, the following data may be specified for each job J_j:

– a *number of operations* m_j;

– a *processing requirement* p_j in the case of single-operation models, or a collection of *processing requirements* p_{ij} in the case of multi-operation models;

– a *release date* r_j, on which J_j becomes available for processing;

– a nondecreasing real *cost function* f_j, measuring the cost $f_j(t)$ incurred if J_j is completed at time t;

– a *due date* d_j and a *weight* w_j, that may be used in defining f_j.

In general, m_j, p_j, p_{ij}, r_j, d_j and w_j have integral values.

3.2. Machine environment

We now describe the first field $\alpha = \alpha_1\alpha_2$ specifying the machine environment. Let $\circ$ denote the empty symbol.

If $\alpha_1 \in \{\circ, P, Q, R\}$, each J_j consists of a single operation that can be processed on any M_i; the processing time of J_j on M_i will be denoted by p_{ij}. The four values are characterized as follows:

– $\alpha_1 = \circ$: *single machine*; $p_{1j} = p_j$;
– $\alpha_1 = P$: *identical parallel machines*; $p_{ij} = p_j$ for all M_i;
– $\alpha_1 = Q$: *uniform parallel machines*; $p_{ij} = p_j/s_i$ for a given *speed* s_i of M_i;
– $\alpha_1 = R$: *unrelated parallel machines*; $p_{ij} = p_j/s_{ij}$ for given job-dependent speeds s_{ij} of M_i.

If $\alpha_1 = O$, we have an *open shop*, in which each J_j consists of a set of operations $\{O_{1j}, \ldots, O_{mj}\}$. O_{ij} has to be processed on M_i during p_{ij} time units, but the order in which the operations are executed is immaterial. If $\alpha_1 \in \{F, J\}$, an ordering is imposed on the set of operations corresponding to each job. If $\alpha_1 = F$, we have a *flow shop*, in which each J_j consists of a chain $(O_{1j}, \ldots, O_{mj})$. O_{ij} has to be processed on M_i during p_{ij} time units. If $\alpha_1 = J$, we have a *job shop*, in which each J_j consists of a chain $(O_{1j}, \ldots, O_{m_j j})$. O_{ij} has to be processed on a given machine μ_{ij} during p_{ij} time units, with $\mu_{i,j} \neq \mu_{i+1,j}$ for $i = 1, \ldots, m_j - 1$.

If α_2 is a positive integer, then m is a constant, equal to α_2; it is specified as part of the problem *type*. If $\alpha_2 = \circ$, then m is a variable, the value of which is specified as part of the problem *instance*. Obviously, $\alpha_1 = \circ$ if and only if $\alpha_2 = 1$.

3.3. Job characteristics

The second field $\beta \subset \{\beta_1, \ldots, \beta_4\}$ indicates a number of job characteristics, which are defined as follows.

(1) $\beta_1 \in \{pmtn, \circ\}$.

$\beta_1 = pmtn$: *Preemption* (job splitting) is allowed: the processing of any operation may be interrupted and resumed at a later time.

$\beta_1 = \circ$: No preemption is allowed.

(2) $\beta_2 = \{prec, tree, \circ\}$.

$\beta_2 = prec$. A *precedence relation* $\rightarrow$ between the jobs is specified. It is derived from an acyclic directed graph G with vertex set $\{1, \ldots, n\}$. If G contains a directed path from j to k, we write $J_j \rightarrow J_k$ and require that J_j is completed before J_k can start.

$\beta_2 = tree$: G is a *rooted tree* with either outdegree at most one for each vertex or indegree at most one for each vertex.

$\beta_2 = \circ$: No precedence relation is specified.

(3) $\beta_3 \in \{r_j, \circ\}$.

$\beta_3 = r_j$: *Release dates* that may differ per job are specified.

$\beta_3 = \circ$: All $r_j = 0$.

(4) $\beta_4 \in \{p_j = 1, p_{ij} = 1, \circ\}$.

$\beta_4 = p_j = 1$: Each job has a *unit processing requirement*. This will occur only if $\alpha_1 \in \{\circ, P, Q\}$.

$\beta_4 = p_{ij} = 1$: Each operation has *unit processing requirement*. This will occur only if $\alpha_1 \in \{O, F, J\}$.

$\beta_4 = \circ$: All p_j or p_{ij} are arbitrary nonnegative integers.

Occasionally, this field will contain additional characteristics such as $m_j \leq 2$ or $p_{ij} \in \{1, 2\}$. The interpretation of these should be obvious.

There are many more types of precedence relations than suggested above. We will encounter generalizations of a rooted tree, such as series–parallel constraints and opposing forests, special cases of a tree, such as intrees, outtrees and chains, and other types, such as interval orders and level orders.

3.4. Optimality criteria

The third field $\gamma \in \{f_{\max}, \Sigma f_j\}$ refers to the optimality criterion. Given a schedule, we can compute for each J_j:

- the *completion time* C_j;
- the *lateness* $L_j = C_j - d_j$;
- the *tardiness* $T_j = \max\{0, C_j - d_j\}$;
- the *unit penalty* $U_j = 0$ if $C_j \leq d_j$, $U_j = 1$ otherwise.

The optimality criteria most commonly chosen involve the minimization of

$$f_{\max} \in \{C_{\max}, L_{\max}\} ,$$

where $f_{\max} = \max_{1 \leq j \leq n} f_j(C_j)$ with $f_j(C_j) = C_j$, L_j, respectively, or of

$$\Sigma\, f_j \in \{\Sigma\, C_j, \Sigma\, T_j, \Sigma\, U_j, \Sigma\, w_jC_j, \Sigma\, w_jT_j, \Sigma w_jU_j\} ,$$

where $\Sigma f_j = \Sigma_{j=1}^{n} f_j(C_j)$ with $f_j(C_j) = C_j$, T_j, U_j, w_jC_j, w_jT_j, w_jU_j respectively.

It should be noted that Σw_jC_j and Σw_jL_j differ by a constant Σw_jd_j and hence are *equivalent*. Furthermore, any schedule minimizing $L_{\max}$ also minimizes $T_{\max}$ and $U_{\max}$, but not *vice versa*.

The optimal value of γ will be denoted by γ^*, and the value produced by an (approximation) algorithm A by $\gamma(A)$. If a known upper bound ρ on $\gamma(A)/\gamma^*$ is best possible in the sense that a class of instances exists for which $\gamma(A)/\gamma^*$ equals or asymptotically approaches ρ, this will be denoted by a dagger (†).

3.5. Three examples

$1 \mid prec \mid L_{\max}$ is the problem of minimizing maximum lateness on a single machine subject to general precedence constraints. It can be solved in polynomial time (Section 4).

$R \mid pmtn \mid \Sigma C_j$ is the problem of minimizing total completion time on an arbitrary number of unrelated parallel machines, allowing preemption. Its complexity is unknown (Section 8).

$J3 \mid p_{ij} = 1 \mid C_{\max}$ is the problem of minimizing maximum completion time in a three-machine job shop with unit processing times. It is NP-hard (Section 14).

3.6. Reducibility among scheduling problems

Each scheduling problem in the class outlined above corresponds to a six-tuple $(u_0, \ldots, u_5)$, where u_i is a vertex of the graph G_i shown in Figure 1 $(i = 0, \ldots, 5)$. For two problems $P = (u_0, \ldots, u_5)$ and $Q = (v_0, \ldots, v_5)$, we write $P \to Q$ if either $u_i = v_i$ or G_i contains a directed path from u_i to v_i, for $i = 0, \ldots, 5$. The reader should verify that $P \to Q$ implies that the decision version of P reduces to the decision version of Q. For example, deciding if $L^*_{\max} \leq k$ can be reduced to the special case where $k = 0$, and this is equivalent to deciding if $\Sigma T^*_j = 0$. The graphs thus define elementary reductions between scheduling problems. It follows that if $P \to Q$ and Q is solvable in polynomial time, then P is solvable in polynomial time, and if $P \to Q$ and P is NP-hard, then Q is NP-hard.

These types of reductions play an instrumental role in the computer program MSPCLASS [Lageweg, Lawler, Lenstra & Rinnooy Kan, 1981, 1982]. The program records the complexity status of scheduling problems on the basis of known results and employing simple inference rules as given above. The main application of MSPCLASS concerns a collection of 4536 problems, which only differs from the class described in this section in that α_2 is restricted to values from $\{1, 2, 3, \circ\}$, $\beta_1 = pmtn$ excludes $\beta_4 = p_{(i)j} = 1$, and β also allows the specification of deadlines, i.e., strict upper bounds on job completion times. At present, 417 of these problems are known to be solvable in polynomial time, 3821 have been proved NP-hard, and 298 are still open. With respect to a

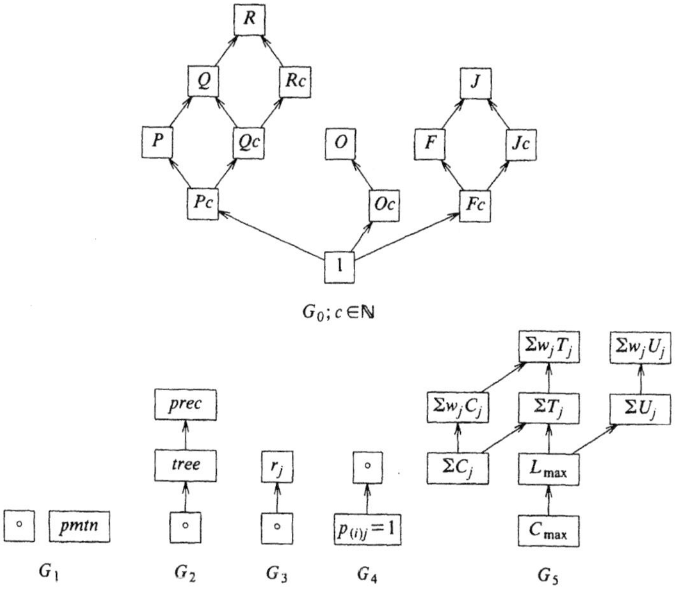

Fig. 1. Problem classification: the graphs G_i $(i = 0, \ldots, 5)$.

unary encoding, 464 are solvable in pseudopolynomial time, 3588 are strongly NP-hard, and 484 are open.

PART II. THE SINGLE MACHINE

The single machine case has been the object of extensive research ever since the seminal work by Jackson [1955] and Smith [1956]. We will survey the principal results, classifying them according to the optimality criterion in question. As a general result, we note that, if all $r_j = 0$, then only schedules without preemption and without machine idle time need be considered [Conway, Maxwell & Miller, 1967].

4. Minmax criteria

4.0. Lawler's algorithm for $1 | prec | f_{max}$

The problem $1 | prec | f_{max}$ has a particularly simple and elegant solution. Note that the cost functions of the jobs can be quite arbitrary and different from one another, provided only that they are nondecreasing.

Let $N = \{1, 2, \ldots, n\}$ be the index set of all jobs, and let $L \subseteq N$ be the index set of jobs without successors. For any subset $S \subseteq N$, let $p(S) = \Sigma_{j \in S}\, p_j$ and let $f^*_{max}(S)$ denote the cost of an optimal schedule for the jobs indexed by S. Clearly, $f^*_{max}(N)$ satisfies the following two inequalities:

$$f^*_{max}(N) \geq \min_{j \in L} f_j(p(N)),$$

$$f^*_{max}(N) \geq f^*_{max}(N - \{j\}) \quad \text{for all } j \in N.$$

Now let J_l with $l \in L$ be such that

$$f_l(p(N)) = \min_{j \in L} f_j(p(N)).$$

We have

$$f^*_{max}(N) \geq \max\{f_l(p(N)), f^*_{max}(N - \{l\})\}.$$

But the right-hand side of this inequality is precisely the cost of an optimal schedule subject to the condition that J_l is processed last. It follows that there exists an optimal schedule in which J_l is in the last position. By repeated application of this rule, one obtains an optimal schedule in $O(n^2)$ time. This algorithm is due to Lawler [1973].

4.1. *Maximum cost*

Lawler's algorithm has been generalized by Baker, Lawler, Lenstra & Rinnooy Kan [1983] to an $O(n^2)$ algorithm for $1 \mid pmtn, prec, r_j \mid f_{max}$. First, the release dates are modified such that $r_j + p_j \leq r_k$ whenever $J_j \rightarrow J_k$. Next, the jobs are scheduled in order of nondecreasing release dates; this creates a number of *blocks* that can be considered separately. From among the jobs without successors in a certain block, a job J_k that yields minimum cost when finishing last is selected, the other jobs in the block are rescheduled in order of nondecreasing release dates, and J_k is assigned to the remaining time intervals. By repeated application of this procedure to each of the resulting subblocks, one obtains an optimal schedule with at most $n-1$ preemptions in $O(n^2)$ time.

Monma [1980] considers a generalization of $1 \| f_{max}$. Let c_j indicate the amount of a resource consumed (or, if $c_j < 0$, contributed) by J_j. The problem is to find a job permutation minimizing the maximum cumulative cost, $\max_j f_{\pi(j)}\ (\sum_{i=1}^{j-1} c_{\pi(i)})$. An NP-hardness proof and polynomial-time algorithms for special cases are presented.

4.2. *Maximum lateness*

Although Lenstra, Rinnooy Kan & Brucker [1977] show that the general $1 \mid r_j \mid L_{max}$ problem is strongly NP-hard, polynomial algorithms exist for the cases that all r_j are equal, all d_j are equal or all p_j are equal, and for the preemptive problem. The first case is solved by a specialization of Lawler's method, known as Jackson's rule [Jackson, 1955]: schedule the jobs in order of nondecreasing due dates. This rule, which minimizes the maximum tardiness as well, is also referred to as the *earliest due date* (*EDD*) rule. Note that, if any sequence completes all jobs by their due dates, an *EDD* sequence does. The second case is solved similarly by scheduling the jobs in order of nondecreasing release dates.

Horn [1974] observes that $1 \mid r_j, p_j = 1 \mid L_{max}$ and $1 \mid pmtn, r_j \mid L_{max}$ are solved by the extended Jackson's rule: at any time, schedule an available job with smallest due date. Frederickson [1983] gives an $O(n)$ algorithm for the case of unit-time jobs. Simons [1978] presents a more sophisticated approach to solve the problem $1 \mid r_j, p_j = p \mid L_{max}$, where p is an arbitrary integer. Let us first consider the simpler problem of finding a feasible schedule with respect to given release dates r_j and deadlines $\bar{d}_j$. If application of the extended Jackson's rule yields such a schedule, we are finished; otherwise, let J_l be the first late job and let J_k be the last job preceding J_l such that $\bar{d}_k > \bar{d}_l$. If J_k does not exist, there is no feasible schedule; otherwise, the only hope of obtaining such a schedule is to postpone J_k by forcing it to yield precedence to the set of jobs currently between J_k and J_l. This is achieved by declaring the interval between the starting time of J_k and the smallest release date of this set to be a forbidden region in which no job is allowed to start and applying the extended Jackson's rule again subject to this constraint. Since at each iteration at least one starting time of the form $r_j + kp$ $(1 \leq j, k \leq n)$ is excluded, at most n^2 iterations will occur and the feasibility question is answered in $O(n^3 \log n)$ time. Garey, Johnson, Simons & Tarjan [1981] give an improved implementation that requires only $O(n \log n)$ time. Bisection search over the possible L_{max} values leads to a polynomial-time algorithm for $1 \mid r_j, p_j = p \mid L_{max}$.

These three special cases as well as the preemptive variant remain well solved in the presence of precedence constraints. It suffices to update release and due dates such that $r_j < r_k$ and $d_j < d_k$ whenever $J_j \rightarrow J_k$, as described by Lageweg, Lenstra & Rinnooy Kan [1976]. Monma [1982] gives a linear-time algorithm for $1 \mid prec, p_j = 1 \mid L_{max}$.

Various elegant enumerative methods exist for solving $1 \mid prec, r_j \mid L_{max}$. Baker & Su [1974] obtain a lower bound by allowing preemption; their enumeration scheme simply generates all active schedules, i.e., schedules in which one cannot decrease the starting time of a job without increasing the starting time of another one. McMahon & Florian [1975] propose a more ingenious approach. Lageweg, Lenstra & Rinnooy Kan [1976] slightly modify this method to obtain very fast solution of quite large problems. Their algorithm makes use of an equivalent formulation in which due dates are replaced by *delivery times* q_j, and if a job completes at time C_j, it is delivered at time $C_j + q_j$; the aim is to minimize $\max_j C_j + q_j$. The role of release times and delivery times is completely symmetric. One can take advantage of this fact and obtain superior performance by interchanging release times and delivery times under certain conditions. Carlier [1982] and Larson, Dessouky & Devor [1985] propose different branching rules, which yield more efficient algorithms for this relatively easy NP-hard problem. Nowicki & Zdrzalka [1986] observe that in the approach suggested by Carlier, the proof of optimality may be somewhat more elusive than originally believed. Nowicki & Smutnicki [1987] provide alternative lower bound procedures. Zdrzalka & Grabowski [1989] consider extensions of these methods to $1 \mid prec, r_j \mid f_{max}$.

Dominance results among the schedules may be used in the obvious way to speed up enumerative procedures. Erschler, Fontan, Merce & Roubellat [1982, 1983] introduce dominance based on the (r_j, d_j) intervals, assuming that the objective is simply to meet all due dates.

Little work has been done on the worst-case analysis of approximation algorithms for single machine problems. For $1 \mid r_j \mid L_{max}$, one must be careful in specifying the problem, in order to obtain reasonable approximation results. First, it is possible that $L^*_{max} = 0$, and any algorithm that may err in such a case will have unbounded relative error. In fact, deciding if $L^*_{max} \leq 0$ is NP-complete, and so it is probably impossible to completely remove this curious technicality. Note that by focusing on the special case that $r_j \geq 0$ and $d_j \leq 0$ for all j, this difficulty is avoided. This is identical to viewing the problem in the delivery time model, since if $q_j = -d_j$, then $C_j + q_j = C_j - d_j$. Kise, Ibaraki & Mine [1979] provide another justification for studying this case, by arguing that the guarantee should be invariant under certain simple transformations of the input data. Six approximation algorithms are considered, and the extended

Jackson's rule (EJ) is shown to guarantee

$$L_{\max}(\mathrm{EJ})/L^*_{\max} \leq 2 . \qquad (\dagger)$$

Potts [1980b] presents an iterative version of the extended Jackson's rule (IJ), and proves that

$$L_{\max}(\mathrm{IJ})/L^*_{\max} \leq \tfrac{3}{2} . \qquad (\dagger)$$

Although interchanging the roles of the release times and delivery times does not improve the performance guarantee of algorithms EJ and IJ, Hall & Shmoys [1992] use it as the essential element of a modification of the latter algorithm (MIJ) that guarantees

$$L_{\max}(\mathrm{MIJ})/L^*_{\max} \leq \tfrac{4}{3} . \qquad (\dagger)$$

The technique of Lageweg, Lenstra & Rinnooy Kan [1976] implies that the results above extend to the case of precedence constraints. Hall & Shmoys [1992] also present two algorithms A_{1k} and A_{2k} that guarantee

$$L_{\max}(A_{lk})/L^*_{\max} \leq 1 + \frac{1}{k} \quad \text{for } l = 1, 2 ; \qquad (\dagger)$$

A_{1k} runs in $O(n \log n + nk^{16k^2+8k})$ time, whereas A_{2k} runs in $O(2^{4k}(nk)^{4k+3})$ time.

5. Total weighted completion time

5.0. *Smith's ratio rule for* $1| |\Sigma w_jC_j$

For the problem $1| |\Sigma w_jC_j$, any sequence is optimal that puts the jobs in order of nondecreasing ratios p_j/w_j [Smith, 1956]. This rule is established by a simple interchange argument. Consider a sequence in which the jobs are not in order of nondecreasing p_j/w_j. Then there is a job J_k that is immediately preceded by a job J_j, with $p_j/w_j > p_k/w_k$. If J_k completes at time C_k, then J_j completes at time $C_k - p_k$. The effect of interchanging these two jobs in the sequence is to decrease its cost by a positive amount:

$$\begin{aligned}&[w_j(C_k - p_k) + w_kC_k] - [w_k(C_k - p_j) + w_jC_k] \\ &= w_kp_j - w_jp_k \\ &= w_jw_k(p_j/w_j - p_k/w_k) > 0 .\end{aligned}$$

Hence the sequence cannot be optimal. This confirms Smith's rule.

In the special case $1 | | \Sigma C_j$, any sequence is optimal that places the jobs in order of nondecreasing p_j. This *shortest processing time* or SPT rule is one of the most celebrated algorithms in sequencing and scheduling. It is often used for more complicated problems, sometimes without much theoretical support for its superior performance.

5.1. Decomposable precedence constraints

Smith's rule can be viewed as an instance of a more general phenomenon. Consider the following very general problem. Given a set of n jobs and a real-valued function f that assigns a value $f(\pi)$ to each permutation π of the job indices, find a permutation π^* such that

$$f(\pi^*) = \min_{\pi} f(\pi) .$$

If we know nothing about the structure of the function f, there is little that we can do, except to evaluate $f(\pi)$ for each of the $n!$ permutations π. However, it may be that we are able to establish that there is a transitive and complete relation $\leq$, a *quasi-total order*, on the index set of the jobs, with the property that for any two jobs J_b, J_c and any permutation of the form $\alpha bc\delta$, we have

$$b \leq c \Rightarrow f(\alpha bc\delta) \leq f(\alpha cb\delta) .$$

If such a *job interchange relation* $\leq$ exists, an optimal permutation π^* can be found by simply ordering the jobs according to $\leq$, with $O(n \log n)$ comparisons of jobs with respect to $\leq$. Smith's rule for $1 | | \Sigma w_j C_j$ and Jackson's rule for $1 | | L_{max}$ can be seen to be special cases.

In fact, there has been a great deal of work in using this general framework to provide polynomial-time algorithms for special classes of precedence constraints. For tree-like precedence constraints, results of Horn [1972], Adolphson & Hu [1973] and Sidney [1975] give $O(n \log n)$ algorithms.

The decomposition approach of Sidney [1975] is applicable to a much broader setting. Most typical is the case of *series–parallel* precedence constraints, for which Lawler [1978a] gives an $O(n \log n)$ algorithm. The crucial observation for each of these cases is that the precedence graph can be broken down into modules, such that an optimal solution for each module can be extended to an optimal solution for the entire instance. (For example, a module can be defined as a set of jobs where each job in the module has the same relation to jobs outside it.) In order to handle precedence constraints, we introduce the notion of a *string interchange relation* that generalizes a job interchange relation by letting b and c, in the implication above, represent disjoint strings of job indices. We will focus on objective functions that admit of a string interchange relation; one such function is $\Sigma\, w_j C_j$.

Given a decomposition tree representing the way in which the modules of the precedence graph are composed, an ordered set of strings is computed for each node in the tree, and the ordering at the root yields the optimal solution. In fact, Buer & Möhring [1983] give an $O(n^3)$ algorithm that computes the decomposition, and Muller & Spinrad [1989] improve the running time to $O(n^2)$. For series-parallel graphs, each leaf of the decomposition tree corresponds to a single job, and each internal node corresponds to either a series operation, where all jobs in the first module must precede all jobs in the second, or a parallel operation, where no precedence constraints are added between the two modules.

The algorithm works from the bottom of the tree upward, merging sets of strings in the appropriate way. The one remaining observation needed is that for a series operation, if the largest string σ_1 in the first set (with respect to $\leqslant$) is bigger than the smallest string σ_2 in the second, then there exists an optimal ordering which contains $\sigma_1\sigma_2$, and so the two strings can be concatenated. By iterating this argument, the two sets of strings can be merged correctly.

Lawler [1978a,b], Monma & Sidney [1979], Monma [1981], Sidney [1981], Lawler & Lenstra [1982] and Monma & Sidney [1987] describe several axiomatic settings for characterizing results of this sort.

Series-parallel graphs can also be viewed as graphs that are iteratively built up by substitution from the two-element chain and from two incomparable elements. Möhring & Radermacher [1985a] generalize this by considering graphs whose prime (undecomposable) modules are of size k, giving an $O(n^{k^2})$ algorithm to minimize, for example, Σw_jC_j subject to such precedence constraints. Sidney & Steiner [1986] improve the running time to $O(n^{w+1})$, where w denotes the maximum width of a prime module, by applying a more sophisticated dynamic programming procedure within the decomposition framework. Monma & Sidney [1987] give a partial characterization of objectives for which this combination of decomposition and dynamic programming can be applied.

5.2. *Arbitrary precedence constraints, release dates and deadlines*

Lawler [1978a] and Lenstra & Rinnooy Kan [1978] show that adding arbitrary precedence constraints results in NP-hardness, even if all $p_j = 1$ or all $w_j = 1$. Potts [1980c, 1985c] considers branch and bound methods for $1 \mid prec \mid \Sigma w_jC_j$ and provides empirical evidence that a simple lower bound heuristic based on Smith's rule pales in comparison to Lagrangean techniques.

Lenstra, Rinnooy Kan & Brucker [1977] show that if release dates are specified, $1 \mid r_j \mid \Sigma C_j$ is already strongly NP-hard. Gazmuri [1985] gives a probabilistic analysis of this problem under the assumption that the processing times and release times are independently and identically distributed. For each of two cases characterized by the relation between expected processing time and expected interarrival time, a heuristic is developed whose relative error tends to 0 in probability.

In the preemptive case, $1 \mid pmtn, r_j \mid \Sigma C_j$ can be solved by a simple extension of Smith's rule [Baker, 1974], but, surprisingly, $1 \mid pmtn, r_j \mid \Sigma w_j C_j$ is strongly NP-hard [Labetoulle, Lawler, Lenstra & Rinnooy Kan, 1984].

If a deadline $\bar{d}_j$ on the completion of each job J_j is introduced, $1 \mid \bar{d}_j \mid \Sigma C_j$ can be solved by another simple extension of Smith's rule [Smith, 1956], but the weighted case $1 \mid \bar{d}_j \mid \Sigma w_j C_j$ is strongly NP-hard [Lenstra, Rinnooy Kan & Brucker, 1977]. Du & Leung [1988b] establish NP-hardness of $1 \mid pmtn, r_j, \bar{d}_j \mid \Sigma C_j$.

For $\mid \; \mid \Sigma w_j C_j$ with either release times or deadlines, several elimination criteria and branch and bound algorithms have been proposed. Potts & Van Wassenhove [1983] apply Lagrangean relaxation to the problem with deadlines, and dualize the constraints $C_j \leqslant \bar{d}_j$. The Lagrangean multipliers are adjusted so that a simple heuristic for the original problem provides an optimal solution to the relaxed problem. Hariri & Potts [1983] consider the variant with release times, and dualize the constraints $C_j \geqslant r_j + p_j$ instead. Rinaldi & Sassano [1977], Bianco & Ricciardelli [1982], and Dessouky & Deogun [1981] give other branch and bound procedures for this problem, based on a variety of lower bound methods and dominance relations. Posner [1985] and Bagchi & Ahmadi [1987] give improvements on the lower bound method of Potts & Van Wassenhove [1983], where in each case, the new heuristic is proved to dominate the previous methods. Belouadah, Posner & Potts [1989] extend this approach and use it within a branch and bound algorithm.

6. Weighted number of late jobs

6.0. *Karp, Lawler & Moore on* $1 \mid \; \mid \Sigma w_j U_j$

Karp [1972] included the decision version of $1 \mid \; \mid \Sigma w_j U_j$ in his list of 21 NP-complete problems. His proof is based on an idea that has been applied to many other scheduling problems.

Recall the NP-complete *partition* problem from Section 2: given n numbers $a_1, \ldots, a_n$ with $\Sigma_{j=1}^{n} a_j = 2b$, does there exist a set $S \subset \{1, \ldots, n\}$ such that $\Sigma_{j \in S} a_j = b$? For any instance of this problem, we define an instance of $1 \mid \; \mid \Sigma w_j U_j$ with n jobs and $p_j = w_j = a_j$, $d_j = b$ $(j = 1, \ldots, n)$. Consider any schedule, where we may assume that all the processing is done in the interval $[0, 2b]$. The jobs that are completed by time b are on time, the others are late, and the $\Sigma w_j U_j$ value of the schedule is equal to the total processing requirement of these late jobs. It follows that, for any schedule, $\Sigma w_j U_j \geqslant b$. Equality can be achieved if and only if there exists a set of jobs of total length b, i.e., if and only if the original instance of the partition problem is a 'yes' instance.

Given the complexity status of the partition problem, we know that $1 \mid \; \mid \Sigma w_j U_j$ is NP-hard in the ordinary sense, and not in the strong sense. In fact, the latter result is unlikely to hold, as the problem is solvable in pseudopolynomial time. This was proved by Lawler & Moore [1969], who proposed a dynamic programming approach.

We may assume that any schedule is of the following form: first, the on-time jobs are processed in order of nondecreasing due dates; next, the late jobs are processed in an arbitrary order. Now suppose that $d_1 \leqslant \cdots \leqslant d_n$, and let $F_j(t)$ denote the minimum criterion value for the first j jobs, subject to the constraint that the total processing time of the on-time jobs is at most t. Initializing the recursion by

$$F_j(t) = \infty \quad \text{for } t < 0\,,\ j = 0, \ldots, n\,,$$

$$F_0(t) = 0 \quad \text{for } t \geqslant 0\,,$$

we have that

$$F_j(t) = \begin{cases} \min\{F_{j-1}(t - p_j), F_{j-1}(t) + w_j\} & \text{for } 0 \leqslant t \leqslant d_j\,, \\ F_j(d_j) & \text{for } t > d_j\,, \end{cases} \quad j = 1, \ldots, n\,.$$

The problem is solved by computing $F_n(\Sigma_j p_j)$, which requires $O(n\Sigma_j p_j)$ time.

6.1. *Further results*

An algorithm due to Moore & Hodgson [Moore, 1968] allows the solution of $1 \mid \mid \Sigma\, U_j$ in $O(n \log n)$ time: jobs are added to the set of on-time jobs in order of nondecreasing due dates, and if the addition of J_j results in this job being completed after d_j, the scheduled job with the largest processing time is marked to be late and removed. Maxwell [1970] gives an alternative derivation of this algorithm based on ideas from linear and integer programming. Sidney [1973] extends the procedure to cover the case in which certain specified jobs have to be on time. The further generalization in which jobs have to meet given deadlines occurring at or after their due dates is shown to be NP-hard by Lawler [1982b]. Lawler [1976a] shows that the Moore-Hodgson algorithm is easily adapted to solve $1 \mid \mid \Sigma w_j U_j$ in $O(n \log n)$ time if processing times and weights are oppositely ordered (i.e., $p_j < p_k \Rightarrow w_j \geqslant w_k$).

Not surprisingly, $1 \mid r_j \mid \Sigma U_j$ is strongly NP-hard, but Lawler [1982b, -] shows how to apply dynamic programming techniques to solve $1 \mid pmtn, r_j \mid \Sigma\, U_j$ in $O(n^5)$ time and $1 \mid pmtn, r_j \mid \Sigma w_j U_j$ in $O(n^3(\Sigma w_j)^2)$ time. Kise, Ibaraki & Mine [1978] provide an $O(n^2)$ algorithm for $1 \mid r_j \mid \Sigma U_j$ in the case that release dates and due dates are similarly ordered (i.e., $r_j < r_k \Rightarrow d_j \leqslant d_k$); Lawler [1982b] shows that a variation of the Moore-Hodgson algorithm solves this problem in $O(n \log n)$ time. Lawler [-] also obtains $O(n \log n)$ solutions for $1 \mid pmtn, r_j \mid \Sigma w_j U_j$ in the case that the (r_j, d_j) intervals are nested and in the case that release dates and processing times are similarly ordered and in opposite order of job weights.

Monma [1982] gives an $O(n)$ algorithm for $1 \mid p_j = 1 \mid \Sigma U_j$. However, Garey & Johnson [1976] prove that $1 \mid prec, p_j = 1 \mid \Sigma U_j$ is NP-hard, and Lenstra & Rinnooy Kan [1980] show that this is true even for *chain*-like precedence constraints.

Villarreal & Bulfin [1983] present a branch and bound procedure for $1| |\Sigma w_j U_j$. Two lower bounds are obtained by applying the algorithms Moore–Hodgson and Lawler as if, respectively, the weights and processing times are identical. (Note that in the case of identical processing times, any set of weights is oppositely ordered.) Potts & Van Wassenhove [1988] give an $O(n \log n)$ algorithm to solve the linear relaxation of a natural integer programming formulation of $1| |\Sigma w_j U_j$. Computational experiments confirm that this is an extremely effective lower bound.

Sahni [1976] gives a pseudopolynomial-time algorithm for $1| |\Sigma w_j U_j$ that requires $O(n\Sigma w_j)$ time and uses this to derive an approximation algorithm A_k with $O(n^3 k)$ running time such that

$$\sum w_j \bar{U}_j(A_k) \Big/ \sum w_j \bar{U}_j^* \geq 1 - \frac{1}{k},$$

where $\bar{U}_j = 1 - U_j$. For reasons similar to those discussed in Section 4.2 for $1|r_j|L_{\max}$, it is easier to design approximation algorithms with respect to this complementary objective. Unlike that case, however, it is possible to decide in polynomial time whether $\Sigma w_j U_j^* = 0$. Gens & Levner [1978] exploit this to give an algorithm B_k with running time $O(n^3 k)$ such that

$$\sum w_j U_j(B_k) \Big/ \sum w_j U_j^* \leq 1 + \frac{1}{k}.$$

By obtaining a preliminary upper bound on the optimum that is within a factor of 2, Gens & Levner [1981] improve the running time of a variant of B_k to $O(n^2 \log n + n^2 k)$. For $1|tree|\Sigma w_j U_j$, Ibarra & Kim [1978] give algorithms D_k of order $O(kn^{k+2})$ with the same worst-case error bound as the algorithm A_k due to Sahni [1976].

7. Total tardiness and beyond

7.0. A branch and bound algorithm for $1| |\Sigma f_j$

Let us first consider the problem with unit processing times, $1|p_j = 1|\Sigma f_j$. In this case, the cost of scheduling J_j in position k is given by $f_j(k)$, irrespective of the ordering of the other jobs. The problem is therefore equivalent to finding a permutation π of $\{1, \ldots, n\}$ that minimizes $\Sigma_j f_j(\pi(j))$. This is a weighted bipartite matching problem, which can be solved in $O(n^3)$ time.

For the case of arbitrary processing times, Rinnooy Kan, Lageweg & Lenstra [1975] applied the same idea to compute a *lower bound* on the costs of an optimal schedule. Suppose that $p_1 \leq \cdots \leq p_n$ and define $t_k = p_1 + \cdots + p_k$ for $k = 1, \ldots, n$. Then $f_j(t_k)$ is a lower bound on the cost of scheduling J_j in position k, and an overall lower bound is obtained by solving the weighted bipartite matching problem with coefficients $f_j(t_k)$.

They also derived a number of *elimination criteria*. These are statements of the following form: if the cost functions and processing times of J_j and J_k satisfy a certain relationship, then there is an optimal schedule in which J_j precedes J_k.

Lower bounds and elimination criteria are used to discard partial schedules that are generated by an *enumeration scheme*. For $1 \mid \mid \Sigma f_j$, it is customary to generate schedules by building them from back to front. That is, at the lth level of the search tree, jobs are scheduled in the $(n-l+1)$th position. The justification for this is that, since the cost functions are nondecreasing, the larger terms of the optimality criterion are fixed at an early stage while the smaller terms are estimated by the lower bound.

7.1. *Further results*

Lawler [1977] gives a pseudopolynomial algorithm for the problem $1 \mid \mid \Sigma T_j$ that runs in $O(n^4 \Sigma p_j)$ time. Recently, Du & Leung [1990] have shown that the problem is NP-hard in the ordinary sense.

Lenstra & Rinnooy Kan [1978] prove that $1 \mid prec, p_j = 1 \mid \Sigma T_j$ is NP-hard, and Leung & Young [1989] show that this is true even for *chain*-like precedence constraints. If we introduce release dates, $1 \mid r_j, p_j = 1 \mid \Sigma w_j T_j$ can be solved as a weighted bipartite matching problem, whereas $1 \mid r_j \mid \Sigma T_j$ is obviously strongly NP-hard.

Lawler [1977] and Lenstra, Rinnooy Kan & Brucker [1977] show that $1 \mid \mid \Sigma w_j T_j$ is strongly NP-hard. Various enumerative solution methods have been proposed for this problem. Elmaghraby [1968] presents the first elimination criteria for the problem, including the observation that any job with due date exceeding the total processing time can be scheduled last in an optimal schedule. Emmons [1969] and Shwimer [1972] develop other elimination criteria, and Rinnooy Kan, Lageweg & Lenstra [1975] extend these to the case of arbitrary nondecreasing cost functions. Rachamadugu [1987] gives an elimination criterion that generates an optimal schedule if there is one in which all jobs are late.

A variety of lower bounds have been studied. As already discussed in Section 7.0, Rinnooy Kan, Lageweg & Lenstra [1975] use a linear assignment relaxation based on an underestimate of the cost of assigning J_j to position k, and Gelders & Kleindorfer [1974, 1975] use a fairly similar relaxation to a transportation problem. Fisher [1976] proposes a method in which the requirement that the machine can process at most one job at a time is relaxed. In this approach, one attaches 'prices' (i.e., Lagrangean multipliers) to each unit-time interval, and looks for multiplier values for which a cheapest schedule does not violate the capacity constraint. The resulting algorithm is quite successful on problems with up to 50 jobs. Potts & Van Wassenhove [1985] observe that a more efficiently computable but weaker bound may be preferable. They apply a multiplier adjustment method similar to the one mentioned in Section 5.2; the constraints $T_j \geq C_j - d_j$ are relaxed while associated prices for violating these constraints are introduced.

Algorithms based on straightforward but cleverly implemented dynamic programming offer a surprisingly good alternative. Baker & Schrage [1978] and Schrage & Baker [1978] suggest compact labeling schemes that can handle up to 50 jobs. Lawler [1979b] gives a more efficient implementation of this approach; Kao & Queyranne [1982] describe carefully designed experiments which confirm that this method is a practical improvement as well. Potts & Van Wassenhove [1982] consider the unweighted problem, and use a combination of the Baker–Schrage algorithm and a decomposition approach implied by the algorithm of Lawler [1977]. Potts & Van Wassenhove [1987] compare the dynamic programming algorithms of Schrage & Baker [1978] and Lawler [1979b], and then consider the relative merits of the decomposition approach when used in a dynamic programming framework or in an algorithm that, as in their previous work, resembles branch and bound.

Abdul-Razaq & Potts [1988] consider $1 \mid \mid \Sigma f_j$ where the costs are no longer assumed to be nondecreasing functions of completion time; however, the constraint that a schedule may not contain idle time is added. Since the straightforward dynamic programming formulation has an unmanageable number of states, a lower bound is computed by recursively solving a formulation with a smaller state space, and then used within a branch and bound procedure.

Using his pseudopolynomial algorithm for $1 \mid \mid \Sigma T_j$ mentioned above, Lawler [1982c] presents a fully polynomial approximation scheme, such that algorithm A_k runs in $O(n^7 k)$ time and guarantees

$$\sum T_j(A_k) \Big/ \sum T_j^* \leq 1 + \frac{1}{k}\,.$$

Fisher & Krieger [1984] study the following general problem: let P_j be a nonincreasing and concave *profit function* of the starting time of J_j; maximize the total profit. They use a heuristic based on a generalization of Smith's rule (GS) to get provably good solutions:

$$\sum P_j(\mathrm{GS}) \Big/ \sum P_j^* \geq \tfrac{2}{3}\,.$$

PART III. PARALLEL MACHINES

Recall from Section 3 the definitions of *identical*, *uniform* and *unrelated* machines, denoted by P, Q and R, respectively.

Section 8 deals with minsum criteria. We will be able to review some interesting polynomial-time algorithms, especially for the minimization of ΣC_j. We then turn to minmax criteria. Section 9 considers the nonpreemptive case with general processing times. The simplest problem of this type, $P2 \mid \mid C_{\max}$, is already NP-hard, and we will concentrate on the analysis of approximation algorithms. Section 10 considers the preemptive case. The situation is much brighter here, and we will mention a number of polynomial-time algorithms for the minimization of $C_{\max}$ and $L_{\max}$, even subject to release dates. Finally, Section 11 deals with the presence of precedence constraints, with an emphasis on unit-time or preemptable jobs. The more general problems in this section are NP-hard and will lead us again to investigate the performance of approximation algorithms. However, several special cases turn out to be solvable in polynomial time.

8. Minsum criteria

8.0. A bipartite matching formulation for $R\,|\,|\,\Sigma C_j$

Horn [1973] and Bruno, Coffman & Sethi [1974] formulated $R\,|\,|\,\Sigma C_j$ as an integer programming problem. The structure of this program is such that it can be solved in polynomial time.

Consider the jobs that are to be performed by a single machine M_i, and for simplicity suppose that these are $J_1, J_2, \ldots, J_l$ in that order. For these jobs we have $\Sigma C_j = lp_{i1} + (l-1)p_{i2} + \cdots + p_{il}$. In general, ΣC_j is a weighted sum of p_{ij} values, where the weight of p_{ij} is equal to the number of jobs to whose completion time it contributes. We now describe schedules in terms of 0–1 variables $x_{(ik),j}$, where $x_{(ik),j} = 1$ if J_j is the kth last job processed on M_i, and $x_{(ik),j} = 0$ otherwise. The problem is then to minimize

$$\sum_{i,k} \sum_{j} k p_{ij} x_{(ik),j}$$

subject to

$$\sum_{i,k} x_{(ik),j} = 1 \quad \text{for } j = 1, \ldots, n\,,$$

$$\sum_{j} x_{(ik),j} \leq 1 \quad \text{for } i = 1, \ldots, m\,,\ k = 1, \ldots, n\,,$$

$$x_{(ik),j} \in \{0, 1\} \quad \text{for } i = 1, \ldots, m\,,\ j, k = 1, \ldots, n\,.$$

The constraints ensure that each job is scheduled exactly once and that each position on each machine is occupied by at most one job. This is a weighted bipartite matching problem, so that the integrality constraints can be replaced by nonnegativity constraints without altering the feasible set. This matching problem can be solved in $O(n^3)$ time.

A similar approach yields $O(n \log n)$ algorithms for $P\,|\,|\,\Sigma C_j$ and $Q\,|\,|\,\Sigma C_j$. In the case of identical machines, ΣC_j is a weighted sum of p_j values, where each weight is an integer between 1 and n, and no weight may be used more than m times. It is obviously optimal to match the smallest weights with the largest processing requirements. This is precisely what the generalized SPT rule of Conway, Maxwell & Miller [1967] accomplishes: schedule the jobs in order of nondecreasing processing times, and assign each job to the earliest available machine.

In the case of uniform machines, ΣC_j is a weighted sum of p_j values, where each weight is of the form k/s_i (k indicating the position and s_i the speed of M_i), and no weight may be used more than once. Once again, we want to select the n smallest of these mn weights and to match the smallest weights with the longest jobs. Horowitz & Sahni [1976] propose to maintain a priority queue of the smallest m unused weights and to build the schedule backwards by assigning the next longest job to the machine associated with the smallest available weight. This algorithm can be implemented to run in $O(n \log n)$ time.

8.1. Unit-length jobs on uniform machines

The problems $Q \mid p_j = 1 \mid \Sigma f_j$ and $Q \mid p_j = 1 \mid f_{\max}$ are easily solved in polynomial time. First, observe that there exists an optimal schedule in which the jobs are executed in the time periods with the n earliest possible completion times. These completion times can be generated in $O(n \log m)$ time: initialize a priority queue with completion times $1/s_i$ ($i = 1, \ldots, m$); at a general step, remove the smallest completion time from the queue and, if this time is k/s_i, insert $(k+1)/s_i$ into the queue. Let $t_i, \ldots, t_n$ denote the n smallest completion times, in nondecreasing order.

$Q \mid p_j = 1 \mid \Sigma f_j$ is now solved by finding an optimal assignment of the jobs to these completion times. This amounts to formulating and solving an $n \times n$ weighted bipartite matching problem with cost coefficients $c_{jk} = f_j(t_k)$; this requires $O(n^3)$ time. Various special cases can be solved more efficiently. Thus $Q \mid p_j = 1 \mid \Sigma w_j C_j$ is solved by assigning the job with the kth largest weight to t_k, and $Q \mid p_j = 1 \mid \Sigma T_j$ is solved by assigning the job with the kth smallest due date to t_k; the time required is $O(n \log n)$, the time needed to sort weights or due dates. $Q \mid p_j = 1 \mid \Sigma w_j U_j$ is solved by considering the completion times from largest to smallest and scheduling, from among all unassigned jobs that would be on time (if any), a job with maximal weight; with appropriate use of priority queues, this can again be done in $O(n \log n)$ time. In the presence of release dates, dynamic programming can be applied to solve $Q \mid r_j, p_j = 1 \mid \Sigma C_j$ in $O(m^2 n^{2m+1} \log n)$ time, which is polynomial only for fixed values of m.

$Q \mid p_j = 1 \mid f_{\max}$ is solved by a method that resembles Lawler's algorithm for $1 \mid \mid f_{\max}$ (see Section 4.0). Consider the completion times from largest to smallest and, at each successive completion time t, schedule a job J_j for which $f_j(t)$ is minimal: this yields an optimal schedule in $O(n^2)$ time. $Q \mid p_j = 1 \mid L_{\max}$ and $Q \mid r_j, p_j = 1 \mid C_{\max}$ can be solved in $O(n \log n)$ time be simply matching the kth smallest due date, or release date, with t_k.

These results are due to Lawler [-], and Dessouky, Lageweg, Lenstra and Van de Velde [1990]. Lawler [1976a] shows that the special case $P \mid p_j = 1 \mid \Sigma U_j$ can be solved in $O(n \log n)$ time.

Complexity results for the precedence-constrained problem $P \mid prec, p_j = 1 \mid \Sigma C_j$ and its special cases will be mentioned in Section 11.1.

8.2. Minsum criteria without preemption

We have seen that $R| |\Sigma C_j$ is solvable in polynomial time. Meilijson & Tamir [1984] show that the SPT rule remains optimal for identical machines that increase in speed over time. On the other hand, if the speed decreases, then the problem is NP-hard.

In the case of arbitrary processing requirements, it seems fruitless to attempt to find polynomial algorithms for more general criteria or for ΣC_j problems with additional constraints, even when there are only two identical machines. $P2| |\Sigma w_j C_j$ is already NP-hard [Bruno, Coffman & Sethi, 1974; Lenstra, Rinnooy Kan & Brucker, 1977], and so is $P2|\mathit{tree}|\Sigma C_j$, for intrees as well as outtrees [Sethi, 1977] and even for chains [Du, Leung & Young, 1991]. The specification of due dates or release dates does not leave much hope either, as both $P2| |C_{\max}$ and $1|r_j|\Sigma C_j$ are NP-hard. In this section, we will therefore be concerned with approximation in polynomial time and with optimization by implicit enumeration.

With respect to $P| |\Sigma w_j C_j$, an obvious idea is to list the jobs according to nondecreasing ratios p_j/w_j, as specified by Smith's rule for the single-machine case (see Section 5.0), and to schedule the next job whenever a machine becomes available. Eastman, Even & Isaacs [1964] show that this largest ratio (LR) rule gives

$$\sum w_j C_j(\mathrm{LR}) - \tfrac{1}{2}\sum_j w_j p_j \geq \frac{1}{m}\Big(\sum_{j=1}^{n}\sum_{k=1}^{j} w_j p_k - \tfrac{1}{2}\sum_{j=1}^{n} w_j p_j\Big). \qquad (\dagger)$$

It follows from this inequality that

$$\sum w_j C_j^* \geq \frac{m+n}{m(n+1)} \sum_{j=1}^{n}\sum_{k=1}^{j} w_j p_k .$$

This lower bound has been the basis for the branch and bound algorithms of Elmaghraby & Park [1974], Barnes & Brennan [1977], and Sarin, Ahn & Bishop [1988]. Kawaguchi & Kyan [1986] have refined the analysis of these bounds to prove that

$$\sum w_j C_j(\mathrm{LR}) \Big/ \sum w_j C_j^* \leq \frac{\sqrt{2}+1}{2} . \qquad (\dagger)$$

Sahni [1976] constructs algorithms A_k (in the same spirit as his approach for $1| |\Sigma w_j U_j$ mentioned in Section 6.1) with $O(n(n^2k)^{m-1})$ running time for which

$$\sum w_j C_j(A_k) \Big/ \sum w_j C_j^* \leq 1 + \frac{1}{k} .$$

For $m = 2$, the running time of A_k can be improved to $O(n^2 k)$.

A general dynamic programming technique of Rothkopf [1966] and Lawler

& Moore [1969] is applicable to special cases of $R| |\Sigma f_j$ and $R| |f_{max}$ in which the following condition is satisfied: it is possible to index the jobs in such a way that the jobs assigned to a given machine can be assumed to be processed in order of their indices. For example, this condition holds in the case of $R| |C_{max}$ (any indexing is satisfactory), $R| |\Sigma w_j U_j$ (index in order of due dates), and $Q| |\Sigma w_j C_j$ (index in order of the ratios p_j/w_j).

Given an appropriate indexing of the jobs, define $F_j(t_1, \ldots, t_m)$ as the minimum cost of a schedule without idle time for $J_1, \ldots, J_j$ subject to the constraint that the last job on M_i is completed at time t_i, for $i = 1, \ldots, m$. Then, in the case of f_{max} criteria,

$$F_j(t_1, \ldots, t_m) = \min_{1 \leq i \leq m} \max\{f_j(t_i), F_{j-1}(t_1, \ldots, t_i - p_{ij}, \ldots, t_m)\},$$

and in the case of Σf_j criteria,

$$F_j(t_1, \ldots, t_m) = \min_{1 \leq i \leq m} (f_j(t_i) + F_{j-1}(t_1, \ldots, t_1 - p_{ij}, \ldots, t_m)).$$

In both cases, the initial conditions are

$$F_0(t_1, \ldots, t_m) = \begin{cases} 0 & \text{if } t_i = 0 \text{ for } i = 1, \ldots, m, \\ \infty & \text{otherwise}. \end{cases}$$

These equations can be solved in $O(mnC^m)$ time, where C is an upper bound on the completion time of any job in an optimal schedule. If the machines are uniform, then only $m-1$ of the values $t_1, \ldots, t_m$ in the equation for $F_j(t_1, \ldots, t_m)$ are independent. This means, for example, that the time bound for $Q| |\Sigma w_j C_j$ can be reduced by a factor of C to $O(mnC^{m-1})$.

One variation of the above technique solves $Q|r_j|C_{max}$, and another variation solves $Q| |\Sigma w_j U_j$ in $O(mn(\max_j d_j)^m)$ time. Still other dynamic programming approaches can be used to solve $P| |\Sigma f_j$ and $P| |f_{max}$ in $O(m \cdot \min\{3^n, n2^n C\})$ time.

8.3. *Minsum criteria with preemption*

A theorem of McNaughton [1959] states that for $P|pmtn|\Sigma w_j C_j$ there is no schedule with a finite number of preemptions which yields a smaller criterion value than an optimal nonpreemptive schedule. The finiteness restriction can be removed by appropriate application of results from open shop theory. It therefore follows that the procedure of Section 8.0 solves $P|pmtn|\Sigma C_j$ in $O(n \log n)$ time, and that $P2|pmtn|\Sigma w_j C_j$ is NP-hard. Du, Leung & Young [1991] extend McNaughton's theorem to the case of chain-like precedence constraints, which implies that $P2|pmtn, tree|\Sigma C_j$ is strongly NP-hard.

McNaughton's theorem does not apply to uniform machines, as can be demonstrated by a simple counterexample. There is, however, a polynomial algorithm for $Q|pmtn|\Sigma C_j$. Lawler & Labetoulle [1978] show that there exists an optimal preemptive schedule in which $C_j \leq C_k$ if $p_j < p_k$. This result is the essence of the correctness proof of the following algorithm of Gonzalez [1977]. First place the jobs in SPT order. Then obtain an optimal schedule by preemptively scheduling each successive job in the available time on the m machines so as to minimize its completion time. This procedure can be implemented to run in $O(n \log n + mn)$ time and yields an optimal schedule with no more than $(m-1)(n-\frac{1}{2}m)$ preemptions. Gonzalez also extends it to cover the case in which ΣC_j is to be minimized subject to a common deadline for all jobs. McCormick & Pinedo [1989] extend this to handle the problem of minimizing $wC_{max} + \Sigma C_j$ for an arbitrary weight $w \geq 0$.

Very little is known about $R \mid pmtn \mid \Sigma C_j$. This remains one of the more vexing questions in the area of preemptive scheduling. One approach has been to apply the techniques of Lawler & Labetoulle [1978] to show that if the optimal *order* of completion times is known, then an optimal solution can be constructed in polynomial time.

The problems $1 \mid pmtn \mid \Sigma w_j U_j$ (see Section 6.0) and $P \mid pmtn \mid \Sigma U_j$ are both NP-hard in the ordinary sense; the latter result is due to Lawler [1983]. Lawler [1979a] also shows that, for any fixed number of uniform machines, $Qm \mid pmtn \mid \Sigma w_j U_j$ can be solved in pseudopolynomial time: $O(n^2(\Sigma w_j)^2)$ if $m=2$ and $O(n^{3m-5}(\Sigma w_j)^2)$ if $m \geq 3$. Hence, $Qm \mid pmtn \mid \Sigma U_j$ is solvable in strictly polynomial time. Lawler & Martel [1989] give an improved algorithm for $m=2$ that runs in $O(n^2 \Sigma w_j)$ time, and also use this algorithm to derive a fully polynomial approximation scheme for $Q2 \mid pmtn \mid \Sigma w_j U_j$. The remaining minimal open problems are $R2 \mid pmtn \mid \Sigma U_j$ and, only with respect to a unary encoding, $P \mid pmtn \mid \Sigma U_j$.

We know from Section 7.1 that $1 \mid pmtn \mid \Sigma T_j$ and $1 \mid pmtn \mid \Sigma w_j T_j$ are NP-hard in the ordinary sense and in the strong sense, respectively. With respect to a unary encoding, $P2 \mid pmtn \mid \Sigma T_j$ is open.

In the presence of release dates, NP-hardness has been established for $P2 \mid pmtn, r_j \mid \Sigma C_j$ [Du, Leung & Young, 1988], $P2 \mid pmtn, r_j \mid \Sigma U_j$ [Du, Leung & Wong, 1989].

9. Minmax criteria without preemption

9.0. The performance of list scheduling for $P \mid \mid C_{max}$

Although $P \mid \mid C_{max}$ is strongly NP-hard [Garey & Johnson, 1978], there are simple procedures to construct schedules that are provably close to optimal. Consider the *list scheduling* (LS) rule, which schedules the next available job in some prespecified list whenever a machine becomes idle.

In the earliest paper on the worst-case analysis of approximation algorithms, Graham [1966] proves that, for any instance,

$$C_{max}(\mathrm{LS})/C^*_{max} \leq 2 - \frac{1}{m}\,. \qquad (\dagger)$$

To see this, let J_l be the last job to be completed in a list schedule, and note that no machine can be idle before time $t = C_{\max}(\text{LS}) - p_l$, when J_l starts processing. Intuitively, the performance guarantee follows from the observation that both t and p_l are lower bounds on the length of any schedule. More formally, we have $\Sigma_{j \neq l} p_j \geqslant mt$ and therefore

$$C_{\max}(\text{LS}) = t + p_l \leqslant \frac{1}{m} \sum_{j \neq l} p_j + p_l = \frac{1}{m} \sum_j p_j + \frac{m-1}{m} p_l .$$

The observations that

$$C^*_{\max} \geqslant \frac{1}{m} \sum_j p_j , \qquad C^*_{\max} \geqslant p_l ,$$

now yield the desired result.

The bound is tight for any value of m, as is shown by the following class of instances. Let $n = m(m-1) + 1$, $p_1 = \cdots = p_{n-1} = 1$, $p_n = m$, and consider the list $(J_1, J_2, \ldots, J_n)$. It is not hard to see that $C_{\max}(\text{LS}) = 2m - 1$ and $C^*_{\max} = m$.

The worst-case analysis also gives insight into the average-case performance of list scheduling. We know that, for any instance,

$$C_{\max}(\text{LS}) / C^*_{\max} \leqslant 1 + (m-1) \max_j p_j \Big/ \sum_j p_j .$$

In order to give a probabilistic analysis of list scheduling, we assume that the processing times $\boldsymbol{p}_j$ are selected from a given probability distribution, and we study the error term under this distribution. (Note that random variables are printed in boldface italic.) For the case that the $\boldsymbol{p}_j$ are independently and uniformly distributed over the interval [0, 1], Bruno & Downey [1986] show that

$$\lim_{n \to \infty} \Pr\Big[\max_j \boldsymbol{p}_j \Big/ \sum_j \boldsymbol{p}_j > 4/n\Big] = 0 .$$

In other words, as long as n grows faster than m, list schedules are asymptotically optimal in probability.

9.1. *Identical machines*

By far the most studied scheduling model from the viewpoint of approximation algorithms is $P \| C_{\max}$. Garey, Graham & Johnson [1978] and Coffman, Lueker & Rinnooy Kan [1988] give easily readable introductions into the techniques involved in, respectively, the worst-case and probabilistic analysis of approximation algorithms.

In the previous section, we have seen that list scheduling is guaranteed to produce a schedule with maximum completion time less than twice the optimal.

Since there always is a list ordering for which this simple heuristic produces an optimal schedule, it is natural to consider refinements of the approach. Graham [1969] shows that, if the jobs are selected in *longest processing time* (LPT) order, then the bound can be considerably improved:

$$C_{\max}(\mathrm{LPT})/C^*_{\max} \leq \frac{4}{3} - \frac{1}{3m} . \qquad (\dagger)$$

A somewhat better algorithm, called *multifit* (MF) and based on a completely different principle, is due to Coffman, Garey & Johnson [1978]. The idea behind MF is to find (by binary search) the smallest 'capacity' that a set of m 'bins' can have and still accommodate all jobs when the jobs are taken in order of nonincreasing p_j and each job is placed into the first bin into which it will fit. The set of jobs in the ith bin will be processed by M_i. Coffman, Garey & Johnsons show that, if k packing attempts are made, the algorithm (denoted by MF_k) runs in time $O(n \log n + kn \log m)$ and satisfies

$$C_{\max}(\mathrm{MF}_k)/C^*_{\max} \leq 1.22 + 2^{-k} .$$

Friesen [1984] subsequently improves this bound from 1.22 to 1.2. Yue [1990] improves it to $\frac{13}{11}$, which is tight. The procedure executed within the binary search 'loop' can be viewed as an approximation algorithm for packing a set of jobs in the fewest number bins of a given capacity. If a more primitive algorithm is used for this, where the jobs are not ordered by decreasing p_j, then all that can be guaranteed is

$$C_{\max}(\mathrm{MF})/C^*_{\max} \leq 2 - \frac{2}{m+1} . \qquad (\dagger)$$

Friesen & Langston [1986] refine the iterated approximation algorithm to provide algorithms MF'_k with running time $O(n \log n + kn \log m)$ (where the constant embedded within the 'big Oh' notation is big indeed) that guarantee

$$C_{\max}(\mathrm{MF}'_k)/C^*_{\max} \leq \tfrac{72}{61} + 2^{-k} . \qquad (\dagger)$$

The following algorithm Z_k is due to Graham [1969]: schedule the k largest jobs optimally, then list schedule the remaining jobs arbitrarily. Graham shows that

$$C_{\max}(Z_k)/C^*_{\max} \leq 1 + \left(1 - \frac{1}{m}\right) \Big/ \left(1 + \left\lfloor \frac{k}{m} \right\rfloor\right) ,$$

and that when m divides k, this is best possible. By selecting $k = m/\varepsilon$, we obtain an algorithm with worst-case performance ratio less than $1 + \varepsilon$. Unfortunately, the best bound on the running time is $O(n^{km})$. Thus, for any fixed number of machines, this family of algorithms is a polynomial approximation scheme. Sahni [1976] has improved this result, by devising algorithms A_k with $O(n(n^2k)^{m-1})$ running time which satisfy

$$C_{\max}(A_k)/C^*_{\max} \leq 1 + \frac{1}{k} .$$

For any fixed number of machines, these algorithms constitute a fully polynomial approximation scheme. For $m = 2$, algorithm A_k can be improved to run in time $O(n^2k)$. As in the cases of $1| \,|\Sigma w_jU_j$ (Section 6.1) and $P| \,|\Sigma w_jC_j$ (Section 8.2), the algorithms A_k are based on a clever combination of dynamic programming and rounding and are beyond the scope of the present discussion.

Hochbaum & Shmoys [1987] use a variation on the multifit approach to provide a polynomial approximation scheme for $P| \,|C_{\max}$, which replaces a (traditional) approximation algorithm in the binary search with a *dual approximation algorithm*. Given a capacity d and a set of jobs to pack, a ρ-dual approximation algorithm ($\rho > 1$) produces a packing that uses *at most* the minimum number of bins of capacity d, but the packing may use bins of capacity ρd. Using a ρ-dual approximation algorithm within binary search for k iterations, one obtains a $(\rho + 2^{-k})$-approximation algorithm for $P| \,|C_{\max}$. Hochbaum and Shmoys further provide a family of algorithms D_k, such that D_k is a $(1 + 1/k)$-dual approximation algorithm and has running time $O((kn)^{k^2})$; Leung [1991] improves the running time to $O((kn)^{k \log k})$. For $k = 5$ and $k = 6$, Hochbaum & Shmoys refine their approach to obtain algorithms with $O(n \log n)$ and $O(n(m^4 + \log n))$ running times, respectively. Since $P| \,|C_{\max}$ is strongly NP-hard, there is no fully polynomial approximation scheme for it unless P = NP.

Several bounds are available which take into account the processing times of the jobs. Recall that the probabilistic analysis discussed in Section 9.0 relies on such a (worst-case) bound for list scheduling. Achugbue & Chin [1981] prove two results relating the performance ratio of list scheduling to the value of $\pi = \max_j p_j / \min_j p_j$. If $\pi \leq 3$, then

$$C_{\max}(\mathrm{LS})/C^*_{\max} \leq \begin{cases} \frac{5}{3} & \text{if } m = 3, 4 , \\ \frac{17}{10} & \text{if } m = 5 , \\ 2 - \dfrac{1}{3\lfloor m/3 \rfloor} & \text{if } m \geq 6 , \end{cases} \qquad (\dagger)$$

and if $\pi \leq 2$,

$$C_{\max}(\mathrm{LS})/C^*_{\max} \leq \begin{cases} \frac{3}{2} & \text{if } m = 2, 3 , \\ \frac{5}{3} - \dfrac{1}{3\lfloor m/2 \rfloor} & \text{if } m \geq 4 . \end{cases} \qquad (\dagger)$$

For the case of LPT, Ibarra & Kim [1977] prove that

$$C_{\max}(\mathrm{LPT})/C^*_{\max} \leq 1 + \frac{2(m-1)}{n} \quad \text{for } n \geq 2(m-1)\pi .$$

Significantly less is known about the worst-case performance of approximation algorithms for other minmax criteria. Gusfield [1984] considers the problem $P \mid r_j \mid L_{\max}$, and proves that for the EDD rule (see Section 4.1),

$$L_{\max}(\mathrm{EDD}) - L^*_{\max} \leq \frac{2m-1}{m} \max_j p_j . \qquad (\dagger)$$

As in the single machine case, it is natural to consider the relative error in the delivery time model. The translation of the previous bound into this setting provides an unnecessarily weak guarantee. By using a simple extension of the argument of Graham [1966], Hall & Shmoys [1989] observe that

$$L_{\max}(\mathrm{LS})/L^*_{\max} < 2 . \qquad (\dagger)$$

They also develop a polynomial approximation scheme for this problem. Carlier [1987] gives an enumerative method for $P \mid r_j \mid L_{\max}$. Simons [1983] shows that an interesting special case, $P \mid r_j, p_j = p \mid L_{\max}$, can be solved in polynomial time. Simons & Warmuth [1989] give an improved $O(mn^2)$ algorithm based on a generalization of the approach of Garey, Johnson, Simons & Tarjan [1981]. No approximation results are known for minimizing $C_{\max}$ with both release times and deadlines; Bratley, Florian & Robillard [1975] give an enumerative method for this problem.

The simple probabilistic analysis of list scheduling that was discussed in Section 8.0 is also just a first step in a series of results in this area. For example, the bounds of Bruno & Downey [1986] were refined and extended to other distributions by Coffman & Gilbert [1985].

Probabilistic analysis also supports the claim that the LPT heuristic performs better than arbitrary list scheduling. Unlike the relative error of list scheduling, the absolute error $C_{\max}(\mathrm{LS}) - C^*_{\max}$ does not tend to 0 as $n \to \infty$ (with m fixed). Coffman, Flatto & Lueker [1984] observe that, if $I(\mathrm{LPT})$ denotes the total idle time in an LPT schedule, then the absolute error is at most $I(\mathrm{LPT})/m$. For processing times selected independently and uniformly from [0, 1], they prove that $\mathrm{E}[\boldsymbol{I}(\mathrm{LPT})] \leq c_m m^2/(n+1)$, where c_m is bounded and $\lim_{m\to\infty} c_m = 1$.

Loulou [1984] and Frenk & Rinnooy Kan [1987] both base their analyses of LPT on the difference $C_{\max}(\mathrm{LPT}) - \Sigma_j\, p_j/m$, which is an upper bound on $C_{\max}(\mathrm{LPT}) - C^*_{\max}$. Loulou shows that, if the processing times are independent and identically distributed with finite mean, then, for any fixed $m \geq 2$, the absolute error of LPT is stochastically smaller than a fixed random variable that does not depend on n. Frenk & Rinnooy Kan consider the general situation where the processing times are independently drawn from a distribution that has finite second moment and positive density at zero. They prove that the absolute error converges to 0 not only in expectation but even almost surely; that is, $\Pr[\lim_{n\to\infty} \boldsymbol{C}_{\max}(\mathrm{LPT}) - \boldsymbol{C}^*_{\max} = 0] = 1$.

Given that the absolute error of the LPT rule approaches 0, a further issue is the rate at which the error converges to 0. Boxma [1984] and Frenk & Rinnooy Kan [1986] show that under a broad range of distributions, the expected absolute error is $O(n^{-c})$ for some positive constant c. Karmarkar & Karp [1982] suggest an entirely different approach, the *differencing method*, and prove that with probability approaching 1, the difference between the completion times of the last and first machines is $O(n^{-c \log n})$ for some positive c. Fischetti & Martello [1987] give a worst-case analysis of this heuristic for $P2 | \, | C_{max}$ and prove that it is a $\frac{7}{6}$-approximation algorithm.

9.2. Uniform machines

Many of the results in the previous section can be generalized to the uniform machine model. The initial work in this area is due to Liu & Liu [1974a,b,c], who consider arbitrary list scheduling as well as a natural extension of the scheme of Graham that optimally schedules the k longest jobs and then uses list scheduling on the remaining jobs. The performance of these algorithms on uniform machines is significantly worse; for example,

$$C_{max}(\mathrm{LS})/C^*_{max} \leq 1 + \max_i s_i / \min_i s_i - \max_i s_i \Big/ \sum_i s_i \,. \qquad (\dagger)$$

The most natural way to implement list scheduling on uniform machines is to assign the next job on the list to any machine that becomes idle. However, this produces schedules without *unforced idleness*, and the optimal schedule might require such idle time. Another implementation LS′ is studied by Cho & Sahni [1980], where the next job in the list is scheduled on the machine on which it will finish earliest. They prove that

$$C_{max}(\mathrm{LS}')/C^*_{max} \leq \begin{cases} (1+\sqrt{5})/2 & \text{for } m = 2\,, \\ (1+(\sqrt{2m-2})/2 & \text{for } m > 2\,. \end{cases}$$

The bound is tight for $m \leq 6$, but in general, the worst known examples have a performance ratio of $\lfloor (\log_2(3m-1)+1)/2 \rfloor$. This approach followed the work of Gonzalez, Ibarra & Sahni [1977], who consider the analogous generalization LPT′ of LPT and show that

$$C_{max}(\mathrm{LPT}')/C^*_{max} \leq 2 - \frac{2}{m+1} \,.$$

Dobson [1984] and Friesen [1987] improve this analysis to obtain an upper bound of $\frac{19}{12}$, and also provide examples that have performance ratio 1.52. Morrison [1988] shows that LPT is better than LS, in that

$$C_{max}(\mathrm{LPT})/C^*_{max} \leq \max\{\max_i s_i/(2 \min_i s_i), 2\} \,. \qquad (\dagger)$$

Friesen & Langston [1983] extend the multifit approach to uniform processors. They prove that, if the bins are ordered in increasing size for each iteration of the binary search, then

$$C_{\max}(\mathrm{MF}_k)/C^*_{\max} \leq 1.4 + 2^{-k},$$

and that there exists an example that has performance ratio 1.341. They also show that the decision to order the bins by increasing size is the correct one, since for decreasing bin sizes there exist examples with performance ratio $\frac{3}{2}$.

Horowitz & Sahni [1976] give a family of algorithms A_k with running time $O(n^{2m}k^{m-1})$ such that

$$C_{\max}(A_k)/C^*_{\max} \leq 1 + \frac{1}{k},$$

so that for any fixed value of m, this is a fully polynomial approximation scheme. Extending their dual approximation approach for identical machines, Hochbaum & Shmoys [1988] give a polynomial approximation scheme, where algorithm D_k has running time $O(mn^{10k^2+3})$ and

$$C_{\max}(D_k)/C^*_{\max} \leq 1 + \frac{1}{k}.$$

For small values of k, the efficiency of this scheme can be improved; Hochbaum & Shmoys provide algorithms with performance guarantee arbitrarily close to $\frac{3}{2}$ that run in $O(n \log n + m)$ time.

The probabilistic results of Frenk & Rinnooy Kan [1986, 1987] also extend to the case of uniform machines. In fact, the naive implementation of the LPT rule (as opposed to the algorithm LPT′ that was discussed above) produces schedules in which the absolute error converges in expectation and almost surely to 0.

9.3. Unrelated machines

Unrelated parallel machine problems are perceived to be significantly harder than uniform machine problems, and results concerning the worst-case analysis of approximation algorithms substantiate this distinction. Lenstra, Shmoys & Tardos [1990] show that it is NP-complete to decide if there is a feasible schedule of length 2 for instances of $R||C_{\max}$. This implies that there does not exist a polynomial-time ρ-approximation algorithm with $\rho < \frac{3}{2}$ unless P = NP. Although this excludes the possibility of a polynomial approximation scheme, Horowitz & Sahni [1976] show that for any fixed number of machines, there is a *fully* polynomial approximation scheme.

Ibarra & Kim [1977] show that a variety of simple algorithms perform discouragingly poorly; in fact, they were only able to prove that these methods were m-approximation algorithms. The first substantial improvement of this bound is due to Davis & Jaffe [1981], who give a variant of a list scheduling algorithm for which

$$C_{\max}(\mathrm{LS}')/C^*_{\max} \leq 2.5\sqrt{m} + 1 + \frac{1}{2\sqrt{m}},$$

and also provide examples that show that this analysis is tight up to a constant factor.

Potts [1985a] proposes an algorithm based on linear programming (LP), the running time of which is polynomial only for fixed m. He proves

$$C_{\max}(\mathrm{LP})/C^*_{\max} \leq 2. \qquad (\dagger)$$

In contrast to the scheme of Horowitz & Sahni, this is a practical algorithm for a modest number of machines, since the space requirements do not grow exponentially in the number of machines. Lenstra, Shmoys & Tardos [1990] extend this approach in two ways. First, they give a modified algorithm LP′ that runs in polynomial time and still satisfies

$$C_{\max}(\mathrm{LP}')/C^*_{\max} < 2. \qquad (\dagger)$$

Second, for a fixed number of machines, they give a polynomial approximation scheme, based on a combination of enumeration of partial schedules and linear programming, which has only modest space requirements.

10. Minmax criteria with preemption

10.0. McNaughton's wrap-around rule for $P \mid pmtn \mid C_{\max}$

McNaughton's [1959] solution of $P \mid pmtn \mid C_{\max}$ is probably the simplest and earliest instance of an approach that has been successfully applied to other preemptive scheduling problems: we first provide an obvious lower bound on the value of an optimal schedule and then construct a schedule that matches this bound.

In this case, we see that the maximum completion time of any schedule is at least

$$\max\Big\{\max_j p_j, \Big(\sum_j p_j\Big)\Big/ m\Big\}.$$

A schedule meeting this bound can be constructed in $O(n)$ time: just fill the machines successively, scheduling the jobs in any order and splitting a job whenever the above time bound is met. The number of preemptions occurring in this schedule is at most $m-1$, and it is possible to design a class of problems for which any optimal schedule has at least this many preemptions. It is not hard to see that the problem of minimizing the number of preemptions is NP-hard.

10.1. Maximum completion time on uniform and unrelated machines

For $Q \mid pmtn \mid C_{\max}$, the length of any schedule is at least

$$\max\left\{\max_{1 \leq k \leq m-1} \sum_{j=1}^{k} p_j \Big/ \sum_{i=1}^{k} s_i, \sum_{j=1}^{n} p_j \Big/ \sum_{i=1}^{m} s_i\right\},$$

where $p_1 \geq \cdots \geq p_n$ and $s_1 \geq \cdots \geq s_m$. This generalizes the lower bound given in the previous section.

Horvath, Lam & Sethi [1977] prove that this bound is met by a preemptive variant of the LPT rule, which, at each point in time, assigns the jobs with the largest remaining processing requirement to the fastest available processors. The algorithm runs in $O(mn^2)$ time and generates an optimal schedule with no more than $(m-1)n^2$ preemptions.

Gonzalez & Sahni [1978b] give a more efficient algorithm. It requires $O(n)$ time, if the jobs are given in order of nonincreasing p_j and the machines in order of nonincreasing s_i; without this assumption, the running time increases only to $O(n + m \log m)$. The procedure yields an optimal schedule with no more than $2(m-1)$ preemptions, which is a tight bound.

Lawler & Labetoulle [1978] show that many preemptive scheduling problems involving independent jobs on unrelated machines can be formulated as linear programming problems. For $R \mid pmtn \mid C_{\max}$, the length of any schedule is at least equal to the minimum value of C subject to

$$\sum_i x_{ij}/p_{ij} = 1 \quad \text{for } j = 1, \ldots, n,$$

$$\sum_i x_{ij} \leq C \quad \text{for } j = 1, \ldots, n,$$

$$\sum_j x_{ij} \leq C \quad \text{for } i = 1, \ldots, m,$$

$$x_{ij} \geq 0 \quad \text{for } i = 1, \ldots, m, \ j = 1, \ldots, n.$$

In this formulation, x_{ij} represents the total time spent by J_j on M_i. The linear program can be solved in polynomial time [Khachiyan, 1979]. A feasible schedule for which $C_{\max}$ equals the optimal value of C can be constructed in polynomial time by applying the algorithm for $O \mid pmtn \mid C_{\max}$, discussed in Section 12.2. This procedure can be modified to yield an optimal schedule with no more than about $7m^2/2$ preemptions. It remains an open question as to whether there is some constant $c > 0$ such that cm^2 preemptions are necessary for an optimal preemptive schedule.

For fixed m, it seems to be possible to solve the linear program in linear time. Certainly, Gonzalez, Lawler & Sahni [1990] show how to solve the special case $R2 | pmtn | C_{max}$ in $O(n)$ time.

10.2. Release dates, due dates, and other complications

Horn [1974] gives a procedure to solve $P | pmtn | L_{max}$ and $P | pmtn, r_j | C_{max}$ in $O(n^2)$ time. Gonzalez & Johnson [1980] give a more efficient algorithm that uses only $O(mn)$ time.

More generally, Horn [1974] shows that the existence of a feasible preemptive schedule with given release dates and deadlines can be tested by means of a network flow model in $O(n^3)$ time. A binary search can then be conducted on the optimal value of L_{max}, with each trial value of L_{max} inducing deadlines that are checked for feasibility by means of the network computation. Labetoulle, Lawler, Lenstra & Rinnooy Kan [1984] show that this yields an $O(n^3 \min\{n^2, \log n + \log \max_j p_j\})$ algorithm.

Other restrictions on allowable preemptive schedules have been investigated. Schmidt [1983] considers the case where the *machines* are only available in certain given time intervals, and shows that the existence of a feasible preemptive schedule can be tested in polynomial time. Rayward-Smith [1987b] studies the situation where a delay of k time units is incurred when a job is preempted from one machine to another. He observes that imposing such delays on identical machines increases C^*_{max} by at most $k - 1$. Thus, for $k = 1$, the problem is solvable in polynomial time by McNaughton's rule. Surprisingly, for any fixed $k \geq 2$, the problem is NP-hard.

In the case of uniform machines, Sahni & Cho [1980] show how to test the existence of a feasible preemptive schedule with given release dates and a common deadline in $O(n \log n + mn)$ time; the algorithm generates $O(mn)$ preemptions in the worst case. More generally, Sahni & Cho [1979b] and Labetoulle, Lawler, Lenstra & Rinnooy Kan [1984] show that $Q | pmtn, r_j | C_{max}$ and, by symmetry, $Q | pmtn | L_{max}$ are solvable in $O(n \log n + mn)$ time, where the number of preemptions generated is $O(mn)$.

The feasibility test of Horn mentioned above has been adapted by Bruno & Gonzalez [1976] to the case of two uniform machines and extended to a polynomial-time algorithm for $Q2 | pmtn, r_j | L_{max}$ by Labetoulle, Lawler, Lenstra & Rinnooy Kan [1984].

Martel [1982] presents a polynomial-time algorithm for $Q | pmtn, r_j | L_{max}$. His method is in fact a special case of a more general algorithm of Lawler & Martel [1982] for computing maximal *polymatroidal* network flows. Federgruen & Groenevelt [1986] give an improved algorithm for the problem by reducing it to the ordinary maximum flow problem; if there are machines of t distinct speeds (and so $t \leq m$), their algorithm runs in $O(tn^3)$ time.

The technique of Lawler & Labetoulle [1978] also yields a polynomial-time algorithm based on linear programming for $R | pmtn, r_j | L_{max}$.

11. Precedence constraints

11.0. An NP-hardness proof for $P \mid prec, p_j = 1 \mid C_{max}$

The first NP-hardness proof for $P \mid prec, p_j = 1 \mid C_{max}$ is due to Ullman [1975]. Lenstra & Rinnooy Kan [1978] show that even the problem of deciding if there exists a feasible schedule of length at most 3 is NP-complete; the proof is given below. This result implies that, for $P \mid prec, p_j = 1 \mid C_{max}$, there is no polynomial ρ-approximation algorithm for any $\rho < \frac{4}{3}$, unless P = NP. Note that it is trivial to decide if a feasible schedule of length 2 exists.

Recall the NP-complete *clique* problem from Section 2: given a graph $G = (V, E)$ and an integer k, does G have a clique (i.e., a complete subgraph) on k vertices? We denote the number of edges in a clique of size k by $l = k(k-1)/2$, and we define $k' = |V| - k$, $l' = |E| - l$. For any instance of the clique problem, we construct a corresponding instance of $P \mid prec, p_j = 1 \mid C_{max}$. The number of machines is given by $m = \max\{k, l + k', l'\} + 1$. We introduce a job J_v for every vertex $v \in V$ and a job J_e for every edge $e \in E$, with $J_v \to J_e$ whenever v is an endpoint of e. We also need dummy jobs X_x $(x = 1, \ldots, m-k)$, Y_y $(y = 1, \ldots, m-l-k')$ and Z_z $(z = 1, \ldots, m-l')$, with $X_x \to Y_y \to Z_z$ for all x, y, z. Note that the total number of jobs is $3m$.

The reduction is illustrated in Figure 2. The basic idea is the following. In any schedule of length 3 for the dummy jobs, there is a certain pattern of idle machines that are available for the vertex and edge jobs. This pattern is chosen such that a complete feasible schedule of length 3 exists if and only if there is a clique of size k.

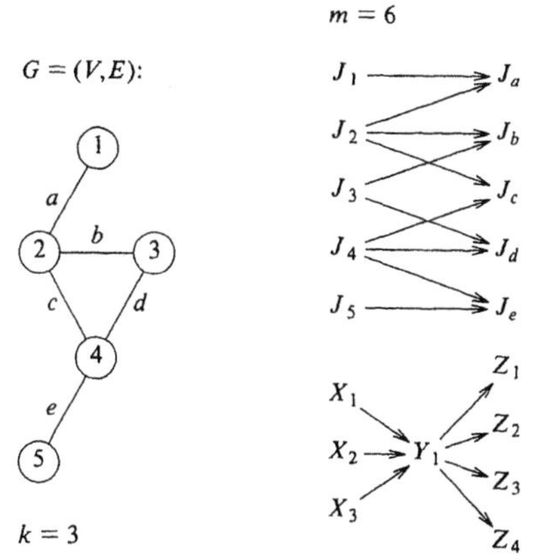

J_2	J_b	J_a
J_3	J_c	J_e
J_4	J_d	Z_1
X_1	J_1	Z_2
X_2	J_5	Z_3
X_3	Y_1	Z_4

(a) (b) (c)

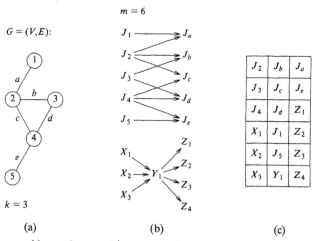

Fig. 2. The clique problem reduces to $P \mid prec, p_j = 1 \mid C_{max}$. (a) Instance of the clique problem. (b) Corresponding instance of $P \mid prec, p_j = 1 \mid C_{max}$. (c) Feasible schedule for $P \mid prec, p_j = 1 \mid C_{max}$.

More precisely, suppose that a clique on k vertices exists. We then schedule the k jobs corresponding to the clique vertices and the $m - k$ jobs X_x in the first time slot. In view of the precedence constraints, we can schedule the l jobs corresponding to the clique edges and the $m - l - k'$ jobs Y_y in the second time slot; we also schedule the k' remaining vertex jobs there. We finally schedule the l' remaining edge jobs and the $m - l'$ jobs Z_z in the third time slot. This is a feasible schedule of length 3.

Conversely, suppose that no clique of size k exists. In any schedule of length 3, exactly k vertex jobs are processed in the first time slot. However, any set of k vertex jobs releases at most $l - 1$ edge jobs for processing in the second time slot. Since at that point only $m - l$ other jobs are available for processing, the schedule cannot be feasible.

11.1. Unit-length jobs on identical machines

We have seen that $P \mid prec, p_j = 1 \mid C_{max}$ is NP-hard. It is an important open question whether this remains true for any constant value of $m \geq 3$. The problem is well solved, however, if the precedence relation is of the *tree* type or if $m = 2$.

Hu [1961] gives a polynomial-time algorithm to solve $P \mid tree, p_j = 1 \mid C_{max}$. Hsu [1966] and Sethi [1976a] give improvements that lead to an $O(n)$ time procedure. We will describe a procedure for the case of an *intree* (each job has at most one successor); an alternative algorithm for the case of an *outtree* (each job has at most one predecessor) is given by Davida & Linton [1976]. The *level* of a job is defined as the number of jobs in the unique path to the root of the precedence tree. At the beginning of each time unit, as many available jobs as possible are scheduled on the m machines, where highest priority is granted to the jobs with the largest levels. Thus, Hu's algorithm is a nonpreemptive *list scheduling* algorithm (cf. Section 9.0). It can also be viewed as a *critical path* scheduling algorithm: the next job chosen is the one which heads the longest current chain of unexecuted jobs. Marcotte & Trotter [1984] show that Hu's algorithm can also be derived from a minmax result of Edmonds [1965] on covering the elements of a matroid by its bases; in this application, the elements correspond to jobs, and a transversal matroid is obtained with bases corresponding to feasible machine histories.

Brucker, Garey & Johnson [1977] show that, if the precedence constraints are in the form of an intree, then Hu's algorithm can be adapted to minimize L_{max}; on the other hand, if the precedence constraints form an outtree, then the L_{max} problem turns out to be NP-hard. Monma [1982] improves the former result by giving a linear-time algorithm.

Garey, Johnson, Tarjan & Yannakakis [1983] consider the case in which the precedence graph is an *opposing forest*, that is, the disjoint union of an inforest and an outforest. They show that if m is arbitrary, then minimizing C_{max} is NP-hard, but if m is fixed, then the problem can be solved in polynomial time. Papadimitriou & Yannakakis [1979] consider the case in which the precedence graph is an *interval order* and give an $O(n+m)$ list scheduling rule that delivers optimal schedules. Bartusch, Möhring & Radermacher [1988a] give an algorithm that unifies many of the special cases previously known to be polynomially solvable.

In addition to proving interesting structural theorems about optimal schedules, Dolev & Warmuth [1984, 1985a,b] give polynomial-time algorithms for a number of special cases of $Pm \mid prec, p_j = 1 \mid C_{\max}$. Dolev & Warmuth [1985b] give an algorithm for opposing forests with substantially improved running time, that also uses substantially more space. In an arbitrary precedence graph, the *level* of a job is the length of the longest path that starts at that job. A *level order* is a precedence graph in which each pair of incomparable jobs with a common predecessor or successor have identical sets of predecessors and successors. Dolev & Warmuth [1985b] also show that level orders can be solved in $O(n^{m-1})$ time. For precedence graphs in which the longest path has at most h arcs, Dolev & Warmuth [1984] give an $O(n^{h(m-1)+1})$ algorithm. Note that the proof given above shows that the problem is already NP-hard for $h = 2$. Dynamic programming can be used to obtain a polynomial-time algorithm for the case where the width of the precedence graph is bounded; this is one of the many polynomially solvable special cases surveyed by Möhring [1989].

Fujii, Kasami & Ninomiya [1969] present the first polynomial-time algorithm for $P2 \mid prec, p_j = 1 \mid C_{\max}$. An undirected graph is constructed with vertices corresponding to jobs and edges $\{j, k\}$ whenever J_j and J_k can be executed simultaneously. An optimal schedule is then derived from a maximum cardinality matching in the graph, and so the algorithm runs in $O(n^3)$ time [Lawler, 1976b].

Coffman & Graham [1972] give an alternative approach that leads to an $O(n^2)$ list scheduling algorithm. First the jobs are labeled in the following way. Suppose labels $1, \ldots, k$ have been applied and S is the subset of unlabeled jobs all of whose successors have been labeled. Then a job in S is given the label $k+1$ if the labels of its immediate successors are *lexicographically minimal* with respect to all jobs in S. The priority list is given by ordering the jobs according to decreasing labels. Sethi [1976b] shows that it is possible to execute this algorithm in time almost linear in n plus the numbers of arcs in the precedence graph, if the graph is given in the form of a *transitive reduction*.

Gabow [1982] presents an algorithm which has the same running time, but which does not require such a representation of the precedence graph. The running time of the algorithm is dominated by the time to maintain a data structure that represents sets of elements throughout a sequence of so-called union-find operations, and Gabow & Tarjan [1985] improve the running time to linear by exploiting the special structure of the particular union-find problems generated in this way. Consider the following procedure to compute a lower bound on the length of an optimal schedule. Delete jobs and precedence constraints to obtain a precedence graph that can be decomposed into t sets of jobs, $S_1, \ldots, S_t$, such that for each pair of jobs $J_k \in S_i$, $J_l \in S_{i+1}$,

J_k precedes J_l; then $\lceil |S_1|/2 \rceil + \cdots + \lceil |S_t|/2 \rceil$ is clearly a lower bound. Gabow's proof implies the duality result that the maximum lower bound that can be obtained in this way is equal to C^*_{max}.

Garey & Johnson [1976, 1977] present a polynomial algorithm for this problem where, in addition, each job becomes available at its *release date* and has to meet a given *deadline*. In this approach, one processes the jobs in order of increasing *modified deadlines*. This modification requires $O(n^2)$ time if all $r_j = 0$, and $O(n^3)$ time in the general case.

The reduction given in Section 11.0 also implies that $P | prec, p_j = 1 | \Sigma C_j$ is NP-hard. Hu's algorithm does not yield an optimal ΣC_j schedule in the case of intrees, but in the case of outtrees, Rosenfeld [-] has observed that critical path scheduling minimizes both C_{max} and ΣC_j. Similarly, Garey [-] has shown that the Coffman–Graham algorithm minimizes ΣC_j as well.

As far as approximation algorithms for $P | prec, p_j = 1 | C_{max}$ are concerned, we have already noted in Section 11.0 that, unless P = NP, the best possible worst-case bound for a polynomial-time algorithm would be $\frac{4}{3}$. The performance of both Hu's algorithm and the Coffman–Graham algorithm has been analyzed.

When critical path (CP) scheduling is used, Chen [1975], Chen & Liu [1975] and Kunde [1976] show that

$$C_{max}(CP)/C^*_{max} \leq \begin{cases} \frac{4}{3} & \text{for } m = 2\,, \\ 2 - \dfrac{1}{m-1} & \text{for } m \geq 3\,. \end{cases} \qquad (\dagger)$$

Lam & Sethi [1977] use the Coffman–Graham (CG) algorithm to generate lists and show that

$$C_{max}(CG)/C^*_{max} \leq 2 - \frac{2}{m} \quad \text{for } m \geq 2\,. \qquad (\dagger)$$

If MS denotes the algorithm which schedules as the next job the one having the greatest number of successors, then Ibarra & Kim [1976] prove that

$$C_{max}(MS)/C^*_{max} \leq \tfrac{4}{3} \quad \text{for } m = 2\,. \qquad (\dagger)$$

Examples show that this bound does not hold for $m \geq 3$.

Finally, we mention some results for related models.

Ullman [1975] and Lenstra & Rinnooy Kan [1978] show that both $P2 | prec, p_j \in \{1, 2\} | C_{max}$ and $P2 | prec, p_j \in \{1, 2\} | \Sigma C_j$ are NP-hard. Nakajima, Leung & Hakimi [1981] give a complicated $O(n \log n)$ algorithm to find the optimal solution for $P2 | tree, p_j \in \{1, 2\} | C_{max}$; for practical purposes, a heuristic due to Kaufman [1974] which has a worst-case *absolute* error of 1, may be more attractive. Du & Leung [1989] give an $O(n^2 \log n)$ algorithm to solve $P2 | tree, p_j \in \{1, 3\} | C_{max}$ to optimality. On the other hand, Du & Leung

[1988a] show that $P|tree, p_j \in \{1, k\}|C_{max}$ (where k is input) is strongly NP-hard, and that $P2|tree, p_j \in \{k^l : l \geq 0\}|C_{max}$ is NP-hard in the ordinary sense for any integer $k > 1$. For $P2|prec, p_j \in \{1, k\}|C_{max}$, Goyal [1977] proposes a generalized version of the Coffman–Graham algorithm (GCG) and shows that

$$C_{max}(\text{GCG})/C^*_{max} \leq \begin{cases} \frac{4}{3} & \text{for } k = 2\,, \\ \frac{3}{2} - \frac{1}{2k} & \text{for } k \geq 3\,. \end{cases} \qquad (\dagger)$$

Rayward-Smith [1987a] considers a model similar to one discussed in Section 10.2, where there is a unit-time communication delay between any pair of distinct processors. For unit-time jobs, the problem is shown to be NP-complete. The performance of a *greedy* (G) algorithm is analyzed, where first a list schedule is generated, and then a local interchange strategy tries to improve the schedule. The algorithm produces schedules such that

$$C_{max}(G)/C^*_{max} \leq 3 - \frac{2}{m}\,. \qquad (\dagger)$$

Approximation algorithms in a similar model are also considered by Papadimitriou & Yannakakis [1990].

11.2. Precedence constraints and no preemption

The list scheduling rule performs surprisingly well on identical machines, even in the presence of precedence constraints. Graham [1966] shows that precedence constraints do not affect its worst-case performance at all; that is,

$$C_{max}(\text{LS})/C^*_{max} \leq 2 - \frac{1}{m}\,. \qquad (\dagger)$$

Now, consider executing the set of jobs twice: the first time using processing times p_j, precedence constraints, m machines and an arbitrary priority list, the second time using processing times $p'_j \leq p_j$, weakened precedence constraints, m' machines and a (possibly different) priority list. Graham [1966] proves that, even then,

$$C'_{max}(\text{LS})/C_{max}(\text{LS}) \leq 1 + \frac{m-1}{m'}\,. \qquad (\dagger)$$

Note that this result implies the previous one. Even when critical path (CP) scheduling is used, Graham [-] provides examples for which

$$C_{max}(\text{CP})/C^*_{max} = 2 - \frac{1}{m}\,.$$

Kunde [1981] shows that for tree-type and chain-type precedence constraints, there are slightly improved upper bounds for CP of $2 - 2/(m+1)$ and $\frac{5}{3}$, respectively. For now, let $C^*_{\max}(pmtn)$ denote the optimal value of $C_{\max}$ if preemption is allowed. Kaufman [1974] shows that for tree-type precedence constraints,

$$C_{\max}(\mathrm{CP}) \leqslant C^*_{\max}(pmtn) + \left(1 - \frac{1}{m}\right) \max_j p_j / \min_j p_j \,. \qquad (\dagger)$$

Du, Leung & Young [1991] prove that $P2 \mid tree \mid C_{\max}$ is strongly NP-hard, even for chains. Graham [-] shows that for general precedence constraints

$$C_{\max}(\mathrm{LS}) / C^*_{\max}(pmtn) \leqslant 2 - \frac{1}{m} \,. \qquad (\dagger)$$

For $P \mid prec, r_j \mid L_{\max}$, Hall & Shmoys [1989] observe that in the delivery time model, the same proof technique again yields

$$L_{\max}(\mathrm{LS}) / L^*_{\max} < 2 \,. \qquad (\dagger)$$

As remarked above, it is an open question whether $Pm \mid prec, p_j = 1 \mid C_{\max}$ (i.e., with m fixed) is solvable in polynomial time. In fact, it is a challenging problem even to approximate an optimal solution appreciably better than a factor of 2 in polynomial time for fixed values of m.

Even less is known about approximation algorithms for uniform machines. Liu & Liu [1974b] also consider $Q \mid prec \mid C_{\max}$ and show that

$$C_{\max}(\mathrm{LS}) / C^*_{\max} \leqslant 1 + \max_i s_i / \min_i s_i - \max_i s_i \Big/ \sum_i s_i \,. \qquad (\dagger)$$

Note that this yields the result of Graham [1966] when all speeds are equal. As above, similar bounds can be proved relative to the preemptive optimum, or relative to an altered problem.

Jaffe [1980a] shows that using all of the machines in list scheduling may be wasteful in the worst case. The arguments of Liu & Liu are generalized to show that by list scheduling on the fastest l machines (LS_l), if $s_1 \geqslant \cdots \geqslant s_m$,

$$C_{\max}(\mathrm{LS}_l) / C^*_{\max} \leqslant \sum_{i=1}^{m} s_i \Big/ \sum_{i=1}^{l} s_i + s_1 / s_l - s_1 \Big/ \sum_{i=1}^{l} s_i \,. \qquad (\dagger)$$

By minimizing this quantity, Jaffe derives an algorithm LS* for which

$$C_{\max}(\mathrm{LS}^*) / C^*_{\max} \leqslant \sqrt{m} + \mathrm{O}(m^{1/4}) \,.$$

This bound is tight up to a constant factor. The surprising aspect of this algorithm is that the decision about the number of machines to be used is made without the knowledge of the processing requirements.

Gabow [1988] considers $Q2 \mid prec, p_j = 1 \mid C_{\max}$ and analyzes two approximation algorithms. The algorithm $P2$, which ignores the machine speeds and finds an optimal solution to the resulting problem on two identical machines, guarantees

$$C_{\max}(P2)/C^*_{\max} \leq 2 - \min\{s_1, s_2\}/\max\{s_1, s_2\} . \qquad (\dagger)$$

The *highest level first* (HLF) algorithm is shown to be slightly better in special cases:

$$C_{\max}(\mathrm{HLF})/C^*_{\max} \leq \begin{cases} \frac{5}{4} & \text{if } \min\{s_1, s_2\}/\max\{s_1, s_2\} = \frac{1}{2}, \\ \frac{6}{5} & \text{if } \min\{s_1, s_2\}/\max\{s_1, s_2\} = \frac{2}{3}. \end{cases} \qquad (\dagger)$$

Gabow also gives an $O((n + a)2^l)$ algorithm to find an optimal solution if $|1/s_1 - 1/s_2| = 1$, where $1/s_1$ and $1/s_2$ are relatively prime integers, a is the number of arcs and l is the number of levels in the precedence graph.

Nothing is known about approximation algorithms for unrelated machines with precedence constraints.

11.3. Precedence constraints and preemption

Ullmann [1976] shows that $P \mid pmtn, prec, p_j = 1 \mid C_{\max}$ is NP-hard, but $P \mid pmtn, tree \mid C_{\max}$ and $P2 \mid pmtn, prec \mid C_{\max}$ can be solved by a polynomial-time algorithm due to Muntz & Coffman [1969, 1970].

The Muntz–Coffman algorithm can be described as follows. Define $l_j(t)$ to be the level of a J_j wholly or partly unexecuted at time t, where the level now refers to the length of the path in the precedence graph with maximum total processing requirement. Suppose that at time t, m' machines are available and that n' jobs are currently maximizing $l_j(t)$. If $m' < n'$, we assign m'/n' machines to each of the n' jobs, which implies that each of these jobs will be executed at speed m'/n'. If $m' \geq n'$, we assign one machine to each job, consider the jobs at the next highest level, and repeat. The machines are reassigned whenever a job is completed or threatens to be processed at a higher speed than another one at a currently higher level. Between each pair of successive reassignment points, jobs are finally rescheduled by means of McNaughton's algorithm for $P \mid pmtn \mid C_{\max}$. Gonzalez & Johnson [1980] give an implementation of the algorithm that runs in $O(n^2)$ time.

Gonzalez & Johnson [1980] have developed a totally different algorithm that solves $P \mid pmtn, tree \mid C_{\max}$ by starting at the roots rather than the leaves of the tree and determines priority by considering the total remaining processing time in subtrees rather than by looking at critical paths. The algorithm runs in $O(n \log m)$ time and introduces at most $n - 2$ preemptions into the resulting optimal schedule.

This approach can be adapted to the case $Q2 \mid pmtn, tree \mid C_{\max}$. Horvath, Lam & Sethi [1977] give an algorithm to solve $Q2 \mid pmtn, prec \mid C_{\max}$ in $O(mn^2)$ time, similar to the result mentioned in Section 10.1.

Lawler [1982a] shows that some well-solvable problems involving the nonpreemptive scheduling of unit-time jobs turn out to have well-solvable counterparts involving the preemptive scheduling of jobs with arbitrary processing times. The algorithms of Brucker, Garey & Johnson [1977] for $P \mid intree, p_j = 1 \mid L_{max}$ and of Garey & Johnson [1976, 1977] for $P2 \mid prec, p_j = 1 \mid L_{max}$ and $P2 \mid prec, r_j, p_j = 1 \mid L_{max}$ (see Section 11.1) all have preemptive counterparts. For example, $P \mid pmtn, intree \mid L_{max}$ can be solved in $O(n^2)$ time. For uniform machines, Lawler shows that $Q2 \mid pmtn, prec \mid L_{max}$ and $Q2 \mid pmtn, prec, r_j \mid L_{max}$ can be solved in $O(n^2)$ and $O(n^6)$ time, respectively. These results suggest a strong relationship between the two models.

It is not hard to see that $R2 \mid pmtn, tree \mid C_{max}$ is NP-hard in the strong sense, even for chains [Lenstra, -].

As to approximation algorithms, Lam & Sethi [1977], much in the same spirit as their work mentioned in Section 11.1, analyze the performance of the Muntz–Coffman (MC) algorithm for $P \mid pmtn, prec \mid C_{max}$. They show

$$C_{max}(\mathrm{MC})/C^*_{max} \leq 2 - \frac{2}{m} \quad \text{for } m \geq 2\,. \tag{†}$$

For $Q \mid pmtn, prec \mid C_{max}$, Horvath, Lam & Sethi [1977] prove that the Muntz–Coffman algorithm guarantees

$$C_{max}(\mathrm{MC})/C^*_{max} \leq \sqrt{3m/2}\,,$$

and examples are given to prove that this bound is tight within a constant factor. Jaffe [1980b] studies the performance of *maximal usage schedules* (MUS) for $Q \mid pmtn, prec \mid C_{max}$, i.e., schedules without unforced idleness in which at any time the jobs being processed are assigned to the fastest machines. It is shown that

$$C_{max}(\mathrm{MUS})/C^*_{max} \leq \sqrt{m} + \tfrac{1}{2}\,,$$

and examples are given for which the bound $\sqrt{m-1}$ is approached arbitrarily closely. A slightly weaker bound on these schedules can also be proved using the techniques of Jaffe [1980a].

PART IV. MULTI-OPERATION MODELS

We now pass on to problems in which each job requires execution on more than one machine. Recall from Section 3 that in an *open shop* (denoted by O) the order in which a job passes through the machines is immaterial, whereas in a *flow shop* (F) each job has the same machine ordering ($M_1, \ldots, M_m$) and in a *job shop* (J) the jobs may have different machine orderings. We survey these problem classes in Sections 12, 13 and 14, respectively. Our presentation focuses on the C_{max} criterion. A few results for other optimality criteria will be briefly mentioned.

Very few multi-operation scheduling problems can be solved in polynomial time; the main well-solvable cases are $F2 | | C_{max}$ [Johnson, 1954], $O2 | | C_{max}$ [Gonzalez & Sahni, 1976], and $O | pmtn | C_{max}$ [Gonzalez & Sahni, 1976; Lawler & Labetoulle, 1978]. General flow shop and job shop scheduling problems have earned a reputation for intractability. We will be mostly concerned with enumerative optimization methods for their solution and, to a lesser extent, with approximation algorithms. An analytical approach to the performance of methods of the latter type is badly needed.

12. Open shops

12.0. Gonzalez & Sahni's algorithm for $O2 | | C_{max}$

The problem $O2 | | C_{max}$ admits of an elegant linear-time algorithm due to Gonzalez & Sahni [1976].

For convenience, let $a_j = p_{1j}$, $b_j = p_{2j}$, $\bar{a} = \Sigma_j a_j$, $\bar{b} = \Sigma_j b_j$. An obvious lower bound on the length of any feasible schedule is given by

$$\max\{\bar{a}, \bar{b}, \max_j a_j + b_j\} .$$

We will show how a schedule matching this bound can be constructed in $O(n)$ time.

Let $A = \{J_j \mid a_j \geq b_j\}$ and $B = \{J_j \mid a_j < b_j\}$. Choose J_r and J_l to be any two distinct jobs, whether in A or B, such that

$$a_r \geq \max_{J_j \in A} b_j , \qquad b_l \geq \max_{J_j \in B} a_j .$$

Let $A' = A - \{J_r, J_l\}$, $B' = B - \{J_r, J_l\}$. We assert that it is possible to form feasible schedules for $B' \cup \{J_l\}$ and for $A' \cup \{J_r\}$ as indicated in Figure 3(a), where the jobs in A' and B' are ordered arbitrarily. In each of these separate schedules, there is no idle time on either machine, from the start of the first operation on that machine to the completion of its last operation.

Suppose $\bar{a} - a_l \geq \bar{b} - b_r$ (the case $\bar{a} - a_l < \bar{b} - b_r$ being symmetric). We then combine the two schedules as shown in Figure 3(b), pushing the jobs in $B' \cup \{J_l\}$ on M_2 to the right. Again, there is no idle time on either machine, from the start of the first operation to the completion of the last operation.

We finally propose to move the processing of J_r on M_2 to the first position on that machine. There are two cases to consider. First, if $a_r \leq \bar{b} - b_r$, then the resulting schedule is as in Figure 3(c); the length of the schedule is $\max\{\bar{a}, \bar{b}\}$. Secondly, if $a_r > \bar{b} - b_r$, then the schedule in Figure 3(d) results; its length is $\max\{\bar{a}, a_r + b_r\}$. Since, in both cases, we have met our lower bound, the schedules constructed are optimal.

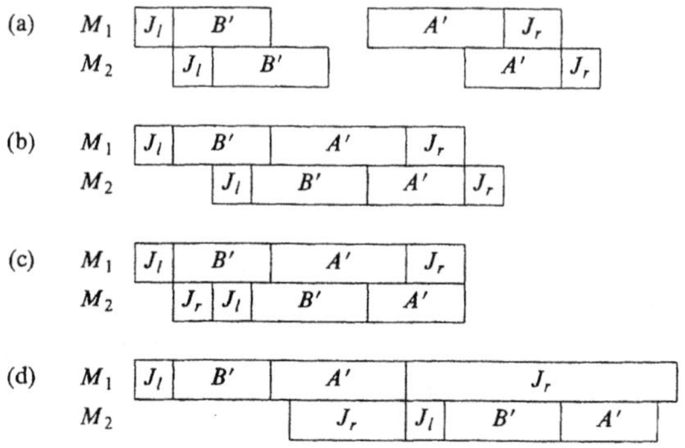

Fig. 3. Solving the two-machine open shop scheduling problem.

12.1. The nonpreemptive open shop

There is little hope of finding polynomial-time algorithms for nonpreemptive open shop scheduling problems beyond $O2| \, |C_{\max}$. Gonzalez & Sahni [1976] show that $O3| \, |C_{\max}$ is NP-hard in the ordinary sense. NP-hardness in the strong sense has been established for $O2| \, |L_{\max}$ and $O2|r_j|C_{\max}$ [Lawler, Lenstra & Rinnooy Kan, 1981], $O2| \, |\Sigma C_j$ [Achugbue & Chin, 1982a], $O2|tree|C_{\max}$ and $O| \, |C_{\max}$ [Lenstra, -], and for a number of m-machine multi-operation problems with 0–1 processing times [Gonzalez, 1982].

We mention a few positive results. Adiri & Aizikowitz [1989] investigate machine dominance, which occurs if $\min_j p_{hj} \geq \max_j p_{ij}$ for some M_h and M_i with $h \neq i$; under this condition, $O3| \, |C_{\max}$ is well solvable. Fiala [1983] uses results from graph theory to develop an $O(m^3n^2)$ algorithm for $O| \, |C_{\max}$ if $\max_i \Sigma_j p_{ij} \geq (16m' \log m' + 5m') \max_{i,j} p_{ij}$, where m' is the roundup of m to the closest power of 2. As to approximation algorithms, Achugbue & Chin [1982a] derive tight bounds on the length of arbitrary schedules and SPT schedules for $O| \, |\Sigma C_j$.

12.2. The preemptive open shop

The result on $O2| \, |C_{\max}$ presented in Section 12.0 also applies to the preemptive case. The lower bound on the schedule length remains valid if preemption is allowed. Hence, there is no advantage to preemption for $m = 2$, and $O2|pmtn|C_{\max}$ can be solved in $O(n)$ time.

More generally, $O|pmtn|C_{\max}$ is solvable in polynomial time as well [Gonzalez & Sahni, 1976]. We had already occasion to refer to this result in Section 10.1. An outline of the algorithm, adapted from Lawler & Labetoulle [1978], follows below.

Let $P = (p_{ij})$ be the matrix of processing times, and let

$$C = \max\left\{\max_j \sum_i p_{ij}, \max_i \sum_j p_{ij}\right\}.$$

Call row i (column j) *tight* if $\Sigma_j p_{ij} = C$ ($\Sigma_i p_{ij} = C$), and *slack* otherwise. Clearly, we have $C^*_{\max} \geq C$. It is possible to construct a feasible schedule for which $C_{\max} = C$; hence, this schedule will be optimal.

Suppose we can find a subset S of strictly positive elements of P, with exactly one element of S in each tight row and in each tight column, and at most one element of S in each slack row and in each slack column. We call such a subset a *decrementing set*, and use it to construct a *partial schedule* of length δ, for some $\delta > 0$. The constraints on the choice of δ are as follows:

- If $p_{ij} \in S$ and row i or column j is tight, then $\delta \leq p_{ij}$.
- If $p_{ij} \in S$ and row i (column j) is slack, then $\delta \leq p_{ij} + C - \Sigma_k p_{ik}$ ($\delta \leq p_{ij} + C - \Sigma_h p_{hi}$).
- If row i (column j) contains no element in S (and is therefore necessarily slack), then $\delta \leq C - \Sigma_k p_{ik}$ ($\delta \leq C - \Sigma_h p_{hj}$).

For a given decrementing set S, let δ be the maximum value subject to these constraints. Then the partial schedule constructed is such that, for each $p_{ij} \in S$, M_i processes J_j for $\min\{p_{ij}, \delta\}$ units of time. We then obtain a matrix P' from P by replacing each $p_{ij} \in S$ by $\max\{0, p_{ij} - \delta\}$, with a lower bound $C - \delta$ on the schedule length for the remaining problem. We repeat the procedure until after a finite number of times, $P' = (0)$. Joining together the partial schedules obtained for successive decrementing sets then yields an optimal schedule for P.

By suitably embedding P in a doubly stochastic matrix and appealing to the Birkhoff–Von Neumann theorem, one can show that a decrementing set can be found by solving a linear assignment problem; see Lawler & Labetoulle [1978] for details. Other networks formulations of the problem are possible. An analysis of various possible computations reveals that $O \mid pmtn \mid C_{\max}$ is solvable in $O(r + \min\{m^4, n^4, r^2\})$ time, where r is the number of nonzero elements in P [Gonzalez, 1979].

Similar results can be obtained for the minimization of maximum lateness. Lawler, Lenstra & Rinnooy Kan [1981] give an $O(n)$ time algorithm for $O2 \mid pmtn \mid L_{\max}$ and, by symmetry, for $O2 \mid pmtn, r_j \mid C_{\max}$. For $O \mid pmtn, r_j \mid L_{\max}$, Cho & Sahni [1981] show that a trial value of $L_{\max}$ can be tested for feasibility by linear programming; bisection search is then applied to minimize $L_{\max}$ in polynomial time.

The minimization of total completion time appears to be much harder. Liu & Bulfin [1985] provide NP-hardness proofs for $O3 \mid pmtn \mid \Sigma C_j$ and $O2 \mid pmtn, \bar{d}_j \mid \Sigma C_j$, where $\bar{d}_j$ is a deadline for the completion of J_j. $O2 \mid pmtn \mid \Sigma C_j$ remains an open problem.

13. Flow shops

13.0. Johnson's algorithm for $F2| \,|C_{max}$

In one of the first papers on deterministic machine scheduling, Johnson [1954] gives an $O(n \log n)$ algorithm to solve $F2| \,|C_{max}$. The algorithm is surprisingly simple: first arrange the jobs with $p_{1j} \leq p_{2j}$ in order of nondecreasing p_{1j}, and then arrange the remaining jobs in order of nonincreasing p_{2j}.

The correctness proof of this algorithm is also straightforward. Notice that the algorithm produces a *permutation schedule*, in which each machine processes the jobs in the same order. An easy interchange argument shows that there exists an optimal schedule that is a permutation schedule. We now make three observations. For a permutation schedule, C_{max} is determined by the processing time of some k jobs on M_1, followed by the processing time of $n+1-k$ jobs on M_2. This implies that, if all p_{ij} are decreased by the same value p, then for each permutation schedule, C_{max} decreases by $(n+1)p$. Finally, if $p_{1j}=0$, then J_j is scheduled first in some optimal schedule, and similarly, if $p_{2j}=0$, then J_j is scheduled last in some optimal schedule. Putting these pieces together, we see that an optimal schedule can be constructed by repeatedly finding the minimum p_{ij} value among the unscheduled jobs, subtracting this value from all processing times, and scheduling the job with a zero processing time. This algorithm is clearly equivalent to the one given above.

13.1. Two or three machines

As a general result, Conway, Maxwell & Miller [1967] observe that there exists an optimal $F| \,|C_{max}$ schedule with the same processing order on M_1 and M_2 and the same processing order on M_{m-1} and M_m. Hence, if there are no more than three machines, we can restrict our attention to permutation schedules. The reader is invited to construct a four-machine instance in which a job necessarily 'passes' another one between M_2 and M_3 in the optimal schedule.

$F3| \,|C_{max}$ is strongly NP-hard [Garey, Johnson & Sethi, 1976]. A fair amount of effort has been devoted to the identification of special cases and variants that are solvable in polynomial time. For example, Johnson [1954] already shows that the case in which $\max_j p_{2j} \leq \max\{\min_j p_{1j}, \min_j p_{3j}\}$ is solved by applying his algorithm to processing times $(p_{1j}+p_{2j}, p_{2j}+p_{3j})$. Conway, Maxwell & Miller [1967] show that the same rule works if M_2 is a *nonbottleneck machine*, i.e., is a machine that can process any number of jobs at the same time. A two-machine variant involves *time lags* l_j, which are minimum time intervals between the completion time of J_j on M_1 and its starting time on M_2 [Mitten, 1958; Johnson, 1958; Nabeshima, 1963; Szwarc, 1968]; these lags can be viewed as processing times on a nonbottleneck machine in between M_1 and M_2, so one has to apply Johnson's algorithm to processing times $(p_{1j} + l_j, l_j + p_{2j})$ [Rinnooy Kan, 1976]. Monma & Rinnooy Kan [1983] put many results of this kind in a common framework. Their discussion includes results for problems with an arbitrary number of machines, such as some of the work by Smith, Panwalkar & Dudek [1975, 1976] on ordered flow shops and by Chin & Tsai [1981] on J-maximal and J-minimal flow shops. In the latter case, there is an M_i for which $p_{ij} = \max_h p_{hj}$ for all j or $p_{ij} = \min_h p_{hj}$ for all j. Achugbue & Chin [1982b] analyze $F3 \| C_{max}$ in which each machine may be maximal or minimal in this sense and derive an exhaustive complexity classification. It should be noted that, in all this work, there is an implicit restriction to permutation schedules. This is justified for special cases of $F3 \| C_{max}$, but not necessarily for its variants. Indeed, the unrestricted $F3 \| C_{max}$ problem with a nonbottleneck M_2 is strongly NP-hard [Lenstra, -].

NP-hardness in the strong sense has also been established for $F2 | r_j | C_{max}$, $F2 \| L_{max}$ [Lenstra, Rinnooy Kan & Brucker, 1977] and $F2 \| \Sigma C_j$ [Garey, Johnson & Sethi, 1976]. Potts [1985b] investigates the performance of five approximation algorithms for $F2 | r_j | C_{max}$. The best one of these, called RJ′, involves the repeated application of a dynamic variant of Johnson's algorithm to modified versions of the problem, and satisfies

$$C_{max}(\mathrm{RJ}')/C^*_{max} \leq \tfrac{5}{3} . \qquad (\dagger)$$

Grabowski [1980] presents a branch and bound algorithm for $F2 | r_j | L_{max}$. Ignall & Schrage [1965], in one of the earliest papers on branch and bound methods for scheduling problems, propose two lower bounds for $F2 \| \Sigma C_i$, Kohler & Steiglitz [1975] report on the implementation of these bounds, and Van de Velde [1990] shows that both bounds can be viewed as special cases of a lower bound based on Lagrangean relaxation.

Gonzalez & Sahni [1978a] and Cho & Sahni [1981] consider the case of preemptive flow shop scheduling. Since preemptions on M_1 and M_m can be removed without increasing C_{max}, Johnson's algorithm solves $F2 | pmtn | C_{max}$ as well. $F3 | pmtn | C_{max}$, $F2 | pmtn, r_j | C_{max}$ and $F2 | pmtn | L_{max}$ are strongly NP-hard. So is $F3 | pmtn | \Sigma C_j$ [Lenstra, -]; $F2 | pmtn | \Sigma C_j$ remains open.

As to precedence constraints, $F2 | tree | C_{max}$ is strongly NP-hard [Lenstra, Rinnooy Kan & Brucker, 1977], but $F2 | tree, p_{ij} = 1 | C_{max}$ and $F2 | tree, p_{ij} = 1 | \Sigma C_j$ are solvable in polynomial time [Lageweg, -]. We note that an interpretation of precedence constraints that differs from our definition is possible. If $J_j \rightarrow' J_k$ only means that O_{ij} has to precede O_{ik}, for $i = 1, 2$, then $F2 | tree' | C_{max}$ and even the problem with series-parallel precedence constraints can be solved in $O(n \log n)$ time [Sidney, 1979; Monma, 1979]. The arguments used to establish this result are very similar to those referred to in Section 5.1 and apply to a larger class of scheduling problems. The general case $F2 | prec' | C_{max}$ is strongly NP-hard [Monma, 1980]. Hariri & Potts [1984] develop a branch and bound algorithm for this problem, using a lower bound based on Lagrangean relaxation.

13.2. Flow shop scheduling

We know from Section 13.1 that, for the general $F \| C_{\max}$ problem, permutation schedules are not necessarily optimal. Nevertheless, in the literature on *enumerative optimization methods* for flow shop scheduling it has become a tradition to assume identical processing orders on all machines and to look for the best permutation schedule.

The usual enumeration scheme generates schedules by building them from front to back. That is, at a node at the lth level of the search tree, a partial schedule $(J_{\sigma(1)}, \ldots, J_{\sigma(l)})$ has been formed and the jobs with index set $S = \{1, \ldots, n\} - \{\sigma(1), \ldots, \sigma(l)\}$ are candidates for the $(l+1)$th position. One then needs to find a lower bound on the length of all possible completions of the partial schedule. Almost all lower bounds developed so far are captured by the following bounding scheme due to Lageweg, Lenstra & Rinnooy Kan [1978].

Let us relax the constraint that each machine can process at most one job at a time, for all machines but at most two, say, M_u and M_v $(1 \leq u \leq v \leq m)$. We then obtain the following problem. Each job J_j $(j \in S)$ has to be processed on five machines N_{*u}, M_u, N_{uv}, M_v, N_{v*} in that order. N_{*u}, N_{uv} and N_{v*} are nonbottleneck machines, of infinite capacity; if $C(\sigma, i)$ denotes the completion time of $J_{\sigma(l)}$ on M_i, then the processing times of J_j $(j \in S)$ on N_{*u}, N_{uv} and N_{v*} are defined by

$$q_{*uj} = \max_{1 \leq i \leq u} \left(C(\sigma, i) + \sum_{h=i}^{u-1} p_{hj} \right),$$

$$q_{uvj} = \sum_{h=u+1}^{v-1} p_{hj},$$

$$q_{v*j} = \sum_{h=v+1}^{m} p_{hj},$$

respectively. M_u and M_v are ordinary machines of unit capacity, with processing times p_{uj} and p_{vj}, respectively. We wish to find a permutation schedule that minimizes $C_{\max}$. We can interpret N_{*u} as yielding release dates q_{*j} on M_u and N_{v*} as setting due dates $-q_{v*j}$ on M_v, with respect to which $L_{\max}$ is to be minimized. Note that we can remove any of the nonbottleneck machines from the problem by underestimating its contribution to the lower bound to be its minimum processing time; valid lower bounds are obtained by adding these contributions to the optimal solution value of the remaining problem.

If we choose $u = v$ and remove both N_{*u} and N_{u*} from the problem, we obtain the *machine-based bound* proposed by Ignall & Schrage [1965]:

$$\max_{1 \leq u \leq m} \left(\min_{j \in S} q_{*uj} + \sum_{j \in S} p_{uj} + \min_{j \in S} q_{u*j} \right).$$

Removal of either N_{*u} or N_{u*} results in a $1 | | L_{max}$ or $1 | r_j | C_{max}$ problem on M_u. Both problems are solvable in $O(n \log n)$ time (see Section 4.2) and provide slightly stronger bounds.

If $u \neq v$, removal of N_{*u}, N_{uv} and N_{v*} yields an $F2 | | C_{max}$ problem, which can be solved by Johnson's algorithm. As pointed out in Section 13.1, we can take N_{uv} fully into account and still solve the problem in $O(n \log n)$ time. The resulting bound dominates the *job-based bound* proposed by McMahon [1971] and is currently the most successful bound that can be computed in polynomial time.

All other variations on this theme lead to NP-hard problems. However, this does not necessarily preclude their effectivity for lower bound computations, as will become clear in Section 14.2.

In addition to lower bounds, one may use elimination criteria in order to prune the search tree. In this respect, particular attention has been paid to conditions under which all completions of $(J_{\sigma(1)}, \ldots, J_{\sigma(l)}, J_j)$ can be eliminated because a schedule at least as good exists among the completions of $(J_{\sigma(1)}, \ldots, J_{\sigma(l)}, J_k, J_j)$. If all information obtainable from the processing times of the other jobs is disregarded, the strongest condition under which this is allowed is the following: J_j can be excluded for the $(l+1)$th position if

$$\max\{C(\sigma kj, i-1) - C(\sigma j, i-1), C(\sigma kj, i) - C(\sigma j, i)\} \leq p_{ij}$$
$$\text{for } i = 2, \ldots, m$$

[McMahon, 1969; Szwarc, 1971, 1973]. Inclusion of these and similar dominance rules can be very helpful from a computational point of view, depending on the lower bound used [Lageweg, Lenstra & Rinnooy Kan, 1978]. It may be worthwhile to consider extensions that, for instance, take the processing times of the unscheduled jobs into account [Gupta & Reddi, 1978; Szwarc, 1978].

A number of alternative and more efficient enumeration schemes has been developed. Potts [1980a] proposes to construct a schedule from the front and from the back at the same time. Grabowski's [1982] *block approach* obtains a complete feasible schedule at each node and bases the branching decision on an analysis of the transformations required to shorten the critical path that determines the schedule length. Grabowski, Skubalska & Smutnicki [1983] extend these ideas to the $F | r_j | L_{max}$ problem.

Not much has been done in the way of worst-case analysis of *approximation algorithms* for the flow shop scheduling problem. It is not hard to see that for any active schedule (AS)

$$C_{max}(AS)/C^*_{max} \leq \max_{i,j} p_{ij} / \min_{i,j} p_{ij} . \qquad (\dagger)$$

Gonzalez & Sahni [1978a] show that

$$C_{max}(AS)/C^*_{max} \leq m . \qquad (\dagger)$$

This bound is tight even for LPT schedules, in which the jobs are ordered according to nonincreasing sums of processing times. They also give an $O(mn \log n)$ heuristic H based on $\lfloor m/2 \rfloor$ applications of Johnson's algorithm, with

$$C_{\max}(H)/C^*_{\max} \leq \lceil m/2 \rceil .$$

Röck and Schmidt [1983] use an aggregation heuristic that first constructs a two-machine instance by combining the first $\lceil m/2 \rceil$ machines to get M_1 and the rest to get M_2, and then applies Johnson's algorithm; the resulting permutation schedule also has a performance ratio of $\lceil m/2 \rceil$. Belov & Stolin [1974] and Sevastyanov [1975] use geometric tools to obtain permutation schedules that are quite close to the overall optimum. The best result along these lines is due to Sevastyanov [1980], who gives an $O(m^2n^2)$ algorithm S to find a schedule which has an absolute error bound that is independent of n:

$$C_{\max}(S) - C^*_{\max} \leq m(m-1) \max_{i,j} p_{ij} .$$

For the formulation and empirical evaluation of various rules for the construction and iterative improvement of flow shop schedules, we refer to Palmer [1965], Campbell, Dudek & Smith [1970], Dannenbring [1977], Nawaz, Enscore & Ham [1983], Turner & Booth [1987], and Osman & Potts [1989]. The current champions are the fast *insertion* method of Nawaz, Enscore & Ham and the less efficient but more effective *simulated annealing* algorithm of Osman & Potts. Simulated annealing is a randomized variant of iterative improvement, which accepts deteriorations with a small and decreasing probability in an attempt to avoid bad local optima and to get settled in a global optimum. In the experiments of Osman & Potts, the neighborhood of a permutation schedule contains all schedules that can be obtained by moving a single job to another position.

13.3. No wait in process

In a variation on the flow shop problem, each job, once started, has to be processed without interruption until it is completed. This *no wait* constraint may arise out of certain job characteristics (such as in the 'hot ingot' problem, where metal has to be processed at a continuously high temperature) or out of the unavailability of intermediate storage in between machines.

The resulting $F \mid no\ wait \mid C_{\max}$ problem can be formulated as a *traveling salesman problem* with cities $0, 1, \ldots, n$ and intercity distances

$$c_{jk} = \max_{1 \leq i \leq m} \left(\sum_{h=1}^{i} p_{hj} - \sum_{h=1}^{i-1} p_{hk} \right) \quad \text{for } j, k = 0, 1, \ldots, n ,$$

where $p_{i0} = 0$ for $i = 1, \ldots, m$ [Piehler, 1960; Reddi & Ramamoorthy, 1972; Wismer, 1972].

For the case $F2|no\ wait|C_{max}$, the traveling salesman problem assumes a special structure, and results due to Gilmore & Gomory [1964] can be applied to yield an $O(n^2)$ algorithm; see Reddi & Ramamoorthy [1972] and also Gilmore, Lawler & Shmoys [1985]. In contrast, $F4|no\ wait|C_{max}$ is strongly NP-hard [Papadimitriou & Kanellakis, 1980], and so is $F3|no\ wait|C_{max}$ [Röck, 1984a]. The same is true for $F2|no\ wait|L_{max}$ and $F2|no\ wait|\Sigma C_j$ [Röck, 1984b], and for $O2|no\ wait|C_{max}$ and $J2|no\ wait|C_{max}$ [Sahni & Cho, 1979a]. Goyal & Sriskandarajah [1988] review complexity results and approximation algorithms for this problem class.

The *no wait* constraint may lengthen the optimal flow shops schedule considerably. Lenstra [-] shows that

$$C^*_{max}(no\ wait)/C^*_{max} < m \quad \text{for } m \geq 2\,. \qquad (\dagger)$$

14. Job shops

14.0. *The disjunctive graph model for* $J|\ |C_{max}$

The description of $J|\ |C_{max}$ in Section 3 does not reveal much of the structure of this problem type. An illuminating problem representation is provided by the disjunctive graph model due to Roy & Sussmann [1964].

Given an instance of $J|\ |C_{max}$, the corresponding disjunctive graph is defined as follows. For every operation O_{ij}, there is a vertex, with a weight p_{ij}. For every two consecutive operations of the same job, there is a (directed) arc. For every two operations that require the same machine, there is an (undirected) edge. Thus, the arcs represent the job precedence constraints, and the edges represent the machine capacity constraints.

The basic scheduling decision is to impose an ordering on a pair of operations on the same machine. In the disjunctive graph, this corresponds to orienting the edge in question, in one way or the other. A schedule is obtained by orienting all of the edges. The schedule is feasible if the resulting directed graph is acyclic, and its length is obviously equal to the weight of maximum weight path in this graph.

The job shop scheduling problem has now been formulated as the problem of finding an orientation of the edges of a disjunctive graph that minimizes the maximum path weight. We refer to Figure 4 for an example.

14.1. *Two or three machines*

A simple extension of Johnson's algorithm for $F2|\ |C_{max}$ allows solution of $J2|m_j \leq 2|C_{max}$ in $O(n \log n)$ time [Jackson, 1956]. Let $\mathcal{J}_i$ be the set of jobs with operations on M_i only ($i = 1, 2$), and let $\mathcal{J}_{hi}$ be the set of jobs that go from M_h to M_i ($\{h, i\} = \{1, 2\}$). Order the latter two sets by means of Johnson's algorithm and the former two sets arbitrarily. One then obtains an optimal

J_j	m_j	μ_{1j}	μ_{2j}	μ_{3j}	μ_{4j}	p_{1j}	p_{2j}	p_{3j}	p_{4j}
J_1	3	M_1	M_2	M_3	—	2	8	4	—
J_2	4	M_2	M_1	M_3	M_4	7	3	6	3
J_3	3	M_1	M_2	M_4	—	5	9	1	—

(a)

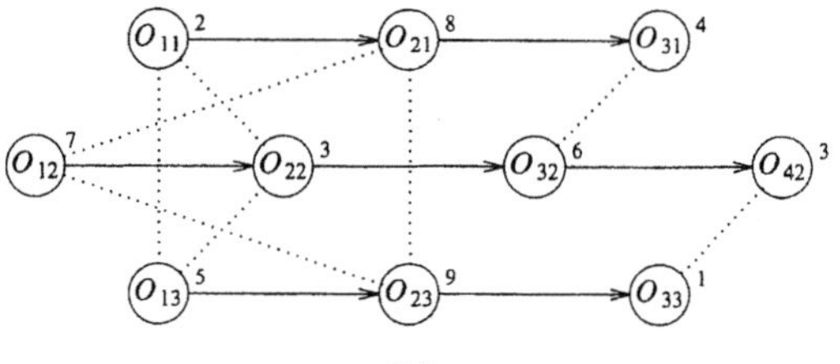

(b)

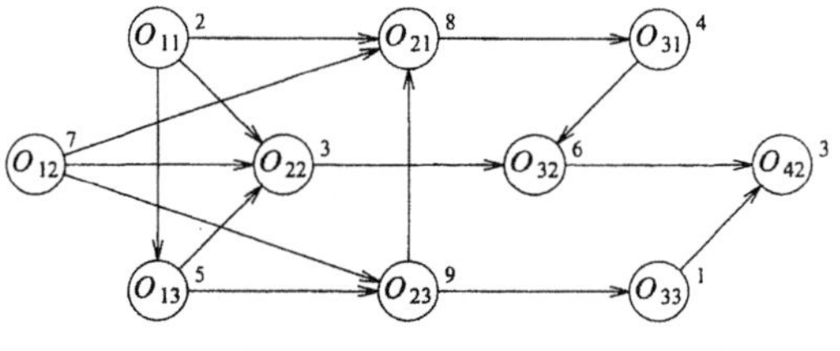

(c)

Fig. 4. A job shop scheduling problem. (a) Instance. (b) Instance, represented as a disjunctive graph. (c) Feasible schedule, represented as an acyclic directed graph.

schedule by executing the jobs on M_1 in the order $(\mathcal{J}_{12}, \mathcal{J}_1, \mathcal{J}_{21})$ and on M_2 in the order $(\mathcal{J}_{21}, \mathcal{J}_2, \mathcal{J}_{12})$.

Hefetz & Adiri [1982] solve another special case, $J2 \mid p_{ij} = 1 \mid C_{\max}$, in time linear in the total number of operations, through a rule that gives priority to the longest remaining job. Brucker [1981, 1982] extends this result to $J2 \mid p_{ij} = 1 \mid L_{\max}$.

This, however, is probably as far as we can get. $J2 \mid m_j \leq 3 \mid C_{\max}$ and $J3 \mid m_j \leq 2 \mid C_{\max}$ are NP-hard [Lenstra, Rinnooy Kan & Brucker, 1977; Gonzalez & Sahni, 1978a], $J2 \mid p_{ij} \in \{1, 2\} \mid C_{\max}$ and $J3 \mid p_{ij} = 1 \mid C_{\max}$ are strongly NP-hard [Lenstra & Rinnooy Kan, 1979], and these results still hold if preemption is allowed. Also, $J2 \mid pmtn \mid \Sigma C_j$ is strongly NP-hard [Lenstra, -]; recall that the corresponding open shop and flow shop problems are open.

14.2. General job shop scheduling

Optimization algorithms for the $J \mid \mid C_{\max}$ problem proceed by branch and bound. We will describe methods of that type in terms of the disjunctive graph $(\mathcal{O}, A, E)$, where $\mathcal{O}$ is the set of operations, A the arc set, and E the edge set.

A node in the search tree is usually characterized by an orientation of each edge in a certain subset $E' \subset E$. The question then is how to compute a lower bound on the value of all completions of this partial solution. Németi [1964], Charlton & Death [1970] and Schrage [1970] are among the researchers who obtain a lower bound by simply disregarding $E - E'$ and computing the maximum path weight in the directed graph $(\mathcal{O}, A \cup E')$. A more sophisticated bound, due to Bratley, Florian & Robillard [1973], is based on the relaxation of the capacity constraints of all machines except one. They propose to select a machine M' and to solve the job shop scheduling problem on the disjunctive graph $(\mathcal{O}, A \cup E', \{\{O_{ij}, O_{i'j'}\} \mid \mu_{ij} = \mu_{i'j'} = M'\})$. This is a single-machine problem, where the arcs in $A \cup E'$ define release times and delivery times for the operations that are to be scheduled on machine M'. This observation has spawned the subsequent work on the $1 \mid r_j \mid L_{\max}$ problem which was reviewed in Section 4.2 and which has led to fast methods for its solution. As pointed out by Lageweg, Lenstra & Rinnooy Kan [1977], the lower bound problem is, in fact, $1 \mid prec, r_j \mid L_{\max}$, since $A \cup E'$ may define precedence constraints among the operations on M'. Again, most other lower bounds appear as special cases of this one, by relaxing the capacity constraint of M' (which gives Németi's longest path bound), by underestimating the contribution of the release and delivery times, by allowing preemption, or by ignoring the precedence constraints. These relaxations, with the exception of the last one, turn an NP-hard single-machine problem into a problem that is solvable in polynomial time.

Fisher, Lageweg, Lenstra & Rinnooy Kan [1983] investigate surrogate duality relaxations, in which either the capacity constraints of the machines or the precedence constraints among the operations of each job are weighted and aggregated into a single constraint. In theory, the resulting bounds dominate the above single-machine bound. Balas [1985] describes a first attempt to obtain bounds by polyhedral techniques.

The usual enumeration scheme is due to Giffler & Thompson [1960]. It generates all active schedules by constructing them from front to back. At each stage, the subset $\mathcal{O}'$ of operations O_{ij} all of whose predecessors have been scheduled is determined and their earliest possible completion times $r_{ij} + p_{ij}$ are calculated. It suffices to consider only a machine on which the minimum value of $r_{ij} + p_{ij}$ is achieved and to branch by successively scheduling next on that machine all operations in $\mathcal{O}'$ for which the release time is strictly smaller than this minimum. In this scheme, several edges are oriented at each stage.

Lageweg, Lenstra & Rinnooy Kan [1977] and Carlier & Pinson [1988] describe alternative enumeration schemes whereby at each stage, a single edge is selected and oriented in either of two ways. Barker & McMahon [1985] branch by rearranging the operations in a critical block that occurs on the maximum weight path.

We briefly outline three of the many implemented branch and bound algorithms for job shop scheduling. McMahon & Florian [1975] combine the Giffler–Thompson enumeration scheme with the $1 \mid r_j \mid L_{\max}$ bound, which is computed for all machines by their own algorithm. Lageweg [1984] applies the same branching rule, computes the $1 \mid prec, r_j \mid L_{\max}$ bound only for a few promising machines using Carlier's [1982] algorithm, and obtains upper bounds with a heuristic due to Lageweg, Lenstra & Rinnooy Kan [1977]. Carlier & Pinson [1988] implement their novel enumeration schemes, the $1 \mid pmtn, prec, r_j \mid L_{max}$ bound (which can be computed in polynomial time), and a collection of powerful elimination rules for which we refer to their paper.

Most *approximation algorithms* for job shop scheduling use a dispatch rule, which schedules the operations according to some priority function. Gonzalez & Sahni [1978a] observe that the performance guarantees for the flow shop algorithms AS and LPT (see Section 13.2) also apply to the case of a job shop. A considerable effort has been invested in the empirical testing of rules of this type [Gere, 1966; Conway, Maxwell & Miller, 1967; Day & Hottenstein, 1970; Panwalkar & Iskander, 1977; Haupt, 1989].

Adams, Balas & Zawack [1988] develop a *sliding bottleneck heuristic*, which employs an ingenious combination of schedule construction and iterative improvement, guided by solutions to single-machine problems of the type described above. They also embed this method in a second heuristic that proceeds by partial enumeration of the solution space.

Matsuo, Suh & Sullivan [1988] and Van Laarhoven, Aarts & Lenstra [1992] apply the principle of *simulated annealing* (see Section 13.2) to the job shop scheduling problem. In the latter paper, the neighborhood of a schedule contains all schedules that can be obtained by interchanging two operations O_{ij} and $O_{i'j'}$ on the same machine such that the arc $(O_{ij}, O_{i'j'})$ is on a maximum weight path. In the former paper, the neighborhood structure is more complex.

14.3. $10 \times 10 = 930$

The computational merits of all these algorithms are accurately reflected by their performance on the notorious 10-job 10-machine problem instance due to Fisher & Thompson [1963].

The single-machine bound, maximized over all machines, has a value of 808. McMahon & Florian [1975] found a schedule of length 972. Fisher, Lageweg, Lenstra & Rinnooy Kan [1983] applied surrogate duality relaxation of the capacity constraints and of the precedence constraints to find lower bounds of 813 and 808, respectively; the computational effort involved did not encourage them to carry on the search beyond the root of the tree. Lageweg [1984] found a schedule of length 930, without proving optimality; he also computed a number of multi-machine lower bounds, ranging from a three-machine bound of 874 to a six-machine bound of 907. Carlier & Pinson [1988] were the first to prove optimality of the value 930, after generating 22 021 nodes and five hours of computing. The main drawback of all these enumerative methods, besides the limited problem sizes that can be handled, is their sensitivity towards particular problem instances and also towards the initial value of the upper bound.

The computational experience with polyhedral techniques that has been reported until now is slightly disappointing in view of what has been achieved for other hard problems. However, the investigations in this direction are still at an initial stage.

Dispatch rules show an erratic behavior. The rule proposed by Lageweg, Lenstra & Rinnooy Kan [1977] constructs a schedule of length 1082, and most other priority functions do worse.

Adams, Balas & Zawack [1988] report that their sliding bottleneck heuristic obtains a schedule of length 1015 in ten CPU seconds, solving 249 single-machine problems on the way. Their partial enumeration procedure succeeds in finding the optimum, after 851 seconds and 270 runs of the first heuristic.

Five runs of the simulated annealing algorithm of Van Laarhoven, Aarts & Lenstra [1992], with a standard setting of the cooling parameters, take 6000 seconds on average and produce an average schedule length of 942.4, with a minimum of 937. If 6000 seconds are spent on deterministic neighborhood search, which accepts only true improvements, more than 9000 local optima are found, the best one of which has a value of 1006. Five runs with a much slower cooling schedule take about 16 hours each and produce solution values of 930 (twice), 934, 935 and 938. In comparison to other approximative approaches, simulated annealing requires unusual computation times, but it yields consistently good solutions with a modest amount of human implementation effort and relatively little insight into the combinatorial structure of the problem type under consideration.

PART V. MORE SEQUENCING AND SCHEDULING

In the preceding sections, we have been exclusively concerned with the class of deterministic machine scheduling problems. Several extensions of this class are worthy of further investigation. A natural extension involves the presence of additional resources, where each resource has a limited size and each job requires the use of a part of each resource during its execution. The resulting *resource-constrained project scheduling* problems are considered in Section 15. We also may relax the assumption that all problem data are known in advance and investigate *stochastic machine scheduling* problems. This class is the subject of Section 16. We will not enter the area of *stochastic project scheduling*, which is surveyed by Möhring & Radermacher [1985b].

15. Resource-constrained project scheduling

15.0. *A matching formulation for* $P2 \mid p_j = 1 \mid C_{\max}$ *with resource constraints*

Consider a single-operation model, and suppose there are l additional resources R_h ($h = 1, \ldots, l$). For each resource R_h, there is a *size* s_h, which is the amount of R_h available at any time. For each resource R_h and each job J_j, there is a *requirement* r_{hj}, which is the amount of R_h required by J_j at all times during its execution. A schedule is *feasible* with respect to the resources if at any time t the index set I_t of jobs being executed at time t satisfies $\Sigma_{j \in I_t} r_{hj} \leq s_h$, for $h = 1, \ldots, l$.

In the case $P2 | p_j = 1 | C_{\max}$, Garey & Johnson [1975] propose to represent the resource constraints by a graph with vertex set $\{1, \ldots, n\}$ and an edge $\{j, k\}$ whenever $r_{hj} + r_{hk} \leq s_h$ for $h = 1, \ldots, l$. That is, vertices j and k are adjacent if and only if J_j and J_k can be processed simultaneously. A matching M in the graph obviously corresponds to a schedule of length $n - |M|$, and an optimal schedule is obtained by computing a maximum cardinality matching.

15.1. Machines and resources

Sequencing and scheduling is concerned with the optimal allocation of scarce resources to activities over time. So far, the resources and the activities have been of a relatively simple nature. It was assumed that an activity, or job, requires at most one resource, or machine, at a time. Also, a machine is able to process at most one job at a time. This unit-capacity is constant, and not affected by its use.

It is obvious that scheduling situations of a more general nature exist. Certain types of resources are depleted by use (e.g., money or energy) or are available in amounts that vary over time, in a predictable manner (e.g., seasonal labor) or in an unpredictable manner (e.g., vulnerable equipment). At one point in time, a resource may be shared among several jobs, and a job may need several resources. The resource amounts required by a job may vary during its processing and, indeed, the processing time itself could depend on the amount or type of resource allocated, as in the case of uniform or unrelated machines.

Through these generalizations, the domain of deterministic scheduling theory is considerably extended. Usually referred to as *resource-constrained project scheduling*, the area covers a tremendous variety of problem types.

15.2. Classification and complexity

To approach this area in the best tradition of deterministic scheduling theory would require the development of a detailed problem classification, followed by a complexity analysis involving polynomial-time algorithms and NP-hardness proofs.

A modest attempt along these lines was made by Blazewicz, Lenstra & Rinnooy Kan [1983]. They consider resource constraints of the type defined in the first paragraph of Section 15.0, and propose to include these in the second field of the problem classification through a parameter $res\lambda\sigma\rho$, where λ, σ, and ρ specify the number of resources, their sizes, and the amounts required. More precisely,

– if λ is a positive integer, then l is a constant, equal to λ; if $\lambda = \cdot$, then l is specified as part of the input;

– if σ a positive integer, then all s_h are constants, equal to σ; if $\sigma = \cdot$, then the s_h are part of the input;

– if ρ is a positive integer, then all r_{hj} have a constant upper bound, equal to ρ; if $\rho = \cdot$, then no such bounds are specified.

Blazewicz, Lenstra & Rinnooy Kan investigate the computational complexity of $Q \mid res \cdots, prec, p_j = 1 \mid C_{\max}$ and its special cases. The resulting exhaustive complexity classification is presented in Figure 5. We have already seen in Section 15.0 that $P2 \mid res \cdots, p_j = 1 \mid C_{\max}$ is solvable by matching techniques. Also note that $P3 \mid res\, 1 \cdot\cdot, p_j = 1 \mid C_{\max}$ is an immediate generalization of the

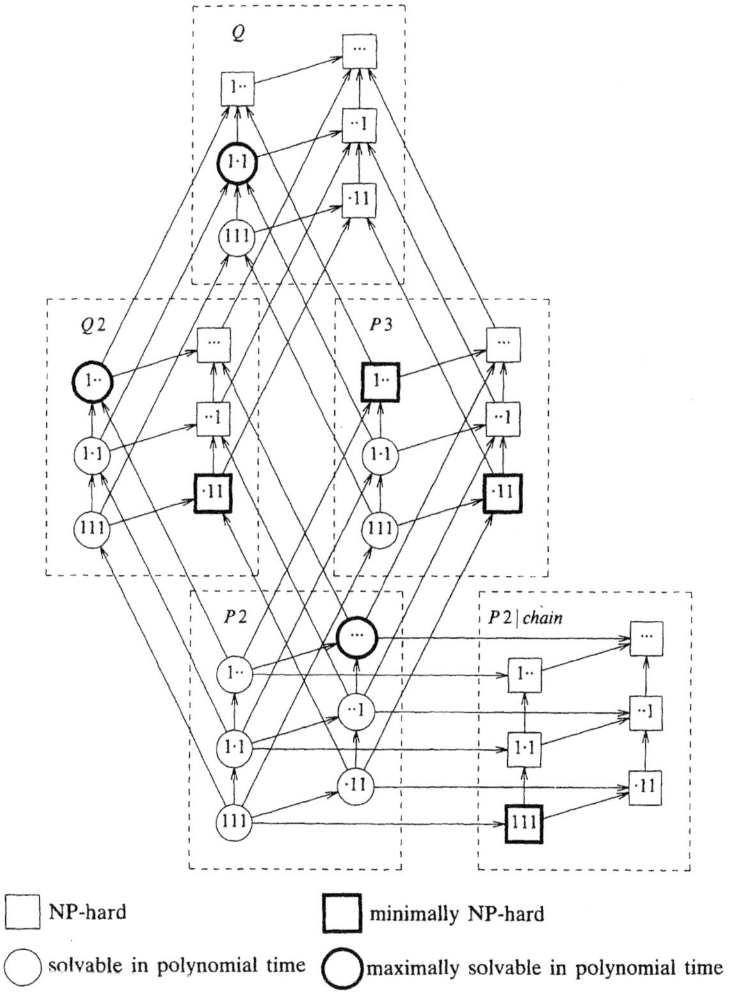

Fig. 5. Complexity of scheduling unit-time jobs on parallel machines subject to resource constraints.

3-partition problem and thereby strongly NP-hard; see Section 2 and Garey & Johnson [1975].

These results are not encouraging, in that virtually all except the simplest resource-constrained project scheduling problems turn out to be NP-hard. In the next section, we abolish the search for special structure and review two optimization models of a fairly general nature.

15.3. Two optimization models

The early literature on optimization and approximation in resource-constrained project scheduling is reviewed by Davis [1966, 1973]. Optimization models are traditionally cast in terms of integer programming. We start by presenting one such formulation, due to Talbot & Patterson [1978] and Christofides, Alvarez-Valdes & Tamarit [1987].

For simplicity, we consider the $P \mid res \cdots, prec \mid C_{\max}$ problem, i.e., $P \mid prec \mid C_{\max}$ with resource constraints as described in the first paragraph of Section 15.0. We also suppose that $m \geqslant n$ and that one job, J_n, succeeds all others. The problem is then to find nonnegative job completion times C_j, which define index sets I_t of jobs executed at time t, such that C_n is minimized subject to precedence constraints and resource constraints:

$$C_j + p_j \leqslant C_k \text{ whenever } J_j \rightarrow J_k ,$$

$$\sum_{j \in I_t} r_{hj} \leqslant s_h \quad \text{for all } R_h \text{ and all } t .$$

To convert the latter set of constraints into linear form, we introduce 0–1 variables y_{jt}, with $y_{jt} = 1$ if and only if $C_j = t$. Obviously, $C_j = \Sigma_t t y_{jt}$, and the resource constraints can be rewritten as

$$\sum_{j=1}^{n} r_{hj} \sum_{u=t}^{t+p_j-1} y_{jt} \leqslant s_h \quad \text{for all } h \text{ and } t .$$

Branch and bound algorithms using bounds based on the linear relaxation, cutting planes, and Lagrangean relaxation of the resource constraints are reasonably effective for problems with up to three resources and 25 jobs.

An entirely different approach was taken by Bartusch, Möhring & Radermacher [1988b]. Recall the formulation of the $J \mid \mid C_{\max}$ problem in terms of a disjunctive graph, where each *edge* corresponds to a pair of operations that cannot be processed simultaneously since they require the same machine. Following earlier work by Balas [1970], Bartusch, Möhring & Radermacher generalize this idea, by defining resource constraints in the form of a family $\mathcal{N} = \{N_1, \ldots, N_l\}$ of *forbidden subsets*. Each N_h is a subset of jobs that cannot be executed simultaneously because of its collective resource requirements; this presupposes constant resource availability over time. In addition, they generalize the traditional precedence constraints of the form

$$C_j + p_j \le C_k \quad \text{whenever } J_j \to J_k$$

to *temporal constraints* of the form

$$C_j + d_{jk} \le C_k \quad \text{for all } J_j, J_k ,$$

where d_{jk} is a (possibly negative) *distance* from J_j to J_k. The resulting model is quite general. It allows for the specification of job release dates and deadlines, of minimal and maximal time lags between jobs, and of time-dependent resource consumption per job.

The investigation of this model leads to structural insights as well as computational methods. This is also true for the related model involving traditional precedence constraints [Radermacher, 1985/6] and for the dual model in which resource consumption is to be minimized subject to a common job deadline [Möhring, 1984]. The approach leads to new classes of polynomially solvable problems that are characterized by the structure of the family of forbidden subsets [Möhring, 1983]. For the general model, it can be shown that for any optimality criterion that is nondecreasing in the job completion times, attention can be restricted to left-justified schedules. Enumerative methods can be designed that, as in the case of $J| \,|C_{\max}$, construct feasible schedules by adding at least one precedence constraint among the jobs in each forbidden subset.

In the case of job shop scheduling, the number of edges is $O(n^2)$. Similarly, the present model is only computationally feasible when the number of forbidden subsets is not too large. It is sufficient if $\mathcal{N}$ contains only those forbidden subsets that are minimal under set inclusion. A branch and bound method that branches by successively considering all possibilities to eliminate a particular forbidden subset and obtains lower bounds by simply computing a longest path with respect to the augmented temporal constraints, compares favorably with the integer programming algorithm of Talbot & Patterson [1978].

16. Stochastic machine scheduling

16.0. List scheduling for $P|\,p_j \sim \exp(\lambda_j)\,|\,\mathrm{E}C_{\max}, \mathrm{E}\Sigma C_j$

Suppose that m identical parallel machines have to process n independent jobs. In contrast to what we have assumed so far, the processing times are not given beforehand but become known only after the jobs have been allocated to the machines. More specifically, each processing time p_j follows an exponential distribution with parameter λ_j, for $j = 1, \ldots, n$. We want to minimize the expected maximum completion time $\mathrm{E}\boldsymbol{C}_{\max}$ or the expected total completion time $\mathrm{E}\Sigma\boldsymbol{C}_j$. (As noted before, random variables are printed in boldface italic.)

Results of Bruno & Downey [1977] for $m = 2$ and of Bruno, Downey & Frederickson [1981] for arbitrary m state that these problems are solved by simple list scheduling policies. The *longest expected processing time* (LEPT) rule, which schedules the jobs in order of nonincreasing values $1/\lambda_j$, minimizes $\mathrm{E}\boldsymbol{C}_{\max}$; the *shortest expected processing time* (SEPT) rule, which schedules the jobs in the reverse order, minimizes $\mathrm{E}\Sigma\boldsymbol{C}_j$.

We will sketch a proof of the optimality of the LEPT rule for minimizing $\mathrm{E}\boldsymbol{C}_{\max}$. This proof, which is due to Weiss & Pinedo [1980], relies on the formulation of the preemptive version of the problem in terms of a semi-Markov decision process. Note, however, that the LEPT rule will never preempt a job, because of the memoryless property of the exponential distribution.

Let $N = \{1, \ldots, n\}$ be the index set of all jobs, and let $F_\pi(S)$ denote the minimum expected maximum completion time for the jobs indexed by $S \subseteq N$ under a scheduling policy π. Consider a policy π that at time 0 selects a set $S_\pi \subseteq N$ to be processed, preempts the schedule at time $t > 0$, and applies the LEPT rule from time t onwards. By time t, a job J_j is completed with probability $\lambda_j t + \mathrm{o}(t)$, and two or more jobs are completed with probability $\mathrm{o}(t)$, for $t \to 0$. It now follows from Markov decision theory that

$$\begin{aligned} F_\pi(N) = t + \sum_{j \in S_\pi} \lambda_j t F_{\mathrm{LEPT}}(N - \{j\}) + \Big(1 - \sum_{j \in S_\pi} \lambda_j t\Big) F_{\mathrm{LEPT}}(N) \\ + \mathrm{o}(t)\,, \quad t \to 0\,. \end{aligned}$$

Without loss of generality, we assume that $|S_\pi| = m < n$. If π is not the LEPT policy, then there exist jobs J_k, J_l with $\lambda_k < \lambda_l$ such that $k \notin S_\pi$, $l \in S_\pi$. Now define another policy π' that at time 0 selects a set $S_{\pi'} = S_\pi \cup \{k\} - \{l\}$ and applies LEPT from time t onwards. We have that

$$\begin{aligned} F_\pi(N) - F_{\pi'}(N) = t[\lambda_k(F_{\mathrm{LEPT}}(N) - F_{\mathrm{LEPT}}(N - \{k\})) \\ - \lambda_l(F_{\mathrm{LEPT}}(N) - F_{\mathrm{LEPT}}(N - \{l\}))] \\ + \mathrm{o}(t)\,, \quad t \to 0\,. \end{aligned}$$

Lengthy but rather straightforward calculations, which are not given here, show that the expression within square brackets is positive. The argument is by induction on n and uses the following simple recursion:

$$F_{\mathrm{LEPT}}(N) = \Big(1 + \sum_{j \in S_{\mathrm{LEPT}}} \lambda_j F_{\mathrm{LEPT}}(N - \{j\})\Big) \Big/ \sum_{j \in S_{\mathrm{LEPT}}} \lambda_j\,,$$

where S_{LEPT} contains the smallest m λ's. It follows that, if t is small enough, then $F_{\pi}(N) > F_{\pi'}(N)$. After at most m interchanges, the policy applied at time 0 is the LEPT rule, and we have that $F_{\pi}(N) > F_{\mathrm{LEPT}}(N)$.

It is interesting to note that, while $P \mid \mid C_{\max}$ is NP-hard, a stochastic variant of the problem is solvable in polynomial time. As observed above, LEPT should be viewed as an algorithm for the preemptive problem, and preemptive scheduling in a deterministic setting is not hard either. Indeed, for the case of uniform machines, Weiss & Pinedo [1980] prove that a preemptive LEPT (SEPT) policy, which allows reallocation of jobs to machines at job completion times, solves $Q \mid pmtn, p_j \sim \exp(\lambda_j) \mid \mathrm{E}C_{\max}$ ($\mathrm{E}\Sigma C_j$).

16.1. Deterministic and stochastic data

The scheduling models discussed in the earlier sections are based on the assumption that all problem data are known in advance. This assumption is not always justified. Processing times may be subject to fluctuations, and job arrivals and machine breakdowns are often random events.

A substantial literature exists in which scheduling problems are considered from a probabilistic perspective. A deterministic scheduling model may give rise to various stochastic counterparts, as there is a choice in the parameters that are randomized, in their distributions, and in the classes of policies that can be applied. A characteristic feature of these models is that the stochastic parameters are regarded as independent random variables with a given distribution and that their realization occurs only after the scheduling decision has been made.

Surprisingly, there are many cases where a simple rule which is merely a heuristic for the deterministic model has a stochastic reformulation which solves the stochastic model to optimality; we have seen an example in the previous section. In the deterministic model, one has perfect information, and capitalizing on it in minimizing the realization of a performance measure may require exponential time. In the stochastic model, one has imperfect information, and the problem of minimizing the expectation of a performance measure may be computationally tractable. In such cases, the scheduling decision is based on distributional information such as first and second moments. In general, however, optimal policies may be dynamic and require information on the history up to the current point in time.

Results in this area are technically complicated; they rely on semi-Markovian decision theory and stochastic dynamic optimization. Within the scope of this section, it is not possible to do full justice to the literature. We present some typical results for the main types of machine environments below, concentrating on scheduling models with random processing times. We refer to Pinedo [1983] for scheduling with random release and due dates, to Pinedo & Rammouz [1988] and Birge, Frenk, Mittenthal & Rinnooy Kan [1990] for single-machine scheduling with random breakdowns, and to the surveys by Pinedo & Schrage [1982], Weiss [1982], Forst [1984], Pinedo [1984], Möhring,

Radermacher & Weiss [1984, 1985], Möhring & Radermacher [1985b] and Frenk [1988] for further information.

16.2. The single machine

In stochastic single-machine scheduling, Gittins' work on *dynamic allocation indices* initiated an important line of research. A prototypical result is the following. One machine has to process n jobs. The job processing times $\boldsymbol{p}_j$ are independent, nonnegative and identically distributed random variables, whose distribution function F has an increasing completion rate $(\mathrm{d}F(t)/\mathrm{d}t)/(1-F(t))$. If job J_j completes at time C_j, then a reward $\alpha_j \mathrm{e}^{-\beta C_j}$ is incurred. The objective is to maximize the *total* expected reward. It is achieved by scheduling the jobs in order of nonincreasing ratios $\alpha_j \mathrm{E}\mathrm{e}^{-\beta \boldsymbol{p}_j}/(1-\mathrm{E}\mathrm{e}^{-\beta \boldsymbol{p}_j})$. This ratio can be interpreted as the expected reward for J_j per unit of expected discounted processing time. The increasing completion rate of F ensures that there is no advantage to preemption.

This result follows from the mathematical theory of *bandit processes*. Subsequent work by Gittins & Glazebrook has led to many extensions. Forst [1984] present a survey of this part of the literature.

Another class of results concerns the situation in which the $\boldsymbol{p}_j$ are independent, nonnegative random variables, and the objective is to minimize the expected *maximum* job completion cost subject to precedence constraints. Hodgson [1977] generalizes the algorithm of Lawler [1973] for $1 \mid prec \mid f_{\max}$ (see Section 4.0) to solve this problem. The result subsumes earlier work involving deterministic due dates, such as the minimization of the maximum probability of lateness [Banerjee, 1965], the maximization of the probability that every job is on time [Crabill & Maxwell, 1969], and the minimization of the maximum expected weighted tardiness [Blau, 1973].

16.3. Parallel machines

Research in stochastic parallel machine scheduling has focused on extending the results quoted in Section 16.0 beyond the realm of exponential distributions. Weber has shown that, as a necessary condition, the processing time distributions have to be consistent in terms of completion rates (i.e., either all decreasing or all increasing) or in terms of likelihood rates (i.e., the log $\mathrm{d}F_j/\mathrm{d}t$ either all convex or all concave). Weiss [1982] reviews this work. Weber, Varaiya & Walrand [1986] show that SEPT minimizes the expected total completion time on identical machines if the processing times are stochastically comparable.

The extension to uniform machines has been explored by Agrawala, Coffman, Garey & Tripathi [1984], Kumar & Walrand [1985], Coffman, Flatto, Garey & Weber [1987] and Righter [1988].

For the case of intree precedence constraints and exponential processing times, Pinedo & Weiss [1985] prove that HLF minimizes the expected maximum completion time on two identical machines if all the jobs at the same level have the same parameter. Frostig [1988] extends this work.

Pinedo & Weiss [1987] investigate the case of identical expected processing times. Their result confirms the intuition that, at least for some simple distributions, the jobs with the largest variance should be scheduled first.

16.4. Multi-operation models

Pinedo's [1984] survey is a good source of information on stochastic shop scheduling. Most work has concentrated on flow shops; Pinedo & Weiss [1984] deal with some stochastic variants of the Gonzalez-Sahni [1976] algorithm for $O2 | | C_{max}$ (see Section 12.0).

Brumelle & Sidney [1982] show that Johnson's [1954] algorithm for $F2 | | C_{max}$ also applies to the exponential case. If $\boldsymbol{p}_{1j} \sim \exp(\lambda_j)$ and $\boldsymbol{p}_{2j} \sim \exp(\mu_j)$, then sequencing in order of nonincreasing $\lambda_j - \mu_j$ minimizes the expected maximum completion time.

For $F | | C_{max}$, it is usually assumed that the $\boldsymbol{p}_{ij}$ are independent random variables whose distributions do not depend on i. Weber [1979] shows that, in the exponential case, any sequence minimizes $\mathrm{E}\boldsymbol{C}_{max}$. Pinedo [1982] observes that, under fairly general conditions, any sequence for which $\mathrm{E}\boldsymbol{p}_{ij}$ is first nondecreasing and then nonincreasing is optimal; as a rule of thumb, jobs with smaller expected processing time and larger variance should come at the beginning or at the end of a schedule, with the others occupying the middle part. These observations carry over to the model in which no intermediate storage is available, so that a job can only leave a machine when its next machine is available. We refer to Foley & Suresh [1986] and Wie & Pinedo [1986] for more recent work on the latter model, and to Boxma & Forst [1986] for a result on a stochastic version of $F | | \Sigma U_j$.

Not surprisingly, job shops pose even greater challenges. The only successful analysis has been carried out by Pinedo [1981] for an exponential variant of $J2 | m_j \leq 2 | C_{max}$ (see Section 14.1).

The results in stochastic scheduling are scattered, and they have been obtained through a considerable and sometimes disheartening effort. In the words of Coffman, Hofri & Weiss [1989], 'there is a great need for new mathematical techniques useful for simplifying the derivation of results'.

Acknowledgements

We gratefully acknowledge the contribution of Leen Stougie to Section 16.0, the comments and suggestions of Leslie Hall, Ben Lageweg, Michael Langston, Joseph Leung, Rolf Möhring, Michael Pinedo, Chris Potts, Steef van de Velde, and Gideon Weiss, and the help of Gerard Kindervater in preparing the figures. The research of the first author was partially supported by the National Science Foundation under grant CCR-8704184. This paper was written when the second author was visiting the Sloan School of Management of the Massachusetts Institute of Technology. The research of the second and fourth author was partially supported by the Presidential Young Investigator Award of the fourth author, with matching support from IBM, Sun Microsystems, and UPS. The research of the fourth author was also supported by Air Force contract AFOSR-86-0078.

References

Abdul-Razaq, T.S., and C.N. Potts (1988). Dynamic programming state-space relaxation for single-machine scheduling. *J. Oper. Res. Soc.* 39, 141–152.

Achugbue, J.O., and F.Y. Chin (1981). Bounds on schedules for independent tasks with similar execution times. *J. Assoc. Comput. Mach.* 28, 81–99.

Achugbue, J.O., and F.Y. Chin (1982a). Scheduling the open shop to minimize mean flow time. *SIAM J. Comput.* 11, 709–720.

Achugbue, J.O., and F.Y. Chin (1982b). Complexity and solution of some three-stage flow shop scheduling problems. *Math. Oper. Res.* 7, 532–544.

Adams, J., E. Balas and D. Zawack (1988). The shifting bottleneck procedure for job shop scheduling. *Management Sci.* 34, 391–401.

Adiri, I., and N. Aizikowitz (1989). Openshop scheduling problems with dominated machines. *Naval Res. Logist.* 36, 273–281.

Adolphson, D., and T.C. Hu (1973). Optimal linear ordering. *SIAM J. Appl. Math.* 25, 403–423.

Agrawala, A.K., E.G. Coffman Jr, M.R. Garey and S.K. Tripathi (1984). A stochastic optimization algorithm minimizing expected flow times on uniform processors. *IEEE Trans. Comput.* 33, 351–356.

Bagchi, U., and R.H. Ahmadi (1987). An improved lower bound for minimizing weighted completion times with deadlines. *Oper. Res.* 35, 311–313.

Baker, K.R. (1974). *Introduction to Sequencing and Scheduling*, Wiley, New York.

Baker, K.R., E.L. Lawler, J.K. Lenstra and A.H.G. Rinnooy Kan (1983). Preemptive scheduling of a single machine to minimize maximum cost subject to release dates and precedence constraints. *Oper. Res.* 31, 381–386.

Baker, K.R., and L.E. Schrage (1978). Finding an optimal sequence by dynamic programming: An extension to precedence-related tasks. *Oper. Res.* 26, 111–120.

Baker, K.R., and G.D. Scudder (1990). Sequencing with earliness and tardiness penalties: A review. *Oper. Res.* 38, 22–36.

Baker, K.R., and Z.-S. Su (1974). Sequencing with due-dates and early start times to minimize maximum tardiness. *Naval Res. Logist. Quart.* 21, 171–176.

Balas, E. (1970). Project scheduling with resource constraints, in: E.M.L. Beale (ed.), *Applications of Mathematical Programming Techniques*, English Univ. Press, London, pp. 187–200.

Balas, E. (1985). On the facial structure of scheduling polyhedra. *Math. Programming Stud.* 24, 179–218.

Banerjee, B.P. (1965). Single facility sequencing with random execution times. *Oper. Res.* 13, 358–364.

Barker, J.R., and G.B. McMahon (1985). Scheduling the general job-shop. *Management Sci.* 31, 594–598.

Barnes, J.W., and J.J. Brennan (1977). An improved algorithm for scheduling jobs on identical machines. *AIIE Trans.* 9, 25–31.

Bartusch, M., R.H. Möhring and F.J. Radermacher (1988a). *M*-machine unit time scheduling: A report of ongoing research, in: A. Kurzhanski, K. Neumann and D. Pallaschke (eds.), *Optimization, Parallel Processing, and Applications*, Lecture Notes in Economics and Mathematical Systems, Vol. 304, Springer, Berlin, pp. 165–212.

Bartusch, M., R.H. Möhring and F.J. Radermacher (1988b). Scheduling project networks with resource constraints and time windows. *Ann. Oper. Res.* 16, 201–240.

Belouadah, H., M.E. Posner and C.N. Potts (1989). A branch and bound algorithm for scheduling jobs with release dates on a single machine to minimize total weighted completion time, Preprint OR14, Faculty of Mathematical Studies, University of Southampton.

Belov, I.S., and J.N. Stolin (1974). An algorithm for the single-route scheduling problem, (in Russian), in: *Mathematical Economics and Functional Analysis*, Nauka, Moscow, pp. 248–257.

Bianco, L., and S. Ricciardelli (1982). Scheduling of a single machine to minimize total weighted completion time subject to release dates. *Naval Res. Logist. Quart.* 29, 151–167.

Birge, J., J.B.G. Frenk, J. Mittenthal and A.H.G. Rinnooy Kan (1990). Single machine scheduling subject to stochastic breakdowns. *Naval Res. Logist.* 37, 661–677.

Blau, R.A. (1973). *N*-job, one machine sequencing problems under uncertainty. *Management Sci.* 20, 101–109.

Blazewicz, J. (1987). Selected topics in scheduling theory. *Ann. Discrete Math.* 31, 1–60.

Blazewicz, J., G. Finke, R. Haupt and G. Schmidt (1988). New trends in machine scheduling. *European J. Oper. Res.* 37, 303–317.

Blazewicz, J., J.K. Lenstra and A.H.G. Rinnooy Kan (1983). Scheduling subject to resource constraints: classification and complexity. *Discrete Appl. Math.* 5, 11–24.

Boxma, O.J. (1984). Probabilistic analysis of the LPT scheduling rule, in: E. Gelenbe (ed.) *Performance '84*, North-Holland, Amsterdam, pp. 475–490.

Boxma, O.J., and F.G. Forst (1986). Minimizing the expected weighted number of tardy jobs in stochastic flow shops. *Oper. Res. Lett.* 5, 119–126.

Bratley, P., M. Florian and P. Robillard (1973). On sequencing with earliest starts and due dates with application to computing bounds for the $(n/m/G/F_{max})$ problem. *Naval Res. Logist. Quart.* 20, 57–67.

Bratley, P., M. Florian and P. Robillard (1975). Scheduling with earliest start and due date constraints on multiple machines. *Naval Res. Logist. Quart.* 22, 165–173.

Brucker, P. (1981). Minimizing maximum lateness in a two-machine unit-time job shop. *Computing* 27, 367–370.

Brucker, P. (1982). A linear time algorithm to minimize maximum lateness for the two-machine, unit-time, job-shop, scheduling problem, in: R.F. Drenick and F. Kozin (eds.), *System Modeling and Optimization*, Lecture Notes in Control and Information Sciences, Vol. 38, Springer, Berlin, pp. 566–571.

Brucker, P., M.R. Garey and D.S. Johnson (1977). Scheduling equal-length tasks under tree-like precedence constraints to minimize maximum lateness. *Math. Oper. Res.* 2, 275–284.

Brumelle, S.L., and J.B. Sidney (1982). The two machine makespan problem with stochastic flow times, Technical Report, Univ. of British Columbia, Vancouver.

Bruno, J.L., E.G. Coffman Jr and R. Sethi (1974). Scheduling independent tasks to reduce mean finishing time. *Comm. ACM* 17, 382–387.

Bruno, J.L., and P.J. Downey (1977). Sequencing tasks with exponential service times on two machines, Technical Report, Department of Electrical Engineering and Computer Science, Univ. of California, Santa Barbara.

Bruno, J.L., and P.J. Downey (1986). Probabilistic bounds on the performance of list scheduling. *SIAM J. Comput.* 15, 409–417.

Bruno, J.L., P.J. Downey and G.N. Frederickson (1981). Sequencing tasks with exponential service times to minimize the expected flowtime or makespan. *J. Assoc. Comput. Mach.* 28, 100–113.

Bruno, J.L., and T. Gonzalez (1976). Scheduling independent tasks with release dates and due dates on parallel machines, Technical Report 213, Computer Science Department, Pennsylvania State University.

Buer, H., and R.H. Möhring (1983). A fast algorithm for the decomposition of graphs and posets. *Math. Oper. Res.* 8, 170–184.

Campbell, H.G., R.A. Dudek and M.L. Smith (1970). A heuristic algorithm for the *n* job, *m* machine sequencing problem. *Management Sci.* 16B, 630–637.

Carlier, J. (1982). The one-machine sequencing problem. *European J. Oper. Res.* 11, 42–47.
Carlier, J. (1987). Scheduling jobs with release dates and tails on identical machines to minimize makespan. *European J. Oper. Res.* 29, 298–306.
Carlier, J., and E. Pinson (1988). An algorithm for solving the job-shop problem. *Management Sci.* 35, 164–176.
Charlton, J.M., and C.C. Death (1970). A generalized machine scheduling algorithm. *Oper. Res. Quart.* 21, 127–134.
Chen, N.-F. (1975). An analysis of scheduling algorithms in multiprocessing computing systems, Technical Report UIUCDCS-R-75-724, Department of Computer Science, Univ. of Illinois at Urbana-Champaign.
Chen, N.-F., and C.L. Liu (1975). On a class of scheduling algorithms for multiprocessors computing systems, in: T.-Y. Feng (ed.), *Parallel Processing*, Lecture Notes in Computer Science, Vol. 24, Springer, Berlin, pp. 1–16.
Cheng, T.C.E., and M.C. Gupta (1989). Survey of scheduling research involving due date determination decisions. *European J. Oper. Res.* 38, 156–166.
Chin, F.Y., and L.-L. Tsai (1981). On *J*-maximal and *J*-minimal flow-shop schedules. *J. Assoc. Comput. Mach.* 28, 462–476.
Cho, Y., and S. Sahni (1980). Bounds for list schedules on uniform processors. *SIAM J. Comput.* 9, 91–103.
Cho, Y., and S. Sahni (1981). Preemptive scheduling of independent jobs with release and due times on open, flow and job shops. *Oper. Res.* 29, 511–522.
Christofides, N., R. Alvarez-Valdes and J.M. Tamarit (1987). Project scheduling with resource constraints: A branch and bound approach. *European J. Oper. Res.* 29, 262–273.
Coffman Jr, E.G. (ed.) (1976). *Computer & Job/Shop Scheduling Theory*, Wiley, New York.
Coffman Jr, E.G., L. Flatto, M.R. Garey and R.R. Weber (1987). Minimizing expected makespans on uniform processor systems. *Adv. in Appl. Probab.* 19, 177–201.
Coffman Jr, E.G., L. Flatto and G.S. Lueker (1984). Expected makespans for largest-fit multiprocessor scheduling, in: E. Gelenbe (ed.), *Performance '84*, North-Holland, Amsterdam, pp. 491–506.
Coffman Jr, E.G., M.R. Garey and D.S. Johnson (1978). An application of bin-packing to multiprocessor scheduling. *SIAM J. Comput.* 7, 1–17.
Coffman Jr, E.G., and E.N. Gilbert (1985). On the expected relative performance of list scheduling. *Oper. Res.* 33, 548–561.
Coffman Jr, E.G., and R.L. Graham (1972). Optimal scheduling for two-processor systems. *Acta Inform.* 1, 200–213.
Coffman Jr, E.G., M. Hofri and G. Weiss (1989). Scheduling stochastic jobs with a two point distribution on two parallel machines. *Probab. Engrg. Inform. Sci.* 3, 89–116.
Coffman Jr, E.G., G.S. Lueker and A.H.G. Rinnooy Kan (1988). Asymptotic methods in the probabilistic analysis of sequencing and packing heuristics. *Management Sci.* 34, 266–290.
Conway, R.W., W.L. Maxwell and L.W. Miller (1967). *Theory of Scheduling*, Addison-Wesley, Reading, MA.
Cook, S.A. (1971). The complexity of theorem-proving procedures, *Proc. 3rd Annual ACM Symp. Theory of Computing*, pp. 151–158.
Crabill, T.B., and W.L. Maxwell (1969). Single machine sequencing with random processing times and random due-dates. *Naval Res. Logist. Quart.* 16, 549–554.
Dannenbring, D.G. (1977). An evaluation of flow shop sequencing heuristics. *Management Sci.* 23, 1174–1182.
Davida, G.I., and D.J. Linton (1976). A new algorithm for the scheduling of tree structured tasks. *Proc. Conf. Inform. Sci and Syst.*, Baltimore, MD, pp. 543–548.
Davis, E., and J.M. Jaffe (1981). Algorithms for scheduling tasks on unrelated processors. *J. Assoc. Comput. Mach.* 28, 721–736.
Davis, E.W. (1966). Resource allocation in project network models – A survey. *J. Indust. Engrg.* 17, 177–188.
Davis, E.W. (1973). Project scheduling under resource constraints – Historical review and categorization of procedures. *AIIE Trans.* 5, 297–313.

Day, J., and M.P. Hottenstein (1970). Review of scheduling research. *Naval Res. Logist. Quart.* 17, 11–39.

Dempster, M.A.H., J.K. Lenstra and A.H.G. Rinnooy Kan (eds.) (1982). *Deterministic and Stochastic Scheduling*, Reidel, Dordrecht.

Dessouky, M.I., and J.S. Deogun (1981). Sequencing jobs with unequal ready times to minimize mean flow time. *SIAM J. Comput.* 10, 192–202.

Dessouky, M.I., B.J. Lageweg, J.K. Lenstra and S.L. Van de Velde (1990). Scheduling identical jobs on uniform parallel machines. *Statist. Neerlandica* 44, 115–123.

Dileepan, P., and T. Sen (1988). Bicriterion static scheduling research for a single machine. *Omega* 16, 53–59.

Dobson, G. (1984). Scheduling independent tasks on uniform processors. *SIAM J. Comput.* 13, 705–716.

Dolev, D., and M.K. Warmuth (1984). Scheduling precedence graphs of bounded height. *J. Algorithms* 5, 48–59.

Dolev, D., and M.K. Warmuth (1985a). Scheduling flat graphs. *SIAM J. Comput.* 14, 638–657.

Dolev, D., and M.K. Warmuth (1985b). Profile scheduling of opposing forests and level orders. *SIAM J. Alg. Disc. Meth.* 6, 665–687.

Du, J., and J.Y.-T. Leung (1988a). Scheduling tree-structured tasks with restricted execution times. *Inform. Process. Lett.* 28, 183–188.

Du, J., and J.Y.-T. Leung (1988b). Minimizing mean flow time with release time and deadline constraints, Technical Report, Computer Science Program, Univ. of Texas, Dallas.

Du, J., and J.Y.-T. Leung (1989). Scheduling tree-structured tasks on two processors to minimize schedule length. *SIAM J. Discrete Math.* 2, 176–196.

Du, J., and J.Y.-T. Leung (1990). Minimizing total tardiness on one machine is NP-hard. *Math. Oper. Res.* 15, 483–495.

Du, J., J.Y.-T. Leung and C.S. Wong (1989). Minimizing the number of late jobs with release time constraints, Technical Report, Computer Science Program, Univ. of Texas, Dallas.

Du, J., J.Y.-T. Leung and G.H. Young (1988). Minimizing mean flow time with release time constraint, Technical Report, Computer Science Program, Univ. of Texas, Dallas.

Du, J., J.Y.-T. Leung and G.H. Young (1991). Scheduling chain-structured tasks to minimize makespan and mean flow time. *Inform. and Comput.* 92, 219–236.

Eastman, W.L., S. Even and I.M. Isaacs (1964). Bounds for the optimal scheduling of n jobs on m processors. *Management Sci.* 11, 268–279.

Edmonds, J. (1965). Minimum partition of a matroid into independent subsets. *J. Res. Nat. Bur. Standards* 69B, 67–72.

Elmaghraby, S.E. (1968). The one-machine sequencing problem with delay costs. *J. Indust. Engrg.* 19, 105–108.

Elmaghraby, S.E., and S.H. Park (1974). Scheduling jobs on a number of identical machines. *AIIE Trans.* 6, 1–12.

Emmons, H. (1969). One-machine sequencing to minimize certain functions of job tardiness. *Oper. Res.* 17, 701–715.

Erschler, J., G. Fontan, C. Merce and F. Roubellat (1982). Applying new dominance concepts to job schedule optimization. *European J. Oper. Res.* 11, 60–66.

Erschler, J., G. Fontan, C. Merce and F. Roubellat (1983). A new dominance concept in scheduling n jobs on a single machine with ready times and due dates. *Oper. Res.* 31, 114–127.

Federgruen, A., and H. Groenevelt (1986). Preemptive scheduling of uniform machines by ordinary network flow techniques. *Management Sci.* 32, 341–349.

Fiala, T. (1983). An algorithm for the open-shop problem. *Math. Oper. Res.* 8, 100–109.

Fischetti, M., and S. Martello (1987). Worst-case analysis of the differencing method for the partition problem. *Math. Programming* 37, 117–120.

Fisher, H., and G.L. Thompson (1963). Probabilistic learning combinations of local job-shop scheduling rules, in: J.F. Muth and G.L. Thompson (eds.), *Industrial Scheduling*, Prentice-Hall, Englewood Cliffs, NJ, pp. 225–251.

Fisher, M.L. (1976). A dual algorithm for the one-machine scheduling problem. *Math. Programming* 11, 229–251.

Fisher, M.L., and A.M. Krieger (1984). Analysis of a linearization heuristic for single-machine scheduling to maximize profit. *Math. Programming* 28, 218–225.

Fisher, M.L., B.J. Lageweg, J.K. Lenstra and A.H.G. Rinnooy Kan (1983). Surrogate duality relaxation for job scheduling. *Discrete Appl. Math.* 5, 65–75.

Foley, R.D., and S. Suresh (1986). Scheduling *n* nonoverlapping jobs and two stochastic jobs in a flow shop. *Naval Res. Logist. Quart.* 33, 123–128.

Forst, F.G. (1984). A review of the static, stochastic job sequencing literature. *Opsearch* 21, 127–144.

Frederickson, G.N. (1983). Scheduling unit-time tasks with integer release times and deadlines. *Inform. Process. Lett.* 16, 171–173.

French, S. (1982). *Sequencing and Scheduling: An Introduction to the Mathematics of the Job-Shop*, Horwood, Chichester.

Frenk, J.B.G. (1988). A general framework for stochastic one-machine scheduling problems with zero release times and no partial ordering, Report 8819, Econometric Institute, Erasmus University, Rotterdam.

Frenk, J.B.G., and A.H.G. Rinnooy Kan (1986). The rate of convergence to optimality of the LPT rule. *Discrete Appl. Math.* 14, 187–197.

Frenk, J.B.G., and A.H.G. Rinnooy Kan (1987). The asymptotic optimality of the LPT rule. *Math. Oper. Res.* 12, 241–254.

Friesen, D.K. (1984). Tighter bounds for the multifit processor scheduling algorithm. *SIAM J. Comput.* 13, 170–181.

Friesen, D.K. (1987). Tighter bounds for LPT scheduling on uniform processors. *SIAM J. Comput.* 16, 554–660.

Friesen, D.K., and M.A. Langston (1983). Bounds for multifit scheduling on uniform processors. *SIAM J. Comput.* 12, 60–70.

Friesen, D.K., and M.A. Langston (1986). Evaluation of a MULTIFIT-based scheduling algorithm. *J. Algorithms* 7, 35–59.

Frostig, E. (1988). A stochastic scheduling problem with intree precedence constraints. *Oper. Res.* 36, 937–943.

Fujii, M., T. Kasami and K. Ninomiya (1969). Optimal sequencing of two equivalent processors. *SIAM J. Appl. Math.* 17, 784–789; Erratum. *SIAM J. Appl. Math.* 20 (1971) 141.

Gabow, H.N. (1982). An almost linear-time algorithm for two-processor scheduling. *J. Assoc. Comput. Mach.* 29, 766–780.

Gabow, H.N. (1988). Scheduling UET systems on two uniform processors and length two pipelines. *SIAM J. Comput.* 17, 810–829.

Gabow, H.N., and R.E. Tarjan (1985). A linear-time algorithm for a special case of disjoint set union. *J. Comput. System Sci.* 30, 209–221.

Garey, M.R. (-). Unpublished.

Garey, M.R., R.L. Graham and D.S. Johnson (1978). Performance guarantees for scheduling algorithms. *Oper. Res.* 26, 3–21.

Garey, M.R., and D.S. Johnson (1975). Complexity results for multiprocessor scheduling under resource constraints. *SIAM J. Comput.* 4, 397–411.

Garey, M.R., and D.S. Johnson (1976). Scheduling tasks with nonuniform deadlines on two processors. *J. Assoc. Comput. Mach.* 23, 461–467.

Garey, M.R., and D.S. Johnson (1977). Two-processor scheduling with start-times and deadlines. *SIAM J. Comput.* 6, 416–426.

Garey, M.R., and D.S. Johnson (1978). Strong NP-completeness results: Motivation, examples and implications. *J. Assoc. Comput. Mach.* 25, 499–508.

Garey, M.R., and D.S. Johnson (1979). *Computers and Intractability: A Guide to the Theory of NP-Completeness*, Freeman, San Francisco.

Garey, M.R., D.S. Johnson and R. Sethi (1976). The complexity of flowshop and jobshop scheduling. *Math. Oper. Res.* 1, 117–129.

Garey, M.R., D.S. Johnson, B.B. Simons and R.E. Tarjan (1981). Scheduling unit-time tasks with arbitrary release times and deadlines. *SIAM J. Comput.* 10, 256–269.

Garey, M.R., D.S. Johnson, R.E. Tarjan and M. Yannakakis (1983). Scheduling opposing forests. *SIAM J. Alg. Disc. Meth.* 4, 72–93.
Garey, M.R., R.E. Tarjan and G.T. Wilfong (1988). One-processor scheduling with symmetric earliness and tardiness penalties. *Math. Oper. Res.* 13, 330–348.
Gazmuri, P.G. (1985). Probabilistic analysis of a machine scheduling problem. *Math. Oper. Res.* 10, 328–339.
Gelders, L., and P.R. Kleindorfer (1974). Coordinating aggregate and detailed scheduling decisions in the one-machine job shop: Part I. Theory. *Oper. Res.* 22, 46–60.
Gelders, L., and P.R. Kleindorfer (1975). Coordinating aggregate and detailed scheduling in the one-machine job shop: II – Computation and structure. *Oper. Res.* 23, 312–324.
Gens, G.V., and E.V. Levner (1978). Approximative algorithms for certain universal problems in scheduling theory. *Engrg. Cybernet.* 16(6), 31–36.
Gens, G.V., and E.V. Levner (1981). Fast approximation algorithm for job sequencing with deadlines. *Discrete Appl. Math.* 3, 313–318.
Gere, W.S. (1966). Heuristics in job shop scheduling. *Management Sci.* 13, 167–190.
Giffler, B., and G.L. Thompson (1960). Algorithms for solving production-scheduling problems. *Oper. Res.* 8, 487–503.
Gilmore, P.C., and R.E. Gomory (1964). Sequencing a one-state variable machine: A solvable case of the traveling salesman problem. *Oper. Res.* 12, 655–679.
Gilmore, P.C., E.L. Lawler and D.B. Shmoys (1985). Well-solvable cases, in: Lawler, Lenstra, Rinnooy Kan & Shmoys [1985], Chapter 4.
Gonzalez, T. (1977). Optimal mean finish time preemptive schedules, Technical Report 220, Computer Science Department, Pennsylvania State University.
Gonzalez, T. (1979). A note on open shop preemptive schedules. *IEEE Trans. Comput.* C-28, 782–786.
Gonzalez, T. (1982). Unit execution time shop problems. *Math. Oper. Res.* 7, 57–66.
Gonzalez, T., O.H. Ibarra, and S. Sahni (1977). Bounds for LPT schedules on uniform processors. *SIAM J. Comput.* 6, 155–166.
Gonzalez, T., and D.B. Johnson (1980). A new algorithm for preemptive scheduling of trees. *J. Assoc. Comput. Mach.* 27, 287–312.
Gonzalez, T., E.L. Lawler and S. Sahni (1990). Optimal preemptive scheduling of two unrelated processors. *ORSA J. Comput.* 2, 219–224.
Gonzalez, T., and S. Sahni (1976). Open shop scheduling to minimize finish time. *J. Assoc. Comput. Mach.* 23, 665–679.
Gonzalez, T., and S. Sahni (1978a). Flowshop and jobshop schedules: Complexity and approximation. *Oper. Res.* 26, 36–52.
Gonzalez, T., and S. Sahni (1978b). Preemptive scheduling of uniform processor systems. *J. Assoc. Comput. Mach.* 25, 92–101.
Goyal, D.K. (1977). Non-preemptive scheduling of unequal execution time tasks on two identical processors. Technical Report CS-77-039, Computer Science Department, Washington State University, Pullman.
Goyal, S.K., and C. Sriskandarajah (1988). No-wait shop scheduling: Computational complexity and approximate algorithms. *Opsearch* 25, 220–244.
Grabowski, J. (1980). On two-machine scheduling with release dates to minimize maximum lateness. *Opsearch* 17, 133–154.
Grabowski, J. (1982). A new algorithm of solving the flow-shop problem, in: G. Feichtinger and P. Kall (eds.), *Operations Research in Progress*, Reidel, Dordrecht, pp. 57–75.
Grabowski, J., E. Skubalska and C. Smutnicki (1983). On flow shop scheduling with release and due dates to minimize maximum lateness. *J. Oper. Res. Soc.* 34, 615–620.
Graham, R.L. (1966). Bounds for certain multiprocessing anomalies. *Bell System Tech. J.* 45, 1563–1581.
Graham, R.L. (1969). Bounds on multiprocessing timing anomalies. *SIAM J. Appl. Math.* 17, 416–429.
Graham, R.L. (-). Unpublished.

Graham, R.L., E.L. Lawler, J.K. Lenstra and A.H.G. Rinnooy Kan (1979). Optimization and approximation in deterministic sequencing and scheduling: A survey. *Ann. Discrete Math.* 5, 287–326.

Graves, S.C. (1981). A review of production scheduling. *Oper. Res.* 29, 646–675.

Gupta, J.N.D., and S.S. Reddi (1978). Improved dominance conditions for the three-machine flowshop scheduling problem. *Oper. Res.* 26, 200–203.

Gupta, S.K., and J. Kyparisis (1987). Single machine scheduling research. *Omega* 15, 207–227.

Gusfield, D. (1984). Bounds for naive multiple machine scheduling with release times and deadlines. *J. Algorithms* 5, 1–6.

Hall, L.A., and D.B. Shmoys (1989). Approximation schemes for constrained scheduling problems, *Proc. 30th IEEE Symp. Foundations of Computer Science*, pp. 134–139.

Hall, L.A., and D.B. Shmoys (1992). Jackson's rule for one-machine scheduling: Making a good heuristic better. *Math. Oper. Res.* 17, 22–35.

Hariri, A.M.A., and C.N. Potts (1983). An algorithm for single machine sequencing with release dates to minimize total weighted completion time. *Discrete Appl. Math.* 5, 99–109.

Hariri, A.M.A., and C.N. Potts (1984). Algorithms for two-machine flow-shop sequencing with precedence constraints. *European J. Oper. Res.* 17, 238–248.

Haupt, R. (1989). A survey of priority rule-based scheduling. *OR Spektrum* 11, 3–16.

Hefetz, N., and I. Adiri (1982). An efficient optimal algorithm for the two-machines unit-time jobshop schedule-length problem. *Math. Oper. Res.* 7, 354–360.

Hochbaum, D.S., and D.B. Shmoys (1987). Using dual approximation algorithms for scheduling problems: Theoretical and practical results. *J. Assoc. Comput. Mach.* 34, 144–162.

Hochbaum, D.S., and D.B. Shmoys (1988). A polynomial approximation scheme for machine scheduling on uniform processors: Using the dual approximation approach. *SIAM J. Comput.* 17, 539–551.

Hodgson, S.M. (1977). A note on single machine sequencing with random processing times. *Management Sci.* 23, 1144–1146.

Horn, W.A. (1972). Single-machine job sequencing with treelike precedence ordering and linear delay penalties. *SIAM J. Appl. Math.* 23, 189–202.

Horn, W.A. (1973). Minimizing average flow time with parallel machines. *Oper. Res.* 21, 846–847.

Horn, W.A. (1974). Some simple scheduling algorithms. *Naval Res. Logist. Quart.* 21, 177–185.

Horowitz, E., and S. Sahni (1976). Exact and approximate algorithms for scheduling nonidentical processors. *J. Assoc. Comput. Mach.* 23, 317–327.

Horvath, E.C., S. Lam and R. Sethi (1977). A level algorithm for preemptive scheduling. *J. Assoc. Comput. Mach.* 24, 32–43.

Hsu, N.C. (1966). Elementary proof of Hu's theorem on isotone mappings. *Proc. Amer. Math. Soc.* 17, 111–114.

Hu, T.C. (1961). Parallel sequencing and assembly line problems. *Oper. Res.* 9, 841–848.

Ibarra, O.H., and C.E. Kim (1976). On two-processor scheduling of one- or two-unit time tasks with precedence constraints. *J. Cybernet.* 5, 87–109.

Ibarra, O.H., and C.E. Kim (1977). Heuristic algorithms for scheduling independent tasks on nonidentical processors. *J. Assoc. Comput. Mach.* 24, 280–289.

Ibarra, O.H., and C.E. Kim (1978). Approximation algorithms for certain scheduling problems. *Math. Oper. Res.* 3, 197–204.

Ignall, E., and L. Schrage (1965). Application of the branch and bound technique to some flow-shop scheduling problems. *Oper. Res.* 13, 400–412.

Jackson, J.R., (1955). Scheduling a production line to minimize maximum tardiness, Research Report 43, Management Science Research Project, Univ. of California, Los Angeles.

Jackson, J.R. (1956). An extension of Johnson's results on job lot scheduling. *Naval Res. Logist. Quart.* 3, 201–203.

Jaffe, J.M. (1980a). Efficient scheduling of tasks without full use of processor resources. *Theoret. Comput. Sci.* 12, 1–17.

Jaffe, J.M. (1980b). An analysis of preemptive multiprocessor job scheduling. *Math. Oper. Res.* 5, 415–421.

Johnson, D.S. (1983). The NP-completeness column: An ongoing guide. *J. Algorithms* 4, 189–203.

Johnson, S.M. (1954). Optimal two- and three-stage production schedules with setup times included. *Naval Res. Logist. Quart.* 1, 61–68.

Johnson, S.M. (1958). Discussion: Sequencing n jobs on two machines with arbitrary time lags. *Management Sci.* 5, 299–303.

Kao, E.P.C., and M. Queyranne (1982). On dynamic programming methods for assembly line balancing. *Oper. Res.* 30, 375–390.

Karmarkar, N., and R.M. Karp (1982). The differencing method of set partitioning, Report UCB/CSD 82/113, Computer Science Division, Univ. of California, Berkeley.

Karp, R.M. (1972). Reducibility among combinatorial problems, in: R.E. Miller, and J.W. Thatcher (eds.) (1972). *Complexity of Computer Computations*, Plenum Press, New York, pp. 85–103.

Karp, R.M. (1975). On the computational complexity of combinatorial problems. *Networks* 5, 45–68.

Kaufman, M.T. (1974). An almost-optimal algorithm for the assembly line scheduling problem. *IEEE Trans. Comput.* C-23, 1169–1174.

Kawaguchi, T., and S. Kyan (1986). Worst case bound of an LRF schedule for the mean weighted flow-time problem. *SIAM J. Comput.* 15, 1119–1129.

Kawaguchi, T., and S. Kyan (1988). Deterministic scheduling in computer systems: A survey. *J. Oper. Res. Soc. Japan* 31, 190–217.

Khachiyan, L.G. (1979). A polynomial algorithm in linear programming. *Soviet Math. Dokl.* 20, 191–194.

Kise, H., T. Ibaraki, and H. Mine (1978). A solvable case of the one-machine scheduling problem with ready and due times. *Oper. Res.* 26, 121–126.

Kise, H., T. Ibaraki, and H. Mine (1979). Performance analysis of six approximation algorithms for the one-machine maximum lateness scheduling problem with ready times. *J. Oper. Res. Soc. Japan* 22, 205–224.

Kohler, W.H., and K. Steiglitz (1975). Exact, approximate and guaranteed accuracy algorithms for the flow-shop problem $n/2/F/\bar{F}$. *J. Assoc. Comput. Mach.* 22, 106–114.

Kumar, P.R., and J. Walrand (1985). Individually optimal routing in parallel systems. *J. Appl. Probab.* 22, 989–995.

Kunde, M. (1976). Beste Schranken beim LP-Scheduling, Bericht 7603, Institut für Informatik und Praktische Mathematik, Universität Kiel.

Kunde, M. (1981). Nonpreemptive LP-scheduling on homogeneous multiprocessor systems. *SIAM J. Comput.* 10, 151–173.

Labetoulle, J., E.L. Lawler, J.K. Lenstra and A.H.G. Rinnooy Kan (1984). Preemptive scheduling of uniform machines subject to release dates, in: Pulleyblank [1984], pp. 245–261.

Lageweg, B.J. (1984). Private communication.

Lageweg, B.J. (-). Unpublished.

Lageweg, B.J., E.L. Lawler, J.K. Lenstra and A.H.G. Rinnooy Kan (1981). Computer aided complexity classification of deterministic scheduling problems, Report BW 138, Centre for Mathematics and Computer Science, Amsterdam.

Lageweg, B.J., J.K. Lenstra, E.L. Lawler and A.H.G. Rinnooy Kan (1982). Computer-aided complexity classification of combinatorial problems. *Commun. ACM* 25, 817–822.

Lageweg, B.J., J.K. Lenstra and A.H.G. Rinnooy Kan (1976). Minimizing maximum lateness on one machine: computational experience and some applications. *Statist. Neerlandica* 30, 25–41.

Lageweg, B.J., J.K. Lenstra and A.H.G. Rinnooy Kan (1977). Job-shop scheduling by implicit enumeration. *Management Sci.* 24, 441–450.

Lageweg, B.J., J.K. Lenstra and A.H.G. Rinnooy Kan (1978). A general bounding scheme for the permutation flow-shop problem. *Oper. Res.* 26, 53–67.

Lam, S., and R. Sethi (1977). Worst case analysis of two scheduling algorithms. *SIAM J. Comput.* 6, 518–536.

Larson, R.E., M.I. Dessouky and R.E. Devor (1985). A forward-backward procedure for the single machine problem to minimize maximum lateness. *IIE Trans.* 17, 252–260.

Lawler, E.L. (1973). Optimal sequencing of a single machine subject to precedence constraints. *Management Sci.* 19, 544–546.

Lawler, E.L. (1976a). Sequencing to minimize the weighted number of tardy jobs. *RAIRO Rech. Opér.* 10(5) Suppl., 27–33.

Lawler, E.L. (1976b). *Combinatorial Optimization: Networks and Matroids*, Holt, Rinehart and Winston, New York.

Lawler, E.L. (1977). A 'pseudopolynomial' algorithm for sequencing jobs to minimize total tardiness. *Ann. Discrete Math.* 1, 331–342.

Lawler, E.L. (1978a). Sequencing jobs to minimize total weighted completion time subject to precedence constraints. *Ann. Discrete Math.* 2, 75–90.

Lawler, E.L. (1978b). Sequencing problems with series parallel precedence constraints, Unpublished manuscript.

Lawler, E.L. (1979a). Preemptive scheduling of uniform parallel machines to minimize the weighted number of late jobs, Report BW 105, Centre for Mathematics and Computer Science, Amsterdam.

Lawler, E.L. (1979b). Efficient implementation of dynamic programming algorithms for sequencing problems, Report BW 106, Centre for Mathematics and Computer Science, Amsterdam.

Lawler, E.L. (1982a). Preemptive scheduling of precedence-constrained jobs on parallel machines, in: Dempster, Lenstra & Rinnooy Kan [1982], pp. 101–123.

Lawler, E.L. (1982b). Scheduling a single machine to minimize the number of late jobs, Preprint, Computer Science Division, Univ. of California, Berkeley.

Lawler, E.L. (1982c). A fully polynomial approximation scheme for the total tardiness problem. *Oper. Res. Lett.* 1, 207–208.

Lawler, E.L. (1983). Recent results in the theory of machine scheduling, in: A. Bachem, M. Grötschel and B. Korte (eds.), *Mathematical Programming: The State of the Art – Bonn 1982*, Springer, Berlin, 202–234.

Lawler, E.L. (-). Unpublished.

Lawler, E.L., and J. Labetoulle (1978). On preemptive scheduling of unrelated parallel processors by linear programming. *J. Assoc. Comput. Mach.* 25, 612–619.

Lawler, E.L., and J.K. Lenstra (1982). Machine scheduling with precedence constraints, in: I. Rival (ed.), *Ordered Sets*, Reidel, Dordrecht, pp. 655–675.

Lawler, E.L., J.K. Lenstra and A.H.G. Rinnooy Kan (1981). Minimizing maximum lateness in a two-machine open shop. *Math. Oper. Res.* 6, 153–158; Erratum. *Math. Oper. Res.* 7 (1982) 635.

Lawler, E.L., J.K. Lenstra and A.H.G. Rinnooy Kan (1982). Recent developments in deterministic sequencing and scheduling: A survey, in: Dempster, Lenstra & Rinnooy Kan [1982], pp. 35–73.

Lawler, E.L., J.K. Lenstra, A.H.G. Rinnooy Kan and D.B. Shmoys (eds.) (1985). *The Traveling Salesman Problem: A Guided Tour of Combinatorial Optimization*, Wiley, Chichester.

Lawler, E.L., J.K. Lenstra, A.H.G. Rinnooy Kan and D.B. Shmoys (1989). Sequencing and scheduling: Algorithms and complexity, Report BS-R8909, Centre for Mathematics and Computer Science, Amsterdam.

Lawler, E.L., and C.U. Martel (1982). Computing maximal 'polymatroidal' network flows. *Math. Oper. Res.* 7, 334–347.

Lawler, E.L., and C.U. Martel (1989). Preemptive scheduling of two uniform machines to minimize the number of late jobs. *Oper. Res.* 37, 314–318.

Lawler, E.L., and J.M. Moore (1969). A functional equation and its application to resource allocation and sequencing problems. *Management Sci.* 16, 77–84.

Lenstra, J.K. (1977). Sequencing by enumerative methods, Mathematical Centre Tracts 69, Centre for Mathematics and Computer Science, Amsterdam.

Lenstra, J.K. (-). Unpublished.

Lenstra, J.K., and A.H.G. Rinnooy Kan (1978). Complexity of scheduling under precedence constraints. *Oper. Res.* 26, 22–35.

Lenstra, J.K., and A.H.G. Rinnooy Kan (1979). Computational complexity of discrete optimization problems. *Ann. Discrete Math.* 4, 121–140.
Lenstra, J.K., and A.H.G. Rinnooy Kan (1980). Complexity results for scheduling chains on a single machine. *European J. Oper. Res.* 4, 270–275.
Lenstra, J.K., and A.H.G. Rinnooy Kan (1984). New directions in scheduling theory. *Oper. Res. Lett.* 2, 255–259.
Lenstra, J.K., and A.H.G. Rinnooy Kan (1985). Sequencing and scheduling, in: O'hEigeartaigh, Lenstra & Rinnooy Kan [1985], pp. 164–189.
Lenstra, J.K., A.H.G. Rinnooy Kan and P. Brucker (1977). Complexity of machine scheduling problems. *Ann. Discrete Math.* 1, 343–362.
Lenstra, J.K., D.B. Shmoys and E. Tardos (1990). Approximation algorithms for scheduling unrelated parallel machines. *Math. Programming* 46, 259–271.
Leung, J.Y.-T. (1991). Bin packing with restricted piece sizes. *Inform. Process. Lett.* 31, 145–149.
Leung, J.Y.-T., and G.H. Young (1989). Minimizing total tardiness on a single machine with precedence constraints, Technical Report, Computer Science Program, Univ. of Texas, Dallas.
Levin, L.A. (1973). Universal sequential search problems. *Problemy Peredachi Informatsii* 9, 115–116. English translation: *Problems Inform. Transmission* 9 (1975) 265–266.
Liu, C.Y., and R.L. Bulfin (1985). On the complexity of preemptive open-shop scheduling problems. *Oper. Res. Lett.* 4, 71–74.
Liu, J.W.S., and C.L. Liu (1974a). Bounds on scheduling algorithms for heterogeneous computing systems, in: J.L. Rosenfeld (ed.), *Information Processing 74*, North-Holland, Amsterdam, pp. 349–353.
Liu, J.W.S., and C.L. Liu (1974b). Bounds on scheduling algorithms for heterogeneous computing systems, Technical Report UIUCDCS-R-74-632, Department of Computer Science, Univ. of Illinois at Urbana-Champaign, 68 pp.
Liu, J.W.S., and C.L. Liu (1974c). Performance analysis of heterogeneous multi-processor computing systems, in: E. Gelenbe and R. Mahl (eds.), *Computer Architectures and Networks*, North-Holland, Amsterdam, pp. 331–343.
Loulou, R. (1984). Tight bounds and probabilistic analysis of two heuristics for parallel processor scheduling. *Math. Oper. Res.* 9, 142–150.
Marcotte, O., and L.E. Trotter Jr (1984). An application of matroid polyhedral theory to unit-execution time, tree-precedence constrained job scheduling, in: Pulleyblank [1984], pp. 263–271.
Martel, C.U. (1982). Preemptive scheduling with release times, deadlines and due times. *J. Assoc. Comput. Mach.* 29, 812–829.
Matsuo, H., C.J. Suh and R.S. Sullivan (1988). A controlled search simulated annealing method for the general jobshop scheduling problem, Working Paper 03-44-88, Graduate School of Business, Univ. of Texas, Austin.
Maxwell, W.L. (1970). On sequencing n jobs on one machine to minimize the number of late jobs. *Management Sci.* 16, 295–297.
McCormick, S.T., and M.L. Pinedo (1989). Scheduling n independent jobs on m uniform machines with both flow time and makespan objectives: A parametric analysis, Department of Industrial Engineering and Operations Research, Columbia University, New York.
McMahon, G.B. (1969). Optimal production schedules for flow shops. *Canad. Oper. Res. Soc. J.* 7, 141–151.
McMahon, G.B. (1971). A study of algorithms for industrial scheduling problems, Ph.D. Thesis, Univ. of New South Wales, Kensington.
McMahon, G.B., and M. Florian (1975). On scheduling with ready times and due dates to minimize maximum lateness. *Oper. Res.* 23, 475–482.
McNaughton, R. (1959). Scheduling with deadlines and loss functions. *Management Sci.* 6, 1–12.
Meilijson, I., and A. Tamir (1984). Minimizing flow time on parallel identical processors with variable unit processing time. *Oper. Res.* 32, 440–446.
Mitten, L.G. (1958). Sequencing n jobs on two machines with arbitrary time lags. *Management Sci.* 5, 293–298.

Möhring, R.H. (1983). Scheduling problems with a singular solution. *Ann. Discrete Math.* 16, 225–239.

Möhring, R.H. (1984). Minimizing costs of resource requirements in project networks subject to a fixed completion time. *Oper. Res.* 32, 89–120.

Möhring, R.H. (1989). Computationally tractable classes of ordered sets, in: I. Rival (ed.), *Algorithms and Order*, Kluwer Academic, Dordrecht, pp. 105–193.

Möhring, R.H., and F.J. Radermacher (1985a). Generalized results on the polynomiality of certain weighted sum scheduling problems. *Methods Oper. Res.* 49, 405–417.

Möhring, R.H., and F.J. Radermacher (1985b). An introduction to stochastic scheduling problems, in: K. Neumann and D. Pallaschke (eds.), *Contributions to Operations Research*, Lecture Notes in Economics and Mathematical Systems, Vol. 240, Springer, Berlin, pp. 72–130.

Möhring, R.H., F.J. Radermacher and G. Weiss (1984). Stochastic scheduling problems I: General strategies. *Z. Oper. Res.* 28, 193–260.

Möhring, R.H., F.J. Radermacher and G. Weiss (1985). Stochastic scheduling problems II: Set strategies. *Z. Oper. Res.* 29, 65–104.

Monma, C.L. (1979). The two-machine maximum flow-time problem with series-parallel precedence constraints: An algorithm and extensions. *Oper. Res.* 27, 792–798.

Monma, C.L. (1980). Sequencing to minimize the maximum job cost. *Oper. Res.* 28, 942–951.

Monma, C.L. (1981). Sequencing with general precedence constraints. *Discrete Appl. Math.* 3, 137–150.

Monma, C.L. (1982). Linear-time algorithms for scheduling on parallel processors. *Oper. Res.* 30, 116–124.

Monma, C.L., and A.H.G. Rinnooy Kan (1983). A concise survey of efficiently solvable special cases of the permutation flow-shop problem. *RAIRO Rech. Opér.* 17, 105–119.

Monma, C.L., and J.B. Sidney (1979). Sequencing with series-parallel precedence constraints. *Math. Oper. Res.* 4, 215–224.

Monma, C.L., and J.B. Sidney (1987). Optimal sequencing via modular decomposition: Characterizations of sequencing functions. *Math. Oper. Res.* 12, 22–31.

Moore, J.M. (1968). An n job, one machine sequencing algorithm for minimizing the number of late jobs. *Management Sci.* 15, 102–109.

Morrison, J.F. (1988). A note on LPT scheduling. *Oper. Res. Lett.* 7, 77–79.

Muller, J.H., and J. Spinrad (1989). Incremental modular decomposition. *J. Assoc. Comput. Mach.* 36, 1–19.

Muntz, R.R., and E.G. Coffman Jr (1969). Optimal preemptive scheduling on two-processor systems. *IEEE Trans. Comput.* C-18, 1014–1020.

Muntz, R.R., and E.G. Coffman Jr (1970). Preemptive scheduling of real time tasks on multiprocessor systems. *J. Assoc. Comput. Mach.* 17, 324–338.

Nabeshima, I. (1963). Sequencing on two machines with start lag and stop lag. *J. Oper. Res. Soc. Japan* 5, 97–101.

Nakajima, K., J.Y.-T. Leung and S.L. Hakimi (1981). Optimal two processor scheduling of tree precedence constrained tasks with two execution times. *Performance Evaluation* 1, 320–330.

Nawaz, M., E.E. Enscore Jr and I. Ham (1983). A heuristic algorithm for the m-machine, n-job flow-shop sequencing problem. *Omega* 11, 91–95.

Németi, L. (1964). Das Reihenfolgeproblem in der Fertigungsprogrammierung und Linearplanung mit logischen Bedingungen. *Mathematica (Cluj)* 6, 87–99.

Nowicki, E., and C. Smutnicki (1987). On lower bounds on the minimum maximum lateness on one machine subject to release date. *Opsearch* 24, 106–110.

Nowicki, E., and S. Zdrzalka (1986). A note on minimizing maximum lateness in a one-machine sequencing problem with release dates. *European J. Oper. Res.* 23, 266–267.

O'hEigeartaigh, M., J.K. Lenstra and A.H.G. Rinnooy Kan (eds.) (1985). *Combinatorial Optimization: Annotated Bibliographies*, Wiley, Chichester.

Osman, I.H., and C.N. Potts (1989). Simulated annealing for permutation flow-shop scheduling. *Omega* 17, 551–557.

Palmer, D.S. (1965). Sequencing jobs through a multi-stage process in the minimum total time – A quick method of obtaining a near optimum. *Oper. Res. Quart.* 16, 101–107.
Panwalkar, S.S., and W. Iskander (1977). A survey of scheduling rules. *Oper. Res.* 25, 45–61.
Papadimitriou, C.H., and P.C. Kannelakis (1980). Flowshop scheduling with limited temporary storage. *J. Assoc. Comput. Mach.* 27, 533–549.
Papadimitriou, C.H., and M. Yannakakis (1979). Scheduling interval-ordered tasks. *SIAM J. Comput.* 8, 405–409.
Papadimitriou, C.H., and M. Yannakakis (1990). Towards an architecture-independent analysis of parallel algorithms. *SIAM J. Comput.* 19, 322–328.
Piehler, J. (1960). Ein Beitrag zum Reihenfolgeproblem. *Unternehmensforsch.* 4, 138–142.
Pinedo, M.L. (1981). A note on the two machine job shop with exponential processing times. *Naval Res. Logist. Quart.* 28, 693–696.
Pinedo, M.L. (1982). Minimizing the expected makespan in stochastic flow shops. *Oper. Res.* 30, 148–162.
Pinedo, M.L. (1983). Stochastic scheduling with release dates and due dates. *Oper. Res.* 31, 559–572.
Pinedo, M.L. (1984). Optimal policies in stochastic shop scheduling. *Ann. Oper. Res.* 1, 305–329.
Pinedo, M.L., and L. Schrage (1982). Stochastic shop scheduling: A survey, in: Dempster, Lenstra & Rinnooy Kan [1982], pp. 181–196.
Pinedo, M.L., and E. Rammouz (1988). A note on stochastic scheduling on a single machine subject to breakdown and repair. *Probab. Engrg. Inform. Sci.* 2, 41–49.
Pinedo, M.L., and G. Weiss (1984). Scheduling jobs with exponentially distributed processing times on two machines with resource constraints. *Management Sci.* 30, 883–889.
Pinedo, M.L., and G. Weiss (1985). Scheduling jobs with exponentially distributed processing times and intree precedence constraints on two parallel machines. *Oper. Res.* 33, 1381–1388.
Pinedo, M.L., and G. Weiss (1987). The 'largest variance first' policy in some stochastic scheduling problems. *Oper. Res.* 35, 884–891.
Posner, M.E. (1985). Minimizing weighted completion times with deadlines. *Oper. Res.* 33, 562–574.
Potts, C.N. (1980a). An adaptive branching rule for the permutation flow-shop problem. *European J. Oper. Res.* 5, 19–25.
Potts, C.N. (1980b). Analysis of a heuristic for one machine sequencing with release dates and delivery times. *Oper. Res.* 28, 1436–1441.
Potts, C.N. (1980c). An algorithm for the single machine sequencing problem with precedence constraints. *Math. Programming Study* 13, 78–87.
Potts, C.N. (1985a). Analysis of a linear programming heuristic for scheduling unrelated parallel machines. *Discrete Appl. Math.* 10, 155–164.
Potts, C.N. (1985b). Analysis of heuristics for two-machine flow-shop sequencing subject to release dates. *Math. Oper. Res.* 10, 576–584.
Potts, C.N. (1985c). A Lagrangean based branch and bound algorithm for single machine sequencing with precedence constraints to minimize total weighted completion time. *Management Sci.* 31, 1300–1311.
Potts, C.N., and L.N. Van Wassenhove (1982). A decomposition algorithm for the single machine total tardiness problem. *Oper. Res. Lett.* 1, 177–181.
Potts, C.N., and L.N. Van Wassenhove (1983). An algorithm for single machine sequencing with deadlines to minimize total weighted completion time. *European J. Oper. Res.* 12, 379–387.
Potts, C.N., and L.N. Van Wassenhove (1985). A branch and bound algorithm for the total weighted tardiness problem. *Oper. Res.* 33, 363–377.
Potts, C.N., and L.N. Van Wassenhove (1987). Dynamic programming and decomposition approaches for the single machine total tardiness problem. *European J. Oper. Res.* 32, 405–414.
Potts, C.N., and L.N. Van Wassenhove (1988). Algorithms for scheduling a single machine to minimize the weighted number of late jobs. *Management Sci.* 34, 843–858.
Pulleyblank W.R. (ed.) (1984). *Progress in Combinatorial Optimization*, Academic Press, New York.

Rachamadugu, R.M.V. (1987). A note on the weighted tardiness problem. *Oper. Res.* 35, 450–452.
Radermacher, F.J. (1985/6). Scheduling of project networks. *Ann. Oper. Res.* 4, 227–252.
Raghavachari, M. (1988). Scheduling problems with non-regular penalty functions: A review. *Opsearch* 25, 144–164.
Rayward-Smith, V.J. (1987a). UET scheduling with unit interprocessor communication delays. *Discrete Appl. Math.* 18, 55–71.
Rayward-Smith, V.J. (1987b). The complexity of preemptive scheduling given interprocessor communication delays. *Inform. Process. Lett.* 25, 123–125.
Reddi, S.S., and C.V. Ramamoorthy (1972). On the flow-shop sequencing problem with no wait in process. *Oper. Res. Quart.* 23, 323–331.
Righter, R., (1988). Job scheduling to minimize expected weighted flowtime on uniform processors. *Syst. and Control Lett.* 10, 211–216.
Rinaldi, G., and A. Sassano (1977). On a job scheduling problem with different ready times: Some properties and a new algorithm to determine the optimal solution, Report R.77-24, Istituto di Automatica, Univ. di Roma.
Rinnooy Kan, A.H.G. (1976). *Machine Scheduling Problems: Classification, Complexity and Computations*, Nijhoff, The Hague.
Rinnooy Kan, A.H.G., B.J. Lageweg and J.K. Lenstra (1975). Minimizing total costs in one-machine scheduling. *Oper. Res.* 23, 908–927.
Röck, H. (1984a). The three-machine no-wait flow shop problem is NP-complete. *J. Assoc. Comput. Mach.* 31, 336–345.
Röck, H. (1984b). Some new results in flow shop scheduling. *Z. Oper. Res.* 28, 1–16.
Röck, H., and G. Schmidt (1983). Machine aggregation heuristics in shop scheduling. *Methods Oper. Res.* 45, 303–314.
Rosenfeld, P. (-). Unpublished.
Rothkopf, M.H. (1966). Scheduling independent tasks on parallel processors. *Management Sci.* 12, 437–447.
Roy, B., and B. Sussmann (1964). Les problèmes d'ordonnancement avec contraintes disjonctives, Note DS no. 9 bis, SEMA, Montrouge.
Sahni, S. (1976). Algorithms for scheduling independent tasks. *J. Assoc. Comput. Mach.* 23, 116–127.
Sahni, S., and Y. Cho (1979a). Complexity of scheduling jobs with no wait in process. *Math. Oper. Res.* 4, 448–457.
Sahni, S., and Y. Cho (1979b). Nearly on line scheduling of a uniform processor system with release times. *SIAM J. Comput.* 8, 275–285.
Sahni, S., and Y. Cho (1980). Scheduling independent tasks with due times on a uniform processor system. *J. Assoc. Comput. Mach.* 27, 550–563.
Sarin, S.C., S. Ahn and A.B. Bishop (1988). An improved branching scheme for the branch and bound procedure of scheduling n jobs on m machines to minimize total weighted flowtime. *Internat. J. Prod. Res.* 26, 1183–1191.
Schmidt, G. (1983). Preemptive scheduling on identical processors with time dependent availabilities, Bericht 83-4, Fachbereich 20 Informatik, Technische Universität Berlin.
Schrage, L. (1970). Solving resource-constrained network problems by implicit enumeration – nonpreemptive case. *Oper. Res.* 18, 263–278.
Schrage, L., and K.R. Baker (1978). Dynamic programming solution of sequencing problems with precedence constraints. *Oper. Res.* 26, 444–449.
Sethi, R. (1976a). Algorithms for minimal-length schedules, in: Coffman [1976], pp. 51–99.
Sethi, R. (1976b). Scheduling graphs on two processors. *SIAM J. Comput.* 5, 73–82.
Sethi, R. (1977). On the complexity of mean flow time scheduling, *Math. Oper. Res.* 2, 320–330.
Sevastyanov, S.V. (1975). On an asymptotic approach to certain problems of scheduling theory (in Russian). *Upravlyaemye Systemy* 14, 40–51.
Sevastyanov, S.V. (1980). Approximation algorithms for Johnson's problem and for the summation of vectors (in Russian), *Upravlyaemye Systemy* 20, 64–73.

Shmoys, D.B., and É. Tardos (1993). Computational complexity of combinatorial problems, in: R.L. Graham, M. Grötschel, and L. Lovász (eds.), *Handbook in Combinatorics*, North-Holland, Amsterdam.

Shwimer, J. (1972). On the N-jobs, one-machine, sequence-independent scheduling problem with tardiness penalties: A branch-and-bound solution. *Management Sci.* 18B, 301–313.

Sidney, J.B. (1973). An extension of Moore's due date algorithm, in: S.E. Elmaghraby (ed.), *Symposium on the Theory of Scheduling and its Applications*, Lecture Notes in Economics and Mathematical Systems, Vol. 86, Springer, Berlin, pp. 393–398.

Sidney, J.B. (1975). Decomposition algorithms for single-machine sequencing with precedence relations and deferral costs. *Oper. Res.* 23, 283–298.

Sidney, J.B. (1979). The two-machine maximum flow time problem with series parallel precedence relations. *Oper. Res.* 27, 782–791.

Sidney, J.B. (1981). A decomposition algorithm for sequencing with general precedence constraints. *Math. Oper. Res.* 6, 190–204.

Sidney, J.B., and G. Steiner (1986). Optimal sequencing by modular decomposition: Polynomial algorithms. *Oper. Res.* 34, 606–612.

Simons, B. (1978). A fast algorithm for single processor scheduling, *Proc. 19th Ann. Symp. Foundations of Computer Science*, pp. 246–252.

Simons, B. (1983). Multiprocessor scheduling of unit-time jobs with arbitrary release times and deadlines. *SIAM J. Comput.* 12, 294–299.

Simons, B., and M. Warmuth (1989). A fast algorithm for multiprocessor scheduling of unit-length jobs. *SIAM J. Comput.* 18, 690–710.

Smith, M.L., S.S. Panwalkar and R.A. Dudek (1975). Flow shop sequencing with ordered processing time matrices. *Management Sci.* 21, 544–549.

Smith, M.L., S.S. Panwalkar and R.A. Dudek (1976). Flow shop sequencing problem with ordered processing time matrices: A general case. *Naval Res. Logist. Quart.* 23, 481–486.

Smith, W.E. (1956). Various optimizers for single-stage production. *Naval Res. Logist. Quart.* 3, 59–66.

Stockmeyer, L.J. (1992). Computational complexity, in: E.G. Coffman Jr, J.K. Lenstra and A.H.G. Rinnooy Kan (eds.), *Handbooks in Operations Research and Management Science; Vol. 3: Computing*, North-Holland, Amsterdam, Chapter 9, pp. 455–517.

Szwarc, W. (1968). On some sequencing problems. *Naval Res. Logist. Quart.* 15, 127–155.

Szwarc, W. (1971). Elimination methods in the $m \times n$ sequencing problem. *Naval Res. Logist. Quart.* 18, 295–305.

Szwarc, W. (1973). Optimal elimination methods in the $m \times n$ sequencing problem. *Oper. Res.* 21, 1250–1259.

Szwarc, W. (1978). Dominance conditions for the three-machine flow-shop problem. *Oper. Res.* 26, 203–206.

Talbot, F.B., and J.H. Patterson (1978). An efficient integer programming algorithm with network cuts for solving resource-constrained scheduling problems. *Management Sci.* 24, 1163–1174.

Turner, S., and D. Booth (1987). Comparison of heuristics for flow shop sequencing. *Omega* 15, 75–78.

Ullman, J.D. (1975). NP-Complete scheduling problems. *J. Comput. System Sci.* 10, 384–393.

Ullman, J.D. (1976). Complexity of sequencing problems, in: Coffman [1976], pp. 139–164.

Van de Velde, S.L., (1990). Minimizing total completion time in the two-machine flow shop by Lagrangian relaxation. *Ann. Oper. Res.* 26, 257–268.

Van Laarhoven, P.J.M., E.H.L. Aarts and J.K. Lenstra (1992). Job shop scheduling by simulated annealing. *Oper. Res.* 40, 113–125.

Villarreal, F.J., and R.L. Bulfin (1983). Scheduling a single machine to minimize the weighted number of tardy jobs. *AIIE Trans.* 15, 337–343.

Weber, R.R. (1979). The interchangeability of $\cdot/M/1$ queues in series. *J. Appl. Probab.* 16, 690–695.

Weber, R.R., P. Varaiya and J. Walrand (1986). Scheduling jobs with stochastically ordered processing times on parallel machines to minimize expected flowtime. *J. Appl. Probab.* 23, 841–847.

Weiss, G. (1982). Multiserver stochastic scheduling, in: Dempster, Lenstra & Rinnooy Kan [1982], pp. 157–179.

Weiss, G., and M.L. Pinedo (1980). Scheduling tasks with exponential service times on non-identical processors to minimize various cost functions. *J. Appl. Probab.* 17, 187–202.

Wie, S.-H., and M.L. Pinedo (1986). On minimizing the expected makespan and flow time in stochastic flow shops with blocking. *Math. Oper. Res.* 11, 336–342.

Wismer, D.A. (1972). Solution of the flowshop-scheduling problem with no intermediate queues. *Oper. Res.* 20, 689–697.

Yue, M. (1990). On the exact upper bound for the multifit processor scheduling algorithm. *Ann. Oper. Res.* 24, 233–259.

Zdrzalka, S., and J. Grabowski (1989). An algorithm for single machine sequencing with release dates to minimize maximum cost. *Discrete Appl. Math.* 23, 73–89.

S.C. Graves et al., Eds., *Handbooks in OR & MS, Vol. 4*

Chapter 10

Hierarchical Production Planning

*Gabriel R. Bitran**
Sloan School of Management, Massachusetts Institute of Technology, Cambridge, MA 02139, U.S.A.

Devanath Tirupati
Department of Management, University of Texas, Austin, TX 78712, U.S.A.

1. Introduction

In general terms, production may be defined as the process of converting raw materials into finished products. Manufacturing systems are typically composed of large numbers of components which have to be managed effectively in order to deliver the final products in right quantities, on time and at an appropriate cost. In systems characterized by multiple products, several plants and warehouses, a wide variety of equipment and operations, production management encompasses a large number of decisions that affect several organizational echelons. To understand the role of Management Science models in supporting those decisions, it is useful to classify them according to the taxonomy proposed by Anthony [1965]. He classifies decisions into three categories: strategic planning, tactical planning and operations control.

Strategic planning decisions are mostly concerned with the establishment of managerial policies and the development of resources to satisfy external requirements in a manner that is consistent with the organizational goals. In the area of production management these decisions relate to the design of production facilities and include the following: (i) location and sizing of new plants, (ii) acquisition of new equipment, (iii) selection of new product lines, and (iv) design of logistic systems.

These decisions are very important because, to a great extent, they define the competitive position of the firm, its growth rate, and eventually, determine its success or failure. Also these decisions, which are made at fairly high managerial levels, involve large investments, have long term implications and are affected by both external and internal information. Thus, any model-based system to support these decisions should have a broad scope, long planning horizon, and recognize the impact of uncertainties and risk attitudes.

*This research has been partially supported by the Leaders for Manufacturing Program.

Tactical planning decisions focus on the resource utilization process. At this stage, after decisions have been made regarding physical facilities, the basic problem to be resolved is the allocation of resources such as capacity, work force availability, storage and distribution resources. Typical decisions in this category include utilization of regular and overtime labor, allocation of capacity to product families, accumulation of seasonal inventories, definition of distribution channels, and selection of transportation alternatives. These decisions involve a medium range planning horizon, and the aggregation of items into product families. In the literature, models addressing these issues are classified as aggregate planning models.

Operations control. Decisions in this category deal with day to day operational and scheduling problems which require complete disaggregation of the information generated at higher levels. Typical decisions at this level include the following: (i) production sequencing and lot sizing at the item level, (ii) assignment of customer orders to individual machines, (iii) inventory accounting and inventory control activities, (iv) dispatching, expediting and processing orders, and (v) vehicle scheduling.

The three types of decisions identified in Anthony's framework – strategic planning, tactical planning and operational control – differ markedly on several dimensions which have important implications in developing a solution approach to address production planning and scheduling problems. Table 1.1,

Table 1.1
Differentiation factors of the three decision categories

Factor	Strategic planning	Management control (tactical planning)	Operational control
Purpose	Management of change, resource acquisition	Resource utilization	Execution, evaluation, and control
Implementation instruments	Policies, objectives, capital investments	Budgets	Procedures, reports
Planning horizon	Long	Medium	Short
Scope	Broad, corporate level	Medium, plant level	Narrow, job shop level
Level of management involvement	Top	Middle	Low
Frequency of replanning	Low	Medium	High
Source of information	Largely external	External and internal	Largely internal
Level of aggregation	Largely aggregated	Moderately aggregated	Largely detailed
Required accuracy	Low	Medium	High
Degree of uncertainty	High	Medium	Low
Degree or risk	High	Medium	Low

reproduced from Hax & Candea [1984], summarizes these differences and contrasts the characteristics of the decisions in these three classes. The interdependence among these classes of decisions is very strong and therefore an integrated approach is required to minimize suboptimization. The development of integrated decision models that deal with all the decisions simultaneously, while attractive in principle, has severe drawbacks. First, these models tend to be very large, and in most practical situations, it would be very difficult, if not impossible, to obtain optimal solutions with reasonable effort. Second, even if computational power and methodological capabilities would permit solution of a large detailed model, the approach is inappropriate because it would not be responsive to the management needs at each level of the organization, and would prevent interaction between models and managers at each organization echelon.

The hierarchical approach to production planning and scheduling recognizes these differences. In this framework, the decisions are decomposed into subproblems, which in some way, within the context of the organizational hierarchy, link the higher level decisions with those of lower level in an effective manner. Decisions that are made at higher level impose constraints on the lower level decisions. In turn, detailed decisions provide the necessary feedback to evaluate the quality of aggregate decision making.

Hierarchical planning provides a framework that has application beyond the areas of production planning and operations management. For example, Winkofsky, Baker & Sweeny [1981] consider this approach in the management of research and development resources. Ruefli & Storbeck [1984] examine hierarchical decision processes in a nonproduction context. In a recent paper, Geoffrion [1987] suggests a hierarchical approach to structured modeling. The aim of structured modeling is to provide a formal mathematical framework and computer based environment for conceiving, representing and manipulating a wide variety of models. The framework of structured modeling uses a hierarchically organized, partitioned, and attributed acyclic graph to represent the structure of a model.

The hierarchical approach to production planning is not a new concept. Early motivation for this approach can be found in Holt, Modigliani, Muth & Simon [1960] and Winters [1962]. However, in this chapter, we focus on recent developments and describe applications of this approach to resolve production planning and scheduling problems. It should also be recognized that a number of other approaches have been proposed to address these problems and are described elsewhere in this handbook. For example, Chapter 7 provides an introduction to production planning, and Chapter 9 is devoted to scheduling. Mathematical programming models and methods are discussed in Chapter 8, Materials Requirement Planning is described in Chapter 11, and Just in Time philosophy and Kanban systems are described in Chapter 12.

This chapter is organized as follows. In the following section we provide the basic ingredients of Hierarchical Production Planning (HPP) systems and describe, in detail, models for single and multi-stage systems. This section (Section 2.2) also contains a discussion of some important issues related to aggregation and disaggregation in hierarchical systems. In Section 3 we describe the role of feedback mechanisms in HPP and discuss two different interpretations of this term. Section 4 is devoted to issues related to uncertainties and the role of stochastic programming models in HPP systems. Finally, we provide some concluding remarks in Section 5.

2. HPP systems

Production planning and scheduling in multiproduct systems has received considerable attention in the operations research literature. The focus of most of this work has been on the analysis of individual components of the overall problem – facilities planning, aggregate capacity planning, inventory control, and detailed scheduling. There are few notable exceptions that provide an integrated solution to these problems. The works of Manne [1958], Dzielinski & Gomory [1965], Lasdon & Terjung [1971] and Zangwill [1966] can be interpreted as efforts to integrate decisions in production planning and scheduling. In this approach, a single detailed model (monolithic formulation) is formulated to determine optimal planning and scheduling decisions. For a detailed discussion of these methods, the reader is referred to Chapter 8 of this volume.

In contrast, in the hierarchical approach to production planning and control the detailed monolithic formulation is replaced by a sequence of models that are consistent with a hierarchy of decisions that have to be made. Aggregate (strategic and tactical) decisions are made first and impose constraints within which more detailed (operational) decisions are made. In turn, the detailed decisions provide the feedback to evaluate the quality of the aggregate decisions. Figure 2.1, from Meal [1984], illustrates the decision hierarchy in the context of production planning and scheduling. Decisions at the higher levels of the hierarchy are invariably based on aggregate models. The success of the hierarchical approach depends, to a large extent, on the consistency between the aggregation and disaggregation procedures, and on the interaction between the models at the different levels. Each hierarchical level has its own characteristics and aggregation methods are typically influenced by a number of factors that include the following:

(i) length of the planning horizon,
(ii) level of detail of the required information and forecasts,
(iii) scope of the planning activity,
(iv) the authority and responsibility of the manager in charge of executing the plan.

Early work using the hierarchical approach was motivated by planning and scheduling problems in discrete parts, batch manufacturing systems [see Hax & Meal, 1975; Bitran & Hax, 1977]. In these applications, end products were aggregated into families and product families were grouped into product types. The upper level models were typically linear and mixed linear integer programs

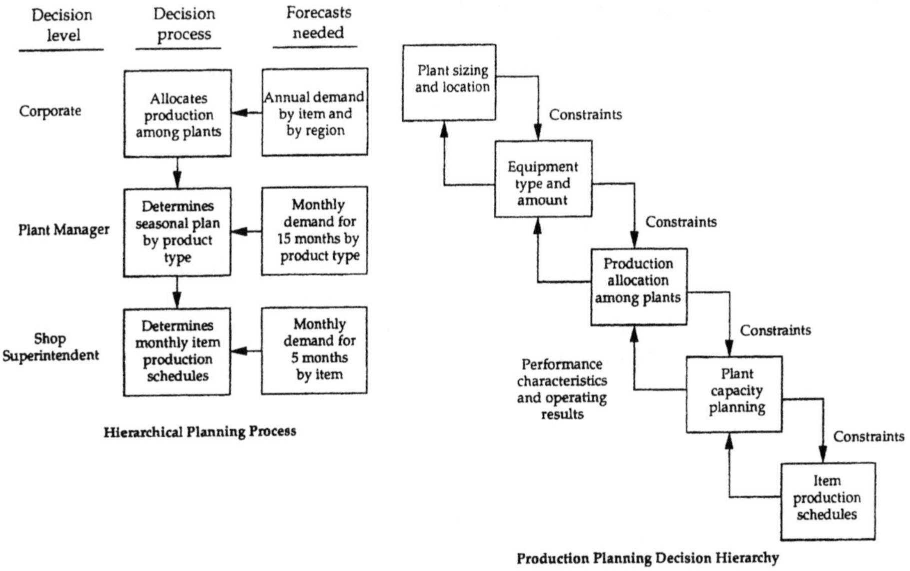

Fig. 2.1. An overview of hierarchical planning approach.

while the lower level models were convex knapsack problems. This approach is described, in detail, later in this section.

The HPP approach, however, is quite general and has been adapted to a wide variety of systems by suitable choice of aggregation and disaggregation schemes and submodels. For example, applications of the approach to a continuous manufacturing process and a job shop can be found in Bradley, Hax & Magnanti [1977, Chapters 6 and 10, respectively].

Axsäter & Jonsson [1984] have used this approach to provide aggregate models for supporting capacity planning decisions in MRP systems. Their model is based on product and machine groups and is designed to provide consistency between machine capacities and the requirements imposed by the detailed schedules derived by the MRP procedure. This paper is discussed in Section 2.4.

Bitran & Tirupati [1988a,b] describes a single stage, parallel machine scheduling application in which resource allocations are determined by an aggregate model. Aggregation in this application is achieved by classifying jobs into product families. The upper level model in this application is a mixed integer, quadratic program that can be interpreted as a machine grouping and aggregate loading problem. As a result, the detailed scheduling problems at the lower level are considerably simplified. Kusiak & Finke [1987] present a hierarchical approach to address the process planning problem in flexible manufacturing systems.

The foregoing discussion indicates that hierarchical planning represents a philosophy to address complex problems, rather than a specific solution technique. In the next section we illustrate this approach by describing, in detail, the method proposed by Hax & Meal [1975], Bitran & Hax [1977] and related work on production planning and scheduling for single stage batch manufacturing systems. This is followed by a discussion of aggregation and disaggregation methods. We note that the single stage model is a simplification of the manufacturing process. In this model the details of the production processes are ignored and the system is modeled as a black box with critical resource(s) that limit its capacity. However, the hierarchical approach is amenable for adaptation to more detailed models. As described in Section 2.2, in more detailed multistage models, we distinguish between different stages of production (such as part production, assembly, etc.) and incorporate resource constraints at each stage.

2.1. Hierarchical planning in single stage systems

Hax and Meal [1975] introduced the concept of hierarchical planning by recognizing the differences between tactical and operational decisions. Tactical decisions are associated with aggregate production planning while operational decisions are an outcome of the disaggregation process. The hierarchical structure proposed by Hax and Meal and subsequently used by Bitran & Hax [1977, 1981] and Bitran, Haas & Hax [1981] is based on three levels of product aggregation described below.

Items are the final products delivered to the customer and represent the highest degree of specificity regarding manufactured products. A given product may generate a large number of items differing in characteristics such as color, packaging, labels, size, accessories etc.

Product types are groups of items that have similar unit costs, direct costs, holding costs per unit period, productivities (labor hours per unit of product) and seasonalities.

Families are groups of items that belong to the same product type and share similar setups. That is, whenever a machine is prepared to produce an item in a family, all other items in the same family can be produced with minor change in setups.

The classification described above can be illustrated by considering the product line of a luggage manufacturer. Products of the same size can be aggregated to define product type. Within a product type, items with the same frame can be produced with a common setup and constitute a product family. Items within a product family are distinguished by characteristics such as color, minor variations in material, etc.

An overview of the planning process is described in Figure 2.2 and essentially consists of three steps, indicated in the figure by boxes 1, 2, and 3. In the first step (box 1) aggregate plans for product types are determined. The planning horizon of this model normally covers a full year to take into consideration the fluctuations of demand requirements for the products. The second step in the process (box 2) results in the disaggregation of the aggregate

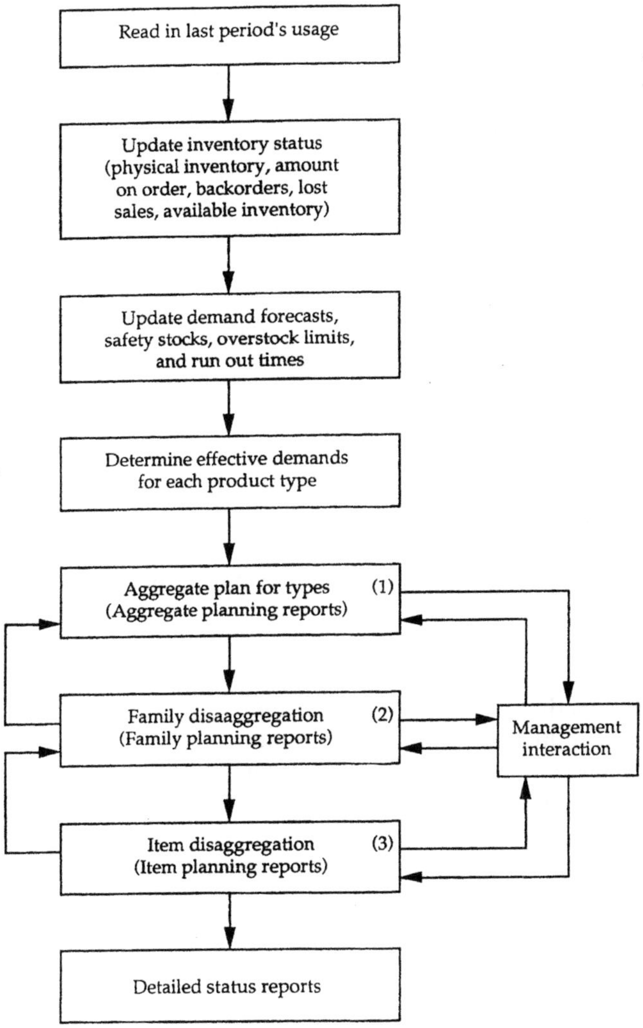

Fig. 2.2. Conceptual overview of hierarchical planning system.

plan for each type to obtain production quantities for each family. Further disaggregation of the family production lots to determine item quantities is performed in the third step (box 3).

It is important to note two features of the process above. First, while the aggregate plan is run every period, only the results for the first period are implemented. Thus the aggregate plan can be viewed as a 'rolling horizon' plan. Second, disaggregation of the aggregate plan (steps 2 and 3) is required only for the first period of the planning horizon. As a consequence, the data collection and data processing is reduced substantially compared to the detailed formulations of the production planning problem.

Hax & Meal [1975] proposed a heuristic to perform the three levels of computations. Bitran & Hax [1977] formalized the hierarchical planning heuristic by suggesting the use of convex knapsack problems to disaggregate the product type and family run quantities into family and item run quantities respectively. This method, referred to as the *regular knapsack method* is described below. To simplify the presentation of these models, in many instances, we assume that the production lead times are zero. This restriction is not necessary. The model formulations and the corresponding results can be modified easily and extended to cases with constant lead times.

Aggregate production planning for product types

The following linear program provides a simple representation of the planning problem at the product type level.

Decision variables

X_{it} = the number of units of product type i to be produced in period t,
I_{it} = the number of units of inventory of type i carried from period t to $t+1$,
R_t, O_t = the regular and overtime hours used during period t respectively.

Parameters

I = number of product types,
T = the length of the planning horizon,
c_{it} = unit production cost (excluding labor),
h_{it} = inventory carrying cost per unit per period,
r_t = regular time cost per manhour,
o_t = overtime cost per manhour,
rm_t, om_t = total availability of regular and overtime hours in period t, respectively,
m_i = hours required to produce one unit of product i,
d_{it} = effective demand for type i in period t. (A definition of effective demand will be given later in this section.)

$$(\mathrm{P}) \quad \min \sum_{i=1}^{I} \sum_{t=1}^{T} (c_{it}X_{it} + h_{it}I_{it}) + \sum_{t=1}^{T} (r_tR_t + o_tO_t)$$

subject to

$$I_{it-1} + X_{it} - I_{it} = d_{it}\,, \quad i = 1, 2, \ldots, I,\ t = 1, 2, \ldots, T\,,$$

$$\sum_{i=1}^{I} m_iX_{it} \leq R_t + O_t\,, \quad t = 1, 2, \ldots, T\,,$$

$$R_t \leq \mathrm{rm}_t\,, \quad t = 1, 2, \ldots, T\,,$$

$$O_t \leq \mathrm{om}_t\,, \quad t = 1, 2, \ldots, T\,,$$

$$X_{it}, I_{it}, R_t, O_t \geq 0\,.$$

Note that in this model, X and I represent respectively production and inventory variables at the aggregate or product type level. Since the cost (c_{it}, h_{it}) and productivity (m_i) parameters are required to be the same for all items within a family, it may be necessary to scale the item quantities in accordance to their resource consumption. In that case X and I represent the corresponding weighted average quantities of items within each family. It is worth noting that this procedure will be exact with a single resource constraint. However, with more than one resource, it would be an approximation.

The formulation above can be modified easily to incorporate many features such as hiring and firing, constant production lead time, back orders, subcontracting, lost sales etc. It is important that, whenever seasonal variations are present in the demand pattern of product types, the planning horizon of (P) covers a full seasonal cycle. It is not necessary to formulate the aggregate problem (P) as a linear program. Any model which adequately represents the practical setting under consideration would suffice. Linear programming is a convenient type of model at this level because of its computational efficiency and the wide availability of computer codes. The shadow price information and sensitivity analysis make such models very flexible and can help identify opportunities for capacity expansion, market penetration, introduction of new products etc.

Manufacturing set up costs are ignored in the aggregate model (P). This is motivated by the fact that often set up costs have a secondary impact on total production costs and need to be considered at the detailed or operational level. When this is not the case the hierarchical approach can be modified as described in Bitran, Haas & Hax [1982] or the highest level problem can be formulated as in Graves [1982].

Advantages of aggregate planning

We now describe in detail some of the advantages of the aggregate approach compared to the detailed monolithic model. These can be broadly classified into three categories.

(i) A major benefit of aggregate planning is the substantial savings in the costs of data collection to support the planning model as well as the reduced computational requirements. In a detailed model a major information system may be needed to collect the demand, productivity parameters, and cost data as well as prepare forecasts for thousands of individual items. Aggregation of items can significantly reduce the cost and effort in demand forecasting and data preparation in addition to reducing the computational costs.

(ii) Another important aspect relates to the accuracy of the data. Unless all items are perfectly correlated, an aggregate forecast of demand will have reduced variance. Given the small number of forecasts required, it is possible to employ more sophisticated techniques such as econometric or time series models, and to obtain judgmental input from the concerned managers. Since the decisions considered in the aggregate model are based on total production quantity rather than item level details, increased forecast accuracy of total demand should improve the decision making process.

(iii) The major advantage of the aggregate approach is in the context of implementation. In a detailed formulation with thousands of items, managers may have difficulties in interacting with the model and comprehending the outputs and may get lost in the details. The aggregate formulation facilitates the managers' understanding of the key tradeoffs involved in the production decisions. At this level of planning, most marketing forecasts are made by product types and manpower decisions are made by broad classes of labor.

A family disaggregation model

The disaggregation model attempts to allocate production quantities of each product type to the families belonging to that type. Coherent disaggregation requires consistency between the allocations among the families and the product type production determined by the aggregate model. In the disaggregation model (Pi) presented below the objective is to determine run quantities for each family so as to minimize the total set up costs. Let

s_j = set up cost for family j,
Y_{j1} = the number of units of family j to be produced in period 1,
d_j = forecast demand for family j,
lb_j, ub_j = lower and upper bounds for Y_{j1},
X_{i1} = production of product type i in period 1 to be allocated among the families (note that X_{i1} is an input parameter for the model and is derived from the aggregate plan),
$J(i)$ = set of families in product type i that will runout in period 1.

$$(\text{P}i)\quad \min \sum_{j\in J(i)} s_j d_j / Y_{j1}$$

$$\text{subject to} \quad \sum_{j\in J(i)} Y_{j1} = X_{i1} ,$$

$$\text{lb}_{j1} \leqslant Y_{j1} \leqslant \text{ub}_{j1}, \quad j \in J(i) .$$

The objective function of Problem (Pi) assumes that the family run quantities are proportional to the set up cost and the annual demand for the family. This assumption which is the basis of the economic order quantity formulation, tends to minimize the average annual set up cost. Observe that the total inventory costs have already been established in the aggregate model and do not appear in Problem (Pi).

The first constraint of (Pi) assures consistency between the aggregate and disaggregate models. The upper and lower bounds on Y in the second constraint are computed as follows:

$$\text{ub}_{j1} = \max\{0, \text{os}_{j1} - \text{ai}_{j1}\} ,$$

$$\text{lb}_{j1} = \max\{0, d_{j1} - \text{ai}_{j1} + \text{ss}_{j1}\} ,$$

where os_{j1}, d_{j1}, ai_{j1}, and ss_{j1} denote respectively the overstock limit, the demand, the available inventory, and the safety stock of family j in period 1. $J(i)$ is initially the set of families in product type i that trigger in period 1, i.e., it is the set of indices j such that $d_{j1} + ss_{j1} - ai_{j1} > 0$. Equivalently $J(i)$ can be defined as the set of families whose runout time is less than one time period. All other families are included in a secondary list and are scheduled only if Problem (Pi) is infeasible and excess capacity is available for product type i. Bitran & Hax [1981] show that the first constraint of (Pi) can be replaced by $\sum_{j \in J(i)} Y_{j1} \leq X_{i1}$ without changing the optimal solution. They also provide an efficient algorithm to solve Problem (Pi).

The above disaggregation approach is motivated by the desire to minimize the set up costs by scheduling only those families that are required to be produced in the period. Hax & Golovin [1978] describe other disaggregation approaches and Bitran, Haas & Hax [1981] provide a comparison of alternate disaggregation procedures. Gabbay [1975] points out that this type of myopic disaggregation could lead to infeasibilities. (This issue is discussed, in detail, later in this section.) Bitran, Haas & Hax [1981] modified the algorithm by introducing a 'Look ahead feasibility' rule to counter the problems of infeasibilities.

An item disaggregation model

Once the quantities Y_{j1} have been determined, it is necessary to allocate this production among items belonging to each family j. For the current planning period all relevant costs have been determined by the previous two stages in the hierarchical process. For example, the inventory holding costs are set by the aggregate plan, while setup costs are determined by the family disaggregation plan. However, the feasible solution chosen will establish the initial conditions for the next period and affect the future costs. It may be observed that the next setup for a family occurs whenever an item in that family is depleted. In order to save setups in future periods, it seems reasonable to distribute the family run quantity among its items in such a way that each item's runout time coincides with the runout time of the family. A direct consequence is that all items will tend to trigger simultaneously. This can be accomplished by solving the following continuous knapsack problem:

$$(\mathrm{Q}_j) \quad \min \sum_{k \in K(j)} \left\{ \left[\left\{ Y_{j1} + \sum_{k \in K(j)} (ai_{k1} - ss_{k1}) \right\} \Big/ \sum_{k \in K(j)} d_{k1} \right] - \left[(Z_{k1} + ai_{k1} - ss_{k1}) / d_{k1} \right] \right\}^2$$

$$\text{subject to} \quad \sum_{k \in K(j)} Z_{k1} = Y_{j1} \,,$$

$$\mathrm{lb}_{k1} \leq Z_{k1} \leq \mathrm{ub}_{k1} \,, \quad k \in K(j) \,,$$

where Z_{k1} is the number of units of item k to be produced in period 1, $K(j)$ is the set of items in family j, d_{k1}, ai_{k1}, ss_{k1}, lb_{k1}, and ub_{k1} represent for item k the same quantities that were discussed for family j in Problem (Pi).

The constraints of Problem (Qj) are similar to those of Problem (Pi) and assure feasibility and consistency during the disaggregation. The two terms inside the square bracket of the objective function represent, respectively, the runout time for family j and the runout time for item k (assuming a perfect forecast). The minimization of the square of the difference will make those quantities as close as possible.

An efficient algorithm to solve (Qj) is presented in Bitran & Hax [1981]. It should be noted that the above formulation does not provide for the presence of minor set ups between item changes within a family production run. In such cases the objective function of (Qj) and the solution procedure should be modified to reflect this fact.

In summary, the hierarchical planning system operates as follows:

(1) An aggregate forecast is generated for each product type for each period in the planning horizon. Since the number of product types is usually small, these forecasts can be produced by using fairly sophisticated models (such as regression analysis) that could be prohibitive at the item level. In addition, these forecasts can be reviewed by experienced managers in order to introduce judgmental inputs which the models cannot capture.

(2) The product type forecasts are disaggregated into item forecasts by estimating the proportion of total type demand corresponding to each item. These proportions can be updated by using exponential smoothing techniques which are appropriate at the detailed level. Item and family forecasts are required for the first period of the planning horizon.

(3) The available inventory for each item is updated. The effective demand for items, families and product type is then computed. (The notion of effective demand is described later in this section.)

(4) The production schedule is then determined by solving the aggregate and disaggregation models described earlier. Computer programs to perform these calculations are described in Hax, Golovin, Bosyj & Victor [1976].

Issues of infeasibility and effective demand

The rolling horizon procedure combined with disaggregation may lead to infeasibilities. This may be illustrated by means of a simple example from Bitran & Hax [1977]. Consider a 3 period problem with one product type and two items. The demand forecasts are assumed to be perfect and are presented in Table 2.1. The table also provides the initial inventory for each item. The aggregate constraints for the problem are

$$I_0 + X_1 - I_1 = d_1 ,$$
$$I_1 + X_2 - I_2 = d_2 ,$$
$$I_2 + X_3 - I_3 = d_3 ,$$
$$X_1, X_2, X_3, I_0, I_1, I_2, I_3 \geq 0 .$$

Table 2.1
Demand

Item	Period t			Initial inventory
	1	2	3	
$k=1$	$d_{11}=5$	$d_{12}=17$	$d_{13}=30$	$I_{10}=9$
$k=2$	$d_{21}=3$	$d_{22}=12$	$d_{23}=30$	$I_{20}=20$
Total	$d_1\ =8$	$d_2\ =29$	$d_3\ =60$	$I_0\ =29$

The detailed constraints are

$$I_{k0}+Z_{k1}-I_{k1}=d_{k1}\,,\quad k=1,2\,,$$
$$I_{k1}+Z_{k2}-I_{k2}=d_{k2}\,,\quad k=1,2\,,$$
$$I_{k2}+Z_{k3}-I_{k3}=d_{k3}\,,\quad k=1,2\,,$$
$$Z_{kt},I_{kt}\geqslant 0\,,\quad k=1,2,\ t=1,2,3\,.$$

Feasibility conditions require that these two constraints are satisfied and that $Z_{1t}+Z_{2t}=X_t$, $t=1,2,3$.

For the data in Table 2.1, the reader can verify that although

$$X_1=8\,,\quad X_2=0\,,\quad X_3=60\,,\quad I_1=29\,,\quad I_2=0\,,\quad I_3=0$$

is a feasible solution to the aggregate problem, it does not have a corresponding disaggregation. The reason for this infeasibility is that the aggregate model ignores the fact that inventory for item 2 cannot be used to satisfy the demand for item 1.

This type of infeasibility can be avoided by working with *effective demands*. If the initial inventory of an item is not zero, the effective demand for the first period is obtained by subtracting the initial inventory from the demand. If the initial inventory is greater than the demand of the first period then the effective demand for that period is zero. The adjustment process is continued until all inventory is used up. The effective demands for the illustrative example are presented in Table 2.2.

Table 2.2
Effective demand

Item	Period t			Initial inventory
	1	2	3	
$k=1$	$d_{11}=0$	$d_{12}=13$	$d_{13}=30$	0
$k=2$	$d_{21}=0$	$d_{22}=0$	$d_{23}=25$	0
Total	$d_1\ =0$	$d_2\ =13$	$d_3\ =55$	0

In general, if d_{kt} is the forecast demand for item k in period t, ai_k is its corresponding initial inventory and ss_k its safety stock, the effective demand $\bar{d}_{kt}$ of item k for period t is given by

$$\bar{d}_{kt} = \begin{cases} \max\left[0, \sum_{m=1}^{t} (d_{km}) - \mathrm{ai}_k + \mathrm{ss}_k\right] & \text{if } \bar{d}_{k,t-1} = 0 \text{ (define } \bar{d}_{k0} = 0\text{)}, \\ d_{kt} & \text{otherwise}. \end{cases}$$

The effective demand for product type i is then given by the sum of the effective demands of all items belonging to that type, i.e.,

$$\bar{d}_{it} = \sum_{k \in K(i)} \bar{d}_{kt} .$$

Even with the use of effective demands, the myopic nature of disaggregation procedure of Bitran and Hax described earlier can give rise to infeasibilities. Their look ahead procedure addresses this issue, but still does not guarantee feasibility. Gabbay [1975] provides a set of feasibility conditions and shows that, if effective demands are used along with these conditions, any feasible solution to the aggregate model generates a feasible solution to the disaggregate model as well. This approach, however, has two drawbacks. First, this approach requires detailed data at the item level for the entire planning horizon which defeats one of the major advantages of the hierarchical approach. Second, the feasibility conditions destroy the knapsack structure of the disaggregation problems and increase the computational complexity. Erschler, Fontan & Merce [1986] address the latter issue and present an equivalent set of feasibility conditions that preserve the knapsack structure of the disaggregation problems. They also interpret the look ahead procedure of Bitran and Hax and show that this procedure is equivalent to imposing the feasibility conditions for two periods – the current period for which disaggregation is required and the following period.

2.2. *Aggregation and disaggregation*

The hierarchical approach described in the previous section should make it clear that aggregation and disaggregation procedures play a crucial role in the success of these methods. This problem is difficult because of the number of factors involved, some of which are not easily quantifiable. In fact, Hax & Meal [1975] provide only guidelines and not a specific procedure for characterizing the product structure of batch production facilities. As described in the previous section, in their framework, items are aggregated to form families and product types. An important consideration in the choice of these procedures is the ability of the disaggregation procedures to obtain feasible solutions at the detailed level. In the previous section we described some of these issues in the context of the Hax and Meal, and Bitran and Hax procedures. In this section we describe other methods that have been reported in the literature for aggregating end items and machines for reducing the size of the planning problem.

The theory of aggregation has been extensively studied in the economic literature. For example, variables like individual prices and incomes are often aggregated into price indices and total incomes. A general overview of this development can be found in Theil [1965], Fisher [1969] and Chipman [1975, 1976]. These aggregation problems are similar to, but not identical to those found in production planning problems.

In the operations research literature a considerable amount of work has been published on the subject of aggregation of linear and mixed integer linear programs. The primary focus of this work has been on the development of bounds, relative to the original large problem, based on the solution of a smaller problem obtained by aggregation of variables and/or constraints. Since linear and mixed integer linear programs are commonly used to model decisions at the upper levels of the hierarchy, these results are of interest. However, we do not provide a review of the related results in this chapter. Instead, we refer the reader to Geoffrion [1977], and Zipkin [1980a,b] and references therein. The problem of disaggregation has also been considered in the context of aggregate planning (for details see Chapter 7 of this volume). Examples of research in this area can be found in Winters [1962] and Zoller [1971]. Ritzman, Krajewski, Berry, Goodman, Hardy & Vitt [1979] present an extensive collection of papers on aggregation and disaggregation in manufacturing and service systems.

Formal approaches to the aggregation problem in the context of hierarchical planning have been considered, among others, by Zipkin [1982] and Axsäter [1981]. We present some key results from these papers to indicate the flavor of the problems and the difficulties involved. In both approaches the aggregation schemes are derived by focusing on the corresponding disaggregation problems.

Zipkin [1982] considers a multi-item problem in which the cost function for item i, $q_i(y_i)$ is defined on (m', ∞) for some $m' < 0$ (possibly $-\infty$). The q_i are assumed to have the following form:

$$q_i(y_i) = -c_i y_i + h_i \int_m^{y_i} H(r/\mu_i)\,\mathrm{d}r\,, \tag{2.1}$$

where y_i = inventory of item i, c_i, h_i, and μ_i are constants, h_i, $\mu_i > 0$; H is the same for all i and continuous and increasing on (m', ∞); and $m > m'$. The functions q_i are continuously differentiable and strictly convex. The objective is to replace the multiple items by a single aggregate product and obtain a closed form expression for the aggregate cost function, $Q(Y)$. The corresponding disaggregation problem is given by

$$Q(Y) = \min_y q(y) \quad \text{s.t.} \quad \sum y_i = Y\,,$$

where y is an I-vector of y_i, $i = 1, 2, \ldots, I$, and

$$q(y) = \sum_{i=1}^{I} q_i(y_i) .$$

Zipkin proposes an approximation for $Q(Y)$, $Q_A(Y)$ which has the same form as (2.1) and is given by

$$Q_A(Y) = -c^0 y + h^0 \int_m^Y H(r/\mu)\,\mathrm{d}r , \quad \text{where } \mu = \sum_{i=1}^{I} \mu_i .$$

The approximation $Q_A(Y)$ is motivated by the desire to define an aggregate problem that is small in size and has the same structure as the detailed problem. It is shown that $Q_A(Y)$ is exact when $c_i = c$ for all i, and H is monomial, i.e., $H(r) = ar^p$ where the constants a and p are either both positive or both negative. The paper provides three methods for determining c^0 and h^0. While the model above has been formulated to describe inventory costs, it can also be used to aggregate production costs. In that case, the variables Y_i represent production quantities and q_i represent production costs.

Zipkin also describes an application of this aggregation scheme to the production smoothing problem of Holt, Modigliani, Muth & Simon [1960] described in Chapter 8 of this volume and extends it to a broader class of polynomial cost functions. It is shown that the model can also be applied to a two stage facility with J components producing I end items. The aggregate problem, in which the I products are partitioned into N groups, is shown to have the same structure as the detailed problem and is formulated in terms of the product groups. For this approach to be effective it is necessary that J and N should be much smaller than I. Furthermore, the items within a group require the same number of each component which appears to be an unduly restrictive condition.

In a more general context of hierarchical planning, Axsäter [1981] considers aggregation procedures in a K item, N machine facility with the following parameters:

I_{kt} = inventory level of item k at end of period t,
I_t = $(I_{1t}, I_{2t}, \ldots, I_{Kt})$,
Z_{kt} = production of item k in period t,
Z_t = $(Z_{1t}, Z_{2t}, \ldots, Z_{Kt})$,
a_{kn} = number of units of item k required to produce one unit of item n,
A = (a_{kn}), $k, n = 1, 2, \ldots, K$,
d_{kt} = demand for item k in period t,
d_t = $(d_{1t}, d_{2t}, \ldots, d_{Kt})$,
m_{kn} = production resources on machine n required to produce one unit of k,
M = (m_{kn}), $k = 1, 2, \ldots, K$, $n = 1, 2, \ldots, N$.

The matrices A and M are nonnegative. Constraints defining the item inventories are given by

$$I_t = I_{t-1} + Z_t - AZ_t - d_t .$$

Axsäter considers two types of aggregation procedures to form K' product groups and N' machine groups to reduce the size of the planning problem. These are referred to as grouping matrices and general linear aggregation. In the first method grouping matrices $R = (r_{ik})$ and $S = (s_{ik})$ in which all columns are unit vectors, are used to define the aggregation in the following manner:

$r_{ik} = 1$ if item k is included in product group i and 0 otherwise ,

$s_{ik} = 1$ if machine k is included in machine group i and 0 otherwise .

Aggregate variables are denoted by $\hat{I}_t$, $\hat{Z}_t$, $\hat{d}_t$. $\hat{A}$ and $\hat{M}$ represent matrices (that correspond to A and M) at the aggregate level and need to be determined. The inventory constraint thus becomes

$$\hat{I}_{t-1} + \hat{Z}_t - \hat{A}\hat{Z}_t - \hat{d}_t = \hat{I}_t .$$

For a given production vector Z_t, true component and capacity requirements are given by RAZ_t and SMZ_t and for consistency between the aggregate and the detailed models we require

$$\hat{A}RZ_t = RAZ_t , \qquad \hat{M}SZ_t = SMZ_t .$$

'Perfect aggregation' refers to an aggregation scheme that ensures consistency between the aggregate and the detailed models for all possible production vectors Z_t. The necessary and sufficient condition for perfect aggregation is given by finding matrices $\hat{A}$ and $\hat{M}$ that satisfy

$$\hat{A}R = RA , \qquad \hat{M}S = SM .$$

Axsäter shows that in general, it is not possible to find perfect aggregation with group matrices and proposes an approximation scheme. This method is motivated by the observation that, while the grouping is static and fixed in the short/medium term, the production vectors are dynamic and vary from period to period. Thus the production vectors can be considered to be stochastic rather than deterministic. Since no single aggregation scheme can be perfect for all realizations of the production vector, a scheme which is perfect in an expected sense may be reasonable. Axsater proposes solution of the following optimization problem (AP) to determine $\hat{A}$ and $\hat{M}$.

$$\text{(AP)} \quad \min_{\hat{A}} \mathrm{E}\{\|(\hat{A}R - RA)Z\|^2\} ,$$
$$\min_{\hat{M}} \mathrm{E}\{\|(\hat{M}S - SM)Z\|^2\}$$
$$\text{subject to} \quad \hat{A}RZ^0 = RAZ^0 \quad \text{and} \quad \hat{M}SZ^0 = SMZ^0 ,$$

where $Z^0 = \mathrm{E}\{Z\}$, and $\mathrm{E}\{\cdot\}$ is the expectation operator.

The constraints of (AP) assure that the aggregation defined by $\hat{A}$ and $\hat{M}$ is perfect in an expected sense while the objective function is the expected value of the squared Euclidean norm. Axsäter shows that a general solution to (AP) is given by

$$\hat{A} = RAR^* + G'G\,, \qquad \hat{M} = SMR^* + G''G\,,$$

where G', G'' are arbitrary matrices of dimension $K' \times K'$ and $K' \times N'$, respectively, and

$$R^* = Z^0Z^{0\mathrm{T}}R^{\mathrm{T}}/Z^{0\mathrm{T}}R^{\mathrm{T}}RZ^0 + (I - Z^0Z^{0\mathrm{T}}R^{\mathrm{T}}R/Z^{0\mathrm{T}}R^{\mathrm{T}}RZ^0)PR^{\mathrm{T}}Q^{\mathrm{t}}\,,$$
$$G = I - RZ^0Z^{0\mathrm{T}}R^{\mathrm{T}}/Z^{0\mathrm{T}}R^{\mathrm{T}}RZ^0 - QQ^{\mathrm{t}}\,,$$
$$Q = (I - RZ^0Z^{0\mathrm{T}}R^{\mathrm{T}}/Z^{0\mathrm{T}}R^{\mathrm{T}}RZ^0)RPR^{\mathrm{T}}(I - RZ^0Z^{0\mathrm{T}}R^{\mathrm{T}}/Z^{0\mathrm{T}}R^{\mathrm{T}}RZ^0)\,,$$
$$Q^t = \text{pseudo-inverse of } Q\,,$$
$$P = \mathrm{E}\{(Z - Z^0)(Z - Z^0)^{\mathrm{T}}\}\,.$$

The procedure above to determine $\hat{A}$ and $\hat{M}$ is computationally reasonable. However, a major drawback is the data requirement. While it is easy to obtain the expected production vectors at the item (detailed) level, it is extremely difficult to estimate the variance/covariance matrix P at this level of detail. In practice, the issue is further complicated because it is necessary to determine the grouping matrices R and S together with $\hat{A}$ and $\hat{M}$.

Axsäter also considers an alternative scheme – general linear aggregation and provides necessary and sufficient conditions to obtain perfect aggregation. However, this procedure does not seem very attractive since it requires assignment of fractions of items to different product groups. For further results on this subject, the reader is referred to Axsäter, Jonsson & Thorsterson [1983], Axsäter & Jonsson [1984], and Axsäter [1986].

The above discussion illustrates some of the difficulties associated with aggregation of items and machines and suggests that the definition of appropriate hierarchies of products and machines, in practice, is still an imprecise science. It also highlights the need to develop easily implementable aggregation methods.

2.3. *Multistage models*

The single stage models described so far in this chapter capture essential features of the hierarchical approach to production planning. Extension of this approach to systems with multiple stages requires coordination between the different stages which introduces an additional dimension of complexity. In this section we discuss some of these issues by focusing on the extensions by Meal [1978] and Bitran, Haas & Hax [1982] for two stage systems. Related work can also be found in Maxwell, Muckstadt, Thomas & Vander Eecken [1983] and

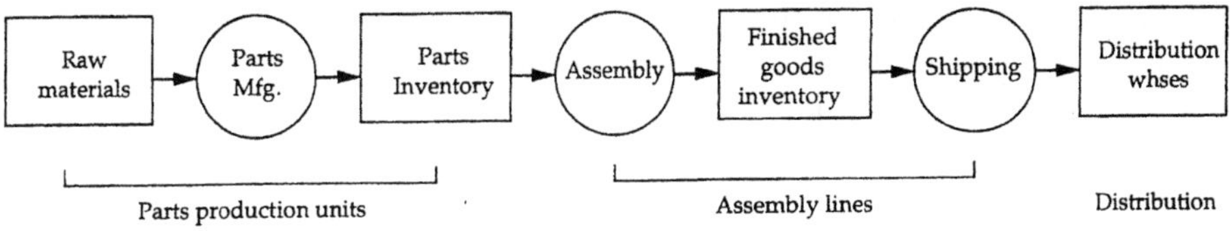

Fig. 2.3. Major stages in the production and distribution system.

Gelders & Van Wassenhove [1982]. Beyond these references, the literature on HPP for multi-stage systems is quite scanty. This area presents potential for further research.

Meal [1978] describes an integrated distribution planning and control system which highlights some of the difficulties encountered in extending the hierarchical approach to multistage systems. A schematic diagram of the system is presented in Figure 2.3. The first two stages model the manufacturing system and correspond to parts production and assembly operations, while the third stage represents the distribution system. The major objective of the planning system is to achieve an integrated control of operations at the three stages. There is no attempt to optimize the decisions at either the aggregate or detailed levels. Figure 2.4 presents an outline of the planning system and describes the data requirements and the flow of control information. It can be observed from this diagram that a two level hierarchical system is used to control the operations in the production stages. The aggregate plan in this system is essentially a manpower plan for a horizon of 9 to 18 months. Unlike

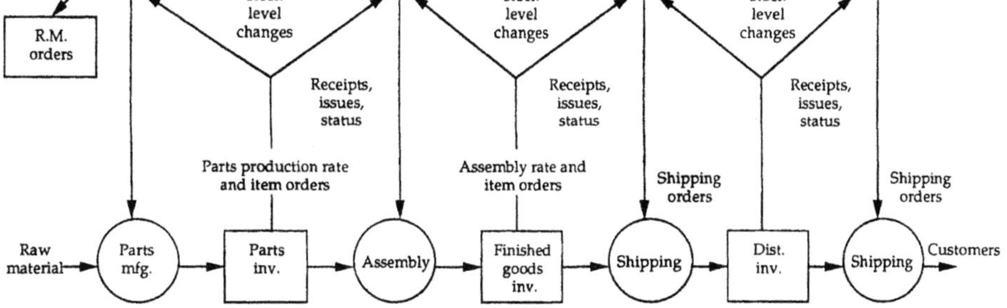

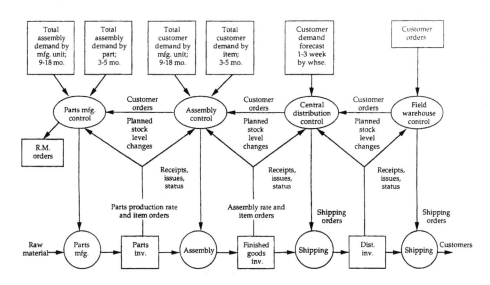

Fig. 2.4. Major information inputs and flow of control information.

the models described in the previous section, in this system there is no mechanism to ensure consistency between the aggregation and disaggregation decisions, except for the imposition of capacity constraints. In this respect, the link between the two hierarchical levels can be considered relatively weak, compared to the previous models. Consistent with the system objectives, detailed schedules (disaggregation decisions) are based on tight coupling between the various stages of the production and distribution system, which is achieved by adopting a base stock control procedure. The inventory levels of the system, however, are determined by the aggregate model and are based on long-term forecasts. Figure 2.5 presents an outline of the two level hierarchical control system for the two production stages.

In contrast to the manufacturing stages, no aggregate planning is done at the distribution stage. This was considered unnecessary in view of the excess capacity available in order processing and shipping activities. Detailed shipping schedules are prepared daily using a 1 to 3 week horizon and are based on a base stock policy. The outline of the control system for this stage is presented in Figure 2.6. Meal [1978] describes several heuristic rules employed in the system to develop aggregate plans and detailed schedules.

Bitran, Haas & Hax [1982] present an extension of the model described in Section 2.1 to a two stage system. The two stages represent respectively, parts

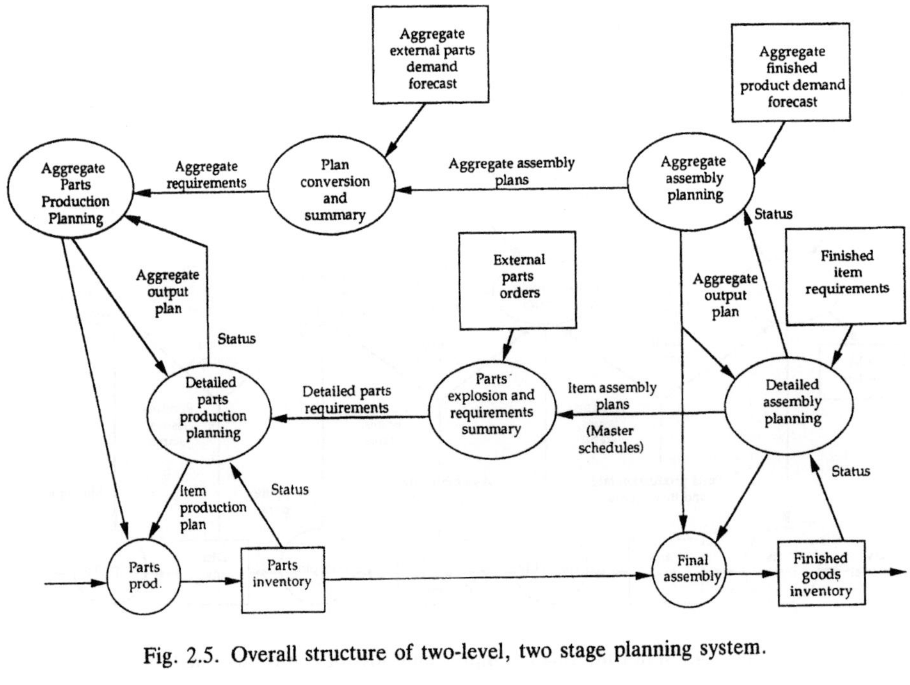

Fig. 2.5. Overall structure of two-level, two stage planning system.

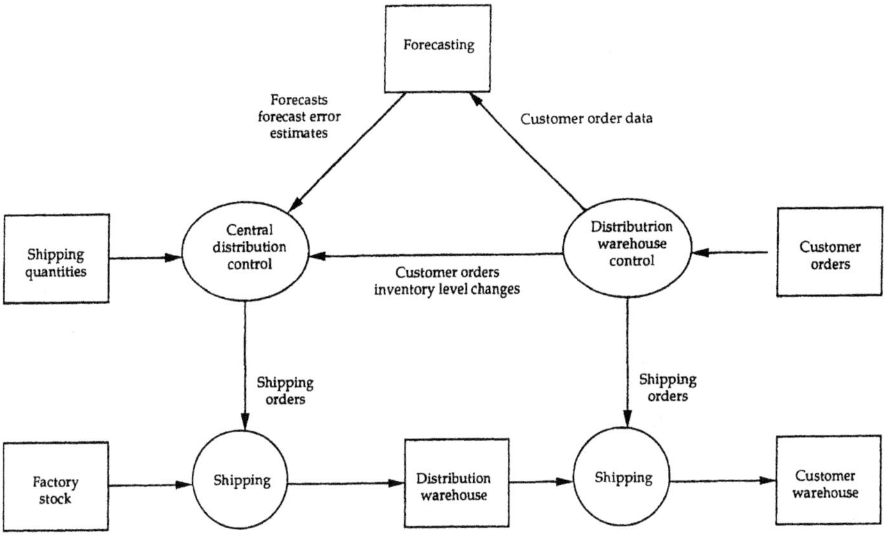

Fig. 2.6. Distribution control system.

production and assembly. Figure 2.7 provides a schematic overview of their approach which may be summarized as follows:

(1) Aggregation of products and parts.

(2) Aggregate planning for the two stages using an integrated model to guarantee appropriate coordination between stages.

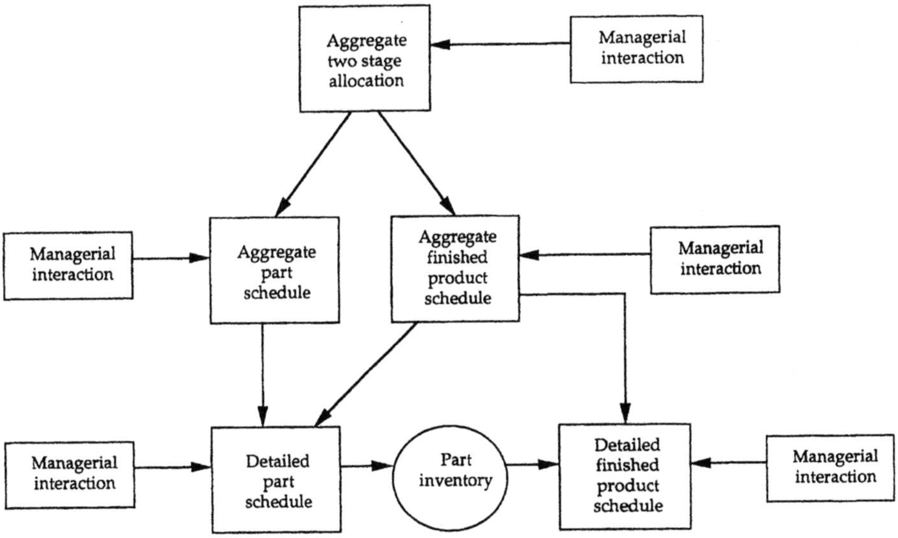

Fig. 2.7. A conceptual overview of a hierarchical production planning system for a fabrication and assembly process.

(3) Aggregate plans for parts and finished products are disaggregated to determine detailed schedules.

(4) Reconcile possible differences at the detailed level via part inventories.

The hierarchy for the assembly stage (end products) is the same as that described in Section 2.1 for single stage systems. At the parts production stage only one level of aggregation is employed and parts are classified into part types. Thus, part items are individual parts required as a component to a product item or having an independent demand as a service spare part. Part types are groups of part items having similar direct production costs per part period, and consume the same amount of resources per part. This particular classification was motivated by the fact that, in the application considered, there was no significant shared setups among the parts. The approach, however, is quite general and can be extended to other two stage systems with different levels or aggregation at each stage.

We introduce the following additional notation to describe the aggregation and disaggregation models (this notation is similar to the one used in Section 2.1 with '^' denoting the corresponding variables at the part production stage):

L = fabrication lead time for parts,
$J(i)$ = the set of indices of product families in product type i,
$N(k)$ = the set of indices of parts in part type k,
$\hat{h}_{kt}$ = holding cost per unit of inventory of part type k from period t to $t+1$,
$\widehat{\mathrm{ss}}_{kt}$ = safety stock for part type k in period t,
$\widehat{\mathrm{os}}_{kt}$ = over stock limit for part type k in period t,
$\hat{r}_{kt}$ = cost of one hour of regular time at the part production stage,
$\hat{o}_{kt}$ = cost of one hour of overtime at the part production stage,
$\hat{m}_k$ = units of labor consumed to produce one unit of part type k,
$(\widehat{\mathrm{rm}})_t$ = availability of regular time in period t at the part production stage,
$(\widehat{\mathrm{om}})_t$ = availability of overtime in period t at the part production stage,
$\hat{D}_{k1}$ = demand of part type k over the runout time,
f_{ijkn} = number of units of part n required by each unit of product family j, $n \in N(k)$, $j \in J(i)$,
f_{ik} = average number of parts of type k required to produce one unit of product type i,
$\hat{s}_k$ = setup cost for parts in part type k,
$\widehat{\mathrm{lb}}_{n1}$, $\widehat{\mathrm{ub}}_{n1}$ = lower and upper bounds on production quantity of part n in period 1,
$\hat{R}_{kt}$ = regular time hours for part type k in period t,
$\hat{O}_{kt}$ = overtime hours for part type k in period t,
$\hat{I}_{kt}$ = inventory of part type k at the end of period t,
$\hat{Q}_{n1}$ = quantity of part n scheduled for production in period 1,
$\widehat{\mathrm{ai}}_{nt}$ = inventory position of part n at time period t (includes the number of parts on order or being fabricated that will become available in period t).

Aggregate production planning for part types and product types

The aggregate model is a linear program similar to the single stage model and is formulated as follows:

$$\text{(TP)}\quad \min \sum_{t=1}^{T}\sum_{i=1}^{I}(h_{it}I_{it}+r_tR_{it}+O_tO_{it})+\sum_{t=1}^{T-L}\sum_{k=1}^{K}(\hat{h}_{kt}\hat{I}_{kt}+\hat{r}_t\hat{R}_{kt}+\hat{o}_t\hat{O}_{kt})$$

subject to

$$I_{i,t-1}+m_i(R_{it}+O_{it})-I_{it}=d_{it}\,,\quad i=1,2,\ldots,I,\ t=1,2,\ldots,T\,, \tag{2.2}$$

$$\sum_{i=1}^{I} R_{it}\leq(\text{rm})_t\,,\quad t=1,2,\ldots,T\,, \tag{2.3}$$

$$\sum_{i=1}^{I} O_{it}\leq(\text{om})_t\,,\quad t=1,2,\ldots,T\,, \tag{2.4}$$

$$\text{ss}_{it}\leq I_{it}\leq \text{os}_{it}\,,\quad i=1,2,\ldots,I,\ t=1,2,\ldots,T\,, \tag{2.5}$$

$$\sum_{k=1}^{K} R_{kt}\leq(\widehat{\text{rm}})_t\,,\quad t=1,2,\ldots,T-L\,, \tag{2.6}$$

$$\sum_{k=1}^{K} O_{kt}\leq(\widehat{\text{om}})_t\,,\quad t=1,2,\ldots,T-L\,, \tag{2.7}$$

$$\widehat{\text{ss}}_{kt}\leq \hat{I}_{kt}\leq \widehat{\text{os}}_{kt}\,,\quad k=1,2,\ldots,K,\ t=1,2,\ldots,T-L\,, \tag{2.8}$$

$$\hat{I}_{k,t-1}+\hat{m}_k(\hat{R}_{kt}+\hat{O}_{kt})-\hat{I}_{kt}=\sum_{i=1}^{I} f_{ik}m_i(R_{i,t+L}+O_{i,t+L})\,,$$

$$k=1,2,\ldots,K,\ t=1,2,\ldots,T-L\,, \tag{2.9}$$

$$R_{it},\,O_{it},\,\hat{R}_{kt},\,\hat{O}_{kt},\,\hat{I}_{kt}\geq 0\,. \tag{2.10}$$

Constraints (2.2) and (2.9) represent the inventory balance for the product and part types, respectively. The product type demand as explained earlier is the net effective demand and the initial inventory I_{k1} is equal to the safety stock ss_{k1}. Constraints (2.9) couple part type requirements and product type production and represent the link between the two stages. The fabrication lead time is modeled as a time lag between initiation of part production and the availability of parts at the assembly stage. Thus part production in period t $[\hat{m}_k(\hat{R}_{kt}+\hat{O}_{kt})]$ is available for assembly in period $t+L$. The right-hand side of (2.9) represents the demand for part type k in the assembly stage in period $t+L$ and defines the demand at the part production stage in period t. The other constraints involve either part types or product types but not both. (2.3) and (2.4) are the regular time and overtime constraints at the assembly stage while (2.6) and (2.7) are the corresponding constraints at the parts production stage. (2.5) and (2.8) reflect upper and lower limits on inventories of product and part types respectively. These limits are defined in a manner similar to those in the single stage model. It may be noted that the parts required for the first L periods of production at the assembly stage (constraint 2.2) are already being manufactured, or have already been ordered. Still, these constraints are included to make the system responsive to forecast changes in each period. This is motivated by the fact that at the parts production stage minor variations can be absorbed by either expediting or by having a supplier make a special delivery.

We note that Problem (TP) is similar to the aggregate problem (P) of Section 2.1 and all remarks pertaining to the advantages and disadvantages of the linear programming formulation apply to (TP) as well. Also, (TP) can be modified to incorporate features such as planned back orders, hiring and layoffs, lost sales and subcontracting. In the same vein, (TP) is also solved with a rolling horizon of length T. At the end of each period, new information becomes available and is used to update the model. Only the results pertaining to the first $L+1$ periods for product types, and the first period for part types are implemented.

A critical parameter in Problem (TP) is the definition of f_{ik}. It is the weighted average of the f_{ijkn} and is defined as

$$f_{ik} = \sum_{j \in J(i)} \sum_{n \in N(k)} \bar{d}_j f_{ijkn} \Big/ \sum_{j \in J(i)} \bar{d}_j ,$$

where $J(i)$ is the set of indices of the product families in product type i, $N(k)$ is the set of indices in part type k, $\bar{d}_j$ is the annual demand of family j. It is important to realize that f_{ik} is a weighted average of the parts required by individual items in the family. Then the solution of the aggregate problem does not assure the existence of a feasible disaggregation, even with perfect forecasts. The authors observe that in practice this is not a critical issue and can be taken care of by using safety stocks to provide protection against variations in the bills of materials. These observations are partly justified by a result which guarantees that, under the following conditions:

(i) perfect forecasts are available,

(ii) initial inventory of every family is zero,

(iii) Problem (TP) is solved just once (it is not solved on a rolling horizon basis),

(iv) the first L constraints of (2.2) are deleted;

the initial inventory of part type k together with the production scheduled by (TP) up to period t is sufficient to satisfy the sum of the demands, corresponding to the interval $[1, t]$, of all parts in part type k for every t, such that $1 \leq t \leq T-L$. This result is easier to understand after reading the disaggregation scheme described below.

Disaggregation procedure

The disaggregation of the aggregate solution to (TP) is achieved in two steps. In the first step product family requirements for the first $L+1$ periods and part requirements for the first period are determined jointly to assure consistency between the two stages, while in the second step the detailed item schedule is developed for the assembly (second) stage.

Step 1. *Product family and part requirements*. Let X_{it} and $\hat{X}_{kt}$ denote the production of product type i and part type k, respectively, in period t, i.e., $X_{it} = m_i\ (R_{it} + O_{it})$, $\hat{X}_{kt} = \hat{m}_k\ (\hat{R}_{kt} + \hat{O}_{kt})$.

The disaggregation model to determine the production quantities and for product families parts is described as follows:

$$\text{(TD)}\quad \min \sum_{t=1}^{L+1} \sum_{i=1}^{I} \sum_{j\in J(i,t)} s_j D_{jt}/Q_{jt} + \sum_{k=1}^{K} \sum_{n\in N(k,1)} \hat{s}_k \hat{D}_{k1}/\hat{Q}_{n1}$$

subject to

$$\sum_{i=1}^{I} \sum_{j\in J(i,t)} f_{ijkn} Q_{jt} \le \widehat{\mathrm{ai}}_{nt} - \widehat{\mathrm{ss}}_{nt}\,,$$

$$k = 1, 2, \ldots, k,\ n \in N(k, t),\ t = 1, 2, \ldots, L + 1\,, \tag{2.11}$$

$$\sum_{i=1}^{I} \sum_{j\in J(i,L+1)} f_{ijkn} Q_{jL+1} \le \widehat{\mathrm{ai}}_{nL+1} - \widehat{\mathrm{ss}}_{nL+1} + \hat{Q}_{n1}\,,$$

$$k = 1, 2, \ldots, K,\ n \in N(k, 1)\,, \tag{2.12}$$

$$\sum_{j\in J(i,t)} Q_{jt} = X_{it}\,,\quad i = 1, 2, \ldots, I,\ t = 1, 2, \ldots, L + 1\,, \tag{2.13}$$

$$\sum_{n\in N(k,1)} \hat{Q}_{n1} = \hat{X}_{k1}\,,\quad k = 1, 2, \ldots, K\,, \tag{2.14}$$

$$\mathrm{lb}_{jt} \le Q_{jt} \le \mathrm{ub}_{jt}\,,\quad j \in J(i, t),\ i = 1, 2, \ldots, I,\ t = 1, 2, \ldots, L + 1\,, \tag{2.15}$$

$$\widehat{\mathrm{lb}}_{n1} \le \hat{Q}_{n1} \le \widehat{\mathrm{ub}}_{n1}\,,\quad n \in N(k, 1),\ k = 1, 2, \ldots, K\,, \tag{2.16}$$

where $J(i, t)$ and $N(k, 1)$ are the set of indices of families in product type i and parts in part type k that are triggered (will run out) in period t and 1 respectively. Similarly to the single stage models of Section 2.1, the objective of the disaggregation procedure is to minimize the set up costs at both stages. The objective function of (TD) assumes that while a set up is required for each part, the set up cost is equal for parts within a part type. Thus $\hat{s}_k$ can be interpreted as the average set up cost for parts within part type k. Constraints (2.11) could have been omitted and the production within the lead time 'frozen'. However, this was not done in Problem (TD) since some corrections can be accommodated in practice either by expediting production or by having special deliveries made by suppliers.

Constraints (2.12) together with (2.11) assure that the part production lots are sufficient to meet part requirements for $L + 1$ periods, (2.13) and (2.14) ensure consistency between the aggregate model and the scheduled lot sizes.

(2.15) and (2.16) impose upper and lower bounds on the production lot sizes. These bounds are defined in the same manner as in single stage models.

Problem (TD) has a convex objective function and linear constraints and is similar to the disaggregation problem (Pi) described in Section 2.1. It can be shown that (TD) can be decomposed into continuous convex knapsack subproblems and each can be solved through procedures similar to those used to solve problem (Pi).

Step 2. *Disaggregation to determine product item requirements*. Once the product family run quantities are determined, the item run quantities are computed by solving a disaggregation problem similar to that encountered in single stage problems [Problem (Qj) of Section 2.1]. The product item run quantities are determined by equalizing the run out time for items within a family.

2.4. *Materials requirement planning (MRP) and HPP*

MRP is perhaps the most commonly used approach to deal with multistage production planning problems and has become a benchmark for evaluation of HPP systems. (For a detailed description of this approach, the reader is referred to Chapter 11 of this volume and references therein.) The basic idea in MRP is to start with a master schedule for the final products, which is then exploded to compute the requirements for all parts. When all the requirements for a given part have been consolidated, an individual production schedule is developed for each item, based on appropriate lot sizing procedures. Typically, MRP systems offer a number of alternative methods for deriving item and part schedules. In most MRP systems, the master schedule is an external input. Thus MRP can be viewed as an information system and a simulation tool that generates proposals for production schedules which managers can evaluate in terms of their feasibility and cost effectiveness. In its present structure, MRP does not deal directly with optimization criteria associated with multilevel production problems. The lack of appropriate support for managers to generate good master schedules usually leads to infeasibilities of schedules due to capacity constraints. This fact is cited as one of the major weaknesses of MRP.

In contrast, the objective in HPP is to develop, at an aggregate level, a joint product type-part type schedule that is consistent and recognizes resource (capacity) limits. The schedule also attempts to minimize the primary costs. Moreover, the aggregate plan is concise and facilitates the understanding of its implications. The disaggregation procedures in HPP focus only on the time periods that cover a lead time, which avoids excessive amount of data and computational work. Bitran, Haas & Hax [1982] contrast the two approaches for a two-stage system and provide a numerical example to illustrate these differences. In this illustration, the master schedule for MRP was determined using the hierarchical procedure of Section 2.1 for single stage systems (end products). The Silver–Meal heuristic was used in developing detailed schedules for parts and items. The two stage model described in Section 2.3 was used to derive the schedules based on the HPP approach. The computational results of that paper suggest that considering explicitly the cost criteria and capacity constraints significantly improves the quality of the production plans.

Axsäter & Jonsson [1984] likewise note the limitations of MRP and suggest that the HPP philosophy can be used to develop systems to support MRP and overcome some of its limitations. They observe that MRP can be considered as a particular form of hierarchical structure, with end products at the highest level and parts and components at the lower levels. They remark that this hierarchy is not suitable in the presence of capacity limitations and suggest that the master schedule for MRP should be developed on the basis of other aggregation methods. Their paper reports simulation results of such a model developed for a Swedish company manufacturing rock drilling equipment. In the aggregate model items and parts are aggregated into three product groups based on number of operations; purchased items, items with at most five operations and the rest with more than five operations. Axsäter and Jonsson examine two alternative methods for aggregation of machine centers into machine groups. In the first method machine groups are based on production load; a utilization of 75% was used as a cut-off to form two machine groups. In the second method, aggregation is based on similarity of product flows. In this method a similarity coefficient s_{ij} between two machines i and j is defined as

$$s_{ij} = \frac{\text{number of items processed on both machines } i \text{ and } j}{\text{number of items processed on machine } i \text{ and/or machine } j} .$$

This measure developed by McAuley [1972] is commonly used in Group Technology and FMS applications in clustering parts and machines. For machine groups I and J containing n_I and n_J machines respectively, the similarity coefficient is defined in an analogous manner as

$$s_{IJ} = \frac{1}{n_I n_J} \sum_{i \in I} \sum_{j \in J} s_{ij} .$$

Axsäter and Jonsson suggest the use of models similar to those described in Section 2.2 for determining aggregation matrices specifying part and capacity requirements for a given grouping scheme. Aggregate production plans are determined sequentially using a hierarchy of objectives. First, aggregate plans for order releases are found by minimizing the sum of echelon stock and undelivered orders. In the second step production of raw materials and parts are determined. The priority of objectives in this step are as follows:

(i) minimize the deviation of machine load from capacity,
(ii) minimize the echelon stock at each stage,
(iii) minimize the net production.

The objective of disaggregation procedures is to obtain order releases for end items and parts that are consistent with the aggregate plans. The authors suggest that the MRP logic may be used in deriving the detailed schedule by modifying the order quantities to maintain consistency between the two levels. However, they adopt a procedure in which order release times are altered at each stage and the MRP logic is not strictly observed. The detailed schedules are derived based on the following priority scheme for order releases.

(i) Items needed to replenish safety stocks of final products.

(ii) Final products with negative slack.

(iii) Orders with earlier starting date according to the MRP system.

Simulation experiments with the two systems indicate that the hierarchical planning approach results in lower costs (statistically significant at 3% level with *t*-test and 7% with Wilcoxon test) compared to the stand alone MRP system. These experiments also examine the impact of alternate methods for aggregation and disaggregation procedures on the quality of the schedules.

The discussion above demonstrates the fact that MRP and HPP concepts are complementary rather than competitive. (Meal, Wachter & Whybark [1987] illustrate this complementarity with an application from the computer industry.) For example, MRP systems can be improved by use of optimization models at the aggregate level to derive good master schedules. Also, HPP methods have been developed for single and two stage systems only and extensions to multistage plants are not easy. The literature on this subject is quite scanty and there is considerable research potential to develop systems that integrate features of both systems.

3. Feedback mechanisms in HPP

An important component of hierarchical systems is the interaction between models at different levels to ensure consistency between the planning and scheduling decisions. 'Feedback' refers to this interaction and represents a critical link between the aggregate and the detailed decisions. This term, however, has been used with different meanings in the context of HPP. For some, feedback refers to the flow of information from the disaggregation problem to the aggregate level at the end of each period. To others it has meant a mechanism like the pricing procedure in generalized programming or like the obtainment of a sequence of convergent dual variables in subgradient algorithms. In this section we review both interpretations and the results presented in the literature. This discussion is primarily based on the models of single stage systems presented in Section 2.1.

In its simplest form the feedback from the detailed level includes the actual realization of the production and demands for each item. The information to the aggregate problem is the inventory levels of the product type. Another component of the feedback, not necessarily from the detailed level, includes revised forecasts of the demand at the product type level. A consequence of this information is the modification of the aggregate plan by resolving Problem (P) in each time period. The solution of the aggregate problem on a rolling horizon basis can thus be interpreted as the manifestation of the feedback mechanism in the Bitran and Hax procedure.

This information flow has other uses as well. For example, the myopic procedure of Section 2.1, for disaggregation of product type quantities into family lot sizes, could lead to infeasibilities. Bitran, Haas & Hax [1981] propose a 'look ahead feasibility rule' to overcome this problem. In this modification the families scheduled for production in a given period are based on (i) the revised aggregate plan, and (ii) the revised demand forecasts for the first two periods. This procedure is still based on knapsack problems and is computationally efficient.

This type of feedback mechanism has cost implications also. It may be recalled that the hierarchical structure of the models presented in Section 2.1 is suitable for systems in which the set up costs are not very significant. In such cases ignoring such costs at the aggregate level is not very critical. Bitran, Haas & Hax [1982] observe that these procedures are effective as long as the set up costs do not exceed 15% of the total production costs. They propose a modification of the regular knapsack method for cases with high set up cost. This heuristic modification adjusts the family run quantities [determined by the solution to Problem (P)] to a value as close as possible to the 'ideal lots' of the corresponding dynamic lot sizing problem. Motivated by computational considerations, the authors propose the use of the Silver–Meal heuristic to determine these ideal lot sizes.

Graves [1982] presents an alternative method to address the feedback question. In this approach 'feedback' between levels corresponds to the pricing procedure of generalized programming methods. Graves first formulates a mixed integer programming model combining the product type planning and family disaggregation decisions. He proposes the use of Lagrangean relaxation to solve the problem. The mixed integer programming model is described as follows:

$$\text{(MM)}\ \min \sum_{t=1}^{T} (o_t O_t + h_{it} I_{it}) + \sum_{j\in J(i)} \sum_{t=1}^{T} s_t \hat{K}_{jt}$$

subject to

$$I_{it-1} + X_{it} - I_{it} = d_{it}\,, \quad i = 1, 2, \ldots, I,\ t = 1, 2, \ldots, T\,, \tag{3.1}$$

$$\sum_{i=1}^{I} m_i X_{it} - O_t \leqslant (\mathrm{rm})_t\,, \quad t = 1, 2, \ldots, T\,, \tag{3.2}$$

$$\sum_{j\in J(i)} \hat{I}_{jt} - I_{it} = 0\,, \quad i = 1, 2, \ldots, I,\ t = 1, 2, \ldots, T\,, \tag{3.3}$$

$$Y_{jt} + I_{jt-1} - I_{jt} = 0\,, \quad j \in J(i),\ i = 1, 2, \ldots, I\,, \tag{3.4}$$

$$Y_{jt} - \hat{m}_j \hat{Y}_{jt} \leqslant 0\,, \quad t = 1, 2, \ldots, T\,, \tag{3.5}$$

$$\hat{Y}_{jt} \in \{0, 1\}\,, \tag{3.6}$$

$$O_t, X_{it}, Y_{jt}, I_{it}, \hat{I}_{jt} \geqslant 0\,, \tag{3.7}$$

where $\hat{I}_{jt}$ and $\hat{Y}_{jt}$ are the additional variables introduced at the family level. $\hat{I}_{jt}$ is the inventory of family j at the end of period t, while $\hat{Y}_{jt}$ is a binary variable associated with the set up of family j in period t.

The objective function of model (MM) minimizes the inventory holding costs, overtime costs and the set up costs. This model assumes that the regular time and other production costs are fixed and hence excluded from the objective function. Constraints (3.1) and (3.2) correspond to the aggregate decisions, while (3.4)–(3.6) correspond to the family disaggregation problem. Constraints (3.3) represent the linking constraints between the two models. Relaxation of constraint (3.3) gives rise to the following dual problem:

(MMD) $\max L(\lambda)$,

$$\text{subject to} \quad Z = \sum_t \Big(o_t O_t + \sum_i h_{it} I_{it}\Big) + \sum_j \sum_t \hat{s}_j \hat{Y}_{jt} ,$$

$$(3.1),\ (3.2),\ (3.4)\text{–}(3.7) ,$$

where

$$L(\lambda) = \min\Big[Z + \sum_{i,t} \lambda_{it}\Big(\sum_j \hat{I}_{jt} - I_{it}\Big)\Big] .$$

The dual problem (MMD) decomposes into subproblems (P′) and (P_i') described below.

$$(\mathrm{P}') \quad \min \sum \Big\{o_t O_t + \sum_i I_{it}(h_{it} - \lambda_{it})\Big\}$$

subject to (3.1), (3.2), (3.7);

$$(\mathrm{P}_i') \quad \min \sum_{j \in J(i)} \sum_{t=1}^{T} s_j \hat{Y}_{jt} + \lambda_{it} \hat{I}_{jt}$$

subject to (3.4)–(3.7) .

Problems (P) and (P′) differ in the definition of the inventory carrying costs. In (P′) the parameter h_{it} is modified to adjust for the dual multiplier of constraint (3.3). Problems (P_i') address the same issue as (P_i), i.e., disaggregation of product types into family lots, but have a different structure. (P_i') decomposes into a set of uncapacitated Wagner–Whitin type lot sizing problems that can be solved efficiently using dynamic programming algorithms. Graves presents an iterative procedure to solve (MMD) and suggests that a heuristic or a branch and bound procedure may be followed to obtain a good feasible solution.

A comparison of the two approaches suggests that the Lagrangean relaxation procedure is likely to provide more cost effective schedules that are likely to be significantly better in cases with high set up costs. However, this should be balanced against the computational requirements and the complexity of the algorithm.

4. HPP and stochastic programming

The hierarchical models described so far in this chapter are primarily deterministic in nature. However, in many real life production situations uncertainties cannot be ignored. In this section we describe three applications of the hierarchical approach to provide an overview of the research in this area. In Section 4.1 we present a job shop design/scheduling problem. This is based on the work by Dempster, Fisher, Jansen, Lageweg, Lenstra & Rinnooy Kan [1980, 1981] and provides a framework for evaluating the hierarchical approach. Section 4.2 is based on the work by Bitran, Haas & Matsuo [1986] and deals with the production planning and scheduling problem in the manufacture of style goods. In Section 4.3 we describe Gershwin's [1987] framework for addressing scheduling and control problems in dynamic manufacturing systems with machine failures, setups and demand changes.

4.1. A job shop design/scheduling problem

Dempster, Fisher, Jansen, Lageweg, Lenstra & Rinnooy Kan [1981] argue that hierarchical models represent a stochastic, multi-level decision process in which decisions at higher levels are often based on aggregate imperfect information. They suggest that such decisions should be based on accurate models of lower level activities that incorporate stochastic parameters to capture the uncertainties in the detailed decisions. They suggest that the objective at each level be the minimization of the current costs plus the expected value of the lower level decisions. The combination of stochastic optimization and scheduling problems makes the resulting formulations very hard to solve. The authors interpret the hierarchical approach as heuristics to solve the global problem. They suggest that the multi-stage stochastic formulation provides a useful framework to evaluate alternative approaches to solve the problem addressed by hierarchical production planning. Their results focus primarily on the analysis and on the development of bounds and heuristics to solve approximately their stochastic programming formulation. In what follows, we illustrate their approach by means of a simple two-level problem described in Dempster, Fisher, Jansen, Lageweg, Lenstra & Rinnooy Kan [1981].

In this simplified example, it is assumed that the number of jobs to be processed is known. The design (higher level) decision consists in determining the number of identical parallel machines to be purchased. At this stage, the job processing times are unknown and are assumed to be random variables with independent distributions. At the detailed level, the number of machines is considered fixed since it is an output of the first stage decisions, and the job processing times are known exactly. The resulting problem is to determine a schedule which minimizes the makespan. (Makespan of a schedule denotes the time required to complete all the jobs.) We use the following notation to describe the model formulations:

n = number of jobs,
c = cost of a single machine,
m = number of machines,
p_j = processing time of job j,

$$p = (p_1, p_2, \ldots, p_n),$$

$C^*(m, \tilde{p})$ = minimum makespan to complete n jobs with m machines and known $\tilde{p}$.

A tilde ($\tilde{}$) above a variable indicates that it is a random variable and E denotes its expected value.

Dempster et al. propose the following two stage stochastic problem to model this situation:

$$\text{(MSP)} \quad Z^* = \min\{cm + \mathrm{E}C^*(m, \tilde{p})\}.$$

The deterministic, parallel machine scheduling problem (with fixed number of machines) to minimize the makespan represents the detailed (second) level optimization problem. This problem, by itself is NP-hard which makes (MSP) also very difficult to solve. The authors propose a two level hierarchical procedure to solve the problem approximately. At the detailed level, schedules are obtained by a list processing heuristic. In this method, jobs are chosen in an arbitrary manner and assigned to machines by a single pass heuristic. Each job is placed on the machine that has the least processing load already assigned. The makespan corresponding to this schedule is denoted by $C^{\mathrm{Ls}}(m, p)$. At the first level an approximate solution to (MSP) is obtained by solving a related problem (MSP) given below.

$$\text{(MSP}') \quad \min_m \{cm + \mathrm{E}\tilde{P}/m\},$$

where $P = \Sigma_{j=1}^n p_j$.

The above approximation is motivated by the facts that P/m represents a lower bound on the makespan and it is asymptotically optimal in the number of jobs. The optimal solution to (MSP′) is given by m^{H} such that $m^{\mathrm{H}} \in \{\lfloor \mathrm{E}\tilde{P}/c \rfloor, \lceil \mathrm{E}\tilde{P}/c \rceil\}$, subject to $m^{\mathrm{H}} \geq 1$, where $\lceil a \rceil$ denotes the smallest integer not less than a and $\lfloor a \rfloor$ denotes the largest integer not greater than a. The overall value realized by this hierarchical approach is then given by

$$Z^{\mathrm{H}} = cm^{\mathrm{H}} + \mathrm{E}C^{\mathrm{Ls}}(m^{\mathrm{H}}, \tilde{P}).$$

It is easy to show that $Z_{\mathrm{H}}/Z^* \leq 1 + \mathrm{E}p_{\max}/(2\sqrt{c\mathrm{E}\tilde{P}})$ where $p_{\max} = \max\{p_j\}$. This result provides bounds on the performance of the hierarchical approach. The bound is reasonable as long as $p_{\max}$ is sufficiently small. The authors also show that if the p_j's have independent and identical distributions with finite second moments, then the hierarchical system is asymptotically optimal in the sense that

$$\lim_{n\to\infty}(\mathrm{E}p_{\max}/\sqrt{\mathrm{E}\tilde{P}}) = 0 \quad \text{and hence} \quad \lim_{n\to\infty}(Z^{\mathrm{H}}/Z^*) = 1 .$$

It is interesting to note that the hierarchical structure proposed for this problem is consistent with the Hax–Meal framework described earlier. At the first level all jobs are replaced by the aggregate processing requirements and complicating details are omitted. The authors conjecture that similar approaches would work well for more complicated systems because the instances for which the higher level assumptions are severely violated occur with decreasingly small probability as the problem grows larger.

A detailed discussion of this approach and extensions to more elaborate models can be found in Dempster, Fisher, Jansen, Lageweg, Lenstra & Rinnooy Kan [1981], Dempster [1982] and Lenstra, Rinnooy Kan & Stongie [1984]. Their research focuses on (i) the development of heuristics to solve the multistage stochastic program and (ii) the derivation of relations between performance measures in related model formulations. A summary of the results relating the performance measures for a two stage decision model is presented in Figure 4.1. In developing these relations, the authors consider, in addition to the exact and approximate formulation based on the hierarchical approach, a third model based on perfect information. This 'omniscient' model represents the best scenario in which all information is known with certainty before the first stage decisions are made and provides a lower bound on the multistage decision model. The following notation would be useful in interpreting the results of Figure 4.1:

x = first stage decisions,
X = set of feasible decisions at the first stage,
$\tilde{w}$ = vector of resource requirements at the second stage,
F = distribution function of w,
W = sample space for w,
$g^*(x, w)$ = cost of optimal decision at the second stage, given the first stage decision x and the realization w of resource requirements,
$f(x)$ = cost of acquisition of x at the first stage,
$Z^*(x, w) = f(x) + g^*(x, w)$.

Figure 4.1 describes the relations between the following three models.
Stochastic program for the two stage decision process.

$$\mathrm{E}Z^* = \mathrm{E}(Z^*(x^*, \tilde{w})) = \min_{x\in X}\{\mathrm{E}(Z^*(x, \tilde{w}))\} .$$

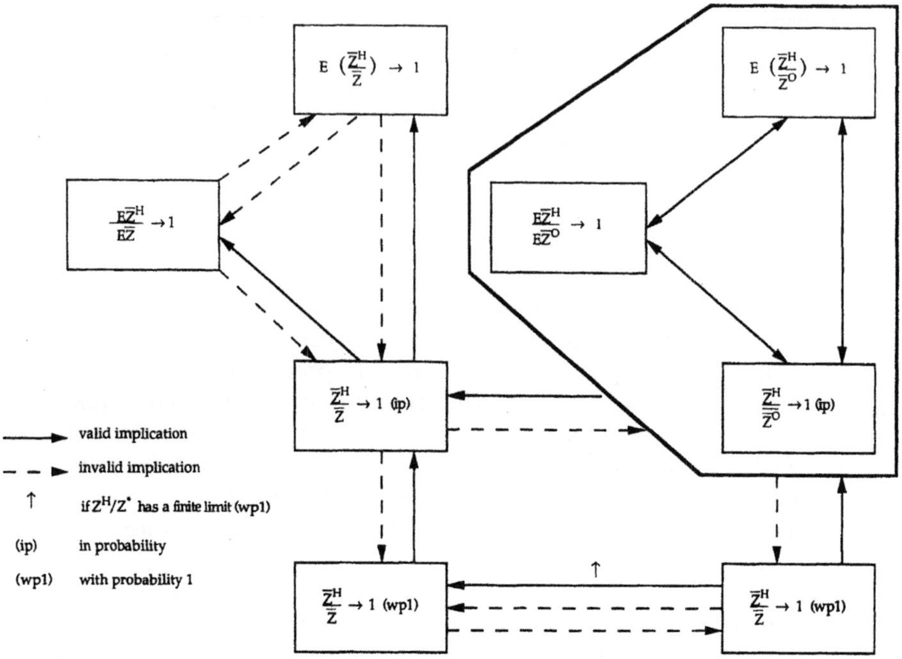

Fig. 4.1. Relations between performance measures.

Omniscient model.

$$Z^0 = Z^*(x^0(w), w) = \min_{x \in X}\{Z^*(x, w)\} .$$

Note that Z^0 (like Z^*) is a function of the resource requirements w and is a random variable. The expectation of Z^0 with respect to w, $\mathrm{E}Z^0$ would be the appropriate measure to compare the performance of this model with that of the stochastic program, $\mathrm{E}Z^*$.

Hierarchical approach. In this model, in the first stage decision, $\mathrm{E}(g^*(x, w))$ is replaced by an estimate $g^{\mathrm{H1}}(x)$, and the first stage decision x^{H} is determined as

$$Z^{\mathrm{H1}}(x^{\mathrm{H}}) = \min_{x \in X}\{Z^{\mathrm{H1}}(x)\} = \min_{x \in X}\{f(x) + g^{\mathrm{H1}}(x)\} .$$

In the second stage x^{H} is given and the requirements w are known. The decisions are made using a detailed model at a cost of $g^{\mathrm{H2}}(x^{\mathrm{H}}, w)$. (The authors observe that while $g^{\mathrm{H2}}(x^{\mathrm{H}}, w)$ could be the result of solving optimally the detailed model, in most cases, the detailed problems are hard. In these cases, $g^{\mathrm{H2}}(x^{\mathrm{H}}, w)$ may be the result of an approximate solution to the second stage model.) Also, the information available at the two decision stages is different, and the functions $g^{H1}(x)$ and $g^{H2}(x^H, w)$ are usually different. The cost of the decisions based on this hierarchical approach is then given by

$$Z^H = f(x^H) + g^{H2}(x^H, w) .$$

Z^H, like Z^0, is a function of w, and EZ^H is the appropriate measure for comparison with EZ^*.

Figure 4.1 presents a summary of results relating to the ratios of cost functions Z^*, Z^H and Z^0 and their expectations. For example, if $Z^H/Z^0 \to 1$ with probability 1 (wp1), then $Z^H/Z^* \to 1$ wp1. However, the converse is not true, and $Z^H/Z^* \to 1$ wp1 does not imply that $Z^H/Z^0 \to 1$ wp1. Similarly, each of the conditions $Z^H/Z^0 \to 1$ in probability (ip), $E(Z^H/Z^0) \to 1$ and $EZ^H/EZ^0 \to 1$ imply that the others are true. Also these conditions imply that the corresponding results hold for Z^H/Z^*. Again, the converse is not true and $Z^H/Z^* \to 1$ ip does not imply that $Z^H/Z^0 \to 1$ ip.

The approach above is most suitable when the higher level decisions are irreversible as in the case of acquisition of machines. For example, in the production planning problems discussed in Sections 2 and 3, the aggregate decisions were flexible in the sense that plans were revised every period. In contrast, the models of Dempster et al. assume that the first stage decisions, once made, cannot be altered (as in the case of purchase of machines).

4.2. Production planning and scheduling with stochastic demand

In the production planning and scheduling models described in Sections 2 and 3 uncertainties occur primarily because of errors in demand estimates. Also, aggregate decisions are somewhat flexible and permit minor changes based on the forecast revisions. The rolling horizon approach to the aggregate problem incorporates this aspect of the problem. A justification for the disaggregation procedure of Section 2 for the case with stochastic demands can be found in Agnihotri [1982]. The author shows that, with stochastic demands, the Bitran and Hax disaggregation procedure provides a lower bound to the family run out time.

Bitran, Haas & Matsuo [1986] explicitly consider uncertainties in demand estimates and forecast revisions while examining production planning and scheduling issues in the manufacture of style goods. Style goods are characterized by a very short selling season and stochastic demand. Because of capacity limitations, manufacturers of style goods usually build up inventory over the year preparing for demand in the selling season. If the demand exceeds on-hand inventory, a shortage cost is incurred, while if the opposite occurs, an overage cost is incurred. Example of style goods can be found in a variety of situations ranging from clothing to consumer durables. The problem is similar to the multi-item newsboy problem with capacity constraints with two additional characteristics described below.

First, the products have a hierarchical structure. That is, individual items are categorized into families. A family is defined as a set of items that share a common setup, consume the same amount of resources per unit, and have the same magnitude of forecast errors. Setup costs are so large that all items within a family must be produced in a single setup. Hence, the production planning decisions consist in determining the sequence in which the product families will be produced and the production lot sizes for items within each family with the objective of minimizing the total cost.

The second feature relates to demand forecasts and revisions during the planning horizon. The mean demand for each family is assumed to be invariant over time. However, demand forecasts for items are revised continuously over the planning horizon. The authors assume that the planners can estimate the improvement in the accuracy of forecasts, perhaps based on historical trends. Forecast accuracy is measured by standard deviation of forecast errors. For example, the volume of a standard line of products can be forecast nearly as accurately in January as in October, while the accuracy of forecasts for new products can be expected to significantly improve over time. Intuition suggests that to take advantage of this characteristic, some standard products should be produced early in the year and the production of families with a potential for large improvement in forecast should be deferred.

Bitran, Haas and Matsuo formulate the problem as a mixed integer stochastic program and propose a two-stage hierarchical approach to solve this difficult problem. The aggregate problem is formulated as a deterministic mixed integer program that provides a lower bound on the optimal solution. The solution to this problem determines the set of product families to be produced in each period. The second level problem may be interpreted as a disaggregation stage where item lot sizes are determined for families scheduled in each period. We now describe the problem in detail.

Notation

i = index for families; n = number of families,
j = index for items; N = number of items,
$J(i)$ = set of indices of items in family i; n_i = number of items in family i,
T = number of time periods in the planning horizon,
m_{jt} = time-t forecast of the demand of item j (this parameter represents the demand forecast for item j at time t and is discussed in detail later),
M_i = mean demand for family i,
X_{jt} = production quantity of item j in period t,
X_{it} = production quantity of family i in period t,
r_{it} = resource consumption for producing one unit of an item in family i in period t,
R_t = resource available in period t,
s_{it} = set up cost for family i in period t,
h_{jt} = inventory holding cost of item j in period t,
v_{jt} = material cost of item j in period t,

v'_{jt} = variable production and inventory holding cost of item j
$= v_{jt} + \Sigma_{k=t}^{T} h_j k$,
P_j = unit selling price of item j,
B_j = loss of goodwill due to shortage of one unit of item j,
G_j = salvage value of item j,
$\delta(X_{jt}) = 1$ if $X_{jt} > 0$,
$= 0$ otherwise,
$d_{\cdot t}$ = N-component vector $(d_{1t}, d_{2t}, \ldots, d_{Nt})$,
$m_{\cdot t}$ = N-component vector $(m_{1t}, \ldots, m_{2t}, \ldots, m_{Nt})$.

Forecasts of item demands and their revisions play an important role in the production planning and scheduling problem examined by Bitran, Haas and Matsuo. The authors make several assumptions in characterizing the demand behavior. These are summarized below:

(1) The demand estimates in period t for items within a family follow a joint normal distribution.

(2) The mean family demand is known in period 1 for all families and does not change over time, i.e.,

$$\sum_{j \in J(i)} m_{jt} = M_i \,, \quad i = 1, 2, \ldots, n, \; t = 1, 2, \ldots, T \,.$$

(3) The demand estimates of items in family i have a covariance matrix $\sigma_{it}^2 \Sigma_i$ in period t for $i = 1, 2, \ldots, n$, $t = 1, 2, \ldots, T$, where Σ_i is an $n_i \times n_i$ correlation coefficient matrix.

(4) The precision of the forecasts are known in period 1, i.e., the standard deviation of forecast errors of items in family i, σ_{it}, is known for $i = 1, 2, \ldots, n$, $t = 1, 2, \ldots, T$ in period 1.

(5) In period t, the demand of items in family i are denoted by random variables $(d_{1t}, d_{2t}, \ldots, d_{n_i t})$ with joint normal distribution

$$\mathrm{N}((m_{1t}, m_{2t}, \ldots, m_{n_i t}), \sigma_{it}^2 \Sigma_i) \,.$$

(6) The forecast accuracy is assumed not to decrease as t increases, i.e.,

$$\sigma_{i1} \geq \sigma_{i2} \geq \cdots \geq \sigma_{iT} \,, \quad i = 1, 2, \ldots, n \,.$$

The above assumptions imply that the forecasts in period t for items in family i, $(m_{1t}, m_{2t}, \ldots, m_{n_i t})$, follow a joint normal distribution with mean $(m_{11}, m_{21}, \ldots, m_{n_i 1})$ and covariance matrix $(\sigma_{i1}^2 - \sigma_{it}^2)\Sigma_i$.

The formulation in Bitran, Haas and Matsuo [1986] applies when the setup costs of producing each family are substantial. The authors assume that each family is setup exactly once in the planning horizon and that all production of a given family occurs during one period. They point out that this assumption is unlikely to be critical when the number of families is much larger than the number of time periods. A consequence of these assumptions is that, for each family i, only one of the X_{it}'s, $t = 1, 2, \ldots, T$, is positive. The cost function can then be formulated in a manner similar to that in a newsboy problem. The overage and underage costs of producing item j in period t are then given by $(v'_{jt} - G_j)$ and $(P_j + B_j - v'_{jt})$, respectively. The cost of producing family i in period t can then be written as follows:

$$\sum_{j \in J(i)} f_{jt}(X_{jt}) + s_{it} ,$$

where

$$f_{jt}(x_{jt}) = \begin{cases} (P_j + B_j - v'_{jt})(d_{jt} - x_{jt}) + v'_{jt} d_{jt} & \text{if } d_{jt} \geqslant x_{jt} , \\ (v'_{jt} - G_j)(x_{jt} - d_{jt}) + v'_{jt} d_{jt} & \text{if } d_{jt} < x_{jt} . \end{cases}$$

The stochastic mixed integer program (P) presented below models the production planning problem as a cost minimization program.

$$\text{(P)} \quad V_{\mathrm{P}} = \min \sum_{t=1}^{T} \mathrm{E}_{m \cdot t | m \cdot 1} \min \mathrm{E}_{d_{\cdot t} | m_{\cdot t}} \sum_{i=1}^{n} \Big\{ \sum_{j \in J(i)} f_{jt}(X_{jt}) + s_{it} \Big\} Y_{it}$$

subject to

$$\sum_{t=1}^{T} Y_{it} = 1 , \quad i = 1, 2, \ldots, n , \tag{4.1}$$

$$\sum_{i=1}^{n} \sum_{j \in J(i)} r_{it} X_{jt} \leqslant R_t , \quad t = 1, 2, \ldots, T , \tag{4.2}$$

$$X_{jt} \leqslant M Y_{it} , \quad j \in J(i) , \quad t = 1, 2, \ldots, T , \quad i = 1, 2, \ldots, n , \tag{4.3}$$

$$Y_{it} \in \{0, 1\} , \quad i = 1, 2, \ldots, n , \quad t = 1, 2, \ldots, T , \tag{4.4}$$

$$X_{jt} \geqslant 0 , \quad j \in J(i) , \quad i = 1, 2, \ldots, n , \quad t = 1, 2, \ldots, T , \tag{4.5}$$

where

$$\Big[\min \mathrm{E}_{d_{\cdot t} | m_{\cdot t}} \Big[\sum_{j \in J(i)} f_{jt}(X_{jt}) \Big] + s_{it} \Big] Y_{it}$$

represents the optimum cost of scheduling family i in period t. Note that at time t, the forecasts are $m_{\cdot t}$ and demands for items in family i follow a joint normal distribution with mean $(m_{it}, m_{2t}, \ldots, m_{n_i t})$ and covariance matrix $(\sigma_{i1}^2 - \sigma_{it}^2)\Sigma_i$. However, in period 1, $m_{\cdot t}$ are random variables (with mean $m_{\cdot 1}$) and the expected cost in period 1 for scheduling family i in period t is given by the expectation of the expression above with respect to $m_{\cdot t}$. Hence the objective function of (P) can be interpreted as the expected cost of the production plan that is based on information available in period 1. The constraints of Problem (P) are rather straightforward. (4.1) ensures that each family is produced exactly once, while (4.2) imposes resource restrictions in each period. (4.3) assures consistency between family and item production schedules.

It is obvious that (P) is a hard problem with little hope for obtaining an optimal solution for most practical cases. Bitran, Haas and Matsuo propose an approximate solution based on a hierarchical approach. In period 1 an aggregate problem (MIP) presented below is solved at the product family level.

$$\text{(MIP)}\ V_{\text{mip}} = \min \sum_{i=1}^{n} \sum_{t=1}^{T} f_{it}(X_{it}) Y_{it}$$
$$\text{subject to} \quad (4.1)\text{–}(4.5),$$

where

$$f_{it}(X_{it}) = \min \mathrm{E}_{d_{\cdot t}|m_{\cdot t}=m_{\cdot 1}} \sum_{j \in J(i)} f_{jt}(X_{jt}) + s_{it}$$
$$\text{subject to} \quad \sum_{j \in J(i)} X_{jt} = X_{it}\,, \quad X_{jt} \geqslant 0\,.$$

The purpose of the aggregate problem (MIP) is to specify the families that need to be produced in each period. The item lot sizes determined by (MIP) are ignored. Instead, the authors propose the solution of the disaggregation problem (SP), given below, in each period.

$$\text{(SP)} \quad v(s_t, m_{\cdot t}) = \min \mathrm{E}_{d_{\cdot t}|m_{\cdot t}} \sum_{i \in S_t} \sum_{j \in J(i)} f_{jt}(X_{jt}) + \sum_{i \in S_t} s_{it}$$
$$\text{subject to} \quad \sum_{i \in S_t} \sum_{j \in J(i)} r_{it} X_{jt} \leqslant R_t\,,$$
$$X_{jt} \geqslant 0\,, \quad j \in J(i),\ i \in S_t\,,$$

where S = set of families scheduled in period t, determined by (MIP).

Bitran, Haas and Matsuo provide extensive justification for the approach described above. They show that V_{mip} is a lower bound on V_{P}. They also demonstrate that if the nonnegativity constraints (4.5) are relaxed, the optimal objective function values for Problems (P) and (MIP) ($V_{\text{p}'}$ and $V_{\text{mip}'}$) are equal. It is further argued that in most applications the nonnegativity constraints are violated with low probability and hence (MIP) should be a good approximation to (P). To obtain detailed schedules (item production quantities), the authors show that Problem (SP) provides a superior solution (a better lower bound) compared to the one obtained by disaggregating the product family lot sizes determined by (MIP). The paper also presents approximate solution procedures for (MIP) and (SP) and provides bounds on the performance of the heuristics.

One of the limitations of the approach described above is the restriction that the production of one family be started and completed during the same period. This constraint seems rather artificial and may become important when the number of families is not very large. In a recent paper, Matsuo [1990] examines a different formulation of the problem and presents solution procedures that eliminate this restriction. He formulates a stochastic sequencing problem that simultaneously determines product sequence and production volumes for the style goods production planning problem. In his formulation time is treated as a continuous variable. Matsuo's solution procedure is also based on the hierarchical approach. In the first stage family lot sizes and sequence are determined by specifying, for each family, the start and finish times of production. In the second stage the family lot sizes are disaggregated. The analysis in this paper is rather involved, but the sequencing rules that are derived are intuitively appealing, elegant and surprisingly simple.

4.3. Production control and scheduling in the presence of machine breakdowns

Gershwin [1987] considers scheduling problems in dynamic manufacturing systems with machine failures, setups, demand changes, etc., and proposes a hierarchical structure based on the frequency of occurrence of different types of events. This framework is based on the assumption that events tend to occur in a discrete spectrum which define the hierarchical levels. For example, the frequency of additions of machines is an order of magnitude smaller than setup decisions, which in turn, occur less frequently than item production. A central assumption in this approach is that activities can be grouped into sets $J_1, J_2, \ldots$ such that for each set J_k, there exists a characteristic frequency f_k satisfying

$$f_1 \ll f_2 \ll \cdots \ll f_k \ll f_{k+1} \ll \cdots .$$

In this framework the hierarchical levels are defined by the frequency of activities (sets J_k). In modeling the decisions at each level, quantities that vary slowly (variables that correspond to higher levels) are treated as static, or constant, and discrete. Quantities that vary much faster (variables at lower levels) are modeled in a way that ignores the variations, for example, replacing fast moving variables by their averages. These ideas may be illustrated by considering a production planning example. In aggregate planning models, the number of machines (variables that correspond to higher level of hierarchy) are considered fixed. Also, in these models, details such as machine breakdowns (lower level variables) are ignored. However, the effect of breakdowns is usually accounted for by factoring an adjustment (based on expected behavior) in available capacity. An interesting feature in this approach is the treatment of capacity. Gershwin makes a distinction between capacities at different hierarchical levels. Figure 4.2, which describes the capacity definitions for an item in a multi-item shop that is modeled with three hierarchical levels, provides an example to clarify this idea. In this example, the terms capacity and production

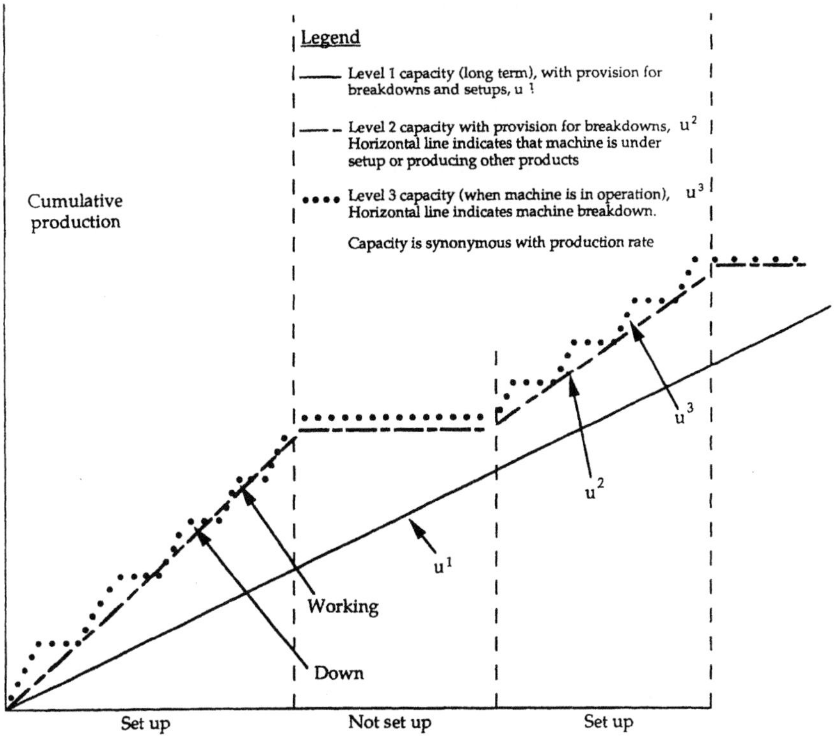

Fig. 4.2.

rate are synonymous. In the figure u^1 is the aggregate production rate (at level 1) that is equal to the demand rate and represents the capacity available for this item. u^2, the capacity at the next level, is the relevant capacity when the setup decisions are considered. At the operational level, when breakdowns occur, the production rate u^3 is higher than u^2 and u^1. Gershwin also distinguishes between controllable variables and activities such as breakdowns and repair that are beyond control.

The objective of this approach is to determine an optimal control strategy at the detailed level. The control strategy is specified by selecting the time to initiate each controllable event. Gershwin proposes the solution of one or two problems at each level to derive the control strategy. These problems are termed as the hedging point strategy and the staircase strategy. In the hedging point strategy problem at level k, the objective is to determine level-k capacities u_j^k, $j \in J_m$, $m > k$, i.e., determine u_j^k for all activities that occur more frequently than f_k. Constraints are imposed by the total capacity available and the decisions at the higher levels. The staircase strategy problem can be interpreted as the allocation of resources among activities at level k, consistent with production rates u^{k-1} determined at the previous level.

Gershwin, Akella & Choong [1985], Kimemia & Gershwin [1983] describe some applications of this approach and discuss the detailed formulation and solution procedures for the staircase and hedging point strategy problems. The two machine, two product example of Figure 4.3 described in Gershwin [1987] can be used to illustrate the basic ideas of this approach. In this example, machine 1 is an unreliable, flexible machine that can produce both parts types 1 and 2. No setups are required to change from product type 1 to 2 or vice versa. Machine 2 is dedicated to production of part type 1 and is totally reliable. The following data is available.

p = failure rate for machine 1,
r = repair rate for machine 1,
t_{ij} = duration of the operation of part type j on machine i (t_{11}, t_{12}, t_{21}),
d_{ij}= demand rates of part type j on machine i (d_{11}, d_{12}, d_{21}).

It is assumed that (i) t_{ij} and $1/d_{ij}$ are of the same order of magnitude, and (ii) $1/r$ and $1/p$ are of the same order of magnitude which is greater than t_{ij}. The state of the system is specified by α, the repair state of machine 1 and x_{11}, x_{12}, and x_{21}, where x_{ij} is the surplus inventory and is defined as the excess of production capacity over the cumulative requirement. An example of a staircase strategy at level 2 for this example is presented in Figure 4.4, which describes the loading decisions as a function of the system state. At level 1, the

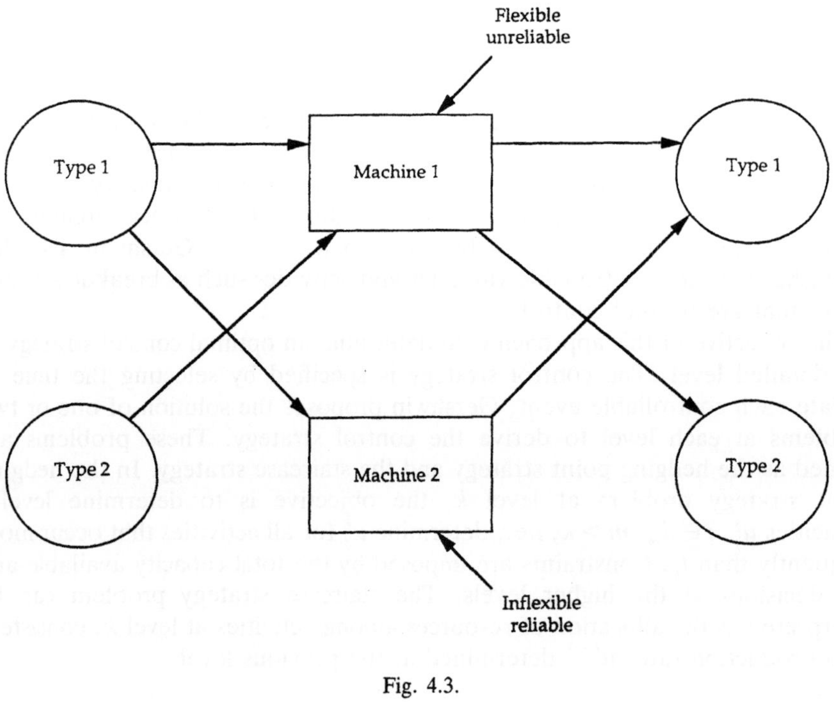

Fig. 4.3.

Level 2: *Staircase strategy*

Loading a Type j part into Machine 1 is eligible if:

1. The number of Type j parts made up to time t on Machine 1 is less than

$$\int_0^t u_{1j}(s)\,ds ,$$

2. Machine 1 is now idle.

Loading a Type 1 part into Machine 2 is eligible if:

1. The number of Type 1 parts made up to time t on Machine 2 is less than

$$\int_0^t u_{21}(s)\,ds ,$$

2. Machine 2 is now idle.

Fig. 4.4.

hedging point strategy problem can be formulated as follows:

$$\min_{u_{ij}} \sum c_{ij}(x, \alpha)u_{ij}$$

$$\begin{aligned} \text{subject to} \quad & t_{11}u_{11} + t_{12}u_{12} \leqslant \alpha , \\ & t_{21}u_{21} \leqslant 1 , \\ & u_{11}, u_{12}, u_{21} \geqslant 0 , \end{aligned}$$

where u_{ij} is the production rate of part type j on machine i (decision variable), $c_{ij}(x, \alpha)$ is the cost of maintaining production rate u_{ij} with the system state (x, α).

The approach described above is a fairly recent development in the application of the hierarchical approach to control and scheduling problems in discrete manufacturing systems. There are several outstanding issues that need to be resolved before the methods can be applied widely. These problems include the following:

(i) Development of methods to model systems in which the time scales for various activities are not widely separated,

(ii) formulating and solving hedging point problems with non-Markov events,

(iii) new formulations and solution procedures for the staircase strategy to obtain loading patterns that are very close to a given rate,

(iv) aggregation issues in modeling higher level activities.

5. Conclusions

In this chapter we have described the basic features of the hierarchical approach in addressing planning and scheduling problems. We have also described some of the models and presented results of general interest in this context. These models span a wide variety of manufacturing environments ranging from continuous processes to discrete systems such as batch and job shops. The approach has been successful on two dimensions. First, the hierarchical framework is attractive to practitioners as evidenced by the several applications that have been reported. Second, considerable amount of research has been generated in developing appropriate models and solution methods.

However, in spite of the developments in the last decade, there is a need for good models that support decisions in more complex environments. We note four areas with potential for further research. First, the problem of aggregation and disaggregation has not been resolved satisfactorily. Second, detailed models have been developed for single and two stage systems only. It is not clear how such models can be extended to more complex systems. Third, the issue of feedback in hierarchical systems has not been explored adequately and merits further research. And finally, except in a few cases, good models have not been developed for systems characterized by uncertainties.

References

Agnihotri, S. (1982). Stochastic allocation rules. *Oper. Res.* 30, 545–555.

Andersson, H., S. Axsäter and H. Jonsson (1981). Hierarchical material requirements planning. *Internat. J. Prod. Res.* 19, 45–57.

Anthony, R.N. (1965). Planning and control systems: A framework for analysis, Harvard University, Graduate School of Business Administration, Cambridge, MA.

Axsäter, S. (1981). Aggregation of product data for hierarchical production planning. *Oper. Res.* 29, 744–756.

Axsäter, S. (1986). Feasibility of aggregate production plans. *Oper. Res.* 34, 796–800.

Axsäter, S., and H. Jonsson (1984). Aggregation and disaggregation in hierarchical production planning. *European J. Oper. Res.* 17, 338–350.

Axsäter, S., H. Jonsson and Thorsterson (1983). Approximate aggregation of product data. *Engrg. Costs Prod. Econom.* 7, 119–126.

Bitran, G.R., and A.C. Hax (1977). On the design of hierarchical production planning systems. *Decision Sci.* 8, 28–55.

Bitran, G.R., and A.C. Hax (1981). Disaggregation and resource allocation using convex knapsack problems. *Management Sci.* 27, 431–441.

Bitran, G.R., E.A. Haas and A.C. Hax (1981) Hierarchical production planning: A single stage system. *Oper. Res.* 29, 717–743.

Bitran, G.R., E.A. Haas and A.C. Hax (1982). Hierarchical production planning: A two stage system. *Oper. Res.* 30, 232–251.

Bitran, G.R., E.A. Haas and H. Matsuo (1986). Production planning of style goods with high set-up costs and forecast revisions. *Oper. Res.* 34, 226–236.

Bitran, G.R., and D. Tirupati (1988a) Planning and scheduling for epitaxial wafer production facilities. *Oper. Res.* 36(1), 34–49.

Bitran, G.R., and D. Tirupati (1988b). Development and implementation of a scheduling system: An application in a wafer fabrication facility. *Oper. Res.* 36(3), 377–395.

Bradley, S.P., A.C. Hax and T.L. Magnanti (1977). *Applied Mathematical Programming*, Addison Wesley, Reading, MA. Chapter 6 based on the technical paper by A.C. Hax, Integration of strategic and tactical planning in the aluminum industry, Working Paper 026-73, September 1973; Operations Research Center, M.I.T.; Chapter 10 based on the paper by R.J. Armstrong and A.C. Hax, A Hierarchical Approach for a Naval Tender Job-Shop Design, Technical Report No. 101, Operations Research Center, M.I.T., Cambridge, MA.

Chipman, J.S. (1975). The aggregation problem in economics. *Suppl. Adv. Appl. Probab.* 7, 72–83.

Chipman, J.S. (1976). Estimation and aggregation in econometrics: An application of the theory of generalized inverses, in: M.Z. Nashed (ed.), *Generalized Inverses and Application*, Academic Press, New York, pp. 549–570.

Dempster, M.A.H. (1982). A stochastic approach to hierarchical planning and scheduling, in: M.A.H. Dempster, J.K. Lenstra and A.H.G. Rinnooy Kan (eds.), *Deterministic and Stochastic Scheduling*, Reidel, Dordrecht, pp. 271–296.

Dempster, M.A.H., M.L. Fisher, L. Jansen, B.J. Lageweg, J.K. Lenstra and A.H.G. Rinnooy Kan (1981). Analytical evaluations of hierarchical planning systems. *Oper. Res.* 29, 707–716.

Doumeingts, G., L. Pun, M. Mondain and D. Breuil (1978). Decision-making systems for production control planning and scheduling. *Internat. J. Prod. Res.* 16, 137–152.

Dzielinski, B.P., and R.E. Gomory (1965). Optimal programming of lot sizes inventory and labor allocations. *Management Sci.* 11(9), 874–890.

Erschler, J., G. Fontan and C. Merce (1986). Consistency of the disaggregation process in hierarchical planning. *Oper. Res.* 34, 464–469.

Fisher, W.D. (1969). *Clustering and Aggregation in Economics*, Johns Hopkins University Press, Baltimore, MD.

Gabbay, H. (1975). Hierarchical approach to production planning, Technical Report No. 120, Operations Research Center, M.I.T., Cambridge, MA.

Gabbay, H. (1979). Optimal aggregation and disaggregation in hierarchical planning, in: L.P. Ritzman, L.J. Krajewski, W.L. Berry, S.H. Goodman, S.T. Hardy and L.D. Vitt (eds.), *Disaggregation: Problems in Manufacturing and Service Organizations*, Martinus Nijhoff, Boston, MA.

Gelders, L.F., and L.N. Van Wassenhove (1982). Hierarchical integration in production planning: Theory and practice. *J. Oper. Management* 3(1), 27–35.

Geoffrion, A.M. (1977). Aggregation theory and its application to modeling in mathematical programming,, Working Paper No. 278, Western Management Science Inst., Univ. of California, Los Angeles, CA.

Geoffrion, A.M. (1987). An introduction to structured modeling. *Management Sci.* 33(5), 547–588.

Gershwin, S.B. (1987). A hierarchical framework for discrete event scheduling in manufacturing systems, LIDS-P-1682, MIT, Presented at the IIASA Workshop in Discrete Event Systems: Models and Applications, Soprun, Hungary.

Gershwin, S.B., R. Akella and Y.F. Choong (1985). Short-term production scheduling of an automated manufacturing facility. *IBM J. Res. Develop.* 29(4), 392–400.

Golovin, J.J. (1975). Hierarchical integration of planning and control, Technical Report No. 116, Operations Research Center, M.I.T., Cambridge, MA.

Graves, S.C. (1982). Using Lagrangian techniques to solve hierarchical production planning problems. *Management Sci.* 28, 260–275.

Hax, A.C. (1976). The design of large scale logistics systems: A survey and an approach, in: W.H. Marlow (ed.), *Modern Trends in Logistics Research*, M.I.T. Press, Cambridge, MA.

Hax, A.C. (1978) Aggregate production planning, in: J. Moder and S.E. Elmaghraby (eds.), *Handbook of Operations Research*, Van Nostrand Reinhold, New York.

Hax, A.C., and D. Candea (1984). *Production and Inventory Management*, Prentice-Hall, Englewood Cliffs, NJ.

Hax, A.C., and J.J. Golovin (1978a). Hierarchical production planning systems, in: A.C. Hax (ed.), *Studies in Operations Management*, North-Holland, Amsterdam.

Hax, A.C., and J.J. Golovin (1978b). Computer based operations management system (COMS), in: A.C. Hax (ed.), *Studies in Operations Management*, North-Holland, Amsterdam.

Hax, A.C., J.J. Golovin, M. Bosyj and T. Victor (1976). COMS: A computer-based operations management system, Technical Report No. 121, Operations Research Center, M.I.T., Cambridge, MA.

Hax, A.C., and N.S. Majluf (1984). The corporate strategic planning process. *Interfaces* 14, 47–60.

Hax, A.C., and H.C. Meal (1975). Hierarchical integration of production planning and scheduling, in: M.A. Geisler (ed.), *Studies in Management Sciences, Vol. 1: Logistics*, Elsevier, New York.

Holt, C.C., F. Modigliani, J.F. Muth and H.A. Simon (1960). *Planning Production, Inventories and Work Force*, Prentice-Hall, Englewood Cliffs, NJ.

Jaikumar, R. (1974). An operational optimization procedure for production scheduling. *J. Comput. Oper.* 1, 191–200.

Kimemia, J., and G.B. Gershwin (1983). An algorithm for the computer control of a flexible manufacturing system. *IIE Trans.* 15(4), 353–362.

Kusiak, A., and G. Finke (1987). Hierarchical approach to the process planning problem. *Discrete Appl. Math.* 18, 175–184.

Lasdon, L.S., and R.C. Terjung (1971). An efficient algorithm for multi-item scheduling. *Oper. Res.* 19(4), 946–969.

Lenstra, J.K., A.H.G. Rinnooy Kan and L. Stougie (1984). A framework for the probabilistic analysis of hierarchical planning systems. *Ann. Oper. Res.* 1, 23–42.

Machulak, G.T., C.L. Moodie and T.J. Williams (1980) Computerized hierarchical production control in steel manufacture. *Internat. J. Prod. Res.* 18, 455–465.

Manne, A.S. (1958). Programming economic lot sizes. *Management Sci.* 4(2), 114–135.

Matsuo, H. (1990). A stochastic sequencing problem for style goods with forecast revisions and hierarchical structure. *Management Sci.* 36(3), 332–347.

Maxwell, W., J.A. Muckstadt, L.J. Thomas and J. Vander Eecken (1983). A modeling framework for planning and control of production in discrete parts manufacturing and assembly systems. *Interfaces* 13, 92–104.

McAuley, J. (1972). Machine grouping for efficient production. *Prod. Engrg.*, February, 53–57.

Meal, H.C. (1975). Manufacturing control and material requirements planning, presented at the 7th Ann. Meeting Inst. Decision Sci., Cincinnati, OH.

Meal, H.C. (1978). A study of multi-stage production planning, in: A.C. Hax (ed.), *Studies in Operations Management*, North-Holland, Amsterdam, Chapter 9.

Meal, H.C. (1984). Putting production decisions where they belong, *Harv. Bus. Rev.* 62(2), 102–111.

Meal, H.C., M.H. Wachter and D.C. Whybark (1987). Material requirements planning in hierarchical production planning systems. *Internat. J. Prod. Res.* 25(7), 947–956.

Mitchell, J.C. (1985). A hierarchical production planning model to allocate scarce resources, AT&T Bell Laboratories, Holmdel, NJ.

Ritzman, L.P., L.J. Krajewski, W.L. Berry, S.H. Goodman, S.T. Hardy and L.D. Vitt, eds. (1979). *Disaggregation Problems in Manufacturing and Service Organizations*, Martinus Nijhoff, Boston, MA.

Ruefli, T.W., and J. Storbeck (1984). NOTE: Removing a self-imposed restriction in modeling hierarchical decision processes. *Management Sci.* 30, 389–392.

Steward, S.M., S.G. Taylor and S.F. Bolander (1985). Progress in integrating and optimizing production plans and schedules. *Internat. J. Prod. Res.* 23, 609f.

Theil, H. (1965). *Linear Aggregation of Economic Relations*, North-Holland, Amsterdam.

Wijngaard, J. (1983). Aggregation in manpower planning. *Management Sci.* 29, 1427–35.

Winkofsky, E.P., N.R. Baker and D.J. Sweeny (1981). A decision process model by R&D resource allocation in hierarchical organizations. *Management Sci.* 27, 268–283.

Winters, P.R. (1962). Constrained inventory rules for production smoothing. *Management Sci.* 8, 470–481.

Zangwill, W. (1966). A deterministic multiproduct multifacility production and inventory model. *Oper. Res.* 14(3).

Zipkin, P. (1980a). Bounds on the effect of aggregating variables in linear programs. *Oper. Res.* 28(2), 403–418.

Zipkin, P. (1980b). Bounds for row-aggregation in linear programming. *Oper. Res.* 28(4), 903–916.

Zipkin, P. (1982). Exact and approximate cost functions for product aggregates. *Management Sci.* 28, 1002–1012.

Zoller, K. (1971). Optimal disaggregation of aggregate production plans. *Management Sci.* 17(8), B533–B549.

Part IV
Additional Topics

S.C. Graves et al., Eds., *Handbooks in OR & MS, Vol. 4*

Chapter 11

Requirements Planning

Kenneth R. Baker
Amos Tuck School of Business, Dartmouth College, Hannover, NH 03755, U.S.A.

1. Basic concepts

Requirements Planning provides a framework for managing production. In the last two decades the most widely used term for this framework has been *material* requirements planning (MRP) because in its earliest versions it focused on managing materials. Later on, the same concepts were applied in situations where it was also important to consider worker-hours. This extension gave rise to procedures for *capacity* requirements planning. Beyond labor and material, further applications dealt with equipment, tooling and other resources. These variations gave rise to the broader term *manufacturing resource planning*, which is often referred to as MRP II. At the core of all these approaches is the logic of material requirements planning, and so we can think of our subject as MRP-based systems for planning and control of production, or simply MRP systems. In this chapter we review this framework, and we examine a number of models appropriate for use with MRP.

It is often useful to think of MRP as primarily a management information system rather than a decision-making system. From this viewpoint an MRP system takes production decisions, records the implications of those decisions in an appropriate data base, and conveys the implications in various reports and signals. It may also collect status information about production. By contrast, the decision-making process itself identifies production situations where a course of action must be determined, considers a number of alternatives, and selects an action according to a particular criterion. The MRP system then helps to formulate and implement those decisions. The distinction between information-gathering and decision-making is helpful because the models we consider attempt to formalize decisions made in production planning and control. The MRP framework provides the context for those decisions.

We can think of this framework as appropriate for the manufacture of complex products. (We usually think in terms of assembling a discrete product from various components, but the ideas have also been applied in process manufacturing and in the provision of services.) The final product is called an *end item*. A generic description of the end item might look like the diagram shown in Figure 1.1. This diagram shows a *product structure*; that is, a

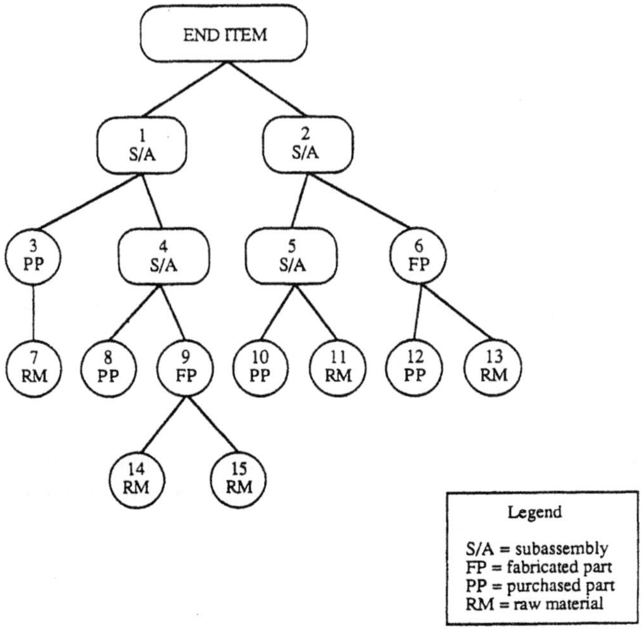

Fig. 1.1. A product structure diagram.

specification of the sequence in which purchased parts, fabricated components, and subassemblies are processed and brought together to form the end item. The end item is said to be at the top level, or level 0, in this diagram. The subassemblies that are brought together directly to form the end item are at level 1, their subassemblies are at level 2, and so on. Moving down the diagram is analogous to reversing the production operations and disassembling the product into its constituent parts. This process terminates at nodes on the diagram corresponding to parts and raw materials that are purchased as inputs.

An important distinction can be drawn between demand for the end item and demand for one of its components. We say that end-item demand is *independent* demand, whereas component demand is *dependent* demand. Independent demand occurs externally, and independent demand quantities are determined by the customer. Dependent demand, by contrast, is derived from the need to assemble an end item, and dependent demand quantities are determined by the technological design of the product. (The distinction is not always complete; in Figure 1.1 there could be independent demand for part 6 – as a spare – as well as dependent demand for the same part required in the end item.) The reason for this distinction is that independent demand is typically uncertain, and we must develop forecasts for it. On the other hand, dependent demand can be derived systematically. In essence, we may *forecast* for meeting independent demand, but we should *plan* for meeting dependent demand. MRP logic tells us how to plan.

Under MRP logic, time is viewed in discrete intervals sometimes called *time buckets*. In some early systems the time buckets corresponded to months, but for most purposes monthly time periods are rather coarse. Sometimes time buckets are weeks, although modern systems often use an even finer time grid. The main implication for modeling is that time is viewed as discrete, and the association of activities with time periods is called *time phasing*.

MRP logic

There are three principal inputs to MRP logic: Master Production Schedule, Bill of Material, and Inventory Status. In computer-based planning and control systems, these are files maintained somewhere in the data base. The Master Production Schedule (MPS) is a time-phased plan for completion of end-items. For the time being we can think of this plan as a schedule for final assemblies. The MPS describes which end-items the production system will build, or more specifically, what quantities of each product will be built in each time bucket.

The Bill of Material (BOM) specifies the makeup for each part in the end item; it is a recipe of ingredients which are necessary to manufacture each component of the final product. It is sometimes referred to as the 'gozinto' file, because it tells what 'gozinto' the final product. Essentially, the BOM provides the information in the product structure diagram (Figure 1.1), sometimes including the 'how' as well as the 'what'. That is, it may contain routing and lead time information, although traditional practice often separates this information into a distinct routing file.

The Inventory Status (INV) file contains current information on the quantities of parts and materials on hand and on order. This information is conceptually straightforward, although in practice this is not always an easy count to maintain accurately.

The three input files thus answer these basic questions:

What are we planning to make (and when will we make it)?

Answer: MPS.

What ingredients do we need to make it?

Answer: BOM.

What do we already have on hand or on order?

Answer: INV.

And from these answers it is not hard to determine:

What must we need to get (and when)?

Answer: Net requirements.

The purpose of MRP logic is to deduce the answer to this last question in a systematic way, determining specific plans for the purchase orders and shop orders that will meet net requirements. It does so with a sequence of steps called *explode*, *net*, *offset*, and *lot size*.

Explosion is the calculation of gross requirements for the components at the next level down the product structure. For example, suppose that the product in the master schedule is a bicycle and that next week's schedule calls for assembly of 20 bicycles. Because the BOM dictates that there are two wheels on a bicycle, the gross requirements for wheels by the end of this week are 40 wheels. Wheels are themselves assemblies, of course, and their requirements can be exploded into components. Since the BOM dictates that there are 36 spokes, one rim, and one tire assembly in each wheel, we can in turn explode the wheel requirements into gross requirements for 1440 spokes, 40 rims, and 40 tire assemblies. In similar fashion, the 40 required tire assemblies can be exploded into gross requirements for tubes, valve stems, and valve caps, while the 1440 spokes can be exploded into gross requirements for steel. In this way, the process of explosion takes the quantity in the MPS, along with information in the BOM, and simulates the disassembly of that quantity into the requisite number of constituent parts and materials. Sometimes a yield adjustment is included in this process. For example, if the rim department produces only 80% of its rims within specifications, then the 40 wheels would be exploded into 50 rims to account for the yield loss.

Netting adjusts gross requirements to account for the quantity already on hand and on order. The net requirements are equal to gross requirements minus the inventory quantity. In the above example, if there are 10 wheels in inventory, then the net requirement for wheels would be 30, instead of 40. Similarly, if there are also 200 spokes in the stockroom, then the net requirement for spokes (based on gross requirements of 1080, derived from net requirements of 30 wheels) would be 880. In other words, gross requirements at a given level of the product structure are netted (and also lot sized) before exploding into requirements at the next level down.

The computations associated with exploding and netting are usually shown in a time-phased format called the *MRP record*. Table 1.1 shows an example for the next six weeks of requirements for wheels.

The first row in this table contains *gross requirements*, defined as the number of wheels that must be on hand at the beginning of each week in order to support production plans at the next higher level of the product structure. In the example, that would refer to the number of bicycles in the master schedule. The next row contains *scheduled receipts*, which are materials due to be received by the beginning of the week, as a result of shop orders or purchase orders that have already been released. The third row gives the *projected on-hand inventory* balance at the end of each week. Note that the initial

Table 1.1
Net requirements in the MRP record

	Time period						
	Current	1	2	3	4	5	6
Gross requirements		80	100	70	80	90	80
Scheduled receipts		0	120	0	0	0	0
Projected on-hand	150	70	90	20	−60	−150	−230
Net requirements		0	0	0	60	90	80

inventory is shown in the column labeled *Current*. (This quantity is obtained from the Inventory Status file.) Each week the new value is found by taking the previous value, adding net receipts, and subtracting gross requirements. Finally, the net requirements are shown in the last row. These are zero unless the inventory balance is negative; in that case, they represent the gross requirements occurring in the week that cannot be met from inventory.

Offsetting determines the timing of order releases, using given information on planned lead times and working backward from the dates at which net requirements occur. Planned lead times are allowances for vendor response time (in the case of purchase orders) and allowances for run time, setup time, move time and queueing (in the case of shop orders). In Table 1.1, suppose that the planned lead time for a production run of wheels is two weeks. Then the order for the next batch of wheels should be released to the wheel department at (the beginning of) week 2 in order to have wheels available to meet the net requirements anticipated in week 4.

Lot sizing determines the batch quantities that will be purchased or produced in order to meet net requirements. Once the lot size is set, it becomes clear which net requirements are to be covered. In the example, if the next batch of wheels contains 130, that quantity will cover not only the net requirements in week 4, but also a portion of the net requirements in week 5. Clearly, an additional lot will be needed in order to cover the remaining net requirements. For the purposes of illustration, assume that this additional lot will also be of size 130. A complete MRP record updates projections for the future in light of plans for lot sizes, as shown in Table 1.2.

In this table, the first four rows are the same as in Table 1.1. The fifth row gives the *planned orders* under the prevailing lot sizing policy. The lots are shown in the week of their release. The final row shows the *planned available inventory*. This is defined as the quantity planned for stock at the end of the week: it is the projected on-hand balance, revised in light of planned orders.

Having constructed the MRP record for wheels, as in Table 1.2, it would then be possible to construct the MRP record for the next level of the product structure, i.e., spokes, rims, and tire assemblies. The method is simply to apply MRP logic to the planned orders of 130 wheels in weeks 2 and 3. The explosion

Table 1.2
Planned orders in the MRP record

	Time period						
	Current	1	2	3	4	5	6
Gross requirements		80	100	70	80	90	80
Scheduled receipts		0	120	0	0	0	0
Projected on-hand	150	70	90	20	−60	−150	−230
Net requirements		0	0	0	60	90	80
Planned orders			130	130			
Planned available		70	90	20	70	110	30

Table 1.3
The MRP record for wheels

	Time period						
	Current	1	2	3	4	5	6
Gross requirements		5	135	135	5	5	5
Scheduled receipts		0	0	0	0	0	0
Projected on-hand	200	195	60	−75	−80	−85	−90
Net requirements		0	0	75	5	5	5
Planned orders			225				
Planned available		195	60	150	145	140	135

step converts these into gross requirements for the end of week 1 (4680 spokes, and 130 rims plus a yield allowance, and 130 tire assemblies). Given a current stock of 200 tire assemblies, and a one-week purchase lead time from a tire company, the MRP record for tire assemblies might appear as shown in Table 1.3, which also includes independent demand for five tire assemblies per week as spare parts.

Together, the exploding, netting, offsetting, and lot sizing procedures determine the size and timing of planned orders for Manufacturing and for Purchasing. In this way, the MRP logic takes the information in the MPS, BOM, and INV files and deduces 'what we need to get and when'. The planned orders, in turn, form the basis of a schedule for the shop and a schedule for suppliers. The essence of this structure is depicted in Figure 1.2. The earliest system designs coupled this core to a 'front end' which provided an interface with customer demand and to a 'back end' which provided an interface with the actual execution of the plans. (Table 1.2 permits a distinction between *planning* and *execution*. The order for 130 to be released in week 2 is only a plan and could still be revised. On the other hand, the scheduled receipts of 120 correspond to an order being executed, having already been released.) However, before these two interfaces can function effectively, there must be some check to make sure that the planned order releases generated by MRP do not make unreasonable demands on capacity.

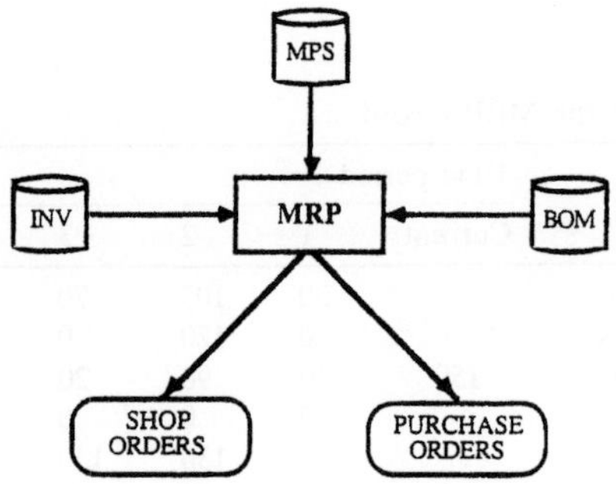

Fig. 1.2. The MRP core.

Capacity analysis

The MRP core, as its name indicates, is clearly materials oriented. Its aim is to bring the right materials (purchased parts, fabricated components, and subassemblies) to the right place in the right quantities at the right time. Consideration must also be given to the labor and equipment requirements of production. There are two standard ways of recognizing capacity, before the MRP logic or after it. Capacity analysis done before the MRP calculations is called *rough cut* capacity planning (RCCP) and is simpler; capacity analysis done after MRP is called *capacity requirements planning* (*CRP*) and is more detailed.

The advantage of RCCP procedures lies in their limited data requirements. For each product in the schedule, it is necessary to know how much capacity is required of each resource. For example, suppose that there are three products and two departments in which labor hours represent a limited resource. In the same spirit as the BOM file, we can construct a Bill of Capacity file, which tells us how many labor hours a product requires in each department. This information allows us to convert the MPS, expressed in terms of product quantities, into a profile of capacity requirements. The next three tables suggest how these calculations might be done. Table 1.4(a) displays the MPS for three end items over a four-week time horizon. Table 1.4(b) provides the Bill of Capacity for each of the three end items, with the standard number of hours required in Departments G and H. Finally, Table 1.4(c) shows the results of the implied multiplication, giving the time-phased capacity requirements in each department.

Now, if regular capacity is 600 hours per week in each department, this analysis tells us that the requirements on Department G are within capacity,

Table 1.4(a)
MPS quantities for three end items

	Week			
	1	2	3	4
End item 1	40	50	60	50
End item 2	50	60	60	80
End item 3	60	50	40	20

Table 1.4(b)
Bills of capacity for three end items

	Department	
	G	H
End item 1	2	6
End item 2	5	4
End item 3	3	1

Table 1.4(c)
Hours required in each department

	Week			
	1	2	3	4
Department G total	510	550	540	560
Department H total	500	590	640	640

but the requirements on Department *H* exceed capacity. Notice that RCCP analysis does not explore how to respond to the capacity problems; it simply provides a signal that the existing plan violates capacity restrictions. The appropriate response might be as simple as scheduling some overtime or using a spare machine, but it is not within the realm of RCCP to consider the alternatives. In other words, RCCP is not a decision-making technique; it is merely a signalling technique.

Although there are alternative ways of performing the details, the main idea is that RCCP is implemented prior to MRP in order to detect capacity violations. We can think of it as a method that simplifies the details of MRP logic as it predicts workloads on different resources. Specifically, there are three aspects of MRP calculations that are not captured by the RCCP approach outlined above. These are lead times, lot sizes, and inventory status.

Lead times are ignored in the sense that workloads implied by the master schedule are not offset to account for the delay in different work centers. Lot sizes are ignored in the sense that the lot size choices to be made in the MRP procedure will affect the amount of time spent in setup and consequently the total workload at a given work center. Finally, inventory status is ignored because RCCP deals only with gross requirements, not net requirements.

Thus, three simplifications are involved in RCCP, corresponding to the netting, offsetting and lot sizing steps in MRP logic. CRP procedures, which are applied after MRP, take these additional steps into account. Using the information of existing open orders and planned order releases produced by MRP logic, CRP computes the workloads implied by a given master schedule at each work center or production resource. If we view RCCP as a form of capacity analysis that simplifies MRP logic while predicting workloads, then we can think of CRP as a more accurate and detailed form. Nevertheless, just like rough-cut procedures, CRP provides a signal that the planned orders will violate capacity; CRP does not invoke a decision-making procedure to resolve the problem.

Although it makes sense to think of CRP as a more accurate substitute for rough-cut planning, CRP itself contains some simplifications. To illustrate, suppose that a particular fabrication operation takes ten hours at Work Center *D*, and that its standard lead time is three weeks. Suppose also that the standard capacity at Work Center *D* is 80 hours per week. It might seem logical to recognize the load due to this operation as 10 hours in Work Center *D* during the last week of the three week lead time. However, this convention could be misleading if, for example, 24 such operations were released simultaneously to an idle Work Center *D*. In that case our convention would indicate an overload of 240 hours in the third week, and no workload in the previous two weeks, when in fact the actual workload would be evenly distributed over the three weeks without violating capacity. In other words, CRP does not represent the detailed scheduling process, so it only approximates the actual workload profile.

MRP systems usually contain both an RCCP module and a CRP module.

The first module tends to catch the more obvious capacity problems, so that the MRP calculations are not wasted on a patently unrealistic master schedule. The second module tends to catch the more subtle problems that are created by MRP logic, but these still require that capacity be adjusted, the master schedule be revised, or the material plan be modified in order to make plans feasible.

Demand management

Many applications of MRP deal with make-to-order (MTO) environments, where customer orders comprise a backlog. A due date negotiated with the customer places the end item in the master schedule, and MRP logic then plans the necessary production. In effect, work does not begin on a custom product until the order is in hand. In this situation the master schedule is comprised of plans for final assembly and delivery to customers.

At the other end of the spectrum, in make-to-stock (MTS) environments, customer orders are filled off the shelf. In this situation demand can only be forecasted, and work must begin before demand is precisely known. Therefore, the master schedule is comprised of demand forecasts, adjusted in light of finished goods inventory. Again, MRP logic plans production.

Additional complications arise when a variety of custom products is assembled from a set of standard components or *modules*. If the number of end items is quite large while the number of modules is small, the Bill of Material is said to have an hourglass shape. In this situation, it may make more sense to develop the master schedule at the level of modules rather than at the level of end items. Therefore, firms often modify the standard MRP approach, mainly for reasons of efficiency in managing data. In the standard approach, with the master schedule oriented to end items, a large number of forecasts must be determined each period, and a large number of bills of material must be maintained in the data base. By comparison, with the master schedule oriented to modules, a smaller number of forecasts and a smaller number of bills is required.

In order to take advantage of the efficiencies of a master schedule oriented to modules, firms divide their planning and control system into two parts, separating the final assembly schedule (FAS) from the master production schedule. The MPS governs the production of modules, while the FAS governs the assembly of end items. The resulting hybrid system is called an assemble-to-order (ATO) strategy. In such a system the MPS is forecast-driven, and modules are built to stock. By contrast, the FAS is order-driven. When a customer order is received, the idea is to obtain the required modules from inventory and simply assemble the end item. The entire manufacturing lead time is split into two portions, the FAS lead time and the MPS lead time. The customer experiences only the FAS lead time, assuming the MPS has built appropriate modules for stock.

When master schedules are based on forecasts, as in MTS and ATO systems, an important role is played by *available-to-promise* (*ATP*) logic. Given that there is an inventory of end items and a master schedule, it is possible to assign certain of the items to customer orders and to designate other items as *available* to meet future demand. When a customer order arrives, a check is made to determine whether the schedule contains enough available items to satisfy the order on time. If so, then the order can be accepted; otherwise, the order will have to be revised or foregone. The ATP system is responsible for this checking and designating function.

The principles of ATP logic can be described with the help of an example containing a single item. Although our example involves a master schedule consisting of end items, as in the typical MTS environment, the concept is also valid for a master schedule consisting of modules, as in the typical ATO environment. In Table 1.5 we represent the existing MPS.

Because other products might be contained in the MPS, suppose that the item of interest is produced every three weeks in lot sizes of 100. The next line of the table shows firm orders that have already been placed. In the three-week interval there is current stock, referred to as Balance On Hand (BOH), and planned production sufficient to meet a demand of 120 units. Since firm orders in this interval total only 105, there is an excess of 15. Therefore, as many as 15 additional items can feasibly be assigned to orders occurring in the weeks covered by the first lot. This quantity is unallocated and remains 'available to promise' for that interval, and the table records this figure in the ATP row. In principle, this information would allow order-entry personnel to know how many items could still be committed to orders that arrive from customers.

In Table 1.6(a) we show a six-week interval, extending through the second MPS lot. Here, orders of 90 in the second three-week interval leave a quantity of 10 available to promise, as shown in the column corresponding to the second MPS lot.

In Table 1.6(b) the scenario is different. There are orders of 110 in the second interval, so that the second lot will not cover all of them. The difference must be made up by committing some of the units in the first lot. To show this relationship, we first enter the incremental value of ATP in the table, as before. Then we add a row to the table for the cumulative value of ATP. Here, the accumulation is from right to left. Thus the ATP quantity is negative for the second lot and just 5 for the first lot.

Table 1.5
Planned orders in the MRP record

	Time period		
	1	2	3
BOH = 20			
MPS quantity	100		
Firm orders	35	40	30
ATP	15		

Table 1.6(a)
Planned orders in the MRP record

	Time period					
	1	2	3	4	5	6
BOH = 20						
MPS quantity	100	0	0	100	0	0
Firm orders	35	40	30	35	25	30
ATP	15			10		

Table 1.6(b)
Planned orders in the MRP record

	Time period					
	1	2	3	4	5	6
BOH = 20						
MPS quantity	100	0	0	100	0	0
Firm orders	35	40	30	35	45	30
ATP (inc)	15			−10		
ATP (cum)	5			−10		

Table 1.7(a) extends the horizon out to week 9. There are 92 orders in the third production interval, so the ATP quantity is 8. Note that the first two production intervals are not affected.

In Table 1.7(b), however, there are 103 orders in the third production interval, and the effect is transmitted back to the first ATP quantity.

Table 1.7(a)
Planned orders in the MRP record

	Time period								
	1	2	3	4	5	6	7	8	9
BOH = 20									
MPS quantity	100	0	0	100	0	0	100	0	0
Firm orders	35	40	30	35	45	30	30	36	26
ATP (inc)	15			−10			8		
ATP (cum)	5			−10			8		

Table 1.7(b)
Planned orders in the MRP record

	Time period								
	1	2	3	4	5	6	7	8	9
BOH = 20									
MPS quantity	100	0	0	100	0	0	100	0	0
Firm orders	35	40	30	35	45	30	30	36	37
ATP (inc)	15			−10			−3		
ATP (cum)	2			−13			−3		

From these examples it is possible to discern a procedure for calculating ATP quantities. Starting at the end of the planning horizon, the ATP quantity is the difference between the size of the last scheduled MPS lot and the number of orders in the corresponding production interval. If this is negative, then the calculation of ATP is extended to include the preceding interval, and so on, until a positive ATP value is encountered. If the ATP quantity is positive, the preceding production interval is considered independently. The purpose of these calculations is to provide guidance for order-acceptance decisions by indicating which deliveries can be supported by the existing master schedule.

Again, the ATP concept can be utilized in either a make-to-stock situation or an assemble-to-order situation, as long as the master schedule is at least partly driven by forecasts. The ATP calculations assure that the master schedule can support the customer orders which are accepted.

Safety stock and safety time

Although MRP logic takes a deterministic view, it is not difficult to incorporate buffers into the basic MRP record. To illustrate how this might be accomplished, we return to the example of Table 1.2. One way of providing protection for uncertainty in demand is to create a buffer of safety stock. In this instance, suppose the buffer is 25 units. Then, in computing the net requirements, we allocate 25 units to the buffer. The revisions to the MRP record are shown in Table 1.8 by adding a new row to the table in order to show the adjusted on-hand balance explicitly. It is the pattern of this adjusted value that determines the timing of planned orders. (Notice that in this case the inclusion of safety stock accelerates the first planned order and alters the *planned available* quantities.)

An alternative strategy is to create safety time, rather than safety stock. In our example, suppose the buffer is one week. Then the planned orders are placed in the schedule as if the lead time were one week longer than the prescribed value of two weeks, as shown in Table 1.9.

Table 1.8
The MRP record adjusted for safety stock

	Time period						
	Current	1	2	3	4	5	6
Gross requirements		80	100	70	80	90	80
Scheduled receipts		0	120	0	0	0	0
Projected on-hand	150	70	90	20	−60	−150	−230
On-hand, adjusted for SS	125	45	65	−5	−85	−175	−255
Net requirements		0	0	5	80	90	80
Planned orders		130		130			
Planned available		70	90	150	70	110	30

Table 1.9
The MRP record adjusted for safety time

	Time period						
	Current	1	2	3	4	5	6
Gross requirements		80	100	70	80	90	80
Scheduled receipts		0	120	0	0	0	0
Projected on-hand	150	70	90	20	−60	−150	−230
Net requirements		0	0	0	60	90	80
Planned orders		130	130				
Planned available		70	90	150	200	110	30

By comparing Tables 1.8 and 1.9 we can see that safety stock and safety time can have different effects on the timing of orders and on the levels of available inventory.

Shop floor control

As plans convert to execution, there is a need for a set of procedures that complement those in the MRP core. The term *Shop Floor Control* refers to this set of procedures, which are generically oriented to *releasing*, *monitoring*, *updating*, and *scheduling*.

The *releasing* procedure essentially checks to see that the planned releases dictated by MRP are feasible. For shop orders involving fabrication this means a check on the availability of raw material; whereas for assembly this means a check on the availability of parts and subassemblies. In both cases, there is also a need to check that capacity is also available, whether in the form of labor, machinery, or tooling. For purchase orders, there may be an analogous check on vendor status to make sure that the release is compatible with supply capability.

The *monitoring* function recognizes the status of orders already released for the purposes of carrying out the MRP steps. There is usually a program to track work-in-process (WIP) in the shop and another to track work being done by vendors. These programs confirm or revise the size and timing of scheduled receipts and the quantities in inventory. Recall that these figures are vital to the precise arithmetic with which MRP generates its plans.

The *updating* function deals with key parameters in the MRP data base. To make sure that these parameters reflect the actual performance of the production system, it is necessary to make periodic checks to see whether realistic data is being used. In this spirit, various programs might review the output of work centers (to confirm capacity standards used in RCCP or CRP), the level of scrap at certain operations (to confirm yield parameters), or the length of shop delays (to confirm lead time parameters).

The need for a *scheduling* procedure derives from the fact that MRP operates on a relatively coarse time grid with an aggregate representation of production capacity. Thus, MRP may dictate that a certain set of fabrication orders be released to a machining department in a given week, but this leaves unresolved details of how jobs will actually flow though the department within that week. A scheduling routine might handle the specific loading of jobs onto machines, the assignment of individual operators to tasks, the setting of dispatching priorities, and the like. Moreover, as conditions change within the time bucket, the scheduling routine may also adapt the schedule to such changes.

Although the logic of releasing, monitoring, and updating programs is generic, shop floor control systems are usually tailored to the specific capabilities of individual shops to collect the requisite information. The scheduling function is often done separately, for at least two reasons. First, the logic of scheduling is not generic, and the uniqueness of the shop must often be taken into account. Second, and more importantly, scheduling is a decision-making procedure, not just an information-gathering procedure. For that reason, many systems aspire to optimize the schedule, and a sophisticated capability – perhaps separate from the main system – is appropriate.

Figure 1.3 depicts a mature planning and control system built around the MRP core. The feedback flow of information from execution to planning is highlighted by arrows. This diagram is intended to illustrate the scope and

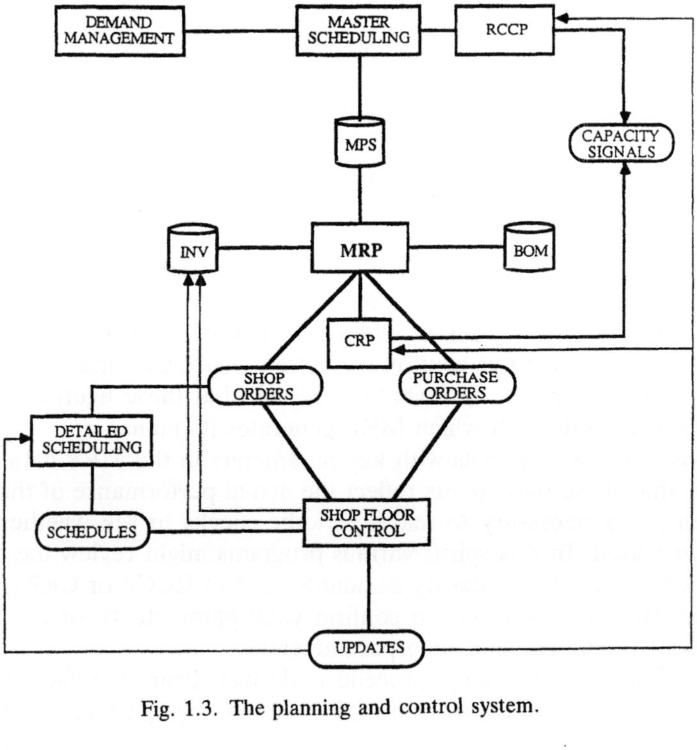

Fig. 1.3. The planning and control system.

organization of a modern planning and control system. It is not a monolithic design, and would clearly need to be adapted, for example, in an FAS/MPS environment. Its main value lies in its use as a guideline for the development of various programs and procedures that could work in concert as a system to plan and control production.

2. Limitations of the MRP framework

The model in Figure 1.3, which most MRP-based systems resemble to some degree, provides an effective framework for managing production. Nevertheless, there are several key weaknesses in the basic MRP framework. These relate to *lot sizes*, *capacity*, *planned lead times*, and *uncertainty*. Most of the models and techniques that have been developed in the MRP setting address these weaknesses, either individually or in combination, and those models are the subject of the sections that follow. In this section we look briefly at the shortcomings of the framework.

Lot sizing is one of the four basic steps in MRP logic. More importantly, it is the only procedure in the system core that involves decision-making rather than information-gathering. As a result, there are alternatives to consider, and different approaches to lot sizing can lead to different plans and performance. In fact, commercially-available MRP software typically comes with one or more of these approaches built in.

It would be desirable to optimize the choice of lot sizes. This means there must be a performance measure for the effect of lot sizes on planned orders. The most common criterion for lot sizing is minimum cost, where cost includes the holding cost of carrying material in stock and the fixed cost of setting up equipment or ordering from a vendor. This focus is no doubt related to the usefulness of the basic Economic Order Quantity (EOQ) model of elementary inventory theory. Apart from the limitations of the specific cost criterion, however, most built-in lot sizing procedures are suboptimal, even for the criterion of minimizing holding cost and fixed cost. The most prominent procedures for lot sizing are surveyed in Section 3.

Capacity is recognized by the RCCP and CRP modules of a standard MRP system. However, those modules are simply information-gathering procedures, and they do not allocate scarce resources when the material plan violates capacity constraints. Instead, they just signal the need to revise the master schedule or to increase capacity. In addition, the logic of the traditional MRP approach is sequential: material plans are made first; then capacity is considered, and an iterative search for a viable schedule follows.

It would be desirable to recognize capacity constraints while building the MPS. Thus the process of master scheduling should be viewed as one of optimizing the use of limited resources while planning the flow of material in production. That is, material and capacity planning should be done somewhat in parallel, rather than in sequence. Master scheduling models with this flavor are described in Section 4.

Planned lead times are treated as given in a standard MRP system. They are parameters stored in the data base. Once specified, the system typically treats them as fixed, although intuition and experience tell us that lead times are always changing.

It would be desirable to treat lead times as dependent on product mix, shop load, and capacity: in short, as dynamic. They should be viewed not as inputs to a scheduling procedure but rather as part of the output. Moreover, lead times are not entirely predictable; they are somewhat probabilistic as well as dynamic. Lead time models with more of this view are covered in Section 5.

Uncertainty is ignored in the standard MRP perspective. All parameters, such as customer demands and material lead times, are treated as if they are known with certainty. This deterministic view oversimplifies reality in a great many environments. Traditional MRP systems recognize that there will be random events in the environment. The simple implication is to insulate the production system by creating buffers for the inputs and outputs of the system at points where it interfaces with the environment, but to avoid any buffers within the system itself. The MRP record can be adapted to reflect safety stock or safety time, but there are few guidelines available for determining the quantity of safety stock or the amount of safety time.

It would be desirable to recognize the costs related to uncertainty and to deploy buffers in a manner designed to minimize these costs. The role of safety stock is considerably more difficult to analyze in multilevel production systems than in pure, single-level inventory systems, but some of the same principles should apply. Some of the models and insights related to buffering strategies are discussed in Section 6.

3. Models for lot sizing

The lot sizing problem arises as part of MRP logic, as discussed earlier, and in traditional systems the problem is addressed level by level. In the single-level version of the problem we are faced with a set of net requirements which are produced by the explosion and netting steps, and we must choose a set of lot sizes. The costs involved are fixed costs and holding costs. This setting is analogous to the classical *Economic Order Quantity* (*EOQ*) model (see Chapter 1). However, the MRP lot sizing problem is posed in discrete time – for a finite horizon – and allows requirements to vary, whereas the EOQ model is posed in continuous time – for an infinite horizon – and assumes constant requirements. For the EOQ model, the optimal lot size is

$$Q = [2Kr/h]^{1/2} , \tag{3.1}$$

where K denotes the fixed cost per order, h denotes the holding cost per period per unit in stock, and r denotes the demand rate. The analysis of the EOQ model reveals several properties of its optimal solution:

(P1) The cost-minimizing lot size is stationary and given by (3.1).

(P2) The optimal policy calls for placing orders at equal intervals, given by $T = Q/r$.

(P3) The optimal policy produces minimum cost per unit of time.

(P4) The optimal policy produces minimum cost per unit of demand.

(P5) Optimization equates average fixed cost per period and average holding cost per period.

(P6) Optimization equates marginal fixed cost per period and marginal holding cost per period.

These properties provide the basic rationale for several of the most popular lot sizing techniques in MRP systems.

In the single-level lot sizing problem of MRP there is a specified time horizon of N periods, a fixed cost incurred for each lot, and a holding cost assessed on inventory level at the end of a period. Because the fixed cost K can represent the cost of a setup or the cost of placing an external order, the problem has the same structure for both shop orders and purchase orders. Let

r_t = net requirement in period t, given for $1 \leq t \leq N$,
Q_t = lot size to be delivered in period t,
I_t = inventory at the end of period t.

The formulation may be stated as follows.

$$\begin{aligned} &\text{minimize} \quad \sum_t [K\,\partial(Q_t) + hI_t] \\ &\text{subject to} \quad I_t = I_{t-1} + Q_t - r_t \quad \text{for } 1 \leq t \leq N\,, \end{aligned} \tag{3.2}$$

where the indicator function $\partial(Q_t) = 1$ if $Q_t > 0$ and $\partial(Q_t) = 0$ otherwise. The model in (3.2) is the discrete-time version of the elementary EOQ model with time-varying demand. An optimal solution can be found by using the algorithm of Wagner & Whitin [1958], as described in Chapter 2. However, the Wagner–Whitin (WW) algorithm has not been widely used in practice. The reason is sometimes said to be the complexity of the dynamic programming procedure involved in the optimization. This argument is not convincing, however, because the detailed lot sizing calculations are usually implemented by software, not by people. A related reason sometimes given is the computational demands of the WW algorithm. This may have some merit, but only in applications of large scale. A better reason has to do with the nature of the WW solution: the optimal policy sometimes has the property that alterations in the requirement schedule for later periods may cause changes in the lot sizes planned for early periods. Similarly, as the planning process rolls forward in time, and new data is appended to the end of the planning interval, there may be changes in the early lot sizes induced by the new information. This type of change is called *nervousness*, a phenomenon that conflicts with the usual desire for stable planning information. Most of the lot sizing procedures used in MRP systems are designed to insulate plans in early periods from revisions occurring in later periods. However, this stability is gained at the expense of guaranteeing that the sum of fixed costs and holding costs will be minimized.

Single-level lot sizing

Several lot sizing procedures have been made available with commercial MRP software; these and others have been studied in the literature. The most important ones provide the stability lacking in the WW algorithm and require fewer computations, but they do not optimize. These procedures are also important because they are building blocks in multilevel lot sizing and in master scheduling algorithms. An overview is given below.

EOQ method. One simple way to adapt the EOQ model to the discrete-time environment is to use the EOQ formula directly, following Property (P1). The main question is what to use as the demand rate r in (3.1). One alternative is to use the average of r_t during the N-period horizon of the model. In principle, this approach calls for the EOQ to be revised each time new information appears, which seems contradictory to the spirit of Property (P1). An alternative is to use a long-run demand forecast, such as the annual demand rate. This would make the EOQ more stable, but it fails to recognize that lot sizing is done against net requirements, whereas the demand rate corresponds to gross requirements. In any event, the main drawback of the EOQ method is that the order quantities do not match requirements for an integral number of periods, thus creating 'remnant' inventories. It is not hard to see that a desirable feature of any lot sizing scheme for (3.2) is to avoid carrying inventory into a period in which an order arrives. (This is sometimes called the *regenerative* property.) Because it lacks this feature, the EOQ method loses credibility as a decision-making procedure.

All of the following methods are structured to avoid remnant inventories. They begin at the first period in which there is a nonzero net requirement. (For present purposes, we can think of this as period 1.) They consider lot sizes that cover requirements through one period, two periods, three periods, and so on, using a specific stopping rule to determine how much to expand the lot size. Once the first lot size is determined, the methods proceed to the first period with uncovered net requirements and repeat the process, continuing in this fashion until the demand over the entire horizon has been covered. Procedures of this type have some stability that the WW algorithm lacks. Specifically, if there is a revision in the final period's requirement, or if an additional period's requirement is appended, then no lot size changes except the last.

POQ method. An easy way to overcome the problem of remnant inventories is to use the *Period Order Quantity* (*POQ*). Following Property (P2), we calculate the optimal time supply T. The stopping rule requires placing orders at this time interval. Specifically, at period 1 the lot size will be $r_1 + r_2 + \cdots +$

r_T. When inventory runs out after period k (where k is some multiple of T), the next lot size will be equal to $r_{k+1} + \cdots + r_{k+T}$.

Notice that the calculation of T, which involves taking a square root, is not likely to result in an integer value. The simplest resolution of this problem is just to round off the calculated value.

LPC method. A more clever way to determine a lot size is to seek the *Least Period Cost* (*LPC*), which is the minimum cost per unit time, following Property (P3). For period 1, a lot size that covers requirements out to period t is $q_{1t} = r_1 + r_2 + \cdots + r_t$. The fixed cost for this lot is K and its holding cost is

$$v_t = h[r_2 + 2r_3 + \cdots + (t-1)r_t] .$$

Thus its cost per unit time is

$$y_t = (K + v_t)/t .$$

The algorithm begins with y_1 (corresponding to q_{11}) and calculates y_2, y_3, etc., until $y_{k+1} > y_k$. Finding this condition, the procedure sets $Q_1 = q_{1k}$. In other words, the procedure locates the first local minimum of cost per unit time. It then fixes the first lot size at this quantity and proceeds to determine the second lot size. This is accomplished by starting over at time $k+1$ and searching for the LPC over periods $k+1$, $k+2, \ldots$ To be precise, the search begins at the first period beyond k where net requirements are positive and continues until all requirements in the N-period horizon are met. Blackburn & Millen [1980] discuss a useful refinement for lumpy demands. They show that it is desirable to consider increasing the lot size to cover any periods immediately following $(k+1)$ with zero requirements, because such zeroes will cause a reduction in the index y_t and perhaps improve on the local optimum found in the basic application of the method.

The LPC method was invented by Silver & Meal [1973] and is more popularly known as the Silver–Meal procedure. It has intuitive appeal, based on Property (P3), and has also been demonstrated to achieve near-optimal costs in a variety of experimental tests.

LUC method. A similar procedure is to seek the *Least Unit Cost* (*LUC*), which is the minimum cost per unit required, following Property (P4). The total holding cost for the first lot is

$$v_t = h[r_2 + 2r_3 + \cdots + (t-1)r_t]$$

as in the LPC method, but a different cost criterion is utilized. The minimum cost per unit is

$$y_t = (K + v_t)/q_{1t} .$$

The LUC method uses this quantity to find a local minimum. That is, the stopping rule dictates that the lot should not be expanded further if $y_{k+1} > y_k$.

The LUC method was devised for some early IBM software, but in experimental tests its cost performance does not rival that of the LPC method.

PPA and LTC methods. The *Part Period Algorithm* (*PPA*) and the *Least Total Cost* (*LTC*) method both relate to Property (P5) for their stopping rules. As in the previous two methods, the holding cost for q_{1t} is

$$v_t = h[r_2 + 2r_3 + \cdots + (t-1)r_t] .$$

The PPA approach calculates v_2, v_3, etc., until $v_{k+1} > K$; then it sets $Q_1 = q_{1k}$. In other words, the stopping rule locates the last period at which holding cost for the lot falls at or below fixed cost. As a result, the fixed cost and the holding cost for the lot will usually be close to equal. The PPA concept was proposed by De Matteis [1968]. The name of the procedure refers to the notion of a part-period, which is an item (i.e., a component part) held for one period. In the expression for v_t above, the quantity in brackets in the number of part-periods. The procedure expands the first lot as long as the number of part-periods does not exceed K/h, which is called the economic part-period (EPP) factor.

The *Least Total Cost* (*LTC*) method, due to Gorham [1968], is similar to PPA except for its stopping rule. Under LTC, the first lot is expanded to q_{1k} or $q_{1,k+1}$ depending on which period leaves the number of part-periods closest to the EPP factor. In this respect, the LTC approach employs the principle of cost balancing embodied in Property (P5). (Sometimes overlooked is the fact that when $v_2 > K$, the rule should not be used if it calls for setting $Q_1 = q_{12}$, because the cost of carrying inventory into period 2 exceeds the cost of incurring the fixed cost in period 2 in order to begin another lot.) In the MRP literature some authors refer to the 'Part Period Balancing' method, and it is sometimes difficult to tell which procedure this name implies. There is, in a sense, more 'balancing' in the LTC method than in the PPA method. The name can therefore be somewhat misleading, and there remains some confusion in the literature about the distinction between PPA and LTC.

IOQ method. A variation on the PPA method is the *Incremental Order Quantity* (*IOQ*) method, which was documented in several papers at approximately the same time. The earliest description of the basic form of the procedure is due to Freeland & Colley [1982], who report that the procedure was in use some 20 years earlier. An alternative name for the procedure is the *Incremental Part Period Algorithm*, because it follows PPA but uses *incremental* holding cost in the stopping rule. In particular, the incremental holding cost associated with q_{1t} is the increase in v_t induced by extending the lot to cover the requirements in period t, or

$$w_t = h(t-1)r_t .$$

The IOQ method calculates w_2, w_3, and so on, until $w_{k+1} > K$; then it sets $Q_1 = q_{1k}$. In other words, the procedure locates the last period at which incremental holding cost for the lot falls at or below fixed cost. It then proceeds in the same fashion as PPA. The intuition for this rule is that we should be willing to pay up to K to add coverage of some future requirement to the current lot. However, any cost beyond K to cover that requirement would be more expensive than placing a separate order later. Although the IOQ method appears to be just a variation on the PPA approach, it does not follow any of the key properties listed above; yet there are situations under which its cost performance is quite good.

MCD method. A procedure anchored to Property (P6) is the *Marginal Cost Difference* (*MCD*) method. Define the marginal setup cost s_t as the change in setup component (of cost per unit time) when the lot size is expanded to cover period $t + 1$ instead of only period t. By expanding the lot size in this way, we incur the setup cost K one time in $(t + 1)$ periods instead of once in t periods. Thus

$$s_t = K/t - K/(t+1)\,.$$

Similarly define the marginal holding cost u_t as the change in the holding component (of cost per unit time) when the lot size is expanded to cover period $t + 1$. Note that this component is essentially the holding rate h multiplied by the average inventory level during this time interval. The inventory level at the start of the interval will be raised by d_{t+1} units, but the inventory level at the end of the interval will still be zero. Thus the increase in the average inventory level is $\frac{1}{2}d_{t+1}$, and we have

$$u_t = \tfrac{1}{2}hd_{t+1}\,.$$

The MCD method calculates successive values of s_t and u_t until $u_{k+1} - s_{k+1} > 0$, then it sets $Q_1 = q_{1k}$. Usually credited to Groff [1979], this procedure is sometimes referred to as *Groff's Marginal Rule*, although it first appeared in White, Donaldson & Lawrie [1974]. The MCD acronym is introduced here for the first time, maintaining the tradition of avoiding the attribution of authorship in the naming of lot sizing methods.

Look-ahead/look-back methods. The original exposition of PPA also proposed an extension involving 'look-ahead' and 'look-back' conditions that can adjust the lot size formed by the basic algorithm. These conditions effectively look back and ahead from the next proposed order to see whether a large requirement falls either one period before or after the order. If so, the order is moved forward or backward (and the lot size adjusted appropriately) to take advantage of the timing of the demand peak. This type of test can be applied recursively. That is, if the look-ahead conditions lead to moving an order ahead, then the look-ahead procedure can be repeated from that new point. In addition, this idea could be appended to methods other than PPA. Therefore, we should view the execution of look-ahead and look-back tests as a generic refinement of the lot sizing procedure, and not necessarily exclusive to PPA.

Although such refinements can provide some small benefit in cost performance, they also lead to some nervousness: the revision of a requirement in a late period may alter the size of the first lot when look-ahead or look-back conditions are used.

Costing. One aspect of the formulation that deserves some discussion is the convention of assessing holding cost on ending inventory (EI) levels. The model ignores the holding cost during the period in which demand is met. If demand occurs at the end of a period, then, in principle, the requirement r_t carries an additional holding cost of hr_t in period t. If demand occurs uniformly over the period, then this additional holding cost is $\frac{1}{2}hr_t$. If demand occurs at the start of a period, then no additional cost is involved. The additional cost, if it applies, may be left out of the model because it is not influenced by the choice of lot sizes. Thus the optimal lot sizes in (3.2), based on EI inventory, will also be optimal if inventory costs are assessed on average inventory (AI) or on starting inventory (SI). However, a constant term would have to be added to the objective function in (3.2) for consistency in the case of AI or SI costing.

Perhaps more importantly, some of the procedures perform differently under alternative costing conventions. In the formulas above, AI costing would require that v_t and w_t be increased by $\frac{1}{2}hr_t$, and SI costing would require that they be increased by hr_t. Wemmerlov [1981] and Heemsbergen [1987] have documented the impact of changing the costing conventions for certain of the methods. A related problem is that experimental tests usually aim at measuring the suboptimality of a method, taken as a percentage of the optimal cost. This latter figure differs, however, depending on the cost convention, so that comparisons of performance between different tests reported in the literature may not be valid if different costing methods are involved.

Experimental studies. Several articles have compared the cost performance of various lot sizing methods. The most recent and comprehensive of these studies are due to Wemmerlov [1982] and Blackburn & Millen [1985a]. These extensive tests show that no one method dominates the others in all cases; however, the LPC and MCD methods tend to be within a few per cent of optimum very consistently. In the large array of test problems there is perhaps a slight edge to MCD. The analytic work of Blackburn & Millen [1985a] shows that the IOQ method can be systematically worse than the LPC and MCD methods when demand is relatively stable and the ratio K/r is large. However, the experimental results in the same article demonstrate that for lumpy demand patterns the IOQ method may actually be the best among the heuristic methods. A related experimental study, due to Benton [1985], compares a few of the same lot sizing procedures when used for purchased parts in the presence of quantity discounts.

Rolling schedules. In practical applications it is seldom the case that an N-period lot sizing problem is solved and the decisions implemented for all N periods. More typically, it is only the first period decisions that are implemented. One period later there will be a new requirement appended to the problem, re-establishing an N-period horizon, and there may also be revisions in some of the existing requirements. These changes give rise to a new

N-period problem, which is solved so that its first period decisions can be implemented. Over time, the decisions that get implemented are not necessarily the decisions emanating from the solution of any single N-period problem; rather they are a sequence of first period decisions emanating from a sequence of related N-period problems. The schedule that results is called a *rolling schedule*.

The relevant practical question in selecting a lot sizing method seems to be which method performs best on a rolling schedule basis? (There is no readily available optimization scheme for this problem; the WW algorithm itself is a heuristic method in a rolling schedule environment.) This question has been addressed by Blackburn & Millen [1980] and by Wemmerlov & Whybark [1986]. In general, their findings are consistent with experiments involving static problems, although for relatively short horizons the nervousness inherent in the WW algorithm seems to cause its performance to deteriorate. For sufficiently long horizons, WW is the dominant method. LPC and MCD, which require less computation, tend to produce costs within a few per cent of WW on average.

All of these results and insights relate to the single-level version of the lot sizing problem. As mentioned earlier, MRP software typically solves the lot sizing problem level by level; therefore, it seems logical to search for a method that will work well for the single-level model. Nevertheless, we should not lose sight of the fact that the broader objective is to determine lot sizes throughout the product structure, for multiple levels. The reason for devoting so much coverage to single-level lot sizing is actually twofold. First, single-level results lay the groundwork for studies of multilevel techniques, as we discuss below. Second, they also play a key role in certain master scheduling algorithms, as we discuss in the next section.

Multilevel lot sizing

In its multilevel version, the lot sizing problem encompasses the entire product structure. At each level the problem resembles (3.2), but with the property that the lot sizes Q_t which form the solution also dictate the requirements for the next level down the product structure. The problem is to find a set of lot sizes at each level that together will minimize the total fixed and holding cost in the system. This problem can be formulated as a very large integer programming model (see Chapter 8), but such a model is beyond the capability of present-day optimization software for most cases of practical size. Among effective heuristic procedures there appear to be four approaches to the problem:

(1) Repeat the use of a single-level method in a single-pass solution.
(2) Develop modified costs and use a single-pass solution.
(3) Use modified costs iteratively in a multi-pass solution.
(4) Proceed forward in time, treating all levels in each time period.

These approaches are outlined in the description that follows.

Single-level method. One very logical way to attack the multilevel problem is to solve it level by level, using one of the relatively successful single-level methods, in a one-pass scheme that cascades down the product structure. A benchmark for this approach would naturally be the use of the WW algorithm at each level. Veral & LaForge [1985] tested this idea in computational experiments using 3200 12-period test problems, each of which contained one end item with an assembly structure. They found that the IOQ method was competitive with the WW algorithm, and that either one improved on POQ by about ten per cent. Blackburn & Millen [1985b] developed 6000 12-period test problems in a broader study, each problem having one end item with an assembly structure. Their results indicated that the WW algorithm was most effective, but not dominant, and that LTC and IOQ were in some cases competitive. The LPC and MCD methods were noticeably less effective in the multilevel setting as compared to their performance in single-level problems. On average, the blanket use of a single-level procedure such as WW achieved costs roughly ten per cent above optimum. There was no strong evidence that mixing different lot sizing methods at different levels could provide a consistent cost advantage.

Cost modification method. Other methods for the multilevel problem build on this basic approach. Blackburn & Millen [1982a] describe a *cost modification* scheme for a single end item whose product structure takes the form of an assembly tree. The idea of cost modification is to alter the fixed cost and holding cost for each item in the product structure and then to solve the lot sizing problem level by level, relying on one of the single-level methods but using the altered costs. The objective is to achieve some degree of interlevel coordination without imposing it explicitly in the form of a constraint.

In a tree structure, each component except the end item has a unique parent into which it gets assembled. Let $p(j)$ denote the parent (or successor) of component j. Similarly, each component has a set of children which get assembled into it (For purchased parts and materials, this set is empty.) Let $C(j)$ denote the set of children (predecessors) for component j. We introduce the following definition:

$$e_j = h_j - \sum_{i \in C(j)} h_i .$$

Here e_j is the echelon (or value-added) holding cost for component j. A nested ordering schedule is considered, in which component j is ordered m_j times for each order of its parent. Then the modified fixed cost and holding cost for component j are given as follows:

$$K'_j = K_j + \sum_{i \in C(j)} (K'_i / m_i) ,$$

$$h'_j = e_j + \sum_{i \in C(j)} m_i e'_i .$$

With the modified cost parameters K' and e' replacing the original parameters K and h, there is an inherent tendency, when the single-level problems are solved independently, for the ordering patterns to match at successive levels. Blackburn & Millen [1982a] give some different ways of finding m_i (see Chapter 2 for similar models), and they show that cost modification schemes produce substantially lower costs than schemes with unmodified costs. Blackburn & Millen [1982b] draw similar conclusions in the case of rolling schedules.

Multi-pass method. A multi-pass procedure for the multilevel problem has been proposed by Graves [1981]. At the heart of the multi-pass procedure is a routine that solves a single-level version of the problem with time-varying unit costs. (In the models discussed so far, the unit cost has been assumed not to vary; hence it has been ignored.) One of the heuristic methods can be used for this purpose, but in his original exposition Graves chose to adapt the WW algorithm. His procedure also assumes that lead times between levels are zero. (This assumption can be made without loss of generality.)

The first step is to determine lot sizes level by level. From this single-pass solution it is possible to compute the marginal cost of meeting one more unit of demand in period t. Let c_{it} denote the original unit cost for component i in time period t. Furthermore, in the single-pass solution, let s_i denote the period in which an order is placed to meet demand for component i in time period t. Then the marginal cost of meeting one additional unit of demand for component i in period t may be written as follows:

$$a_{it} = c_{it} + h_i(t - s_i) .$$

The next step is to calculate a_{it} for each component i at the bottom level. Then, for component j at the next level up the tree, a modified cost is substituted for the original unit cost c_{jt}. The modified cost is

$$c'_{jt} = c_{jt} + \sum_{i \in C(j)} a_{it} .$$

Next, these modified costs are used to solve the single-level problem for this level, using the generalized WW algorithm. The solution makes it possible to compute marginal costs at this level. Then these costs are imbedded in the modified costs one level further up the tree, and a new single-level solution is produced there. The procedure continues toward the top of the product structure, but it need not stop there. The procedure can iterate through multiple passes until it converges. Graves discusses convergence properties more specifically in his article, along with alternative ways of sequencing the levels.

The multi-pass procedure thus employs some of the same cost modification ideas that appear in the better single-pass procedures. Experimental tests were conducted on 250 test problems, each with a single assembled product and 12 periods of given demand. The results indicate that the multi-pass procedure found optimal solutions in more than 80% of the problems, and its average cost error was well within 1% of optimum. Perhaps the most promising feature of the multi-pass procedure is that it can be applied in cases where the product structure is not a tree. This is the most realistic situation for multilevel lot sizing, because there may be several end items in the schedule, and there may be commonality among components. The cost modification schemes of Blackburn and Millen are not designed for nontree structures, so in these situations the multi-pass procedure may be the best alternative solution technique available.

The parallel heuristic. For multilevel lot sizing problems with tree structures, the best computational results among heuristic solution procedures have been achieved by the *parallel heuristic* due to Afentakis [1987]. The parallel heuristic finds a solution for the 1-period problem for all levels, then it uses this information to find a solution to the 2-period problem, then the 3-period problem, and so on, always building up a solution from solutions to smaller-length problems. In essence, the algorithm proceeds period by period rather than level by level.

At every stage the solutions exhibit two properties. First, they consist of *regenerative* schedules for each component. In other words, for component i, the solutions will satisfy $I_{i,t-1}Q_t = 0$. Second, they are *nested* schedules. This means that for $i = p(j)$ we must have $Q_{it} > 0$ whenever $Q_{jt} > 0$. The regenerative property allows us to express the solution for each component as a string of zeroes and ones. The ones tell us the periods in which an order is placed, and the zeroes that immediately follow tell us what future requirements are covered by that order. For example, in a four-period problem the string $(1, 0, 1, 1)$ implies three orders, with the first order covering requirements for periods 1 and 2, and the remaining orders covering imminent requirements.

The parallel heuristic contains two phases. The first (generation) phase identifies a small set of alternative schedules for each component, and the second (optimization) phase finds the best combination of the alternatives. For component i at period t, alternatives are generated as follows. On hand are the strings representing previously-computed solutions for periods $k < t$. Let s_k denote the last period in which an order is placed (the last place in the string where a one appears) in the k-period solution. Maintaining the string in periods prior to s_k, complete the string by placing a single one in just one of the remaining periods s_k, $s_k + 1, \ldots, t$. (This procedure generates $t - s_k + 1$ candidates.) Repeat this generation step for all $k < t$, discarding any duplicate candidates that may be encountered.

The optimization phase is implemented after all of the t-period alternatives are generated for each of the components. This phase tests to see which combinations of alternatives comprise nested schedules, and among these, which combination has the minimum cost. The individual component schedules in this solution constitute the t-period alternatives considered when the algorithm goes on to seek the $(t + 1)$-period solution.

The full solution obtained for the N-period horizon is not guaranteed to be optimal because the limited number of alternatives at each intermediate stage may omit the true optimum. Nevertheless, the computational results reported by Afentakis are remarkable. In ninety 12-period test problems containing up to 50 components and as many as 15 levels, the parallel heuristic found a solution that was always within 1% of the optimum. The solutions produced by the cost modification method were as much as 6% above optimal, although they were slightly faster to obtain. In addition, the parallel heuristic exhibited modest computational requirements on test problems containing as many as 200 components with 45 levels.

Extensions. As the foregoing discussion indicates, great progress has been made in developing knowledge and methodology for solving lot sizing problems, at least for the criterion of minimizing the sum of setup and holding costs. The basic paradigm begins with the solution of static, single-level problems. Then comes verification that the same ideas work well in a rolling schedule environment. Next comes the extension to multiple levels. In practice, we can expect that lot sizing problems may have additional cost elements in the objective function, such as quality, handling, storage, learning, and smoothing. Nevertheless, the basic paradigm provides us with a framework to include these considerations as well as setup and holding costs. In addition, another important topic is the extension of uncapacitated lot sizing techniques to situations where there are capacity constraints. Some steps in this direction are described in the next section.

4. Models for master scheduling

Although master production scheduling is one of the most common functions within an MRP system, there is little consensus on the nature of the master scheduling problem. Moreover, the emphasis in master scheduling seems to vary according to whether the system is functioning in a make-to-order, make-to-stock, or assemble-to-order mode. In this section we look at two different perspectives on the subject.

One perspective views the master scheduling problem as a lot sizing problem with known demands. In this view, the problem amounts to selecting lot sizes for the last production step (usually the final assembly operation), in the face of a trade-off between setup costs for production runs and inventory costs for finished goods. In essence, the problem is a complicated version of the single-level lot sizing problem considered in the previous section. Two complications distinguish the master scheduling problem: first, multiple products are involved, and second, there is limited production capacity serving the various products to be scheduled. This limited capacity must be allocated among the product lot sizes, and for this reason the problem cannot be solved by considering the individual products separately.

An alternative perspective views master scheduling as a problem in demand management. In this view, the problem arises at the interface between production planning and customer demand when at least some production is initiated on the basis of demand forecasts. The operation of an assemble-to-order system is a good example. In an ATO setting, once the module stock is determined and demands are known, the problem involves assigning of modules to end items in order to fill specific customer orders. Before demands are known, a schedule must be determined for module production. In addition, customer demands must be managed by available-to-promise logic. If there were only one end item and only one module, this would be a classical inventory problem with uncertain demand. However, the multiproduct nature of master scheduling, together with the commonality inherent in the typical ATO product structure, make this a complicated allocation problem.

Multiproduct lot sizing

We can treat multiproduct lot sizing as a mathematical programming problem. Using the subscripts i and t to represent product and time period, respectively, let

x_{it} = production quantity,
I_{it} = inventory at end of t,
y_{it} = setup indicator (0 or 1),
a_i = production hours per unit,
d_{it} = demand,
h_i = holding cost,
K_i = setup cost,
C_t = production hours available.

Then the basic formulation might take the form shown below.

$$\begin{aligned} \text{minimize} \quad & \sum_i \sum_t (K_i y_{it} + h_i I_{it}) \\ \text{subject to} \quad & I_{i,t-1} + x_{it} - I_{it} = d_{it} \quad \text{for all } (i, t)\,, \\ & \sum_i a_i x_{it} \leq C_t \quad \text{for all } t\,, \\ & x_{it} - y_{it} \sum_t d_{it} \leq 0 \quad \text{for all } (i, t)\,, \\ & x_{it} \geq 0,\ I_{it} \geq 0,\ \text{and } y_{it} = 0 \text{ or } 1\,. \end{aligned} \tag{4.1}$$

This basic model can be extended to include consideration of overtime production, subcontracting, backlogging of demand, and explicit setup times. In the formulation of (4.1) production capacity is represented as limited production time, presumably for the final assembly operation. However, the limited capacity could represent a bottleneck at some other stage of the system.

For problems of practical dimensions, this model contains a large number of variables and constraints, making the computational demands on an optimization procedure somewhat prohibitive. However, it appears possible to solve this problem very efficiently using the heuristic method of Maes and Van Wassenhove [1986], which is known as the ABC method.

To set the stage for the ABC method, assume that we are given the demand matrix d_{it}, the capacities C_t, and the cost parameters K_i and h_i. The problem is to fill out the matrix of x_{it} values, where the columns correspond to the time periods and the rows to the various products. The lot sizing step of the ABC method calls for filling out this matrix in a one-pass procedure. Once a unit of demand is assigned to production in a particular period, this assignment is not revised. Each lot size is developed by first including a quantity sufficient to meet imminent demand and then possibly expanding the lot size to meet some portion of future demand. Three modules influence the precise details of the lot sizing step:

(A) The rule that orders the products for consideration.

(B) The criterion that determines whether adding a future demand is desirable.

(C) The strategy that governs the search of future demands.

A specification of each module constitutes a variation of the algorithm; hence, the ABC name. Maes and van Wassenhove discuss alternative choices for each module, thus generating several variations of the ABC method.

In module (A) a specific rule determines the order in which the products will be considered. Several plausible alternatives exist, including the following:

(A1) Largest POQ based on average demand, i.e., ordered by $[2K_i/d_ih_i]^{1/2}$.

(A2) Largest EPP, i.e., ordered by K_i/h_i.

(A3) Largest EPP per hour of production, i.e., ordered by K_i/a_ih_i.

(A4) Smallest cost in the comparable EOQ model, i.e., ordered by $[2K_id_ih_i]^{1/2}$.

In each of these calculations, d_i represents an average value for the planning horizon.

In module (B) a specific rule determines whether it is desirable to expand a particular lot to include some future demand quantity for the same product. This type of rule is analogous to the stopping rule used in a single-level lot sizing method. Therefore, some plausible alternatives include the more effective methods discussed in the previous section:

(B1) MCD.

(B2) LPC.

(B3) IOQ.

(B4) PPA.

Although Maes and Van Wassenhove were not aware of the MCD method, they did suggest each of the other methods.

In module (C) a specific rule determines the order in which future demands will be considered under the criterion in module (B). Maes and Van Wassenhove suggest the following:

(C1) East.

(C2) South.

(C3) Southeast.

The east rule considers the d-matrix row by row. In other words, the possible covering of all future demand for a given product is examined before any other product is addressed. The South rule considers the d-matrix column by column. In other words, the possible covering of all demand in period t is examined before any later demand is addressed. The Southeast rule is a hybrid. The products are first grouped according to the length of their POQ values. The group with the longest POQ is considered first, and their demands are examined according to the South rule. Then the next group is considered using the South rule, and so on.

By selecting a module from each of the three lists, Maes and Van Wassenhove created a distinct variation of the ABC method. From the illustrative lists given above, there would be 48 (=4 × 4 × 3) variations, although in their original work Maes and Van Wassenhove considered a total of 72.

There are two additional routines in the solution method. The first relates to feasibility considerations. A naive approach to lot sizing might encounter some difficulty because demand may exceed capacity in certain of the periods. If adequate provisions are not made early to build inventory for these periods, then the one-pass procedure will fail when it encounters large demands. Fortunately, it is possible to anticipate in advance how much inventory must be built.

Define R_t as the required excess to be on hand at the end of period t, expressed in terms of production hours. This quantity can be computed recursively at the outset of the solution procedure, beginning with the last period N of the horizon:

$$R_N = 0\,,$$

$$R_t = \max\Big(\sum_i a_i d_{i,t+1} + R_{t+1} - C_{t+1}, 0\Big) \quad \text{for } 1 \leq t \leq N-1\,.$$

Now suppose that at some point in the procedure we choose to add the demand d_{ik} to some early lot size, x_{it}, where $k > t$. The number of production hours to be added is $p_{ik} = a_i d_{ik}$. Working backward from period k, we then update the data as follows for periods $t \leq s < k$:

$$p_{is} = \min(R_{s+1}, p_{i,s+1})\,,$$
$$R_s \leftarrow R_s - p_{is}\,. \tag{4.2}$$

Pulling in the demand d_{ik} to be part of the lot size x_{it} contributes p_{is} hours to the required excess R_s in each of the periods from t to k; hence the update in (4.2). In period t, where the lot size is being formed, we must have the following condition met:

$$C_t - a_i d_{ik} \geq R_t - p_{it} . \tag{4.3}$$

The right-hand side of this inequality corresponds to (4.2): it measures the remaining excess that will subsequently have to be accumulated in period t to assure feasibility in later periods. The left-hand side measures the remaining number of hours that will be available in period j after the quantity d_{ik} is added to the current lot size x_{it}. Thus (4.3) must be checked and satisfied before expanding the lot size.

We can now outline the logic for selecting a lot size x_{it} in period t, assuming that lot sizes have already been chosen for periods 1 through $(t-1)$. The ordering rule in effect [such as (A1)] determines which product to consider. First, x_{it} must be large enough to meet net demand in period t. (Net demand might be zero if d_{it} was zero originally, or if earlier lots created sufficient inventory to cover demand in period t.) Second, x_{it} can be expanded if the criterion in use [such as (B1)] indicates that it is desirable to pull in demand d_{ik} for some future period k and if the feasibility condition in (4.3) is satisfied. The search strategy in effect [such as (C1)] dictates whether consideration will next be given to demand in another period for the same product or to demand for a different product.

The final routine in the procedure is comprised of some 'clean-up' steps, which are invoked after an entire plan has been constructed. The first step combines two successive lots for the same product when costs do not increase and capacity is available. The second step pushes inventory into the future, to avoid situations in which a lot size is scheduled for a period and inventory for the same product is also carried into that period. Although these are obvious adjustments, the main steps in the ABC method do not make them automatically.

In their original study, Maes and Van Wassenhove applied the ABC method in solving 360 test problems containing 12 products and 12 periods. They recommended the (A1)/(B2)/(C3) variation as the best single combination in their study. They also examined a procedure that produces solutions using ten variations of the ABC method and choosing the best. This heuristic procedure performed better on average (and faster) than several other methods proposed in the literature. The flexibility of the ABC method makes it an important benchmark for algorithms that schedule the lot sizes of multiple products in the presence of a single bottleneck capacity.

Mathematical programming models. The ABC method is only a heuristic procedure and does not guarantee an optimal solution. For the purposes of optimization, the power of mathematical programming can be exploited in solving problems similar to the formulation in (4.1). Recent advances are described by Barany, Van Roy & Wolsey [1984], Thizy & Van Wassenhove [1983], Trigeiro [1987], and Trigeiro, Thomas & McClain [1989]. The last of these three papers also explores the implications of including explicit provisions for setup time as well as setup cost. Chapter 8 covers some of the optimization approaches that can be viewed as models for master scheduling.

Demand management

As introduced earlier, the assemble-to-order (ATO) environment divides scheduling into two parts: the Master Production Schedule (MPS) which governs the production of modules, and the Final Assembly Schedule (FAS) which governs the production of end items. Because the MPS is forecast-driven, there are inevitably some discrepancies between the modules produced for the forecast and the modules actually required in the FAS. This type of mismatch is typical of inventory problems involving demand forecasts, and there are two basic costs to trade off, the cost of overstocking and the cost of understocking.

The cost of overstocking is the carrying charge on excess module inventory, but larger stock levels provide greater assurance that the right materials will be available to meet demand on time. Nevertheless, in the ATO environment, it might be difficult to meet all demand, even when stock levels are plentiful. In times of peak demand, capacity restrictions in final assembly may limit the rate at which end items can be produced. Therefore, the recognition of capacity constraints or capacity choices might also be pertinent in some representations of the problem.

The cost of understocking is the penalty for not being able to meet demand on schedule. Without the incentive to fill orders on time the solution would be to hold no module stock and simply to use an MTO strategy. Therefore, it is important to recognize that customer orders have timing as well as quantity requirements, and we can think of each order as having a due date. The cost of understocking is the delay penalty incurred when an order cannot be filled by its due date. This penalty can be represented in two basic ways. In one setting demand can be backordered, and the penalty may reflect such factors as the opportunity cost of delayed revenues and the incremental costs of premium shipment or other contractual penalties. In the other setting demand cannot be backordered, so an order is rejected upon arrival when the planning system determines that it cannot be met on time. For this setting the penalty is lost profit.

In order to structure a basic framework for thinking about this problem, assume that there is a known MPS which, along with initial inventory levels, determines how much of each module will be available in each period for an N-period horizon. In addition, customer demands are known throughout the planning horizon, with backorders permitted. There are then two types of costs to be balanced: the holding cost associated with carrying surplus modules in inventory and the penalty cost associated with delayed response to a customer order.

Suppose there are m module types and n product types. Define the given information (obtained from the master production schedule and the bill of material) as follows:

Q_{kt} = quantity of module k in the MPS at period t,

g_{kj} = number of modules of type k required to assemble order j.

The decision variables in the problem are the following:

$y_{jt} = 1$ if order j is assembled and delivered in period t, and 0 otherwise,

I_{kt} = inventory of module k after period t.

(Here we represent each order individually, so that if multiple orders for a given type were demanded, we would represent each order with a distinct index j.) Next, let h_k denote the holding cost per period for module k stock, and let p_{jt} denote the penalty cost if order j is satisfied in period t. We assume that assembly and delivery of an order occur in the same period. Were capacity infinite, that would be a reasonable assumption, because it would always be preferable to hold inventory in the (cheaper) form of components than in the form of end items. Suppose, however, that there is a capacity restriction for the assembly operation. In this case there could be circumstances in which we would like to assemble an order early but not deliver it. The model can still capture the effect of this option by treating such an order as if it were delivered upon assembly and by assessing a penalty cost via p_{jt} that reflects the holding cost for the order.

Let C_t denote the number of assembly hours available in period t, and let a_j denote the number of hours required by order j. A formulation of the problem as a mixed integer program is shown below.

$$\begin{aligned}
\text{minimize} \quad & \sum_k \sum_t h_k I_{kt} + \sum_j \sum_t p_{jt} y_{jt} \\
\text{subject to} \quad & I_{kt} = I_{k,t-1} + Q_{kt} - \sum_j g_{kj} y_{jt} \quad \text{for all } (k, t)\,, \\
& \sum_j a_j y_{jt} \leq C_t \quad \text{for all } t\,, \\
& \sum_t y_{jt} = 1 \quad \text{for all } t\,.
\end{aligned} \tag{4.4}$$

In this model the specific set of customer orders and the MPS quantities are given. However, there is no reason for knowledge of these two kinds of information to span the same horizons. Instead, we might assume that the MPS is known for N periods, but customer orders are known only for L periods, where $L < N$. In this situation, the order data would be collected and allocation decisions would be made for the first L periods. At that time, new order information would become available, and the next L-period analysis could be carried out. We call L the *accumulation period*, and it would seem to be intuitive that a longer accumulation period should ultimately lead to better decisions.

Taking this basic structure as a starting point, the model can be enriched in several directions. One direction involves specialization, particularly in the nature of the objective function. For example, the penalty cost p_{jt} could be structured to represent the cost of tardiness, if customer orders have corresponding due dates, or the cost of lost sales, if demand is not captive. Another direction involves generalization of the trade offs in the model. For example, the formulation could be extended to recognize the possibility of overtime decisions, incorporating the associated costs in the objective function.

Investigations of ATO decision-making have been limited. Guerrero [1991] focuses on the implementation of available-to-promise (ATP) logic using a model containing one product and one component module. He assumes that customer orders have an early and a late due date. The latter is a deadline, which must be met if the order is to be accepted. The early due date is the first period at which delivery will be accepted. He also assumes that some speculative orders can be scheduled for the FAS in anticipation of future demand.

To perform the allocation decisions analogous to those modeled above, Guerrero invokes ATP logic. The steps are as follows:

(1) Collect arriving orders for an accumulation period of length L.

(2) Rank the orders by a priority rule.

(3) Assign components to orders using ATP logic.

For the objective of service level (percentage of orders accepted) Guerrero finds that the greatest leverage on this measure comes from implementing Step (3) by assigning orders as late as possible, that is, as close as possible to the order's late due date, and by implementing Step (2) by giving priority to the most urgent late due date.

King & Benton [1987] examine a more basic aspect of the ATO framework, namely the procedure that generates the master scheduling decisions. In particular, they compare two approaches, one based on covering sets and the other based on superbills. They conclude that the use of superbills is more effective at minimizing lead times, and they identify the major external factors that influence lead time performance.

At a longer-run level, the problem is to select the MPS quantities as decisions, in the face of uncertainty about orders. It would seem appropriate to view the master scheduling decision as if it were a multiproduct newsvendor problem: a supply decision – selecting the build quantities in the master schedule – must be made before the demand outcome – customer orders for final assemblies – is known. The problem is complicated by commonality among components of different end items and by the fact that the ultimate matching of known demand with available supply – as in the optimization model of (4.4) – is more complex than the simple matching of the newsvendor model. For the time being, such complexity has limited researchers to simulation studies of specialized cases.

McClelland [1988] compares alternative master scheduling approaches in a situation where demand is forecast-driven. One alternative is to associate the MPS with end-items, as in the traditional MTO or MTS structure, while another is to associate the MPS with subassemblies, as in the ATO structure. Two primitive forms of RCCP are also studied. One form examines aggregate capacity at the level of the MPS; the other involves disaggregation by individual end items (if the MPS is built at the end-item level) or by individual subassemblies (if the MPS is built at the subassembly level). In each case, capacity is recognized at only the level at which the MPS is constructed. McClelland finds no dominant type of MPS strategy: the various alternatives seem to balance customer service levels with inventory levels in different ways. Not surprisingly, there is some evidence that the explicit consideration of backlog and capacity conditions can improve the accuracy of promises made to customers. In addition, there is some evidence that the safety stock strategy should be co-ordinated with the MPS strategy.

In general, it seems fair to say that relatively little research is available on models for the decisions involved in demand management. This appears to be a topic for which we shall have to rely on future research to produce the same kinds of insights that we have been able to gain from lot sizing and capacity models.

5. Models for capacity and lead times

In many MRP-based planning and control systems, even those purchased as relatively standard software, the modules for capacity planning are often among the last to be implemented. The difficulty is related in part to the fact that standard data on capacity, compared to standard data on material, is less likely to exist in usable form. When it comes to documenting the capacity requirements for an end item, there is seldom a specification as clear as the Bill of Material is for material requirements. Indeed, the very flexibility that may account for a firm's competitive strength often makes it impossible to document capacity requirements in the same unique way that a product structure diagram can specify material needs. Thus one difficulty in developing a capacity planning module for a production system may be the lack of precise standards.

However, there seems to be another reason for the fact that capacity-oriented tools have been put on line much less quickly than material-oriented tools in MRP systems: the basic capacity tools offered with most standard MRP systems are just too primitive. Although RCCP and CRP are in widespread use, they are only partial measures. They provide warnings that loads and capacities are in conflict, but they do not provide guidance for resolving the conflict. Their representation of capacity is not linked to lead time parameters, and they ignore queueing effects entirely. The more recent capacity models in the literature begin to recognize some of these factors in capacity analysis.

Input/output models

The formal description of Input/Output (I/O) modeling by Karni [1982] provides some useful insight into the relationship between capacity and lead times. Recall that in the traditional MRP model, the lead time is a parameter stored on the data base. It is not necessarily linked automatically to decisions about capacity levels. The I/O model provides this link at a particular work center by tracing its status over time. Let

C = capacity of the work center,
R_t = work released (input) to the work center during period t,
P_t = production (output) from the work center during period t.

The planned releases R_t are determined by MRP over an N-period horizon and are assumed to occur at the start of the period. The production levels P_t are determined within the I/O model and are assumed to occur throughout the period. All of these variables are measured in common units such as hours.

In addition, let Q_t denote the queue at the work center, measured at the beginning of time period t and prior to the release of work. We can then write the following consistency relations:

$$P_t = \min(C, Q_{t-1} + R_t)\,, \tag{5.1}$$

$$Q_t = Q_{t-1} + R_t - P_t\,. \tag{5.2}$$

The first of these states that production can be at most equal to the work available in the period or the capacity; the second accounts for changes in queue size.

Finally, let W_t denote the work in process (WIP) at the given work center. Then, by definition, we have:

$$W_t = Q_{t-1} + R_t = Q_t + P_t \tag{5.3}$$

and we can define the lead time at the work center to be L_t, where

$$L_t = W_t / C\,. \tag{5.4}$$

Notice that this definition does not prescribe that the lead time be an integer number of periods. In addition, the lead time is indexed by the time subscript, to recognize the fact that lead time might vary at the work center. Obviously, that could be the case if releases to the work center fluctuate over time. In this sense, the I/O model provides a more realistic, and thus more appealing representation of lead time than the constant parametric value normally used in the MRP record.

The relationships in (5.1)–(5.4) are simple equations that can easily be displayed on a spreadsheet. The spreadsheet can then be used to examine two questions. First, given the pattern of planned releases R_t and a specific capacity level C, what lead time will be achieved? Second, given the lead time (perhaps from the MRP data base) what minimum capacity must be put in place to support the lead time?

To illustrate these analyses, consider the six-week example in Table 5.1, displayed as it might appear in spreadsheet format.

Table 5.1
An example of input/output relationships

	Period						
	0	1	2	3	4	5	6
Capacity		36	36	36	36	36	36
Input		20	30	60	20	40	40
Production		30	30	36	36	36	36
Queue	10	0	0	24	8	12	16
WIP		30	30	60	44	48	52
Lead time		0.83	0.83	1.67	1.22	1.33	1.44

Assuming that capacity is set at 36 hours per week, the model tells us that the lead time will fluctuate but will not exceed 1.67 weeks. Therefore, if the lead time for this work center is specified as 2 weeks on the MRP record, that figure would be consistent with the load for the six-week horizon. If we wanted to know how much lower the capacity level could drop without violating the 2-week lead time standard, then we could easily search over potential values of capacity. In this example we would find that a lead time of 2 weeks could be achieved with a capacity of 32 hours. Thus the I/O model permits us to choose capacity so that pre-specified lead times are satisfied.

The spreadsheet can also be utilized to identify capacity levels that are feasible with respect to other conditions that might be imposed. For example, suppose we require that the queue length never exceed 20 hours. Then the capacity of 36 hours is infeasible because, as Table 1.7 shows, it would lead to a queue length of 24 hours at the end of week 3. A direct search will reveal that the 20-hour limit cannot be achieved unless the capacity is at least 40 hours.

Using this framework, Karni [1981a] formulates the problem of selecting the optimal capacity level. In the Karni model there are costs associated with capacity, production levels, and queue sizes. The problem is to choose capacity so as to minimize the total of these costs, subject to constraints on the minimum, maximum, or final values of the variables Q_t, W_t, and L_t. Once the spreadsheet has been set up, this problem can be solved by direct enumeration of the feasible capacity levels. Karni also discusses two extensions. In one, there are several sources of capacity (e.g., regular time, overtime, and subcontracting), each in limited amounts and at different unit costs. In the second extension, there is a convex cost function corresponding to each source.

In a generalization, Karni [1981b] allows the capacity level to be selected independently in each period. In this setting there is no reason to have idle capacity, and it is unnecessary to distinguish between the cost of capacity and the cost of production. In order to solve the general case, Karni proposes a dynamic programming approach. Let $G(P_t)$ denote the cost of production at output level P_t, and let h denote the holding cost for in-process inventory level Q_t. At stage t the state variable is the queue size Q_{t-1} at the end of the previous period. Let $F_t(Q)$ denote the minimum cost for periods t through N, given that $Q_{t-1} = Q$. Then the basic recursion is as follows:

$$F_t(Q) = \min[G(P) + h(Q + R_t - P) + F_{t+1}(Q + R_t - P)], \qquad (5.5)$$

where the minimum is taken over feasible values of the production level P. The recursion starts with $F_{N+1}(Q) = 0$ and ultimately calculates $F_1(Q_0)$.

The calculations dictated by (5.5) can be simplified in certain special cases. Karni provides simple algorithms for continuous and discrete capacity alternatives with convex costs. Notice, however, that the solution need not meet all demand unless a constraint is imposed on final queue length. Karni therefore discusses variations of the model in which restrictions are placed on queue lengths, giving rise to a specialized form of the dynamic programming approach in (5.5).

Capacity variations and lead time

The Input/Output model recognizes the dynamic link between capacity and lead time, but it takes a deterministic viewpoint. The next step is to recognize the effect of uncertainty on lead times. We can think of the MRP lead time parameter as a planned lead time, whereas the actual lead time tends to vary around the plan. This variation occurs because of uncertainty within the production system and in its environment, and in the execution phase various measures are taken to overcome the effects of this uncertainty. One such measure is prioritization of a dispatch list, which attempts to maintain the progress of individual jobs according to their planned lead times. Priority dispatching is not very effective, however, at anticipating how jobs will interact and progress downstream, so its ability to control progress is limited. Another measure in this category is Input/Output control, which attempts to stabilize loads at work centers by adjusting the mechanism for releasing work. However, I/O techniques can be difficult to adapt at work centers other than so-called 'gateway' operations because inputs at some work centers are determined by outputs at others.

A third measure, if the option exists, is the variation of production rates in response to variation in loads. Graves [1986] suggests a model with flexible production rates that will permit a trade-off between smooth flow and low WIP levels. Although the complete details of the modeling approach are not repeated here, the basic premises can be outlined.

Let the subscripts i and t represent work center and time period, respectively. One key part of the model relates production rate to the amount of work in queue. The equation is

$$P_{it} = \alpha_i Q_{it}, \qquad (5.6)$$

where α_i is a proportionality factor. In particular, $1/\alpha_i$ represents the number of periods, on average, that work requires to move through the work center. For example, when $\alpha_i = 0.25$, that means that one-fourth of the work in queue is processed in any period. On average, therefore, work spends four periods at the work center before moving to the next operation. Equation (5.6) might be viewed as a descriptive equation, to the extent that production planners in actual systems attempt to shift capacity to locations where load is heavy; but we can also think of it as a prescriptive equation: that is, planners *should* preserve the integrity of the planned lead time by shifting capacity toward heavily-loaded locations.

A companion equation accounts for the increases and decreases in WIP:

$$Q_{it} = Q_{i,t-1} + A_{it} - P_{it} , \tag{5.7}$$

where A_{it} represents the amount of work that arrives at work center i in period t. If we substitute (5.7) into (5.6), we obtain a smoothing equation:

$$P_{it} = (1 - \alpha_i)P_{i,t-1} + \alpha_i A_{it} . \tag{5.8}$$

Finally, Graves represents the arriving work as follows.

$$A_{it} = \sum_j q_{ij} P_{j,t-1} + \varepsilon_{it} , \tag{5.9}$$

where q_{ij} is the proportion of work that comes to work center i when it leaves j, and ε_{it} is a term that captures not only the mean arrival rate from outside of the system but also the variability of work flow. By making assumptions about the stochastic behavior of ε_{it}, Graves ultimately relates the variation in production levels to the size of WIP. The key planning parameter in this relation is the smoothing constant α_i. As α_i is reduced, the planned lead time at work center i rises, but the variability in production level drops. This lower variability means first, that there are fewer occasions when the shop must resort to overtime or other emergency capacity measures and, second, that smaller amounts of work are past due.

Capacity utilization, lot sizes, and lead times

In the basic MRP model lead times and lot sizes are input parameters. Moreover, they are independent parameters in the sense that they are not formally linked, and either parameter may be changed by itself. There is no provision in the MRP model for tracing the effects of modified lot sizes on component lead times. Most practitioners would find this to be an oversimplification: logic and experience tell us that a part's lead time will be affected if its lot size is changed. In addition, there are dependencies between parts. If a substantial change is made in the lot size of component i, then the lead time of component j may well be altered. Thus the true relation between lot size and lead time is more complex than depicted in the basic MRP model.

On another front, the capacity models in most MRP systems are based on average-case behavior. When using averages, capacity analyses indicate that utilization can grow toward 100% without having an impact on lead times or WIP levels. Again, logic and experience tell a different story. When utilization approaches 100%, lead times and WIP increase. (Sometimes the cause and effect are not always clear. Many a shop foreman being measured on utilization strives for high WIP levels in order to guarantee that utilization will be high.) Long lead times and high WIP levels are signs of congestion, and we know that, when there is variability in the system, congestion increases as demand approaches capacity. An average-case analysis would not suggest that a problem exists until the 100% level is exceeded. Thus the true relation between capacity and lead time cannot be fully captured without recognizing the variation that lies behind the averages.

These observations account for criticism of the basic MRP model on the ground that it does not recognize the complicated relation between capacity utilization, lot sizes, and component lead times. Until recently, the only means of modeling this relation was through simulation, but the advent of specialized queueing models has contributed new insights into lead time performance. The purpose of a queueing model is to relate queueing delays (hence lead times) to demand, capacity, and lot sizes in a shop. The essence of the approach is to decompose the shop by machine centers into separate nodes, and then to analyze the behavior of queues at each node. Although it is approximate, the queueing approach recognizes the following properties:

- The lot size of a product affects its lead time.
- The lot size of one product affects the lead times of other products.
- A change in product mix influences lead times.
- An increase in utilization causes an increase in lead times.

The queueing viewpoint, as exemplified in the exposition of Karmarkar, Kekre, Kekre & Freeman [1985], prescribes two aggregate effects that should be present in any lead time model. First, as lot sizes increase, lead times should also increase. This is called the *batching effect*. For example, consider the delay created by lot sizing for a batch of 10 parts. Once processing begins, the first part must wait for the other nine parts before proceeding. The last part must wait for the first nine before getting access to the operation. Suppose the batch size is doubled, to 20. Now each part must wait for 19 other parts during processing. The idea is that larger batch sizes will cause longer delays of parts waiting for the rest of the batch to be completed.

The second effect works in the opposite direction. As lot sizes decrease, lead times will eventually increase, first gradually, then more dramatically. This is called the *saturation effect*. When lot sizes are reduced, there will be more lots in the shop, provided that demand stays the same. With more lots there will be more time spent in setup, and relatively less time available for processing. As a result, demand becomes a relatively larger proportion of effective capacity, and congestion increases. According to basic queueing concepts, as demand approaches capacity the level of congestion will rise, first gradually and then sharply, toward saturation levels.

Combining the two effects, the queueing viewpoint proposes that the aggregate behavior of lead time as a function of lot size should resemble the U-shaped function shown in Figure 5.1. What remains is to flesh out the analytical details of this function. The exposition that follows illustrates how this can be done.

A representative machine center in the shop is modeled as a single server queueing system that serves n different products. Assuming random arrivals and an arbitrary distribution of service time, we can use the M/G/1 queueing model to describe lead time at the queue. The conventional formula for this quantity is

$$W = \frac{(\lambda/\mu)^2 + \lambda^2\sigma^2}{2\lambda(1-\lambda/\mu)} + \frac{1}{\mu}, \tag{5.10}$$

where λ denotes the mean arrival rate, μ denotes the mean service time, and σ^2 denotes the variance of service time.

In our situation product j is described by the following parameters:

d_j = demand rate,
p_j = production rate,
s_j = setup time,

and the decision to be made is its lot size, denoted Q_j. If we think of the customers in the queue as batches, then the mean arrival rate of batches is

$$\lambda = \sum_{j=1}^{n} \frac{d_j}{Q_j}$$

and the mean service time for the batches is the weighted average given by

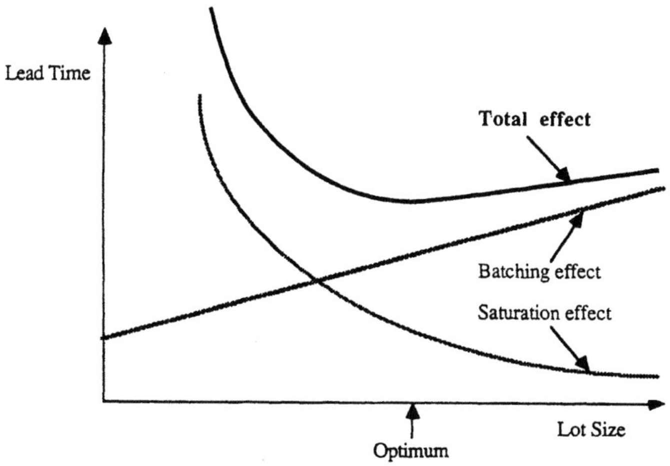

Fig. 5.1. The effect of lot size on lead time.

$$\mu = \sum_{j=1}^{n} \lambda_j(s_j + p_jQ_j) \Big/ \sum_{j=1}^{n} \lambda_j ,$$

where $\lambda_j = d_j/Q_j$ is the arrival rate for batches of product j. Finally, the variance of service times is

$$\sigma^2 = \Big(\sum_{j=1}^{n} \lambda_j(s_j + p_jQ_j)^2 \Big/ \sum_{j=1}^{n} \lambda_j\Big) - \frac{1}{\mu^2} .$$

In order to calculate the lead time, we substitute the expressions for λ, μ, and σ^2 into (5.10). This substitution gives us a multivariate version of the function described in Figure 5.1. In particular, W is a (nonlinear) function of the n lot size choices $q_1, Q_2, \ldots, Q_n$ with a well-behaved minimum for Q_j values that do not cause the system to saturate ($\lambda < \mu$).

As an example, suppose there are four products with the parameters described in Table 5.2. The formula for W in (5.10) can easily be set up in a spreadsheet model, and a trial and error search will get close to the optimum in no more than a few minutes. Alternatively, a multidimensional search routine will reveal that the minimal value of W is about 1.29 weeks, with lot sizes of (roughly)

$$Q_1 = 60 , \qquad Q_2 = 1300 , \qquad Q_3 = 400 , \qquad Q_4 = 500 .$$

This kind of analysis can, in principle, be extended to a multi-operation shop. In that case the lead time for a given component can be found by summing the lead times at the individual machine centers on its routing. In addition, the analysis can be extended to machine centers with several machines in parallel by using parallel-server queueing models. Notice that queueing models of this sort have the desired characteristics. They relate lead time to lot size choices, and they provide for the lot size of product i to influence the lead time for product j. Thus they specify how lead times will change with product mix. By reflecting production capacity in production rates, queueing models represent effective capacity by intrinsically providing for saturation if the arrival rate should equal or exceed the service rate.

Queueing models of this sort can be used in a variety of ways in connection with a standard planning and control system. For example, in the shorter term,

Table 5.2

Product no.	Demand (weekly)	Setup (Hrs)	Run time (Hrs/1000)
1	100	3	30
2	500	15	45
3	50	6	75
4	250	24	150

a queueing model can be used with the MRP system to generate meaningful lead time estimates for a given set of lot sizes, so that offsets for order releases can be calculated with due recognition of shop load, product mix, and capacity. Furthermore, in situations where it is strategically important to reduce WIP and enhance responsiveness, lead times can be minimized by searching for the optimal combination of lot sizes. In the medium term, a queueing model can help perform 'what if' analysis on changes in product mix and volume. For various scenarios the model would suggest alterations in lot sizes or overtime schedules in order to cope with anticipated changes. In the longer term, a queueing model might be useful in evaluating the lead time and WIP consequences of purchasing additional machines or otherwise investing in new capacity. Thus the queueing model could be used to support and extend the MRP system.

6. Models for deploying buffers

The MRP model is deterministic, but reality is not. Therefore, safety stocks are deployed in actual MRP systems to provide a buffer against uncertainty. However, there is relatively little analytic justification of the buffering procedures that are used in practice, and there is a need for models to illuminate several aspects of the problem. First, we must answer the question of where in the product structure the buffer should be held. Second, even in the cases where that answer is known (or assumed), we must answer the question of how much buffer is desirable. For both questions, 'where' and 'how much', our knowledge is limited.

The classical view in the MRP literature was that safety stock could be held at the level of end items, to provide a cushion for uncertainty about external demand, and at the level of purchased material, to provide a cushion for uncertainty about external supply. Traditionalists argued that buffers were not necessary at any stage of production in between. Nevertheless, the more prevalent view today is that there may be good reasons to hold buffers within the product structure. One reason for this view stems from the fact that some sources of uncertainty, such as process yields, arise within the stages of manufacture. A more compelling reason, even for demand uncertainty, is that there are intrinsic economic trade-offs to be addressed.

As the buffer is pushed upstream, away from the end-item level, the associated holding cost drops. In addition, if there is any commonality at all, the flexibility of the buffer improves. On the other hand, as the buffer is pushed downstream, toward the end-item level, the lead time to the customer drops. As a result, there is less delay imposed on the customer, even though the holding cost is higher. Therefore, the economic trade-off in holding safety stock leads naturally to the question of where to deploy the buffer.

A related question is what form the buffer should take. The two primary forms are safety stock, which is a quantity buffer, and safety time, which is a time buffer. Either one can be incorporated in the MRP record, as shown earlier, but the challenge is still to determine the optimal quantity of safety stock or the optimal amount of safety time, whichever is utilized.

An answer to the question of where to place buffers is just a starting point. We also need methodologies that will provide help with the details of sizing the buffers. Experts in this field have inherited the paradigm of multilevel inventory systems or distribution networks. To some extent the same principles and insights apply, but they must be extended to recognize the special features of buffers for multilevel production systems.

One key feature is the assembly structure in the typical bill of material. In the traditional models of inventory theory there is no need to co-ordinate two or more inputs at an assembly point. Hence, there is no risk of staging delay. However, as Schmidt & Nahmias [1985] have shown with a two-level model, it is quite difficult to adapt the results of existing inventory theory (see Chapter 3) to assembly structures. The prospects for techniques that optimize multistage assembly models are not promising.

Another feature is the existence of component commonality in product structures of related end items. Although commonality provides the opportunity to exploit statistical economies of scale, it also poses the problem of allocating safety stock among common and unique components. As shown by Baker, Magazine & Nuttle [1986], the optimal allocation may be somewhat counterintuitive, and the calculations are difficult in all but the simplest cases. Again, the prospects for optimizing techniques are not promising.

Location of buffers

There are no general normative results on the proper location of buffers. The few insights we have come from specialized studies, and these are primarily concerned with buffering aimed at uncertainty in external demand. Moreover, the simplified MRP systems represented in these studies hardly capture the generality that we ultimately seek.

For example, De Bodt and Van Wassenhove [1983a] develop a simulation model for a three-level assembly structure and investigate the exchange curve reflecting the trade-off between inventory cost and customer service level. Their very limited investigation suggests that it is desirable to hold safety stock at several levels in the product structure.

McClelland & Wagner [1988] use a simulation model for a different three-level assembly structure to investigate this question in greater detail. They also examine the trade-off between inventory cost and customer service level, and a special feature of their design is the recognition of demand variance as an experimental factor. For a moderate level of variance, they find that *diversified* policies, which distribute the buffer among levels, dominate single-level policies. For a high level of variance, their findings are similar except at lower levels of inventory, where a slight advantage is gained by holding the buffer at the subassembly level. (Recalling McClelland's related work discussed in

Section 4, this result may simply be a function of the fact that master scheduling is done at the subassembly level.) Similar results are obtained whether the buffer is held in the form of safety stock or in the form of safety time.

Yano & Carlson [1988] develop an analytic model for a simple product structure involving one end-item and two subassemblies. Their model has an objective function comprised of expected holding and penalty costs, with some approximation involved in its derivation. They search for optimal values of this objective function, using a heuristic procedure, and then examine the nature of the safety stock policies thus deduced. They find that in most cases it is not desirable to hold safety stock for the components.

At this stage, researchers have come to clear, but different, conclusions about the location of buffers. More work is needed to understand the reasons for the differences encountered thus far.

Pipeline hedging

The term *hedging* refers to a buffering tactic that provides a cushion for uncertainty. The best known hedging tactic is the creation of safety stocks for finished goods in the face of uncertainty about demand. Figure 6.1 shows an example three-level product, with lead time and value-added cost displayed at

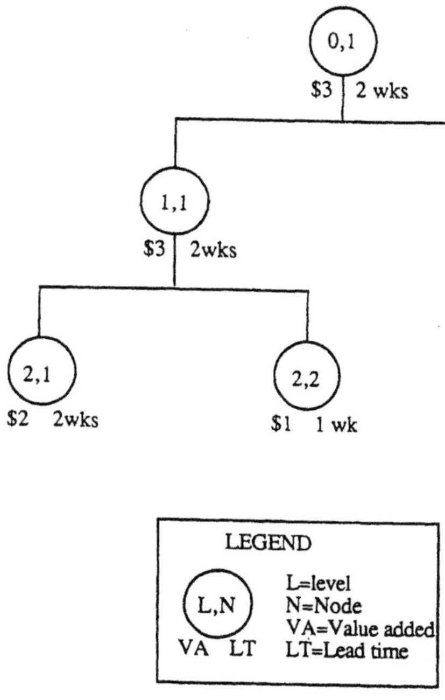

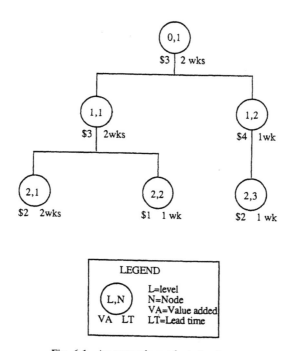

Fig. 6.1. An example product structure.

each node of the product structure. In particular, the total manufacturing lead time for this end item is 6 weeks. For the purposes of this example, assume that shop orders are placed and deliveries are made at the start of a week, while external demand occurs throughout the week. In other words, an order is placed in week 1 before demand in week 1 is known precisely.

Suppose that weekly demand for this product follows a normal distribution with mean 1000 and standard deviation 100, and suppose that the safety stock policy calls for 2-*sigma coverage*. This means that the safety stock is set equal to twice the standard deviation of demand during the exposure period.

In order to understand the length of the exposure period, suppose that an order for a replenishment lot is placed at the beginning of week 1. The end items in that order will not be available until the start of week 7. At the start of week 2, another order can be placed, and those end items will be available at the start of week 8. Thus, once we place an order at the start of week 1, that order (and those already in the pipeline) will have to provide protection through the end of week 7. Therefore, the exposure period is seven weeks, consisting of the six-week lead time and a one-week review interval. The standard deviation of demand during the exposure period is therefore equal to the standard deviation of weekly demand (100), multiplied by $\sqrt{7}$, or 264.5.

At the start of this exposure period, there must be enough stock on hand (or on order) to cover the demand forecast for weeks 1–7, and also to provide a cushion for uncertainty during the same period. In our example, there must be 7000 units on hand (or on order) to cover the forecast, plus 529 units of safety stock. In summary, if we hedged by holding a safety stock of finished goods, then we would plan to hold 529 units (worth $7935) as a buffer quantity.

The concept of pipeline hedging is based on the notion that the buffer need not be maintained only in the form of end items; it can instead be distributed among the stages of the product structure, throughout the manufacturing pipeline. The idea is formalized by Miller [1979] and discussed further by Wijngaard & Wortmann [1985]. We next describe an example of this technique, using a 98% target service level. In the case of a Normal distribution, this target roughly corresponds to 2-sigma coverage.

Suppose we had extensive inventories at level 1. How much safety stock would we need to hold downstream at level 0? To answer this question, we note that the exposure period is 3 weeks for end item $(0, 1)$, consisting of two weeks of lead time plus the one week review period. Therefore, a 2-sigma policy will require a safety stock of 346.

Given a safety stock of 346 end items, suppose next that we had extensive inventories at level 2. How much safety stock would we need to hold downstream at level 1? For component $(1, 1)$ the exposure period is 5 weeks, consisting of four weeks of lead time plus one week review period. Therefore, we need a safety stock of 447. However, there are already 346 units contained in the safety stock of end items; therefore, we need only the difference of $447 - 346 = 101$ units of safety stock for component $(1, 1)$. Similarly, for component $(1, 2)$ the exposure period is 4 weeks, implying a need for a total safety stock of 400. Again, some of this safety stock is already contained in the end-item buffer, and the net safety stock is only $400 - 346 = 54$ units.

Given the safety stocks at levels 0 and 1, how much do we need upstream at level 2? We answer this question in a similar way, by identifying the lead time for the component, calculating the implied total safety stock, and netting out the buffer already in place at higher levels. Thus,

$$\text{for } (2,1) \quad \text{SS} = 529 - 447 = 82\,,$$

$$\text{for } (2,2) \quad \text{SS} = 490 - 447 = 43\,,$$

$$\text{for } (2,3) \quad \text{SS} = 447 - 400 = 47\,.$$

In summary, the distribution of safety stock throughout the manufacturing pipeline yields the following pattern:

Component:	(0, 1)	(1, 1)	(1, 2)	(2, 1)	(2, 2)	(2, 3)
Stock:	346	101	54	82	43	47

The total number of units in safety stock is 673, with a value of \$6421. Compared to the strategy of carrying the entire buffer at the end-item level, the pipeline strategy involves a larger number of units in the buffer, but they represent less investment.

Actually, this model is only an approximation, because at each stage of the analysis we made the assumption that the upstream node has sufficient inventory to cover all replenishment orders emanating from the downstream node. In fact, the stock at every node is limited, which means that it will not be guaranteed to cover all replenishment orders. Nevertheless, the assumption of total upstream coverage appears to be a reasonable first cut. We return to this assumption later on.

In order to accommodate a pipeline hedge within the structure of the MRP record, we introduce the following elements:

Gross requirements	= Demand forecast, or else exploded downstream requirements.
Cumulative hedge	= Safety stock for the cumulative exposure period.
Incremental hedge	= Difference between successive values of cumulative hedge.
Scheduled receipts	= As usually defined in MRP systems.
On hand	= As usual in MRP; in equilibrium, on hand = safety stock.
Net requirements	= From MRP logic, but based on including the incremental hedge.
Planned orders	= From MRP logic, but with hedge included in future orders.

These elements are illustrated in Table 6.1, where no lot sizing occurs, and

Table 6.1
MRP records for the example with provisions for pipeline hedging

Item (0, 1)		1	2	3	4	5	6	7	8
Requirements		1000	1000	1000	1000	1000	1000	1000	1000
Cum. hedge		200	283	346	400	447	490	529	529
Incr. hedge		200	83	63	54	47	43	39	0
Sch. receipts		1000	1000						
On hand	346	146	63						
Net req'ts.				1000	1054	1047	1043	1039	1000
Pl. orders		1000	1054	1047	1043	1039	1000		

Item (1, 1)		1	2	3	4	5	6
Requirements		1000	1054	1047	1043	1039	1000
Sch. receipts		1000	1000				
On hand	101	101	47				
Net req'ts.				1000	1043	1039	1000
Pl. orders		1000	1043	1039	1000		

Item (2, 1)		1	2	3	4	5	6
Requirements		1000	1043	1039	1000		
Sch. receipts		1000	1000				
On hand	82	82	39				
Net req'ts.				1000	1000		
Pl. orders		1000	1000				

Item (2, 2)		1	2	3	4	5	6
Requirements		1000	1043	1039	1000		
Sch. receipts		1000	1000				
On hand	43	43					
Net req'ts.			1000	1039	1000		
Pl. orders		1000	1039	1000			

Item (1, 2)		1	2	3	4	5	6
Requirements		1000	1054	1047	1043	1039	1000
Sch. receipts		1000					
On hand	54	54					
Net req'ts.			1000	1047	1043	1039	1000
Pl. orders		1000	1047	1043	1039	1000	

Item (2, 3)		1	2	3	4	5
Requirements		1000	1047	1043	1039	1000
Sch. receipts		1000				
On hand	47	47				
Net req'ts.			1000	1043	1039	1000
Pl. orders		1000	1043	1039	1000	

each lot size is equal to the imminent net requirements. In the portion of the table for level 0, which represents the MPS, the cumulative hedge is tabulated explicitly, along with the incremental hedge. The quantity in the incremental hedge is treated as if it were a demand requirement in some future period. This adjustment is sometimes called *demand overplanning*. The existence of the incremental hedge in the MPS causes stock to be held in the required quantity at each intermediate stage in the pipeline, simply by following MRP logic.

In Table 6.1 the demand forecast is taken to be stable at 1000 per week. In addition, a set of compatible starting conditions is assumed: all scheduled receipts are 1000 per week, and the initial stock on hand is equal to the desired safety stock. This constitutes an equilibrium state for the model. Specifically, if demand each week is equal to the forecast of 1000, then the MRP records will be unchanged week to week. One consequence of this observation is that even though the MPS overstates the forecast by including the incremental hedge in the requirements, the actual order release quantities will be equal to the forecast of 1000 each week as long as demand is equal to the forecast. Therefore, the overstatement implied by including the incremental hedge in the MPS is reflected in planned orders but not in actual releases.

In summary, the pipeline hedging strategy for safety stocks requires that the exposure period be determined for each node in the product structure. (This would typically be the manufacturing lead time at that node plus the review interval.) Next, there must be a distribution for demand during this exposure period. Given a target service level, this specifies a percentile of the demand distribution, which in turn allows us to specify the quantity of stock that must exist as a buffer between the node being analyzed and the customer. By netting out safety stock already in place downstream, we can calculate the requirement for safety stock at the given node.

Let i represent a node in the product structure for which we wish to calculate the required safety stock SS_i using the pipeline hedging strategy. Let θ denote the target service level, expressed as a fraction, and let $S(i)$ denote the set of all nodes in the product structure that lie downstream from node i. In network terminology, $S(i)$ is the successor set for i. Finally, let $F_i(y)$ represent the cumulative distribution function for demand during the exposure period that applies to node i. Then the required level of safety stock that must be in the system at node i or downstream from it is given by B_i, where

$$F(B_i) = \theta$$

and the quantity to be deployed at node i itself is given by

$$\mathrm{SS}_i = B_i - \sum_{j \in S(i)} \mathrm{SS}_j .$$

The pipeline hedging model is important for several reasons. First, it provides explicitly for safety stock to be deployed at each node in the product structure. More generally, safety stock could be deployed selectively at specified nodes in the product structure, and the model could be modified accordingly. Second, pipeline hedging can easily be incorporated within the existing format of MRP records, as illustrated in Table 6.1. Third, pipeline hedging provides a rational technique for calculating the buffer sizes, although the derivation requires that at each node we ignore the possibility of upstream stockouts.

The pipeline hedging model also has some drawbacks. First, it is driven by a target service level as a measure of performance. A more fundamental analysis would be to represent the trade-off between the cost of safety stock and the cost of stockouts, and thus allow the desired service level to be produced by optimization rather than by policy. Second, the approximation of no upstream stockouts may be unrealistic if the target service level is not extremely close to 100%. In fact, one could argue that this assumption tends to isolate the various levels of the product structure when the crux of the problem is to understand the cascading interaction among the different levels under conditions of uncertain demand. Finally, the model does not give normative information about where to deploy buffers, only how to size them.

Optimization. As indicated above, a more ambitious step would be to represent the trade-off of holding and penalty costs in an optimization model. This can be done, in principle, within the framework of dynamic programming, as suggested by Lambrecht, Muckstadt & Luyten [1984]. However, such an approach becomes unwieldy for practical size problems because of the large state space required. Approximate models, based on heuristic decomposition of the optimization problem, are proposed by Lambrecht, Muckstadt & Luyten [1984] and by Yano & Carlson [1988]. In both cases however, the heuristic procedures are tested in an exploratory way and involve no large scale data sets.

Total upstream coverage. As indicated above, the assumption of total upstream coverage simplifies the development of the pipeline hedging model. It also permits useful forms of decomposition in heuristic optimization approaches. To go beyond this simplification, a model should represent the realistic implications of a stockout at some level. However, the price for doing so may be considerable analytic difficulty.

One approach is to say that safety stock is not meant to cover demand variation beyond a certain level. When extreme forecast errors occur, the response does not come by means of safety stock, but rather by scheduling overtime, by expediting, or by negotiating with the customers affected. In this context, safety stock is intended only to provide protection against 'normal' variations; the other measures are available for dealing with more extreme variations. This approach is exemplified in the work of Simpson [1958], which deals with the location of buffers in a setting where each stage in the system faces a service level requirement imposed by the adjacent downstream stage.

Another approach is to say that when safety stock is depleted there is a delay in satisfying demand and, furthermore, that the length of delay varies with the size of the stockout. Hanssmann [1959] takes this approach and models the impact of this delay on the demand rate. However, to make this type of approach tractable, Hanssmann suppresses the randomness in the length of the delay.

Wijngaard & Wortmann [1985] add to this discussion. They point out that there can be at least three distinct types of buffers in an MRP system: finished goods safety stock resulting from demand overplanning, component safety stock resulting from explicit provision for interstage buffers, and work in process resulting from explicit policies governing the size of queues. Moreover, each of these buffers may be controlled by a different organizational unit. Finished goods inventories are determined by the Master Scheduling function, which is responsible for demand management. Component safety stocks are determined by the Material Coordination (MRP) function, which is responsible for coping with uncertainties in supply quantities and timing, in addition to changes in the MPS. WIP levels are determined by the Shop Floor Control function, which is responsible for implementing changes in the schedule as the material plan gets updated. Thus, while it might be an interesting analytic problem to distinguish the benefits and overlaps in these distinct buffers, the more relevant practical problem may be the organizational one of encouraging the various functions to set consistent and nonredundant policies.

Buffers and lot sizing

A fundamental assumption in most buffering analysis is that uncertainty is resolved after material is in the pipeline. If the forecast is too low and the buffer inadequate, then the result is a stockout. Economic analysis of desirable buffer sizes must therefore consider such costs of stocking out as backorder penalties or lost profits. A different perspective is taken in the work of De Bodt and Van Wassenhove [1983b], who assume that demand in period 1 becomes known at the start of period 1, and that an order may be placed at that point in time to satisfy demand in period 1. In effect, they consider a situation in which the uncertainty is resolved sufficiently early that a replenishment order can still be placed to avoid a stockout. In this setting, they examine the effects of forecast uncertainty on single-level lot sizing and propose a framework for computing an optimal buffer size. Although their results are mainly specialized to the LPC lot sizing procedure (which is discussed in Section 3 above), their model should be robust if a different procedure is used instead.

A simplified version of the De Bodt–Van Wassenhove model follows. The effect of having too small a buffer is that an order is placed earlier than planned in the LPC calculations; hence, the fixed ordering cost tends to be incurred more frequently than would be the case without forecast errors. To illustrate the analysis in a special case, assume that forecast errors are small enough in comparison with demands that an order would have to be placed no more than one period earlier than planned and no later than planned. Let TBO denote the average time between orders using average demand. (Equivalently, this is the optimal period order quantity.) Let B denote the size of the buffer. Then the forecast error E, accumulated over (TBO-1) periods, will cause an order to be placed early if it exceeds the buffer size. Let the probability of this event be α, where

$$\alpha = P(E > B) .$$

This probability can be obtained from normal tables under the assumption that E is the sum of (TBO-1) independently distributed error terms, each of which follows a Normal distribution. The incremental cost per period due to using a buffer includes the additional carrying cost of the buffer and the expected increase in cost (relative to the deterministic case) of more frequent ordering than planned. De Bodt and Van Wassenhove derive a function for this incremental cost, which in our special case, takes the form

$$C(B) = h(B + d\alpha \text{ TBO})/(\text{TBO} - \alpha) ,$$

where d represents mean demand. The function $C(B)$ can be minimized by a one-dimensional search.

Although the derivation is predicated on the use of LPC lot sizing, we might expect that the other effective methods of lot sizing have very similar order sizes and frequencies, and that an optimal buffer for LPC would be close to optimal for some slightly different method. Based on their research, De Bodt and van Wassenhove conclude that buffering can be very effective when the cost of ordering is small or when the variance of forecast error is small.

Other sources of uncertainty

In the literature on buffering procedures the predominant emphasis has been on measures to deal with uncertainty in demand. In a complex production and inventory system, however, there are other sources of uncertainty, and work has begun on developing appropriate models.

Yield uncertainty. When yield problems are a factor, adjustments can be made in lot sizes to compensate for the effects of uncertain yield. As a first step, consider the single-level lot sizing problem with uncertain yields. In particular, suppose that a planned order results in a number of nondefectives given by a binomial distribution with parameters q and p, where q is the initial size of the lot and p is the average proportion of good items. In other words, the distribution of the number of usable items in a batch of size q has a mean of qp and a variance of $qp(1-p)$ and can be approximated by a Normal distribution. As discussed earlier, MRP logic would deal with this situation by multiplying all net requirements by a factor of $1/p$.

Mazzola, McCoy & Wagner [1987] describe a heuristic procedure for this problem in which the first step is to solve the lot sizing problem as if yields were perfect. The Wagner–Whitin algorithm (or any of the lot sizing schemes discussed in Section 3) will provide a set of lot sizes Q_j desired net of yield effects. The next step is to adjust the lot sizes in order to account for yield. Suppose that a service level of α is given. (In their original exposition, MMW develop a model that permits backlogging, and the desired service level is determined in the optimization. However, the service level could also be specified a priori, as a policy parameter.) For period j this means that the following condition must be met:

$$qp - z[qp(1-p)]^{1/2} \geq Q_j\,, \tag{6.1}$$

where z is an appropriately chosen factor from the standard Normal table. Based on some experimentation, MMW found that a good choice of the z-value was the standard Normal deviate associated with a percentile of $\frac{1}{2}\alpha$. Solving (6.1) as an equality provides the lot size:

$$q_j = Q_j/p + z/2p[z(1-p) + z\{(1-p)[4Q_j + z^2(1-p)^2]\}^{1/2}]\,. \tag{6.2}$$

Although the justification for selecting z is not intuitive it is instructive to see that (6.2) always adjusts the typical MRP value (Q_j/p) upward.

MMW report on computational tests with their heuristic method, showing that in many cases it achieves total costs within 1% of optimum. (The optimal cost can be computed using a computationally-demanding dynamic programming procedure.)

Lee & Yano [1988] consider a serial system with uncertain yield at each stage and a single period. Their model can be viewed as appropriate for an intermediate level of the product structure. In this case, the series of stages represents as a set of operations that must be done on a particular component, and 'demand' is the net requirement generated by the next higher level in the Bill of Material. The objective is to minimize total expected cost, consisting of variable production cost, disposal cost, and shortage cost. Lee and Yano give a dynamic programming formulation of the problem, and they demonstrate that, under mild restrictions, the optimal policy consists of a critical number S_j for each state j. If the incoming quantity is greater than S_j, then the batch size should be reduced to S_j; otherwise, the entire incoming quantity should comprise the batch.

Lead time uncertainty. Another factor is uncertainty in planned lead times. Suppose that we think of a simple queueing model as representing lead time at an individual machine center. The waiting time distribution for the queueing model provides a probabilistic description of lead time delay at the machine center. Using this distribution we can select a planned lead time that can be met a given percent of the time. Let $F(x)$ represent the cumulative distribution function of waiting time at the queue (i.e., actual lead time at the work center), and let θ denote the required probability that actual lead time is within planned lead time. To achieve this 'service level' we set $F(t) = \theta$, and solve for the planned lead time t.

The analysis can be aimed at cost minimization rather that service level. Again, let t denote the planned lead time and let L denote the actual lead time of a job. Suppose there are three components of cost, as represented in the following cost function:

$$g(t) = c_T(L - t)^+ + c_E(t - L)^+ + c_P t\,. \tag{6.3}$$

Here, c_T represents the unit cost of tardiness, incurred if the actual lead time exceeds the planned lead time. Similarly, c_E represents the unit cost of earliness. If there were only these two cost components, the minimization of expected cost would be given by solution of the critical fractile equation:

$$F(t) = c_T/(c_T + c_E)\,. \tag{6.4}$$

The third term in (6.3) allows for a cost due to a slow response. If there were only one production stage, we could think of t as representing a planned response time offered to an arriving customer. Presumably, there is some economic cost, possibly intangible, for offering a protracted response. Assuming that $c_P < c_T$, the critical fractile solution is adjusted to reflect the fact that the benefit of offering a quick response partly offsets the increased risk of tardiness:

$$F(t) = (c_T - c_P)/(c_T + c_E)\,. \tag{6.5}$$

A generalization has been offered by Seidmann & Smith [1981]. Suppose that there is a response time R that is normally tolerated by the market, so that the third cost component is not incurred unless the planned lead time exceeds R. The cost function becomes

$$g(t) = c_T(L - t)^+ + c_E(t - L)^+ + c_P(1 - R)^+\,. \tag{6.6}$$

If R is quite large, then (6.4) dictates the optimal value of t; if R is quite small, then (6.5) dictates the optimal value of t; and in some cases, for certain intermediate values of R the optimal choice is to set $t = R$.

This queueing approach has been extended beyond single-stage models by Yano [1987a,b]. However, the analysis relies heavily on the availability of queueing results for waiting time distributions. For these results to be in reasonably tractable form, it is usually necessary to assume that the queue discipline (priority rule) is first-come first-served. This assumption restricts the usefulness of the model severely.

A more important limitation, from a conceptual point of view, is that these models represent variability that is intrinsic to the production process. However, unlike yield uncertainty, which does tend to be intrinsic to a production process, lead time uncertainty is related to other decisions, such as lot size and capacity. Thus, the approaches of Graves [1986] and of Karmarkar, Kekre, Kekre & Freeman [1985], reviewed in the previous section, seem to be broader attempts to capture the relevant complexity of lead time uncertainty.

7. Summary

MRP-based systems provide a framework for managing production, and they serve as extensive information systems for production planning and control. For the most part, however, they do not have the capability to analyze decision alternatives. This is where operations research models come in. They formalize the trade-offs and criteria faced by decision makers who are operating within the MRP framework, and they provide the analysis on which good decisions can be based.

This chapter identified four main areas in which MRP systems typically have shortcomings and where supplementary models can provide effective decisions support. The first of these dealt with lot sizing. Heuristic procedures for single-level lot sizing have been tested extensively, and discernable conclusions have emerged. The insights gained from this testing have influenced the development of multilevel lot sizing models. These models feature built-in devices for coordinating the decisions made for different levels in the product structure.

The second area dealt with master scheduling, where two model-based perspectives were presented. The first views master scheduling as constrained, multiproduct lot sizing, giving rise to models that generalize the lot sizing results discussed earlier. The second perspective applies in situations where the strategy is assemble-to-order. In this arena, some preliminary modeling steps have been taken to represent the important trade-offs and to pose the optimization problems involved.

The third area dealt with capacity planning, where models can go beyond the MRP system response of merely signalling violations. Input/Output models provide some understanding of the relationship between work center capacities and production lead times. Such models can be useful when a deterministic view of reality will suffice. More sophisticated tools for capacity analysis recognize the effects of variability, and they illuminate the lead time consequences of decisions made with respect to capacity and lot size.

The fourth area dealt with buffering techniques. Most of the attention by model builders has been focused on the analysis of demand uncertainty, and in particular, on techniques for hedging with safety stock within the product structure. Some progress has also been made in building models that capture the effects of yield and lead time uncertainty.

Perhaps the most striking aspect of operators research models is that they supplement a typical MRP system on a piecemeal basis. They carve out one area at a time where the MRP system is incomplete and provide analytic support for the decision maker. It would appear that this will be the pattern for the foreseeable future; integrative models that encompass lot sizing, master scheduling, capacity, and buffering would appear to be well beyond the capability of the current state of the art.

Acknowledgement

Helpful comments on an earlier draft of this chapter were provided by James Freeland, Arthur Hill, Paul Zipkin and Stephen Graves.

References

Afentakis, P. (1987). A parallel heuristic algorithm for lot sizing in multistage production systems. *IIE Trans.* 19(1), 34–42.

Baker, K.R., M.J. Magazine and H.L.W. Nuttle (1986). The effect of commonality on safety stock in a simple inventory model. *Management Sci.* 32(8), 982–988.

Barany, I., T.J. Van Roy and L.A. Wolsey (1983). Strong formulations for multi-item capacitated lot-sizing. *Management Sci.* 30(10), 1255–1261.

Benton, W.C. (1985). Multiple price breaks and alternative purchase lot-sizing procedures in material requirements planning systems. *Internat. J. Prod. Res.* 23(5), 1025–1047.

Berry, W.L., T.G. Schmitt and T.E. Vollmann (1982). Capacity planning techniques for manufacturing control systems: Information requirements and operational features. *J. Oper. Management* 3(1), 13–25.

Blackburn, J.D., and R.A. Millen (1980). Heuristic lot-sizing performance in a rolling-schedule environment. *Decision Sci.* 11(4), 691–701.

Blackburn, J.D., and R.A. Millen (1982a). Improved heuristics for multi-stage requirements planning systems. *Management Sci.* 28(1), 44–56.

Blackburn, J.D., and R.A. Millen (1982b). The impact of a rolling schedule in a multi-level MRP system. *J. Oper. Management* 2(2), 125–135.

Blackburn, J.D., and R.A. Millen (1985a). A methodology for predicting single-stage lot-sizing performance: Analysis and experiments. *J. Oper. Management* 5(4), 433–448.

Blackburn, J.D., and R.A. Millen (1985b). An evaluation of heuristic performance in multi-stage lot-sizing systems. *Internat. J. Prod. Res.* 23(5), 857–866.

De Bodt, M.A., and L.N. Van Wassenhove (1983a). Lot sizes and safety stocks in MRP: A case study. *Prod. Invent. Management* 24, 1–16.

De Bodt, M.A., and L.N. Van Wassenhove (1983b). Cost increases due to demand uncertainty in MRP lot sizing. *Decision Sci.* 14, 345–361.

DeMatteis, J.J. (1968). The part-period algorithm. *IBM Syst. J.* 7(1), 30–39.

Freeland, J.R., and J.L. Colley Jr (1982). A simple heuristic method for lot-sizing in a time-phase reorder system. *Prod. Invent. Management* 23, 15–22.

Gorham, T. (1968). Dynamic order quantities. *Prod. Invent. Management* 9, 75–81.

Graves, S.C. (1981). Multilevel lot sizing: An iterative approach, in: L.B. Schwarz (ed.), *Multilevel Production/Inventory Control Systems: Theory and Practice*, North-Holland, Amsterdam, pp. 237–256.

Graves, S.C. (1986). A tactical planning model for a job shop. *Oper. Res.* 34(4), 522–533.

Graves, S.C. (1988). Safety stocks in manufacturing systems. *J. Manuf. Oper. Management* 1(1), 67–101.

Groff, G.K. (1979). A lot-sizing rule for time phased component demand. *Prod. Invent. Management* 20, 47–53.

Guerrero, H.H. (1991). Demand management strategies for assemble-to-order production environments, *Internat. J. Prod. Res.* 29(1), 39–51.

Hanssmann, F. (1959). Optimal inventory location and control in production and distribution networks. *Oper. Res.* 7(9), 483–498.

Heemsbergen, B.L. (1987). The part-period algorithm and least-total-cost heuristics in single-level discrete-demand lot sizing. *Prod. Invent. Management* 28, 1–9.

Karmarkar, U.S., S. Kekre, S. Kekre and S. Freeman (1985). Lot-sizing and lead-time performance in a manufacturing cell. *Interfaces* 15(2), 1–9.

Karni, R. (1981a). Capacity requirements planning-optimal work station capacities. *Internat. J. Prod. Res.* 19(5), 595–611.

Karni, R. (1981b). Dynamic algorithms for input-output planning of work-station loading. *AIIE Trans.* 13(4), 333–342.
Karni, R. (1982). Capacity requirements planning – A systematization. *Internat. J. Prod. Res.* 20(6), 715–739.
King, B.E., and W.C. Benton (1987). Alternative master production scheduling techniques in an assemble-to-order environment. *J. Oper. Management* 7(2), 179–201.
Lambrecht, M.R., J.A. Muckstadt and R. Luyten (1984). Protective stocks in multi-stage production systems. *Internat. J. Prod. Res.* 22(6), 1001–1025.
Lambrecht, M.R., R. Luyten and J. Vander Eecken (1984). Protective inventories and bottlenecks in production systems. *European J. Oper. Res.* 22, 319–328.
Lee, H.L., and C.A. Yano (1988). Production control in multistage systems with variable yield losses. *Oper. Res.* 36, 269–278.
Maes, J., and L.N. Van Wassenhove (1986). A simple heuristic for the multi item single level capacitated lotsizing problem. *Oper. Res. Lett.* 4(6), 265–273.
Mazzola, J.B., W.F. McCoy and H.M. Wagner (1987). Algorithms and heuristics for variable-yield lot sizing. *Naval Res. Logist.* 34, 67–86.
McClelland, M.K. (1988). Order promising and the master schedule. *Decision Sci.* 19(4), 858–879.
McClelland, M.K., and H.W. Wagner (1988). Location of inventories in the MRP environment. *Decision Sci.* 19(3), 535–553.
Miller, J.G. (1979). Hedging the master schedule, in: L.P. Ritzman et al. (eds.), *Disaggregation Problems in Manufacturing and Service Organizations*, Martinus Nijhoff, Boston, MA, pp. 237–256.
Schmidt, C.P., and S. Nahmias (1985). Optimal policy for a two-stage assembly system under random demand. *Oper. Res.* 33(5), 1130–1145.
Seidmann, A., and M.L. Smith (1981). Due date assignment for production systems. *Management Sci.* 27(5), 571–581.
Silver, E.A., and H.C. Meal (1973). A heuristic for selecting lot size quantities for the case of a deterministic time-varying demand rate and discrete opportunities for replenishment. *Prod. Invent. Management* 14, 64–74.
Simpson, K.F. (1958). In-process inventories. *Oper. Res.* 6, 863–873.
Thizy, J.M., and L.N. Van Wassenhove (1987). A subgradient algorithm for the multi-item capacitated lot-sizing problem. *IIE Trans.* 17(4), 308–313.
Trigeiro, W.W. (1987). A dual-cost heuristic for the capacitated lot sizing problem. *IIE Trans.* 19(1), 67–72.
Trigeiro, W.W., L.J. Thomas and J.O. McClain (1989). Capacitated lot sizing with setup times. *Management Sci.* 35(3), 353–366.
Veral, E.A., and R.L. LaForge (1985). The performance of a simple incremental lot-sizing rule in a multilevel inventory environment. *Decision Sci.* 16(1), 57–72.
Wagner, H.M., and T. Whitin (1958). Dynamic version of the economic lot size model. *Management Sci.* 5(1), 89–96.
Wemmerlov, U. (1981). The ubiquitous EOQ – Its relation to discrete lot sizing heuristics. *Internat. J. Oper. Prod. Management* 1(3), 161–179.
Wemmerlov, U. (1982). A comparison of discrete, single stage lot-sizing heuristics with special emphasis on rules based on the marginal cost principle. *Engrg. Costs Prod. Econ.* 7, 45–53.
Wemmerlov, U., and D.C. Whybark (1984). Lot-sizing under uncertainty in a rolling schedule environment. *Internat. J. Prod. Res.* 22(3), 467–484.
White, D.J., W.A. Donaldson and N. Lawrie (1974). *Operational Research Techniques, Vol. 2*, Business Books, London.
Wijngaard, J., and J.C. Wortmann (1985). MRP and inventories. *European J. Oper. Res.* 20, 283–293.
Yano, C.A. (1987a). Planned leadtimes for serial production systems. *IIE Trans.* 19(3), 300–307.
Yano, C.A. (1987b). Stochastic leadtimes in two-level assembly systems. *IIE Trans.* 19(4), 371–378.
Yano, C.A., and R.C. Carlson (1988). Safety stocks for assembly systems with fixed production intervals. *J. Manuf. Oper. Management* 1(2), 182–201.

S.C. Graves et al., Eds., *Handbooks in OR & MS, Vol. 4*

Chapter 12

The Just-in-Time System

Harry Groenevelt

William E. Simon Graduate School of Business Administration, University of Rochester, Rochester, NY 14627, U.S.A.

1. Introduction

In the last years, the term 'Just-in-Time' or 'JIT' and many of its near synonyms such as Zero Inventory, Stockless Production, World Class Manufacturing, etc., have become household words in repetitive manufacturing organizations all over the world. Low inventory is one of the most visible characteristics of many successful production organizations in Japan and increasingly elsewhere, and is arguably one of the reasons for the continuing strong competitive position of Japanese corporations. Competitive success has drawn attention to Japanese operations management techniques with their heavy emphasis on inventory reduction. JIT has received an extraordinary amount of attention in trade and professional journals, and a large number of books have been written on JIT and its various elements, see Deming [1982, 1986], Goldratt & Cox [1986], Hall [1981, 1983, 1987], Juran [1988], Monden [1983, 1986], Ohno [1988a,b], Schonberger [1982, 1986, 1900], Shingo [1985, 1989]. Many of its techniques are being implemented in factories all over the world. At last count (taken a couple of years ago), more than 1000 articles had appeared in English language journals alone in the preceding 10 years.

Even though the term JIT is by now commonplace, it is not so easy to define. The term JIT describes the attempt to produce items only when they are needed, in the smallest possible quantities and with minimal waste of human and natural resources. Stated in this way, Material Requirement Planning (MRP) systems aim to achieve JIT, and of course every production manager has it as one of his primary objectives.

In a narrow sense then, the term JIT simply denotes an emphasis on inventory reduction. In a broad sense, the term JIT is also used to describe a management philosophy that fosters change and improvements through inventory reduction. Used in the latter sense, the term JIT can encompass a host of management techniques such as continuous improvement, worker involvement, setup and lot size reduction, and quality control. Whether a broad or a narrow definition of JIT is employed or not, an essential characteristic of any serious inventory reduction effort is the effect it is likely to have on all aspects of a production organization. Hence, to determine the scope of this chapter, a broad definition of the term JIT will be assumed.

In some ways, JIT represents a break with manufacturing management practices of the recent past. At the risk of oversimplification, one could say that during the sixties and seventies management focused more on equipment and labor utilization and less on material flow. Hence, inventories at the various stages of manufacture were allowed to be built up if this would contribute to a more efficient use of other resources. One can view JIT as a reaction to this trend that refocuses attention on material flows. To achieve more efficient flow, local improvements (such as setup time reduction, quality improvements, and preventive maintenance) can often be made. In addition, closer coordination between various production resources and departments becomes necessary. The active cooperation of accounting, finance, marketing, personnel, purchasing, and sales departments is needed as well as that of production, quality control, production engineering, distribution, etc. To substantially reduce inventories, companies need to take an integrative approach, because many or all of the factors involved in the production process are affected. In some cases, the entire supply chain or a large section thereof can be taken as the range of application of inventory reduction techniques. The purpose is to improve coordination between a plant and its supply and distribution networks. In some cases, such coordination extends across ownership boundaries as well.

In a JIT environment every part of an organization has a well defined, operational objective: implement improvements that allow reductions in inventory or equivalently lead time.[1] Cooperation between different departments is facilitated by this common goal. This provides greater cohesion in the firm and allows a firm to be controlled in a more decentralized manner. Lead time is a performance indicator that is easy to track for any sub-unit within the organization. The reader is referred to Chapter 6 for a thorough discussion of lead time related issues.

Another change from the recent past involves increased worker involvement and responsibility. This is also a natural consequence of reduced inventories. Every step in the production process becomes more critical as local disruptions have more severe effects on the other steps. Hence, more decisions need to be made on the spot, and workers need to be trained and motivated. Labor relations become more critical as workers acquire more skills and responsibilities (and are thus harder to replace). The goals of reducing inventory and improving material flow can serve as local objectives for evaluating alternative courses of action. Since these are system-wide goals, they will tend to encourage cooperation and identification with the system.

JIT is in many ways an empirical phenomenon. JIT's popularity is partially due to the competitive success of some of its most visible proponents. Many developments within JIT are fueled by continuing experimentation in factories

[1] Inventory and lead time are closely related via Little's Law, see also Chapter 6.

rather than by theoretical research. A reconsideration of the role of traditional analytical models like the Economic Order Quantity (EOQ) model and MRP in the light of recent practices in manufacturing is therefore appropriate. In the traditional production literature, the models are often trade-off models, like EOQ, safety stock models and many scheduling models, or feasibility seeking models, like MRP and many other scheduling systems. These analytical models and systems focus on only a limited set of issues at a time. The EOQ model focuses on the lot sizing decision, MRP systems handle the order release and lot sizing functions, and safety stock calculations take only random demand or random supply, and holding and backordering costs into account in setting safety stock levels. In addition, these models tend to ignore uncertainty and contingencies. Sub-optimization is therefore a very real danger in using these analytical methods. Integrative models can partially overcome this problem. Examples of this trend are hierarchical planning models (see Chapter 11), the production/inventory models of Zipkin [1986], vehicle routing and inventory models of Federgruen & Zipkin [1984] and others (see Chapter 4), the push towards MRP-II and Capacity Requirements Planning (CRP). Many reports in the popular press and in trade journals suggest that in many situations an inventory reduction program can yield substantial dividends. This does not mean that traditional models have lost their relevance, but that their results must be interpreted with care and augmented with common sense and practical experience. The models still provide important insights and render effective assistance in decision-making. However, their use always needs to be evaluated and verified in the larger context of the application. As can be seen from the rest of this chapter, JIT has already stimulated a large number of papers that reinterpret and extend traditional operations management models.

This chapter has two goals. The first is to give an overview of JIT. To do good applied research it is necessary that one understands the various JIT elements and their interrelationships. Familiarity with and a thorough understanding of the practical issues cannot be achieved without making plant visits, doing case studies, and reviewing the literature, especially the trade journals and the various texts. The second goal of this chapter is to provide a summary of current active research issues in JIT. An exhaustive review of the JIT literature is beyond the scope of this chapter. The list of references at the end of this chapter, although quite extensive, is anything but complete. Further reviews of the JIT literature can be found in Sohal, Keller & Fouad [1989], Im [1989], and Moras, Jalali & Dudek [1991].

The remainder of this chapter is organized as follows. Section 2 contains a brief history of Just-in-Time and a general survey of the literature. More detailed reviews of specific papers are deferred until the discussion of individual topics later in the chapter. Section 3 describes the general concepts of Just-in-Time and discusses each of the critical elements that are often part of Just-in-Time implementations. Section 4 reviews the benefits and drawbacks of Just-in-Time in particular situations, and considers organizational and implementation problems. The Kanban system is the topic in Section 5. Section

5.1 details the mechanics of various types of Kanban systems. In Section 5.2 various models and methods that have been proposed to select the operating parameters of Kanban systems will be discussed, and the relationship between Kanban and other production control systems is the topic of Section 5.3. In particular the relationship between Kanban and MRP has received considerable attention in the literature. A very important aspect of Just-in-Time systems is the philosophy of gradual process improvement and learning. Section 6 surveys the literature in this area. The chapter is concluded in Section 7 with some crystal ball gazing and an attempt to identify future research directions.

2. A brief history of Just-in-Time

The concept of Just-in-Time is well-established in many process industries such as steel, chemicals, glass, paper, oil refineries, and on assembly lines. Work-in-process inventory is routinely kept to a minimum in such systems. However, the widespread application of inventory reduction techniques to the production of discrete products and the extension of JIT ideas to the production of discrete parts feeding into assembly lines is relatively new. One can trace back the origins of Just-in-Time in this environment to at least Henry Ford, who said 'We have found that in buying materials it is not worthwhile to buy for other than immediate needs . . . if transportation were perfect and an even flow of materials could be assured it would not be necessary to carry any stock whatsoever' [see Ford, 1924, p. 143]. However, the systematic application of JIT ideas did not progress much until 1950, when Toyota started experimenting. Between then and the mid 1970s, the Toyota group of corporations in Japan developed many of the production ideas and methods discussed in this chapter. The main proponents of JIT within Toyota were Taiichi Ohno, whose climb through the manufacturing ranks at Toyota was accompanied by a spread of the basic JIT ideas, and Shigeo Shingo, see Ohno [1982], and Shingo [1989]. In this period, JIT was very much an empirical development, and to some extent confined within the Toyota corporation and its family of suppliers. During the oil crisis starting in 1973, which hit Japan especially hard, it was evident that Toyota was doing very well compared with its main competitors in Japan. Hence there was a broad effort in Japan to copy Toyota's system with its track record of success against the more traditional systems that were in use in other corporations, see Suzaki [1985]. Since then, starting in the late 1970s, elements of the JIT system have spread to other parts of the world, its popularity stimulated by the successes of the early Japanese adopters. Just-in-Time has become a household world in many corporations in the United States and Europe. Early adopters in the United States include subsidiaries of Japanese manufacturers such as Kawasaki, Honda, Nissan, and Toyota, see Sepehri [1985]. Among the native American companies that started JIT programs are Goodyear, Harley Davidson, General Electric, and Hewlett

Packard, IBM, and Xerox, see Schonberger [1984], Schonberger & Schniederjans [1984], Sepehri [1986], Sepehri & Walleigh [1986], Walleigh & Sepehri [1986]. JIT is now widely known, and implementation efforts have become increasingly numerous. JIT is affecting factory floors, production scheduling and engineering departments, purchasing departments [see Ansari, 1986; Ansari & Modarress, 1987; Giunipero & Keiser, 1987; Macbeth, 1988; Robinson & Timmerman, 1987; Schonberger & Gilbert, 1983], data processing [see Justis, 1981; Cole, 1985], and accounting departments [see Heard, 1984; Seglund & Ibarreche, 1986; Tatikonda, 1988]. JIT concepts also find application in service organizations [see Savage-Moore, 1988; Conant, 1988, Feather & Cross, 1988; Groenevelt, 1990].

The literature on Just-in-Time is already very voluminous, and it is not possible to give a complete bibliography here. Instead, an attempt is made to describe it in general terms. References to specific papers are provided throughout the chapter when specific issues are discussed. These references are without exception to articles or books that have appeared in the English language. A large body of Japanese language literature exists on Just-in Time, and fortunately an important subset of this literature continues to be translated into English.

The literature on Just-in-Time can be classified into five general categories. These are general descriptions and case studies, simulation studies, analytical studies, survey reports, and papers with general observations, theories, and commentaries. Of course, many papers contain elements of several or all of these categories, so classification of all referenced papers is quite difficult, and will not be attempted. Here the literature is discussed in general terms and more detailed descriptions will be given later in the chapter where appropriate.

Many of the early papers on Just-in-Time fall in the category of general descriptions and case studies. They primarily document existing conditions and problems and as such form a valuable basis for formulating targeted research questions. Examples of publications in this category are Barrett [1988], Conant [1988], Clutterbuck [1978], Feather & Cross [1988], Finch & Cox [1986], Giunipero & Keiser [1987], Groenevelt & Karmarkar [1988], Hayes [1981], Monden [1981a,b,c,d], Nakane & Hall [1983], Sepehri [1985, 1987], Savage-Moore [1988], Sepehri & Walleigh [1986], Sugimoro, Kusunoki, Cho & Uchikawa [1977], and Walleigh & Sepehri [1986]. Most of the papers in this category will not be discussed in any detail in this chapter.

Many simulation studies have appeared to date, particularly to study the operation of Kanban systems. For a discussion of these the reader is referred to Section 5.2.

There are also a number of analytical studies in the literature, and to date these fall into two categories. One attempts to model the operation of Kanban or closely related systems, and this category is discussed in Section 5.2. The other category involves primarily process improvement and learning models and is discussed in Section 6.

A couple of surveys have been done on JIT. Ansari [1986] and Ansari &

Modarress [1987] discuss the results of a survey on Just-in-Time purchasing techniques, and Crawford, Blackstone & Cox [1988] surveyed implementation and operating problems in Just-in-Time environments. The results of these surveys are briefly discussed in Section 4.

A host of papers contain general observations on, give explanations for observed phenomena, or comment on developments in Just-in-Time. There are too many of these to enumerate, but many of them are referenced below.

3. What is Just-in-Time?

There is a certain amount of confusion over what exactly constitutes a Just-in-Time system. Just-in-Time can be defined as the ideal of having exactly the necessary amount of material available where it is needed and when it is needed. In some sense this is precisely what MRP systems try to accomplish (with varying degrees of success), and what assembly lines closely approximate. However, the term Just-in-Time is most frequently used to describe the pursuit of this ideal in repetitive parts manufacturing. To more completely characterize Just-in-Time in this environment, the basic elements of Just-in-Time will be described here.

The various elements of a Just-in-Time program that are often cited include the following: a pull method of coordination of the production stages, setup time reduction, lot size reduction, production smoothing, standardized operations, flexible workers and facilities, a group technology or cellular layout, an emphasis on quality control activities, and continual improvement efforts. Each of these is briefly reviewed below. Other overviews of Just-in-Time elements are given by Hall [1983], Monden [1981a,b,c,d, 1983], Nellemann & Smith [1982], Schonberger [1982, 1986], etc.

Many Just-in-Time programs involve a pull method of coordination between the various stages of production. A pull method is characterized by the fact that a production activity at a stage is initiated to replace a part used by a downstream stage, whereas in a push system production takes place in anticipation of a future need, see Monden [1983], Hall [1983], and Schonberger [1982, 1986]. There are a number of ways of implementing a pull system, the most popular of which (in the context of Just-in-Time) is the Kanban system, to the extent that the term Kanban has become a synonym for Just-in-Time. This is misleading, as there are many other ways possible to efficiently implement the real time coordination needed in low inventory pull systems, and it is quite feasible in certain situations to approach the ideal of Just-in-Time production with push systems (systems where production activity at a stage is initiated in response to a work order). The Kanban system and other systems for implementing Just-in-Time will be discussed in Section 5 of this chapter.

A vital part of every Just-in-Time program is the reduction of setup times and lot sizes. These two go hand-in-hand, as can be shown with a variety of models. Assume that a cyclic schedule is followed in a given production step, and that demand rates and production times are constant. Assume further that no breakdowns or other interruptions will ever occur. Let

T = cycle time (days),
τ_i = setup time for item i (days),
D_i = demand rate for item i (units/day),
P_i = production rate for item i (units/day),
Q_i = lot size for item i (units).

Clearly, during every cycle a total of $Q_i = D_i T$ units of item i need to be produced to meet demand. Including the setup, this takes $\tau_i + D_i T/P_i$ time units. Hence the cycle time T needs to be chosen so that $T \geq \Sigma\, (\tau_i + D_i T/P_i)$, or $T \geq \Sigma\, \tau_i/(1 - \Sigma\, D_i/P_i)$. In this simple example, lot sizes and corresponding work-in-process inventories are directly proportional to setup times, and inversely proportional to the fraction of time available for setups $= (1 - \Sigma\, D_i/P_i)$.

In the presence of variability in demand rate and production rate, simple queueing models show that inventory is still proportional to setup times [see Zipkin, 1986; Karmarkar, 1987; and Karmarkar, Kekre & Kekre, 1985, or Chapter 6]. It is also noteworthy that in both these examples there are strong interactions between all products: lot sizes cannot be set independently.

Many actions can be taken to reduce setup times. In some cases setups may be eliminated altogether by eliminating the operation, by using dedicated equipment, by redesigning the process to combine several setups into one, or by redesigning parts to reduce the number of part types. A useful technique to reduce the remaining setup times is to separate the internal setup from the external setup. The internal setup consists of those actions that can only be taken when the machine is stopped. The external setup consists of all other actions associated with the setup. One can often reduce setups considerably by simply making sure that the machine is actually stopped only during the internal setup and is operating during the external setup. Additional reductions can be obtained by moving as many setup activities as possible from the internal setup to the external setup. Finally, various techniques can be used to eliminate the adjustment process, which not only reduces setup times but also reduces scrap. See Hall [1983], Hay [1987], Monden [1981d, 1983], Schonberger [1982] and Shingo [1985, 1989] for more detailed discussions of setup reduction techniques.

Since the objective is to obtain a regular flow of product with very little inventory, it is important that a level production schedule is used in all departments. To prevent shortages when little inventory is present capacity must match peak demand. When peak demand is high relative to average demand, this would be expensive. To illustrate the possible effect of leveling the production schedule on inventory, consider the approximate G/G/1 waiting time formula $W = (c_s^2 + c_a^2)\lambda E^2[S]/2(1 - \lambda E[S])$, where c_s^2 is the (squared) coefficient of variation of the service time, and c_a^2 is the (squared) coefficient of variation of the inter-arrival times. By driving both c_s^2 and c_a^2 to zero, one can operate at very close to full utilization with small lead times and hence with low work-in-process inventories. This is in effect what happens in paced assembly lines. Note that leveling the production schedule will indeed force c_a^2 down. In Section 5.2.1 an approach that attempts to level loads on all departments simultaneously by appropriate scheduling of final assembly will be described.

The concept of standardized operations is an important element of Just-in-Time as well. Under this concept, the precise actions required to accomplish a given production task efficiently are described in full detail (often using graphs and figures), and their time requirements are determined. Tasks so described include all actions required to operate equipment: loading/unloading, changeovers, adjustments, etc. The standardized operations charts are displayed near the equipment, clearly visible to workers and managers. Doing this systematically throughout the plant achieves a number of important objectives. First, it reduces variability in production times (it brings down c_s^2 in the example of the previous paragraph), and thereby helps bring about a smooth flow of product, see Monden [1984]. It assists in determining the number of workers needed to achieve the required production rate, which helps achieve balance between the various processes. It is used to determine the minimum amount of inventory necessary to support production. In addition, the standardization increases the repeatability and consistency of production, thereby enhancing safety and improving quality. Finally, it enforces documentation and makes specific knowledge about production processes easier to transfer.

Just-in-Time implies that work never has to wait long for a processing step. One can say that the service levels in a Just-in-Time facility are very high. Of course, this can be achieved by operating at a low level of utilization (i.e. with excess capacity), but it would be expensive to do so. To achieve the desired service levels it is highly desirable to be able to reallocate capacity to where it is needed most. This means flexible equipment, proper layout of equipment, and cross-training of workers. Equipment must be capable of producing several different parts if volume and equipment cost do not allow dedicated equipment, and it must be possible to convert it quickly when model changes are implemented. Setup times must be small enough to make frequent changeovers feasible. Equipment should be laid out so that it is easy to increase or decrease capacity by adding or removing workers in response to changes in demand volume. This is only feasible if sufficient numbers of workers are cross-trained. A program of frequent job rotation is necessary to maintain workers' skills on specific processes.

The concepts of Group Technology (GT) and Cellular Manufacturing (CM) date back at least to a 1925 article by Flanders, see Snead [1988, p. 17]. However, GT did not really catch on in the United States, and the development of GT took place in the USSR in the 1950s, in Western Europe and especially Japan in the 1970s [see Suresh & Meredith, 1985]. Group Technology concepts form an integral part of JIT by reducing transportation delays, making small transportation lots feasible and by fostering a climate that stimulates setup reductions.

To achieve the full benefits of production in small lots one needs frequent conveyance of material. With traditional functionally oriented layouts of equipment in the plant this requires too much time and transportation equipment, and it is difficult to coordinate the movements. Cellular Manufacturing layouts alleviate these problems to a considerable extent. In such layouts, the production equipment is clustered into cells of dissimilar machines capable of doing all of the processing for a limited set of similar parts. This type of layout cuts down on the need for material handling and reduces transportation times, makes control of inventory easier, and allows quicker feedback on quality and other problems. In case job routings are very similar within the cell, it can be set up as a flow line with very limited work-in-process, greatly reduced lead time, and purely visual coordination, see Monden [1981d]. Equipment choice and utilization are affected significantly when cellular layouts are used. More but simpler, slower, and smaller machines are preferred over big, fast and expensive machines. This has an effect on technology choice as well, see Schonberger [1983b]. In production planning the emphasis is usually on worker utilization and less on machine utilization. If an expensive machine is unavoidable, the layout should be such that it can be kept busy, i.e., some spare capacity is designed into the other parts of the cell [see McManus, 1980]. The somewhat wider concept of Group Technology offers a number of additional advantages in the areas of product design rationalization and standardization (especially when combined with CAD/CAM), production planning, costing, etc. Suresh & Meredith [1985] discuss the use of GT in the context of Computer Integrated Manufacturing (CIM) and JIT, and they stress that many of the JIT objectives (such as cross-training of workers) make sense in a cellular layout but not in a functional layout. Black [1983] discusses the design of cells in their various forms: manned, fixed automated and flexible automated. Schonberger [1983b] discusses the cellular production concept in the context of JIT and notes that it is superior to the Kanban system as a tool to achieve Just-in-Time production. Kanban can then be used to link separate cells together. He cites several success stories of cellular, product oriented plants. Monden [1983, Chapter 8] gives a detailed description of the very flexible layouts developed by Toyota. Welke & Overbeeke [1988] describe the use of Group Technology at Deere & Co. Huang & Houck [1985] and DeVries, Harvey & Tipnes [1976] give bibliographies of the Group Technology literature; see also Seidmann [1988] for a discussion of recent additions to the literature.

An emphasis on improving quality is a vital part of any Just-in-Time implementation effort. Poor quality leads to rework and scrap, which immediately cause extra expenses and disruptions preventing a smooth product flow. Ideally, every worker checks his own work and is held responsible for its quality. Workers are given the responsibility and the authority to stop production if a problem develops. Automatic monitoring devices are used with automated production equipment to prevent the mass production of defects. Rapid feedback should be established by making a worker do his own rework, and responsibility for quality and process improvements should be delegated to the workers that use the equipment. This means that all workers have to be trained in at least elementary techniques of quality control. In Japan, all workers are trained in the use of the so called 'Seven Tools': cause and effect (Ishikawa) diagrams, graphs, Pareto diagrams, histograms, control charts, scatter diagrams, nomograms, see Ryan [1988]. By delegating these activities to the workers, feedback is faster and specialized inspection stations can be largely avoided. Only when quality of production and reliability of equipment are sufficiently improved it is possible to run smoothly with drastically reduced inventory. One tool to propagate quality improvement activities is the formation of Quality Circles. These consist of workers involved with a particular process. Frequently, they pick specific quality problems to study and help remedy, and they also have the freedom to take initiatives such as organizing lectures, visits to other facilities, etc. There is a voluminous literature on the organizational and technical aspects of quality control. See Crosby [1984] for an introduction to quality control in Just-in-Time settings. The reader is referred to Crosby [1979], Deming [1982, 1986], Juran [1988], Ryan [1988], Schonberger [1986, Chapter 7] and Chapter 13 of this volume for more details on quality management.

Successful Just-in-Time programs operate under the assumption that improvement is always possible, and provide incentives for all production workers to actively engage in improvement activities. Examples are Quality Circles and employee suggestion programs. Under Toyota's suggestion plan workers crank out hundreds of thousands of suggestions per year, and millions of dollars are paid out every year in rewards. How many of these suggestions resulted in genuine improvements is open to debate, see Cole [1985]. There can be little doubt however of their considerable cumulative value to Toyota. Often problems are exposed by deliberately reducing work-in-process inventory. After resolving the problems identified, inventory is reduced even further, exposing a new set of problems, etc. This process is often illustrated with a picture of rocks (problems) covered by water (inventory): lowering the water level will expose the rocks so that they can be chipped away, see Hall [1983, p. 13].

The application of Just-in-Time to the purchasing of parts and raw materials deserves separate mention. In many cases Just-in-Time techniques can and should be extended to suppliers, i.e., parts and raw materials supplied by outside vendors are delivered frequently in small quantities at the time they are needed. However, geographical and ownership considerations often make special provisions necessary. Sourcing decisions will not solely be made based on price. Instead, considerations like long term stability of the supplier, ability of the supplier to cooperate on problem resolution, willingness and ability to make frequent deliveries, and quality of the parts supplied become important factors. Since more effort is involved in evaluating potential suppliers, fewer will be used, so single sourcing becomes more prevalent, and existing suppliers have the inside track to obtain additional work. More effort is involved in switching suppliers, hence longer term relationships develop.

It will be clear that there are significant advantages in using nearby suppliers since it is often easier to coordinate with and control them. Transportation costs are also likely to be lower. However, it is not impossible to use JIT principles with remote suppliers. Four major modes of transporting materials can be distinguished (see Figure 1): direct from supplier to customer (A), from supplier to consolidation warehouse to customer (B), from supplier to consolidation warehouse to staging warehouse to customer (C), and from supplier to staging warehouse to customer (D). At the consolidation warehouse, shipments from several remote or overseas suppliers are consolidated for shipment either directly to the customer or to the staging warehouse. At the staging warehouse shipments are broken down for frequent small deliveries to the customer plant. Shipment modes should be chosen so that there are frequent shipments along all links of the network and inventory buildups are kept to a minimum. In many cases it is better to ship a mixed load container every week from a given consolidation point to the staging warehouse than to ship one container per month from each of four different suppliers.

There are two keys to Just-in-Time supplier logistics: taking control of inbound deliveries and establishing quick feed-back loops. Taking control of inbound deliveries means that the customer determines the time windows for all deliveries to be made (and these time windows can be as narrow as 15 minutes or half an hour), the customer determines the packaging, the precise amounts, and sometimes even the order in which the materials are loaded on the truck or in the container. In most cases this will mean that the customer arranges for pickup at the supplier and transportation from supplier to customer. To economically accomplish small deliveries from remote suppliers may require a staging warehouse where bulk shipments can be broken down, counted and checked and from which small Just-in-Time deliveries can be made to the factory floor. If necessary, materials can be re-packed into totes or containers fit for immediate use in the customer's plant. The supplier is not responsible for transportation. His responsibility is limited to having the shipment ready for pickup at the agreed upon date and time. To establish fast

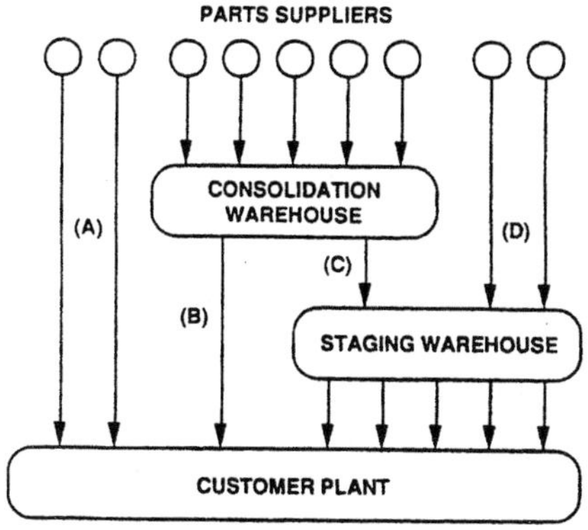

Fig. 1. Supplier shipping modes.

feedback, ideally one would count and check the shipment as soon as possible after pickup. If a freight consolidator is used to combine shipments from several remote suppliers, the consolidator could be used to inspect shipments. In this fashion, feedback to the supplier of intercontinental or transcontinental shipments can be given almost immediately, instead of two weeks or more later, and frequent small shipments can be made economically. In addition, the customer has the chance to stop or delay other incoming shipments immediately if problems are reported. Hence the important properties of Just-in-Time systems with nearby suppliers (fast feedback, balance in production) can be emulated in carefully designed Just-in-Time parts logistics systems with remote suppliers. It is mainly a matter of carefully monitoring and controlling the flow of parts on their way to the plant. This requires a good information and communications system (besides reliable transportation links), but such systems are definitely feasible. A number of Japanese manufacturers successfully supply assembly plants in the United States with parts from Japan in a Just-in-Time fashion. For other reports on long distance JIT supply systems see Giunipero & O'Neal [1988] who report on a case of multiple JIT deliveries per day at distances of up to 900 miles to automobile assembly plants in Michigan, Macbeth, Baxter, Ferguson & Neil [1988] who report on JIT deliveries from Italy to Scotland, and Stowe [1986].

The advantages and disadvantages of Just-in-Time, and some of the problems and obstacles often encountered during Just-in-Time implementation are considered next.

4. Benefits, risks, and limitations of Just-in-Time

As the previous sections show, substantial reductions in inventory require changes in all aspects of the production system: methods, standards, layout, material handling, job content, job descriptions, management-labor relationship, etc., are affected. In return for the effort to make those changes, certain benefits stand to be reaped by the organization. Some of the often cited benefits of Just-in-Time production include reduced inventories, reduced floor space requirements, reduced lead times, reduced scrap and rework rates, higher quality, better utilization of workers and equipment, increased worker satisfaction, increased flexibility, easier automation, ability to keep schedules, and establishment of a different incentive system. All of these ultimately translate reduced costs, higher quality finished products, and the ability to compete better.

On the other hand, Just-in-Time also requires numerous adjustments in support activities both within and outside the firm. The cost accounting system needs to be adapted, capital budgeting procedures are affected, financial justification procedures need to be changed, and personnel evaluation procedures, worker and management incentive systems are all affected by JIT. Outside the firm, suppliers need to be persuaded to cooperate by changing delivery patterns, packing methods, shipping modes, etc., and customers may need to provide information on their production plans and level their schedules to smooth out the demand.

To successfully implement a Just-in-Time program, all these changes need to be made. This cannot be done instantaneously, and so long term commitment by top management is needed, as well as the support of key lower people in the organization. Next the benefits obtainable with a successful JIT program, the risks that are involved, and the limitations of JIT and the factors that influence the outcome of a JIT implementation effort are considered in more detail.

According to JIT proponents, the organization derives multiple benefits from reducing inventories through a series of connected changes. Reductions in setup times and lot sizes lead to proportional reductions in inventories. Inventory reductions have a number of beneficial effects. First is reduced inventory carrying charges. However, in many cases these carrying charges are but a small fraction of total manufacturing costs, and secondary benefits may be more significant. Warehouse and floor space needs are reduced. Material handling and inventory control costs are reduced. Reduced inventory also means reduced lead times and quicker reactions to changes in demand patterns, market opportunities, and competitive threats. Forecasts can be more accurate since lead times are shorter, so less finished goods inventories will be needed. In some cases production to order may become possible. This and the reduced work-in-process inventories help contain obsolescence costs in an environment with shorter product life cycles. Shorter lead times also provide faster feedback in case of quality problems and thus help reduce scrap losses and rework costs.[2] By reducing inventory, bottlenecks become more visible: a stage in front of which work queues build up frequently is a bottleneck. By redeploying the work force, changes in methods and procedures, changes in layout, etc., such imbalances can often be eliminated, and better utilization of people and equipment is achieved. Because problems of all types are more acute when less inventory is around to alleviate them, and because of the faster feedback, diagnosis of problems is facilitated. There is less physical space separating workers, and this and the institution of cellular layouts enhance team spirit and cooperation. Workers now know their immediate customers and suppliers, and small problems can be ironed out quickly, sometimes without management intervention. Management becomes more efficient as well and factory overhead is reduced.

The above-mentioned benefits do not automatically accrue. To actually achieve all of them, active participation of many people and departments in the organization is required. Such participation needs to be encouraged by changes in the reward system (compensation, performance evaluation, promotions, etc.). Whether widespread participation can be obtained is a question that cannot be answered in general, but that should figure prominently in any deliberation on the desirability of JIT.

[2] Lead time related issues are also discussed in Chapter 6.

JIT affects most functional areas within the organization in one way or another. The additional flexibility in manufacturing furnished by shorter lead times and a cross-trained workforce provides the organization with marketing opportunities. In addition, shorter product life cycles can be sustained by manufacturing, and by speeding up product development additional market opportunities may become available. Of course this will require more intimate cooperation between marketing, product development and manufacturing. A very important competitive weapon in many industries is the speed and frequency of model changes, see Stalk [1988]. Many interesting issues regarding the organization of product development teams remain to be investigated.

Marketing, distribution and sales departments have an opportunity to capitalize on the higher quality and shorter lead times and translate them into better customer service and higher sales. The advantages of shortened manufacturing lead times can be squandered in the sales and distribution system if information and product flows are not streamlined there as well. When finished product quality levels go up substantially, the role of field service organizations may have to be redefined.

Personnel management needs to adjust to a reduced number of job classifications, changing job qualifications, and increased training requirements. Performance evaluation criteria for managers often need to be changed. Production managers should not be evaluated on output alone, but also on the rate of quality improvement, on meeting cross-training targets, and interaction with workers, peers, superiors and customers. Frequency of layoffs and hiring should go down, since replacing a cross-trained worker is time consuming and expensive.

The accounting department has to develop new ways of measuring activities on the factory floor. In many cases it will no longer be economical to track the multitude of material handling transactions involving small quantities of product in the inventory system. In fact, it is not necessary to do so any more because the very limited amounts of inventory make visual control possible. A change from a functional to a cellular layout also makes the use of traditional cost centers ineffective.

The finance department often has to make changes in the areas of budgeting, capital investment justification procedures, etc. In addition, considerable investment in equipment and training may be required at the start of a Just-in-Time program.

Changes are often necessary in quality control as well. Instead of making the quality control department responsible for quality, under JIT it becomes, as Schonberger [1986] says, everybody's business. The emphasis switches from detection to prevention of defects. Traditional batch inspection techniques become very inefficient when production takes place in small batches. Instead, process control and fail-safing techniques need to be applied. Rapid feedback is established when little inventory is present, and this allows workers to rapidly diagnose and eliminate many quality problems. The logical locus of responsibility for process control and improvements is now with the workers, and not in inspection or quality control departments. Inspection procedures for incoming materials similarly need to be changed when JIT is extended to part suppliers. Direct incoming material inspection is replaced by vendor qualification programs involving quality audits at the vendor's plant, etc. Hence quality control personnel assume the role of educators in simple quality control techniques and facilitators of improvement activities initiated by production workers. They may also become involved in vendor qualification activities.

Finally, the role of management changes. As workers assume more responsibility, first line supervisors become team leaders. The emphasis shifts from monitoring the output from individual workers to facilitating production and improvement activities by teams. When quality and equipment reliability improve, management spends less time fighting these fires and more time is available to cultivate and develop the workforce and the business. Fewer managers may be needed, and the number of layers of management may be reduced.

To maximize the probability of success of a JIT program, it is also necessary to put proper incentive systems in place that encourage employees and management to implement the desired changes, and to redefine areas of responsibility throughout the organization. This is an often overlooked but essential part, and it can be extremely difficult. It requires significant changes in existing business systems and demands substantial adjustments from personnel, many of who have vested interests in the status quo. If this aspect is not handled carefully, a key employee or group of employees may be antagonized and the organization can be damaged substantially.

The extension of Just-in-Time to the purchasing function requires special effort in many cases. The supplier needs to become more flexible in making multiple small deliveries with narrow time windows, and a high quality level is imperative. This may require considerable investment in production processes and training by the supplier. To compensate the supplier, the purchasing firm guarantees a certain volume of purchases, and informs the supplier early of future production plans. The purchasing firm also attempts to level its production schedule to make JIT deliveries possible without significant buffer inventories.

The potential benefits to the purchasing firm are clear: it is assured of a reliable supplier of high quality material at a reasonable price. The purchaser is relieved of the need to hold raw material inventory, and in advanced situations incoming parts counting and inspection can be eliminated. Additional material handling can be avoided by using standardized containers filled at the supplier ready for use at the customer plant.

On the other hand, by sole sourcing and reducing inventories the purchaser increases his dependence on the supplier, at least in the short run, and a disruption of the supply of a single part may quickly lead to widespread stoppages.

The benefits of JIT purchasing to the supplier may also be substantial. They include a certain level of guaranteed demand, a more stable demand pattern, and possibly an inside track on future business.

The supplier becomes more dependent on a single customer for orders, increasing vulnerability to pressure for price and other concessions. In addition, by making investments in people and processes that will only pay for themselves when sales volumes are sufficient, the entire organization may be jeopardized.

The extension of JIT across firms thus creates mutual dependencies between supplier and customer, and hence incentives to cooperate to resolve problems and increase efficiency. In the best case, both benefit and become more competitive and profitable. Cooperation is extended to areas such as quality control and product development. In the worst case, one or both can be seriously affected by a break in the relationship.

Frequently, JIT purchasing is attempted when the customer is a large corporation and the supplier a small subcontractor. It is then possible for the customer to impose strict conditions on the supplier that may lead to real hardship. Especially when the discrepancy between the ordering quantity communicated to the supplier and the actual requirements differ substantially, there is the risk of imposing cost on the supplier in the form of a need for extra inventories, unnecessary overtime, and extra capacity. Ultimately, this would result in higher costs for parts and thus hurt the combined competitiveness of supplier and customer. As described in Monden [1983, Chapter 3], such problems led to questions about Toyota's Kanban system in the Diet, the Japanese parliament, in 1977. To alleviate these problems Toyota (i) uses a level production schedule during the month, (ii) tries to keep the discrepancies to less than 10%, (iii) provides suppliers with advance notice about model changes, and (iv) encourages suppliers to reduce their own production lead times by providing education.

Geographical distance between supplier and customers limits the potential for achieving Just-in-Time deliveries. Transportation delays are to some extent unavoidable, and a trade-off needs to be made between transportation cost and transportation time. Demand information communicated to the supplier should cover at least the supplier's production lead time plus the transportation lag, and when a significant volume change occurs, earlier warning is necessary. It is also necessary to control the actual transportation system more tightly to avoid early and late deliveries, and when large distances have to be bridged, this can be more difficult and costly. A sketch of a supplier logistics control system that could be used for this purpose is given in the previous section.

For a discussion of the issues involved in implementing Just-in-Time purchasing, see Schonberger & Gilbert [1983]. Schonberger & Ansari [1984] emphasize the quality benefits obtainable with Just-in-Time purchasing. Ansari [1986] and Ansari & Modarress [1987] report on surveys to identify and quantify the benefits of Just-in-Time purchasing. In a case study, Giunipero & Keiser [1987] document the advantages obtained with Just-in-Time purchasing in a non-manufacturing environment. Giunipero & O'Neil [1988] list obstacles to Just-in-Time procurement and discuss ways to overcome them. Macbeth, Baxter, Ferguson & Neil [1988] conclude from a study of British and U.S. owned plants in Scotland that geographical proximity does not free a supplier from the need to be competitive on a world wide basis, since customers attempt to compare suppliers using 'total all in cost' or acquisition cost. Robinson & Timmerman [1987] describe a case study of a JIT vendor analysis system that provides performance feedback to vendors. Das & Goyal [1989] describe an implementation from the vendor's viewpoint. Monden [1983, Chapter 3] discusses the Kanban system used at Toyota to coordinate part deliveries from its suppliers immediately to the points of use in the Toyota factories.

It is difficult to outline the limitations of JIT precisely. Even in situations where JIT principles do not seem to apply at present, that may change. As an example, consider Benetton. By reducing production lead time and improving the collection of demand information, they are able to adjust production quantities of fashionable clothing during the season. This gives Benetton a cost advantage over traditional manufacturers who have to fix production quantities before the selling season starts.

Limitations certainly apply to individual elements of JIT. A customized JIT program will have to be designed to fit the particular circumstances of an organization, and a cost/benefit analysis may indicate that JIT is not appropriate.

A number of authors sound notes of caution. Evidence of resistance to change (if any evidence is needed) can be found in Wilson [1985], who advises American management to be extremely cautious about adopting JIT techniques and specifically cautions against reducing inventory levels quickly to avoid severe stockout costs. Zipkin [1991] warns against an idealistic view of JIT. He argues that in many cases substantial investments are required to prepare for inventory cuts, and that inventories should not be cut arbitrarily without them. Similar warnings can be found in a number of other publications. Moyes [1988] sees dangers in the wholesale adoption of a foreign system, in particular regarding workers' expectations and supplier/customer relations, and he worries that the stability of the entire economy will suffer from the absence of the cushioning factor of buffer inventories. He observes that each of the elements of the Just-in-Time philosophy yield benefits if applied by itself and therefore advocates adopting only those that fit the socio-economic environment.

The majority of published reports on JIT implementations are positive. Bockerstette [1988] gives a summary of the pre-implementation work that needs to be done to establish a base of reference for future JIT activities. Barrett [1988] describes a successful Just-in-Time implementation at a division of Lockheed. Berry [1987] lists successes in the automative industry. Burnham [1987] discusses implementation issues and lists a number of actual implementations in major U.S. manufacturing companies. Many other references on JIT implementations are available in the literature.

Finch & Cox [1986] discuss the problems faced by small manufacturers in implementing JIT. Their conclusion is that the elements of JIT should be considered individually in light of the particular manufacturing situation, because some may not be applicable. In other words, they advocate tailoring the JIT approach to the specific small production environment. Finch [1986], Williams & Tice [1984], and Inman & Mehra [1990] also discuss the application of JIT techniques to small businesses. Dicasali [1986] argues for the application of JIT techniques to job shops. He notes that there are operations within job shops that are essentially repetitive in nature and these are natural areas of application. In some cases it is also possible to make the nature of some operations more repetitive by increasing component commonality and a judicious use of out-sourcing.

Although the majority of published reports on JIT implementations are favorable, it would be misleading to consider only reported case studies to estimate the success rate of JIT programs: failures are probably less likely to be reported on. Surveys can partially overcome this bias. Crawford, Blackstone & Cox [1988] give the results of a survey on implementation problems among 35 U.S. corporations. The most important conclusions are that enough resources must be provided for education and training to overcome the cultural resistance to change, that preparation in the form of a focus on effective preventive maintenance and quality control programs has a beneficial impact on JIT implementation efforts, and that interdepartmental implementation teams should be employed.

Under optimal circumstances, JIT can have significant benefits in the form of increased profitability and competitiveness. To increase the success probability, the implementation of JIT needs to be adjusted to the circumstances. Even then, the success of a JIT program is not at all guaranteed, and starting one still implies significant risks. More theoretical and empirical research into various implementations is desirable.

5. The Kanban system

5.1. A description of the basic system

One of the most visible aspects of some Just-in-Time programs is the so-called Kanban system. Kanban is the Japanese word for visual record or card, and in the Kanban system cards are used to authorize production or transportation of a given amount of material. The Kanban contains information about the type and amount of material it represents, the operation (production or transportation) that it authorizes, and where the material is to be stored. The Kanban should not be confused with a routing sheet or shop ticket or similar paper that often accompanies a lot through the factory in other systems. A Kanban relates to only one operation, and is recycled after use. Usually, parts are stored in special containers that can hold a fixed amount of material. In the basic Kanban system, there always has to be a Kanban attached to each full container, and partially filled containers are not allowed. Production and transportation cannot take place without authorization in the form of a Kanban. The Kanban system effectively limits the amount of in-process inventories, and it coordinates production and transportation of consecutive stages of production in assembly-line fashion, even when the stages are separated in space. Toyota uses the Kanban system to coordinate the deliveries of materials from some outside suppliers. The Kanban system appears to be best suited for discrete part production feeding an assembly line.

Below follows a description of the mechanics of the Kanban system. A number of similar descriptions have appeared in the literature, see Monden [1981a,b, 1983], Hall [1983], Sugimori, Kusunoki, Cho & Uchikawa [1977], Schonberger [1983a], Karmarkar [1986a]. Buzacott [1989] gives a detailed framework for the comparison of the mechanics of Kanban and MRP systems. In the next subsection analytical and simulation models of Kanban systems are reviewed. The section on the Kanban system is concluded with a discussion of the relationships between Kanban and MRP systems.

A number of variants and adaptations of the Kanban system have been developed. First the Two Card Kanban system is described in detail, and then some variations are discussed. Figure 2 depicts the basic mechanics of a Two Card Kanban system. The Two Card system employs two types of Kanban cards: Production or P-Kanbans and Transportation or T-Kanbans. As the

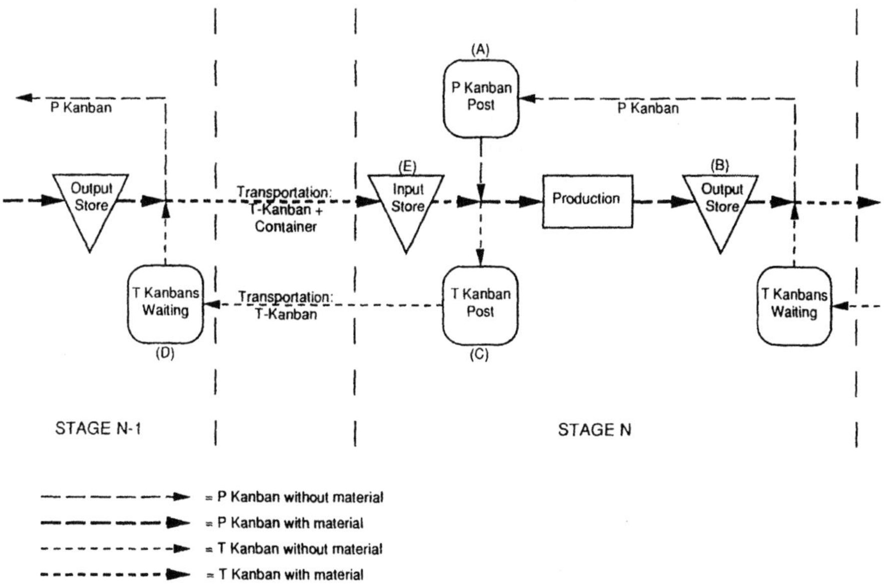

Fig. 2. Flow of parts and Kanbans in a Two Card Kanban system.

names indicate, the P-Kanban authorizes production of a fixed amount of product, and the T-Kanban authorizes transportation of a fixed amount of product. Let us first consider the activities that take place within a production cell. When a P-Kanban is not attached to its standard amount of product, it signals the need to replenish the output store with a standard lot. All such Kanbans are given visibility by posting them on a board (A). In this way, they form a representation of the queue of work waiting to be performed in the cell, readily visible to production workers and management. When production of the lot starts, the P-Kanban is taken from the board. Upon completion, the finished lot is placed in the output store with the P-Kanban attached (B). When the parts are removed from the output store, the P-Kanban is detached and again posted on the board and becomes the release order for the next lot. The movements of a T-Kanban are similar, except that the operation authorized is transportation, and the T-Kanban circulates between two consecutive stages of the production process. Depending on the implementation, there can be several queues of detached T-Kanbans: in the downstream cell there can be a queue of cards waiting to be taken over to the supplying work cell upstream (C), and in the supplying work cell there can be a queue of detached T-Kanbans waiting for product to be attached to, or waiting for transportation (D). After transportation, the inputs remain in the input store (E) with the T-Kanbans attached, until they are used in production. In principle, responsibility for transportation of Kanbans and materials can be given to the upstream cell, to the downstream cell, or to a third party.

The basic rules of the Kanban system are now as follows: (i) there can be no production without authorization in the form of a P-Kanban; (ii) there can be no transportation without authorization in the form of a T-Kanban; (iii) there is no material without a Kanban attached. The result is that the successive stages of production are linked in approximately assembly-line fashion. After an interruption somewhere in the chain, the stages downstream soon run out of raw material to work on, and stations upstream from any stopped station will soon run out of detached P-Kanbans to authorize production. Hence the system forces all production steps to be nearly synchronized. It is important to note that the speed of propagation of interruptions depends on the numbers of Kanbans in circulation at each stage, since this directly controls the amount of inventory by rule (iii). Hence the Kanban system behaves very much like an asynchronous assembly line in its response to interruptions in the regular flow of product.

Unlike assembly lines, the Kanban system is very flexible in a number of respects:

- By displaying the cards, visibility is given to in-process inventories. Inventory reduction can be achieved by simply pulling detached cards from circulation. If card counts are monitored and controlled, the only means of avoiding interruptions in the flow of parts is through process and method improvements. These in turn allow further inventory and lead time reductions.
- A cell or stage can produce a number of different parts or products. Each

part will simply have its own P-Kanbans. By displaying the detached P-Kanbans on the board, the cell scheduler (and everyone else) has a perfect picture of the current load, and sequencing decisions are easy to make.

• If the supplier cell is near the user cell, the supplier's output buffer and the user's input buffer can be combined, and the T-Kanban between the two can be eliminated. If setup times are sufficiently reduced, the two cells can be combined and controlled with a single P-Kanban.

• By combining the production runs for several Kanbans it is possible to combine production for several P-Kanbans to produce larger batches, as pointed out by Karmarkar [1991]. Hence, when multiple Kanbans are waiting, a temporary increase in throughput can be achieved by eliminating some setups altogether.

• In addition, the product flow does not have to be linear: a cell or stage can receive inputs from several upstream facilities, as well as produce outputs destined for several downstream facilities. Upstream and downstream facilities can be located quite far apart while effective real time coordination is maintained. Of course transportation times and costs are negatively affected when facilities are far apart.

• The transportation function can be organized in a number of ways. One can make pickups every hour or half hour (this is called the fixed interval system) or after a predetermined number of T-Kanbans has been detached (fixed quantity system). One can make the supplier responsible for making deliveries or the customer responsible for picking up his own material. Alternatively, it is possible to centralize the transportation function and institute internal 'bus routes' within the plant. Just-in-Time shipments from outside suppliers can be combined into outside 'bus routes' to achieve more frequent deliveries at affordable costs.

For a Kanban system to work well, a number of requirements have to be fulfilled. The Kanban system performs best when setup times are small, demand for parts is steady and has sufficient volume, the equipment is reliable and defect rates are low.

Items with large setup times are more difficult to manage with the Kanban system. The reason is that large setup times require large lot sizes, and large lot sizes inflate lead times and in-process inventories. As a result, parts of the system that are far from a disturbance (such as a machine breakdown, or extra demand caused by scrap losses) can no longer react in a timely fashion. Note that such information is transmitted by physical movement of material and Kanbans. Safety stock or costly over-capacity becomes necessary, and the system loses its Just-in-Time characteristics and becomes harder to control. Therefore, an emphasis on bringing down setup times is an important component of Just-in-Time programs.

Items with large demand fluctuations cause similar problems. This has important implications for production scheduling. It is desirable to employ level production schedules in all stages of the system, see also Section 5.2.1. A related issue is that demand fluctuations have a tendency to become amplified from one stage to the next when timing and size of replenishment orders are based on locally observed demands as in a pull system, see Hall [1981, pp. 25–27], Kimura & Terada [1981], Tabe, Maramatsu & Tanaka [1980], and below. A Kanban system is also ineffective in achieving Just-in-Time production for items with low volume, i.e., less than a day's worth of consumption per container. Since at each stage of manufacture there is at least some inventory for a product, too much in-process inventory would accumulate for items that require only infrequent production. Such items may be better controlled with a push system such as MRP. Toyota's rule of thumb is that the container capacity should not exceed 10% of a day's usage [Hall, 1981].

Reliable equipment and low scrap and rework rates are necessary in all Just-in-Time systems, as discussed earlier. Without them the ability to execute production plans is severely impaired in the absence of a large amount of safety stock.

In the single card Kanban system described by Schonberger [1983a] the transportation of materials is still controlled by T-Kanbans. However, the P-Kanbans to control production within a cell are absent. Their role is filled by a production schedule provided on a regular basis by central production planning. The amount of product in the input stores is kept strictly limited to just one or two containers. Hence this system has a strong similarity to a conventional push system, with pull elements added to coordinate the transportation of parts. Such a system can work in a Just-in-Time mode only when production lead times are short and it is easy to create detailed production schedules for the different production cells from the final assembly schedule. The relationships between Kanban and push systems is discussed more fully in Section 5.3 below.

To conclude this subsection, it should be noted that many other methods besides cards could be and have been used to perform the coordination and control functions necessary in Just-in-Time systems. In some cases it may be possible to do away with any formal control mechanism whatsoever by appropriately laying out the production facilities and establishing standard flow patterns. In other cases, containers themselves might play the role of P-Kanbans, stocking areas marked off on the floor can serve as P-Kanbans, electronic communications or voice or light signals can be used to communicate the need for more parts and replace T-Kanbans. One could imagine an automated factory controlled in a decentralized fashion by 'electronic' Kanbans, etc. Indeed, Monden [1983, p. 33] describes the use of a limit switch that functions as an 'electric' Kanban, and Seidmann [1988] describes an application of controlling flexible machining cells in this fashion.

Spearman, Hopp & Woodruff [1990] propose an interesting alternative to Kanban. Their Constant Work-in-Process (CONWIP) system aims at keeping the work-in-process inventory in a production line constant by releasing orders to a production line as jobs are completed. This system provides for more flexibility in distributing the available work-in-process inventory than the two card Kanban system. Spearman, Hopp & Woodruff [1989] develop a hierarchical planning methodology for CONWIP systems.

It is also possible to use Kanban systems in situations that do not fit the traditional 'part production for assembly' pattern. Groenevelt & Karmarkar [1988] describe a so-called dynamic Kanban system with several unusual features. Customer demands directly drive the system. Finished product inventories are controlled through a Kanban controlled base stock system. When customer demands cannot be satisfied from stock, special 'hot' Kanbans are created which are destroyed again as soon as the finished product is shipped. To account for seasonality and to handle large orders, extra cards are introduced into the system ahead of time. The system provides for visibility of the load on the shop, facilitates scheduling of the bottleneck operation, and enables control of finished product inventories. In addition, it provides incentives for setup time reduction at the bottleneck operation and process improvements.

5.2. Models for Kanban systems

5.2.1. Leveling production schedules

Level production schedules are highly desirable in Kanban systems, as argued above. Since the final assembly schedule determines production schedules for all of the preceding operations, it is advisable to smooth out the loads by appropriate scheduling of final assembly. This implies level (constant rate) final assembly schedules for all products. This can be achieved with mixed model assembly, i.e., the assembly line has the capability to produce different models one unit at a time in any order desired. The following example is adapted from Monden [1983]. Monthly demand data are given in Table 1. By evenly dividing the total demand by the 20 working days in the month, the desired daily output for each type is obtained. Available production time per day is 480 minutes $\times$ 2 shifts = 960 minutes, so the desired cycle time is 0.96 minutes per unit. Final production should now be scheduled so that 10 units are made every 9.6 minutes: 4 of type A, 3 of type B, 2 of type C, and 1 of type D. Even within the 9.6 minutes, demand can be further smoothed by spreading out the 4 units of type A as evenly as possible, etc. Finally, one could come up with a final assembly schedule of A-B-A-C-B-A-D-A-B-C repeated 100 times during the day. Such extreme smoothing is desirable if not

Table 1
Data for production smoothing example

Model	Monthly demand (units)	Average daily output (units)	Output every 9.6 minutes (units)
A	8000	400	4
B	6000	300	3
C	4000	200	2
D	2000	100	1
Total	20 000	1000	10

all types place equal loads on all production stages. If, e.g., type D requires a unique processing step, and if all type D units were produced at the end of the day, the load on this processing step would be very uneven over the course of a single day, making necessary either a full day's worth of safety stock or a push type mechanism that cannot be provided by the pure Kanban system. (Of course it would be possible to add such elements if absolutely necessary, see below.) If the product line contains many different models and options the final assembly sequencing problem can become quite unwieldy. The problem can be formulated as follows.[3] Let

Q_i = number of units of product i to be produced,
$Q = \Sigma_i Q_i$ = total number of units to be produced,
a_{ij} = number of units of part j required to assemble one unit of product i,
$a_j = \Sigma_i a_{ij} Q_i$ = total number of units of part j required,

$$x_{ij} = \begin{cases} 1 & \text{if a unit of product } i \text{ occupies the } k\text{th position in the assembly sequence ,} \\ 0 & \text{otherwise .} \end{cases}$$

A feasible assembly sequence if fixed by selecting a 0–1 matrix (x_{ik}) such that

$$\sum_k x_{ik} = Q_i \quad \text{for all } i , \tag{1}$$

and

$$\sum_i x_{ik} = 1 \quad \text{for all } k . \tag{2}$$

The desirability of a sequence is a function of the numbers

$$D_{kni} = \sum_{m=k+1}^{n} x_{im} - (n-k)\frac{Q_i}{Q} , \quad 0 \leq k < n \leq Q, \text{ for all } i , \tag{3}$$

and

$$d_{knj} = \sum_{m=k+1}^{n} \sum_i a_{ij} x_{im} - (n-k)\frac{a_j}{Q} , \quad 0 \leq k < n \leq Q, \text{ for all } j . \tag{4}$$

Note that D_{kni} denotes the difference between the actual number of units of product i assembled from position $k+1$ through position n and the number of units that would be assembled under a perfectly smooth production schedule. Similarly, d_{knj} denotes the difference between the actual number of units of part j required for assembly of the units produced from position $k+1$ through position n and the number that would be required under a perfectly smooth

[3] This formulation assumes that the assembly times for all products are identical. A generalization to nonidentical assembly times is straightforward but somewhat cumbersome.

production schedule. The problem is to minimize a suitable function of (D_{kni}) and (d_{knj}) subject to (1)–(4). Monden [1981c, 1983, Appendix 2] describes Toyota's heuristic approach that greedily selects the product i for position k that minimizes $\Sigma_j d_{0kj}^2$ given the sequence for positions $1, \ldots, k-1$. To reduce the numerical work involved, one could consider only major subassemblies and divide the entire planning horizon in a number of smaller parts. Miltenburg [1989] gives several heuristics for the assembly sequencing problem with objective function $\Sigma_{k=1}^{Q} \Sigma_i D_{0ki}^2$, and Miltenburg & Sinnamon [1989] discuss algorithms for the general problem. Kubiak & Sethi [1991] point out that Miltenburg's assembly sequencing problem can be reformulated as an assignment problem. Inman & Bulfin [1991] propose setting due dates for each unit to be produced on the assembly line and then minimizing either the sum of the squared deviations or the sum of the absolute deviations from the due dates. If all jobs have the same processing time, the Earliest Due Date (EDD) algorithm is optimal for both objectives.

5.2.2. Choosing the operating parameters

For each part in the Kanban system two basic parameters have to be set: the capacity of the container (which is equal to the amount of product that the Kanban corresponds to), and the number of containers to be used. The choice of container capacity is often influenced by physical considerations. Small containers increase the total handling required and the transportation costs, containers that are too large make special material handling provisions necessary. Very few studies exist that consider the container size explicitly. Karmarkar & Kekre [1989] formulate several queueing models to investigate the effect of the container capacity on the throughput performance of single and dual card Kanban stages. They also model a two stage Kanban system as a two-dimensional Markov chain. Their conclusion is that the impact of the container capacity on system performance is substantial. This conclusion is similar to the one reached by Shen [1987] in a simulation study. From a simulation study Kimura & Terada [1981] conclude that the Kanban size has an impact on the amplification of load and inventory variations through the stages of the system. They conclude that the Kanban size should be small relative to the daily demand. This phenomenon is also observed for an MRP type push system with forecast errors [see Tabe, Maramatsu & Tanaka [1980], and the preferred system depends on the magnitude of these errors.[4]

On the other hand, several authors discuss the decision of how many Kanbans to have. Monden [1983, Appendix 1] details the procedures to select the number of Kanbans used at Toyota for the various withdrawal systems. He notes that the formulas are only used as a starting point: the supervisors are told to try to reduce the number of cards, one at a time, as process improvements are made. Sugimori, Kusunoki, Cho & Uchikawa [1977] and

[4] See below for additional simulation studies reporting on amplification.

Monden[1983] give the standard formula used by Toyota to set the number of withdrawal Kanbans used. Let

n = the number of Kanbans,
D = demand (in units of product) per day,
L = average lead time for the Kanban,
c = the capacity of a container (in units of product),
α = a safety coefficient.

Then $n = DL(1 + \alpha)/c$. In the case of transportation Kanbans, the average lead time L is the time that elapses between a T-Kanban being placed on the T-Kanban post (C) and its return to the input store (E), see Figure 2. Hence L is determined primarily by the frequency of pickups and the transportation time. In case of production Kanbans, the lead time depends on the actual production time and on the length of the queue of work represented by Kanbans on the P-Kanban post (A), see Figure 2. Monden [1983, Appendix 1] notes that it is Toyota's practice to largely leave the number of withdrawal Kanbans the same when the demand rate changes and to adjust the frequency of pickups instead. The parameter α is viewed by management as an index of the shop's capability to improve the process. Rees, Philipoom, Patrick, Taylor III & Huang [1987] discuss a methodology to adjust the number of Kanbans using demand forecasts and estimated lead time distributions. Philipoom, Rees, Taylor III & Huang [1987] investigate the influence of several factors on the number of Kanbans required through a simulation model. The factors investigated include the production rate, the variability of processing times, the utilization, and the autocorrelation of processing times. Huang, Rees & Taylor III [1983] simulate a Kanban system to investigate its appropriateness in typical American production environments. It is found that variability in processing times and demand rates are amplified in a multi-stage setting, and that enough excess capacity has to be available to avoid bottlenecks. In a comment, Monden [1984] points out that these factors are variables under management control, and should be subject to improvement. Jordan [1988] uses a Markov chain model to analyze the same system. Muramatsu, Ishii & Takahashi [1985] simulate push and pull control systems and find that their pull system does not lead to amplification of variability, while the push system does. Deleersnyder, Hodgson, Muller(-Malek) & O'Grady [1989] develop a discrete time Markov chain model to determine the number of Kanbans that should be used in a Kanban controlled serial production system when machine reliability, demand variability, and end item safety stocks are taken into account. Using a deterministic approach, Miyazaki, Ohta & Nishiyama [1988] determine average inventory levels for fixed interval and supplier Kanban systems, give formulae to determine the minimum numbers of Kanbans required, and derive an algorithm to obtain the optimal order interval. Bitran & Chang [1987] formulate a deterministic multi-stage, multi period, capacitated mathematical programming model to determine the number of Kanbans required in a tree-structured assembly context. Since uncertainty does not figure in their model, they advise managers to adjust the number of Kanbans obtained from the model to consider the potential uncertainties in demand and machine breakdowns.

Buzacott [1989] gives a detailed description of Kanban and MRP systems as linked queueing networks with blocking. The differences between Kanban, Kanban with backorders, and MRP can be characterized in terms of the blocking mechanisms, and the models can be used to identify surplus Kanban cards. Seidmann [1988] gives a dynamic programming formulation to obtain the optimal buffer sizes (number of Kanbans) in a system consisting of an automated manufacturing cell supplying parallel finishing machines with random processing times. Coordination is achieved through an (electronic) pull system. Zipkin [1989] presents an exact analysis of a two stage production system controlled by a modified Kanban scheme that allows backorders and extra inventories for the finished products. Demands and processing times are random and product differentiation occurs only at the second stage. Mitra & Mitrani [1990] present a decomposition approach to a similar system that does not allow extra finished product inventories, an assumption that is subsequently relaxed in Mitra & Mitrani [1991]. Other simulation studies are found in Ebrahimpour & Fathi [1985], Lee [1987], Lee & Seah [1988], and Schroer, Black & Zhang [1984].

It should be pointed out that many authors have investigated the behavior of serial production lines with random processing times or unreliable machines. Some of the models mentioned previously in this subsection fall within this category. The rationale for singling them out for discussion here is that they incorporate part of the mechanics of Kanban systems. For surveys of the literature on serial production lines, see Conway, Maxwell, McClain & Thomas [1988] or Gershwin & Schick [1983].

5.3. Kanban and MRP

It is not surprising that many authors have compared Kanban and MRP systems. Both systems are designed to coordinate order release and shop floor control functions on a factory-wide or even larger scale, with the intent of minimizing work-in-process inventories. Both systems can be used to manage purchasing. Rice & Yoshikawa [1982] find many similarities between the Kanban system and MRP. Both are 'Just-in-Time' systems in the sense that they attempt to minimize work-in-process, both require participation and cooperation, both focus on shop floor control, adapting to schedule changes, and communicating timely information. Both Kanban and MRP are systems that require many controls and procedures to be in place before they can be implemented successfully, and both systems benefit (like any planning and control system would) from quality control improvement efforts.

Capacity planning in Kanban systems also shows some similarities with capacity planning in MRP systems. If a level production schedule is used (see above), then it is a simple matter to calculate the required production rate for each item at each stage of processing by using a single level bill of materials. The required production rates are then compared with available capacity, and adjustments are made in the deployment of the workforce, purchasing plans, etc. Since the schedule is kept constant for a certain amount of time, these adjustments need to be made only occasionally. There is no need for lead time offsetting, the generation of detailed production orders, or formal tracking, monitoring and dispatching systems. Because the lead times are short, the Kanbans handle material coordination, and a problem will manifest itself by quickly halting production.

There are also radical differences between MRP and Kanban systems. MRP operates in a centralized fashion, where Kanban is much more decentralized. In MRP systems all information is kept in a central database, maintained and updated by a computer. Production schedules incorporating information from all production, engineering, purchasing, sales, and marketing departments are thrashed out, and all of this information is centrally available. In addition, order releases are cut, purchase orders are triggered, and progress is tracked by the central system. MRP is a 'push' system: order releases are based on future demands or requirements.

By contrast, in Kanban systems, less information is stored centrally. Most detailed information is scattered across the factory floor and not available real time in a centralized system. The Kanban cards have the functions of production orders and move tickets. New orders are generated automatically, without intervention by management or a central system, when withdrawals are made from an inventory store located next to the machine or cell that replenishes the inventory. The Kanban system is therefore a 'pull' system. Progress throughout all processes is easily tracked, since work-in-process is so limited that an interruption in the smooth flow of products soon triggers a widespread halt in production in all connected processes. Adherence to the Final Assembly Schedule by the entire system (including vendor facilities) is easily verified by monitoring output from the final assembly line.

A second major difference is the time scale with which the two systems accomplish coordination. MRP sets production schedules with discrete time buckets that are typically a week long. Schedules are then updated once a week in a revolving fashion, and the necessary change orders are generated to inform those involved of the changes. This rather large time bucket implies that production lead times will be on the order of weeks or months.

Kanban approaches continuous time control much closer, with time lags measured in hours and minutes rather than weeks. Contingencies can be dealt with locally, and the Kanban mechanisms transmit the necessary adjustments to those remote production stages that are affected.

A third major difference involves the way in which both systems deal with changes and uncertainty. When using MRP systems, planners tend to react to temporary bottlenecks and uncertainty by increasing the planned lead time between order release and completion. This creates queues of work-in-process on the factory floor and further inflates lead times. More sophisticated systems may have capabilities to smooth out the work load better over time by varying the lead time and/or adjusting the Master Production Schedule. However, the smoothing out of the work load can be done only by time buckets (weeks), and additional provisions are needed for time spans of less than the bucket length.

In systems controlled with Kanban the emphasis is on smoothing out the work-load over time in all time scales varying in length from minutes up to several months, and on eliminating bottlenecks by a balanced deployment of the work force. Uncertainty is reduced by achieving high quality levels and high equipment reliability. This is made possible by extensive cross-training, small setup times, continual improvement efforts by workers, extensive preventive maintenance, etc.

These differences have profound consequences for the way in which the systems tend to evolve. In MRP systems the tendency is to try to solve problems by modifying or expanding the MRP system. For instance, late deliveries from vendors, quality problems, and equipment breakdowns are accommodated by rescheduling and expediting, activities well supported by the existing MRP systems. This has the effect of reducing the urgency of tackling the real underlying problems, and improving the capabilities of the production system. Lead times are considered fixed, so there is no need to try to reduce them.

The natural tendency to increase inventories to alleviate problems is probably just as strong in Kanban systems as in MRP systems. However, in Kanban systems the amount of inventory can be kept under tight control, and an alert management has a better chance of focusing attention on process and other improvements and away from inventory increases.

Several authors have compared the two approaches to production control. Krajewski, King, Ritzman & Wong [1987] perform extensive simulation experiments to compare the influence of the manufacturing environment on the performance of Kanban and MRP systems. Factors used to describe the environment include: (i) customer influence – forecast error for standard products, forecast error for special products, proportion of special products, (ii) vender influence – vendor quality, average lead times, lead time variability, (iii) buffer mechanisms – capacity slack, safety stock and lead time, short releases, (iv) product structure – shape of the Bill of Materials (BOM), number of levels of BOM, commonality, (v) facility design – routing pattern, shop emphasis on fabrication or assembly, length of routings, (vi) process – scrap, equipment failures, worker flexibility, capacity imbalances, and (vii) inventory – accuracy, end item lot sizing, component lot sizing. Each of the seven factors was assigned a high and a low setting, and a one-eighth replicate of a complete factorial experiment was performed to assess the impact on the three performance measures: labor requirements, inventory, and past due demand. The results largely confirm the existing intuitions. They indicate that the degree of performance improvement obtained by installing a Kanban system depends on the environment, and that the significant factors are inventory, process and product structure. Kanban applied to an environment with large lot sizes and setup times does not produce the inventory reductions normally associated with it. The process factors proved to have a high impact on service performance, in the directions expected. The product structure affects inventory and service performance in reverse directions: inventory performance is better with a pyramid product structure, shallow bill of materials and low commonality, while service performance is worse. Nevertheless, Kanban performed well with either product structure. To assess the question whether it is the environment or the Kanban system that produces the attractive results, a limited comparison with two reorder point systems was performed, one with daily and one with weekly review of the inventory positions. The results seem to indicate that there is not much difference. The conclusion that suggests itself is that Kanban is not attractive because it is the best system for any given environment, but rather that it is a good way of improving the environment, because it facilitates instead of obstructs improvements.

Several authors point out that MRP and Kanban are not necessarily alternatives, but that elements of both systems can be present in the same factory. According to Belt [1987], the Kanban approach integrates succeeding processing steps seamlessly, so that their interface becomes virtually invisible and requires no special intervention. On the other hand, MRP handles interfaces explicitly, and it is a company-wide system that does a lot more than detailed scheduling and shop-floor control. He therefore pleads for a judicious implementation of Kanban principles while maintaining overall coordination with an MRP system. Bose & Rao [1988] discuss some of the issues involved in integrating 'islands' of Just-in-Time into advanced MRP systems. The single card Kanban system described by Schonberger [1983a] integrates MRP type production planning with a Kanban controlled pull material delivery system, and is implemented in several Japanese plants. Karmarkar [1986b] discusses a similar hybrid system where Kanban cards are generated by the MRP system at the cell level. He proposes various strategies to deal with scrap losses, lead time variations, etc. Many of the incentives to reduce inventories inherent in the standard Kanban system are maintained. The system is appropriate for repetitive batch manufacturing where lot identity does not have to be maintained. Karmarkar [1989] compares the approaches of push (MRP) and pull (Kanban) systems to the various functions of a production control system such as order release, information flow, batching policies, and proposes a variety of hybrid approaches to production control. Schonberger [1983c] compares JIT with various types of MRP as well as other manufacturing control systems. Karmarkar & Shivdasani [1986] review different push and pull approaches to batch manufacturing control and advocate the use of 'custom design' systems depending on the characteristics of the production task at hand.

6. Models for Just-in-Time

Various models have been proposed to investigate the improvement and learning processes the Just-in-Time system seeks to foster. A number of authors have studied the relationship between traditional operations management models and Just-in-Time. Probably the best known model in operations management is the Economic Order Quantity (EOQ) model that attempts to set lot sizes to obtain an optimal trade-off between setup costs and inventory holding costs. Let d be the product demand per unit time, K the cost of setting up production or of placing an outside order, and h the cost of holding a unit of inventory per unit time. Then the optimal production quantity, Q^*, and the minimum per period setup plus holding cost C^* are given by

$$Q^* = \sqrt{2Kd/h}\,, \qquad C^* = \sqrt{2Khd}\,.$$

It is often pointed out that both the optimal production quantity Q^* and the minimum cost C^* are insensitive to small changes in the parameters of the EOQ model [see the basic text books by Moskowitz & Wright, 1979; Hax & Candea, 1984; McClain & Thomas, 1985], implying that it does not pay much to invest in reducing setup costs K. The result is that traditionally K was considered fixed in applications of the EOQ model, and the potential benefits of substantial reductions in K were largely overlooked.

Schonberger & Schniederjans [1984] point out that in addition the per unit holding cost h is usually underestimated: the interest and administrative costs that traditionally make up h should be augmented with shop-floor material storage and handling costs, the foregone benefits from improvement activities, and the costs involved in uneven workloads. When the necessary improvements have been made to reduce K (by improving setup methods, by using nearby suppliers or otherwise) and when the correct value is used for the holding cost h, Schonberger and Schniederjans claim that the optimal lot size Q^* equals one.

The models in Porteus [1985, 1986b] incorporate the possibility of investing in setup cost reduction. Here the undiscounted case [Porteus, 1985] is briefly summarized. It is assumed that a reduction of the setup cost to a value of K requires a total investment $a(K)$, and without discounting this translates into a per period cost of $ia(K)$, where i is the per period opportunity cost of capital. It is assumed that $a(K_0) = 0$, where K_0 is the setup cost before process improvement, and $a(K)$ is assumed to be convex. The decision variables are now both the ultimate setup cost and the lot size. For a given setup cost K the optimal lot size is of course given by

$$Q(K) = \sqrt{2Kd/h}\,,$$

with per period inventory holding plus setup cost $C(K) = \sqrt{2Khd}$, and it remains to select the setup cost K to minimize $ia(K) + C(K)$, the sum of a convex and a concave function. To obtain an explicit solution, Porteus assumes a particular form for the cost of reducing the setup cost: $a(K) = \theta \ln(K/K_0)$, $0 < K \leq K_0$. In other words, it costs a fixed amount to reduce the setup cost by a fixed percentage. The result is that investments in reducing setup costs are worthwhile only if $K_0hd > 2(\theta i)^2$, so if the product of demand, current setup cost and holding cost rate are high enough compared with the price paid to achieve a given percentage reduction of K. Other things equal, this implies that a high volume firm should invest more in setup reduction than a low volume firm. In the case that a positive investment is worthwhile, the optimal lot size is given by $2\theta i/h$, independent of the demand rate. Hence the optimal per period holding cost for each lot is a constant $2\theta i$. As Porteus remarks, this result is consistent with the practice to use a standard container in the Kanban system, regardless of the product being made. Indeed, a standard container will hold a larger number of small pieces, and if h is positively correlated with the size of a piece, the use of standard containers becomes even more plausible. In case investment is warranted, it will yield increasing marginal returns at first, but diminishing marginal returns for higher levels of investment.

In Porteus [1986a] the nondiscounted EOQ model with investments to reduce setup cost from Porteus [1985] is extended to incorporate quality effects and investments in process quality improvements. It is assumed that during the production of a single unit the production process starts producing defective parts with a fixed probability $q > 0$. All remaining units of the lot will be defective, since the problem is assumed not to be detected until after the entire lot is produced. Each defective unit can be reworked at a cost of $c_R > 0$. It is not hard to calculate the expected number of defects in a lot as a function of the lot size (note that this is strictly increasing), and find (approximate) values for the lot size that minimizes the per period inventory holding plus setup plus rework cost, and the minimal per period cost. The option of investing in process improvement is added in a fashion analogous to adding investing in setup cost reduction in Porteus [1985] by stipulating that it costs $a(q; q_0) = \gamma \ln(q/q_0)$, $0 < q \leq q_0$ to reduce the probability of the process turning bad on a single unit from q_0 to q. The results are similar as those in Porteus [1985] for investing in setup time reduction: there is a critical demand rate above which it is profitable to invest in process quality. When both investment opportunities (process quality and setup cost reduction) exist simultaneously, the optimal policy has one of four structures. When the demand rate is low enough neither investment opportunity is profitable, and when the demand is high enough, it is best to invest in both simultaneously. In between there is a region where it is profitable to invest in one but not the other, depending on the other parameters (especially γ and θ).

By way of a numerical example, it is shown that when both investment opportunities are available simultaneously the optimal combination of setup cost K and quality level q is somewhere in between the setup cost and quality level combinations optimal for each opportunity considered separately.

The Porteus models allow only a one time investment in process improvement along a single dimension. A stochastic dynamic programming model incorporating multiple small investments in improving quality and reducing setup costs is given by Fine & Porteus [1989]. The model again uses the EOQ model as its base, and assumes that improvements achieved (measured in units of a fixed percentage reduction in setup cost or fraction defectives) are an increasing random function of the amounts invested. The 'last chance' policy, i.e., the policy that assumes that no further improvements can be made in the future, reveals a great deal about the optimal policy. The optimal policy invests in improvements only when the last chance policy does, and the optimal policy never invests more than the last chance policy. If improvement along only one dimension is possible, there is a 'target' state such that both the optimal and the last chance policy invest as long as this state has not been reached and invest nothing after it has been reached. When improvement in both dimensions is considered, there is a set of target states with this property. If uncertainty in the improvement process is decreased, the target state(s) increase and the total return increases.

Zangwill [1987a,b] considers investments in setup reduction in the context of dynamic lot sizing models. Zangwill [1987a] investigates the effect of reducing setup costs in the classical dynamic lot size model, see Wagner & Whitin [1958]. In this model demands and setup costs can vary from period to period, and the variable production cost is given by a concave function of the number of units produced in a period. It is well known that for this model an optimal production schedule exists such that if production takes place in a given period, no inventory is carried over from the previous period. Consequently, if there is production in a period t, then the production amount equals the total demand for an integral number of consecutive periods $t, t+1, \ldots, s$. Zangwill shows by example that when the setup costs are reduced unevenly, it is possible that total inventory will increase (even though total costs will go down) in an optimal production schedule. When setup costs are reduced evenly (by the same amount in each period) it can be shown that the number of periods in which inventory will be held will go down (even though total inventory costs can still go up). What is more important, he shows that the minimal total cost as a function of the amount of an even setup reduction (evenly applied over all setups) is concave. This implies that setup cost reductions have increasing marginal returns. Zangwill goes on to show that, when setup costs are stationary and variable production costs linear and stationary, total inventory cost is a nonincreasing function of an even setup cost reduction.

Zangwill [1987b] develops a procedure for identifying the stages that will never need to hold inventories in a series facility dynamic lot size model with deterministic demand. This information can be useful for designing the layout of the facilities and for scheduling purposes. In addition, he emphasizes that the key parameter determining whether inventory will be held at a particular stage is the ratio of setup cost over incremental holding cost at the stage, and not just setup cost alone. Bielecki & Kumar [1988] show that even when a production stage is not perfectly reliable it can be optimal not to have any inventory to buffer it from the next stage based on inventory holding cost alone. This occurs when the stage is reliable enough, because in that case neither holding nor shortage cost will be incurred during a significant fraction of the time.

The above discussed lot sizing models assume zero setup times. As pointed out by Karmarkar [1987], in many cases setup costs are used to represent the opportunity cost of setup times. This implies that they are subject to change over time as the utilization of production resources changes. The qualitative results in these models therefore need to be interpreted carefully. In addition, the previously cited papers consider only the benefits of reductions in certain costs (determined by the underlying model of the manufacturing system). But as pointed out by their authors and elsewhere [see Hall, 1983; Monden, 1983; Shingo, 1989, 1985, etc.], many other benefits might be obtained, such as a favorable impact of setup reduction on quality, an increase in capacity due to less setup time and rework, etc.

With the exception of the Fine and Porteus model, the learning models discussed so far in this section assume that all improvements desired will be obtained immediately, whereas in the real world many improvements are implemented one at a time over a considerable period. However, at this point they are among the few models incorporating both a learning/improvement process and specific production decisions in whatever form, even though the nature of the improvement process is rather abstract. Some dynamic learning models are considered next.

Fine [1986] formulates several models incorporating the effects of quality conformance efforts into general learning curve models. The models treat time continuously and the solution technique used is calculus of variations. This allows qualitative results to be obtained. At each moment the firm makes two decisions: the quality conformance level (measured as the fraction of nondefectives q) and the instantaneous production rate. It is assumed that the firm faces a stationary downward sloping demand curve, so by selecting the production rate the firm also selects the price. The cost of achieving a given quality conformance level is the sum of two separate terms: appraisal and prevention costs that increase with q and approach infinity when q approaches 1, and failure costs that decrease with q and approach infinity when q approaches 0. Hence, without learning effects the firm would choose the (unique) conformance level q^* that minimizes the sum of these terms. This is in essence the economics of quality model of Lundvall & Juran [1974], and it conflicts with the zero defects notion espoused by Crosby [1979] and Deming [1982]. In Fine's first model, per unit production costs decrease with quality-weighted cumulative experience, so if the firm selects higher quality conformance levels, it will progress down the experience curve faster. In this model, the optimal conformance level decreases over time, but is always greater than q^*. As Fine remarks, this may be characteristic of the approach taken to quality by many firms, but it contradicts the zero defects philosophy of relentless pursuit of the cause of every defect. In the second model, per unit production cost is constant, but instead the appraisal and prevention cost function decreases as quality-weighted cumulative experience accumulates. In this model the optimal conformance level increases over time and is always greater than q^*. This model resolves the quality is costly versus quality is free conflict: it is still costly to achieve a very high quality level in the short term, but in the long term a firm can reach a competitive position of low cost and high quality.

Fine [1988] uses a stochastic dynamic programming formulation to investigate the amount of inspection of the production system that should be performed when such inspection enhances learning. Specifically, it is assumed that each time an inspection finds the system 'out of control', not only will it be brought under control, but also improvements will be undertaken that permanently decrease the probability that the system will go out of control during the next period. In addition, the process has a greater likelihood of producing a defective unit when it is out of control than when it is in control. It is assumed that 100% inspection is performed on the units produced, and the posterior probability of the system being out of control is updated constantly. It is costly to produce defective units, and inspection of the production system also costs money. Under the optimal policy one should inspect the station only if the probability that the station is out of order (given the output obtained from the system since the last inspection) exceeds a critical level that depends on the current propensity for the system to go out of control.

Tapiero [1987] gives a stochastic dynamic programming formulation to decide how much inspection to perform on the outputs of a production process when experience accumulates through inspection. He incorporates both learning and forgetting, and his formulation allows various sampling plans. Due to the generality of the model it is impossible to obtain structural results, but depending on the assumptions regarding the experience building process, and the relative costs of inspection and of shipping defective product, various policies such as always full inspection, full inspection until experience reaches a certain level, or no inspection can be optimal.

As the discussion of these papers indicates, the general area of modeling improvement processes in a Just-in-Time context is only just starting to be developed. Some general insights have been obtained, but it appears that the effects of specific improvement actions and specific operational decisions are hard to incorporate in one model. An empirical foundation for these models also appears to be substantially missing. This area remains a potentially fruitful field of research.

7. Research issues and future developments

In view of the heavy emphasis on actual practice and implementation in the development of JIT, it is not surprising that most of the early publications on JIT are primarily written by and for practitioners. More recently, JIT has received its share of attention in the academic literature, and there is now a substantial and growing body of theory on JIT. The scope for additional research on JIT remains ample. In particular, there is a lack of empirical studies based on solid industry data. Another category that is currently underrepresented is research that integrates several areas. Such research is all the more important because JIT brings so many separate areas closer together.

A sample of individual areas of particular interest follows:

- *Material handling*. In existing models of Kanban systems this aspect is often ignored. The typical assumption is that transportation is instantaneous. In other words, transportation mechanisms and organizational setup are modeled in a rudimentary way or not at all.
- *Work cell layout and design*. Much work has already been done in this area. However, with rapidly changing technical capabilities and increasing flexibility many interesting research topics remain.
- *Part supplier logistics*. Many theoretical issues regarding long distance JIT deliveries are still unresolved, see Section 3. Existing logistics models often ignore the impact of the logistics system on production. Questions regarding the optimization of the feedback mechanisms, how to consolidate, and how to choose the shipment mode still deserve further study.
- *Customer interfaces*. The ultimate goal of JIT is to react to final customer demands instead of trying to predict them. The influence of customers on production will continue to grow, and manufacturing facilities will acquire more of the characteristics of service facilities. Novel information systems and production control systems will be developed to deal with this aspect.
- *Quality control*. Many new ideas for controling quality are being developed. The emphasis in this area will shift eventually from training workers to developing better quality tools for managers. Analysis of use and effectiveness of these and other new tools yet to be created will be a fruitful topic of research.
- *Maintenance*. With the increased use of flexible automation, preventive maintenance will be more critical and will require more resources. New strategies for dealing with problems will have to be devised and analyzed.
- *Production planning*. The existing JIT production planning models deal mainly with smoothing production schedules (see Section 5.2.1). Issues like manpower planning and redeployment, and product development will become even more important.
- *Production control*. New approaches to production control and monitoring continue to be developed, and many issues relating to existing procedures are still open. This will continue to be an area of interest.
- *Improvement/learning*. Improvement and learning models (see Section 6) are still quite rudimentary. Many interesting questions remain unresolved, and particularly empirical work needs to be done in this area.

The Just-in-Time approach to production is likely to remain an important paradigm in many industries. Applications will continue to spread, and new techniques will continue to be developed and existing ones refined. Our understanding of many detailed empirical and theoretical issues related to JIT is still quite fragmented and incomplete, and much useful research and development work can still be done, both in industry and in research institutions.

References

Ansari, A. (1986). Survey identifies critical factors in implementation of Just in Time purchasing techniques. *Ind. Eng.* 18(10), 44–50.

Ansari, A., and B. Modarress (1987). The potential benefits of Just-in-Time purchasing for U.S. manufacturing. *Prod. Invent. Management* 28(2), 30–36.

Barret, J. (1988). IE's at CalComp are integrating JIT, TQC and employee involvement for 'World Class Manufacturing'. *Ind. Eng.* 20(9), 26–32.

Berry, B. (1987). Sagas of success: Making Just-in-Time work. *Automotive Industries* 167, 72–74.

Belt, B. (1987). MRP and Kanban – A possible synergy? *Prod. Invent. Management* 28(1), 71–80.

Bielecki, T., and P.R. Kumar (1988). Optimality of zero-inventory policies for unreliable manufacturing systems. *Oper. Res.* 36(4), 532–541.

Bitran, G., and L. Chang (1987). A mathematical programming approach to a deterministic Kanban system. *Management Sci.* 33(4), 427–441.

Black, J.T. (1983). Cellular manufacturing systems reduce setup time, make small lot production economical. *Ind. Eng.* 15(11), 36–48.

Bockerstette, J.A. (1988). Misconceptions abound concerning Just-in-Time operating philosophy. *Ind. Eng.* 20(9), 54–58.

Bose, H.J., and A. Rao (1988). Implementing JIT with MRP II creates hybrid manufacturing environment. *Ind. Eng.* 20(9), 49–53.

Burnham, J.M. (1987). Some conclusions about JIT manufacturing. *Prod. Invent. Management* 28(3), 7–11.

Buzacott, J.A. (1989). Queueing models of Kanban and MRP controlled production systems. *Engrg, Costs Prod. Econom.* 17, 3–20.

Clutterbuck, D. (1978). What makes Japanese car manufacturers so productive? *Internat. Management* 33(4), 17–20.

Cole, R.E. (1985). Target information for competitive performance. *Harv. Bus. Rev.* 3(3), 100–109.

Conant, R.G. (1988). JIT in a mail order operation reduces processing time from four days to four hours. *Ind. Eng.* 20(9), 34–37.

Conway, R., W. Maxwell, J.O. McClain and L.J. Thomas (1988). The role of work-in-process inventory in serial production lines. *Oper. Res.* 36(2), 229–241.

Crawford, K.M., J.H. Blackstone and J.F. Cox (1988). A study of JIT implementation and operating problems. *Internat. J. Prod. Res.* 26(9), 561–568.

Crosby, P.B. (1979). *Quality is Free*, McGraw-Hill, New York.

Crosby, P.B. (1984). The Just in Time manufacturing process: Control of quality and quantity. *Prod. Invent. Management* 25(4), 21–34.

Das, C., and S.K. Goyal (1989). A vendor's view of the JIT manufacturing system. *Internat. J. Oper. Prod. Management* 9(8), 106–111.

Deleersnyder, J.-L., T.J. Hodgson, H. Muller(-Malek) and P.J. O'Grady (1989). Kanban controlled pull system – An analytic approach. *Management Sci.* 35(9), 1079–1091.

Deming, W.E. (1982). *Quality, Productivity, and Competitive Position*, M.I.T. Center for Advanced Engineering Study.

Deming, W.E. (1986). *Out of the Crisis*, M.I.T. Center for Advanced Engineering Study.

DeVries, M.F., S.M. Harvey and V.A. Tipnes (1976). *Group Technology: An Overview and Bibliography*, Metcut Research Associates, Inc., Cincinnati, OH.

Dicasali, R.L. (1986). Job shops can use repetitive manufacturing methods to facilitate Just in Time production. *Ind. Eng.* 18(6), 48–52.

Ebrahimpour, M., and B.M. Fathi (1985). Dynamic simulation of a Kanban production inventory system. *Internat. J. Oper. Prod. Management* 5(1), 5–14.

Feather, J.G., and K.F. Cross (1988). Workflow analysis, Just in Time techniques simplify administrative process in paperwork operation. *Ind. Eng.* 20(1), 32–40.

Federgruen, A., and P. Zipkin (1984). A combined vehicle routing and inventory allocation problem. *Oper. Res.* 32(5), 1019–1037.

Finch, B.J. (1986). Japanese management techniques in small manufacturing companies: A strategy for implementation. *Prod. Invent. Management* 27(3), 30–38.
Finch, B.J., and J.F. Cox (1986). An examination of Just-in-Time management for the small manufacturer: With an illustration. *Internat. J. Prod. Res.* 24(2), 329–342.
Fine, C. (1986). Quality improvement and learning in productive systems. *Management Sci.* 32(10), 1301–1315.
Fine, C. (1988). A quality control model with learning effects. *Oper. Res.* 36(3), 437–444.
Fine, C., and D. Bridge (1986). Managing quality improvement, in: M. Sepehri (ed.), *Quest for Quality*, Industrial Engineering and Management Press, Atlanta, GA.
Fine, C.H., and E.L. Porteus (1989). Dynamic process improvement. *Oper. Res.* 37(4), 580–591.
Ford, H. (1924). *My Life and Work*, Heinemann, London.
Gershwin, S.B., and I.C. Schick (1983). Modeling and analysis of three-stage transfer lines with unreliable machines and finite buffers. *Oper. Res.* 31(2), 354–380.
Goldratt, E.M., and J. Cox (1986). *The Goal*, North River Press, Croton-on-Hudson, NY.
Giunipero, L.C., and E.F. Keiser, Jr. (1987). JIT purchasing in a non-manufacturing environment: A case study. *J. Purchasing Materials Management* 23(4), 19–25.
Giunipero, L.C., and C. O'Neal (1988). Obstacles to JIT procurement. *Indust. Marketing Management* 17, 35–41.
Groenevelt, C.J. (1990). Applying Japanese management tips to patient accounts. *Healthcare Financial Management* 44(4), 46–54.
Groenevelt, H., and U.S. Karmarkar (1988). A dynamic Kanban system case study. *Prod. Invent. Management* 29(2), 46–51.
Hall, R.W. (1981). *Driving the Productivity Machine: Production Planning and Control in Japan*, APICS, Falls Church, VA.
Hall, R.W. (1983). *Zero Inventories*, Dow, Jones-Irwin, Homewood, IL.
Hall, R.W. (1987). *Attaining Manufacturing Excellence*, Dow, Jones-Irwin, Homewood, IL.
Hax, A.C., and D. Candea (1984). *Production and Inventory Management*, Prentice-Hall, Englewood Cliffs, NJ.
Hay, E.J. (1987). Any machine set-up time can be reduced by 75%. *Ind. Eng.* 19(8), 62–67.
Hayes, R. (1981). Why Japanese factories work. *Harv. Bus. Rev.* 59(4), 56–66.
Heard, J.A. (1984). *JIT Accounting*, APICS 1984 Readings in Zero Inventory, APICS, Falls Church, VA, pp. 20–23.
Huang, P.Y., and B.L.W. Houck (1985). Cellular manufacturing: An overview and bibliography. *Prod. Invent. Management* 26(4), 83–93.
Huang, P.Y., L.R. Rees and B.W. Taylor III (1983). A simulation analysis of the Japanese Just-in-Time technique (with Kanbans) for a multiline, multistage production system. *Decision Sci.* 14(3), 326–344.
Im, J.H. (1989). Lessons from Japanese production management. *Prod. Invent. Management* 30(3), 25–29.
Inman, R., and S. Mehra (1990). The transferability of Just-in-Time concepts to American small businesses. *Interfaces* 20(2), 30–37.
Inman, R.I., and R.L. Bulfin (1991). Sequencing JIT mixed-model assembly lines. *Management Sci.* 37(7), 901–904.
Jordan, S. (1988). Analysis and approximation of a JIT production line. *Decision Sci.* 19(3), 672–681.
Juran, J.M. (1988). *Juran on Planning for Quality*, Free Press, New York.
Justis, R.T. (1981). America feasts on Japanese management delicacies. *Data Management* 19, 30–31, 43.
Karmarkar, U.S. (1986a). Kanban systems, Working Paper Nr. QM8612, William E. Simon Graduate School of Business Administration, University of Rochester, Rochester, NY.
Karmarkar, U.S. (1986). Integrating MRP with Kanban/pull systems, Working Paper Nr. QM8615, William E. Simon Graduate School of Business Administration, University of Rochester.

Karmarkar, U.S. (1987). Lot sizes, lead times and in-process inventories. *Management Sci.* 33(3), 409–418.

Karmarkar, U.S. (1989). Getting control of Just-in-Time. *Harv. Bus. Rev.* 67(5), 122–131.

Karmarkar, U.S. (1991). Push, pull and hybrid control schemes. *Tijdschrift voor Economie en Management* 26, 345–363.

Karmarkar, U.S., and S. Kekre (1989). Batching policy in Kanban systems. *J. Manuf. Syst.* 8, 317–328.

Karmarkar, U.S., S. Kekre and S. Kekre (1985). Lot sizing in multi-item, multi-machine job shops. *IIE Trans.* 17, 290–298.

Karmarkar, U., and I.M. Shivdasani (1986). Alternatives for batch manufacturing control, Working Paper Nr. QM8613, William E. Simon Graduate School of Business Administration, University of Rochester, Rochester, NY.

Kimura, O., and H. Terada (1981). Design and analysis of pull system, a method of multi-stage production control. *Internat. J. Prod. Res.* 19(3) 241–253.

Krajewski, L.J., B.E. King, L.P. Ritzman and D.S. Wong (1987). Kanban, MRP, and shaping the manufacturing environment. *Management Sci.* 33(1), 39–57.

Kubiak, W., and S. Sethi (1991). A note on 'Level schedules for mixed-model assembly lines in Just-in-Time production systems'. *Management Sci.* 37(1), 121–122.

Lee, L.C. (1987). Parametric appraisal of the JIT system. *Internat. J. Prod. Res.* 25(10), 1415–1429.

Lee, L.C., and K.H.W. Seah (1988). JIT and the effects of varying process and set up times. *Internat. J. Oper. Prod. Management* 8(1), 19–35.

Lundvall, D.M., and J.M. Juran (1974). Quality costs, in: J.M. Juran (ed.), *Quality Control Handbook, 3rd ed.*, McGraw-Hill, New York.

Macbeth, D.K., L.F. Baxter, N. Ferguson and G.C. Neil (1988). Buyer–vendor relationships with Just-in-Time: Lessons from U.S. multinationals. *Ind. Eng.* 20(9), 38–41.

McClain, J.O., and L.J. Thomas (1985). *Operations Management*, Prentice-Hall, Englewood Cliffs, NJ.

McManus, J. (1980). Some lessons from a decade of group technology. *Prod. Engineer* 59(11), 40–42.

Miltenburg, J. (1989). Level schedules for mixed-model assembly lines in Just-in-Time production systems. *Management Sci.* 35(2), 192–207.

Miltenburg, G.J., and G. Sinnamon (1989). Scheduling mixed-model multi-level Just-in-Time production systems. *Internat. J. Prod. Res.* 27(9), 1487–1509.

Mitra, D., and I. Mitrani (1990). Analysis of a Kanban discipline for cell coordination in production lines I. *Management Sci.* 36(12), 1548–1566.

Mitra, D., and I. Mitrani (1991). Analysis of a Kanban discipline for cell coordination in production lines II: Stochastic demands. *Oper. Res.* 39(5), 807–823.

Miyazaki, S., H. Ohta and N. Nishiyama (1988). The optimal operation planning of Kanban to minimize the total operation cost. *Internat. J. Prod. Res.* 26(10), 1605–1611.

Monden, Y. (1981a). What makes the Toyota production system really tick? *Ind. Eng.* 13(1), 36–46.

Monden, Y. (1981b). Adaptable Kanban system helps Toyota maintain Just-in-Time production. *Ind. Eng.* 13(5), 20–30.

Monden, Y. (1981c). Smoothed production lets Toyota adapt to demand changes and reduce inventory. *Ind. Eng.* 13(8), 42–51.

Monden, Y. (1981d). How Toyota shortened supply lot production time, waiting time, and conveyance time. *Ind. Eng.* 13(9), 22–30.

Monden, Y. (1983). *Toyota Production System: Practical Approach to Production Management*, Industrial Engineering and Management Press, Atlanta, GA.

Monden, Y. (1984). A simulation analysis of the Japanese Just-in-Time technique (with Kanbans) for a multiline, multistage production system; A comment. *Decision Sci.* 15(3), 445–447.

Monden, Y. (ed.) (1986). *Applying Just-In-Time: The American/Japanese Experience*, Industrial Engineering and Management Press, Atlanta, GA.

Moras, R.G., M.R. Jalali and R.A. Dudek (1991). A categorized survey of the JIT literature. *Prod. Planning and Control* 2(4), 322–334.
Moskowitz, H., and G.P. Wright (1979). *Operations Research Techniques for Management*, Prentice-Hall, Englewood Cliffs, NJ.
Moyes, J. (1988). The dangers of JIT. *Management Accounting* 66(2) 22–24.
Muramatsu, R., K. Ishii and K. Takahashi (1985). Some ways to increase flexibility in manufacturing systems. *Internat. J. Prod. Res.* 23(2), 691–703.
Nakane, J., and R.W. Hall (1983). Management specs for stockless production. *Harv. Bus.. Rev.* 61(3), 84–91.
Nellemann, D.O., and L.F. Smith (1982). Just-in-Time vs. Just-in-Case borrowed back from Japan. *Prod. Inv.* 23(2), 12–21.
Ohno, T. (1982). How the Toyota production system was created. *Japan. Econom. Stud.* 10(4), 83–101.
Ohno, T. (1988a). *Toyota Production System: Beyond Large-Scale Production*, Productivity Press, Cambridge, MA.
Ohno, T. (with S. Mito) (1988b). *Just-In-Time for Today and Tomorrow*, Productivity Press, Cambridge, MA.
Philipoom, P.R., L.P. Rees, B.W. Taylor III and P.Y. Huang (1987). An investigation of the factors influencing the number of Kanbans required in the implementation of the JIT technique with Kanbans. *Internat. J. Prod. Res.* 25(3), 457–472.
Porteus, E. (1985). Investing in reduced setups in the EOQ model. *Management Sci.* 31(8), 998–1010.
Porteus, E. (1986a). Optimal lot sizing, process quality improvement and setup cost reduction. *Oper. Res.* 34(1), 137–144.
Porteus, E. (1986b). Investing in new parameter values in the discounted EOQ model. *Naval. Res. Logist. Quart.* 33, 39–48.
Rees, L.P., P.R. Philipoom, R. Patrick, B.W. Taylor III and P.Y. Huang (1987). Dynamically adjusting the number of Kanbans in a Just-in-Time production system using estimated values of leadtime. *IIE Trans.* 19(2), 199–207.
Rice, J.W., and T. Yoshikawa (1982). A comparison of Kanban and MRP concepts for the control of repetitive manufacturing systems. *Prod. Invent. Management* 23(1), 1–13.
Robinson, M.A., and J.C. Timmerman (1987). How vendor analysis supports JIT manufacturing. *Management Accounting* 69(6), 20–24.
Ryan, T.P. (1988). *Statistical Methods for Quality Improvement*, Wiley, New York.
Savage-Moore, W. (1988). The evolution of a Just-in-Time environment at Northerm Telecom Inc.'s Customer Service Center. *Ind. Eng.* 20(9), 60–63.
Schonberger, R.J. (1982). *Japanese Manufacturing Techniques: Nine Hidden Lessons in Simplicity*, Free Press, New York.
Schonberger, R.J. (1983a). Applications of single-card and dual-card Kanban. *Interfaces* 13(4), 56–67.
Schonberger, R.J. (1983b). Plant layout becomes product-oriented with cellular, Just-in-Time production concepts. *Ind. Eng.* 15(11), 66–71.
Schonberger, R.J. (1983c). Selecting the right manufacturing inventory system: Western and Japanese approaches. *Prod. Invent. Management* 24(2), 33–44.
Schonberger, R.J. (1984). Just in Time production systems: Replacing complexity with simplicity in manufacturing management. *Ind. Eng.* 16(10), 52–63.
Schonberger, R.J. (1986). *World Class Manufacturing*, Free Press, New York.
Schonberger, R.J. (1990). *Building a Chain of Customers: Linking Business Functions to Create a World Class Company*, Free Press, New York.
Schonberger, R.J., and A. Ansari (1984). Just-in-Time purchasing can improve quality. *J. Purchasing Mat. Management* 20(1), 2–7.
Schonberger, R.J., and J.P. Gilbert (1983). Just-in-Time purchasing: A challenge for U.S. industry. *California Management Rev.* 26(1), 54–68.

Schonberger, R.J., and M.J. Schniederjans (1984). Reinventing inventory control. *Interfaces* 14(3), 76–83.

Schroer, B.J., J.T. Black and S.X. Zhang (1984). Microcomputer analyzes 2 card Kanban system for 'Just in Time' small batch production. *Ind. Eng.* 16(6), 54–65.

Seglund, R., and S. Ibarreche (1986). Just-in-Time: The accounting implications, in: Y. Monden (ed.), *Applying Just-in-Time: The American/Japanese Experience*, Industrial Engineering and Management Press, Atlanta, GA, pp. 118–120.

Seidmann, A. (1988). Regenerative pull (Kanban) production control policies. *European J. Oper. Res.* 35, 401–413.

Sepehri, M. (1985). How Kanban system is used in an American Toyota motor facility. *Ind. Eng.* 17(2), 51–56.

Sepehri, M. (1986). *Just-In-Time, Not Just in Japan*, The Library of American Production – APICS, Falls Church, VA.

Sepehri, M. (1987). Manufacturing revitalization at Harley Davidson Motor Co. *Ind. Eng.* 19(8), 86–93.

Sepehri, M. and R. Walleigh (1986). Quality and inventory control go hand in hand at Hewlett Packard's computer systems division. *Ind. Eng.* 18(2), 44–51.

Shen, H.N. (1987). Simulation of a two stage Kanban system using SLAM, Working Paper Nr. CMOM 87-02, William E. Simon Graduate School of Business Administration, University of Rochester, Rochester, NY.

Shingo, S. (1989). *A Study of the Toyota Production System from an Industrial Engineering Viewpoint, revised edition*, Productivity Press, Cambridge, MA.

Shingo, S. (1985). *Revolution in Manufacturing: The SMED System*, Productivity Press, Cambridge, MA.

Snead, C.S. (1988). *Group Technology: Foundation for Competitive Manufacturing*, Van Nostrand Reinhold, New York.

Sohal, A.S., A.Z. Keller and R.H. Fouad (1989). A review of literature relating to JIT. *Internat. J. Oper. Prod. Management* 9(3), 15–25.

Spearman, M.L., W.J. Hopp and D.L. Woodruff (1989). A hierarchical control architecture for constant work-in-process (CONWIP) production systems. *J. Manuf. Oper. Management* 2(3), 147–171.

Spearman, M.L., W.J. Hopp and D.L. Woodruff (1990). CONWIP: A pull alternative to Kanban. *Int. J. Prod. Res.* 28(5), 879–894.

Stalk, G. (1988). Time – The next source of competitive advantage. *Harv. Bus. Rev.* 66(4), 41–51.

Stowe, L. (1986). A remote Just-in-Time supplier success story, *Proceedings of the 1986 Annual Conference*, Association for Manufacturing Excellence.

Sugimori, Y., Kusunoki, F. Cho and S. Uchikawa (1977). Toyota production system and Kanban system: Materialization of Just-in-Time and Respect-for-Human system. *Internat. J. Prod. Res.* 15(6), 553–564.

Suresh, N.C., and J.R. Meredith (1985). Achieving factory automation through group technology principles. *J. Oper. Management* 5(2), 151–167.

Suzaki, K. (1985). Work in process management: An illustrated guide to productivity improvement. *Prod. Invent. Management* 26(3), 101–110.

Tabe, T., R. Muramatsu and Y. Tanaka (1980). Analysis of production ordering quantities and inventory variations in a multi-stage production ordering system. *Internat. J. Prod. Res.* 18(2), 245–257.

Tapiero, C. (1987). Production learning and quality control. *IIE Trans.* 19(4), 362–370.

Tatikonda, M.V. (1988). Just-in-Time and modern manufacturing environments: Implications for cost accounting. *Prod. Invent. Management* 29(1), 1–5.

Wagner, H.M., and T. Whitin (1958). Dynamic version of the economic lot size model. *Management Sci.* 5, 89–96.

Walleigh, R., and M. Sepehri (1986). HP Division programs reduce cycle times, set stage for ongoing process improvements. *Ind. Eng.* 18(2), 44–51.

Welke, H.A., and J. Overbeeke (1988). Cellular manufacturing: A good technique for implementing Just-in-Time and total quality control. *Ind. Eng.* 20(11), 36–41.
Williams, J.R., and H.S. Tice (1984). A program for communicating Just-in-Time concepts to smaller manufacturing vendors, *Annual international Conference of the American production and inventory control society*, pp. 170–173.
Wilson, G.T. (1985). Kanban scheduling – Boon or bane? *Prod. Invent. Management* 26(3), 134–142.
Zangwill, W.I. (1987a). Eliminating inventory in a series facility production system. *Management Sci.* 33(9), 1150–1164.
Zangwill, W.I. (1987b). From EOQ towards ZI. *Management Sci.* 33(10), 1209–1223.
Zipkin, P.H. (1986). Models for design and control of stochastic, multi-item batch production systems. *Oper. Res.* 34, 91–104.
Zipkin, P.H. (1989). A Kanban-like production control system: Analysis of simple models, Research Working Paper Nr. 89-1, Columbia Business School, Columbia University, New York.
Zipkin, P.H. (1991). Does manufacturing need a JIT revolution? *Harv. Bus. Rev.* 69(1), 40–50.

S.C. Graves et al., Eds., *Handbooks in OR & MS, Vol. 4*

Chapter 13

Scientific Quality Management and Management Science

Peter J. Kolesar

The Deming Center for Quality Management, Graduate School of Business, Columbia University, New York, NY 10027, U.S.A.

1. Purpose and objections

This chapter deals with quality and quality management from the viewpoint of the management scientist. Our main focus is on the mathematical modelling and statistical research base of the scientific quality control movement. We introduce, survey and critique the technical literature in these areas and offer suggestions for fruitful future research directions. Although the primary emphasis of the chapter is on research we offer en route comments and suggestions on practice. This is an essay on research written from the perspective of a practitioner who has major concerns about the relationship between research on quality control and actual and future practice.

Our goal is to encourage more practically oriented research by management scientists on quality related problems and issues. The views of the author stem from personal experience implementing statistical quality control on the shop floor in several industries, as a researcher contributing to the technical literature, as a university teacher of statistical quality control and reliability, and most recently as a consultant to the senior management of some major U.S. firms on the design and implementation of total quality management efforts and as an examiner for the Malcolm Baldrige National Quality Award.

The chapter opens with a brief discussion of the re-emerging role of quality as a central feature in the competitive strategy of modern firms. We then survey and critique the research literature in three major areas of quality control. We close with some advice to those interested in practicing what is coming to be called 'Total Quality Management' or TQM.

2. The re-emerging strategic role of quality

We begin with the observation that quality has become a unifying theme of the business strategies of many firms in recent years. Companies as diverse as Xerox, Motorola, Ford, Corning Glass, Milliken, Proctor and Gamble,

ALCOA and American Express have, in the 1980s, adopted corporate visions with quality as the guiding strategic theme. In these companies, as in many others, the corporate quality visions and missions are not simply slogans that decorate the corporate newspaper or the walls of conference rooms. They have, in each of the firms listed above, been followed by concerted efforts to remake the systems, procedures, processes and even the culture by which these companies attack their internal and external quality problems and opportunities. Such quality thrusts have been backed by the investment of considerable time, energy and capital and are fundamentally different in magnitude and in kind from the localized and piecemeal roles that quality management played in corporate strategies in the 1960s or 70s.

Why this intensified emphasis on quality? Dominant among the several reasons, is that many such firms face competitors who have very successfully emphasized quality. One particular set of competitors, the Japanese, have demonstrated in industry after industry that they are ready, willing and able to supply superior quality – and at competitive prices. The German camera industry, the Swiss watch industry, and the U.S. consumer electronics and automobile industries, are but a few examples of the overwhelming penetration the Japanese are capable of. The nearly fatal losses suffered by legendary western names like RCA in color television, Omega in fine watches, Triumph and Harley-Davidson in motorcycles, Caterpillar in earth moving equipment, General Motors and Jaguar in automobiles, Kodak, Rollei and Leica in cameras and Xerox in copiers indicate that even the great quality leaders of yesteryear are very vulnerable. By 1984, in that most American of U.S. industries, automobiles, there was a $30 billion trade imbalance with Japan, despite a restrictive set of voluntary quotas on Japanese auto exports to the U.S. Where they once were confined to the low-cost subcompact niche of the market, the Japanese manufacturers' quality posture had, by the early 1980s, permitted them to charge premium prices and, as this is being written in 1991, they are implementing with apparent success a challenge to the German auto manufacturers in the luxury end of the market. Evidence of the international dimension of the challenge in the automobile industry is the very strong pressures within the European community to maintain extensive trade barriers against the Japanese for the rest of the century. Moreover, Japanese automobile and consumer electronics manufacturers are demonstrating in their North American manufacturing operations that they can achieve the same levels of quality and productivity far from home. The most startling example is the case of NUMMI, a joint Toyota-General Motors venture in which Toyota took over a closed GM plant in California and with few changes of technology transformed it from the worst to the best performer in the system. One is reminded of the refrain in the song from musical comedy *Annie Get Your Gun*: 'Anything we can do they can do better!' Faced with this challenge firms like Xerox, Corning, Motorola and Ford that compete head to head with powerful Japanese rivals have little choice but to respond to the quality challenge.

It would be a counterproductive oversimplification to assert that quality management is the sole force explaining this striking Japanese industrial success. It is, however, clear to most thorough observers that quality is central to any understanding of what has happened in Japan since 1950. See for example the books of Halberstam [1986], Jacobson & Hillkirk [1986], Schonberger [1982], Ableggen & Stalk [1986], Hayes & Wheelwright [1984], Clark & Fujimoto [1989] and Prestowitz [1988], which delineate a variety of factors – including quality – which contribute to Japanese success. In a cogent and prescient 1966 speech the American quality 'guru' Joseph Juran forecast quite accurately the Japanese quality strategy and its success and characterized the situation as a 'Quality Crisis for the West' [Juran, 1979]. It is our thesis that notwithstanding other forces at play, and without being simplistic or simple-minded about it, quality is a central factor and the importance of quality as a business strategy can only increase as firm after firm, east or west, whether industrial commodity supplier or producer of consumer goods, high or low technology, goods or services provider, etc. adopt the methods of modern quality management.

Quality is so central and is becoming more so due to four primary factors:

(1) Quality refocuses the firm back on the basic reason for its existence which is to serve and thereby satisfy or, as modern jargon puts it, 'delight' its customers. Too many western firms lost their customer focus during recent decades. Among the many explanations for this we must include the size and complexity of the megacorporation. With its tens of thousands of employees, thousands of individual products, hundreds of locations, perhaps millions of customers, it is not easy or natural to maintain intimate and ongoing relationships with customers. Worse, it was felt by many senior managers that quality could be delegated to the drones in the factory and that success is actually measured (only) by short run financial performance. Many financially oriented and trained managers rose to the top leadership of companies in which they had never personally experienced product creation or customer contact.

(2) Quality and productivity are positively correlated. Contrary to what many managers, economists, and engineers have thought, quality and costs are not always antagonistic since as quality increases productivity typically increases also. Why so? 'Less scrap, less rework' [Deming, 1986], 'It is not quality that costs, it is all the things you do because you don't have quality in the first place' [Crosby, 1979]. This is particularly true when we focus on those aspects of quality that relate to *conformance* to a particular design. Too many have thought of quality as the difference between a Cadillac and a Chevrolet rather than focusing on quality within the class 'Cadillac' or within the class 'Chevrolet'.

(3) The very affluence and bounty of modern life coupled with the provision of unparalleled levels of quality by suppliers of some products has made consumers ever more demanding across the board. The complexity of modern life is another factor: there are too many things – e.g., electric motors, in our lives to permit the old standards of quality or reliability.

(4) In a number of ways higher technology makes higher quality necessary.

The incredible pace of change of technology and its concomitant ever shorter product life cycles places a premium on designing quality into products and processes to start with. No firm today has the luxury of learning how to achieve quality the old fashioned way – by trial and error. Computerization and integration of production processes have also made higher quality possible and necessary. What technology makes possible today, it makes necessary tomorrow. The pace of modern production systems contributes to the urgency. When we make them so fast, we simply can't afford to make any bad. When we use just-in-time inventory policies, all incoming materials and components *have* to be correct all the time. Thus, as society becomes more demanding and processes become more interrelated, faster and highly automated, both the necessity and possibility of zero-defects quality levels are enhanced.

3. A brief history of scientific quality management

What is quality management? In particular what is its scientific, theoretical and methodological content and how does all this relate to what we know of as 'Management Science'? Our very encapsulated history of modern scientific quality management must begin at Bell Laboratories when in the mid-1920s the physicist Walter Shewhart was asked to study how variation in production processes caused quality problems and what could be done about it [Godfrey, 1986; Duncan, 1986]. This research was prompted by a variation in production processes so severe that specifications for components used in AT&T's first great U.S. national telephone network were not being met consistently. Shewhart was charged with examining the problem of quality control from a scientific viewpoint.

Some variation, thought Shewhart, seemed inherent in all physical processes, but what part of it is controllable? Perhaps, he reasoned, it was futile or even counterproductive to fight all variation. That part of manufacturing variation due to minor differences in raw material properties or dimensions, small eccentricities of bearings, modest fluctuations in voltages and so forth, Shewhart called *common cause variation*. With a given production process or fixed product design he reasoned that little could be done to reduce this category of inherent variation save for a fundamental re-design or re-engineering. On the other hand, Shewhart postulated that some fraction of the variation experienced in manufacturing was perhaps manageable, indeed extraneous to the process itself. It was his thesis that special cause variation added unnecessarily and uneconomically to production costs and to quality problems. Indeed, all too often on top of what he had termed common cause variation there was, Shewhart found, another substantial, uneconomic, and often readily detectable and correctable component of variation due to special or *assignable causes* such as distinctly different operator behaviors one from another, substantial lot to lot quality variations in incoming materials, performance differences between apparently identical machines, etc. Shewhart characterized processes that, although fluctuating in the quality of their outputs, exhibited only common cause variation as being 'in statistical control'. His agenda, simply put, was to improve quality and productivity by first bringing such processes into statistical control, and once they were there keep them in control. To achieve this would require diagnosis of the state of the process, identification of assignable causes of variation, elimination of the causes, and finally ongoing monitoring of the process to avoid regression to the out of control state. To these ends he invented a set of simple tools that he called 'statistical control charts'. This line of research, which Shewhart began in 1924, reached a very full development and elucidation in his seminal and remarkable 1931 book, *Economic Control of Quality of Manufactured Product*. It is not an exaggeration to say that nearly 60 years later most practitioners doing statistical process control still apply Shewhart's ideas and tools essentially off-the-shelf as he set them out in 1931.

The philosophical and scientific foundations of Shewhart's thinking about quality, first captured in his 1931 classic, were further developed in an influential 1939 monograph that was edited very actively and influenced heavily by W. Edwards Deming [Shewhart, 1939]. In this work Shewhart (and Deming) fully express a paradigm of production management as a scientific problem. They relate the classical scientific process of hypothesis, experiment and test-of-hypothesis to the production management sequence of product and process specification, production and inspection. Moreover, Deming and Shewhart saw both the scientific and production management processes as never-ending cycles. Although in these pre-cybernetic days they did not explicitly use the word *feedback*, the concept permeates their writing and thinking, and the tools they proposed. Indeed, in this 1939 monograph Shewhart explicitly and powerfully captures these ideas in a diagram that later became known as the Deming cycle and that would prove to have a profound impact on management practices throughout Japan (Figure 3.1) [Imai, 1986; Ishikawa, 1985; Deming, 1986].

Thus, in one bold conceptual stroke the management of quality acquired a scientific and statistical foundation. Shewhart had identified and succinctly defined a central quality management problem, formulated a mathematical model of it and created a tool for its solution. We find in his work, in effect, a formulation and implementation of management science in the area of quality that predates by some 20 years the creation of the field of management science as we know it. Starting in the 1950s and continuing to the present day, a substantial theoretical literature was produced on this Shewhartian theme of statistical process control, much of it done by management scientists. It is our view, to be elaborated on later, that this stream of post-Shewhart work, these refinements and elaborations of his ideas, has had almost no impact on practice.

Quite simultaneously with Shewhart's process control work other researchers at Bell Laboratories, most notably Harold Dodge and Harry Romig began to put the problem of product quality inspection on a sound statistical basis

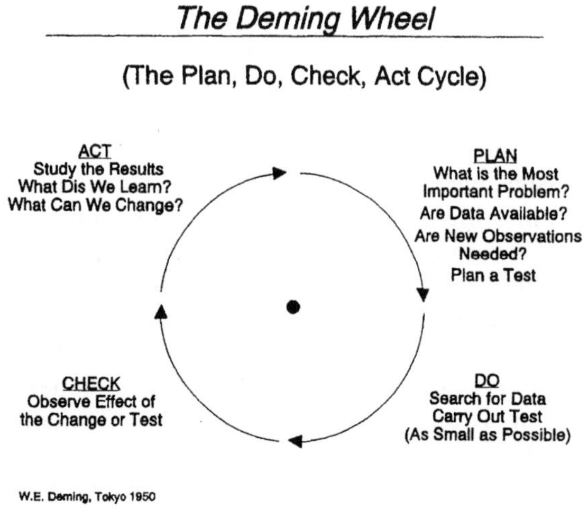

Fig. 3.1. The Deming/Shewhart cycle.

[Dodge & Romig, 1929, 1959]. Here the issues are fundamentally different from those treated by Shewhart's statistical process control methods. Whereas Shewhart wanted to control and improve the production process itself, Dodge and Romig sought to identify efficient procedures for deciding whether an already produced 'lot', perhaps containing some individual items that did not conform to specification was still in the aggregate, acceptable to the customer. The Shewhartian control chart was designed to be used in real time process monitoring by production managers and engineers on the production site. On the other hand, the Dodge and Romig sampling plans were to be used typically many miles or days away from the actual production site, when a customer needed to decide on a mass basis if the already made items were acceptable in the aggregate. Dodge and Romig's customer was typically the next production stage or another plant, warehouse, etc. inside the AT&T production or distribution system. They asked the question: 'What is the smallest amount of evidence needed in order to make a rational decision about whether or not to use this lot of goods?' The essence of their answer was to use the framework of statistical test of hypothesis as developed by Neyman & Pearson [1933] and Fisher [1925]. The Dodge and Romig approach was to balance the classical type I and type II errors which measure the consequences to the producer and consumer of acting erroneously on the lot, with the costs of inspection. This seminal approach led to institutionalization of statistical quality sampling plans of great diversity. For the initial paper see Dodge & Romig [1929]. (We give other references in a later section.) Many variations followed and statistical sampling plans have gained frequent use by industry and governments, world-wide. Theoreticians modified and further refined the Dodge–Romig approach and development of new techniques and implementation of existing ones surged during World War II. On the theoretical side the work of the Statistical Research Group at Columbia University, sponsored by the U.S. War Department was particularly fruitful – among its theoretical products was the concept and first applications of sequential sampling methods [Wallis, 1980; Wald, 1947]. It is an interesting sidelight to note that sequential analysis was classified as a U.S. military secret until after the war. An influential outgrowth of this work was the world famous military standard sampling plans including the bellwether MIL STD 105D that is much in use to this day. See Duncan [1986] and Schilling [1982].

While research and implementation of statistical acceptance sampling plans continue to the present, the reputation and influence of the statistical sampling side of quality management has been seriously diminished by the allegation – perhaps most forcefully expressed by Deming – that this work, in which he once participated [Deming, 1950], is on the whole a terrible blunder, an error of the third kind for it solves the wrong problem [Deming, 1986]! In sum, the modern (read here Japanese) view is: Don't try to efficiently sort out the good from the bad, thereby at best eking out marginal gains while at worst implicitly condoning poor quality, rather use your scientific, statistical and managerial tools to improve the process and product itself: prevent, don't correct. The old AT&T motto is to be made operative: *Do it right the first time*. This is a very substantial difference in philosophy and in approach and the controversy surrounding it is perhaps relevant to many management scientists for as we look at other parts of our literature, it appears that we too have sometimes worked on the wrong problems. In a plenary address to a TIMS 1984 International Meeting in Australia, Deming himself used the imagery that we 'fiddle while Rome burns'.

During World War II the U.S. military sponsored a substantial statistical quality control training effort that was very much influenced by and partially staffed with workers from the Quality Assurance Department at Bell Labs, the home of Shewhart, Dodge and Romig [see Duncan, 1986]. Some locally successful implementations resulted, but there is some uncertainty and controversy about the actual impact . . . the legendary grand wartime successes of statistical quality control may be more myth than fact. A key participant and architect of this training effort was Deming who, after the war, finding no domestic audience took his learning to Japan [Deming, 1951; Mann, 1986] where he had been preceded by trainers from Bell Labs whose message was similar [Hopper, 1982, 1985; Kobayashi, 1986].

An important post-war outgrowth of the statistical quality control movement was an important research effort on the mathematical and statistical foundations of electronic system reliability [AGREE, 1957; Zelen, 1963]. Reliability can be viewed as the study of how performance (quality) changes over the life of the product. Since much reliability theory focuses on length of useful life and related statistical characteristics this research endeavor has many commonalities with aspects of actuarial and biological statistics. Reliability is an important area of both theoretical and practical work and deserves considerable attention, but it would take us too far afield to treat it here. There is a heavy management science/operations research flavor to much of this work. For basic references see Barlow & Proschan [1965, 1975], Mann, Schafer & Singpurwalla [1974].

An additional stream of research and application of statistical and scientific tools for quality management that must be briefly mentioned here, even though it falls into a methodological area not often seen as the province of management scientists, is the study of statistically planned experimentation for product and process improvement. The basic research on statistical design of experiments also began in the 1930s with British researchers playing the seminal role. The enormously influential work on experimental design and the analysis of variance led by R.A. Fisher and other British statisticians was originally motivated by problems in agricultural experimentation, but their methods were soon to be applied in British industry. The work of W. Gosset (aka Student) at the Guinness Brewery, of H.C. Tippett in the textile industry and O.L. Davies and others at Imperial Chemical Industries on the application of formal statistical experimental design techniques for process improvement proved path breaking and influential on both sides of the Atlantic [see Fisher, 1935; Davies, 1956, Tippett, 1950]. But, except for an enduring stream of applications in process industries or particular applications within R&D labs, these powerful experimental design techniques were largely ignored by the rest of western industry, until propelled to reconsider them by numerous examples of their successful use and extension by the Japanese in the 1980s. It should be noted that a major advance in experimental design methods for the early screening stages of a study that would eventually prove to be uncommonly influential in practice was the work of two British ORMS workers, Plackett & Burman [1946]. In the 1980s variants on these methods were being heavily 'marketed' in Japan and in North America by the Japanese statistician Taguchi [1983, 1987] whose ideas we will discuss later on.

Thus, we have a brief history of scientific statistical quality management up to about 1950. In summary, the key aspects were:

(1) A recognition that variability is itself a key aspect of, indeed frequently is a root cause of quality problems, and that probabilistic and statistical tools must be used in managing for improved quality.

(2) The recognition by leading researchers, if not by practitioners, that the problem of quality management can be approached properly by making close parallels to the scientific method itself.

(3) The creation of effective models and methods for reducing and controlling variation in production processes through statistical process control charts and related tools.

(4) The creation of a large body of theory and practical methods for sampling inspection of products.

(5) The occasional borrowing of statistical experimental design techniques for application in quality and productivity improvement efforts.

The stage was set for next advances in quality management.

4. 1950 and beyond: Total quality management

Three Americans, W. Edwards Deming, Joseph Juran and Armand Feigenbaum, played crucial roles in extending the scope and impact of quality management beyond simple mechanistic and localized applications on the factor floor of the tools just discussed. The plain fact is that up till 1950 there was more bark than bite to the scientific quality management movement. Deming, profiting from the highly visible and well thought of experiences of U.S. industry with statistical quality control during World War II, brought together a set of remarkable insights in his now legendary 1950 Tokyo lectures on quality [Deming, 1951]. Given to some 50 leading Japanese industrialists, Deming set the stage for the next 40 years of quality progress in Japan by emphasizing, in addition to some rather standard Shewhart-like messages on statistical control and control charts, that:

(1) Quality would be the basis of future international industrial competition. It could be the key competitive advantage of Japanese industry if only they would effectively employ the methods of statistical quality control he was about to teach them. He predicted significant improvements in their world competitive position within five years. The Japanese, he would later remark, proved him wrong. Within only 2 years substantial results were obtained.

(2) Quality and productivity improvements go hand-in-hand. His own simple proof: higher quality equals less scrap and rework.

(3) To effectively manage for quality, quality must become everyone's job and it therefore is a senior management responsibility. Deming had seen that a crucial impediment to the success of the American efforts on quality during World War II was the lack of involvement of senior management. This recommendation which might today appear a triviality or obvious was a substantial break in the tradition for the 1950s quality was treated by U.S. management as a problem to be handed down to the folks in the trenches, to the quality technicians and production workers. It was in these 1950 Tokyo lectures that Deming relentlessly employed his flow chart view of the enterprise to impress on senior management its role as the architect of the system (social and technological) in which the product, and hence its quality is created. See Figure 4.1.

(4) To improve quality efficiently, quality problems had to be approached more effectively than by the trial and error methods of the past. Deming advocated a modified version the scientific method for quality problem solving that he called the Shewhart or Plan-Do-Check-Act Cycle. See Figure 3.1. The Japanese would soon call it the Deming wheel and apply it more broadly than even Deming might have hoped for. See Ishikawa [1986], Imai [1986], and Mizuno [1988]. By 1967 for example, employing the P-D-C-A cycle on *all* significant managerial problems was made corporate policy by the Toyota Motor Company's board of directors. Today one can hardly visit any Japanese company that is renowned for total quality management without seeing concrete evidence of the use of a Deming-like problem solving approach [Toyota

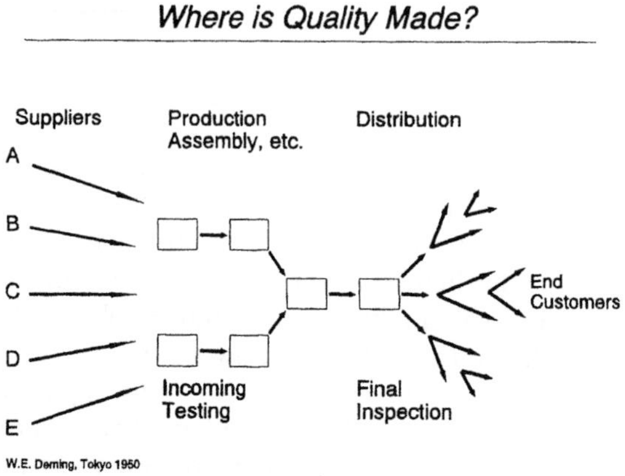

Fig. 4.1. The Deming process flow view of the enterprise.

Motor Corporation, 1988]. (We cannot help noting that, as of 1986, not a single American textbook on quality even mentioned this concept.)

Deming's impact in Japan was immediate. Successful applications of basic statistical methods including Shewhart control charts were reported within a year and the now world famous Deming Prize for quality was first awarded by the Union of Japanese Scientists and Engineers in 1952. In 1954 Deming was followed to Japan by Joseph Juran, who just three years earlier had produced the first edition of the now classic *The Quality Control Handbook* [Juran, 1951]. Juran had been a member of the 1926 AT&T team that undertook the initial implementation of many of statistical quality control tools developed by Shewhart, and Dodge and Romig at the Western Electric Hawthorne Works in Chicago. Juran's Japanese lectures focused on the managerial aspects of implementing quality. He did much to organize and systematize an approach to make quality happen – to turn sound ideas into sound practice and to make the practice consistent throughout the organization. Juran also offered a diagrammatic view of the role of quality in the organization through his 'spiral of quality progress' which emphasizes the role of quality at each stage of the cycle of product development – from market research through design, process development and engineering to production inspection, distribution (logistics) to customers, and back to market research (see Figure 4.2). It is possible to view the 'Juran spiral' as another elaboration and refinement of Shewhart's original cycle of 'design it, make it, sell it' [Shewhart, 1939]. As product life cycles shorten and the pace of product and process competition increases the urgency of managing for quality in the design and development phases becomes ever more crucial. Both Deming and Juran focused Japanese management's attention on high leverage points in the 'quality system' – at the upstream activities of design and purchasing and on the fundamental management responsibilities of creating and monitoring the quality management system itself. Japanese

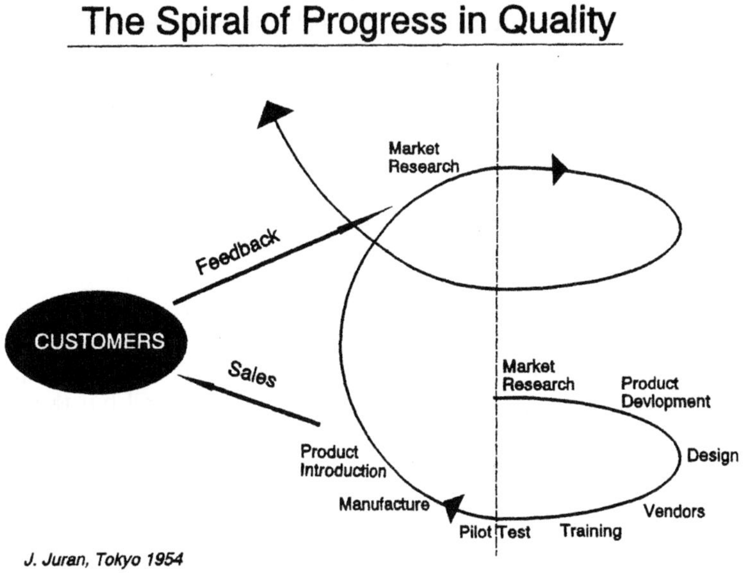

Fig. 4.2. Juran's spiral of progress in quality.

commentators freely acknowledge that both Deming and Juran were very influential and helpful.

The third American who greatly influenced Japanese thinking was Armand Feigenbaum who as corporate quality control director at General Electric had developed the concept of 'total quality control'. This is a somewhat ill-chosen phrase, for he did not mean control, rather he extended the purview of quality management activities from a simple focus on quality control on the shop floor or in the quality control department to an integration of product quality development, quality assurance and quality improvement through a systematic linking of marketing, engineering, production and service functions, Feigenbaum [1961]. Not many U.S. firms acted on this unifying vision, but across the Pacific it did not take long for the Japanese to get the message and to implement and develop Feigenbaum's ideas more fully. Indeed, the thinking of Deming, Juran and Feigenbaum, while not identical, is similar and, generally, complementary. The Japanese borrowed from all and added their own twists. By the 1980s in Japan TQC was being spoken of as standing for *total quality creation* and it described a broad range of activities, tools and attitudes used in every part of the organization [Kano, 1987]. It focused on creating quality in all activities, both goods and services – internal as well as external. Indeed, its scope became so broad that in many Japanese firms it is nearly impossible to differentiate those activities that are quality management from the rest of what management does. The ultimate development has been called CWQC – company-wide quality control. See Mizuno [1988], Imai [1986], and Ishikawa [1985]. Similar agendas are now emerging in the West, particularly in the

United States. The framework of the U.S. Malcolm Baldrige National Quality Award is very much TQC influenced [NIST, 1991; De Carlo & Sterett, 1990].

5. Management science and statistical process control

The pioneering work of Shewhart cited earlier had given heuristic answers to a number of important practical questions. For better or worse, the rules of thumb he proposed in the 1930s are, as mentioned earlier, still being implemented today with little if any modification. This is so despite a steady stream of research that attempts to address and resolve a number of technical questions that Shewhart left open. The survey papers of Gibra [1975], Montgomery [1980] and Vance [1983] do a fine job of covering all but the latest of this long stream of literature. We shall not attempt to replicate such a detailed review here – particularly since it is our judgement that the vast majority of this work sheds little light on actual problems and leads to few useful advances in either theory or practice.

Here in a nutshell is the problem that Shewhart proposed and how he 'solved' it. Consider a process whose outputs may be enumerated in time order of production and whose quality can be measured and forms a sequence of random variables (a stochastic process) X_t, $t = 1, 2, \ldots$. We suppose that there is a natural, and for the sake of argument, desirable or at least acceptable state of the physical production system under which the X_t form a sequence of independent identically distributed random variables with some (typically unknown) distribution function, $F_0(x)$. When the system is in this state, 0, it is said to be in 'statistical control' and the quality fluctuations or variations described by the distribution $F_0(x)$ are thought to be beyond our understanding or influence. These variations are termed the results of a system of 'common chance causes' per Shewhart [1931, 1939]. We presume that when the process is in this desirable state no special actions are required on management's part, indeed there is the strong presumption that any attempted special action – typically termed tinkering or tampering with the system – will actually cause its performance to deteriorate. For provocative distributions on this point see Deming [1986] and Walton [1986].

However, the process does not stay in this natural state forever. Some combination of forces, be it a change in a particular causal variable, 'Murphy's Law', the third law of thermodynamics, or the like, causes the system to deteriorate, say at a particular time epoch τ, to another state whose output X_t has distribution $F_1(t)$, $t = \tau, \tau + 1, \ldots$. The distribution $F_1(x)$ is different from and inferior to $F_0(x)$ in quality. The underlying managerial and inferential dilemma is that the factors causing the change are not themselves observable, so whoever manages the process must *infer* whether a process change has occurred by examining only the output variables, X_t. In sum, we see the result, not the cause. And we see only through the dark glass of variation which clouds our ability to properly diagnose what is happening – to separate signal from noise. There are many possible scenarios for the future evolution of the process. The simplest of these is that at time t the process having shifted to this particular unsatisfactory distribution of output, $F_1(x)$ will stay there forevermore unless we diagnose the shift and take appropriate corrective action. The simplicity of this model is particularly attractive to researchers and has received most of the attention in the literature. More realistic, in the author's experience, are actual systems whose output stochastic processes become non-stationary in quite complex ways that are frustratingly hard to describe mathematically. For example, it is not infrequent to experience situations in which the process feeds back on itself and thus becomes highly autocorrelated, or situations in which the process due to external environmental influences cycles slowly through a series of very different states, situations in which the process continually and steadily deteriorates further and further, etc. These phrases describe control problems that are near to impossible to model, let alone solve – exactly. Of course, real world managers and engineers must grope with such problems or 'messes' all the time, regardless of how intractable they are mathematically. They settle for any reasonable solution such as those obtained by following the traditional Shewhart suggestions. Optimality is not a dominant concern to them. A rudimentary view of other possible sample paths for such processes and a broad view of the how to implement Shewhart's tools may be found in the Western Electric *Statistical Quality Control Handbook* [Small, 1956].

So, returning to the main line of our discussion, the essential problem is that the process manager observes a subsequence of the X_t and from the observed sequence must diagnose whether the system is in state 0, has moved to a worse state, or is moving among various less desirable states. If the latter is judged to be the case, the manager is responsible to act to bring the system back to state 0. In the parlance of statistical quality control this is called removing the 'assignable' cause – the reason for the change of state. It is presumed that the change is detectable and correctable. In practice this is quite an heroic assumption and corrective action is itself no small task. Managers and engineers sorely need help here, for it is usually much easier to tell when a process has gone out of control than to either identify the cause or to do something to correct it.

Now for Shewhart's solution to the diagnosis problem. He proposed collecting data on the variable X_t in subsets of size n in such a fashion that homogeneity of conditions within each subset was maximal while there was simultaneously ample opportunity for assignable cause variation to appear via between-subset inhomogeneity. The disparity of variance between and within subsets would be used to reveal whether the system state had shifted from state 0. A modern technique for doing this would be through an analysis of variance or components of variance analysis – techniques not available in 1924. For Shewhart the behavior of each subgroup was summarized by two statistics: the subgroup mean $\bar{x}$ and the subgroup range R. Supposing that at the outset of the process control effort little would be known in exactitude about process behavior or its statistical parameters, Shewhart proposed using the averages of a set of N subgroup means and N subgroup ranges to 'define' hypothetical or tentative system parameters describing state 0. These parameters, called the grand mean, $\bar{\bar{X}}$ and the average range $\bar{R}$, he viewed as estimates of the central tendency and variation of the process, respectively. To these he added the now traditional 3 sigma control limits for both the subgroup averages and ranges, to wit $\bar{\bar{X}} \pm 3\sigma_{\bar{x}}$ and $\bar{R} \pm 3\sigma_R$ where both $\sigma_{\bar{x}}$ and σ_R were estimated from $\bar{R}$ under the supposition that the process was in control and that $F_0(x)$ was normal [Duncan, 1986]. Shewhart proposed a simple diagnostic rule: as long as successive group means and ranges fall within the 3 sigma control limits of $\bar{\bar{X}}$ and $\bar{R}$, do nothing. That is, act as if state 0 pertains. Indeed, accept $\bar{\bar{X}}$ and $\bar{R}$ as reasonable estimates of the process parameters. When a point falls outside of the control limits on either the $\bar{X}$ or R chart, act as if the process has deviated from state 0. There are two implications – one operational and one statistical. The operator, manager or engineer must seek out the assignable cause and act on the process to return it to state 0. Second, statistically we cannot be confident of our parameter estimates since it appears that the process is not stationary. Shewhart would recommend discarding the offending data and reestimating $\bar{\bar{X}}$ and $\bar{R}$.

Shewhart and his followers suggested rules of thumb for implementing his procedures. Among his suggestions were: The control limits should always be at 3 sigma from the center on both $\bar{X}$ and R charts, the group sizes should be 4 to 6, one subgroup should be sampled each hour, usually consisting of items essentially adjacent in order of production, and at least $N = 20$ subgroups should be used to estimate $\bar{\bar{X}}$ and R. Other writers reinforced and amplified upon these heuristics. See Small [1956], Ishikawa [1976], and Juran [1988]. It is not inaccurate to observe that the control chart when employed in this fashion is, in effect, an heuristical ongoing test of the hypothesis that the sequence X_t, $t = 1, 2, \ldots$, is in fact i.i.d., and thus it is rough and ready analysis of variance.

Girschick & Rubin [1952] were the first to see the problem as requiring optimization from a cost minimization framework, but it was not until Duncan's work [1956] that a serious optimization version of the problem was first solved – at least to a close approximation. In his remarkable and seminal work Duncan analyzed the following model. When in the control (desired) state, the random variable X_t is normally distributed with mean μ_0 and variance σ_0^2. It stays in state 0 for an exponentially distributed length of time whose mean duration is $1/\lambda$. Then the process jumps to the undesirable state, 1, where it has mean $\mu_1 = \mu_0 \pm \Delta\sigma_0$ and variance $\sigma_1^2 = \sigma_0^2$. Here $\Delta > 0$ is a measure of how much worse or off-target the process has gotten. The process remains in this state until the shift is detected and corrected. Duncan wishes to determine the sampling interval, sample size, and the control limits (in multiples of σ_0) which minimize the long run average cost per unit time. He includes a penalty cost rate for time spent in the undesirable state, the cost of testing and sampling, the consequences of a false diagnosis of a process shift when one has not really occurred, and a cost of correcting the out of control condition when it is at last detected. He assumes all parameters are known and uses a renewal theory approach and a numerical approximation to develop optimal solutions. Over the years since 1956 a large number of other authors have worked variations on Duncan's theme. See Montgomery [1980], Gibra [1975], and Vance [1983] for an extensive set of references. (A clear exposition of the theme of optimization of control chart design is contained in Chapter 10 of the basic textbook of Montgomery [1991], the only text to treat the issue at all.) Qualitatively, this body of research indicates that the optimal sample size depends strongly on the magnitude of the shift to be detected, that optimal sampling frequency depends strongly on the cost penalty rate in the undesirable state and on the expected length of time spent in the desirable state before a shift occurs, and that the control limits depend strongly on the cost of sampling and on the costs of finding and correcting process shifts as well as on the penalty for falsely diagnosing a process shift. For some specifics see Montgomery [1991].

Lorenzen & Vance [1986] unified a good deal of this work. Such research continues to the present with the paper of Tagaras & Lee [1988] being typically sound work in the long stream of variations on the theme of Duncan. They build on the basic Duncan model to analyze situations in which there are a multiplicity of possible process shifts. They assume three possibilities: in control with parameters μ_0, σ_0^2 as above, out of control with parameters $\mu_0 \pm \Delta_1\sigma_0$, σ_0^2, and out of control with parameters $\mu_0 \pm \Delta_2\sigma_0$, σ_0^2. The occurrence times of the two types of process shifts are exponential random variable with parameters λ_1 and λ_2, respectively. They optimize over a reasonable but simplified set of control chart designs.

An alternative stream of research looked at related problems with the complication that the process states evolve according to a Markov chain, but with the simplification there is generally no error in detecting what the state actually is. Here the state space is also more complex, there being many bad states with movements away from state 0 typically being monotonically worse. The dilemma is to achieve a balance between the costs and frequency of resetting the process to state 0 and the costs of being in a less desirable state. These models can often be discussed somewhat interchangeably as optimal control, or optimal maintenance, or optimal replacement problems. The literature is large. (See Pierskalla & Voelker [1976] and Monahan [1982] for surveys.) For typical research see Derman [1963], Kolesar [1966], Ross [1971] and Tijms & Van der Schonten [1984]. The results of these analyses show that only under very orderly assumptions about process parameters and dynamics are the optimal strategies of simple structure. Fine [1986, 1988] strains to put the maintenance literature into a continuous learning scenario and gets similar mathematical structural results but no managerial engineering insights.

Sadly enough, this research has had essentially zero impact on practice for both good and bad reasons. Let us consider why.

(1) First, is the entrenchment of the Shewhart methods by reasons of their simplicity, robustness and proven effectiveness in actual applications. The Shewhart methods can be implemented manually, can be taught to workers

with the most modest educational backgrounds, require no prior knowledge of process parameters, and have a record of 'working' in an enormous variety of industries and applications. Moreover, the formal Shewhart charts and rules are easily modified in practice by heuristics that make them still more effective. One would have to forcefully demonstrate considerable advantage to replace them with something that is in fact more complex and is seen by practitioners as being incomprehensible.

(2) Second, is the inaccessibility of the new models to the practitioner community. None of the theoreticians who develop these methods has extended serious efforts to proselytize their techniques. The results remain tucked away in journals that practitioners do not read and are expressed in language that is not understood. With the sole exception of Duncan's [1986] and Montgomery's [1991] statistical quality control texts, none of the many SPC texts or treatises even mention these results.

(3) The alternative methods are optimal only for very carefully specified scenarios that are not likely to describe reality. In addition, their use requires knowledge of the parameters of both the 'in' and 'out-of-control' states that is not likely to be available to practitioners – certainly not at start-up of SPC activities when methods get set.

(4) To a considerable extent the new models make an error of the third kind: they solve the wrong problem. There are several levels of meaning latent in this remark. First, the motivating problems are invariably put in a renewal theory setting: the process jumps from one known state to another, stays there until the change is detected and then is reset. The process then continues afresh from the reset point. There are few interesting real world processes amenable to applications of such models and most of those usually use monitoring and detection methods that are more subtle than the simple Shewhart rules that these new optimal control chart models compete with. Second, this very type of scenario almost denies the possibility for improvement or root cause removal. The process is restarted afresh and nothing is learned. These models are thus at variance with the modern TQM philosophy of continuous improvement. Third, among the most important applications of Shewhart control chart methods are situations where diagnosis is of the essence. The process is in a rather completely uncontrolled state and the charts are used together with other tools to diagnose and eliminate the problems over an extended period of time and with much effort. For some insight on how control charts are used in the diagnostic effort see the books of Ott [1975] and Wheeler & Chambers [1986]. A recent approach to creating robust methods but still in a Shewhart theme through 'trimmed estimators' is the work of Rocke [1989].

(5) Somewhat related to the above points is the fact that the Shewhart control chart is a multi-purpose tool. This is little understood even by practitioners who tend to blur the vital distinctions between the several uses of control charts as:

(a) A substitute for an ANOVA model that generates a robust estimate of pure (common cause) randomness. Again, see Rocke [1989] and its predecessors which do work along these lines.

(b) A diagnostic tool for the early stages of bringing processes into some semblance of control.

(c) A monitoring device for processes that have already been brought into control but now need to be kept there. (The proposed models deal exclusively with very special cases of this problem.)

(6) The few suggestions emanating from the models in some of the literature are not likely to be persuasive or inspiring to practicing managers or engineers. Consider an example cited in the otherwise excellent paper of Lorenzen & Vance [1986] to illustrate the use and value of their model and algorithm: a foundry produces 84 castings per hour and the quality issue is the rate of cooling of the castings. (Although details are not given in the paper we presume that the rate of cooling affects the propensity of the castings to crack or distort). It is explained in the paper that samples of molten metal are taken periodically and the cooling curve is recorded. It is not explained how but it is indicated that these curves are then characterized as conforming or not to the desired state. Such samples cost about $4 each and take five minutes to do. When the process is in control the defect rate is about 1%, whereas when the process is out of control it is about 11%. A defect costs about $100. Once in control, the process stays there an exponential amount of time – about 50 hours average, and it takes about 45 minutes and about $1000 to fix the out of control condition which, by the way, it is related in the paper says is due to a build up of the carbon-silicate content of the molten metal. The correction consists of flushing out the system. What control scheme should be used? Lorenzen and Vance state that their algorithm derives an optimal plan which takes a sample of 20 castings every 2.88 hours and uses 3.3 sigma control limits – which they say is equivalent to stopping the process if 2 or more of the twenty samples are defective. This recommendation appears to this writer, to be not workable – the 20 samples would take 100 minutes to carry out. The authors go on to make a case for their analysis by alleging that the great Japanese statistician Ishikawa would recommend a foolish procedure of taking a sample of size 250 every 8 hours using the traditional 3 sigma limits [Ishikawa, 1976]. One doubts that the ever practical Dr. Ishikawa would agree with either proposal – Lorenzen and Vance's own or their interpretation of him. The model proposed by Lorenzen and Vance seems to be physically unsound. In particular, it would be surprising if carbon-silicate build-up occurred according to a process even remotely connected to the Poisson. The word build-up is a giveaway that accumulation must be happening. Could accumulation be Poisson? One supposes this is possible but doubts it. More likely a time to failure distribution that has an increasing failure rate needs to be used. See Banerjee & Rahim [1988] for one such model.

(7) The analyses often over-simplify to the point of being simplistic the manner in which practitioners actually employ control charts. Specifically, most analyses presume that only a single chart such as an $\bar{X}$ chart is being employed.

In practice $\bar{X}$ charts are typically accompanied by R charts which aid greatly in the diagnosis. Indeed, some practitioners' advice is to never use an $\bar{X}$ chart without an R chart. It is recommended by this author that simple run charts also be used in parallel with $\bar{X}$ and R charts. Hunter [1986, 1990] has recommended that exponentially smoothed moving average charts might also be used in conjunction with $\bar{x}$ charts. Saniga [1989, 1991] does treat the $\bar{X}$ and R charts as a pair. Moreover, practitioners do not base their diagnoses only on points falling outside control limits but also on patterns among the most recent points plotted. When used in this more complex, but admittedly difficult to analyze fashion, control charts are considerably more powerful than is revealed in the theoretical papers. Champ & Woodall [1987] analyze performance of $\bar{X}$ charts using the Western Electric rules which are perhaps the most frequently employed supplementary procedures. Saniga [1991] has produced a computer program that, rather than optimizing, can evaluate type 1 and type 2 errors, etc., for joint $\bar{X}$, R charts under reasonably flexible conditions.

(8) In many applications of control charts on-line process control is the essence of the problem. For example, consider industries such as metals, paper and chemicals where on-line sensors measure key process variables in real-time, or where data is rapidly fed back from laboratories to be used to key adjustments of such process parameters as temperatures, pressures, additive flow rates, and the like. Such variables can be changed continuously over time – partially in response to the varying character of input materials or environmental conditions that may be out of control, that is nonstationary. This invites explicit feedback-control modelling which the classic SQC approach does not provide. Moreover as testing, data gathering and data analysis technologies improve it is increasingly possible to measure key variables on-line and in real-time, and on the entire stream of production. *Sampling* is of decreasing importance. The typical models reported in the SQC literature do not address these problems. (The author has recently visited a peanut butter plant in which every single one of the billions of roasted peanuts is automatically inspected for color and kicked out of the production line if appropriate.)

So, what is needed is a marriage between the Shewhart statistical process control paradigm and its management science derivatives, and the differential equations feed-back loop approach of the engineering process control theoretician. Some researchers are beginning to work on this interface. The papers of Hunter [1986], Montgomery & Friedman [1989], and Alwan & Roberts [1989] are indications of what is necessary to incorporate concepts of traditional statistical process control from Shewhart through Duncan and his successors with time series analysis in the spirit of Box & Jenkins [1976] or Kalman filtering with the classical proportional-integrative-differential control theory approach of process engineers. A paper of Lucas & Saccucci [1990] focuses on the simplest of ARIMA (Box–Jenkins) models, the exponentially weighted moving average chart, and compares it to cumulative sum chart methods. This paper plus the discussion that follows in the same issue of the *Technometrics* delineate the current state of the art. Spurrier & Thomas [1990] deal explicitly with detecting cycles by using periodograms. It is comforting that the recent literature is moving in practical directions. For some other relevant papers see Montgomery & Mastrangelo [1991], Collani [1987], Rocke [1989], Iglewicz & Hoaglin [1987], J.R. King [1989], Roth [1988], and Saniga [1991].

6. Management science and sampling inspection

In this section we consider the following dilemma. A supplier has shipped our firm a quantity of items which we shall call the 'lot', consisting of raw materials, components, or the like that are to be used in manufacturing our finished product. We are uncertain about the quality of the goods received, and consequently are also uncertain about whether or not they should be used as is. They now sit in our warehouse and we imagine three possible courses of action:

(1) Notwithstanding our concern and uncertainty we could pass the lot into the production system without further ado.

(2) We could subject the items in the lot to a 100% inspection, use those that are acceptable, and return, discard or rework as appropriate those that are defective.

(3) We could take a random sample of the items in the lot, subject this sample to inspection and on the basis of the quality of the sample make a decision about what to do with the rest of the lot – use it, discard it, do a 100% inspection, etc.

As alluded to earlier, there is a continuing and long history of mathematical/statistical study of this problem, the most important stream of which commenced in the late 1920s at Bell Laboratories with Dodge being the initiator and key investigator, Dodge [1928]. The majority of that body of research focuses attention on how to execute the third option effectively, that is, how to carry out sampling inspection. Indeed, there are a number of books exclusively devoted to this topic [see, for example, Dodge & Romig, 1959; Shilling, 1982, and Hald, 1981]. For some history see Duncan [1986], Wallis [1980], and Godfrey [1986].

It is remarkable that today, some forty years after this burst of wartime activity, which was acclaimed as having made vital contributions to the Allied War efforts, there is a decided movement away from sampling inspection. Indeed, it is clear that the current thrust of modern quality management is to push toward employing the first of the actions listed above – use the items without further ado, essentially relying on the supplier to assure proper quality. This is the essence of the thinking behind just-in-time (JIT) inventory strategies. The purchasing or consuming enterprise does not passively rely on the supplier, instead the burden is deliberately placed on the supplier to assure that the materials conform to requirements and that proper quantities arrive at the producer's facility immediate to their use. Indeed, in most cases the supplier is expected to provide 100% compliance or 'zero defects'. Moreover, the modern TQM purchaser helps the supplier meet these objectives. (Toyota, Ford, Motorola and Xerox are among the firms with noteworthy vendor certification and assistance programs. They educate and train their suppliers, audit their quality management efforts and processes and work with them to solve quality problems. They invite suppliers to participate in new product or process design.) Testing of incoming materials by the consuming organization is thought of as wasteful and redundant, and, worse, too late to be really helpful. In the stripped down operations of the best of today's plants there is neither the time nor the facility to do such testing, nor is there the space or time available to hold the materials while the checking is being carried out.

Notwithstanding the JIT philosophy – ideology, if you will – there are clearly situations that call for sampling inspections or for 100% testing such as when the consequences of using nonconforming materials are catastrophic or simply well out of proportion to the cost of testing. Moreover, if there is a high enough proportion of defectives in the typical shipment and no alternative supplier, one would naturally revert to a complete vetting of the shipment before use. But what of sampling inspection? Has it no role?

Two of Deming's famous '14 Points for Management' are specifically targeted to the relations between consuming and supplying enterprises:

Point 3. Cease dependence on inspection to achieve quality. Eliminate the need for inspection on a mass basis by building quality into the product in the first place.

Point 4. End the practice of awarding business on the basis of price tag. Instead, minimize total cost. Move toward a single supplier for any one item, on a long term relationship of loyalty and trust.

Thus, Deming's advice is to push toward long term high quality relationships between vendor and user with eliminating the need for incoming inspection as a long term goal. In the meanwhile, some testing or sampling may be necessary, but Deming indicates that these circumstances should be few and far between. In Chapter 15 of *Out of the Crisis*, [Deming, 1986] 'Plan for minimum average total cost for test of incoming materials and final product' he makes very forceful arguments that in most situations sampling inspection is not called for, and the consumer should decide on option (1) or (2) depending on a simple breakeven analysis. Deming gives a variety of problem formulations. The simplest, which captures the essence of the problem is as follows: Consider a single product which is to be used as a component of system we assemble. The product is supplied in lots of size n, and p denotes the average fraction defective (probability of a defective item) in the stream of such lots. Let k_1 be the cost to inspect one part, and let k_2 be the cost to dismantle, repair, reassemble or otherwise dispose of an assembly that fails because a defective part was used. The expected cost of not inspecting the incoming lot and instead passing it directly into production is npk_2, whereas the expected cost of doing a 100% inspection is nk_1. Clearly, the former cost increases with p until the costs are equal at the 'breakeven quality' p_0, defined by the equations

$$np_0k_2 = nk_1 , \qquad p_0 = k_1/k_2 .$$

Based on this model, Deming suggests that rules for achieving minimum total cost are as follows:

Case 1. If the worst lot received always has $p \leqslant k_1/k_2$ no inspection should be carried out. The parts are to be used as is.

Case 2. If the best lot received always has $p > k_1/k_2$ the lot should be subjected to 100% inspection prior to use.

Of course, the catch is that we typically do not know the value of p. If we did, these problems would be trivial, but it may be argued that frequently in practice the shipments are either very very good or very bad. Deming admits that if one is uncertain about whether Case 1 or Case 2 applies, sampling inspection may be necessary, particularly if the vendor's manufacturing process is not in statistical control. He cites the work of his student Orsini [1982] who developed heuristic sampling plans that appear to work reasonably in such situations of uncertainty or as she calls it, 'chaos'. Chapter 14 of Duncan's classic text [1986] on statistical quality control amplifies on the concept of breakeven quality and also refers to the writing of Hald [1981] on this subject.

To a generation of quality control workers brought up under the statistical sampling plan style of thinking, the Deming arguments for 'all or nothing inspection' are startling. Management scientists, on the other hand may be more receptive to these ideas since our own literature on stochastic optimization models is replete with examples in which 'all or nothing' or nonrandomized strategies are indeed optimal. A thorough investigation of conditions under which all or nothing acceptance sampling strategies are optimal is clearly called for. The paper by Lorentzen [1985] makes a beginning.

Before discussing what to do when sampling inspection *is* called for, we ask a sharp question that rocks our intuition about the effectiveness of sampling inspection. *Question*: can sampling inspection effectively sort out relatively good from relatively bad lots? Most practitioners would appear to think so, yet the answer is no, at least not if the process producing the lots is statistically stable, that is, 'in-control'. An answer to this question was first provided by Mood [1943] and is contained in Deming [1986] and Duncan [1986]. The argument goes as follows. Consider a population of M items p which are defective. From this population a *lot* of size N is drawn at random, and then from this lot a further *sample* of size n is drawn at random. (All sampling is done without replacement.)

It is clear that if such random sampling were repeated over and over, the sequence of lots and samples produced would be in control in the Shewhart sense and the expected proportion of defectives in both lots and samples would be p. Yet, our intuition is that some of these lots will, as a matter of chance, have a high and some a low proportion of defectives and that the follow-on sampling inspection could distinguish among those lots. That is, it makes sense to use the data from such samples to sort out the good from the bad lots. Thus by, say, discarding 'bad' lots we would improve the quality downstream. The samples with high proportions of defectives would indicate lots with high proportion of defectives, etc.

Let D_L and D_S be the random variables, the number of defectives in the lot and the sample, respectively. Let D_R be the number of defectives *remaining* in the lot after the sample is withdrawn, i.e., $D_R = D_L - D_S$. Mood [1943] showed that

$$P\{D_R = r \cap D_S = s\} = \left[\binom{N-n}{r} q^{N-n-r} p^r\right]\left[\binom{n}{s} q^{n-s} p^s\right]$$

which neatly factors into two hypergeometric terms and shows that contrary to our intuition the samples and the remainder are independent random variables. *Moral*: if a process is strictly in control in the sense of binomial sampling, then sampling inspection is completely ineffective in sorting out relatively good from relatively bad lots. Conversely, sampling inspection will only be truly effective as a screening tool if the input process is out of control. Yet, when the production process is out of control the real job is to improve it, to get it into control, etc. The proper approach to this task is organized root cause focused problem solving at the production site using tools like control charts, designed experiments, and the like, not sampling inspection. Sampling inspection data are typically taken too many miles or weeks away from the production site and are next to useless for this purpose – too little, and too late.

Coming back to the main theme, the fundamental acceptance sampling problem is as follows. We have before us a specific lot of N distinct items. We are able to sample at random from the lot, examine or inspect each item in the sample and produce thereby either a characterization that the item is acceptable (defect free) or not, or an actual measurement of a quality characteristic usually considered as a random variable X. This dichotomy of data types gives rise to two broad classes of sampling inspection models. The former case in which items are simply classified as good or bad is called *attribute* sampling, while the latter case where measurements are recorded is called *variables* sampling. Another categorization of sampling models and techniques depends how the data is gathered. Specifically on whether a single sample is taken or on whether multiple samples are taken one after another. In the extreme case of sequential sampling, samples are taken and examined one at a time until a conclusion can be reached.

What then are the practical considerations that guide the choice of which type of sampling system to employ? The first decision, whether to use attribute or variables plans, is based largely on the following considerations:

(1) Many quality characteristics cannot possibly be *measured*; one must rely on a 'judgment' or characterization and thus, attribute sampling is called for. This is often the case for physical appearance, taste, the quality of a 'service', and the like.

(2) Even when variables may be measured, there are cases where so many variables matter and where they may be intercorrelated in complex ways, so that to record an overall quality appraisal one must in the final analysis simply designate the item as good or bad on an aggregate basis. For example, there are more than 10 key quality characteristics of a simple 'commodity product'

such as 42 pound liner board, the type of brown kraft paper used in making corrugated cartons. Among the quality characteristics for this product are gauge (thickness), basis weight (density), moisture content, tensile strength (in several directions), color, puncture strength, and many others. Thus, we may be compelled to use attribute sampling for overall quality even though each of the above variables can be measured.

(3) Though there may be a dominant measurable variable of interest it may be so expensive to actually measure that we prefer to use a go, no-go gauge to identify good and bad items. Again, this leads to using attribute sampling.

(4) We may face a dominant measurable quality characteristic whose probability distribution is not one of the handful of distributions for which the statistics of sampling plans have been worked out. By and large, practitioners have been limited to variables plans that assume random variables follow the normal distribution. (Montgomery [1985] has written on the sensitivity of sampling plan performance to the exact shape of the underlying distribution.) Again, as a fall back when the distribution is not normal the practical method may be attribute sampling.

(5) If a single measurable variable is the dominant quality characteristic and if it follows a standard probability distribution such as the normal, then much more information is obtained per item tested from variables rather than attribute data. In particular, one can estimate the entire probability distribution of quality, not just the proportion of bad product. This is a major impetus toward variables sampling. Variables sampling, if based on appropriate assumptions, is usually far more efficient than attribute sampling.

As to deciding whether to use single, multiple or sequential sampling two considerations dominate:

(1) Much incoming and in-process sampling and testing is done in the complex environment of the warehouse, shipping dock or production floor. Often many different items from many suppliers must be dealt with. Moreover, the work is often done by relatively unsophisticated employees. Thus, simplicity in sampling procedures, tests, etc. can be essential. This drives toward taking a single sample, once and for all. (By the way, in practice even obtaining a single sample that is reasonably close to random can be quite a challenge. Imagine a warehouse with 200 tons of duplicator paper in 500 sheet reams, 20 reams to a carton, 30 cartons to a pallet piled 5 pallets high. Try to take a truly random sample of 100 sheets of paper without turning the warehouse upside down!)

(2) If sampling and testing is itself very costly, or if the testing is destructive or damaging and the items are costly it is of interest to minimize the amount of testing done. In principle, multiple sampling plans offer testing economies, however, the reduction in sample size from single to double sampling is in most cases quite modest. If sampling efficiencies are really needed it makes sense to go directly to full sequential sampling in which items are tested one at a time, and as each piece of evidence accumulates one answers a tri-partite question. Is there enough evidence to accept? To reject? Or must we take one more

sample? See Wald [1947], or Duncan [1986]. It should be noted that quite different considerations and sampling procedures apply when the characteristic being measured is a lifetime or reliability. See Mann, Schafer & Singpurwalla [1974] and Nelson [1982] for some details on 'life testing'.

To illustrate the basic statistical and economic considerations of acceptance sampling consider what is arguably the simplest case: single attribute sampling from a fixed lot. The scenario that started this section applies. The questions are:

(1) How large should the sample be? Call this number n.

(2) How many defective items are permitted in the sample before we reject[1] the (remainder) of the lot? Call the (maximum) acceptable number of defects c.

Assuming that there are N items in the lot, of which a proportion p are bad (Np is the number of bad items in the lot), the probability that the lot will be accepted is given exactly by the hypergeometric distribution for the random variable X, the number of bad items found in the sample:

$$\mathrm{P}\{\text{lot is accepted}\} = \mathrm{P}\{X \leqslant c\} = \sum_{k=0}^{c} \frac{\binom{Np}{k}\binom{N(1-p)}{n-k}}{\binom{N}{n}} . \tag{1}$$

This probability may be viewed as a function of the proportion of defectives in the lot. In these terms it is called the operating characteristic or OC function of the plan and it plays the central role in the classical (Dodge–Romig, etc.) theory of acceptance sampling. The basic design dilemma is to pick n and c to balance three considerations:

(1) The cost of the sampling and measurement itself.

(2) The economic consequences of rejecting from further use good items because of decisions arrived at through the sampling process.

(3) The economic consequences of admitting to further use bad items because of decisions arrived at through the sampling process.

If the economics of the problem were clearly enough understood and if it were possible and sensible to postulate (or estimate from past data) a prior distribution of the quality of the lots, that is, a distribution of p itself, this problem could be solved – using the terminology of statistical decision theory – as a Bayesian decision problem. Indeed while there has been a substantial literature on Bayesian sampling, there has been little implementation. Fundamental papers are by Guthrie & Johns [1959] and Hald [1960] while a more recent paper including a workable algorithm for determination of optimal plans by Lorentzen [1985] also connects this Bayesian stream of work to the all or

[1] 'Rejection' might mean that the lot is returned to the supplier, sold for scrap or the like. It might also mean 100% inspection with bad items discarded, or it might mean bad items are replaced. The latter was called 'rectification' by Dodge and Romig. Thus the word reject has different interpretations depending on the context.

nothing sampling ideas of Deming that were mentioned earlier. See Duncan [1986] for other references. A particularly novel empirical Bayes approach was developed at Bell Laboratories by Hoadley and others. It is now being implemented for the former AT&T Bell operating Telephone companies with the assistance of Bellcore. See Hoadley [1981], Hoadley & Boswell [1985], and Brush, Hoadley & Saperstein [1990]. In an attempt to get free of the logical and empirical morass of making a priori assumptions about the distribution of p, Collani [1984] has proposed a mini–max regret objective and derived sampling plans that he argues compare favorably to standard procedures.

To practitioners, the non-economic, or at least not explicitly economic, viewpoint first proposed by Dodge has been dominant since its introduction in the 1920s right up to the present. The Dodge approach is essentially that of classical statistical hypothesis testing and, as we shall see, has close parallels to the Neyman–Pearson framework of testing hypotheses. In this framework, it is proposed that the users of the sampling plan – both supplier and purchaser – agree on a probability of defectives that is so low that the vast majority of lots having no more than that 'target' probability defective should be passed by the sampling plan. Such a number is typically called the 'acceptable quality level' or AQL. Lots with proportion of defectives exactly at the AQL should have a high probability, say $1 - \alpha$ of being passed (typical practice has been to set $1 - \alpha = 0.95$). The reader will recognize α as the type I error probability of classic Neyman–Pearson hypothesis testing. The users also identify a quality level that is so poor that most lots this bad or worse should be rejected. This proportion of defectives is variously called the lot tolerance per cent defective (LTPD) or the unacceptable quality level, UQL. Lots whose proportion defectives are exactly at the LTPD should have probability β of being passed. Practice has been less consistent on choice of β than of $1 - \alpha$ but typical values are about 0.05 to 0.10. We recognize β as the Neyman–Pearson type II error probability. The design problem of choosing n and c can be approached by trial and error using equation (1) or more efficiently by approximating (1) by the Poisson distribution and then resorting to readily available tables such as Grubbs [1949] or Bowker & Lieberman [1955]. Entire volumes of sampling plans have been produced whose charts and tables facilitate the process of choosing the plan to implement.

This opens up another level of discussion about acceptance sampling. Up to this point we have focused the discussion on a single lot. The question is *what are we to do with these items*? Use them, return them, dispose of them, fix them, etc.? No other lots or items are under explicit consideration. Deming [1950, Chapter 7, 1953] calls this an analytical study. But, now suppose that we view this lot as one of an endless stream of such lots from the same supplier. How should we behave? The famous, or depending on one's viewpoint, infamous Military Standard Sampling Plan 105D (MIL-STD 105D) first developed for the U.S. military at the close of World War II and now extended to an international standard as ANSI/ASQC Z1.4 [1981] attempts to answer this question by an elaborate sampling procedure or scheme in which the user sequences through a series of sampling plans depending on the history of quality provided by the supplier. The overall sampling schemes are keyed to an AQL and a lot size N. (The producer's risk $1 - \alpha$ is essentially fixed at 0.95 for all these plans.) The sampling plan starts using what is called 'normal' inspection levels and stays at this level until there is built up a history point toward significantly higher or lower quality than the AQL. At this level one employs a specific sample size n and acceptance number c. If a history of rejected lots shows lower quality than the AQL, the plan changes to a tighter level of inspection that typically involves both a larger sample size and a smaller acceptance number, thus yielding a higher producer's risk. If a history of steadily accepted lots shows higher quality, MIL-STD 105D calls for less sampling and a lower producer's risk is permitted. In both cases the changed inspection levels persist until evidence indicates another change back to normal, or that the situation has gotten so bad that all acceptance of the vendor's product is terminated. Thus, MIL-STD 105D is implicitly a feedback system. See Schilling [1982, 1985] for discussion of details. Many criticisms have been made of these plans, among the most telling of which is that of Deming [1986] who gives a simple example where use of MIL-STD 105D considerably increases costs over either 100% screening or no testing at all. For statistical appraisals of the performance of the MIL-STD 105D series see Liebesman [1979] and Brush, Cautin & Lewin [1981]. Some of the key criticisms of the MIL-STD plans are:

(1) The plans do not have a clearly stated economic objective, do not explicitly optimize anything, and as the Deming example shows they can be distinctly not optimal.

(2) The entire MIL-STD structure plan is rather complex and many (if not most) firms that claim to be implementing it are in fact only picking out in a rather willy nilly fashion seemingly convenient parts of the plan with little understanding of the overall implications of their actions.

(3) The design of the plans reflects an archaic viewpoint of an adversarial relationship between supplier and consumer. It does not facilitate cooperative working together. The MIL-STD plans incorporate an attitude of punishment which reflects and institutionalizes the historical deep mistrust between government procurement agencies and their suppliers. This is no model for modern quality management.

(4) As Mood [1943] and others show such sampling plans cannot work if the supplier's process is in control and worse they also cannot really be effective if the supplier's process is out of control because the testing is done at the wrong place and time and is not intimately linked to SPC or process improvement or capability studies.

(5) The plans focus on sorting out or fixing up bad products, not on process improvement and causal diagnosis.

There is one more very telling argument to be made against employing acceptance sampling plans in the decades to come. We are clearly entering a world of unprecedented increases in quality and reliability expectations, standards and requirements. Whereas in the 1930s when Dodge and Roming began their pioneering work on acceptance sampling it was reasonable to speak of acceptance quality levels of say 1%, such a quality level is at present completely unacceptable in many industries. The spirit of contemporary goals in the electronics industry is captured by the 'Six-Sigma' quality thrust of Motorola, Inc. which is pushing that company to achieve defect rates of just 3.4 parts per million across the board by 1992 [Therrien, 1989; Harry & Stewart, 1988]. Consider for a moment that a 10% AQL is 1000 parts per million! Moreover, the tightest AQL contained in the MIL-STD 105D tables is 0.01% which is 10 parts per million. With a lot of size 10 000 and a Motorola-like six-sigma defect rate of 3.4 parts per million, a sample of size 1000 would have an expected defect rate of 0.0034 and the probability of finding at least one defective of only $1 - e^{-0.0034} \approx 0.0034$. If the process went out of control to a defect rate ten times the AQL, namely 34 parts per million the detection rate would be approximately 0.034. Thus, the expected number of lots until we saw a single defective and thereby could diagnose a change in quality would be 1/0.034 or 29 lots at best. Conclusion: sampling inspection cannot possibly work in the world of parts per million AQLs. The Motorola Six Sigma theme is rapidly gaining acceptance by many other firms. Among notable adherents are Procter and Gamble, and IBM.

In summary, we must remark that although there are many interesting academic research issues in the area of acceptance sampling, and acceptance sampling was once a useful part of scientific quality control in the past, it no longer seems to have much relevance to the actual practice of modern quality management. Acceptance sampling makes the error of the third kind: elegant solutions to the wrong problem.

7. Design, experimentation and the ideas of Taguchi

The previous sections of this chapter have considered in turn the activities of statistical process control (SPC) and acceptance sampling, and the mathematical models and analysis that support them. Our judgements have been first that SPC is a vital quality management activity, but that with some exceptions it is the simplest and earliest of models that are most useful, and second that acceptable sampling, notwithstanding the great deal of research done and the long history of activity, is no longer a very productive approach to quality control and will be increasingly deemphasized in coming years.

The reader then might be asking 'Well then, how *do* you make quality happen?' Deming asks and then answers this question as follows about midway in the course of his standard 4 day seminar on quality. The enterprise must, he says:

(1) Create new and improved products.
(2) Create new and improved processes.

(3) Modify and improve existing products.

(4) Modify and improve existing processes.

Indeed, what else is there to quality management, or, as Kano [1987] puts it, total quality creation? Other answers invariably can be interpreted as activities, systems, or tools that serve to support these four basic agendas. Notice that both SPC and acceptance sampling mainly support agenda item 4 to the exclusion of the others. Indeed, within agenda item 4 they focus on the subagendas of control, monitoring and fix-up. Notice also that the agendas are presented above in what is, intuitively to this writer at least, a priority or hierarchical order. In reviewing their forty years of progress on quality management some Japanese quality experts now say that they spent roughly 10 years in an excessive emphasis on SPC and activity 4, doing what were essentially micro improvements to existing processes. The say 'Excessive emphasis' because though this agenda pays off, it is not now in their judgment where the high leverage is [Sullivan, 1986]. The biggest leverage, it appears, is in attainment of quality through design of new products and processes and fundamental improvements to existing products and processes. It must be remarked that the decreasing product life cycles place even more emphasis on design than ever before. Thus, we see in current Japanese quality management theory and efforts an extraordinary emphasis on such design and planning activity. See, e.g., Ableggen & Stalk [1986], Box, Jenkins, Kacker, Nair, Phadke, Shoemaker & Wu [1988], Kano [1987], and Akao [1990].

Two tools appear to play particularly important roles in these design and improvement activities. First, we must consider the experimental design methods mentioned briefly in the introduction to this chapter. Box, Jenkins, Kacker, Nair, Phadke, Shoemaker & Wu [1988] report on the very high level of experimental design activity seen in many Japanese firms. Though the key ideas, concepts and tools were invented in the west and first implemented here, the Japanese have been much more persistent and systematic about actually applying them to product design and improvement. Experimental design is a specialized branch of statistics that we cannot delve deeply into here, however the ideas of Taguchi on experimentation and product design are so novel and influential in Japan and increasingly in the West that it is appropriate to summarize them. For basic expositions of Taguchi's central ideas see Taguchi [1983, 1987], Taguchi & Clausing [1990] and Phadke [1989]. Taguchi's ideas are considered controversial in some circles and the reader will also benefit from considering critiques made by writers such as Box [1988], Pignatiello & Ramberg [1986], and Ryan [1988].

The essence of Taguchi's ideas is as follows. First, he defines quality as conformance to optimal or ideal parameters. Thus, picking up on our earlier discussion of quality of the commodity 42 pound liner-board, Taguchi would take the position that there are optimal 'set-points' or targets for the chief quality characteristics we mentioned earlier such as gage, moisture content, tensile strength, etc. Moreover, Taguchi argues that any deviation from these optimal targets causes *society* a loss. This is a rather broad and idealistic viewpoint. Can it be acted on? To Taguchi society is the totality of players and affected parties including the producer of the liner-board, the convertor or manufacturer who uses it to make the cartons, the auto parts manufacturer who uses the carton to package his goods, the shipper who transports the cartoned products, the merchant who sells the products, the ultimate customer of the product contained in the carton, and the community that must dispose of the used carton, etc. In an effort to make the loss concept operational, Taguchi estimates or models them in terms of a quadratic loss function that is zero at exact conformance to the target. To many management scientists this will seem an old idea. Quadratic and other loss functions are, after all, nothing new – the concept goes back at least as far as Gauss. Yet, this idea, as popularized and propagandized first throughout Japanese industry, and now throughout U.S. industry, appears to be having considerable impact. It focuses more management and engineering attention on the issue of identification of optimal targets. In fact, in too many industries product and process targets have evolved or migrated over time and are now based on data, needs and traditions that may no longer apply. Too frequently they do not actually reflect true customer requirements. In many cases their optimality of appropriateness is now being questioned for the first time in years, and the resulting problems are being successfully attacked, yielding substantial quality improvements. Hence, the Taguchi charge to examine and focus on optimal set-points is very useful and refreshing. Taguchi's focus on the quadratic loss function also underscores the importance of reducing variation in quality characteristics. Through Taguchi's quadratic loss curves, it is easy to drive home to management the seriousness of variation by graphing the convex increasing losses as variation from target increases, both in the sense of bias (average error from target) and deviations about the average (variance). The Taguchi viewpoint discourages dependence on the traditional, but very imperfect and increasingly unsatisfactory concept that all product that falls inside specifications is good and equally so, while all product that falls outside specifications is bad and equally so. These are, one might say, obvious points for they have been made before in many forums. But under the influence of a 'Taguchi movement' they are increasingly being *acted* upon.

From this basic concept of quality losses due to deviation from optimal targets, Taguchi draws some important managerial and engineering conclusions. He reasons that deviations from optimal target values could occur because:

(1) The product was not manufactured on target.

(2) The product deteriorated or changed over time or with use.

(3) Variations in the environment in which the product is used actually require variations in target values.

He then postulates three broad product development stages: product design, process design and actual manufacturing. (We should remember that according to the Shewhart–Deming view of the world these should not be independent stages, but interrelated and cyclic activities.) Taguchi then asks how activities of these stages can impact the aforementioned three sources of variation, and displays his answer in the following matrix.

Source of variation (*deviation from optimal*)

	Environmental factors	Product deterioration	Manufacturing variations
Product design	×	×	×
Process design			×
Manufacturing			×

Here × marks where quality management activities can have a substantial impact on a source of variation. Two conclusions are evident. First, that product design can, if done from the proper viewpoint, impact all three categories of variation. We must note that until recently product design got almost *no* emphasis in the quality management literature. Second, that manufacturing control, SPC, etc., can only impact manufacturing variations, and these may or may not be a particularly important category. Over the last 40 years this area has gotten almost all of the attention of the western quality management literature, and redirection of emphasis is clearly called for, and some industrial design engineers are quoted to the effect that these ideas are revolutionary. At the time of writing major U.S. firms including AT&T, Xerox, and Ford among many others are intensively experimenting with incorporating elements of Taguchi's ideas into their product and process design activities.

A third emphasis that Taguchi draws from this framework is the importance of product and process designs that are 'robust against', i.e., relatively insensitive to variation in the environments in which they are used or operate. These might be actual environmental conditions like ambient temperature or humidity, or properties of incoming materials, or perhaps most importantly, characteristics of the user. Taguchi's reasoning continues along the lines that one must be *systematic* about achieving product and process designs that are optimal. Consequently a major aspect of his thinking and work centers on the use of statistical experimental design methods and other tools for both product and process design as well as for both product and process improvement – reminding us again of the total Deming agenda for quality improvement and creation. (Taguchi was by the way an early winner of the Japanese Deming Prize for individual contributions to quality management.) There is nothing startlingly novel in his proposal – what is startling is how intensively major Japanese firms have acted on it. Taguchi's writings are replete with Japanese examples, and the proceedings of conferences sponsored by the American Supplier Institute of Dearborn, Michigan which is dedicated to disseminating Taguchi methods in North America has many U.S. implementations. Building out of the classic ideas that originated with Fisher, Taguchi has also given experimental design methods a novel and important twist. He forcefully makes the observation, also made by others, that it is frequently easier to control or adjust the mean or target value of a product of process characteristic than it is to control or reduce its variance. He then uses this insight into the physical design and improvement processes as a key to modifying strategies for carrying out experiments and interpretations of the data derived from them. Specifically, he first proposes that in the early stages of product design – but after initial prototype work has been done – the focus should be on designs that control or minimize variation per se, rather than on designs that seek optimal target values. This is a definite reversal of the usual design criteria and sequence. Taguchi's recommendation derives from the viewpoint that variation is 'an enemy' that it is so hard to deal with that one should seek a low variation region of the design space early in the design process, and then later on deal with the relatively, and one hopes, easier problem of setting optimal target levels. There is not, nor can there be any proof that this design scheme will always work, but there are some persuasive examples. See Kacker & Shoemaker [1986], Phadke [1986, 1989], and Lin & Kacker [1985]. Taguchi suggests that researchers begin with massive 'screening experiments' aimed at determining at the outset which design parameters matter most. He typically suggests doing this via designs employing orthogonal arrays, and finally he suggests inducing environmental variation into the experimental design in a controlled way.

Several researchers have been pursuing what may be more rigorous approaches that achieve these aims. See, e.g., the work of Leon, Shoemaker & Kacker [1987], Box [1988], and Kacker, Lagergren & Filliben [1991]. Indeed, it is in the details of how Taguchi proposes to go about experimentation that his work becomes controversial. To say more here would take us too far afield. Some key references pro and con have been cited earlier and should be studied carefully by anyone proposing to use Taguchi methods. New contributions to the literature appear frequently. Notwithstanding these criticisms, Taguchi has made a powerful contribution to contemporary thinking on quality control and design.

We close this section with a related quality design issue that can be posed by asking several vital questions:

(1) How to determine what the key customer satisfaction issues are?

(2) How to translate those into a preliminary design – into internal specs?

(3) How to disseminate this information throughout those parts of the organization that need to act on it?

Many firms have, they will admit, very imperfect, informal and ineffective ways of doing the above. Several Japanese firms, in the late 1970s created a procedure and some specific tools that facilitate all this. The package is called Quality Function Deployment (QFD) and, as with Taguchi methods, at the time of writing in 1991, QFD is all the rage in the United States. For some basic references see Hauser & Clausing [1988], Kogure & Yoji [1983] and R. King [1989].

The problem that QFD proposes to attack may be expressed in MS/OR modelling terms as follows. Assume that there are m quality characteristics that describe product quality to the customer. (Of course, the product might be either a good or a service.) For an automobile, we might think of characteristics like acceleration, fuel consumption, durability of paint, luxury of interior, quietness of ride, maximum load, etc. Denote these (dependent) variables by y_i, $i = 1, \ldots, m$. Assume further, that there are n design variables or choices at the disposal of the firm. For an automobile these may include elements such as number and bore of the cylinders, the amount of insulation in the door frames, the gage of sheet metal used on the hood, the thickness of a crank shaft, etc. Denote these (independent) variables by x_j, $j = 1, \ldots, n$. Further assume, that there exist functions linking the dependent and independent variables, namely

$$y_i = f_i(x_1, \ldots, x_n)\,, \quad i = 1, \ldots, m\,.$$

Now suppose further, that a rather remarkable situation pertains, namely that:

(1) The important dependent variables have all been identified, and are expressed in terms that are clearly understood by, and relevant to the customer. The Japanese originators of QFD write of these as being expressed in 'the voice of the customer'.

(2) The important design or independent variables or choices have indeed all been identified, and moreover the response functions linking the dependent and independent variables are all known.

(3) The correlations, interactions, incompatibilities or interrelations between the independent variables are also all known and quantified.

(4) The dependent variables, which represent quite different, sometimes competing factors e.g., acceleration, fuel economy, smoothness of ride, etc. have all been prioritized in terms of customer preferences, and constraints have been placed on some of these, and others perhaps have been combined to form an overall measure of merit say,

$$z = \sum_{i=1}^{m} a_i y_i\,.$$

(5) The firm has identified its several competitors' choices of both the x's and y's.

If this wonderful state of affairs existed, and if the knowledge above was shared by marketing, product design, process engineering, procurement, production, etc., then the design of the product, the design of the process to create it, and the management of the production process would be greatly facilitated. Indeed, we might even find some significant amount of actual optimization being done in the design process – MS/OR workers on the alert! As anyone who has worked in the real world will testify, sadly enough this situation – such detailed knowledge – does not usually pertain, except in very rare situations and perhaps, even then only for sub-components. Indeed, typically not even condition (1) is met fully enough.

QFD is an organized approach to obtaining better information for design, albeit often with much less precision than is implied by our formalistic mathematical notation. QFD is also a process for organizing and enabling the enterprise to act on this information. Typically, a QFD study results in a matrix whose rows are the y_i (often the y_i are only expressed qualitatively), whose columns are x_j, whose contents are simply indications of whether or not a particular x_j has *any* influence in a particular y_i, and some notion of the strength and direction of that relationship. To this basic QFD matrix is added other rows or columns containing indications of customer priorities on the y's and the design positions already taken by the competitors with respect to the x's. To this is added a lower triangular matrix indicating the nature of any correlations that exist between pairs of x's. The resulting 'ikon' is called a 'house of quality because of its houselike shape' [Hauser & Clausing, 1988]. The creation of such a house of quality by an interdisciplinary and cross functional team is seen as a major tool in improving product quality, in reducing design cycle time, in reducing last minute design changes, etc.

8. Some closing remarks

Although the main purpose of this chapter has been to examine the scientific content of quality management from the viewpoint of the researcher in management science it is appropriate to take a brief foray into the domain of practice. How should an enterprise implement total quality management and statistical process control or quality improvement?

The first macro question would require a chapter of its own to treat, even in summary. See for example Deming [1986], Godfrey & Kolesar [1988], and Juran [1989]. As indicated earlier, there has evolved since 1950 a new philosophy and many new systems and tools for total quality management, the many dimensions of which are captured in the books of Ishikawa [1985], Garvin [1987], Imai [1986], Deming [1986] and Juran [1951, 1989], among others. Examination of these works will lead the reader to a few observations that may be troubling. First, the scope of total quality management (TQM) is so broad and all-encompassing that it is difficult at times to see it as pertaining more particularly to quality than to any other managerial concern. What has evolved out of the ideas of Deming, Juran, Ishikawa, Taguchi, Mizuno and others is in effect a total philosophy of, and new systems and tools for management. The framework of the Baldrige National Quality Award reflects this to a considerable extent.

Second, although a scientific focus is dominant in TQM, and although there is a tremendous emphasis on facts and data, and although there is an almost ritualistic use of statistical displays of data and analyses, there is not a very heavy emphasis on what has traditionally been seen as statistical quality control. The type of control chart and acceptance sampling work that features so heavily in research discussed here are component tools rather than the cornerstones of TQM.

What one finds in examining the literature of TQM and the companies that practice it are a number of key characteristics. We take the Toyota Motor Corporation and Xerox Corporation as prototypical TQC companies. We describe many of the key TQM features as they appear in Xerox or Toyota literature and programs.

(1) A company-wide dedication to the concept of quality which is defined as 'totally satisfying customer needs and expectations'. Toyota, for example, says this: 'the customer always comes first', while Xerox says: 'Xerox is a quality company. Quality is the fundamental business principle of Xerox. Quality means providing our external and internal customers with innovative products and services that fully satisfy their requirements'.

(2) Quality concerns are a fully integrated and central aspect of the overall business planning for the enterprise. Companies such as Toyota and Hewlett–Packard have elaborate systems to do this planning. Xerox is developing such. These systems bear names such as 'Quality Policy Deployment' or 'Hoshin-Planning'.

(3) There is a very strong emphasis on using factual data to support decision making, and such data is incorporated into very formalistic, if you will, ritualized problem-solving processes based on the Deming 'Plan-Do-Check-Act Cycle'. Both Toyota and Xerox have done so.

(4) There is a very heavy emphasis on involving all employees at all levels and in all functions in quality improvement, quality control and quality planning activities. Social mechanisms are used to support this. One is the use of formal problem-solving tools mentioned above. A second is the practice of doing much of this work in teams. A third is the heavy use of the concepts of quality on the *internal* customer relationships for all activities within the enterprise. This gives even the humblest of employees the ability to contribute and permits no function to opt out. Quality is no longer just the job of manufacturing.

(5) The focus of TQM is on prevention of quality problems, on designing them out of products and the processes that create them, and on planning for quality. By planning for quality is meant the complete range of managerial activities by which products, processes, systems and procedures and resources are put in place to create quality [Juran, 1989; Holden, 1986].

(6) There is a strongly-held belief at the heart of most TQM approaches that quality and productivity are not antithetical, that higher quality results in lower costs, that in the extreme articulation of the case 'quality is free' [Deming, 1986; Garvin, 1988; Crosby, 1979]. This philosophy drives toward a policy of continual improvements as opposed to the old-fashioned 'if it ain't broke, don't fix it', a goal of zero-defects, six-sigma quality or error-free work as contrasted to acceptable quality levels (AQL) that are tradeoffs of cost of quality

improvements contrasted to quality gains. Fine [1986] attempts to capture and explain the spirit of continual improvement mathematically – the first piece of management science research to attack the new TQM paradigms.

We close with two observations about the challenge that TQM makes to management science. First, and perhaps simplest, is that within our traditional domain of statistical quality control we should cast aside our preconceptions of what constitutes acceptable research and address the actual control problems of today. The most current literature is moving in those directions. Yet some trends in the current literature are not likely to yield anything more than mathematical formalisms. Of concern are efforts to use traditional management science methods or models and 'tack them onto' a quality scenario. While we have respect for the mathematical abilities of the authors, it is our considered opinion that more papers in the spirit of Porteus [1986], Fine [1988], and Lee & Rosenblatt [1987] will not advance the actual state of quality management in either the short or long run. We should resist those elegant formalizations that are 'made-up' problems and work on issues that really matter for the present, or those that are *likely* to matter in the future. It is certain that we will be able to rise to that challenge. Second, is for management scientists to move beyond control problems and attempt through our unique approach of mathematical modelling to put other TQM approaches onto a more scientific basis than they currently have.

References

Ableggen, J., and G.C. Stalk (1986). *Kaisha, The Japanese Corporation*, Basic Books, New York.

AGREE (1957). *Reliability of Military Electronic Equipment*, (*Advisory Group on Reliability of Electronic Equipment*) *The AGREE Report*, U.S. Government Printing Office, Washington, DC.

Akao, Y. (ed.) (1990). *Quality Function Deployment*, The Productivity Press, Cambridge, MA.

Alwan, L.C., and H.V. Roberts (1989). Time series modelling for statistical process control, in: J. Keats and N. Hubele (eds.), *Statistical Process Control in Automated Manufacturing*, Marcel Dekker, New York, pp. 45–66.

ANSI/ASQC Z1.4 (1981). *Sampling Procedures and Tables for Inspection by Attributes*, American Society for Quality Control, Milwaukee, WI.

Banerjee, P., and M. Rahim (1988). Economic design of $\bar{X}$ control charts under Weibull shock models. *Technometrics* 30(4), 407–414.

Barker, T.B. (1986). Quality engineering by design: Taguchi's philosophy. *Quality Progr.* 19, 32–42.

Barlow, R.E., and F. Proschan (1965). *Mathematical Theory of Reliability*, Wiley, New York.

Barlow, R.E., and F. Proschan (1975). *Statistical Theory of Reliability and Life Testing Probability Models*, Holt, Rinehart and Winston, New York.

Bowker, A., and G. Lieberman (1955). *Handbook of Industrial Statistics*, Prentice-Hall, Englewood Cliffs, NJ.

Box, G.E.P., and G.M. Jenkins (1976). *Time Series Analysis: Forecasting and Control*, Holden-Day, San Francisco, CA.

Box, G.E.P., G.M. Jenkins, R. Kacker, K. Nair, M. Phadke, A. Shoemaker and C.F. Wu (1988). On quality practice in Japan. *Quality Progr.* 21, 37–41.

Box, G.E.P. (1988). Signal to nosie ratios, performance criteria and transformations. *Technometrics* 30, 1–17.
Brush, G., H. Cautin and B. Lewin (1981). Outgoing quality distributions for MIL-STD-105D sampling plans. *J. Quality Tech.* 13, 254–263.
Brush, G., B. Hoadley and B. Saperstein (1990). Estimating outgoing quality using the quality measurement plan. *Technometrics* 32, 31–44.
Champ, C., and W. Woodall (1987). Exact results for Shewhart control charts with supplementary runs rules. *Technometrics* 29(4), 393–399.
Clark, K., and T. Fujimoto (1989). Lead time in automobile product development: Explaining the Japanese advantage. *J. Engrg. Tech. Management* 6, 25–58.
Collani, E.V. (1984). A sampling system for inspection by attributes, in: H.J. Lentz (ed.), *Frontiers in Statistical Quality Control*, Physica-Verlag, Würzburg, pp. 11–24.
Collani, E.V. (1987). Economic control of continuously monitored production processes. *Rep. Statist. Appl. Res.* 34(2), 1–18.
Crosby, P. (1979). *Quality is Free*, McGraw-Hill, New York.
Davies, O.L. (1956). *Design and Analysis of Industrial Experiments, 2nd edition*, Hafner, New York.
DeCarlo, N., and W.K. Sterett (1990). History of the Malcolm Baldrige national quality award. *Quality Prog.* 23, 21–27.
Deming, W.E. (1950). *Some Theory of Sampling*, Wiley, New York; reprinted: Dover, New York, 1966.
Deming, W.E. (1951). *Elementary Principles of The Statistical Control of Quality*, Nippon Kagaku Gijutsu Remmi, Tokyo.
Deming, W.E. (1953). On the distinction between enumerative and analytic surveys. *JASA* 48, 244–255.
Deming, W.E. (1986). Out of the crisis, MIT, Center for Advanced Engineering Studies, Cambridge, MA.
Derman, C. (1963). On optimal replacement rules when changes of state are Markovian, in: R. Bellman (ed.), *Mathematical Optimization Techniques*, Univ. of California Press, Berkeley, CA, pp. 201–210.
Dodge, H.F. (1928). Using inspection data to control quality. *Manuf. Ind.* 16, 515–519, 613–615.
Dodge, H.F., and H.G. Romig (1929). A method of sampling inspection. *Bell Syst. Tech. J.* 24, 613–631.
Dodge, H.F., and H.G. Romig (1959). *Sampling Inspection Tables – Single and Double Sampling, 2nd edition*, Wiley, New York.
Duncan, A.J. (1956). The economic design of $\bar{X}$ charts used to maintain current control of a process. *J. Amer. Statist. Assoc.* 51, 228–242.
Duncan, A.J. (1986). *Quality Control and Industrial Statistics, 5th edition*, Irwin, Homewood, IL.
Feigenbaum, A.F. (1961). *Total Quality Control*, McGraw-Hill, New York.
Fine, C. (1986). Quality improvement and learning in production systems. *Management Sci.* 32, 1301–1315.
Fine, C. (1988). A quality control model with earning effects. *Oper. Res.* 36, 437–444.
Fisher, R.A. (1925). *Statistical Methods for Research Workers*, Oliver & Boyd, Edinburgh; 14th edition: Hafner, New York, 1970.
Fisher, R.A. (1935). *The Design of Experiments*, Oliver & Boyd, Edinburgh; 9th edition: Hafner, New York, 1971.
Garvin, D. (1987). *Managing Quality*, The Free Press, New York.
Gibra, I.N. (1975). Recent developments in control chart techniques. *J. Quality Tech.* 7, 183–192.
Girschick, M.A., and H. Rubin (1952). A Bayes approach to a quality control model. *Ann. Math. Statist.* 23, 114–125.
Godfrey, A.B. (1986). The history and evolution of quality at AT&T. *AT&T Tech. J.* 65(2), 9–20.
Godfrey, A.B., and P. Kolesar (1988). The role of quality in achieving world class competitiveness, in: M.K. Starr (ed.), *Global Competitiveness*, Norton, New York.

Gnedenko, B.V., Y.K. Belyayev and A.D. Solovyev (1969). *Mathematical Methods of Reliability Theory*, Academic Press, NY.

Grubbs, F. (1949). On designing single sampling inspection plans. *Ann. Math. Statist.* 20, 256.

Guthrie, D., and M.V. Johns (1959). Bayes acceptance sampling processes for large lots. *Ann. Math. Statist.* 30, 896–925.

Halberstam, D. (1986). *The Reckoning*, Morrow, New York.

Hald, A. (1960). The compound hypergeometric distribution and a system of single sample inspection based on prior distributions and costs. *Technometrics* 2, 275–340.

Hald, A. (1981). *Statistical Theory of Sampling Inspection by Attributes*, Academic Press, New York.

Harry, M., and R. Stewart (1988). *Six Sigma Mechanical Design Tolerancing*, Motorola Government Electronics Group, Scottsdale, AZ, 60 pp.

Hauser, J.R., and D. Clausing (1988). The house of quality. *Harv. Bus. Rev.*, May–June, 63–73.

Hayes, R., and S. Wheelwright (1984). *Restoring Our Competitive Edge: Competing Through Manufacturing*, Wiley, New York.

Hoadley, B. (1981). The quality measurement plan. *Bell Syst. Tech. J.* 60, 215–273.

Hoadley, B., and G. Boswell (1985). GMPIUSP: A modern alternative to MIL STD 105D. *Naval Res. Logist. Quart.* 32, 95–112.

Holden, C. (1968). New Toyota-GM plant is U.S. model for Japanese management. *Science* 233, 31–34.

Hopper, K. (1982). Creating Japan's new industrial management: The Americans as teachers. *Human Resources Quart.* 21(2–3), 13–34.

Hopper, K. (1985). Quality, Japan and the US; the first chapter. *Quality Prog.* 18, 34–41.

Hunter, J.S. (1985). Statistical design applied to product design. *J. Quality Tech.* 17(4), 210–221.

Hunter, J.S. (1986). The exponentially weighted moving average. *J. Quality Tech.* 18(4), 203–209.

Hunter, J.S. (1990). A one point plan equivalent to the Shewhart chart with western electric rules. *Quality Engrg.* 2, 13–20.

Iglewicz, B., and D. Hoaglin (1987). Use of box plots for process evaluation. *J. Quality Tech.* 19, 180–190.

Imai, M. (1986). *Kaizen: The Key to Japan's Competitive Success*, Random House Business Division, New York.

Ishikawa, K. (1976). *Guide to Quality Control*, Asian Productivity Organization (availability through the American Society for Quality Control, Milwaukee, WI).

Ishikawa, K. (1985). *Total Quality Control The Japanese Way*, Prentice-Hall, Englewood Cliffs, NJ.

Jacobson, G., and J. Hillkirk (1986). *Xerox, American Samurai*, Macmillan, New York.

Juran, J. (ed.) (1951). *The Quality Control Handbook* (4th edition, 1988), McGraw-Hill, New York.

Juran, J. (1979). Japanese and western quality – A contrast, Parts I and II. *Quality*, January and February.

Juran, J. (1989). *Juran On Planning for Quality*, The Free Press, New York.

Kacker, R.N. (1985). Off-line quality control, parameter design, and the Taguchi method. *J. Quality Tech.* 17, 189–210.

Kacker, R.N., and A. Shoemaker (1986). Robust design: A cost effective method for improved manufacturing. *AT&T Tech. J.* 65, 39–50.

Kacker, R.N., E. Lagergren and J. Filliben (1991). Taguchi's fixed-element arrays are fractional factorials. *J. Quality Tech.* 23, 107–116.

Kano, N. (1987). TQC as total quality creation. *Proc. Internat. Conf. on Quality Control, Tokyo*, JUSE, Tokyo, 143–148.

King, J.R. (1989). Nontraditional control charting. *Quality Engrg.* 1(3), 229–245.

King, R. (1989). *Better Designs in Half the Time: Quality Function Deployment*, GOAL, Lawrence, MA.

Kobayashi, K. (1986). Quality management at NEC corporation. *Quality Prog.* 19, 18–23.

Kogure, M., and A. Yoji (1983). Quality function deployment and CWQC in Japan. *Quality Prog.* 16, 25–29.

Kolesar, P. (1966). Minimum cost replacement under Markovian deterioration. *Management Sci.* 12, 694–706.

Lawler, J.F. (1982). *Statistical models and methods for lifetime data*, Wiley, New York.

Lee, H., and M.J. Rosenblatt (1987). Simultaneous determination of production cycle and inspection schedules in a production system. *Management Sci.* 33, 1125–1136.

Leon, R.V., A.C. Shoemaker and R.N. Kacker (1987). Performance measures independent of adjustment. *Technometrics* 29, 253–265.

Lieberman, G.J. (1965). Statistical process control and the impact of automatic process control. *Technometrics* 7(3), 283–292.

Liebesman, B.S. (1979). The use of MIL-STD-105D to control average outgoing quality. *J. Quality Teach.* 11, 36–43.

Lin, K., and R.N. Kacker (1985). Wave soldering optimization by orthogonal array design method. *Electronic Packaging and Production*, February, 108–115.

Lorenzen, T. (1985). Minimum cost sampling plans using Bayesian methods. *Naval Res. Logist. Quart.* 32, 57–70.

Lorenzen, T., and L.C. Vance (1986). The economic design of control charts: A unified approach. *Technometrics* 28(1), 3–10.

Lucas, J.M., and M. Saccucci (1990). Exponentially weighted moving average control schemes: Properties and enhancements – With commentaries. *Technometrics* 32, 1–29.

Mann, N., R.E. Schafer and N. Singpurwalla (1974). *Methods for Statistical Analysis of Reliability and Life Data*, Wiley, New York.

Mann, N. (1986). *The Keys to Excellence: The Story of the Deming Philosophy*, Prestwick Books, Los Angeles, CA.

Mizuno, S. (1988). *Company Wide Total Quality Control*, Asian Productivity Organization (available through ASQC, Milwaukee, WI).

Monahan, G. (1982). A survey of partially observable Markov decision processes. *Management Sci.* 28, 1–16.

Montgomery, D.C. (1980). The economic design of control charts: A review and literature survey. *J. Quality Tech.* 12, 75–87.

Montgomery, D.C. (1985). The effect of nonnormality on variables sampling plans. *Naval Res. Logist. Quart.* 32, 27–34.

Montgomery, D.C. (1991). *Introduction to Statistical Quality Control, 2nd edition*, Wiley, New York.

Montgomery, D.C., and D.J. Friedman (1989). Statistical process control in a computer integrated manufacturing environment, in: J. Keats and N. Hubele (eds.), *Statistical Process Control in Automated Manufacturing*, Marcel Dekker, New York, pp. 67–88.

Montgomery, D.C., and C. Mastrangelo (1971). Some statistical process control methods for autocorrelated data. *Technometrics* 23, 179–193.

Mood, A.M. (1943). On the dependence of sampling inspection plans upon population distributions. *Ann. Math. Statist.* 14, 415–425.

Nelson, W. (1982). *Applied Life Data Analysis*, Wiley, New York.

Neyman, J., and E.S. Pearson (1933). On the problem of the most efficient tests of statistical hypothesis. *Philos. Trans. Roy. Soc. (A)* 231, 289–337.

NIST (1991). *1991 Application Guidelines: Malcolm Baldrige National Quality Award*, National Institute of Standards and Technology, Gaithersburg, MD.

Orsini, J.N. (1982). Simple rules to reduce the total cost of inspection and correction of product in a state of chaos, Ph.D. Dissertation, New York University.

Ott, E. (1975). *Process Quality Control: Troubleshooting and Interpretation of Data*, McGraw-Hill, New York.

Phadke, M. (1986). Design optimization case studies. *AT&T Tech. J.* 65, 51–68.

Phadke, M. (1989). *Quality Engineering Using Robust Design*, Prentice-Hall, Englewood Cliffs, NJ.

Pierskalla, W., and J. Voelker (1986). A survey of maintenance models: The control and surveillance of deteriorating systems. *Naval Res. Logist. Quart.* 23, 353–388.

Pignatiello, J.J., and J. Ramberg (1988). Discussion of the Taguchi method. *J. Quality Tech.* 17, 198–206.

Plackett, R., and J.P. Burman (1946). The design of optimum multifactorial experiments. *Biometrica* 33, 305–325, 328–332.
Port, O. (1987). The push for quality; a business week special report. *Business Week*, June 8, 130–143.
Porteus, E.L. (1986). Optimal lot sizing, process quality improvement and setup cost reduction. *Oper. Res.* 34, 137–144.
Prestowitz, C. (1988). *Trading Places: How We Allowed Japan to Take the Lead*, Basic Books, New York.
Rocke, D. (1989). Robust control charts. *Technometrics* 31(2), 173–184.
Ross, S. (1971). Quality control under Markovian deterioration. *Management Sci.* 17, 587–596.
Roth, G. (1988). The statistical process control life cycle. *Quality Engrg.* 1(2), 117–126.
Ryan, T. (1988). Taguchi's approach to experimental design: Some concerns. *Quality Progr.* 21(5), 34–37.
Saniga, E. (1989). Economic statistical control chart designs with application to $\bar{X}$ and R charts. *Technometrics* 31, 313–320.
Saniga, E. (1991). Joint statistical design of $\bar{X}$ and R control charts. *J. Quality Tech.* 23, 156–162.
Schilling, E.G. (1982). *Acceptance Sampling in Quality Control*, Marcel Dekker, New York.
Schilling, E.G. (1985). New ANSI Versions of MIL-STD-414 and MIL-STD-105D. *Naval Res. Logist. Quart.* 32, 5–9.
Schonberger, R.J. (1982). *Japanese Manufacturing Techniques*, The Free Press, New York.
Shewhart, W.A. (1931). *Economic Control of Quality of Manufactured Products*, Van Nostrand, New York.
Shewhart, W.A. (1939). *Statistical Methods From the Viewpoint of Quality Control* (edited by W.E. Deming), The Graduate School of the Department of Agriculture, Washington; reprinted: Dover, New York, 1986.
Small, B. (ed.) (1956). *AT&T Statistical Quality Control Handbook*, AT&T Technical Publication, Indianapolis.
Spurrier, J., and L. Thomas (1990). Control charts for detecting cyclical behavior. *Technometrics* 32(2), 163–172.
Sullivan, L. (1986). The seven stages in company wide quality. *Quality Prog.* 19, 77–83.
Tagaras, G., and H.L. Lee (1988). Economic design of control charts with different control limits for different assignable causes. *Management Sci.* 34(11), 1247–1366.
Taguchi, G. (1983). *Introduction to Quality Engineering, Designing Quality into Products and Processes*, Asian Productivity Organization (available through the American Supplier Institute, Dearborn, MI).
Taguchi, G. (1987). *System of Experimental Design* (in 2 volumes), American Supplier Institute, Dearborn, MI.
Taguchi, G., and D. Clausing (1990). Robust quality. *Harv. Bus. Rev.* 90(1), 65–75.
Therrien, L. (1989). Motorola: The rival Japan respects. *Business Week*, November 13, 108–121.
Tijms, H., and F. Van der Schonten (1984). A Markovian decision algorithm for optimal inspections and revisions in a maintenance system with partial information. *European J. Oper. Res.* 21, 245–253.
Tippett, H. (1950). *Technological Applications of Statistics*, Wiley, New York.
Toyota Motor Corporation (1988). *Handbook on Quality Control*, Toyota City, Japan.
Vance, L.C. (1983). A bibliography of statistical quality control chart techniques 1970–1980. *J. Quality Tech.* 15, 59–62.
Wald, A. (1947). *Sequential Analysis*, Wiley, New York.
Wallis, W.A. (1980). The statistical research group, 1942–45. *JASA* 75(370), 320–335.
Walton, M. (1986). *The Deming Management Method*, Dodd, Mead, NY.
Wheeler, D.J., and D.S. Chambers (1986). *Understanding Statistical Process Control*, Statistical Process Controls, Inc., Knoxville, TN.
Yoji, A., T. Ohfuji and T. Naoi (1987). Survey and reviews on quality function deployment in Japan. *Proc. Internat. Conf. on Quality Control, Tokyo*, JUSE, Tokyo, 171–176.
Zelen, M. (1963). *The Statistical Theory of Reliability*, Univ. of Wisconsin Press, Madison, WI.

S.C. Graves et al., Eds., *Handbooks in OR & MS, Vol. 4*

Chapter 14

Developments in Manufacturing Technology and Economic Evaluation Models

Charles H. Fine

Sloan School of Management, Massachusetts Institute of Technology, Cambridge, MA 02139, U.S.A.

This paper describes recent developments in technologies for automated, integrated manufacturing and theoretical models for the economic evaluation of those technologies. This chapter attempts to be broad and serve several purposes: (1) to provide an introduction to technologies for manufacturing automation, (2) to discuss the managerial challenges to adopting those technologies, (3) to provide conceptual underpinnings for considering economic evaluation of manufacturing technology investments, and (4) to review the literature on theoretical models of economic evaluation of manufacturing technology and develop a framework for that literature.

1. Introduction

Driven by international competition and aided by application of computer technology, manufacturing firms persistently pursued two principal trajectories during the 1980s: automation and integration. Automation is the substitution of machine for human function; integration is the reduction of buffers between physical or organizational entities. With the aims of reducing their needs for low-skilled labor and liberating human resources for knowledge work, firms have automated away simple, repetitive, or unpleasant functions in their offices, factories, and laboratories. To improve quality, cost, and responsiveness to their customers, firms are reducing the physical, temporal, and organizational buffers between productive entities in their operations. Such buffer reduction has been implemented by the elimination of waste, the substitution of information for inventory, the insertion of computer technology, or some combination of these.

In most process industries, automation and integration have been critical trends for decades. However, in discrete goods manufacture in most of the Western world, significant movement in these directions is a recent phenomenon. In many cases, factory automation and integration require significant capital outlays. Therefore, the advent of new computerized manufacturing technology for automation and integration has also spawned a flurry of scholarly research into the development of models for economic evaluation of investment opportunities in these technologies.

The goal of this chapter is to examine the contributions of the model-based theoretical work from management science and operations research (and to some extent, economics) for use in evaluation of technology investments to support automation and integration. Toward that end, Section 2 begins by describing in some detail the trends toward automation and integration in manufacturing as well as the technological hardware and software that has been evolving to support and accelerate these trends. Section 3 discusses a number of management challenges and opportunities created by these technologies, ranging from the adjustments required by the human resource system in response to significant technological change, to the economic evaluation of these technologies. Section 4 provides a broad framework for the technology evaluation problem and a brief discussion of manufacturing performance evaluation models and their relationship to the economic evaluation literature. Section 5 provides some historical perspective on relevant literature from the field of economics, and then surveys recent modeling work on economic evaluation models for technology adoption. Most of the modeling work done on technology evaluation that is surveyed in this section seems to have been driven by two of the effects of investment in the new technologies described in Section 2: (1) the increased flexibility provided by these systems, and (2) the increased capital intensiveness and the resulting change in the firm's cost structure arising from the new investments. Section 7 briefly describes some related empirical work. Section 7 discusses the usefulness of the modeling literature for the economic evaluation of new manufacturing technology and presents a research agenda for the area.

2. A description of the new manufacturing technologies

This section describes the technology that is supporting automation and integration in manufacturing. Some of this technology, such as Computer-Aided Design (CAD) and robotics, is reasonably well established and productively employed in many locations. Other technologies, Computer-Integrated Manufacturing (CIM), for example, are still primarily in the future plans of most firms. Despite these differences, all of the technologies described below are expected to play important roles in international competitiveness in the coming decade.

2.1. Automation in manufacturing

As characterized, for example, by Toshiba [1986], automation in manufacturing can be divided into thee categories: factory automation, engineering automation, and planning and control automation. Automation in these three areas can occur independently, but coordination among the three drives opportunities for computer-integrated manufacturing, discussed below.

2.1.1. Factory automation

Although software plays a critical role, factory automation is typically described by the technological hardware used in manufacturing: robots, Numerically Controlled (NC) machine tools, automated inspection systems, and automated material handling systems. Increasingly, these technologies are used in integrated systems, known as manufacturing cells or Flexible Manufacturing Systems (FMSs).

The term *robot* refers to a piece of automated equipment, typically programmable, that can be used for moving material to be worked on (pick and place) or assembling components into a larger device. Robots are also used to substitute for direct human labor in the use of tools or equipment, as is done, for example, by a painting robot, or a welding robot, which both positions the welder and welds joints and seams. Robots can vary significantly in complexity, from simple single-axis programmable controllers to sophisticated multi-axis machines with microprocessor control and real-time, closed-loop feedback and adjustment.

A *Numerically-Controlled (NC) machine tool* is a machine tool that can be run by a computer program that directs the machine in its operations. A stand-alone NC machine needs to have the workpieces, tools, and NC programs loaded and unloaded by an operator. However, once an NC machine is running a program on a workpiece, it requires significantly less operator involvement than a manually-operated machine. A Computer Numerically-Controlled (CNC) tool typically has a small computer dedicated to it, so that programs can be developed and stored locally. In addition, some CNC tools have automated parts loading and tool changing. CNC tools typically have real-time, on-line program development capabilities, so that operators can implement engineering changes rapidly. A Distributed Numerically-Controlled (DNC) system consists of numerous CNC tools linked together by a larger computer system that downloads NC programs to the distributed machine tools. Such a system is necessary for the ultimate integration of parts machining with production planning and scheduling.

Automated inspection of work can be achieved with, for example, vision systems or pressure-sensitive sensors. Inspection work tends to be tedious and prone to errors, so it is a good candidate for automation. However, automated inspection (especially with diagnosis capability) tends to be very difficult and expensive. This situation, where automated inspection systems are expensive to develop, but human inspection is error-prone, demonstrates the value of very high reliability in automated manufacturing systems: in such systems, inspection and test strategies can be developed to exploit the high-reliability features, with the potential to reduce significantly the total cost of manufacture and test.

Automated material handling systems move workpieces among work centers, storage locations, and shipping points. These systems may include automated guided vehicles, conveyor systems, or systems of rails. By connecting separate points in the production system, automated material handling systems serve an integration function, reducing the time delays between different points in the production process. These systems force process layout designers to depict clearly the path of each workpiece and often make it economical to transport workpieces in small batches, providing the potential for reduced wait times and idleness.

A *Flexible Manufacturing System* (FMS) is a computer-controlled system that connects automated workstations with a material handling system to provide a multi-stage automated manufacturing capability for a wider range of parts than is typically made on a highly-automated transfer line. These systems provide flexibility because both the operations performed at each work station and the routing of parts among work stations can be varied with software controls. The promise of FMS technology is to provide the capability for flexibility approaching that available in a job shop with equipment utilizations approaching what can be achieved with a transfer line. In fact, an FMS is a technology intermediate to these two extremes, but good management can help in pushing both frontiers simultaneously [Jaikumar, 1986].

Automated factories can differ significantly with respect to their strategic purpose and impact. Two examples may be instructive. In Osaka, Japan, Matsushita Electric Industrial Company has a plant that produces video cassette recorders (VCRs). The heart of the operation features a highly automated robotic assembly line with 100-plus work stations. Except for a number of trouble-shooting operators and process improvement engineers, this line can run, with very little human intervention, for close to 24 hours per day, turning out any combination of 200VCR models. As of August 1988, the facility was underutilized, and Matsushita was poised to increase production, by running the facility more hours per month, as demand materialized. The marginal costs of producing more output are quite low. As a consequence, Matsushita could price very aggressively against any potential new competitor attempting to enter into the VCR business. Thus, Matsushita seems to have achieved strong product-market benefits from its automated factory.

As a second example, consider Plant III in General Electric's Aircraft Engine Group in Lynn, Massachusetts. This fully automated plant machines a small set of parts that are used by the Aircraft Engine Group's assembly plant. In contrast to Matsushita's plant, which provides strategic advantage in the VCR *product* market, the strategic advantage provided by GE's plant seems to address its *labor* market. Plant III's investment is now sunk. Eventually, it will run around the clock at very high utilization rates with a very small crew. As volume is ramped up, GE has the ability to use Plant III's capacity and cost structure as leverage with its unionized labor force which is currently making many of the parts that could be transferred to Plant III. Thus, factory automation can address a variety of types of strategic needs, from product market considerations to labor market concerns. (However, the work of Kukatilaka & Marks [1988] illustrates how the type of strategy employed by GE may not always be beneficial to the firm.)

2.1.2. *Engineering automation*

From analyzing initial concepts to finalizing process plans, engineering functions that precede and support manufacturing are becoming increasingly automated. *Computer-Aided Design* (CAD), sometimes used as an umbrella term for computer-aided drafting, computer-aided engineering analysis, and computer-aided process planning, eliminates significant amounts of the drudgery from engineering design work, so that engineers can concentrate more of their time and energy being creative and evaluating a wider range of possible design ideas.

Computer-aided drafting is a software tool that increases productivity in the drafting and drawing functions of the engineer. The technology permits engineers to make incremental modifications to drawings or to try many 'what if' conceptual experiments with great ease. *Computer-aided engineering* allows the user to apply necessary engineering analysis, such as finite element analysis, to proposed designs during the drawing-board stage. This capability can reduce dramatically the time-consuming prototype workup and test stages of the product development process. *Computer-aided process planning* helps to automate the manufacturing engineer's work of developing process plans for a product, once it has been designed.

In many respects, engineering automation is very similar to factory automation. Both phenomena can improve dramatically labor productivity and both increase the proportion of knowledge work for the remaining employees. However, for many companies, the economic payback structure and the justification procedures for the two technologies can be quite different. This difference stems from a difference in the scale economies of the two types of technologies. In many settings, the minimum efficient scale for engineering automation is quite low. Investment in an engineering workstation can often be justified whether or not it is networked and integrated into the larger system. The first-order improvement of the engineer's productivity is sufficient. For factory automation, the reverse is more frequently the case. The term 'island of automation' has come to connote a small investment in factory automation that, by itself, provides a poor return on investment. Many firms believe that factory automation investment must be well integrated and widespread in the operation before the strategic benefits of quality, lead time, and flexibility manifest themselves. This issue is discussed further in later sections.

2.1.3. *Planning and control automation*

Planning and control automation is most closely associated with *Material Requirements Planning* (MRP) and its descendants. Classical MRP develops production plans and schedules by using product bills of materials and production lead times to explode customer orders and demand forecasts netted against current and projected inventory levels. MRP II systems (second-generation MRP) are manufacturing resource planning systems that build on the basic MRP logic, but also include modules for shop floor control, resource requirements planning, inventory analysis, forecasting, purchasing, order processing, cost accounting, and capacity planning in various levels of detail. [See Baker, 1991, Chapter 11 in this Volume] for more on MRP and related issues.

The economic considerations for investment in planning and control automation are more similar to those for investment in factory automation than those for engineering automation. The returns from an investment in an MRP II system can only be estimated by analyzing the entire manufacturing operation, as is also the case for factory automation. The *integration* function of the technology provides a significant portion of the benefits.

2.2. *Integration in manufacturing*

Four important movements in the manufacturing arena are pushing the implementation of greater integration in manufacturing: Just-in-Time manufacturing (JIT), Design for Manufacturability (DFM), Quality Function Deployment (QFD), and Computer-Integrated Manufacturing (CIM). Of these, CIM is the only one directly related to computer technology. JIT, DFM, and QFD, which are organization management approaches, are not inherently computer-oriented and do not rely on any new technological developments. Therefore, in later sections, they will not be addressed. I describe them briefly here because they are important to the changes that many manufacturing organizations are undertaking and because their integration objects are consonant with those of CIM. In fact, many believe that the three should be implemented before CIM to avoid automating inefficient practices that these approaches will ameliorate or eliminate.

2.2.1. *Management tools for integration*

JIT embodies the idea of pursuing streamlined or continuous-flow production for the manufacture of discrete goods. Central to the philosophy is the idea of reducing manufacturing setup times, variability, inventory buffers, and lead times in the entire production system, from vendors through to customers, in order to achieve high product quality (conformity), fast and reliable delivery performance, and low costs. The reduction of time and inventory buffers between work stations in a factory, and between a vendor and its customers, creates a more integrated production system. People at each work center develop a better awareness of the needs and problems of their predecessors and successors. This awareness, coupled with a cooperative work culture, can help significantly with quality improvement and variability reduction. Schonberger [1982], Hall [1983], Karmarkar [1989], Zipkin [1990], and Groenevelt [1991, Chapter 12 in this Volume] are interesting and useful references on JIT.

Investment in technology, that is, machines and computers, is not required for the implementation of JIT. Rather, JIT is a management technology that relies primarily on persistence in pursuing continuous incremental improvement in manufacturing operations. JIT is important because it accomplishes some of the same integration objectives achieved by CIM, without significant capital investment. Just as it is difficult to quantify the costs and benefits of investments in (hard) factory automation, it is also difficult to quantify costs and benefits of a 'soft' technology such as JIT. Some recent models have attempted to do such a quantification [Fine & Porteus, 1989], but that body of work has not yet been widely applied.

Design for Manufacturability (sometimes called concurrent design or simultaneous engineering), is a set of concepts related to pursuing closer communication and cooperation among design engineers, process engineers, and manufacturing personnel. In many engineering organizations, traditional product development practice was to have product designers finish their work before process designers could even start theirs. Products developed in such a fashion would inevitably require significant engineering changes as the manufacturing engineers struggled to find a way to produce the product in volume at low cost with high uniformity. Good introductory references to DFM are Nevins, Whitney et al. [1989], and Ulrich, Sartorius, Pearson & Jakiela [1990].

Closely related to Design for Manufacturability is the concept of Quality Function Deployment (QFD) which requires increased communication among product designers, marketing personnel, and the ultimate product users. In many organizations, once an initial product concept was developed, long periods would pass without significant interaction between marketing personnel and the engineering designers. As a result, as the designers confronted a myriad of technical decisions and tradeoffs, they would make choices with little marketing or customer input. Such practices often lead to long delays in product introduction because redesign work was necessary once the marketing people finally got to see the prototypes. QFD formalizes interaction between marketing and engineering groups throughout the product development cycle, assuring that design decisions are made with full knowledge of all technical and market tradeoff considerations. Good introductory references to QFD are Hauser & Clausing [1988] and Eureka & Ryan [1988].

Taken together, Design for Manufacturability and Quality Function Deployment promote integration among engineering, marketing, and manufacturing to shorten the total product development cycle and to improve the quality of the product design, as perceived by both the manufacturing organization and the customers who will buy the product. Like JIT, Design for Manufacturability and Quality Function Deployment are not primarily technological in nature. However, computer technologies such as computer-aided design can be useful for fostering engineering/manufacturing/marketing integration. In a sense, such usage can be considered as the application of Computer-Integrated Manufacturing concepts for implementing these policy choices.

2.2.2. Computer-Integrated Manufacturing

Computer-Integrated Manufacturing (CIM) refers to the use of computer technology to link together all functions related to the manufacture (and design) of a product. In usage by many authors, CIM refers to both the hardware of factory automation discussed above as well as the software and information systems to control and link together the islands of factory automation. For clarity, I depart from this tradition by using the term CIM to mean only the information and control systems.

Because its intent is so all-encompassing, even describing CIM in a meaningful way can be difficult. One analysis of interest is by Clark, Henderson, & Jaikumar [1989], who classify CIM technologies by whether they handle information to be used locally or system-wide, and by whether the information is to be used for managing ongoing operations or for operations improvement. Other helpful references are Rembold, Blume, & Dillman [1985], Gerelle & Stark [1988], and Browne, Harhen, & Shivnan [1988].

A relatively simple conceptual model [Fine, Koefoot, McCan & Spitz, 1989] that attempts to cover the principal information needs and flows in a manufacturing firm is described below. The model consists of two types of system components: departments that supply and/or use information, and processes that transform, combine, or manipulate information in some manner. The ten departments in the model are:

1. production (shop floor operations),
2. purchasing (procurement, vendor management),
3. sales/marketing/distribution,
4. industrial and manufacturing engineering,
5. product design engineering,
6. materials management and production planning,
7. controller/finance/accounting,
8. plant and corporate management,
9. quality assurance,
10. maintenance.

The ten processes that transform, combine, or manipulate information are:

1. cost analysis,
2. inventory analysis,
3. product line analysis,
4. quality analysis,
5. workforce analysis,
6. master scheduling,
7. material requirements planning,
8. plant and equipment investment,
9. process design and layout,
10. manufacturability analysis.

Based on field studies at several firms, we have developed information flow maps that capture the principal information flows among these departments and information processes. Our expectation is that such information flow maps can aid the development of a conceptual blueprint for CIM design, and can aid in visualizing the scope and function requirements for a CIM information system. In particular, individual user requirements as well as database requirements at a given site become more evident after the model has been worked up for that site. In addition, applying the model in a collection of sites sheds light on how an information systems vendor might develop a generic shell for CIM systems.

Design and implementation of a computer system to link together all of these information suppliers, processors, and users is typically a long, difficult, and expensive task. Such a system must serve the needs of a diverse group of users, and must typically bridge a variety of different software and hardware subsystems. The economic benefits from such a system come from faster and more reliable communication among employees within the organization and the resulting improvements in product quality and lead times.

Since many of the benefits of a CIM system are quite difficult to quantify, the decision to pursue a CIM program must be based on a long term, strategic commitment to improve manufacturing capabilities. Traditional return-on-investment evaluation procedures that characterize the decision-making processes of many U.S. manufacturing concerns typically will not justify the tremendous amount of capital and time required to pursue CIM aggressively. [Although, see Kaplan, 1986.] Despite the high cost and uncertainty associated with CIM implementation, most large U.S. mnufacturing companies are investing some resources to explore the feasibility of using computerized information systems to integrate the various functions of their organizations. Some observers [Harhalakis, Mark, Johri & Cochrane, 1988] believe that existing CAD and MRP II systems will form the foundation of future CIM systems. The challenge will be to link these information systems islands together to encompass all of the requirements represented by the ten departments and ten information processes listed above.

The remainder of this paper focuses attention primarily on factory automation, engineering automation, and CIM, defining the latter as: the computer-based information system to support integration of the entire manufacturing system. I will sometimes refer to factory automation, engineering automation, and CIM, collectively, as 'the new manufacturing technologies'.

3. Challenges in implementing the new manufacturing technologies

For firms that decide to make a major commitment to CIM and factory automation, significant effort is required to adjust to the changes that take place throughout the organization. This section briefly discusses five management challenges created by these new manufacturing technologies.

3.1. *Design and development of CIM systems*

Because of their ambitious integration objectives, CIM systems entail large, complex information systems. Ideally, the design process should start with the enunciation of the CIM mission, followed by a statement of specific goals and tasks. A top-down design approach insures that the hardware and software components are engineered into a cohesive system. In addition, since the foundation of CIM consists of an integrated central database plus distributed databases, database design is critical.

Since many people in the organization will be responsible for entering data into the system, they must understand how their functions interact with the entire system. Users' needs must be considered at the design stage, and systems for checking database accuracy and integrity must be included. In addition, hardware and software standardization must also be considered at the system design stage. At many companies, computing and database capabilities have come from a wide variety of vendors whose products are not particularly compatible. Either retooling, or developing systems to link these systems together, will require significant resources. Obviously, designing a system that will be recognized as a success, both inside and outside the organization, is a formidable challenge.

3.2. Human resource management system

As mentioned above, significant adjustment is required for an organization to coalesce behind the implementation of new factory automation and CIM technology. If the new technology is installed in an existing plant, then layoffs are often one consequence of the change. Reductions in force are inevitably associated with morale problems for the remaining employees who may view the layoffs as a sign of corporate retreat rather than revitalization. Furthermore, workforce problems are not typically limited to simply laying off a set number of people and then just moving forward with the remaining group. CIM and automation technologies, as well as a general increased level of competition, typically place significantly greater skill demands on the organization. Retraining and continuous education must be the rule for firms that hope to be competitive with these technologies; the firm must undergo a cultural and organizational transformation.

Requirements for retraining and continuous education are at least as stringent for managers and engineers who work with these new technologies as for the factory workers on the plant floor. Designing automated factories, managing automated factories, and designing products for automated factories all require supplemental knowledge and skills compared with those required for a traditional, labor-intensive plant. Senior managers, who must evaluate CIM technologies, ex ante and ex post, and evaluate the people who work with them, also can benefit significantly from education about the technologies.

Case-based research by Graham & Rosenthal [1986] has addressed human resource policies for assuring that FMS installations achieve their goals with respect to integration, intelligence, and immediacy (reduced lead times). Their findings might be paraphrased as, 'To get intelligence and integration out, you must put intelligence and integration in.' More specifically, the FMS project team must be drawn from a wide range of functions in the firm and the team must be endowed with ample software engineering talent, even if the firm is purchasing a 'turnkey' FMS. In addition, they found that most firms underestimate the amount of skill, training, breadth, responsibility, and commitment required by FMS factory operators and system controllers. Finally, the authors suggest that there is a significant learning curve to be traversed for FMS implementation and that, because every firm has a unique culture and organization to some degree, only experience, persistence, and experimentation can assure eventual success.

3.3. Product development system

Factory automation and CIM can make product designers' jobs more difficult. Human-driven production systems are infinitely more adaptable than automated manufacturing systems. When setting requirements for a manually built product, a designer can afford some slack in the specifications, knowing that the human assemblers can either accommodate unexpected machining or assembly problems as they occur, or at least can recognize problems and communicate them back to the designer for redesign.

In an automated setting, designers cannot rely on the manufacturing system to discover and recover from design errors. There are severe limits to the levels of intelligence and adaptability that can be designed into automated manufacturing systems, so product designers must have either intimate knowledge of the manufacturing system or intimate communication with those who do. Developing such a design capability in the organization is difficult, but necessary for world-class implementation of the manufacturing system. Ulrich & Fine [1990] discuss the use of product attribute-driven cost models as one type of tool to support rapid, effective product development by giving design engineers instant feedback on the cost, yield, and manufacturability implications of their design options.

Managing new product development has become an area of significant research activity. Clark, Chew & Fujimoto [1987], Clark [1989], Clark & Fujimoto [1989a,b] have conducted extensive studies of product development for automobiles on three continents. Their research shows significant variability in firms' product development performance as measured by total development lead time and total engineering hours to complete a new product. Their results suggest that better performance can be achieved by having product development project managers with significant organizational power ('heavyweight' project managers) and by using component and subsystem suppliers to do some of the development work. Eppinger, Whitney, Smith & Gebala [1990] and Black, Fine, & Sachs [1990] illustrate the design structure matrix as one tool to support coordination complex development projects by the heavyweight project manager. Fine, Johnson, & Maggs [1990] provide guidance on managing customer supplier partnerships for product development projects. In particular, they find that the compatibility of databases, information systems, and communication protocols can influence the success of such joint product development projects. Such needs for compatibility can best be addressed if anticipated at the design stage of the information systems.

3.4. *Managing dynamic process improvement*

In most well-run, labor-intensive manufacturing systems, continuous improvement results from a highly motivated workforce that constantly strives to discover better methods for performing its work. In a highly automated factory, there are few workers to observe, test, experiment with, think about, and learn about the system and how to make it better. As a consequence, some observers claim that factory automation will mean the end of the learning curve as an important factor in manufacturing competitiveness. Such an assertion runs counter to a very long history of progress in industrial productivity, resulting from a collection of radical technological innovations, each followed by a long series of incremental improvements that help perfect the new technology. According to Rosenberg [1982, p. 68], '. . . a large portion of the total growth in productivity takes the form of a slow and often invisible accretion of individually small improvements in innovations.' Rosenberg goes on to cite several empirical studies, including that of Hollander [1965] who sought to explain the sources of cost reduction in du Pont's rayon plants. In Rosenberg's [1982, p. 68] words, Hollander found that, "the cumulative effect of minor technical changes on cost reduction was actually greater than the effect of major technical change." In essence, any radical innovation may be thought of as a first pass innovation which will require much work before it reaches its maximum potential. Fine & Porteus [1989] develop an optimizing model linking this observation with the continuous improvement philosophies of Just-in-Time and Total Quality Management.

To presume that factory automation and CIM will reverse this historic pattern is premature at best, and potentially very misleading to managers and implementers of these technologies. Because these technologies are so new and so complex, one cannot expect to capture all of the relevant knowledge or exploit all of the potential capability at the system design stage. If a firm assumes that once in place, the technology will not be subject to very much improvement, it will evaluate, design, and manage the system much differently than under the assumption that much benefit can be achieved by learning more about how best to use the system once it is in place. One might expect to observe self-fulfilling prophecies in this regard. Even though an automated factory has far fewer people (potential innovators) in it, firms investing in this technology would be wise to assure that those people who are present are trained to discover, capture, and apply as much new knowledge as possible.

3.5. *Development of evaluation and control systems*

Once a technology investment choice has been implemented, managers typically want to track the efficacy of that investment. Much has been written recently [e.g., Kaplan 1983; Cooper & Kaplan 1988a,b; Berliner & Brimson 1988] on the difficulties of measuring manufacturing performance with traditional cost accounting methods. The problems stem, in part, from the fact that most modern manufacturing systems are far more complex than the traditional cost accounting model used to measure and monitor them. Kaplan [1984] describes how that model was developed at a time when most firms had one product, one technology, much labor, manual information systems, and little capital investment, compared with today's firms.

Firms need better models to improve their control and evaluation systems. Problems also arise because many cost accounting methods can be manipulated to make current results look good at the expense of future results. In addition, in many firms, cost accounting reports on operations are too late and too aggregated to be of use for operations control and improvement [Kaplan, 1988].

Increasingly, firms are using multidimensional measures of manufacturing performance. Rather than depending on just a profitability summary statistic, measures on quality, cost of quality, lead times, delivery performance, and total factor productivity are being utilized to evaluate performance. Despite this trend, firms could benefit from more research on how, for example, to set standards for productivity and learning rates in a highly automated, integrated environment. The work of Clark & Hayes [1985] provides an example of this type of research.

4. A framework for technology evaluation

Thomas [1988] focuses on the *politics* of technological change with two case studies of manufacturing technology justification and adoption at an aerospace manufacturer. In those cases, the personal objectives of the proposers and implementers of new technology played at least as important a role in determining what technologies were championed and adopted as did the corporate strategic and organizational objectives. His findings suggest that economic considerations serve primarily as a *constraint* on what new technology proposals will be brought to top management for approval, rather than as the *objective*. From this perspective, the models of the type described in Section 5 would be more likely to be used for the *justification* of new technology by proponents who have already made up their minds, rather than for the *evaluation* of technology by dispassionate technocrats. On the other hand, high-level corporate manufacturing managers might be more likely to be concerned primarily with the economic and competitive effects of proposed technology investments, and so would be more interested in impartial *evaluation* of the technology.

In the concluding section of this chapter, I argue that the models described in Section 5 can be useful in either the justification or the evaluation mode, even though most of them are presented in the tone of objective evaluation. This section adopts the latter tone as well.

To avoid severe oversights and missed opportunities, manufacturing technology decisionmaking by a firm must be preceded by manufacturing strategy formulation. Describing a process for the latter is beyond the scope of this chapter, but useful references include Skinner [1985], Hayes & Wheelwright [1984], Fine & Hax [1985], Buffa [1984], Gunn [1987], and Hayes, Wheelwright and Clark [1988]. A firm's manufacturing strategy will include goals and objectives with respect to cost, quality, lead times, and flexibility, which, in turn can help guide general objective setting for technology acquisition. Since, for a given industry, the low cost technology may be quite different from the short lead time technology, for example, bypassing the manufacturing strategy formulation step can lead to myopic (or disastrous) decisions.

Three different levels of models can be usefully employed in the technology evaluation process: (1) multiattribute models for including the very wide range of strategic, economic, operational, and organizational variables that are affected by a given technology adoption decision, (2) economic models (of the type surveyed in the next section) for conceptually and analytically relating strategic and operational factors to financial outcomes, and (3) performance evaluation models for detailed analysis of the operational implications of different technology decisions. The relationships among these models are often likely to be hierarchical: the performance evaluation models provide operating characteristics of a technology to the economic models which, in turn, calculate and pass the economic consequences of those operating characteristics up to the multiattribute model. All of these model results are likely to be used in the political setting of multi-person decisionmaking.

A number of researchers [e.g., Falkner, 1986; Falkner & Benhajla, 1989; Meredith & Suresh, 1986] have noted the usefulness of using multiattribute decision methods for examining simultaneously the many issues to be considered in technology evaluation. As an example, Arbel & Seidmann [1984], using the analytical hierarchy process of Saaty [1980], divide benefits from FMS investment into the categories of (1) economic, (2) production (operational), and (3) organizational, and then develop subcategories and sub-subcategories, each of which may be associated with one or more of these three categories. Among the considerations and criteria for investments in new manufacturing technology that ought to be included in a full multiattribute evaluation model are: cost, capacity, ability to meet tolerances, flexibility (in its myriad of meanings), compatibility with existing systems, installability and installation time, upgradability, serviceability, maintainability, fit with strategy, fit with technical and human capabilities, fit with culture, etc.

For firms that state their objectives in terms of economic variables such as sales, profits, and return on equity, stating technology objectives in terms of economic outcomes is quite natural. And, in principle, most operational objectives ultimately could be expressed in terms of economic outcomes. In fact, one of the goals of economic modeling is to relate operational variables, such as flexibility, with economic outcomes. However, trying to develop one economic model of technology choice to relate every relevant consideration and to its financial consequences is an unrealistic and probably hopeless task. Therefore, a large multiattribute model is useful as a vehicle for simultaneously including the very wide range of strategic, economic, operational and organizational implications of a manufacturing technology investment decision.

In this hierarchical technology evaluation framework, economic models would ideally be developed to feed directly the needs of the multiattribute model. However, since few, if any, of the economic models were developed with this framework in mind, the fit is not perfect. Nevertheless, I will describe their use as though they could be used this way, as I believe they can with only minor additional effort. Among existing economic models for technology evaluation, some are presented primarily as contributions to a conceptual understanding of some aspects of technology and economics, whereas others are cast primarily as computational tools to actually quantify the qualitative phenomena addressed by the more theoretical models. Development of these two types of models to address a certain phenomenon may often be iterative. Someone might work on an application in industry and find that existing theory gives insufficient guidance on how to analyze the problem. This observation might lead to attempts to develop the missing theory. Those results can then be included into the next application, which, in turn, reveals more opportunities for theoretical development. Typically this process seems to have occurred in a haphazard way, with many people working independently and simultaneously on different aspects of a problem, and with some cross-fertilization with other research domains, such as cost accounting, finance, and mathematical programming.

In the published literature, the theoretical models have had the lion's share of the journal space, reflecting perhaps, the preferences of editorial reviewers, the training of management faculty, the differences in incentives for publication by academicians and practitioners, and the desire for confidentiality by industrial firms who have applied available theory to their problems. A discussion of these issues is far outside the scope of this chapter, however, raising the point has three purposes. First, it explains why the work described in Section 5 is primarily theoretical. Second, it exposes a shortcoming in the development of the field that can best be remedied by looking at the above-mentioned issues. Finally, it points to the wealth of opportunity for doing future work on applications in industry.

As discussed earlier, investments in factory automation and CIM move a firm in the direction of more automation and integration. The economic modeling literature has focused primarily on two derivative effects of these characteristics: (1) the flexibility of the manufacturing operation, and (2) the capital intensiveness of the operation.

Flexibility has become a popular topic for manufacturing academicians and a very frequently used term in the lexicon of those interested in manufacturing. Hyun & Ahn [1990] and Sethi & Sethi [1990] provide excellent surveys of the rapidly growing literature on manufacturing flexibility. The importance of manufacturing flexibility for firm competitiveness has become apparent over the past decade as the rate of economic and technological change has accelerated and as many consumer and industrial markets have become increasingly internationalized. As a consequence of this increased competition, product life cycles shorten as each firm tries to keep up with the new offerings of a larger group of industrial rivals. To survive, companies must respond quickly and flexibly to competitive threats. The discussion in Section 5 pays particular attention to evaluating the flexibility component of the new manufacturing technologies. However, that literature is less effective in identifying when factory automation and CIM increase flexibility and when they decrease it. In general, flexible automation provides flexibility within the range of anticipated needs, but can prove inflexible if asked to perform outside originally established parameters. Piore [1986] provides a useful distinction between technologies for flexible mass production and flexible craft production. The former (with FMS as the prototypical example) provides product mix flexibility for a certain set of products, whereas the latter provides the flexibility to respond to a wider range of demands, but perhaps higher labor content and variable costs relative to making the same type of products with an FMS.

By definition, the capital intensiveness of an operation is increased when manufacturing automation on a large scale replaces humans with machines. Such a transformation has two important effects. First, the resulting change in cost structure, from one with low fixed investment and high unit variable costs, to one with high fixed investment and low variable costs, can affect significantly a firm's ability to weather competitive challenges. Models capturing this characteristic are discussed in Section 5. Second, the changes in both employment levels and work responsibilities brought about by automation require significant organizational adjustment.

4.2. Manufacturing performance evaluation models

An important set of models, related to models for economic evaluation of technology, are manufacturing performance evaluation models. These models are used to analyze the physical performance, rather than the economic performance, of a manufacturing system or technology. Typically, such models capture the flow of parts and products in a system and predict means and/or variances of measures such as production rate, inventories, lead times, and queueing times. Queueing network models are the basis for perhaps the largest bulk of this type of work. Simulation provides another methodology used for manufacturing system performance analysis. Buzacott & Yao [1986] provide many references for work on performance evaluation that has been applied to modeling flexible manufacturing systems. Suri, Sanders & Kamath [1991, Chapter 5 in this Volume] describe this literature.

One would expect that the outputs from performance evaluation models of manufacturing systems could be used as inputs for cash flow analysis and economic models. However, the two literatures, performance evaluation and economic evaluation, have not grown up that way. Rather, most economic models are formulated at a much more aggregate level than the performance evaluation models, and there has been little intersection in the literatures.

Despite this separate development, each area has been quite productive in its own right. Both have made valuable contributions. In addition, there has been some cross-fertilization. Fu, Falkner, Suri & Garlid [1987] provide one notable example of a paper that develops a performance model of a manufacturing system, and uses the output of that model directly in a cash flow analysis. Although their analysis does not include a great number of the issues treated in the economic evaluation literature, it begins to fill a gap where more work is needed.

5. Economic evaluation models for technology adoption

The bulk of this section is devoted to modeling work from the management science and operations research literatures that addresses technology adoption. Much of this literature takes the perspective of an optimizing firm or firms and asks what investments should be made given the environment and available opportunities. I have organized this literature into two major categories (see Table 1). The first of these addresses the optimal *timing* of investment in new technology. This literature assumes that the best available technology is known and available to all firms, and confines itself to determining when, or at what rate, this technology should be adopted. I have subdivided this work into the following categories: (1) consideration of a one-time innovation, (2) choosing from a stream of innovations, and (3) technology acquisition over time. The second category of models addresses the question of *what* technology should be adopted. Models in this group typically assume that multiple technological options are available to firms, who must choose among them. A number of these works have been spawned by the advent of new computerized manufacturing technology. I have subdivided this work as follows: (1) choosing among technologies with different cost structures, (2) technology adoption with

Table 1
Categorization of economic models for technology evaluation

I. Optimal timing of investment
   1. One-time innovation,
   2. Choosing from a stream of innovations,
   3. Technology acquisition over time;

II. What technology should be adopted
   1. Technologies with different cost structures,
   2. Technology adoption with network externalities: Standards and compatibility,
   3. Evaluating flexible technologies
      a. Flexibility as a hedge against uncertainty,
      b. Interactions between flexibility and inventory,
      c. Flexibility as a strategic, competitive factor;

III. Single-firm optimization versus game-theoretic.

network externalities: standards and compatibility, and (3) evaluating *flexible* manufacturing technologies. I have further subdivided the flexibility-related papers into three groups, based on the economic phenomena they consider: (a) flexibility as a hedge against uncertainty, (b) interactions between flexibility and inventory, (c) flexibility as a strategic variable that influences competitors' actions.

A second way to categorize the theoretical technology adoption literature is to divide the models by whether they take the perspective of a single firm optimizing its technology portfolio or of several firms who will noncooperatively reach an equilibrium in technology strategies. Although game-theoretic models do not have as long a history in the analysis of technology adoption as do single-firm models, in many industry settings the technology decisions of firms are interdependent, so that a firm cannot prudently ignore the plans and reactions of its rivals while planning its own technological course. The game-theoretic models attempt to reflect this reality of technological and market interdependence. Historically, the game-theoretic models have been influenced by literature in economics as well as from management science and operations research, so I have included in the beginning of this section a brief review of some of the important works from the former. Kreps & Spence [1984], Fudenberg & Tirole [1986], and Tirole [1988] provide excellent introductions to the relevant game-theoretic literature. In the coverage that follows, I have limited myself primarily to work that focuses on technology choice and adoption. Therefore, the optimization models surveyed by Luss [1982], for example, that exclusively treat capacity expansion models, are barely touched on.

In the descriptions of individual papers that follow, I have not attempted to record completely the formulation(s) and results of each work. Rather, I have tried to provide a guide to this literature to direct the interested reader in fruitful directions. In some cases, where I have summarized only one formulation or a single result from a paper, I have done so based in part on what I found to be the most interesting about a paper or on what seems to have contributed to a line of thought addressed or continued by others.

5.1. *Historical perspective from the economics literature*

One conceptual approach related to the problem of economic evaluation of new technology is to examine the forces that drive innovation in an economy and drive firms to adopt those innovations in the form of new technological acquisitions. The work of Schumpeter [1943], which has been enormously influential in this area, introduces the concept of 'creative destruction', whereby the discovery and adoption of a new, better innovation effectively destroys the old technology by rendering it obsolete. Schumpeter asserted that innovation competition was far more important to firm success and industrial progress than was the classic notion of price competition. Attendant to these ideas are the hypotheses that large, profitable, market-dominating firms are (1) most able to afford the investments to develop new technologies, and (2) most likely to be the drivers of innovation, creative destruction, and industrial progress.

Kamien & Schwartz [1982], in their excellent survey of the literature spawned by Schumpeter's work, discuss three reasons why firms with monopoly power are likely to develop a disproportionate fraction of important innovations. First, profitable firms have the financial capability to underwrite types of risky research projects that small firms could not convince outside lenders or investors to fund. Second, large firms, by virtue of their hiring of large numbers of researchers, are more likely to discover and nourish the intellectual stars who develop pathbreaking innovations. Third, incumbent large firms have significant existing bases of skills and assets, for example in marketing, sales, and manufacturing, likely to be complementary to and necessary for the exploitation of new innovations. By making it easier for such large firms to profit by new discoveries, these pre-existing assets provide significant incentives to invest in research projects. Teece [1986] elaborates on the implications of this third point, focusing on its implications for firms who might think they can survive as concept innovators without having the complementary capabilities in manufacturing necessary to deliver their concepts to the market as competitive products. This line of thinking illustrates very well the concept of economies of scope and why such economies can be important for understanding successful or unsuccessful adoption of innovations. Milgrom & Roberts [1990] provide additional insight on this concept.

Arrow [1962] provides one important reason (related distantly to the 'fat cat effect' of Fudenberg & Tirole [1984]) that large firms may not be so likely to innovate in their industries. Suppose the possibility exists in an industry to develop a new technology, either product or process, that delivers monopoly power to its developer. Then the payoff to a 'fat cat' incumbent of developing this technology is only the *difference* between its present profits and the total potential profits achievable through using the innovation. However, if a new entrant develops the technology, its payoff is the *entire* monopoly profit from the new technology. Therefore, the new entrant has a much higher return on its research investment, if it develops the new technology. This argument is countered, to some extent, by Schmalensee [1983] and Gilbert & Newberry [1982] who suggest that an entrant's potential profits provide an incumbent incentive to innovate in order to prevent the loss of its entire market position. Empirical work by Mansfield [1968], Mansfield, Rapaport, Romeo, Villani, Wagner & Husic [1971], Mansfield, Rapaport, Romeo, Villani, Wagner & Husic [1977] suggests that larger firms do not account for a disproportionate share of innovations. Lippman & McCardle [1987] provide theoretical support for those findings based on a model of information acquisition. Fudenberg & Tirole [1986] provide an excellent discussion of this 'persistence of monopoly' debate. Bresnahan [1985] finds evidence in the market for plain paper copiers that Xerox may have suffered from the 'fat cat' effect leading to its dramatic loss of market share in the mid 1970s.

Rosenberg [1982], provides an excellent examination of economic forces that affect firms' decisions to adopt new technologies. Of particular interest are his discussions of the effects on technology adoption outcomes of technological expectations and the role of multi-industry technological interdependence: firms that anticipate significant technological improvement in the near future, may not invest in the state-of-the-art processes even in projects that are clearly superior to those presently in use. Rosenberg suggests that adoption rates will be slow when the rate of technological change is fast, and adoption rates will increase when the rate of change slows. (In the single-firm model of Balcer & Lippman [1984], described below, a high pace of technological development does lead firms to postpone adoption of the best available technology.) With respect to interindustry effects, developments in one field, aeronautics or factory automation, for example, must often await technological progress in other fields, materials or microelectronics, for example. In addition, adoption may not come at the time of innovation, but rather, when the innovation becomes profitable.

5.2. Optimal timing of new technology investments

The models discussed below all address timing of the adoption of a new technology. In most cases, a new technology is characterized as having lower operating costs than previous technologies. I have divided the optimal timing literature into three principal groups. One group assumes that only one innovation, with uncertain payoff, is available. In these models, the firm sequentially collects information until it decides whether or not to adopt. In another group, there is a constant stream of innovations that only can be adopted with lumpy, periodic acquisitions. In this case, a firm must decide the intervals at which to abandon its old technology and acquire the latest innovation. The third group examines the optimal rate at which to acquire new technology, assuming that new technology acquisition takes place continuously over time, rather than at discrete time intervals.

5.2.1. Consideration of a one-time innovation

As an example of the first group, McCardle [1985] analyzes an optimal stopping model where a firm has the option to adopt a single, exogenously-given technology with unknown profitability. The firm can sequentially collect costly information to refine its priors on the likely profitability of the innovation. McCardle characterizes the form of the optimal process for gathering information and deciding whether to adopt the technology, and examines how this policy is affected by changes in model parameters. Jensen [1982] presents a similar model where delaying the decision to adopt explicitly costs the firm in terms of foregone benefits from using the new technology. (Although McCardle's model does not explicitly capture these delay costs, his model could easily be reformulated so that the information collection costs included delay costs.) Jensen also provides comparative statics for his model and emphasizes how firms that differ with respect to their prior beliefs about the technology will adopt a 'good' technology at different times. This result is consistent with the commonly observed diffusion of technology adoption times in industry.

Neither of the above models considers the aspect of competition, although both mention its potential importance on firms' adoption decisions. Mamer & McCardle [1987] analyze a two-firm, game-theoretic version of McCardle's earlier paper. The model is essentially a two-stage game: in the first stage, each firm independently collects information about the likely profitability of the innovation. In the second stage, the firms simultaneously decide whether to adopt the technology, each knowing only its own information collection outcome. Two cases are compared: the firms produce substitute products or they produce complementary products. In the substitutes case, adoption is less likely because firms require the signals about the benefits of the technology to be especially good, since competition will reduce the extent that the firm will benefit. One aspect of this model, relative to those to be discussed shortly, is that firms make their adoption decisions independently and simultaneously, so that temporal competition is absent. That is, in this model there are no benefits to a firm from adopting first and preempting its competitor(s). Thus, this model actually only addresses *whether* each firm should adopt the technology, rather than *when* each firm should adopt.

5.2.2. *Choosing from a stream of innovations*

The second group of models on when to adopt has evolved out of the capital replacement and equipment replacement literatures. Hotelling [1925] and Preinrich [1940] each worked on the problem of determining the 'optimal economic life' of capital equipment for a single firm. Meyer [1971], who reviews both models, points out that each is computationally quite burdensome, and each neglects the possibility of technological improvement in successive generations.

Terborgh [1949] remedies both of these complaints with a dynamic, deterministic, constant-demand-rate model that assumes that a firm's current technology depreciates over time such that its operating costs increase at a rate b, whereas the best available new technology is improving such that the lowest available operating costs are decreasing at a rate a. Therefore, the 'inferiority gap' of the currently installed technology versus the best available technology grows at the rate $a + b$. With this formulation, Terborgh derives the optimal replacement policy, which dictates adopting the new technology at fixed intervals, every time the inferiority gap exceeds a certain critical value.

Several researchers have built on the basic ideas from Terborgh's work combined with the work on capacity expansion stimulated by Manne [1961] and surveyed by Luss [1982]. Hinomoto [1965] formulates a deterministic model in which both capacity requirements and technology productivity may vary. He provides conditions on optimal timing and sizing of new facilities, as well as on production levels in those facilities. Klincewicz & Luss [1985] analyze optimal adoption timing when demand is growing linearly and an improved technology is available. Other papers of interest in this area are Chand & Sethi [1982] and the survey by Pierskalla & Voelker [1976].

Meyer [1971] extends Terborgh's model by assuming that the rate of change in the inferiority gap is stochastic. As with Terborgh's analysis, the solution for Meyer's model is also to adopt the newest technology every time the inferiority gap exceeds a critical number. However, since the change in $a + b$ is stochastic, the intervals between adoption times are random variables. The relationship between Terborgh's model and Meyer's model is similar to the relationship between the EOQ inventory model and the (s, S) inventory model.

The stochastic dynamic programming model of Balcer & Lippman [1984] provides an excellent extension of Meyer's work, including an analysis of how technological expectations can affect a firm's adoption decisions. The model assumes that an exogenous, stochastic stream of new technologies becomes available to a firm over time. At any point in time the likelihood of the discovery of an improved technology depends on (1) the current state of technology, (2) the inherent 'discovery potential' at that time, and (3) the length of time since the last innovation. As above, their results show that the optimal adoption policy takes the form of a cutoff policy, i.e., adopt the new technology if and only if the technological lag (inferiority gap) exceeds a cutoff, which is a function of the time since the last innovation and the current discovery potential. The innovative aspect of the Balcer–Lippman analysis is their demonstration that if the pace of technological progress (i.e., the discovery potential) increases (decreases) then the cutoff increases (decreases) causing a slower (faster) rate of adoption, thus confirming the intuition of Rosenberg [1982] mentioned above.

Two observations on this model may be of interest. First, Balcer and Lippman discuss how a preemptive announcement of a new technology could cause a buyer to revise upward its estimate of the discovery potential and postpone its adoption decision. They cite IBM's August 1964 announcement of its (then nonexistent) model 360/91 just before the delivery of CDC's model 6600 as a possible example of an attempt to influence customers' estimates of the discovery potential, so that they would postpone their decisions to buy the CDC machine. This example suggests how sellers of technology can influence their customers' evaluations of their technological options, an issue that is also addressed in the standards and compatibility literature, discussed below. Second, the result that adoption should be postponed when the rate of technical change is fast is derived in a model without competition. Hayes & Jaikumar [1988] suggest that such delay may not be possible in a world in which rapid change is the rule and the competition is moving rapidly with new technology adoption. That observation is addressed to some extent by some of the game-theoretic models described below. However, development of a full game-theoretic version of the Balcer–Lippman model, addressing this issue, would be a valuable contribution to the literature.

The game-theoretic literature on optimal timing of technology adoption focuses primarily on issues of preemption, the advantages of being first to adopt the newest technology, and diffusion, the temporal 'spreading out' of adoption dates. Barzel [1968] was one of the first to describe and model the intuition that, in a multifirm environment, competition to preempt one's rivals would lead to earlier adoption of new technologies that would be observed in a monopolistic industry. Stimulated by Barzel [1968], Kamien & Schwartz [1982] developed a large body of work on decision-theoretic models that provided some of the groundwork for the game-theoretic work that followed. With the maturation of game-theoretic modeling in economics, Reinganum [1981a, b] used a precommitment equilibrium analysis to derive adoption times in a model where (1) all firms are ex ante identical, (2) no firm has incentive to adopt at or before time zero, (3) firms experience decreasing returns in the rank of adoption, and (4) in finite time, adoption becomes a dominant strategy for each firm. Any equilibrium to her model exhibits diffusion in adoption times. However, the analysis is subject to the criticism that noncredible threats are required to achieve the equilibria she derived.

Fudenberg & Tirole [1985] derive perfect equilibria for Reinganum's model: in a duopoly market, in equilibrium, both firms earn equal profits. There are two ways in which this may occur: either one firm will preempt and adopt early while the other adopts very late (and possibly never), or both may wait until they can adopt simultaneously and be profitable. In either case this *rent equalization* result obtains because very early adoption in the first case is very costly, following from Reinganum's assumption (2) above. Analysis for three or more firms becomes quite complex, but the authors do demonstrate that rent equalization will not occur in the three-firm case. Throughout their analysis, firms' motives are toward early adoption (relative to when a monopolist would adopt) to preempt the competition. Tirole [1988] demonstrates how the structure of industry payoffs could also drive firms to delay adoption, perhaps indefinitely, to maximize profits.

5.2.3. Technology acquisition over time

In the third group, addressing the optimal rate of dynamic technology adoption, several models of interest have been developed by Gaimon. These deterministic models capture more of the operational detail of technological change, compared with the models described above. For example, Gaimon [1986a] models the details of production and inventory costs, and how they are affected by new technology. The model by Gaimon [1986b] examines aspects of how automation affects the capital/labor mix utilized. The effect of automation on labor productivity is considered by Gaimon [1985]. These papers seem to be aimed more directly at practitioners than the work described above, because they suggest how specific automation projects may be modeled and optimized.

Building on some of the features in Gaimon's deterministic model formulations, Monahan & Smunt [1979] develop a Markov decision model in which interest rates and technological progress are random variables. In their model, in each period the firm chooses the fraction of its technology which is to be automated, in order to minimize the expected costs of production, inventory, and financing for its automation investments. Monahan & Smunt [1987] describe a decision support system that incorporates this model.

In the game-theoretic domain, Fudenberg & Tirole [1983] derive perfect equilibria for a model of Spence [1979] on the optimal rate of new technology adoption when preemption incentives are present. In this model, competing firms expand their capital stocks as fast as possible, attempting to achieve as much market share as possible, while denying it to competitors. The Fudenberg–Tirole analysis clearly shows the advantage of being an early adopter or a fast adopter: the leader can expand beyond the level that would be expected in a symmetric outcome, leaving the follower with a small share (or none) of the market.

To summarize, the work on optimal timing of technology adoption has raised a number of important issues for the economic evaluation of new manufacturing technology. In particular, firms must be concerned with (1) the processes that generate the magnitude of technology lag (i.e., the rates of capital depreciation and technological innovation), (2) expectations about these processes, and (3) how competitors' adoption decisions and preemption incentives affect payoffs from new technology investment.

5.3. Models to analyze what new technology to adopt

Most of the work analyzing what technology to adopt is relatively recent. Some of these models were stimulated specifically by the advent of computer-driven innovations in manufacturing and other application areas, such as telecommunications. The models of this section fall into three groups. The first group consists of several models that allow firms to choose among technologies that differ with respect to their cost structure. These models address the issues of capital intensiveness, mentioned in Section 2, as a characteristic of firms that have invested heavily in factory automation. The second group examines technology adoption when standards setting and technological compatibility play an important role in firms' decisions on which technology to adopt. The third group models technologies that differ with respect to their manufacturing flexibility, another important characteristic of factory automation mentioned earlier.

5.3.1. Choosing among technologies with different cost structures

The models concerning cost structure choice address a range of issues. Lederer & Singhal [1988] present empirical evidence that FMS and other new manufacturing technologies have lower fixed period costs and lower unit variable costs than conventional technologies. Then they use the capital asset pricing model to show how cost structure affects the correct discount rate to use. The empirical evidence presented suggests that FMS is less risky than conventional technology and should be evaluated with a lower discount rate. Their model shows how correct risk adjustment, in turn, influences a firm's ultimate technology choice.

Cohen & Halperin [1986] develop a single-product, dynamic, stochastic model that allows a firm to choose among technologies that differ with respect to cost structure. Each technology is characterized by three parameters: the purchase cost, the fixed per-period operating cost, and the variable per-unit production cost. Their principal result gives conditions sufficient to guarantee that an optimal technology sequence exhibits nonincreasing variable costs. That result could be interpreted as giving conditions under which each successive technology acquisition by a firm will feature more automation (and capital intensiveness) than the previous one.

In a related model, where demand deterministically follows the classic product life cycle pattern, Fine & Li [1988] show conditions under which a firm would switch from a labor intensive (low fixed costs, high variable costs) technology to a capital-intensive (high fixed costs, low variable costs) technology, as well as conditions in which no switch occurs or the reverse switch occurs. As a foundation for extending this model to the more complex stochastic, game-theoretic settings, Fine & Li [1989] develop a stochastic, game-theoretic model of exit from an industry in the declining stages of its product life cycle. More work is required to fully explore the implications of a model that combines the features of both these papers.

In what might be considered a stripped-down game-theoretic version of the Cohen–Halperin or the Fine–Li [1988] model, Spence [1977, 1979] and Dixit [1979, 1980] develop a model of cost structure choice where one firm can move first and commit itself to the market by sinking its investment into a low-variable-cost technology, significantly reducing (or eliminating) the profit opportunities of its rival who moves second. Related work by De Groote [1988] shows how observability by one's competitor(s) of the cost structure of one's technology influences technology investment and production output decisions. In particular, in one of the four cases examined (products are substitutes and market competition is in terms of strategic substitutes), if a firm knows that its cost structure will be learned by its rival(s), it will choose a low cost technology to discourage rivals from competing aggressively. Such results provide strategic motivation both for investing in a technology that locks in low variable costs, as in the automated Matsushita VCR factory mentioned in Section 2, and for letting observers into the factory to see the automation running.

5.3.2. Technology adoption with network externalities: Standards and compatibility

When technologies exhibit increasing returns in the number of firms adopting, then a single firm will typically make its technology choices only after consideration of what technologies others are likely to adopt. As pointed out by Arthur [1988], such positive network externalities can arise from a number of sources. For example, if an innovation is viewed as particularly risky when it is first developed, a firm will view it as less risky if many other firms are adopting. Pure technological compatibility, as with computers and software, or with video recording and playing equipment, will also affect adoption decisions. There may also be economies of scale associated with the manufacture, service, distribution of a technology, such that significant benefits accrue from adopting the technology with the largest market share. Historically, in the computer business, for example, 'no one ever got fired by buying IBM.'

In the model of Farrell & Saloner [1985], if a new technology is developed, and each industry participant knows that this technology is viewed as superior by all other industry participants, then each firm will independently decide to adopt the new technology. However, if the technology preferences of others are unknown, then a superior technology may not be adopted because no single firm has the confidence to adopt it without knowing that others will follow. In other cases with unknown preferences a few firms may prefer the new technology to such a degree that they adopt independent of the others. This can start a 'bandwagon effect', leading the rest of the industry to follow suit.

Farrell & Saloner [1986] present a more extensive model in which equilibrium adoption decisions depend upon the size of the installed base of the old technology, when the new technology is introduced, how quickly the network benefits of the new technology are realized, and the relative superiority of the new technology. Their analysis shows that a technology preannouncement, like that of the 1964 IBM model 360/91 mentioned by Balcer & Lippman [1984], can lead an industry to eventually adopt the newly announced technology when it would not have been adopted absent the announcement, and when the industry would have been better off staying with the old technology.

5.3.3. Evaluating flexible *manufacturing technologies*

As mentioned earlier, flexibility is an important characteristic of CIM and factory automation. This section focuses particularly on papers that address the flexibility component of technology. Interest in the management science community for analyzing manufacturing flexibility has followed the increasing interest, viability, and use of flexible manufacturing systems by industry. This new interest has spurred a significant amount of work, both in the economics of flexibility and on the design, planning, and control of flexible manufacturing systems. For examples of the extent and breadth of this work, see Hyun & Ahn [1990], Sethi & Sethi [1990], Stecke & Suri [1984, 1986], Adler [1985], and Buzacott & Yao [1986]. As will become evident below, different researchers have chosen to model different aspects of flexibility.

Hutchinson [1976] and Hutchinson & Holland [1982] developed some of the earliest modeling work that considered the economics of FMSs. The two models are similar, so only the latter is described. The objective of the Hutchinson and Holland model is to determine when an FMS would be economically superior to a transfer line. They assume that FMSs have higher variable costs, but exhibit two types of flexibility: capacity can be added incrementally rather than all at once, and capacity can be converted to produce more than one product. The model assumes that industry demand follows a classic product life cycle pattern over time: demand starts low, increases over time to some peak, and then decreases as the product goes into its decline stage. The authors simulate manufacturing system performance for a stochastic product stream, first assuming that all technologies are inflexible transfer lines, and again, assuming that all technologies are FMSs. The 192 simulation runs suggest that the value of flexible systems relative to transfer lines, increases as the rate of new product introductions and the maximum capacity of FMSs increase, and deceases in the interest rate and the average volume per part produced.

Fine & Li [1988] developed an analytical model that builds on the Hutchinson–Holland idea of flexibility playing an important role in manufacturing a portfolio of products in different stages of their life cycles. The Fine–Li model assumes that the firm can choose to invest in two generic types of technology: dedicated technology that can only produce the one product and flexible technology that can produce more than one product. The model captures an intertemporal economies-of-scope incentive for investing in flexible technology and illustrates how high interest rates can dull this incentive. In addition, the paper discussed how optimal utilization of flexible technology may exhibit use of the technology for a narrow range of products in some time intervals and for a wide range of products at other times.

The remainder of the models described here are divided into three groups, based on the economic phenomena they consider: (1) flexibility as a hedge against uncertainty, (2) interactions between flexibility and inventory, (3) flexibility as a strategic variable that influences competitors' actions. An important motivation for some of this work has been to improve the set of conceptual and capital budgeting tools available to managers who make technology investment decisions. Kulatilaka [1984] surveys the capital budgeting issues related to evaluating manufacturing automation projects.

5.3.4. *Flexibility as a hedge against uncertainty*

In group (1), the model of Kulatilaka [1988], building on capital budgeting concepts from finance theory, provides a versatile tool for valuing the flexibility of flexible technology. His stochastic dynamic program can be used to calculate a value of the ability of FMSs to cope with a range of types of uncertainty. The paper also illustrates the optimal operational use of flexible technology as it switches into its various possible modes of operation, and use of the model for making other operating decisions such as the timing of temporary shutdowns and project abandonment.

Also addressing the use of flexible technology as a hedge against uncertainty, Fine & Freund [1986, 1990] develop a two-stage stochastic quadratic programming model in which a firm chooses a capacity and technology portfolio from among dedicated technologies, each of which can manufacture only one product, and a flexible technology that can manufacture all products. The firm makes its technology and capacity decisions in the first period, then observes an outcome of random demand, and then makes production decisions, constrained by its earlier capital investments. Flexible capacity has value because product demand quantities and mix are unknown at the time of investment.

The paper derives necessary and sufficient conditions for acquiring flexible capacity, characterizes optimal technology investment portfolios, and develops comparative statics results to explore the sensitivity of optimal technology acquisitions to the technology purchase costs and the demand probability distributions. A two-product example illustrates that flexible technology has its maximum (minimum) value when product demands are perfectly negatively (positively) correlated.

The above analysis has been extended in several directions. Gupta, Buzacott, & Gerchak [1988], noting that the Fine–Freund model characterizes technologies as either completely flexible or completely inflexible, develop a flexibility parameter that spans these extremes. They characterize optimal investment decisions when the firm can also choose the degree of flexibility achieved. He & Pindyck [1989] use the options pricing methodology from the finance literature to develop a dynamic model of flexible versus dedicated technology choice. Their model captures the irreversible character of technology investment, which has been studied by Pindyck [1988]. The authors derive conditions to evaluate when flexible technology maximizes the firm's market value. Independently, Triantis & Hodder [1989] have also used the contingent claims pricing methodology to value an investment in a flexible manufacturing system.

5.3.5. Interactions between flexibility and inventory

In group (2), the work addresses how flexible technology affects three types of inventories, differentiated by the economic motive for holding them: cycle stocks, safety stocks, and seasonal stocks. One aspect of the cycle stock issue relates to the flexibility provided by investing in reduced production setup or changeover times and costs. Porteus [1985] extends the standard EOQ framework to investigate investments to reduce setup costs. Porteus [1986] extends this framework to also investigate the interactions between investments to reduce setup costs and to improve process quality. Karmarkar & Kekre [1987] use an EPQ-like model to analyze the tradeoff between owning one large, flexible machine that cycles between two products, and two small, machines, each dedicated to a single product. Total capital costs for the single large machine are lower than for the two small machines, but the large-machine option generates lost capacity due to changeover downtime and inventory holding costs due to cycle stocks. The authors provide conditions to show when each option dominates the other. Vander Veen & Jordan [1989] develop an n-product, m-machine version of this model, where part allocation decisions must also be taken into account. They present an algorithm to optimize both the investment decisions and the production cycling decisions.

A number of useful extensions to these models would be quite interesting to pursue. First, unlike most of the other technology investment models described here, the models of both Karmarkar–Kekre and Vander Veen–Jordan annualize the investment costs, rather than treating them as one lump sum that must be sunk in order for production to commence. As pointed out by Pindyck

[1988], for example, irreversibility is an important strategic characteristic of a capital investment decision. Therefore the sunk investment character of technology acquisition ought to be taken into account in developing a model that realistically captures both the operational and strategic characteristics of technology investment. A second interesting extension to these models would be to allow a range of technology options that vary with respect to the changeover costs associated with them, as is done by Porteus [1985], combined with the questions asked by Karmarkar–Kekre and Vander Veen–Jordan. Then the models would allow optimizing over what might be considered to be a flexibility parameter, as is done by Gupta, Buzacott, & Gerchak [1988].

Graves [1988] presents a model to analyze the interaction between safety inventories and the production rate flexibility of a manufacturing station. He provides a method for calculating the required safety stock level as a function of the rate flexibility and the mix flexibility. He finds that inventories are much more sensitive to volume flexibility than to mix flexibility. Although he does not endow his model with cost and revenue parameters to enable economic optimization of inventory and flexibility, the model sets the stage for such an analysis to be performed.

Caulkins & Fine [1990] develop a model to explore the interaction between product-flexible manufacturing technology and seasonal inventories. Initial intuition might suggest that inventories and flexible capacity should be substitutes: the optimal amount of product-flexible capacity to acquire should increase in the cost of holding interperiod inventory because flexible capacity can help smooth production for products with demands that are countercyclical to each other. (The classic case of building one factory to produce both lawn mowers and snow blowers, two seasonal products whose manufacturing requirements are similar and whose demands exhibit such a pattern, illustrates this point.) However, the analysis shows that flexible capacity and inventory can be either substitutes or complements, depending upon demand patterns. The paper also points out significant opportunities for more work needed on this problem and on its relationship to a stochastic version of the model where safety stocks are also held.

5.3.6. Flexibility as a strategic variable that influences competitors' actions

To date, there are only a few game-theoretic models that analyze the competitive dynamics involving flexible manufacturing technology. Considering the wealth of observers who tout the *strategic* benefits of flexible manufacturing systems, this shortage is a little surprising. Thus, this area may be a growth area in the field. As the survey below illustrates, the subject area is quite rich with opportunity.

Gaimon [1989] uses a two-firm, continuous-time model to compare how firms' technology acquisition strategies compare under the assumptions of open-loop or closed-loop dynamics. The decision variables for each firm are the price charged, the rate of acquisition of new technology, and total capacity from old and new technology. The results show that firms charge higher prices, acquire less new technology, but less total capacity, and earn higher profits in the closed-loop game. Gaimon also analyzes the case when one firm is an 'open-loop player' who must commit at the start of the game to an entire technology and price strategy, and the other firm is a 'closed-loop player' who dynamically adjusts technology and price variables in response to his rival's actions. In equilibrium, the open-loop player, who can commit to an aggressive strategy, outperforms the closed-loop player who, to his detriment, has the flexibility to contract as his rival expands. Gaimon draws the analogy to the worldwide automobile manufacturing industry, where Japanese (open-loop) no-layoff policies serve to make firms unable to adjust their production downward, while the U.S. companies have the (closed-loop) flexibility to shut down plants and lay off workers. Thus, in this setting, flexibility (to shrink) makes a firm worse off than if it had a technology that committed it to high output.

Tombak [1988b] presents a continuous-time spatial competition model in which each firm can choose between staying with its old, inflexible transfer line or switching to a flexible manufacturing system. The intuition from the model can be illustrated with the two-firm case. For any time during which one firm has switched to the FMS, and its competitor has not, the market share of the first firm will grow at the expense of the second firm, thus giving each firm incentive to preempt its rival. In the n-firm case, this result also holds, leading Tombak to conclude that technology adoption will occur in 'swarms', as predicted by Schumpeter [1939].

Fine & Pappu [1990] present a supergame model whose results complement those of both Gaimon and Tombak. (See, e.g., Kreps & Spence [1984] and Fudenberg & Tirole [1986] for explanations and examples of supergames.) The Fine–Pappu model assumes that there are two firms and two markets. Initially, each firm has a monopoly in its own market. The existence of flexible technology gives each firm a relatively inexpensive avenue for invading its rival's market. Two possible types of equilibria are possible. In one, each firm buys the flexible technology, invades its rival's market, and ends up with duopoly profits in both markets, earning lower total profits than it would from monopoly profits in one market. In the other equilibrium, each firm buys the flexible technology, but stays only in its own market, deterred from invading its rival's market by the credible threat that such entry will be met with a retaliatory invasion, but needing the flexible technology to credibly threaten such retaliation if invaded itself. In both types of equilibria, the existence of flexible technology makes both firms worse off. Each would earn higher profits if flexible technology did not exist. As in Gaimon's model, flexibility, in addition to an inability to commit to a certain course of action (in this case, not to invade a rival's market), makes a firm worse off. However, firms are worse off because they cannot costlessly sustain a monopoly position. As a result, in the cases when both firms produce for both markets, the competition makes consumers better off. With a related, but different formulation, Roller & Tombak [1990] also find that consumers are made better off when flexible automation is adopted by firms.

To summarize, the modeling literature on what technology to adopt has exploded in recent years. To date the literature has focused primarily on the areas of cost structure, compatibility, and flexibility. These models have enriched significantly our understanding of technology evaluation and adoption. I believe that the modeling literature that addresses flexibility is especially useful because formulating a formal model forces concreteness in thinking for a concept that is notorious for having been subject to a great deal of nonconcrete writing and thinking. Although none of these models individually come even close to addressing all of the facets of flexibility discussed in the literature described in Section 4, collectively, they can contribute materially to an understanding of the issues related to investing in flexibility through new technology.

6. Empirical work on technology evaluation and adoption

This section briefly describes some empirical research related to the theoretical research described above. Due to the recency of the development of much of the work described above and to the lags in technology transfer to new ideas from academia to industry, limited information is available to evaluate the utility to industry of many of the models described. In addition, many of the papers have been written primarily for a theory-oriented academic audience, and have not trickled down, through publication of applications, to the practitioner literature.

There is, however, an extensive empirical research literature on technology adoption that predates the development of most of the technology described in Section 2. Reviewing that literature is beyond the scope of this work. However, Kamien & Schwartz [1982] and Rosenberg [1982] each include a chapter with significant coverage of this literature. In the FMS domain, empirical work is much more scarce, but a few relevant papers are described here.

Tombak [1988a] has pursued the question of whether flexibility has an important effect on firm performance. Based on a sample of 1455 business units from the extensive PIMS (Profit Impact on Marketing Strategy) database, he develops a regression model which finds flexibility to be an important explanatory variable for firm performance. Using two other databases that cover 410 European and 168 U.S. firms, Tombak & De Meyer [1988] find that managers use flexible manufacturing systems to accommodate variability in their inputs and to enable them to produce a wider variety of outputs. Based on a sample of 60 FMSs installed in Japan and 35 in the United States, Jaikumar [1986] finds that Japanese firms are much farther along in the application of the technology and that the flexibility offered by the technology is an important strategic variable for them. Overall, the available evidence is consistent with the hypothesis that flexibility has become an important concern for a significant number of manufacturing firms.

Gerwin [1981] presents an excellent case study of one firm's process of evaluating an FMS investment opportunity. In this case, the Net Present Value

(NPV) investment tool was the only quantitative model used, but champions of the FMS investment attempted to quantify case flow items that typically would be considered intangible, and left out of the analysis. Little formal analysis was employed in evaluating the flexibility component of the FMS, but subjectively this flexibility seems to play a significant role in convincing the decisionmakers of the merits of the FMS over the transfer line alternative. Since this case study predates the development of many of the models described above, and since this was one of the early FMS implementations in the United States, one would not have expected extensive sophisticated analysis reflecting the concepts described above. Additional case studies and industrial perspectives may be found in Meredith [1986].

7. Overview and conclusions

This section evaluates the potential usefulness of the modeling literature for the economic evaluation of new manufacturing technology and presents a research agenda for the area.

7.1. Evaluation of the existing literature on technology adoption models

Rogers [1983] lists five attributes of innovations that may affect the rate at which adoption occurs: (1) relative advantage, (2) compatibility, (3) complexity, (4) trialability, and (5) observability. Relative advantage is the direct difference in profitability brought about by the new technology. Compatibility of a new technology can refer either to organizational issues or technical issues. Complexity refers to the degree of difficulty in understanding and using an innovation. Trialability is the ease with which one can experiment with a new technology, before making an adoption commitment. Observability is the degree of transparency of the innovation's results to any observer. If a technology's benefits are self-evident, firms will perceive less risk in their technology decisionmaking.

Most of the technology adoption models discussed here deal only with relative advantage. Exceptions are the Farrell and Saloner papers on compatibility and the De Groote work on observability. (Although, De Groote's observability effect, which influences a rival's evaluation of potential profit opportunities, is different from that of Rogers.) The ideas of trialability and experimentation are explored by Bohn [1988], but not in the context of the economic evaluation of new technologies. That work, however, could serve as a useful launching point for analysis of trialability as it affects technology adoption decisions. Therefore, considering Rogers' list, significantly more work could be done to develop models for attributes (2)–(5). In addition, there are many open questions, some of which have been alluded to above just in consideration of relative advantage of the new manufacturing technologies.

Overall, the technology evaluation and adoption literature is in a state of rapid innovation, reflecting perhaps the rapid rate of change of technological options in industry. If one accepts the analysis of Balcer & Lippman [1984], then in such a period, potential adopters of these methods are advised to take a wait-and-see posture, with the expectation that this rate of innovation will slow and some consolidation and formation of dominant practice will arise. (As mentioned above, this prescription assumes that one's rivals will not develop a lock on the market in the meantime.)

This literature review suggests that a consolidation has not yet occurred for technology evaluation models (although the work of Fudenberg & Tirole [1986] and Tirole [1988] contribute significantly to such eventual consolidation in the game-theoretic literature). Since the rate of innovation is still high, consolidation into a few dominant models and paradigms may not be on the immediate horizon.

Despite the state of flux for this research area, some speculation as to the usefulness of this literature is possible. First, these models may help teachers and practitioners refine their intuition about the economics of new technology investment. Aside from direct use by practitioners, the models described here might also be expected to be used in two other domains: education of management and engineering students and development of decision support systems. Casual observation suggests that a number of schools are beginning to teach the concepts and models described here, so that some faculty interested in technology evaluation problems find these models to be useful. Some new methods and ideas in management do not become widely used until a generation of students who have learned these ideas in school moves high enough in organizations so that they have decisionmaking power. So judging this channel for potential utilization and application would be premature. A potential route for near-term application of these models is in the development of decision support systems that would be used by practitioners. The Monahan–Smunt [1987] system is an example of this type of outlet for these models.

Since virtually all of the models discussed in Section 5 have profits or costs as their objectives rather than as constraints, one might be inclined to conclude that they are of little practical use for this technology justification process. However, the findings of Thomas [1988], mentioned in Section 4, if they stand the test of further research at other sites, may bode well for the type of modeling work surveyed above because such work provides technology champions more powerful tools for making their cases to top management. Historically, cost and headcount reductions have been the principal vehicles for justifying investment in new technology. At many firms, if a potential benefit from a new investment cannot be quantified, then it is considered as an afterthought for borderline projects that don't quite make the hurdle rate. The models discussed above can be used as tools for quantifying and including a much wider range of corporate objectives into the formal proposals to top management, thus expanding the feasible set of projects. (Some field research, including that of Thomas [1988], suggests that managers manipulate the numbers to pass the hurdle rate for whatever projects they deem desirable. Even in the presence of this practice, better models can expand the set of projects where the numbers can credibly be made to look desirable, thus providing utility to technology champions.)

Thomas' research also suggests that high-level managers responsible for approving technology investment proposals are not always as well informed as they might be about those technological options and their economic implications. Exposure to the theory discussed above might also be helpful for such managers to better judge, or at least question, the projects they receive to review.

7.2. Research agenda

The existing modeling literature discussed in this chapter has great potential in two areas; (1) development of a more unified theory of the economics of technology evaluation and (2) helping practitioners make better investment decisions. With respect to developing a unified theory, work is required in several areas. First, Rogers [1983] paper on five attributes of innovations could serve as an excellent guide to issues that have not been modeled or explored sufficiently. In addition, case-based sources might be used to discover other important aspects of the technology evaluation problem that have not been modeled. Second, the industry interdependence characteristics of technological advance, described by Rosenberg [1982], whereby adoption of an innovation in one industry often must await some technological development in another industry, has not been captured well by the existing modeling literature. Third, work is needed to take the many features of technology adoption decisions, each of which has been modeled separately, and knit them together to as great an extent as possible. The Balcer & Lippman [1984] paper did an excellent job of this for the single-firm, optimal adoption timing literature, and might potentially serve as a base from which to build a game-theoretic model. Additional features such as product life cycles, flexibility, compatibility, asymmetric information, and inventories might also eventually be included. Developing one tractable model to include all of these features may be impossible, but learning how these different features of technology adoption decisions interact is an important goal for deepening our understanding of the problem.

Hayes, Wheelwright, & Clark [1988] make a strong case for firms to do as much technology development in-house as possible to minimize information leaks about the firm's process technology, to develop and maintain competence in strategically critical technologies, and to assure a proper fit between the firm's new technology and its existing strategy, people, and capital assets. Such technology investments may go through a significantly different evaluation process. I have seen no 'make or buy' models for technology acquisition decisions, and I believe this represents a gap in the existing theory.

Falkner [1989] has observed that CIM technology is rarely adopted except with the introduction of a new product. (Although, General Electric's Plant

III, mentioned in Section 2, is one exception to this.) Falkner's observation suggests that models that simultaneously encompass both product and technology decisions could be much more useful than models that consider only technology choice problems. This would seem to be a fruitful line for future research.

To move toward helping practitioners make better investment decisions, and toward helping theoreticians build better models, theoreticians and practitioners must communicate, and, in the best of all worlds, work together on real problems. Achieving this goal is often difficult because the two groups are typically separated by organizational walls, different mindsets and different timetables. However, for some who have tried it, such joint efforts have proven rewarding and productive.

Acknowledgement

This chapter was improved significantly by helpful comments from Paul Adler, John Caulkins, Xavier de Groote, Steven Eppinger, Chuck Falkner, Ken Farrar, Rebecca Henderson, Chuck Holloway, Bob Kaplan, Phil Lederer, Steve Lippman, Don Rosenfield, Avi Seidmann, Rajan Suri, Mikhel Tombak, Marcie Tyre, Karl Ulrich, Larry Wein, Steve Wheelwright, Paul Zipkin, and especially Steve Graves. The author gratefully acknowledges these debts and takes responsibility for the remaining shortcomings.

References

Adler, P. (1985). Managing flexibility: A selective review of the challenges of managing the new production technologies' potential for flexibility, Report to the Organization for Economic Co-operation and Development, Stanford Dept. of Industrial Engineering and Engineering Management.

Arbel, A., and A. Seidmann (1984). Performance evaluation of flexible manufacturing systems. *IEEE Trans. Systems, Man, Cybernet.* 14(4), 606–617.

Arrow, K. (1962). Economic welfare and the allocation of resources to innovation, in: R. Nelson (ed.), *The Rate and Direction of Inventive Activity*, Universities-National Bureau Conference Series, No. 14, Arno Press, New York.

Arthur, W.B. (1988). Competing technologies: An overview, in: G. Dosi et al. (eds.), *Technical Change and Economic Theory*, Columbia University Press, New York.

Baker, K.R. (1991). Requirements planning, in: S.C. Graves, A.H.G. Rinnooy Kan, and P.H. Zipkin (eds.), *Logistics of Production and Inventory*, Handbooks in Operations Research and Management Science, Vol. 4, North-Holland, Amsterdam, Chapter 11.

Balcer, Y., and S.A. Lippman (1984). Technological expectations and adoption of improved technology. *J. Econom. Theory* 34, 292–318.

Barzel, Y. (1968). Optimal timing of innovations. *Rev. Econom. Statist.* 348–355.

Berliner, C., and J.A. Brimson eds. (1988). *Cost Management for Today's Advanced Manufacturing*, Harvard Business School Press, Boston, MA.

Black, T., C.H. Fine and E. Sachs (1990). A method for systems design using precedence relationships: An application to automotive Brake systems, MIT Sloan School WP#3208-90-MS.

Bohn, R.E. (1988). Noise and learning in semiconductor manufacturing, Working Paper, Harvard Business School, May.
Bresnahan, T.F. (1985). Post-entry competition in the plain paper copier market. *Amer. Econom. Rev.* 75(2), 15–19.
Browne, J., J. Harhen and J. Shivnan (1988). *Production Management Systems: A CIM Perspective*, Addison-Wesley, Reading, MA.
Buffa, E.S. (1984). *Meeting the Competitive Challenge: Manufacturing Strategies for U.S. Companies*, Dow, Jones-Irwin, New York.
Buzacott, J.A., and D.D. Yao (1986). Flexible manufacturing systems: A review of analytical models. *Management Sci.* 32(7), 890–905.
Caulkins, J.P., and C.H. Fine (1990). Seasonal inventories and the use of product-flexible manufacturing technology. *Ann. Oper. Res.* 26, 351–375.
Chand, S., and S. Sethi (1982). Planning horizon procedures for machine replacement models with several possible replacement alternatives. *Naval. Res. Logist. Quart.* 29(3), 483–493.
Clark, K.B. (1989). Project scope and project performance: The effect of parts strategy and supplier involvement on product development. *Management Sci.* 35(10), 1247–1263.
Clark, K.B., W.B. Chew and T. Fujimoto (1987). Product development in the world auto industry. *Brookings Papers on Economic Activity* 3, 729–771.
Clark, K.B., and T. Fujimoto (1989a). Overlapping problem solving in product development, in: K. Ferdows (ed.), *Managing International Manufacturing*, North-Holland, Amsterdam.
Clark, K.B., and T. Fujimoto (1989b). Lead time in automobile product development: Explaining the Japanese advantage. *J. Engrg. Tech. Management* 1, 1–34.
Clark, K.B., and R.H. Hayes (1985). Exploring the sources of productivity differences at the factory level, in: K.B. Clark, R.H. Hayes and C. Lorenz (eds.), *The Uneasy Alliance: Managing the Productivity–Technology Dilemma*, Harvard Business School Press, Boston, MA, pp. 151–188.
Clark, K.B., R. Henderson and R. Jaikumar (1989). A perspective on computer integrated manufacturing tools, Draft, Harvard Business School.
Cohen, M.A., and R.M. Halperin (1986). Optimal technology choice in a dynamic-stochastic environment. *J. Oper. Management* 6(3), 317–331.
Cooper, R., and R.S. Kaplan (1988a). How cost accounting systematically distorts product costs. *Management Accounting*, April, 20–30.
Cooper, R., and R.S. Kaplan (1988b). Measure costs right: Make the right decisions. *Harv. Bus. Rev.* 66(5), 96–105.
De Groote, X. (1988). The strategic choice of production processes, Ph.D. Dissertation, Graduate School of Business, Stanford University.
Dixit, A. (1979). A model of duopoly suggesting a theory of entry barriers. *Bell J. Econom.* 10, 20–32.
Dixit, A. (1980). The role of investment in entry deterrence. *Econom. J.* 90, 95–106.
Eppinger, S.E., D.E. Whitney, R.P. Smith and D.A. Gebala (1990). Organizing the tasks in complex design projects, MIT Sloan School WP#3083-89-MSA.
Eureka, W.E., and N.E. Ryan (1988). *The Customer-Driven Company: Managerial Perspectives on QFD*, The ASI Press, Dearborn, MI.
Falkner, C. (1986). Multi-attribute decision analysis for justifying flexible automation, *Proceedings of the IEEE International Conference on Robotics and Automation*, pp. 1815–1820.
Falkner, C. (1989). Personal communication.
Falkner, C.H., and S. Benhajla (1989). Multi-attribute decision models in the justification of CIM systems. *Engrg. Econom.*
Farrell, J., and G. Saloner (1985). Standardization, compatibility, and innovation. *Rand J. Econom.* 16(1), 70–83.
Farrell, J., and G. Saloner (1986). Installed base and compatibility: Innovation, product preannouncements, and predation. *Amer. Econom. Rev.* 76(5), 940–955.
Fine, C.H., and R.M. Freund (1986). Economic analysis of product-flexible manufacturing systems investment decisions, in: K.E. Stecke and R. Suri (eds.), *Proceedings of the Second ORSA/TIMS Conference on Flexible Manufacturing Systems*, Elsevier, Amsterdam.

Fine, C.H., and R.M. Freund (1990). Optimal investment in product-flexible manufacturing capacity. *Management Si.* 36(4), 449–466.
Fine, C.H., and A.C. Hax (1985). Manufacturing strategy: A methodology and an illustration. *Interfaces* 15(6), 28–46.
Fine, C.H., J. Johnson and V. Maggs (1990). Product development and customer-supplier partnerships: An in-depth case study and a new framework, Working Paper, MIT Leaders for Manufacturing program.
Fine, C.H., E. Koefoot, S. McCan and D. Spitz (1989). An information system model for comptuer-integrated manufacturing, Draft, Sloan School of Management, MIT.
Fine, C.H., and L. Li (1988). Technology choice, product life cycles, and flexible automation. *J. Manuf. Oper. Management* 1(4), 372–396.
Fine, C.H., and L. Li (1989). Equilibrium exit in stochastically declining industries. *Games Econom. Behav.* 1(1), 40–59.
Fine, C.H., and S. Pappu (1990). Flexible manufacturing technology and product-market competition, MIT Sloan School, WP #31350-90-MSA.
Fine, C.H., and E.L. Porteus (1989). Dynamic process improvement. *Oper. Res.* 37(4), 580–591.
Fu, B., C. Falkner, R. Suri and S. Garlid (1989). Combining economic analysis and system modeling to evaluate test strategies for circuit board assembly lines, in: J.A. Edosomwan and A. Ballakur (eds.), *Productivity and Quality Improvement in Electronics Assembly*, McGraw-Hill, New York. pp. 479–506.
Fudenberg, D., and J. Tirole (1983). Capital as a commitment: Strategic investment to deter mobility. *J. Econom. Theory* 31, 227–256.
Fudenberg, D., and J. Tirole (1984). The fat-cat effect, the puppy-dog ploy, and the lean and hungry look. *Amer. Econom. Rev.* 74, 361–366.
Fudenberg, D., and J. Tirole (1985). Preemption and rent equalization in the adoption of new technology. *Rev. Econom. Stud.* 52, 383–401.
Fudenberg, D., and J. Tirole (1986). *Dynamic Models of Oligopoly*, Harwood, New York.
Gaimon, C. (1985). The optimal acquisition of automation to enhance the productivity of labor. *Management Sci.* 31(9), 1175–1190.
Gaimon, C. (1986a). The continuous acquisition of automation to reduce production and in-process inventory costs, in: A. Kusiak (ed.), *Studies in the Management Sciences and Systems*, Vol. 12, North-Holland, New York. pp. 29–44.
Gaimon, C. (1986b). An impulsive control approach to deriving the optimal dynamic mix of manual and automatic output. *European J. Oper. Res.* 24, 360–368.
Gaimon, C. (1989). Dynamic game results on the acquisition of new technology. *Oper. Res.* 37(3), 401–425.
Gerelle, E., and J. Stark (1988). *Integrated Manufacturing: Strategy, Planning, and Implementation*, McGraw-Hill, New York.
Gerwin, D. (1981). Control and evaluation in the innovation process: The case of flexible manufacturing systems. *IEEE Trans. Engrg. Management* 28(3), 62–70.
Gilbert, R., and D. Newberry (1982). Preemptive patenting and the persistence of monopoly. *Amer. Econom. Rev.* 72, 514–526.
Graham, M.B.W., and S.R. Rosenthal (1986). Flexible manufacturing systems require flexible people. *Human Systems Management* 6, 211–222.
Graves, S.C. (1988). Safety stocks in manufacturing systems. *J. Manuf. Oper. Management* 1(1), 67–101.
Groenevelt, H. (1991). The Just-in-Time system, in: S.C. Graves, A.H.G. Rinnooy Kan and P.H. Zipkin (eds.), *Logistics of Production and Inventory*, Handbooks in Operations Research and Management Science, Vol. 4, North-Holland, Amsterdam, Chapter 12.
Gunn, T.G. (1987). *Manufacturing for Competitive Advantage: Becoming a World Class Manufacturer*, Ballinger, Boston, MA.
Gupta, D., J.A. Buzacott and Y. Gerchak (1988). Economic analysis of investment decisions in flexible manufacturing systems, Working Paper, Department of Management Sciences, University of Waterloo, Waterloo, Ont.
Hall, R. (1983). *Zero Inventories*, Dow, Jones-Irwin, Homewood, IL.

Harhalakis, G., L. Mark, A. Johri and B. Cochrane (1988). MRP II and CAD are foundation for CIM systems. *CIM Rev.*, Fall, 14–17.

Hauser, J., and D. Clausing (1988). The house of quality. *Harv. Bus. Rev.* 66(3), 63–73.

Hayes, R.H., and R. Jaikumar (1988). Manufacturing's crisis: New technologies, obsolete organizations. *Harv. Bus. Rev.* 66(5), 77–85.

Hayes, R.H., and S.C. Wheelwright (1984). *Restoring our Competitive Edge: Competing Through Manufacturing*, Wiley, New York.

Hayes, R.H., S.C. Wheelwright and K.B. Clark (1988). *Dynamic Manufacturing*, Free Press, New York.

He, H., and R.S. Pindyck (1989). Investments in flexible production capacity, Working Paper MIT-EL 89-001WP, Center for Energy Policy Research, MIT.

Hinomoto, H. (1985). Capacity expansion with facilities under technological improvement. *Management Sci.* 11(5), 581–592.

Hollander, S. (1965). *The Sources of Increased Efficiency: A Study of DuPont Rayon Plants*, MIT Press, Cambridge, MA.

Hotelling, H. (1925). A general mathematical theory of depreciation. *J. Amer. Statist. Assoc.* 20, 340–353.

Hutchinson, G.K. (1976). Production capacity: CAM vs. transfer line. *IIE*, September, 30–35.

Hutchinson, G.K., and J.R. Holland (1982). The economic value of flexible automation. *J. Manuf. Syst.* 1(2), 215–228.

Hyun, J., and B. Ahn (1990). Flexibility revisited: Review, unifying frameworks and strategic implications, Working Paper, Management Science Dept., Korea Advanced Institute of Science and Technology.

Jaikumar, R. (1986). Postindustrial manufacturing. *Harv. Bus. Rev.* 64(6), 69–76.

Jensen, R. (1982). Adoption and diffusion of an innovation of uncertain profitability. *J. Econom. Theory* 27, 182–193.

Kamien, M.I., and N.L. Schwartz (1982). *Market Structure and Innovation*, Cambridge University Press, Cambridge, U.K.

Kaplan, R.S. (1983). Measuring manufacturing performance: A new challenge for managerial accounting research. *Accounting Rev.* 58(4), 686–705.

Kaplan, R.S. (1984). The evolution of management accounting. *Accounting Rev.* 59(3), 390–418.

Kaplan, R.S. (1986). Must CIM be justified by faith alone? *Harv. Bus. Rev.* 64(2), 87–95.

Kaplan, R.S. (1988). One cost system is not enough, *Harv. Bus. Rev.* 66(1), 61–66.

Karmarkar, U.S. (1989). Getting control of Just-in-Time. *Harv. Bus. Rev.* 67(5), 122–131.

Karmarkar, U.S., and S. Kekre (1987). Manufacturing configuration, capacity and mix decisions considering operational costs. *J. Manuf. Syst.* 6, 315–324.

Klincewicz, J.G., and H. Luss (1985). Optimal timing decisions for the introduction of new technologies. *European J. Oper. Res.* 20, 211–220.

Kreps, D.M., and A.M. Spence (1984). Modeling the role of history in industrial organization and competition, in: G. Feiwel (ed.), *Contemporary Issues in Modern Microeconomics*, Macmillan, London.

Kulatilaka, N. (1984). Financial, economic and strategic issues concerning the decision to invest in advanced automation. *Internat. J. Prod. Res.* 22(6), 949–968.

Kulatilaka, N. (1988). Valuing the flexibility in flexible manufacturing systems. *IEEE Trans. Engrg. Management* 35(4), 250–257.

Kulatilaka N., and S.G. Marks (1988). The strategic value of flexibility: Reducing the ability to compromise. *Amer. Econom. Rev.* 78(3), 574–580.

Lederer, P.J., and V.S. Singhal (1988). Effect of cost structure and demand risk in the justification of new technologies. *J. Manuf. Oper. Management* 1(4), 339–371.

Lippman, S., and K. McCardle (1987). Does cheaper, faster, or better imply sooner in the timing of innovation decisions? *Management Sci.* 33(8), 1058–1064.

Luss, H. (1982). Operations research and capacity expansion problems: A survey. *Oper. Res.* 30(5), 907–947.

Mamer, J.W., and K.F. McCardle (1987). Uncertainty, competition, and the adoption of new technology. *Management Sci.* 33(2), 161–177.

Manne, A.S. (1961). Capacity expansion and probabilistic growth. *Econometrica* 29(4), 632–649.

Mansfield, E. (1968). *Industrial Research and Technological Innovation*, Norton, New York.

Mansfield, E., J. Rapaport, A. Romeo, E. Villani, S. Wagner and F. Husic (1977). *The Production and Application of New Industrial Technology*, Norton, New York.

Mansfield, E., J. Rapaport, J. Schnee, S. Wagner and M. Hamburger (1971). *Research and Innovation in the Modern Corporation*, Norton, New York.

McCardle, K.F. (1985). Information acquisition and the adoption of new technology. *Management Sci.* 31(11), 1372–1389.

Meredith, J. (ed.) (1986). *Justifying New Manufacturing Technology*, Industrial Engineering and Management Press, Atlanta, GA.

Meredith, J.R., and N. Suresh (1986). Justification techniques for advanced manufacturing technologies. *Internat. J. Prod. Res.* 24(5), 1043–1057.

Meyer, R.A. (1971). Equipment replacement under uncertainty. *Management Sci.* 17(11), 750–758.

Milgrom, P.R., and D.J. Roberts (1990). The economics of modern manufacturing: Technology, strategy, and organization. *Amer. Econom. Rev.* 80(3), 511–528.

Monahan, G.E., and T.L. Smunt (1987). A multi-level decision support system for the financial justification of automated flexible manufacturing systems. *Interfaces* 17, 29–40.

Monahan, G.E., and T.L. Smunt (1989). Optimal acquisition of automated flexible manufacturing processes. *Oper. Res.* 37(2), 288–300.

Nevins, J.L., D.E. Whitney et al. (1989). *Concurrent Design of Products and Processes*, McGraw-Hill, New York.

Pierskalla, W.P., and J.A. Voelker (1976). A survey of maintenance models: The control and surveillance of deteriorating systems. *Naval. Res. Logist. Quart.* 23(3), 353–388.

Pindyck, R.S. (1988). Irreversible investment, capacity choice, and the value of the firm. *Amer. Econom. Rev.* 78, 969–985.

Piore, M.J. (1986). Corporate reform in American manufacturing and the challenge to economic theory, Working Paper, MIT Dept. of Economics.

Porteus, E.L. (1985). Investing in reduced setups in the EOQ model. *Management Sci.* 31, 998–1010.

Porteus, E.L. (1986). Optimal lot sizing, process quality improvement, and setup cost reduction. *Oper. Res.* 34, 137–144.

Preinreich, G. (1940). The economic life of industrial equipment. *Econometrica* 8, 12–44.

Reinganum, J.M. (1981a). On the diffusion of new technology: A game theoretic approach. *Rev. Econom. Stud.*, 395–405.

Reinganum, J.M. (1981b). Market structure and the diffusion of new technology. *Bell J. Econom.* 12(2), 618–624.

Rembold, U., C. Blume and R. Dillmann (1985). *Computer-Integrated Manufacturing Technology and Systems*, Marcel Dekker, New York.

Rogers, E. (1983). Attributes of innovations and their rate of adoption, in: *The Diffusion of Innovations*, Macmillan, New York, Chapter 6.

Roller, L.H., and M.M. Tombak (1990). Strategic choice of flexible production technologies and welfare implications. *J. Indust. Econom.* 38(4), 417–431.

Rosenberg, N. (1982). *Inside the Black Box: Technology and Economics*, Cambridge University Press, Cambridge, U.K.

Saaty, T.L. (1980). *The Analytical Hierarchy Process*, McGraw-Hill, New York.

Schmalensee, R. (1983). Advertising and entry deterrence. *J. Political Economy* 90, 636–653.

Schonberger, R.J. (1982). *Japanese Manufacturing Techniques*, Free Press, New York.

Schumpeter, J. (1939). *Business Cycles*, Vol. 1, McGraw-Hill, New York.

Schumpeter, J. (1943). *Capitalism, Socialism, and Democracy*, Unwin University Books, London.

Sethi, A.K., and S.P. Sethi (1990). Flexibility in manufacturing: A survey. *Internat. J. Flexible Manuf. Syst.* 2, 289–328.

Skinner, W. (1985). *Manufacturing: The Formidable Competitive Weapon*, Wiley, New York.

Spence, A.M. (1977). Entry, capacity, investment and oligopolistic pricing. *Bell J. Econom.* 8, 534–544.

Spence, A.M. (1979). Investment strategy and growth in a new market. *Bell J. Econom.* 10, 1–19.
Stecke, K.E., and R. Suri (1984). *Proceedings of the First ORSA/TIMS Conference on Flexible Manufacturing Systems*, Ann Arbor, MI.
Stecke, K.E., and R. Suri (1986). *Proceedings of the Second ORSA/TIMS Conference on Flexible Manufacturing Systems*, Elsevier, New York.
Suri, R., J. Sanders and M. Kamath (1991). Performance evaluation of production networks, in: S.C. Graves, A.H.G. Rinnooy Kan and P.H. Zipkin (eds.), *Logistics of Production and Inventory*, Handbooks in Operations Research and Management Science, Vol. 4, North-Holland, Amsterdam, Chapter 5.
Teece, D.J. (1986). Profiting from technological innovation: Implications for integration, collaboration, licensing, and public policy. *Res. Policy* 15(6), 285–305.
Terborgh, G. (1949). *Dynamic Equipment Policy*, McGraw-Hill, New York.
Thomas, R.J. (1988). The politics of technological change: An empirical study, MIT Sloan School WP#2035-88, July.
Tirole, J. (1988). *The Theory of Industrial Organization*, MIT Press, Cambridge, MA.
Tombak, M.M. (1988a). The importance of flexibility in manufacturing, Insead Working Paper No. 88/33, Fontainbleau, France.
Tombak, M.M. (1988b). A strategic analysis of investment in flexible manufacturing systems. *European J. Oper. Res.*
Tombak, M.M., and A. De Meyer (1988). Flexibility and FMS: An empirical analysis. *IEEE Trans. Engrg. Management* 35(2), 101–107.
Toshiba (1986). A Guide to OME Works, Company Brochure, Toshiba.
Triantis, A.J., and J.E. Hodder (1989). Valuing flexibility as a complex option, Working Paper, Stanford University, Department of Industrial Engineering and Engineering Management, April.
Ulrich, K.T., and C.H. Fine (1990). Cost estimation tools to support product design, *Proceedings of the ASME Manufacturing International Conference*, March, Atlanta, GA.
Ulrich, K., D. Sartorius, S. Pearson and M. Jakiela (1990). Connecting product design decisions to manufacturing system performance, Working Paper, MIT Sloan School.
Vander Veen, D.J., and W.C. Jordan (1989). Analyzing trade-offs between machine investment and utilization. *Management Sci.* 35(10), 1215–1226.
Zipkin, P. (1990). How simple, really, is the Just-in-Time system?, Working Paper, Graduate School of Business, Columbia University.

Subject Index

Printed and bound by CPI Group (UK) Ltd, Croydon, CR0 4YY
08/05/2025
01865023-0003